# 1985 CATHOLIC ALMANAC

Felician A. Foy, O.F.M.
EDITOR

Rose M. Avato
ASSOCIATE EDITOR

**Our Sunday Visitor, Inc.**
HUNTINGTON • INDIANA

ACKNOWLEDGMENTS: NC News Service, for
coverage of news and documentary texts; *The
Documents of Vatican II,* ed. W. M. Abbott
(Herder and Herder, America Press: New York
1966), for quotations of Council documents;
*Annuario Pontificio* (1984); *Statistical Yearbook
of the Church* (1981); *The Official Catholic
Directory* (P. J. Kenedy & Sons, 1984); *The Papal
Encyclicals,* 5 vols., ed. C. Carlen (McGrath
Publishing: Wilmington, NC 1981); The United
States Catholic Mission Assoc. (1233 Lawrence
St. N.E., Washington, D.C. 20017), for U.S.
foreign-mission compilations and statistics;
*Catholic Press Directory* (1984); *CCCB 1984
Directory* (Canadian Conference of Catholic
Bishops; Ottawa, Ont. 1984), for Canadian
Catholic statistics; other sources as credited in
particular entries.

1985 Catholic Almanac

ISBN 0-87973-255-5
Library of Congress Catalog Card No. 73-641001
International Standard Serial Number (ISSN) 0069-1208

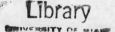

# TABLE OF CONTENTS

## PAPAL VISIT TO THE DOMINICAN REPUBLIC AND PUERTO RICO

At the time of writing, Pope John Paul was preparing for the 24th foreign trip of his pontificate — to the Dominican Republic and Puerto Rico, Oct. 10 to 13, 1984 — to help launch a nine-year evangelization program designed to develop and enrich the life of faith among Latin Americans.

The central event of the trip was expected to be the Pontiff's meeting with Latin American bishops Oct. 11 in Santo Domingo. He intended to join them in inaugurating a "novena of years" leading up to a 500th-year commemoration in 1992 of Christopher Columbus' first voyage to the New World and the subsequent arrival of Christianity.

Indications were that the Holy Father would make evangelization and the deepening of the region's Catholic roots the major theme of talks and actions during his visit.

The Council of Latin American Bishops said in a statement connected with the visit and their evangelization program that the prelates wanted the nine years of reflection, prayer and study to focus on the future as well as the past of the people and the faith of the region.

The statement took note of North-South polarization and economic imbalance as something that, "until now, has found no satisfactory solution." Also noted was the decision of the Church in Latin America to assume a "preferential option for the poor" in direct response to the fact of poverty there and in many other areas of the world. The bishops added that the world must respond to "the immense cry for (economic and social) justice raised by more than half of humanity."

The statement echoed Pope John Paul's frequent affirmation that universal peace is impossible without justice. He touched on the issue during his first trip to Santo Domingo in 1979, when he stopped there overnight on the way to Mexico. He said then that contemporary evangelization means a "renewed transmission of faith" and an invitation to build a just society that is open to God.

The scheduled papal agenda in Santo Domingo included meeting with bishops, government officials and representatives of other churches, the celebration of an outdoor Mass, a Liturgy of the Word, and a visit to the Santo Domingo cathedral, the oldest church in the Western World.

During a seven-hour stop in San Juan, Puerto Rico, Oct. 12, the Pope planned to celebrate Mass in the city's main plaza, and to meet with bishops, clergy, seminarians, and men and women religious.

On the first leg of the trip, the Pope was scheduled to make an overnight stop at Zaragoza, Spain, Oct. 10 and 11. While there, he intended to visit the Basilica of Our Lady of Pilar, the site of a legendary appearance of Mary to St. James the Apostle in 40 A.D.

---

## PUBLICATION HISTORY

The *Catholic Almanac* originated remotely from *St. Anthony's Almanac*, a 64-page annual with calendar, feature and devotional contents, published by the Franciscans of Holy Name Province from 1904 to 1929.

Completely revised and enlarged, the publication was issued under the title, *The Franciscan Almanac*, by *The Franciscan Magazine* from 1931 to 1933, and by St. Anthony's Guild from 1936 to 1971. From 1940 to 1969, its title was *The National Catholic Almanac*. The present title was adopted in 1969. The 1959 to 1971 editions were produced jointly by St. Anthony's Guild and Doubleday & Co., Inc.

The *Catholic Almanac* was acquired in 1971 by Our Sunday Visitor, Inc., Huntington, IN 46750.

## POPE JOHN PAUL IN ASIA AND OCEANIA

On the 21st foreign trip of his pontificate, May 2 to 12, 1984, Pope John Paul visited South Korea, Papua New Guinea, the Solomon Islands and Thailand.

The key event of the 25,000-mile tour was the canonization of 103 martyrs in connection with the celebration of the 200th anniversary of the coming of Catholicism in Korea.

### MAY 2

#### Fairbanks

The Alitalia DC-10 carrying the Holy Father and his party landed at Fairbanks, Alaska, at about 10:00 a.m., some 10 hours after departing from Rome.

During the refueling stop of more than two hours, the Pope met with President and Mrs. Reagan, on their way home from China, and several members of the U.S. hierarchy.

The President called the Pope "a minister of peace and love," and pledged American support in the "quest for human rights and world peace."

The Pope was greeted by about 10,000 people. He did a walk-through of 250 handicapped persons in the airport terminal building. During a brief prayer service, he spoke about missionary work and its effects in Alaska.

Over the Pacific en route to Seoul, he prayed for the 269 persons killed in the South Korean airliner that was shot down Sept. 1, 1983.

### MAY 3

#### Seoul

On arrival at Seoul-Kimbo International Airport before midafternoon, the Pope told those who greeted him, including President Chun Doo-hwan, of South Korea, that he came "as your friend and as an apostle of peace."

Hope and Praise: "I pray that your beloved fatherland, now tragically divided into two for over a generation, will be reunited as one family, not through confrontation and hostility, but through dialogue, mutual trust and brotherly love, giving the lie to a world more and more given to mistrust, hatred and the violence of arms."

He looked forward to "a more human society of true justice and peace, where all life is upheld as sacrosanct, where to live is to work for the good of others, where to govern is to serve, where no one is used as a tool, no one left out and no one downtrodden, where all can live in real brotherhood."

He praised "the marvelous flowering of the Christian faith in Korea," noting that his visit commemorated the 200th anniversary of the coming of Catholicism to Korea.

Visit to Martyrs' Shrine: His first stop in Seoul was at the shrine where the remains of 25 of the martyrs of Korea are buried. While venerating them, he prayed the Our Father with 100 of their descendants.

He had a private meeting with the president after the visit to the martyrs' sanctuary.

He celebrated Mass at the seminary in Seoul before a congregation of students for the priesthood. He said their number was symbolic of the vitality of the Church in the country: "Nine hundred strong . . . you are a consolation and a great promise for the Church."

Meeting with Bishops: With bishops in the evening, he said: "On behalf of the universal Church, I express gratitude through you, the bishops, to the whole Church in Korea for the achievements of two centuries. . . . I willingly bless all of your systematic and sustained efforts on behalf of the family, the program of evangelization of neighbor, the building up of the parish and community, the consolidation of the diocese and, finally, the ecclesial solidarity on the national and universal level."

### MAY 4

#### Kwangju — Sorokdo — Seoul

At Mass late in the morning in Mudung Municipal Stadium in Kwangju, the Holy Father baptized and confirmed 72 adults. With them especially in mind, he addressed the congregation of 65,000 people on life in Christ.

Life in Christ: " 'Dying to sin' and 'being alive to God in Christ Jesus' is a commitment for your whole life, and it requires effort for the future. It means keeping yourselves free, by God's grace, from hatred and rancor. It means pardoning those who may have sinned against you. It means being reconciled to one another and to God in forgiveness and love. But forgiveness is an act which is greater than our poor hearts: it belongs to God alone. I am keenly aware of the deep wounds that pain your hearts and souls from personal experiences and from recent tragedies, which are difficult to overcome from a merely human point of view, especially for those of you from Kwangju. Precisely for this reason the grace of reconciliation has been granted to you in baptism. It is a gift of the mercy of God manifested in Jesus Christ, who suffered, died and rose again for us.

"This part of Christ's saving message is particularly relevant for those who are haunted by the memory of the unfortunate events of this place. (The reference was to riots in 1980 in which security forces broke up demonstrations against the imposition of martial law; the death toll was higher than the official figure of 170 persons.) But now you have been conformed to the image and likeness of Christ through baptism, and each one of you is called to follow the example of Christ, the authentic peacemaker and perfect model for reconciliation. By accepting the consequences of our baptismal commitment, we become instruments of reconciliation and peace in the midst of dissension and hatred. In this way, as effective signs of Christ's healing power working through us, we can ease the pain of injured hearts that are filled with anxiety and bitterness. At the same time, we can offer hope to those who suffer from oppression, and thus become instruments of Christian liberation and signs of true freedom."

"You are 72 in number. You symbolize the hundred thousand or more Koreans who, by the grace of God, are baptized each year into life with Christ and become his witnesses. As Jesus once sent out 72 of his disciples, two by two, to spread the good news of salvation, so you too will be sent out today to be his heralds. The gift of Christ's life is a gift to be shared with others in gratitude, so that all may have fullness of life."

**With Lepers:** At the leprosarium on Sorokdo Island late in the afternoon, the Pope had an emotional encounter with some 700 of the people there. While greeting them and giving them his blessing, he urged them to heed the example of Christ who "suffered entirely for others, giving himself in unending love."

**Obstacles to Peace:** Back in Seoul in the evening, the Pope spoke about this subject at a meeting with members of the diplomatic corps.

Lack of trust between individuals, groups, nations and alliances is perhaps the greatest obstacle to the achievement of a constructive dialogue for peace.

Genuine peace is ever more elusive. "The available structures of dialogue . . . have shown themselves to be extremely fragile and vulnerable."

But, "would it not be a crime to remain silent when what is needed is an effective appeal for a real 'conversion of heart' on the part of individuals, governments and nations?"

Peace "is threatened wherever the human spirit is oppressed by poverty or constrained by socio-political or ideological dictates." It is threatened by East-West tensions, by the growing contrast between developed and developing nations. It is threatened wherever fundamental rights are trampled upon.

The Pope renewed his support for unification between communist-ruled North Korea and U.S.-aligned South Korea: "In your diplomatic service in Korea, you can see how contrasting ideologies and the passions they unleash give rise to intense suffering. The anguish and pain of a divided Korea are emblematic of a divided world that lacks trust and fails to achieve reconciliation in brotherly love. They are a symbol of a world situation that cries out for a response."

The Holy Father told the diplomats there is "serious need for re-thinking basic policies and priorities. At this time in history, there is a great need for wisdom."

## MAY 5

### Taegu—Pusan—Seoul

The Pope ordained 38 men from 12 dioceses to the priesthood at a morning Mass attended by 50,000 people in the Citizens' Stadium in Taegu. He told them they were called to play a role in society similar to the one Christ played in his day.

**Role of Priests:** "Jesus is where the Gospel shows him to us: in poverty, humility and vulnerability at his birth; sharing the joys and sorrows of his people; close to the daily life of the men and women of his land; blessing the children; in conversation with the young; compassionate to all."

In 20 years the number of priests in Korea increased from 250 to more than 1,000. The nation's four seminaries were filled to capacity.

**Address to Workers:** Late in the afternoon at Pusan's Sogang Airport, the Pope addressed 200,000 industrial workers, farmers and fishermen.

He told them they should "work together in fraternal love to show that a more just sharing of the world's goods means access to these goods, especially through a just wage."

The worker is more important than the product of his or her work. "Even the biggest city, the most complicated computer, the greatest nation, is only something made by man and is meant to serve man, to benefit man."

"Unfortunately, the whole issue of work has often been looked at from the viewpoint of conflict between 'capital' and 'labor': a conflict that has vast social, ideological and political implications. This conflict has been a great tragedy for humanity and a source of suffering for untold millions of individual human beings and families.

"I well realize that the relationship between employers and employees in the context of your Korean cultural and social traditions has its own special characteristics, and that it is not true that the way to better relationships is to be found in a simplistic application of standards and methods devised elsewhere — still less by imposing alien ideological systems which have allowed flagrant injustices to persist, or have created new ones, threatening the very peace of the world.

"Justice requires that ways be found to give workers a greater share in the organizational aspects of production and in profits, and I am pleased to know that initiatives have been taken in this direction. Justice also requires that the workers themselves benefit from the success of the enterprise in which they work, and that they have the satisfaction of knowing that through diligent and conscientious work they are thereby contributing to the social development of their country."

The Pope returned to Seoul for two evening meetings at Sogang University, a Jesuit institution.

**Bearing witness to Christ:** Addressing several thousands of priests and Religious, men and women, he urged them to "bear witness to what it means to be blessed by God," by being, living and working in the spirit of the Beatitudes.

He also said: "I invite all of you to join me today in expressing gratitude to God and in praising him for the many vocations to the priesthood and Religious life which have characterized the Church in Korea in recent years. Here is a sign of the vitality of your faith; it is likewise a sign of the power of Christ's paschal mystery and the efficacy of his precious blood. Indeed, the Church in your land cannot even be imagined without your vital presence in parishes, schools, hospitals and other specialized fields of apostolic endeavor. And your service offers great hope for the future, not only for the Church in your land but for other countries as well which will receive missionaries from Korea. The universal Church counts on your missionary contribution.

"I encourage you to pray for more vocations, and to try continually to foster them among the people whom you serve. Ask the Korean martyrs to intercede for this special intention, which is so important for the future of the Church. And may your lives which are an incarnation of the Beatitudes be eloquent signs of the presence of Jesus Christ in the world."

At a gathering of several hundred intellectuals, the Pontiff praised scientific and cultural achievements for their possibility of revealing God's greatness and of bringing about a deeper appreciation of the human person. He said that, following the example of the first Christians in Korea, the Church should "adopt an attitude of exchange and of understanding with the cultural identity of the people."

## MAY 6
### Seoul

On his last full day in Korea, the Pope dedicated the cathedral in Seoul and the nation to Mary, canonized 103 martyrs, and addressed leaders of non-Christian religions, representative Protestants, delegates to a national pastoral council and a gathering of youths.

**The Martyrs of Korea:** The central event of the celebration of the bicentennial of Catholicism in Korea and of the Pope's visit to the country was the canonization of 103 martyrs who were killed during persecutions in the mid-1800s. The canonization was the first ever outside of Rome in modern church history. It occurred during a Mass attended by about 800,000 people in Youido Plaza.

The Holy Father, in an English-Korean homily, recounted the stories of some of the martyrs, 92 of whom were lay people from nearly every walk of life, 47 women and 45 men; the other 11 were 10 French priests and the first native Korean priest.

**The Church in Korea:** In sketching the beginning and development of the Church in Korea, the Pope said:

"The truth about Jesus Christ also reached Korean soil. It came by means of books brought from China. And, in a most marvelous way, divine grace soon moved your scholarly ancestors first to an intellectual quest for the truth of God's word and then to a living faith in the risen Savior.

"Yearning for an ever greater share in the Christian faith, your ancestors sent one of their own (Yi Sung Hun) in 1784 to Peking, where he was baptized. From this good seed was born the first Christian community in Korea, a community unique in the history of the Church by reason of the fact that it was founded entirely by lay people. This fledgling Church, so young and yet so strong in faith, withstood wave after wave of fierce persecution. Thus, in less than a century, it could already boast of some 10,000 martyrs. The years 1791, 1801, 1827, 1839, 1846 and 1866 are forever signed with the holy blood of your martyrs and engraved in your hearts.

"Even though the Christians in the first half-century had only two priests from China to assist them, and these only for a time, they deepened their unity in Christ through prayer and fraternal love; they disregarded social classes and encouraged religious vocations. And they sought ever closer union with their bishop in Peking and the pope in faraway Rome.

"After years of pleading for more priests to be sent, your Christian ancestors welcomed the first French missionaries in 1836. Some of these, too, are numbered among the martyrs who gave their lives for the sake of the Gospel, and who are being canonized today in this historic celebration.

"The splendid flowering of the Church in Korea today is indeed the fruit of the heroic witness of the martyrs. Even today, their undying spirit sustains the Christians in the Church of Silence in the north of this tragically divided land."

**With Religious Leaders:** In the afternoon, the Pope met with 12 Buddhist, Confucian and other non-Christian leaders. He expressed "high esteem for the millennia of precious cultural heritage and admirable traditions" of such religions. He called "reverence for life and nature, (and) the quest for truth and harmony noble hallmarks of (their) spiritual tradition" that will lead Korea "through turbulent times." He appealed to people of differing religious and ethical beliefs "to foster genuine fraternal dialogue and to give special consideration to what human beings have in common and to what promotes fellowship among them."

He also met with 15 leaders of Protestant denominations, with whom he noted the importance of working together toward full religious unity.

At the opening session of the National Pastoral Congress of South Korean Catholics, he told 900 delegates, clergy and lay persons: "The first Christians (in Korea) had no wealth, no prestige, no power, not even church buildings, but, like Jesus himself, and because they were filled with his spirit, they bore witness to the good news by their own life, attracting the multitudes to conversion."

"While remaining completely true to their own identity . . . they were able to be perfectly united to the universal Church," he added, in an apparent reference to difficulties of the Church in China.

**It's Youths' Turn:** The last event of the day was an address to a crowd of 8,000 young working people, college and high school students at the Seoul Sports Palace.

After observing that young people have questions to be answered about themselves, the Church and the relationship of the Church to their lives, he said:

"It is now your turn to embrace this heritage (of the Church) in its fullness and to pass it on to those to come. For this reason, it is important for you to feel at home in the Church, to take your place in the Church, especially by becoming more and more involved in the life of your parish communities and in the works of the apostolate. 'Let your light shine before men, that they may see your good works and give glory to your Father who is in heaven' (Mt. 5:16).

"Let the world know that you have chosen the path of truth, goodness and compassion, honesty and love, pardon and reconciliation where necessary, and openness to all. Yes, the path of generosity, personal discipline and prayer. And, when someone asks why you live this way, you will answer, 'Because of my faith in Jesus Christ.' "

## MAY 7

### Seoul-Papua New Guinea

Before leaving Seoul, the Pope made a final plea for the reunification of South and North Korea: "I remember with profound regret, sympathy and sorrow those of your parents and children, brothers and sisters, friends and relatives in the North who could not share the joy of your celebrations."

**A Shepherd's Visit:** The Holy Father arrived late in the afternoon at Port Moresby, Papua New Guinea, and was welcomed at the airport by a lively crowd of 3,500 people and a group of tribal dancers. He received an official greeting from Sir Kingford Dibela, governor general of the island.

In a brief address — delivered in a combination of English, Pidgin and Motu — the Pope said he came primarily as the chief shepherd of the Church "to encourage and strengthen my brothers and sisters in the practice of the faith."

He celebrated Mass in the evening in Hubert Murray Stadium before a gathering of 40,000 people. He appealed for more native vocations to the priesthood and religious life in a homily, saying that the Church "gradually grows toward maturity as indigenous sons and daughters take up and respond to the divine call of the Gospel . . . by embracing vocations to the ministerial priesthood and consecrated life."

## MAY 8

### Mt. Hagen-Port Moresby

The Pope flew from Port Moresby to Mt. Hagen for a mid-morning Mass attended by more than 150,000 people, some of whom had walked in pilgrimage for weeks to be with the Holy Father in this first-of-its-kind celebration in the highlands of Papua New Guinea. The Holy Father said the Mass in pidgin, the common language of the 700 tribes of the country.

Despite their diversity, the Pope said they had a common bond in their Catholic faith.

He said in his homily: "I pray that . . . divine love will be ever more revealed to you and among you; that it will lead you safely into the future; that it will enable you to walk through this life here on earth . . . never losing sight of eternal life and eternal communion with God."

Back in Port Moresby, the Pope met with people who were ill, youths, catechists, priests and religious, and the governor. He made a point of telling those who were ill that "suffering is not a punishment from God, nor something caused by witchcraft or evil spirits."

**Role of an Episcopal Conference:** At a meeting with members of the Bishops' Conference of Papua New Guinea and the Solomon Islands, he said their joint action was an expression of the unity of the Church in the region. He spoke about the tasks of an episcopal conference, the role of the laity in the Church, and the needs of families.

Conferences "should strive to address the major pastoral problems affecting the life of the Church. . . . Joint pastoral documents give opportunities to present the official doctrine of the Church in clear and understandable terms while taking into consideration concrete situations and problems." It is also important for bishops to "face together questions of the social order, such as human work, political ethics, alcoholism, bureaucratic corruption," and other subjects.

## MAY 9

### Solomon Islands-Port Moresby

In the morning, the Holy Father flew from Port Moresby to Guadalcanal, where thousands of islanders gave him a spectacular welcome at an athletic field transformed into the scene of a jubilant native festival.

In a brief address of greeting, he expressed to the people his admiration "for the harmony and good will which you have been able to achieve in this one nation." He urged Catholics, who comprised about 20 per cent of the population, to "stand firm in the message of the Gospel" received from missionaries who first came to the Solomons just before the middle of the 19th century.

Governor General Sir Baddeley Devesi welcomed the Pope with word that the nation's cabinet had voted the previous week to establish diplomatic relations with the Vatican.

After leaving the festive scene at the athletic field, the Pope visited Holy Cross Cahedral overlooking the capital city of Honiara. Afterwards, he lunched with the four bishops of the Solomons, met with the governor at his home and with inmates at the Rove Prison.

After Mass in a large open field, he entrusted the Church and the nation to Mary and prayed for those of the nation and others — among them 2,000 Americans and 25,000 Japanese — who died on Guadalcanal in some of the fiercest fighting of World War II.

The Pope returned to Port Moresby in the evening.

## MAY 10

### Bangkok

In Thailand after a flight from Port Moresby, the Pope was greeted by the crown prince at the airport and formally welcomed by King Bhumibol Adulyadej at the Grand Palace.

The king paid tribute to the missionaries who brought not only the Catholic faith but also western culture to Thailand.

**Thai Tolerance:** The Pope, on his part, told the king that the "history of Thai freedom and Thailand's legendary spirit of tolerance are a reminder of the deepest aspirations of the human family to live in peace, harmony and brotherhood." He added that the hospitality given to hundreds of thousands of refugees from neighboring countries "makes me feel at home in this great land of yours."

With Vasana Tara, the supreme Buddhist patriarch of Thailand, the Pope made his own the patriarch's wish that religious leaders might "cooperate and coordinate in bringing peace and happiness to mankind."

**Catholics and Buddhism:** The Holy Father celebrated Mass in the evening at Bangkok's National Stadium before a gathering of 35,000 Catholics. Their relationship to Buddhism, the religion of 95 per cent of the population, and peace were subjects of his address.

"You find yourselves in a world where the majority of your fellow citizens embrace Buddhism, that complex of religious beliefs and philosophical ideas which profoundly influences your identity as a nation," he said.

Reminding the people that the Church rejects nothing that is true and holy in non-Christian traditions, he added: "Your cultural heritage as Thai people is intimately linked to the indigenous Buddhist tradition, which provides a fertile terrain for the seed of God's word, proclaimed by Jesus Christ, to take root and grow."

Regarding peace, he said: "As people who are enriched by the Buddhist tradition of your country, you are endowed with a special sensitivity to the renunciation of violence in the vindication of personal rights."

**Message to Vietnamese:** As the plane bearing the Pope flew near Vietnam on the way from Papua New Guinea to Thailand, the Vatican released a statement — broadcast by Veritas Radio in the Philippines — in which he expressed "my good will and sentiments of peace, my encouragement and my cordial best wishes" to all Vietnamese. "I pray that you will always have practical opportunities for professing and living your faith. The guarantee of these opportunities does honor to a country, manifests its concern for justice and favors the realization of the spiritual values so necessary for its development."

He pledged international Catholic support for the work of rebuilding the war-torn country.

## MAY 11
### Bangkok

On the last busy day of his trip, the Holy Father visited a refugee camp; met at the cathedral with priests, Religious and catechists; celebrated Mass at the major seminary and ordained a number of men to the priesthood; met with government officials, diplomats and bishops; and, finally, departed for Rome near midnight.

**Counsel to Refugees:** At Phanat Nikhom, a camp for persons in transit to host countries, he told Indochinese refugees: "I wish to share with you your sufferings, your hardships, your pain, so that you may know that someone cares for you, sympathizes with your plight, and works to help you find relief, comfort and a reason for hope."

He advised refugees to "remain firmly rooted in your respective cultures, from which the world can learn much and come to appreciate you in your uniqueness." He also suggested: "Take every opportunity offered you to study a language and perfect a skill in order to be able to adapt socially to the country which will open its door to you and be enriched by your presence."

Refugees and their problems were also the subjects of papal remarks at a meeting in the evening with government officials and diplomats.

**An Abnormal Condition:** "The fact remains," he said, "that it is something repugnant and abnormal for hundreds of thousands of human beings to have to leave their own countries because of their race, ethnic origin, political convictions or religion, or because they are in danger of violence or even death from civil strife or political turmoil."

He thanked Thailand and many agencies and international organizations — especially the Office of the U.N. High Commissioner for Refugees — for their hospitality to refugees. At the same time, he said: "Resettlement alone can never be the final answer to these peoples' plight. They have a right to go back to their roots, to return to their native lands."

In the final analysis, the problem cannot be solved "unless the conditions are created whereby genuine reconciliation may take place: reconciliation between nations, between various sectors of a given national community, within each ethnic group and between ethnic groups themselves."

**Responsibilities of Bishops:** At his last meeting of the tour, with the bishops of Thailand, he said: "As bishops, you are called upon to help your people face many issues that affect their lives as individuals and as members of a family and of society."

"This great treasure (of the Catholic faith and life in Christ) must be presented in an especially dynamic way to the young people of the Church. It is they who are assailed most by the problems of the modern world; it is they who need a particular grace from Christ to endure the Christian combat with temptation and sin. In Christ, the young people can find the answers to the deep questions that are at the basis of all Christian choices. How greatly they need the pastoral support of their bishops, together with their priests, in order to develop and persevere in their Christian vocation.

"In speaking of the young people and their needs, we cannot ignore the formidable problem of narcotics in the world today, as well as the causes of this phenomenon and the means needed to face this crisis of humanity. The whole human community must be mobilized to confront this issue. But here the Church has a specific task of educating to human dignity, to the respect of self, to the values of the spirit, to the search for that true joy which abides in the heart and not in the passing exhilaration of the senses."

"Above all, the power of Christ's word, presented through the ministry of the bishops, offers to all the young the deep solution to all the many problems that touch their consciences as they strive to live the life of Christ."

*This trip, the Pope's second to Asia, was his first to Korea with its growing Catholic population. It marked the beginning of the third century of the Church there.*

## ECUMENICAL PILGRIMAGE TO SWITZERLAND

Pope John Paul, addressing a general audience three days after returning from his June 12 to 17, 1984, trip to Switzerland, called it an ecumenical pilgrimage in keeping with the theme of the Second Vatican Council's *Decree on Ecumenism.* It was the 22nd foreign trip of his pontificate.

He said the trip emphasized the necessity of "an unceasing exchange of ideas and theological dialogue" with other Christian churches. Also necessary is "common witness to Christ," despite "the reality of the division" among Christian churches.

The Pope said that, in meetings with Swiss Catholics, frank questions were raised about such sensitive church issues as the role of women in ministry, clerical celibacy and the laicization of priests. All of the meetings, he declared, were "cordial, well prepared, permeated with a sense of realism and, at the same time, by a sincere concern for the mission of the Gospel in a society that is suffering the influx of secularization."

### JUNE 12

Pope John Paul gave a strong stamp of approval to ecumenism when he visited the World Council of Churches headquarters in Geneva and called for greater cooperation between the Catholic Church and the WCC, especially in efforts for peace and justice.

"We should meet together more and more in all fields where human beings, because of the burden of their environment, experience great difficulties on the social, ethical or religious levels, in living according to the dignity of their vocation," the Pope said.

### Ecumenism, a Firm Commitment

The Pope declared that the Church's engagement in the ecumenical movement is irreversible.

At the same time, he added, the Church "entered on the hard ecumenical task bringing with it a conviction" about the role of the bishop of Rome. "It is convinced that in the ministry of the bishop of Rome it has preserved the visible pole and guarantee of unity in full fidelity to the apostolic tradition and to the faith of the Fathers."

The Pope encouraged participants in the ecumenical movement to discuss this point.

He also emphasized things Christians have in common, among them baptism, reverence for the word of God, prayer, and a rediscovery of the "whole role of the Holy Spirit."

He reiterated, however, the doctrinal opposition to sharing the Eucharist until full unity among Christians is restored. He called for common prayer. Although "it is not yet possible for us to celebrate the Eucharist together and communicate at the same table."

The Holy Spirit, he said, "knows how to find new ways as soon as there is question of moving together toward a unity at once founded on truth and respectful of the rich diversity of really Christian values."

### Shared Vision

"Despite our separations and the frequent differences in methods of operation, we often meet on the level of social thought and action, and we witness to one and the same vision, based on the same reading of the Gospel," the Pope said.

(He did not say how the Catholic Church and WCC differ on methods of achieving peace and justice. However, in an NC interview earlier in the year, Msgr. Basil Meeking, an official of the Vatican Secretariat for Promoting Christian Unity, said disagreement over means toward social change was a sore point between the Vatican and WCC.

("There is a tendency of the WCC to make specific statements about specific issues," said Msgr. Meeking, coordinator of Catholic Church relations with the WCC.

("The Catholic Church style is to point out principles of ethical and moral concern without making specific applications of them. The Vatican leaves specific applications to the local church," he said.)

Cardinal Johannes Willebrands, head of the Christian Unity Secretariat, and the Rev. Philip Potter, a Methodist minister and general secretary of the WCC since 1972, issued a joint statement regretting the divisions which still exist among Christian churches.

"We pray that the Holy Spirit, dwelling in those who believe, may illuminate our minds and prepare our hearts so that the remaining obstacles to full communion among Christians may be overcome," they said.

"We long for such a communion based on one baptism, united in confessing the one apostolic faith, served by one apostolic ministry and expressed in a common celebration of the Eucharist, to the glory of God and for the salvation of humankind."

Cardinal Willebrands and Mr. Potter also called for cooperation in social efforts.

"This will mean an effort to give more effective expression to initiatives of social collaboration, engaging closely the partners on both sides, seeking to take up some of the most pressing issues together, especially the concern for world peace," they said.

### Significant Step

Vatican officials stressed the significance of the visit and saw it as an important ecumenical step and a logical follow-up to Pope John Paul's other major endorsements of ecumenism: the November, 1979, meeting with Ecumenical Orthodox Patriarch Dimitrios I in Istanbul, Turkey; the November, 1980, meeting with the Council of the Evangelical Lutheran Church in West Germany; and the May, 1982, meeting with Anglican Archbishop Robert Runcie of Canterbury, England.

"From the beginning of my ministry as Bishop of Rome, I have insisted that the engagement of the Catholic Church in the ecumenical movement is irreversible and that the search for unity was one of its pastoral priorities," the Pope told the WCC.

The WCC ceremony during the papal visit included a prayer service in which male and female ministers read the Scriptures.

## Unity Theme

The Pope stressed the theme of unity from the moment he landed in security-conscious Switzerland where an armored personnel carrier escorted the papal plane as it taxied down the runway.

"The challenge of modern times to mankind and to all of Christianity makes Christians feel even more painfully the unhappy divisions and polarizations that today, as in the past, separate us," he said to a sparse airport crowd kept at a distance from him.

"In a more and more secularized society, all Christians are called upon to give a common witness for Christ," he added.

The Pope noted that this call for unity was appropriate in a country which witnesses to unity in diversity by maintaining a strong regional identity, claiming four official languages — Italian, German, French and Romansch — yet still stands as one nation.

"This pilgrimage is taking me to a country where the plurality of linguistic tradition does not impair the common identity of the Swiss nor their cohesion, but contributes to the richness of their cultural patrimony," he said.

## Mass and Meeting with Orthodox

Unity within the Catholic Church was the theme of the Pope's remarks at an outdoor Mass in Lugano in the Italian-speaking region of Switzerland.

Speaking to an enthusiastic congregation, he declared that "a local church cannot exist unless it is in communion with the others, unless it is open to the sufferings and joys of the other local churches, unless it seeks to be in harmony with them."

Unlike other papal trips outside Italy, the Pope was greeted and guarded by Swiss Guards in their ceremonial dress.

Noting the guards dressed in the uniform designed by Michelangelo, he recalled that "through many centuries, young Swiss citizens have served the successor of Peter in his many apostolic duties, faithfully and even at the cost of their lives."

The Pope also noted Switzerland's neutral status in world politics through which, he said, the country "has secured long years of peace and social progress, and also has made possible the expansion of humanitarian work, especially in times of international conflict."

At the end of the day, the Pope visited the Orthodox Center at Chambesy to express solidarity with the Orthodox Churches with which the Catholic Church had grown closer in recent years with the formation of a joint theological dialogue commission.

"Our churches are now engaged in a dialogue expressing itself both in theological study and in ever more intensive fraternal relations, in mutual intercession and a spirit of solidarity that go on growing, thanks to the almost total communion of faith existing between us," the Pope said.

He expressed hope that "soon the blessed day will dawn when we shall be able to share the same Eucharistic bread and drink from the same chalice."

## JUNE 13

The Pope's second day in Geneva began with a visit to St. Nicholas Cathedral, the gothic structure named for the patron of Switzerland, St. Nicholas of Flue, who left wife, family and farm to live as a hermit for 20 years.

After visiting the cathedral, the Pope went to the larger Church of the Cordeliers to meet with Religious who greeted him with enthusiastic applause and cheers. He joined them in the Morning Prayer of the Liturgy of the Hours, and told them not to become discouraged by declining numbers of priests and Religious.

The decrease "is by no means a fatality and should never lead to despair," he said. He called for renewal of religious life and praised the commitment of Religious to serve others through a life 'where obedience and fraternal community are discreet countersigns to the excesses of an often capricious sterile independence."

## Science and Culture

Science, its potential and limits, was the subject of an address by Pope John Paul to faculty members and students at the University of Fribourg.

"If science is the work of reason," he said, "it is not by distrusting it that the crisis of contemporary culture will be overcome. On the contrary, it is important to put trust in the immense scientific effort of mankind. Its increasing discoveries are an enrichment of the patrimony of truths, and thereby correspond to the Creator's design."

While expressing support for the work of science, the Pope criticized the scientistic ideology "which persists in affirming the self-sufficiency of the scientific project, as if it could give satisfaction on its own to all the essential questions which man asks."

He added: "A thoughtless transformation" of the world (by science and technology without regard for ethical and moral limits) runs grave risks." But, "ever more numerous scientists are becoming conscious of their human responsibility and are convinced that there cannot be science without conscience."

## Theologians and Their Work

Also at the University of Fribourg, the Pope addressed an assembly of Swiss Catholic theology professors.

"The theologian," he said, "is the servant of God's truth, he participates in the Church in the great act of tradition which goes on throughout history."

The scope of the freedom of theologians, their relationship to the teaching authority of the Church, the handling of controversial questions and the value of drawing from other fields of contemporary study were among points discussed by the Pope.

He told them they should approach controversial issues with discretion and not publicize private opinions as if they were official teachings of the Church. He added that they must work in union with the bishops and with himself.

Theologians "are not called to be judges, but to be loyal colleagues of those who, through their office, have the duty of unity for all," he said. "Theologians must also be able to accept the fact that, from their level, they cannot solve all the problems that are presented to them."

He cautioned theologians about making their work public before it has been properly evaluated.

Theological research "would therefore profit from being reviewed by other scholars beyond the boundaries of a particular theological school or country before being presented to the general public," he said.

"One must be careful not to confuse those believers who are less instructed in questions of faith by presenting them with theses which are not officially recognized and are at times still immature and insufficiently nuanced," he added.

At a press conference after the meeting, Bishop Henri Schwery, president of the Swiss Bishops' Conference, and five of the professors who attended the meeting said that issues brought up by the theologians were the shortage of priests, the possibility of ordaining women, and the role of women in the Church. Dominican Father John Dominic Barthelemy, professor of Old Testament at the University of Fribourg, said the Pope made no response to these issues.

### Mission of Lay People

The Pope met the largest crowd of the day when 30,000 people attended an outdoor Mass at Fribourg's La Poya Park under sunny skies.

In his homily, he asked Catholics to reach out to others, especially to those who come to their country from foreign lands.

Major points in the address were the roles lay people can play in promoting Christian unity, in furthering social justice and in carrying out a Christian mission in the world.

"God let you be born in the midst of the world. . . . This is your world, where God put you and where he wants you to be," he said.

He stressed the vocation of lay persons to service, with humility, gentleness, love, patience and pardon.

This vocation means "receiving the other (person) as a gift from God, as a brother in Christ, with his thirst for life, love, dignity. It means respecting him, trying to understand him, appreciating his value and his needs, making room for him in our little universe, getting the necessary aid for him and accepting his aid."

"Put yourselves in service to one another," the Pope said.

"Serve your neighbor. Serve the foreigners. Serve the poorest," he said.

He also spoke of Christian unity, the theme which marked most of the speeches of the previous day when he visited the World Council of Churches in Geneva.

"We must progress so that, in recognizing Jesus as Lord and Savior, the only founder of their church, Christians will come to live in a communion of faith and deep and visible charity, aspiring to share the same bread of life," he said.

### Diplomats, Jews, Youths

The Pope alluded again to the plight of foreign workers in his meeting with the diplomatic corps.

"The influx of foreign manpower also awakens reflections on the working conditions and on the conditions of family life of such workers," he said.

During the meeting, he asked the diplomats to help ease world tensions.

"It belongs to your scope of duties to intervene in the burning and numerous problems that are troubling the whole world at the moment," the Pope said. "You know them well. Every one of them is able to endanger the fragile and wavering peace: already existing regional conflicts; the armaments race; proliferation of nuclear weapons; famine, drought and any sort of misery in various parts of the world; disregard for human rights; ideological tensions."

The Pope also attended a brief meeting with representatives of the Jewish community which comprised 0.3 per cent of Switzerland's population. He urged the Jewish leaders to work for a "peace founded on justice, respect for the rights of all."

Robert Braunschweig, president of the Swiss Federation of Jewish Communities, praised the improving relations between Catholics and Jews, and expressed "hope for the day when normal relations will exist between the Vatican State and the State of Israel, so that the exchange of diplomatic representatives becomes a matter of fact."

In the evening, the Pope met a large group of French-speaking young people at a hockey stadium. They presented a discussion agenda which included the themes of a female priesthood, celibacy, the role of Church in politics, more lay involvement in liturgical life, and the future of mankind.

"I cannot give an answer to everything in the space of a few moments," the pope said. He asked catechists, priests and bishops to discuss these issues with the young people.

### JUNE 14

The Pope praised ecumenical efforts while maintaining the stance of the Church against intercommunion between Catholics and Protestants, at a meeting with the Swiss Protestant Evangelical Association in the village of Kehrsatz.

"We may not give a false sign," he said.

### Intercommunion

Shared communion is the goal of unity, not the means toward it, he said, addressing the group of Protestant leaders. He acknowledged the pain of separation felt by Christians of different denominations who want to pray together at the Eucharist, but said that to agree to intercommunion just to avoid pain would be delusionary.

"It would be of no use to do away with pain of separation if we do not remedy the cause of this pain, which is precisely the separation itself," he said.

Catholic and Protestant churches differ on substantial doctrinal issues, such as the role of the Church as the mediator between God and man and the role of the ministry. Intercommunion is one of the most controversial practical issues between Catholics and Protestants.

## Legacy of Division

"We cannot forget that the work of (the Reformers — Luther, Zwingli and others) remains a permanent point of contention between us and makes our church divisions something still present," the Pope said.

"On the other hand, no one can deny that the elements of the theology and spirituality of each one of them maintains the deep ties between us," he added.

The Pope called for "the frank acknowledgement of reciprocal wrongs and errors committed in the way of reacting toward each other when, indeed, each one wanted to make the Church more faithful to the will of God."

"Perhaps the day will come, and I hope it will be soon," he added, "when Swiss Catholics and Protestants will be able to write the history of that troubled and complex period together and with an objectivity rooted in deep fraternal charity."

On another subject, the Pope said that questions on women's rights and dignity should be part of discussion among churches. "We may hope that they lead to a common clarification and formation of opinion," he said. Many who attended the ecumenical meetings saw the visit of the Pope as a step forward for ecumenism.

### Reactions

Bishop Pierre Mamie of Lausanne, Geneva and Fribourg told NC News that prior to the visit of the Pope, Protestants had a stereotyped attitude about the Pope and Catholics.

"Their seeing him here in his human simplicity is a major step toward reconciliation," he added.

Protestant religious leaders echoed his sentiments at a press conference following the papal visit.

A Baptist minister reported that a layman asked the Pope why the Church could not take the small step of allowing intercommunion for the sake of ecumenism.

Cardinal Johannes Willebrands, head of the Vatican Secretariat for Promoting Christian Unity, responded for the Pope and said that for Catholics intercommunion was the biggest step, added the Baptist minister.

Before the Pope's visit, Msgr. Aloys Klein, a staff member of the Christian unity secretariat, told NC News that tensions existed between Catholic and Protestant churches in Switzerland, where Protestants had recently blocked Catholic efforts to establish dioceses in Geneva and Zurich.

He noted, however, that, after 50 years of work between the churches, there had been progress.

"Catholics and Evangelical Christians in Switzerland," he said, "have been able to agree on mutual recognition of baptism in one another's churches, to develop a pastoral care program for

mixed marriages, and to present common statements on treatment of foreign workers living in Switzerland."

Later the same day, the Pope went by helicopter to the tiny village of Flueli, home of Switzerland's nation saint, Nicholas of Flue.

At a Mass on the meadow of the farm where Brother Klaus lived and worked with his wife and 10 children before going to a nearby ravine to live as a hermit, the Pope urged the Swiss to spread peace to the world.

In his homily, he urged the Swiss to be ethical in the use of their powerful economy and banking system.

He said that Switzerland, a major arms exporter, should make sure that its financial system contributes to peace rather than war and injustice.

"As a democratically constituted society, you must watch vigilantly over all that goes on in this powerful world of money," he said.

"The world of finance, too, is a world of human beings," the Pope said, "subject to the consciences of us all.

"Ethical principles apply to it too," the Pope said.

## JUNE 15

On the fourth day of his visit, Pope John Paul was presented with a list of 10 concerns compiled by a number of Swiss priests concerning, among other things, clerical celibacy, the role of women in the Church and the tightening of Vatican policy on laicization of priests.

In response, he wondered if the issues were of concern to only a few priests and other persons.

### Celibacy

"I have read and I have listened attentively to all the questions and concerns which you set out with frankness. I received them with seriousness," said the Pope. "I do not know whether they correspond to the thinking and the cares of the majority of clergy in Switzerland, to whom I wish to speak."

(Under Pope John Paul II, few requests for laicizations have been granted, and the requirements for granting laicization, dispensation from the active ministry, have been tightened.)

During his address to the priests, the Pope defended celibacy.

"Celibacy is not simply a juridical addition to the sacrament of orders," he said. "It is a commitment of the person, taken in full maturity, to Christ and the Church."

"Dispensations, even if they are possible, must not be allowed to suppress, diminish, or threaten with oblivion the character of this commitment. In a sense, fidelity to a state of life that one has accepted is required for the dignity of the very person," he said.

### Pastoral Problems

In his talk to priests and in an earlier one the same day to the Swiss bishops, the Pope called on clergy to be faithful to church authorities and told the bishops that "to speak collegially is to stress your entire solidarity" with the Pope.

The Pope also told the bishops that they should be merciful when faced with pastoral problems, such as those faced by Catholics who have divorced and remarried outside the church and so cannot participate in the Eucharist. He said, however, that there are not always solutions to pastoral problems.

"With respect to certain questions posed by Christian people, it has to be accepted — despite the attitude of mercy which must inspire us in imitation of the mercy of God — that some of them can find no satisfactory solution because the situation creating the problem stands in the way," he said.

"I am thinking of certain cases involving remarriage after divorce, involving priests or involving mixed marriages," he added.

"Whatever the problem may be, the people involved must be helped to find a deeper spiritual attitude which has its own value as a witness to truth," he said.

The Pope's visit to the primarily Catholic, German-speaking region was not entirely marked by confrontations.

He met the most enthusiastic reception of the first four days of his trip in the town of Einsiedeln, to which pilgrims from all over Switzerland come to pray at the Benedictine abbey, which was celebrating its 1,050th anniversary.

About 2,500 persons warmly applauded the Pope when he entered the abbey church to lead them in the Church's Morning Prayer. Thousands of others stood outside the imposing baroque monastery the evening before, waiting to see the Pope who spent the night there.

### JUNE 16

The Pope devoted a major effort of the day to urging better treatment for foreign seasonal workers and calling on the country to continue being a haven for refugees.

### Seasonal Workers, Refugees

Foreign seasonal workers should be guaranteed "housing and schools, allowances and social security which ensure peace of mind for the individual and for families," Pope John Paul said before an audience of approximately 15,000 foreigners living in Switzerland.

Swiss law prevented the families of seasonal workers from staying in the country longer than three months at a time. The workers themselves, who were an important element of the Swiss tourist, construction and agriculture industries, were limited to nine-month stays each year. They were barred from seeking Swiss citizenship as long as they retained seasonal status.

(Swiss bishops had expressed concern over laws affecting foreign workers and had voiced disappointment over the defeat of initiatives to improve their living and working conditions.)

In his talk to the foreign community in Lucerne, the Pope also urged Switzerland to continue its tradition as a haven for refugees, "particularly at the moment when she could open new ways for the worldwide effort that is being made to discover a

soution to the grave problem of refugees."

(About 8,000 foreigners sought asylum in Switzerland in 1983. Of those, 2,000 were accepted.)

### "Be Patient with the Church"

The Pope told German-speaking and Romansch-speaking Swiss that their country's neutral status did not isolate it from the world's political upheavals.

He said "human beings feel less and less safe" because of "international conflicts between East and West, and North and South. Colossal technological progress and its possible misuse, as conventional and atomic armaments, threaten to put the survival of the human race itself into question."

The Pope suggested that the security-conscious country, "a refuge of peace and prosperity," might not be as secure as it seemed because of its internal decay.

He cited a "decay of values, the downfall of ethical norms, anxiety over the future, the feeling of meaninglessness."

The Pope also said that criticism of the Church must be fair and stem "from great love."

"Be patient with the Church" because it is "a human church" comprised of imperfect men, he said.

The Holy Father celebrated Mass in the latter part of the afternoon in Allmend.

### JUNE 17

Pope John Paul II stressed obedience to papal authority and endorsed liturgical renewal June 17 in Sion, a town less than 12 miles away from Econe, home of the suspended Archbishop Marcel Lefebvre, the dissident leader of a movement opposed to ecumenical and liturgical reforms of the Second Vatican Council.

The stress on obedience came during a Mass at Sion's airport where he ordained nine men to the priesthood and recalled the priest's promise of obedience to his bishop and to the pope.

"By being obedient to these two, the priest lives in community with the whole church," the Pope said.

### Love the Actual Church

During the outdoor Mass, attended by 80,000 people, the Pope said that the Church is not perfect but added that the priest must love "not only the Church of the past nor a Church that does not yet exist, but the concrete, actual Church, whose wrinkles and spots must be removed through his humble assistance."

During his visit to Notre Dame du Glarier in Sion, the Pope defended liturgical reforms.

"May you all be attentive in preparing worthy liturgical services, services in which the people actively participate according to the norms and the orientation of the church today, and thus be prepared, through beauty, contemplation and fervor, to enter the mystery of Christ," the Pope said to the priests, Religious and laity in the cathedral.

The Pope also delighted sports enthusiasts when he blessed their skier's flag and recalled his own mountain ventures.

The Pope departed from the Sion airport shortly before 5:00 p.m. He arrived at Rome two hours later, at the end of the 22nd foreign pastoral trip of his pontificate.

## POPE JOHN PAUL IN CANADA

### Human Life and Faith Issues

*(By Jerry Filteau, NC News Service)*
Pope John Paul II repeatedly condemned threats to human life and dignity as he toured Canada Sept. 9 to 20, 1984. Just as often, he called for a renewed faith as the most needed response to such threats.

Abortion, the arms race and stark issues of global economic injustice were the targets of ringing papal denunciations.

In messages directed more specifically to Catholics in Canada, Pope John Paul encouraged them to recover the roots of their faith, not to separate faith from their life in modern society, and to infuse Canadian culture with the values of faith.

He urged lay persons to be active witnesses to the faith in their lives and to attend Mass regularly and receive the sacraments of penance and the Eucharist frequently.

He asked nuns to live their life of consecration fully as a witness of the Gospel to the world.

Priests were called on to strengthen their people's sacramental life and formation in an adult faith.

Speaking to the nation's bishops in Ottawa, Canada's capital, on the last day, the Pope urged a broad range of pastoral ministry, asking them to teach and instill faith in their people.

### Itinerary

Pope John Paul's 12-day trip across Canada was one of the longest of his 23 trips abroad as Pope, matched only by his 1980 trip to Brazil.

Starting with three days in French-speaking Quebec Province, chiefly in Quebec City and Montreal, the Pope then moved on to the Maritime Provinces of Newfoundland, New Brunswick and Nova Scotia.

On Sept. 14, he began a long westward sweep that took him to Toronto, then into Manitoba, Alberta, the Northwest Territories and British Columbia near the shores of the Pacific. He flew back east Sept. 19 to spend a day and a half in Ottawa before returning to Rome.

Weather was a constant factor in the trip. Although the Pope arrived under clear, calm skies in Quebec, gray skies and rain plagued most of his first week.

Then came strong winds in Canada's central plains and western mountains. The bad weather brought good-natured papal jokes about rain as a sign of baptism and wind as the breath of the Holy Spirit.

There was no joking, however, when heavy fog in Fort Simpson, Northwest Territories, forced the Pope to cancel one of the focal points of his trip, a third and climactic meeting with Native Americans. Unable to land there and participate personally in the ceremonies, he was forced to tape his message of support for Native American cultures and their oft-denied political rights. As he left Canada, he said he had attached "great importance to this encounter" and hoped to meet with those he had missed on another occasion. He then joked that, as he was leaving Canada, he had just invited himself to a second visit.

### Seen by Hundreds of Thousands

Despite the frequent bad weather, hundreds of thousands of Canadians turned out to see the Pope, especially along motorcade routes from one event to the next and at the outdoor Masses he celebrated almost every day of the trip.

For the millions of Canadians who were unable to see the Pontiff in person, Canadian television carried several hours of live coverage daily, plus nightly wrap-ups, on French and English channels.

For many, especially children and the sick and handicapped, the highlight of the trip was a few personal words and a direct touch, kiss or caress from the Pope. At most major stops, he had at least one meeting with young people or with the sick and handicapped, so that he met with those groups more frequently in Canada than he had in any other country he had visited.

### Matters of Concern

**Ecumenism:** Ecumenism was another highlight of the papal trip. Representatives of other Christian churches were frequently guests of honor at papal events and met with the Pope, even though the events were not specifically ecumenical. At his one major ecumenical meeting, the Pope strongly encouraged the high degree of collaboration among Canadian churches and challenged them to do even more.

**Native Peoples:** In speeches at his two meetings with Native Americans and in the broadcast text of his cancelled meeting, the Pope strongly endorsed in principle their political efforts to redress past injustices. He backed their desires to regain control of their cultural heritage and their children's education, to be assured a sufficient land base and economic base for their development, and to achieve a greater degree of self-government.

The Pope also urged, however, that the native peoples work for those goals in a spirit of dialogue and love, with an eye toward the common good as well as their own good.

Twice he apologized for past insensitivities of the Church in dealing with native cultures, and de-

---

*The Pope began Sept. 10 with a visit to the Francois-Charon Center in Quebec. He spoke about the spiritual dimensions of suffering and appealed to more than 700 handicapped persons to offer their prayers and sufferings for him and the Church.*

clared that the Church is now seeking to rectify those past mistakes.

**Place Human Needs First:** One of the strongest papal messages on social justice issues came during the Sept. 12 visit to the small fishing town of Flatrock, Newfoundland, where Pope John Paul called for "a re-structuring of the economy" to place human needs before profits, questioned the concentration of power over food production and distribution in the hands of large corporations, and challenged the morality of policies that accept unemployment as a cost for economic goals. He also urged worker participation in employer decision-making through unions, cooperatives or "joint ownership or partnership," and suggested that new approaches are needed to international trade, food aid and Third World development.

**Challenge of Technology:** Earlier in Quebec and subsequently in Toronto, the Pope challenged presuppositions of a growing "technological mentality which challenges Gospel values."

Technology, he told leaders of Canadian churches in Toronto Sept. 14, runs the risk of becoming "an autonomous force" guided by "the logic or profit" and the "pursuit or maintenance of power.'

"United in the name of Christ, we need to ask critical questions and assert basic moral principles which have a bearing on technological development," the Pope said.

**Rich-Poor Gap:** In Edmonton, Alberta, Sept. 17, the Pope denounced the rich-poor gap between the world's developed North and underdeveloped South.

"This poor South will judge the rich North . . . those people who take these goods away from them, amassing to themselves the imperialistic monopoly of economic and political supremacy at the expense of others," he declared.

Near Winnipeg, Manitoba, the day before, the Pope had warned sharply against "the split between the Gospel and culture" — and on Sept. 18 in Vancouver, British Columbia, he linked the whole range of social issues he had been discussing as part of the "many threats to life which exist in our technological society."

**Total Respect for Life:** Calling abortion an "unspeakable crime" and "incalculable danger to all humanity," the Pope declared that "the sacredness of human life" must be proclaimed and defended against all onslaughts.

"If the weak are vulnerable from the time of conception, then they are vulnerable in old age, and they are vulnerable before the might of an aggressor and the power of nuclear weapons," he said.

"Life from conception onwards must be defended against all that attacks it, such as hunger and war; it must be healed of what weakens or dishonors it, such as disease and the abuse of alcohol and of drugs; it must be protected from what degrades it, such as violence, subhuman living conditions, unworthy working conditions."

Speaking to government officials and diplomats in Ottawa Sept. 19, the Pope struck out again at threats to human life and dignity. He said it is a lack of "the ethical dimensions" of society and culture which underlies the arms race, wars, abortion, experimentation on human embryos, starvation and malnourishment in the world. He said the ethical gap also underlies the lack of basic health care, ill effects of rapid urbanization and losses of human liberty, including freedom of religion.

### New Vision of Humanity Needed

"A new vision of humanity" is needed to "produce the political will" that can resolve such problems, the Pope said.

He climaxed his series of appeals for social justice at his final Mass in Canada, where, speaking on the theme of peace, he declared that "to build peace we must establish justice. . . . The way to justice and peace begins with the redemption of the world which Christ accomplished by the power of his cross and resurrection."

Twice during his trip, the Pope also linked respect for life and the dignity of the human being in an atmosphere of love with church teaching on the sacredness and indissolubility of marriage and on the need for the conjugal act to be open always to new life.

The papal attacks on social ills — from divorce, contraception and abortion to the arms race and a wide range of economic injustice and the cultural injustices to Native Americans — dominated media coverage of the papal trip.

Less easy for news media to explain, but of equal or greater importance for the Church's response to such issues, was the persistent papal teaching that the Gospel's message of love, redemption and the sacredness of the human person must infuse culture if that culture is to deal adequately with the ills that afflict its people.

**Appeal to Youths:** He urged young people in Montreal not to drop out of society out of discouragement, but instead to find the hope and courage in the Gospel to take an active role in society and try to change it.

Speaking to Catholic educators in Newfoundland, he defended Catholic schools and declared that education is not only a matter of "intellectual development" but of formation in "the meaning of life." It is impossible in this context, he said, to "ignore the centrality of God in the believer's outlook on life. . . . We cannot leave God at the schoolhouse door."

**Faith and Culture:** To various ethnic Canadian groups, the Pope stressed the value of retaining their cultural heritage and roots, insisting frequently on the role the Catholic faith has played in the development of those cultures.

Even as he apologized to Native Americans for past missionary mistakes, he stressed that the Gospel itself was not at fault. He told Indians in the Huronia region north of Toronto that the Gospel, "far from destroying their (native peoples') authentic values and customs, had the power to purify and uplift the cultural heritage which they had received."

It is only through the Gospel commandment of love, he told ethnically diverse Manitobans, that there can be an "atmosphere of respect for cultural diversity" and a "lasting and effective multicultural community."

## ADDRESS AT MEETING WITH BISHOPS

*(By Agostino Bono, NC News Service)*

In a Sept. 20 speech to Canada's bishops, Pope John Paul II reiterated church opposition to contraception and said that the conjugal act has the twofold purpose of expressing love and being open to procreation.

In a wide-ranging speech on the last day of his Canadian visit, the Pope also criticized the practice of abortion, asked priests to spend more time hearing private confessions, and praised the Canadian bishops for their social stands and ecumenical activities.

He also asked the bishops to link faith and culture, and to infuse Christian values in the economic, scientific and technological fields.

### Family Life and Sexual Morality

The Pope spoke strongly in defense of church teachings on family life issues which, he said, will not change "despite frequently passionate opinions to the contrary."

The Pope said the "dignity of family life" is being attacked by "a generalized tendency to hedonism." He cited widespread use of abortion, broken homes, divorce, people living together without being married, and use of contraception.

"Many have recourse to contraceptive means instead of respecting, in self-control and a mutually agreed effort, the double finality of the conjugal act: love and openness to life," the Pope said.

"There is without a doubt an ignorance of the theology of the body, of the magnificent plan of God for conjugal union, of the necessity of an asceticism in order to deepen a love which is truly worthy of the man and woman," he said.

"Despite frequently passionate opinions to the contrary, it is expected that the Church would help to save human love and respect for life," he added.

"Sex education, the preparation of young people for marriage and support for family life should be . top priorities here," the Pope said.

### Sacramental Ministry and Practice

Regarding confession, the Pope said "it is the right of each penitent" to be personally absolved after "personal confession of one's sins to a priest."

"In the last few years, this centuries-old practice of the Church has been neglected," he said.

"Help your priests to give priority to this ministry, after the Eucharist, but before many other activities which are less important," the Pope said.

He praised general absolution which leads Catholics "to celebrate together the mercy of God and the grace of reconciliation."

"But the communal renewal must never lead to abandoning the personal act of the penitent and personal absolution," he added.

The Pope exhorted Catholics to "frequent reception" of private confession and Communion.

"We pastors must do all we can to restore a sense of the Lord's Day and of the Eucharist, and to see that our liturgies are carefully prepared and characterized by the active participation of the faithful," he said in a country where the bishops estimate that less than 50 percent of the Catholics attend Mass weekly.

At a press conference following the meeting, Bishop John O'Mara of Thunder Bay, Ontario, said the Pope "was positive in his whole assessment of the Canadian Church."

"The Pope emphasized the formation of our people, the importance of the sacraments, and that there is always need for deeper conversion," said Bishop O'Mara.

### Social Teachings

Bishop Bernard Hubert of Saint-Jean-Longueuil said the bishops had a problem with the lack of acceptance of their social teachings.

The Pope's speech to the bishops strongly supported their social stands.

"The values of honesty, justice, the dignity of man and woman, work, aid, charity, social love and solidarity with the poor and the disinherited in the face of the new economic and cultural situations claim your attention," the Pope said.

"You seek to respond in faith to the new questions posed by the sciences, technology, and the sometimes disturbing developments of human biology. I understand and approve this preoccupation," he added.

Pope John Paul also praised the bishops' work "in the important field of ecumenism."

### Religious Freedom

The bishops also were asked to overcome a "conspiracy of silence" about abuse of religious freedom in many countries.

"This fundamental freedom of the practice of one's faith is abused every day in vast regions; it is a most grave violation which dishonors humanity," he said.

The Pope praised the courage of people facing religious persecution.

"It awakens Christians who are half asleep in an easy life, enjoying all the freedoms, and at times too worried about problems which are, all things considered, quite relative in comparison with this essential one," said Pope John Paul.

---

*The Pope met with two groups of young Canadians Sept. 11. First, he greeted individually many in a gathering of 2,600 near-teens. Afterwards, at Montreal's Olympic Stadium, he spent two hours with an enthusiastic, cheering throng of some 60,000.*

*He addressed questions many had written him before his visit. Then he urged them: "Have the courage to resist the dealers in deception who make capital of your hunger for happiness, and who make you pay dearly for a moment of artificial paradise."*

## FAITH MUST BE ACTIVE IN MODERN SOCIETY

*(By Agostino Bono, NC News)*

During his 12-day tour of Canada, Pope John Paul challenged Catholics to renew their Christian faith if they are to effectively influence the rapidly changing values of secularized, industrialized and pluralistic societies.

He delivered the message in a country where the bishops estimate that less than 50 per cent of Catholics attend Mass weekly, yet where the Church is an active social critic. He stressed that all church social actions must be rooted in an active faith.

This witness, he said, is vital for the infusing of Christian values in societies confronted with ethical challenges posed by technological and scientific advances.

The Pope issued a strong call for Christian ecumenism in raising ethical and moral questions about economics, technology, science and culture — especially in pluralistic nations where Christianity is only one of many voices seeking to influence society.

### New Missionary Effort

This challenge involves "a new missionary effort" which respects Canadian pluralism while making faith a key element of cultural development, the Pope said. "The Church is no longer alone in suggesting answers or attitudes; it sometimes feels on the margin of things; some go so far as to speak of its being 'in exile.' "

Yet the Church has much to offer society, especially now when rapid changes, especially technological changes, are causing a "crisis of values," the Pope said. The world is witnessing a "deep-seated process of changes, one which heralds the appearance of a new culture, of a new society."

"United in the name of Christ, we need to ask critical questions and assert basic moral principles which have a bearing on technological development," he told leaders of other Christian churches.

"The needs of the poor must take priority over the desires of the rich, the rights of the workers over the maximization of profits, the preservation of the environment over uncontrolled industrial expansion, production to meet social needs over production for military purposes," he said.

### Necessity of Faith

The Pope repeatedly praised the Canadian bishops for their stands on war and peace issues, the need for economic reforms and defense of Indian rights. Yet he warned that these positions, to be an effective Christian witness, must come from a deep faith.

"Efforts in sharing, justice and charity — which one can call 'social love' — run the risk of becoming simple philanthropy if they are not rooted in the spiritual energy to which I have made reference," he said in a Mass homily in Moncton, New Brunswick.

"Today it is necessary, in the first place, to revive the faith which, for a certain number, has been shaken and questioned," he added.

"Do not allow religious ignorance to stand side by side with the prestige of secular knowledge," the Pope said.

At a Sept. 20 meeting with the Catholic bishops, the Pope punctuated that theme: "All the ethical reflections and the questions which we can and must raise as pastors before the human, social and cultural problems of our times . . . are subordinated to the proclamation of salvation in Jesus Christ," he said.

### What's Expected of the Church

"If the world no longer dares to speak about God, it expects from the Church — and especially from the bishops and from the priests — a word which witnesses to God with strength and conviction, in a persuasive and adapted language, without ever reducing the greatness of the message to the expectation of the listeners," the Pope told the bishops.

During Mass homilies and talks to lay groups, he repeatedly stressed that faith must be active.

"Everyone is called to active participation in the public worship of God's great majesty," the Pope told one lay group.

Much of the Pope's stress on faith came from his concern that affluent western societies are replacing God with a yearning for possessions, said Bishop Remi De Roo, chairman of the Canadian Bishops' Social Affairs Committee.

"In democratic societies, there is a danger that freedom is associated with things we have," he said as he assessed the Pope's message during the Canadian visit.

Pope John Paul, on his last day in Canada, asked Catholics to look for inspiration to Catholics who hold on to their faith in the many countries where there is no religious freedom.

"Their courage in the faith helps in a mysterious way the whole Church. It awakens Christians who are half asleep in an easy life, enjoying all the freedoms, and at times too worried about problems which are, all things considered, quite relative in comparison with this essential one," the Pope said.

### CANADIAN NUN BEATIFIED

*The Holy Father beatified Mother Marie-Leonie Paradis Sept. 11 during a Mass attended by 300,000 people at Jarry Park, Montreal.*

*Blessed Leonie was born in 1840 in the Diocese of Saint Jean, Quebec, joined the Holy Cross Sisters in Indiana in 1870 and 10 years later founded the Little Sisters of the Holy Family.*

*Following is an excerpt from the Pope's homily.*

To this living record of saints and blessed which has been in this land for centuries, a new name is being added, that of Sister Marie-Leonie Paradis.

This woman is one of you, humble among the humble, and today she takes her place among those whom God has lifted up to glory. I am happy that, for the first time, this beatification is taking place in Canada, her homeland.

Born of simple, poor and virtuous parents, she soon grasped the beauty of religious life and committed herself to it through her vows with the Marist Order of the Holy Cross. She never once questioned that gift of God, not even during the difficult periods of community life in New York and in Indiana.

When she was appointed to serve in a college in Memramcook in Acadia, the richness of her religious life drew young women to her who also wanted to dedicate their lives to God. With them and thanks to the understanding of Bishop Larocque of Sherbrooke, she founded the Congregation of the Little Sisters of the Holy Family which is still thriving and is still very much appreciated.

### She Came To Serve

Never doubting her call, she often asked: "Lord, show me your ways," so that she would know the concrete form of her service in the Church. She found and proposed to her spiritual daughters a special kind of commitment: the service of educational institutions, seminaries and priests' homes.

She never shied away from the various forms of manual work which is the lot of so many people today and which held a special place in the Holy Family and in the life of Jesus of Nazareth himself. It was there that she saw the will of God for her life. It was in carrying out these tasks that she found God.

In the sacrifices which were required and which she offered in love, she experienced a profound joy and peace. She knew that she was one with Christ's fundamental attitude: he had "come not to be served, but to serve." She was filled with the greatness of the Eucharist and with the greatness of the priesthood at the service of the Eucharist. That is one of the secrets of her spiritual motivation.

Yes, God looked upon the holiness of his humble servant, Marie-Leonie, who had been inspired by Mary's openness and receptivity. And henceforth, from age to age, her congregation and the Church will call her blessed.

### The Gift and Contribution of Religious

This new beatification of a Canadian nun reminds us how much religious communities in every sector of ecclesial and social life have contributed to Canada. They have done this through contemplative prayer, education, assistance to the poor, work in hospitals and apostolic involvement of all kinds. It is a great gift. And if, today, the concrete forms of service can be different and evolve according to need, the religious vocation as such remains a marvelous gift of God.

It is a witness without parallel, a prophetic charism essential to the Church, not only because of the immeasurable services for which the sisters are responsible, but because, first of all, it signifies the gratuity of love in a spousal gift to Christ, in a total consecration to his redemptive work.

I would ask this of all the Christians gathered here:

Are the Canadian people still able to appreciate this gift?

Do they help religious women to find and to strengthen their vocation?

And you, dear Sisters, do you appreciate the greatness of the call of God and the fundamentally evangelical lifestyle which corresponds to that gift?

### Forms of Service by Lay People

I also address myself in this Mass to all the Christian people of Montreal, Quebec and Canada. Brothers and sisters: seek the Lord; seek his will; listen to the one who calls each of you by name in order to entrust a mission in you, so that you can bear his light within the Church and society.

You are the Christian laity, baptized and confirmed. And you wish to live as sons and daughters of God.

In the body of the Church there are many charism, many forms of activity for developing your talents in the service of others. God sends you to serve your brothers and sisters who are suffering, in distress, in search of him. By our prayers and deeds each day, may the love of God, the justice of God and hope find their place in the earthly city, in all your places of work, leisure and research. Having had the experience of God yourselves, contribute to building a fraternal world which is open to God.

I address this message to all people; but, since I am beatifying a woman today, I address it especially to women.

### The Call of Women

Like all the baptized, you are called to holiness in order to sanctify the world according to your vocation in the plan of God, who created humanity as "man and woman." Together with men, bring into the heart of your families, bring into the heart of this society, the human and Christian capacities with which God has endowed your femininity and which you will be able to develop according to your rights and duties to the very degree that you are united with Christ, the source of holiness.

The Lord counts on you so that human relations may be permeated with the love that God desires. The ways of accomplishing this service may differ from that chosen by Blessed Sister Marie-Leonie. But — in the most evangelical sense which transcends the opinions of this world — it is always a question of service, which is indispensable for humanity and the Church.

---

*The idea that a faith-infused culture is needed to deal with contemporary problems was one of the main themes of Pope John Paul's first eight days in Canada.*

*"To detach culture from its link to the Gospel commandment of love would be to make impossible the multicultural interplay which is characteristic of Canada," he said.*

# THE HISPANIC PRESENCE: CHALLENGE AND COMMITMENT

## Pastoral Letter of the U.S. Bishops

*Following are excerpts from the pastoral letter on Hispanic ministry approved by the United States hierarchy in November, 1983. Copyright© 1984 by the National Conference of Catholic Bishops and the U.S. Catholic Conference, it was released Jan. 10.*

*These excerpts are from the text circulated by the NC Documentary Service, Origins, Jan. 19, 1984 (Vol. 13, No. 32).*

### A CALL TO HISPANIC MINISTRY

At this moment of grace we recognize the Hispanic community among us as a blessing from God. We call upon all persons of good faith to share our vision of the special gifts which Hispanics bring to the body of Christ, his pilgrim Church on earth (1 Cor. 12:12-13).

Hispanics exemplify and cherish values central to the service of Church and society. Among these are:

• profound respect for the dignity of each person, reflecting the example of Christ in the Gospels;

• deep and reverential love for family life, where the entire extended family discovers its roots, its identity and its strength;

• a marvelous sense of community that celebrates life through "fiesta";

• loving appreciation for God's gift of life and an understanding of time which allows one to savor that gift;

• authentic and consistent devotion to Mary, the Mother of God.

The pastoral needs of Hispanic Catholics are indeed great; although their faith is deep and strong, it is being challenged and eroded by steady social pressures to assimilate. Yet the history, culture and spirituality animating their lively faith deserve to be known, shared and reinforced by us all. Their past and present contributions to the faith life of the Church deserve appreciation and recognition.

Let us work closely together in creating pastoral visions and strategies which, drawing upon a memorable past, are made new by the creative hands of the present.

### URGENT PASTORAL IMPLICATIONS

We urge all U.S. Catholics to explore creative possibilities for responding innovatively, flexibly and immediately to the Hispanic presence. Hispanics and non-Hispanics should work together, teach and learn from one another, and together evangelize in the fullest and broadest sense. Non-Hispanic clergy — especially Religious, priests and bishops who have been at the forefront of the Hispanic apostolates — are needed more than ever to serve with the Hispanic people.

### The Church's Mission and the Hispanic Presence

From an ecclesial perspective, evangelization, which is the Church's central mission and purpose, consists not just in isolated calls to individual conversion but in an invitation to join the People of God. This is reflected in the Hispanic experience of evangelization, which includes an important communitarian element expressed in an integral or "holistic" vision of faith and pastoral activity carried out in community.

This experience is summed up in the concept of the *pastoral de conjunto*, a pastoral focus and approach to action arising from reflection among the agents of evangelization.

**A. Liturgy:** Universal in form, our Church respects and fosters the spiritual adornments and gifts of the various races and peoples in its liturgical life. As applied to the Hispanic presence, this requires making provision for Spanish and bilingual worship according to the traditions and customs of the people being served.

**B. Renewal of Preaching:** The recasting and proclamation of the word in powerful, new, liberating images are unavoidable challenges for Hispanic ministry.

**C. Catechesis:** Like initial evangelization, catechesis must start where the hearer of the Gospel is. In the case of Hispanics, this suggests not merely the use of Spanish but also an active dialogue with their culture and their needs. Since religious education is a lifelong process for the individual, parishes should provide an atmosphere for catechesis which in every respect encourages the ongoing formation of adults as well as children. Such efforts will match the effectiveness of grade-level programs for children among the English-speaking and explore new methods in adult catechesis.

**D. Vocation and Formation of Lay Ministers:** Adequate training must have a high priority in Hispanic ministry. In planning such training the goals of enhancing pluralism and catholicity will suggest the means. Formation should aim to incorporate the knowledge and practical experience necessary to minister effectively, while also fostering a serious commitment of service.

**E. Vocations to Priestly, Religious Ministries:** The scarcity of Hispanic priests, religious sisters, brothers and permanent deacons is one of the most serious problems facing the Church in the United States.

We encourage seminaries to provide courses in Spanish, Hispanic culture and religiosity, and Hispanic pastoral ministry for seminarians, priests, Religious, permanent deacons and all pastoral ministers.

We commit ourselves to fostering Hispanic vocations. Bishops, priests, Religious and laity now must aggressively encourage Hispanic youth to consider the priestly or religious vocation. We call upon Hispanic parents to present the life and work of a priest or Religious as a highly desirable vocation for their children and to take rightful pride in having a son or daughter serve the Church in this way. Without their strong support, the Church will not have the number of Hispanic priests and Religious needed to serve their communities.

**F. Catholic Education:** Catholic educators in the United States . . . must turn their skills to responding to the educational needs of Hispanics.

We recommend adaptations which respond adequately to the Hispanic presence in our schools. Curricula should provide opportunities for bilingual education; teachers should be familiar with the Spanish language and should respect and understand Hispanic culture and religious expression. At the same time, care must be taken to ensure that bilingual education does not impede or unduly delay entrance into the political, socio-economic and religious mainstream because of inability to communicate well in the prevalent language.

The Church must also become an advocate for the many young Hispanics who attend public schools, doing all it can to ensure that provision is made for their needs. Particular attention should be given to those who have dropped out of school, whether Catholic or public, and who need remedial education or assistance in developing technical skills.

**G. Communications:** For the most part, the church press and electronic media lag in the area of Hispanic ministry.

This suggests the need for greater efforts toward planned and systematic programming and regular coverage of issues relevant to the Hispanic community.

**H. Effective Ecumenism:** The Lord Jesus prayed for the unity of his followers; yet the division of the churches is a major obstacle to evangelization. This is underlined in the United States by instances of active proselytizing among Hispanics carried on in an anti-ecumenical manner by Protestant sects. A variety of fundamentalist groups divide Hispanics and their families with their preaching, which reflects an anti-Catholic spirit hardly emanating from the Gospel of Jesus Christ.

Our response as Catholics is not to attack or disparage brothers and sisters of other Christian traditions, but to live the Gospel more authentically in order to present the Catholic Church as the fullness of Christianity and thus nourish the faith of our Hispanic peoples. Other Christian churches have been part of the history of salvation. Prayer, dialogue and partnership in efforts of common concern remain high on the Catholic agenda. In the Hispanic context, however, the Catholic Church and its tradition have played the major historical role of inculturation of the Gospel; the Church is committed to continuing this mission.

**I. Hispanic Youth:** Hispanic youths and young adults with leadership qualities must be offered opportunities for religious education, biblical studies, catechesis and special training, so that their vocations to serve the Church will flourish. Such programs should take into account the fact that these youths will develop best in familiar, warm environments.

**J. Family:** The tradition of commitment to family is one of the distinguishing marks of Hispanic culture. Although there are variations among Mexican-Americans, Puerto Ricans, Cubans and other

Hispanics, there are shared family values and culture attributes among all Hispanics.

In our pastoral planning . . . we must not take for granted the continued strength and unity of the Catholic Hispanic family. Hispanic nuclear families are already experiencing the same social pressures faced by other groups. The unity of the Hispanic family is threatened in particular by the uprooting caused by mobility, especially from a rural to an urban lifestyle and from Latin American countries to our own; by poverty, which a high proportion of Hispanic families endure; and by pressures engendered by the process of assimilation, which often leads to generation gaps within the family and identity crises in young people.

There is an urgent need for pastoral ministries that will prepare our people well for married life, for parenthood and for family counseling and religious education. We make a special plea for measures to assist Hispanic families which are "hurting," as well as the divorced, the separated, single parents and victims of parental or spouse abuse.

**K. Migrants:** As noted, Hispanics are highly mobile and are found in both urban and rural settings. As a result, they tend to escape the attention and care of the urban church. This underlines the need for adaptations in pastoral care, particularly in the case of migrant workers.

Abuses of farmworkers are notorious, yet they continue to go unrelieved. Conditions are worsening in many regions. Men and women are demoralized to the point where the riches of Hispanic culture, strong family ties and the profound faith-life are sometimes lost. We denounce the treatment of migrants as commodities — cheap labor — rather than persons. We urge others to do the same. Economic conditions often require children to be part of the labor force. Along with the other problems associated with mobility, their education suffers. In the same vein, we find deplorable the abuse of the rights of undocumented workers. All this makes it imperative for the Church to support the right of migrant farmworkers to organize for the purpose of collective bargaining.

Experience in the Hispanic apostolate suggests the need for mobile missionary teams and various forms of itinerant ministries. Dioceses and parishes in the path of migrant streams also have a responsibility to support this work and coordinate the efforts of sending and receiving dioceses.

**L. Social Justice and Social Action:** The integral evangelization described earlier as the central focus of the pastoral strategy we envisage will be incomplete without an active component of social doctrine and action.

We call attention to those social concerns which most directly affect the Hispanic community, among them: voting rights, discrimination, immigration rights, the status of farmworkers, bilingualism and pluralism. These are social justice issues of paramount importance to ministry with Hispanics and to the entire Church.

As it engages in social teaching, the Church embraces the quest for justice as an eminently religious task. Persons engaged in this endeavor must be involved with, informed by and increasingly led by those who know from experience the paradoxical blessings of poverty, prejudice and unfairness. Accordingly, we urge Hispanics to increase their role in social action and non-Hispanics increasingly to seek out Hispanics in a true partnership.

**M. Prejudice and Racism:** Within our memory, Hispanics in this country have experienced cruel prejudice. So extensive has it been in some areas that they have been denied basic human and civil rights. Even today Hispanics, blacks, the recent Southeast Asian refugees and native Americans continue to suffer from such dehumanizing treatment — treatment which makes us aware that the sin of racism lingers in our society. Despite great strides in eliminating racial prejudice, both in our country and in our Church there remains an urgent need for continued purification and reconciliation. It is particularly disheartening to know that some Catholics hold strong prejudices against Hispanics and others, and deny them the respect and love due their God-given human dignity.     This is evident even in some parish communities where one finds a reluctance among some non-Hispanics to serve with Hispanics or to socialize with them at parochial events. We appeal to those with this unchristian attitude to examine their behavior in the light of Jesus' commandment of love and to accept their Hispanic brothers and sisters as full partners in the work and life of their parishes.

We urge those who employ Hispanics to provide them with safe and decent working conditions and to pay them salaries which enable them to provide adequately for their families. The inhuman condition of pervasive poverty forced on many Hispanics is at the root of many social problems in their lives. Decent working conditions and adequate salaries are required by justice and basic fairness.

**N. Ties with Latin America:** Hispanics in our midst are an as-yet untapped resource as a cultural bridge between North and South in the Americas. The wellspring of Hispanic culture and faith is historically and geographically located in Latin America. For this reason, a dynamic response to the Hispanic presence in the United States will necessarily entail an ever greater undrstanding of and linkage with Latin American society and church.

**O. Popular Catholicism:** Hispanic spirituality is an example of how deeply Christianity can permeate the roots of a culture. In the course of almost 500 years in the Americas, Hispanic people have learned to express their faith in prayer forms and traditions that were begun and encouraged by missionaries and passed from one generation to the next.

Hispanic spirituality places strong emphasis on the humanity of Jesus, especially when he appears weak and suffering, as in the crib and in his passion and death. This spirituality relates well to all that is symbolic in Catholicism: ritual, statues and images, holy places and gestures. It is also a strongly devotional spirituality. The Blessed Virgin Mary, especially under the titles of Our Lady of Guadalupe (Mexico), Our Lady of Providence (Puerto Rico) and Our Lady of Charity (Cuba), occupies a privileged place in Hispanic popular piety.

A closer dialogue is needed between popular and official practice, lest the former lose the guidance of the Gospel and the latter lose the active participation of the unsophisticated and the poorest among the faithful. An ecclesial life vibrant with a profound sense of the transcendent, such as is found in Hispanic popular Catholicism, can also be a remarkable witness to the more secularized members of our society.

**P. Comunidades Eclesiales de Base:** Hispanics in the Americas have made few contributions to the Church more significant than the *comunidades eclesiales de base* (basic ecclesial communities). The small community has appeared on the scene as a ray of hope in dealing with dehumanizing situations that can destroy people and weaken faith. A revitalized sense of fellowship fills the Church in Latin America, Africa, Europe and Asia with pastoral joy and hope. The Synod of Bishops in 1974 witnessed an outpouring of such hope from Latin American pastors, who saw in *comunidades eclesiales de base* a source of renewal in the Church. Since these communities are of proven benefit of the Church, we highly encourge their development.

The *comunidad eclesial de base* is neither a discussion or study group nor a parish. It is "the first and fundamental ecclesiastical nucleus, which on its own level must make itself responsible for the richness and expansion of the faith, as well as of the worship of which it is an expression." It should be an expression of a Church that liberates from personal and structural sin; it should be a small community with personal relationships; it should form part of a process of integral evangelization; and it should be in communion with other levels of the Church. The role of the parish, in particular, is to facilitate, coordinate and multiply the *comunidades eclesiales de base* within its boundaries and territories. The parish should be a community of communities. The ideal *comunidad eclesial de base* is a living community of Christians whose active involvement in every aspect of life is nourished by profound commitment to the Gospel.

**Q. Other Possibilities:** We urge U.S. Catholics to use their best creative talents to go boldly beyond these first steps, which are merely prerequisites for effective action.

One opportunity for creative action arises from the presence of Hispanics in the U.S. military. We encourage the Military Vicariate to explore new means of integral evangelization, with particular attention to this Hispanic presence.

Similarly, as those in prison ministry know, incarcerated Hispanics are in dire need of attention. There is a need for pastoral ministers to assist in this area.

Among Hispanics there are also handicapped persons whose special needs are compounded by many of the problems we have described. According to estimates, nearly two million Hispanic Catholics have one or more disabling conditions, including blindness, deafness, mental retardation, learning disabilities and orthopedic impairments. There is a serious need for programs of ministry which encourage participation by disabled Hispanic Catholics.

## STATEMENT OF COMMITMENT

While conscious of the many ethnic and racial groups who call legitmately upon our services and resources, and grateful for the present significant, if limited, outreach to the Hispanic people of the United States, we commit ourselves and our pastor associates to respond to the call to Hispanic ministry. Awareness of the good works of the past and present must not make us slow to read the signs of the times. Our preparations today will make it easier to carry out tomorrow's task.

**Commitment to Catholicity:** The universal character of the Church involves both pluralism and unity.

The gospel teaching that no one is a stranger in the Church is timeless.

Our commitment to Hispanic ministry therefore leads us, as teachers, to invite all Catholics to adopt a more welcoming attitude toward others. Hispanics, whose presence in this land is antedated only by that of native Americans, are called to welcome their brothers and sisters, the descendants of other European immigrants. Similarly, the latter are called to embrace Hispanic newcomers from Latin America. Where all are freed from attitudes of cultural or ethnic dominance, the gifts of all will enrich the Church and give witness to the Gospel of Jesus Christ.

**Commitment to Respond to Temporal Needs:** We . . . pledge to raise our voices and go on raising them, as leaders in defense of the human dignity of Hispanics. We remind our pastoral associates that their work includes the effort to gain for Hispanics participation in the benefits of our society. We call all U.S. Catholics to work not just for Hispanics but with them, in order to secure their empowerment in our democracy and the political participation which is their right and duty. In this way, we deepen our preferential option for the poor which, according to Jesus' example and the Church's tradition, must always be a hallmark of our apostolate.

**Commitment of Resources:** Also part of our commitment, as shepherds and stewards of the common resources of the Church, is the pledge to harness these resources for Hispanic ministry.

## Convocation for the III Encuentro

We ask our Hispanic peoples to raise their prophetic voices to us once again, as they did in 1972 and 1977, in a *III Encuentro Nacional Hispano de Pastoral* so that together we can face our responsibilities well. We call for the launching of an *encuentro* process, from *comunidades eclesiales de base* and parishes, to dioceses and regions, and to the national level, culminating in a gathering of representatives in Washington, D.C. in August, 1985.

## Conclusion

As we continue our pilgrimage together with our Hispanic brothers and sisters, we frame our commitment in the same spirit as our brother bishops of Latin America.

• We call upon the entire Catholic Church in the United States — laity, Religious, deacons and priests — to join us in our pledge to respond to the presence of our Hispanic brothers and sisters.

• We honor and rejoice in the work that has taken place before us, and we pledge our best efforts to do even better henceforth.

• We envisage a new era of ministry with Hispanics, enriched by the gifts of creativity placed providentially before us and by the Spirit of Pentecost, who calls us to unity, to renewal and to meeting the prophetic challenge posed by the Hispanic presence.

• We commit ourselves to engage in a thorough, conscientious and continuing pastoral effort to enhance the catholicity of the Church and the dignity of all its members.

• We look hopefully to the greater blessings Hispanics can bring to our local churches.

## WHAT WE HAVE SEEN AND HEARD: PASTORAL LETTER OF BLACK BISHOPS

*This NC News account was circulated before the text of the letter became generally available.*

The black community in the Catholic Church in the United States has come of age but racism remains the major obstacle to evangelization, said the 10 black Catholic bishops of the U.S. in their first pastoral letter.

The letter, entitled "What We Have Seen and Heard", said racism "still festers within our Church as within our society. This stain of racism . . . is a scandal to many, but for us it must be the opportunity to work for the Church's renewal as part of our task of evangelization."

The bishops said the time has come to proclaim the richness of the heritage of American black Catholics and to accept the challenge to "share the gift of our blackness with the Church in the United States."

They said, however, that the contribution of blacks and other minorities is hindered by the fact that they still remain absent from many aspects of Catholic life and are only meagerly represented on the decision-making level.

The demand of black Catholics for recognition and leadership roles in the task of evangelization is not a call for separatism but "a pledge of our commitment to the Church and to share in her witnessing to the love of Christ," the bishops said.

### Evangelization and Social Justice

They linked evangelization to social justice. "Our own history has taught us that preaching to the poor and to those who suffer injustice without concern for their plight and the systemic cause of their plight is to trivialize the Gospel and mock the Cross. To preach to the powerful without denouncing oppression is to promise Easter without Calvary, forgiveness without conversion, and healing without cleansing the wound."

Numerous opportunities for evangelization exist within the black community, according to the bishops. They called attention to the need to encourage vocations, saying the duty lies especially with black priests and Religious who have contact with youth to serve as role models.

They urged recruitment of permanent deacons. "Many permanent deacons continue to pursue their occupations in the workaday world and in family life. This gives them access to opportunities for evangelization in places where a priest or Religious might find entry difficult. This is particularly true for black deacons in the black community where many of the clergy are not black."

### Responsibility of Lay Persons

The work of evangelization is also the responsibility of the laity. Their role must be better understood, and "that which is understood in theory must lead to practical plans for action and even structural change."

The Catholic school has been, and remains, one of the chief vehicles of evangelization within the black community, the bishops said, but inner-city schools continue to disappear and black vocational recruitment lacks sufficient support.

The bishops called for programs for youth because "black youth are especially vulnerable in our modern society. Today's youth in the black community undergo many pressures. Especially in our urban areas — where disillusionment and despair, desires and drugs, passion and poverty entrap the young. Adults and mature youths dedicated to Christ are needed to counsel, to inspire and to motivate those whom Jesus loved and placed first in his kingdom."

The black family is assailed on all sides, the bishops said. They called abortion another form of subjugation and urged more day care centers, jobs, good schools "and all else that a just society should offer its people."

The letter was dated September 9, the feast day of St. Peter Claver, the 17th century Spanish Jesuit missionary to black slaves in South America.

The letter was signed by Bishop Joseph L. Howze of Biloxi and Auxiliary Bishops: James P. Lyke of Cleveland, Harold R. Perry of New Orleans, Eugene A. Marino of Washington, Joseph A. Francis of Newark, N.J.; Emerson J. Moore of New York; Moses B. Anderson of Detroit, Walton D. Gregory of Chicago, J. Terry Steib of St. Louis; and John H. Ricard of Baltimore.

*Contributing to the development of the contents of the pastoral letter were the experiences of the bishops themselves. These experiences reflected those of individuals and groups like the National Office for Black Catholics and other associations.*

## THEOLOGY OF LIBERATION

*Following are excerpts from an Instruction on Certain Aspects of the "Theology of Liberation" released by the Congregation for the Doctrine of the Faith Sept. 3, 1984, with the approval of Pope John Paul. Several subheads and lead lines have been added. The text was circulated by the NC Documentary Service, Origins, Sept. 13, 1984 (Vol. 14, No. 13).*

*A summary of the instruction follows these excerpts.*

Liberation is first and foremost liberation from the radical slavery of sin. Its end and its goal is the freedom of the children of God, which is the gift of grace. As a logical consequence, it calls for freedom from many different kinds of slavery in the cultural, economic, social and political spheres, all of which derive ultimately from sin and so often prevent people from living in a manner befitting their dignity. To discern clearly what is fundamental to this issue and what is a byproduct of it, is an indispensable condition for any theological reflection on liberation.

### Purpose

The present instruction has a limited and precise purpose: to draw the attention of pastors, theologians and all the faithful to the deviations and risks of deviation, damaging to the faith and to Christian living, that are brought about by certain forms of liberation theology which use, in an insufficiently

critical manner, concepts borrowed from various currents of Marxist thought.

This warning should in no way be interpreted as a disavowal of all those who want to respond generously and with an authentic evangelical spirit to the "preferential option for the poor." It should not at all serve as an excuse for those who maintain an attitude of neutrality and indifference in the face of the tragic and pressing problems of human misery and injustice. It is, on the contrary, dictated by the certitude that the serious ideological deviations which it points out tend inevitably to betray the cause of the poor.

### LIBERATION: A CHRISTIAN THEME

The expression, "theology of liberation," refers first of all to a special concern for the poor and the victims of oppression, which in turn begets a commitment to justice. Starting with this approach, we can distinguish several often contradictory ways of understanding the Christian meaning of poverty and the type of commitment to justice which it requires. As with all movements of ideas, the "theologies of liberation" present diverse theological positions. Their doctrinal frontiers are badly defined.

### BIBLICAL FOUNDATIONS

New Testament revelation teaches us that sin is the greatest evil, since it strikes man in the heart of his personality. The first liberation, to which all others must make reference, is that from sin.

Unquestionably, it is to stress the radical character of the deliverance brought by Christ and offered to all, be they politically free or slaves, that the New Testament does not require some change in the political or social condition as a prerequisite for entrance into this freedom. However, the Letter to Philemon shows that the new freedom procured by the grace of Christ should necessarily have effects on the social level.

**"Social Sin":** Consequently, the full ambit of sin, whose first effect is to introduce disorder into the relationship between God and man, cannot be restricted to "social sin." The truth is that only a correct doctrine of sin will permit us to insist on the gravity of its social effects.

Nor can one localize evil principally or uniquely in bad social, political or economic "structures" as though all other evils came from them so that the creation of the "new man" would depend on the establishment of different economic and sociopolitical structures. To be sure, there are structures which are evil and which cause evil and which we must have the courage to change. Structures, whether they are good or bad, are the result of man's actions, and so are consequences more than causes. The root of evil, then, lies in free and responsible persons who have to be converted by the grace of Jesus Christ in order to live and act as new creatures in the love of neighbor and in the effective search for justice, self-control and the exercise of virtue.

To demand, first of all, a radical revolution in social relations and then to criticize the search for personal perfection is to set out on a road which leads to the denial of the meaning of the person and his transcendence, and to destroy ethics and its foundation, which is the absolute character of the distinction between good and evil. Moreover, since charity is the principle of authentic perfection, that perfection cannot be conceived without an openness to others and a spirit of service.

The Church's magisterium (teaching authority) has frequently expressed her desire to awaken Christian consciences to a sense of justice, social responsibility and solidarity with the poor and the oppressed, and to highlight the present urgency of the doctrine and imperatives contained in Revelation.

**Pillars of Authentic Liberation:** Following Paul VI, who had insisted on the distinctive character of the Gospel message, a character which is of divine origin, John Paul II, in his address at Puebla, recalled the three pillars upon which any authentic theology of liberation will rest: truth about Jesus Christ, truth about the Church and truth about mankind.

## NEW INTERPRETATION OF CHRISTIANITY

Faced with the urgency of sharing bread, some are tempted to put evangelization into parentheses, as it were, and postpone it until tomorrow: first the bread, then the word of the Lord. It is a fatal error to separate these two and even worse to oppose the one to the other. In fact, the Christian perspective naturally shows they have a great deal to do with one another.

To some it even seems that the necessary struggle for human justice and freedom in the economic and political sense constitutes the whole essence of salvation. For them, the Gospel is reduced to a purely earthly gospel.

The different theologies of liberation are situated between the preferential option for the poor forcefully reaffirmed without ambiguity after Medellin at the conference of Puebla on the one hand, and the temptation to reduce the Gospel to an earthly gospel on the other.

We noted above that an authentic theology of liberation will be one which is rooted in the word of God, correctly interpreted.

But, from a descriptive standpoint, it helps to speak of theologies of liberation, since the expression embraces a number of theological positions or even sometimes ideological ones, which are not simply different but more often incompatible with one another.

**Developments under Discussion:** In this present document, we will only be discussing developments of that current of thought which, under the name, "theology of liberation," proposes a novel interpretation of both the content of faith and of Christian existence which seriously departs from the faith of the church and, in fact, actually constitutes a practical negation.

Concepts uncritically borrowed from Marxist ideology and recourse to theses of a biblical hermeneutic marked by rationalism are at the basis of the new interpretation which is corrupting whatever was authentic in the generous initial commitment on behalf of the poor.

## MARXIST ANALYSIS

The thought of Marx is such a global vision of reality that all data received from observation and analysis are brought together in a philosophical and ideological structure, which predetermines the significance and importance to be attached to them. The ideological principles come prior to the study of the social reality and are presupposed in it. Thus, no separation of the parts of this epistemologically unique complex is possible. If one tries to take only one part, say, the analysis, one ends up having to accept the entire ideology. That is why it is not uncommon for the ideological aspect to be predominant among the things which the "theologians of liberation" borrow from Marxist authors.

The warning of Paul VI remains fully valid today: Marxism as it is actually lived out poses many distinct aspects and questions for Christians to reflect upon and act on. However, it would be "illusory and dangerous to ignore the intimate bond which radically unites them, and to accept elements of the Marxist analysis without recognizing its connections with the ideology, or to enter into the practice of class struggle and of its Marxist interpretation while failing to see the kind of totalitarian society to which this process slowly leads."

## INCOMPATIBLE TENETS

To the extent that they remain fully Marxist,

these currents continue to be based on certain fundamental tenets which are not compatible with the Christian conception of humanity and society. In this context certain formulas are not neutral, but keep the meaning they had in the original Marxist doctrine. This is the case with the "class struggle." This expression remains pregnant with the interpretation that Marx gave it, so it cannot be taken as the equivalent of "severe social conflict," in an empirical sense. Those who use similar formulas, while claiming to keep only certain elements of the Marxist analysis and yet to reject this analysis taken as a whole, maintain at the very least a serious confusion in the minds of their readers.

Let us recall the fact that atheism and the denial of the human person, his liberty and his rights, are at the core of Marxist theory. This theory, then, contains errors which directly threaten the truths of the faith regarding the eternal destiny of individual persons. Moreover, to attempt to integrate into theology an analysis whose criterion of interpretation depends on this atheistic conception is to involve oneself in terrible contradictions. What is more, this misunderstanding of the spiritual nature of the person leads to a total subordination of the person to the collectivity and thus to the denial of the principles of a social and political life which is in keeping with human dignity.

### Ideological Core

This all-embracing conception thus imposes its logic and leads the "theologies of liberation" to accept a series of positions which are incompatible with the Christian vision of humanity. In fact, the ideological core borrowed from Marxism which we are referring to exercises the function of a determining principle. It has this role in virtue of its being described as "scientific," that is to say, true of necessity.

In this core we can distinguish several components.

According to the logic of Marxist thought, the "analysis" is inseparable from the praxis and from the conception of history to which this praxis is linked. The analysis is for the Marxist an instrument of criticism, and criticism is only one stage in the revolutionary struggle. This struggle is that of the proletarian class, invested with its mission in history.

Consequently, for the Marxist, only those who engage in the struggle can work out the analysis correctly.

The only true consciousness, then, is the partisan consciousness. There is no truth, they pretend, except in and through the partisan praxis.

**Class Struggle:** For the Marxist, the praxis and the truth that comes from it are partisan praxis and truth because the fundamental structure of history is characterized by class struggle. There follows, then, the objective necessity to enter into the class struggle, which is the dialectical opposite of the relationship of exploitation, which is being condemned. For the Marxist, the truth is a truth of class: There is no truth but the truth in the struggle of the revolutionary class.

**Fundamental Law:** The fundamental law of history, which is the law of the class struggle, implies that society is founded on violence. To the violence which consititutes the relationship of the domination of the rich over the poor, there corresponds the counterviolence of the revolution, by means of which this domination will be reversed.

The class struggle is presented as an objective, necessary law. Upon entering this process on behalf of the oppressed, one "makes" truth, one acts "scientifically." Consequently, the conception of the truth goes hand in hand with the affirmation of necessary violence, and so, of a political amorality. Within this perspective, any reference to ethical requirements calling for courageous and radical institutional and structural reforms makes no sense.

The fundamental law of class struggle has a global and universal character. It is reflected in all the spheres of existence: religious, ethical, cultural and institutional.

The very nature of ethics is radically called into question because of the borrowing of these theses from Marxism. In fact, it is the transcendent character of the distinction between good and evil, the principle of morality, which is implicitly denied in the perspective of the class struggle.

### THEOLOGICAL APPLICATION OF THIS CORE

The positions here in question are often brought out explicitly in certain of the writings of "theologians of liberation." In others, they follow logically from their premises. In addition, they are presupposed in certain liturgical practices, as for example a "eucharist" transformed into a celebration of the people in struggle, even though the persons who participate in these practices may not be fully conscious of it. We are facing, therefore, a real system, even if some hesitate to follow the logic to its conclusion. As such, this system is a perversion of the Christian message as God entrusted it to his Church. This message in its entirety finds itself then called into question by the "theologies of liberation."

**Class Struggle Divides the Church:** It is not the fact of social stratification with all its inequity and injustice, but the theory of class struggle as the fundamental law of history which has been accepted by these "theologies of liberation" as a principle. The conclusion is drawn that the class struggle thus understood divides the Church herself, and that in light of this struggle even ecclesial realities must be judged.

The claim is even made that it would maintain an illusion with bad faith to propose that love in its universality can conquer what is the primary structural law of capitalism.

According to this conception, the class struggle is the driving force of history. History thus becomes a central notion. It will be affirmed that God himself makes history. It will be added that there is only one history, one in which the distinction between the history of salvation and profane history is no longer necessary.

**Temporal Messianism:** Thus there is a tendency to identify the kingdom of God and its growth with the human liberation movement and to make history itself the subject of its own development, as a process of the self-redemption of man by means of the class struggle.

Along these lines, some go so far as to identify God himself with history and to define faith as "fidelity to history," which means adhering to a political policy which is suited to the growth of humanity, conceived of as a purely temporal messianism.

As a consequence, faith, hope and charity are given a new content: They become "fidelity to history," "confidence in the future" and "option for the poor." This is tantamount to saying they have been emptied of their theological reality.

A radical politicization of faith's affirmations and of theological judgments follows inevitably from this new conception.

Every affirmation of faith or of theology is subordinated to a political criterion which in turn depends on the class struggle, the driving force of history.

As a result, participation in the class struggle is presented as a requirement of charity itself. The desire to love everyone here and now, despite his class, and to go out to meet him with the non-violent means of dialogue and persuasion, is denounced as counterproductive and opposed to love.

As far as the Church is concerned, this system would see her only as a reality interior to history, herself subject to those laws which are supposed to govern the development of history in its immanence. The Church, the gift of God and mystery of faith, is emptied of any specific reality by this reductionism. At the same time, it is disputed that the participation of Christians who belong to opposing classes at the same eucharistic table still makes any sense.

**Church of the Class:** But the "theologies of liberation," which reserve credit for restoring to a place of honor the great texts of the prophets and of the Gospel in defense of the poor, go on to a disastrous confusion between the poor of the Scripture and the proletariat of Marx. In this way they pervert the Christian meaning of the poor, and they transform the fight for the rights of the poor into a class fight within the ideological perspective of the class struggle. For them, the "church of the poor" signifies the church of the class which has become aware of the requirements of the revolutionary struggle as a step toward liberation and which celebrates this liberation in its liturgy.

But the "theologies of liberation" of which we are speaking mean by church of the people a church of the class, a church of the oppressed people whom it is necessary to "conscientize" in the light of the organized struggle for freedom. For some, the people, thus understood, even become the object of faith.

**Challenge to the Nature of the Church:** Building on such a conception of the church of the people, a critique of the very structures of the Church is developed. It is not simply the case of fraternal correction of pastors of the Church whose behavior does not reflect the evangelical spirit of service and is linked to old-fashioned signs of authority which scandalize the poor. It has to do with a challenge to the sacramental and hierarchical structure of the Church, which was willed by the Lord himself. There is a denunciation of members of the hierarchy and the magisterium as objective representatives of the ruling class which has to be opposed. Theologically, this position means that ministers take their origin from the people, who therefore designate ministers of their own choice in accord with the needs of their historic revolutionary mission.

## A NEW HERMENEUTIC

For these theologians start out with the idea, more or less consciously, that the viewpoint of the oppressed and revolutionary class, which is their own, is the single, true point of view. Theological criteria for truth are thus relativized and subordinated to the imperatives of the class struggle. In this perspective, orthodoxy, or the right rule of faith, is substituted by the notion of orthopraxy as the criterion of the truth.

For the "theologies of liberation" . . . the social doctrine of the Church is rejected with disdain. It is said that it comes from the illusion of a possible compromise, typical of the middle class, which has no historic destiny.

**Politicalization:** The new hermeneutic inherent in the "theologies of liberation" leads to an essentially political rereading of the scriptures.

Likewise, one places oneself within the perspective of a temporal messianism, which is one of the most radical of the expressions of secularization of the kingdom of God and of its absorption into the immanence of human history.

In giving such priority to the political dimension, one is led to deny the radical newness of the New Testament and, above all, to misunderstand the Person of our Lord Jesus Christ, true God and true Man, and thus the specific character of the salvation he gave us, that is, above all, liberation from sin, which is the source of all evils.

In setting aside the authoritative interpretation of the Church, one is at the same time departing from tradition. In that way one is robbed of an essential theological criterion of interpretation. Without a critical eye, one returns to the opposition of the "Jesus of History" vs. the "Jesus of Faith."

**New Meaning to Creeds:** Of course, the creeds of the faith are literally preserved, especially the Chalcedonian Creed, but a new meaning is given to them which is a negation of the faith of the Church. On one hand, the Christological doctrine of tradition is rejected in the name of class; on the other hand, one claims to meet again the "Jesus of history" coming from the revolutionary experience of the struggle of the poor for their liberation.

Faith in the Incarnate Word, dead and risen for all men, and whom "God made Lord and Christ" is denied. In its place is substituted a figure of Jesus who is a kind of symbol who sums up in himself the requirements of the struggle of the oppressed.

An exclusively political interpretation is thus given to the death of Christ. In this way its value for salvation and the whole economy of redemption is denied.

When the same hermeneutical criterion is applied to the life and to the hierarchical constitution of the Church, the relationship between the hierarchy and the "base" becomes the relationship of obedient domination to the law of the struggle of the classes. Sacramentality, which is at the root of the ecclesial ministries and which makes of the Church a spiritual reality which cannot be reduced to a purely sociological analysis, is quite simply ignored.

This inversion of symbols is likewise verified in the area of the sacraments. The Eucharist is no longer to be understood as the real sacramental presence of the reconciling sacrifice and as the gift of the body and blood of Christ. It becomes a celebration of the people in their struggle.

## ORIENTATIONS

It is only when one begins with the task of evangelization understood in its entirety that the authentic requirements of human progress and liberation are appreciated. This liberation has as its indispensable pillars: the truth about Jesus the Savior, the truth about the Church and the truth about man and his dignity.

The acute need for radical reforms of the structures which conceal poverty and which are themselves forms of violence should not let us lose sight of the fact that the source of injustice is in the hearts of men.

An effective defense of justice needs to be based on the truth of mankind, created in the image of God and called to the grace of divine sonship. The recognition of the true relationship of human beings to God constitutes the foundation of justice to the extent that it rules the relationships between people.

The overthrow by means of revolutionary violence of structures which generate violence is not *ipso facto* the beginning of a just regime. . . . Millions of our own contemporaries legitimately yearn to recover those basic freedoms of which they were deprived by totalitarian and atheistic regimes which came to power by violent and revolutionary means, precisely in the name of the liberation of the people.

**Mythical Objective of Class Struggle:** The class struggle as a road toward a classless society is a myth which slows reform and aggravates poverty and injustice.

One of the conditions for necessary theological correction is giving proper value to the social teaching of the Church. This teaching is by no means closed. It is, on the contrary, open to all the new questions which are so numerous today.

## TRUTHS AT ISSUE

In this full presentation of Christianity, it is proper to emphasize those essential aspects which the "theologies of liberation" especially tend to misunderstand or to eliminate, namely: the transcendence and gratuity of liberation in Jesus Christ, true God and true Man; the sovereignty of grace; and the true nature of the means of salvation, especially of the Church and the sacraments. One should also keep in mind the true meaning of ethics, in which the distinction between good and evil is not relativized, the real meaning of sin, the necessity for conversion and the universality of the law of fraternal love.

## SUMMARY

*This is the official summary by the Sacred Congregation for the Doctrine of the Faith of its Instruction on Certain Aspects of the "Theology of Liberation":*

I. By "theology of liberation" is meant a theological and pastoral movement which, starting from Latin America, has now spread to large sections of the Church in every part of the Third World. There are many priests, men and women Religious, and pastoral workers who often refer to it, but who do not always have the ability to be quite clear about what "liberation theology" means.

### Some Erroneous Ideas

There have been from the beginning of this movement some theologians who have popularized a number of ideas which are seriously in error as far as the faith is concerned. For that reason a clarification on the part of the magisterium (teaching authority of the Church) appeared necessary.

II. With this purpose in mind, the document distinguishes between the *aspiration* of poor people for economic social and political conditions which are in keeping with the dignity of the human person, and, on the other hand, the *theological expressions* of that yearning.

The theological expression of this aspiration is in itself quite a legitimate thing and is one of the characteristic *signs of our times.* Among these expressions, however, there are some which are authentic, some which are ambiguous and some which actually seriously endanger the faith and the doctrinal and moral life of Christians.

### Several Forms

The "theology of liberation" takes several forms and it is not always possible to distinguish clearly between them. This is because this "theology" is expressed in all kinds of ways, in books and articles, for example, or in pamphlets and in homilies and newspapers where it is often reduced to simplistic phrases.

For this reason, the document itself does not directly cite the principal authors and works in the field of "liberation theology." Such citations would have run the risk of giving the impression that some partiular authors were being criticized while those not mentioned were not.

### Christian Theme of Liberation

III. It seemed necessary that the document address the issue in a positive manner. After all, *liberation is a Christian theme which has found-*

ations in both the Old and New Testament. The Christian has a specific kind of liberty (cf. Gal 5:1ff). Christ is our Liberator. He has freed us from sin and from servitude to the Law and the flesh, characteristic of sinful man. Likewise, "liberation theology" can be taken in a completely positive way as long as it accentuates certain aspects of the Mystery of Salvation, and does not do away with a theology of that Mystery.

## Three Central Points

In recent documents, the magisterium has repeatedly made this clear. The address of the Holy Father at Puebla focuses on the three central points of any authentic theology of liberation: the *Truth about Jesus Christ,* the *Truth about the Church* and the *Truth about Mankind.* In this perspective, the *preferential option for the poor* takes on its proper meaning, which is rooted in the Gospel, and becomes fully legitimate.

IV. It is in the name of this option, interpreted in a seriously distorted way, that some theologians have disseminated their erroneous opinions, to which the document wishes to call the attention of pastors and the faithful.

## Elements of Marxist Analysis

At the basis of the errors in question, there is the desire to struggle effectively against the poverty of people, and the idea, quite right in itself, that any effective struggle first requires a scientific analysis of the causes of poverty. The error lies precisely in the identification of this scientific analysis with the "Marxist analysis," without critical study.

There is not sufficient consciousness of the fact that this analysis essentially depends on ideological presuppositions which are incompatible with the faith. One is then shut up within a certain logic which necessarily ends up in a distortion of Christianity, whether or not the particular authors are aware of it.

The document presents a certain number of ideological presuppositions.

**Novel Concept of Truth:** The first, which establishes the direction of the whole, is the novel conception of the *truth.* In Marxism, scientific analysis is linked to *praxis,* which is itself dependent on a conception of *history,* whose motivating principle is the *class struggle.*

Consequently, the true consciousness is the partisan consciousness. There is no truth except in and through the revolutionary *praxis.* By means of various adaptations of the language, the radical liberation theologians adopt a similar conception of the truth, characterized by relativism and the primary importance of action.

**Class Struggle the Fundamental Law:** The class struggle is presented as the objective fundamental law of history. The concept of history is one of the key concepts of the new theologies of liberation which are directly influenced by the themes of Marxism which have not been able to be critically examined from a theological point of view. Consequently, these theologians are drawn toward an immanentism and an historicism which even affects their understanding of God.

Thus, it will be affirmed that there is only one history, and the distinction between the history of salvation and profane history is rejected. It will be maintained that God has made himself into history and history is thus divinized. Likewise the struggle is divinized which is carried on in his name. In this way, everything is reduced to political criteria.

**Church of the Class:** In light of the above, expressions such as *Church of the poor* or *Church of the people* come to mean *Church of the class.* Thus, the unity of the Church which has its source in the grace of God is denied. Some go so far as to say that it makes no sense for Christians who are separated by the class struggle to share the same Eucharistic table. It is in terms of the class struggle that the positions taken by the hierarchy are discredited in advance.

## Influence on Theology

V. The influence of the Marxist conception is also felt in the way in which theology is understood and also how its proper methodology is conceived.

**New Rule of Faith:** The criterion of orthopraxy is substituted for orthodoxy. In other words, the new rule of faith is engagement in the struggle for the liberation of the poor, in the Marxist sense.

**Everything Politicized:** The method of interpretation, the hermeneutic, conforms to the presuppositions presented. The reading of scripture becomes essentially, and often exclusively, a political reading. Both the *Exodus* and the Magnificat are interpreted in this way. The radical newness of the New Testament is thereby removed.

**False View of Jesus and the Sacraments:** Still without theological critique, the opposition seen by rationalist exegesis between the "Jesus of History" and the "Jesus of Faith" is accepted. The death of Christ is given a political interpretation as well, so that its universal redemptive value is denied. And even if the creeds are literally preserved, a new and different meaning is attached to them. They are reduced to the level of symbols of the struggle of the poor for their liberation.

**Sacraments:** The sacraments equally become pure symbols of the struggle of the people for liberation.

## Movement Needs Evaluation

VI. In conclusion, the document spells out the need for an urgent re-evaluation of a movement which, while professing to help the poor, will inevitably bring them a new kind of poverty, the spiritual poverty of the loss of faith, and lead them into new kinds of servitude.

The major imperative for catechesis is the presentation of the Good News, the source of joy, in its totality.

It is equally important to restore the meaning of ethics and the absolute and transcendent value of the distinction between good and evil, as well as the meaning of liberation from sin, the effect of the gift of the Holy Spirit. The totally politicized notion of Christianity to which these theologians lead is the abolition of both the mysteries of faith and of Christian moral living.

# POLITICS AND RELIGION

*Following is the text of a statement on politics and religion issued Aug. 9, 1984, by Bishop James W. Malone of Youngstown, president of the U.S. Catholic Conference. The statement was circulated by NC News Service. Subheads have been added.*

As an agency of the Catholic bishops of the United States, the U.S. Catholic Conference speaks on public policy issues, but it does not take positions for or against political candidates. This point needs emphasizing lest, in the present political context, even what we say about issues be perceived an an expression of political partisanship.

Bishops are teachers. In regard to public issues, they exercise their teaching role by defining the content of moral principles and indicating how they apply to specific problems. The bishops' principal role in the public arena is described in this statement of the Second Vatican Council:

"By preaching the truth of the Gospel and shedding light on all areas of human activity through her teaching and the example of the faithful, the Church shows respect for the political freedom and responsibility of citizens to foster these values. She also has the right to pass moral judgments, even on matters touching the political order, whenever basic personal rights or the salvation of souls makes such judgments necessary." *(Pastoral Constitution on the Church in the Modern World, No. 76)*

## Moral Dimensions of Policy Issues

In view of the bishops' teaching role, the Catholic Conference focuses its attention on policy issues involving significant moral dimensions. By analyzing and taking positions on such issues, the conference seeks to establish a framework of moral guidance for use by Catholics and other persons of good will in making their decisions on political candidates and parties.

The conference's views on many current issues are spelled out in such documents as the statement on political responsibility issued earlier this year by the USCC Administrative Board and USCC's testimony to the platform committees of the two major parties. These are public documents, which I commend to the attention of anyone who wishes to know where we stand. (See the following article.)

The political responsibility statement urges Catholics and others to involve themselves in the political process. It also sets forth specific positions which the bishops have taken on issues. These range from protecting human life from the attack of abortion, to safeguarding human life from the devastation of nuclear war; they extend to the enhancement of life through promoting human rights and satisfying human needs like nutrition, education, housing, and health care for the poor. The platform testimony explains our view of the interdependence of these issues, and why belief in the unique dignity of the human person leads the bishops to take positions on them all, with particular emphasis upon abortion and nuclear war.

## Fundamental Human Rights

The Catholic Conference's policy positions express the Catholic moral tradition. With regard to many issues, of course, there is room for sincere disagreement by Catholics and others who share our moral convictions, over how moral principles should be applied to the current facts in the public policy debate. But with regard to the immorality of the direct taking of innocent human life (e.g., by abortion or by direct attacks on non-combatants in war), our views are not simply policy statements of a particular Catholic organization, the United States Catholic Conference. They are a direct affirmation of the constant moral teaching of the Catholic Church, enunciated repeatedly over the centuries, as in our day, by the highest teaching authority of the Church.

We seek, however, not only to address Catholics and others who share our moral convictions, but to make a religiously informed contribution to the public policy debate in our pluralistic society. When we oppose abortion in that forum, we do so because a fundamental human right is at stake — the right to life of the unborn child. When we oppose any such deterrence policies as would directly target civilian centers or inflict catastrophic damage, we do so because human values would be violated in such an attack. When we support civil rights at home and measure foreign policy by human rights criteria, we seek to do so in terms all people can grasp and support.

## Personal Morality and Public Policy

In proclaiming authentic Catholic moral teaching, therefore, we recognize at the same time the need to join the public policy debate in a way which attempts to convince others of the rightness of our positions. As the Catholic Conference seeks to observe this prescription itself, so it urges other participants in the policy debate to do the same. It would be regrettable if religion as such were injected into a political campaign through appeals to candidates' religious affiliations and commitments. We reject the idea that candidates satisfy the requirements of rational analysis in saying their personal views should not influence their policy decisions; the implied dichotomy — between personal morality and public policy — is simply not logically tenable in any adequate view of both. This position would be as unacceptable as would be the approach of a candidate or officeholder who pointed to his or her personal commitments as qualification for public office, without proposing to take practical steps to translate these into policies and practical programs. This is true of all candidates of all parties.

It is our hope, in short, that the political debate in the months ahead will illuminate policy approaches. Policy proposals should be evaluated from a moral perspective; we have done this and will continue to do so. We encourage others to do the same.

## U.S. CATHOLIC CONFERENCE VIEWS ON PUBLIC ISSUES

*The following recommendations on issues of the 1984 presidential election campaign were presented to the platform committees of the Democratic and Republican parties by the U.S. Catholic Conference. The recommendations, in full form, were contained in a statement — "Political Responsibility: Choices for the 1980s" — issued by the Administrative Board of the conference Apr. 3, 1984.*

*The following excerpts from the full texts of the recommendations were prepared by Liz S. Armstrong, national affairs writer, NC News Service.*

### Abortion

Abortion directly destroys an unborn human being and thus violates the right to life. A legal system which permits abortion contradicts the principle that human rights are inherent and inalienable. Thus, the 1973 Supreme Court decisions on abortion, and subsequent decisions which rely on them, should be reversed, while society's resources should be directed to solving the problems for which abortion is mistakenly proposed as a solution.

Restoration of legal protection to the lives of the unborn requires an amendment to the Constitution.

Public funding policies should encourage childbirth over abortion. Specifically, we oppose all public funding of abortion in programs for medical care and other services.

We support legal equity for women and reject efforts to link abortion "rights" to this objective. Women's equity measures should be scrutinized and, where necessary, amended so that their legitimate and important goals are not exploited as vehicles for abortion and abortion funding.

### Arms Control and Disarmament

Our pastoral letter, "The Challenge of Peace: God's Promise and Our Response," condemns the counter-city or counter-population use of nuclear weapons; rejects the notion of waging limited nuclear war, because of the risk of escalation to all-out nuclear war; and questions the moral acceptability of policies that contemplate the initiation of nuclear war to repel a conventional attack, as is the case in NATO strategy.

Our judgment of "strictly conditional moral acceptance" of nuclear deterrence" means that the deployment of certain kinds of new weapons systems not clearly essential to deterrence should be avoided. Moreover, we recommend a bilateral, verifiable and negotiated halt to all new nuclear weapons deployment, while urging intensified negotiations to achieve reductions in the nuclear arsenals of the superpowers and a comprehensive test ban treaty.

### Crime

Crime and violence are major and legitimate concerns for many. We support strong and effective action to control handguns, leading to their eventual elimination from society.

We oppose the use of capital punishment. A return to the death penalty can only lead to further erosion of respect for life.

### Economic Assistance

We have called on the Congress and the (Reagan) administration to increase substantially the United States' contribution to (the International Development Agency of the World Bank).

We also support emergency food relief to sub-Saharan Africa. While Congress and the administration have responded to this need for emergency food relief, it is likely that further assistance will be essential.

### Education

We advocate policies to improve the educational opportunities available to economically disadvantaged persons and minorities, including bilingual education.

We also support . . . constitutionally acceptable means of providing tax assistance for the education of children in non-public schools, in order to guarantee the free exercise of parental rights in choosing educational opportunities for their children.

### Employment and Income

Our nation should provide jobs for those who can work and a decent income for those who cannot. Current policies fall short of these goals.

Present levels of unemployment, although down from the extreme levels of two years ago, are still too high.

Full employment should be a basic element of just economic policy; we call for efforts to achieve this essential goal. This will entail a national guarantee that no one seeking work will be denied the opportunity to earn a livelihood.

We reaffirm our support for the right of workers to join together to bargain collectively with their employers and ask that protection of this right be extended to those whose rights are currently unprotected, especially farm laborers.

We support a comprehensive reform of the welfare system, which will provide an adequate income base for all Americans and replace the present system of fragmented programs. Current federal policy, which permits states to discriminate against married couples with children, is anti-family and should be abandoned.

Mandatory workfare programs are an unacceptable alternative to training and real jobs with fair compensation.

### Food and Agricultural Policy

The right to eat follows from the right to life. We support a national policy aimed at securing this right, including nutrition programs which help meet the needs of hungry and malnourished Americans, especially children, the poor, the unemployed, and the elderly.

The United States should support the maintenance of an agricultural system based on small and moderate-sized family farms both at home and abroad.

## Health Care

Adequate health care is a basic human need to which society must respond according to its best ability. Budget cuts, rising health costs and high unemployment have deprived millions of adequate preventive and acute care.

While our goal remains a comprehensive national health insurance program, we strongly urge that immediate attention be given to meeting the basic health needs of the poor, half of whom are ineligible for Medicaid under current standards.

## Housing

National housing policy should: (1) provide sufficient resources and programs to meet the housing needs of low- and moderate-income families; (2) ensure the adequate production of new low-income housing; (3) seek to preserve existing housing stock and support neighborhoods by opposing "redlining" and encouraging rehabilitation and reinvestment in central cities; (4) encourage monetary policy and credit allocation systems that provide a sustained supply of affordable credit for housing production; (5) focus effort on the special needs of low-income families, Blacks, Hispanics, rural people, the elderly and the handicapped; (6) support the integral participation of housing consumers and tenants in decisions regarding housing at neighborhood, community and national levels; and (7) promote equal housing opportunity within a framework of cultural pluralism.

## Human Rights

The dignity of the human person requires the defense and promotion of human rights in global and domestic affairs. With respect to human rights internationally, there is a pressing need for the United States to pursue a double task: to strengthen and expand international mechanisms by which human rights can be protected and promoted, and to take seriously the human rights dimensions of U.S. foreign policy.

We also support a policy which gives greater weight to the protection of human rights in the conduct of U.S. affairs. The pervasive presence of U.S. power in many parts of the world creates a responsibility to use that power in the service of human rights.

## Immigration

We support immigration reform legislation which, among other things, provides a generous legalization program for undocumented aliens and preserves the traditional U.S. policy of giving priority to family reunification. At the same time, we are deeply concerned about the potential im-

pact of proposed employer sanctions for hiring undocumented aliens upon U.S. citizens and legal aliens of Hispanic origin. We are also concerned about the possible expansion of the present H-2 temporary workers program into a system of guestworkers which would erode labor standards and compound the problems of domestic farmworkers.

## Mass Media

Communication media should be responsive to the public interest. . . . We oppose legislative initiatives in Congress which would remove the accountability of broadcasters and the owners of cable systems to the communities they are licensed and franchised to serve.

We support the concept of universal telephone service at a cost which all Americans can afford.

## Regional Conflicts

**Central America:** The United States should play a creative diplomatic role in supporting dialogue leading to cessation of hostilities, a negotiated end to the conflicts, and an internationally guaranteed process of political and social reform and economic reconstruction. Under no reasonably foreseeable circumstances can direct intervention of military personnel in the region on the part of the United States or any other outside power be justified.

We have consistently supported substantial economic assistance for the countries of Central America. . . . Military assistance to El Salvador should be conditioned upon compliance with established human rights criteria.

We oppose covert aid to forces seeking to overthrow the present government of Nicaragua by violence. We favor resumption of significant bilateral economic assistance to Nicaragua, conditioned on compliance with established human rights criteria. We urge new efforts at political engagement.

**Middle East:** In the Middle East, the quest for peace continues and the relevant parties (the international community, the United Nations, the regional parties) bear distinct yet interdependent responsibilities.

**Southern Africa:** South Africa has long been of grave moral concern to the world because of its internal racial policies and its occupation of Namibia-Southwest Africa. . . . It has become a threat to the entire area of southern Africa.

U.S. foreign policy and its influence on corporate activity in South Africa should be directed toward needed change in South Africa and in its relations with neighboring states.

## ABORTION-RELATED COURT DECISIONS

*Following is a chronological list of abortion-related decisions handed down by the U.S. Supreme Court and other courts since Jan. 22, 1973.*

• In Roe v. Wade, the Court ruled, 7 to 2, Jan. 22, 1973: (1) During the first three months of pregnancy a woman's right to privacy is paramount. Ac-

cordingly, she has an unrestricted right to abortion with the consent and cooperation of a physician. (2) In the second trimester, the principle controlling legislation on abortion is the health or welfare of the mother, understood in the widest possible sense. (3) In the "state subsequent to viability," the controlling principles are the State's "interest in the potentiality of human life" and "the preservation of the life or health of the mother." These rulings canonized the absolutely private right of a woman to have an abortion and denied to the unborn the right to life.

• In Dole v. Bolton, also decided Jan. 22, 1973, the Court ruled, 7 to 2, against restrictions on facilities that could be used in performing abortions.

• In Danforth v. Planned Parenthood, the Court ruled, 6 to 3, July 1, 1976, against the constitutionality of state laws requiring spousal (in the case of a married woman) or parental (in the case of a minor) consent for an abortion.

### Restrictive Amendment

• (The first of several versions of the Hyde Amendment was adopted by Congress Sept. 30, 1976, in an appropriations measure for the Department of Labor and the Department of Health, Education and Welfare. The amendment provided for limiting federal funding of abortions under Medicaid to cases of danger to the life of a mother and to cases of rape or incest reported in a required manner. See below.)

• An injunction against the amendment was issued Oct. 22, 1976, by U.S. District Court Judge John F. Dooling Jr., in a suit originally filed by Cora McRae.

• In Maher v. Roe, the Court ruled, 6 to 3, June 20, 1977, that the Constitution does not require states to pay for non-therapeutic (elective) abortions and does not require public hospitals to provide them.

• The Court set aside June 19, 1977, Judge Dooling's injunction against the Hyde Amendment and ordered him to restudy his ruling of the previous October in the light of its decision in Maher v. Roe.

• Funding restrictions of the Hyde Amendment went into effect Aug. 4, 1977, and the McRae case went back to the Dooling courtroom.

• The Court ruled, 6 to 3, Jan. 9, 1979, in Colautti v. Franklin against the constitutionality of a 1974 Pennsylvania law because of its vagueness about the timing of fetal viability. The decision had the effect of meaning that a woman exercising a legal right to have an abortion had the right to a dead fetus and that the doctor performing the abortion could not be charged civilly or criminally for the death of the fetus.

• In Bellotti v. Baird, the Court ruled, 8 to 1, July 2, 1979, against the constitutionality of a Massachusetts law requiring a minor to consult with her parents before having an abortion. In the absence of parental consent (which the Court ruled in 1976 was not required) or parental consultation (not required either), a court could clear the way for the abortion of a minor judged to be mature enough to have one.

• Judge Dooling ruled Jan. 15, 1980, against the constitutionality of the Hyde Amendment but stayed enforcement of his decision to permit an appeal to the Supreme Court.

• The Court responded Feb. 19, 1980, to Judge Dooling's action with a one-sentence order requiring federal and state governments to provide Medicaid funding for abortions deemed "medically necessary." The Court also agreed to rule on the constitutionality of the Hyde Amendment, in connection with another case (Williams v. Zbaraz) that originated in Illinois.

### Hyde Amendment Constitutional

• In Harris v. McRae, the Court, with a 5-to-4 decision June 30, 1980, upheld the constitutionality of the Hyde Amendment and its restrictions on Medicaid abortion funding. The decision overturned the Dooling ruling, of Jan. 15, 1980.

While deciding that neither the federal government nor state governments are required to provide funding for "medically necessary" abortions, the Court noted that "abortion is inherently different from other medical procedures because no other medical procedure involves the purposeful termination of a potential life."

The Hyde Amendment provided: "None f the funds provided for in this paragraph shall be used to perform abortions except where the life of the mother would be endangered if the fetus were carried to term; or except for such medical procedures necessary for the victims of rape or incest, where such rape or incest has been reported promptly to a law enforcement agency or public health service."

About two-thirds of the states dropped elective abortion funding from their Medicaid programs after the 1977 decision of the Supreme Court.

### Additional Decisions

• The Supreme Court, by a 6-to-3 vote in H.L. v. Matheson, upheld Mar. 23, 1981, the constitutionality of a Utah law requiring physicians to notify the parents of an unmarried, immature minor daughter seeking an abortion.

• With another 6-to-3 vote in Gary-Northwest Indiana Woman v. Orr, the Court ruled Apr. 27, 1981, that states may outlaw the performance of abortions outside of hospitals for women more than three months pregnant.

• The Court struck down, 6 to 3, June 15, 1983, major provisions of a Dayton, O., ordinance regulating the practice of abortion; in so doing, it reaffirmed its key decisions of 1973 against any such constraints.

The Court also struck down a Missouri law requiring that abortions after 12 weeks of pregnancy be performed in hospitals.

At the same time, the Court upheld two Missouri laws: one requiring the presence of a second physician during abortions after viability, the other requiring a pathology report for each abortion performed.

• The Pennsylvania Commonwealth Court ruled Mar. 9, 1984, that a 1980 state law prohibiting public funding of abortion violated the equal protection clause of the state's constitution and equal rights amendment.

• The 3rd U.S. Circuit Court of Appeals struck down May 31, 1984, some regulatory provisions of Pennsylvania's Abortion Control Act, but upheld the requirement that a child born alive through abortion be protected.

Statistics on legal abortions performed in the U.S. each year from 1972 to 1979 provide reliable indices of the magnitude of the challenge facing right-to-life proponents. The rising numbers of abortions and years, as reported by the Center for Disease Control, U.S. Department of Health and Human Services, were: 586,760 (1972), 615,831 (1973), 763,476 (1974), 854,853 (1975), 988,267 (1976), 1,079,430 (1977), 1,157,776 (1978), 1,251,921 (1979), 1,297,606 (1980). Another source reported 1,573,800 abortions in 1982.

The total number of abortions performed annually worldwide is estimated in the range of 30 to 35 million.

### Charges Against the Church

The Catholic Church is the largest and strongest institutional opponent of abortion, because of its firm teaching and practice on the subject, and also because of the number of its members who are against it.

Because this is so in a cultural climate favoring abortion and moral liberalism, the Church has been accused and charged with:

• dominating the pro-life movement;
• trying to force its views on others who do not share its faith;
• violating a peculiar interpretation of the principle of separation of Church and state.

These accusations have been implicit and explicit in reporting of the abortion controversy ever since it began.

The Church insists, however, on its right to speak and act on moral issues on an equal basis with others who claim rights of conscience and freedom to influence others in a society which is subject not only to the laws of man but, above all, to universal moral law.

## IN VITRO FERTILIZATION

*The bishops of the metropolitan area of Victoria, Australia, locale of the most advanced experiments in fertilization "in vitro," sent a letter on the subject to the In Vitro Fertilization Committee of Melbourne Jan. 16, 1984. Following are excerpts from the letter, with appropriate subheads.*

*The text was published in the May 14 English edition of "L'Osservatore Romano."*

We, the Catholic bishops of Victoria, believe in the human dignity and the human rights of every human being without exception. We insist especially on the dignity and rights of those who have no one to speak out or lobby for them.

We therefore categorically condemn any *using* of a human embryo, or of any other human being, as a mere means to others' ends and purpose, however admirable — e.g., for scientific experiment or as therapeutic source material.

### I. FOUR GENERAL PRINCIPLES

#### Medical Science and Government

1. The Catholic Church looks on science as one of the great friends of mankind, and Medical Science as one of the very greatest.

She acknowledges that the development of Government Interventionism has produced many great advances in justice and well-being, both of the individual and of Society.

#### Politics

2. The Catholic Church therefore rejoices in the genuine advances of modern Science and modern Politics. However, she does not do so uncritically. Like all good things, they can be misused. The great achievements of Science and Political Interventionism must not render them immune from the rational scrutiny of social conscience and moral principle.

The Church is delighted when Science fosters and furthers man's mastery and employment of creation; but she is well aware that Science, like every other good thing, can be used against, as well as for, human interests and human rights.

The same is true of Political Interventionism.

The Church recognizes that the development of lobbies and organized interest groups can quite properly serve perfectly proper ends. But, as Political Interventionism grows, so does the temptation to use it *for* the vocal, the powerful and the politically adroit, *at the expense* of the voiceless and the impotent. It is a noble thing for a political party, whether in Government or Opposition, to champion the voiceless and friendless; it is a shameful thing for it to decide not to do so because it calculates that more will be gained politically in ignoring their dignity and rights, and siding with some group which wants to *use* them for its own ends and purposes, however worthy.

#### Moral Obligation and Law

3. Not every moral obligation need be, or should be, enforced by secular law; not every immoral act or practice need be, or should be, forbidden by it. But serious human rights should be realistically protected by secular law, and systematic violations of them should be strictly forbidden by it.

#### Role of Law

4. Sound Law has an educative role in a just society. It indicates what sorts of conduct further human dignity and human rights, and what sorts of conduct militate against them.

It is therefore not enough for legislators mechanically to follow the public opinion polls or the most vocal or powerful lobby. We have full-time parliamentarians and we pay them reasonable salaries, so that they can seriously study the implications and the likely consequences of proposed legislation; and, first and foremost, its foreseeable impact on the human dignity and rights of those likely to be affected.

This is not the quickest way to short-term media applause; but it is the very stuff of authentic statesmanship. One thinks of the recent performance of the British House of Commons. The public opinion polls were all running heavily in favour of re-introducing capital punishment; yet the Commons voted decisively against it. By such action, and by the subsequent explanation and argument which is open to energetic politicians, they can gradually turn public opinion around. The great majority of people are amenable to reason and persuasion when it is brought home to them that human dignity and rights are at stake.

## II. SPECIFIC POINTS

### The Embryo Is Human

1. *The embryo is a human being.* An ovum is not. A gamete is not. But once the marvel, the irreversible marvel of human conception has occurred, the new life conceived is a separate human individual: an organism of human origin possessing within itself everything needed to organize its own development, growth, multiplication and differentiation, given only nutrition and the right environment. Robert Edwards, one of the world's first successful pair of IVF practitioners, describes the embryo as "magnificently organized, switching on its own biochemistry." Edwards sums up the truth in one pregnant phrase: even at the pre-implantation stage, he says, the embryo is *"a microscopic human being — one in its very earliest stages of development."*

### Human Dignity and Rights

2. Every human being is endowed with human dignity and human rights: *every* human being — microscopic or macroscopic, infantile or adult or senile, Caucasian or Negroid or Asiatic. Every human life is objectively, intrinsically valuable. It is valuable *objectively*: not just by virtue of the value subjectively perceived in it by others, or of its own subjective desire or self-valuation. It is valuable *intrinsically*, for its own sake: not for its role in others' lives or any function it may fulfill in or for society. A sustained commitment to this truth as non-negotiable is basic to a consistently egalitarian democracy.

### Law's Business To Protect

3. It is therefore the Law's business to protect every human being, regardless of colour, size or stage of development. Serious violations of any human being's dignity or rights must be forbidden by law. This is true, of course, when the violation is occasional or episodic: *a fortiori,* when the violation is planned and systematic.

### Freezing Is Wrong

"Freezing" a living human embryo is abrupting that marvellous process to which as a living human being it is strictly entitled for its own sake: that process which involves becoming "magnificently organized, switching on its own biochemistry, increasing in size, and preparing itself quickly for life in the womb." Rudely, deliberately it is to be ruthlessly stopped from so preparing itself. If this is done with a view to eventual implantation, it confronts the same grave objections raised in our earlier submissions. If it is done in order to lay up human material to be used in experimentation ·or therapy, it constitutes a gross violation of human dignity and a denial of the right to life itself.

Therefore:

• Using a living human embryo simply as an object of scientific experimentation is a gross violation of human dignity.

• Using a human embryo as a mere source of therapeutic material is a gross violation of *the* human right, an explicit denial of the truth that every human life is intrinsically, objectively valuable. It is a direct case of treating a human being as a mere means to others' ends and purposes.

"Rattle his bones over the stones, he's only a pauper that nobody owns."

At least the pauper was getting the essential dignity of human burial, though some of the accidental niceties were missing. The little embryo is to be denied every essential of human dignity, including even the right to continued existence, and reduced to the status of therapeutic resource material.

• To legalize a programme of freezing embryos intended to serve these ends is therefore quite unacceptable.

## III. LEGISLATIVE DUTY

Every human being has rights to human life and human dignity. Every legislature has the duty to protect those rights.

We recognize that, increasingly, legislators are being subjected to various pressures to break away from that principle, or to erode it with euphemisms. The terminally ill; the senile, whose life is "a burden to others and meaningless to themselves;" physically impaired or mentally retarded babies — all of these, under some re-description or other, are held to have a less than 100 per cent right to life.

### Pressure against the Unborn

Eleven years ago, a young American philosopher published an article called "Abortion and Infanticide." He declared that, "if it could be shown that there is no moral objection to infanticide, the happiness of society could be significantly and justifiably increased." He proceeded to argue that, not only the unborn, but the infant baby also, has no serious right to life unless it "possess the concept of a self as a continuing subject of experiences, and that it believes that it is itself such an entity." He now holds a distinguished Australian university chair, and his article has been expanded into a book recently published by one of the most prestigious university presses in the world. Past experience suggests that there will soon be a pressure group urging that "society" and legislatures acquiesce in this view, and nervous politicians will be sniffing the wind to see which way it is blowing.

### Speaking for the Unborn

We realize that few voices have been raised on behalf of a human being which is never going to be allowed to run its natural term; but that only convinces us that Catholic bishops, at least, must not desert their cause. It is easy to say "Me too" on behalf of victims who are championed by fashionable or powerful lobbies or media. We speak out for the unborn, not out of any romantic attachment to quixotry, but because the Catholic Church believes in the human dignity and the human rights of every human being without exception. These tiny creatures are not Catholics or Protestants or Jews: they are just human beings.

## Danger of Denial of Rights

Whenever there is Interventionist Government, groups which cannot organize support for their interests are liable to suffer encroachments on or denial of their human rights and dignity. In South Africa, it happens to blacks and coloureds; in the Soviet Union, to Jews and religious activists; in many Latin-American countries, to the landless farm labourers. Here in Australia, it is the unborn: and we are confident that, as more and more

people realize that the embryo is a human being, public opinion will demand that every embryo be accorded human status. A recent ABC television programme of Our World presented a Swedish film showing the development of human life before and after implantation; for many people all over Australia, it proved to be an exercise in raising their consciousness of the marvel of human existence before birth.

The primary criterion for judging a legislature or a government is: faithful and efficacious commitment to human dignity and human rights. By that criterion, we in Victoria have to say: If a government protects forests even at the cost of causing unemployment, yet legalizes the systematic violation of the dignity and rights of the human embryo, it has lost its way.

## INNOVATIVE FORCE OF REVISED CODE OF CANON LAW

*Following are excerpts from an address delivered by Pope John Paul to personnel of the Sacred Roman Rota Jan. 26, 1984, at the beginning of the new judicial year.*

*These excerpts are from the text published in the Feb. 13, 1984, English edition of "L'Osservatore Romano."*

The fruit of a long, patient and careful work, enriched by various consultations with the episcopate which have given it a particular note of collegiality, it (the revised Code of Canon Law) represents an authoritative guide for the application of the Second Vatican Council, and could even be considered, as I said on another occasion, the last Council document. In promulgating it, I expressed the hope that it "will prove to be an efficacious means in order that the Church may progress in conformity with the spirit of the Second Vatican Council, and may be ever more suited to carry out its office of salvation in this world."

### Observance of the Law

The fulfillment of this hope of mine depends for the most part on how the new Canon Law is received and observed. As my venerated predecessor, Paul VI, said while speaking to an International Congress of Canonists:

"It must, nevertheless, be added that the advantages envisaged in the reform of Canon Law will not be effectively secured unless, and to the extent that, the laws are observed in practice by the People of God. For however relevant or well-drafted ecclesiastical legislation may be, if it should be disregarded in practice, or should be challenged or rejected, it will unfortunately remain barren and useless, and deprived of all profit and efficacy. Hence it follows that the drive toward reform, unsupported by the practical observance of the laws, will be weakened and short-lived, and it will certainly be less genuine and assured."

### Vatican II Perspective

The Code is a new law and is to be evaluated primarily in the perspective of the Second Vatican Council, to which it is intended to conform fully.

Knowledge is followed almost spontaneously by *fidelity* which . . . is the judge's first and most important duty to the law.

Fidelity is, above all, the sincere, honest and unconditional acceptance of the law legitimately promulgated; which, in its turn, must be seen as the pondered expression of the *office of government* entrusted to the Church by Christ, and therefore a concrete manifestation of the will of God.

Such a recommendation of fidelity addressed to persons who, like you (Rota personnel), are not only distinguished experts of the law, but who by training and profession have a fundamental orientation of adherence to the law, would seem completely superfluous. Nevertheless, two considerations induce me to make such a recommendation.

### Time for Implementation

The first derives from the particular situation of *the drafting of the law* which we have lived through for more than twenty years.

In that period, a critical attitude in regard to drafts or schemata of law was spontaneous, I would say almost a duty, especially in the case of experts and specialists. Its purpose was to point out defects and deficiencies with the intention of improving them. Such an attitude could then have been very useful and constructive for a more accurate and perfect formulation of the law.

But today, after the promulgation of the Code, it cannot be forgotten that the period of *drafting* is over and that now, the law, even with its possible limitations and defects, is a *choice* already made by the legislator after careful reflection and which therefore demands full adherence. Now it is no longer a time for discussion, but for implementation.

### Innovative Force of the Law

The other consideration also derives from a similar motivation.

Knowledge of the Code just abrogated and long familiarity with it could lead some to a kind of identification with the laws contained in it, which would be considered better and therefore worthy of nostalgic regret, with the knowledge of a kind of negative "foreknowledge" of the new Code, which would be read almost exclusively in the perspective of the former. And this not merely for those parts which repeat almost literally the previous law, but also for those which are objectively real innovations.

This attitude, even though psychologically understandable, may be pushed to the extent of almost annulling the innovative force of the new Code which, however, in the sector of court procedure must make itself particularly visible. As you can well understand, it is a question of a subtly insidious attitude, since it seems to find justification in the second rule of juridical interpretation contained in Canon 6 of the Code of 1917 and in the principle of legislative continuity characteristic of Canon Law.

### Flexible Procedures

In the reform of canonical procedural law, an effort was made to meet a very frequent criticism, and one which was not completely without foundation, concerning the slowness and excessive length of trials. Therefore, accepting a deeply felt need, without wishing to impair or in the slightest way to diminish the necessary guarantees offered by the course and formalities of court procedure, it was sought to render the administration of justice more flexible and functional by simplifying procedures, speeding up the formalities, shortening the terms, increasing the discretional powers of the judge, etc.

This effort must not be rendered vain by delaying tactics or by a lack of care in studying cases, by an attitude of inertia which cautions against entering the new track, by lack of expertise in applying the procedures.

### Interpretation and Jurisprudence

Another important aspect of the relationship of the judge with the law revolves around the *interpretation* of it. In a strict sense, the true, authentic interpretation which declares the general meaning of the law for the entire community is reserved to the legislator, according to the well-known principle: *"Unde ius prodiit, interpretatio quoque procedat"* ("The source of the law is the source also of interpretation").

Nevertheless, the judge plays a very important role in deciding the meaning of the law. Above all, the sentence represents an authentic interpretation of the law for the parties. By applying it to the particular case, the judge makes an interpretation which, although it does not have general value, binds the parties with the same force of the law.

But the interpretative power is to be placed, above all, in the formation of *jurisprudence*, that is, of that ensemble of concordant sentences which, without having the absoluteness of the ancient *"auctoritas rerum perpetuo similiter iudicatarum"* ("The authority of cases always decided in the same way"), nevertheless plays a notable role in filling possible *lacunae* in the law.

The value of the Rota jurisprudence in the Church has always been noteworthy, given the knowledge and experience of the judges and the authority they enjoy as papal judges. Canon 19 of the new Code expressly confirms this.

## CONTENTS OF THE CODE

*Following is a general index of the contents of the revised Code of Canon Law.*

### Book I, General Norms
(Canons 1-203)

Canons in this book cover: church laws in general, custom and law, general decrees and instructions, administrative acts, statutes, physical and juridical persons, juridical acts, the power of governing, ecclesiastical offices, prescription (rights having the force of law), the reckoning of time.

### Book II, The People of God
(Canons 204-746)

Canons in Part I cover: the obligations and rights of all the faithful, the obligations and rights of lay persons, sacred ministers and clerics, personal prelatures and associations of the faithful.

Canons in Part II cover the hierarchic constitution of the Church under the headings: the supreme authority of the Church and the college of bishops, particular churches and the authority constituted in them, councils of particular churches and the internal order of particular churches.

Canons in Part III cover institutes of consecrated life and societies of apostolic life.

### Book III, The Teaching Office of the Church
(Canons 747-833)

Canons under this heading cover: the ministry of the divine word, the missionary action of the Church, Catholic education, the instruments of social communication and books in particular, and the profession of faith.

### Book IV, The Sanctifying Office of the Church
(Canons 834-1253)

Canons under this heading cover: each of the seven sacraments — baptism, confirmation, the Eucharist, penance, anointing of the sick, holy orders and matrimony; other acts of divine worship including sacramentals, the Liturgy of the Hours, ecclesiastical burial; the veneration of saints, sacred images and relics; vows and oaths.

### Book V, Temporal Goods of the Church
(Canons 1254-1310)

Canons under this heading cover: the acquisition and administration of goods, contracts and the alienation of goods, wills and pious foundations.

### Book VI, Sanctions in the Church
(Canons 1311-1399)

Canons in Part I cover crimes and penalties in general: the punishment of crimes in general, penal law and penal precept, persons subject to penal sanctions, penalties and other punishments, the application and cessation of penalties.

Canons in Part II cover penalties for particular crimes: crimes against religion and the unity of the Church; crimes against the authorities of the Church and the liberty of the Church; the usurpation of church offices and crimes in exercising office; false accusation of a confessor; crimes against special obligations; crimes against human life and liberty; a general norm regarding the punishment of external violations of divine and canon law not specifically covered in the Code.

## Book VII, Procedures

(Canons 1400-1752)

Judicial proceedings are the principal subjects of canons under this heading: tribunals and their personnel, parties to proceedings, details regarding litigation and the manner in which it is conducted, special proceedings — with emphasis on matrimonial cases.

# JERUSALEM: APOSTOLIC LETTER

*This is the text of the apostolic letter entitled "Redemptionis Anno" (Year of the Redemption) in which Pope John Paul appealed for international guarantees to protect Jerusalem as a city sacred to Christians, Jews and Moslems, while also stating support for a homeland for Palestinians and peace and security for Jews in Israel. The letter was published in the Apr. 19, 1984, edition of "L'Osservatore Romano."*

*This English translation of the Latin text, by "L'Osservatore Romano," was circulated by the NC Documentary Service, Origins, May 24, 1984 (Vol. 14, No. 2).*

As the Jubilee Year of Redemption draws to a close, my thoughts go to that place where Europe, Asia and Africa meet and in which the redemption of the human race was accomplished "once and for all" (Rom. 6:10; Heb. 7:27; 9:12; 10:10).

It is the land which we call holy, indeed the land which was the earthly homeland of Christ, who walked about it that "preaching the Gospel of the kingdom and healing every disease and every infirmity" (Mt. 4:23).

This year especially I was pleased to be touched by the same sentiment and the same joy as my predecessor Pope Paul VI when he visited the Holy Land and Jerusalem in 1964.

### City of Jesus and Biblical Revelation

Although I cannot be there physically, I nevertheless feel that I am spiritually a pilgrim in that land where our reconciliation with God was brought about, to beg the Prince of Peace for the gift of redemption and of peace which is so earnestly desired by the hearts of people, families and nations — in a special way, by the nations which inhabit this very area.

I think especially of the City of Jerusalem where Jesus, offering his life, "has made us both one, and has broken down the dividing wall of hostility . . . bringing the hostility to an end" (Eph. 2:14, 16).

Before it was the City of Jesus the Redeemer, Jerusalem was the historic site of the biblical revelation of God, the meeting place, as it were, of heaven and earth, in which more than in any other place the word of God was brought to men.

### City of Christians, Jews, Moslems

Christians honor it with a religious and intent concern because there the words of Christ so often resounded, there the great events of the redemption were accomplished: the passion, death and resurrection of the Lord. In the City of Jerusalem, the first Christian community sprang up and remained throughout the centuries a continual ecclesial presence despite difficulties.

Jews ardently love it and in every age venerate its memory, abundant as it is in many remains and monuments from the time of David, who chose it as the capital, and of Solomon, who built the temple there. Therefore, they turn their minds to it daily, one may say, and point to it as the sign of their nation.

Moslems also call Jerusalem "holy," with a profound attachment that goes back to the origins of Islam and springs from the fact that they have there many special places of pilgrimage and for more than a thousand years have dwelt there almost without interruption.

Besides these exceptional and outstanding testimonies, Jerusalem contains communities of believers full of life whose presence the peoples of the whole world regard as a sign and source of hope — especially those who consider the Holy City to be in a certain way their spiritual heritage and a symbol of peace and harmony.

### Symbol of Unity

Indeed, insofar as it is the homeland of the hearts of all the spiritual descendants of Abraham, who hold it very dear, and the place where, according to faith, the created things of earth encounter the infinite transcendence of God, Jerusalem stands out as a symbol of coming together, of union and of universal peace for the human family.

The Holy City therefore strongly urges peace for the whole human race, especially for those who worship the one great God, the merciful Father of the peoples. But it must be acknowledged that Jerusalem continues to be the cause of daily conflict, violence and partisan reprisals.

This situation and those considerations cause these words of the prophet to spring to the lips: "For Zion's sake I will not keep silent, and for Jerusalem's sake I will not rest until her vindication goes forth as brightness and her salvation as a burning torch" (Is. 62:1).

I think of and long for the day on which we shall all be so "taught by God" (Jn. 6:45) that we shall listen to his message of peace and reconciliation. I think of the day on which Jews, Christians and Moslems will greet each other in the City of Jerusalem with the same greeting of peace with which Christ greeted the disciples after the resurrection: "Peace be with you" (Jn. 20:19).

## Papal Concern

The Roman pontiffs, especially in this century, have witnessed with an ever anxious solicitude the violent events which have afflicted Jerusalem for many decades, and they have followed closely with watchful care the declarations of the United Nations which have dealt with the fate of the Holy City.

On many occasions the Holy See has called for reflection and urged that an adequate solution be found to this difficult and complex situation. The Holy See has done this because she is concerned for peace among peoples no less than for spiritual, historical and cultural reasons of a nature eminently religious.

The entire human race, and especially the peoples and nations who have brothers in faith in Jerusalem — Christians, Jews and Moslems — have reason to feel involved in this mattter and to do everything possible to preserve the unique and sacred character of the city. Not only the monuments or the sacred places, but the whole historical Jerusalem and the existence of religious communities, their situation and future cannot but affect everyone and interest everyone.

## Special Statute Wanted

Indeed, there should be found, with good will and farsightedness, a concrete and just solution by which different interests and aspirations can be provided for in a harmonious and stable form, and be safeguarded in an adequate and efficacious manner by a special statute internationally guaranteed so that no party could jeopardize it.

## Critical Question for Middle East

I also feel it an urgent duty, in the presence of the Christian communities, of those who believe in the one God and who are committed to the defense of fundamental human values, to repeat that the question of Jerusalem is fundamental for a just peace in the Middle East. It is my conviction that the religious identity of the city, and particularly the common tradition of monotheistic faith, can pave the way to promote harmony among all those who in different ways consider the Holy City their own.

I am convinced that the failure to find an adequate solution to the question of Jerusalem and the resigned postponement of the problem only compromise further the longed-for peaceful and just settlement of the crisis of the whole Middle East.

It is natural in this context to recall that in the area two peoples, the Israelis and the Palestinians, have been opposed to each other for decades in an antagonism that appears insoluble.

The Church which looks at Christ the Redeemer and sees his image in the face of every man, invokes peace and reconciliation for the peoples of the land that was his.

## Israelis and Palestinians

For the Jewish people who live in the State of Israel and who preserve in that land such precious testimonies to their history and their faith, we must ask for the desired security and the due tranquility that is the prerogative of every nation and condition of life and progress for every society.

The Palestinian people, who find their historical roots in that land and who for decades have been dispersed, have the natural right in justice to find once more a homeland and to be able to live in peace and tranquility with the other peoples of the area.

All the peoples of the Middle East, each with its own heritage of spiritual values, will not be able to overcome the tragic events in which they are involved — I am thinking of Lebanon, so sorely tried — unless they discover again the true sense of their history, which through faith in the one God calls them to live together peacefully in mutual cooperation.

## Appeal

I want, therefore, to draw the attention of politicians, of all those who are responsible for the destiny of peoples, of those who are in charge of international organizations, to the plight of the City of Jerusalem and of the communities who live there. In fact, it escapes no one that the different expressions of faith and of culture present in the Holy City can and should be an effective aid to concord and peace.

On this Good Friday, when we solemnly recall the passion and death of the Savior, we invite you all, revered brothers in the episcopate and all priests, men and women religious, and the faithful of the whole world, to include among the special intentions of your prayers the petititon for a just solution to the problem of Jerusalem and the Holy Land, and for the return of peace to the Middle East.

As this Jubilee Year of Redemption draws to a close, a year which we have celebrated with great spiritual joy whether in Rome or in all the dioceses of the universal Church, Jerusalem has been the ideal goal, the natural place to which we direct our thoughts of love and thankfulness for the great gift of the redemption which the Son of Man accomplished for all people in the Holy City.

## Prayer for Reconciliation

And, since the fruit of the redemption is the reconciliation of man with God and of every man with his brothers, we ought to pray that also in Jerusalem, in the Holy Land of Jesus, those who believe in God may find reconciliation and peace after such sorrowful divisions and strife.

This peace proclaimed by Jesus Christ in the name of the Father who is in heaven thus makes Jerusalem the living sign of the great ideal of unity, of brotherhood and of agreement among peoples, according to the illuminating words of the Book of Isaiah: "Many peoples shall come and say: 'Come, let us go up to the mountain of the Lord, to the house of the God of Jacob; that he may teach us his ways and that we may walk in his paths' " (Is. 2:3).

Finally, we gladly impart our Apostolic Blessing.

Given in Rome at St. Peter's on Good Friday, April 20, 1984, the sixth year of our pontificate.

# PAPAL MESSAGE ON WORLD POPULATION

*Following is the text of an address by Pope John Paul II to Rafael M. Salas, secretary general of the International Conference on Population and director of the United Nations Fund for Population Activities. The address was delivered during a June 7, 1984, audience at the Vatican.*

*The text, released by the Vatican, was circulated by NC News Service. Subheads have been added.*

1. This conference, to be held in Mexico City in August, 1984, provides an opportunity for a re-examination of many important issues related to population growth or decline some 10 years after the World Population Conference in 1974. The Holy See has followed the discussions of population during these years, and has studied the implications of the demographic factors for the entire human family.

It is readily apparent that the worldwide population situation is very complex and varies from region to region. Behind the demographic facts there are many interrelated issues that have to do with improving the circumstances of living so that people can live in dignity, justice and peace; so that they can exercise the God-given right to form families, to bear and bring up children; and so that they can pursue their eternal destiny, which is union with the loving God who has created them. Thus, the Catholic Church takes positive note of the concern for improving systems of education and health care, recognizing the roles of aging persons, obtaining greater opportunities for people to be active participants in the development process, and in constructing a new global economic system based on justice and equity.

## Dignity of Persons

2. The Church recognizes the role of governments and of the international community to study and to face with responsibility the population problem in the context of and with a view to the common good of individual nations and of all humanity. But demographic policies must not consider people as mere numbers, or only in economic terms, or with any kind of prejudice. They must respect and promote the dignity and the fundamental rights of the human person and of the family.

The "dignity of the human person" — of each and every person — and his or her uniqueness and capacity to contribute to the well-being of society are of primary importance to the Church when entering into discussions about population. For the Church believes that human dignity is based on the fact that God has created each person, that we have been redeemed by Christ, and that, according to the divine plan, we shall rejoice with God forever. The Church must always stand as a sign and safeguard of the transcendent character of the human person, restoring hope to those who might otherwise despair of anything better than their present lot. This conviction of the Church is shared

by others, is in harmony with the most secret desires of the human heart, and responds to the deepest longings of the human person. The dignity of the person, then, is a value of universal importance, one that is upheld by people of differing religious, cultural and national backgrounds. This emphasis on the value of the person demands respect for human life, which is always a splendid gift of God's goodness.

## The Church Stands for Life

Against the pessimism and selfishness which cast a shadow over the world, the Church stands for life and calls for ever greater efforts to correct those situations that endanger or diminish the value and appropriate enjoyment of human life. Thus, I recall the words of my apostolic exhortation *Familiaris Consortio,* which reflects the consensus of the 1980 world Synod of Bishops on the family in the modern world.

"The Church is called upon to manifest anew to everyone, with clear and stronger conviction, her will to promote human life by every means and to defend it against all attacks, in whatever condition or state of development it is found.

"Thus, the Church condemns as a grave offense against human dignity and justice all those activities of governments or other public authorities which attempt to limit in any way the freedom of couples in deciding about children. Consequently, any violence applied by such authorities in favor of contraception or, still worse, of sterilization and procured abortion, must be altogether condemned and forcefully rejected; likewise to be denounced as gravely unjust are cases where, in international relations, economic help given for the advancement of peoples is made conditional on programs of contraception, sterilization and procured abortion."

## Negative Effects of Contraception

The experiences and trends of recent years clearly emphasize the profoundly negative effects of contraceptive programs. These programs have increased sexual permissiveness and promoted irresponsible conduct, with grave consequences especially for the education of youth and the dignity of women. The very notion of "responsible parenthood" and "family planning" has been violated by the distribution of contraceptives to adolescents.

Moreover, from contraceptive programs a transition has in fact often been made to the practice of sterilization and abortion, financed by governments and international organizations.

## Importance of the Family

3. The Church stresses the importance of the family, which is "the natural and fundamental group unit of society and is entitled to protection by society and the state" (cf. "Universal Declaration of Human Rights").

At the request of the international Synod of Bishops, the Holy See itself has issued a "Charter on the Rights of the Family" in which it "urges all states, international organizations, and all interested institutions and persons to promote respect for those rights and to secure their effective recognition and observance."

In this document, the family is recognized as "a community of love and solidarity which is uniquely suited to teach and transmit cultural, ethical, social, spiritual and religious values, essential to the well-being of its own members and of society." The family is truly a community of persons bound together by love, by mutual concern, by commitments to the past and to the future. While the primary members of the family are the spouses and their children, it is important to maintain an awareness of the family as a community where the different generations come together, and whose strength it is to provide a place of identity and security for relatives and for those who are assimiliated into it.

## Value of Children

The family has a unique and irreplaceable role in handing on the gift of life and in providing the best environment for the education of children and their introduction into society. It is in the family, primarily, that the child finds love and acceptance from the moment of conception and throughout the process of growth and development. Insecurity about the future should not diminish our hope and joy in children. Now, more than ever before, we must reaffirm our belief in the value of the child and in the contributions that today's children can make to the entire human family. As I said before the United Nations General Assembly:

"In the presence of the representatives of so many nations of the world gathered here, I wish to express the joy that we all find in children, the springtime of life, the anticipation of the future history of each of our present earthly homelands. No country on earth, no political system can think of its own future otherwise than through the image of these new generations that will receive from their parents the manifold heritage of values, duties and aspirations of the nation to which they belong and of the whole human family. Concern for the children, even before birth, from the first moment of conception and then throughout the years of infancy and youth, is the primary and fundamental test of the relationship of one human being to another."

## Parental Decision

4. Yet we all know that the spouses' decision in favor of childbearing and childrearing is not always easy and often occasions sacrifice. The Church is realistically aware of this, and her teaching on responsible parenthood concerns married couples — who, alone, have the right to procreation — to assist them in making what must be a free, informed and mutual decision regarding the spacing of births and the size of the family. This decision should be based on their prayerful and generous appreciation of their association with God in the work of creation, and of their re-

sponsibilities to themselves, to their children, to their family and to society.

It should be a decision that is based on morally acceptable methods of spacing or limiting births, about which it is the right and duty of the Church to speak. On the other hand, it is the role of governments and of international organizations to assist married couples by creating a socio-economic order conducive to family life, childbearing and childrearing, and by providing accurate information on the demographic situation so that couples may properly assess their duties and their capabilities.

## Women, Aged

5. Special attention should be given to the role of women in modern society. Improving the status of women is important. In this regard, we should not overlook the contributions that women make in the home and in their unique capacity to nurture the infant and guide the child in the earliest phase of education. This particular contribution of women is often ignored or diminished in favor of economic considerations or employment opportunities, and sometimes even in order to decrease the number of children. Continued efforts should be made to ensure the full integration of women in society, while giving due recognition to their important social role as mothers. This should include maternal and child health care, proper maternal leave, and family income supplements.

The Church is also aware of the initiatives in favor of the aging. . . . The number of aging persons is increasing in most countries. Their needs are often overlooked, and also the contribution they make to society. They bring experience, wisdom and a special patience to the solution of human problems, and they can and should be active members of contemporary society.

## Population and Development

6. Much attention is given to the relationship of population to development. It is widely recognized that a population policy is only one part of an overall development strategy. Once again, the Church emphasizes that the needs of families should be a primary consideration in development strategies, that families should be encouraged to assume responsibility for transforming society and be active participants in the development process. Yet, development itself should be more than a pursuit of material benefits; it should involve a more comprehensive approach that respects and satisfies the spiritual as well as the material needs of each person and of the whole of society.

In a word, development strategies should be based on a just, worldwide socio-economic order directed toward an equitable sharing of created goods, respectful stewardship of the environment and natural resources, and a sense of moral responsibility and cooperation among nations in order to achieve peace, security and economic stability for all. Above all, development should not be interpreted simply in terms of population control, nor should governments or international agencies make development assistance dependent on the achievement of family planning goals.

At this time, Mr. Secretary General, I would appeal to you and through you to all those participating in the 1984 International Conference on Population, to face the issues of population with renewed confidence in the human person, and in the power that moral and spiritual values have to contribute to the true solution of human problems in our day. May God himself assist you to fulfill this important task.

## CONFERENCE ACTION

A seven-member Vatican delegation to the International Population Conference Aug. 6 to 14, 1984, in Mexico City declined to endorse its World Plan of Action because of its support for contraception and other objectionable policies.

Bishop Jan Schotte, head of the delegation, said the plan included "some valuable proposals with regard to development, the important role of the family, migration and aging," but: The Vatican could not approve "the sections that assert for individuals, including unmarried adolescents, the prerogatives that belong to married couples in regard to sexual intimacy and parenthood."

The bishop said that the Vatican based its stand on "its understanding of the nature of the human person and the sacredness of life, marriage and sexuality."

One positive achievement of the conference was its endorsement of an amendment stating that abortion should not be promoted as a method of family planning. The amendment was supported by the delegations of the Vatican, the United States and several Latin American nations.

The purpose of the conference was to review and update developments stemming from the international population conference held in Bucharest in 1974.

## CHARTER OF THE RIGHTS OF THE FAMILY

*Following are the 12 articles of the "Charter of the Rights of the Family" developed in accord with recommendations emanating from the 1980 assembly of the Synod of Bishops.*

*The English-language text of the entire document, released by the Vatican Nov. 24, 1983, was circulated by the NC Documentary Service, Origins, Dec. 15, 1983 (Vol. 13, No. 27).*

The Holy See, having consulted the bishops' conferences, now presents this "Charter of the Rights of the Family" and urges all states, international organizations, and all interested institutions and persons to promote respect for these rights, and to secure their effective recognition and observance.

### Article 1

All persons have the right to the free choice of their state of life and thus to marry and establish a family or to remain single.

### Article 2

Marriage cannot be contracted except by the free and full consent of the spouses duly expressed.

### Article 3

The spouses have the inalienable right to found a family and to decide on the spacing of births and the number of children to be born, taking into full consideration their duties toward themselves, their children already born, the family and society, in a just hierarchy of values and in accordance with the objective moral order which excludes recourse to contraception, sterilization and abortion.

### Article 4

Human life must be respected and protected, absolutely, from the moment of conception.

### Article 5

Since they have conferred life on their children, parents have the original, primary and inalienable right to educate them; hence, they must be acknowledged as the first and foremost educators of their children.

### Article 6

The family has the right to exist and to progress as a family.

### Article 7

Every family has the right to live freely its own domestic religious life under the guidance of the parents, as well as the right to profess publicly and to propagate the faith, to take part in public worship and in freely chosen programs of religious instruction, without suffering discrimination.

### Article 8

The family has the right to exercise its social and political functions in the construction of society.

### Article 9

Families have the right to be able to rely on an adequate family policy on the part of public authorities in the juridical, economic, social and fiscal domains, without any discrimination whatsoever.

### Article 10

Families have a right to a social and economic order in which the organization of work permits the members to live together and does not hinder the unity, well-being, health and the stability of the family, while offering also the possibility of wholesome recreation.

### Article 11

The family has the right to decent housing, adequate for family life and commensurate to the number of the members, in a physical environment that provides the basic services for the life of the family and the community.

### Article 12

The families of migrants have the right to the same protection as that accorded other families.

## OCTOBER 1983

### VATICAN

**The Rosary** — Recitation of the Rosary is needed to fight the "spirit of error and evil" in the world, declared the Holy Father before 100,000 people attending Mass in St. Peter's Square on World Marian Day, Oct. 2. "The Rosary," he said, "is full of greater purposes than in the past. It is not a matter of asking for great victories, like those at Lepanto and Vienna (in 1571 and 1683, respectively), over anti-Christian Turkish forces), but rather of asking Mary to make us brave combatants against the spirit of error and evil."

**Pius XII and World War II** — Pope Pius XII, "a strenuous defender and passionate servant of peace," wrote and worked tirelessly to prevent the terrible Second World War from breaking out. Later, he did everything (he could) to reduce the harmful and tragic effects of the monstrous conflict." So stated Pope John Paul Oct. 8 during ceremonies marking the 25th anniversary of his predecessor's death. Cardinal Siri rebutted criticism of Pope Pius for allegedly doing nothing to prevent the 1944 massacre of 335 Italians by Nazi soldiers in Rome. He said the Pope knew about the episode "only when everything was already decided and at least partly carried out." He also quoted the Pontiff as having said: "Some have spoken out of place, and the reaction to what they said was another 200,000 dead."

On Sept. 30, the Italian Supreme Court ruled that a book by American Robert Katz had defamed the Pope by portraying him as able but unwilling to prevent the massacre.

**Natural Family Planning** — As he witnessed the marriages of 38 couples from nine countries Oct. 9 in St. Peter's Basilica, the Holy Father told them to "recognize the rhythms of human fertility" and to follow them in "responsible parenthood," treating the mystery of life with the greatest respect."

**Self-Knowledge through Faith in God** — Man's desire to know himself is part of a deeper spiritual need that is satisfied only by faith in God, declared the Pope Oct. 12 before a general audience of 80,000 people in St. Peter's Square. He warned against the interpretation of human experience in exclusively sociological or psychological terms. "Man always runs the risk of making errors of perspective. These errors make him forget his own nature as a being made in God's image, and then leave him in the most desolate of desperations or, worse, in the most hardened cynicism."

**Franciscan Priest Canonized** — Pope John Paul canonized Capuchin Father Leopold Mandic on Oct. 16, the fifth anniversary of his election to the papacy. The newly declared saint was born in 1866 in Croatia (now Yugoslavia), spent most of his priestly life in Padua, Italy, and died in 1942. The Pope said of him: "St. Leopold didn't leave behind theological or literary works. He didn't fascinate us with his culture. He didn't found social institutions. For those who knew him, he was nothing but

a poor monk, small and sickly," whose pastoral mission and gift was hearing confessions.

**World Hunger** — The solution to the problem of hunger in the world is the formation of "an international economic order that is truly more just and more fraternal," said the Pope in a letter marking the third annual World Food Day, Oct. 16. Addressing the U.N. Food and Agriculture Organization, he praised U.N. efforts to relieve the hunger of "millions of human beings," especially in Africa, Asia and Latin America.

**Teaching Mission of Bishops** — This was the subject of remarks by the Pope at a meeting Oct. 22 with a group of bishops from the United States. He said: "It is as a minister of God's word, acting in the power of the Holy Spirit and through the charism of his episcopal office, that the bishop manifests Christ to the world, makes Christ present in the community, and effectively communicates Christ to all who open wide their hearts. . . . The (Second Vatican) Council declares that the episcopal office of teaching in the Church is conferred by episcopal consecration and can be exercised only in hierarchical communion with the head and members of the college of bishops." They have the responsibility of defending the word of God "against whatever would compromise its purity and integrity." He also said bishops should realize that "the present or 'current' teaching of the Church does not admit of a development that is either a reversal or a contradiction" of doctrine.

**World Mission Day** — The aim of the missionary is the "liberation of souls, through the blood of Christ," declared the Pope on World Mission Day, Oct. 23. Addressing 239 missionaries about to depart on foreign assignments, he said: "The work of the missionary is not a battle against people, to subjugate them. Rather, it is a battle for people. It has its motivation in love toward people still imprisoned by error, misery and evil." The Pontiff also appealed for greater spiritual and material support for missionary endeavors in all fields.

**Genetic Manipulation** — The Pope told 160 medical experts Oct. 29 that genetic engineering "must respect the fundamental dignity of human beings" because human dignity transcends a person's biological condition. "Genetic manipulation becomes arbitrary and unjust when it reduces (human) life to an object, when it forgets that it has to do with a human subject, capable of intelligence and freedom, that should be respected, whatever its limitations might be." The Pontiff's address was to participants in the just concluded 35th general assembly of the World Medical Association held in Venice.

**The Pope Also:**

• Congratulated Polish labor leader Lech Walesa for winning the Nobel Peace Prize, in a message Oct. 5

• Was "deeply saddened" by the bombing attack

in which 19 people, including four South Korean cabinet ministers, were killed Oct. 9 in Rangoon.

• Praised the Knights of Columbus Oct. 17 for their efforts "to foster among the laity a better understanding of their irreplaceable role in the Church, something so greatly praised by the Second Vatican Council."

• Called the massacres of more than 200 U.S. and French troops Oct. 23 in Lebanon and the U.S. invasion of Grenada signs of distrust among world leaders which can cause wars.

• Expressed sadness at the deaths of more than 1,000 persons in the Oct. 30 earthquake in Turkey.

• Met privately: U.S. Secretary of Defense Caspar Weinberger, Oct. 3; U.S. Attorney General William French Smith, Oct. 13; Spanish Prime Minister Felipe Gonzalez, Oct. 15; Swedish Prime Minister Olof Palme, the first Swedish head of government to visit a pope, Oct. 18.

**Vatican Briefs:**

• Nearly 1.5 million people toured Vatican museums in the first nine months of 1983.

• The Secretariat for Promoting Christian Unity announced Oct. 8 the appointment of Maryknoll Sister Joan Delaney to work with the Commission on World Mission and Evangelism, World Council of Churches.

• The Vatican formally accepted Oct. 18 the gift of the Shroud of Turin, regarded by many as the burial cloth of Christ, which had been willed to Pope John Paul II by former King Umberto, head of the House of Savoy.

• The manner in which local churches can provide for the pastoral and other needs of migrants and refugees was the central subject of discussion during the sixth plenary assembly of the Pontifical Commission for the Ministry of Migration and Tourism, Oct. 25 to 27.

### Synod of Bishops

Pope John Paul, presiding Oct. 29 at the closing session of the month-long, 1983 assembly of the Synod of Bishops, said that the "crisis of penance in its diverse forms must be a source of anxiety." He spoke about the fundamental importance of penance and reconciliation in the mission of the Church, and the need for the sacrament of penance in the lives of the faithful.

The Pontiff also disclosed to the more than 200 bishops in attendance that he had sent urgent appeals several days earlier to the heads of government in the United States and the Soviet Union calling for negotiation and dialogue pointed toward an end to the arms race.

Sixty-three propositions, the product of synodal deliberations, were presented to the Pope for his consideration in drafting a statement on the theme of the Synod, "Reconciliation and Penance in the Mission of the Church."

(See separate entry, Synod of Bishops.)

### NATIONAL

**Society Desensitized to Abortion** — Contemporary society has become desensitized and indifferent to abortion and its anti-life mentality, declared Father John Powell in an address to 500 participants in the Sept. 30 to Oct. 2 Pennsylvania Pro-Life Convention. The author of *Abortion: The Silent Holocaust* said the process toward desensitization was outlined in an editorial written by five physicians for a medical publication in 1970. The editorial set forth a "new ethic" based on the major premise that the quality of life supercedes the sanctity of life.

**Court Decisions** — The U.S. Supreme Court let stand Oct. 3 a 1977 Rhode Island law providing bus transportation for children attending parochial and private as well as public schools.

In Newark, a federal judge struck down Oct. 24 a New Jersey statute mandating a minute of silence in public school classrooms. U.S. District Court Judge Dickinson R. Debevoise called the law "an obvious attempt to cross the forbidden line" of separation of church and state.

**Death of Cardinal Cooke** — Cardinal Terence Cooke, archbishop of New York and bishop of Catholics in the U.S. armed forces since 1968, died of acute leukemia Oct. 6. A week before his death, the 62-year-old prelate, who was chairman of the Bishops' Committee for Pro-Life Activities, issued a statement to be read in parishes of the archdiocese on Oct. 9. In it, he said: "Life is no less beautiful when it is accompanied by illness or weakness, hunger or poverty, mental or physical handicaps, loneliness or old age."

**Seminary Personnel and Students** — Bishop John Marshall of Burlington, in a letter addressed to U.S. bishops and seminary rectors in August, informed them of the insistence of the Congregation for Catholic Education that:

• "Spiritual directors of seminarians must be priests. Laity and non-priest Religious, whether men or women, are not to be appointed to this task."

• "Students other than seminarians are not generally to be admitted to the academic program" of seminaries.

• "Professors, as a general rule, should be priests. . . . The congregation accepts the possibility of the appointment of laymen or laywomen, religious brothers or sisters, as faculty for certain disciplines which cannot be readily taught by priests, but this is always to be done in a limited degree."

The norms stated in the letter, which was reported belatedly, appeared to be at odds with practices in a number of U.S. seminaries. They also seemed against recommendation made four years earlier by a task force of the National Federation of Spiritual Directors, which favored a role for women in programs of spiritual direction and formation of students for the priesthood.

Bishop Marshall was in charge of a seminary review project ordered by the Congregation for Catholic Education.

**Fund for Religious Education Supplement** — Father Edward J. Slattery, president of the Catholic Church Extension Society, announced the creation of a $1 million grant fund for the production and distribution of a new weekly religious education supplement for Catholic newspapers. It was reported that the first issue of the four-page

"Faith Today," to be produced by the National Catholic News Service, would be ready for distribution to participating newspapers in January, 1984.

**Hyde Amendment Passed** — Congress gave final approval Oct. 20 to a one-year extension of the Hyde Amendment permitting federal funding of abortion only in cases of danger to the life of the mother.

**Skepticism about Nuclear Arms** — U.S. representatives of the Catholic Church and the World Alliance of Reformed Churches (Presbyterian and Congregational) "have registered in their recent statements an increasing skepticism about the nuclear arms race and a strong affirmation that the issue is, at heart, not simply a technical-strategic one but equally a moral one. The national debate, both sides believe, can only be illuminated by the involvement of an aware citizenry. The churches, then, have a clear responsibility to enter the public debate and to educate their congregations to participate actively in the decision-making process concerning it." So stated Eugene J. Fisher, executive secretary of the Secretariat for Catholic-Jewish Relations, National Conference of Catholic Bishops, at the conclusion of an Oct. 20-22 meeting at Princeton Theological Seminary.

**Sentenced for Transporting Illegal Aliens** — Father Thomas Davis and parish secretary Maria Elena Requejo of St. Francis Xavier Church, Laredo, Tex., were sentenced late in the month to a year of probation after pleading guilty to a charge of transporting illegal aliens the previous Sept. 29. Father Davis said: "I had a certain apprehension" about transporting the aliens "because of the law, but my compassion and concern about these people were greater. You have to do something as a Christian. . . . We're caught between the laws of man and the laws of God, and I chose the laws of God." Bishop Rene Gracida called Father Davis' action "a serious mistake of judgment" and "a dangerous, counterproductive activity to be engaged in."

**National Briefs:**
• Individuals and groups in at least 45 states and 17 foreign countries reported participation in the International Rosary March Oct. 2, "in petition for world peace" and deliverance "from nuclear war."
• Seton Hill Sister of Charity Melanie DiPietro, an associate in a Pittsburgh law firm, was appointed to a six-year term on the Pennsylvania Board of Public Welfare.
• The Church has "no apologies to make for failing to fit a political label" when it takes controversial stands on abortion and the nuclear arms race, declared Archbishop James A. Hickey of Washington Oct. 2 during a Red Mass celebrated for public officials, diplomats and members of the legal profession.
• The Religious Heritage of America presented its Clergyman of the Year Award to Cardinal John J. Krol of Philadelphia Oct. 10. The interfaith organization also presented a Faith and Freedom Award to Sister Elizabeth Thoman, executive di-

rector of the Los Angeles Center for Communications Ministry.
• Increasing poverty in the U.S. was called Oct. 18 "a conscious result of current government policy," by Father Thomas J. Harvey, executive director of the National Conference of Catholic Charities.
• Archbishop Joseph T. Ryan, while praying for the more than 200 Marines killed Oct. 23 in the suicide bombing of their headquarters in Beirut, called the attack a "moment of human tragedy."
• The U.S. invasion of Grenada Oct. 25 raised questions, doubts and criticism from a number of bishops and other religious leaders.

### NCC Lectionary Criticized

The National Council of Churches released Oct. 14 *An Inclusive Language Lectionary* of scriptural readings purged of as many male expressions as possible in language about God, Christ and human beings. The purpose of the reworking of the text of the *Revised Standard Version of the Bible* was to eliminate such terminology as well as other expressions considered in some quarters to be discriminatory and pejorative for any one of several reasons. The book, which had no official authority, was intended for "experimental and voluntary use."

The lectionary was the subject of immediate criticism.

Bruce Metzger of Princeton Seminary objected: "The changes in language pertaining to the deity are tatamount to rewriting the Bible. In my view as a Christian and as a scholar, such changes are altogether unacceptable. To explain that God transcends differences of gender is the work of the religious educator, not the Bible translator."

An unnamed Catholic scriptural scholar said he was concerned because of reports that changes affected not only style but also, and more importantly, matters of doctrinal substance.

Msgr. Richard Malone, executive director of the Committee on Doctrine, National Conference of Catholic Bishops, said a major thrust of the "inclusive" language project was an attempt "to ignore Jesus' masculinity."

### INTERNATIONAL

**Probe of Massacres Sought** — The Maronite bishops of Lebanon called Oct. 3 for an international investigation into what they said were massacres of Christians in the Chouf Mountain region of their country. They also appealed for the delivery of relief supplies for civilians in the area. They said atrocities there recalled "the darkest epochs of barbarism."

**Walesa, Nobel Medalist** — Lech Walesa, founder of the outlawed Solidarity labor union in Poland, was named winner of the 1983 Nobel Peace Prize for his "contribution, made with considerable personal sacrifice, to ensure the workers' right to establish their own organizations." The Nobel Committee announced the award Oct. 5 in Oslo.

**Genocide in Guatemala** — In a 21-page report issued Oct. 11, Archbishop James M. Hayes, of Halifax and several Anglican churchmen in Canada accused the Guatemalan government of genocide. The report said that the numbers of disappearances and assassinations were high and that pro-government death squads had "again unleashed a dramatic wave of violence. . . . These attacks are so extensive that they merit the definition of genocide."

**Nuclear War the Major Issue** — The nuclear dilemma is the most serious ethical issue confronting educators, said Father Theodore M. Hesburgh, president of the University of Notre Dame, Oct. 13 in Toronto. Addressing a joint meeting of the American Council on Education and the Association of Universities and Colleges of Canada, he said: "If we do not learn and teach our students how to cope with this primordial nuclear problem, we need not worry about all the others. . . . After total nuclear conflagration, all human problems are moot."

**Unborn Not Protected** — An unborn child is not a person in the legal sense and is not protected by the Canadian constitution, ruled Judge W. R. Matheson Oct. 13 in Regina, Saskatchewan. Although "rapid advances in medical science may make it socially desirable that some legal status be extended to fetuses," he stated, "it is the prerogative of Parliament and not the courts to . . . extend to the unborn all legal rights possessed by a living person."

**Convictions Upheld** — Vatican Radio reported Oct. 13 that an appeals court in Czechoslovakia had upheld the convictions of two Franciscan priests, Fathers Jiri Mazanec and Frantisek Pometio, and sentenced them to prison terms of eight months and six months, respectively. The priests were found guilty in July on charges of "anti-state activities" that included publishing a theological magazine, accepting a novice into their order and celebrating Mass in the presence of other priests.

In another development, a communist newspaper in eastern Slovakia charged that the Pope and other church leaders were seeking to "exploit religion and abuse religious feelings . . . for ideological operations of contemporary imperialism, including the endeavor to incite counter-revolution in the countries of real socialism."

**Church Property in Malta** — Archbishop Joseph Mercieca of Malta, in a suit filed Oct. 16, challenged the constitutionality of a law authorizing the government to expropriate almost all church-owned property not used for purposes of worship and to use proceeds from the expropriation for educational purposes. The suit claimed that the law violated constitutional provisions regarding freedom of religion, freedom against discrimination and freedom from expropriation without due compensation.

**Political Solution in El Salvador** — Two Salvadoran prelates — Auxiliary Bishop Gregorio Rosa Chavez and Bishop Marco Rene Revelo — told the Kissinger Commission on Central America that church personnel favored a political rather than a military solution to the civil war in their country. An agency of the Archdiocese of San Salvador reported that more than 47,000 people had been killed in four years of conflict.

**Bishop Attacked, Masses Cancelled** — Members of a pro-government group physically attacked Auxiliary Bishop Bosco Vivas of Managua Oct. 30 and forced the cancellation of Sunday Masses in at least eight churches in Nicaragua. The reason for the group's action appeared to be the opposition of the bishops to the military draft policy of the Sandinist government. The episcopal conference, in a statement issued in August, said the policy "follows the general lines of all totalitarian-type legislation," and expressed fear that under the plan "the army becomes converted into an obligatory center of political indoctrination in favor of the Sandinist Party."

**South African Priest Detained** — The president of the South African Bishops' Conference protested "in the strongest possible terms" the detention of its secretary general, Father Smangaliso Mkhatshwa, for undisclosed reasons. The black priest, an opponent of the government policy of apartheid, and the leader of the Catholic Students' Association were arrested by police Oct. 30 after attending a prayer service. The student was released by the following day but there was no report concerning the whereabouts of Father Mkhatshwa. Archbishop Denis E. Hurley said the conference was "experiencing deep anxiety" about his situation. "The anxiety," he said, "confirms how detestable a political situation becomes when the rule of law is discarded and people disappear into detention without trace."

**International Briefs:**

• Bishop John M. Sherlock of London, Ontario, and Bishop Jean-Guy Hamelin of Rouyn-Noranda, Quebec, were elected president and vice president, respectively, of the Canadian Conference of Catholic Bishops.

• The United Nations Educational, Scientific and Cultural Organization announced Oct. 7 that Pax Christi International, a worldwide Catholic peace organization, had won its 1983 prize for peace education.

• The bishops of Chile renewed Oct. 15 an appeal for dialogue between the military government and its civilian opposition, for the purpose of ending months of violence. The country, after 10 years of military rule, was in serious economic trouble and civil disorder.

### Jesuit General Congregation

The 33rd general congregation in the history of the Society of Jesus was concluded Oct. 25 with the release of a policy statement entitled "Companions of Jesus Sent into the World of Today." In it, the congregation pledged continuity in the Jesuits' service of faith and promotion of justice, urged members of the society "to a more profound sense of obedience to and collaboration with the pope and local bishops," and counseled against engagement in "a merely secular activism."

The congregation, in session since Sept. 2, elected Father Peter-Hans Kolvenbach to succeed Father Pedro Arrupe as superior general of the society.

Attending the congregation were more than 200 representatives of nearly 27,000 Jesuits.

# NOVEMBER 1983

## VATICAN

**For Justice in Guatemala** — The Pope urged 14 bishops of Guatemala Nov. 5 to promote justice and the common good, "above all, for the poorest people." He also cautioned them against confusing "authentic evangelization with subversion." He said the Church has to confront "persistent structures of social injustice" but should nevertheless keep itself "above the confrontations of political groups and parties. . . . The Church's choice of nonviolence does not signify passivity, nor silent complicity with sin, injustice and suffering," but represents "an active commitment to justice and peace."

**Family Rights and Values** — Pope John Paul, in a speech to 1,000 participants in the seventh annual International Congress on the Family, said that parents have the right and duty to educate their children "in conformity with their moral and religious convictions," and in schools or other institutions of their choice. He called on governments to support parental rights, and said also that moral and sex education rightfully belongs under the "attentive guidance" of parents.

**Luther Anniversary** — Pope John Paul marked the 500th anniversary of the birth of Martin Luther, Nov. 10, with a letter addressed to Cardinal Johannes Willebrands, head of the Secretariat for Promoting Christian Unity. He welcomed the observance as "a fraternal invitation . . . to common (Catholic-Lutheran) effort toward a deeper and more complete picture of the historical events as well as a critical discussion of the manifold legacy of Luther. . . . It has . . . become clear that the breach of church unity may solely be attributed neither to lack of comprehension on the part of bishops of the Catholic Church nor to lack of understanding of true Catholicism on Luther's side, however much such an element may have played its part. The decisions taken reached back much further. In the dispute over the relationship between faith and tradition were involved basic problems of right interpretation and acceptance of Christian belief. Their power to split the Church is not to be explained by purely historical understanding." He added that historical clarification of the causes and results of the Reformation have to be complemented by "the dialogue of faith . . . in the spirit befitting its fundamentals: in loyalty to the faith give to us, which includes penitence and readiness to learn by listening."

**Lay Persons' Influence** — The "distinctive Christian responsibility" of lay men and women involves participation in social and economic life, military affairs, science, the arts and the mass media. They "are able to exert a great influence on culture and make a special contribution to its evangelization. They can do this particularly in the fields of science, literature and art." So stated the Holy Father at a Nov. 11 meeting with Australian bishops.

**Appeal to Scientists** — In an address Nov. 12 to the Pontifical Academy of Sciences, the Pope asked scientists to work in "laboratories of life" for peace and the improvement of living conditions. Noting that people are living in "a grave moment in history," he said: "Faced with this great patient (humanity) in danger of death, scientists, in collaboration with all other members of the world of culture and with the social institutions, must carry out the work of salvation analogous to that of the doctor who has sworn to use all his powers to heal the sick." He said he was seeking "for the success of the only war that must be fought: the war against hunger, disease and the death of millions of human beings whose quality and dignity of life could be helped and promoted with seven per cent of the amount spent each year for the incessant and threatening rearmament of the richest nations." He asked scientists to help in the process of building peace by directing their research toward "the promotion of justice" and by resisting efforts to "exploit (their) research and discoveries against justice and peace."

**Incentive for Peace** — "The frightening specter of nuclear holocaust" is an incentive to work for peace, declared the Pope Nov. 19 in an address to members of the private North Atlantic Treaty Organization. "While nations are naturally preoccupied with the requirement of their own defense, the seemingly endless instances of discord and unrest in the world, and especially the frightening specter of nuclear holocaust, are powerful incentives to continue the unrelenting search for practical and enduring means of achieving peace. . . . The Church engages in this pursuit, furthermore, not in a secondary or extraneous way, but in faithful compliance with the exhortation of the Lord himself."

**Anti-Family Campaign** — The Pope urged the bishops of Puerto Rico Nov. 24 to take measures against "powerful and highly destructive private and public forces that militate against the family." In addition to a "divorce mentality," the forces included movements in favor of sterilization, contraception and abortion.

In an address to bishops of Panama earlier in the month, the Pontiff said: "The systematic application of plans conceived and financed from abroad, ranging from artificial birth control and sterilization to those aimed at legalizing abortion, have a negative effect on the health of the family."

**Negative Stance regarding Masons** — In a statement released Nov. 26 with the approval of Pope John Paul, the Congregation for the Doctrine of the Faith declared, in part: "The Church's negative position on Masonic associations . . . remains unaltered, since their principles have always been regarded as irreconcilable with the Church's doctrine. Hence, joining them remains prohibited by the Church. Catholics enrolled in Masonic associations are involved in serious sin and may not approach Holy Communion."

**The Pope Also:**

• Said on All Saints' Day that participation in the communion of saints "requires a daily effort to correspond fully with the divine vocation and to reach our future glory."

• Told a general audience on All Souls' Day: "We should take up with our loved ones, in the intimacy of our hearts, the dialogue that death should not cut off."

• Praised the "total faithfulness" to Christ and the Church of Pius XII and John XXIII on the 25th anniversaries of their respective death and election.

• Urged a group of European Catholic legislators Nov. 10 to be guided by their faith in dealing with issues of peace and justice.

• Met privately with: Haitian Ambassador Pierre Pompee, Nov. 14; Tanzanian Ambassador Ahmed Du Diria Hassan, Nov. 17; Lebanese President Amin Gemayel, Nov. 26.

### Vatican Briefs:

• The Pontifical Academy of Sciences called for the diversion of funds for arms to programs and projects for the relief of hunger in the world, in a statement issued Nov. 16.

• The Pontifical Mission for Palestine reported Nov. 21 that since 1948 it had contributed more than $150 million in funds, goods and services to Palestinian refugees.

• High-stakes gambling that damages the gambler and his family is morally unacceptable, said an editorial in the Nov. 22 issue of *L'Osservatore Romano.*

• A 12-article Charter of the Rights of the Family was issued by the Holy See Nov. 24.

### Canon Law

The revised Code of Canon Law for the Latin Rite, promulgated by Pope John Paul Jan. 25, went into effect Nov. 27. This code, superceding the one in effect since 1918, marked the completion of the last major reform in the Church stemming from the Second Vatican Council.

The revised Code is shorter (1,752 canons) than the one it replaces (2,414 canons).

It is more pastoral and flexible, as well as more theologically oriented than the former Code. And it gives greater emphasis than its predecessor to a number of significant facets and concepts in church life.

One of them, along with the hierarchical constitution of the Church, is the underlying notion of the *communio* or community of all members of the Church.

Another is the central significance of the sacraments and their far-reaching ramifications in the lives of the people of God.

The Code provides for greater participation by lay persons in the teaching, sanctifying and governing missions of the Church.

Of general relevance and interest are the canons which deliniate the rights and obligations of all the faithful and lay persons in particular.

### NATIONAL

**Bishops Asked To Help Religious** — In a letter dated Oct. 3 and released this month through the Institute on Religious Life, Mother Teresa of Cal-

cutta asked bishops of the U.S. to help Religious "love, obey and remain faithful to the Church and the Vicar of Christ." The letter was "more or less" timed for release with similar letters by members of the institute urging bishops to share the Pope's concern for religious communities in the U.S. This concern prompted the Holy Father in June to name Archbishop John R. Quinn of San Francisco to head a special commission to help bishops work with Religious. Mother Teresa said in her letter: "There has been much disturbance in the religious life of sisters, all due to misguided advice and zeal. . . . Like in many laywomen, so also in our Religious, the ambition to be equal to men in all things, even in the priesthood, has taken away that peace and joy of being one with Jesus and his Church."

**Investigation in Seattle** — In a statement released Oct. 26, Archbishop James A. Hickey of Washington announced that he had been appointed by the Vatican to go to Seattle to "visit with Archbishop Hunthausen at length and to explore the views and opinions of informed members of the clergy, Religious and laity," so that the Holy See might evaluate reports concerning the archbishop in his ministry.

In a statement issued after his Nov. 2 to 8 visit, Archbishop Hickey said: "I have observed the progress made in the Archdiocese of Seattle and have gained, I believe, an insight into a range of viewpoints. I heard from so many who expressed admiration for Archbishop Hunthausen as a man of Gospel values, a bishop deeply committed to Christ and to the Church. Concerns and criticism expressed to me have been discussed with the archbishop. We are confident that these can be resolved in a spirit of mutual understanding and in harmony with the teaching and direction of the Church."

The specific concerns and criticism mentioned in the statement were not disclosed.

During his visit, Archbishop Hickey conferred not only with Archbishop Hunthausen but also with more than 60 priests, Religious and lay persons.

**Reactions to Grenada Invasion** — While at least one Catholic churchman in Grenada joined other religious leaders in praise of the U.S. invasion, there was some criticism of the action in this country. Cardinal Joseph L. Bernardin of Chicago had "serious reservations" about it. The Justice and Peace Commission of the Archdiocese of Baltimore said the invasion appeared to be an unethical exercise in military intervention. Father Ronald N. Carignan, president of the Conference of Major Superiors of Men Religious, called the invasion a cause for "deep concern."

**Lectionary Repudiated** — Orthodox delegates to the Nov. 9 to 11 meeting of the governing board of the National Council of Churches repudiated *An Inclusive Language Lectionary* recently produced by the council's Division of Education and Ministry. "The lectionary (because of its use of sex-neutral and similar terms) implies a false theology and substantially alters crucial biblical witness to the church's understanding of God — Father, Son and Holy Spirit," said a statement read by Greek Orthodox Father Gregory Wingenbach of Monassen, Pa. "The lectionary's effect is to distort fundamental Christian doctrines and our witness to non-Christians. For example, by designating God as father and mother, by changing Jesus' own scriptural witness to his nature and being, and by effectively denying the Christological and Trinitarian witness of the Council of Nicaea, one practical effect of the proposed lectionary is to disavow the world and national councils' hard-won consensus on the apostolic faith of Christians."

**Evangelization Called For** — At a Mass marking the 250th anniversary of Old St. Joseph's Church in Philadelphia, Msgr. John P. Foley suggested that Catholics should celebrate the gift of religious liberty with a nationwide evangelization effort keyed to "personal practice, public advocacy and popular proclamation" of the faith. The editor of the *Catholic Standard and Times* observed that most of the growth of the Church in this country had come "from immigration and reproduction, not from evangelization and conversion."

**Luther Anniversary** — Catholics joined Lutherans and other Protestants in observances marking the 500th anniversary of the birth, Nov. 10, 1483, of Martin Luther. One of the principal celebrations was the Martin Luther Jubilee, a series of conferences, programs and related events held Nov. 6 to 12 in Washington.

**Bishops Meet with Women** — One hundred bishops and 50 women took part in a Nov. 12 and 13 meeting in Washington. Heavy emphasis on feminist demands for radical changes in various areas of church practice prompted Auxiliary Bishop Austin B. Vaughan of New York to call the meeting "stacked."

Demands for radical changes were also the substance of a "Woman Church Speaks" meeting Nov. 11 to 13 in the Chicago suburb of Rosemont.

**Swaggart Show Dropped** — Atlanta television stations WAGA and WANX dropped the Rev. Jimmy Swaggart's daily, paid-time TV program following complaints by Catholics that he was attacking the Church. The Atlanta archdiocesan *Georgia Bulletin* said in editorials Nov. 10 and 17: "It really is surprising that TV evangelist Jimmy Swaggart, in this day and age, would be so blatantly and disgustingly anti-Catholic in many of his programs. . . . Mr. Swaggart's style is . . . a continuation of . . . divisive hatred that has no place within the arena of a loving, building community of faith." The paper called his message "the Swaggart gospel of hate."

**U.S.-Vatican Relations** — A bill lifting a century-old ban on U.S. diplomatic relations with the Vatican was signed into law by President Reagan Nov. 22. (For background regarding relations before 1867, see separate article.)

**National Briefs:**

• John E. McCarthy, director of Migration and Refugee Services, U.S. Catholic Conference, was elected to a third consecutive term as president of the International Catholic Migration Commission.

• Sister Mary Hennessey, staff member of the Diocese of Worcester, was named director of ministerial studies at Harvard Divinity School.

• Ninety-three dioceses participated in the 33rd annual clothing drive of Catholic Relief Services. The 1983 drive resulted in the collection of seven million pounds of clothing for needy persons overseas.

• On the last weekend of the month, Philadelphia became the last archdiocese in the country to have Saturday evening Masses for fulfilling the Sunday Mass obligation.

## NCCB-USCC Meeting

Bishops attending the annual meeting of the National Conference of Catholic Bishops and the United States Catholic Conference Nov. 14 to 17 in Washington took the following actions;

• approved continuing observance of six holy days of obligation;

• approved and issued a pastoral letter on Hispanic ministry;

• issued a statement on liturgical developments, marking the 20th anniversary of the constitution on the subject produced by the Second Vatican Council;

• approved a budget of $23.9 million for the forthcoming year;

• elected Bishop James A. Malone of Youngstown and Archbishop John L. May of St. Louis to three year terms, respectively, as president and vice president of the conferences.

(For detailed coverage, see 1983 Meeting of U.S. Bishops.)

## INTERNATIONAL

**"No" to Nuclear Weapons** — Franciscan superiors from the United States, Canada, Ireland and Italy, at a meeting in Cochrane, Alberta, condemned the development, testing and deployment of nuclear weapons and the planned installation of cruise and Pershing missiles in Western Europe. Father Alan McCoy of Oakland, Calif., said that "stationing cruise weapons in Europe . . . will put a nuclear confrontation on a hair-trigger."

**Islamic Penalties in Sudan** — While supporting the government's call for moral reform, Archbishop Gabriel Subeir Wako of Khartoum expressed concern over the adoption of the Islamic penal code in the nation. A report on a pastoral letter issued in September said that objection was raised because provisions of the code were degrading, too severe, and could "dull the moral and humane feelings of the nation." The archbishop also said that Christians were the objects of discrimination even before the code went into effect.

**Church Threatened in Central America** — The Catholic Church "is and will continue to be persecuted as long as it does not accommodate itself to the caprices of totalitarian systems, whether of the right or the left." So stated Archbishop Arturo Rivera Damas of San Salvador in a homily at Mass Nov. 13. He said priests in Guatemala and El Salvador were threatened by "irrational violence" and that the Marxist-oriented government of Nicaragua was harassing the Church.

**Sandinistas Crippling the Church** — "Christians in Nicaragua today confront a government that is committed to manipulating, dividing and crippling the Church," although it claims to be supportive of religion and includes priests in cabinet-level positions. "The Sandinista leaders want a Marxist-Leninist Nicaragua. They created their movement with that dream in mind; they fought for it; and now they are working to make it a reality." So stated Humberto Belli, a Nicaraguan Catholic who left the country in 1982, in a 51-page criticism of the regime.

**Priest Arrested, Others Warned in Poland —** Father Henryk Jankowski, the parish priest of Solidarity leader Lech Walesa, accused Polish authorities Nov. 15 of conducting a "campaign against me." He made the accusation after being interrogated by police for alleged "abuse of the freedom of conscience and of religion" in connection with sermons linked by authorities with antigovernment demonstrations.

In another development, the government called on Cardinal Jozef Glemp to silence about 69 "antisocialist" priests.

**Pastoral Restrictions in Czechoslovakia —** Vatican Radio reported Nov. 22 that the government of Czechoslovakia had tightened restrictions on hospital visits by priests. The station said that red tape, requiring priests to get permission beforehand from a patient's physician and to file documentation on each visit, made it difficult for priests to provide pastoral care and comfort to sick persons and their families. "The long and complicated procedure" caused such delays that some patients died before a priest could visit them.

**Jesuit Loyalty Pledged, Defects Acknowledged —** At his first press conference since becoming superior general of the Society of Jesus, Father Peter-Hans Kolvenbach reaffirmed Nov. 25 the Jesuits' loyalty to the Pope and agreed with the Holy Father that the order, like others, had "defects." He said the defects included "certain secularizing practices and attitudes, sacrificing prayer for activity that is simply too humanitarian, and adopting socio-political modes of behavior that are determined by criteria that are not always evangelical in nature."

**Appeal for Rights in the Philippines —** The bishops of the Philippines asked President Ferdinand Marcos for "full re-establishment of civil rights, honest elections, freedom of the press," and a willingness to listen to the needs of the people. In a pastoral letter read in churches Nov. 27, they warned of a "bloody revolution" if repressive violations of basic rights were not ended, and said that graft and corruption had weakened the government's credibility. "We ask," the bishops said, "only that the common good of 60 million Filipinos be placed above the petty and narrow interests of any political family or party."

**Bethlehem University To Reopen —** Israeli military officials agreed late in the month to reopen Vatican-affiliated Bethlehem University Dec. 5, a month short of the 60-day closure ordered Nov. 2 in the wake of student disturbances. Christian Brother Thomas Scanlan, vice chancellor of the university, said Nov. 25 while announcing the reopening: "It was made clear that any recurrence of violent demonstration or disturbances of the public order would evoke stiff penalties to the university in the future." The school had been closed following conflict over a Palestinian folklore exhibit in late October.

**International Briefs:**

• Assessing five years of experience under a liberal abortion law, the Italian Movement for Life reported that abortions in Italy had become a widespread means of birth limitation among married women who already had children.

• Religion in Cuba was reported to be dying from indifference rather than persecution, according to an article in the Nov. 14 editon of the *Washington Post;* the article was based on the views of a priest, a rabbi and several lay persons in Cuba.

• Mother Teresa of Calcutta was awarded the Order of Merit by Queen Elizabeth II of England Nov. 18, for her work with the poor, sick and abandoned.

• The government news agency Tass reported that Father Sigitas Tamkevicius went on trial Nov. 29 in the Lithuanian capital, Vilna, on charges of slandering the state and using church funds for the support of underground publications reporting violations of human rights. He was the second Lithuanian priest to go on trial in 1983; Father Alfonsas Svarinskas, before him, was sentenced to seven years' imprisonment after conviction on similar charges.

### Nuclear Deterrence

Nuclear deterrence under strict conditions and as a temporary step toward disarmament was emerging "as the most widely accepted view of the Roman Catholic Church," said Cardinal George Basil Hume in an article in the Nov. 17 edition of *The Times* of London. British bishops, at the same time, said in a statement: "In spite of claims about the need for a balance in deterrence, the coming of the cruise (missile) is seen by many, not as a bargaining factor but as an additional obstacle to progress in the vital disarmament talks in Geneva."

The bishops of France, by an overwhelming vote of 93 to 2 Nov. 8, approved a 5,000-word statement in which they condemned total pacifism and unilateral disarmament while declaring that "nuclear deterrence is still legitimate. . . . It still serves peace to discourage the aggressor by forcing him into the beginning of prudence through an appropriate fear."

Austrian university groups and church leaders were critical of the U.S. bishops' pastoral letter on war and peace, reported American pacifist Gordon Zahn Nov. 27 after a 10-day trip to Austria. He said: "Claiming to speak from the standpoint of their national experience of occupation by Soviet forces . . . and the more recent events which have made their country a haven for refugees from communist oppression, they obviously felt it was naive of me — and presumably our bishops as well — to reject or even question the need to maintain the existing balance of terror."

## DECEMBER 1983

### VATICAN

**Prayer and Sensitivity of the Church** — Only the Church at prayer, the Pope told 15 U.S. bishops Dec. 3, "can show herself sufficiently sensitive to the needs of the sick, the suffering, the lonely — especially in the great urban centers — and the poor everywhere. . . . The Church as a community of service has first to feel the weight of the burden carried by so many individuals and families, and then strive to alleviate these burdens. The discipleship that the Church discovers in prayer she expresses in deep interest for Christ's brethren in the modern world and for their many different needs. . . . In prayer, the Church is confirmed in her solidarity with the weak who are oppressed, the vulnerable who are manipulated, the children who are exploited, and everyone who is in any way discriminated against."

**Justice and the Gospel** — Theologians must work harder to link the quest for justice with the message of Christ, the Pope told members of the International Theological Commission Dec. 5. He said that the connection made by the Second Vatican Council between the dignity of the human person and the doctrine of Christ as Redeemer "has not yet been well inserted into theology," nor has it been well applied. The concept of Christ's "living for others" must animate the Christian quest for justice, he added. At the same time, he criticized a "false horizontalism" based on a brotherhood of man which is not related to the Fatherhood of God and the role of the Son of God made Man.

**Feminism and Religious Life** — In June-July conversations with 10 representatives of religious institutes of women, the Pope expressed "his conviction that we must deepen our understanding of the women's movements in order to understand the problems of religious life." He acknowledged positive as well as negative aspects of feminism, and said that reactions of women "against the abuses of men are justified." He also said:

• Women Religious should receive adequate remuneration for their work.

• "Bishops have stated that the presence of women Religious is an element without which it would be difficult to build a local church."

• There is a "crisis in maternity" in the Western World, and "physical and spiritual" maternity are intimately linked to the identity of women.

These and other related views of the Pope and women Religious were contained in a report circulated by the nuns early in December.

**Mary, Image of the Church** — In an address before 25,000 people in St. Peter's Square Dec. 11, Pope John Paul said Mary reflects the living image of the Church. "Placed at the meeting of the Old and New Covenants, Mary is the end of the messianic church of Israel and the beginning of the Church born with Christ. With Mary, therefore, are concluded the promises, the plans, the prophecies and the spirituality of the Old Testament church. The New Testament church begins, without stain or wrinkle, in the fullness of the grace of the Holy Spirit." In Mary, the Church reaches its "highest perfection, without the shadow of sin" (a reference to her Immaculate Conception).

**Visit to Lutherans** — The Holy Father made the first-ever papal visit to a Lutheran congregation Dec. 11. Addressing 500 persons during a prayer service at the Evangelical Lutheran Church in Rome, he said: "On this 500th anniversary of the birth of Martin Luther, we seem to discern the distant dawn of the advent of a recomposition of our unity and community. . . . We desire unity. We are working for unity without letting ourselves be discouraged by the difficulties we find along the way."

The Pope prefaced his remarks by saying: "The gift of this meeting moves me from the bottom of my heart. I wanted this meeting to occur exactly in Advent. It is an outstanding occasion to look together to the Lord and wait upon the God of our salvation. . . .

"I have come because the Spirit of God is calling us to search for the full unity of Christians through ecumenical dialogue. We know of the difficult history of the Evangelical-Lutheran community in Rome, its beginning marked with care and its development through light and shade in the conditions of this city. The question comes before us all the more pressingly: 'May we — in spite of all human weakness, in spite of the insufficiencies of the past centuries — mistrust the grace of the Lord, which has been revealed in these latter days through the word of the Holy Spirit, that which we have received through the Council?' *(Decree on Ecumenism.)*

"So we find ourselves, even with the apparent divisions in doctrine and life, still bound together most deeply in the solidarity of all Christians."

The Pontiff concluded with: "Let us follow the call to reconciliation with God and each other. Christ, the ruler of all, is not only over us, but he is also among us, the *Kyrios,* who was, who is and who shall be in eternity."

**Educators and Evangelization** — The Pope called on 1,000 European university professors and administrators Dec. 15 to offer "intellectual charity" to students, colleagues and social institutions, and to contribute culturally to religious education and evangelization. "You should not merely be intellectuals who reflect, evaluate and contemplate truth, isolated in individualistic ivory towers. You, too, are integrally involved in a prophetic task of forming consciences capable of saying 'no' to death, hatred, violence, terror, error, evil and degradation."

**Confessional Ministry** — Priests "must give priority" to the ministry of the confessional, the Holy Father told a group of U.S. priests Dec. 16. "As priests, we are charged with being Christ's ambassadors of reconciliation. . . . In allowing penitents the opportunity to personally confess their sins to the Lord, you mediate one of the most profoundly religious moments of forgiveness and joy." In this "deeply intimate" encounter, Christ "has chosen us, his priests, to be the only ones to forgive sins in his name. . . . This ministry, therefore, is uniquely ours and is one to which we must give priority."

In a related talk, the Pontiff told a group of Mexican bishops Dec. 1 that the abuse of general absolution was "an attack against the true dignity of the sacrament of penance.

**Meeting with Agca** — Two days after Christmas, in Rome's top-security Rebibbia Prison, the Holy Father met and spoke for 20 minutes with the man who tried to kill him on May 13, 1981. After the meeting of reconciliation with Mehmet Ali Agca, the Pope said: "I have spoken to a brother who has my complete trust. What was said is a secret that will remain between him and me."

**The Pope Also:**
• Met with Foreign Minister Bohuslav Chnoupek of Czechoslovakia Dec. 2; it was the first papal meeting with a high Czechoslovakian official since the end of World War II.
• Prayed that the world's decision-makers would seek to solve their problems through dialogue rather than resort to violence, during a visit Dec. 8 to Rome's Spanish Steps, the site of a statue of Mary commemorating the proclamation of the dogma of the Immaculate Conception in 1854.
• Called on a general audience of 4,000 people Dec. 21 to "throw open the doors" of their lives to Christ during the days before Christmas.
• Renewed the pledge of the Church to work for world peace with "governments as well as the man on the street," in an address Dec. 22 to 32 cardinals and members of the Roman Curia.

**Vatican Briefs:**
• The Congregation for Catholic Education issued Dec. 1 a document entitled "Educational Guidance in Human Love: Outlines for Sex Education."
• Msgr. Mariano Oles, a staff member of the Congregation for Bishops, said late in the month: "The Vatican's business is the Church, whether or not the Church is clandestine is irrelevant." He made the comment in reference to remarks about church-state relations by Vladmini Janku, Czechoslovakian minister of religious affairs.

### Christmas Message

Pope John Paul, in an impassioned Christmas appeal, urged nations to stop spending enormous sums of money and talent on sophisticated weapons while thousands upon thousands of men, women and children were dying of hunger and laboring under the burden of all kinds of suffering. He delivered the message before 80,000 people in St. Peter's Square after celebrating Masses in St. Peter's Basilica. At its conclusion, he extended Christmas greetings in 44 languages to television viewers in 35 countries.

In praying for the blessing of God, the Pope said, in part: "Look upon our world of today, with its hopes and disappointments, with its high aspirations and its vile deeds, with its noble ideals and its humiliating compromises. Impel individuals and peoples to break down the wall of selfishness, of arrogance and hate, in order to open themselves to

fraternal respect for all human beings, near or far, because they are . . . brothers and sisters in Christ. . . . Assist your Church in her efforts on behalf of the poor, the neglected and the suffering."

### NATIONAL

**Report Classified** — While commemorative services marked the third anniversary of the murders of four U.S. women missionaries in El Salvador, the State Department announced that a new report on the investigation into the circumstances of their deaths had been marked "classified" and would not, therefore, be made public. Release of the report, it was said, could jeopardize trials pending against five ex-Salvadoran National Guardsmen being held in the case. Critics of the investigation charged that U.S. and Salvadoran authorities had not adequately pursued evidence that the murders may have been ordered by high Salvadoran officials.

**Vatican Relations Opposed** — A half-page advertisement in the Dec. 5 edition of *The Washington Post,* sponsored by the Seventh Day Adventist Church, called on President Reagan not to appoint an ambassador to the Vatican, "for the sake of the nation, for the sake of the church."

**Vatican Art in San Francisco** — Between Nov. 19 and Dec. 6, approximately 135,000 people viewed 237 works of Vatican art on exhibit at the M.H. de Young Memorial Museum. The exhibit, shown earlier in New York and Chicago, was to continue until Feb. 19, 1984.

**"Seamless Garment" of Life Issues** — The Church's position on nuclear arms, abortion and capital punishment make up a "seamless garment" of issues that Catholics should address together rather than separately, Cardinal Joseph L. Bernardin said Dec. 6 in an address at Fordham University. He emphasized the importance of developing a "consistent ethic of life in our culture," declaring: "I believe the Catholic moral tradition has something valuable to say in the face of the multiple threats to the sacredness of life today, and I am convinced that the Church is in a position to make a significant defense of life in a comprehensive and a consistent manner."

**Nun Killed in Peru** — Cardinal Bernardin joined Cardinal Juan Landazuri Ricketts of Lima in asking for an impartial investigation into events surrounding the death of Sister Joan Sawyer. The Columban missionary from Chicago was killed Dec. 14 when police fired on an ambulance in which she and three other sisters engaged in prison ministry were held hostage by inmates attempting to escape from Lurigancho Prison in Lima. One other nun was wounded and eight prisoners were killed by gunfire. The Peruvian government announced that charges of negligent homicide were filed Dec. 26 against two prison officials and seven police officers in connection with the death of the nun.

**Hunger in the U.S.** — The U.S. Catholic Conference and other church agencies urged the federal government Dec. 22 to increase federal funding to fight hunger. The agencies cited statistics on the increased burden borne by religious and other voluntary groups as hungry individuals and families — hurt by recession, unemployment and cutbacks in federal assistance — flocked to breadlines. The agencies said that private efforts could not meet the massive needs of the hungry. Walter Grazer, a U.S. Catholic Conference staff member, said: "While the Church will continue to do its utmost with our limited resources to continue to serve those who are hungry, we simply do not have the resources to meet the need or fill the gap created by the budget reductions enacted in the federal food programs over the last two years."

While voluntary agencies were extending their efforts to provide food and housing for the needy, presidential advisor Edwin Meese said he had never seen "any authoritative figures that there are hungry children in America." In related remarks, he inferred that many, if not most, people seeking food relief were freeloaders. Some persons with first-hand knowledge of the needs and circumstances of the poor called his comments "outrageous," "scandalous" and "an insult to the poor."

**Priest Shortage** — By the year 2000, the number of active diocesan priests in the U.S. might decline by as much as 50 per cent and most priests will be in the 46 to 75 age bracket. The predictions were based on a study conducted under the auspices of the Center for Youth Studies at the Catholic University of America.

**Interfaith Developments** — Communion in Christ, the role of creeds with respect to church unity, the relationship of the church to suffering and the church as the sign of the world God wills, were among subjects under discussion at the first international meeting of representatives of the Catholic Church and the Disciples of Christ. The meeting, first in a projected seven-year series, was held in Venice.

The Anglican-Roman Catholic Dialogue marked four years of work with the publication Dec. 22 of a statement entitled "Images of God: Reflections on Christian Anthropology." The 9,000-word document:
• cited masculine and feminine images of God;
• rejected inferior social norms or roles for women;
• rejected discrimination against homosexually-oriented persons but declared homosexual activity "morally wrong";
• praised celibacy and consecrated virginity as an "eschatological witness" complementing and supporting "the love between married persons";
• noted some sharing of belief with respect to Mary and the saints.

**National Briefs:**
• Religious and political leaders in Utah joined Bishop William K. Weigand in proclaiming Dec. 4 to 10 as Peace Week in the Diocese of Salt Lake City.
• The Catholic League for Civil and Religious Rights urged Sen. Ernest F. Hollings of South Carolina to apologize for calling the bishops of the U.S. "a bunch of kids" because of their support of tuition tax credit legislation that would benefit Catholic schools.

• Charles H. Keating, Jr., chairman of the board of Continental Homes, announced that the company would donate $1 million over a 10-year period to the St. Vincent de Paul Society of Maricopa County, Ariz., to help homeless people.

### Leading 1983 News Stories

Forty-two editors of newspapers subscribing to NC News Service rated the following as the 10 leading stories of 1983.
1. The U.S. bishops' pastoral letter, "The Challenge of Peace: God's Promise and Our Response," for the second time.
2. The revised Code of Canon Law, in effect as of Nov. 27.
3. U.S.-Vatican tensions regarding priests and religious in politics and the rejection of efforts in support of the ordination of women.
4. Visits of Pope John Paul to Central America and Haiti, Poland, France and Austria.
5. Release of a document on justification by the Catholic-Lutheran dialogue group.
6. Abortion developments, including the U.S. Supreme Court ruling against an Akron, O., ordinance regulating the practice of abortion, and defeat by the Senate of a proposed constitutional amendment against abortion.
7. Controversy over the intent and mission of a papal commission appointed to investigate and improve relations between bishops and religious.
8. The 1983 assembly of the Synod of Bishops, with its theme, "Reconciliation and Penance in the Mission of the Church."
9. U.S. Supreme Court decision upholding tuition tax deductions in Minnesota and Senate defeat of a tuition tax credit bill.
10. Charter of the Rights of the Family.
Pope John Paul was voted the leading newsmaker of the year, followed by Cardinal Joseph L. Bernardin, new archbishop of Chicago and leader in the development of the bishops' pastoral letter on war and peace, and Lech Walesa, Nobel laureate for peace.

### INTERNATIONAL
**Lay Persons in Evangelization** — Christianity has made little headway in contacts with Asian religions because the Church has neglected to use lay persons for this purpose, according to Auxiliary Bishop Alan de Lastic of Calcutta. "Evangelization has all along been undertaken exclusively by the clergy and the Religious. The laity have not been utilized to fulfill their mission," he told delegates to the Dec. 2 to 6 conference of Asian Catholic lay persons in Hong Kong. He said emphasis should be placed on lay formation: "So much is spent on the training of priests and Religious. Why can't we spend more on training the lay person for the lay apostolate?"

**Lithuanian Priest Sentenced** — Father Sigitas Tamkevicius, found guilty of "anti-state activities," was sentenced to six years in a Soviet labor camp, reported Tass Dec. 7. A founder in 1978 of the Catholic Committee for the Defense of Believers' Rights, he joined Father Alfonsas Svarinskas as the second priest sent to prison since 1972. While on trial, Father Tamkevicius refused to answer questions about the committee and denied that its activities were illegal.

**Lefebvre Criticism** — Dissident French Archbishop Marcel Lefebvre's latest public statement Dec. 9 included criticism not only of Pope John Paul's commitment to the quest for Christian unity, but also of the revised Code of Canon Law, the concept and practice of collegiality, and various doctrinal and liturgical developments since the Second Vatican Council. The archbishop made his comments at a press conference in Olten, Switzerland. He was suspended from the exercise of orders in 1976 for ordaining priests without due authorization and had a record of opposition to enactments of the Second Vatican Council.

**Catholic Teacher Training Curtailed** — The bishops of England and Wales expressed "profound disappointment" at the decision of Secretary of State for Education Sir Keith Joseph to proceed with plans to withdraw teacher training from De La Salle College in Manchester, one of eight such teacher training colleges. The bishops said the college was a "vital part" of teacher training for the whole country, and added that the decision of Sir Keith "could put all voluntary colleges in jeopardy."

**Abortion Legalized in Spain** — Despite the opposition of the bishops, the Spanish Senate followed the lead of the lower house in Parliament in voting to legalize abortion in cases of rape, severe fetal malformation or danger to the life of a mother.

**Nobel Medal Donation** — Peace prize winner Lech Walesa donated his Nobel medal to the Shrine of Our Lady of Czestochowa a few days after his wife and son accepted it in his name on Dec. 10. Walesa and his party were harassed by police Dec. 13 while on their way from Czestochowa to their home in Gdansk.

**Date of the Crucifixion** — Oxford University scientists Colin J. Humphreys and W.G. Waddington, writing in the Dec. 22 edition of the British science magazine *Nature,* said they had pinpointed the date of the crucifixion of Christ as April 3 in the year 33. They said they based their conclusion on astronomical calculations and biblical and historical references. They were able to reconstruct the Jewish calendar at the time and to date a lunar eclipse which scriptural and other sources suggested followed the crucifixion.

**Conciliation Sought in Poland** — Cardinal Jozef Glemp urged priests in Poland to stay out of politics and called for tolerance between the communist government and its opponents in the ranks of the Solidarity labor movement. "We understand that the word 'conciliation' has lost its true meaning and that today it does not refer to any program," the cardinal said in a Christmas message with reference to current tension between the government and Solidarity. "Poland must be saved. . . . In all the opposing sides, the instinct of self-preservation must be revived. . . . We in Poland must limit dissatisfaction, reciprocal accusations and actions that harm fellow men." He also said

that "the episcopate will warn priests not to deal in politics."

**Chinese Bishop and Priest Jailed** — Seventy-six-year-old Bishop Peter Joseph Fan of Baoding and his vicar general were each sentenced to 10 years in prison by Chinese authorities, the German Catholic news agency KNA reported Dec. 28. The agency said the bishop was accused of secretly ordaining bishops and priests, of maintaining relations with the Vatican, and of receiving money from outside the country. He had received an earlier lengthy prison sentence for refusing to collaborate with the government-sponsored Patriotic Association of Chinese Catholics. Charges against the vicar general, Msgr. Huo Pin Chang, were not specified in the report.

**An Unconstitutional Prayer** — Vatican Radio reported Dec. 28 that Father Filip Pavic, pastor of St. Nicholas Parish in Metkovic, Yugoslavia, had been sentenced to 50 days in jail for publishing a prayer to recently canonized St. Leopold Mandic. The prayer was held to be unconstitutional because of its opposition to Marxist materialism. The simple text was: "St. Leopold Bogdan Mandic, pray to God with all the other saints and blessed Croatians for our parish, for all our people, so that the theory and practice of materialism will not take possession of them."

**International Briefs:**

• Women with expertise in canon law can be appointed members of church tribunals in Colombia under new rules adopted in November by the nation's episcopal conference. The conference also set the minimum age for the marriage of Catholics at 18, in line with civil law regarding the age for marriage.

• An article in the Dec. 9 edition of *Rud e Pravo,* a Czechoslovakian daily newspaper, attacked the Church, and especially the Jesuits, for anti-communist positions.

• Three missionary priests were arrested Dec. 14 in Santiago for participating in protests against the torture of political prisoners in Chile.

• The Chilean Bishops' Conference, noting that torture is "a grave offense against human dignity," leveled the penalty of excommunication against those who practice torture and those who help them do so.

### Death Squads

Government inaction against death squads considered responsible for killing and/or threatening to kill people believed to have ties with guerrillas was the target of a Sunday homily Dec. 4 by Archbishop Arturo Rivera Damas of San Salvador. He also criticized political violence by guerrillas fighting to overthrow the U.S.-backed government of El Salvador. "If this war is unjustified," he said, "much less justified is the death-squad violence on the one hand, and the sabotage and executions, much less frequent, by the other side. The difference is that the left is combatted and the right is not."

The archbishop said that, in the five days before he delivered his homily, death squads murdered 17 persons and kidnapped 30 others.

# JANUARY 1984

## VATICAN

**New Canon Law Commission** — Pope John Paul, in a document issued on his own initiative and dated Jan. 2, established a new Pontifical Commission for the Authentic Interpretation of the Code of Canon Law in effect since Nov. 27, 1983. At the same time, he abolished the Pontifical Commission for the Revision of the Code of Canon Law and the Pontifical Commission for the Interpretation of the Decrees of the Second Vatican Council.

Features of the revised Code were among subjects covered by the Pope in an address Jan. 26 to members of the Sacred Roman Rota. He called attention to the innovative force of the Code and the flexibility of norms for conducting various kinds of procedures. He also spoke about the application of scientific findings in cases concerning the ability of persons to contract marriage in a valid manner.

**Opus Dei** — Meeting Jan. 15 with 32 regional leaders of the international association, the Pope said: "I hope that you who are Opus Dei become more Opus Dei and take Opus Dei in every direction of the human and created world. . . . Perhaps in this formula ("Work of God," for the Christianization of society) there is the theological reality, the essence, the nature itself of the vocation of the age in which we live and in which you have been called by the Lord."

**Christian Unity** — "The fact that Christians are praying together for the gift of perfect unity is already a gift of God; it is the first dawn of unity," the Holy Father told 6,000 people attending a general audience Jan. 18 at the start of the Week of Prayer for Christian Unity. He stressed baptism as "the foundation of all unity, that which we have and that which we hope for." Christ's suffering on the cross is also a call to unity in redemption from sin and death. The Pontiff added: "If our behavior or acts of omission perpetuate divisions or place obstacles in the way of reconciliation, we become accomplices in prolonging the wounds of Christianity."

The Pope met during the week with Bishop Josiah Kibira and the Rev. Carl Mau, president and secretary general, respectively, of the World Lutheran Federation. He ended the week Jan. 25 at an ecumenical liturgical celebration during which he was joined by Lutheran, Anglican and Greek Orthodox churchmen in scriptural readings and prayers.

**Apocalypse** — "It is necessary to create a new knowledge in humanity — and especially in the leaders of nations — in order to avoid what would be not a war but nuclear destruction, the Apocalypse," declared the Pope in an address to 17 world-famous scientists Jan. 23. The scientists, in turn, asked the Holy Father to add his voice to the chorus of concern over the dangers of a "nuclear winter," the phenomenon marked by darkness and cold which would destroy much of the earth as a result of even limited nuclear war.

**Basis of Human Dignity** — The attempt to define fundamental human rights and values should be based on the incarnation and redemptive death of Christ, the Pope told 8,000 people at a general audience Jan. 25. When Christ became flesh, he "assumed the humanity of every person, starting with the poorest and the most abandoned. . . . At that point, he became joined with each person in order to guarantee that person's dignity. . . . The full realization of man's dignity comes only in the dynamism of love that brings one person to another," and thus opens him to God.

**Information Can Improve Understanding** — "A greater circulation of ideas and information in human society can promote not only better understanding but also a removal of obstacles — mistrust, suspicion, incomprehension, discrimination, injustice — that still hinder the way to peace and solidarity between individuals and peoples." So stated the Pope at a Holy Year meeting with journalists Jan. 27. "In a pluralistic world like ours, characterized by an unprecedented technological revolution, it is evident that the tools of social communication — if used for distorted goals or, worse, if bent to the logic of whatever power — can provoke profound damage to the connective fabric of society." On the other hand, the same tools "can have a decisive (beneficial) importance for the future of humanity. . . . This is a choice that should be constantly kept in mind in efforts toward a new world order of information and communication."

### The Pope Also:

• Ordained nine bishops Jan. 6, on celebrating the solemnity of the Epiphany, and baptized a number of infants from seven countries Jan. 8.

• Promised that the Church would do all it could to combat economic disparity and hunger caused by drought in African nations.

• Told members of a U.S. Congressional delegation Jan. 19 that they should "favor unhesitatingly all initiatives which aim at strengthening the family in American society," as means of counteracting drug abuse.

• Said that Christians should work for justice based on Gospel values rather than political ideologies, at a meeting with Costa Rican bishops Jan. 26.

### Vatican Briefs:

• The English translation of a report, "Penance and Reconciliation" — produced by the International Theological Commission in 1982 in preparation for the 1983 assembly of the Synod of Bishops — was released early in the month.

• The Vatican announced approval by the Pope of "The Eucharist and the Christian Family" as the theme of the 43rd International Eucharistic Congress to be held Aug. 11 to 18, 1985, in Nairobi, Kenya.

• As of Jan. 10, 107 countries — nearly three times as many as in 1939 — had diplomatic relations with the Holy See.

## Peace Day Homily

Pope John Paul brought a series of peace pleas to a climax Jan. 1 by asking for a resumption of East-West talks on arms limitation and for action to relieve hunger in the world. He made the twin appeal during a Mass celebrating the solemnity of Mary, Mother of God, and the 17th observance of the annual church-sponsored World Day of Peace. The Pope said, in part:

"The relations between East and West have reached a radical opposition of positions, with the interruption — which we all hope is temporary and as brief as possible — of negotiations on the reduction of nuclear and conventional weapons. Meanwhile, mutual distrust increases the fateful effects of ideological struggles and exacerbates already grave local conflicts by which various nations . . . are daily stained with blood."

"In the other direction, between North and South, the gap that separates the rich countries from the poor countries, already serious for many years, has been further widened with the recent economic crisis. . . . The most worrisome feature is represented by the resulting contrasts in the condition of humanity. In the rich countries, health and nourishment improve, whereas in the poor countries the means of nourishment for survival are lacking and the mortality rate soars, especially among infants."

"The threat of nuclear disaster and the plague of hunger appear on the horizon as terrifying as the deadly horsemen of the Apocalypse: each of them (is) the fruit of complex phenomena of the economic, political, ideological and moral orders which, at their root, are also the sources of constantly interacting violence."

## NATIONAL

**No General Absolution** — Bishop William J. Connare announced Jan. 5 that general absolution was prohibited in the Diocese of Greensburg because the conditions under which it might be allowed did not exist there. He said: "The mere gathering of a large number of penitents, for example at a penance service or on a pilgrimage, is not sufficient cause for granting general absolution. Proper planning for such services should include providing an adequate number of priest confessors."

**Women of Faith** — About 100 Jewish, Catholic and Protestant women took part in the Women of Faith in the '80s Conference Jan. 8 to 10 at Marymount College of Virginia. Subjects of discussion included racism and classism, sexism, anti-Semitism in international politics, women in religious and ethnic communities, economics, justice and peace.

**Vatican Relations** — The establishment of full diplomatic relations between the United States and the Vatican was announced jointly Jan. 10. The Vatican, in a brief statement, said the two countries, "desirous of developing mutually friendly relations already existing," had decided to establish relations at the level of an embassy at the Holy See and an apostolic nunciature in Washington.

William A. Wilson was subsequently named U.S. Ambassador to the Holy See; Archbishop Pio Laghi was named Apostolic Pro-Nuncio to the United States. (See U.S.-Vatican Relations for additional coverage.)

**Division of Opinion** — A number of right-to-life advocates took exception to Cardinal Joseph L. Bernardin's "seamless garment" concept of a pro-life position linking opposition to abortion with nuclear war, capital punishment and other threats to life. They contended that abortion is such an important issue that it should be opposed on its own and not in combination with other causes.

**Church Impact on Public Policy** — A significant tenet of the U.S. constitutional tradition calling for the separation of church and state "holds a paradoxical place in the public mind." So stated Cardinal Bernardin Jan. 16 during a symposium at the Divinity School of the University of Chicago. "There seems to be an inverse relationship between the readiness of people to invoke the principle and their capacity to understand it clearly," he said. The phrase is most often used "to tell religious bodies to keep quiet." But, "my reading of the constitutional principle — and the theology which affirms its truth — is that the separation of church and state is designed to provide religious organizations space to speak." Central to the public role of the church is the "task of trying to shape a well-formed public opinion which both provides positive direction and sets moral limits for power." The cardinal assessed the current impact of public opinion on U.S. nuclear arms policy and policy in Central America. He said: "It is easier to prevent certain policy choices than it is to shape a redirection of policy." The cardinal's address was one in a series sponsored by the school.

**Week of Prayer** — Interfaith services in dioceses and parishes across the country marked observance of the Week of Prayer for Christian Unity, Jan. 18 to 25. Backgrounding the observance were signs of progress in ecumenical dialogues and in cooperative works of social concern by members of different religious bodies. (See separate article for coverage of Ecumenism.)

**Deacon Won't Run, Ex-Nun Will** — Permanent deacon John Keefe cancelled plans to run for the office of trustee of Bellows Falls., Vt., after learning that church officials preferred that deacons not seek political office.

Arlene Violet, who ran for political office in 1982 while a Sister of Mercy, announced Jan. 19 that she had left her religious community in order to run as a Republican candidate for the office of attorney general of Rhode Island. Earlier, Bishop Louis E. Gelineau of Providence turned down her request for a dispensation from her religious obligations so she could seek public office. "The Code of Canon Law clearly states," he said Jan. 4, "that priests and Religious 'are forbidden to assume public offices which entail a participation in the exercise of civil power.' . . . It is incorrect for a Religious to think that one so consecrated can abandon that life 'temporarily' to serve in a public office."

**Two New Archbishops** — Episcopal appointments of more than usual public interest were those of Archbishop Bernard F. Law to Boston, Jan. 24, and Archbishop John J. O'Connor to New York, Jan. 31. Archbishop Law was known for his significant engagement in interfaith relations. Archbishop O'Connor was a former Navy chaplain with a record of 27 years of service and the rank of rear admiral.

It was also announced Jan. 31 that the Military Vicariate, headed up to that time by the archbishop of New York, would henceforth be under the separate jurisdiction of its own bishop.

**Nestle Boycott Suspended** — The International Nestle Boycott Committee suspended Jan. 26 its U.S. boycott of Nestle S.A. because of the corporation's "commitment" to follow the World Health Organization's code for the marketing of infant formula. Nestle had been accused, by boycotting Catholic and other groups, of improper marketing in underdeveloped nations where, critics charged, infants were threatened by formula because mothers were unable to use it properly due to inadequate supplies of safe water, lack of education and other problems.

**Corporate Responsibility** — The Interfaith Center on Corporate Responsibility reported Jan. 27 that church-related groups and agencies had filed 82 stockholder resolutions with 69 companies in efforts to influence corporate policies and practices. Nuclear energy production and use, the militarization of space and the effect of lending practices on underdeveloped nations were among the subjects of resolutions.

**"A Flash of Hell"** — Music videos shown nationally on the MTV cable channel seem "like a flash of hell," said Jesuit Father Morton Hill of Morality in Media. He made the comment after the National Coalition on Television Violence issued a report in which it said that more than half of MTV's videos featured violence or strongly suggested violence, and that 35 per cent of the violence shown was sexual in nature. Father Hill said "kids are eating this stuff up."

**National Briefs:**
• The anti-Catholic daily, paid-time TV program of the Rev. Jimmy Swaggart, which had been cancelled by two Atlanta stations in November, was being aired by cable SuperStation WTBS.

• National Migration Week, sponsored by the U.S. Bishops' Committee on Migration and Tourism, was observed Jan. 9 to 14.

• Three South Carolina women were recipients of the papal Benemerenti Medal for outstanding work in their respective fields: Helen N. Merritt, a public elementary school principal of Greenville; Dr. Patricia A. Carter, a gynecologist of Charleston; and Margaret Bayly, a social worker for Catholic Charities of Charleston.

• Nellie Gray, founder and president of March for Life, presented the Outstanding Life Award to U.S. Surgeon General Dr. C. Everett Koop at the March for Life Rose Dinner Jan. 23 in Washington.

• Msgr. John Tracy Ellis received Jan. 24 the Theodore M. Hesburgh Award of the Association for Catholic Colleges and Universities for his outstanding contribution to Catholic higher education.

**March for Life**

Fifty-thousand persons from states across the nation converged on Washington Jan. 23 to take part in the 11th annual March for Life in protest against the 1973 pro-abortion decisions of the U.S. Supreme Court. The intent of the march was also to mobilize opinion and generate action against the death-by-abortion of approximately 1.5 million unborn children a year.

For the first time in the history of the march, 30 of its leaders met with the President, Ronald Reagan, who voiced his support for its purposes. He also designated Jan. 22, the actual date of the court decisions, as National Sanctity of Human Life Day.

Related anti-abortion demonstrations were held in many U.S. cities.

(See other entries for additional coverage of developments related to Abortion.)

**INTERNATIONAL**

**Nuclear Deterrence** — A policy of nuclear deterrence is legitimate if it is "purely defensive," Cardinal Carlo Martini said during one of many New Year's Day peace demonstrations in Italy. In an address to 5,000 young people in Milan, he rejected what he described as an attitude of "fatalism," and said: "We have to dare to take the realistic position of purely defensive deterrence," emphasizing that such deterrence must be understood as "modern legitimate defense."

**Socialism in Zimbabwe** — The bishops of Zimbabwe, in a pastoral letter issued Jan. 1, pledged that they would support a form of socialism based on Christian values but would oppose Marxism. "In Zimbabwe," they said, "socialism is understood to mean equality, regardless of race, creed or sex, and an equitable distribution of land, health-care and education for all, regardless of income. It means fair wages, a life-style of self-reliance as well as of sharing, the promotion of cooperative ways of production and a national policy of reconciliation. . . . To the extent that the government has in fact begun to implement these policies, we have expressed our full support. . . . We acknowledge that socialism has inherited some elements from Christianity, but we also know that some forms of socialism do not agree with Christianity."

**Unchristian Guatemala** — "As a U.S. citizen, I was ashamed of our government's role in Guatemala and our identification with a corrupt government that is oppressive, immoral and every bit as unchristian as a communist state." So stated Bishop Elden F. Curtiss of Helena on his return from a trip to the Central American nation. He accused the U.S. government of having greater concern for U.S. business interests than for the rights of the majority of Guatemalans. He said the U.S. government "has supported a policy which has actually helped to destroy moderate leadership in Guatemala," that "we have ignored the systematic slaughter of emerging Indian leaders," that the U.S. is widely criticized "as the main oppressor of the people because of its political and economic policies."

**Violence in Peru** — The bishops of Peru condemned indiscriminate violence, calling it particularly unjustifiable when it takes place "in the name of the authorities of the country." The Jan. 15 statement referred to stepped-up military action against the subversive movement, *Sendero Luminoso*. The prelates complained that the government was acting not only against guerrillas but also against church personnel engaged in social activism.

**The Church in Cambodia** — Father Rogatien Rondineau, a French missionary with 20 years of experience in the country, called the situation of the Church in Cambodia "the worst in the world." Speaking in Philadelphia, he said the decline of the Church in Cambodia was due to actions of the 1975-79 Pol Pot communist regime which imprisoned and murdered thousands of people, incuding 3,000 Catholics. He also said that the Holy Father was "very concerned about the situation" because there were no priests, bishops or Religious in the country. "Even the churches have been demolished to the ground," said Father Rondineau.

**Displaced Persons in Central America** — Father Michael Campbell-Johnston, founder of the Jesuit Refugee Service, estimated that there were more than a million displaced persons in Central America, some within their own strife-torn countries and others in refuge in neighboring nations. "The most serious problem," he said, was "that of displaced persons in El Salvador (300,000 or more) and Guatemala (more than 500,000)."

**U.N. Emphasis on Contraception** — The Holy See was concerned about strong United Nations emphasis on contraception as a solution to world population growth, according to Msgr. James McHugh, special advisor to the Vatican's U.N. Observer Mission. He made the statement Jan. 24 at a meeting of a U.N. committee preparing the agenda for the World Population Conference to be held in August, 1984, in Mexico City. He said: "The Holy See . . . notes that population policies should place an emphasis on the dignity of the human person and of the couple. Population policies should treat the two persons, that is, the couple, as active participants in the development process, not as the object of fertility control programs that are directed primarily, and sometimes almost exclusively, to the limitation of birth. . . . The Holy See is opposed to the use of abortion as a method of birth control, as well as the constant and almost exclusive emphasis on contraception and sterilization to lower the birth rate as a necessary prerequisite for development."

**Ova Donation Unacceptable** — Vatican Radio reported Jan. 24 that Archbishop Frank Little of Melbourne had called morally unacceptable the donation of human ova for use in test-tube fertilization. He said the practice directly offends persons, erodes the dignity of marriage and leaves important questions unanswered. One major concern, he commented, is identification of the eventual child's real (biological) parents.

**Bishops' Stance in Poland** — The Polish bishops pledged Jan. 27 to continue defending political prisoners but at the same time asked people to cooperate with the government to ease social tensions and to overcome economic problems. They said: "Many working people feel embittered. Some of them are in prison despite the fact that they believe they served a just cause. Many have been sacked from work or discriminated against. . . . The Church has not reduced its efforts to eliminate these harmful phenomena because this is part of its mission. But the Church also teaches that people should protect the good of society, which the state represents."

**Abortion in Portugal** — The Portuguese Parliament passed a bill Jan. 27 eliminating legal penalties for abortions in cases of fetal deformity, pregnancy following rape and danger to a mother's life. The law was sponsored by the ruling Socialist Party. Prior to passage, the bishops of the country issued a pastoral letter in which they reiterated the Church's moral opposition to abortion and urged Parliament to reject the bill.

**International Briefs:**

• Two weeks after the bombing of a London department store, Bishop Cahal Daly of Down and Connor called the Irish Republican Army's use of violence immoral and counterproductive, reported Vatican Radio Jan. 3.

• Cardinal Ugo Poletti, papal vicar for the Diocese of Rome, opened a new cafeteria for the poor Jan. 6.

• More than 1,000 Miskito Indians fled from Nicaragua to Honduras in December because their leaders feared fighting in Nicaragua would lead to a "slaughter," said Capuchin Father Wendelin Shafer who accompanied the Indians.

• Instead of enacting easier divorce laws, the Canadian government should emphasize reconciliation procedures to help married couples stay together. So stated Bishop John Sherlock, president of the nation's episcopal conference, in a letter to Minister of Justice Mark MacGuigan.

### Restricted Freedom in Cuba

"There is currently freedom of religion and worship in Cuba," according to a report prepared by the Inter-American Commission on Human Rights of the Organization of American States. This freedom, however, "is limited in terms of dissemination by two fundamental restrictions: the use of the mass communications media and education."

The early hostility in church-state relations (for some years after the beginning of the Castro regime in 1959) has given way to ideological competition, in which the government has, and uses, the vast resources it has at its command to actively promote the official Marxist-Leninist philosophy.

"There is no religious persecution; the restrictions to which certain religious groups have been subjected, including imprisonment of some of their members, can be traced to the impact of their actions on the political system and not to the fact of professing a religious belief as such.

"Nevertheless, indirect restrictions continue to constrain believers, leading to discrimination against them in various central aspects of the life and politics of Cuban society."

# FEBRUARY 1984

## VATICAN

**"Man above Things"** — The Church and civil society should work together to place "man above things," the Holy Father told a group of Italian political leaders Feb. 2. He said: "One cannot speak too much about the vital and fundamental theme of the primacy of man above things. Man often, voluntarily or involuntarily, becomes for various reasons a slave of things, an instrument of ideologies and systems — he himself becomes a thing in the hands of other men." The primacy of man means the "priority of being over having."

**Vatican Role in World Affairs** — While accepting the diplomatic credentials of Finnish Ambassador Kaario Juhana Yrjo-Koskinen, the Pope said Feb. 9 that the role of the Vatican in world affairs is to promote an atmosphere of trust among nations. "The moral and spiritual authority of the Holy See is directed, beyond the technical aspects of negotiations, to the spirit which should inspire them and permit them to bear fruit. What the Holy See seeks to promote is an atmosphere of trust."

**Death of Andropov** — Pope John Paul sent condolences to the Soviet leadership on the death Feb. 9 of Soviet President Yuri Andropov. He designated Jerome Lejeune, a member of the Pontifical Academy of Sciences, as his personal representative at the funeral.

**Suffering and Redemption** — These were the themes of an apostolic letter entitled *Salvifici Doloris* and released Feb. 10. In it, the Pope said: "Suffering has a special value in the eyes of the Church. It is something good, before which the Church bows down in reverence with all the depth of her faith in the redemption." The passion of Christ is the key to understanding suffering. His death on the cross brought an end to "definitive suffering," i.e., the loss of eternal life. With his sacrifice, suffering "entered into a completely new dimension and a new order . . . linked to love." By sharing in the suffering of Christ, people participate in the redemption and become mature enough to enter the Kingdom of God. Suffering, thus, has a "creative" and redemptive character.

**Work** — It is not just a means of earning a living but is intended also "for the purpose of building a more just and peaceful society, for furthering the cause of truth and brotherhood," said the Pope during a general audience Feb. 15. "Human work is a participation in the kingship of Christ. . . . We are helping to bring to completion God's designs for the created world."

**"Persuasive Pope"** — The Pope was "articulate and most persuasive" about the need to reduce world tensions caused by nuclear weapons, said Vice President George Bush Feb. 15 after a 50-minute private meeting with the Holy Father.

**Climate of Permissiveness** — The Pope told 1,500 French pilgrims Feb. 20 that Western society is a milieu in which "religious indifference, materialism, doubt, unbelief and the climate of permissive morality unsettle Christians. . . . Despite the good will and generosity that remain and that sometimes express themselves with force and intelligence, this environment risks stifling or extinguishing the faith of numerous young people and adults." In such a climate there is need for courage in the face of "indifference, lack of understanding and derision."

**Moral Criteria in Politics** — The Pope offered the services of the Vatican in international peace efforts and cited the need for moral criteria in making political decisions, at a meeting Feb. 24 with Austrian Ambassador Hans Pasch. He said the Holy See "shares with Austria the distinctive sign of neutrality which in a particular way permits it to place itself objectively at the service of the international community and to offer its mediation and its concrete collaboration." The Pontiff also said: "Political responsibilities, in the end, must be evaluated according to moral criteria."

**Renewal of Promises** — Four thousand priests from dozens of countries joined Pope John Paul in renewing their promises of dedication and service to God, the Church and people. The renewal took place Feb. 24 in connection with a Holy Year celebration marking the 1,950th anniversary of the redemption.

**Visit to Bari** — Christian unity, "the mature fruit of the spirit," was the theme of an address delivered by the Pope before Greek Orthodox leaders during a visit to Bari Feb. 26. "The only way to reach this unity," he said, is through growth "of mind and heart which every encounter presupposes." The Holy Father also prayed for persons suffering religious persecution, especially those in Albania.

**Taiwanese Bridge Church** — Catholics in Taiwan should act as a "bridge church" for the people of mainland China, and should promote essential cultural values despite "the momentary separations of history," said the Pope Feb. 28 while meeting with seven bishops of Taiwan. "It is to you Catholics of Taiwan and the diaspora that is entrusted this wonderful task of being a bridge church for your mainland compatriots."

**The Pope Also:**

• Told a general audience Feb. 1 that, to gain peace in the world, the logic of society must be changed to allow truth to defeat falsehood.

• Dedicated part of a new 20-room underground section of the Vatican Library, Feb. 7.

• At a meeting with bishops of El Salvador Feb. 24, said he shared their concern over the continuing "deaths, attacks and displacement of thousands of Salvadorans."

• Praised a group of Catholic college and high school students Feb. 25 for having "come out into the open" as people of faith.

• Called on the Catholics of Lithuania to "persevere in the faith" Feb. 29, a few days before the 500th anniversary of the death of their patron, St. Casimir.

**Vatican Briefs:**

• The Congregation for Religious and Secular Institutes issued decrees Feb. 2 concerning: (1) the conformity of constitutions of religious institutes with provisions of the Code of Canon Law, and (2) the temporary vows of Religious.

• The Vatican and Italy signed Feb. 18 a new concordat on church-state relations, replacing the Lateran Pacts in effect since 1929. (See separate entry.)

## Martyrs Beatified

The Holy Father presided Feb. 19 at ceremonies of beatification for 99 persons — priests, women religious, lay women — martyred for the faith in 1794 in France, and for missionary Father Giovanni Mazzucconi who was killed in 1855 in what is now Papua New Guinea.

Father Mazzucconi was the first martyr of the Pontifical Institute for Foreign Missions.

The other 99 persons beatified were all from the Diocese of Angers: 12 priests, four laymen, 3 nuns and 80 laywomen. All were victims of the anti-religious rage of the French Revolution.

Pope John Paul said during the ceremony that the beatification should be a motive of joy as well as a lesson of faith for everyone.

"These martyrs invite us to think of the multitude of believers who even today suffer persecution throughout the world in a more subtle manner, less conspicuous but at the same time every bit as serious, because it results in the lack of religious liberty, discrimination, impossibility of self-defense, imprisonment, civil death. . . . Their trials have much in common with those of the beatified.

"We must ask for ourselves the courage of faith, of indomitable fidelity to Jesus Christ, to his Church, in the time of trial as well as in everyday life. Our world, very often indifferent or ignorant, asks an unequivocal witness of the disciples of Christ, which is equivalent to proclaiming as did the martyrs whom we celebrate today: 'Jesus Christ is the living God.' Prayer and the Eucharist are essential for us to live his life; devotion to Mary preserves us as his disciples.

The French Revolution was the violent counterpart of the Age of Enlightenment's intellectual attack on the Church.

## NATIONAL

**Military Chaplains** — U.S. District Judge Joseph M. McLaughlin ruled Feb. 2 in New York that government funding for military chaplains ($85 million a year) does not violate the U.S. Constitution. "Affording the opportunity for worship without coercion preserves the religious neutrality of the government," while failure to provide chaplains could prevent military personnel from exercising their religious freedom. A case brought in 1979 by Harvard law students Joel Katcoff and Allen Wieder had contended that government funding for chaplains constituted an establishment of religion.

**Embryo-Transfer Baby** — Moral objections related to the birth of the first embryo-transfer baby, a boy in January, were sketched by Richard Doerflinger, legislative assistant in the U.S. bishops's Office for Pro-Life Activities. The objections were to artificial insemination, surrogate motherhood, depersonalization of the conjugal act of procreation, and unwarranted risks to embryonic life. Doerflinger called the embryo-transfer procedure a kind of "technologized adultery."

**Purpose of Seattle Study** — The Vatican-ordered study of Archbishop Raymond Hunthausen was made "precisely because we did not want to give uncritical acceptance to extremist viewpoints," said Cardinal Joseph Ratzinger, prefect of the Congregation for the Doctrine of the Faith, in a letter to the Seattle prelate. The letter did not describe specific complaints that led to the investigation carried out in November, 1983, but did make a general reference to a need "to overcome specific problems" which had been encountered.

**Cluster Plan** — The Diocese of Superior announced that 80 communities and 30 to 50 priests would be affected by a proposed redistribution of priests and a clustering arrangement of parishes. No churches would be closed, it was said, but 15 parishes would be required "to relinquish regular weekend liturgies and some other services," and many more would "need to consolidate efforts and share programs." A shortage of priests was the principal reason for development of the cluster proposal.

**Moral Theology** — Two hundred and 40 bishops of North and Central America and the Caribbean area attended a Feb. 6 to 9 workshop on a variety of subjects suggested by the theme, "Bishops, Theologians and the Moral Life of the Church." Rules and limits to be observed by theologians in dealing with authoritative teachings of the Church were outlined by Cardinal Joseph Ratzinger, prefect of the Congregation for the Doctrine of the Faith. He said also that bishops and theologians both play key roles in "forging a balance between external progress and morality." The bishop must be "a learner and a critical partner" of the theologian. The bishop's task is the "transmission of the faith"; the theologian's, "dialogue between the world of faith and the mindset of the world at large."

**Episcopal Priest Ordained** — Father Larry D. Lossing, a former Episcopal priest, was ordained a Catholic priest Feb. 11 in St. Louis. He was the 12th former Episcopal clergyman so ordained since 1982. It was also reported that 70 former Episcopal priests were awaiting action on their requests for ordination to the priesthood in the Catholic Church.

**Aid for Hungry in Africa** — Auxiliary Bishop T. Francis Murphy of Baltimore urged the U.S. Feb. 21 to take "immediate action" to send emergency food aid to starving people in 24 African countries. Speaking for the U.S. Catholic Conference at a news conference in Washington, he said the bishops of the U.S. were supportive of legislative and private efforts to provide emergency relief aid.

**"White Train" Protests** — Twelve bishops along "white train" routes for nuclear warhead transport called such shipments a violation of international law, the Gospel and teaching contained in the 1983 pastoral letter of the U.S. bishops on peace and war. The bishops said Feb. 22 that they would join in prayer vigils and non-violent protests against the shipments, and urged people to "give prayerful consideration to joining in these vigils." Two of the bishops were Archbishop Raymond Hunthausen of Seattle and Bishop Leroy Matthiesen of Amarillo.

**Capital Punishment** — The U.S. Senate voted 63 to 32 Feb. 22 to restore the death penalty for such federal crimes as terrorism, assassination or attack on a president, murder on federal property and kidnapping. A statement by a spokesman for the U.S. Catholic Conference, Msgr. Daniel F. Hoye, called the action "a deeply troubling sign," and said that "restoring the death penalty would mark a major erosion of our society's respect for the sanctity of human life." Action on the bill was pending in the House of Representatives.

**Christopher Awards** — "A Chorus Line," the longest-running Broadway show, and the Rev. Fred Rogers, a Protestant minister and star of "Mr. Rogers' Neighborhood," were the recipients of Christopher Awards Feb. 23. Also honored with awards were the producers, directors and writers of 12 television specials, two motion pictures and 15 books. The awards, presented since 1949, recognize the achievement of artistic excellence in books, films and television specials "affirming the highest values of the human spirit."

**Embassy Move Opposed** — The U.S. Catholic Conference urged rejection Feb. 23 of a bill sponsored by Senator Daniel Patrick Moynihan of New York that would move the U.S. embassy in Israel from Tel Aviv to Jerusalem. Conference staff member Father J. Bryan Hehir, in testimony before the Senate Foreign Relations Committee, linked the conference's position with the Vatican's concern for preserving Jerusalem's international religious character and with repeated papal opposition to unilateral moves that could exacerbate already serious tensions in the Middle East.

**National Briefs:**
• "Catholic Schools: Beacons of Hope" was the theme of Catholic Schools Week, Jan. 29 to Feb. 4.
• Bishop Anthony J. Bevilacqua, chairman of the U.S. bishops' migration committee, said Feb. 7 that the detention of Haitian and other asylum-seekers was "morally unacceptable" and contrary to the long-standing parole policy of the Immigration and Naturalization Service.
• The Communications Department of the U.S. Catholic Conference announced Feb. 9 approval of funding ($1,426,953) for 24 media projects in 1984.
• Archbishop Ignatius J. Strecker of Kansas City, Kan., urged Congress Feb. 29 to adopt a comprehensive food and agricultural policy in which farmers would be adequately compensated, consumers would get quality and affordable food, the hungry would be fed, and land would be protected for future generations.
• Honored: Professional basketball star Julius Irving, "Dr. J," named 1984 recipient of the Father Flanagan Award for Service to Youth; Father J. Bryan Hehir, staff member of the U.S. Catholic Conference, with a five-year MacArthur Fellowship worth $216,000, for his work for human rights and arms control, and his contribution to the devel-

opment of the U.S. bishops' 1983 pastoral letter on war and peace.

## Problems and Need for Hope

The Church must meet the challenges of society by giving people a reason to hope, declared Belgian Cardinal Godfried Danneels in an interview early in the month in Washington.

The principal problems facing the Church in the U.S., Canada and the nations of Western Europe, he said, were a shortage of priests and vocations to the priesthood, issues of moral theology, catechetics, points of doctrine, evangelization, relations with the Holy See, and questions regarding the influence of the Church on people.

The cardinal observed that the Church had a stronger identity in the secular culture of the U.S. than in the traditionally Catholic countries of Western Europe.

## INTERNATIONAL

**Nuclear Deployment a Crime** — "We declare unanimously that the production, installation and use of nuclear arms are a crime against humanity and must be considered condemned both from the ethical and theological points of view." This was the central message in a pastoral letter issued by three bishops in Czechoslovakia, according to a Feb. 8 report by Kathpress, the Austrian Catholic news agency. The prelates said the world is threatened with annihilation when nuclear weapons fall into the hands of leaders who seek world domination and "fail to respect fundamental human rights." The letter was issued as the Soviet Union was in the process of installing medium-range nuclear missiles in Czechoslovakia and East Germany.

**Protest against Restrictions on Priests** — Austria's Kathpress reported that young people in Bratislava, Czechoslovakia, had written letters of protest against government restrictions placed on two Jesuit priests because of allegedly "unfriendly acts against the state." The government accused Father Peter Homolka of sympathy with the outlawed Solidarity labor movement in Poland. Father Jozef Rybansky was charged with illegal propagation of "religious teaching in schools."

**Archbishop Offers Resignation but Won't Quit** — As he turned 75 on Feb. 7 and submitted a letter of resignation as head of the Archdiocese of Olinda-Recife, Brazil, Archbishop Helder Camara said he would continue his efforts to help the poor in developing countries. "I don't plan to slow down," he said as he announced plans to work for the renegotiation of Third World debt payments to banks in North America and Europe.

**Church-State Relations in Romania** — Three major barriers remained standing in the way of any significant improvement in relations:
• persistent government hostility toward religion and religious values;
• the Hungarian or German descent of most of the Catholics;
• opposition by the Romanian Orthodox hierarchy.

**Marcos and His Opponents** — Cardinal Jaime Sin of Manila accused both President Ferdinand Marcos of the Philippines and his opponents of being inflexible in their political demands. Speaking Feb. 9, he said that Marcos was inflexible in regarding his opposition as being interested only in toppling his government. At the same time, the cardinal called opposition leaders "rigid and unbending" in their demand for Marcos' resignation from office. He suggested the possibility of some kind of reconciliation through the medium of honest elections.

**Priests in Nicaraguan Government** — Bishop Pablo Antonio Vega, president of the nation's bishops' conference, criticized priest officeholders in the Sandinista government and warned them of possible sanctions if they did not leave their positions. They were Fathers: Miguel D'Escoto, M.M., foreign minister; Ernesto Cardenal, cultural minister; Fernando Cardenal, S.J., director of the Sandinista Youth Movement; Edgar Parrales, ambassador to the Organization of American States; and Alvaro Arguello, member of the Council of State. Bishop Vega said: "It appears that they are more in love with the political ministry than with the priestly ministry. Today, I don't know how many of them are willing to accept the dictates of the new canon law (against clerics in public office when this involves sharing in the exercise of civil power). There has not yet been an official pronouncement but, if nothing happens, we will have to apply the code; and they know this."

**Education Policies in Spain** — The bishops' Commission for Education accused the government of trying to impose an agnostic vision of the world on public school students. Specifically, the commission objected to the purchase of a controversial sex education book for school libraries in Andalusia and a directive by the Province of Asturias which said that prayers must be limited to religion classes. The commission also criticized government interpretations of existing legislation which "set precedents for administrative decisions about public education that are inspired by secular agnostic views and aimed at the submission of priests and legitimate social institutions — in this case the Church — to the very powerful action of the state."

**Catholic Schools Threatened in Malta** — The government of Malta informed directors of Catholic schools Feb. 12 that the schools must offer their services free of charge, and that failure to comply with this order by Feb. 29 would result in takeover of the schools by the government beginning in October. The action was part of a series of measures supported by Socialist Prime Minister Dom Mintoff in an effort to secularize Catholic schools and confiscate church property. More than 90 per cent of the population of 320,000 was Catholic.

**Peace Center in Northern Ireland** — In Belfast, a city known for violence and political tension, the Irish Council of Churches and the Catholic Commission for Justice and Peace opened a peace education resource center Feb. 22. Auxiliary Bishop Dermot O'Mahony of Dublin, commission president, said during the opening ceremony that a year of peace education for children aged 8 to 12 years had overcome prejudice and removed misunderstanding more effectively than any other means.

**Journalists Criticized** — Some Western journalists concentrate "on the political influence" of the Church in Poland rather than its efforts to make "good triumph over evil," said Cardinal Jozef Glemp late in the month in an interview with *Niedziela*, the weekly publication of the Diocese of Czestochowa. He denied that there was internal discord in the Church in Poland, despite demonstrations in the Warsaw suburb of Ursus against his transfer to a rural parish of Father Mieczyslaw Nowak, an outspoken supporter of the outlawed Solidarity labor union movement.

**Albanian Charge against the Pope** — Pope John Paul's call for religious freedom for the people of Albania, made during a visit to Bari Feb. 26, was called "fascist" by the nation's official newspaper. An article in *Zeri I Popullit* said: "Albania is not Poland, and the Albanian people know well the Pope's limitations, as they know of so many of the actions of his predecessors who approved of fascism." The newspaper also accused the Pope of taking part in some kind of anti-Albania campaign allegedly supported by the Central Intelligence Agency. During his visit to Bari, the Holy Father had prayed for the people of Albania who, he said, "cannot openly express their faith, a fundamental right of the human person." In 1967, Albania declared itself "the first atheistic state in the world."

**International Briefs:**

• No significant change in Soviet policy toward religion was expected with the succession to power of Konstantin U. Chernenko following the death Feb. 9 of President Yuri V. Andropov.

• Christian and Moslem leaders in Lebanon put forth Feb. 22 a hopeful but futile three-point plan for peace and the unconditional release of all prisoners.

• The National Catholic Radio of Ecuador, aided by funds from the United States and Canada, began broadcasting Feb. 16.

## Catholics in China

"The Catholic Church in China is divided in two," said exiled Archbishop Dominic Tang of Canton during an interview in Honolulu. "On the one side is the Chinese Catholic Patriotic Association, with bishops, seminaries and churches. On the other side is the vast majority of Catholics who remain faithful to the Pope."

"Many faithful priests, bishops and Religious are in prison. . . . Catholics loyal to the Holy Father have no church. They can go to the Patriotic Church to receive the sacraments, but they are not happy with the arrangement."

More than 200 churches that were open were "all under the control of the Chinese Catholic Patriotic Association, ruled by the communist government. Patriotic Catholics are not allowed to owe allegiance to the Pope."

Archbishop Tang was arrested in 1958 and spent the next 22 years in prison without being charged or having a trial. His residence was in Hong Kong.

# MARCH 1984

## VATICAN

**Contraception** — Pope John Paul called on priests to be faithful to the Church's teaching against contraception Mar. 1. Addressing 110 Italian priests attending a seminar on natural family planning, he said: "With simple and humble firmness, be faithful to the magisterium (teaching authority) of the Church on a point of decisive importance for the destiny of mankind." The teaching of the Church on responsible parenthood "is nothing else than that which the original plan of the Creator has impressed on the humanity of man and of woman. . . . It would be a grave error to conclude that the norm taught by the Church (against artificial contraception) is in itself only an 'ideal' which ought then to be adapted, proportioned, scaled down, as it is said, to the concrete possibilities of man according to a "weighing of the various goods in question. . . . Our pastoral charity toward spouses consists in being always available to offer them pardon for their sins through the sacrament of penance, not in diminishing in their eyes the greatness and the dignity of their conjugal love."

**Development Fund for Africa** — Using more than $9.2 million donated by West German Catholics, the Pope started a development fund for people in the drought-ridden and famine-plagued Sahel region of Africa. Establishment of the John Paul II Foundation was announced Mar. 6 by Cardinal Bernardin Gantin, president of Cor Unum, the pontifical commission for coordinating international relief activities.

**Lent's Meaning and Practices** — With the austere sign of ashes, "the Church calls us to spiritual renewal through the more fervent practice of prayer, sacrifice and works of charity," said the Pope before 23,000 persons at a general audience on Ash Wednesday. During Lent, he encouraged people "to receive more frequently the sacrament of penance." He also urged Catholics to translate their penitential sacrifices into "real action" against hunger and for peace and human dignity.

**Control of Evolution** — Scientists have the power to control evolution for good or for evil, declared the Pope Mar. 10 in an address to participants in a conference on the scientific work of Augustinian Father Gregor Mendel, the Father of Genetics. "Today," said the Pope, "man has started to have the power in his hands to control his own evolution. The measure and the effects of such control, good or bad, will depend not so much on his science as on his wisdom."

**St. Paola Frassinetti** — The Holy Father canonized Mar. 11 Paola Frassinetti (1809-1882), foundress of the Sisters of St. Dorothy in 1834. Her life "affirmed the identity and dignity of women, which the Church has always protected and sustained for the moral betterment of society, and for the coming of the reign of Christ," the Pontiff said during a homily at Mass.

**A Good Confession** — A good confession means facing one's sins squarely and looking for the reasons behind them, Pope John Paul said Mar. 14 during a weekly general audience. "To receive the sacrament of penance worthily, we must take time to become aware of our sins and of the intentions and motives which underlie them." Regarding an examination of conscience, he said "it is not merely an exercise of psychological introspection. Rather, it is a prayerful effort to bring ourselves face to face with the moral law and to stand humbly in the presence of the Lord."

**Holy Year Events: Workers, Families, Handicapped** — Addressing 25,000 persons attending a Holy Year event for Workers Mar. 18, the Pope said: "The principle of solidarity must be given a primary position in human life, social life and international life. . . . Even struggle — just, social struggle — must be subordinated at all times to the principle of solidarity, because struggle alone causes nothing but war."

Marriage commitment was the theme of the Pope's address Mar. 25 at a Mass attended by 150,000 people in St. Peter's Square. "Matrimony is a great sacrament which . . . consecrates man and woman as dispensers of reciprocal love and as co-workers with the Creator in the work of transmitting life."

At a celebration intended to arouse "the conscience of the community, especially Christians, regarding their attitude toward the handicapped," the Holy Father said Mar. 31: "We do not consider a handicap as something dramatic and unnatural . . . but rather as a condition of weakness which induces Christians and civil society to show their level of faith and of humanity."

**Racism** — The Pope called it an evil that "disfigures our era," during a weekly general audience Mar. 21. "In a time in which public opinion is particularly sensitive to the respect for and promotion of human rights, the manifold evil of discrimination disfigures our era. It negates the fundamental equality of all men . . . which, above all, is rooted in God."

**Dispute over Crucifixes** — The Pope expressed "profound solidarity" Mar. 21 with the Polish bishops in their dispute with the government over the public display of crucifixes in schools. "Catholic society desires that the cross be found in places of education of the youth. The good of the country requires tranquillity, and this requires respect for the civil rights of believers."

**Anti-Semitism** — Pope John Paul condemned anti-Semitism during a meeting Mar. 22 with representatives of the Anti-Defamation League of B'nai B'rith. "The Catholic Church, even before the Second Vatican Council, condemned such ideology and practice as opposed not only to the Christian profession but also to the dignity of the human person created in the image of God." He encouraged increased understanding between Catholics and Jews, declaring that, in "knowing each other, we discover still more what brings us together for a deeper concern for humanity at large."

**Pro-Nuncio to the U.S.** — The Pope announced

Mar. 26, jointly with the White House, the appointment of Archbishop Pio Laghi as the first papal ambassador to the United States in 117 years. The appointment was made three weeks after the U.S. Senate confirmed William A. Wilson as the first modern-day U.S. ambassador to the Holy See.

**The Pope Also:**

• Prayed for the people of Lithuania during Vatican celebrations Mar. 3 and 4 marking the 500th anniversary of the death of St. Casimir, patron saint of that country and Poland.

• Made his annual Lenten retreat, Mar. 11 to 17.

• At a meeting with senior citizens Mar. 23, said: "According to the divine plan, every single human being is a life in growth, from the first spark of existence to the last breath. Nobody has the right to say 'enough.' You should not stop nor consider yourselves in decline."

• Decried the use of chemical weapons, in violation of the Geneva Protocol of 1925, in the war between Iran and Iraq.

**Vatican Briefs:**

• It was estimated that the Holy See would have a 1984 budget deficit of approximately $31 million, by the Council of Cardinals for the Study of the Organizational and Economic Problems of the Holy See.

• It is evident that the judges who condemned Galileo Galilei in 1683 acted "certainly in good faith, but wrongly." So stated Archbishop Paul Poupard in an introduction to a series of essays dealing with the action against the scientist. It was thought at the time that his thesis — that the earth revolves around the sun — contradicted Scripture and threatened belief in the centrality of people as redeemed by Christ.

### Redemptionis Donum

The Holy Father called men and women Religious "a special treasure of the Church," in an apostolic exhortation entitled *Redemptionis Donum* ("Gift of Redemption"). The document, made public Mar. 29, was described as a "spiritual meditation" by Archbishop Augustin Mayer, O.S.B., secretary of the Congregation for Religious and Secular Institutes. Its contents highlighted the personal nature of God's call to Religious, the meaning and role of the evangelical counsels (poverty, chastity and obedience), and the role of Religious in the Church.

### NATIONAL

**Lenten Themes** — Penance, reconciliation and peace-making efforts were key themes in the messages and exhortations of bishops across the country at the beginning of Lent, Mar. 7. Many bishops called attention to the fact that the range of penitential practices is far more extensive than the requirements of abstinence on Fridays of Lent and of fast and abstinence on Ash Wednesday and Good Friday. They called for frequent attendance at Mass and reception of the sacraments of penance and the Eucharist, along with direct actions of an apostolic nature to achieve peace — individually, in the family and community — combat injustice and meet the needs of the poor and suffering. Operation Rice Bowl went into effect in various dioceses, to result in contributions — achievable by saving on meals during Lent — for feeding the needy in this country and abroad.

**Ambassador to the Holy See** — By a vote of 81 to 13 Mar. 7, the Senate confirmed the nomination of William Wilson as U.S. Ambassador to the Holy See.

**Ruling against Haitians** — A federal appeals court ruling — that Haitians seeking political asylum have no constitutional right to challenge U.S. immigration decisions — drew criticism from Miami church leaders, including Archbishop Edward A. McCarthy. He said the Feb. 28 ruling may run "counter to a higher law of humanity." The decision, by the 11th U.S. Circuit Court of Appeals in Atlanta, reversed an earlier ruling that the Immigration and Naturalization Service unlawfully discriminated against Haitians.

**Anti-Catholic Posters** — Posters warning of "Vatican ownership and manipulation" of major U.S. media were reported appearing on buildings, telephone poles and at bus stops in several cities. The posters, first noticed Feb. 12 in Des Moines, claimed that the Vatican secretly owned *Time, Newsweek, People, Life,* ABC, CBS, NBC, the Hearst newspaper chain, *The New York Times* and *The Los Angeles Times,* as well as local newspapers, television and radio stations. "The Vatican uses these magazines to exalt and exonerate themselves (sic) from crimes that they have done and are currently doing," and uses the media "to smear and malign who they will secretly," the posters charged. The posters were seen in Nashville and Clarksville, Tenn.,; Evansville, Ind.; St. Louis and Cape Girardeau, Mo.; New Orleans, La.; Louisville, Ky.; Tulsa, Okla.; Charlotte, N.C.; and Jackson, Miss. No one claimed responsibility for the posters.

**Outrage at New York Times Inferences** — Several days before his installation as head of the Archdiocese of New York, Archbishop John J. O'Connor said Mar. 13 he was "outraged" at inferences in a *New York Times* editorial that he was anti-Semitic and condemnatory of women who had abortions. The editorial referred to remarks by the archbishop in an NBC-TV interview Mar. 11. In response to the editorial, he said in a *Times* interview Mar. 14: "I very sincerely believe that an abortion mentality, structured and legalized in this country, does not differ in essence from that mentality that legalized putting Jews to death in Nazi Germany."

Regarding women who have abortions, he said in the TV interview: "I think objectively it is gravely sinful. A human life has been taken. But I don't condemn the individual who acts out of confusion and desperation."

The archbishop also mentioned politicians and the stance of many of them on abortion: "I have absolutely no tolerance, I must confess, for those politicians, political figures or political campaigners, who . . . deliberately and intentionally exploit the political potential of this issue, try to sit on the fence with this business of 'I personally am opposed to abortion but, after all, we must have a choice.' "

**New Ways Ministry** — Responding to criticism concerning his treatment of New Ways Ministry, Archbishop James A. Hickey of Washington said he had refused to approve the ministry because it is "ambiguous and unclear with regard to the morality of homosexual activity." He said in a statement Mar. 13 that, while New Ways Ministry presents the Church's teaching on homosexuality, it "also presents as viable options other opinions which hold that it is morally permissible for homosexuals to live together in a sexually active, stable relationship." The archbishop said he had made known his objections to New Ways directors Father Robert Nugent and Sister Jeannine Gramick. The latest objections to the archbishop's position came from the National Coalition of American Nuns and the National Assembly of Religious Women.

**Prayer Amendments Downed** — The U.S. Senate rejected Mar. 20 a proposed constitutional amendment to allow organized spoken prayers in public schools. The vote 56 to 44, was "short of the two-thirds majority required for passage."

By a vote of 81 to 15 on Mar. 15, the Senate defeated an amendment providing that "nothing in this Constitution shall be construed to prohibit individual or group silent prayer or silent reflection in public schools."

**Nativity Scene Not Unconstitutional** — The U.S. Supreme Court ruled 5 to 4 Mar. 25 that the First Amendment does not mandate "complete separation of church and state" and, therefore, that the sponsorship of a Christmas nativity scene by the city of Pawtucket, R.I., is not unconstitutional. The case, Lynch v. Donnelly, involved a nativity scene included in a display of Christmas symbols sponsored by Pawtucket in a park owned by a nonprofit group.

The U.S. Constitution "affirmatively mandates accommodation, not merely tolerance, of all religions and forbids hostility toward any," Chief Justice Warren Burger wrote in the majority opinion. A lower court had found that the city's sponsorship of the nativity scene represented an effort to endorse and promulgate religious beliefs. "An absolute approach in applying the establishment clause is simplistic and has been uniformly rejected by the Court," Burger wrote. He said the Court was satisfied that Pawtucket had a secular purpose for including the nativity scene, "that the city has not impermissibly advanced religion, and that including the creche does not create excessive entanglement between religion and government." The city, said Burger, "has principally taken note of a significant historical religious event long celebrated in the Western World." The main dissenting opinion by Justice William Brennan said there was nothing in history or in the creche's setting to offset "the plain fact that Pawtucket's action amounts to an impermissible governmental endorsement of a particular faith."

Later in the year, a lower court found unconstitutional the display of another nativity scene in a different set of circumstances.

**National Briefs:**

• The Catholic Home Study Institute, based in Leesburg, Va., received approval as a pontifical institute for religious instruction from the Congregation for the Clergy.

• Even greater than the need for people to work with the poor is the need for Catholics "who sit in the pews" to listen to the experiences of the poor, said the Catholic Committee of the South in a report entitled "The Best Ones To Speak It Are the Ones That Live It."

• Pollster George Gallup, speaking at the annual Religion in American Life Dinner Mar. 28 in New York, said a majority of Americans reported that religion was more important to them at this time than it was five years earlier.

## ERA and Abortion

Judge John A. MacPhail of the Commonwealth Court in Harrisburg ruled Mar. 9 that a 1980 Pennsylvania law restricting public funding of abortion violated the constitution and equal rights amendment of the state. The ruling was handed down in a suit (Fischer v. Commonwealth of Pennsylvania) filed by Planned Parenthood of Southeastern Pennsylvania and other pro-abortion plaintiffs; they argued that limiting Medicaid funding of abortion to cases of rape, incest and danger to the life of a mother was a form of sex discrimination.

Howard J. Fetterhoff, executive director of the Pennsylvania Catholic Conference, called the decision "very disappointing to everyone who is trying to protect unbon children." He said the ruling "would seem to suggest that the (proposed federal) ERA can . . . be used to guarantee a right to abortion."

Douglas Johnson, legislative director for the National Right to Life Committee, said of the decision: "Pro-ERA groups have been playing a dishonest game with Congress — claiming that ERA has nothing to do with abortion, but at the same time arguing exactly the opposite in the state courts." The Pennsylvania ruling, he added, "demonstrates how the proposed federal ERA would result in tax-funded abortion on demand."

## INTERNATIONAL

**Priest Won't Run** — Father Bob Ogle, a member of the Canadian parliament since 1979, announced Mar. 1 that he would not seek reelection after being told that he would not be exempted from a church law prohibiting priests from the exercise of civil power in political office. He had been informed by Archbishop Angelo Palmas, pro-nuncio to Canada, that a dispensation from the law granted him by Bishop James Mahoney of Saskatoon was "not esteemed justified."

**Decline in Religious Liberty** — "Persecution of all religion has continued unabated," and there has been "an absolute decline in degree to which religious liberty is permitted in the Soviet Union." So stated the Rev. Michael Bourdeaux, winner of the 1984 Templeton Prize for Progress in Religion. The Anglican clergyman, a specialist on religion in communist countries, was head of the Center for the Study of Religion and Communism in London

**War Toll in Beirut** — Violence and destruction in Beirut were so extensive that they affected virtually every resident directly or indirectly, according to Joseph Curtin, Catholic Relief Services director in Lebanon. He said Mar. 6 that many people in the city had family members who had been killed, wounded or kidnapped. The need for housing was acute; about 500,000 people had been displaced and there was no significant housing construction in progress or prospect.

**Two Views of Nicaragua** — "The Sandinista government, through its ideology and method, is a Marxist-Leninist government," said Bishop Pablo Antonio Vega, president of the bishops' conference, in an interview in the Mar. 9 edition of the Italian national Catholic newspaper, *Avvenire.* "In its daily praxis, the government does not act in an exclusively totalitarian manner," but there is "total domination of the people."

Father Cesar Jerez, vice president of the Jesuit-run Central American University in Nicaragua, said Catholics in the country were marked by a "conflictive unity" in which they had no serious doctrinal disputes but disagreed in their attitudes toward the government. In an address Mar. 22 at Georgetown University, he spoke about a three-way split among Catholics: those who considered the government to be communist; those opposed because "establishment of a Marxist regime will bring about more evil than good"; those who held "the position that a Christian presence within the revolutionary process is possible" and "are willing to risk being a critical presence inside the revolution."

**Defense of Rights in Argentina** — The Church defended human rights under the previous military government with more energy than any other national institution, declared Cardinal Juan Carlos Aramburu of Buenos Aires in response to criticism that the bishops had been relatively silent about abuses. The Church "manifested itself as being more energetic and more concrete than other entities existing in the country," he said in mid-March. "In fact, the hierarchy has published (relevant) documents in a book where it can be seen how, repeatedly and in a severe tone, it spoke of the severe problems which affected the nation." It was estimated that as many as 30,000 people, seized by security forces of the military regime, had disappeared since 1976.

**Bishops against Violence** — Archbishop Arturo Rivera Damas of San Salvador criticized the murder of civilians by death squads and said that fighting in El Salvador's four-year civil war was useless and dangerous, Vatican Radio reported Mar. 12. He called Salvadorans to a "total conversion" to improve conditions in the country.

The bishops of Angola condemned the hatred that had provoked civil war, resulting in "kidnappings, dislocations of whole groups of people, destruction of families, illness, death, and the presence of foreign troops" in the country.

As civil strife increased in Chile, two archbishops called for negotiations to end violence. Archbishop Juan Francisco Fresno of Santiago asked all parties Mar. 25 to negotiate an agreement to end the "spiral of violence." On the same day, Archbishop Jose Manuel Santos of Concepcion called violence "illegitimate" and "counterproductive."

**Churches Must Help** — The churches in Britain and Ireland must help to bring about the change in atmosphere necessary for the success of peace initiatives in Northern Ireland, said Cardinal George Basil Hume Mar. 17. Rather than confrontation and violence, he suggested dialogue as the way to the solution of problems there. He added, however, that "dialogue remains totally ineffective unless it is accompanied on all sides by a real change of heart, that is, by honest admission of mistakes made and wrongs done; by a readiness to forgive; and also by the will to proceed to positive and even radical action. . . . Churches must help to build up trust and confidence, to help people forget the past and create a new future out of present initiatives of spiritual renewal and Christian forgiveness."

**International Briefs:**

• Dutch millionaire Piet Derksen announced Mar. 2 that he was going to sell shares in his sports equipment company and donate the estimated $150 million in proceeds to missionary projects helping the sick and poor.

• In preparation for the Holy Year celebration for families Mar. 25, the French bishops' conference issued a document early in the month upholding the rights and importance of the family.

• Auxiliary Bishop Luciano Mendes of Sao Paolo, Brazil, called on government officials Mar. 13 to avoid including in health programs means of birth control "which are contrary to ethical and religious principles."

• Archbishop Helder Camara of Olinda-Recife, Brazil, announced the creation of The Work of Brother Francis, a foundation to help the poor and to counteract violence.

• Father Joseph Krasovec was sentenced to a month in jail and a five-year suspended sentence for giving a conference on atheism that was critical of government authorities in Yugoslavia, reported Vatican Radio Mar. 15.

### Father Karl Rahner, Theologian

Eighty-year-old Jesuit Father Karl Rahner, one of the outstanding theologians of the century, died of a heart attack Mar. 30 in Innsbruck, Austria.

A seminal thinker of great depth and vision, he authored between 1,000 and 1,500 published works; taught at universities in Munich, Munster and Innsbruck; served on the theological commission and other advisory bodies of the Second Vatican Council; contributed significantly to the formulation of conciliar documents on the Church, revelation and other subjects; was one of the original appointees to the International Theological Commission.

Throughout his life, Father Rahner moved easily back and forth from highly theoretical works in theology to popular writings on the spiritual life, prayer and devotion, and — sometimes with deep but loyal and constructive criticism — trends and issues facing the Church.

# APRIL 1984

## VATICAN

**Canonization Causes** — The Holy Father issued decrees Apr. 7 advancing the causes of:

• Francesco Febres Cordero, known as Blessed (Christian) Brother Michael, of Ecuador (1854-1910);

• Father Federico Albert, founder of the Vincentian Sisters of the Immaculate Conception, of Italy (1820-1876);

• Father Ciriaco Elia Chavara, co-founder of the Congregation of Carmelite Brothers of Mary Immaculate, of India (1805-1872);

• Maria Carmela Gonzalez Ramos Garcia Rieto, known as Maria Carmela of the Child Jesus, foundress of a religious institute, of Spain (1834-1899).

• Virginia Centurione Bracelli, foundress of the Sisters of Our Lady of Refuge on Mt. Calvary, of Italy (1587-1651).

**Right to Defense** — Pope John Paul upheld Apr. 8 the right of a country to use arms to defend human rights and preserve peace. At the same time, the Church favors "maintaining the primacy of political efforts founded on reason, conviction and values over the use of military force," he said during a Holy Year Mass in St. Peter's Square for more than 10,000 military personnel from 24 countries.

**U.S. Ambassador Welcomed** — The Pope accepted Apr. 9 at the credentials of William A. Wilson, U.S. ambassador to the Holy See. As he did so, the Pontiff said that, in collaboration with the United States, "the Holy See envisions a useful and respectful exchange of ideas on world peace and development, and on the conditions essential to their attainment, beginning with the need to protect freedom, promote justice and vindicate truth against every attempted manipulation."

**Roman Curia Officials** — Appointments to key posts in the Roman Curia, made by Pope John Paul, were announced Apr. 9. Among them were those of Msgr. John Foley, editor of *The Catholic Standard and Times* of Philadelphia, to be president of the Pontifical Commission for Social Communications, and of African Cardinal Bernardin Gantin, to be prefect of the Congregation for Bishops. These and other appointments were made to replace officials who had completed five-year terms in office or who had resigned for reason of age or health.

**Confession for Conversion** — Confession is an important means to conversion, the Pope told 60,000 persons at a general audience Apr. 11. While observing that people do not have to rely solely on the sacrament of penance for the forgiveness of venial sins, he said they should still go to confession because "the faithful reception of sacramental confession offers us the grace of conversion, helps us to grow in humble awareness of our need for pardon, and brings us to a greater trust in God, who is rich in mercy."

**Holy Year Celebration for Youths** — The Holy Father welcomed more than 50,000 young people from 40 or more countries to the Vatican Apr. 11 at the start of a five-day Holy Year celebration. Three days later, in the largest single gathering of the Holy Year, 250,000 youths converged on the Vatican at the end of a march from two starting points in Rome. The size and enthusiasm of the gathering prompted the Pope to say: "What a marvelous spectacle this assembly makes in the setting of this (St. Peter's) Square! Who says that the youths of today have lost their sense of values?"

Addressing the young people Apr. 14, the Pope said: "In a very real sense, the 21st century, which is rapidly approaching, belongs to you. I ask you, therefore, to think carefully about the choices in life which you have to make. . . . In a world which often seems to be dominated by death, be ready to choose life, and whatever promotes life and goodness in society. . . . Relying on the Spirit's presence within you, stand up against violence and evil, and seek to bring peace and new hope."

**Liberation Theology** — Some expressions of liberation theology are "fully legitimate, even necessary, . . . others are open to criticism," and still others are, "in the final analysis, unacceptable." So stated Cardinal Joseph Ratzinger, prefect of the Congregation for the Doctrine of the Faith, Apr. 13 at a Vatican press conference. He was very critical of forms of liberation theology which "use Marxist analysis as a scientific instrument to interpret not only history and social and economic reality, but also the Bible and the Christian message." Reviewed during the conference were subjects discussed by representatives of the Doctrinal Congregation and the Latin American bishops' conferences Mar. 26 to 30 in Bogota: relations between bishops and Religious, cooperation between bishops and theologians, ecumenism, pastoral issues and moral problems.

**Role of Priests** — In his annual Holy Thursday message to priests, the Pope urged them to become more and more aware of their role in reconciling people with one another and with God, particularly through the celebration of Mass and the hearing of confessions. He told priests: "We are more necessary than ever, because Christ is more necessary than ever."

**Martyrs of Modern Times** — They were subjects of the Pope's remarks during a general audience Apr. 25. "This is the hour in which many of our brothers in faith pay a dear price for their witness. . . . They are the martyrs of modern times, . . . victims of totalitarian systems" which deny them "the most elementary freedom to express openly their religious faith. . . . With their courage, they constitute a warning and an example in their many sacrifices and deprivations."

**The Suffering of Children** — "The scandalous imbalances which exist within our society are reflected in a particular way among our children," declared the Pope Apr. 26 in an address to 500 members of the United Nations Children's Emergency Fund. "While in one sector of our world children are suffering the lack of the most elementary human necessities, in other sectors children from the earliest age are being inserted into a society based on consumerism, possession and even waste." The purpose of the conference at which the Pope spoke was to find ways and means of preventing the deaths of 40,000 children a day from malnutrition and disease in Third World countries.

**Charismatics and the Local Church** — The mission of charismatics lies in participation in their local churches, the Holy Father told 300 participants in the fifth international conference of leaders of the Catholic charismatic renewal Apr. 30. "The Church's mission is to proclaim Christ to the world. And you share effectively in this mission insofar as your groups and communities are rooted in the local churches, in your dioceses and parishes. . . . It is at the sacramental heart of the Church, and at the sacramental heart of your local churches, that your life as baptized and confirmed Christians can be ceaselessly renewed."

**The Pope Also:**

• Named St. John Capistran patron of military chaplains. The Franciscan priest was with the Christian army in its successful defense of Belgrade against invading Turks in 1456.

• Said Catholic schools should be free from governmental interference, at a meeting Apr. 5 with members of the Congregation for Catholic Education.

• Praised an interdisciplinary approach to medical care which highlights the spiritual nature of people, in an address Apr. 27 to cancer researchers.

**Vatican Briefs:**

• Walter Persegati, secretary and treasurer, reported Apr. 3 that Vatican museums had received more than $1 million from the 14-month exhibit in the U.S. of "The Vatican Collections: The Papacy and Art." The exhibit was viewed by more than two million people.

• A manifesto presented Apr. 12 at a Vatican symposium declared that the Olympic Games should not be manipulated by nations for political purposes.

**Easter Ends Holy Year**

Pope John Paul brought observances of the Jubilee Year of the Redemption to an end Apr. 22 with the closing of the Holy Door of St. Peter's Basilica, following the celebration of Mass and the imparting of his Easter blessing "To the City and the World."

The Mass and related ceremonies were witnessed by more than 300,000 people and were seen via television by viewers in 36 countries. The Holy Father voiced his Easter greetings in 46 languages to people throughout the world.

In his Easter message, he expressed thanks to God for the grace of the Holy Year which marked the 1950th anniversary of the Redemption. He also called for an end to the world's "feverish preparation" for war, and lamented the discrepancy between "the wealth that comes from material and technical progress" and the "extreme poverty and penury paid for with the deaths through hunger or thirst of millions of men, women and children."

*Il Tempo,* a daily newspaper of Rome, estimated that "no less than 15 million tourists" visited Rome during the Holy Year period of Mar. 25, 1983, to Apr. 22, 1984.

**NATIONAL**

**Ruling against School Prayer** — The U.S. Supreme Court rejected Apr. 2 an Alabama law allowing teacher-led prayers in public schools but agreed to study a related state law permitting a moment of silence in the schools. The Court affirmed without dissent a ruling by the 11th U.S. Circuit Court of Appeals which said the prayer law was in violation of the Constitution.

**Voice of Pain** — "Church: Women and Men Relating," was the theme of an Apr. 3 and 4 conference at the College of St. Catherine in St. Paul. Archbishop John R. Roach, addressing the closing session, said that men in positions of authority in the Church must learn to listen to what he called women's "voice of pain." Organizers of the conference refused to schedule Mass during proceedings "because it is male-centered."

**Protection of Life** — The first joint statement of New York state bishops under the leadership of Archbishop John J. O'Connor called for an end to "legalized permissive abortion," and urged public officials to "stand up for the sacredness of every human life." They identified the protection of all human life as the "top priority of our age," and added: "How can we respect the lives of the elderly, the handicapped and the poor, how can we draw back in horror from the prospect of nuclear destruction, while we continue to destroy human life before it emerges from the mother's womb?" The statement questioned the logic and consistency of officeholders who say they are "personally opposed" to abortion but refuse to oppose it in their official capacities.

**Hispanic Priorities** — Delegates to a conference in Rosemont, Ill., selected "The Hispanic Presence Is Raising Our Prophetic Voices" as the theme of the Third Encuentro to be held in 1985 in Washington. They also drew up a list of priorities for study and action, including: evangelization, bilingual and multicultural education, social justice and leadership formation.

**Pro-Nuncio Laghi** — Archbishop Pio Laghi, papal pro-nuncio to the United States, presented his diplomatic credentials to President Reagan Apr. 13. "This is a historical event for me," he told newsmen afterwards; "I'm so very moved."

**Report on the Electronic Church** — The authors of a report on religious television, the electronic church, said at a New York news conference Apr. 16:

• It does not take people away from local churches. Viewers continue to participate in and provide financial support to their local congregations.

• It wins few new converts and has a smaller-than-estimated national audience of 13.3 million people.

The study was conducted by the Annenberg School of Communications at the University of Pennsylvania and the Gallup Organization. It was commissioned by the Ad Hoc Committee on Electronic Church Research, a coalition of church and independent religious agencies including the U.S. Catholic Conference, the National Council of Churches and National Religious Broadcasters.

**Hispanics Are Targets of Raids** — Bishop Roger M. Mahony of Stockton said the U.S. Supreme Court's 7-2 decision of Apr. 17, to allow sweeping Immigration and Naturalization Service searches of factories for illegal aliens, made Hispanics targets of discrimination. The majority opinion, he noted, "portrays the most idealistic scenario. . . . Raids are portrayed as informal, friendly walk-throughs. In my experience, that is not the case — uniformed officers block the doors, sometimes guns are drawn, people panic." The bishop told NC News he was disappointed with the decision: "I had hoped the Supreme Court would lay down some guidelines that would give more protection to the dignity of the workers and the rights of the workers."

**F.E.L. vs. Chicago Archdiocese** — A federal jury ordered the Chicago Archdiocese, Apr. 19 to pay nearly $3.2 million in damages to F.E.L. Publications, Ltd., a religious music publisher that had sued the archdiocese in 1976 over alleged illegal reproduction of copyrighted music in parishes. The six-member jury of the U.S. District Court in Chicago awarded F.E.L. $190,400 for copyright infringements by parishes between 1973 and 1976, plus $2 million in actual damages and $1 million in punitive damages for illegal interference in the publishing firm's business. Evidence before the court included more than 1.4 million unauthorized copies of F.E.L. songs in songsheets or homemade parish hymnals printed and distributed by 238 parishes. The key point in the suit for damages, beyond the actual copyright infringements, was the fact that, when F.E.L. first filed suit in 1976, the archdiocese banned even legitimate use of F.E.L. music throughout the archdiocese. By also sending copies of that order to bishops throughout the country, F.E.L. said, the archdiocese encouraged other bishops to take a similar course of action.

**NCEA Convention** — Approximately 15,000 educators attended the 81st annual convention of the National Catholic Educational Association Apr. 23 to 26 in Boston. Proceedings were focused on the effectiveness of Catholic schools, their values and role in education for peace. The convention theme was "Freedom, Our Heritage — Peace, Our Challenge."

**Struggle against Violence** — Cardinal Timothy Manning called on Catholics of the Los Angeles Archdiocese to involve themselves personally in the struggle to eliminate violence. In a 1,600-word pastoral letter entitled "Violence: God's Image Marred," released Apr. 27, he said: "We must challenge, assail and denounce those elements in our world that nurture the seeds of violence." He added: "Our focus is the more immediate local and personal forms of violence."

**Priests, Politics and Injustice** — Priests should stay out of politics, but must speak out against injustice even if so doing brings accusations that they are becoming political. So stated Jesuit Superior General Father Peter-Hans Kolvenbach in a CBS-TV interview released Apr. 29. The main reason the Church does not want a priest to become involved in politics is because a priest must serve as a "minister of reconciliation. . . . As a politician (however), he has to choose one part and then be against another part. That can be very strongly, that can be very weakly; but it will always be one against another," according to the nature of politics as distinguished from a ministry of reconciliation.

**Nun Leaving To Run** — Sister Elizabeth Morancy, a four-term Rhode Island state representative, announced Apr. 29 her decision to leave the Sisters of Mercy in order to continue her political career rather than comply with church law against political office holding by Religious as well as priests.

**National Briefs:**

• Francis X. Doyle became the first layman to serve as associate general secretary of the National Conference of Catholic Bishops and the U.S. Catholic Conference, Apr. 1.

• The Catholic Golden Age Foundation established Apr. 5 a $1 million endowment at The Catholic University of America's Center for the Study of Pre-Retirement and Aging.

• Five more Episcopal clergymen were ordained to the Catholic priesthood in the early part of the month, bringing to 18 the number of men so ordained, since 1982.

• U.S. Catholics contributed more than $40 million in 1983 to the worldwide general fund of the Society for the Propagation of the Faith.

• A book, fourth in a series, containing 64 pastoral letters and official statements by the U.S. bishops between 1975 and 1983, was published by the U.S. Catholic Conference.

### Imprimaturs Removed

Paulist Press announced Apr. 16 that it had halted circulation of its adult catechism, *Christ Among Us,* at the request of the Congregation for the Doctrine of the Faith. The book by Anthony T. Wilhelm, a former Paulist priest, had been called "not suitable as a catechetical text" by Cardinal Joseph Ratzinger, prefect of the congregation. The *imprimatur* for the book (permission to publish) was withdrawn by Archbishop Peter Gerety of Newark.

Archbishop Raymond G. Hunthausen of Seattle announced Apr. 24 the removal of his *imprimatur* from another Paulist publication, *Sexual Morality,* by Sulpician Father Philip S. Keane. The removal was made at the request of the Doctrinal Congregation, which informed the archbishop that "an *imprimatur* is to be granted only to those works which completely agree with official church teaching."

### INTERNATIONAL

**Torture** — "Torture in the Eighties," issued by Amnesty International Apr. 3, cited allegations of torture or ill treatment in 98 countries. The report was based on evidence gathered from victims of torture, witnesses, doctors, medical and court records, and former security agents. It said the often-systematic application of cruelty by authorities was "usually part of the state-controlled machinery to suppress dissent." Countries cited in the report included El Salvador, Guatemala, Argentina, the Soviet Union, Poland, Iran and the Philippines.

**Appeal for Help of Churches** — The government of Zambia, reversing an earlier decision, asked Christian churches to resume administration of the schools and hospitals which they had directed prior to the country's declaration of independence in 1964, *L'Osservatore Romano* reported in its Apr. 3-4 edition. The need for church-related personnel to cope with the educational and medical needs of the people prompted the government to make the appeal.

**Laws against Pornography** — The Canadian Conference of Catholic Bishops called for tougher legal measures against pornography and prostitution. "Pornography must not be allowed to spread its heinous message of sexual aggression, torture and disregard for the other person and his or her body," the bishops said in a brief presented Apr. 6 to a special governmental committee.

**Pledge and Decision in South Africa** — A pledge by the Mariannhill Missionaries to raise $25 million for the development of the town of St. Wendolin's played a key role in the decision of the government of South Africa not to relocate its 12,000 Black residents. Piet Koornhof, who announced the decision in Parliament Apr. 11, said the residents would be given freehold property rights.

**Mother Teresa in China?** — "We are trying to get into China," Mother Teresa of Calcutta told Cardinal Agostino Casaroli Apr. 14 at the Vatican. She spoke of hope that her Sisters of Charity might be allowed admission to the country and opportunity to serve the poorest of the aged poor.

At the same time, Mother Teresa said the community had 250 houses in 35 countries, and 132 requests from bishops for the establishment of houses in their dioceses.

**Atrocities in Zimbabwe** — The Zimbabwean bishops' Justice and Peace Commission, in a statement issued Apr. 18, defended a report in which the bishops accused government forces of killing, raping and torturing villagers in the southern Province of Matabeleland. The statement said the bishops and the commission were "concerned only with protecting innocent people against brutality, the violation of human rights and starvation." Prime Minister Robert Mugabe charged that the bishops were playing politics and acting in support of rebels fighting against the government.

**Catholic Schools in Danger** — The Parliament of Malta passed a bill Apr. 19 providing that all secondary education should be free and that, if private schools should charge fees, the government would take them over and run them at the expense of the owners. Nearly all private schools in Malta were Catholic. National Party leader Eddie Fenech Admi said the Socialist-sponsored bill, passed 32 to 31, was against the wishes of the people and the rights of the Church; also, that it violated the letter and spirit of the constitution.

**Negotiations Wanted in Nicaragua** — The Sandinista government should open negotiations with guerrillas, stated the bishops of Nicaragua in a joint pastoral letter Apr. 22. "If this does not happen," they said, "there will be no chance for an agreement, and our people, especially the poorest among them, will continue suffering and dying. ... It is not always honest to justify internal aggressions and violence on aggressions from outside" (meaning U.S. support of guerrillas and government charges of impending U.S. invasion). Interior Minister Tomas Borge rejected the bishops' proposal Apr. 25, calling it "a criminal suggestion."

**Sharing of Resources** — Representatives of more than a million men and women Religious appealed for a just distribution of the world's resources in a statement released Apr. 27 in Rome. "We are convinced that peace will be created only when there is a just distribution of the earth's resources. ... We appeal, therefore, to all people, but especially to our own members, to use and share the world's goods responsibly and to create an awareness of the interdependence of all, of the sacredness of life, and of the need for tolerance and respect." This was the central thrust of a statement issued by members of the Commission on Justice and Peace of the International Union of General Superiors (of women Religious) and the Union of General Superiors (of men Religious).

**International Briefs:**

• Archbishop Arturo Rivera Damas said in a homily Apr. 1 that El Salvador's death squads were active again and that, as a result, "fear is hovering over the people here."

• Forty-eight representatives of the Catholic, Anglican and Reformed churches in England and Wales took part in an ecumenical weekend of prayer and recollection Apr. 6 to 9 at Canterbury.

• Seventy-seven organizations of peace- and justice-seeking Catholics and Protestants were listed in a 22-page directory entitled "Peace and Reconciliation Projects in Ireland." The largest and oldest organizations was Corrymeela, founded in 1965, with 120 members and 1,000 associates.

### The Crucifix War

The crucifix war in Poland ended Apr. 6 with announcement by the director of the agricultural school in Mietno that a crucifix could be displayed in the school, that students could war crucifixes in school, and that parents would not be required to sign pledges acknowledging that public education is secular in nature.

The dispute erupted after crucifixes were removed from the school in December, 1983, in selective compliance with a government directive that was not applied to factories and other buildings. Student protests, coupled with wider expressions of opposition by thousands of people, including the bishops, led to the compromise settlement.

The basic issue in the affair was the significance of the crucifix as a symbol of the faith of the people, to which the communist regime remained adamantly opposed.

# MAY 1984

## VATICAN

**Unemployment** — The Holy Father spoke about this and related subjects before a general audience of 30,000 people May 1, the feast of St. Joseph the Worker. Unemployment, he said, is caused by many factors, including product saturation, inflation, competition and technological changes which eliminate jobs. "Another problem is the danger that man may become a slave of those machines that he himself has invented and constructed. It is necessary . . . to control and guide technology, which otherwise is placed against man." He also criticized "professional alienation" by which work loses its significance and becomes "mere merchandise."

**Peace Talks Urged** — The Pope asked the people of Lebanon to resume peace talks aimed at establishing unity and democratic processes in their country. He also urged bishops throughout the world to support peace efforts and to pray for the survival of Christianity in Lebanon. The appeals were contained in separate messages dated May 1 and released May 5.

**"What Are Your Plans?"** — Pope John Paul addressed this question to young people May 13 in a message for the 21st World Day of Prayer for Vocations to the priesthood and religious life. "What will you do with your life?" he asked. "Have you ever thought of committing your existence totally for Christ? Do you think that there can be anything greater than to bring Jesus to people and people to Jesus" in and through the priesthood and religious life?

**Anniversary of Shooting** — Three years to the day of the attempt on his life by Ali Mehmet Agca, the Pope said May 13: "On this anniversary so significant to me, my thoughts go to Fatima to renew to Mary the expression of my affection and my gratitude for her maternal protection."

**No Contact with North Korea** — Four days after returning to Rome from his 21st pastoral trip outside Italy, the Pope lamented a lack of contact with North Korean Christians. "Together with the entire Korean nation, I feel the sad fact of the separation of North Korea from South Korea," he told 35,000 people at a general audience May 16. "Unfortunately, we cannot set up any contact with Christians in North Korea. Therefore, we recommend them even more to the prayers of the whole Church."

In related comment, Father Mong Um-kim said that, despite persecution, the number of North Korean Catholics had increased from 50,000 in 1945 to 200,000. Father Mong reported this estimate in the April edition of the Italian magazine, *30 Giorni.* He was the head of a South Korean commission working for the Church in the North.

**Biblical Studies** — The Pope called attention to the importance of biblical scholarship May 17 in an address marking the 75th anniversary of the Pontifical Institute for Biblical Studies. Study of the Bible "is essentially an ecclesiastical service," he told students, faculty members and friends of the institute. (For excerpts from the address, see separate entry.)

**Athletic Competition** — Loyalty, honesty, perseverance, generosity, teamwork and other qualities among athletes should serve as a "springboard" toward a spiritual level, helping them to "overcome all frivolous behavior which leads to a gray existence deprived of ideals," the Pope told 400 participants in an Italian sports congress May 18. In comparing Christian life to a sports event and spiritual formation to athletic training, he said: "In fact, all Christian life is like a race or a tournament not for the conquest of a corruptible crown but, as St. Paul says, for the conquest of an incorruptible crown."

**Guard Purity of Doctrine** — A major task of bishops is "to protect the purity of doctrine, safeguarding the treasure Christ has entrusted to us so that we can make it fruitful." So stated the Pope at a meeting Mar. 24 with 12 bishops of Peru. "It is your duty," he said, "to be attentive to any doctrinal or pastoral deviations, and thus avoid damage to the faith of believers."

**Morality and Media** — These were the subjects of remarks by the Pope May 24 at an audience with Italian Catholic cinema operators. The spreading phenomenon of pornography, he said, should worry everyone "concerned with promoting human dignity and the moral formation of younger generations."

**Trip to Viterbo** — The Holy Father visited Viterbo, 50 miles north of Rome, May 27. While in the city, which was a refuge and residence for several popes in the 12th and 13th centuries, he visited 150 prison inmates and 50 drug addicts, took part in a celebration honoring the local patron, St. Rose of Viterbo, and asked for prayers for Soviet dissident Andrei Sakharov and his wife.

**Prayer for Unity** — The Holy Father appealed for prayer for Catholic-Orthodox unity May 30, the starting date of a third round of ecumenical discussions by a 60-member joint commission of Catholic and Orthodox representatives. "May common study, the prayer of all, and frank and loyal dialogue overcome all the difficulties still existing, in order to reestablish full unity of the churches," he said at a general audience in St. Peter's Square.

**Ordinations** — The Pope ordained 77 priests from 19 countries in St Peter's Basilica May 31, Ascension Thursday. He told the newly ordained: "Christ shares with you in a very special way the power that was given to him alone in heaven and on earth. . . . Through the Eucharist, that power of Christ — the offering of himself for the life of the world — is shared daily by the Church."

**The Pope Also:**

• Designated May 19 the theme of the 1986 assembly of the Synod of Bishops: "The Mission of the Laity in the Church and in the World."

• Announced his support for a declaration for a halt in the testing, production and deployment of nuclear weapons. The declaration was signed May

22 by representatives of Argentina, India, Mexico, Sweden, Tanzania and Greece.

• Said the recently completed 1983-84 Jubilee Year of the Redemption should stimulate new spiritual and pastoral initiatives, in a letter to bishops throughout the world.

**Vatican Briefs:**

• Twenty-three recruits were inducted May 6 into the Swiss Guards, raising the number in the corps to 101.

• Bishop Jan Schotte, vice president of the Justice and Peace Commission, criticized the "racist ideology" of the South African government and praised local church efforts to proclaim the Gospel "without artificially and unjustly imposed separations." He did so in an article published in the May 5 edition of *L'Osservatore Romano.*

• An editorial in the May 17 edition of *L'Osservatore Romano* said the candidacy of Italian Father Gianni Baget Bozzo for membership in the European Parliament was "in opposition to canon laws that forbid priests to take an active part in party politics."

### Second Trip to Asia

On his second trip to Asia, May 2 to 12, Pope John Paul visited South Korea, Papua New Guinea, the Solomon Islands and Thailand. A highlight of the pastoral tour was the canonization of 103 victims of 19th-century persecutions which took a toll of 10,000 lives in Korea.

(See separate entry.)

### NATIONAL

**Anti-Semitism** — Anti-Semitism is incompatible with Catholicism, declared Archbishop John J. O'Connor May 2 in an address to participants in the 78th annual meeting of the American Jewish Committee in New York. He said the declaration of the Second Vatican Council on Catholic-Jewish relations is "obligatory in conscience on all Catholics." The archbishop also stated his support for the security of Israel, agreed with a suggestion that the Palestine Liberation Organization must be distinguished from the Palestinian people, pledged that he would work with Jews on issues of social justice, and expressed hope that improvements in understanding might enable Jews and Catholics to work together for the unborn.

**State ERA Support Withheld** — Pending clear legislative or judicial declaration that no link exists between abortion and equal rights for all citizens, "we must withdaw our support of the proposed Equal Rights Amendment that will face Maine voters this fall," declared two Portland diocesan officials in a statement published in the May 3 edition of the NC Documentary Service, Origins.

**More Bigotry** — A new anti-Catholic pamphlet, "The Pope's Secrets," published by the Tony and Susan Alamo Christian Foundation, claimed that the Vatican controls the United Nations, the White House, Congress, the Supreme Court, the Internal Revenue Service, the FBI and other law enforcement agencies, and most of network radio and television. It also claimed that Jesuits carried out the assassinations of Abraham Lincoln and John F. Kennedy. The pamphlet appeared about two months after posters claiming that the Vatican owns and controls much of the news media began showing up around the country.

**Charismatic Renewal** — The U.S. charismatic renewal movement is strong but could become too "spiritualized," said Kevin Ranaghan, leader of the People of Praise Covenant Community of 3,000 members in five dioceses. The chief danger of charismatic communities is that they "become so spiritualized as to lose the fundamental Catholic teachings about the works of charity and works of justice," he observed after attending the fifth international meeting of leaders of the movement Apr. 30 to May 5 in Rome.

**Vatican Art** — Nearly 40 works of art from Vatican and other collections were features of the Vatican Pavilion at the 1984 Louisiana World Exposition which opened May 12. Archbishop Philip M. Hannan of New Orleans, speaking at preview ceremonies May 6, said the art treasures were "an inspiration for all persons, because beauty ultimately leads us to God." Masterpieces by Raphael, Caravaggio and El Greco were among the works on display. The pavilion theme was "Jesus Christ Our Redeemer in Art: Ages, Images and Impact."

**NFPC Convention** — More than 200 priests, including 122 voting delegates, attended the annual meeting of the National Federation of Priests' Councils May 13 to 17 in San Antonio. Discussion topics included sacramental life, the role and importance of priests' councils, and a variety of resolutions on pastoral and other subjects. Father Richard Hynes, 37, of Newark was elected to a two-year term as president.

**Moon Appeal Rejected** — The U.S. Supreme Court rejected May 14 the request of the Rev. Sun Myung Moon to hear an appeal of his 1982 conviction for failing to pay taxes on $50,000 in stock earnings and some $112,000 in interest on a $1.6 million bank account set up in his name through the Unification Church. Mr. Moon's request for an appeal was backed by Bishop Ernest F. Unterkoefler of Charleston, S.C., the Catholic League for Religious and Civil Rights, the National Council of Churches and other denominational groups. These supporters, who said they did not necesssarily agree with the tenets of the Unification Church, claimed he was a victim of religious persecution and that the action against him could set a precedent for attacks against any church which, like his, allots financial and administrative control to one person or a hierarchy.

**Letter on Economy by Laymen** — The American Catholic Committee, a New York-based group formed in 1982 to analyze issues "from the fullness of Catholic tradition," announced May 16 the formation of a 27-member commission to write a "Letter of the Laity on Catholic Social Teaching and the U.S. Economy." It was said the letter would be a kind of parallel to the letter on the economy being prepared by a U.S. bishops' committee headed by Archbishop Rembert Weakland of Milwaukee. The laymen's letter-writing committee was chaired by former Secretary of the Treasury William Simon.

**Interracial Council Anniversary** — Voluntary agencies need to redouble their efforts as a response to national "regression" in concern for social justice, former New York Mayor Robert Wagner said May 15 at the 50th anniversary dinner of the Catholic Interracial Council of New York. The New York council, founded May 20, 1934, served as a prototype of other social justice councils across the country.

**Anti-Pornography Law** — Franciscan Father Bruce Ritter said a new anti-pornography law signed by President Reagan May 21 would have a "chilling impact" on the child pornography industry. Father Ritter, founder of Covenant House in New York City, a shelter for runaways and victims of sexual exploitation, said the law would give prosecutors more clout against pornographers.

**Press Convention** — About 500 journalists attended sessions of the May 23 to 25 joint convention of the Catholic Press Association and the Associated Church Press. During the meeting, Father Owen F. Campion, editor of *The Tennessee Register*, was installed for a three-year term as CPA president. Msgr. George Higgins, columnist and defender of worker rights, was awarded the St. Francis de Sales Award. *Our Sunday Visitor* won first place in the "general excellence" category for national newspapers.

In a related development, the *1984 Catholic Press Directory* reported that in 1983 the circulation of U.S. Catholic newspapers declined by 173,000 while the circulation of U.S. and Canadian Catholic magazines increased by more than 2.3 million.

**Ruling on Abortion Law** — The 3rd U.S. Circuit Court of Appeals ruled May 31 against requirements of Pennsylvania's Abortion Control Act which:

• permitted higher state employee insurance rates for abortion;

• called for doctors to provide detailed information on the condition of the fetus;

• provided for a 24-hour waiting period before abortion;

• demanded that a second physician be present to try to save an abortion child,

The court upheld:

• a requirement that a child born alive be protected;

• a demand that abortion clinics provide public reports of ownership;

• a requirement that a minor get the consent of a parent, or a court order, in order to have an abortion.

**National Briefs:**

• John E. McCarthy, a leading figure in U.S. Catholic immigration work for 35 years, was named May 15 director emeritus of Migration and Refugee Services, U.S. Catholic Conference.

• Sister Frances A. Mlocek, I.H.M., was appointed May 23 director of finance for the National Council of Catholic Bishops and the U.S. Catholic Conference.

• Silvio Mayo, the first U.S. deacon named to

such a post, was appointed chancellor of the Salt Lake City Diocese.

• Martin Work ended 40 years of professional service to the Church with the announcement of his retirement May 30. He had been head of the National Council of Catholic Men, an attendant at the Second Vatican Council and, immediately prior to his retirement, an adviser to Archbishop James Casey of Denver.

### Catholic Statistics

The *1984 Official Catholic Directory* reported, as of Jan. 1, that there were 52,392,934 Catholics in the United States. The figure was more than 300,000 higher than the one reported for the previous year.

Los Angeles was the largest archdiocese, with 2,373,021 Catholics; Chicago had 2,368,316.

There were 57,891 priests (an increase of 21 for the year), 392 bishops (an increase of 22), 6,702 permanent deacons (an increase of 636), 118,027 Sisters (a decline of 2,672) and 7,596 Brothers (a decline of 62).

(For detailed listings, see statistical tables in various categories.)

### INTERNATIONAL

**Apparitions under Study** — Vatican Radio reported May 1 that a commission had been set up and was conducting an investigation of alleged apparitions of Mary to six young people at Medjugorje, Yugoslavia. The reported apparitions began June 24, 1981, in a field outside the town and continued in a small chapel in St. James Church. Father Tomislav Vlasic, one of four Franciscans assigned to the church, said that messages reportedly from Mary to the "seers" could be described as urging "peace through conversion." The investigative commission said in a report: "The commission cannot approve of the fact that priests and lay people are organizing pilgrimages to Medjugorje and that the public display of the 'seers' is being promoted in the churches, before an authoritative judgment has been made on the authenticity of the visions."

**Kidnapped Missionaries Released** — Five nuns, two priests and a brother, kidnapped by guerrillas Dec. 18, 1983, in Angola, were released by their captors Apr. 26, according to a report issued by their superiors early in May. The Sisters were Franciscan Missionaries of Mary, the men were Divine Word Missionaries. The superior of the nuns said they wanted to return to their mission in Cacolo, despite political and other troubles there.

**Conflict in Nicaragua** — Conflict between the Church and the government in Nicaragua sharpened following the release at Easter of a pastoral letter in which the bishops called for a dialogue of all Nicaraguans, including the guerrillas, for peace. Government spokesmen called the bishops "traitors" and "false prophets." The regime also blocked the radio broadcast of a letter signed by thousands of persons in support of the bishops. The letter, read May 6 in churches throughout the country, said:

"We want to show proof of the total support of

the bishops' pastoral letter on the theme of reconciliation. We believe dialogue to be a civilized path to peace. We also wish to demonstrate our protest against the attacks on bishops of the Episcopal Conference of Nicaragua, especially the Archbishop of Managua, Msgr. Miguel Obando y Bravo. We also think the Nicaraguans in armed opposition to the government should participate in this dialogue."

**Peace Moves Endorsed** — Representatives of Western and Soviet-bloc Christian churches urged that political activities replace the threat of nuclear destruction as means for preserving global peace. Nations should renounce force, seek mutual security and promote social justice, they said at a May 7 to 10 conference in Loccum, West Germany. Bishop Matthew H. Clark of Rochester and Auxiliary Bishop Joseph Sullivan of Brooklyn were among participants in the conference.

**Templeton Prize Winner** — Anglican clergyman Michael Bourdeaux, founder and director of Keston College, noted for studies of religion in communist countries, was awarded the Templeton Prize for Progress in Religion May 15 in London. He said in an acceptance speech that the West should press the Soviet Union on the issue of religious and human rights: "For the Soviet Union to grant real religious liberty, would bring world peace substantially closer. This thought horrifies those who hold power in the Kremlin, but the reality might not harm them so much as they think."

**First Decade of Bethlehem University** — Vatican Radio reported May 17 that Bethlehem University had completed and celebrated its first decade of operation. The West Bank institution, closed several times by the Israeli government — three times in 1983, once in 1982, twice in 1980 — was founded in 1973 during the pontificate of Paul VI. It was administered by Brothers of the Christian Schools and was supported financially by the Congregation for Eastern Churches. It had an enrollment of about 1,200 students — 40 per cent Christian, 60 per cent Moslem — and offered a variety of academic and vocational programs.

**Paul VI Award to Father Von Balthasar** — Giuseppe Camadini, president of the Brescia-based Paul VI Institute, announced May 22 that the Paul VI International Award would be presented June 23 to Swiss theologian Father Hans Urs Von Balthasar for his contribution to "the research and knowledge of religion." He said the 78-year-old theologian, in 75 books and hundreds of articles, had "integrated theological reflection with a great understanding of the age and real originality." He called his work "courageous" and "rooted in the faith."

**"Publicity Stunt" and "Lies"** — A church historian and a priest of Milan sharply repudiated new allegations by an American Jewish agency that church officials may have knowingly aided in the 1947-48 escape of Walter Rauff, a former Nazi SS officer accused of murdering thousands of Jews. In Rome, Jesuit Father Robert Graham called the accusation a "publicity stunt." In Milan, Msgr. Giuseppe Bicchierai, a central figure in the allegations, said they were lies: "It is impossible that either Cardinal Schuster or I would have helped Rauff escape." On the basis of what he knew, he added: "Charges or insinuations that the Church aided Rauff in his escape are lies." The allegations, like those published in the Jan. 26, 1983, edition of *The New York Times,* were made by Rabbi Marvin Hier, dean of the Simon Wiesenthal Center, Los Angeles, at a May 9 press conference in New York.

Rauff died of lung cancer May 14 at his home in Santiago, Chile.

**Low Mass Attendance in Italy** — Diocesan statistics indicated that only 20 per cent of Catholics in Italy attended Sunday Mass regularly, and that the percentage of attendance was even lower in large cities. The low attendance figures were called "a phenomenon worse than atheism" by Archbishop Mariano Magrassi of Bari, president of the bishops' liturgical commission. Addressing a plenary assembly of the Italian Bishops' Conference May 10, he said the decrease in attendance was contributing to a "large scale growth in the number of non-believers and non-practicing Catholics."

**International Briefs:**

• Bishop John Baptist Wu of Hong Kong expressed worry about the future of the Church in Hong Kong after the scheduled 1997 handing over of the British colony to communist China.

• Catholic Relief Services reported the spread of drought and starvation across 24 of Africa's 54 countries in the Sub-Sahara area extending from the southern edge of the Sahara Desert to the southern tip of the continent. The agency said it had sent $7 million worth of emergency aid into Africa this year; $5 million worth of the aid was supplied by the U.S. government.

• In a letter released May 25, Archbishop Juan Fresno Larrain of Santiago pledged continuing church support for relatives of persons who had disappeared after being detained by security forces during the 11-year-old military regime headed by Gen. Augusto Pinochet.

### Church Harassed in Malta

An amendment to Malta's education law, prohibiting Catholic schools from charging tuition, was called one more step in harassment of the Church, by Father Joseph Borg, head of the archdiocesan press office.

During an interview May 12 in Rome, he said: "The theologians have been kicked out of the university. Catholic hospitals have been forced to close down. Church broadcasting has been severely limited. The government has passed laws which allow it to confiscate church property and investments. The bishops have been refused permission to visit the prisons. And we have been refused permission to build churches. . . . The government wants to do away with the advance of the Church in Malta."

He added that free schooling is not the primary concern of the government: "This is clearly not a question of money but of ideology. The government wants control of the schools. It is a question of controlling the minds of the chidlren."

# JUNE 1984

## VATICAN

**First State Visit to Italy** — Pope John Paul paid his first visit as head of state to Italian President Sandro Pertini June 2 at the Quirinale Palace. He said the new concordat between the Vatican and Italy would make it possible for church and state officials to meet "in the spirit of loyal friendship and open trust."

**Two-Way Potential of the Media** — In a message for Communications Day, June 3, the Pope said modern means of communication have a tremendous positive potential for evangelization, but: "Unfortunately, in our time the mass media are often used against man." In many countries, "freedom of expression is confused with license." Urging personnel in the communications industry to "always be inspired by the criteria of truth and justice," he said: "Do not corrupt society, especially young people, by complacent and insistent repetition of evil, of violence and of denigration of morality, carrying out works of ideological manipulation, planting seeds of division. Do not mock human values, do not ignore them, do not interpret them according to ideological schemes."

**Flawed Family Planning Programs** — The Pope was critical of certain government family planning programs during a meeting June 7 with Rafael Salas, executive director of the U.N. Fund for Population Activities. Contraceptive programs "have increased sexual permissiveness and promoted irresponsible conduct with grave consequences, especially for the education of youth and the dignity of women," he said. "The very notion of responsible parenthood" has been violated by distributing contraceptives to adolescents. Such programs have often led "to the practice of sterilization and abortion, financed by governments and international organizations."

**Suffering, That Others May Know** — "I would energetically exhort all the faithful to make full use of suffering in its myriad forms, uniting it to the sacrifice of the cross for evangelization; that is, for the redemption of those who do not know Christ." So stated the Holy Father in a message for World Mission Day to be observed Oct. 21. In the message released June 9, he challenged Christians to understand the plight of others, and spoke of "the suffering that daily strikes many parts of humanity, anguishing from sickness, from hunger, from persecutions, and deprived of fundamental and inalienable rights, such as liberty." He called on everyone to work for the alleviation of suffering.

**Corpus Christi Procession** — The Pope walked more than a mile along one of central Rome's busiest streets June 21, carrying aloft in a monstrance the Eucharistic Host in a procession marking the solemnity of the institution of the Eucharist. Nearly 10,000 people formed the procession as half again as many watched along the way.

**Knights of Malta** — Pope John Paul encouraged the Knights of Malta to continue their tradition of charity at a meeting June 26 with members of the order's highest council. He praised their work on behalf of the poor, noting that they ran leprosariums, medical dispensaries, blood banks and homes for the aged in various places in Africa, Asia and Latin America. He called the work, supported by some 10,000 Knights throughout the world, "a testimony of faith, because it is exercised in the name of the universal fatherhood of God and in the application of the Gospel."

**Support for the Bishops of Poland** — The Pope voiced support June 27 for the call by the bishops of Poland for an end to political repression and for the release of political prisoners. "I strongly desire for my homeland," he said at a general audience, "the healing of the situation and an appropriate climate in all sectors of public life."

**Defense of Catholic Education** — In a strong defense of religious education, the Pope declared flatly June 28 that "the Church has not only the right but also the duty to have its schools." He called Catholic schools essential for the full development of young Catholics and said they "must not be obstructed or reduced" to state control. He added: "I address, in particular, my fellow bishops who, in various nations of Europe and the world, find themselves in particular situations of difficulty, which must be confronted with calm and firmness. I take an active, personal part in their concerns, their efforts and their activity in this area." The Pontiff did not mention them by name, but Malta, France and Spain were countries in which there were "particular situations of difficulty," created by government efforts to control or eliminate Catholic schools.

**Threat to the Ethical Basis of Medicine** — In an address June 28 at Gemelli Polyclinic Hospital, Pope John Paul said that medical sciences loses its ethical basis when it participates in the "manipulation of human life." The moral basis of medicine is threatened "when it is called on to suppress conceived life, where it is used to eliminate the dying, where it is induced to intervene in the design of the Creator in the life of the family, or where it gives in to the temptation of the manipulation of human life." In such cases, the Pope said, medicine "loses its vision and its authentic goal of helping the least fortunate and the most sick." The Holy Father spent 77 days in Gemelli Hospital after being shot May 13, 1981.

### The Pope Also:

• Called on governments and individuals to work toward an equal distribution of the world's resources, June 4.

• Asked June 10 for mutual understanding as a step toward ending religious violence between Indian troops and Sikhs in Punjab.

• Joined European leaders in an expression of condolence at the death June 11 of Enrico Berlinguer, head of the Italian Communist Party for 12 years.

• Outlined his concern for Christian unity in meetings late in the month with Syrian Orthodox

Patriarch Moran Mar Ignatius Zakka I Iwas, members of the Catholic-Orthodox dialogue group, and Catholic bishops from Greece.

**Vatican Briefs:**

• In a two-line statement issued June 12, the Vatican Press Office criticized as "fantastic and absurd" allegations in a book by a British author that Pope John Paul I was murdered and that high-ranking church officials may have been involved in the plot. The statement said of *In God's Name*, written by David Yallop: "It provokes shock and disapproval that hypotheses like these can ever be formulated in a book — hypotheses that whoever is familiar with the facts and the people (involved) must find fantastic and absurd."

• Archbishop Francis Arinze, pro-president of the Secretariat for Non-Christians, conveyed greetings to Moslems throughout the world and wishes for "happiness, prosperity and peace," at the end of Ramadan, their annual month-long period of prayer and fasting.

### A Necessary Ecumenical Pilgrimage

Pope John Paul called his visit to Switzerland June 12 to 17, the 22nd pastoral trip of his pontificate outside Italy, a necessary ecumenical pilgrimage.

Its ecumenical nature was highlighted in meetings at the Geneva headquarters of the World Council of Churches, with a joint working group of Swiss Catholic and Protestant churches, and with representatives of the Swiss Reformed Church. The meetings, he said on his return to the Vatican, showed "the reality of the division" among Christian churches, along with the desire for "common witness to Christ." Meetings with Catholic clergy and some youths brought forth evidence also of division within the Church on such subjects as celibacy, the role of women in ministry and points of theological opinion.

All the meetings, said the Holy Father, were "permeated with a sense of realism and, at the same time, by a sincere concern for the mission of the Gospel in a society that is suffering the influx of secularism."

(See separate entry for an account of the trip.)

### NATIONAL

**Peace Demonstrations** — Catholics took part in ecumenical services and demonstrations for peace over the Pentecost weekend. A spokesman for Sojourners, an interfaith Christian community which helped organize the activities, said there were more than 200 demonstrations in at least 40 states. In one such event in Washington, more than 200 people conducted a prayer service in front of locked doors at the Department of Energy, the U.S. agency responsible for the production and transportation of nuclear warheads.

**No Compromise on Homosexuality** — Archbishop John J. O'Connor said June 8 that the Archdiocese of New York would not compromise church teaching on homosexuality even if it meant giving up millions of dollars of government money for its social service agencies. He said he would support laws against discrimination on the basis of

sexual orientation if the term was defined to mean only an inclination, not active practice or teaching, of homosexuality. "By orientation," he stated, "we mean an inclination, but some states have interpreted it to include active homosexuality and the teaching of homosexuality. There is a tremendous difference between an inclination and the argument that heterosexuality is only one preference. The word 'orientation' is filled with pitfalls." At issue in the archbishop's remarks was a 1981 executive order of Mayor Ed Koch requiring funded agencies to pledge they would not discriminate in hiring on the basis of "sexual orientation or affectional preference."

**GE Stock Sold** — Twenty-six Catholic religious orders announced June 10 sale of their General Electric Co. stock — 49,000 shares worth an estimated $2.4 million — to protest the company's continued production of nuclear warhead components. The orders belonged to the Interfaith Center on Corporate Responsibility, founded in 1970. Members used shareholder resolutions, legal actions, public hearings and consumer pressure to fight corporate practices contributing, in their view, to social injustice.

**Views of Visitors to the U.S.S.R.** — Catholic participants in an interfaith seminar-tour of the Soviet Union, June 8 to 21, returned with mixed impressions about religious life there. "A sign of hope to me was that, in individual contacts with people on the side, they said the situation for religion was the best it had been in their lifetime," said Benedictine Sister Mary Catherine Shambour, one of the 226 visitors from the U.S. Mary Frances Ford of Blomington, Minn., said that, on the basis of her contact with a priest in Russia, she thought it would be misleading to take his word, "excellent," as a description of the religious situation in general. Some of the views expressed by those on the tour, which was sponsored by the National Council of Churches, were considered naive, misleading and a disservice to their religious commitment. The American Jewish Committee was critical of the "rosy picture" they painted.

**Eucharistic Devotion** — Archbishop James A. Hickey of Washington called for a revival of Eucharistic devotion in a letter he asked priests of the archdiocese to read at Masses on June 24, the Sunday for the U.S. celebration of the solemnity of Corpus Christi. "To think that some of our youngsters have been raised without ever hearing of Benediction, much less experiencing it, is shocking," he said. He called adoration of the Lord in the Eucharist a source of strength and courage "to confront personal and social evil," encouraged the practices of exposition of the Blessed Sacrament and nocturnal adoration, and urged that churches make provision to be open as much as possible for people to stop in for prayer and meditation.

**Liberation Theology** — An international group of theologians, members of the editorial board of Concilium, issued a "vigorous protest" against attacks on liberation theology, asserting that "any premature intervention by higher authorities (of the Church) risks stifling the Spirit." They said theology needs "freedom of research and expression" to reflect on Christian liberation movements among the poor and minorities.

The statement was apparently directed primarily at Cardinal Joseph Ratzinger, prefect of the Congregation for the Doctrine of the Faith. The cardinal was on record in praise of some elements of the "extraordinarily complex phenomenon of liberation theology," and also in criticism of liberation theologians who "have made their own fundamental Marxist option." Among theologians named as unacceptable by the cardinal were: Peruvian Father Gustavo Gutierrez, a member of the Concilium board; Jesuit Father Jon Sobrino, a Spaniard working in El Salvador, and Hugo Assman, a Brazilian ex-priest and acknowledged Marxist who claimed his thinking was still influenced by Christianity.

**Cruise Deployment and MX under Attack —** Cardinal Joseph L. Bernardin of Chicago and Archbishop John J. O'Connor of New York, at a congressional hearing June 26, criticized deployment of U.S. Pershing and cruise missiles in Western Europe and the "MIRVing" of nuclear weapons. They also asked for a reconsideration of deployment of the MX missile, said they were disturbed by proposals for major increases in spending for nuclear weapons systems, and expressed skepticism over the proposed "star wars," space-based defense system.

They said in prepared testimony that "the Church does not embrace pacifism as a public position." Rather, "it believes that some uses of force are justified in the defense of freedom, independence and human dignity. The Church continues to employ the just war criteria to establish limits to the permissible use of force."

Quoting the U.S. bishops' 1983 pastoral letter on peace and war, the prelates said: "It is imperative 'to prevent any use of nuclear weapons and to hope that our leaders will resist the notion that nuclear conflict can be limited, contained, or won in any traditional sense.' "

**Spending Rule Broken —** The U.S. Supreme Court declared July 26 that laws limiting the amount charities can spend on fund raising violate the constitutional right of free speech. The 5-to-4 ruling against a 1976 Maryland law affected similar percentage limits on fund raising by charitable organizations in up to 24 states and in many cities and counties across the nation.

**Meetings —** Meetings during the month included those of the following organizations.

• National Right to Life Convention, June 7 to 9 in Kansas City, Mo. Dr. John Willke was elected president of the committee. Cardinal Bernardin assured delegates that addressing a broad range of pro-life issues would not weaken the anti-abortion movement.

• Catholic Health Association, June 10 to 13 in St. Louis. Speakers noted that more coordination of the nation's resources is needed to serve a growing elderly population.

• Washington, D.C., Office of Black Catholics, June 10 to 15. Good liturgy should incorporate elements of the culture of participants, said Auxiliary Bishop Wilton Gregory of Chicago.

• Catholic Theological Society of America, June 13 to 16 in Washington. Father Avery Dulles, S. J., speaking on "The World Church" theme, said: "The emergence of the world Church sets the main agenda for Catholicism in the decades to come." The John Courtney Murray Award was presented to Monika Hellwig of the Georgetown University faculty.

• National Council for Catholic Evangelization, first meeting, in the middle of the month in Chicago. Father Patrick Brennan, director of the Office of Evangelization, Chicago, was elected president. It was reported that more than 900 organizations, parishes and individuals had joined the council in its first year of operation.

• National Catholic Young Adult Ministry Association, leadership convention, in Buffalo. The theme of the meeting was "The Heart of the Matter: Catholic Identity and Strategies for Ministry with Young Adults.

**National Briefs:**

• James A. Doyle, executive director of the Catholic Press Association for 26 years, was named a Knight of St. Gregory by Pope John Paul June 12.

• Auxiliary Bishop Thomas W. Lyons of Washington presented Bibles to Catholic Senators at the Capitol June 27 in a ceremony marking the conclusion of the observance of the Year of the Bible.

• Migration and Refugee Services, U.S. Catholic Conference, took responsibility for resettling 11 of the 26 Cuban political prisoners released by Fidel Castro at the urging of the Rev. Jesse Jackson.

### Stability in the Church

Working in a deliberate and systematic manner, Pope John Paul has "restored the Church to stability," British historian Paul Johnson declared in an address at a conference in New York called "American Catholics Look to the 21st Century."

Johnson took issue with the claim that the Pope had tried to reverse the direction of the Church since the time of Pope John XXIII. Rather, he said, John Paul had "applied the brakes" to a movement that "got out of hand" in the 1970s. John Paul was elected to the papacy when the Church was "shellshocked" from a decade of radical experiments in liturgy, moral and theological questioning, clergy turning to "political activism," challenge to the Church's teaching authority, declining vocations to the priesthood and religious life, and diminishing attendance at worship.

The Pope's strategy for the restoration of stability, Johnson said, was focused on "orthodoxy, discipline and hierarchy."

### INTERNATIONAL

**Funding for Ontario Schools.** — The Ontario government announced June 12 that it would grant full public funding to Catholic schools in the province in a phased program due to go into effect in September, 1985. The schools, officially called "separate," had been publicly funded through the eighth grade since 1867; ninth and 10th grades received partial funding, but there was no funding for grades 11 through 13. The new funding program made Catholic schools "fully a part of the public school system," said Chris Asseff, executive director of the Ontario Separate School Trustees' Association.

**Bishops for Civilian Rule** — The bishops of Nigeria became the first influential national group to call for the reestablishment of democratic government since army officers ousted President Shehu Shagari Dec. 31, 1983. They also urged the government to stop promoting the idea that politics and politicians are corrupt. "It would not be in the lasting interest of our nation to confirm the impression that we can never rule ourselves well through elected leaders," they said. "That many of our politicians betrayed the trust placed in them does not make politics any less a sacred duty of service to the people."

**What Kind of End for Apartheid?** — A black South African priest who had been penalized for opposing racial discrimination said the Church was seeking peaceful change in South Africa, but that the white-ruled government would decide whether apartheid would end quietly. "Change will come, must come," said Father Smangaliso Mkahtshwa, secretary general of the Southern African Catholic Bishops' Conference. But "the Pretoria regime will to a large extent be the deciding factor" regarding the type of change to come. "Our hope is that peaceful means will be found." But, if the government "uses violence" to suppress the movement for change, then people will resist, he said.

**Smuggling Charges** — Vatican Radio reported June 15 that three young Czechoslovakian men were facing trial for allegedly smuggling religious literature into Poland. Kathpress, the Austrian Catholic news agency, said the arrests were part of a campaign by the Czechoslovakian government to uncover an underground religious information network.

**Family Planning Program under Review** — Colombia's top health official denied a cardinal's charge that the country was subsidizing mass sterilization, but indicated that a former program may have paid for sterilizations by private doctors; he also said the government had begun a review of its family planning policies. Health Minister Jaime Arias announced, in the wake of criticism by Cardinal Alfonso Lopez Trujillo of Medellin, that health workers in family planning would be trained in natural methods of birth regulation approved by the Church.

The New York-based Population Council said that 41,000 Colombians, mostly women, were sterilized under government-supported birth control programs in 1980.

**Repression in Poland** — The bishops of Poland pleaded June 18 for a relaxation of political repression in the country, saying they were worried that "a number of new arrests for political reasons" would result in "new tensions." They said: "Curing that situation requires creating a new political climate that would remove the sources of tensions and repressions."

Three days later, Cardinal Jozef Glemp told a congregation of 20,000 people that atheism was a minority view in Poland. He added: "we hope the state's religious policy does not revert to state atheism. . . . Mass atheism makes citizens more docile to the directives of authorities" and leads to "social degradation."

**Protest against Education Bill in France** — About a million people marched in France June 24 to protest passage by the National Assembly of an education reform measure which would cut state funding for Catholic and other private schools if half of their teachers did not become civil servants after 11 years. The bill still required approval by the Senate. At issue was the Socialist government's effort to get control of private education.

**Christian-Moslem Tension in Sudan** — A campaign by the government of Sudan to establish Moslem law as the law of the land, coupled with new economic and political tensions over oil and other resources in the southern part of the country, was reported to be threatening Christian-Moslem reconciliation in process since 1972. Archbishop Gabriel Subeir Wako of Khartoum was on record with a call to Catholics to "take part in whatever is good for the country," and to "cooperate with all men of good will, irrespective of their religion." He also said that Sudanese Catholics must "stand up for Christian principles to the best of (their) ability."

**Lefebvre Ordinations** — Dissident Archbishop Marcel Lefebvre ordained 25 priests June 29 at the headquarters of his Priestly Society of St. Pius X in Econe, Switzerland. Archbishop Lefebvre was suspended from the legitimate exercise of holy orders in 1976 for ordaining priests without appropriate authority. Before and since then, he was also adamant in opposition to enactments of the Second Vatican Council. Overtures for reconciliation with the Church were fruitless.

**International Briefs:**

• Dutch businessman Piet Derksen of Rotterdam, who made a fortune in sporting goods and family recreation parks, donated $1 million to help finance a worldwide retreat for priests to be held Oct. 5 to 9 at the Vatican.

• A group of northern Italian terrorists turned over three suitcases full of weapons and ammunition to Cardinal Carlo Maria Martini of Milan. The weapons and ammunition were left at the archdiocesan office June 13.

### Salvadoran Guardsmen Sentenced

Five former Salvadoran National Guardsmen were sentenced June 18 to 30 years in prison, with no possibility of parole, for the murder of four American Catholic churchwomen. The sentences were the maximum allowed under Salvadoran law, according to a U.S. State Department specialist.

The four women — Maryknoll Sisters Ita Ford and Maura Clark, Ursuline Sister Dorothy Kazel and lay volunteer Jean Donovan — were found shot to death Dec. 2, 1980, along a country road 15 miles from the San Salvador airport. After more than three years, suspicion still lingered in some quarters that high-ranking Salvadoran military officers were involved in the murders.

# JULY 1984

## VATICAN

**Christian-Jewish Stereotypes** — Religious education should be free of stereotypes about Christians and Jews, Pope John Paul told 20 directors of the International Council of Christians and Jews July 6. He said he identified himself with the group's concern "that the images which each of us projects of the other should be really free of stereotypes and prejudices, that they should respect the other's identity." He noted the importance of teaching history accurately, "given the sad and entangled common history of Jews and Christians — a history which is not always taught or transmitted correctly."

**Apartheid Denounced** — The Pope denounced apartheid, South Africa's policy of rigid racial segregation, calling it an offense against human dignity and a possible threat to regional and world peace. He also criticized July 7 the forced removal of black people to tribal homelands established by the government, and appealed for the rapid establishment of independence for Namibia, a territory administered by South Africa. Addressing the U.N. Special Committee against Apartheid, the Pontiff said: "Every form of discrimination based on race, whether occasionally or systematically practiced, and whether it is aimed at individuals or whole racial groups, is absolutely unacceptable." Apartheid must be changed, he added, "so that other catastrophic consequences can be avoided in the future, for the true good of all who live in the region and for the sake of world peace."

**Encouragement to Czechs** — During a Sunday Angelus message July 8, the Pope prayed that Catholics in Czechoslovakia might be given the strength to give "clear witness" to their faith. He spoke two days after the conclusion of talks between Vatican and Czechoslovakian representatives concerning tense church-state relations in the country. It was reported that the talks were "frank and constructive," but did not result in any concrete resolutions.

**Qualities of a Confessor** — A good confessor should possess "patience, punctuality, discretion, delicacy of manner and of speech, a willing tendency to converse, breadth of mind and heart," the Holy Father told a group of priests July 9. He said such attributes free priests "from the danger of falling into that lack of delicacy, of goodness, of respect for conscience, of affability, of devotion, which at times can put off those who come to the sacrament with the hope and the expectation of finding there a concrete manifestation of the One whom they know to be 'rich in mercy.' " He said the ministry of the confessional is one "which permits so many humble, good and wise priests to be artisans of the renewal of consciences, of the rejuvenation of the Christian community."

**Expulsion of Priests from Nicaragua** — The Pope said July 11 that he deplored the expulsion of 10 foreign priests from Nicaragua, and that the action "added to the trials already suffered" by the Church in that country. The government announced the expulsion of the priests July 9 because, it was alleged, they planned to "provoke a confrontation" between the Church and the state. The action by the government followed a protest march led by Archbishop Miguel Obando Bravo of Managua in support of a Nicaraguan priest accused of aiding rebels. *L'Osservatore Romano* editorialized July 11 that "the painful episode is a further confirmation of a June 22 communique of the executive commission of the Nicaraguan Bishops' Conference which denounced and lamented the campaign under way for years to undermine the Church."

**Message to Lutherans** — The Pope sent greetings July 22 to participants in the Seventh General Assembly of the Lutheran World Federation in Budapest. "May the works of the assembly bear good fruit and contribute to the reestablishment of full unity between all Christians," he said. He also called attention to the "rich theological dialogue" since the Second Vatican Council between the Secretariat for Promoting Christian Unity and the Lutheran World Federation.

**Appeal for Unity of Chinese Catholics** — In a message marking the 125th anniversary of the evangelization of Taiwan, the Pope appealed for the union of the Catholics of Taiwan with the Catholics of mainland China, who were divided between those loyal to the Pope and those belonging to the government-sponsored Patriotic Association of Chinese Catholics. The Pontiff said: "I ardently hope that it may soon be possible to reestablish everywhere, also in an outward manner, that unity and communion which are essential to our condition as Catholics and which have always characterized our common faith." The message, addressed to the head of the Regional Episcopal Conference of China, was published in the July 23 edition of *L'Osservatore Romano*.

**Amnesty and Social Reform** — The Pope said July 25 that he hoped amnesty for 652 political prisoners, declared July 21, would be a step toward social reform in Poland, based on principles agreed to in the 1980 accords between the later-outlawed trade union, Solidarity, and the government. He also praised the bishops for their policy of dialogue with the government: "I know that the Polish episcopate makes constant, untiring efforts so that the principle of dialogue, announced by the Church, can become a fruitful basis for internal peace."

**Refugees** — In a message to a U.N. Conference on African Refugees held in Geneva July 9 to 11, the Pope said they had an inalienable right to a place in their homelands, and that the international community should assist in their financial support while they are in exile.

At a meeting July 27 with several U.S. bishops involved in ministry to refugees, the Pope said the flight of refugees from Marxist countries was an argument against the repressive policies of the governments of those nations.

**The Pope Also:**
- Told the nine bishops of Sri Lanka July 5 that he supported their efforts for peace between the major ethnic groups in their country.
- Said Religious are called to be signs of God's love in a contemporary world marked by "materialism and moral confusion," in a letter to the National Congress of Religious in Scotland.
- In a message to the National Congress of German Catholics meeting in Munich, urged: "Do not hesitate to take on the uncomfortable task of defending life, even unborn life," and of testifying in word and action for "the dignity of the person and his inalienable rights."
- Began a working vacation July 11 at Castel Gandolfo.
- Enjoyed skiing on 11,000-foot high Mt. Adamello in northern Italy July 16 and 17.

**Vatican Briefs:**
- Announced July 2 was the decision of the Vatican Bank to make an immediate, discounted, lump-sum payment of approximately $240 million to creditors of Italy's failed Banco Ambrosiano. The Vatican called the payment a "voluntary contribution," and said it should not be seen as an admission of responsibility for the failure of the bank.
- The three-hundred-year-old Vatican Observatory announced the establishment of an observation station in Tucson, Arizona.

**Talks on Humanae Vitae**

The Holy Father began July 11 a series of talks at weekly general audiences on the encyclical letter, *Humanae Vitae,* concerning marital relations and birth regulation. He also ordered arrangements for briefing sessions by theologians after the talks, a move indicative of his view of the importance of the talks and of his desire for their proper understanding and reporting by journalists.

(For coverage of essential elements of the talks, see under *Humanae Vitae.*)

**NATIONAL**

**Anti-Catholic Bigotry** — The Anti-Defamation League of B'nai B'rith said July 3 that the nationwide anti-Catholic campaign being waged by Christian fundamentalist Tony Alamo was "preposterous and obscene." The agency's research report also said that, in addition to the "blatant biogtry against Catholicism" in millions of pamphlets distributed around the country by Alamo followers in recent months, Alamo had "also disseminated propaganda reflecting anti-Semitism."

**Death Row Population** — The number of inmates on death rows in prisons across the country increased 13 per cent in 1983 to a record 1,202 according to a Justice Department report issued July 8. Also reported:
- Nine persons were executed in the first six months of 1984.
- Twenty persons were executed since the U.S. Supreme Court reinstated the death penalty in 1976.
- Thirty-eight states had death penalty laws.
- The total number of executions since 1930 by

civil and military authorities was 4,039.

The U.S. bishops as a body and individual bishops in several states have issued statements opposed to capital punishment as currently applied in this country.

**Instructional Programs Unconstitutional** — The U.S. 2nd Court of Appeals ruled July 10 against the constitutionality of a New York City program that sent public school teachers into church-related schools to provide remedial instruction. The program, which had helped about 20,000 students in 250 schools in poor neighborhoods, was praised by the court but was found to be in violation of the First Amendment's ban against governmental involvement in religion.

**No Fetus Burial by Church Group** — NC News reported July 11 the June 29 decision of the California Court of Appeals of the Second District, that 16,433 aborted fetuses discovered two years earlier in an abandoned storage container could not be buried by a Catholic group in a public cemetery. Burial of the fetuses by the local chapter of the Catholic League for Religious and Civil Rights would create "excessive entanglement" of church and state, the court said. The three-member court held that the league was an extension of the Catholic Church and that the burial would have been a distinct religious rite.

**Pirate Attacks on Boat People** — Migration and Refugee Services, U.S. Catholic Conference, reported that pirate attacks on boats loaded with Vietnamese refugees had increased in severity at the same time that $5 million approved by Congress to combat piracy in Southeast Asian waters went unused. The report estimated that almost half of all refugee boats arriving in Thailand were attacked by Thai fishermen.

**Denial of Funds for Abortion** — The White House issued a policy statement saying it would deny U.S. population control aid to non-governmental groups which "perform or actively promote" abortion, but it may continue to give funds to nations in which abortion is part of its population control program. It was thought that policy would cut U.S. funding of the International Planned Parenthood Federation by more than $10 million a year.

**Different Creche Decisions** — Between March and July, two separate rulings raised questions about the constitutionality of Christmas nativity scenes erected by cities. The U.S. Supreme Court decided Mar. 5 that a nativity scene in Pawtucket, R.I., was constitutional because it had other Christmas displays with it, and also because the Constitution "affirmatively mandates accommodation, not merely tolerance, of all religions and forbids hostility toward any." On July 23, a U.S. District Court ruled that a nativity scene in Birmingham, Mich., was unconstitutional because it was placed alone on public property with the use of public funds.

**Papal "Biography" a Fraud** — *God's Broker,* supposedly a biography of Pope John Paul II by Antoni Gronowicz, was withdrawn from circulation late in the month by its publisher. Julian M. Snyder, president of Richardson and Snyder Publishing Co., called the book a "total fraud." The Vatican Press Office blasted the credentials of the author with a statement originally issued May 31. Father Romeo Panciroli said of Gronowicz: "He is not recognized in Polish circles around the Pope. He asked for but was not granted a private audience with the Pope. He was admitted only one or two times in a group or in a general audience. Therefore, it is completely false that he had 200 hours of conversation with the Pope as he asserted."

**"Baby Doe" Legislation** — The Senate unanimously approved July 26 legislation making any failure to provide treatment or nourishment to a severely deformed infant with a chance for life a form of child abuse. Differences with a similar bill approved by the House of Representatives in March remained to be worked out.

The government's role in such a case had been at issue in national debate since 1972, when an Indiana baby with Down's Syndrome died of starvation after his parents rejected surgery to correct a malformed esophagus. The legislation would provide that non-complying states could lose federal funds earmarked for the prevention of child abuse. It would not require treatment for an infant who was "chronically and irreversibly" in a coma, nor when treatment would be "futile," "nearly futile," "merely prolonging dying," or could not improve or correct all of the life-threatening conditions. The legislation was supported by pro-life groups and opposed by the American Medical Association, which contended that it would put government officials, instead of parents and doctors, in charge of deciding which deformed babies would die and which ones would live.

**Immigration Reform** — James M. Hoffman, assistant director of immigration affairs for the U.S. Catholic Conference, called immigration reform legislation morally necessary July 26. He made the remark as legislation sponsored by Senator Alan K. Simpson of Wyoming and Representative Romano Mazzoli of Kentucky remained stalled over differences between bills in the two chambers of Congress. At issue were guest worker provisions reminiscent of the former bracero program, sanctions against employers of undocumented aliens, and the cutoff date for amnesty for illegal aliens. Hispanic groups were generally dissatisfied with the legislative proposals.

**Meetings** — Meetings during the month included those of the following groups.
• Worldwide Marriage Encounter, June 29 to July 1 in Chicago.
• Byzantine Catholics, 25th annual convention, July 5 to 8 in Washington.
• Couple to Couple League, July 6 in Baltimore.
• National Association of Priest Pilots, July 9 to 11 in Stacyville, Iowa.
• Catholic Daughters of the Americas, July 15 to 20 in Houston, on the theme, "Family Unity: The Strength of the Nation."
**National Briefs:**
• Franciscan Sister Margaret Mary Moddé was named to head the Department of Canon Law in

the Division of Legal Services of the Catholic Health Association.
• Mercy Sister Faith Marie Mauro was appointed representative for Youth and Young Adult Ministry for the Department of Education, U.S. Catholic Conference.
• A Catholic communications organization funded by the Milwaukee-based De Rance Foundation launched a new satellite television network in an effort "to foster Christian doctrine" throughout North America. Santa Fe Communications aimed to call "Catholics everywhere to a basic love for Jesus Christ and the Church."
• The Archdiocese of New Orleans inaugurated public television station WLAE-TV July 8.
• Michael Kirwan, a friend of the "street people" of Washington, was named recipient of the Good Samaritan Award of the National Catholic Development Conference.

### Washington Post Report on Papal Plot

After nearly three years of work, Italian investigators had only a weak case for the alleged Bulgarian connection in Mehmet Ali Agca's 1981 attempt to kill Pope John Paul II, said *The Washington Post* July 22. In a lengthy report from Rome, foreign correspondent Michael Dobbs said that contradictions or lack of corroborating evidence marred key points in confessions made by Agca. Those confessions, in which Agca claimed he was working under orders from the Bulgarian secret service, were the core of the assassination plot investigation.

Dobbs' story, based on interviews and analysis of a leaked prosecutor's report, said that some Italian magistrates thought the state had built a "convincing case" but one that would be hard to prove in court. Others remained skeptical of the whole plot theory.

### INTERNATIONAL

**Aid for African Refugees** — Caritas Internationalis asked public and private international agencies to increase aid to five million refugees in Africa. The plea was made at a July 9 to 11 U.N.-sponsored conference in Geneva. The Caritas delegation said aid programs should go beyond the immediate material needs of the refugees to include long-range plans and projects for helping them to develop economic self-sufficiency in their host countries and to aid local communities that receive them.

**Priests Cleared of Murder Charge** — Two Columban Fathers, whose murder trial ended when charges were dismissed, said July 10 in Manila that they had been framed by the Philippine military because they had campaigned against violations of human rights by the government. Reuters, the British news agency, reported that Fathers Brian Gore of Australia and Niall O'Brien of Ireland were freed early in the month after a 15-month court battle. The judge in the case said that evidence brought forward against them was insufficient to prove, "beyond a reasonable doubt," a connection with the ambush slaying of Mayor Pablo Sola of Kabankalan in 1982.

**End of the "Savary Project"** — French Prime Minister Pierre Mauroy and his cabinet resigned, July 17, partly because President Francois Mitterand announced July 12 abandonment of a controversial plan, the "Savary Project," to increase state control of Catholic and other private schools. Among those who resigned was Education Minister Alain Savary who had sponsored and staked his political reputation on the plan. Country-wide protests against the measure in June led to its withdrawal from consideration for adoption.

**Unacceptable Embryo Experimentation** — Cardinal Basil Hume of Westminster declared July 19 that Catholic teaching condemns a special British government committee's recommendation to legalize experimentation on human embryos developed in scientific laboratories. He said: "The moral teaching of our Church will not allow Catholics to accept the proposals that experimentation on embryos should be permitted in the first 14 days. We have particular and profound moral objections to procedures which work, or are considered to work, to the detriment and even the destruction of individuals. Catholics recognize the importance of research into factors which contribute to infertility and inherited disorders, but the freedom to experiment on and then destroy human embryos can never be morally justified."

The cardinal said Catholics "would welcome long-overdue restrictions" recommended by the commission on artificial insemination in which sperm or eggs are supplied to a childless couple by an outside donor. But the Church still maintains "absolute moral objections" to the practice.

Cardinal Hume also said that Catholics would support proposals to outlaw surrogate motherhood.

**Amnesty and Farm Program in Poland** — The Polish government declared amnesty July 21 for 652 political prisoners, an action for which the bishops, with the support of the Pope, had waged a strong campaign. The amnesty included four senior advisors to Solidarity, the outlawed labor union, underground activists who come out of hiding and confess their activities, and 36,000 common criminals. Not covered in the amnesty program were persons held in connection with acts of high treason, espionage and sabotage. Church leaders were pleased with the announcement of amnesty, but cautioned that the pardon alone would not bring about national reconciliation.

In another action, the government agreed July 25 to let the Church run a unique fund for private farmers, with heavy reliance on contributions from church and public sources in western nations. The agreement was reached after the regime withdrew its demand for a voice in administration of the program.

**Explosive Factors in Latin America** — "Unemployment, inflation and the foreign debt are three elements that, when put together, become highly explosive" factors in economic and political developments in Latin America, according to Argentine Archbishop Antonio Quarracino, president of the Latin American Bishops' Council. He also said in a report published in the July 26 edition of

*L'Osservatore Romano:* "In the panorama of today's Latin America, the possibility of overcoming poverty seems always to be further away."

**Marcos' Criticism of His Critics** — President Ferdinand Marcos again accused church personnel of meddling in government affairs, in an apparent reference to vocal Catholic critics of violations of human rights in the Philippines. He made the accusation in a speech delivered on July 27. The most recent criticism was that contained in a pastoral letter prepared for delivery in churches on July 22. In it, the bishops criticized Marcos for the deployment of undercover marshals who, they said, had killed 45 people in Manila since the previous month.

**International Briefs:**

• The communist government of China completed restoration of the grave of Jesuit Father Matteo Ricci, who introduced the Catholic faith and contributed to the development of culture in China in the 16th century. The grave had been damaged by Red Guards during the Cultural Revolution of the 1960s.

• The Rev. Emilio Castro, a Uruguayan Methodist minister, was elected July 12 as secretary general of the World Council of Churches.

• Bishop Castor Sekwa of Shinyanga launched a food relief program to avoid famine in his drought-stricken diocese in western Tanzania. "We have reached a time when the first duty is to feed the starving, the hungry, the needy," he said.

• The Japanese Bible Society reported that the Bible was the best-selling book (1.1 million copies) in Japan in 1983.

### Relations Worsen in Nicaragua

Events during the month signaled a worsening of church-state relations in Nicaragua.

Archbishop Miguel Obando Bravo of Managua led a march of protest July 9 against the arrest and detention since June 20 of Father Luis Amado Pena for trial on allegations that he had supplied weapons and ammunition to guerrillas and had conspired against the government. The archbishop said the priest was framed and that a videotape of alleged evidence was fabricated. The opposition newspaper in Managua was not permitted to publish a report on the march.

Ten foreign priests were expelled from the country after the march, in which they allegedly took part. Reasons for the expulsions were allegations that they had violated laws of the country and had provoked confrontation with the government.

Throughout the month, Jesuit Father Fernando Cardenal refused to comply with church law and the order of his Jesuit superior general not to accept cabinet rank in the government as education minister.

With these and related events as background, Archbishop Obando Bravo said in an interview July 21: "I want to say very clearly that this government is totalitarian. I was never on the side of Somoza. But these people, the Sandinistas, are more unjust because they trample on the dignity of the people."

# AUGUST 1984

## VATICAN

**Tribute to Paul VI** — The Pope praised Pope Paul VI Aug. 5, the eve of the sixth anniversary of his death. He said: "This Pope left to the Church and to the world a precious inheritance of examples and teachings. We should always be aware of this, and grateful. . . . He loved the Church intensely, and with no less intensity he loved, exalted and defended man. He loved and esteemed his age, and ardently wanted to announce to it the message of Christ."

**Canon Law** — The revised Code of Canon Law which went into effect Nov. 27, 1983, marks "a new stage in bringing about that interior renewal" which the Second Vatican Council intended "and for which we continue to work and pray." This was the substance of a letter addressed by the Pope Aug. 10 to the Fifth International Canonists' Congress in Ottawa. The new code, he said, is an "indispensable instrument" of the Church's life and vitality, and: "Canon lawyers must be aware of their grave responsibilities in the task of consolidating the life of the Church at every level, according to the spirit of the Gospel, overcoming uncertainity and banishing laxity in the observance of a discipline which, by reason of its ordination to the life and mission of the Church, is truly sacred and salvific." (See separate entries.)

**Visit to Fano** — The Pope visited the fishing port of Fano 136 miles northeast of Rome Aug. 12. While there, he addressed a group of priests and religious, celebrated Mass before a gathering of 100,000 people, and dined with 800 fishermen at dockside. In a homily, he urged his listeners to follow the example of St. Peter, a fisherman, and to look to Christ as the source of salvation and inspiration. "It is not easy," he acknowledged, "to coherently live the faith in the environment of modern society, filled with materialism and permissiveness."

**The Assumption of Mary** — "On this feast of the Assumption of the Blessed Virgin Mary, we pray that she, who was assumed body and soul into heaven, will be our powerful intercessor before God." This was the petition of Pope John Paul Aug. 15 in a brief address to tourists at Castel Gandolfo.

**"The Eucharist and the Christian Family"** — In a letter on this theme of the 43rd International Eucharistic Congress, the Holy Father noted: "The Chrisian family has a special vocation to be witness to the Gospel in the contemporary world. From the Eucharist, it will draw the strength needed to fulfill such a task. . . . What strikes one immediately in considering the Eucharistic mystery is that, from the very beginning of the Church, it has been lived in a dimension of community." The scriptural terms — "home, family, supper" — evoke such a setting. And, "the fact that the Eucharist is celebrated today in the temple should not stop us from seeing the deepest connection that runs between the sacrament of the Body and Blood of the Lord and that first and vital cell of society,

the family." The Pontiff's letter, dated Aug. 15, was addressed to Cardinal Opilio Rossi, president of the Permanent Committee for International Eucharistic Congresses. The 43rd congress was scheduled to be held in August, 1985, in Nairobi, Kenya. (See separate entry.)

**Lay Participation in the Liturgy** — This was the theme of a letter addressed by the Pope Aug. 18 to participants in the 35th Italian National Liturgical Week. The message, noting in particular the work of lectors, acolytes, cantors and extraordinary ministers of the Eucharist, said the Church affirms the diversity of functions in liturgical celebrations. The Holy Father urged lay ministers to deeper study of their ministries so that, "aware of their functions for a more worthy, efficient and fruitful celebration of the liturgy, they might offer a generous increase in the liturgical life of the Church."

**Danger of Nuclear Winter** — Pope John Paul urged an international meeting of scientists Aug. 19 to help free the world from the grave risks of new nuclear weapons and the catastrophic "nuclear winter" their use could bring. He did so in a letter sent in his name to participants in a week-long seminar in Erice, Sicily. The message said: "The theme of nuclear winter and the new defense systems calls attention once again to the many grave consequences to which the use of nuclear weapons exposes all humanity. . . . It is his (Pope John Paul's) hope that this gathering will further the mutual respect and confidence between peoples upon which peace must be built. . . . May this experience of active collaboration likewise contribute to a deeper understanding of the interconnection between the problems which confront humanity today, and help awaken within the community of nations a lively sense of man's dignity, his common future and spiritual destiny." Attendants at the seminar included representatives from the United States, the Soviet Union and China.

**Morality of Marital Relations** — In the sixth of a series of talks on marital relations and birth regulation, the Holy Father said Aug. 22: "In accordance with the true nature of marriage, as an authentic communion of persons, the conjugal act signifies not only mutual love but also an openness to the transmission of new life. As such, the marriage act cannot be deprived of its full meaning by separating artifically the unitive aspect from the procreative aspect. This is so since a conjugal act which lacks an essential element of its own intimate structure ceases to be an act of love in its fullest sense."

**No Trip to Lithuania** — The Pope said Aug. 23 that he and Secretary of State Cardinal Agostino Casaroli had tried without success to visit Lithuania this year. He did not say specifically why he was unable to make the visit. It was thought, however, that the Pope wanted it known publicly that he had asked for and had not received permission to travel to the Baltic nation. The Holy Father made the unusual statement in a message to Lithuanians during concluding ceremonies of the 500th anniversary celebration of the death of St. Casimir, patron saint of Lithuania and Poland.

**Use of the Bible** — "The faithful are called to serve God's revelation, rather than to use the Word to further their own ideas, however lofty they may be." So declared the Pope Aug. 23 in a message to the General Assembly of the World Catholic Federation for the Biblical Apostolate. He also said: "One cannot forget that the Word is entrusted to the Church, and that the Church's teaching office bears responsibility for authentically interpreting its message." The Bible "may inspire various forms of response," but "care must always be taken to avoid permitting the revealed Word to serve a particular theology."

**The Church Is Committed to Life** — The Pope told Peter Hermes, West German ambassador to the Vatican, that the Church is committed to fundamental values regarding life and human rights. "In modern, pluralistic society, the Church is especially committed to its prophetic role," he said. It seeks "the promotion and the defense of fundamental spiritual and ethical values." For that reason, the Church must oppose any action which "threatens the fundamental values and rights of mankind."

It was estimated that 91,000 abortions were performed in West Germany in 1982.

**Spiritual Formation** — The Pope told 350 participants in the World Congress of Secular Institutes Aug. 28 that spiritual formation never ends. "None of us has reached the perfection to which we are called. Each of us is always in formation, always on the way," he said. Regarding spiritual advisors, he said they "can and should become agents and instruments" of formation while showing "respect for the mysterious action of grace."

**The Pope Also:**

• In a letter addressed to Archbishop Michael Coppenrath of Papeete, marked the 150th anniversary of the arrival of the first missionaries in Polynesia.

• Said resolutions of major world issues must emphasize human dignity, rights and freedoms, in a message to the fourth interfaith World Conference on Religion and Peace, held Aug. 23 to 30 in Nairobi.

**Vatican Briefs:**

• New emphasis on Islamic law in some Moslem countries was viewed as a threat to improved relations achieved by Catholics and Moslems over the previous 20 years, according to an article in the Aug. 15 edition of *L'Osservatore Romano.*

• *L'Osservatore Romano,* in its Aug. 22 edition, condemned as "a satanic market" a reported international traffic in human fetuses for scientific research and use in the cosmetic industry.

• American Archbishop John Foley was named president of the Council for the administration of the Vatican Television Center, Aug. 21.

**For the Poor but Not Their Revolt**

"The solidarity of the Church with the poor, with the victims of unjust laws or unjust social and economic structures, goes without saying," declared the Pope Aug. 22, in a message sent to the first general assembly of bishops from Lesotho, Swaziland, Zimbabwe, Botswana, South Africa and Namibia.

"But," he added, "the forms in which this solidarity is realized cannot be dictated by an analysis based on class distinctions and class struggle. The Church's task is to call all men and women to conversion and reconciliation without opposing groups, without being 'against' anyone."

## NATIONAL

**Vietnamese Adapting Well** — Most of the Vietnamese refugee families which came to the United States since 1975 were adapting to American life and beginning to reap its benefits, according to a Vietnamese-American priest. "We are learning what it means to be Americans in an American church," said Father John Nghi, founding director of the New Orleans Vietnamese Apostolate and secretary general of the July 26 to 29 conference of the Vietnamese Catholic Federation in the United States. He said: "A lot of refugees have resettled in many dioceses across the country. We have the same faith. We have the same doctrine. We have felt very much welcome here from the very beginning." He said there were 120 Vietnamese parishes in the U.S.

Migration and Refugee Services, U.S. Catholic Conference, played a major role in resettling a large percentage of the refugees in this country.

**Two Anglicans Ordained** — Two more married former Anglican clergymen were ordained Catholic priests under special rules in force only in the United States. They were Father Patrick Sutton, ordained Aug. 4 in Baltimore, and Father Patrick Eastman, ordained Aug. 14 in Tulsa. The total number of Anglican clergymen so ordained was 22.

**Fetus a Person in Vehicular Homicide** — The Massachusetts State Supreme Court ruled 4 to 3 Aug. 16 that a viable fetus is a person, and that a driver causing its death may be prosecuted for vehicular homicide. The court said: "An offspring of a human parent cannot reasonably be considered to be other than a human being, and therefore a person, first within and then in normal course outside the womb." The eight-and-one-half-month-old fetus, whose mother was struck by a car in 1982, "was viable at the time of the incident and died as a result of internal injuries caused by the impact of the vehicle," said the court.

A spokesman for Massachusetts Citizens for Life praised the decision "for recognizing the existence and value of unborn human life. . . . By including viable, unborn children under the vehicular homicide law's definition of 'person,' the court takes a step forward in logic and compassion. . . . It is ironic, however, that on one hand the law upholds a woman's right to kill even viable fetuses, while on the other hand the law imposes criminal sanctions for the taking of life before birth."

**Lay People To Run High School** — A report from Milwaukee said that an archdiocesan high school forced to close in May because of low enrollment would reopen in September under the auspices of a lay group made up of alumni and parents. The parent-alumni organization bought the school and its contents as well as the accompanying rectory and convent for $375,000 provided by an anonymous benefactor. Carol Rauen, president of the sponsoring organization, said the curriculum of Messmer High School would be four-year college preparatory with a complete basic educational program, and would be "theologically sound." The school, it was said, would not be part of the archdiocesan system.

**Tension Accelerating in Nicaragua** — Church-state tension in Nicaragua was said to be "accelerating rapidly" by Archbishop John R. Roach of St. Paul-Minneapolis on his return from meetings Aug. 19 to 22 with church and government leaders, including junta president Daniel Ortega. "I will only say at this moment that the situation in Nicaragua is very desperate. The civil war is devastating and is causing great hunger and very serious health problems. The situation is incredibly complex, and any attempt to simplify it is to underestimate the reality."

**Doyle Honored** — James A. Doyle, executive director of the Catholic Press Association since 1958, was invested as a Knight of St. Gregory at a Mass and related ceremonies Aug. 26 in Rockville Centre, N.Y. During the proceedings honoring Doyle, Bishop John R. McGann said in an address that the Church should not overlook the continuing vital role of the print medium in its efforts to extend communications in radio and television.

**Schools Cited for Excellence** — Thirty-three Catholic schools were among the 262 American junior and senior high schools cited for educational excellence by President Reagan Aug. 27.

Earlier in the month, U.S. Secretary of Education Terrell H. Bell said the value-oriented education offered by Catholic schools made them a "treasured national resource among all American schools. With their long record of contributions to the national goal of excellence in education, Catholic schools have served as a pillar in the structure of quality education."

**Serra Bicentennial** — Initial ceremonies for the celebration of the 200th anniversary of the death of Father Junipero Serra were held Aug. 28 at San Carlos Borromeo Mission in Carmel, Calif., where the Franciscan missionary is buried. In 35 years of missionary work, he founded the first Catholic mission in California in 1769 at San Diego, established a string of 20 other missions and brought more than 5,000 persons into the Church. It was hoped that the bicentennial observance would evoke a crusade of prayer for his canonization.

**Meetings** — Organizations holding meetings during the month were the following.
• Tekakwitha Conference, Aug. 1 to 5 in Phoenix.
• The Knights of Columbus, Supreme Council, Aug. 7 to 9 in Denver.
• The National Assembly of Religious Women, Aug. 9 to 12 in Cleveland.
• The American Catholic Correctional Chaplains' Association, Aug. 19 to 23 in San Antonio.
• The Conference of Major Superiors of Men, Aug. 19 to 24 in Atlanta.
**National Briefs:**
• Gregory F. Pierce of Brooklyn was elected president of the National Center for the Laity in Chicago.
• More than 100 stores in western Washington and nearby states stopped selling a number of "adult" magazines after members of Holy Family Parish in Kirkland, Wash., and a local citizens' group threatened them with a boycott.
• Bishop Charles V. Grahmann of Victoria, Tex., was named the 1984 recipient of the Father Paul Kaletta Award of the National Catholic Stewardship Council.
• The National Catholic Rural Life Conference announced that "Thanksgiving: A Season of Reflection and Praise" would be the theme of its 1984 fall period of prayer.

### Religion and Politics

Bishop James W. Malone, president of the U.S. Catholic Conference, issued a conference statement Aug. 9 which warned against the use of religion in a partisan political manner while criticizing the position that religious convictions should not influence public policy decisions. The statement named no names but was perceived as referring to Democratic vice presidential candidate Geraldine Ferraro and New York Governor Mario Cuomo, Catholics, who said they were personally opposed to abortion but would not support steps to ban it. (See separate entry, same title.)

### INTERNATIONAL

**Officers Named** — Three bishops joined other human rights activists in naming 896 military officers Aug. 2 involved in thousands of disappearances during eight years of military rule in Argentina. The list was presented to the Senate to prevent the promotion of any of the officers named thereon. Rights organizations estimated that eight thousand to 10,000 people had disappeared without a trace. The hierarchy had criticized the military privately and publicly for the deaths of innocent people and the disappearances of thousands during the anti-guerrilla "dirty war."

**End of Abuse of the Church Sought** — L'Osservatore Romano carried a report in its Aug. 5 edition which said the bishops of Nicaragua had asked the government to stop abusing the Church. They called for an end to "insults against the person of Archbishop Miguel Obando Bravo and of other bishops, priests and Catholic faithful." The archbishop was already on record to the effect that there was "a state of persecution in Nicaragua."

Father Ernesto Cardenal, minister of culture and one of four priests refusing to give up key posts in the government, said the archbishop was simply voicing right-wing opposition to the Sandinista regime.

Later in the month, Msgr. Julian Herranz reiterated Aug. 27 the Holy See's opposition to government office-holding by the four priests, and said that not even a dispensation from the local bishops could supersede that opposition. He referred to a statement of Aug. 10 which said the priests "know perfectly that the church authority has been insisting since 1979 that they leave positions that are incompatible with the priestly mission." Msgr. Herranz was secretary of the Pontifical Commission for the Interpretation of the Code of Canon Law.

**Social Reform in Guatemala** — Archbishop Prospero Penados del Barrio of Guatemala City said in an interview early in the month that he was trying to involve the Church more and more in social reform while keeping his distance from the nation's military regime. "The Church cannot confine itself to preaching a spiritual message without doing anything to put that message into practice," he said. "Military authorities have told me that the Church should only preach, and not act. (But) without good works, faith has no life." Regarding relations with the government, he added: "I want to maintain a certain distance. We need to be in constant dialogue with the authorities, but never be united with them, much less submit to them."

**Population Conference** — A seven-member Vatican delegation to the International Population Conference Aug. 6 to 14 in Mexico City declined to endorse its World Plan of Action because of its support for contraception and other objectionable policies. One positive achievement of the conference was its endorsement of an amendment stating that abortion should not be promoted as a method of family planning. The amendment had the support of the U.S. delegation. (See separate entry.)

**School Conflict in Malta** — Archbishop Joseph Mercieca asked a Maltese civil court Aug. 10 to overturn a law prohibiting Catholic and other private secondary schools from charging tuition. He also said that all Catholic schools in the nation would reopen in September, despite an Aug. 1 government order closing eight schools which refused to comply with the law.

**Problems, but Growth in Africa** — Despite enormous problems, the Church in Africa was growing, said American Archbishop John L. May, recently returned from Kinshasa and attendance at a meeting of 80 bishops of Africa. Problems reported early in the month included: widespread poverty and illiteracy, "despotic" governments, tribal factions, language barriers, rigid racial segregation in South Africa and resurgent Islam in the North. Factors indicative of growth were increases in the appointment of native bishops and in the number of students for the priesthood, adaptation of the liturgy to native cultures, and concern and moves regarding economic development and social justice.

**Error about Civilian Deaths** — Tutela Legal, the human rights office of the San Salvador Archdiocese, said Aug. 16 that it had substantially over-estimated the number of civilians killed during an army operation of Dec. 31, 1983.

**South African Election Criticized** — Archbishop Denis Hurley, chairman of the Southern Africa Bishops' Conference, sharply criticized his country's Aug. 23 parliamentary election, calling it "a weak substitute for authentic democratic evolution." The white minority remained in complete control of the government and its policies of rigid racial discrimination. The election was part one of a two-phased process for determining mixed-race and Indian representation in parliament; blacks, comprising about 72 per cent of the population, had rights neither to vote nor to be represented.

**Violations of Rights in Mozambique** — The Marxist government, in control since the achievement of independence from Portugal in 1975, was violating human rights at a "great cost in human life," said Archbishop Jaime Pedro Goncalves, president of the Mozambique Bishops' Conference, Aug. 27 at a press conference in Harare, Zimbabwe. "The major suffering of a large part of our people is caused by the privation of fundamental human rights as a consequence of atheistic and materialistic ideologies, which continue to be applied at a great cost in human life. . . . We recognize the good things that governments do, even under difficult conditions, but we also ask that Africa be permitted to grow according to its own forms and cultural values, and that these not be manipulated in favor of an unacceptable ideology."

**International Briefs:**
• The World Lutheran Federation suspended Aug. 1 two white South African churches for failure to reject the nation's system of rigid racial segregation.
• Casa Alianza in Guatemala City, founded by Franciscan Father Bruce Ritter of New York's Covenant House, was in its fifth year of operation.

### "Patriotic" Church in Vietnam

A Vatican report on the Church in Vietnam indicated "deep concern" over what it described as the government's attempt to establish a parallel, pro-government Catholic Church. The report by Fides, an agency of the Congregation for the Evangelization of Peoples, said a number of recent accounts reaching the West from a variety of sources, revealed "a situation of substantial restriction of freedom and even persecution of the Catholic Church. . . . What deeply concerns Vietnamese church leaders and Catholics at this moment is the so-called 'Committee for the Solidarity of Patriotic Vietnamese Catholics.' "

Fides cited press reports saying that the communist government held the first convention of "patriotic" Catholics in November, 1983, in Hanoi, and had subsequently organized the parallel church on local levels despite strong criticism from the bishops.

The Fides report cited a document obtained from a regional governmental office which listed measures to be taken by authorities against the Church:
• suspending authorization for the ordination of new priests, except in special cases;
• controlling priestly activities. and limiting them to the territory assigned to each priest;
• requiring reports from bishops about religious ceremonies attended and diocesan visits made;
• suspending from ministerial functions priests and others who had been convicted by Vietnamese courts, even after their release from prison;
• reducing the membership of parish organizations to seven people or less.

## SEPTEMBER 1984

### VATICAN

**Pseudo-Values** — Pope John Paul, on a one-day visit to the Italian hill town of Alatri, told thousands of people Sept. 2 to resist pseudo-values of the 20th century. "The Christian life is, above all, self-sacrifice," he said. "In this way, our lives — perhaps hidden, monotonous or insignificant in the eyes of the others — become extraordinarily precious to God." The Christian life thus becomes "a form of denial of the errors and ideas that go against the word of God." The Christian should respond with eternal values "to the pseudo-values that the mentality of this century would like to set in opposition against perfect revelation," he said.

**Euthanasia Proponents "Inhuman"** — People and groups who promote euthanasia are "absurd and inhuman," said the Pope Sept. 6 as he told Catholics they should oppose legalized mercy killing. Christians must "do more than simply condemn euthanasia, or stand in the way of (its) eventual spread and legalization. . . . The basic problem, above all, is to succeed in aiding men of our time to become aware of the inhumanity of certain aspects of the dominant culture and to rediscover the more precious values which are hidden." He called for "the presence and incisive involvement of Catholics in all national and international centers and organizations which make extremely important decisions for the direction of society."

**Sanctions Face Nicaraguan Priests** — The Pope, en route to Canada Sept. 9, said that canonical sanctions would be imposed on four Nicaraguan priests if they refused to leave jobs in the government. The four were Fathers: Fernando Cardenal, S.J., minister of education, and his brother, Ernesto, minister of culture; Miguel d'Escoto, M.M., foreign minister; and Edgar Parrales, ambassador to the Organization of American States. A delegation of Nicaraguan officials met with Cardinal Agostino Casaroli, papal secretary of state, Sept. 6 and 7 for discussions on church-state relations, but no report was issued on the outcome.

**Drug Traffic** — The Pope called drug traffic Sept. 11 an "underground river" which had poisoned the lives of young people and was a main factor in the "general decadence" of contemporary society. He also restated opposition to the use of substitute drugs in the treatment of addiction: "The possibility of recovery and redemption from this heavy slavery has been concretely proven, and it is significant that this has been done with methods that rigorously exclude any concession for legal or illegal substitute drugs." The Pope made the remarks in an address to participants in an international convention of drug therapists.

### Visit to Canada

Pope John Paul, on the 23rd foreign trip of his pontificate, crisscrossed Canada Sept. 9 to 20. During the tour, he:
• touched down in almost every province;
• addressed thousands of people on a wide range of subjects — from the need for living and active faith and a new vision of humanity to essential moral obligations, issues pertaining to many aspects of human rights, ecumenism and ethnic diversity;
• consecrated Canada and its people to Mary at the nation's principal Marian sanctuary at Cap-de-la-Madeleine;
• held the first beatification ever on Canadian soil.
(See separate article.)

Four days before the Pope took off for Canada, the Vatican announced that he planned to visit the Dominican Republic and Puerto Rico Oct. 11 to 13.

**Vatican Consultation Increasing** — Officials and Religious living and working in Rome told an NC News interviewer that greater Vatican consultation with local churches was a major change in its operating style. They traced the change to the rationale and development in practice of the principle of collegiality stated by the Second Vatican Council. Another reason was the need for consultation because of the complexity and variety of issues faced by the Church on local, national and international levels, such as human needs and rights, doctrinal and disciplinary problems. The Holy See "wants to be with the local churches" on these matters, said one official.

**Instruction on Liberation Theology** — The Congregation for the Doctrine of the Faith issued Sept. 3 an Instruction on Certain Aspects of the "Theology of Liberation." The instruction was critical of Marxist elements considered to be incompatible with Catholic teaching. Some such elements are usable, but only under strict conditions, declared Cardinal Joseph Ratzinger, prefect of the congregation, at a press conference Sept. 3. He said: "The system of Marx has developed in opposition to Christianity, in opposition to the thirst for God and for his hope. This does not exclude the presence of some valid and usable elements. But this (use) requires a much stronger vigilance and a much more conscious critique" than for elements borrowed from other non-Christian philosophies. There were some mixed reactions to the instruction. (See separate entry for excerpts and a summary of the Instruction.)

### INTERNATIONAL

**Death of Cardinal Slipyi** — Ukrainian Cardinal Josyf Slipyi, who spent 18 years in Soviet prisons and labor camps before being exiled to Rome, died at age 92 Sept. 7.

Pope John Paul, in a telegram addressed to Ukrainian Catholics, said the cardinal had given "a singular and shining witness to faith in Christ, even in difficulties and in suffering that was endured with exemplary dignity." The cardinal was called "a symbol of faithfulness, sacrifice, constancy and courage" by Archbishop Miroslav Lubachivsky, his successor as the ranking prelate of Ukrainian Catholics.

Until his death, Cardinal Slipyi was a staunch defender of the prerogatives of Ukrainian Catholics.

**"Popular Church" in Nicaragua** — Bishop Pablo Antonio Vega, president of the Nicaraguan Bishops' Conference, said Sept. 7 at an interview in Rome that ex-priests and ex-Religious were helping the Sandinista government form an opposition "popular church." He said they had the support of and were paid directly or indirectly by the government.

**Vatican Intervention in Religious Institute** — The Vatican appointed new administrators of the European branch of the U.S.-based Sisters of St. Francis "to restore peace and harmony," a Vatican official told NC News Sept. 7. The action by the Congregation for Religious and Secular Institutes followed a May 28 decision to suspend the authority of the U.S. community over its European province because of a conflict between the provincial superior and the superior general concerning authority.

**Court Finding against Malta Government** — The Constitutional Court of Malta declared Sept. 24 that the Devolution of Certain Church Properties Act passed in June, 1983, to permit government take-over of church property, was unconstitutional. (See related earlier entries.)

## NATIONAL

**Cuomo Address on Religion and Politics** — New York Governor Mario Cuomo, in an address at the University of Notre Dame, warned Sept. 13 that attempting to legislate against abortion in the current political climate would be an imposition of personal views, would not work, and would endanger religious freedom.

Commentators differed in their evaluations of the speech. Jesuit Father Charles M. Whelan, professor of law at Fordham University, called it "an American classic." Msgr. James T. McHugh, a staff member of the National Conference of Catholic Bishops and the U.S. Catholic Conference, represented another view with the statement that Cuomo "introduced more confusion and more chaos into an ongoing debate about the relationship of religion and politics than one could think possible in an hour's speech."

It was clear that the Governor's viewpoint was different from the one expressed in a statement on religion and politics issued by Bishop James W. Malone on Aug. 9 on behalf of the U.S. Catholic Conference:

"We reject the idea that candidates satisfy the requirements of rational analysis in saying their personal views should not influence their policy decisions; the implied dichotomoy — between personal morality and public policy — is simply not logically tenable in any adequate view of both."

(See separate entry, Religion and Politics.)

**Hyde Address on Religion and Politics** — Religious values still belong in politics, and it is up to Catholic politicians to put them there, Republican Representative Henry Hyde of Illinois told law students and faculty members at the University of Notre Dame Sept. 24. He delivered the speech 11 days after New York Governor Mario Cuomo spoke at the university and warned that injecting religion into politics would endanger religious liberty.

Hyde said the current debate about the role of religion in politics was of interest to Catholics not only as participants but also as defendants. "Our citizenship is on trial," he said. "We are accused of 'imposing our views' and 'forcing our beliefs' on the community. Our bishops are accused of 'violating constititional separation of church and state.' "

He said that assertions of violating the church-state balance create the assumption that abortion is a "religious" issue, raises suspicions against most Catholics who oppose abortion, and intimidates Catholics, making them ashamed to speak out.

Hyde said Catholics in public life should do more than just abide by their oath of office. They must, he declared, use the office to "make it clear that abortion is not a Catholic issue, but rather a moral and civil rights issue, a humanitarian issue of the first importance."

Alluding to Governor Cuomo's statement that public morality depends on a consensus view of right and wrong, Hyde said: "You will note that consensus is a highly selective requirement applying only to abortion legislation. No consensus was demanded before adopting the Civil Rights Act of 1964 or fair housing legislation. These were right, and their proponents helped create a consensus by advocacy and example, and by understanding that the law is an excellent teacher."

He added that Catholics did not import pro-life attitudes but found them here. When Catholic immigrants arrived in the 19th century, the states already had laws restricting abortion for reasons not at all religious.

"The Catholic Church," he said, "has introduced nothing foreign or novel. It has merely been the most important institution to insist on the moral consensus the (U.S. Supreme) Court assaulted" with its pro-abortion decisions of Jan. 22, 1973.

**Nurses Shun Abortions** — George Maroney, administrator of Memorial Hospital in Carbondale, Ill., told doctors Sept. 7 they would have to supply their own help for abortions or do the procedures elsewhere. He did so because the 24 operating room nurses at the hospital objected to abortions on moral grounds. It was thought that their refusal marked the first time an entire operating room staff said they did not want to participate in abortions.

**Decision against Executive Order 50** — A decision by Judge Alvin Klein of the New York State Supreme Court upheld the contention of the New York Archdiocese that Mayor Ed Koch lacked authority to forbid hiring discrimination against homosexuals by groups providing contractual services to New York City. At issue was the Mayor's Executive Order 50 which required agencies receiving city social service funds to sign agreements not to discriminate in hiring on the basis of "sexual orientation or affectional preference."

(See earlier entry concerning the archdiocese's objection to the order.)

(See many related entries under John Paul II in the Index.)

Cardinal-Archbishop Karol Wojtyla of Cracow was elected Bishop of Rome Oct. 16, 1978, on the seventh or eighth ballot cast on the second day of voting at a conclave of 111 cardinals. He chose the name John Paul II and was invested with the pallium, the symbol of his papal office, Oct. 22 in ceremonies attended by more than 250,000 persons in St. Peter's Square.

The 263rd successor of St. Peter as Bishop of Rome and Supreme Pastor of the Universal Church, he is the first non-Italian Pope since Adrian VI (1522-23), the first Polish Pope in the history of the Church, and the youngest at the time of his election since Pius IX (1846-78).

## Early Career

Karol Wojtyla was born May 18, 1920, in Wadowice, Poland.

He began higher studies at the age of 18, with major interests in poetry and theater arts. Forced to suspend university courses because of the outbreak of World War II, he went to work in a stone quarry and a chemical plant, thereby earning the later designation of himself as the "Worker Cardinal."

He started studies for the priesthood in 1942 in the underground seminary of Cracow, whose operations had been banned after the Nazi invasion of Poland.

Ordained to the priesthood Nov. 1, 1946, he was immediately sent to Rome for studies at the Angelicum University, where he earned a doctorate in ethics.

Back home in Poland, he worked as an assistant pastor in a village parish and as a chaplain to university students while continuing studies at the Catholic University of Lublin. He was awarded another doctorate there, in moral theology.

He began writing about this time, and eventually produced more than 100 articles and several books on ethical and other themes. Phenomenology was one of his fields of expertise.

University teaching came next, in 1953, with appointment in 1954 to the position of lecturer and later to the chair of ethics at the Catholic University of Lublin, the most prestigious institute of higher learning in Poland.

## Bishop and Cardinal

He was ordained Auxiliary Bishop of Cracow Sept. 28, 1958, became vicar capitular in 1962 after the death of Apostolic Administrator Eugeniusz Baziak, and was appointed Archbishop Jan. 13, 1964. He was the first residential head of the see since the death of Cardinal Adam Sapieha in 1951. Between then and 1964 the archdiocese was run by administrators because the communist government refused to permit the appointment and ministry of a residential bishop.

Archbishop Wojtyla attended all sessions of the Second Vatican Council from 1962 to 1965, and was one of the writers of the *Pastoral Constitution on the Church in the Modern World.* He also contributed input to the *Declaration on Religious Freedom* and the *Decree on the Instruments of Social Communication.*

His efforts to put into effect the directives of the council induced him to write a book, *Foundations of Renewal,* in 1972 and to start that same year an archdiocesan synod he saw concluded as Pope during his visit to Poland in 1979.

He was inducted into the College of Cardinals June 26, 1967, as one of the younger members, and subsequently served actively in the Congregation for the Sacraments and Divine Worship, the Congregation for the Clergy, and the Congregation for Catholic Education.

He also served as a theological consultant to Pope Paul VI.

He attended assemblies of the Synod of Bishops as a representative of the Polish Bishops' Conference and was a member of the Synod's permanent council.

From the beginning of his priestly career, and especially during his episcopate, the Cardinal was vigorous in the defense of human and religious rights, the rights of workers, and rights to religious education.

Close to Cardinal Wyszynski and in company with his fellow bishops, he negotiated the tightrope of Catholic survival in a country under communist control. With them, and as their spokesman at times, he was stalwart in resisting efforts of the regime to impose atheism, materialism and secularism on the people and culture of Poland.

## Active Pope

Since the beginning of his pontificate, John Paul has been active as Bishop of Rome, with frequent visits to parishes and institutions of the diocese for the celebration of Mass and participation in other events. During these visits, as well as others to places of pilgrimage and historic significance in Italy, he has had perhaps more personal contact with the faithful than any other Pope. The number of attendants at weekly general audiences at the Vatican and Castel Gandolfo has been unprecedented.

Unprecedented also has been the attention focused on him during and in connection with his 23 pastoral trips to 44 foreign countries between January, 1979, and the latter part of September, 1984.

## Extensive Travels

**Pastoral Pilgrimages:** His first three, in 1979, were to the Dominican Republic and Mexico, Poland, Ireland and the United States.

He traveled to Turkey at the end of November, 1979, to meet with Orthodox Ecumenical Patriarch Dimitrios I. With him, he announced the establishment of a joint commission of theologians to begin formal dialogue in quest of the union of the Roman Catholic and Orthodox Churches.

He made four trips in 1980.

While touring six African nations in May, he

spoke about Africanization of the Church, the cultural values of African peoples and the independence they should have from alien influences of other countries.

In France for an address before the United Nations Educational, Scientific and Cultural Organization also in May, he delineated with great clarity the stance of the Church on a wide variety of subjects, with special emphasis on its role in a secularized state, society and culture.

During a 13-city tour of Brazil in July, the Pope declared that the Church is on the side of the poor, appealed for across-the-board respect for human rights by governments and people of influence, called for measures of economic and social reform, and indicated his approval of non-violent social activism for the good of all peoples. He attended a plenary assembly of the bishops of the country and took part in opening ceremonies of a national Eucharistic congress.

His eighth and ninth pastoral pilgrimages were to West Germany, Nov. 15 to 19, 1980, and to the Philippines and Japan, Feb. 16 to 27, 1981. While in the Philippines, he beatified six 17th century martyrs of Japan.

Plans for additional trips in 1981 to Lourdes, for participation in the 42nd International Eucharistic Congress, and to Switzerland had to be cancelled because of the attack on the Pope's life in May.

The Pope made six trips outside of Italy by mid-September, 1982, to: the African nations of Nigeria, Benin, Gabon and Equatorial Guinea, Feb. 12 to 19; six cities of Portugal, May 12 to 15, as well as the shrine of Our Lady of Fatima where he consecrated the world to the Blessed Virgin Mary; nine major cities of Great Britain, May 28 to June 2; Argentina, June 11 and 12; Switzerland, June 15.

The 15th foreign trip of his pontificate was to the tiny Republic of San Marino, Aug. 29, when he also made his 28th pastoral visit to an Italian city other than Rome, Rimini.

The Holy Father visited Spain Oct. 31 to Nov. 9, 1982, to take part in celebrations marking the 400th anniversary of the death of St. Teresa of Jesus (Avila), Carmelite mystic and reformer, and the first woman Doctor of the Church. He made a two-day trip to Sicily the following Nov. 20 and 21.

In 1983, the Pope visited eight nations of Central America — Costa Rica, Nicaragua, Panama, El Salvador, Guatemala, Honduras, Belize and Haiti — Mar. 2 to 9. He revisited Poland June 16 to 23 to take part in the observance of the 600th anniversary of the arrival in the country of the icon of Our Lady of Czestochowa. He made a devotional pilgrimage to the Marian shrine at Lourdes Aug. 14 and 15, and joined in the celebration of *Katholikentag* in Austria Sept. 10 to 13.

The Pope made three trips in 1984, to: South Korea, Papua New Guinea, the Solomon Islands and Thailand, May 2 to 12; Switzerland, June 12 to 17; Canada, Sept. 9 to 20. (See separate entries for detailed coverage.)

### Key Writings

**Encyclicals:** The homilies and addresses delivered by the Pope on these trips were the equivalent of doctrinal, pastoral and social encyclical letters on a wide variety of subjects, all related to the key document of the first year of his pontificate. That was the formal encyclical, *Redemptor Hominis,* a treatise on Christian anthropology dealing with the divine and human aspects of redemption and the mission of the Church to carry on a dialogue of salvation with all peoples.

Two other encyclicals published within less than a year of each other were *Dives in Misericordia* ("Rich in Mercy"), issued Dec. 2, 1980, and *Laborem Exercens,* on work as a "way of sanctification," whose publication was announced Sept. 13, 1981.

**Apostolic Exhortation:** The Pope published a lengthy exhortation on the family, *Familiaris Consortio,* in December, 1981. It is an extensive synthesis of the theology of the family based not only on traditional doctrinal background but also on recommendations that emanated from the 1980 assembly of the Synod of Bishops.

Writings published in 1984 included two apostolic letters — on suffering, *Salvifici Doloris,* and on Jerusalem (see separate entry for text); an apostolic exhortation, *Redemptionis Donum,* addressed to and about Religious; and a "Charter of the Rights of the Family" (see separate entry).

### Various Items

**Doctrinal Concern:** In December, 1980, the Pope directly confronted the controversial writings of Father Hans Kung by giving his approval to a declaration by the Congregation for the Doctrine of the Faith that he could not be regarded as a Catholic theologian.

On Aug. 6, 1983, he authorized release by the Doctrinal Congregation of a letter to bishops throughout the world in refutation of unorthodox views — especially those of Father Edward Schillebeeckx, O.P. — concerning "The Minister of the Eucharist."

The Holy Father regarded as extremely important a series of talks begun at general audiences in the summer of 1984 on marriage and sexual morality, explaining and firmly supporting traditional doctrine, with emphasis on teaching contained in the encyclical letter, *Humanae Vitae,* by Pope Paul VI.

He approved an Instruction on Certain Aspects of the "Theology of Liberation" that was issued by the Congregation for the Doctrine of the Faith Sept. 3. (See separate entry for excerpts and a summary.)

In talks at the Vatican and in various places visited during trips abroad, the Pope has repeatedly spoken about the role and service of theologians in the Church.

These actions, along with various other statements and indications of attitude, mark John Paul as a pastor of decisive leadership for doctrinal orthodoxy and church discipline.

**Canon Law:** The Pope was deeply involved in the work of completing the revision of the Code of Canon Law, which he ordered into effect as of Nov. 27, 1983. He called it, in effect, the final act of the

Second Vatican Council. He emphasized its innovative force in an address Jan. 26, 1984, to personnel of the Sacred Roman Rota. (See separate entry.)

**Causes of Saints:** In 1984, the Pope canonized St. Paola Frassinetti, foundress of the Sisters of St. Dorothy, and 103 Korean martyrs who were killed during persecutions in the mid-1800s. He beatified 99 persons who were martyred for their faith during the French Revolution. While visiting Canada, he beatified Sister Marie-Leonie Paradis, foundress of the Little Sisters of the Holy Family.

**Synods:** The Holy Father convoked three of them in 1980.

With the Dutch bishops at the Vatican for a particular synod in January, he called for measures to cope with differences among the prelates, polarization among the people and action to remedy doctrinal and disciplinary irregularities. Later reports indicated that results of the synod were less than satisfactory.

Meeting with Ukrainian bishops in March, he named a successor to Cardinal Josyf Slipyi as the ranking Ukrainian bishop and turned down demands of some Ukrainians for a patriarchate.

With more than 200 delegates from episcopal conferences around the world, he held the fifth ordinary assembly of the Synod of Bishops.

He designated "Reconciliation and Penance in the Mission of the Church" as the theme of the 1983 assembly of the Synod. (See separate entry.)

**Holy Year:** The Holy Father proclaimed a Jubilee celebration of the 1950th anniversary of the Redemption from the Solemnity of the Annunciation of the Lord Mar. 25, 1983, to Easter Sunday, Apr. 22, 1984. (See separate entry.)

**Cardinals:** In June, 1979, the Holy Father inducted 14 new cardinals into the Sacred College, raising its membership at that time to 135. A second group was inducted into the Sacred College Feb. 3, 1983, at which time the total membership was 138.

**Meetings with Bishops:** In relations with the hierarchy since becoming Pope, John Paul has met with groups of bishops making required *ad limina* visits to the Vatican, for first-hand reports and admonitions regarding conditions in dioceses all over the world. He has also met with assemblies of bishops in the countries he has visited.

**Ecumenism:** He met with Anglican Archbishop Robert Runcie at the Canterbury Cathedral during his visit to Great Britain in May, 1982. The two prelates prayed together, renewed their baptismal promises and issued a joint statement in which they announced the formation of a new joint Catholic-Anglican theological commission for a second phase of interfaith dialogue.

Ever since the beginning of his pontificate, the Pope has maintained contact with Orthodox leaders and officials of other churches and religious bodies, and has encouraged interfaith relations at all levels.

While visiting the headquarters of the World Council of Churches in Geneva June 12, 1984, the Pope said the Church's engagement in the quest for religious unity is irreversible. At the same time, he mentioned two points of extreme significance in Catholic doctrine and practice.

The Church, he said, "entered on the hard ecumenical task bringing with it a conviction" about the role of the bishop of Rome. "It is convinced that in the ministry of the bishop of Rome it has preserved the visible pole and guarantee of unity in full fidelity to the apostolic tradition and to the faith of the Fathers."

He also reiterated doctrinal opposition to sharing the Eucharist until full unity is achieved. "It is not yet possible for us to celebrate the Eucharist together and communicate at the same table."

Nevertheless, he placed emphasis on things Christians have in common, among them, baptism, reverence for Scripture, prayer, a rediscovery of the "whole role of the Holy Spirit," and cooperation in work for social justice and human rights.

He had several contacts with leaders of separated Eastern churches in 1984. One of them was with the Syrian Orthodox patriarch, with whom he issued a statement on the doctrine of the Incarnation. (See separate entry.)

**Audiences and Addresses:** The Pope has delivered hundreds of addresses at general and private audiences and on special occasions. All of them have characteristically been grounded in doctrinal essentials coupled with relevance to the people being addressed or the events being commemorated.

**World Affairs:** In 1984, the Pope agreed to a new concordat with Italy, regulating church-state relations. He agreed also to the establishment of diplomatic relations with the United States. It was reported that at least 16 nations — among them predominantly Protestant Great Britain, Sweden, Norway and Denmark — had established diplomatic relations with the Vatican in the previous three years.

On his travels as well as at the Vatican, the Pope has been an outstanding advocate of human rights and dignity, of respect for life, of peace, of nuclear and conventional disarmament, of reconciliation among nations, of aid and relief for distressed peoples and nations, of people first and things second in all areas of life.

**Near Tragedy:** The Pope narrowly escaped death May 13, 1981, when he was fired upon at close range by Mehmet Ali Agca as he entered St. Peter's Square to address a general audience. Wounded more seriously than realized at first, he underwent emergency surgery and remained in Gemelli Polyclinic Hospital until June 3. On release, he stayed at the Vatican until June 20 when he was hospitalized a second time, until Aug. 14.

Agca told reporters July 8, 1983, that the Bulgarian secret service and the KGB were involved in his attempt on the life of the Pope, but did not allege that Soviet agents took direct part in the shooting. Some evidence seemed to support theories that he did not act alone and that Bulgarian and Soviet agents were implicated in the action. Hard and convincing evidence appeared to be missing, however, despite exhaustive investigation by Italian authorities.

## FIRST CENTURY

**Early 30's:** First Christian Pentecost: gathering together of the Christian community, outpouring of the Holy Spirit, preaching of St. Peter to Jews in Jerusalem, baptism and aggregation of some 3,000 persons to the Christian community.

St. Stephen, deacon, was stoned to death at Jerusalem; he is venerated as the first Christian martyr.

**34:** St. Paul, formerly Saul the persecutor of Christians, was converted, baptized and joined to the college of Apostles. After three major missionary journeys, he was martyred in 64 or 67 at Rome.

**39:** The Gentile Cornelius and his family were baptized by St. Peter.

**42:** Persecution of Christians in Palestine broke out during the rule of Herod Agrippa; St. James the Greater, the first Apostle to die, was beheaded in 44; St. Peter was imprisoned for a short time; many Christians fled to Antioch and elsewhere.

At Antioch, the followers of Christ were first called Christians.

**49:** Christians at Rome, who were considered members of a Jewish sect, were adversely affected by a decree of Claudius which forbade Jewish worship there.

**51:** The Council of Jerusalem, in which all the Apostles participated under the presidency of St. Peter, decreed that circumcision, dietary regulations, and various other prescriptions of Mosaic Law were not obligatory for Gentile converts to the Christian community. The decree was issued in opposition to Judaizers who contended that observance of the Mosaic Law in its entirety was necessary for salvation.

**64:** Persecution under Nero. The emperor, accusing Christians of starting a fire which destroyed half of Rome, inaugurated the era of major Roman persecutions.

**64 or 67:** Martyrdom of St. Peter at Rome during the Neronian persecution. He established his see and spent his last years there after preaching in and around Jerusalem, establishing a see at Antioch, and presiding at the Council of Jerusalem.

**70:** Destruction of Jerusalem by Titus.

**88-97:** Pontificate of St. Clement I, third successor of St. Peter as bishop of Rome, one of the Apostolic Fathers. The *First Epistle of Clement to the Corinthians*, with which he has been identified, was addressed by the Church of Rome to the Church at Corinth, the scene of irregularities and divisions in the Christian community.

**95:** Domitian persecuted Christians, principally at Rome.

**c. 100:** Death of St. John, Apostle and Evangelist, marking the end of the Age of the Apostles and the first generation of the Church.

## SECOND CENTURY

**c. 107:** St. Ignatius of Antioch was martyred at Rome. He was the first writer to use the expression, "the Catholic Church."

**112:** Emperor Trajan, in a rescript to Pliny the Younger, governor of Bithynia, instructed him not to search out Christians but to punish them if they were publicly denounced and refused to do homage to the Roman gods. This rescript set a pattern for Roman magistrates in dealing with Christians.

**117-138:** Persecution under Hadrian. Many *Acts of Martyrs* date from this period.

**c. 125:** Spread of Gnosticism.

**c. 155:** St. Polycarp, bishop of Smyrna and disciple of St. John the Evangelist, was martyred.

**c. 156:** Beginning of Montanism.

**161-180:** Reign of Marcus Aurelius. His persecution, launched in the wake of natural disasters, was more violent than those of his predecessors.

**165:** St. Justin, an important early Christian writer, was martyred at Rome.

**c. 180:** St. Irenaeus, bishop of Lyons and one of the great early theologians, wrote *Adversus Haereses*. He stated that the teaching and tradition of the Roman See was the standard for belief.

**196:** Easter Controversy.

The *Didache*, written in the second century, was an important record of Christian belief, practice and government in the first century.

Latin was introduced in the West as a liturgical language.

The Catechetical School of Alexandria, founded about the middle of the century, increased in importance.

## THIRD CENTURY

**202:** Persecution under Septimius Severus, who wanted to establish one common religion in the Empire.

**206:** Tertullian, a convert since 197 and the first great ecclesiastical writer in Latin, joined the heretical Montanists. He died in 230.

**215:** Death of Clement of Alexandria, teacher of Origen and a founding father of the School of Alexandria.

**217-235:** St. Hippolytus, the first antipope. He was reconciled to the Church while in prison during persecution in 235.

**232-254:** Origen established the School of Caesarea after being deposed in 231 as head of the School of Alexandria; he died in 254. A scholar and voluminous writer, he was one of the founders of systematic theology and exerted wide influence for many years.

**c. 242:** Manichaeism originated in Persia.

**249-251:** Persecution under Decius. Many of those who denied the faith *(lapsi)* sought readmission to the Church at the end of the persecution in 251. Pope St. Cornelius had correspondence with St. Cyprian on the subject and ordered that *lapsi* were to be readmitted after suitable penance.

**250-300:** Neo-Platonism of Plotinus and Porphyry gained followers.

**251:** Novatian, an antipope, was condemned at Rome.

**256:** Pope St. Stephen I upheld the validity of

baptism administered by heretics, in the Rebaptism Controversy.

**257:** Persecution under Valerian, who attempted to destroy the Church as a social structure.

**258:** St. Cyprian, bishop of Carthage, was martyred.

**c. 260:** St. Lucian founded the exegetical School of Antioch.

Pope St. Dionysius condemned teachings of Sabellius and the Marcionites.

St. Paul of Thebes became a hermit.

**261:** Gallienus issued an edict of toleration which ended general persecution for nearly 40 years.

**c. 266:** Sabellianism was condemned and Paul of Samosata deposed.

**c. 292:** Diocletian divided the Roman Empire into East and West. The division emphasized political, cultural and other differences between the two parts of the Empire and influenced the Church in the East and West. The prestige of Rome began to decline.

## FOURTH CENTURY

**303:** Persecution broke out under Diocletian. It ended in the West in 306 but continued for 10 years in the East; it was particularly violent in 304.

**305:** St. Anthony of Heracles established a foundation for hermits near the Red Sea in Egypt.

**c. 306:** The first local legislation on clerical celibacy was enacted by a council held at Elvira, Spain; bishops, priests, deacons and other ministers were forbidden to have wives.

**310:** St. Hilarion established a foundation for hermits in Palestine.

**311:** An edict of toleration issued by Galerius at the urging of Constantine and Licinius officially ended persecution in the West; some persecution continued in the East.

**313:** The *Edict of Milan* issued by Constantine and Licinius recognized Christianity as a lawful religion and the legal freedom of all religions in the Roman Empire.

**314:** The Council of Arles condemned Donatism in Africa and declared that baptism by heretics was valid.

**318:** St. Pachomius established the first foundation of the cenobitic (common) life, as compared with the solitary life of hermits in Upper Egypt.

**325:** The Ecumenical Council of Nicaea (I), first of its kind in the history of the Church, condemned Arianism; see separate entry.

**326:** Discovery of the True Cross on which Christ was crucified.

**337:** Baptism and death of Constantine.

**c. 342:** Beginning of a 40-year persecution in Persia.

**343-344:** A local Council of Sardica reaffirmed doctrine formulated by Nicaea I and declared that bishops had the right of appeal to the pope as the highest authority in the Church.

**361-363:** Julian the Apostate waged an unsuccessful campaign against the Church in an attempt to restore paganism as the religion of the Empire.

**c. 365:** Persecution under Valens in the East.

**c. 376:** Beginning of the barbarian invasion in the West.

**379:** Death of St. Basil, the Father of Monasticism in the East. His writings contributed greatly to the development of rules for the religious life.

**381:** The Ecumenical Council of Constantinople (I); see separate entry.

**382:** The *Decree of Pope St. Damasus* listed the Canon of Sacred Scripture.

**382-c. 406:** St. Jerome translated the Old and New Testaments into Latin. His work is called the Vulgate Version of the Bible.

**396:** St. Augustine became bishop of Hippo in North Africa.

**397:** A local Council of Carthage published the Canon of Sacred Scripture.

## FIFTH CENTURY

**410:** Visigoths sacked Rome.

**411:** Donatism was condemned by a council at Carthage.

**430:** St. Augustine, bishop of Hippo for 35 years, died. He was a strong defender of orthodox doctrine against Manichaeism, Donatism and Pelagianism. The depth and range of his writings made him a dominant influence in Christian thought for many centuries.

**431:** The Ecumenical Council of Ephesus; see separate entry.

**432:** St. Patrick arrived in Ireland. By the time of his death in 461 most of the country had been converted, monasteries founded and the hierarchy established.

**438:** The *Theodosian Code,* a compilation of decrees for the Empire, was issued by Theodosius II. It had great influence on subsequent civil and ecclesiastical law.

**449:** The Robber Council of Ephesus, which did not have ecclesiastical sanction, declared itself in favor of the opinions of Eutyches who contended that Christ had only one nature.

**451:** The Ecumenical Council of Chalcedon; see separate entry.

**452:** Pope St. Leo the Great persuaded Attila the Hun to spare Rome.

**455:** Vandals sacked Rome. The decline of imperial Rome dates approximately from this time.

**484:** Patriarch Acacius of Constantinople was excommunicated for signing the *Henoticon,* a unity law published by Emperor Zeno in 482 to end the turmoil associated with the Monophysite heresy. The document capitulated to the heresy. The excommunication triggered a 35-year-long schism.

**494:** Pope St. Gelasius I declared in a letter to Emperor Anastasius that the pope had power and authority over the emperor in spiritual matters.

**496:** Clovis, King of the Franks, was converted and became the defender of Christianity in the West. The Franks became a Catholic people.

## SIXTH CENTURY

**520 and later:** Irish monasteries flourished as centers for spiritual life, missionary training and scholarly activity.

**529:** The Second Council of Orange condemned Semi-Pelagianism.

**c. 529:** St. Benedict founded the Monte Cassino Abbey. Some years before his death in 543 he wrote a monastic rule which exercised tremendous influence on the form and style of religious life. He is called the Father of Monasticism in the West.

**533:** John II became the first pope to change his name. The practice did not become general until the time of Sergius IV (1009).

**533-534:** Emperor Justinian promulgated the *Corpus Juris Civilis* for the Roman world. Like the *Theodosian Code,* it influenced subsequent civil and ecclesiastical law.

**c. 545:** Death of Dionysius Exiguus who was the first to date history from the birth of Christ, a practice which resulted in use of the B.C. and A.D. abbreviations. His calculations were at least four years late.

**553:** The Ecumenical Council of Constantinople (II); see separate entry.

**585:** St. Columban founded an influential monastic school at Luxeuil. He died in 615.

**589:** The most important of several councils of Toledo was held. The Visigoths renounced Arianism, and St. Leander began the organization of the Church in Spain.

**590-604:** Pontificate of Pope St. Gregory I the Great. He set the form and style of the papacy which prevailed throughout the Middle Ages; exerted great influence on doctrine and liturgy; was strong in support of monastic discipline and clerical celibacy; authored writings on many subjects. Gregorian Chant is named in his honor.

**596:** Pope St. Gregory I the Great sent St. Augustine of Canterbury and 40 monks to do missionary work in England.

**597:** St. Columba died. He founded an important monastery at Iona, established schools and did notable missionary work in Scotland.

By the end of the century, monasteries of nuns were common; Western monasticism was flourishing; monasticism in the East, under the influence of Monophysitism and other factors, was losing its vigor.

## SEVENTH CENTURY

**613:** St. Columban established the influential monastery of Bobbio in northern Italy.

**622:** The Hegira (flight) of Mohammed from Mecca to Medina signalled the beginning of Islam, which, by the end of the century, claimed almost all of the southern Mediterranean area.

**629:** Emperor Heraclius recovered the True Cross from the Persians.

**649:** A Lateran Council condemned two erroneous formulas *(Ecthesis* and *Type)* issued by emperors Heraclius and Constans II as means of reconciling Monophysites with the Church.

**664:** Actions of the Synod of Whitby advanced the adoption of Roman usages in England, especially regarding the date for the observance of Easter. (See Easter Controversy.)

**680-681:** The Ecumenical Council of Constantinople (III); see separate entry.

**692:** Trullan Synod. Eastern-Church discipline on clerical celibacy was settled, permitting marriage before ordination to the diaconate and continuation in marriage afterwards, but prohibiting marriage following the death of the wife thereafter. Anti-Roman canons contributed to East-West alienation.

During the century, the monastic influence of Ireland and England increased in Western Europe; schools and learning declined; regulations regarding clerical celibacy became more strict in the East.

## EIGHTH CENTURY

**711:** Moslems began the conquest of Spain.

**726:** Emperor Leo III, the Isaurian, launched a campaign against the veneration of sacred images and relics; called Iconoclasm (image-breaking), it caused turmoil in the East until about 843.

**731:** Pope Gregory III and a synod at Rome condemned Iconoclasm, with a declaration that the veneration of sacred images was in accord with Catholic tradition.

Venerable Bede issued his *Ecclesiastical History of the English People.*

**732:** Charles Martel defeated the Moslems at Poitiers, halting advance by them in the West.

**744:** The Monastery of Fulda was established by St. Sturmi, a disciple of St. Boniface.

**754:** A council of more than 300 Byzantine bishops endorsed Iconoclast errors. This council and its actions were condemned by the Lateran Synod of 769.

Stephen II (III) crowned Pepin ruler of the Franks. Pepin twice invaded Italy, in 754 and 756, to defend the pope against the Lombards. His land grants to the papacy, called the Donation of Pepin, were later extended by Charlemagne (773) and formed part of the States of the Church.

**c. 755:** St. Boniface (Winfrid) was martyred. He was called the Apostle of Germany for his missionary work and organization of the hierarchy there.

**781:** Alcuin was chosen by Charlemagne to organize a Palace School, which became a center of intellectual leadership.

**787:** The Ecumenical Council of Nicaea (II); see separate entry.

**792:** A council at Ratisbon condemned Adoptionism.

The famous *Book of Kells* ("The Great Gospel of Columcille") dates from the early eighth or late seventh century.

## NINTH CENTURY

**800:** Charlemagne was crowned Emperor by Pope Leo III on Christmas Day.

Egbert became king of West Saxons. He unified England and strengthened the See of Canterbury.

**813:** Emperor Leo V, the Armenian, revived Iconoclasm, which persisted until about 843.

**814:** Charlemagne died.

**843:** The Treaty of Verdun split the Frankish kingdom among Charlemagne's three grandsons.

**844:** A Eucharistic controversy involving the writings of St. Paschasius Radbertus, Ratramnus and Rabanus Maurus occasioned the development of terminology regarding the doctrine of the Real Presence.

**846:** The Moslems invaded Italy and attacked Rome.

**847-852:** Period of composition of the *False Decretals,* a collection of forged documents attributed to popes from St. Clement (88-97) to Gregory II (715-731). The *Decretals,* which strongly supported the autonomy and rights of bishops, were suspect for a long time before being repudiated entirely about 1628.

**848:** The Council of Mainz condemned Gottschalk for heretical teaching regarding predestination. He was also condemned by the Council of Quierzy in 853.

**857:** Photius displaced Ignatius as patriarch of Constantinople. This marked the beginning of the Photian Schism, a confused state of East-West relations which has not yet been cleared up by historical research. Photius, a man of exceptional ability, died in 891.

**865:** St. Ansgar, Apostle of Scandinavia, died.

**869:** St. Cyril died and his brother, St. Methodius (d. 885), was ordained a bishop. The Apostles of the Slavs devised an alphabet and translated the Gospels and liturgy into the Slavonic language.

**869:** The Ecumenical Council of Constantinople (IV); see separate entry.

**871-c. 900:** Reign of Alfred the Great, the only English king ever anointed by a pope at Rome.

### TENTH CENTURY

**910:** William, Duke of Aquitaine, founded the Benedictine Abbey of Cluny, which became a center of monastic and ecclesiastical reform.

**915:** Pope John X played a leading role in the expulsion of Saracens from central and southern Italy.

**955:** St. Olga, of the Russian royal family, was baptized.

**962:** Otto I, the Great, crowned by Pope John XII, revived Charlemagne's kingdom, which became the Holy Roman Empire.

**966:** Mieszko, first of a royal line in Poland, was baptized; he brought Latin Christianity to Poland.

**989:** Vladimir, ruler of Russia, was baptized. Russia was subsequently Christianized by Greek missionaries.

**993:** John XV was the first pope to decree the official canonization of a saint (Ulrich) for the universal Church.

**997:** St. Stephen became ruler of Hungary. He assisted in organizing the hierarchy and establishing Latin Christianity in that country.

**999-1003:** Pontificate of Sylvester II (Gerbert of Aquitaine), a Benedictine monk and the first French pope.

### ELEVENTH CENTURY

**1009:** Beginning of lasting East-West schism in the Church, marked by dropping of the name of Pope Sergius IV from the Byzantine diptychs (the listing of persons prayed for during the liturgy). The deletion was made by Patriarch Sergius II of Constantinople.

**1012:** St. Romuald founded the Camaldolese Hermits.

**1025:** The Council of Arras, and other councils later, condemned the Cathari (Neo-Manichaeans, Albigenses).

**1027:** The Council of Elne proclaimed the Truce of God as a means of stemming violence. The truce involved armistice periods of varying length, which were later extended.

**1038:** St. John Gualbert founded the Vallombrosians.

**1043-1059:** Constantinople patriarchate of Michael Cerularius, the key figure in a controversy concerning the primacy of the papacy. His and the Byzantine synod's refusal to acknowledge this primacy in 1054 widened and hardened the East-West schism in the Church.

**1047:** Pope Clement II died. He was the only pope ever buried in Germany.

**1049-54:** Pontificate of St. Leo IX, who inaugurated a movement of papal, diocesan, monastic and clerical reform.

**1055:** Condemnation of the Eucharistic doctrine of Berengarius.

**1059:** A Lateran Council issued new legislation regarding papal elections. Voting power was entrusted to the Roman cardinals.

**1066:** Death of St. Edward the Confessor, King of England from 1042 and restorer of Westminster Abbey.

Defeat, at Hastings, of Harold by William I, who subsequently exerted strong influence on the life style of the Church in England.

**1073-1085:** Pontificate of St. Gregory VII (Hildebrand). A strong pope, he carried forward programs of clerical and general ecclesiastical reform and struggled against Henry IV and other rulers to end the evils of lay investiture. He introduced the Latin liturgy in Spain and set definite dates for the observance of ember days.

**1077:** Henry IV, excommunicated and suspended from the exercise of imperial powers by Gregory VII, sought absolution from the Pope at Canossa. Henry later repudiated this action and in 1084 forced Gregory to leave Rome.

**1079:** The Council of Rome condemned Eucharistic errors of Berengarius, who retracted.

**1084:** St. Bruno founded the Carthusians.

**1097-1099:** The first of several Crusades undertaken between this time and 1265. Recovery of the Holy Places and gaining free access to them for Christians were the original purposes, but these were diverted to less worthy objectives in various ways. Results included: a Latin Kingdom of Jerusalem, 1099-1187; a military and political misadventure in the form of a Latin Empire of Constantino-ple, 1204-1261; acquisition, by treaties, of visiting rights for Christians in the Holy Land. East-West economic and cultural relationships increased during the period. In the religious sphere, actions of the Crusaders had the effect of increasing the alienation of the East from the West.

**1098:** St. Robert founded the Cistercians.

### TWELFTH CENTURY

**1108:** Beginnings of the influential Abbey and School of St. Victor.

**1115:** St. Bernard established the Abbey of Clairvaux and inaugurated the Cistercian Reform.

**1118:** Christian forces captured Saragossa, Spain; the beginning of the Moslem decline in that country.

**1121:** St. Norbert established the original monastery of the Praemonstratensians near Laon, France.

**1122:** The Concordat of Worms (Pactum Callixtinum) was formulated and approved by Pope Callistus II and Emperor Henry V to settle controversy concerning the investiture of prelates. The concordat provided that the emperor could invest prelates with symbols of temporal authority but had no right to invest them with spiritual authority, which came from the Church alone, and that the emperor was not to interfere in papal elections. This was the first concordat in history.

**1123:** The Ecumenical Council of the Lateran (I), the first of its kind in the West; see separate entry.

**1139:** The Ecumenical Council of the Lateran (II); see separate entry.

**1140:** St. Bernard met Abelard in debate at the Council of Sens. Abelard, whose rationalism in theology was condemned for the first time in 1121, died in 1142 at Cluny.

**1148:** The Synod of Rheims enacted strict disciplinary decrees for communities of women religious.

**1152:** The Synod of Kells reorganized the Church in Ireland.

**1160:** Gratian, whose *Decretum* became a basic text of canon law, died.

Peter Lombard, compiler of the *Four Books of Sentences,* a standard theology text for nearly 200 years, died.

**1170:** St. Thomas Becket, archbishop of Canterbury, who clashed with Henry II over Church-state relations, was murdered in his cathedral.

**1171:** Pope Alexander III reserved the process of canonization of saints to the Holy See.

**1179:** The Ecumenical Council of the Lateran (III); see separate entry.

**1184:** Waldenses and other heretics were excommunicated by Pope Lucius III.

## THIRTEENTH CENTURY

**1198-1216:** Pontificate of Innocent III, during which the papacy reached its medieval peak of authority, influence and prestige in the Church and in relations with civil rulers.

**1208:** Innocent III called for a crusade, the first in Christendom itself, against the Albigensians.

**1209:** Verbal approval was given by Innocent III to a rule of life for the Order of Friars Minor, started by St. Francis of Assisi.

**1212:** The Second Order of Franciscans, the Poor Clares, was founded.

**1215:** The Ecumenical Council of the Lateran (IV); see separate entry.

**1216:** Formal papal approval was given to a rule of life for the Order of Preachers, started by St. Dominic.

The Portiuncula Indulgence was granted by the Holy See at the request of St. Francis of Assisi.

**1221:** The Third Order of St. Francis for lay persons was founded.

**1226:** Death of St. Francis of Assisi.

**1245:** The Ecumenical Council of Lyons (I); see separate entry.

**1247:** Preliminary approval was given by the Holy See to a Carmelite rule of life.

**1270:** St. Louis IX, king of France, died. Beginning of papal decline.

**1274:** The Ecumenical Council of Lyons (II); see separate entry.

Death of St. Thomas Aquinas, Doctor of the Church, of lasting influence; see separate entry.

**1280:** Pope Nicholas III, who made the *Breviary* the official prayer book for clergy of the Roman Church, died.

**1281:** The excommunication of Michael Palaeologus by Pope Martin IV ruptured the union effected with the Eastern Church in 1274.

## FOURTEENTH CENTURY

**1302:** Pope Boniface VIII issued the bull *Unam Sanctam,* concerning the unity of the Church and the temporal power of princes, against the background of a struggle with Philip IV of France; it was the most famous medieval document on the subject.

**1308-1378:** For a period of approximately 70 years, seven popes resided at Avignon because of unsettled conditions in Rome and other reasons; see separate entry.

**1311-1312:** The Ecumenical Council of Vienne; see separate entry.

**1321:** Dante Alighieri died a year after completing the *Divine Comedy.*

**1324:** Marsilius of Padua completed *Defensor Pacis,* a work condemned by Pope John XXII as heretical because of its denial of papal primacy and the hierarchical structure of the Church, and for other reasons. It was a charter for conciliarism.

**1337-1453:** Period of the Hundred Years' War, a dynastic struggle between France and England.

**1338:** Four years after the death of Pope John XXII, who had opposed Louis IV of Bavaria in a years-long controversy, electoral princes declared at the Diet of Rhense that the emperor did not need papal confirmation of his title and right to rule. Charles IV later (1356) said the same thing in a *Golden Bull,* eliminating papal rights in the election of emperors.

**1347-1350:** The Black Death swept across Europe, killing perhaps one-fourth to one-third of the total population; an estimated 40 per cent of the clergy succumbed.

**1374:** Petrarch, poet and humanist, died.

**1378:** Return of the papacy from Avignon to Rome.

Beginning of the Western Schism; see separate entry.

## FIFTEENTH CENTURY

**1409:** The Council of Pisa, without canonical authority, tried to end the Western Schism but succeeded only in complicating it by electing a third claimant to the papacy; see Western Schism.

**1414-1418:** The Ecumenical Council of Constance ended the Western Schism; see separate entry.

**1431:** St. Joan of Arc was burned at the stake.

**1431-1449:** The Council of Basle, which began with convocation by Pope Martin V in 1431, turned into an anti-papal forum of conciliarists seeking to subject the primacy and authority of the pope to the overriding authority of an assembly of bishops. It was not an ecumenical council.

**1438:** The Pragmatic Sanction of Bourges was enacted by Charles VIII and the French parliament to curtail papal authority over the Church in France, in the spirit of conciliarism. It found expression in Gallicanism and had effects lasting at least until the French Revolution.

**1438-1443:** The Ecumenical Council of Florence affirmed the primacy of the pope in opposition to conciliarism and effected a measure of union with separated Eastern Christians; see separate entry.

**1453:** The fall of Constantinople to the Turks.

**c. 1456:** Gutenberg issued the first edition of the Bible printed from movable type, at Mainz, Germany.

**1476:** Pope Sixtus IV ordered observance of the feast of the Immaculate Conception on Dec. 8 throughout the Church.

**1492:** Columbus discovered the Americas.

**1493:** Pope Alexander VI issued a *Bull of Demarcation* which determined spheres of influence for the Spanish and Portuguese in the Americas.

The Renaissance, a humanistic movement which originated in Italy in the 14th century, spread to France, Germany, the Low Countries and England. A transitional period between the medieval world and the modern secular world, it introduced profound changes which affected literature and the other arts, general culture, politics and religion.

### SIXTEENTH CENTURY

**1512-1517:** The Ecumenical Council of the Lateran (V); see separate entry.

**1517:** Martin Luther signalled the beginning of the Reformation by posting 95 theses at Wittenberg. Subsequently, he broke completely from doctrinal orthodoxy in discourses and three published works (1519 and 1520); was excommunicated on more than 40 charges of heresy (1521); remained the dominant figure in the Reformation in Germany until his death in 1546.

**1519:** Zwingli triggered the Reformation in Zurich and became its leading proponent there until his death in combat in 1531.

**1524:** Luther's encouragement of German princes in putting down the two-year Peasants' Revolt gained political support for his cause.

**1528:** The Order of Friars Minor Capuchin was approved as an autonomous division of the Franciscan Order; like the Jesuits, the Capuchins became leaders in the Counter-Reformation.

**1530:** The *Augsburg Confession* of Lutheran faith was issued; it was later supplemented by the *Smalcald Articles* approved in 1537.

**1533:** Henry VIII divorced Catherine of Aragon,

married Anne Boleyn, was excommunicated. In 1534 he decreed the Act of Supremacy, making the sovereign the head of the Church in England, under which Sts. John Fisher and Thomas More were executed in 1535. Despite his rejection of papal primacy and actions against monastic life in England, he generally maintained doctrinal orthodoxy until his death in 1547.

**1536:** John Calvin, leader of the Reformation in Switzerland until his death in 1564, issued the first edition of *Institutes of the Christian Religion*, which became the classical text of Reformed (non-Lutheran) theology.

**1540:** The constitutions of the Society of Jesus (Jesuits), founded by St. Ignatius of Loyola, were approved.

**1541:** Start of the 11-year career of St. Francis Xavier as a missionary to the East Indies and Japan.

**1545-1563:** The Ecumenical Council of Trent formulated statements of Catholic doctrine under attack by the Reformers and mobilized the Counter-Reformation; see separate entry.

**1549:** The first *Book of Common Prayer* was issued by Edward VI. Revised editions were published in 1552, 1559 and 1662 and later.

**1553:** Start of the five-year reign of Mary Tudor who tried to counteract actions of Henry VIII against the Roman Church.

**1555:** Enactment of the Peace of Augsburg, an arrangement of religious territorialism rather than toleration, which recognized the existence of Catholicism and Lutheranism in the German Empire and provided that citizens should adopt the religion of their respective rulers.

**1558:** Beginning of the reign of Elizabeth I, during which the Church of England took on its definitive form.

**1559:** Establishment of the hierarchy of the Church of England, with the consecration of Matthew Parker as archbishop of Canterbury.

**1563:** The first text of the *39 Articles* of the Church of England was issued. Also enacted were a new Act of Supremacy and Oath of Succession to the English throne.

**1570:** Elizabeth I was excommunicated. Penal measures against Catholics subsequently became more severe.

**1571:** Defeat of the Turkish armada at Lepanto staved off the invasion of Eastern Europe.

**1577:** The *Formula of Concord*, the classical statement of Lutheran faith, was issued; it was, generally, a Lutheran counterpart of the canons of the Council of Trent. In 1580, along with other formulas of doctrine, it was included in the *Book of Concord*.

**1582:** The Gregorian Calendar, named for Pope Gregory XIII, was put into effect and was eventually adopted in most countries: England delayed adoption until 1752.

### SEVENTEENTH CENTURY

**1605:** The Gunpowder Plot, an attempt by Catholic fanatics to blow up James I of England and the houses of Parliament, resulted in an anti-Catholic

Oath of Allegiance; the Oath was condemned by Pope Paul V in 1606.

**1610:** Death of Matteo Ricci, outstanding Jesuit missionary to China, pioneer in cultural relations between China and Europe.

Founding of the first community of Visitation Nuns by Sts. Francis de Sales and Jane de Chantal.

**1611:** Founding of the Oratorians.

**1613:** Catholics were banned from Scandinavia.

**1625:** Founding of the Congregation of the Mission (Vincentians) by St. Vincent de Paul. He founded the Sisters of Charity in 1633.

**1642:** Death of Galileo, scientist, who was censured by the Congregation of the Holy Office for supporting the Copernican theory of the sun-centered planetary system.

Founding of the Sulpicians by Jacques Olier.

**1643:** Start of publication of the Bollandist *Acta Sanctorum*, a critical work on lives of the saints.

**1648:** Provisions in the Peace of Westphalia, ending the Thirty Years' War, extended terms of the Peace of Augsburg (1555) to Calvinists and gave equality to Catholics and Protestants in the 300 states of the Holy Roman Empire.

**1649:** Oliver Cromwell invaded Ireland and began a severe persecution of the Church there.

**1653:** Pope Innocent X condemned five propositions of Jansenism, a complex theory which distorted doctrine concerning the relations between divine grace and human freedom. Jansenism was also a rigoristic movement which seriously disturbed the Church in France, the Low Countries and Italy in this and the 18th century.

**1673:** The Test Act in England barred from public office Catholics who would not deny the doctrine of transubstantiation and receive Communion in the Church of England.

**1678:** Many English Catholics suffered death as a consequence of the Popish Plot, a false allegation by Titus Oates that Catholics planned to assassinate Charles I, land a French army in the country, burn London, and turn over the government to the Jesuits.

**1682:** The four articles of the *Gallican Declaration*, drawn up by Bossuet, asserted political and ecclesiastical immunities of France from papal control. The articles, which rejected the primacy of the pope, were condemned in 1690.

**1689:** The Toleration Act granted a measure of freedom of worship to other English dissenters but not to Catholics.

## EIGHTEENTH CENTURY

**1704:** Chinese Rites — involving the Christian adaptation of elements of Confucianism, veneration of ancestors and Chinese terminology in religion — were condemned by Clement XI. An earlier ban was issued in 1645; a later one, in 172.

**1720:** The Passionists were founded by St. Paul of the Cross.

**1724:** Persecution in China.

**1732:** The Redemptorists were founded by St. Alphonsus Liguori.

**1738:** Freemasonry was condemned by Clement XII and Catholics were forbidden to join, under penalty of excommunication; the prohibition was repeated by Benedict XIV in 1751 and by later popes.

**1760's:** Josephinism, a theory and system of state control of the Church, was initiated in Austria; it remained in force until about 1850.

**1764:** Febronianism, an unorthodox theory and practice regarding the constitution of the Church and relations between Church and state, was condemned for the first of several times. Proposed by an auxiliary bishop of Trier using the pseudonym Justinus Febronius, it had the effects of minimizing the office of the pope and supporting national churches under state control.

**1773:** Clement XIV issued a brief of suppression against the Jesuits, following their expulsion from Portugal in 1759, from France in 1764 and from Spain in 1767. Political intrigue and unsubstantiated accusations were principal factors in these developments. The ban, which crippled the Society, contained no condemnation of the Jesuit constitutions, particular Jesuits or Jesuit teaching. The Society was restored in 1814.

**1778:** Catholics in England were relieved of some civil disabilities dating back to the time of Henry VIII, by an act which permitted them to acquire, own and inherit property. Additional liberties were restored by the Roman Catholic Relief Act of 1791 and subsequent enactments of Parliament.

**1789:** Religious freedom in the United States was guaranteed under the First Amendment to the Constitution.

Beginning of the French Revolution which resulted in: the secularization of church property and the Civil Constitution of the Clergy in 1790; the persecution of priests, religious and lay persons loyal to papal authority; invasion of the Papal States by Napoleon in 1796; renewal of persecution from 1797-1799; attempts to dechristianize France and establish a new religion; the occupation of Rome by French troops and the forced removal of Pius VI to France in 1798.

This century is called the age of Enlightenment or Reason because of the predominating rational and scientific approach of its leading philosophers, scientists and writers with respect to religion, ethics and natural law. This approach downgraded the fact and significance of revealed religion. Also characteristic of the Enlightenment were subjectivism, secularism and optimism regarding human perfectibility.

## NINETEENTH CENTURY

**1809:** Pope Pius VII was made a captive by Napoleon and deported to France where he remained in exile until 1814. During this time he refused to cooperate with Napoleon who sought to bring the Church in France under his own control.

The turbulence in church-state relations in France at the beginning of the century recurred in connection with the Bourbon Restoration, the July Revolution, the second and third Republics, the Second Empire and the Dreyfus case.

**1814:** The Society of Jesus, suppressed since 1773, was restored.

**1817:** Reestablishment of the Congregation for the Propagation of the Faith (Propaganda) by Pius VII was an important factor in increasing missionary activity during the century.

**1820:** Years-long persecution, during which thousands died for the faith, ended in China. Thereafter, communication with the West remained cut off until about 1834. Vigorous missionary work got under way in 1842.

**1822:** The Pontifical Society for the Propagation of the Faith, inaugurated in France by Pauline Jaricot for the support of missionary activity, was established.

**1829:** The Catholic Emancipation Act relieved Catholics in England and Ireland of most of the civil disabilities to which they had been subject from the time of Henry VIII.

**1832:** Gregory XVI, in the encyclical *Mirari Vos*, condemned indifferentism, one of the many ideologies at odds with Christian doctrine which were proposed during the century.

**1833:** Start of the Oxford Movement which affected the Church of England and resulted in some notable conversions, including that of John Henry Newman in 1845, to the Catholic Church.

Frederick Ozanam founded the Society of St. Vincent de Paul in France. The society, whose objective was works of charity, became worldwide.

**1848:** The *Communist Manifesto*, a revolutionary document symptomatic of socio-economic crisis, was issued.

**1850:** The hierarchy was reestablished in England and Nicholas Wiseman made the first archbishop of Westminster. He was succeeded in 1865 by Henry Manning, an Oxford convert and proponent of the rights of labor.

**1853:** The Catholic hierarchy was reestablished in Holland.

**1854:** Pius IX proclaimed the dogma of the Immaculate Conception in the bull *Ineffabilis Deus*.

**1858:** The Blessed Virgin Mary appeared to St. Bernadette at Lourdes, France; see separate entry.

**1864:** Pius IX issued the encyclical *Quanta Cura* and the *Syllabus of Errors* in condemnation of some 80 propositions derived from the scientific mentality and rationalism of the century. The subjects in question had deep ramifications in many areas of thought and human endeavor; in religion, they explicitly and/or implicitly rejected divine revelation and the supernatural order.

**1867:** The first volume of *Das Kapital* was published. Together with the Communist First International, formed in the same year, it had great influence on the subsequent development of Communism and Socialism.

**1869:** The Anglican Church was disestablished in Ireland.

**1869-1870:** The First Vatican Council; see separate entry.

**1870-1871:** Victor Emmanuel II of Sardinia, crowned king of Italy after defeating Austrian and papal forces, marched into Rome in 1870 and expropriated the Papal States after a plebiscite in which Catholics, at the order of Pius IX, did not vote. In 1871, Pius IX refused to accept a Law of Guarantees. Confiscation of church property and hindrance of ecclesiastical administration by the regime followed.

**1871:** The German Empire, a confederation of 26 states, was formed. Government policy launched a Kulturkampf whose May Laws of 1873 were designed to annul papal jurisdiction in Prussia and other states and to place the Church under imperial control. Resistance to the enactments and the persecution they legalized forced the government to modify its anti-Church policy by 1887.

**1878:** Beginning of the pontificate of Leo XIII, who was pope until his death in 1903. Leo is best known for the encyclical *Rerum Novarum*, which greatly influenced the course of Christian social thought and the labor movement. His other accomplishments included promotion of a revival of Scholastic philosophy and the impetus he gave to scriptural studies.

**1881:** The first International Eucharistic Congress was held in Lille, France.

Alexander II of Russia died. His policies of Russification — as well as those of his two predecessors and a successor during the century — caused great suffering to Catholics, Jews and Protestants in Poland, Lithuania, the Ukraine and Bessarabia.

**1882:** Charles Darwin died. His theory of evolution by natural selection, one of several scientific highlights of the century, had extensive repercussions in the faith-and-science controversy.

**1889:** The Catholic University of America was founded in Washington, D.C.

**1893:** The U.S. apostolic delegation was set up in Washington, D.C.

## TWENTIETH CENTURY

**1901:** Restrictive measures in France forced the Jesuits, Benedictines, Carmelites and other religious orders to leave the country. Subsequently, 14,000 schools were suppressed; religious orders and congregations were expelled; the concordat was renounced in 1905; church property was confiscated in 1906. For some years the Holy See, refusing to comply with government demands for the control of bishops' appointments, left some ecclesiastical offices vacant.

**1903:** Start of the 11-year pontificate of St. Pius X. He initiated the codification of canon law, 1904; removed the ban against participation by Catholics in Italian national elections, 1905; issued decrees calling upon the faithful to receive Holy Communion frequently and daily, and stating that children should begin receiving the Eucharist at the age of seven, 1905 and 1910, respectively; ordered the establishment of the Confraternity of Christian Doctrine in all parishes throughout the world, 1905; condemned Modernism in the decree *Lamentabili* and the encyclical *Pascendi*, 1907.

**1908:** The United States and England, long under the jurisdiction of the Congregation for the Propagation of the Faith as mission territories, were removed from its control and placed under the common law of the Church.

**1910:** Laws of separation were enacted in Portugal, marking a point of departure in church-state relations.

**1911:** The Catholic Foreign Mission Society of America — Maryknoll, the first U.S.-founded society of its type — was established.

**1914:** Start of World War I, which lasted until 1918.

Start of the eight-year pontificate of Benedict XV. Much of his pontificate was devoted to seeking ways and means of minimizing the material and spiritual havoc of World War I. In 1917 he offered his services as a mediator to the belligerent nations, but his pleas for settlement of the conflict went unheeded.

**1917:** The Blessed Virgin Mary appeared to three children at Fatima, Portugal; see separate entry.

A new constitution, embodying repressive laws against the Church, was enacted in Mexico. Its implementation resulted in persecution in the 1920's and 1930's.

Bolsheviks seized power in Russia and set up a communist dictatorship. The event marked the rise of Communism in Russian and world affairs. One of its immediate, and lasting, results was persecution of the Church, Jews and other segments of the population.

**1918:** The *Code of Canon Law*, in preparation for more than 10 years, went into effect in the Western Church.

**1919:** Benedict XV stimulated missionary work through the decree *Maximum Illud*, in which he urged the recruiting and training of native clergy in places where the Church was not firmly established.

**1922:** Beginning of the 17-year pontificate of Pius XI. He subscribed to the Lateran Treaty, 1929, which settled the Roman Question created by the confiscation of the Papal States in 1871; issued the encyclical *Casti Connubii*, 1930, an authoritative statement on Christian marriage; resisted the efforts of Benito Mussolini to control Catholic Action and the Church, in the encyclical *Non Abbiamo Bisogno*, 1931; opposed various Fascist policies; issued the encyclicals *Quadragesimo Anno*, 1931, developing the social doctrine of Leo XIII's *Rerum Novarum*, and *Divini Redemptoris*, 1937, calling for social justice and condemning atheistic Communism; condemned anti-Semitism, 1937.

Ireland was partitioned. All but two of the predominantly Catholic counties were included in the southern part of the country, which eventually attained the status of an independent republic in 1949.

**1926:** The Catholic Relief Act repealed virtually all legal disabilities of Catholics in England.

**1931:** Leftists proclaimed Spain a republic and proceeded to disestablish the Church, confiscate church property, deny salaries to the clergy, expel the Jesuits and ban teaching of the Catholic faith. These actions were preludes to the civil war of 1936-1939.

**1933:** Emergence of Adolf Hitler to power in Germany. By 1935 two of his aims were clear, the elimination of the Jews and control of a single national church. Persecution decimated the Jews over a period of years. The Church was subject to repressive measures, which Pius XI protested futilely in the encyclical *Mit Brennender Sorge* in 1937.

**1936:** A three-year civil war broke out in Spain between the leftist Loyalists and forces led by Francisco Franco. The Loyalists were defeated and one-man, one-party rule was established. A number of priests, religious and lay persons fell victims to Loyalist persecution.

**1939:** Start of World War II, which lasted until 1945.

Start of the 19-year pontificate of Pius XII; see separate entry.

**1940:** Start of a decade of communist conquest in more than 13 countries, resulting in conditions of persecution for a minimum of 60 million Catholics as well as members of other faiths; see various countries.

Persecution diminished in Mexico through non-enforcement of anti-religious laws still on record.

**1950:** Pius XII proclaimed the dogma of the Assumption of the Blessed Virgin Mary.

**1954:** St. Pius X was canonized.

**1957:** The communist regime of China attempted to start a national schismatic church.

**1958:** Beginning of the five-year pontificate of John XXIII; see separate entry.

**1962:** The Second Vatican Council began the first of four sessions; see separate entry.

**1963:** Beginning of 15-year pontificate of Paul VI; see separate entry.

**1978:** Thirty-four-day pontificate of John Paul I; see separate entry.

Beginning of pontificate of John Paul II; see separate entry.

**1983:** The revised *Code of Canon Law* was promulgated and placed in effect.

## HERESIES

Heresy is the formal and obstinate denial or doubt by a baptized person, who remains a nominal Christian, of any truth which must be believed as a matter of divine and Catholic faith. Formal heresy involves deliberate resistance to the authority of God who communicates revelation through Scripture and tradition and the teaching authority of the Church. Obstinate refusal to accept the infallible teaching of the Church constitutes the canonical crime of heresy.

Formal heretics automatically incur the penalty of excommunication (Canon 1364 of the Code of Canon Law). Material heretics are those who, in good faith and without formal obstinacy, do not accept articles or matters of divine and Catholic faith.

Heresies have been significant not only as disruptions of unity of faith but also as occasions for the clarification and development of doctrine.

Heresies from the beginning of the Church to the 13th century are listed below.

**Judaizers:** Early converts from Judaism who claimed that members of the Church had to observe all the requirements of Mosaic Law as well as the obligations of Christian faith. This view was condemned by the Council of Jerusalem held in 51 under the presidency of St. Peter (Acts 15:28).

**Gnosticism:** A combination of elements of Platonic philosophy and Eastern mystery religions which claimed that its secret-knowledge principle gave its adherents a deeper insight into Christian doctrine than divine revelation and faith. One Gnostic thesis denied the divinity of Christ; others denied the reality of his humanity, calling it mere appearance **(Docetism, Phantasiasm).**

**Modalism:** A general term covering propositions **(Monarchianism, Patripassianism, Sabellianism)** that the Father, Son and Holy Spirit are not really distinct divine Persons but are only three different modes of being and self-manifestation of the one God. Various forms of Modalism, which appeared in the East in the second century and spread westward, were all condemned.

**Marcionism:** A Gnostic creation named for its author, who claimed there was total opposition and no connection at all between the Old Testament and the New Testament, between the God of the Jews and the God of the Christians; and that the canon of Scripture consisted only of portions of Luke's Gospel and 10 epistles of Paul. Marcion was excommunicated in 144 at Rome, and his tenets were condemned again by a Roman council about 260. The heresy was checked at Rome by 200 but persisted for several centuries in the East and had some adherents as late as the Middle Ages.

**Montanism:** A form of extremism preached about 170 by Montanus of Phrygia, Asia Minor. Its principal tenets were: an imminent second coming of Christ, denial of the divine nature of the Church and its power to forgive sin, excessively rigorous morality. The heresy was condemned by Pope St. Zephyrinus (199-217). Tertullian was one of its victims.

**Novatianism:** A heresy of excessive rigorism named for its author, a priest of Rome and antipope. Its principal tenet was that persons who fell away from the Church under persecution and or those guilty of serious sin after baptism could not be absolved and readmitted to communion with the Church. The heresy, condemned by a Roman synod in 251, slowly subsided in the West and died in the East by the end of the seventh century.

**Subordinationism, Adoptionism:** Christological errors and logical antecedents of Arianism. The key tenet was that Christ, while the most excellent of creatures, was subordinate to God whose Son he was by adoption rather than by nature. First proposed at Rome late in the second century, it was condemned by Pope St. Victor in 190 and again in the following century, in 785 by Pope Adrian I, in 794 by a council of Frankfurt, and in 1177 by Pope Alexander III.

**Arianism:** Denial of the divinity of Christ, the most devastating of the early heresies, authored by Arius of Alexandria, a priest, and condemned by the Council of Nicaea I in 325. Arians and several kinds of **Semi-Arians** propagandized their tenets widely, raised havoc in the Church for several centuries, and established their own hierarchies and churches.

**Macedonianism:** Denial of the divinity of the Holy Spirit, who was said to be a creature of the Son. Condemned by the Council of Constantinople I in 381. Macedonians were also called **Pneumatomachists,** enemies of the Spirit; and **Marathonians,** after the name of one of their leaders, a bishop of Nicomedia.

**Nestorianism:** Denial of the real unity of divine and human natures in the single divine Person of Christ, proposed by Nestorius, patriarch of Constantinople. He also held that Mary could not be called the Mother of God *(Theotokos);* that is, of the Second Person of the Trinity made Man. Condemned by the councils of Ephesus in 431 and Chalcedon in 451.

**Monophysitism:** Denial of Christ's human nature; also called **Eutychianism,** after the name of one of its leading advocates. The heresy was condemned by the Council of Chalcedon in 451.

**Monothelitism:** Denial of the human will of Christ. Severus of Antioch and Sergius, patriarch of Constantinople, were leading advocates of the heresy, which was condemned by the Council of Constantinople III in 681.

**Priscillianism:** A fourth century amalgamation of elements from various sources — Sabellianism, Arianism, Docetism, Pantheism, belief in the diabolical nature of marriage, corruption of Scripture. The heresy was condemned by a council of Braga in 563 on 17 different counts.

**Donatism:** A development of the error at the heart of the third century **Rebaptism Controversy** (baptism conferred by heretics is invalid because persons deprived of grace are incapable of being ministers of grace to others). Followers of Donatus the Great asserted throughout the fourth century that sacraments administered by sinners were invalid. Condemnation of the heresy is traced to Pope St. Stephen I (254-257) and the principle that sacraments have their efficacy from Christ, not from their human ministers.

**Pelagianism:** Denial of the supernatural order of things, proposed by Pelagius (360-420), a Breton monk. Proceeding from the assumption that Adam had a natural right to supernatural life, the theory held that man could attain salvation through the efforts of his own free will and natural powers. The theory involved errors concerning the nature of original sin, the meaning of grace and other matters. St. Augustine opposed the heresy, which was condemned by the Council of Ephesus in 431. **Semi-Pelagianism** was condemned by a council of Orange in 529.

**Iconoclasm:** An image-breaking campaign which resulted from an edict issued by Eastern Emperor Leo the Isaurian in 726, that the veneration of images, pictures and relics was idolatrous. The theoretical basis of the heresy was the Monophysite error which denied the humanity of Christ. It was denounced several times before its condemnation by the Council of Nicaea II in 787.

**Berengarian Heresy:** Denial of the Real Presence of Christ under the appearances of bread and wine, the first clear-cut Eucharistic heresy; proposed by Berengarius of Tours (c. 1000-1088). The heresy was condemned by various synods and finally by a council held at Rome in 1079.

**Waldensianism:** Claimed by Peter Waldo, a merchant of Lyons, to be a return to pure Christianity, the heresy rejected the hierarchical structure of the Church, the sacramental system and other doctrines. Its adherents were excommunicated in 1184 and their tenets were condemned several times thereafter.

**Albigensianism, Catharism:** Related errors based on the old **Manichaean** assumption that two supreme principles of good and evil were operative in creation and life, and that the supreme objective of human endeavor was liberation from evil (matter). The heresy denied the humanity of Christ, the sacramental system and the authority of the Church (and state), and endorsed a moral code which threatened seriously the fabric of social life in southern France and northern Italy in the 12th and 13th centuries. The heresy was condemned by councils of the Lateran III and Lateran IV in 1179 and 1215.

## ECUMENICAL COUNCILS

An ecumenical council is an assembly of the college of bishops, with and under the presidency of the pope, which has supreme authority over the Church in matters pertaining to faith, morals, worship and discipline.

The Second Vatican Council stated: "The supreme authority with which this college (of bishops) is empowered over the whole Church is exercised in a solemn way through an ecumenical council. A council is never ecumenical unless it is confirmed or at least accepted as such by the successor of Peter. It is the prerogative of the Roman Pontiff to convoke these councils, to preside over them, and to confirm them" *(Dogmatic Constitution on the Church,* No. 22).

### Pope Presides

The pope is the head of an ecumenical council; he presides over it either personally or through legates. Conciliar decrees and other actions have binding force only when confirmed and promulgated by him. If a pope dies during a council, it is suspended until reconvened by another pope. An ecumenical council is not superior to a pope; hence, there is no appeal from a pope to a council.

Collectively, the bishops with the pope represent the whole Church. They do this not as democratic representatives of the faithful in a kind of church parliament, but as the successors of the Apostles with divinely given authority, care and responsibility over the whole Church.

Council participants with a deliberative vote are: cardinals, including those who are retired; residential patriarchs, primates, archbishops and bishops, even if they are not yet consecrated; abbots and certain other prelates, an abbot primate, abbot superiors of monastic congregations and heads of exempt clerical religious; titular bishops, on invitation. Experts in theology and canon law may be given a consultative vote. Others, including lay persons, may address a council or observe its actions, but may not vote.

Basic legislation concerning ecumenical councils is contained in the Code of Canon Law. Basic doctrinal considerations were stated by the Second Vatican Council in the *Dogmatic Constitution on the Church.*

### Background

Ecumenical councils had their prototype in the Council of Jerusalem in 51, at which the Apostles under the leadership of St. Peter decided that converts to the Christian faith were not obliged to observe all the prescriptions of Old Testament law (Acts 15). As early as the second century, bishops got together in regional meetings, synods or councils to take common action for the doctrinal and pastoral good of their communities of faithful. The expansion of such limited assemblies to ecumenical councils was a logical and historical evolution, given the nature and needs of the Church.

Emperors were active in summoning or convoking the first eight councils, especially the first five and the eighth. Among reasons for intervention of this kind were the facts that the emperors regarded themselves as guardians of the faith; that the settlement of religious controversies, which had repercussions in political and social turmoil, served the cause of peace in the state; and that the emperors had at their disposal ways and means of facilitating gatherings of bishops. Imperial actions, however, did not account for the formally ecumenical nature of the councils.

Some councils were attended by relatively few bishops, and the ecumenical character of several was open to question for a time. However, confirmation and de facto recognition of their actions by popes and subsequent councils established them as ecumenical.

### Role in History

The councils have played a highly significant role in the history of the Church by witnessing to and defining truths of revelation, by shaping forms of worship and discipline, and by promoting measures for the ever-necessary reform and renewal of Catholic life. In general, they have represented attempts of the Church to mobilize itself in times of crisis for self-preservation, self-purification and growth.

The first eight ecumenical councils were held in the East; the other 13, in the West. The majority of separated Eastern Churches — e.g., the Orthodox — recognize the ecumenical character of the first seven councils, which formulated a great deal of basic doctrine. Nestorians, however, acknowledge only the first two councils; the Monophysite Armenians, Syrians, and Copts acknowledge the first three.

### The 21 Councils

The 21 ecumenical councils in the history of the Church are listed below, with indication of their names or titles (taken from the names of the places where they were held); the dates; the reigning and/or approving popes; the emperors who were instrumental in convoking the eight councils in the East; the number of bishops who attended, when available; the number of sessions; the most significant actions.

**1. Nicaea I,** 325: St. Sylvester I (Emperor Constantine I); attended by approximately 300 bishops; sessions held between May 20 or June 19 to near the end of August. Condemned Arianism, which denied the divinity of Christ; contributed to formulation of the Nicene Creed; fixed the date of Easter; passed regulations concerning clerical discipline; adopted the civil division of the Empire as the model for the organization of the Church.

**2. Constantinople I,** 381: St. Damasus I (Emperor Theodosius I); attended by approximately 150 bishops; sessions held from May to July. Condemned various brands of Arianism, and Macedonianism which denied the divinity of the Holy Spirit; contributed to formulation of the Nicene Creed; approved a canon which made the bishop of Constantinople the ranking prelate in the East, with primacy next to that of the pope. Doubt about the ecumenical character of this council was resolved by the ratification of its acts by popes and the Council of Chalcedon.

**3. Ephesus,** 431: St. Celestine I (Emperor Theodosius II); attended by 150 to 200 bishops; five sessions held between June 22 and July 17. Condemned Nestorianism, which denied the real unity of the divine and human natures in the Person of Christ; defined *Theotokos* ("Bearer of God") as the title of Mary, Mother of the Son of God made Man; condemned Pelagianism, which reduced the supernatural to the natural order of things.

**4. Chalcedon,** 451: St. Leo I (Emperor Marcian); attended by approximately 600 bishops; 17 sessions held between Oct. 8 and Nov. 1. Condemned: Monophysitism, also called Eutychianism, which denied the humanity of Christ by holding that he had only one, the divine, nature; and the Monophysite Robber Synod of Ephesus, of 449.

**5. Constantinople II,** 553: Vigilius (Emperor Justinian I); attended by 165 bishops; eight sessions held between May 5 and June 2. Condemned the *Three Chapters*, Nestorian-tainted writings of Theodore of Mopsuestia, Theodoret of Cyrus and Ibas of Edessa.

**6. Constantinople III,** 680-681; St. Agatho, St. Leo II (Emperor Constantine IV); attended by approximately 170 bishops; 16 sessions held between Nov. 7, 680, and Sept. 16, 681. Condemned Monothelitism, which held that there was only one will, the divine, in Christ; censured Pope Honorius I for a letter to Sergius, bishop of Constantinople, in which he made an ambiguous but not infallible statement about the unity of will and/or operation in Christ. Constantinople III is also called the Trullan Council because its sessions were held in the domed hall, Trullos, of the imperial palace.

**7. Nicaea II,** 787: Adrian I (Empress Irene); attended by approximately 300 bishops; eight sessions held between Sept. 24 and Oct. 23. Condemned: Iconoclasm, which held that the use of images was idolatry; and Adoptionism, which claimed that Christ was not the Son of God by nature but only by adoption. This was the last council regarded as ecumenical by Orthodox Churches.

**8. Constantinople IV,** 869-870: Adrian II (Emperor Basil I); attended by 102 bishops; six sessions held between Oct. 5, 869, and Feb. 28, 870. Condemned Iconoclasm; condemned and deposed Photius as patriarch of Constantinople; restored Ignatius to the patriarchate. This was the last ecumenical council held in the East. It was first called ecumenical by canonists toward the end of the 11th century.

**9. Lateran I,** 1123: Callistus II; attended by approximately 300 bishops; sessions held between Mar. 18 and Apr. 6. Endorsed provisions of the Concordat of Worms concerning the investiture of prelates: approved reform measures in 25 canons.

**10. Lateran II,** 1139: Innocent II; attended by 900 to 1,000 bishops and abbots; three sessions held in April. Adopted measures against a schism organized by antipope Anacletus; approved 30 disciplinary measures and canons, one of which stated that holy orders is an invalidating impediment to marriage.

**11. Lateran III,** 1179: Alexander III; attended by at least 300 bishops; three sessions held between Mar. 5 and 19. Enacted measures against the Waldenses and Albigensians; approved reform decrees in 27 canons; provided that popes be elected by two-thirds vote of the cardinals.

**12. Lateran IV,** 1215: Innocent III; sessions held between Nov. 11 and 30. Ordered annual confession and Communion; defined and made first official use of the term "transubstantiation"; adopted measures to counteract the Cathari and Albigensians; approved 70 canons.

**13. Lyons I,** 1245: Innocent IV; attended by approximately 150 bishops; three sessions held between June 28 and July 17. Confirmed the deposition of Emperor Frederick II; approved 22 canons.

**14. Lyons II,** 1274: Gregory X; attended by approximately 500 bishops; six sessions held between May 7 and July 17. Accomplished a temporary reunion of separated Eastern Churches with the Roman Church; issued regulations concerning conclaves for papal elections; approved 31 canons.

**15. Vienne,** 1311-1312: Clement V; attended by 132 bishops; three sessions held between Oct. 16, 1311, and May 6, 1312. Suppressed the Knights Templar; enacted a number of reform decrees.

**16. Constance,** 1414-1418: Gregory XII, Martin V; attended by nearly 200 bishops, plus other prelates and many experts; 45 sessions held between Nov. 5, 1414, and Apr. 22, 1418. Took successful action to end the Western Schism; rejected the teachings of Wycliff; condemned Hus as a heretic. One decree, passed in the earlier stages of the council, asserted the superiority of an ecumenical council over the pope; this was later rejected.

**17. Florence** (also called Basel-Ferrara-Florence), 1438-1445: Eugene IV; attended by many Latin-Rite and Eastern-Rite bishops; preliminary sessions were held at Basel and Ferrara before definitive work was accomplished at Florence. Reaffirmed the primacy of the pope against the claims of Conciliarists that an ecumenical council is superior to the pope; formulated and approved decrees of union — with the Greeks, July 6, 1439; with the Armenians, Nov. 22, 1439; with the Jacobites, Feb. 4, 1442. These decrees failed to gain general or lasting acceptance in the East.

**18. Lateran V,** 1512-1517: Julius II, Leo X; 12 sessions held between May 3, 1512, and Mar. 16, 1517. Stated the relation and position of the pope with respect to an ecumenical council; acted to counteract the Pragmatic Sanction of Bourges and exaggerated claims of liberty by the French Church; condemned erroneous teachings concerning the nature of the human soul; stated doctrine concerning indulgences. The council reflected concern for abuses in the Church and the need for reforms but failed to take decisive action in the years immediately preceding the Reformation.

**19. Trent,** 1545-1563: Paul III, Julius III, Pius IV; 25 sessions held between Dec. 13, 1545, and Dec. 4, 1563. Issued a great number of decrees concerning doctrinal matters opposed by the Reformers, and mobilized the Counter-Reformation. Definitions covered the rule of faith, the nature of justification, grace, faith, original sin and its effects, the seven sacraments, the sacrificial nature of the Mass, the veneration of saints, use of sacred images, belief in purgatory, the doctrine of indulgences, the jurisdiction of the pope over the whole Church. Initiated many reforms for renewal in the liturgy and general discipline in the Church, the promotion of religious instruction, the education of the clergy through the foundation of seminaries, etc. Trent ranks with Vatican II as the greatest ecumenical council held in the West.

**20. Vatican I,** 1869-1870: Pius IX; attended by approximately 800 bishops and other prelates; four public sessions and 89 general meetings held between Dec. 8, 1869, and July 7, 1870. Defined papal primacy and infallibility in a dogmatic constitution on the Church; covered natural religion, revelation, faith, and the relations between faith and reason in a dogmatic constitution on the Catholic faith. The council suspended sessions Sept. 1 and was adjourned Oct. 20, 1870.

### Vatican II

The Second Vatican Council, which was forecast by Pope John XXIII Jan. 25, 1959, was held in four sessions in St. Peter's Basilica.

Pope John convoked it and opened the first session, which ran from Oct. 11 to Dec. 8, 1962. Following John's death June 3, 1963, Pope Paul VI reconvened the council for the other three sessions which ran from Sept. 29 to Dec. 4, 1963; Sept. 14 to Nov. 21, 1964; Sept. 14 to Dec. 8, 1965.

A total of 2,860 Fathers participated in council proceedings, and attendance at meetings varied between 2,000 and 2,500. For various reasons, including the denial of exit from Communist-domi-

nated countries, 274 Fathers could not attend.

The council formulated and promulgated 16 documents — two dogmatic and two pastoral constitutions, nine decrees and three declarations — all of which reflect its basic pastoral orientation toward renewal and reform in the Church. Given below are the Latin and English titles of the documents and their dates of promulgation.

• *Lumen Gentium* (Dogmatic Constitution on the Church), Nov. 21, 1964.

• *Dei Verbum* (Dogmatic Constitution on Divine Revelation), Nov. 18, 1965.

• *Sacrosanctum Concilium* (Constitution on the Sacred Liturgy), Dec. 4, 1963.

• *Gaudium et Spes* (Pastoral Constitution on the Church in the Modern World), Dec. 7, 1965.

• *Christus Dominus* (Decree on the Bishops' Pastoral Office in the Church), Oct. 28, 1965.

• *Ad Gentes* (Decree on the Church's Missionary Activity), Dec. 7, 1965.

• *Unitatis Redintegratio* (Decree on Ecumenism), Nov. 21, 1964.

• *Orientalium Ecclesiarum* (Decree on Eastern Catholic Churches), Nov. 21, 1964.

• *Presbyterorum Ordinis* (Decree on the Ministry and Life of Priests), Dec. 7, 1965.

• *Optatam Totius* (Decree on Priestly Formation), Oct. 28, 1965.

• *Perfectae Caritatis* (Decree on the Appropriate Renewal of the Religious Life), Oct. 28, 1965.

• *Apostolicam Actuositatem* (Decree on the Apostolate of the Laity), Nov. 18, 1965.

• *Inter Mirifica* (Decree on the Instruments of Social Communication), Dec. 4, 1963.

• *Dignitatis Humanae* (Declaration on Religious Freedom), Dec. 7, 1965.

• *Nostra Aetate* (Declaration on the Relationship of the Church to Non-Christian Religions), Oct. 28, 1965.

• *Gravissimum Educationis* (Declaration on Christian Education), Oct. 28, 1965.

The key documents were the four constitutions, which set the ideological basis for all the others. To date, the documents with the most visible effects are those on the liturgy, the Church, Church in the world, ecumenism, the renewal of religious life, the life and ministry of priests, the lay apostolate.

The main business of the council was to explore and make explicit dimensions of doctrine and Christian life requiring emphasis for the full development of the Church and the better accomplishment of its mission in the contemporary world.

## CONSTITUTION ON THE LITURGY

A statement commemorating the 20th anniversary of the Second Vatican Council's *Constitution on the Sacred Liturgy* was issued by the bishops of the United States in November, 1983.

The statement discussed the role liturgy should play in the spiritual life of Catholics; liturgical formation of lay persons as well as the clergy; renewal of the sacraments; liturgical adaptation to

diverse cultures, which it called a theological necessity; ecumenical angles to liturgical renewal, and other subjects.

"Liturgical flexibility and adaptation," the statement said, "have made it possible for the Church's proclamation of the Good News to challenge our times with a realistic chance for a hearing and an impact."

*Information includes the name of the pope, in many cases his name before becoming pope, his birthplace or country of origin, the date of accession to the papacy, and the date of the end of reign which, in all but a few cases, was the date of death. Double dates indicate times of election and coronation.*

*Source: "Annuario Pontificio."*

St. Peter (Simon Bar-Jona): Bethsaida in Galilee; d. c. 64 or 67.

St. Linus: Tuscany; 67-76.

St. Anacletus (Cletus): Rome; 76-88.

St. Clement: Rome; 88-97.

St. Evaristus: Greece; 97-105.

St. Alexander I: Rome; 105-115.

St. Sixtus I: Rome; 115-125.

St. Telesphorus: Greece; 125-136.

St. Hyginus: Greece; 136-140.

St. Pius I: Aquileia; 140-155.

St. Anicetus: Syria; 155-166.

St. Soter: Campania; 166-175.

St. Eleutherius: Nicopolis in Epirus; 175-189.

Up to the time of St. Eleutherius, the years indicated for the beginning and end of pontificates are not absolutely certain. Also, up to the middle of the 11th century, there are some doubts about the exact days and months given in chronological tables.

St. Victor I: Africa; 189-199.

St. Zephyrinus: Rome; 199-217.

St. Callistus I: Rome; 217-222.

St. Urban I: Rome; 222-230.

St. Pontian: Rome; July 21, 230, to Sept. 28, 235.

St. Anterus: Greece; Nov. 21, 235, to Jan. 3, 236.

St. Fabian: Rome; Jan. 10, 236, to Jan. 20, 250.

St. Cornelius: Rome; Mar., 251, to June, 253.

St. Lucius I: Rome; June 25, 253, to Mar. 5, 254.

St. Stephen I: Rome; May 12, 254, to Aug. 2, 257.

St. Sixtus II: Greece; Aug. 30, 257, to Aug. 6, 258.

St. Dionysius: July 22, 259, to Dec. 26, 268.

St. Felix I: Rome; Jan. 5, 269, to Dec. 30, 274.

St. Eutychian: Luni; Jan. 4, 275, to Dec. 7, 283.

St. Caius: Dalmatia; Dec. 17, 283, to Apr. 22, 296.

St. Marcellinus: Rome; June 30, 296, to Oct. 25, 304.

St. Marcellus I: Rome; May 27, 308, or June 26, 308, to Jan. 16, 309.

St. Eusebius: Greece; Apr. 18, 309 or 310, to Aug. 17, 309 or 310.

St. Melchiades (Miltiades): Africa; July 2, 311, to Jan. 11, 314.

St. Sylvester I: Rome; Jan. 31, 314, to Dec. 31, 335. (Most of the popes before St. Sylvester I were martyrs.)

St. Marcus: Rome; Jan. 18, 336, to Oct. 7, 336.

St. Julius I: Rome; Feb. 6, 337, to Apr. 12, 352.

Liberius: Rome; May 17, 352, to Sept. 24, 366.

St. Damasus I: Spain; Oct. 1, 366, to Dec. 11, 384.

St. Siricius: Rome; Dec. 15, or 22 or 29, 384, to Nov. 26, 399.

St. Anastasius I: Rome; Nov. 27, 399, to Dec. 19, 401.

St. Innocent I: Albano; Dec. 22, 401, to Mar. 12, 417.

St. Zozimus: Greece; Mar. 18, 417, to Dec. 26, 418.

St. Boniface I: Rome; Dec. 28 or 29, 418, to Sept. 4, 422.

St. Celestine I: Campania; Sept. 10, 422, to July 27, 432.

St. Sixtus III: Rome; July 31, 432, to Aug. 19, 440.

St. Leo I (the Great): Tuscany; Sept. 29, 440, to Nov. 10, 461.

St. Hilary: Sardinia; Nov. 19, 461, to Feb. 29, 468.

St. Simplicius: Tivoli; Mar. 3, 468, to Mar. 10, 483.

St. Felix III (II): Rome; Mar. 13, 483, to Mar. 1, 492.

He should be called Felix II, and his successors of the same name should be numbered accordingly. The discrepancy in the numerical designation of popes named Felix was caused by the erroneous insertion in some lists of the name of St. Felix of Rome, a martyr.

St. Gelasius I: Africa; Mar. 1, 492, to Nov. 21, 496.

Anastasius II: Rome; Nov. 24, 496, to Nov. 19, 498.

St. Symmachus: Sardinia; Nov. 22, 498, to July 19, 514.

St. Hormisdas: Frosinone; July 20, 514, to Aug. 6, 523.

St. John I, Martyr: Tuscany; Aug. 13, 523, to May 18, 526.

St. Felix IV (III): Samnium; July 12, 526, to Sept. 22, 530.

Boniface II: Rome; Sept. 22, 530, to Oct. 17, 532.

John II: Rome; Jan. 2, 533, to May 8, 535.

John II was the first pope to change his name. His given name was Mercury.

St. Agapitus I: Rome; May 13, 535, to Apr. 22, 536.

St. Silverius, Martyr: Campania; June 1 or 8, 536, to Nov. 11, 537 (d. Dec. 2, 537).

St. Silverius was violently deposed in March, 537, and abdicated Nov. 11, 537. His successor, Vigilius, was not recognized as pope by all the Roman clergy until his abdication.

Vigilius: Rome; Mar. 29, 537, to June 7, 555.

Pelagius I: Rome; Apr. 16, 556, to Mar. 4, 561.

John III: Rome; July 17, 561, to July 13, 574.

Benedict I: Rome; June 2, 575, to July 30, 579.

Pelagius II: Rome; Nov. 26, 579, to Feb. 7, 590.

St. Gregory I (the Great): Rome; Sept. 3, 590, to Mar. 12, 604.

Sabinian: Blera in Tuscany; Sept. 13, 604, to Feb. 22, 606.

Boniface III: Rome; Feb. 19, 607, to Nov. 12, 607.

St. Boniface IV: Abruzzi; Aug. 25, 608, to May 8, 615.

St. Deusdedit (Adeodatus I): Rome; Oct. 19, 615, to Nov. 8, 618.

Boniface V: Naples; Dec. 23, 619, to Oct. 25, 625.

Honorius I: Campania; Oct. 27, 625, to Oct. 12, 638.

Severinus: Rome; May 28, 640, to Aug. 2, 640.

John IV: Dalmatia; Dec. 24, 640, to Oct. 12, 642.

Theodore I: Greece; Nov. 24, 642, to May 14, 649.

St. Martin I, Martyr: Todi; July, 649, to Sept. 16, 655 (in exile from June 17, 653).

St. Eugene I: Rome; Aug. 10, 654, to June 2, 657.

St. Eugene I was elected during the exile of St. Martin I, who is believed to have endorsed him as pope.

St. Vitalian: Segni; July 30, 657, to Jan. 27, 672.

Adeodatus II: Rome; Apr. 11, 672, to June 17, 676.

Donus: Rome; Nov. 2, 676, to Apr. 11, 678.

St. Agatho: Sicily; June 27, 678, to Jan. 10, 681.

St. Leo II: Sicily; Aug. 17, 682, to July 3, 683.

St. Benedict II: Rome; June 26, 684, to May 8, 685.

John V: Syria; July 23, 685, to Aug. 2, 686.

Conon: birthplace unknown; Oct. 21, 686, to Sept. 21, 687.

St. Sergius I: Syria; Dec. 15, 687, to Sept. 8, 701.

John VI: Greece; Oct. 30, 701, to Jan. 11, 705.

John VII: Greece; Mar. 1, 705, to Oct. 18, 707.

Sisinnius: Syria; Jan. 15, 708, to Feb. 4, 708.

Constantine: Syria; Mar. 25, 708, to Apr. 9, 715.

St. Gregory II: Rome; May 19, 715, to Feb. 11, 731.

St. Gregory III: Syria; Mar. 18, 731, to Nov., 741.

St. Zachary: Greece; Dec. 10, 741, to Mar. 22, 752.

Stephen II (III): Rome; Mar. 26, 752, to Apr. 26, 757.

After the death of St. Zachary, a Roman priest named Stephen was elected but died (four days later) before his consecration as bishop of Rome, which would have marked the beginning of his pontificate. Another Stephen was elected to succeed Zachary as Stephen II. (The first pope with this name was St. Stephen I, 254-57.) The ordinal III appears in parentheses after the name of Stephen II because the name of the earlier elected but deceased priest was included in some lists. Other Stephens have double numbers.

St. Paul I: Rome; Apr. (May 29), 757, to June 28, 767.

Stephen III (IV): Sicily; Aug. 1 (7), 768, to Jan. 24, 772.

Adrian I: Rome; Feb. 1 (9), 772, to Dec. 25, 795.

St. Leo III: Rome; Dec. 26 (27), 795, to June 12, 816.

Stephen IV (V): Rome; June 22, 816, to Jan. 24, 817.

St. Paschal I: Rome; Jan. 25, 817, to Feb. 11, 824.

Eugene II: Rome; Feb. (May), 824, to Aug., 827.

Valentine: Rome; Aug. 827, to Sept., 827.

Gregory IV: Rome; 827, to Jan., 844.

Sergius II: Rome; Jan., 844 to Jan. 27, 847.

St. Leo IV: Rome; Jan. (Apr. 10), 847, to July 17, 855.

Benedict III: Rome; July (Sept. 29), 855, to Apr. 17, 858.

St. Nicholas I (the Great): Rome; Apr. 24, 858, to Nov. 13, 867.

Adrian II: Rome; Dec. 14, 867, to Dec. 14, 872.

John VIII: Rome; Dec. 14, 872, to Dec. 16, 882.

Marinus I: Gallese; Dec. 16, 882, to May 15, 884.

St. Adrian III: Rome; May 17, 884, to Sept., 885. Cult confirmed June 2, 1891.

Stephen V (VI): Rome; Sept., 885, to Sept. 14, 891.

Formosus: Portus; Oct. 6, 891, to Apr. 4, 896.

Boniface VI: Rome; Apr., 896, to Apr., 896.

Stephen VI (VII): Rome; May, 896, to Aug., 897.

Romanus: Gallese; Aug., 897, to Nov., 897.

Theodore II: Rome; Dec., 897, to Dec., 897.

John IX: Tivoli; Jan., 898, to Jan., 900.

Benedict IV: Rome; Jan. (Feb.), 900, to July, 903.

Leo V: Ardea; July, 903, to Sept., 903.

Sergius III: Rome; Jan. 29, 904, to Apr. 14, 911.

Anastasius III: Rome; Apr., 911, to June, 913.

Landus: Sabina; July, 913, to Feb., 914.

John X: Tossignano (Imola); Mar., 914, to May, 928.

Leo VI: Rome; May, 928, to Dec., 928.

Stephen VII (VIII): Rome; Dec., 928, to Feb., 931.

John XI: Rome; Feb. (Mar.), 931, to Dec., 935.

Leo VII: Rome; Jan. 3, 936, to July 13, 939.

Stephen VIII (IX): Rome; July 14, 939, to Oct., 942.

Marinus II: Rome; Oct. 30, 942, to May, 946.

Agapitus II: Rome; May 10, 946, to Dec., 955.

John XII (Octavius): Tusculum; Dec. 16, 955, to May 14, 964 (date of his death).

Leo VIII: Rome; Dec. 4 (6), 963, to Mar. 1, 965.

Benedict V: Rome; May 22, 964, to July 4, 966.

Confusion exists concerning the legitimacy of claims to the pontificate by Leo VIII and Benedict V. John XII was deposed Dec. 4, 963, by a Roman council. If this deposition was invalid, Leo was an antipope. If the deposition of John was valid, Leo was the legitimate pope and Benedict was an antipope.

John XIII: Rome; Oct. 1, 965, to Sept. 6, 972.

Benedict VI: Rome; Jan. 19, 973, to June, 974.

Benedict VII: Rome; Oct. 974, to July 10, 983.

John XIV (Peter Campenora): Pavia; Dec., 983, to Aug. 20, 984.

John XV: Rome; Aug., 985, to Mar., 996.

Gregory V (Bruno of Carinthia): Saxony; May 3, 996, to Feb. 18, 999.

Sylvester II (Gerbert): Auvergne; Apr. 2, 999, to May 12, 1003.

John XVII (Siccone): Rome; June, 1003, to Dec., 1003.

John XVIII (Phasianus): Rome; Jan., 1004, to July, 1009.

Sergius IV (Peter): Rome; July 31, 1009, to May 12, 1012.

The custom of changing one's name on election to the papacy is generally considered to date from the time of Sergius IV. Before his time, several popes had changed their names. After his time, this became a regular practice, with few exceptions; e.g., Adrian VI and Marcellus II.

Benedict VIII (Theophylactus): Tusculum; May 18, 1012, to Apr. 9, 1024.

John XIX (Romanus): Tusculum; Apr. (May), 1024, to 1032.

Benedict IX (Theophylactus): Tusculum; 1032, to 1044.

Sylvester III (John): Rome; Jan. 20, 1045, to Feb. 10, 1045.

Sylvester III was an antipope if the forcible removal of Benedict IX in 1044 was not legitimate.

Benedict IX (second time): Apr. 10, 1045, to May 1, 1045.

Gregory VI (John Gratian): Rome; May 5, 1045, to Dec. 20, 1046.

Clement II (Suitger, Lord of Morsleben and Hornburg): Saxony; Dec. 24 (25), 1046, to Oct. 9, 1047.

If the resignation of Benedict IX in 1045 and his removal at the December, 1046, synod were not legitimate, Gregory VI and Clement II were antipopes.

Benedict IX (third time): Nov. 8, 1047, to July 17, 1048 (d. c. 1055).

Damasus II (Poppo): Bavaria; July 17, 1048, to Aug. 9, 1048.

St. Leo IX (Bruno): Alsace; Feb. 12, 1049, to Apr. 19, 1054.

Victor II (Gebhard): Swabia; Apr. 16, 1055, to July 28, 1057.

Stephen IX (X) (Frederick): Lorraine; Aug. 3, 1057, to Mar. 29, 1058.

Nicholas II (Gerard): Burgundy; Jan. 24, 1059, to July 27, 1061.

Alexander II (Anselmo da Baggio): Milan; Oct. 1, 1061, to Apr. 21, 1073.

St. Gregory VII (Hildebrand): Tuscany; Apr. 22 (June 30), 1073, to May 25, 1085.

Bl. Victor III (Dauferius; Desiderius): Benevento; May 24, 1086, to Sept. 16, 1087. Cult confirmed July 23, 1887.

Bl. Urban II (Otto di Lagery): France; Mar. 12, 1088, to July 29, 1099. Cult confirmed July 14, 1881.

Paschal II (Raniero): Ravenna; Aug. 13 (14), 1099, to Jan. 21, 1118.

Gelasius II (Giovanni Caetani): Gaeta; Jan. 24 (Mar. 10), 1118, to Jan. 28, 1119.

Callistus II (Guido of Burgundy): Burgundy; Feb. 2 (9), 1119, to Dec. 13, 1124.

Honorius II (Lamberto): Fiagnano (Imola); Dec. 15 (21), 1124, to Feb. 13, 1130.

Innocent II (Gregorio Papareschi): Rome; Feb. 14 (23), 1130, to Sept. 24, 1143.

Celestine II (Guido): Citta di Castello; Sept. 26 (Oct. 3), 1143, to Mar. 8, 1144.

Lucius II (Gerardo Caccianemici): Bologna: Mar. 12, 1144, to Feb. 15, 1145.

Bl. Eugene III (Bernardo Paganelli di Montemagno): Pisa; Feb. 15 (18), 1145, to July 8, 1153. Cult confirmed Oct. 3, 1872.

Anastasius IV (Corrado): Rome; July 12, 1153, to Dec. 3, 1154.

Adrian IV (Nicholas Breakspear): England; Dec. 4 (5), 1154, to Sept. 1, 1159.

Alexander III (Rolando Bandinelli): Siena; Sept. 7 (20), 1159, to Aug. 30, 1181.

Lucius III (Ubaldo Allucingoli): Lucca; Sept. 1 (6), 1181, to Sept. 25, 1185.

Urban III (Uberto Crivelli): Milan; Nov. 25 (Dec. 1), 1185, to Oct. 20, 1187.

Gregory VIII (Alberto de Morra): Benevento; Oct. 21 (25), 1187, to Dec. 17, 1187.

Clement III (Paolo Scolari): Rome; Dec. 19 (20), 1187, to Mar., 1191.

Celestine III (Giacinto Bobone): Rome; Mar. 30 (Apr. 14), 1191, to Jan. 8, 1198.

Innocent III (Lotario dei Conti di Segni); Anagni; Jan. 8 (Feb. 22), 1198, to July 16, 1216.

Honorius III (Cencio Savelli): Rome; July 18 (24), 1216, to Mar. 18, 1227.

Gregory IX (Ugolino, Count of Segni): Anagni; Mar. 19 (21), 1227, to Aug. 22, 1241.

Celestine IV (Goffredo Castiglioni): Milan; Oct. 25 (28), 1241, to Nov. 10, 1241.

Innocent IV (Sinibaldo Fieschi): Genoa; June 25 (28), 1243, to Dec. 7, 1254.

Alexander IV (Rinaldo, Count of Segni): Anagni; Dec. 12 (20), 1254, to May 25, 1261.

Urban IV (Jacques Pantaléon): Troyes; Aug. 29 (Sept. 4), 1261, to Oct. 2, 1264.

Clement IV (Guy Foulques or Guido le Gros): France; Feb. 5 (15), 1265, to Nov. 29, 1268.

Bl. Gregory X (Teobaldo Visconti): Piacenza; Sept. 1, 1271 (Mar. 27, 1272), to Jan. 10, 1276. Cult confirmed Sept. 12, 1713.

Bl. Innocent V (Peter of Tarentaise): Savoy; Jan. 21 (Feb. 22), 1276, to June 22, 1276. Cult confirmed Mar. 13, 1898.

Adrian V (Ottobono Fieschi): Genoa: July 11, 1276, to Aug. 18, 1276.

John XXI (Petrus Juliani or Petrus Hispanus): Portugal; Sept. 8 (20), 1276, to May 20, 1277.

Elimination was made of the name of John XX in an effort to rectify the numerical designation of popes named John. The error dates back to the time of John XV.

Nicholas III (Giovanni Gaetano Orsini): Rome; Nov. 25 (Dec. 26), 1277, to Aug. 22, 1280.

Martin IV (Simon de Brie): France; Feb. 22 (Mar. 23), 1281, to Mar. 28, 1285.

The names of Marinus 1 (882-84) and Marinus II (942-46) were construed as Martin. In view of these two pontificates and the earlier reign of St. Martin I (649-55), this pope was called Martin IV.

Honorius IV (Giacomo Savelli): Rome; Apr. 2 (May 20), 1285, to Apr. 3, 1287.

Nicholas IV (Girolamo Masci): Ascoli; Feb. 22, 1288, to Apr. 4, 1292.

St. Celestine V (Pietro del Murrone): Isernia; July 5 (Aug. 29), 1294, to Dec. 13, 1294; d. 1296. Canonized May 5, 1313.

Boniface VIII (Benedetto Caetani): Anagni; Dec. 24, 1294 (Jan. 23, 1295), to Oct. 11, 1303.

Bl. Benedict XI (Niccolo Boccasini): Treviso; Oct. 22 (27), 1303, to July 7, 1304. Cult confirmed Apr. 24, 1736.

Clement V (Bertrand de Got): France; June 5 (Nov. 14), 1305, to Apr. 20, 1314. (First of Avignon popes.)

John XXII (Jacques d'Euse): Cahors; Aug. 7 (Sept. 5), 1316, to Dec. 4, 1334.

Benedict XII (Jacques Fournier): France; Dec. 20, 1334 (Jan. 8, 1335), to Apr. 25, 1342.

Clement VI (Pierre Roger): France; May 7 (19), 1342, to Dec. 6, 1352.

Innocent VI (Etienne Aubert): France; Dec. 18 (30), 1352, to Sept. 12, 1362.

Bl. Urban V (Guillaume de Grimoard): France; Sept. 28 (Nov. 6), 1362, to Dec. 19, 1370. Cult confirmed Mar. 10, 1870.

Gregory XI (Pierre Roger de Beaufort): France; Dec. 30, 1370 (Jan. 5, 1371), to Mar. 26, 1378. (Last of Avignon popes.)

Urban VI (Bartolomeo Prignano): Naples; Apr. 8 (18), 1378, to Oct. 15, 1389.

Boniface IX (Pietro Tomacelli): Naples; Nov. 2 (9), 1389, to Oct. 1, 1404.

Innocent VII (Cosma Migliorati): Sulmona; Oct. 17 (Nov. 11), 1404, to Nov. 6, 1406.

Gregory XII (Angelo Correr): Venice; Nov. 30 (Dec. 19), 1406, to July 4, 1415, when he voluntarily resigned from the papacy to permit the election of his successor. He died Oct. 18, 1417. (See The Western Schism.)

Martin V (Oddone Colonna): Rome; Nov. 11 (21), 1417, to Feb. 20, 1431.

Eugene IV (Gabriele Condulmer): Venice; Mar. 3 (11), 1431, to Feb. 23, 1447.

Nicholas V (Tommaso Parentucelli): Sarzana; Mar. 6 (19), 1447, to Mar. 24, 1455.

Callistus III (Alfonso Borgia): Jativa (Valencia); Apr. 8 (20), 1455, to Aug. 6, 1458.

Pius II (Enea Silvio Piccolomini): Siena; Aug. 19 (Sept. 3), 1458, to Aug. 15, 1464.

Paul II (Pietro Barbo): Venice; Aug. 30 (Sept. 16), 1464, to July 26, 1471.

Sixtus IV (Francesco della Rovere): Savona; Aug. 9 (25), 1471, to Aug. 12, 1484.

Innocent VIII (Giovanni Battista Cibo): Genoa; Aug. 29 (Sept. 12), 1484, to July 25, 1492.

Alexander VI (Rodrigo Borgia): Jativa (Valencia); Aug. 11 (26), 1492, to Aug. 18, 1503.

Pius III (Francesco Todeschini-Piccolomini): Siena; Sept. 22 (Oct. 1, 8), 1503, to Oct. 18, 1503.

Julius II (Giuliano della Rovere): Savona; Oct. 31 (Nov. 26), 1503, to Feb. 21, 1513.

Leo X (Giovanni de' Medici): Florence; Mar. 9 (19), 1513, to Dec. 1, 1521.

Adrian VI (Adrian Florensz): Utrecht; Jan. 9 (Aug. 31), 1522, to Sept. 14, 1523.

Clement VII (Giulio de' Medici): Florence; Nov. 19 (26), 1523, to Sept. 25, 1534.

Paul III (Alessandro Farnese): Rome; Oct. 13 (Nov. 3), 1534, to Nov. 10, 1549.

Julius III (Giovanni Maria Ciocchi del Monte): Rome; Feb. 7 (22), 1550, to Mar. 23, 1555.

Marcellus II (Marcello Cervini): Montepulciano; Apr. 9 (10), 1555, to May 1, 1555.

Paul IV (Gian Pietro Carafa): Naples; May 23 (26), 1555, to Aug. 18, 1559.

Pius IV (Giovan Angelo de' Medici): Milan; Dec. 25, 1559 (Jan. 6, 1560), to Dec. 9, 1565.

St. Pius V (Antonio-Michele Ghislieri): Bosco (Alexandria); Jan. 7 (17), 1566, to May 1, 1572. Canonized May 22, 1712.

Gregory XIII (Ugo Buoncompagni): Bologna; May 13 (25), 1572, to Apr. 10, 1585.

Sixtus V (Felice Peretti): Grottammare (Ripatransone); Apr. 24 (May 1), 1585, to Aug. 27, 1590.

Urban VII (Giovanni Battista Castagna): Rome; Sept. 15, 1590, to Sept. 27, 1590.

Gregory XIV (Niccolo Sfondrati): Cremona; Dec. 5 (8), 1590, to Oct. 16, 1591.

Innocent IX (Giovanni Antonio Facchinetti): Bologna; Oct. 29 (Nov. 3), 1591, to Dec. 30, 1591.

Clement VIII (Ippolito Aldobrandini): Florence; Jan. 30 (Feb. 9), 1592, to Mar. 3, 1605.

Leo XI (Alessandro de' Medici): Florence; Apr. 1 (10), 1605, to Apr. 27, 1605.

Paul V (Camillo Borghese): Rome; May 16 (29), 1605, to Jan. 28, 1621.

Gregory XV (Alessandro Ludovisi): Bologna; Feb. 9 (14), 1621, to July 8, 1623.

Urban VIII (Maffeo Barberini): Florence; Aug. 6 (Sept. 29), 1623, to July 29, 1644.

Innocent X (Giovanni Battista Pamfili): Rome; Sept. 15 (Oct. 4), 1644, to Jan. 7, 1655.

Alexander VII (Fabio Chigi): Siena; Apr. 7 (18), 1655, to May 22, 1667.

Clement IX (Giulio Rospigliosi): Pistoia; June 20 (26), 1667, to Dec. 9, 1669.

Clement X (Emilio Altieri): Rome; Apr. 29 (May 11), 1670, to July 22, 1676.

Bl. Innocent XI (Benedetto Odescalchi): Como; Sept. 21 (Oct. 4), 1676, to Aug. 12, 1689.

Alexander VIII (Pietro Ottoboni): Venice; Oct. 6 (16), 1689, to Feb. 1, 1691.

Innocent XII (Antonio Pignatelli): Spinazzola; July 12 (15), 1691, to Sept. 27, 1700.

Clement XI (Giovanni Francesco Albani): Urbino; Nov. 23, 30 (Dec. 8), 1700, to Mar. 19, 1721.

Innocent XIII (Michelangelo dei Conti): Rome; May 8 (18), 1721, to Mar. 7, 1724.

Benedict XIII (Pietro Francesco — Vincenzo Maria — Orsini): Gravina (Bari); May 29 (June 4), 1724, to Feb. 21, 1730.

Clement XII (Lorenzo Corsini): Florence; July 12 (16), 1730, to Feb. 6, 1740.

Benedict XIV (Prospero Lambertini): Bologna; Aug. 17 (22), 1740, to May 3, 1758.

Clement XIII (Carlo Rezzonico): Venice; July 6 (16), 1758, to Feb. 2, 1769.

Clement XIV (Giovanni Vincenzo Antonio — Lorenzo — Ganganelli): Rimini; May 19, 28 (June 4), 1769, to Sept. 22, 1774.

Pius VI (Giovanni Angelo Braschi): Cesena; Feb. 15 (22), 1775, to Aug. 29, 1799.

Pius VII (Barnaba — Gregorio — Chiaramonti): Cesena; Mar. 14 (21), 1800, to Aug. 20, 1823.

Leo XII (Annibale della Genga): Genga (Fabriano); Sept. 28 (Oct. 5), 1823, to Feb. 10, 1829.

Pius VIII (Francesco Saverio Castiglioni): Cingoli; Mar. 31 (Apr. 5), 1829, to Nov. 30, 1830.

Gregory XVI (Bartolomeo Alberto — Mauro — Cappellari): Belluno; Feb. 2 (6), 1831, to June 1, 1846.

Pius IX (Giovanni M. Mastai Ferretti): Senigallia; June 16 (21), 1846, to Feb. 7, 1878.

Leo XIII (Gioacchino Pecci): Carpineto (Anagni); Feb. 20 (Mar. 3), 1878, to July 20, 1903.

St. Pius X (Giuseppe Sarto): Riese (Treviso); Aug. 4 (9), 1903, to Aug. 20, 1914. Canonized May 29, 1954.

Benedict XV (Giacomo della Chiesa): Genoa; Sept. 3 (6), 1914, to Jan. 22, 1922.

Pius XI (Achille Ratti): Desio (Milan); Feb. 6 (12), 1922, to Feb. 10, 1939.

Pius XII (Eugenio Pacelli): Rome; Mar. 2 (12), 1939, to Oct. 9, 1958.

John XXIII (Angelo Giuseppe Roncalli): Sotto il Monte (Bergamo); Oct. 28 (Nov. 4). 1958, to June 3, 1963.

Paul VI (Giovanni Battista Montini): Concessio (Brescia); June 21 (June 30), 1963, to Aug. 6, 1978.

John Paul I (Albino Luciani): Forno di Canale (Belluno); Aug. 26 (Sept. 3), 1978, to Sept. 28, 1978.

John Paul II (Karol Wojtyla): Wadowice, Poland; Oct. 16 (22), 1978.

## ANTIPOPES

*This list of men who claimed or exercised the papal office in an uncanonical manner includes names, birthplaces and dates of alleged reigns.*

Source: "Annuario Pontificio."

St. Hippolytus: Rome; 217-235; was reconciled before his death.

Novatian: Rome; 251.

Felix II: Rome; 355 to Nov. 22, 365.

Ursinus: 366-367.

Eulalius: Dec. 27 or 29, 418, to 419.

Lawrence: 498; 501-505.

Dioscorus: Alexandria; Sept. 22, 530, to Oct. 14, 530.

Theodore: ended alleged reign, 687.

Paschal: ended alleged reign, 687.

Constantine: Nepi; June 28 (July 5), 767, to 769.

Philip: July 31, 768; retired to his monastery on the same day.

John: ended alleged reign, Jan., 844.

Anastasius: Aug., 855, to Sept., 855; d. 880.

Christopher: Rome; July or Sept., 903, to Jan., 904.

Boniface VII: Rome; June, 974, to July, 974; Aug., 984, to July, 985.

John XVI: Rossano; Apr., 997, to Feb., 998.

Gregory: ended alleged reign, 1012.

Benedict X: Rome; Apr. 5, 1058, to Jan. 24, 1059.

Honorius II: Verona; Oct. 28, 1061, to 1072.

Clement III: Parma; June 25, 1080 (Mar. 24, 1084), to Sept. 8, 1100.

Theodoric: ended alleged reign, 1100; d. 1102.

Albert: ended alleged reign, 1102.

Sylvester IV: Rome; Nov. 18, 1105, to 1111.

Gregory VIII: France; Mar. 8, 1118, to 1121.

Celestine II: Rome; ended alleged reign, Dec., 1124.

Anacletus II: Rome; Feb. 14 (23), 1130, to Jan. 25, 1138.

Victor IV: Mar., 1138, to May 29, 1138; submitted to Pope Innocent II.

Victor IV: Montecelio; Sept. 7 (Oct. 4), 1159, to Apr. 20, 1164; he did not recognize his predecessor (Victor IV, above).

Paschal III: Apr. 22 (26), 1164, to Sept. 20, 1168.

Callistus III: Arezzo; Sept., 1168, to Aug. 29, 1178; submitted to Pope Alexander III.

Innocent III: Sezze; Sept. 29, 1179, to 1180.

Nicholas V: Corvaro (Rieti); May 12 (22), 1328, to Aug. 25, 1330; d. Oct. 16, 1333.

*Four antipopes of the Western Schism:*

Clement VII: Sept. 20 (Oct. 31), 1378, to Sept. 16, 1394.

Benedict XIII: Aragon; Sept. 28 (Oct. 11), 1394, to May 23, 1423.

Alexander V: Crete; June 26 (July 7), 1409, to May 3, 1410.

John XXIII: Naples; May 17 (25), 1410, to May 29, 1415.

Felix V: Savoy; Nov. 5, 1439 (July 24, 1440), to April 7, 1449; d. 1451.

## AVIGNON PAPACY

Avignon was the residence of a series of French popes from Clement V to Gregory XI (1309-77). Prominent in the period were power struggles over the mixed interests of Church and state with the rulers of France (Philip IV, John II), Bavaria (Lewis IV), England (Edward III); factionalism of French and Italian churchmen; political as well as ecclesiastical turmoil in Italy, a factor of significance in prolonging the stay of popes in Avignon. Despite some positive achievements, the Avignon papacy was a prologue to the Western Schism which began in 1378.

## WESTERN SCHISM

The Western Schism was a confused state of affairs which divided Christendom into two and then three papal obediences from 1378 to 1417.

It occurred some 50 years after Marsilius theorized that a general (not ecumenical) council of bishops and other persons was superior to a pope and nearly 30 years before the Council of Florence stated definitively that no kind of council had such authority.

It was a period of disaster preceding the even more disastrous period of the Reformation.

Urban VI, following transfer to Rome of the 70-year papal residence at Avignon, was elected pope Apr. 8, 1378, and reigned until his death in 1389. He was succeeded by Boniface IX (1389-1404), Innocent VII (1404-1406) and Gregory XII (1406-1415). These four are considered the legitimate popes of the period.

Some of the cardinals who chose Urban pope, dissatisfied with his conduct of the office, declared that his election was invalid. They proceeded to elect Clement VII, who claimed the papacy from 1378 to 1394. He was succeeded by Benedict XIII.

Prelates seeking to end the state of divided papal loyalties convoked the Council of Pisa which, without authority, found Gregory XII and Benedict XIII, in absentia, guilty on 30-odd charges of schism and heresy, deposed them, and elected a third claimant to the papacy, Alexander V (1409-1410). He was succeeded by John XXIII (1410-1415).

The schism was ended by the Council of Constance (1414-1418). This council, although originally called into session in an irregular manner, acquired authority after being convoked by Gregory XII in 1415. In its early irregular phase, it deposed John XXIII whose election to the papacy was uncanonical anyway. After being formally convoked, it accepted the abdication of Gregory in 1415 and dismissed the claims of Benedict XIII two years later, thus clearing the way for the election of Martin V on Nov. 11, 1417. The Council of Constance also rejected the theories of John Wycliff and condemned John Hus as a heretic.

---

## THE AMERICAN COLLEGE, LOUVAIN

The American College was founded by the bishops of the United States in 1857 as a residence and house of formation for U.S. seminarians and graduate students pursuing courses in theology and related subjects at The Catholic Universities of Leuven and Louvain-la-Neuve (dating from 1425) in Belgium.

The college is administered by an American rector and staff, and operates under the auspices of a special committee of the National Conference of Catholic Bishops. Bishop Eusebius J. Beltran of Tulsa is chairman of the committee. The present rector, the 11th, is Father John J. Costanzo of Pueblo, Colo. The address is: The American College, University of Louvain, Naamsestraat 100, 3000 Leuven, Belgium.

The current enrollment of The American College includes students from more than 40 dioceses in the U.S., Canada, Europe and the Third World countries.

# TWENTIETH CENTURY POPES

## LEO XIII

Leo XIII (Gioacchino Vincenzo Pecci) was born May 2, 1810, in Carpineto, Italy. Although all but three years of his life and pontificate were of the 19th century, his influence extended well into the 20th century.

He was educated at the Jesuit college in Viterbo, the Roman College, the Academy of Noble Ecclesiastics, and the University of the Sapienza. He was ordained to the priesthood in 1837.

He served as an apostolic delegate to two States of the Church, Benevento from 1838 to 1841 and Perugia in 1841 and 1842. Ordained titular archbishop of Damietta, he was papal nuncio to Belgium from January, 1843, until May, 1846; in the post, he had controversial relations with the government over education issues and acquired his first significant experience of industrialized society.

He was archbishop of Perugia from 1846 to 1878. He became a cardinal in 1853 and chamberlain of the Roman Curia in 1877. He was elected to the papacy Feb. 20, 1878. He died July 20, 1903.

**Canonizations:** He canonized 18 saints and beatified a group of English martyrs.

**Church Administration:** He established 300 new dioceses and vicariates; restored the hierarchy in Scotland, set up an English, as contrasted with the Portuguese, hierarchy in India; approved the action of the Congregation for the Propagation of the Faith in reorganizing missions in China.

**Encyclicals:** He issued 86 encyclicals, on subjects ranging from devotional to social. In the former category were *Annum Sacrum,* on the Sacred Heart, in 1899, and 11 letters on Mary and the Rosary.

**Interfaith Relations:** He was unsuccessful in unity overtures made to Orthodox and Slavic Churches. He declared Anglican orders invalid in the apostolic bull *Apostolicae Curae* Sept. 13, 1896.

**International Relations:** Leo was frustrated in seeking solutions to the Roman Question arising from the seizure of church lands by the Kingdom of Italy in 1870. He also faced anticlerical situations in Belgium and France and in the Kulturkampf policies of Bismarck in Germany.

**Social Questions:** Much of Leo's influence stemmed from social doctrine stated in numerous encyclicals, concerning liberalism, liberty, the divine origin of authority; socialism, in *Quod Apostolici Muneris,* 1878; the Christian concept of the family, in *Arcanum,* 1880; socialism and economic liberalism, relations between capital and labor, in *Rerum Novarum,* 1891. Two of his social encyclicals were against the African slave trade.

**Studies:** In the encyclical *Aeterni Patris* of Aug. 4, 1879, he ordered a renewal of philosophical and theological studies in seminaries along scholastic, and especially Thomistic, lines, to counteract influential trends of liberalism and Modernism. He issued guidelines for biblical exegesis in *Providentissimus Deus* Nov. 18, 1893, and established the Pontifical Biblical Commission in 1902.

In other actions affecting scholarship and study, he opened the Vatican Archives to scholars in 1883 and established the Vatican Observatory.

**United States:** He authorized establishment of the apostolic delegation in Washington, D.C. Jan. 24, 1893. He refused to issue a condemnation of the Knights of Labor. With a document entitled *Testem Benevolentiae,* he eased resolution of questions concerning what was called an American heresy in 1899.

## ST. PIUS X

St. Pius X (Giuseppe Melchiorre Sarto) was born in 1835 in Riese, Italy.

Educated at the college of Castelfranco and the seminary at Padua, he was ordained to the priesthood Sept. 18, 1858. He served as a curate in Trombolo for nine years before beginning an eight-year pastorate at Salzano. He was chancellor of the Treviso diocese from November, 1875, and bishop of Mantua from 1884 until 1893. He was cardinal-patriarch of Venice from that year until his election to the papacy by the conclave held from July 31 to Aug. 4, 1903.

**Aims:** Pius' principal objectives as pope were "to restore all things in Christ, in order that Christ may be all and in all," and "to teach (and defend) Christian truth and law."

**Canonizations, Encyclicals:** He canonized four saints and issued 16 encyclicals. One of the encyclicals was issued in commemoration of the 50th anniversary of the proclamation of the dogma of the Immaculate Conception of Mary.

**Catechetics:** He introduced a whole new era of religious instruction and formation with the encyclical *Acerbo Nimis* of Apr. 15, 1905, in which he called for vigor in establishing and conducting parochial programs of the Confraternity of Christian Doctrine.

**Catholic Action:** He outlined the role of official Catholic Action in two encyclicals in 1905 and 1906. Favoring organized action by Catholics themselves, he had serious reservations about interconfessional collaboration.

He stoutly maintained claims to papal rights in the anticlerical climate of Italy. He authorized bishops to relax prohibitions against participation by Catholics in some Italian elections.

**Church Administration:** With the motu proprio *Arduum Sane* of Mar. 19, 1904, he inaugurated the work which resulted in the Code of Canon Law; the code was completed in 1917 and went into effect in the following year. He reorganized and strengthened the Roman Curia with the apostolic constitution *Sapienti Consilio* of June 29, 1908. While promoting the expansion of missionary work, he removed from the jurisdiction of the Congregation for the Propagation of the Faith the Church in the United States, Canada, Newfoundland, England, Ireland, Holland and Luxembourg.

**International Relations:** He ended traditional

prerogatives of Catholic governments with respect to papal elections, in 1904. He opposed anti-Church and anticlerical actions in several countries: Bolivia in 1905, because of anti-religious legislation; France in 1906, for its 1901 action in annulling its concordat with the Holy See, and for the 1905 Law of Separation by which it decreed separation of Church and state, ordered the confiscation of church property, and blocked religious education and the activities of religious orders; Portugal in 1911, for the separation of Church and state and repressive measures which resulted in persecution later.

In 1912 he called on the bishops of Brazil to work for the improvement of conditions among Indians.

**Liturgy:** "The Pope of the Eucharist," he strongly recommended the frequent reception of Holy Communion in a decree dated Dec. 20, 1905; in another decree, *Quam Singulari,* of Aug. 8, 1910, he called for the early reception of the sacrament by children. He initiated measures for liturgical reform with new norms for sacred music and the start of work on revision of the *Breviary* for recitation of the Divine Office.

**Modernism:** Pius was a vigorous opponent of "the synthesis of all heresies," which threatened the integrity of doctrine through its influence in philosophy, theology and biblical exegesis. In opposition, he condemned 65 of its propositions as erroneous in the decree *Lamentabili* July 3, 1907; issued the encyclical *Pascendi* in the same vein Sept. 8, 1907; backed both of these with censures; and published the Oath against Modernism in September, 1910, to be taken by all the clergy. Ecclesiastical studies suffered to some extent from these actions, necessary as they were at the time.

Pius followed the lead of Leo XIII in promoting the study of scholastic philosophy. He established the Pontifical Biblical Institute May 7, 1909.

His death, Aug. 20, 1914, was hastened by the outbreak of World War I. He was beatified in 1951 and canonized May 29, 1954. His feast is observed Aug. 21.

## BENEDICT XV

Benedict XV (Giacomo della Chiesa) was born Nov. 21, 1854, in Pegli, Italy.

He was educated at the Royal University of Genoa and Gregorian University in Rome. He was ordained to the priesthood Dec. 21, 1878.

He served in the papal diplomatic corps from 1882 to 1907; as secretary to the nuncio to Spain from 1882 to 1887, as secretary to the papal secretary of state from 1887, and as undersecretary from 1901.

He was ordained archbishop of Bologna Dec. 22, 1907, and spent four years completing a pastoral visitation there. He was made a cardinal just three months before being elected to the papacy Sept. 3, 1914. He died Jan. 22, 1922. Two key efforts of his pontificate were for peace and the relief of human suffering caused by World War I.

**Canonizations:** Benedict canonized three saints; one of them was Joan of Arc.

**Canon Law:** He published the Code of Canon Law, developed by the commission set up by St.

Pius X, June 28, 1917; it went into effect the following year.

**Curia:** He made great changes in the personnel of the Curia. He established the Congregation for the Oriental Churches May 1, 1917, and founded the Pontifical Oriental Institute in Rome later in the year.

**Encyclicals:** He issued 12 encyclicals. Peace was the theme of three of them. In another, published two years after the cessation of hostilities, he wrote about child victims of the war. He followed the lead of Leo XIII in *Spiritus Paraclitus,* Sept. 15, 1920, on biblical studies.

**International Relations:** He was largely frustrated on the international level because of the events and attitudes of the war period, but the number of diplomats accredited to the Vatican nearly doubled, from 14 to 26, between the time of his accession to the papacy and his death.

**Peace Efforts:** Benedict's stance in the war was one of absolute impartiality but not of uninterested neutrality. Because he would not take sides, he was suspected by both sides and the seven-point peace plan he offered to all belligerents Aug. 1, 1917, was turned down. The points of the plan were: recognition of the moral force of right; disarmament; acceptance of arbitration in cases of dispute; guarantee of freedom of the seas; renunciation of war indemnities; evacuation and restoration of occupied territories; examination of territorial claims in dispute.

**Relief Efforts:** Benedict assumed personal charge of Vatican relief efforts during the war. He set up an international missing persons bureau for contacts between prisoners and their families, but was forced to close it because of the suspicion of warring nations that it was a front for espionage operations. He persuaded the Swiss government to admit into the country military victims of tuberculosis.

**Roman Question:** Benedict arranged a meeting of Benito Mussolini and the papal secretary of state, which marked the first step toward final settlement of the question in 1929.

## PIUS XI

Pius XI (Ambrogio Damiano Achille Ratti) was born May 31, 1857, in Desio, Italy.

Educated at seminaries in Seviso and Milan, and at the Lombard College, Gregorian University and Academy of St. Thomas in Rome, he was ordained to the priesthood in 1879.

He taught at the major seminary of Milan from 1882 to 1888. Appointed to the staff of the Ambrosian Library in 1888, he remained there until 1911, acquiring a reputation for publishing works on palaeography and serving as director from 1907 to 1911. He then moved to the Vatican Library, of which he was prefect from 1914 to 1918. In 1919, he was named apostolic visitor to Poland in April, nuncio in June, and was made titular archbishop of Lepanto Oct. 28. He was made archbishop of Milan and cardinal June 13, 1921, before being elected to the papacy Feb. 6, 1922. He died Feb. 10, 1939.

**Aim:** The objective of his pontificate, as stated in the encyclical *Ubi Arcano,* Dec. 23, 1922, was to establish the reign and peace of Christ in society.

**Canonizations:** He canonized 34 saints, including the Jesuit Martyrs of North America, and conferred the title of Doctor of the Church on Sts. Peter Canisius, John of the Cross, Robert Bellarmine and Albertus Magnus.

**Eastern Churches:** He called for better understanding of the Eastern Churches in the encyclical *Rerum Orientalium* of Sept. 8, 1928, and developed facilities for the training of Eastern-Rite priests. He inaugurated steps for the codification of Eastern-Church law in 1929. In 1935 he made Syrian Patriarch Tappouni a cardinal.

**Encyclicals:** His first encyclical, *Ubi Arcano,* in addition to stating the aims of his pontificate, blueprinted Catholic Action and called for its development throughout the Church. In *Quas Primas,* Dec. 11, 1925, he established the feast of Christ the King for universal observance. Subjects of some of his other encyclicals were: Christian education, in *Rappresentanti in Terra,* Dec. 31, 1929; Christian marriage, in *Casti Connubii,* Dec. 31, 1930; social conditions and pressure for social change in line with the teaching in *Rerum Novarum,* in *Quadragesimo Anno,* May 15, 1931; atheistic Communism, in *Divini Redemptoris,* Mar. 19, 1937; the priesthood, in *Ad Catholici Sacerdotii,* Dec. 20, 1935.

**Missions:** Following the lead of Benedict XV, Pius called for the training of native clergy in the pattern of their own respective cultures, and promoted missionary developments in various ways. He ordained six native bishops for China in 1926, one for Japan in 1927, and others for regions of Asia, China and India in 1933. He placed the first 40 mission dioceses under native bishops, saw the number of native priests increase from about 2,600 to more than 7,000 and the number of Catholics in missionary areas more than double from nine million.

In the apostolic constitution *Deus Scientiarum Dominus* of May 24, 1931, he ordered the introduction of missiology into theology courses.

**Interfaith Relations:** Pius was negative to the ecumenical movement among Protestants but approved the Malines Conversations, 1921 to 1926, between Anglicans and Catholics.

**International Relations:** Relations with the Mussolini government deteriorated from 1931 on, as indicated in the encyclical *Non Abbiamo Bisogno,* when the regime took steps to curb liberties and activities of the Church; they turned critical in 1938 with the emergence of racist policies. Relations deteriorated also in Germany from 1933 on, resulting finally in condemnation of the Nazis in the encyclical *Mit Brennender Sorge,* March, 1937. Pius sparked a revival of the Church in France by encouraging Catholics to work within the democratic framework of the Republic rather than foment trouble over restoration of a monarchy. Pius was powerless to influence developments related to the civil war which erupted in Spain in July, 1936, sporadic persecution and repression by the Calles regime in Mexico, and systematic persecution of the Church in the Soviet

Union. Many of the 10 concordats and two agreements reached with European countries after World War I became casualties of World War II.

**Roman Question:** Pius negotiated for two and one-half years with the Italian government to settle the Roman Question by means of the Lateran Agreement of 1929. The agreement provided independent status for the State of Vatican City; made Catholicism the official religion of Italy, with pastoral and educational freedom and state recognition of Catholic marriages, religious orders and societies; and provided a financial payment to the Vatican for expropriation of the former States of the Church.

## PIUS XII

Pius XII (Eugenio Maria Giovanni Pacelli) was born Mar. 2, 1876, in Rome.

Educated at the Gregorian University and the Lateran University, in Rome, he was ordained to the priesthood Apr. 2, 1899.

He entered the Vatican diplomatic service in 1901, worked on the codification of canon law, and was appointed secretary of the Congregation for Ecclesiastical Affairs in 1914. Three years later he was ordained titular archbishop of Sardis and made apostolic nuncio to Bavaria. He was nuncio to Germany from 1920 to 1929, when he was made a cardinal, and took office as papal secretary of state in the following year. His diplomatic negotiations resulted in concordats between the Vatican and Bavaria (1924), Prussia (1929), Baden (1932), Austria and the German Republic (1933). He took part in negotiations which led to settlement of the Roman Question in 1929.

He was elected to the papacy Mar. 2, 1939. He died Oct. 9, 1958, at Castel Gandolfo after the 12th longest pontificate in history.

**Canonizations:** He canonized 34 saints, including Mother Frances X. Cabrini, the first U.S. citizen-Saint.

**Cardinals:** He raised 56 prelates to the rank of cardinal in two consistories held in 1946 and 1953. There were 57 cardinals at the time of his death.

**Church Organization and Missions:** He increased the number of dioceses from 1,696 to 2,048. He established native hierarchies in China (1946), Burma (1955) and parts of Africa, and extended the native structure of the Church in India. He ordained the first black bishop for Africa.

**Communism:** In addition to opposing and condemning Communism on numerous occasions, he decreed in 1949 the penalty of excommunication for all Catholics holding formal and willing allegiance to the Communist Party and its policies. During his reign the Church was persecuted in some 15 countries which fell under communist domination.

**Doctrine and Liturgy:** He proclaimed the dogma of the Assumption of the Blessed Virgin Mary Nov. 1, 1950 (apostolic constitution, *Munificentissimus Deus.*)

In various encyclicals and other enactments, he provided background for the *aggiornamento* introduced by his successor, John XXIII: by his formulations of doctrine and practice regarding the

Mystical Body of Christ, the liturgy, sacred music and biblical studies; by the revision of the Rites of Holy Week; by initiation of the work which led to the calendar-missal-breviary reform ordered into effect Jan. 1, 1961; by the first of several modifications of the Eucharistic fast; by extending the time of Mass to the evening. He instituted the feasts of Mary, Queen, and of St. Joseph the Worker, and clarified teaching concerning devotion to the Sacred Heart.

His 41 encyclicals and nearly 1,000 public addresses made Pius one of the greatest teaching popes. His concern in all his communications was to deal with specific points at issue and/or to bring Christian principles to bear on contemporary world problems.

**Peace Efforts:** Before the start of World War II, he tried unsuccessfully to get the contending nations — Germany and Poland, France and Italy — to settle their differences peaceably. During the war, he offered his services to mediate the widened conflict, spoke out against the horrors of war and the suffering it caused, mobilized relief work for its victims, proposed a five-point program for peace in Christmas messages from 1939 to 1942, and secured a generally open status for the city of Rome. After the war, he endorsed the principles and intent of the United Nations and continued efforts for peace.

**United States:** Pius appointed more than 200 of the 265 American bishops resident in the U.S. and abroad in 1958, erected 27 dioceses in this country, and raised seven dioceses to archiepiscopal rank.

## JOHN XXIII

John XXIII (Angelo Roncalli) was born Nov. 25, 1881, at Sotte il Monte, Italy.

He was educated at the seminary of the Bergamo diocese and the Pontifical Seminary in Rome, where he was ordained to the priesthood Aug. 10, 1904.

He spent the first nine or 10 years of his priesthood as secretary to the bishop of Bergamo and as an instructor in the seminary there. He served as a medic and chaplain in the Italian army during World War I. Afterwards, he resumed duties in his own diocese until he was called to Rome in 1921 for work with the Society for the Propagation of the Faith.

He began diplomatic service in 1925 as titular archbishop of Areopolis and apostolic visitor to Bulgaria. A succession of offices followed: apostolic delegate to Bulgaria (1931-1935); titular archbishop of Mesembria, apostolic delegate to Turkey and Greece, administrator of the Latin vicariate apostolic of Istanbul (1935-1944); apostolic nuncio to France (1944-1953). On these missions, he was engaged in delicate negotiations involving Roman, Eastern-Rite and Orthodox relations; the needs of people suffering from the consequences of World War II; and unsettling suspicions arising from wartime conditions.

He was made a cardinal Jan. 12, 1953, and three days later was appointed patriarch of Venice, the position he held until his election to the papacy

Oct. 28, 1958. He died of stomach cancer June 3, 1963.

John was a strong and vigorous pope whose influence far outmeasured both his age and the shortness of his time in the papacy.

**Second Vatican Council:** John announced Jan. 25, 1959, his intention of convoking the 21st ecumenical council in history to renew life in the Church, to reform its structures and institutions, and to explore ways and means of promoting unity among Christians. Through the council, which completed its work two and one-half years after his death, he ushered in a new era in the history of the Church.

**Canon Law:** He established a commission Mar. 28, 1963, for revision of the Code of Canon Law. The revised Code was promulgated in 1983.

**Canonizations:** He canonized 10 saints and beatified Mother Elizabeth Ann Seton, the first native of the U.S. ever so honored. He named St. Lawrence of Brindisi a Doctor of the Church.

**Cardinals:** He created 52 cardinals in five consistories, raising membership of the College of Cardinals above the traditional number of 70; at one time in 1962, the membership was 87. He made the college more international in representation than it had ever been, appointing the first cardinals from the Philippines, Japan and Africa. He ordered episcopal ordination for all cardinals. He relieved the suburban bishops of Rome of ordinary jurisdiction over their dioceses so they might devote all their time to business of the Roman Curia.

**Eastern Rites:** He made all Eastern-Rite patriarchs members of the Congregation for the Oriental Churches.

**Ecumenism:** He assigned to the Second Vatican Council the task of finding ways and means of promoting unity among Christians. He established the Vatican Secretariat for Promoting Christian Unity June 5, 1960. He showed his desire for more cordial relations with the Orthodox by sending personal representatives to visit Patriarch Athenagoras I June 27, 1961; approved a mission of five delegates to the General Assembly of the World Council of Churches which met in New Delhi, India, in November, 1961; removed a number of pejorative references to Jews in the Roman-Rite liturgy for Good Friday.

**Encyclicals:** Of the eight encyclicals he issued, the two outstanding ones were *Mater et Magistra* ("Christianity and Social Progress"), in which he recapitulated, updated and extended the social doctrine stated earlier by Leo XIII and Pius XI; and *Pacem in Terris* ("Peace on Earth"), the first encyclical ever addressed to all men of good will as well as to Catholics, on the natural-law principles of peace.

**Liturgy:** In forwarding liturgical reforms already begun by Pius XII, he ordered a calendar-missal-breviary reform into effect Jan. 1, 1961. He authorized the use of vernacular languages in the administration of the sacraments and approved giving Holy Communion to the sick in afternoon hours. He selected the liturgy as the first topic of major discussion by the Second Vatican Council.

**Missions:** He issued an encyclical on the mis

140 20th Century Popes

sionary activity of the Church; established native hierarchies in Indonesia, Vietnam and Korea; and called on North American superiors of religious institutes to have one-tenth of their members assigned to work in Latin America by 1971.

**Peace:** John spoke and used his moral influence for peace in 1961 when tension developed over Berlin, in 1962 during the Algerian revolt from France, and later the same year in the Cuban missile crisis. His efforts were singled out for honor by the Balzan Peace Foundation. In 1963, he was posthumously awarded the U.S. Presidential Medal of Freedom.

## PAUL VI

Paul VI (Giovanni Battista Montini) was born Sept. 26, 1897, at Concesio in northern Italy.

Educated at Brescia, he was ordained to the priesthood May 29, 1920. He pursued additional studies at the Pontifical Academy for Noble Ecclesiastics and the Pontifical Gregorian University. In 1924 he began 30 years of service in the Secretariat of State; as undersecretary from 1937 until 1954, he was closely associated with Pius XII and was heavily engaged in organizing informational and relief services during and after World War II.

He was ordained archbishop of Milan Dec. 12, 1954, and was inducted into the College of Cardinals Dec. 15, 1958. He was elected to the papacy June 21, 1963, two days after the conclave began. He died of a heart attack Aug. 6, 1978.

**Second Vatican Council:** He reconvened the Second Vatican Council after the death of John XXIII, presided over its second, third and fourth sessions, formally promulgated the 16 documents it produced, and devoted the whole of his pontificate to the task of putting them into effect throughout the Church. The main thrust of his pontificate — in a milieu of cultural and other changes in the Church and the world — was toward institutionalization and control of the authentic trends articulated and set in motion by the council.

**Canonizations:** He canonized more saints, 84, than any other pope. They included groups of 22 Ugandan martyrs and 40 martyrs of England and Wales, as well as two Americans — Elizabeth Ann Bayley Seton and John Nepomucene Neumann.

**Cardinals:** He created more cardinals, 137, than any other pope and gave the Sacred College a more international complexion than it ever had before. He limited participation in papal elections to 120 cardinals under the age of 80.

**Collegiality:** He established the Synod of Bishops in 1965 and called it into session five times. He stimulated the formation and operation of regional conferences of bishops, and of consultative bodies on other levels.

**Creed and Holy Year:** On June 30, 1968, he issued a Creed of the People of God in conjunction with the celebration of a Year of Faith. He proclaimed and led the observance of a Holy Year from Christmas Eve of 1974 to Christmas Eve of 1975.

**Diplomacy:** He met with many world leaders, including Soviet President Nikolai Podgorny in

1967, Marshal Tito of Yugoslavia in 1971 and President Nicolas Ceausescu of Rumania in 1973. He worked constantly to reduce tension between the Church and the intransigent regimes of Eastern European countries by means of a detente type of policy called Ostpolitik. He agreed to significant revisions of the Vatican's concordat with Spain and initiated efforts to revise the concordat with Italy. More then 40 countries established diplomatic relations with the Vatican during his pontificate.

**Encyclicals:** He issued seven encyclicals, three of which are the best known. In *Populorum Progressio* ("Development of Peoples") he appealed to wealthy countries to take "concrete action" to promote human development and to remedy imbalances between richer and poorer nations; this encyclical, coupled with other documents and related actions, launched the Church into a new depth of involvement as a public advocate for human rights and for humanizing social, political and economic policies. In *Sacerdotalis Caelibatus* ("Priestly Celibacy") he reaffirmed the strict observance of priestly celibacy throughout the Western Church. In *Humanae Vitae* ("Of Human Life") he condemned abortion, sterilization and artificial birth control, in line with traditional teaching and in "defense of life, the gift of God, the glory of the family, the strength of the people."

**Interfaith Relations:** He initiated formal consultation and informal dialogue on international and national levels between Catholics and non-Catholics — Orthodox, Anglicans, Protestants, Jews, Moslems, Buddhists, Hindus, and unbelievers. He and Greek Orthodox Patriarch Athenagoras I of Constantinople nullified in 1965 the mutual excommunications imposed by their respective churches in 1054.

**Liturgy:** He carried out the most extensive liturgical reform in history, involving a new Order of the Mass effective in 1969, a revised church calendar in 1970, revisions and translations into vernacular languages of all sacramental rites and other liturgical texts.

**Ministries:** He authorized the restoration of the permanent diaconate in the Roman Rite and the establishment of new ministries of lay persons.

**Peace:** In 1968, he instituted the annual observance of a World Day of Peace on New Year's Day as a means of addressing a message of peace to all the world's political leaders and the peoples of all nations. The most dramatic of his many appeals for peace and efforts to ease international tensions was his plea for "No more war!" before the United Nations Oct. 4, 1965.

**Pilgrimages:** A "Pilgrim Pope," he made pastoral visits to the Holy Land and India in 1964, the United Nations and New York City in 1965, Portugal and Turkey in 1967, Colombia in 1968, Switzerland and Uganda in 1969, and Asia, Pacific islands and Australia in 1970. While in Manila in 1970, he was stabbed by a Bolivian artist who made an attempt on his life.

**Roman Curia:** He reorganized the central administrative organs of the Church in line with provisions of the apostolic constitution, *Regimini Ecclesiae Universae*, streamlining procedures for more effective service and giving the agencies a more international perspective by drawing officials and consultors from all over the world. He also instituted a number of new commissions and other bodies. Coupled with curial reorganization was a simplification of papal ceremonies.

## JOHN PAUL I

John Paul I (Albino Luciani) was born Oct. 17, 1912, in Forno di Canale (now Canale d'Agordo) in northern Italy.

Educated at the minor seminary in Feltre and the major seminary of the Diocese of Belluno, he was ordained to the priesthood July 7, 1935. He pursued further studies at the Pontifical Gregorian University in Rome and was awarded a doctorate in theology. From 1937 to 1947 he was vice rector of the Belluno seminary, where he taught dogmatic and moral theology, canon law and sacred art. He was appointed vicar general of

his diocese in 1947 and served as director of catechetics.

Ordained bishop of Vittorio Veneto Dec. 27, 1958, he attended all sessions of the Second Vatican Council, participated in three assemblies of the Synod of Bishops (1971, 1974 and 1977), and was vice president of the Italian Bishops' Conference from 1972 to 1975.

He was appointed archbishop and patriarch of Venice Dec. 15, 1969, and was inducted into the College of Cardinals Mar. 5, 1973.

He was elected to the papacy Aug. 26, 1978, on the fourth ballot cast by the 111 cardinals participating in the largest and one of the shortest conclaves in history. The quickness of his election was matched by the brevity of his pontificate of 33 days, during which he delivered 19 addresses. He died of a heart attack Sept. 28, 1978.

## JOHN PAUL II

See separate entry.

## CANONIZATIONS BY LEO XIII AND HIS SUCCESSORS

Canonization is an infallible declaration by the pope that a person who suffered martyrdom and/or practiced Christian virtue to a heroic degree is in glory with God in heaven and is worthy of public honor by the universal Church and of imitation by the faithful.

(See Canonization entry in Glossary.)

### Leo XIII
(1878-1903)

**1881:** Clare of Montefalco, virgin (d. 1308); John Baptist de Rossi, priest (1698-1764); Lawrence of Brindisi, doctor (d. 1619).

**1883:** Benedict J. Labre (1748-1783).

**1888:** Seven Holy Founders of the Servite Order; Peter Claver, priest (1581-1654); John Berchmans (1599-1621); Alphonsus Rodriguez, lay brother (1531-1617).

**1897:** Anthony M. Zaccaria, founder of Barnabites (1502-1539); Peter Fourier, co-founder of Augustinian Canonesses of Our Lady (1565-1640).

**1900:** John Baptist de La Salle, founder of Christian Brothers (1651-1719); Rita of Cascia (1381-1457).

### St. Pius X
(1903-1914)

**1904:** Alexander Sauli, bishop (1534-1593); Gerard Majella, lay brother (1725-1755).

**1909:** Joseph Oriol, priest (1650-1702); Clement M. Hofbauer, priest (1751-1820).

### Benedict XV
(1914-1922)

**1920:** Gabriel of the Sorrowful Mother (1838-1862); Margaret Mary Alacoque, virgin (1647-1690); Joan of Arc, virgin (1412-1431).

### Pius XI
(1922-1939)

**1925:** Therese of Lisieux, virgin (1873-1897); Peter Canisius, doctor (1521-1597); Mary Magdalen

Postel, foundress of Sisterhood of Christian Schools (1756-1846); Mary Magdalen Sophie Barat, foundress of Society of the Sacred Heart (1779-1865); John Eudes, founder of Eudist Fathers (1601-1680); John Baptist Vianney (Curé of Ars), priest (1786-1859).

**1930:** Lucy Filippini, virgin (1672-1732); Catherine Thomas, virgin (1533-1574); Jesuit North American Martyrs (see Index); Robert Bellarmine, bishop-doctor (1542-1621); Theophilus of Corte, priest (1676-1740).

**1931:** Albert the Great, bishop-doctor (1206-1280) (equivalent canonization).

**1933:** Andrew Fournet, priest (1752-1834); Bernadette Soubirous, virgin (1844-1879).

**1934:** Joan Antida Thouret, foundress of Sisters of Charity of St. Joan Antida (1765-1826); Mary Michaeli, foundress of Institute of Handmaids of the Blessed Sacrament (1809-1865); Louise de Marillac, foundress of Sisters of Charity (1591-1660); Joseph Benedict Cottolengo, priest (1786-1842); Pompilius M. Pirotti, priest (1710-1756); Teresa Margaret Redi, virgin (1747-1770); John Bosco, founder of Salesians (1815-1888); Conrad of Parzham, lay brother (1818-1894).

**1935:** John Fisher, bishop-martyr (1469-1535); Thomas More, martyr (1478-1535).

**1938:** Andrew Bobola, martyr (1592-1657); John Leonardi, founder of Clerics Regular of the Mother of God (c. 1550-1609); Salvatore of Horta, lay brother (1520-1567).

### Pius XII
(1939-1958)

**1940:** Gemma Galgani, virgin (1878-1903); Mary Euphrasia Pelletier, foundress of Good Shepherd Sisters (1796-1868).

**1943:** Margaret of Hungary, virgin (d. 1270) (equivalent canonization).

**1946:** Frances Xavier Cabrini, foundress of Missionary Sisters of the Sacred Heart (1850-1917).

**1947:** Nicholas of Flue, hermit (1417-1487); John of Britto, martyr (1647-1693); Bernard Realini, priest (1530-1616); Joseph Cafasso, priest (1811-1860); Michael Garicoits, founder of Auxiliary Priests of the Sacred Heart (1797-1863); Jeanne Elizabeth des Ages, cofoundress of Daughters of the Cross (1773-1838); Louis Marie Grignon de Montfort, founder of Montfort Fathers (1673-1716); Catherine Laboure, virgin (1806-1876).

**1949:** Jeanne de Lestonnac, foundress of Religious of Notre Dame of Bordeaux (1556-1640); Maria Josepha Rossello, foundress of Daughters of Our Lady of Pity (1811-1880).

**1950:** Emily de Rodat, foundress of Congregation of the Holy Family of Villefranche (1787-1852); Anthony Mary Claret, bishop, founder of Claretians (1807-1870); Bartolomea Capitanio (1807-1833) and Vincenza Gerosa (1784-1847), foundresses of Sisters of Charity of Lovere; Jeanne de Valois, foundress of Annonciades of Bourges (1461-1504); Vincenzo M. Strambi, bishop (1745-1824); Maria Goretti, virgin-martyr (1890-1902); Mariana Paredes of Jesus, virgin (1618-1645).

**1951:** Maria Domenica Mazzarello, co-foundress of Daughters of Our Lady Help of Christians (1837-1881); Emilie de Vialar, foundress of Sisters of St. Joseph "of the Apparition" (1797-1856); Anthony M. Gianelli, bishop (1789-1846); Ignatius of Laconi, lay brother (1701-1781); Francis Xavier Bianchi, priest (1743-1815).

**1954:** Pius X, pope (1835-1914); Dominic Savio (1842-1857); Maria Crocifissa di Rosa, foundress of Handmaids of Charity of Brescia (1813-1855); Peter Chanel, priest-martyr (1803-1841); Gaspar del Bufalo, founder of Missioners of the Most Precious Blood (1786-1837); Joseph M. Pignatelli, priest (1737-1811).

**1958:** Herman Jóseph, O. Praem., priest (1150-1241) (equivalent canonization).

### John XXIII
(1958-1963)

**1959:** Joaquina de Vedruna de Mas, foundress of Carmelite Sisters of Charity (1783-1854); Charles of Sezze, lay brother (1613-1670).

**1960:** Gregory Barbarigo, bishop (1625-1697) (equivalent canonization); John de Ribera, bishop (1532-1611).

**1961:** Bertilla Boscardin, virgin (1888-1922).

**1962:** Martin de Porres, lay brother (1579-1639); Peter Julian Eymard, founder of Blessed Sacrament Fathers (1811-1868); Anthony Pucci, priest (1819-1892); Francis Mary of Camporosso, lay brother (1804-1866).

**1963:** Vincent Pallotti, founder of Pallottine Fathers (1795-1850).

### Paul VI
(1963-1978)

**1964:** Charles Lwanga and Twenty-One Companions, Martyrs of Uganda.

**1967:** Benilde Romancon, lay brother (1805-1862).

**1969:** Julia Billiart, foundress of Sisters of Notre Dame de Namur (1751-1816).

**1970:** Maria Della Dolorato Torres Acosta, foundress of Servants Sisters of Mary (1826-1887); Leonard Murialdo, priest, founder of Congregation of St. Joseph (1828-1900); Therese Couderc, foundress of Congregation of Our Lady of the Cenacle (1805-1885); John of Avila, preacher and spiritual director (1499-1569); Sts. Nicholas Tavelic, Deodatus of Aquitaine, Peter of Narbonne and Stephen of Cuneo, martyrs (d. 1391); Forty English and Welsh Martyrs (d. 16th cent.).

**1974:** Teresa of Jesus Jornet Ibars, foundress of Little Sisters of Abandoned Aged (1843-1897).

**1975:** Vicenta Maria Lopez y Vicuna, foundress of Institute of Daughters of Mary Immaculate (1847-1890); Elizabeth Bayley Seton, foundress of Sisters of Charity in the U.S. (1774-1821); John Masias, Dominican brother-missionary (1585-1645); Oliver Plunket, archbishop-martyr (1629-1681); Justin de Jacobis, missionary bishop (1800-1860); John Baptist of the Conception, priest, reformer of the Order of the Most Holy Trinity (1561-1613).

**1976:** Beatrice da Silva, foundress of Congregation of the Immaculate Conception of the BVM (1424 or 1426-1490); John Ogilvie, Scottish Jesuit martyr (1579-1615).

**1977:** Rafaela Maria Porras y Ayllon, foundress of Handmaids of the Sacred Heart (1850-1925); John Nepomucene Neumann, bishop (1811-1860); Sharbel Makhlouf, Maronite Rite monk (1828-1898).

### John Paul II
(1978- )

**1982:** Crispin of Viterbo, Capuchin brother (1668-1750); Maximilian Kolbe, Conventual Franciscan priest (1894-1941); Marguerite Bourgeoys, foundress of Congregation of Notre Dame (1620-1700); Jeanne Delanoue, foundress of Sisters of St. Anne of Providence of Saumur, France (1666-1736).

**1983:** Leopold Mandic, Capuchin priest (1866-1942).

**1984:** Paola Frassinetti, foundress of Sisters of St. Dorothy (1809-1892); 103 Korean Martyrs (d. 1791, 1801, 1827, 1839, 1846, 1866); Michele Febres Cordero, of the Brothers of the Christian Schools (1854-1910).

### English and Welsh Martyrs

Forty Martyrs of England and Wales, victims of persecution from 1535 to 1671, were canonized by Pope Paul Oct. 25, 1970.

The martyrs were prosecuted and executed as traitors for refusal to comply with laws enacted by Henry VIII and Elizabeth I regarding supremacy (the sovereign was proclaimed the highest authority of the Church in England, acknowledgment of papal primacy was forbidden), succession and the prohibition of native-born to study for the priesthood abroad and return to England for practice of the ministry.

John Houghton, prior of the London Charterhouse, was the first of his group to die (1535) for opposing Henry's Acts of Supremacy and Succession. Cuthbert Mayne (d. 1577) was the protomartyr of the English seminary at Douay. Margaret Clitherow (d. 1586) and Swithun Wells (d. 1591) were executed for sheltering priests. Richard Gwyn (d. 1584), poet, was the protomartyr of Wales.

John Almond, Edmund Arrowsmith, Ambrose Barlow, John Boste, Alexander Briant, Edmund Campion, Philip Evans, Thomas Garnet, Edmund Gennings;

Philip Howard, John Jones, John Kemble, Luke Kirby, Robert Lawrence, David Lewis, Ann Line, John Lloyd;

Henry Morse, Nicholas Owen, John Paine, Polydore Plasden, John Plessington, Richard Reynolds, John Rigby, John Roberts;

Alban Roe, Ralph Sherwin, Robert Southwell, John Southworth, John Stone, John Wall, Henry Walpole, Margaret Ward, Augustine Webster and Eustace White.

## PAPAL ENCYCLICALS — BENEDICT XIV (1740) TO JOHN PAUL II

(Source: *The Papal Encyclicals* (5 vols.), Claudia Carlen, I.H.M.; a Consortium Book, © McGrath Publishing Co., Wilmington, N.C. Used with permission.)

An encyclical letter is a pastoral letter addressed by a pope to the whole Church. In general, it concerns matters of doctrine, morals or discipline. Its formal title consists of the first few words of the official text. A few encyclicals, notably *Pacem in Terris* by John XXIII and *Ecclesiam Suam* by Paul VI, have been addressed to "all men of good will"

An encyclical epistle, which is like an encyclical letter in many respects, is addressed to part of the Church, that is, to the bishops and faithful of a particular country or area. Its contents may concern other than doctrinal, moral or disciplinary matters of universal significance; for example, the commemoration of historical events, conditions in a certain country.

The authority of encyclicals was stated by Pius XII in the encyclical *Humani Generis* Aug. 12, 1950.

"Nor must it be thought that what is contained in encyclical letters does not of itself demand assent, on the pretext that the popes do not exercise in them the supreme power of their teaching authority. Rather, such teachings belong to the ordinary magisterium, of which it is true to say: 'He who hears you, hears me' (Lk. 10:16); for the most part, too, what is expounded and inculcated in encyclical letters already appertains to Catholic doctrine for other reasons. But if the supreme pontiffs in their official documents purposely pass judgment on a matter debated until then, it is obvious to all that the matter, according to the mind and will of the same pontiffs, cannot be considered any longer a question open for discussion among theologians."

The following list contains the titles and indicates the subject matter of encyclical letters and epistles. The latter are generally distinguishable by the limited scope of their titles or contents.

### Benedict XIV
#### (1740-1758)
**1740:** *Ubi Primum* (On the duties of bishops), Dec. 3.

**1741:** *Quanta Cura* (Forbidding traffic in alms), June 30.

**1743:** *Nimian Licentiam* (To the bishops of Poland: on validity of marriages), May 18.

**1745:** *Vix Pervenit* (To the bishops of Italy: on usury and other dishonest profit), Nov. 1.

**1748:** *Magnae Nobis* To the bishops of Poland: on marriage impediments and dispensations), June 29.

**1749:** *Peregrinantes* (To all the faithful: proclaiming a Holy Year for 1750), May 5.

*Apostolica Constitutio* (On preparation for the Holy Year), June 26.

**1751:** *A Quo Primum* (To the bishops of Poland: on Jews and Christians living in the same place), June 14.

**1754:** *Cum Religiosi* (To the bishops of the States of the Church: on catechesis), June 26.

*Quod Provinciale* (To the bishops of Albania: on Christians using Mohammedan names), Aug. 1.

**1755:** *Allatae Sunt* (To missionaries of the Orient: on the observance of Oriental rites), July 26.

**1756:** *Ex Quo Primum* (To bishops of the Greek rite: on the Euchologion), Mar. 1.

*Ex Omnibus* (To the bishops of France: on the apostolic constitution, *Unigenitus)*, Oct. 16.

### Clement XIII
#### (1758-1769)
**1758:** *A Quo Die* (Unity among Christians), Sept. 13.

**1759:** *Cum Primum* (On observing canonical sanctions), Sept. 17.

*Appetente Sacro* (On the spiritual advantages of fasting), Dec. 20.

**1761:** *In Dominico Agro* (On instruction in the faith), June 14.

**1766:** *Christinae Reipublicae* (To bishops of Austria: on the dangers of anti-Christian writings), Nov. 25.

**1768:** *Summa Quae* (To the bishops of Poland: on the Church in Poland), Jan. 6.

### Clement XIV
#### (1769-1774)
**1769:** *Decet Quam Maxime* (To the bishops of Sardinia: on abuses in taxes and benefices), Sept. 21.

*Inscrutabili Divinae Sapientiae* (To all Christians: proclaiming a universal jubilee), Dec. 12.

*Cum Summi* (Proclaiming a universal jubilee), Dec. 12.

**1774:** *Salutis Nostrae* (To all Christians: proclaiming a universal jubilee), Apr. 30.

### Pius VI
#### (1775-1799)
**1775:** *Inscrutabile* (On the problems of the pontificate), Dec. 25.

**1791:** *Charitas* (To the bishops of France: on the civil oath in France), Apr. 13.

### Pius VII
#### (1800-1823)
**1800:** *Diu Satis* (To the bishops of France: on a return to Gospel principles), May 15.

## Leo XII
(1823-1829)

**1824:** *Ubi Primum* To all bishops: on Leo XII's assuming the pontificate), May 5.

*Quod Hoc Ineunte* (Proclaiming a universal jubilee), May 24.

**1825:** *Charitate Christi* Extending jubilee to the entire church), Dec. 25.

## Pius VIII
(1829-1830)

**1829:** *Traditi Humilitati* (On Pius VIII's program for the pontificate), May 24.

## Gregory XVI
(1831-1846)

**1832:** *Summo Iugiter Studio* (To the bishops of Bavaria: on mixed marriages), May 27.

*Cum Primum* (To the bishops of Poland: on civil obedience), June 9.

*Mirari Vos* (On liberalism and religious indifferentism), Aug. 15.

**1833:** *Quo Graviora* (To the bishops of the Rhineland: on the "pragmatic Constitution"), Oct. 4.

**1834:** *Singulari Nos* (On the errors of Lammenais), June 25.

**1835:** *Commissum Divinitus* (To clergy of Switzerland: on Church and State), May 17.

**1840:** *Probe Nostis* (On the Propagation of the Faith), Sept. 18.

**1841:** *Quas Vestro* (To the bishops of Hungary: on mixed marriages), Apr. 30.

**1844:** *Inter Praecipuas* (On biblical societies), May 8.

## Pius IX
(1846-1878)

**1846:** *Qui Pluribus* (On faith and religion), Nov. 9.

**1847:** *Praedecessores Nostros* (On aid for Ireland), Mar. 25.

*Ubi Primum* (To religious superiors: on discipline for religious), June 17.

**1849:** *Ubi Primum* (On the Immaculate Conception), Feb. 2.

*Nostis et Nobiscum* (To the bishops of Italy: on the Church in the Pontifical States), Dec. 8.

**1851:** *Exultavit Cor Nostrum* (On the effects of jubilee), Nov. 21.

**1852:** *Nemo Certe Ignorat* (To the bishops of Ireland: on the discipline for clergy), Mar. 25.

*Probe Noscitis Venerabiles* (To the bishops of Spain: on the discipline for clergy), May 17.

**1853:** *Inter Multiplices* (To the bishops of France: pleading for unity of spirit), Mar. 21.

**1854:** *Neminem Vestrum* (To clergy and faithful of Constantinople: on the persecution of Armenians), Feb. 2.

*Optime Noscitis* (To the bishops of Ireland: on the proposed Catholic university for Ireland), Mar. 20.

*Apostolicae Nostrae Caritatis* (Urging prayers for peace), Aug. 1.

**1855:** *Optime Noscitis* (To the bishops of Austria: on episcopal meetings), Nov. 5.

**1856:** *Singulari Quidem* (To the bishops of Austria: on the Church in Austria), Mar. 17.

**1858:** *Cum Nuper* (To the bishops of Sicily: on care for clerics), Jan. 20.

*Amantissimi Redemptoris* (On priests and the care of souls), May 3.

**1859:** *Cum Sancta Mater Ecclesia* (Pleading for public prayer), Apr. 27.

*Qui Nuper* (On Pontifical States), June 18.

**1860:** *Nullis Certe Verbis* (On the need for civil sovereignty), Jan. 19.

**1862:** *Amantissimus* (To bishops of the Oriental rite: on the care of the churches), Apr. 8.

**1863:** *Quanto Conficiamur Moerore* (To the bishops of Italy: on promotion of false doctrines), Aug. 10.

*Incredibili* (To the bishops of Bogota: on persecution in New Granada), Sept. 17.

**1864:** *Maximae Quidem* (To the bishops of Bavaria: on the Church in Bavaria), Aug. 18.

*Quanta Cura* (Condemning current errors), Dec. 8.

**1865:** *Meridionali Americae* (To the bishops of South America: on the seminary for native clergy), Sept. 30.

**1867:** *Levate* (On the afflictions of the Church), Oct. 27.

**1870:** *Respicientes* (Protesting the taking of the Pontifical States), Nov. 1.

**1871:** *Ubi Nos* (To all bishops: on Pontifical States), May 15.

*Beneficia Dei* (On the twenty-fifth anniversary of his pontificate), June 4.

*Saepe Venerabiles Fratres* (On thanksgiving for twenty-five years of pontificate), Aug. 5.

**1872:** *Quae in Patriarchatu* (To bishops and people of Chaldea: on the Church in Chaldea), Nov. 16.

**1873:** *Quartus Supra* (To bishops and people of the Armenian rite: on the Church in Armenia), Jan. 6.

*Etsi Multa* (On the Church in Italy, Germany and Switzerland), Nov. 21.

**1874:** *Vix Dum a Nobis* (To the bishops of Austria: on the Church in Austria), Mar. 7.

*Omnem Sollicitudinem* (To the bishops of the Ruthenian rite: on the Greek-Ruthenian rite), May 13.

*Gravibus Ecclesiae* (To all bishops and faithful: proclaiming a jubilee for 1875), Dec. 24.

**1875:** *Quod Nunquam* (To the bishops of Prussia: on the Church in Prussia), Feb. 5.

*Graves ac Diuturnae* (To the bishops of Switzerland: on the Church in Switzerland), Mar. 23.

## Leo XIII
(1878-1903)

**1878:** *Inscrutabili Dei Consilio* (On the evils of society), Apr. 21.

*Quod Apostolici Muneris* (On socialism), Dec. 28.

**1879:** *Aeterni Patris* (On the restoration of Christian philosophy), Aug. 4.

**1880:** *Arcanum* (On Christian marriage), Feb. 10.

*Grande Munus* (On Sts. Cyril and Methodius), Sept. 30.

*Sancta Dei Civitas* (On mission societies), Dec. 3.

**1881:** *Diuturnum* (On the origin of civil power), June 29.

*Licet Multa* (To the bishops of Belgium: on Catholics in Belgium), Aug. 3.

**1882:** *Etsi Nos* (To the bishops of Italy: on conditions in Italy), Feb. 15.

*Auspicato Concessum* (On St. Francis of Assisi), Sept. 17.

*Cum Multa* (To the bishops of Spain: on conditions in Spain), Dec. 8.

**1883:** *Supremi Apostolatus Officio* (On devotion to the Rosary), Sept. 1.

**1884:** *Nobilissima Gallorum Gens* (To the bishops of France: on the religious question), Feb. 8.

*Humanum Genus* (On Freemasonry), Apr. 20.

*Superiore Anno* (On the recitation of the Rosary), Aug. 30.

**1885:** *Immortale Dei* (On the Christian constitution of states), Nov. 1.

*Spectata Fides* (To the bishops of England: on Christian education), Nov. 27.

*Quod Auctoritate* (Proclamation of extraordinary Jubilee), Dec. 22.

**1886:** *Iampridem* (To the bishops of Prussia: on Catholicism in Germany), Jan. 6.

*Quod Multum* (To the bishops of Hungary: on the liberty of the Church), Aug. 22.

*Pergrata* (To the bishops of Portugal: on the Church in Portugal), Sept. 14.

**1887:** *Vi e Ben Noto* (To the bishops of Italy: on the Rosary and public life), Sept. 20.

*Officio Sanctissimo* (To the bishops of Bavaria: on the Church in Bavaria), Dec. 22.

**1888:** *Quod Anniversarius* (On his sacerdotal jubilee), Apr. 1.

*In Plurimis* (To the bishops of Brazil: on the abolition of slavery), May 5.

*Libertas* (On the nature of human liberty), June 20.

*Saepe Nos* (To the bishops of Ireland: on boycotting in Ireland), June 24.

*Paterna Caritas* (To the Patriarch of Cilicia and the archbishops and bishops of the Armenian people: on reunion with Rome), July 25.

*Quam Aerumnosa* (To the bishops of America: on Italian immigrants), Dec. 10.

*Etsi Cunctas* (To the bishops of Ireland: on the Church in Ireland), Dec. 21.

*Exeunte Iam Anno* (On the right ordering of Christian life), Dec. 25.

**1889:** *Magni Nobis* (To the bishops of the United States: on the Catholic University of America), Mar. 7.

*Quamquam Pluries* (On devotion to St. Joseph), Aug. 15.

**1890:** *Sapientiae Christianae* (On Christians as citizens), Jan. 10.

*Dall'Alto Dell'Apostolico Seggio* (To the bishops and people of Italy: on Freemasonry in Italy), Oct. 15.

*Catholicae Ecclesiae* (On slavery in the missions), Nov. 20.

**1891:** *In Ipso* (To the bishops of Austria: on episcopal reunions in Austria), Mar. 3.

*Rerum Novarum* (On capital and labor), May 15.

*Pastoralis* (To the bishops of Portugal: on religious union), June 25.

*Pastoralis Officii* (To the bishops of Germany and Austria: on the morality of dueling), Sept. 12.

*Octobri Mense* (On the Rosary), Sept. 22.

**1892:** *Au Milieu des Sollicitudes* (To the bishops, clergy and faithful of France: on the Church and State in France), Feb. 16.

*Quarto Abeunte Esaeculo* (To the bishops of Spain, Italy, and the two Americas: on the Columbus quadricentennial), July 16.

*Magnae Dei Matris* (On the Rosary), Sept. 8.

*Inimica Vis* (To the bishops of Italy: on Freemasonry), Dec. 8.

*Custodi di Quella Fede* (To the Italian people: on Freemasonry), Dec. 8.

**1893:** *Ad Extremas* (On seminaries for native clergy), June 24.

*Constanti Hungarorum* (To the bishops of Hungary: on the Church in Hungary), Sept. 2.

*Laetitiae Sanctae* (Commending devotion to the Rosary), Sept. 8.

*Non Mediocri* (To the bishops of Spain: on the Spanish College in Rome), Oct. 25.

*Providentissimus Deus* (On the study of Holy Scripture), Nov. 18.

**1894:** *Caritatis* (To the bishops of Poland: on the Church in Poland), Mar. 19.

*Inter Graves* (To the bishops of Peru: on the Church in Peru), May 1.

*Litteras a Vobis* (To the bishops of Brazil: on the clergy in Brazil), July 2.

*Iucunda Semper Expectatione* (On the Rosary), Sept. 8.

*Christi Nomen* (On the propagation of the Faith and churches), Dec. 24.

**1895:** *Longinqua* (To the bishops of the United States: on Catholicism in the United States), Jan. 6.

*Permoti Nos* (To the bishops of Belgium: on social conditions in Belgium), July 10.

*Adiutricem* (On the Rosary), Sept. 5.

**1896:** *Insignes* (To the bishops of Hungary: on the Hungarian millennium), May 1.

*Satis Cognitum* (On the unity of the Church), June 29.

*Fidentem Piumque Animum* (On the Rosary), Sept. 20.

**1897:** *Divinum Illud Munus* (On the Holy Spirit), May 9.

*Militantis Ecclesiae* (To the bishops of Austria, Germany, and Switzerland: on St. Peter Canisius), Aug. 1.

*Augustissimae Virginis Mariae* (On the Confraternity of the Holy Rosary), Sept. 12.

*Affari Vos* (To the bishops of Canada: on the Manitoba school question), Dec. 8.

# 146

**1898:** *Caritatis Studium* (To the bishops of Scotland: on the Church in Scotland), July 25.

*Spesse Volte* (To the bishops, priests, and people of Italy: on the suppression of Catholic institutions), Aug. 5.

*Quam Religiosa* (To the bishops of Peru: on civil marriage law), Aug. 16.

*Diuturni Temporis* (On the Rosary), Sept. 5.

*Quum Diuturnum* (To the bishops of Latin America: on Latin American bishops' plenary council), Dec. 25.

**1899:** *Annum Sacrum* (On consecration to the Sacred Heart), May 25.

*Depuis le Jour* (To the archbishops, bishops, and clergy of France: on the education of the clergy), Sept. 8.

*Paternae* (To the bishops of Brazil: on the education of the clergy), Sept. 18.

**1900:** *Omnibus Compertum* (To the Patriarch and bishops of the Greek-Melkite rite: on unity among the Greek Melkites), July 21.

*Tametsi Futura Prospicientibus* (On Jesus Christ the Redeemer), Nov. 1.

**1901:** *Graves de Communi Re* (On Christian democracy), Jan. 18.

*Gravissimas* (To the bishops of Portugal: on religious orders in Portugal), May 16.

*Reputantibus* (To the bishops of Bohemia and Moravia: on the language question in Bohemia), Aug. 20.

*Urbanitatis Veteris* (To the bishops of the Latin church in Greece: on the foundation of a seminary in Athens), Nov. 20.

**1902:** *In Amplissimo* (To the bishops of the United States: on the Church in the United States), Apr. 15.

*Quod Votis* (To the bishops of Austria: on the proposed Catholic University), Apr. 30.

*Mirae Caritatis* (On the Holy Eucharist), May 28.

*Quae ad Nos* (To the bishops of Bohemia and Moravia: on the Church in Bohemia and Moravia), Nov. 22

*Fin dal Principio* (To the bishops of Italy: on the education of the clergy), Dec. 8.

*Dum Multa* (To the bishops of Ecuador: on marriage legislation), Dec. 24.

## Saint Pius X
### (1903-1914)

**1903:** *E Supremi* (On the restoration of all things in Christ), Oct. 4.

**1904:** *Ad Diem Illum Laetissimum* (On the Immaculate Conception), Feb. 2.

*Iucunda Sane* (On Pope Gregory the Great), Mar. 12.

**1905:** *Acerbo Nimis* (On teaching Christian doctrine), Apr. 15.

*Il Fermo Proposito* (To the bishops of Italy: on Catholic Action in Italy), June 11.

**1906:** *Vehementer Nos* (To the bishops, clergy, and people of France: on the French Law of Separation), Feb. 11.

*Tribus Circiter* (On the Mariavites or Mystic Priests of Poland), Apr. 5.

*Pieni l'Animo* (To the bishops of Italy: on the clergy in Italy), July 28.

*Gravissimo Officio Munere* (To the bishops of France: on French associations of worship), Aug. 10.

**1907:** *Une Fois Encore* (To the bishops, clergy, and people of France: on the separation of Church and State), Jan. 6.

*Pascendi Dominici Gregis* (On the doctrines of the Modernists), Sept. 8.

**1909:** *Communium Rerum* (On St. Anselm of Aosta), Apr. 21.

**1910:** *Editae Saepe* (On St. Charles Borromeo), May 26.

**1911:** *Iamdudum* (On the Law of Separation in Portugal), May 24.

**1912:** *Lacrimabili Statu* (To the bishops of Latin America: on the Indians of South America), June 7.

*Singulari Quadam* (To the bishops of Germany: on labor organizations), Sept. 24.

## Benedict XV
### (1914-1922)

**1914:** *Ad Beatissimi Apostolorum* (Appeal for peace), Nov. 1.

**1917:** *Humani Generis Redemptionem* (On preaching the Word of God), June 15.

**1918:** *Quod Iam Diu* (On the future peace conference), Dec. 1.

**1919:** *In Hac Tanta* (To the bishops of Germany: on St. Boniface), May 14.

*Paterno Iam Diu* (On children of central Europe), Nov. 24.

**1920:** *Pacem, Dei Munus Pulcherrimum* (On peace and Christian reconciliation), May 23.

*Spiritus Paraclitus* (On St. Jerome), Sept. 15.

*Principi Apostolorum Petro* (On St. Ephrem the Syrian), Oct. 5.

*Annus Iam Plenus* (On children of central Europe), Dec. 1.

**1921:** *Sacra Propediem* (On the Third Order of St. Francis), Jan. 6.

*In Praeclara Summorum* (To professors and students of fine arts in Catholic institutions of learning: on Dante), Apr. 30.

*Fausto Appetente Die* (On St. Dominic), June 29.

## Pius XI
### (1922-1939)

**1922:** *Ubi Arcano Dei Consilio* (On the peace of Christ in the Kingdom of Christ), Dec. 23.

**1923:** *Rerum Omnium Perturbationem* (On St. Francis de Sales), Jan. 26.

*Studiorum Ducem* (On St. Thomas Aquinas), June 29.

*Ecclesiam Dei* (On St. Josaphat), Nov. 12.

**1924:** *Maximam Gravissimamque* (To the bishops, clergy, and people of France: on French diocesan associations), Jan. 18.

**1925:** *Quas Primas* (On the feast of Christ the King), Dec. 11.

**1926:** *Rerum Ecclesiae* (On Catholic missions), Feb. 28.

*Rite Expiatis* (On St. Francis of Assisi), Apr. 30.

*Iniquis Afflictisque* (On the persecution of the Church in Mexico), Nov. 18.

**1928:** *Mortalium Animos* (On religious unity), Jan. 6.

*Miserentissimus Redemptor* (On reparation to the Sacred Heart), May 8.

*Rerum Orientalium* (On the promotion of Oriental studies), Sept. 8.

**1929:** *Mens Nostra* (On the promotion of Spiritual Exercises), Dec. 20.

*Quinquagesimo Ante* (On his sacerdotal jubilee), Dec. 23.

*Rappresentanti in Terra* (On Christian education), Dec. 31.

**1930:** *Ad Salutem* (On St. Augustine), Apr. 20.

*Casti Connubii* (On Christian marriage), Dec. 31.

**1931:** *Quadragesimo Anno* (Commemorating the fortieth anniversary of Leo XIII's *Rerum novarum:* on reconstruction of the social order), May 15.

*Non Abbiamo Bisogno* (On Catholic Action in Italy), June 29.

*Nova Impendet* (On the economic crisis), Oct. 2.

*Lux Veritatis* (On the Council of Ephesus), Dec. 25.

**1932:** *Caritate Christi Compulsi* (On the Sacred Heart), May 3.

*Acerba Animi* (To the bishops of Mexico: on persecution of the Church in Mexico), Sept. 29.

**1933:** *Dilectissima Nobis* (To the bishops, clergy, and people of Spain: on oppression of the Church in Spain), June 3.

**1935:** *Ad Catholici Sacerdotii* (On the Catholic priesthood), Dec. 20.

**1936:** *Vigilanti Cura* (To the bishops of the United States: on motion pictures), June 29.

**1937:** *Mit Brennender Sorge* (To the bishops of Germany: on the Church and the German Reich), Mar. 14.

*Divini Redemptoris* (On atheistic communism), Mar. 19.

*Nos Es Muy Conocida* (To the bishops of Mexico: on the religious situation in Mexico), Mar. 28.

*Ingravescentibus Malis* (On the Rosary) Sept. 29.

### Pius XII
### (1939-1958)

**1939:** *Summi Pontificatus* (On the unity of human society), Oct. 20.

*Sertum Laetitiae* (To the bishops of the United States: on the 150th anniversary of the establishment of the hierarchy in the United States), Nov. 1.

**1940:** *Saeculo Exeunte Octavo* (To the bishops of Portugal and its colonies: on the eighth centenary of the independence of Portugal), June 13.

**1943:** *Mystici Corporis Christi* (On the Mystical Body of Christ), June 29.

*Divino Afflante Spiritu* (On promoting biblical studies, commemorating the fiftieth anniversary of *Providentissimus Deus),* Sept. 30.

**1944:** *Orientalis Ecclesiae* (On St. Cyril, Patriarch of Alexandria), Apr. 9.

**1945:** *Communium Interpretes Dolorum* (To the bishops of the world: appealing for prayers for peace during May), Apr. 15.

*Orientales Omnes Ecclesias* (On the 350th anniversary of the reunion of the Ruthenian Church with the Apostolic See), Dec. 23.

**1946:** *Quemadmodum* (Pleading for the care of the world's destitute children), Jan. 6.

*Deiparae Virginis Mariae* (To all bishops: on the possibility of defining the Assumption of the Blessed Virgin Mary as a dogma of faith), May 1.

**1947:** *Fulgens Radiatur* (On St. Benedict), Mar. 21.

*Mediator Dei* (On the sacred liturgy), Nov. 20.

*Optatissima Pax* (Prescribing public prayers for social and world peace), Dec. 18.

**1948:** *Auspicia Quaedam* (On public prayers for world peace and solution of the problem of Palestine), May 1.

*In Multiplicibus Curis* (On prayers for peace in Palestine), Oct. 24.

**1949:** *Redemptoris Nostri Cruciatus* (On the holy places in Palestine), Apr. 15.

**1950:** *Anni Sacri* (On the program for combatting atheistic propaganda throughout the world), Mar. 12.

*Summi Maeroris* (On public prayers for peace), July 19.

*Humani Generis* (Concerning some false opinions threatening to undermine the foundations of Catholic doctrine), Aug. 12.

*Mirabile Illud* (On the crusade of prayers for peace), Dec. 6.

**1951:** *Evangelii Praecones* (On the promotion of Catholic missions), June 2.

*Sempiternus Rex Christus* (On the Council of Chalcedon), Sept. 8.

*Ingruentium Malorum* (On reciting the Rosary), Sept. 15.

**1952:** *Orientales Ecclesias* (On the persecuted Eastern Church), Dec. 15.

**1953:** *Doctor Mellifluus* (On St. Bernard of Clairvaux, the last of the fathers), May 24.

*Fulgens Corona* (Proclaiming a Marian Year to commemorate the centenary of the definition of the dogma of the Immaculate Conception), Sept. 8.

**1954:** *Sacra Virginitas* (On consecrated virginity), Mar. 25.

*Ecclesiae Fastos* (To the bishops of Great Britain, Germany, Austria, France, Belgium, and Holland: on St. Boniface), June 5.

*Ad Sinarum Gentem* (To the bishops, clergy, and people of China: on the supranationality of the Church), Oct. 7.

*Ad Caeli Reginam* (Proclaiming the Queenship of Mary), Oct. 11.

**1955:** *Musicae Sacrae* (On sacred music), Dec. 25.

**1956:** *Haurietis Aquas* (On devotion to the Sacred Heart), May 15.

*Luctuosissimi Eventus* (Urging public prayers for peace and freedom for the people of Hungary), Oct. 28.

*Laetamur Admodum* (Renewing exhortation for prayers for peace for Poland, Hungary, and especially for the Middle East), Nov. 1.

*Datis Nuperrime* (Lamenting the sorrowful events in Hungary and condemning the ruthless use of force), Nov. 5.

**1957:** *Fidei Donum* (On the present condition of the Catholic missions, especially in Africa), Apr. 21.

*Invicti Athletae* (On St. Andrew Bobola), May 16.

*Le Pelerinage de Lourdes* (Warning against materialism on the centenary of the apparitions at Lourdes), July 2.

*Miranda Prorsus* (On the communications field: motion picture, radio, television), Sept. 8.

**1958:** *Ad Apostolorum Principis* (To the bishops of China; on Communism and the Church in China), June 29.

*Meminisse Juvat* (On prayers for persecuted Church), July 14.

### John XXIII
(1958-1963)

**1959:** *Ad Petri Cathedram* (On truth, unity, and peace, in a spirit of charity), June 29.

*Sacerdotii Nostri Primordia* (On St. John Vianney), Aug. 1.

*Grata Recordatio* (On the Rosary: prayer for the Church, missions, international and social problems), Sept. 26.

*Princeps Pastorum* (On the missions, native clergy, lay participation), Nov. 28.

**1961:** *Mater et Magistra* (On Christianity and social progress), May 15.

*Aeterna Dei Sapientia* (On fifteenth centenary of the death of Pope St. Leo I: the see of Peter as the center of Christian unity), Nov. 11.

**1962:** *Paenitentiam Agere* (On the need for the practice of interior and exterior penance), July 1.

**1963:** *Pacem in Terris* (On establishing universal peace in truth, justice, charity, and liberty), Apr. 11.

### Paul VI
(1963-1978)

**1964:** *Ecclesiam Suam* (On the Church), Aug. 6.

**1965:** *Mense Maio* (On prayers during May for the preservation of peace), Apr. 29.

*Mysterium Fidei* (On the Holy Eucharist), Sept. 3.

**1966:** *Christi Matri* (On prayers for peace during October), Sept. 15.

**1967:** *Populorum Progressio* (On the development of peoples), Mar. 26.

*Sacerdotalis Caelibatus* (On the celibacy of the priest), June 24.

**1968:** *Humanae Vitae* (On the regulation of birth), July 25.

### John Paul II
(1978-     )

**1979:** *Redemptor Hominis* (On redemption and the dignity of the human race), Mar. 4.

**1980:** *Dives in Misericordia* (On the mercy of God), Nov. 30.

**1981:** *Laborem Exercens* (On human work), Sept. 14.

## 43rd INTERNATIONAL EUCHARISTIC CONGRESS

"The Eucharist and the Christian Family," the theme of the 43rd International Eucharistic Congress, was called "truly fundamental" by Pope John Paul in a letter addressed Aug. 15, 1984, to Cardinal Opilio Rossi, president of the Permanent Committee for International Eucharistic Congresses. The Congress was scheduled to be held Aug. 11 to 18, 1985, in Nairobi, Kenya, under the general supervision of the committee headed by Cardinal Rossi.

In his letter, the Pope said: "The Christian family has a special vocation, to be a witness to the Gospel in the contemporary world. From the Eucharist it will draw the strength which the fulfillment of such a task demands."

### A Peak Moment

He expressed hope that the Congress "may be a peak moment in the life of the Church, so that the Christian family may draw from it those lights and helps which it particularly needs today."

### For Greater Understanding

The Holy Father prayed that, "thanks to this awaited ecclesial event, there may be an ever greater understanding of the essential value of the Eucharist for the salvation and sanctification of

the family, and the indispensable role of the family for evangelization and for the coming of the kingdom of God which has its anticipation and its center in the Eucharist."

The Pope's message had special reference to the Eucharist, the Paschal Meal; The Eucharist, Sacrament of the Family; and The Eucharist, Source of the Family Apostolate. These themes, in the view of one African commentator, are in close accord with the significance of the family in African tribal and social life. They are also closely related to the setting in which the Eucharist was celebrated in the early Church.

Public demonstrations of faith in the Eucharist are part and parcel of these congresses. Combining liturgical services, other public ceremonies, subsidiary meetings, different kinds of instructional and inspirational elements, they are unified by central themes and serve to increase understanding of and devotion to Christ in the Eucharist, and to relate this liturgy of worship and witness to daily life.

The first international congress held in Africa took place at Carthage in 1930, 49 years after the first one at Lille, France, as a result of the efforts of Marie Marthe Tamisier of Touraine, Msgr. Louis Gaston de Segur and Philibert Vrau.

# HIERARCHY OF THE CATHOLIC CHURCH

## ORGANIZATION AND GOVERNMENT

As a structured society, the Catholic Church is organized and governed along lines corresponding mainly to the jurisdictions of the pope and bishops. The pope is the supreme head of the Church. He has primacy of jurisdiction as well as honor over the entire Church.

Bishops, in union with and in subordination to the pope, are the successors of the Apostles for care of the Church and for the continuation of Christ's mission in the world. They serve the people of their own dioceses, or local churches, with ordinary authority and jurisdiction. They also share, with the pope and each other, in common concern and effort for the general welfare of the whole Church.

Bishops of exceptional status are Eastern-Rite patriarchs who, subject only to the pope, are heads of the faithful belonging to their rites throughout the world.

Subject to the Holy Father and directly responsible to him for the exercise of their ministry of service to people in various jurisdictions or divisions of the Church throughout the world are: resident archbishops and metropolitans (heads of archdioceses), diocesan bishops, vicars and prefects apostolic (heads of vicariates apostolic and prefectures apostolic), certain abbots and prelates, apostolic administrators. Each of these, within his respective territory and according to the provisions of canon law, has ordinary jurisdiction over pastors (who are responsible for the administration of parishes), priests, Religious and lay persons.

Also subject to the Holy Father are titular archbishops and bishops, religious orders and congregations of pontifical right, pontifical institutes and faculties, papal nuncios and apostolic delegates.

Assisting the pope and acting in his name in the central government and administration of the Church are cardinals and other officials of the Roman Curia.

## THE HIERARCHY

The ministerial hierarchy is the orderly arrangement of the ranks and orders of the clergy to provide for the spiritual care of the faithful, the government of the Church, and the accomplishment of the Church's total mission in the world. Persons belong to this hierarchy by virtue of ordination and canonical mission.

The term hierarchy is also used to designate an entire body or group of bishops; for example, the hierarchy of the Church, the hierarchy of the United States.

**Hierarchy of Order:** Consists of the pope, bishops, priests and deacons. Their purpose, for which they are ordained to holy orders, is to carry out the sacramental and pastoral ministry of the Church.

**Hierarchy of Jurisdiction:** Consists of the pope and bishops by divine institution, and other church officials by ecclesiastical institution and mandate, who have authority to govern and direct the faithful for spiritual ends.

### The Pope

His Holiness the Pope is the Bishop of Rome, the Vicar of Jesus Christ, the successor of St. Peter, Prince of the Apostles, the Supreme Pontiff who has the primacy of jurisdiction and not merely of honor over the universal Church, the Patriarch of the West, the Primate of Italy, the Archbishop and Metropolitan of the Roman Province, the Sovereign of the State of Vatican City, Servant of the Servants of God.

### Cardinals

(See Index)

### Patriarchs

Patriarch, a term which had its origin in the Eastern Church, is the title of a bishop who, second only to the pope, has the highest rank in the hierarchy of jurisdiction. He is the incumbent of one of the sees listed below. Subject only to the pope, an Eastern-Rite patriarch is the head of the faithful belonging to his rite throughout the world. The patriarchal sees are so called because of their special status and dignity in the history of the Church.

The Council of Nicaea (325) recognized three patriarchs — the bishops of Alexandria and Antioch in the East, and of Rome in the West. The First Council of Constantinople (381) added the bishop of Constantinople to the list of patriarchs and gave him rank second only to that of the pope, the bishop of Rome and patriarch of the West; this action was seconded by the Council of Chalcedon (451) and was given full recognition by the Fourth Lateran Council (1215). The Council of Chalcedon also acknowledged patriarchal rights of the bishop of Jerusalem.

Eastern Rite patriarchs are as follows: one of Alexandria, for the Copts; three of Antioch, one each for the Syrians, Maronites and Greek Melkites (the latter also has the personal title of Greek Melkite patriarch of Alexandria and of Jerusalem). The patriarch of Babylonia, for the Chaldeans, and the patriarch of Sis, or Cilicia, for the Armenians, should be called, more properly, *Katholikos* — that is, a prelate delegated for a universality of causes. These patriarchs are elected by bishops of their rites: they receive approval and the pallium, symbolic of their office, from the pope.

Latin Rite patriarchates were established for Antioch, Jerusalem, Alexandria and Constantinople during the Crusades; afterwards, they became patriarchates in name only. Jerusalem, however, was reconstituted as a patriarchate by Pius IX, in virtue of the bull *Nulla Celebrior* of July 23, 1847. In 1964, the Latin titular patriarchates of Constantinople, Alexandria and Antioch, long a bone of contention in relations with Eastern Rites, were abolished.

As of July 1, 1984, the patriarchs in the Church were:

The Pope, Bishop of Rome, Patriarch of the West; Cardinal Stephanos I Sidarouss, C.M., of Alexandria, for the Copts; Ignace Antoine II Hayek, of Antioch, for the Syrians; Maximos V Hakim, of Antioch, for the Greek Melkites (he also has the titles of Alexandria and Jerusalem for the Greek Melkites); Cardinal Antoine Khoraiche, of Antioch, for the Maronites; Giacomo Beltritti, of Jerusalem, for the Latin Rite; Paul II Cheikho, of Babylon, for the Chaldeans; Jean Pierre XVIII Kasparian, of Cilicia, for the Armenians.

The titular patriarchs (in name only) of the Latin Rite were: Cardinal Antonio Ribeiro, of Lisbon; Cardinal Marco Cé of Venice and Archbishop Raul Nicolau Goncalves of the East Indies (Archbishop of Goa and Daman, India). The patriarchate of the West Indies has been vacant since 1963.

### Archbishops, Metropolitans

**Archbishop:** A bishop with the title of an archdiocese.

**Metropolitan Archbishop:** Head of the principal see, an archdiocese, in an ecclesiastical province consisting of several dioceses. He has the full powers of bishop in his own archdiocese and limited supervisory jurisdiction and influence over the other (suffragan) dioceses in the province.

**Titular Archbishop:** Has the title of an archdiocese which formerly existed in fact but now exists in title only. He does not have ordinary jurisdiction over an archdiocese.

**Archbishop ad personam:** A title of personal honor and distinction granted to some bishops. They do not have ordinary jurisdiction over an archdiocese.

**Primate:** A title of honor given to the ranking prelate of some countries or regions.

### Bishops

**Diocesan Bishop:** A bishop in charge of a diocese.

**Coadjutor Bishop:** An assistant bishop to a diocesan bishop, with right of succession to the see.

**Titular Bishops:** A bishop with the title of a diocese which formerly existed in fact but now exists in title only; an assistant bishop to a diocesan bishop.

**Episcopal Vicar:** An assistant, who may or may not be a bishop, appointed by a residential bishop as his deputy for a certain part of a diocese, a determined type of apostolic work, or the faithful of a certain rite.

**Eparch, Exarch:** Titles of bishops of Eastern-Rite churches.

**Nomination of Bishops:** Nominees for episcopal ordination are selected in several ways. Final appointment and/or approval in all cases is subject to decision by the pope.

In the U.S., bishops periodically submit the names of candidates to the archbishop of their province. The names are then considered at a meeting of the bishops of the province, and those receiving a favorable vote are forwarded to the pro-nuncio for transmission to the Holy See. Bishops are free to seek the counsel of priests, religious and lay persons with respect to nominees.

Eastern-Rite churches have their own procedures and synodal regulations for nominating and making final selection of candidates for episcopal ordination. Such selection is subject to approval by the pope.

The Code of Canon Law concedes no rights or privileges to civil authorities with respect to the election, nomination, presentation or designation of candidates for the episcopate.

**Ad Limina Visit:** Diocesan bishops and military vicars are obliged to make a periodic *ad limina* visit ("to the threshold" of the Apostles) to the tombs of Sts. Peter and Paul, have audience with the Holy Father, consult with appropriate Vatican officials and present a written report on conditions in their jurisdictions. The most recent regulations concerning the formalities and scheduling of visits by bishops from various countries, generally every five years, were issued by the Congregation for Bishops in a decree dated Nov. 27, 1975.

### Others with Ordinary Jurisdiction

Some members of the clergy, with jurisdiction like that of diocesan bishops, are pastors of the people of God in territories (prelatures and abbacies, not under the jurisdiction of diocesan bishops.

**Vicar Apostolic:** Usually a titular bishop who has ordinary jurisdiction over a mission territory.

**Prefect Apostolic:** Has ordinary jurisdiction over a mission territory.

**Apostolic Administrator:** Usually a bishop appointed to administer an ecclesiastical jurisdiction temporarily. Administrators of lesser rank are also appointed for special and more restricted supervisory duties.

**Vicar General:** A bishop's deputy for the administration of a diocese. Such a vicar does not have to be a bishop.

### Honorary Prelates

Honorary prelates belonging to the Pontifical Household are: Apostolic Prothonotaries, Honorary Prelates of His Holiness, and Chaplains of His Holiness. Their title is Reverend Monsignor.

---

### 1984 COMMEMORATIONS

Bishop Frederic Baraga (d. 1868), missionary to Indians in Michigan, was honored June 29 with the issue of a commemorative U.S. postal card. The bicentennial celebration of the death of Franciscan Father Junipero Serra, missionary in California, began Aug. 28.

# SYNOD OF BISHOPS

The Synod of Bishops was chartered by Pope Paul VI Sept. 15, 1965, in a document he issued on his own initiative under the title, *Apostolica Sollicitudo*. Provisions of this *motu proprio* are contained in Canons 342 to 348 of the Code of Canon Law. According to major provisions of the Synod charter:

• The purposes of the Synod are: "to encourage close union and valued assistance between the Sovereign Pontiff and the bishops of the entire world; to insure that direct and real information is provided on questions and situations touching upon the internal action of the Church and its necessary activity in the world of today; to facilitate agreement on essential points of doctrine and on methods of procedure in the life of the Church."

• The Synod is a central ecclesiastical institution, permanent by nature.

• The Synod is directly and immediately subject to the Pope, who has authority to assign its agenda, to call it into session, and to give its members deliberative as well as advisory authority.

• In addition to a limited number of ex officio members and a few heads of male religious institutes, the majority of the members are elected by and representative of national or regional episcopal conferences. The Pope reserved the right to appoint the general secretary, special secretaries and no more than 15 per cent of the total membership.

The Pope is president of the Synod.

The secretary general is Archbishop Jozef Tomko of Czechoslovakia.

## FIRST MEETING, 1967

The Synod met for the first time from Sept. 29 to Oct. 29, 1967, in Vatican City. Its objectives, as stated by Pope Paul, were "the preservation and strengthening of the Catholic faith, its integrity, its force, its development, its doctrinal and historical coherence."

One result of synodal deliberations was a recommendation to the Pope to establish an international commission of theologians to assist the Congregation for the Doctrine of the Faith and to broaden approaches to theological research. The commission was subsequently set up by Pope Paul in 1969.

## EXTRAORDINARY SESSION

The second Synod of Bishops, meeting in extraordinary session Oct. 11 to 28, 1969, opened the door to wider participation by the bishops with the Pope and each other in the government of the Church.

Proceedings were oriented to three main points: (1) the nature and implications of collegiality; (2) the relationships of bishops and their conferences to the Pope; (3) the relationships of bishops and their conferences to each other.

Three proposals approved and moved for action provided for regular meetings of the Synod at two-year intervals (later extended to three years), staff organization and operations of the general secretariat in the interim between meetings, and openness of the synodal agenda to suggestions by bishops.

Between the second and third meetings of the Synod, an advisory council of 15 members (12 elected, three appointed by the Pope) was formed to provide the secretariat with adequate staff for carrying on liaison with episcopal conferences and for drawing up the agenda of synodal meetings.

## SECOND GENERAL ASSEMBLY

The ministerial priesthood and justice in the world were the principal topics of discussion at the third and longest meeting, the Second General Assembly of the Synod, Sept. 30 to Nov. 6, 1971.

**The Priesthood:** In its report on the priesthood, the Synod described difficulties experienced by priests, stated traditional doctrinal principles on the priesthood, and drew from these principles a set of guidelines for priestly life and ministry in the mission of Christ and the Church, and in the communion of the Church.

The report emphasized the primary and permanent dedication of priests in the Church to the ministry of word, sacrament and pastoral service as a full-time occupation.

**Justice in the World:** In connection with "The Mission of the People of God To Further Justice in the World," a synodal report reviewed a wide range of existing injustices; cited the social-justice imperatives of the Gospel; called for the practice of justice throughout the Church and for greater efforts in education and ecumenical collaboration for justice; and outlined an eight-point program for international action.

The assembly observed: Action on behalf of justice and participation in the transformation of the world fully appear to us as a constitutive dimension of the preaching of the Gospel; or, in other words, of the Church's mission for the redemption of the human race and its liberation from every oppressive situation."

## THIRD ASSEMBLY

"Evangelization of the Modern World" was the theme of the third assembly of the Synod, Sept. 27 to Oct. 26, 1974. Its major product was a general statement on the subject, covering the need for it and its relationship to efforts for total human liberation from personal and social evil.

The statement reconfirmed "that the mandate to evangelize all men constitutes the essential mission of the Church," that "the duty to proclaim the Gospel belongs to the whole people of God," and that "this work demands incessant interior conversion on the part of individual Christians and continual renewal of our communities and institutions."

**Liberation:** Regarding the relationship between evangelization and human liberation, the bishops said:

"Faithful to her evangelizing mission, the Church, as a truly poor, praying and fraternal community, can do much to bring about the integral salvation or the full liberation of men. She can draw from the Gospel the most profound reasons and ever new incentives to promote generous dedication to the service of all men — the poor especially, the weak and the oppressed — and to eliminate the social consequences of sin which are translated into unjust social and political structures.

"The Church does not remain within merely political, social and economic limits (elements which she must certainly take into account) but leads towards freedom under all its forms — liberation from sin, from individual or collective selfishness — and to full communion with God and with men who are like brothers. In this way the Church, in her evangelical way, promotes the true and complete liberation of all men, groups and peoples."

### SYNOD '77

"Catechetics in Our Time, with Special Reference to Children and Young People," was the theme of the fourth assembly, Sept. 30 to Oct. 29, 1977. Its major products were a "Message to the People of God," the first synodal statement issued since inception of the body, and two documents presented to Pope Paul — a set of 34 propositions and some 900 suggestions regarding the substance of the propositions and the message on catechetics.

The propositions covered six general subjects in considerable detail: the importance of catechetical renewal, the theme of authentic catechesis, the mode of authentic catechizing, the necessity of catechesis for all Christians, the community as the context and milieu of catechesis, attitudes and other factors affecting catechesis.

The "Message to the People of God" consisted of three parts, dealing with: the world, young people and catechesis; the manifestation of salvation in Christ; catechesis as the task of all people in the Church.

### FIFTH ASSEMBLY

"The Role of the Christian Family in the Modern World" was the theme of the fifth assembly, Sept. 26 to Oct. 25, 1980. Its major products were "A Message to Christian Families in the Modern World" and a proposal for a "Charter of Family Rights."

In the message to families, the bishops said: "Today the family is sometimes obliged to choose a way of life that goes contrary to modern culture in such matters as sexuality, individual autonomy and material wealth. In the face of sin and failure, it gives witness to an authentically Christian spirit."

The message criticized unjust structures which increase poverty in the world, the "spiritual emptiness" of materialistic cultures, and disregard for the rights of families by some governments and international agencies.

It reaffirmed the indissolubility of marriage and the contents of the Encyclical *Humanae Vitae* (see separate entry), and urged those who find it hard to live up to "the difficult but loving demands" of Christ not to be discouraged.

In response to recommendations of the fifth general assembly, Pope John Paul issued a charter on family rights late in 1983.

## SYNOD '83

"Penance and Reconciliation in the Mission of the Church" was the theme of the sixth general assembly of the Synod of Bishops held Sept. 29 to Oct. 29, 1983, at the Vatican.

### 63 Propositions

Sixty-three propositions related to this theme were developed in 28 sessions of the entire assembly and in numerous relatively small language-group meetings. At the end of the assembly, they were presented to Pope John Paul for consideration in his preparation of a final document on the Synod.

The propositions, in the words of a summary released by the Vatican, "can be divided into three sections:

• "The first part illustrates the Church's mission of reconciliation at its roots and in its public expressions.

• "The second part looks at the current situation.

• "The third part sets out the paths to be followed for a wide-ranging renewal of the practice" of penance and reconciliation.

Backgrounding the propositions were synodal discussions of a wide variety of subjects, including: personal sin and so-called systemic or institutional sin; the nature of serious sin; the diminished sense of sin and of the need of redemption, related to decline in the administration and reception of the sacrament of penance; general absolution; individual and social reconciliation; violence and violations of human rights; reconciliation as the basis of peace and justice in society.

### Synodal and Papal Statements

In a statement issued Oct. 27, two days before the end of the assembly, the Synod stressed the need of the world to become, increasingly, "a reconciled community of peoples," and said that "the Church, as sacrament of reconciliation to the world, has to be an effective sign of God's mercy."

The Synod called for interreligious effort and cooperation in a tireless quest for peace and disarmament, and urged those with power in society "to summon up the necessary will to give us a more just and peaceful society."

Pope John Paul, in a closing address, spoke of the fundamental place of penance and reconciliation in Christian life. He also acknowledged the "vivid preoccupation for world peace" manifested by participants in the Synod. He told them he had sent "a pressing appeal" to U.S. and Soviet leaders, "asking them not to turn away from negotiation as the only way to . . . put an end to the arms race, which keeps the whole of contemporary humanity in apprehension."

The Pope referred, finally, to the value of the Synod as an advisory body, and said: "Perhaps collegial pastoral responsibility could be expressed in the Synod even more fully. Nonetheless, one must note that, in the form in which it exists and presently operates . . . it renders an enormous service to the Church."

The Holy Father attended most of the sessions of the Synod but spoke only at the beginning and end of the assembly.

His presiding legates during the sessions were Cardinals Joseph Cordeiro of Karachi, Joseph Ratzinger, prefect of the Congregation for the Doctrine of the Faith, and Timothy Manning of Los Angeles.

## U.S. Participants

Eleven Americans were among the 244 participants in the assembly; 221 were voting delegates.

Four delegates were elected by the bishops of the United States: Cardinal Joseph Bernardin of Chicago; Archbishop John Roach of St. Paul-Minneapolis, president of the National Conference of Catholic Bishops; Archbishop Patrick Flores of San Antonio, and Auxiliary Bishop Austin Vaughan of New York.

Cardinal Manning and Archbishop Edmund Szoka of Detroit were also delegates, chosen by the Pope himself.

Cardinal William Baum, prefect of the Congregation for Catholic Education and former archbishop of Washington, was an ex officio member of the Synod.

Two representatives of religious orders were Fathers John Vaughn, Franciscan minister general, and Paul M. Boyle, head of the Passionists.

Father Carl Peter attended as a non-voting theological expert; he was dean of the School of Religious Studies, Catholic University of America, and a member of the International Theological Commission.

Gerald Hughes of Dallas, an official in the Cursillo movement, was a non-voting observer.

During proceedings of the assembly, Cardinal Bernardin was reelected to the 12-member council of the Synod.

# ROMAN CURIA

The Roman Curia consists of the Secretariat of State, the Sacred Council for the Public Affairs of the Church, ten congregations, three tribunals, three secretariats, and a complex of commissions, councils and offices which administer church affairs at the highest level.

## Background

The Curia evolved gradually from advisory assemblies or synods of the Roman clergy with whose assistance the popes directed church affairs during the first 11 centuries. Its original office was the Apostolic Chancery, dating from the fourth century. The antecedents of its permanently functioning agencies and offices were special commissions of cardinals and prelates. Its establishment in a form resembling what it is now dates from the second half of the 16th century.

Pope Paul VI gave the following short account of the background of the Curia in the apostolic constitution *Regimini Ecclesiae Universae* ("For the Government of the Universal Church"), dated Aug. 15, 1967.

"The Roman Pontiffs, successors to Blessed Peter, have striven to provide for the government of the Universal Church by making use of experts to advise and assist them.

"In this connection, we should remember both the Presbyterium of the City of Rome and the College of Cardinals of the Holy Roman Church which in the course of centuries evolved from it. Then, little by little, as we know, out of that office (Apostolic Chancery) which was set up in the fourth century to transmit papal documents, many offices developed; to these was added the Auditorium, which was a well-developed tribunal in the 13th century and which was more thoroughly organized by John XXII (1316-1334).

"With an increase in the volume of things to be dealt with, bodies or commissions of cardinals selected to treat of specific questions began to be more efficiently organized in the 16th century, from which eventually arose the congregations of the Roman Curia. It is to the credit of our predecessor Sixtus V that, in the constitution *Immensa Aeterni Dei* of Jan. 22, 1588, he arranged the sacred councils in an orderly manner and wisely described the structure of the Roman Curia.

"With the progress of time, however, it happened that some of them became obsolete, others had to be added, and others had to be restructured. This is the work our predecessor St. Pius X set out to do with the constitution *Sapienti Consilio* of June 29, 1908. Its provisions, a lasting testimony to that wise and ingenious pastor of the Church, were with a few changes incorporated into the Code of Canon Law."

### Reorganization

Pope Paul initiated a four-year reorganization study in 1963 which resulted in the constitution *Regimini Ecclesiae Universae*. The document was published Aug. 18, 1967, and went into full effect in March, 1968.

While the study was under way, the Pope took preliminary steps toward curial reorganization by reorienting and changing the title of the Sacred Congregation of the Holy Office (to the Sacred Congregation for the Doctrine of the Faith) and by appointing a number of non-Italians to key curial positions.

The stated purposes of the reorganization were to increase the efficiency of the Curia and to make it more responsive to the needs and concerns of the Universal Church. The pursuit of these objectives involved various modifications.

### Curial Departments

• The Office of the Pope, including the Papal

Secretariat or Secretariat of State and the Council for the Public Affairs of the Church.

• Nine congregations, instead of twelve as formerly. The functions of the Sacred Congregation of Ceremonies were transferred to the Prefecture of the Pontifical Household; the duties of the Sacred Congregation for Extraordinary Ecclesiastical Affairs were taken over by the Sacred Council for the Public Affairs of the Church; the Sacred Congregation of the Basilica of St. Peter was reduced in rank. In 1969, the Sacred Congregation of Rites was phased out of existence and its functions were assigned to the Sacred Congregation for the Causes of Saints and the Sacred Congregation for Divine Worship.

The Congregation for the Sacraments and Divine Worship, established in 1975 to replace the Congregation for the Discipline of the Sacraments and the Congregation for Divine Worship, was made two separate congregations in 1984.

• Three secretariats, the Council of the Laity and the Pontifical Commission on Justice and Peace.

• Three tribunals.

• Six offices, including the former Apostolic Chancery (abolished in 1973) and Apostolic Chamber, and the newly constituted Prefecture of Economic Affairs, Prefecture of the Pontifical Household, Administration of the Patrimony of the Apostolic See, and Central Statistics Office. Functions of the former Apostolic Datary and the Secretariats of State, of Briefs to Princes, and of Latin Letters were transferred to the Secretariat of State.

### Operational Procedures

• The papal secretary or secretary of state has authority to take initiative in coordinating and expediting business through meetings and other cooperative procedures.

• Officials of departments have five-year terms of office, which may be renewed. Terms end automatically on the death of a pope. The five-year terms of consultors are renewable.

• Diocesan bishops as well as full-time curial personnel have membership in curial departments, in accordance with provisions of the decree *Pro Comperto Sane* of Aug. 6, 1967. Seven diocesan bishops hold five-year membership in each congregation, with full rights to participation in the more important plenary assemblies scheduled once a year. They are also entitled to take part in routine meetings whenever they are in Rome. Three general superiors of male religious institutes hold similar membership in the Sacred Congregation for Religious and Secular Institutes.

• Lay persons are eligible to serve as consultors to curial departments.

• Close liaison with episcopal conferences is required. They should be given prior notice of forthcoming curial decrees affecting them in any special way.

• In line with customary procedure, matters in which the competence of two or more departments is involved are handled on a cooperative basis, with mutual consultation and decision.

• Although Latin remains the official language of the Curia, communication in any of the widely known modern languages is acceptable.

• Informational and financial services are centralized in the Central Statistics Office and the Prefecture of Economic Affairs, respectively.

• Heads of curial departments are required to notify the pope before conducting any serious or extraordinary business.

• Authority to act and decide on many matters belongs to departmental officials in virtue of delegation from the pope. Some matters, however, have to be referred to the pope for final decision.

### Internationalization

As of July 1, 1984, principal officials of the Roman Curia (cardinals unless indicated otherwise) were from the following countries: Italy (Baggio, Caprio, Casaroli, Oddi, Palazzini, Opilio Rossi, Sabattani, Abp. Dadaglio); Germany (Ratzinger, Abp. Mayer, Bp. Cordes); United States (Baum, Abp. Foley, Abp. Marcinkus); France (Etchegaray, Abp. Poupard); India (Parecattil, Abp. Lourdusamy); Argentina (Pironio); Belgium (Abp. Hamer); Benin (Gantin); Brazil (Agnelo Rossi); Canada (Abp. Gagnon); Ireland (Abp. Ryan); Netherlands (Willebrands); Nigeria (Abp. Arinze); Poland (Rubin); Ukraine (Abp. Marusyn); Venezuela (Abp. Castillo Lara).

### DEPARTMENTS

**Secretariat of State:** Provides the pope with the closest possible assistance in the care of the universal Church and in dealings with all departments of the Curia.

The cardinal secretary is the key coordinator of curial operations. He has authority to call meetings of the prefects of all departments for expediting the conduct of business, for consultation and intercommunication. He handles: any and all matters entrusted to him by the pope, and ordinary matters which are not within the competence of other departments; some relations with bishops; relations with representatives of the Holy See, civil governments and their representatives, without prejudice to the competence of the Council for the Public Affairs of the Church.

The cardinal secretary has been likened to a prime minister or head of government because of the significant role he plays in coordinating curial operations at the highest level.

The secretariat has two offices for preparing and writing letters for the pope (functions formerly performed by the Secretariat of Briefs to Princes and the Secretariat of Latin Letters), and a Central Statistics Office.

It also handles work formerly done by the Apostolic Datary (the dating and countersigning of papal documents, and the management of church benefices), and the Apostolic Chancery, abolished in 1973 (care of the pope's leaden seal and the Fisherman's Ring).

It has supervisory duties over the Commission for the Instruments of Social Communication, two Vatican publications, *Acta Apostolicae Sedis* and *Annuario Pontificio,* and the Vatican Personnel Office.

The Prefecture of Vatican City is answerable to the secretary of state.

OFFICIALS: *Cardinal Agostino Casaroli, secretary of state; Most Rev. Eduardo Martinez Somalo, undersecretary and secretary of the Cifra.*

**Council for the Public Affairs of the Church:** Handles diplomatic and other relations with civil governments. With the Secretariat of State, it supervises matters concerning nunciatures and apostolic delegations. It also has supervision of the Pontifical Commission for Russia.

OFFICIALS: *Cardinal Agostino Casaroli, prefect, secretary of state; Most Rev. Achille Silvestrini, secretary.*

BACKGROUND: Originated by Pius VI in 1793 as the Congregation for Extraordinary Affairs from the Kingdom of the Gauls; given wider scope by Pius VII, July 19, 1814; formerly called the Sacred Congregation for Extraordinary Ecclesiastical Affairs.

## CONGREGATIONS

**Sacred Congregation for the Doctrine of the Faith:** Has responsibility to safeguard the doctrine of faith and morals.

Accordingly, it examines doctrinal questions; promotes studies thereon; evaluates theological opinions and, when necessary and after prior consultation with concerned bishops, reproves those regarded as opposed to principles of the faith; examines books on doctrinal matters and can reprove such works, if the contents so warrant, after giving authors the opportunity to defend themselves.

It examines matters pertaining to the Privilege of Faith (Petrine Privilege) in marriage cases, and safeguards the dignity of the sacrament of penance.

It has working relations with the Pontifical Biblical Commission (see separate entry).

In 1969, Pope Paul set up a Theological Commission (see separate entry) as an adjunct to the congregation, to provide it with the advisory services of additional experts in theology and allied disciplines.

OFFICIALS: *Cardinal Joseph Ratzinger, prefect; Most Rev. Alberto Bovone, secretary.*

BACKGROUND: At the beginning of the 13th century, legates of Innocent III were commissioned as the Holy Office of the Inquisition to combat heresy; the same task was entrusted to the Dominican Order by Gregory IX in 1231 and to the Friars Minor by Innocent IV from 1243 to 1254. On July 21, 1542 (apostolic constitution *Licet*), Paul III instituted a permanent congregation of cardinals with supreme and universal competence over matters concerning heretics and those suspected of heresy. Pius IV, St. Pius V and Sixtus V further defined the work of the congregation. St. Pius X changed its name to the Congregation of the Holy Office.

Paul VI, in virtue of the motu proprio *Integrae*

*Servandae* of Dec. 7, 1965, began reorganization of the Curia with this body, to which he gave the new title, Sacred Congregation for the Doctrine of the Faith. Its orientation is not merely negative, in the condemnation of error, but positive, in the promotion of orthodox doctrine. The right of appeal, judicial representation, and the consultation of their proper regional conference of bishops, are assured to persons accused of unorthodox doctrine. The office for the censorship of books and the Roman Index of Prohibited Books were abolished.

**Sacred Congregation for the Oriental Churches:** Has competence in matters concerning the persons and discipline of Eastern Rite Churches. It has jurisdiction over territories in which the majority of Christians belong to Oriental Rites (i.e., Egypt, the Sinai Peninsula, Eritrea, Northern Ethiopia, Southern Albania, Bulgaria, Cyprus, Greece, Iran, Iraq, Lebanon, Palestine, Syria, Jordan, Turkey, Afghanistan, the part of Thrace subject to Turkey); also, over minority communities of Orientals no matter where they live.

To assure adequate and equal representation, it has as many offices as there are rites of Oriental Churches in communion with the Holy See.

It is under mandate to consult with the Secretariat for Promoting Christian Unity on questions concerning separated Oriental Churches, and with the Secretariat for Non-Christians, especially in relations with Moslems.

It has a special commission on the liturgy and an Oriental Church Information Service.

OFFICIALS: *Cardinal Wladyslaw Rubin, prefect; Most Rev. Miroslav Stefan Marusyn, secretary.*

*Members include all Eastern Rite patriarchs and the president of the Secretariat for Promoting Christian Unity. Consultors include the secretary of the same secretariat.*

BACKGROUND: Special congregations for the affairs of the Greek and other Oriental Churches were founded long before this body was created by Pius IX Jan. 6, 1862 (apostolic constitution *Romani Pontifices*), and united with the Sacred Congregation for the Propagation of the Faith. The congregation was made autonomous by Benedict XV May 1, 1917 (motu proprio *Dei Providentis*), and given wider authority by Pius XI Mar. 25, 1938 (motu proprio *Sancta Dei Ecclesia*). John XXIII appointed six patriarchs, five of Eastern Rites and one of the Roman Rite, to the congregation and gave them the same rights as cardinals belonging to the body, in March, 1963. Paul VI named representatives of all Eastern-Rite bodies to serve as consultors of the congregation, in November, 1963.

**Sacred Congregation for Bishops,** formerly called the Sacred Consistorial Congregation: Has functions related in one way or another to bishops and the jurisdictions in which they serve.

Its concerns are: the establishment and changing of dioceses, provinces, military vicariates and other jurisdictions; providing for the naming of bishops and other prelates; studying things concerning the persons, work and pastoral activity of bishops; providing for the care of bishops when they leave office; receiving and studying reports on the conditions of dioceses; general supervision of the holding and recognition of particular councils and conferences of bishops; publishing and circulating pastoral norms and guidelines through conferences of bishops.

It supervises the Pontifical Commission for Latin America and the Pontifical Commission for Migration and Tourism.

*OFFICIALS: Cardinal Bernardin Gantin, prefect; Most Rev. Lucas Moreira Neves, O.P., secretary.*

*Ex officio members are the prefects of the Council for the Public Affairs of the Church, and of the Congregations for the Doctrine of the Faith, for the Clergy, and for Catholic Education. The substitute secretaries and undersecretaries of these curial departments are ex officio consultors.*

BACKGROUND: Established by Sixtus V Jan. 22, 1588 (apostolic constitution *Immensa*); given an extension of powers by St. Pius X June 20, 1908, and Pius XII Aug. 1, 1952 (apostolic constitution *Exsul Familia*).

**Sacred Congregation for the Sacraments:** Supervises the discipline of the sacraments without prejudice to the competencies of the Congregation for the Doctrine of the Faith and other curial departments.

*OFFICIALS: Most Rev. Augustin Mayer, pro-prefect; Most Rev. Lajos Kada, secretary.*

BACKGROUND: Instituted by St. Pius X, June 29, 1908, as the Congregation for the Discipline of the Sacraments; replaced by the Congregation for the Sacraments and Divine Worship by Paul VI (apostolic constitution, *Constans novis studium*, July 11, 1975); reestablished as a separate congregation by John Paul II in an autograph letter dated April 5, 1984.

**Sacred Congregation for Divine Worship:** Has general competence over the ritual and pastoral aspects of divine worship in the Roman and other Western rites.

*OFFICIALS: Most Rev. Augustin Mayer, pro-prefect; Most Rev. Virgilio Noe, secretary.*

BACKGROUND: Established by Paul VI, May 8, 1969, to replace the Congregation of Rites instituted by Pope Sixtus V in 1588; united with Congregation for the Discipline of the Sacraments by Paul VI in 1975; reestablished as a separate congregation by John Paul II in an autograph letter dated Apr. 5, 1984.

**Sacred Congregation for the Causes of Saints:** Handles matters connected with beatification and canonization causes (in accordance with revised procedures decreed in 1983), and the preservation of relics.

*OFFICIALS: Cardinal Pietro Palazzini, prefect; Most Rev. Traian Crisan, secretary.*

BACKGROUND: Established by Sixtus V in 1588 as the Congregation of Rites; affected by legislation of Pius XI in 1930; title changed and functions defined by Paul VI, 1969 (apostolic constitution

*Sacra Rituum Congregatio*). The Congregation was restructured and canonization procedures revised by John Paul II in 1983 (apostolic constitution *Divinus Perfectionis Magister*).

**Sacred Congregation for the Clergy,** formerly called the Sacred Congregation of the Council: Handles matters concerning the persons, work and pastoral ministry of clerics who exercise their apostolate in a diocese. Such clerics are diocesan deacons and priests, and religious who are engaged in ordinary parochial ministry in a diocese. It carries on its work through three offices.

One office promotes the spiritual growth and formation as well as the professional competence of priests by encouraging the establishment and operation of pastoral institutes and other study opportunities; oversees the general discipline of the clergy, the establishment and conduct of pastoral councils and senates of priests, and resolves controversies among clerics; has a mandate to draw up a set of general principles to direct a better distribution of priests for pastoral service.

A second office, in view of its primary concern for preaching of the word of God, encourages effective apostolic programs and methods, with special emphasis on catechetical and other forms of religious training and formation for the faithful.

A third office has supervisory responsibility over church property and the temporalities of priestly life; among its functions are efforts to provide for the support of the clergy through suitable salary scales, pensions, security and health insurance programs, and other measures.

*OFFICIALS: Cardinal Silvio Oddi, prefect; Most Rev. Maximino Romero de Lema, secretary.*

BACKGROUND: Established by Pius IV Aug. 2, 1564 (apostolic constitution *Alias Nos*), under the title, Sacred Congregation of the Cardinals Interpreters of the Council of Trent; affected by legislation of Gregory XIII and Sixtus V.

**Sacred Congregation for Religious and Secular Institutes,** formerly known as the Sacred Congregation of Religious or for the Affairs of Religious: Has dual competence over institutes of religious, together with societies of the common life without vows, and secular institutes.

One section deals with the affairs of all religious institutes and societies of the common life, and their members. It has authority in matters related to the establishment, general direction and suppression of institutes; general discipline in line with their rules and constitutions; the movement toward renewal and adaptation of institutes in contemporary circumstances; the setting up and encouragement of councils and conferences of major religious superiors for intercommunication and other purposes.

A second section has the same competence over the affairs and members of secular institutes as the first has over religious.

*OFFICIALS: Most Rev. Jerome Hamer, pro-prefect; Most. Rev. Vincenzo Fagiolo, secretary.*

BACKGROUND: Founded by Sixtus V May 27, 1586, with the title, Sacred Congregation for Consultations of Regulars (apostolic constitution *Romanus Pontifex*); confirmed by the apostolic constitution *Immensa* Jan. 22, 1588; made part of the Congregation for Consultations of Bishops and other Prelates in 1601; made autonomous by St. Pius X in 1908.

**Sacred Congregation for Catholic Education,** formerly known as the Sacred Congregation of Seminaries and Universities: Has supervisory competence over institutions and works of Catholic education.

It carries on its work through three offices.

One office handles matters connected with the direction, discipline and temporal administration of seminaries, and with the education of diocesan clergy, religious and members of secular institutes.

A second office oversees Catholic universities, faculties of study and other institutions of higher learning inasmuch as they depend on the authority of the Church; encourages cooperation and mutual assistance among Catholic institutions, and the establishment of Catholic hospices and centers on campuses of non-Catholic institutions.

A third office is concerned in various ways with all Catholic schools below the college-university level, with general questions concerning education and studies, and with the cooperation of conferences of bishops and civil authorities in educational matters.

The congregation supervises Pontifical Works for Priestly Vocations.

*OFFICIALS: Cardinal William Wakefield Baum, prefect; Most Rev. Antonio M. Javierre Ortas, S.D.B., secretary.*

BACKGROUND: The title and functions of the congregation were defined by Benedict XV Nov. 4, 1915; Pius XI, in 1931 and 1932, and Pius XII, in 1941 and 1949, extended its functions. Its work had previously been carried on by two other congregations erected by Sixtus V in 1588 and Leo XII in 1824.

**Sacred Congregation for the Evangelization of Peoples** (for the Propagation of the Faith): Directs and coordinates missionary work throughout the world.

Accordingly, it has competence over those matters which concern all the missions established for the spread of Christ's kingdom. These include: fostering missionary vocations; providing for the training of missionaries in seminaries; assigning missionaries to fields of work; establishing ecclesiastical jurisdictions and proposing candidates to serve them as bishops and in other capacities; encouraging the recruitment and development of indigenous clergy; mobilizing spiritual and financial support for missionary activity.

In general, the varied competence of the congregation extends to most persons and affairs of the Church in areas classified as mission territories.

To promote missionary cooperation, the congregation has a Supreme Council for the Direction of Pontifical Missionary Works. Subject to this council are the general councils of the Missionary Union of the Clergy, the Society for the Propagation of the Faith, the Society of St. Peter the Apostle

for Native Clergy, the Society of the Holy Childhood, the International Center of Missionary Animation and the *Fides* news agency.

*OFFICIALS: Most Rev. Dermot Ryan, pro-prefect; Most Rev. D. Simon Lourdusamy, secretary.*

The heads of the Secretariats for Promoting Christian Unity, for Non-Christians, and for Non-Believers are ex officio members of the congregation.

BACKGROUND: Originated as a commission of cardinals by Gregory XIII and modified by Clement VIII to promote the reconciliation of separated Eastern Christians; erected as a stable congregation by Gregory XV June 22, 1622 (apostolic constitution *Inscrutabili*).

## TRIBUNALS

**Sacred Apostolic Penitentiary:** Has jurisdiction for the internal forum only (sacramental and non-sacramental). It issues decisions on questions of conscience; grants absolutions, dispensations, commutations, sanations and condonations; has charge of non-doctrinal matters pertaining to indulgences.

*OFFICIALS: Most Rev. Luigi Dadaglio, pro-major penitentiary; Msgr. Luigi de Magistris, regent.*

BACKGROUND: Origin dates back to the 12th century; affected by the legislation of many popes; radically reorganized by St. Pius V in 1569; jurisdiction limited to the internal forum by St. Pius X; Benedict XV annexed the Office of Indulgences to it Mar. 25, 1917.

**Apostolic Signatura:** The principal concerns of this supreme court of the Church are to resolve questions concerning juridical procedure and to supervise the observance of laws and rights at the highest level. It decides the jurisdictional competence of lower courts and has jurisdiction in cases involving personnel and decisions of the Rota. It is the supreme court of the State of Vatican City.

*OFFICIALS: Cardinal Aurelio Sabattani, prefect; Most Rev. Zenon Grocholewski, secretary.*

BACKGROUND: A permanent office of the Signatura has existed since the time of Eugene IV in the 15th century; affected by the legislation of many popes; reorganized by St. Pius X in 1908 and made the supreme tribunal of the Church.

**Sacred Roman Rota:** The ordinary court of appeal for cases appealed to the Holy See. It is best known for its competence and decisions in cases concerning the validity of marriage.

*OFFICIAL: Msgr. Arturo De Jorio, dean.*

BACKGROUND: Originated in the Apostolic Chancery; affected by the legislation of many popes; reorganized by St. Pius X in 1908 and further revised by Pius XI in 1934.

## SECRETARIATS

**Secretariat for Promoting Christian Unity:** Handles relations with members of other Christian ecclesial communities; deals with the correct interpretation and execution of the principles of ecumenism; initiates or promotes Catholic ecumenical groups and coordinates on national and international levels the efforts of those promoting Christian unity; undertakes dialogue regarding ecumenical questions and activities with churches and ecclesial communities separated from the Apostolic See; sends Catholic observer-representatives to Christian gatherings, and invites to Catholic gatherings observers of other churches; orders into execution conciliar decrees dealing with ecumenical affairs.

The Commission for Catholic-Jewish Relations is attached to the secretariat.

It has two offices, for the West and for the East. Each office is under the immediate direction of a delegate.

The prefects of the Congregation for the Oriental Churches and of the Congregation for the Evangelization of Peoples are ex officio members of the secretariat. Consultors include the secretaries of these two departments.

OFFICIAL: Cardinal Johannes Willebrands, president.

BACKGROUND: Established by John XXIII June 5, 1960, as a preparatory secretariat of the Second Vatican Council; raised to commission status during the first session of the council in the fall of 1962; this status confirmed Jan. 3, 1966.

**Secretariat for Non-Christians:** Is concerned with persons who are not Christians but profess some kind of religious faith. Its function is to promote studies and dialogue for the purpose of increasing mutual understanding and respect between Christians and non-Christians.

The Commission for Catholic-Moslem Relations is attached to the secretariat.

The prefect of the Congregation for the Evangelization of Peoples is an ex officio member of the secretariat.

OFFICIALS: Most Rev. Francis Arinze, pro-president; Very Rev. Marcello Zago, O.M.I., secretary.

BACKGROUND: Established by Paul VI May 19, 1964.

**Secretariat for Non-Believers:** Studies the background and philosophy of atheism, and initiates and carries on dialogue with non-believers.

OFFICIAL: Most Rev. Paul Poupard, pro-president.

BACKGROUND: Established by Paul VI Apr. 9, 1965.

## COUNCILS, COMMISSIONS

**Laity, Pontifical Council for:** Instituted on an experimental basis by Paul VI Jan. 6, 1967; given permanent status Dec. 10, 1976 (motu proprio Apostolatus Peragendi); its competence covers the apostolate of the laity in the Church and the discipline of the laity as such. Members are mostly lay people from different parts of the world and involved in different apostolates. The council is headed by a cardinal. The Council for the Family is attached to the Council while retaining its own identity. Cardinal Eduardo Pironio, president.

**Justice and Peace, Pontifical Commission:** Instituted by Paul VI Jan. 6, 1967, on an experimen-

tal basis; reconstituted and made a permanent body Dec. 10, 1976 (motu proprio Iustitiam et Pacem). Holy See's organization for examining and studying (from the point of view of doctrine, pastoral practice and the apostolate) problems connected with justice and peace and awakening the sensitivity of the people of God to their responsibility in these areas. Cardinal Roger Etchegaray, president.

**Authentic Interpretation of the Code of Canon Law, Pontifical Commission:** Established by John Paul II (motu proprio, Recognito iuris canonici codice, Jan. 2, 1984) to interpret canons of the revised Code of Canon Law and other universal laws of the Church. Most Rev. Rosalio Jose Castillo Lara, pro-president.

**Revision of the Code of Oriental Canon Law:** Reconstituted by Paul VI in 1972 to replace a former commission dating from July 17, 1935, "to prepare . . . the reform of the Code of Oriental Canon Law, both in the sections already published by . . . four motu proprios" (1,950 canons concerning marriage; processes; religious, church property and terminology; Eastern Rites and persons), "and in the remaining sections which have been completed but not published" (the balance of a total of 2,666 canons); Cardinal Joseph Parecattil, president.

**Social Communications:** Instituted on an experimental basis by Pius XII in 1948; reorganized three times in the 1950's; made permanent commission by John XXIII Feb. 22, 1959; name changed to present title Apr. 11, 1964; authorized to implement the Decree on the Instruments of Social Communication promulgated by the Second Vatican Council; under supervision of the Secretariat of State and the Council for the Public Affairs of the Church; Most Rev. John P. Foley, president; Most Rev. Martin J. O'Connor and Most Rev. Andrzej M. Deskur, presidents emeriti.

**Latin America, Commission:** Instituted by Pius XII Apr. 19, 1958; placed under supervision of the Congregation for Bishops July, 1969; Cardinal Sebastiano Baggio, president.

**Migration and Tourism, Commission:** Instituted by Paul VI Mar. 19, 1970, for pastoral assistance to migrants, nomads, tourists, sea and air travelers; placed under the general supervision and direction of the Congregation for Bishops; Cardinal Sebastiano Baggio, president.

**Cor Unum, Council:** Instituted by Paul VI July 15, 1971, to provide informational and coordinating services for Catholic aid and human development organizations and projects on a worldwide scale; Cardinal Roger Etchegaray, president.

**Family, Pontifical Council:** Instituted by John Paul II May 9, 1981, replacing the Committee for the Family established Jan. 11, 1973, for "promoting the pastoral care of the family . . . by putting into effect the teachings and directives of the ecclesiastical magisterium, so that Christian families may carry out the educative, evangelizing and apostolic mission to which they have been called"; has special relations with the Pontifical Council for the Laity. Most Rev. Edouard Gagnon, P.S.S., pro-president.

**Theological Commission:** Instituted by Paul VI Apr. 11, 1969, as an advisory adjunct of no more than 30 theologians to the Congregation for the Doctrine of the Faith; Cardinal Joseph Ratzinger, president. (See separate entry.)

**Biblical Commission:** Instituted by Leo XIII Oct. 30, 1902; completely restructured by Paul VI June 27, 1971; Cardinal Joseph Ratzinger, president. (See separate entry.)

**Revision and Emendation of the Vulgate, Pontifical Commission:** Established in 1983 by John Paul II to replace the Abbey of St. Jerome instituted by Pius XI in 1933.

**Sacred Archeology, Commission:** Instituted by Pius IX Jan, 6, 1852; Most Rev. Gennaro Verolino, president.

**Historical Sciences, Committee:** Instituted by Pius XII Apr. 7, 1954, as a continuation of a commission dating from 1883; Msgr. Michele Maccarrone, president.

**Ecclesiastical Archives of Italy, Commission:** Instituted by Pius XII Apr. 5, 1955; Most Rev. Martino Giusti, president.

**Sacred Art in Italy, Commission:** Instituted by Pius XI Sept. 1, 1924; Most Rev. Giovanni Fallani, president.

**Sanctuaries of Pompei, Loreto and Bari, Cardinalatial Commission:** Originated by Leo XIII for Sanctuary of Pompei, Loreto placed under commission in 1965, St. Nicholas of Bari, 1980; under supervision of the Congregation for the Clergy; Cardinal Opilio Rossi, president.

**Russia, Commission:** Instituted by Pius XI Apr. 6, 1930, to handle all ecclesiastical affairs of the country; placed under supervision of the Congregation for Extraordinary Ecclesiastical Affairs (now the Council for the Public Affairs of the Church) in 1934, with jurisdiction limited to clergy and faithful of the Roman Rite; under supervision of the Council for the Public Affairs of the Church; Most Rev. Achille Silvestrini, president.

**Catholic-Jewish Relations, Commission:** Instituted by Paul VI, Oct. 22, 1974, to promote and foster relations of a religious nature between Jews and Christians; attached to the Secretariat for Christian Unity; Cardinal Johannes Willebrands, president.

**Catholic-Moslem Relations, Commission:** Instituted by Paul VI, Oct. 22, 1974, to promote, regulate and interpret relations between Catholics and Moslems; attached to the Secretariat for Non-Christians; Most Rev. Francis Arinze, pro-president.

**State of Vatican City, Commission:** Cardinal Sebastiano Baggio, president; Most Rev. Paul Marcinkus, pro-president.

**Protection of the Historical and Artistic Monuments of the Holy See, Commission:** Instituted by Pius XI in 1923, reorganized by Paul VI in 1963; Most Rev. Giovanni Fallani, president.

**Preservation of the Faith, Erection of New Churches in Rome:** Instituted by Pius XI Aug. 5, 1930, to replace a commission dating from 1902; Cardinal Ugo Poletti, president.

**Roman Curia, Commission for Discipline:** Most Rev. Rosalio Jose Castillo Lara, president.

**Works of Religion, Commission:** Instituted by Pius XII June 27, 1942, to bank and administer funds for works of religion; replaced an earlier administration established by Leo XIII in 1887; Most Rev. Paul C. Marcinkus, president.

**Council of Cardinals for Study of Organizational and Economic Problems of the Holy See:** Council established in 1981 by Pope John Paul II; composed of 15 cardinals — residential archbishops — from countries outside of Italy.

**Culture, Pontifical Council:** Established in 1982 by Pope John Paul II to facilitate contacts between the saving message of the Gospel and the plurality of cultures. Cardinal Gabriel-Marie Garrone, head of presidential committee; Most Rev. Paul Poupard, president of executive committee.

## OFFICES

**Prefecture of the Economic Affairs of the Holy See:** A financial office which coordinates and supervises administration of the temporalities of the Holy See.

*OFFICIALS: Cardinal Giuseppe Caprio, president; Msgr. Giovanni Angelo Abbo, secretary.*

BACKGROUND: Established by Paul VI Aug. 15, 1967.

**Apostolic Chamber:** Administers the temporal goods and rights of the Holy See between the death of one pope and the election of another, in accordance with special laws.

*OFFICIALS: Cardinal Paolo Bertoli, chamberlain of the Holy Roman Church; Most Rev. Ettore Cunial, vice-chamberlain.*

BACKGROUND: Originated in the 11th century; reorganized by Pius XI in 1934.

**Administration of the Patrimony of the Apostolic See:** Handles the estate of the Apostolic See under the direction of papal delegates acting with ordinary or extraordinary papal authorization.

*OFFICIALS: Cardinal Agnelo Rossi, president; Most Rev. Lorenzo Antonetti, secretary.*

BACKGROUND: Some of its functions date back to 1878; established by Paul VI Aug. 15, 1967.

**Prefecture of the Pontifical Household:** Oversees the papal chapel — which is at the service of the pope in his capacity as spiritual head of the Church — and the pontifical family — which is at the service of the pope as a sovereign. It arranges papal audiences, has charge of preparing non-liturgical elements of papal ceremonies, makes all necessary arrangements for papal visits and trips outside the Vatican, and settles questions of protocol connected with papal audiences and other formalities.

*OFFICIALS: Most Rev. Jacques Martin, prefect; Msgr. Dino Monduzzi, regent.*

BACKGROUND: Established by Paul VI Aug. 15, 1967, under the title, Prefecture of the Apostolic Palace; it supplanted the Sacred Congregation for Ceremonies founded by Sixtus V Jan. 22, 1588. The office was updated and reorganized under the present title by Paul VI, Mar. 28, 1968.

**Central Statistics Office:** Compiles. systematizes and analyzes information on the status and condition of the Church and the needs of its pastoral ministry, from parish to top levels.

The office is one of the organs of the Secretariat of State.

BACKGROUND: Established by Paul VI Aug. 15, 1967.

**Aid Office:** Distributes alms and aid to the aged, sick, handicapped and other persons in need.

OFFICIAL: Most Rev. Antonio M. Travia, director.

BACKGROUND: The office originated as a charitable office in the time of Bl. Gregory X (1271-1276).

**Vatican II Archives:** Preserves the acts and other documents of the Second Vatican Council.

**Personnel:** Set up by Paul VI May 9, 1971, to handle personnel relations in the offices and other agencies of the Vatican.

OFFICIAL: Msgr. Michele Buro.

## THEOLOGICAL COMMISSION

Establishment with experimental status of a Theological Commission as an adjunct to the Congregation for the Doctrine of the Faith was announced by Pope Paul VI Apr. 28, 1969. The move had been recommended by the Second Vatican Council and was proposed by the Synod of Bishops in 1967. The commission was removed from experimental status in virtue of a *motu proprio* of John Paul II dated Aug. 6, 1982, and effective the following Oct. 1.

The purpose of the commission is to provide the Doctrinal Congregation with the consultative and advisory services of theologians and scriptural and liturgical experts representative of various schools of thought. The international membership is restricted to 30, and the ordinary term of membership is five years (renewable).

### Membership

The commission is headed by Cardinal Joseph Ratzinger, prefect of the Doctrinal Congregation. Msgr. Philippe Delhaye of Belgium is secretary. Members appointed to five-year terms in 1980 and listed in the 1984 edition of *Annuario Pontificio* were as follows.

Barnabas Ahern, C.P. (U.S.); Juan Alfaro, S.J. (Spain); Catalino Arevalo (Philippines); Hans Urs von Balthasar (Switzerland); Carlo Caffara (Italy); Giuseppe Colombo (Italy); Ives Congar, O.P. (France); Wilhelm Ernst (West Germany); Pierre Eyt (France); Ivan Fucek (Yugoslavia); Ferenc Gal (Hungary); Edouard Hamel, S.J. (Canada); Walter Kasper (West Germany); Hachem Elie Khalife, O.L.M. (Lebanon); Bishop Bonaventure Kloppenburg, O.F.M. (Brazil); Michael Ledwith (Ireland); Bishop Karl Lehmann (West Germany); Jorge Medina Estevez (Chile); Bp. John Onaiyekan (Nigeria); Carl Peter (U.S.); Candido Pozo, S.J. (Spain); Walter Principe, C.S.B. (Canada); Ignacy Rozycki (Poland); Heinz Schurmann (West Germany); Bernard Sesboue, S.J. (France); John Thornhill (Australia); Cipriano Vagaggini, O.S.B. (Italy); Christophe von Schonborn, O.P. (Switzerland); Jan Walgrave, O.P. (Belgium).

### Meetings

The commission met for the first time Oct. 6 to 8, 1969, for organizational purposes and the assignment of subcommissions to studies on the priesthood, the theology of hope, unity of faith and pluralism in theology, the criteria of moral knowledge, and collegiality.

Week-long general assemblies, for discussion and decision on subjects of individual and group research have been held annually, except in 1978, since 1969.

Twenty-six members attending the second meeting, Oct. 5 to 10, 1970, discussed reports on the priestly ministry and collegiality. Views were exchanged about the question of ordaining married men, but marriage was ruled out for already ordained priests wanting to continue in the ministry. With respect to collegiality, no doubt was raised about the pope's authority to act independently in the Church; the consensus, however, was that he would be prudent to engage in wide consultation before acting.

By early 1971, the commission prepared the basis of a feasible working paper on the priesthood for the Synod of Bishops, which met for the third time in the fall. The ordination of women was one of the subjects covered, but it did not figure significantly in discussion by the commission because the issue was not considered urgent. Agreement was reported on two points: tradition militated against ordination but permitted a form of diaconal ordination with a rite and purpose distinctive and proper to women.

### Various Studies

Pluralism in theology — concerning different ways of treating, presenting and expressing in practice the unity of faith — was the main subject under consideration at the fourth general assembly Oct. 5 to 11, 1972. The topic had been under study since the first meeting of the commission in 1969.

The October, 1973, meeting, attended by 21 members, completed work on a statement concerning apostolic succession and ordination to holy orders. The necessary sacramental sign of both, the statement said, is the imposition of hands by successors of the Apostles acting in accord with the intention of the Church.

The results of research on Christian morality were discussed at the 1974 meeting, and several articles on the subject were published in 1975.

The majority of members attending the Sept. 25 to Oct. 1, 1975, meeting approved a number of conclusions concerning the relationship between "the mandate given to the ecclesiastical magisterium (the teaching authority of the Church) to protect divine revelation and the task given to theologians to investigate and explain the doctrine of the faith." These conclusions were published by the U.S. Catholic Conference in April, 1977.

Christian salvation and human progress, centering on the nature of and relationship between evangelization and human liberation, was the subject of the meeting held Oct. 4 to 9, 1976. The subject was connected with earlier consideration of the matter by the Synod of Bishops, and also with the contents and tenor of the *Pastoral Constitution on the Church in the Modern World* issued by the Second Vatican Council.

The meeting of Dec. 1 to 6, 1977, focused attention on pastoral aspects of Christian marriage and agreed on a summary of conclusions which: (1) reaffirmed the indissolubility of marriage and the stance of the Church against divorce; (2) declared that the Church should not witness the marriage of Catholics who have rejected the faith.

Various aspects of Christology have been under consideration since 1979.

The 1982 meeting was devoted entirely to the preparation of material related to the sacrament of reconciliation, the theme of the 1983 assembly of the Synod of Bishops; its report, "Penance and Reconciliation," was released in English translation in January, 1984.

Progress was reported on continuing studies in 1983-1984.

## BIBLICAL COMMISSION

The Pontifical Biblical Commission, which has been instrumental in directing the course of Catholic biblical scholarship, was established by Leo XIII Oct. 30, 1902, with the apostolic letter *Vigilantiae Studiique*, at a time when biblical studies were open to great promise as well as to the serious threat of Modernism.

The commission was ordered to promote biblical studies; to safeguard the correct interpretation of Scripture, in the pattern of the rule of faith and against the background of sound scholarship; to state positions which had to be held by Catholics on biblical questions; to indicate questions requiring further study and/or those which were open to the judgment of competent scholars. The commission was also authorized — by St. Pius X in 1904, Pius XI in 1924 and 1931, and Pius X II in 1942 — to set up standards for biblical studies and to grant degrees in Sacred Scripture.

The commission issued 23 decrees or decisions between 1905 and 1953; letters on the scientific study of the Bible (1941) and the Pentateuch (1948); instructions on teaching Scripture in seminaries (1950), biblical associations (1955), and the historical truth of the Gospels (1964).

### Authority of Decisions

Pope St. Pius X stated the authority of decisions of the commission in the letter *Illibatae*, which he issued June 29, 1910, on his own initiative:

"All are bound in conscience to submit to the decisions of the Pontifical Biblical Commission pertaining to doctrine, whether already issued or to be issued in the future, in the same way as to the decrees of the Sacred Congregations (of the Roman Curia) approved by the Pontiff; nor can they avoid the stigma both of disobedience and temerity or be free from grave sin who by any spoken or written words impugn these decisions."

Decisions of the commission regarding points of doctrine are not infallible of themselves. They require religious assent, however, so long as there is no positive evidence that they are wrong. They do not close the door to continuing investigation and study.

### New Norms

The commission was reorganized June 27, 1971, in line with directives issued by Paul VI on his own initiative under the title *Sedula Cura*.

Fifteen new norms changed its structure from a virtually independent office of cardinals aided by lifetime consultors into a group consisting ordinarily of 20 biblical scholars with five-year terms (renewable) linked with the Congregation for the Doctrine of the Faith. Functionally, however, it remains the same.

The commission:

• receives questions and studies topics referred to it by a variety of sources, from the pope to Catholic universities and biblical associations;

• is required to meet in plenary session at least once a year and to submit conclusions reached in such meetings to the pope and the Congregation for the Doctrine of the Faith;

• is under directive to promote relationships with non-Catholic as well as Catholic institutes of biblical studies;

• is to be consulted before any new norms on biblical matters are issued;

• retains its authorization to confer academic degrees in biblical studies.

### Membership

Cardinal Joseph Ratzinger, prefect of the Congregation for the Doctrine of the Faith, is president of the commission.

The May 14, 1984, English edition of *L'Osservatore Romano* reported that Pope John Paul had appointed the following members to the commission: Auxiliary Bishop Monsengwo Pasinya of Kisangani, Msgr. Josef Schreiner and Fathers: John F. McHugh, Domingo Munoz Leon, Gianfranco Ravasi, Giuseppe Segalla, Marcel Dumais, O.M.I., Joseph Fitzmyer, S.J. (U.S.), Jan Lambrecht, S.J., Joao Evangelista Martins Terra, S.J., J. Pathrapankal, C.M.I., Albert Vanhoye, S.J.

### Recent Studies

Since its plenary assembly of April, 1980, the commission has focused attention on the hermeneutic problem in Christology, i.e., the interpretation of what Scripture says about the nature and mission of Jesus.

At its 1979 meeting, the commission initiated a study of acculturation in the Old and New Testaments. The purpose of the study, as stated by Pope John Paul, was "to establish the distinction" between what is culturally conditioned (language, manner of expression, historical circumstances) "and what must always retain its value" (truth relating to salvation) in the words and events used to communicate divine revelation in the Bible.

*Pope John Paul, in an address late in the summer of 1984, cautioned people against reading their own interpretation into the Bible rather than accepting the authentic meaning.*

## COLLEGE OF CARDINALS

Cardinals are chosen by the pope to serve as his principal assistants and advisers in the central administration of church affairs. Collectively, they form the Sacred College of Cardinals. Provisions regarding their selection, rank, roles and prerogatives are detailed in Canons 349 to 359 of the Code of Canon Law.

The college evolved gradually from synods of Roman clergy with whose assistance popes directed church affairs in the first 11 centuries. The first cardinals, in about the sixth century, were priests of the leading churches of Rome who were assigned liturgical, advisory and administrative duties with the Holy See, and the regional deacons of Rome.

For all cardinals except Eastern patriarchs, membership in the college involves aggregation to the clergy of Rome. This aggregation is signified by the assignment to each cardinal, except the patriarchs, of a special or titular church in Rome.

### History of the College

The Sacred College of Cardinals was constituted in its present form and categories of membership in the 12th century. Before that time the pope had a body of advisers selected from among the bishops of dioceses neighboring Rome, priests and deacons of Rome. The college was given definite form in 1150, and in 1179 the selection of cardinals was reserved exclusively to the pope. Sixtus V fixed the number at 70, in 1586. John XXIII set aside this rule when he increased membership at the 1959 and subsequent consistories. The number of cardinals reached an all-time high of 145 under Paul VI in 1973. The number of cardinals entitled to participate in papal elections was limited to 120.

In 1567 the title of cardinal was reserved to members of the college; previously it had been used by priests attached to parish churches of Rome and by the leading clergy of other notable churches. The Code of Canon Law promulgated in 1918 decreed that all cardinals must be priests. Previously there had been lay cardinals (e.g., Cardinal Giacomo Antonelli, d. 1876, Secretary of State to Pius IX). John XXIII provided in the motu proprio *Cum Gravissima* Apr. 15, 1962, that cardinals would henceforth be bishops; this provision is included in the revised Code of Canon Law.

Pope Paul VI placed age limits on the functions of cardinals in the apostolic letter *Ingravescentem Aetatem*, dated Nov. 21, 1970, and effective as of Jan. 1, 1971. At 80, they cease to be members of curial departments and offices, and become ineligible to take part in papal elections. They retain membership in the College of Cardinals, however, with relevant rights and privileges.

### Three Categories

The three categories of members of the college are cardinal bishops, cardinal priests and cardinal deacons.

**Cardinal bishops** include the six titular bishops of the suburban sees of Rome and Eastern patriarchs.

First in rank are the titular bishops of the suburban sees, neighboring Rome: Ostia, Palestrina, Porto and Santa Rufina, Albano, Velletri, Frascati, Sabina and Poggio Mirteto. The dean of the college holds the title of the See of Ostia as well as his other suburban see. These cardinal bishops are engaged in full-time service in the central administration of church affairs in departments of the Roman Curia.

Full recognition is given in the revised Code of Canon Law to the position of Eastern patriarchs as the heads of ancient liturgies and of sees of apostolic origin. Because of their patriarchal dignity and titles, which antedate the dignity and titles of cardinals, they are not aggregated to the Roman clergy and are not, like other cardinals, given title to Roman churches. The patriarchs are assigned rank among the cardinals in order of seniority, following the suburban titleholders.

**Cardinal priests,** who were formerly in charge of leading churches in Rome, are bishops whose dioceses are outside Rome.

**Cardinal deacons,** who were formerly chosen according to regional divisions of Rome, are titular bishops assigned to full-time service in the Roman Curia.

The dean and sub-dean of the college are elected by the cardinal bishops — subject to approval by the pope — from among their number. The dean, or the sub-dean in his absence, presides over the college as the first among equals.

### Selection and Duties

Cardinals are selected by the pope and are inducted into the college in appropriate ceremonies.

Cardinals under the age of 80: elect the pope when the Holy See becomes vacant (see Papal Election), and are major administrators of church affairs, serving in one or more departments of the Roman Curia. Cardinals in charge of agencies of the Roman Curia and Vatican City are asked to submit their resignation from office to the Pope on reaching the age of 75. All cardinals enjoy a number of special rights and privileges. Their title, while symbolic of high honor, does not signify any extension of the powers of holy orders. They are called princes of the Church.

A **cardinal in pectore** is one whose selection has been made by the pope but whose name has not been disclosed; he has no title, rights or duties until such disclosure is made, at which time he takes precedence from the time of the secret selection.

## CONFERRAL OF PALLIUMS

Three Americans were among 11 new archbishops who received palliums from Pope John Paul II June 29, 1984, in a historic ceremony: John J. O'Connor of New York, Bernard Law of Boston, Daniel Kucera of Dubuque. The historical note: it was the first time in modern church history that the vestment, symbolic of authority over an archdiocese, was conferred personally by a pope.

# BIOGRAPHIES OF CARDINALS

*Biographies of the cardinals, as of Aug. 1, 1984, are given below in alphabetical order. For historical notes, order of seniority and geographical distribution of cardinals, see separate entries.*

*An asterisk indicates cardinals ineligible to take part in papal elections.*

**Alfrink,\* Bernard Jan:** b. July 5, 1900, Nijkerk, Netherlands; ord. priest Aug. 15, 1924; professor of Sacred Scripture at Utrecht major seminary, 1933; consultor to Pontifical Biblical Commission, Rome, 1944; professor at Catholic University of Nijmegen, 1945; ord. titular archbishop of Tiana and coadjutor archbishop of Utrecht, July 17, 1951; archbishop of Utrecht, 1955-75; cardinal Mar. 28, 1960; titular church, St. Joachim. Archbishop emeritus of Utrecht.

**Antonelli,\* Ferdinando Giuseppe, O.F.M.:** b. July 14, 1896, Subbiano, Italy; solemnly professed in Order of Friars Minor, Apr. 7, 1914; ord. priest July 25, 1922; taught church history, 1928-32, and Christian archeology, 1932-65, at Antonianum; rector magnificus of Antonianum, 1937-43, 1953-59; definitor general of Friars Minor, 1939-45; held various offices in Roman Curia; secretary of Congregation of Rites, 1965-69, and Congregation for Causes of Saints, 1969-73; ord. titular archbishop of Idicra, Mar. 19, 1966; cardinal Mar. 5, 1973; titular church, San Sebastian (on the Palatine).

**Aponte Martinez, Luis:** b. Aug. 4, 1922, Lajas, Puerto Rico; ord. priest Apr. 10, 1950; parish priest at Ponce; ord. titular bishop of Lares and auxiliary of Ponce, Oct. 12, 1960; bishop of Ponce, 1963-64; archbishop of San Juan, Nov. 4, 1964; cardinal Mar. 5, 1973; titular church, St. Mary Mother of Providence (in Monteverde). Archbishop of San Juan, member of:
Congregation: Causes of Saints.

**Aramburu, Juan Carlos:** b. Feb. 11, 1912, Reduccion, Argentina; ord. priest in Rome, Oct. 28, 1934; ord. titular bishop of Plataea and auxiliary of Tucuman, Argentina, Dec. 15, 1946; bishop, 1953, and first archbishop, 1957, of Tucuman; titular archbishop of Torri di Bizacena and coadjutor archbishop of Buenos Aires, June 14, 1967; archbishop of Buenos Aires, Apr. 22, 1975; cardinal May 24, 1976; titular church, St. John Baptist of the Florentines. Archbishop of Buenos Aires, ordinary for Eastern Rite Catholics in Brazil without ordinaries of their own rites, member of:
Congregations: Oriental Churches, Catholic Education.
Office: Prefecture of Economic Affairs.

**Arns, Paulo Evaristo, O.F.M.:** b. Sept. 14, 1921, Forquilhinha, Brazil; ord. priest Nov. 30, 1945; held various teaching posts; director of *Sponsa Christi*, monthly review for religious, and of the Franciscan publication center in Brazil; ord. titular bishop of Respetta and auxiliary of Sao Paulo, July 3, 1966; archbishop of Sao Paulo, Oct. 22, 1970; cardinal Mar. 5, 1973; titular church, St. Anthony of Padua (in Via Tuscolana). Archbishop of Sao Paulo, member of:

Congregations: Sacraments, Divine Worship; Secretariat: Non-Believers.

**Bafile,\* Corrado:** b. July 4, 1903, L'Aquila, Italy; practiced law in Rome for six years before beginning studies for priesthood; ord. priest Apr. 11, 1936; served in Vatican secretariat of state, 1939-59; ord. titular archbishop of Antiochia in Pisidia, Mar. 19, 1960; apostolic nuncio to Germany, 1960-75; pro-prefect of Congregation for Causes of Saints, July 18, 1975; cardinal May 24, 1976; deacon, S. Maria (in Portico); prefect of Congregation for Causes of Saints, 1976-80.

**Baggio, Sebastiano:** b. May 16, 1913, Rosa, Italy; ord. priest Dec. 21, 1935; ord. titular bishop of Ephesus, July 26, 1953; served in Vatican diplomatic corps, 1953-69; nuncio to Chile, apostolic delegate to Canada, nuncio to Brazil; cardinal Apr. 28, 1969; archbishop of Cagliari, 1969-73; entered order of cardinal bishops as titular bishop of Velletri, Dec. 12, 1974; prefect of Congregation for Bishops, 1973-84. President of Pontifical Commission for Vatican City, 1984, member of:
Council for Public Affairs of Church;
Congregations: Doctrine of the Faith, Religious and Secular Institutes, Catholic Education, Evangelization of Peoples;
Commissions: Authentic Interpretation of Code of Canon Law, Latin America (President), Migration and Tourism (President), Sanctuaries of Pompei, Loreto, and Bari;
Office: Patrimony of Holy See.

**Ballestrero, Anastasio Alberto, O.C.D.:** b. Oct. 3, 1913, Genoa, Italy; professed in Order of Discalced Carmelites, 1929; ord. priest June 6, 1936; provincial, 1942-48, and superior general, 1955-67, of Carmelites; author of many books on Christian life; ord. archbishop of Bari, Feb. 2, 1974; archbishop of Turin, Aug. 1, 1977; cardinal June 30, 1979; titular church, S. Maria (sopra Minerva). Archbishop of Turin, member of:
Council for Public Affairs of the Church;
Congregations: Bishops, Religious and Secular Institutes.

**Baum, William Wakefield:** b. Nov. 21, 1926, Dallas, Tex.; moved to Kansas City, Mo., at an early age; ord. priest May 12, 1951; executive director of U.S. bishops commission for ecumenical and interreligious affairs, 1964-69; attended Second Vatican Council as *peritus* (expert adviser); ord. bishop of Springfield-Cape Girardeau, Mo., Apr. 6, 1970; archbishop of Washington, D.C., 1973-80; cardinal May 24, 1976; titular church, Holy Cross (on the Via Flaminia). Prefect of Congregation for Catholic Education, 1980, grand chancellor of Pontifical Gregorian University, and member of:
Council for Public Affairs of the Church;
Congregations: Doctrine of the Faith, Bishops, Oriental Churches, Religious and Secular Institutes, Evangelization of Peoples;
Secretariat: Non-Believers;
Office: Administration of Patrimony of Holy See;
Commissions: Council for Laity, Authentic Interpretation of Code of Canon Law.

**Beras Rojas, Octavio Antonio:** b. Nov. 16, 1906, Seibo, Dominican Republic; ord. priest Aug. 13, 1933; founded national Catholic youth movement; ord. titular archbishop of Euchaitae and coadjutor archbishop of Santo Domingo, Aug. 12, 1945; archbishop of Santo Domingo, 1961-81; cardinal May 24, 1976; titular church, San Sisto. Archbishop emeritus of Santo Domingo.

**Bernardin, Joseph L.:** b. Apr. 2, 1928, Columbia, S.C.; ord. priest Apr. 26, 1952; ord. titular bishop of Lugara and auxiliary bishop of Atlanta, Ga., Apr. 26, 1966; general secretary, 1968-72, and president, 1974-77, of NCCB/USCC; archbishop of Cincinnati, 1972-82; archbishop of Chicago, July 10, 1982, installed Aug. 25, 1982; cardinal Feb. 2, 1983; titular church, Jesus the Divine Worker. Archbishop of Chicago, member of:
Congregations: Sacraments, Divine Worship, Evangelization of Peoples;
Secretariat: Christian Unity.

**Bertoli, Paolo:** b. Feb. 1, 1908, Poggio Garfagnana, Italy; ord. priest Aug. 15, 1930; entered diplomatic service of the Holy See, serving in nunciatures in Yugoslavia, France, Haiti and Switzerland; ord. titular archbishop of Nicomedia, May 11, 1952; apostolic delegate to Turkey (1952-53), nuncio to Colombia (1953-59), Lebanon (1959-60), France (1960-69); cardinal Apr. 28, 1969; prefect of Congregation for Causes of Saints, 1969-73; entered order of cardinal bishops as titular bishop of Frascati, June 30, 1979. Chamberlain (Camerlengo) of Holy Roman Church, 1979, member of:
Council for Public Affairs of Church:
Congregations: Doctrine of the Faith, Bishops, Oriental Churches, Evangelization of Peoples;
Secretariat: Non-Believers;
Tribunal: Apostolic Signatura;
Commission: Latin America, State of Vatican City.

**Brandao Vilela, Avelar:** b. June 13, 1912, Vicosa, Brazil; ord. priest Oct. 27, 1935; professor and spiritual director at diocesan seminary at Aracaju; ord. bishop of Petrolina, Oct. 27, 1946; archbishop of Teresina, Nov. 5, 1955; established 20 social centers and a radio station; introduced agrarian reform of church properties; erected the Institute of Catechetics: archbishop of Sao Salvador da Bahia, Mar. 25, 1971; president of CELAM, 1967-72; co-president of Medellin Conference, 1968; cardinal Mar. 5, 1973; titular church, Sts. Boniface and Alexius. Archbishop of Sao Salvador da Bahia, member of:
Congregations: Clergy, Causes of Saints;
Commission: Latin America.

**Bueno y Monreal,* Jose Maria:** b. Sept. 11, 1904, Zaragoza, Spain; ord. priest Mar. 19, 1927; ord. bishop of Jaca, Mar. 19, 1946; bishop of Vitoria, May 13, 1950; titular archbishop of Antioch in Pisidia and coadjutor archbishop of Seville, Oct. 27, 1954; archbishop of Seville, 1957-82; cardinal Dec. 15, 1958; titular church, Sts. Vitus, Modestus and Crescentia. Archbishop emeritus of Seville.

**Caprio, Giuseppe:** b. Nov. 15, 1914, Lapio, Italy; ord. priest Dec. 17, 1938; served in diplomatic missions in China (1947-51, when Vatican diplomats were expelled by communists), Belgium (1951-54),

and South Vietnam (1954-56); internuncio in China with residence at Taiwan, 1959-67; ord. titular archbishop of Apollonia, Dec. 17, 1961; pro-nuncio in India, 1967-69; secretary, 1969-77, and president, 1979-81, of Administration of Patrimony of Holy See; substitute secretary of state, 1977-79; cardinal June 30, 1979; deacon, St. Mary Auxiliatrix in Via Tuscolana. President of Prefecture of Economic Affairs of the Holy See, 1981, member of:
Council for Public Affairs of Church;
Congregations: Bishops, Oriental Churches, Causes of Saints, Evangelization of Peoples.

**Carberry,* John J.:** b. July 31, 1904, Brooklyn, N.Y.; ord. priest July 28, 1929; ord. titular bishop of Elis and coadjutor bishop of Lafayette, Ind., July 25, 1956; bishop of Lafayette, Nov. 20, 1957; bishop of Columbus, Ohio, Jan. 16, 1965; archbishop of St. Louis, Mo., 1968-79; cardinal Apr. 28, 1969; titular church, St. John Baptist de Rossi (Via Latina). Archbishop emeritus of St. Louis.

**Carpino, Francesco:** b. May 18, 1905, Palazzolo Acreide, Italy; ord. priest Aug. 14, 1927; ord. titular archbishop of Nicomedia and coadjutor archbishop of Monreale, Apr. 8, 1951; archbishop of Monreale, 1951-61; titular archbishop of Sardica, Jan. 19, 1961; assessor of Consistorial Congregation, 1961; pro-prefect of Congregation of the Council, Apr. 7, 1967; cardinal June 26, 1967; archbishop of Palermo, 1967-70; entered order of cardinal bishops as titular bishop of Albano, Jan. 27, 1978. Referendary of the Congregation of Bishops, 1970, and member of:
Council for Public Affairs of the Church;
Congregation: Causes of Saints;
Tribunal: Apostolic Signatura.

**Carter, Gerald Emmett:** b. Mar. 1, 1912, Montreal, Canada; ord. priest May 22, 1937; engaged in pastoral and teaching ministry in Montreal; founder and president of St. Joseph Teachers' College and co-founder and director of Thomas More Institute for adult education; ord. titular bishop of Altiburo and auxiliary bishop of London, Ont., Feb. 2, 1962; bishop of London, Ont., 1964-78; vice president, 1971-73, and president, 1975-77, of Canadian Conference of Catholic Bishops; archbishop of Toronto, Apr. 27, 1978; cardinal June 30, 1979; titular church, St. Mary (in Traspontina). Archbishop of Toronto, member of:
Congregation: Evangelization of Peoples;
Secretariats: Christian Unity, Non-Christians.

**Casaroli, Agostino:** b. Nov. 24, 1914, Castel San Giovanni, Italy; ord. priest May 27, 1937; entered service of Vatican secretariat of state, 1940; undersecretary, 1961-67, of the Congregation for Extraordinary Ecclesiastical Affairs, and secretary, 1967-79, of its successor the Council for Public Affairs of the Church; ord. titular archbishop of Cartagina, July 16, 1967; chief negotiator for the Vatican with East European communist governments; missions included visits to Hungary, Yugoslavia, Poland, Czechoslovakia, Bulgaria; headed Vatican delegations to several UN conferences and the Helsinki Conference (1975); Pro-Secretary of State and Pro-Prefect of Council for Public Affairs of the Church, Apr. 28, 1979; cardinal June 30, 1979; titular church, the Twelve Apostles; presi-

dent, 1981-84, of Administration of Patrimony of Holy See and Pontifical Commission for Vatican City. Secretary of State and prefect of Council for Public Affairs of the Church, July 1, 1979 (given increased responsibility in government of Vatican City State, 1984), member of:
Congregations: Doctrine of the Faith, Bishops;
Secretariat: Non-Believers;
Commissions: Authentic Interpretation of Code of Canon Law, Revision of Oriental Code of Canon Law, Institute for Works of Religion.

**Casoria, Giuseppe:** b. Oct. 1, .1908, Acerra, Italy; ord. priest Dec. 21, 1930; jurist; Roman Curia official from 1937; under-secretary, 1959-69, and secretary, 1969-73, of Congregation for Sacraments and Divine Worship; secretary of Congregation for Causes of Saints, 1973-81; ord. titular archbishop of Vescovia, Feb. 13, 1972; pro-prefect of Congregation for Sacraments and Divine Worship, 1981-83; cardinal Feb. 2, 1983; deacon, St. Joseph on Via Trionfale. Prefect of Congregation for Sacraments and Divine Worship, 1983-84. Member of:
Congregations: Doctrine of the Faith, Oriental Churches, Causes of Saints;
Commissions: Authentic Interpretation of Code of Canon Law, Revision of Oriental Code of Canon Law.

**Cé, Marco:** b. July 8, 1925, Izano, Italy; ord. priest Mar. 27, 1948; taught sacred scripture and dogmatic theology at seminary in his home diocese of Crema; rector of seminary, 1957; presided over diocesan liturgical commission, preached youth retreats; ord. titular bishop of Vulturia, May 17, 1970; auxiliary bishop of Bologna, 1970-76; general ecclesiastical assistant of Italian Catholic Action, 1976-78; patriarch of Venice, Dec. 7, 1978; cardinal June 30, 1979; titular church, St. Mark. Patriarch of Venice, member of:
Congregations: Clergy, Catholic Education.

**Ciappi, Mario Luigi, O.P.:** b. Oct. 6, 1909, Florence, Italy; ord. priest Mar. 26, 1948; papal theologian from 1955, serving Pius XII, John XXIII and Paul VI; ord. titular bishop of Misenum June 18, 1977; cardinal June 27, 1977; deacon, Our Lady of the Sacred Heart. Pro-theologian of pontifical household, member of:
Congregation: Causes of Saints;
Tribunal: Apostolic Signatura.

**Civardi, Ernesto:** b. Oct. 21, 1906, Fossarmato, Italy; ord. priest June 29, 1930; assistant rector of Pontifical Lombard Seminary in Rome; held various curial offices; undersecretary, 1953-67, and secretary, 1967-79, of the Congregation for Bishops (known as the Consistorial Congregation until 1967); ord. titular archbishop of Sardica, July 16, 1967; secretary of College of Cardinals, 1967-79; filled office of secretary at 1978 conclaves which elected Popes John Paul I and John Paul II; cardinal June 30, 1979; deacon, St. Theodore. Member of:
Congregations: Causes of Saints, Evangelization of Peoples;
Tribunal: Apostolic Signatura.

**Colombo,\* Giovanni:** b. Dec. 6, 1902, Caronno, Italy; ord. priest May 29, 1926; rector of Milan Seminary, 1953; ord. titular bishop of Filippopoli

and auxiliary bishop of Milan, Dec. 7, 1960; archbishop of Milan, 1963-79; cardinal Feb. 22, 1965; titular church, Sts. Sylvester and Martin. Archbishop emeritus of Milan.

**Confalonieri,\* Carlo:** b. July 25, 1893, Seveso, Italy; ord. priest Mar. 18, 1916; private secretary to Pius XI for 17 years, to Pius XII for two years; ord. archbishop of L'Aquila, May 4, 1941; transferred to titular archbishopric of Nicopoli al Nesto, Feb. 22, 1950; cardinal Dec. 15, 1958; titular bishop of suburban see of Palestrina, Mar. 14, 1972, when he entered order of cardinal bishops, and Ostia, Dec. 12, 1977, when he was named dean of College of Cardinals; prefect of Congregation for Bishops, 1967-73; sub-dean of college of cardinals, 1974-77. Archpriest of Patriarchal Liberian Basilica, dean of College of Cardinals, Dec. 12, 1977.

**Cooray,\* Thomas B., O.M.I.:** b. Dec. 28, 1901, Periyamulla Negombo, Ceylon (now Sri Lanka); ord. priest June 23, 1929; ord. titular archbishop of Preslavo, Mar. 7, 1946; coadjutor archbishop of Colombo, Sri Lanka, 1946-47; succeeded as archbishop of Colombo, July 26, 1947 (retired 1976); cardinal Feb. 22, 1965; titular church, Sts. Nereus and Achilleus. Archbishop emeritus of Colombo, Sri Lanka.

**Cordeiro, Joseph:** b. Jan. 19, 1918, Bombay, India; ord. priest Aug. 24, 1946; served in educational and other diocesan posts at Karachi, Pakistan; ord. archbishop of Karachi, Aug. 24, 1958, the first native-born prelate in that see; cardinal Mar. 5, 1973; titular church, St. Andrew Apostle. Archbishop of Karachi, member of:
Congregation: Religious and Secular Institutes;
Secretariat: Non-Christians;
Commission: Pontifical Council Cor Unum.

**Corripio Ahumada, Ernesto:** b. June 29, 1919, Tampico, Mexico; ord. priest Oct. 25, 1942, in Rome, where he remained until almost the end of World War II; taught and held various positions in local seminary of Tampico, 1945-50; ord. titular bishop of Zapara and auxiliary bishop of Tampico, Mar. 19, 1953; bishop of Tampico, 1956-67; archbishop of Antequera, 1967-76; archbishop of Puebla de los Angeles, 1976-77; archbishop of Mexico City and primate of Mexico, July 19, 1977; cardinal June 30, 1979; titular church, Mary Immaculate al Tiburtino. Archbishop of Mexico City, member of:
Congregations: Sacraments, Divine Worship, Clergy, Catholic Education;
Commission: Latin America.

**Danneels, Godfried:** b. June 4, 1933, Kanegem, Belgium; ord. priest Aug. 17, 1957; professor of liturgy and sacramental theology at Catholic University of Louvain, 1969-77; ord. bishop of Antwerp Dec. 18, 1977; app. archbishop of Mechelen-Brussel, Dec. 19, 1979; installed Jan. 4, 1980; elected member of general secretariat of Synod of Bishops, 1981; cardinal Feb. 2, 1983; titular church, St. Anastasia. Archbishop of Mechelen-Brussel, military vicar of Belgium, member of:
Council for Public Affairs of the Church;
Congregations: Doctrine of the Faith, Bishops, Evangelization of Peoples, Catholic Education.

**Darmojuwono, Justin:** b. Nov. 2, 1914, Godean, Indonesia; ord. priest May 25, 1947; ord. archbishop of Semarang, Apr. 6, 1964 (resigned July 3, 1981, for health reasons); cardinal June 26, 1967; titular church, Most Holy Names of Jesus and Mary. Archbishop emeritus of Semarang. Member of: Congregations: Sacraments, Divine Worship.

**De Araujo Sales, Eugenio:** b. Nov. 8, 1920, Acari, Brazil; ord. priest Nov. 21, 1943; ord. titular bishop of Tibica and auxiliary bishop of Natal, Aug. 15, 1954; archbishop of Sao Salvador, 1968-71; cardinal Apr. 28, 1969; titular church, St. Gregory VII. Archbishop of Rio de Janeiro (1971), ordinary for Eastern Rite Catholics in Brazil without ordinaries of their own rites, member of:
Council for Public Affairs of the Church;
Congregations: Bishops, Oriental Churches, Clergy, Evangelization of Peoples, Catholic Education;
Commissions: Social Communications, Council for Culture.

**Dearden, John Francis.:** b. Oct. 15, 1907, Valley Falls, R. I.; ord. priest Dec. 8, 1932; ord. titular bishop of Sarepta and coadjutor bishop of Pittsburgh, May 18, 1948; bishop of Pittsburgh, Dec. 22, 1950; archbishop of Detroit, 1958-80; first president of the National Conference of Catholic Bishops and the United States Catholic Conference, 1966-71; cardinal Apr. 28, 1969; titular church, St. Pius X (alla Balduina). Archbishop emeritus of Detroit, member of:
Congregations: Sacraments, Divine Worship.

**De Furstenberg,\* Maximilien:** b. Oct. 23, 1904, Heerlen, Netherlands; ord. priest Aug. 9, 1931; ord. titular archbishop of Palto and apostolic delegate to Japan, Apr. 25, 1949; internuncio, 1952, when Japan established diplomatic relations with the Vatican; apostolic delegate to Australia, New Zealand and Oceania, Feb. 11, 1960; nuncio to Portugal, 1962-67; cardinal June 26, 1967; titular church, Most Sacred Heart of Jesus (a Castro Pretorio); prefect of the Congregation for the Oriental Churches, 1969-73. Grand Master of Equestrian Order of Holy Sepulchre of Jerusalem, member of:
Council for Public Affairs of Church;
Congregations: Bishops, Causes of Saints, Evangelization of Peoples;
Commissions: State of Vatican City, Institute for Works of Religion.

**De Lubac,\* Henri, S.J.:** b. Feb. 20, 1896, Cambrai, France; entered Society of Jesus, October, 1913; ord. priest Aug. 22, 1927; taught fundamental theology and history of religions at the Theology Faculty of Lyons from 1929 to the early 50s when he was dismissed because of misunderstanding of his book *The Supernatural*, intended to re-emphasize the doctrine on supernatural destiny; reinstated to his teaching post by Pope John XXIII; chief consultor of preparatory theological commission for Vatican II and *peritus* for Council itself; appointed member of International Theological Commission by Paul VI; cardinal Feb. 2, 1983, with permission to decline episcopal ordination; deacon, St. Mary in Domnica.

**do Nascimento, Alexandre:** b. Mar. 1, 1925, Malanje, Angola; ord. priest Dec. 20, 1952, in Rome; professor of dogmatic theology in major seminary of Luanda, Angola; editor of *O*

*Apostolada,* Catholic newspaper; forced into exile in Lisbon, Portugal, 1961-71; returned to Angola, 1971; active with student and refugee groups; professor at Pius XII Institute of Social Sciences; ord. bishop of Malanje, Aug. 31, 1975; archbishop of Lubango and apostolic administrator of Onjiva, Feb. 3, 1977; held hostage by Angolan guerrillas, Oct. 15 to Nov. 16, 1982; cardinal Feb. 2, 1983; titular church, St. Mark in Agro Laurentino. Archbishop of Lubango, apostolic administrator of Onjiva, member of:
Congregation: Evangelization of Peoples.

**Duval,\* Leon-Etienne:** b. Nov. 9, 1903, Chenex, France; ord. priest Dec. 18, 1926; ord. bishop of Constantine, Algeria, Feb. 11, 1947; archbishop of Algiers, Feb. 3, 1954; cardinal Feb. 22, 1965; titular church, St. Balbina. Archbishop of Algiers.

**Ekandem, Dominic Ignatius:** b. 1917, Ibiono, Nigeria; ord. priest Dec. 7, 1947; ord. titular bishop of Gerapoli di Isauri and auxiliary bishop of Calabar, Feb. 7, 1954, the first Nigerian to become a bishop; first bishop of Ikot Ekpene, Mar. 1, 1963; cardinal May 24, 1976; titular church, San Marcello. Bishop of Ikot Ekpene, superior of mission "sui juris" of Abuja, member of:
Congregation: Evangelization of Peoples.

**Enrique y Tarancon, Vicente:** b. May 14, 1907, Burriana, Spain; ord. priest Nov. 1, 1929; ord. bishop of Solsona, Mar. 24, 1946; bishop of Oviedo, Apr. 12, 1964; archbishop of Toledo, 1969-71; cardinal Apr. 28, 1969; titular church, St. John Chrysostom; archbishop of Madrid, 1971-83. Archbishop emeritus of Madrid.

**Etchegaray, Roger:** b. Sept. 25, 1922, Espelette, France; ord. priest July 13, 1947; deputy director, 1961-66, and secretary general, 1966-70, of French Episcopal Conference; ord. titular bishop of Gemelle di Numidia and auxiliary bishop of Paris, May 27, 1969; archbishop of Marseilles, Dec. 22, 1970; prelate of Mission de France, 1975-82; president of French Episcopal Conference, 1979-81; cardinal June 30, 1979; titular church, St. Leo I. Archbishop of Marseilles, President of Pontifical Commission for Justice and Peace and the Pontifical Council *Cor Unum*, 1984, member of:
Congregations: Evangelization of Peoples, Catholic Education;
Secretariat: Christian Unity;
Commission: Social Communications.

**Flahiff, George B., C.S.B.:** b. Oct. 26, 1905, Paris, Ont., Canada; ord. priest Aug. 17, 1930; professor of medieval history at the University of Toronto and Pontifical Institute of Medieval Studies in Toronto, 1934-54; superior general of Basilian Fathers, 1954; ord. archbishop of Winnipeg, May 31, 1961 (retired 1982); president of Canadian Conference of Bishops, 1963-65; cardinal Apr. 28, 1969; titular church, St. Mary della Salute (Primavalle). Archbishop emeritus of Winnipeg, member of:
Congregation: Religious and Secular Institutes.

**Florit,\* Ermenegildo:** b. July 5, 1901, Fagagna, Italy; ord. priest Apr. 11, 1925; taught Sacred Scripture at Lateran University from 1929; prorector of Lateran University and Institute of Civil and Canon Law, 1951-54; ord. titular archbishop of Hieropolis and coadjutor archbishop of Florence,

Sept. 12, 1954; archbishop of Florence, 1962-77; cardinal Feb. 22, 1965; titular church, Queen of the Apostles. Archbishop emeritus of Florence.

**Freeman, James Darcy:** b. Nov. 19, 1907, Sydney, Australia; ord. priest July 13, 1930; ord. titular bishop of Ermopoli minore and auxiliary of Sydney, Jan. 24, 1957; bishop of Armidale, 1968-71; archbishop of Sydney, 1971-83; cardinal Mar. 5, 1973; titular church, St. Mary Queen of Peace. (in Ostia Mare). Archbishop emeritus of Sydney, member of;
Congregation: Catholic Education.

**Gantin, Bernardin:** b. May 8, 1922, Toffo, Dahomey (now Benin): ord. priest Jan. 14, 1951; ord. titular bishop of Tipasa di Mauritania and auxiliary bishop of Cotonou, Feb. 3, 1957; archbishop of Cotonou, 1960-71; associate secretary (1971-73) and secretary (1973-75) of Congregation for Evangelization of Peoples; vice-president (1975) and president (1976-84) of Pontifical Commission for Justice and Peace; cardinal June 27, 1977; deacon, Sacred Heart of Christ the King; transferred to order of priests June 25, 1984. Prefect of Congregation for Bishops, 1984, member of:
Council for Public Affairs of the Church;
Congregations: Doctrine of the Faith, Bishops, Causes of Saints, Evangelization of Peoples, Oriental Churches, Religious and Secular Institutes, Catholic Education;
Secretariats: Non-Believers, Non-Christians;
Tribunal: Apostolic Signatura;
Commissions: Social Communications, Pontifical Council *Cor Unum*, Institute for Works of Religion, Sanctuaries of Pompeii, Loreto and Bari.

**Garrone,\* Gabriel-Marie:** b. Oct. 12, 1901, Aix-les-Bains, France; ord. priest Apr. 11, 1925; captain during World War II, cited for bravery, taken prisoner; rector of major seminary of Chambery, 1947; ord. titular archbishop of Lemno and coadjutor of Toulouse, June 24, 1947; archbishop of Toulouse, 1956-66; titular archbishop of Torri di Numidia and pro-prefect of Congregation of Seminaries and Universities, Mar. 24, 1966; cardinal June 26, 1967; titular church, St. Sabina; prefect of Congregation for Catholic Education, 1968-80. Former prefect of Congregation for Catholic Education, head of presidential committee of Pontifical Council for Culture.

**Glemp. Jozef:** b. Dec. 18, 1928, Inowroclaw, Poland; assigned to forced labor on German farm in Rycerzow during Nazi occupation; ord. priest May 25, 1956; studied in Rome, 1958-64, receiving degree in Roman and canon law from Pontifical Lateran University; secretary of primatial major seminary at Gniezno on his return to Poland, 1964; spokesman for secretariat of primate of Poland and chaplain of primate for archdiocese of Gniezno, 1967; ord. bishop of Warmia, Apr. 21, 1979; archbishop of Gniezno, July 7, 1981, with title of archbishop of Warsaw and primate of Poland; cardinal Feb. 2, 1983; titular church, St. Mary in Trastevere. Archbishop of Gniezno and Warsaw, primate of Poland, member of:
Congregation: Oriental Churches.

**Gonzalez Martin, Marcelo:** b. Jan. 16, 1918, Villanubla, Spain; ord. priest June 29, 1941; taught theology and sociology at Valladolid diocesan seminary; founded organization for construction of houses for poor; ord. bishop of Astorga, Mar. 5, 1961; titular archbishop of Case Mediane and coadjutor of Barcelona, Feb. 21, 1966; archbishop of Barcelona, 1967-71; archbishop of Toledo, Dec. 3, 1971; cardinal Mar. 5, 1973; titular church, St. Augustine. Archbishop of Toledo, member of:
Congregations: Clergy, Evangelization of Peoples.

**Gouyon, Paul:** b. Oct. 24, 1910, Bordeaux, France; ord. priest Mar. 13, 1937; ord. bishop of Bayonne, Oct. 7, 1957; titular archbishop of Pessinonte and coadjutor archbishop of Rennes, Sept. 6, 1963; archbishop of Rennes, Sept. 4, 1964; cardinal Apr. 28, 1969; titular church, Nativity of Our Lord Jesus Christ. (Via Gallia). Archbishop of Rennes, member of:
Congregation: Causes of Saints;
Secretariat: Non-Believers.

**Gray, Gordon Joseph:** b. Aug. 10, 1910, Edinburgh, Scotland; ord. priest June 15, 1935; ord. archbishop of Saint Andrews and Edinburgh, Sept. 21, 1951; chairman of International Committee for English in the Liturgy; cardinal Apr. 28, 1969; titular church, St. Clare. Archbishop of Saint Andrews and Edinburgh, member of:
Congregations: Clergy, Evangelization of Peoples, Sacraments, Divine Worship;
Commission: Social Communications.

**Guerri, Sergio:** b. Dec. 25, 1905, Tarquinia, Italy; ord. priest Mar. 30, 1929; ord. titular archbishop of Trevi, Apr. 27, 1969; cardinal Apr. 28, 1969; titular church, Most Holy Name of Mary; pro-president of Pontifical Commission for State of Vatican City, 1968-81. Member of:
Congregations: Causes of Saints, Evangelization of Peoples;
Commission: Patrimony of Holy See.

**Guyot, Jean:** b. July 7, 1905, Bordeaux, France; ord. priest June 29, 1932; held various offices in Bordeaux diocese; ord. titular bishop of Helenopolis and coadjutor of Constance, May 4, 1949; bishop of Constance, 1950-66; archbishop of Toulouse, 1966-78; invested with Legion of Honor by French government; cardinal Mar. 5, 1973; titular church, Saint Agnes Outside the Walls. Archbishop emeritus of Toulouse.

**Hoeffner, Joseph:** b. Dec. 24, 1906, Horhausen, Germany; ord. priest Oct. 30, 1932; ord. bishop of Munster, Sept. 14, 1962; titular archbishop of Aquileia and coadjutor archbishop of Cologne, Jan. 6, 1969; archbishop of Cologne, Feb. 23, 1969; cardinal Apr. 28, 1969; titular church, St. Andrew of the Valley. Archbishop of Cologne, member of:
Congregations: Religious and Secular Institutes, Evangelization of Peoples, Catholic Education;
Secretariat: Non-Believers;
Office: Prefecture of Economic Affairs.

**Hume, George Basil, O.S.B.:** b. Mar. 2, 1923, Newcastle-upon-Tyne, England; began monastic studies at Benedictine Abbey of St. Laurence at Ampleforth, 1941; made solemn perpetual vows as Benedictine, 1945; ord. priest July 23, 1950; abbot of Ampleforth, 1963-76; ord. archbishop of Westminster, Mar. 25, 1976; cardinal May 24, 1976;

titular church, S. Silvestro (in Capite). Archbishop of Westminster, member of:
Congregation: Religious and Secular Institutes;
Secretariat: Christian Unity.

**Jubany Arnau, Narciso:** b. Aug. 12, 1913, Santa Coloma de Farnes, Spain; ord. priest July 30, 1939; professor of law at Barcelona seminary; served on ecclesiastical tribunal; ord. titular bishop of Ortosia and auxiliary of Barcelona, Jan. 22, 1956; bishop of Gerona, 1964-71; archbishop of Barcelona, Dec. 3, 1971; cardinal Mar. 5, 1973; titular church, San Lorenzo (in Damaso). Archbishop of Barcelona, member of:
Congregations: Sacraments, Divine Worship, Religious and Secular Institutes.

**Khoraiche, Antoine Pierre:** b. Sept. 20, 1907, Ain-Ebel, Lebanon; ord. priest Apr. 12, 1930; ord. titular bishop of Tarsus and auxiliary bishop of Sidon of the Maronites, Oct. 15, 1950; bishop of Sidon, Nov. 25, 1957; elected patriarch of Antioch for Maronites, Feb. 3, 1975, granted ecclesial communion by Paul VI, Feb. 15, 1975; advocate of reconciliation among various Lebanese ethnic and religious groups and withdrawal of foreign troops from country; cardinal Feb. 2, 1983. Patriarch of Antoioch for Maronites (residence in Beirut), member of:
Congregation: Oriental Churches;
Commission: Revision of Code of Oriental Canon Law.

**Kim, Stephan Sou Hwan:** b. May 8, 1922, Tae Gu, Korea; ord. priest Sept. 15, 1951; ord. bishop of Masan, May 31, 1966; archbishop of Seoul, Apr. 9, 1968; cardinal Apr. 28, 1969; titular church, St. Felix of Cantalice (Centocelle). Archbishop of Seoul, apostolic administrator of Pyeong Yang, member of:
Congregation: Evangelization of Peoples;
Secretariat: Non-Christians.

**Kitbunchu, Michael Michai:** b. Jan. 25, 1929, Samphran, Thailand; ord. priest Dec. 20, 1959, in Rome; rector of metropolitan seminary in Bangkok, 1965-72; ord. archbishop of Bangkok, June 3, 1973; cardinal Feb. 2, 1983, the first from Thailand; titular church, St. Laurence in Panisperna. Archbishop of Bangkok, member of:
Congregation: Evangelization of Peoples.

**Koenig, Franz:** b. Aug. 3, 1905, Rabenstein, Lower Austria; ord. priest Oct. 28, 1933; ord. titular bishop of Livias and coadjutor bishop of Sankt Poelten, Aug. 31, 1952; archbishop of Vienna, May 10, 1956; cardinal Dec. 15, 1958; titular church, St. Eusebius; president of Secretariat for Non-Believers, 1965-80. Archbishop of Vienna, ordinary for faithful of Byzantine Rite living in Austria.

**Krol, John Joseph:** b. Oct. 26, 1910, Cleveland, Ohio; ord. priest Feb. 20, 1937; ord. titular bishop of Cadi and auxiliary bishop of Cleveland, Sept. 2, 1953; archbishop of Philadelphia, Feb. 11, 1961, installed Mar. 22, 1961; cardinal June 26, 1967; titular church, St. Mary (della Merced) and St. Adrian Martyr; vice-president, 1966-72, and president, 1972-74, of NCCB/USCC. Archbishop of Philadelphia, member of:
Congregations: Oriental Churches, Clergy;
Office: Prefecture of Economic Affairs.

**Kuharic, Franjo:** b. Apr. 15, 1919, Pribic, Yugoslavia; ord. priest July 15, 1945; ord. titular bishop of Meta and auxiliary bishop of Zagreb, May 3, 1964; apostolic administrator of archdiocese of Zagreb, 1968-70; archbishop of Zagreb, June 16, 1970; cardinal Feb. 2, 1983; titular church, St. Jerome of the Croats. Archbishop of Zagreb, member of:
Council for Public Affairs of the Church;
Congregations: Bishops, Clergy;
Secretariat: Non-Believers.

**Landazuri Ricketts, Juan, O.F.M:** b. Dec. 19, 1913, Arequipa, Peru; entered Franciscans, 1933; ord. priest Apr. 16, 1939; ord. titular archbishop of Roina and coadjutor archbishop of Lima, Aug. 24, 1952; archbishop of Lima, May 2, 1955; cardinal Mar. 19, 1962; titular church, St. Mary (in Aracoeli). Archbishop of Lima, member of:
Congregations: Clergy, Religious and Secular Institutes.

**Lebrun Moratinos, Jose Ali:** b. Mar. 19, 1919, Puerto Cabello, Venezuela; ord. priest Dec. 19, 1943; ord. titular bishop of Arado and auxiliary bishop of Maracaibo, Sept. 2, 1956; first bishop of Maracay, 1958-62; bishop of Valencia, 1962-72; titular archbishop of Voncaria and coadjutor archbishop of Caracas, Sept. 21, 1972; archbishop of Caracas, May 24, 1980; cardinal Feb. 2, 1983; titular church, St. Pancratius. Archbishop of Caracas, member of:
Council for Public Affairs of Church;
Congregations: Bishops, Catholic Education.

**Leger,\* Paul Emile, S.S.:** b. Apr. 26, 1904, Valleyfield, Quebec, Canada; ord. priest May 25, 1929; rector Canadian College, Rome, 1947; ord. archbishop of Montreal, Apr. 26, 1950; cardinal Jan. 12, 1953; titular church, St. Mary (of the Angels); resigned as archbishop of Montreal (Apr. 20, 1968) to become missionary to lepers, retired 1979. Archbishop emeritus of Montreal.

**Lekai, Laszlo:** b. Mar. 12, 1910, Zalalovo, Hungary; ord. priest Oct. 28, 1934; professor of philosophy and dogmatic theology at major seminary at Veszprem; arrested and imprisoned by Nazis during World War II; engaged in pastoral work and held diocesan offices after the war; ord. titular bishop of Girus Tirasii and apostolic administrator of Esztergom, Mar. 16, 1972; archbishop of Esztergom and primate of Hungary, Feb. 12, 1976; cardinal May 24, 1976; titular church, S. Teresa (on the Corso d'Italia). Archbishop of Esztergom, member of:
Congregation: Catholic Education.

**Lopez Trujillo, Alfonso:** b. Nov. 8, 1935, Villahermosa, Colombia; ord. priest Nov. 13, 1960, in Rome; returned to Colombia, 1963; taught at major seminary; was pastoral coordinator for 1968 International Eucharistic Congress in Bogota; vicar general of Bogota, 1970-72; ord. titular bishop of Boseta (with personal title of archbishop), Mar. 25, 1971; auxiliary bishop of Bogota, 1971-72; secretary-general of CELAM, 1972-78; helped organize 1979 Puebla Conference in which Pope John Paul II participated; app. coadjutor archbishop of Medellin, 1978; archbishop of Medellin, Jan. 2, 1979; president of CELAM, 1979-83; cardinal Feb. 2,

1983; titular church, St. Prisca. Archbishop of Medellin, member of:
Congregations: Doctrine of the Faith, Sacraments, Divine Worship, Evangelization of Peoples;
Secretariat: Non-Believers;
Commissions: Social Communications, Latin America, Pontifical Council *Cor Unum.*.

**Lorscheider, Aloisio, O.F.M.:** b. Oct. 8, 1924, Linha Geraldo, Brazil; received in Franciscan Order, Feb. 1, 1942; ord. priest Aug. 22, 1948; professor of theology at the Antonianum, Rome, and director of Franciscan international house of studies; ord. bishop of Santo Angelo, Brazil, May 20, 1962; archbishop of Fortaleza, Mar. 26, 1973; president of CELAM, 1975-79; cardinal May 24, 1976; titular church, S. Pietro (in Montorio). Archbishop of Fortaleza, member of:
Congregations: Religious and Secular Institutes, Clergy;
Secretariat: Non-Believers.

**Lustiger, Jean-Marie:** b. Sept. 16, 1926, Paris, France, of Polish-Jewish parents who emigrated to France after World War I; taken in by Catholic family in Orleans when his parents were deported during Nazi occupation (his mother died in 1943 at Auschwitz); convert to Catholicism, baptized Aug. 25, 1940; active in Young Christian Students during university days; ord. priest Apr. 17, 1954; ord. bishop of Orleans, Dec. 8, 1979; archbishop of Paris, Jan. 31, 1981; cardinal Feb. 2, 1983; titular church, Sts. Marcellinus and Peter. Archbishop of Paris, ordinary for Eastern-Rite faithful without ordinaries of their own, member of:
Council for Public Affairs of Church;
Congregations: Sacraments, Divine Worship, Bishops, Oriental Churches, Clergy, Religious and Secular Institutes.

**McCann, Owen:** b. June 29, 1907, Woodstock, South Africa; ord. priest Dec. 21, 1935; ord. titular bishop of Stettorio and vicar apostolic of Cape Town, May 18, 1950; first archbishop of Cape Town, Jan. 11, 1951; opponent of apartheid policy; cardinal Feb. 22, 1965; titular church, St. Praxedes. Archbishop of Cape Town, member of:
Congregation: Evangelization of Peoples.

**Macharski, Franciszek:** b. May 20, 1927, Cracow, Poland; ord. priest Apr. 2, 1950; engaged in pastoral work, 1950-56; continued theological studies in Fribourg, Switzerland, 1956-60; taught pastoral theology at the Faculty of Theology in Cracow; app. rector of archdiocesan seminary at Cracow, 1970; ord. archbishop of Cracow, Jan. 6, 1979, by Pope John Paul II; cardinal June 30, 1979; titular church, St. John at the Latin Gate. Archbishop of Cracow, member of:
Council for Public Affairs of Church;
Congregations: Bishops, Clergy, Catholic Education;
Secretariat: Non-Believers.

**Malula, Joseph:** b. Dec. 17, 1917, Kinshasa, Zaire; ord. priest June 9, 1946; ord. titular bishop of Attanaso and auxiliary bishop of Kinshasa, Sept. 20, 1959; archbishop of Kinshasa. July 7, 1964; cardinal Apr. 28, 1969; titular church, Ss. Pro-

tomartyrs (Via Aurelia Antica). Archbishop of Kinshasa.

**Manning, Timothy:** b. Nov. 15, 1909, Ballingeary, Ireland; completed studies for the priesthood at St. Patrick's Seminary, Menlo Park, Calif.; ord. priest June 16, 1934; became American citizen, Jan. 14, 1944; ord. titular bishop of Lesvi and auxiliary of Los Angeles, Oct. 15, 1946; first bishop of Fresno, 1967-69; titular archbishop of Capri and coadjutor of Los Angeles, May 26, 1969; archbishop of Los Angeles, Jan. 21, 1970; cardinal Mar. 5, 1973; titular church, Santa Lucia. Archbishop of Los Angeles, member of:
Congregation: Religious and Secular Institutes.

**Marella,\* Paolo:** b. Jan. 25, 1895, Rome, Italy; ord. priest Feb. 23, 1918; aide in Congregation for Propagation of the Faith; on staff of apostolic delegation, Washington, D.C., 1923-33; ord. titular archbishop of Doclea, Oct. 29, 1933; apostolic delegate to Japan, 1933-48, to Australia, New Zealand and Oceania, 1948-53; nuncio to France, 1953-59; cardinal Dec. 14, 1959; entered order of cardinal bishops as titular bishop of Porto and Santa Rufina, Mar. 14, 1972; president of Secretariat for Non-Christians, 1967-73. Archpriest emeritus of St. Peter's Basilica, sub-dean of College of Cardinals, 1977.

**Martini, Carlo Maria, S.J.:** b. Feb. 15, 1927, Turin, Italy; entered Jesuits Sept. 25, 1944; ord. priest July 13, 1952, at the age of 25; biblical scholar; seminary professor, Chieti, Italy, 1958-61; professor and later rector, 1969-78, of Pontifical Biblical Institute; rector of Pontifical Gregorian University, 1978-79; author of theological, biblical and spiritual works; ord. archbishop of Milan, Jan. 6, 1980, by Pope John Paul II; cardinal Feb. 2, 1983; titular church, St. Cecilia. Archbishop of Milan, member of:
Council for Public Affairs of the Church;
Congregations: Doctrine of the Faith, Bishops, Catholic Education, Religious and Secular Institutes, Evangelization of Peoples.

**Marty,\* Francois:** b. May 18, 1904, Pachins, France; ord. priest June 28, 1930; ord. bishop of Saint-Flour, May 1, 1952; titular archbishop of Emesa and coadjutor archbishop of Rheims, Dec. 14, 1959; archbishop of Rheims, May 9, 1960; archbishop of Paris, 1968-81; cardinal Apr. 28, 1969; titular church, St. Louis of France. Archbishop emeritus of Paris, member of:
Congregation: Clergy.

**Maurer,\* Jose Clemente, C.SS.R.:** b. Mar. 13, 1900, Puttlingen, Germany; ord. priest Sept. 19, 1925; assigned to Bolivian missions, 1926; became a Bolivian citizen; ord. titular bishop of Cea and auxiliary bishop of La Paz, Apr. 16, 1950; archbishop of Sucre, 1951-83; cardinal June 26, 1967; titular church, Most Holy Redeemer and St. Alphonsus. Archbishop emeritus of Sucre.

**Meisner, Joachim:** b. Dec. 25, 1933, Breslau, Silesia, Germany (present-day Wroclaw, Poland); ord. priest Dec. 22, 1962; regional director of Caritas; ord. titular bishop of Vina and auxiliary of apostolic administration of Erfurt-Meiningen, E. Germany, May 17, 1975; app. bishop of Berlin, Apr. 22, 1980, installed May 17, 1980 (resides in East

Berlin); cardinal Feb. 2, 1983; titular church, St. Prudenziana. Bishop of Berlin, member of:
Congregations: Sacraments, Divine Worship, Catholic Education.
Secretariat: Non-Believers.

**Miranda y Gomez,\* Miguel Dario:** b. Dec. 19, 1895, Leon, Mexico; ord. priest Oct. 28, 1918; ord. bishop of Tulancingo, Dec. 8, 1937; titular archbishop of Selimbra and coadjutor archbishop of Mexico City, Dec. 20, 1955; archbishop of Mexico City, 1956-77; served as president of the Latin American Bishops' Council (CELAM); cardinal Apr. 28, 1969; titular church, Our Lady of Guadalupe (Montemario). Archbishop emeritus of Mexico City.

**Munoz Duque, Anibal:** b. Oct. 3, 1908, Santa Rosa de Osos, Colombia; ord. priest Nov. 19, 1933; ord. bishop of Soccoro y San Gil, May 27, 1951; bishop of Bucaramango, 1952-59; archbishop of Nueva Pamplona, 1959-68; titular archbishop of Cariana and coadjutor archbishop of Bogota, 1968; archbishop of Bogota, 1972-84; cardinal Mar. 5, 1973; titular church, St. Bartholomew. Archbishop emeritus of Bogota, military vicar, member of:
Congregations: Sacraments, Divine Worship, Catholic Education.

**Munoz Vega,\* Pablo, S. J.:** b. May 23, 1903, Mira, Ecuador; ord. priest July 25, 1933; ord. titular bishop of Ceramo and auxiliary bishop of Quito, Mar. 19, 1964; archbishop of Quito, June 23, 1967; cardinal Apr. 28, 1969; titular church, St. Robert Bellarmine. Archbishop of Quito.

**Nasalli Rocca di Corneliano,\* Mario:** b. Aug. 12, 1903, Piacenza, Italy; ord. priest Apr. 9, 1927; ord. titular archbishop of Anzio, Apr. 20, 1969; cardinal Apr. 28, 1969; titular church, St. John the Baptist.

**Nsubuga, Emmanuel:** b. Nov. 5, 1914, Kisule, Uganda; ord. priest Dec. 15, 1946; ord. bishop of Kampala, Oct. 30, 1966; cardinal May 24, 1976; titular church, S. Maria Nuova. Archbishop of Kampala, member of:
Congregation: Evangelization of Peoples.

**O'Boyle,\* Patrick A.:** b. July 18, 1896, Scranton, Pa.; ord. priest May 21, 1921; executive director of War Relief Services, NCWC, 1943; ord. archbishop of Washington, Jan. 14, 1948 (retired, 1973); cardinal June 26, 1967; titular church, St. Nicholas (in Carcere). Archbishop emeritus of Washington.

**Oddi, Silvio:** b. Nov. 14, 1910, Morfasso, Italy; ord. priest May 21, 1933; ord. titular archbishop of Mesembria, Sept. 27, 1953; served in Vatican diplomatic corps, 1953-69; apostolic delegate to Jerusalem, Palestine, Jordan and Cyprus, internuncio to the United Arab Republic, and nuncio to Belgium and Luxembourg; cardinal Apr. 28, 1969; titular church, St. Agatha of the Goths. Pontifical legate for Patriarchal Basilica of St. Francis of Assisi, prefect of Sacred Congregation for the Clergy, 1979, chamberlain of the Sacred College of Cardinals, 1984, member of:
Council for Public Affairs of Church;
Congregations: Bishops, Oriental Churches, Causes of Saints, Evangelization of Peoples;
Tribunal: Apostolic Signatura;
Commissions: Authentic Interpretation of Code

of Canon Law, State of Vatican City, Sanctuaries of Pompei, Loreto and Bari.

**O'Fiaich, Tomas:** b. Nov. 3, 1923; Crossmaglen, Ireland; ord. priest July 6, 1948; lecturer, 1953, and professor, 1959, of modern history at Maynooth College; vice president, 1970, and president, 1974, of Maynooth; prolific author of scholarly works; recognized authority on early Irish Christianity; ord. archbishop of Armagh and primate of All Ireland, Oct. 2, 1977; pledged to work for the cause of peace in Northern Ireland; outspoken in his condemnation of violence; cardinal June 30, 1979; titular church, St. Patrick. Archbishop of Armagh, primate of All Ireland, member of:
Council for Public Affairs of Church;
Congregations: Bishops, Clergy, Catholic Education, Evangelization of Peoples;
Secretariat: Christian Unity.

**Otunga, Maurice:** b. January, 1923, Chebukwa, Kenya; son of pagan tribal chief; baptized 1935, at age of 12; ord. priest Oct. 3, 1950, at Rome; taught at Kisumu major seminary for three years; attaché in apostolic delegation at Mombasa, 1953-56; ord. titular bishop of Tacape and auxiliary of Kisumu, Feb. 25, 1957; bishop of Kisii, 1960-69; titular archbishop of Bomarzo and coadjutor of Nairobi, Nov. 15, 1969; archbishop of Nairobi, Oct. 24, 1971; cardinal Mar. 5, 1973; titular church, St. Gregory Barbarigo. Archbishop of Nairobi, military vicar of Kenya, 1981, member of:
Congregations: Sacraments, Divine Worship, Religious and Secular Institutes, Evangelization of Peoples, Catholic Education.

**Palazzini, Pietro:** b. May 19, 1912, Piobbico, Pesaro, Italy; ord. priest Dec. 6, 1934; assistant vice-rector of Pontifical Major Roman Seminary and vice-rector and bursar of Pontifical Roman Seminary for Juridical Studies; professor of moral theology at Lateran University; held various offices in Roman Curia; secretary of Congregation of Council (now Clergy), 1958-73; ord. titular archbishop of Caesarea in Cappadocia, Sept. 21, 1962; author of numerous works on moral theology and law; cardinal Mar. 5, 1973; titular church, St. Jerome. Prefect of Congregation for Causes of Saints, 1980, member of:
Congregations: Oriental Churches, Sacraments and Divine Worship, Clergy;
Tribunal: Apostolic Signatura;
Commission: Authentic Interpretation of Code of Canon Law.

**Pappalardo, Salvatore:** b. Sept. 23, 1918, Villafranca Sicula, Sicily; ord. priest Apr. 12, 1941; entered diplomatic service of secretariat of state, 1947; ord. titular archbishop of Miletus, Jan. 16, 1966; pro-nuncio in Indonesia, 1966-69; president of Pontifical Ecclesiastical Academy 1969-70; archbishop of Palermo, Oct. 17, 1970; cardinal Mar. 5, 1973; titular church, St. Mary Odigitria of the Sicilians. Archbishop of Palermo, member of:
Council for Public Affairs of Church;
Congregations: Bishops, Oriental Churches, Clergy, Catholic Education.

**Parecattil, Joseph:** b. Apr. 1, 1912, Kidangoor, India; ord. priest Aug. 24, 1939; ord. titular bishop of Aretusa for Syrians and auxiliary bishop of

Ernakulam, Nov. 30, 1953; archbishop of Ernakulam (Syro-Malabar Rite), 1956-84; appointed one of seven members of Pope Paul VI's advisory council for Eastern Rite churches, 1968; cardinal Apr. 28, 1969; titular church, Our Lady Queen of Peace (Monte Verde). Archbishop emeritus of Ernakulam of the Syro-Malabar Rite, member of:
Congregation: Oriental Churches;
Secretariat: Non-Christians;
Commission: Revision of Oriental Code of Canon Law (President).

**Parente,\* Pietro:** b. Feb. 16, 1891, Casalnuovo, Monterotaro, Italy; ord. priest Mar. 18, 1916; director of Archiepiscopal Seminary at Naples, 1916-26; rector of Pontifical Urban College of Propagation of the Faith, 1934-38; Consultor of the Congregations of the Holy Office, Council, Propagation of the Faith, and Seminaries and Universities; ord. archbishop of Perugia, Oct. 23, 1955; titular archbishop of Tolemaide di Tebaide, Oct. 23, 1959; assessor (1959-65) and secretary (1965-67) of Congregation of Holy Office (now Doctrinal Congregation); cardinal June 26, 1967; titular church, St. Lawrence (in Lucina).

**Paupini, Giuseppe:** b. Feb. 25, 1907, Mondavio, Italy; ord. priest Mar. 19, 1930; ord. titular archbishop of Sebastopolis in Abasgia, Feb. 26, 1956; served in Vatican diplomatic corps, 1956-69; internuncio to Iran, 1956-57; nuncio to Guatemala and El Salvador, 1957-58, nuncio to Colombia, 1959-69; cardinal Apr. 28, 1969; titular church, All Saints Church; major penitentiary 1973-84. Member of:
Congregation: Causes of Saints;
Commission: State of Vatican City.

**Pellegrino,\* Michele:** b. Apr. 25, 1903, Centallo, Italy; ord. priest Sept. 19, 1925; ord. archbishop of Turin, Oct. 17, 1965 (resigned 1977); cardinal June 26, 1967; titular church, Most Holy Name of Jesus. Archbishop emeritus of Turin.

**Picachy, Lawrence Trevor, S.J.:** b. Aug. 7, 1916, Lebong, India; ord. priest Nov. 21, 1947; dean, 1950-54, and then rector, 1954-60, of St. Francis Xavier University College, Calcutta; ord. bishop of Jamshedpur, Sept. 9, 1962; archbishop of Calcutta, May 29, 1969; cardinal May 24, 1976; titular church, Sacred Heart of Mary. Archbishop of Calcutta.

**Pironio, Eduardo:** b. Dec. 3, 1920, Nueve de Julio, Argentina; ord. priest Dec. 5, 1943; taught theology at Pius XII Seminary of Mercedes diocese, 1944-59; vicar general of diocese 1958-60; attended Second Vatican Council as *peritus*; ord. titular bishop of Ceciri, May 31, 1964; apostolic administrator of diocese of Avellaneda, 1967-72; secretary general 1967-72, and president, 1973-75, of CELAM; bishop of Mar del Plata, 1972-75; titular archbishop of Thiges and pro-prefect of Sacred Congregation for Religious and Secular Institutes, Sept. 20, 1975; cardinal May 24, 1976; deacon, Sts. Cosmas and Damian. Prefect of the Sacred Congregation for Religious and Secular Institutes, 1976-84. President of Pontifical Council for the Laity, 1984, member of:
Council for Public Affairs of the Church,

Congregations: Bishops, Sacraments, Divine Worship, Catholic Education, Oriental Churches;
Commissions: Latin America, Authentic Interpretation of Code of Canon Law.

**Poletti, Ugo:** b. Apr. 19, 1914, Omegna, Italy; ord. priest June 29, 1938; served in various diocesan offices at Novara; ord. titular bishop of Medeli and auxiliary of Novaro, Sept. 14, 1958; president of Pontifical Mission Aid Society for Italy, 1964-67; archbishop of Spoleto, 1967-69; titular archbishop of Cittanova, 1969; served as second viceregent of Rome, 1969-72; pro-vicar general of Rome, 1972, following the sudden death of Cardinal Dell'Acqua; cardinal Mar. 5, 1973; titular church, Sts. Ambrose and Charles. Vicar general of Rome, 1973, archpriest of Patriarchal Lateran Archbasilica, 1973, grand chancellor of Lateran University, member of:
Congregations: Clergy, Sacraments, Divine Worship, Oriental Churches, Religious and Secular Institutes;
Commission: Council for the Laity.

**Poma, Antonio:** b. June 12, 1910, Villanterio, Italy; ord. priest Apr. 15, 1933; ord. titular bishop of Tagaste and auxiliary bishop of Mantova, Dec. 9, 1951; bishop of Mantova, Sept. 8, 1954; titular archbishop of Gerpiniano and coadjutor archbishop of Bologna, July 16, 1967; archbishop of Bologna, Feb. 12, 1968 (resigned Feb. 11, 1983); cardinal Apr. 28, 1969; titular church, St. Luke (a Via Prenestina). Archbishop emeritus of Bologna, member of:
Congregation: Clergy.

**Primatesta, Raul Francisco:** b. Apr. 14, 1919, Capilla del Senor, Argentina; ord. priest Oct. 25, 1942, at Rome; taught at minor and major seminaries of La Plata; contributed to several theology reviews; ord. titular bishop of Tanais and auxiliary of La Plata, Aug. 15, 1957; bishop of San Rafael, 1961-65; archbishop of Cordoba, Feb. 16, 1965; cardinal Mar. 5, 1973; titular church, St. Mary Sorrowful Virgin. Archbishop of Cordoba, Argentina, member of:
Congregations: Clergy, Religious and Secular Institutes, Sacraments, Divine Worship, Evangelization of Peoples.

**Ratzinger, Joseph:** b. Apr. 16, 1927, Marktl am Inn, Germany; ord. priest June 29, 1951; professor of dogmatic theology at University of Regensburg, 1969-77; member of International Theological Commission, 1969-80; ord. archbishop of Munich-Freising, May 28, 1977 (resigned Feb. 15, 1982); cardinal June 27, 1977; titular church, St. Mary of Consolation (in Tiburtina). Prefect of Congregation for Doctrine of the Faith, 1981, member of:
Council for Public Affairs of the Church;
Congregations: Bishops, Sacraments, Divine Worship, Oriental Churches, Clergy, Evangelization of Peoples, Causes of Saints, Catholic Education;
Tribunal: Apostolic Signatura;
Secretariat: Christian Unity;
Commissions: Authentic Interpretation of Code of Canon Law, Revision of Oriental Code of Canon Law, Biblical (President), Theological (President).

**Razafimahatratra, Victor, S.J.:** b. Sept. 8, 1921, AmbanitsilenaRanomasina, Madagascar; entered Society of Jesus, 1945; ord. priest July 28, 1956; rector of Fianarantsoa Minor Seminary, 1960-63; superior of Jesuit residence at Ambositra, 1963-69; rector of Tananarive Major Seminary, 1969-71; ord. bishop of Farafangana, Apr. 18, 1971; archbishop of Tananarive, Apr. 10, 1976; cardinal May 24, 1976; titular church, Holy Cross in Jerusalem. Archbishop of Tananarive, member of:
Congregation: Evangelization of Peoples.

**Ribeiro, Antonio:** b. May 21, 1928, Gandarela di Basto, Portugal; ord. priest July 5, 1953; professor of fundamental theology at major seminary at Braga; ord. titular bishop of Tigillava and auxiliary of Braga, Sept. 17, 1967; patriarch of Lisbon, May 10, 1971; cardinal Mar. 5, 1973; titular church, St. Anthony of Padua (in Rome). Patriarch of Lisbon, military vicar, member of:
Congregations: Clergy, Catholic Education;
Commission: Social Communications.

**Righi-Lambertini, Egano:** b. Feb. 22, 1906, Casalecchio di Reno, Italy; ord. priest May 25, 1929; entered service of secretariat of state, 1939; served in diplomatic missions in France (1949-54), Costa Rica (1955), England (1955-57); first apostolic delegate to Korea, 1957-60; ord. titular archbishop of Doclea, Oct. 28, 1960; apostolic nuncio in Lebanon, 1960-63, Chile, 1963-67, Italy, 1967-69; France, 1969-79; while nuncio in France he also served as special envoy at the Council of Europe, 1974-79; cardinal June 30, 1979; deacon, St. John Bosco in Via Tuscolana. Member of:
Council for Public Affairs of the Church;
Congregations: Bishops, Causes of Saints;
Secretariat: Non-Christians;
Office: Administration of Patrimony of Holy See;
Commission: Sacred Art in Italy (Honorary President).

**Rossi, Agnelo:** b. May 4, 1913, Joaquim Egidio, Brazil; ord. priest Mar. 27, 1937; ord. bishop of Barra do Pirai, Apr. 15, 1956; archbishop of Ribeirao Preto, 1962-64; archbishop of Sao Paulo, 1964-70; cardinal Feb. 22, 1965; titular church, Mother of God; entered order of cardinal bishops as titular bishop of Sabina and Poggia Mirteto June 25, 1984; prefect of Congregation for Evangelization of Peoples, 1970-84. President of Administration of Patrimony of the Holy See, 1984, grand chancellor of Pontifical Urban University, member of:
Council for Public Affairs of Church;
Congregations: Clergy, Doctrine of Faith, Bishops, Oriental Churches, Causes of Saints, Religious and Secular Institutes, Catholic Education;
Secretariats: Christian Unity, Non-Christians;
Commissions: Revision of Oriental Code of Canon Law, Institute for Works of Religion.

**Rossi, Opilio:** b. May 14, 1910, New York, N.Y.; holds Italian citizenship; ord. priest for diocese of Piacenza, Italy, Mar. 11, 1933; served in nunciatures in Belgium, The Netherlands and Germany, 1938-53; ord. titular archbishop of Ancyra, Dec. 27, 1953; nuncio in Ecuador, 1953-59, Chile, 1959-61, Austria, 1961-76; cardinal May 24, 1976; deacon, S.

Maria Liberatrice (on the Monte Testaccio). Member of:
Council for Public Affairs of the Church;
Congregations: Bishops, Oriental Churches, Sacraments, Divine Worship, Religious and Secular Institutes, Clergy, Causes of Saints, Evangelization of Peoples;
Tribunal: Apostolic Signatura;
Commissions: Authentic Interpretation of Code of Canon Law, Sanctuaries of Pompeii, Loreto and Bari.

**Roy, Maurice:** b. Jan. 25, 1905, Quebec, Canada; ord. priest June 12, 1927; chief of chaplains of Canadian Armed Forces during World War II; ord. bishop of Trois Rivieres, May 1, 1946; military vicar, 1946-81; archbishop of Quebec, 1947-81; primate of Canada, Jan. 25, 1956; cardinal Feb. 22, 1965; titular church, Our Lady of the Most Holy Sacrament and the Holy Canadian Martyrs; president of Council for the Laity and the Pontifical Commission for Justice and Peace (1967-76). Archbishop emeritus of Quebec, member of:
Congregation: Clergy.

**Rubin, Wladyslaw:** b. Sept. 20, 1917, Toki, Poland; seminary studies interrupted during World War II when he was arrested and deported to labor camp; completed studies at St. Joseph's University in Beirut; ord. priest in Beirut June 30, 1946, and served Polish community there; sent to Rome for further studies, 1949; chaplain for Polish refugees in Italy, 1953-58; rector of Polish College in Rome, 1959-64; ord. titular bishop of Serta, primate of Poland's delegate for emigration and auxiliary of Gniezno, Nov. 29, 1964; established contact with Polish emigrants throughout the world; secretary general of Synod of Bishops, 1967-79; cardinal June 30, 1979; deacon, St. Mary in Via Lata. Prefect of Congregation for Oriental Churches, 1980, member of:
Congregations: Doctrine of the Faith, Causes of Saints; Religious and Secular Institutes, Evangelization of Peoples, Catholic Education;
Tribunal: Apostolic Signatura;
Secretariat: Christian Unity;
Commissions: Revision of Oriental Code of Canon Law.

**Rugambwa, Laurean:** b. July 12, 1912, Bukongo, Tanzania; ord. priest Dec. 12, 1943; ord. titular bishop of Febiano and vicar apostolic of Lower Kagera, Feb. 10, 1952; bishop of Rutabo, Mar. 25, 1953; cardinal Mar. 28, 1960; titular church, St. Francis of Assisi (a Ripa); bishop of Bukoba, 1960-68. Archbishop of Dar-es-Salaam, 1968, member of:
Congregation: Causes of Saints.

**Sabattani, Aurelio:** b. Oct. 18, 1912, Casal Fiumanese, Italy; ord. priest July 26, 1935; jurist; served in various assignments in his native diocese of Imola and as judge and later an official of the regional ecclesiastical tribunal of Bologna; called to Rome in 1955 as prelate auditor of the Roman Rota; ord. titular archbishop of Justinian Prima, July 25, 1965; prelate of Loreto, 1965-71; secretary of Supreme Tribunal of Apostolic Signatura and consultor of Secretariat of State, 1971; pro-prefect of Apostolic Signatura, 1982-83; cardinal Feb. 2,

1983; deacon, St. Apollinaris. Prefect of Apostolic Signatura, 1983, archpriest of St. Peter's Basilica, 1983, member of:
Council for Public Affairs of the Church;
Congregations: Bishops, Oriental Churches;
Commission: Authentic Interpretation of Code of Canon Law.

**Salazar Lopez, Jose:** b. Jan. 12, 1910, Ameca, Mexico; ord. priest May 26, 1934, in Rome; instrumental in building of new seminary at Guadalajara, the largest in Mexico; vice-rector and later rector of seminary; ord. titular bishop of Prusiade and coadjutor bishop of Zamora, Aug. 20, 1961; bishop of Zamora, 1967-70; archbishop of Guadalajara, Feb. 21, 1970; cardinal Mar. 5, 1973; titular church, Santa Emerentia. Archbishop of Guadalajara, member of:
Congregations: Sacraments and Divine Worship, Clergy.

**Satowaki,\* Joseph Asajiro:** b. Feb. 1, 1904, Shittsu, Japan; ord. priest Dec. 17, 1932; served in various pastoral capacities in Nagasaki archdiocese after his ordination; apostolic administrator of Taiwan (then a Japanese possession), 1941-45; director of Nagasaki minor seminary, 1945-57; vicar general of Nagasaki, 1945; ord. first bishop of Kagoshima, May 3, 1955; archbishop of Nagasaki, Dec. 19, 1968; cardinal June 30, 1979; titular church, St. Mary of Peace. Archbishop of Nagasaki, member of:
Secretariat: Non-Christians.

**Scherer,\* Alfred Vicente:** b. Feb. 5, 1903, Bom Principio, Brazil; ord. priest Apr. 3, 1926; ord. archbishop of Porto Alegre, Feb. 23, 1947 (retired Aug. 29, 1981); cardinal Apr. 28, 1969; titular church, Our Lady of La Salette. Archbishop emeritus of Porto Alegre, Brazil.

**Sensi, Giuseppe Maria:** b. May 27, 1907, Cosenza, Italy; ord. priest Dec. 21, 1929; entered Vatican diplomatic service; served in nunciatures in Hungary, Switzerland, Belgium and Czechoslovakia, 1934-49; ord. titular archbishop of Sardes, July 24, 1955; apostolic nuncio to Costa Rica, 1955; apostolic delegate to Jerusalem, 1956-62; nuncio to Ireland, 1962-67, and Portugal, 1967-76; cardinal May 24, 1976; deacon, SS. Biagio e Carlo (ai Catinari). Member of:
Commission: State of Vatican City.

**Sidarouss,\* Stephanos I, C.M.:** b. Feb. 22, 1904, Cairo, Egypt; ord. priest July 2, 1939; ord. titular bishop of Sais, Jan. 25, 1948; auxiliary to the patriarch of Alexandria for the Copts, 1948-58; patriarch of Alexandria, May 10, 1958; cardinal Feb. 22, 1965. Patriarch of Alexandria for the Copts, member of:
Congregation: Oriental Churches;
Secretariat: Christian Unity;
Commission: Revision of Code of Oriental Canon Law.

**Silva Henriquez, Raul, S.D.B.:** b. Sept. 27, 1907, Talca, Chile; ord. priest July 3, 1938; ord. bishop of Valparaiso, Nov. 29, 1959; archbishop of Santiago de Chile, 1961-83; cardinal Mar. 19, 1962; titular church, St. Bernard (alle Terme). Archbishop emeritus of Santiago de Chile.

**Sin, Jaime L.:** b. Aug. 31, 1928, New Washington,

Philippines; ord. priest Apr. 3, 1954; diocesan missionary in Capiz, 1954-57; app. first rector of the St. Pius X Seminary, Roxas City, 1957; ord. titular bishop of Obba and auxiliary bishop of Jaro, Mar. 18, 1967; apostolic administrator of archdiocese of Jaro, June 20, 1970; titular archbishop of Massa Lubrense and coadjutor archbishop of Jaro, Jan. 15, 1972; archbishop of Jaro, Oct. 8, 1972; archbishop of Manila, Jan. 21, 1974; cardinal May 24, 1976; titular church, S. Maria (ai Monti). Archbishop of Manila, member of:
Council for Public Affairs of the Church;
Congregations: Bishops, Sacraments, Divine Worship, Clergy, Evangelization of Peoples, Catholic Education;
Secretariat: Non-Christians;
Commission: Social Communications;
Office: Prefecture of Economic Affairs.

**Siri, Giuseppe:** b. May 20, 1906, Genoa, Italy; ord. priest Sept. 22, 1928; ord. titular bishop of Liviade and auxiliary bishop of Genoa, May 7, 1944; archbishop of Genoa, May 14, 1946; cardinal Jan. 12, 1953; titular church, St. Mary (della Vittoria). Archbishop of Genoa, apostolic administrator of Bobbio, member of:
Congregations: Clergy, Catholic Education.

**Slipyi or Slipyj,\* Josyf (Kobernyckyj-Dyckowskyj):** b. Feb. 17, 1892, Zazdrist in the Ukraine; ord. priest Sept. 30, 1917; ord. titular archbishop of Serre, Dec. 22, 1939; coadjutor archbishop of Lwow for the Ukrainians, 1939-44; archbishop of Lwow, Nov. 1, 1944; imprisoned 1945-63 for unspecified crimes; released by Soviets and allowed to go to Rome in February, 1963; named major archbishop by Paul VI, 1963; cardinal Feb. 22, 1965; titular church, St. Athanasius. Major Archbishop of Lwow of the Ukrainians (not permitted to exercise his office; he resides in Vatican City).

**Suenens,\* Leo Josef:** b. July 16, 1904, Brussels, Belgium; ord. priest Sept. 4, 1927; ord. titular bishop of Isinda, Dec. 16, 1945; auxiliary bishop of Mechelen, 1945-61; archbishop of Mechelen-Brussels, 1961-79; cardinal Mar. 19, 1962; titular church, St. Peter in Chains. Archbishop emeritus of Mechelen-Brussels, member of:
Congregation: Causes of Saints;

**Taofinu'u, Pio, S.M.:** b. Dec. 9, 1923, Falealupo, W. Samoa; ord. priest Dec. 8, 1954; joined Society of Mary, 1955; ord. bishop of Apia (Samoa and Tokelau), May 29, 1968, the first Polynesian bishop; cardinal Mar. 5, 1973; titular church, St. Humphrey (on the Janiculum). Archbishop of Samoa-Apia and Tokelau (Oct 10, 1982), apostolic administrator of Samoa-Pago Pago, superior of mission "sui juris" of Funafuti, member of:
Congregation: Causes of Saints.

**Thiandoum, Hyacinthe:** b. Feb. 2, 1921, Poponguine, Senegal; ord. priest Apr. 18, 1949; studied at Gregorian University, Rome, 1951-53; returned to Senegal, 1953; ord. archbishop of Dakar, May 20, 1962; cardinal May 24, 1976; titular church, S. Maria (del Popolo). Archbishop of Dakar, member of:
Congregations: Clergy, Religious and Secular Institutes;
Commission: Social Communications.

**Tomasek,\* Frantisek:** b. June 30, 1899, Studenka, Moravia, Czechoslovakia; ord. priest July 5, 1922; professor of pedagogy and catechetics at the theology faculty of Olomouc, 1934-39; resumed academic activity after liberation in 1945; author, *Catechism of the Catholic Religion;* ord. titular bishop of Butus and auxiliary of Olomouc, Oct. 13, 1949; only Czech bishop to attend Second Vatican Council; apostolic administrator of Prague, Feb. 18, 1965; cardinal May 24, 1976 (*in pectore*); solemnly proclaimed at June 27, 1977, consistory; titular church, Sts. Vitalis, Valeria, Gervase and Protase. Archbishop of Prague, 1978, member of:
Congregation: Clergy.

**Trinh van-Can, Joseph-Marie:** b. Mar. 19, 1921, Trac But, Vietnam; ord. priest Dec. 3, 1949; held various offices in Hanoi archdiocese; ord. titular bishop of Ela (with personal title of archbishop) and coadjutor archbishop of Hanoi, June 2, 1963; archbishop of Hanoi, Nov. 27, 1978; cardinal June 30, 1979; titular church, St. Mary in Via. Archbishop of Hanoi, member of:
Congregation: Evangelization of Peoples.

**Ursi, Corrado:** b. July 26, 1908, Andria, Italy; ord. priest July 25, 1931; vice-rector and later rector of the Pontifical Regional Seminary of Molfetta, 1931-51; ord. bishop of Nardo, Sept. 30, 1951; archbishop of Acerenza, Nov. 30, 1961; archbishop of Naples, May 23, 1966; cardinal June 26, 1967; titular church, St. Callistus. Archbishop of Naples, member of:
Congregation: Catholic Education.

**Vaivods,\* Julijans:** b. Aug. 18, 1895, Vorkova, Latvia; ord. priest Apr. 7, 1918; chaplain of various schools, 1918-23; wrote and published catechetical books and theatrical works for youth; vicar general of Liepaja, 1944; apostolic activity curtailed by political situation, he resumed writing; publications denounced as hostile to regime, he was tried and sentenced to two years' exile, 1958-60; released early but not permitted to exercise his priestly ministry for a time; vicar general of Riga, 1962; attended Vatican II, 1964; ord. titular bishop of Macriana Maior and apostolic administrator of archdiocese of Riga and diocese of Liepaja, Nov. 18, 1964, in Rome; cardinal Feb. 2, 1983; titular church, SS. Quattro Coronati. Apostolic administrator of Riga and Liepaja.

**Volk,\* Hermann:** b. Dec. 27, 1903, Steinheim, Germany; ord. priest Apr. 2, 1927; professor of dogmatic theology at University of Muenster; ord. bishop of Mainz, June 5, 1962 (retired Dec. 27, 1982); cardinal Mar. 5, 1973; titular church, Saints Fabian and Venanzio (at Villa Fiorelli). Archbishop emeritus of Mainz, member of:
Secretariat: Christian Unity.

**Willebrands, Johannes:** b. Sept. 4, 1909, Bovenkarspel, The Netherlands; ord. priest May 26, 1934; ord. titular bishop of Mauriana, June 28, 1964; secretary of Secretariat for Christian Unity, 1960-69; cardinal Apr. 28, 1969; titular church, St. Sebastian (alle Catacombe); archbishop of Utrecht, 1975-83. President of Secretariat for Christian Unity, 1969, member of:
Congregations: Doctrine of Faith, Sacraments,

Divine Worship, Oriental Churches, Catholic Education, Evangelization of Peoples;
Commission: Revision of Oriental Code of Canon Law.

**Williams, Thomas Stafford:** b. Mar. 20, 1930, Wellington, New Zealand; ord. priest Dec. 20, 1959, in Rome; studied in Ireland after ordination, receiving degree in social sciences; served in various pastoral assignments on his return to New Zealand; missionary in Western Samoa to 1976; ord. archbishop of Wellington, New Zealand, Dec. 20, 1979; cardinal Feb. 2, 1983; titular church, Jesus the Divine Teacher at Pineda Sacchetti. Archbishop of Wellington, member of:
Congregation: Evangelization of Peoples;
Secretarist: Non-Christians.

**Yago, Bernard:** b. July, 1916, Pass, Ivory Coast; ord. priest May 1, 1947; ord. archbishop of Abidjan, May 8, 1960, by Pope John XXIII in St. Peter's Basilica, becoming the first native member of the hierarchy of Ivory Coast; cardinal Feb. 2, 1983; titular church, St. Chrysogonus. Archbishop of Abidjan, member of:
Congregation: Evangelization of Peoples;
Secretariat: Christian Unity.

**Zoungrana, Paul, P.A.:** b. Sept. 3, 1917, Ouagadougou, Upper Volta; ord. priest May 2, 1942, in the Missionaries of Africa; ord. archbishop of Ouagadougou at St. Peter's Basilica by John XXIII, May 8, 1960; cardinal Feb. 22, 1965; titular church, St. Camillus de Lellis. Archbishop of Ouagadougou, member of:
Congregations: Religious and Secular Institutes, Evangelization of Peoples.

## CATEGORIES OF CARDINALS

*(As of Aug. 27, 1984.)*

Information below includes categories of cardinals and dates of consistories at which they were created. Seniority or precedence usually depends on order of elevation, except in the case of cardinal bishops whose seniority depends on date of appointment to suburban see.

Two of these cardinals were named by Pius XII (consistory of Jan. 12, 1953); 9 by John XXIII (consistories of Dec. 15, 1958, Dec. 14, 1959, Mar. 28, 1960, and Mar. 19, 1962); 83 by Paul VI (consistories of Feb. 22, 1965, June 26, 1967, Apr. 28, 1969, Mar. 5, 1973, May 24, 1976, and June 27, 1977); 32 by John Paul II (consistories of June 30, 1979, and Feb. 2, 1983).

### Order of Bishops

Titular Bishops of Suburban Sees: Carlo Confalonieri, Dean (Dec. 15, 1958); Paolo Marella (Dec. 14, 1959); Sebastiano Baggio (Apr. 28, 1969); Francesco Carpino (June 26, 1967); Paolo Bertoli (Apr. 28, 1969); Agnelo Rossi (Feb. 22, 1965).

Eastern Rite Patriarchs: Stephanos I Sidarouss, C.M. (Feb. 22, 1965); Antoine Pierre Khoraiche (Feb. 2, 1983).

### Order of Priests

**1953** (Jan. 12): Giuseppe Siri, Paul Emile Leger, S.S.
**1958** (Dec. 15): Jose M. Bueno y Monreal, Franz Koenig.

**1960** (Mar. 28): Bernard Jan Alfrink, Laurean
Rugambwa.
**1962** (Mar. 19): Juan Landazuri Ricketts,
O.F.M., Raul Silva Henriquez, S.D.B., Leo Josef
Suenens.
**1965** (Feb. 22): Josyf Slipyi, Thomas B.
Cooray, Maurice Roy, Owen McCann, Leon-Etienne Duval,
Ermenegildo Florit, Paul Zoungrana, Giovanni
Colombo.
**1967** (June 26): Gabriel Garrone, Patrick
O'Boyle, Maximilien de Furstenberg, Jose
Clemente Maurer, C.SS.R., Pietro Parente, John
J. Krol, Corrado Ursi, Justin Darmojuwono,
Michele Pellegrino.
**1969** (Apr. 28): Alfredo Vicente Scherer, Gordon
J. Gray, Silvio Oddi, Miguel Dario Miranda y
Gomez, Giuseppe Paupini, Joseph Parecattil, John
F. Dearden, Francois Marty;
George Flahiff, Paul Gouyon, Vicente Enrique y
Tarancon, Joseph Malula, Pablo Muñoz Vega, S.J.,
Antonio Poma;
John J. Carberry, Stephan Sou Hwan Kim,
Eugenio de Araujo Sales, Joseph Hoeffner,
Johannes Willebrands, Mario Nasalli Rocca di
Corneliano, Sergio Guerri.
**1973** (Mar. 5): Antonio Ribeiro, Avelar Brandao
Vilela, Joseph Cordeiro, Anibal Muñoz Duque,
Pietro Palazzini, Luis Aponte Martinez, Raul
Francisco Primatesta, Salvatore Pappalardo,
Ferdinando Giuseppe Antonelli, Marcelo Gonzalez
Martin, Louis Jean Guyot, Ugo Poletti, Timothy
Manning, Maurice Otunga, Jose Salazar Lopez,
Paulo Evaristo Arns, James Darcy Freeman,
Narciso Jubany Arnau, Hermann Volk, Pio
Taofinu'u.
**1976** (May 24): Octavio Beras Rojas, Juan
Carlos Aramburu, Hyacinthe Thiandoum, Emmanuel
Nsubuga, Lawrence Trevor Picachy,
Jaime L. Sin, William W. Baum, Aloisio
Lorscheider, Laszlo Lekai, George Basil Hume,
O.S.B., Victor Razafimahatratra, Frantisek
Tomasek, Dominic Ekandem.
**1977** (June 27): Joseph Ratzinger, Bernardin
Gantin.
**1979** (June 30): Agostino Casaroli, Marco Ce,
Joseph-Marie Trinh van-Can, Ernesto Corripio
Ahumada, Joseph Asajiro Satowaki, Roger
Etchegaray, Anastasio Alberto Ballestrero,
O.C.D., Tomas O'Fiaich, Gerald Emmett Carter,
Franciszek Macharski.
**1983** (Feb. 2): Bernard Yago, Franjo Kuharic,
Jose Ali Lebrun Moratinos, Joseph L. Bernardin,
Michael Michai Kitbunchu, Alexandre do
Nascimento, Alfonso Lopez Trujillo, Godfried
Danneels, Thomas Stafford Williams, Carlo Maria
Martini, Jean-Marie Lustiger, Jozef Glemp, Julijans
Vaivods, Joachim Meisner.

### Order of Deacons

**1976** (May 24): Opilio Rossi, Giuseppe Maria
Sensi, Corrado Bafile, Eduardo Pironio.
**1977** (June 27): Luigi Ciappi.
**1979** (June 30): Giuseppe Caprio, Egano Righi-
Lambertini, Ernesto Civardi, Wladyslaw Rubin.
**1983** (Feb. 2): Aurelio Sabattani, Giuseppe
Casoria, Henri de Lubac.

### Ineligible To Vote

As of Aug. 27, 1984, 29 of the 126 cardinals were
ineligible to take part in a papal election in line
with the apostolic letter *Ingravescentem
Aetatem* effective Jan. 1, 1971, which limited the
functions of cardinals after completion of their
80th year.
Cardinals affected were: Alfrink, Antonelli,
Bafile, Carberry, Colombo, Confalonieri, Cooray,
de Lubac, Duval, Florit, Garrone Leger, Marella
Marty, Maurer, Miranda y Gomez, Munoz Vega,
Nasalli Rocca di Corneliano, O'Boyle, Parente,
Pellegrino, Satowaki, Scherer, Sidarouss, Slipyi,
Suenens, Tomasek, Vaivods, Volk.
Two more cardinals were due to become ineligible
to vote by the end of 1984: Jose Maria Bueno
y Monreal, after Sept. 11; Maximilien de
Furstenberg, after Oct. 23.
Cardinals completing their 80th year in 1985:
Maurice Roy, Jan. 25; Francesco Carpino, May 18;
Jean Guyot, July 7; Franz Koenig, Aug. 3; George
Flahiff, Oct. 26; Sergio Guerri, Dec. 25.

### DISTRIBUTION OF CARDINALS

*As of Aug. 27, 1984, there were 126 cardinals
from more than 50 countries or areas. Listed
below are areas, countries, number and last
names.*

#### Europe — 66

**Italy** (33): Antonelli, Bafile, Baggio,
Ballestrero, Bertoli, Caprio, Carpino, Casaroli,
Casoria, Cé, Ciappi, Civardi, Colombo, Confalonieri,
Florit, Guerri, Marella, Martini, Nasalli
Rocca di Corneliano, Oddi, Palazzini, Pappalardo,
Parente, Paupini, Pellegrino, Poletti, Poma,
Righi-Lambertini, Rossi, Sabattani, Sensi, Siri,
Ursi.
**France** (7): De Lubac, Etchegaray, Garrone,
Gouyon, Guyot, Lustiger, Marty.
**Germany** (4): Hoeffner, Meisner, Ratzinger,
Volk.
**Spain** (4): Bueno y Monreal, Enrique y Tarancon,
Gonzalez Martin, Jubany Arnau.
**Netherlands** (3): Alfrink, De Furstenberg,
Willebrands.
**Poland** (3): Glemp, Macharski, Rubin.
**Belgium** (2): Danneels, Suenens.
One from each of the following countries: Austria,
Koenig; Czechoslovakia, Tomasek; England,
Hume; Hungary, Lekai; Ireland, O'Fiaich; Latvia
(USSR), Vaivods; Portugal, Ribeiro; Scotland,
Gray; Ukraine (now in USSR), Slipyi; Yugoslavia,
Kuharic.

#### Asia — 11

**India** (2): Parecattil, Picachy.
One from each of the following countries: Indonesia,
Darmojuwono; Japan, Satowaki; Korea,
Kim; Lebanon, Khoraiche; Pakistan, Cordeiro;
Philippines, Sin; Sri Lanka, Cooray; Thailand, Kitbunchu,
Vietnam, Trinh van-Can.

#### Oceania — 3

Australia, Freeman; New Zealand, Williams;
Pacific Islands (Samoa), Taofinu'u.

## Africa — 14

One from each of the following countries: Algeria, Duval; Angola, do Nascimento; Benin, Gantin; Egypt, Sidarouss; Ivory Coast, Yago; Kenya, Otunga; Madagascar, Razafimahatratra; Nigeria, Ekandem; Senegal, Thiandoum; South Africa, McCann; Tanzania, Rugambwa; Uganda, Nsubuga; Upper Volta, Zoungrana; Zaire, Malula.

## North America — 15

United States (7): Baum, Bernardin, Carberry, Dearden, Krol, Manning, O'Boyle.

Canada (4): Carter, Flahiff, Leger, Roy.

Mexico (3): Corripio Ahumada, Miranda y Gomez, Salazar Lopez.

Puerto Rico (1): Aponte Martinez.

## Central and South America — 17

Brazil (6): Arns, Brandao Vilela, De Araujo Sales, Lorscheider, Rossi, Scherer.

Argentina (3): Aramburu, Pironio, Primatesta.

Colombia (2): Lopez Trujillo, Munoz Duque.

One from each of the following countries: Bolivia, Maurer; Chile, Silva Henriquez; Dominican Republic, Beras Rojas; Ecuador, Munoz Vega, S.J.; Peru, Landazuri Ricketts; Venezuela, Lebrun Moratinos.

## Cardinals of U.S.

As of Aug. 27, 1984, U.S. cardinals, years of elevation and sees.

Patrick A. O'Boyle, 1967, Washington (retired 1973); John J. Krol, 1967, Philadelphia; John F. Dearden, 1969, Detroit (retired 1980); John J. Carberry, 1969, St. Louis (retired 1979); Timothy Manning, 1973, Los Angeles; William W. Baum, 1976, Washington, D.C. (1973-80); prefect of Congregation for Catholic Education, 1980; Joseph L. Bernardin, 1983, Chicago.

Deceased cardinals of the United States,. Data: years of elevation, sees, years of birth and death.

John McCloskey, 1875, New York, 1810-1885; James Gibbons, 1886, Baltimore, 1834-1921; John Farley, 1911, New York, 1842-1918; William O'Connell, 1911, Boston, 1859-1944; Dennis Dougherty, 1921, Philadelphia, 1865-1951; Patrick Hayes, 1924, New York, 1867-1938; George Mundelein, 1924, Chicago, 1872-1939; John Glennon, 1946, St. Louis, 1862-1946; Edward Mooney, 1946, Detroit, 1882-1958;

Francis Spellman, 1946, New York, 1889-1967; Samuel Stritch, 1946, Chicago, 1887-1958; James F. McIntyre, 1953, Los Angeles, 1886-1979; John O'Hara, C.S.C., 1958, Philadelphia, 1888-1960; Richard Cushing, 1958, Boston, 1895-1970; Albert Meyer, 1959, Chicago, 1903-1965; Aloysius Muench, 1959, Fargo (and papal nuncio), 1889-1962; Joseph Ritter, 1961, St. Louis, 1892-1967; Francis Brennan, 1967, official of Roman Curia, 1894-1968; John P. Cody, 1967, Chicago 1907-1982; John J. Wright, 1969, prefect of Congregation for Clergy, 1909-1979; Humberto S. Medeiros, 1973, Boston, 1915-1983; Terence J. Cooke, 1969, New York, 1921-1983; Lawrence J. Shehan, 1965, Baltimore, 1898-1984.

# REPRESENTATIVES OF THE HOLY SEE

Papal representatives and their functions were the subject of a document entitled *Sollicitudo Omnium Ecclesiarum* which Pope Paul VI issued on his own initiative under the date of June 24, 1969.

## Delegates and Nuncios

Papal representatives "receive from the Roman Pontiff the charge of representing him in a fixed way in the various nations or regions of the world.

"When their legation is only to local churches, they are known as apostolic delegates. When to this legation, of a religious and ecclesial nature, there is added diplomatic legation to states and governments, they receive the title of nuncio, pro-nuncio, and internuncio."

[An apostolic nuncio has the diplomatic rank of ambassador extraordinary and plenipotentiary. Traditionally, because the Vatican diplomatic service has the longest uninterrupted history in the world, a nuncio has precedence among diplomats in the country to which he is accredited and serves as dean of the diplomatic corps on state occasions. Since 1965 pro-nuncios, also of ambassadorial rank, have been assigned to countries in which this prerogative is not recognized.]

(Other representatives, who are covered in the Almanac article, Vatican Representatives to International Organizations, are clerics and lay persons "who form . . . part of a pontifical mission attached to international organizations or take part in conferences and congresses." They are variously called delegates or observers.)

"The primary and specific purpose of the mission of a papal representative is to render ever closer and more operative the ties that bind the Apostolic See and the local churches.

"The ordinary function of a pontifical representative is to keep the Holy See regularly and objectively informed about the conditions of the ecclesial community to which he has been sent, and about what may affect the life of the Church and the good of souls.

"On the one hand, he makes known to the Holy See the thinking of the bishops, clergy, religious and faithful of the territory where he carries out his mandate, and forwards to Rome their proposals and their requests; on the other hand, he makes himself the interpreter, with those concerned, of the acts, documents, information and instructions emanating from the Holy See."

## Service and Liaison

Representatives, while carrying out their general and special duties, are bound to respect the autonomy of local churches and bishops. Their service and liaison responsibilities include the following:

• **Nomination of Bishops:** To play a key role in compiling, with the advice of ecclesiastics and lay persons, and submitting lists of names of likely candidates to the Holy See with their own recommendations.

• **Bishops:** To aid and counsel local bishops without interfering in the affairs of their jurisdictions.

• **Episcopal Conferences:** To maintain close relations with them and to assist them in every possible way. (Papal representatives do not belong to these conferences.)

• **Religious Communities of Pontifical Rank:** To advise and assist major superiors for the purpose of promoting and consolidating conferences of men and women religious and to coordinate their apostolic activities.

• **Church-State Relations:** The thrust in this area is toward the development of sound relations with civil governments and collaboration in work for peace and the total good of the whole human family.

The mission of a papal representative begins with appointment and assignment by the pope and continues until termination of his mandate. He acts "under the guidance and according to the instructions of the cardinal secretary of state and prefect of the Council for the Public Affairs of the Church, to whom he is directly responsible for the execution of the mandate entrusted to him by the Supreme Pontiff." Normally, representatives are required to retire at the age of 75.

## NUNCIOS AND DELEGATES

(Sources: *Annuario Pontificio, L'Osservatore Romano, Acta Apostolicae Sedis,* NC News Service.)

Data, as of July 1, 1984, country, rank of legation (corresponding to rank of legate unless otherwise noted), name of legate (archbishop unless otherwise noted) as available.

**Delegate for Papal Representatives:** Archbishop Giovanni Coppa. The post was established in 1973 to coordinate papal diplomatic efforts throughout the world. The office entails responsibility for "following more closely through timely visits the activities of papal representatives . . . and encouraging their rapport with the central offices" of the Secretariat of State and the Council for the Public Affairs of the Church.

**Africa, Southern** (Botswana, South Africa, Namibia, Swaziland): Pretoria, South Africa, Apostolic Delegation; Edward Cassidy (also Pro-Nuncio to Lesotho).

**Algeria:** Algiers, Nunciature; Gabriel Montalvo, Pro-Nuncio (He is also Pro-Nuncio to Tunisia and Apostolic Delegate to Libya.)

**Angola:** Luanda, Apostolic Delegation; Fortunato Baldelli (also Apostolic Delegate to Sao Tome and Principe).

**Antilles:** Apostolic Delegation; Paul Fouad Tabat (resides in Port of Spain, Trinidad).

**Argentina:** Buenos Aires, Nunciature; Ubaldo Calabresi.

**Australia:** Canberra, Nunciature; Luigi Barbarito, Pro-Nuncio.

**Austria:** Vienna, Nunciature; Mario Cagna.

**Bahamas:** Nunciature; Paul Fouad Tabat, Pro-Nuncio (resides in Port of Spain, Trinidad).

**Bangladesh:** Dacca, Nunciature; Luigi Accogli, Pro-Nuncio (also serves as Apostolic Delegate to Burma.)

**Barbados:** Nunciature; Paul Fouad Tabat, Pro-Nuncio (resides in Port of Spain, Trinidad).

**Belgium:** Brussels, Nunciature; Angelo Pedroni (also Nuncio to Luxembourg and European Community).

**Belize:** Paul Fouad Tabat, Pro-Nuncio (resides in Port-of-Spain, Trinidad).

**Benin** (formerly Dahomey): Nunciature; Ivan Dias, Pro-Nuncio (resides in Accra, Ghana).

**Bolivia:** La Paz, Nunciature; Alfio Rapisarda.

**Botswana:** See Africa, Southern.

**Brazil:** Brasilia, Nunciature; Carlo Furno.

**Brunei:** See Malaysia and Brunei.

**Burma:** See Bangladesh.

**Burundi:** Bujumbura, Nunciature; Bernard Jacqueline, Pro-Nuncio.

**Cameroon:** Yaounde, Nunciature; Donato Squicciarino, Pro-Nuncio (also Pro-Nuncio to Gabon Republic and Equatorial Guinea).

**Canada:** Ottawa, Nunciature; Angelo Palmas, Pro-Nuncio.

**Cape Verde, Republic of:** Nunciature; Luigi Dossena, Pro-Nuncio (resides in Dakar, Senegal).

**Central African Republic:** Bangui, Nunciature; Giovanni Bulaitis, Pro-Nuncio (also Pro-Nuncio to Congo and Apostolic Delegate to Chad).

**Chad:** Apostolic Delegation; Giovanni Bulaitis (resides in Bangui, Central African Republic).

**Chile:** Santiago, Nunciature; Angelo Sodano.

**China:** Taipei (Taiwan), Nunciature.

**Colombia:** Bogota, Nunciature; Angelo Acerbi.

**Congo Republic:** Brazzaville, Nunciature; Giovanni Bulaitis, Pro-Nuncio (resides in Bangui, Central African Republic).

**Costa Rica:** San Jose, Nunciature (also Nuncio to El Salvador).

**Cuba:** Havana, Nunciature; Giulio Einaudi, Pro-Nuncio.

**Cyprus:** Nicosia, Nunciature; Carlo Curis, Pro-Nuncio (also Apostolic Delegate to Jerusalem).

**Denmark:** Copenhagen, Nunciature; Luigi Bellotti, Pro-Nuncio (also Pro-Nuncio to Finland, Iceland, Norway and Sweden).

**Djibouti:** See Red Sea Region.

**Dominica:** Nunciature: Paul Fouad Tabet, Pro-Nuncio (resides in Port-of-Spain, Trinidad).

**Dominican Republic:** Santo Domingo, Nunciature; Blasco Francisco Collaco (also Apostolic Delegate to Puerto Rico).

**Ecuador:** Quito, Nunciature; Vincenzo Farano.

**Egypt:** Cairo, Nunciature; Giovanni Moretti, Pro-Nuncio.

**El Salvador:** San Salvador, Nunciature (also Nuncio to Costa Rica).

**Equatorial Guinea:** Santa Isabel, Nunciature; Donato Squicciarino, Pro-Nuncio (resides in Yaounde, Cameroon).

**Ethiopia:** Addis Ababa, Nunciature; Thomas White, Pro-Nuncio.

**Fiji:** Nunciature; Antonio Magnoni, Pro-Nuncio (resides in New Zealand).

**Finland:** Helsinki, Nunciature; Luigi Bellotti, Pro-Nuncio (resides in Denmark).

**France:** Paris, Nunciature; Angelo Felici.

**Gabon:** Libreville, Nunciature; Donato Squicciarino, Pro-Nuncio (resides in Yaounde, Cameroon).

**Gambia:** Nunciature; Pro-Nuncio (resides in Monrovia, Liberia).

**Germany:** Bonn, Nunciature; Guido Del Mestri.

**Ghana:** Accra, Nunciature; Ivan Dias, Pro-Nuncio (also Pro-Nuncio to Benin and Togo).

**Great Britain:** London, Nunciature; Bruno Heim, Pro-Nuncio (also papal representative to Gibraltar).

**Greece:** Athens, Nunciature; Giovanni Mariani, Pro-Nuncio.

**Grenada:** Nunciature.

**Guatemala:** Guatemala City, Nunciature; Oriano Quilici.

**Guinea:** Conakry, Apostolic Delegation (resides in Monrovia, Liberia).

**Guinea-Bissau:** Apostolic Delegation; Luigi Dossena (resides at Dakar, Senegal).

**Haiti:** Port-au-Prince, Nunciature; Paolo Romeo.

**Honduras:** Tegucigalpa, Nunciature; Andrea Cordero Lanza di Montezemolo. (also Nuncio to Nicaragua).

**Iceland:** Nunciature; Luigi Bellotti, Pro-Nuncio (resides in Denmark).

**India:** New Delhi, Nunciature; Agostino Caccavillan, Pro-Nuncio.

**Indonesia:** Jakarta, Nunciature; Pablo Puente, Pro-Nuncio.

**Iran:** Teheran, Nunciature; Giovanni De Andrea, Pro-Nuncio.

**Iraq:** Baghdad, Nunciature; Luigi Conti, Pro-Nuncio (also Pro-Nuncio to Kuwait).

**Ireland:** Dublin, Nunciature; Gaetano Alibrandi.

**Italy:** Rome, Nunciature; Romolo Carboni.

**Ivory Coast:** Abidjan, Nunciature; Justo Mullor Garcia (also Pro-Nuncio to Niger and Upper Volta).

**Jamaica:** Nunciature; Paul Fouad Tabat, Pro-Nuncio (resides in Port of Spain, Trinidad).

**Japan:** Tokyo, Nunciature; William A. Carew, Pro-Nuncio.

**Jerusalem, Palestine, Jordan, Israel:** Jerusalem, Apostolic Delegation; Carlo Curis (also Pro-Nuncio to Cyprus).

**Kenya:** Nairobi, Nunciature; Clemente Faccani, Pro-Nuncio.

**Korea:** Seoul, Nunciature; Francesco Monterisi, Pro-Nuncio.

**Kuwait:** Al Kuwait, Nunciature; Luigi Conti, Pro-Nuncio (resides in Baghdad, Iraq).

**Laos:** Apostolic Delegation; Renato Raffaele Martino (resides in Bangkok, Thailand).

**Lebanon:** Beirut, Nunciature; Luciano Angeloni.

**Lesotho:** Maseru, Nunciature; Edward Cassidy, Pro-Nuncio (resides in Pretoria, S. Africa).

**Liberia:** Monrovia, Nunciature; Pro-Nuncio (also Pro-Nuncio to Gambia and Apostolic Delegate to Guinea and Sierra Leone).

**Libya:** Apostolic Delegation; Gabriel Montalvo (resides in Algiers, Algeria).

**Luxembourg:** Nunciature; Angelo Pedroni (resides in Brussels, Belgium).

**Madagascar:** Tananarive, Nunciature; Sergio Sebastiani, Pro-Nuncio (also Pro-Nuncio to Mauritius and Apostolic Delegate to Reunion).

**Malawi:** Lilongwe, Nunciature; Georg Zur, Pro-Nuncio (resides in Zambia).

**Malaysia and Brunei:** Apostolic Delegation; Renato Raffaele Martino (resides in Bangkok, Thailand).

**Mali:** Nunciature; Luigi Dossena, Pro-Nuncio (resides in Dakar, Senegal).

**Malta:** La Valletta, Nunciature.

**Mauritania:** Nouakchott, Apostolic Delegation; Luigi Dossena (resides in Dakar, Senegal).

**Mauritius:** Port Louis, Nunciature; Sergio Sebastiani, Pro-Nuncio (resides in Tananarive, Madagascar).

**Mexico:** Mexico City, Apostolic Delegation; Girolamo Prigione.

**Morocco:** Rabat, Nunciature; Pro-Nuncio.

**Mozambique:** Maputo, Apostolic Delegation; Francesco Colasuonna (also Pro-Nuncio to Zimbabwe).

**Namibia:** See Africa, Southern.

**Netherlands:** The Hague, Nunciature; Bruno Wustenberg, Pro-Nuncio.

**New Zealand:** Wellington, Nunciature; Antonio Magnoni, Pro-Nuncio. (He is also Pro-Nuncio to Fiji and Apostolic Delegate to Pacific Islands).

**Nicaragua:** Managua, Nunciature; Andrea Cordero Lanza di Montezemolo (also Nuncio to Honduras).

**Niger:** Niamey, Nunciature; Justo Mullor Garcia, Pro-Nuncio (resides in Abidjan, Ivory Coast).

**Nigeria:** Lagos, Nunciature; Pro-Nuncio.

**Norway:** Nunciature; Luigi Bellotti, Pro-Nuncio (resides in Denmark).

**Pacific Islands:** Apostolic Delegation; Antonio Magnoni (resides in New Zealand).

**Pakistan:** Islamabad, Nunciature; Emanuele Gerada, Pro-Nuncio.

**Panama:** Panama, Nunciature; Jose Sebastian Laboa.

**Papua New Guinea:** Port Moresby; Nunciature; Francesco De Nittis, Pro-Nuncio. (He is also Apostolic Delegate to western and southern Solomon Islands.)

**Paraguay:** Asuncion, Nunciature; Joseph Mees.

**Peru:** Lima, Nunciature; Mario Tagliaferri.

**Philippines:** Manila, Nunciature; Bruno Torpigliani.

**Portugal:** Lisbon, Nunciature; Salvatore Asta.

**Puerto Rico:** See Dominican Republic.

**Red Sea Region** (Somalia, Djibouti, part of Arabian Peninsula): Apostolic Delegation (resides in Khartoum, Sudan).

**Reunion:** See Madagascar.

**Rhodesia:** See Zimbabwe.

**Rwanda:** Kigali, Nunciature. Giovanni Battista Morandini, Pro-Nuncio.

**Sao Tome and Principe:** See Angola.

**Senegal:** Dakar, Nunciature; Luigi Dossena, Pro-Nuncio (also Pro-Nuncio to Cape Verde and Mali; Apostolic Delegate to Guinea-Bissau, and Mauritania.)

**Seychelles Islands:** Diplomatic relations established 1984.

**Sierra Leone:** Apostolic Delegation (resides in Monrovia, Liberia).

**Singapore:** Nunciature; Renato Raffaele Martino, Pro-Nuncio (resides in Bangkok, Thailand).

**Solomon Islands:** Apostolic Delegation; Francesco De Nittis (resides in Port Moresby, Papua New Guinea).

**Somalia:** See Red Sea Region.

**South Africa:** See Africa, Southern.

**Spain:** Madrid, Nunciature; Antonio Innocenti.

**Sri Lanka:** Colombo, Nunciature; Ambrose De Paoli, Pro-Nuncio.

**Sudan:** Khartoum, Nunciature; Pro-Nuncio (also Apostolic Delegate to Red Sea Region).

**Swaziland:** See Africa, Southern.

**Sweden:** Nunciature; Luigi Bellotti, Pro-Nuncio (resides in Denmark).

**Switzerland:** Bern, Nunciature; Ambrogio Marchioni.

**Syria** (Syrian Arab Republic): Damascus, Nunciature; Nicola Rotunno, Pro-Nuncio.

**Tanzania:** Dar-es-Salaam, Nunciature; Gian Vincenzo Moreni, Pro-Nuncio.

**Thailand:** Bangkok, Nunciature; Renato Raffaelo Martino, Pro-Nuncio (also Pro-Nuncio to Singapore and Apostolic Delegate to Laos, Malaysia and Brunei).

**Togo:** Lome, Nunciature; Ivan Dias, Pro-Nuncio (resides in Accra, Ghana).

**Trinidad and Tobago:** Port of Spain, Trinidad, Nunciature; Paul Fouad Tabat, Pro-Nuncio (also Pro-Nuncio to Bahamas, Barbados, Belize, Dominica, Jamaica and Apostolic Delegate to Antilles).

**Tunisia:** Tunis, Nunciature; Gabriel Montalvo, Pro-Nuncio (resides in Algiers, Algeria).

**Turkey:** Ankara, Nunciature; Pro-Nuncio.

**Uganda:** Kampala, Nunciature; Karl Joseph Rauber, Pro-Nuncio.

**United States of America:** Washington, D.C., Nunciature; Pio Laghi, Pro-Nuncio.

**Upper Volta:** Ouagadougou, Nunciature; Justo Mullor Garcia, Pro-Nuncio (resides in Abidjan, Ivory Coast).

**Uruguay:** Montevideo, Nunciature; Franco Brambilla.

**Venezuela:** Caracas, Nunciature; Luciano Storero.

**Vietnam and Cambodia:** Apostolic Delegation.

**Yugoslavia:** Belgrade, Nunciature; Michele Cecchini, Pro-Nuncio.

**Zaire:** Kinshasa-Gombe, Nunciature; Giuseppe Uhac, Pro-Nuncio.

**Zambia:** Lusaka, Nunciature; Georg Zur, Pro-Nuncio (also Pro-Nuncio to Malawi).

**Zimbabwe:** Nunciature; Francesco Colasuonno, Pro-Nuncio (is also Apostolic Delegate to Mozambique).

**European Community:** Brussels, Belgium, Nunciature; Angelo Pedroni, Nuncio.

### Pro-Nuncio to U.S.

The representative of the Pope to the Church in the United States is Archbishop Pio Laghi, pro-nuncio. Archbishop Laghi was born May 21, 1922, in Castiglione, Italy. Ordained to the priesthood Apr. 20, 1946, he entered the Vatican diplomatic service in 1952. He served in Nicaragua, the U.S. (as secretary of the apostolic delegation, 1954-61) and India. He was recalled to Rome and served on the Council for the Public Affairs of the Church. He was appointed to the titular see of Mauriana and received episcopal ordination June 22, 1969. He was apostolic delegate to Jerusalem and Palestine, 1969-74, and apostolic nuncio to Argentina, 1974-80. On Dec. 10, 1980, he was appointed apostolic delegate to the United States and permanent observer to the Organization of American States.

He was named first pro-nuncio in 1984 when the U.S. and the Vatican reestablished diplomatic relations (See Index: U.S.-Vatican Relations).

The U.S. Apostolic Nunciature is located at 3339 Massachusetts Ave. N.W., Washington, D.C. 20008.

From 1893 to 1984, papal representatives to the Church in the U.S. were apostolic delegates (all archbishops): Francesco Satolli (1893-1896), Sebastiano Martinelli, O.S.A. (1896-1902), Diomede Falconio, O.F.M. (1902-1911), Giovanni Bonzano (1911-1922), Pietro Fumasoni-Biondi (1922-1933), Amleto Cicognani (1933-1958), Egidio Vagnozzi (1958-1967); Luigi Raimondi (1967-1973); Jean Jadot (1973-1980); Pio Laghi (1980-84).

## DIPLOMATS AT VATICAN

(Sources: *Annuario Pontificio, L'Osservatore Romano, Acta Apostolicae Sedis,* NC News Service. As of July 1, 1984.)

The dean of the diplomatic corps at the Vatican is Ambassador Joseph Amichia of Ivory Coast (from 1971) who succeeded to the post in 1983.

**Algeria:** Abdelmalek Benhalyles, Ambassador.

**Argentina:** Jose Maria Alvarez de Toledo, Ambassador.

**Australia:** Sir Peter Lawler, Ambassador.

**Austria:** Hans Pasch, Ambassador.

**Bahamas:** Ambassador.

**Bangladesh:** Ali Kaiser Hasan Morshed, Ambassador.

**Barbados:** Ambassador.

**Belgium:** Eugene Rittweger de Moor, Ambassador.

**Belize:** Rodolfo Inocente Castillo, Ambassador.

**Benin** (formerly Dahomey): Ambassador.

**Bolivia:** Carlos Romero Alvarez Garcia, Ambassador.

**Brazil:** Antonio Correa do Lago, Ambassador.

**Burundi:** Egide Nkuriyin Goma, Ambassador.

**Cameroon:** Enoch Kwayeb, Ambassador.

**Canada:** Pierre Dumas, Ambassador.

**Cape Verde, Republic of:** Viriato de Barros, Ambassador.

**Central African Republic:** Albert Sato, Ambassador.

**Chile:** Hector Riesle Contreras, Ambassador.

**China** (Taiwan): Chow Shu-Kai, Ambassador.

**Colombia:** Miguel Escobar Mendez, Ambassador.

**Congo Republic:** Jean-Pierre Nonault, Ambassador.

**Costa Rica:** Enrique Obregon Valverde, Ambassador.
**Cuba:** Manuel Estevez Perez, Ambassador.
**Cyprus:** Polys Modinos, Ambassador.
**Denmark:** Hans Erik Thrane, Ambassador.
**Dominica:** Ambassador (relations established in 1981).
**Dominican Republic:** Victor Gomez Berges, Ambassador.
**Ecuador:** Jorge Salvador Lara, Ambassador.
**Egypt:** Mostafa Kamal El-Diwani, Ambassador.
**El Salvador:** Prudencio Llach Schonenberg, Ambassador.
**Equatorial Guinea:** Ambassador (relations established 1981).
**Ethiopia:** Ambassador.
**Fiji:** Ratu Josua Brown Toganivalu, Ambassador.
**Finland:** Kaarlo Yrjo-Koskinen, Ambassador.
**France:** Xavier Daufresne de la Chavalier, Ambassador.
**Gabon:** Ambassador.
**Gambia, The:** Ambassador.
**Germany:** Walter Gehlhoff, Ambassador.
**Ghana:** Joseph Quao Cleland, Ambassador.
**Great Britain:** Mark Evelyn Heath, Ambassador.
**Greece:** Christos Rokofollis, Ambassador.
**Grenada:** Ambassador.
**Guatemala:** Jose Alejandro Deutschmann Miron, Ambassador.
**Haiti:** Pierre Pompee, Ambassador.
**Honduras:** Oscar Acosta, Ambassador.
**Iceland:** Niels P. Sigurdsson, Ambassador.
**India:** Thomas Abraham, Ambassador.
**Indonesia:** Hardiman Sastrapoespita, Ambassador.
**Iran:** Seyed Hadi Khosrovshahian, Ambassador.
**Iraq:** Abdul Wadood Y.M. Al-Jaddoua, Ambassador.
**Ireland:** Francis A. Coffey, Ambassador.
**Italy:** Claudio Chelli, Ambassador.
**Ivory Coast:** Joseph Amichia, Ambassador.
**Jamaica:** Keith Johnson, Ambassador.
**Japan:** Teruhiko Nakamuro, Ambassador.
**Kenya:** John Kamau Kimani, Ambassador.
**Korea:** Joa Soo Kim, Ambassador.
**Kuwait:** Essa Ahmad Al-Hamad, Ambassador.
**Lebanon:** Nasri Salhab, Ambassador.
**Lesotho:** Mokheseng Rtekateka, Ambassador.
**Liberia:** Harry Fumba Moniba, Ambassador.
**Lithuania:** Stasys Lozoraitis, Jr., first secretary.
**Luxembourg:** Jean Wagner, Ambassador.
**Madagascar:** Salomon Rahatoka, Ambassador.
**Malawi:** Ambassador.
**Mali:** Yaya Diarra, Ambassador.
**Malta:** Paolo Farrugia, Ambassador.
**Mauritius:** Ambassador.

**Monaco:** Cesar Charles Solamito, Ambassador.
**Morocco:** Youssef Ben Abbes, Ambassador.
**Nepal:** Ambassador.
**Netherlands:** Johan Anthony Beelaerts Van Blokland, Ambassador.
**New Zealand:** John G. McArthur, Ambassador.
**Nicaragua:** Ricardo Agustin Peter Silva, Ambassador.
**Niger:** Ambassador.
**Nigeria:** Isaac Jemide Sagay, Ambassador.
**Norway:** Torbjorn Kristoffer Christiansen, Ambassador.
**Order of Malta:** Christophe de Kallay, Ambassador.
**Pakistan:** Fazli Raziq, Ambassador.
**Panama:** Jaime Ingram Jaen, Ambassador.
**Papua New Guinea:** Peter Ipu Paipul, Ambassador.
**Paraguay:** Juan Livieres Argana, Ambassador.
**Peru:** Jorge Nicholson Sologuren, Ambassador.
**Philippines:** Bienvenido R. Tantoco, Sr., Ambassador.
**Portugal:** Helder de Mendonca Cunha, Ambassador.
**Rwanda:** Callixte Hatungimana, Ambassador.
**San Marino:** Dr. Giovanni Galassi, Minister.
**Senegal:** Joseph Mathiam, Ambassador.
**Seychelles:** Diplomatic relations established 1984.
**Singapore:** Chiang Hai Ding, Ambassador.
**Spain:** Nuno Aguirre de Carcer y Lopez de Sagredo, Ambassador.
**Sri Lanka:** Nadaraja Balasubramaniam, Ambassador.
**Sudan:** Sayed Yousif Mukhtar Yousif, Ambassador.
**Sweden:** Gunnar Johan Ljungdahl, Ambassador.
**Syria** (Arab Republic): Adib Daoudy, Ambassador.
**Tanzania:** Ahmed Diria Hassan, Ambassador.
**Thailand:** Owart Suthiwart-Narueput, Ambassador.
**Togo:** Vigniko A. Amedegnato, Ambassador.
**Trinidad and Tobago:** Maurice Oscar St. John, Ambassador.
**Tunisia:** Abdelmadjid Chaker, Ambassador.
**Turkey:** Sulhi Dislioglu, Ambassador.
**Uganda:** James Nagai Obua-Otoa, Ambassador.
**United States:** (1984): William A. Wilson, Ambassador.
**Upper Volta:** Ambassador.
**Uruguay:** Carlos Maria Romero, Ambassador.
**Venezuela:** Luciano Joguera Mora, Ambassador.
**Yugoslavia:** Zvonimir Stenek, Ambassador.
**Zaire:** Tshimbalanga Shala-Dibwe, Ambassador.
**Zambia:** Peter Dingiswayo Zuze, Ambassador.
**Zimbabwe:** Ambassador.

---

## JOHN XXIII CENTER

The John XXIII Ecumenical Center was established in 1951 (as the Russian Center) by Father Feodor Wilcock, S.J., in cooperation with Fordham University. It is sponsored by the Jesuit Conference of the United States as a center for study as well as for apostolic and ecumenical activity with Eastern Christians, Catholics and Orthodox, in America. It publishes *Diakonia*, conducts special seminars and conferences, sponsors the John XXIII Summer Institute and its degree in the study of Eastern Christian traditions.

Father John F. Long, S.J., is superior and director of the center, located at 2502 Belmont Ave., Bronx, N.Y 10458.

# U.S. — VATICAN RELATIONS

The United States and the Vatican announced Jan. 10, 1984, the establishment of full diplomatic relations, thus ending a gap of 117 years in their relations. The announcement followed action by the Congress in November, 1983, to end a prohibition on diplomatic relations enacted in 1867.

William A. Wilson, a Catholic and President Ronald Reagan's personal representative to the Vatican since February, 1981, was confirmed as the U.S. ambassador by the Senate on Mar. 7, 1984; he presented his credentials to Pope John Paul on Apr. 9. Archbishop Pio Laghi, apostolic delegate to the U.S. since 1980, was named pro-nuncio by the Pope on Mar. 26.

## Nature of Relations

The nature of relations was described in nearly identical statements by John Hughes, a State Department spokesman, and the Vatican.

Hughes said: "The United States of America and the Holy See, in the desire to further promote the existing mutual friendly relations, have decided by common agreement to establish diplomatic relations between them at the level of embassy on the part of the United States of America, and nunciature on the part of the Holy See, as of today, Jan. 10, 1984."

The Vatican statement said: "The Holy See and the United States of America, desiring to develop the mutual friendly relations already existing, have decided by common accord to establish diplomatic relations at the level of apostolic nunciature on the side of the Holy See and of embassy on the side of the United States beginning today, Jan. 10, 1984."

The establishment of relations was criticized as a violation of the separation-of-church-and-state principle by spokesmen for the National Council of Churches, the National Association of Evangelicals, the Baptist Joint Committee on Public Affairs, Seventh Day Adventists, Americans United for Separation of Church and State, and the American Jewish Congress.

Their view was not shared by the Reagan administration.

## Not a Religious Issue

Bishop James W. Malone, president of the U.S. Catholic Conference, said in a statement: "This matter has been discussed at length for many years. It is not a religious issue but a public policy question which, happily, has now been settled in this context."

Russell Shaw, a conference spokesman, said the decision to send an ambassador to the Vatican was not a church-state issue and "confers no special privilege or status on the Church."

## Earlier Relations

Official relations for trade and diplomatic purposes were maintained by the United States and the Papal States while the latter had the character of and acted like other sovereign powers in the international community.

Consular relations developed in the wake of an announcement, made by the papal nuncio in Paris to the American mission there Dec. 15, 1784, that the Papal States had agreed to open several Mediterranean ports to U.S. shipping.

U.S. consular representation in the Papal States began with the appointment of John B. Sartori, a native of Rome, in June, 1797. Sartori's successors as consuls were: Felix Cicognani, also a Roman, and Americans George W. Greene, Nicholas Browne, William C. Sanders, Daniel LeRoy, Horatio V. Glentworth, W.J. Stillman, Edwin C. Cushman, David M. Armstrong.

Consular officials of the Papal States who served in the U.S. were: Count Ferdinand Lucchesi, 1826 to 1829, who resided in Washington; John B. Sartori, 1829 to 1841, who resided in Trenton, N.J.; Daniel J. Desmond, 1841 to 1850, who resided in Philadelphia; Louis B. Binsse, 1850 to 1895, who resided in New York.

U.S. recognition of the consul of the Papal States did not cease when the states were absorbed into the Kingdom of Italy in 1871, despite pressure from Baron Blanc, the Italian minister. Binsse held the title until his death Mar. 28, 1895. No one was appointed to succeed him.

## Diplomatic Relations

The U.S. Senate approved a recommendation, made by President James K. Polk in December, 1847, for the establishment of a diplomatic post in the Papal States. Jacob L. Martin, the first charge d'affaires, arrived in Rome Aug. 2, 1848, and presented his credentials to Pius IX Aug. 19. Martin, who died within a month, was succeeded by Lewis Cass, Jr. Cass became minister resident in 1854 and served in that capacity until his retirement in 1858.

John P. Stockton, who later became a U.S. Senator from New Jersey, was minister resident from 1858 to 1861. Rufus King was named to succeed him but, instead, accepted a commission as a brigadier general in the Army. Alexander W. Randall of Wisconsin took the appointment. He was succeeded in August, 1862, by Richard M. Blatchford who served until the following year. King was again nominated minister resident and served in that capacity until 1867 when the ministry was ended because of objections from some quarters in the U.S. and failure to appropriate funds for its continuation. J. C. Hooker, a secretary, remained in the Papal States until the end of March, 1868, closing the ministry and performing functions of courtesy.

## Personal Envoys

Myron C. Taylor was appointed by President Franklin D. Roosevelt in 1939 to serve as his personal representative to Pope Pius XII and continued serving in that capacity during the presidency of Harry S. Truman until 1951. Henry Cabot Lodge was named to the post by President Richard M. Nixon in 1970, served also during the presidency of Gerald Ford, and represented President Carter at the canonization of St. John Neumann in 1977.

Miami attorney David Walters, a Catholic, served as the personal envoy of President Jimmy Carter to the Pope from July, 1977, until his resignation Aug. 16, 1978. He was succeeded by Robert F. Wagner, also a Catholic and former mayor of New York, who served from October, 1978, to the end of the Carter presidency in January, 1981. William A. Wilson, a California businessman and Catholic, was appointed by President Ronald Reagan in February, 1981, to serve as his personal envoy to the Pope.

None of the personal envoys had diplomatic status.

President Harry S. Truman nominated Gen. Mark Clark to be ambassador to the Vatican in 1951, but withdrew the nomination at Clark's request because of controversy over the appointment.

None of Truman's three successors — Dwight D. Eisenhower, John F. Kennedy or Lyndon B. Johnson — had a personal representative to the Pope.

## VATICAN CITY

The State of Vatican City (Stato della Citta del Vaticano) is the territorial seat of the papacy. The smallest sovereign state in the world, it is situated within the city of Rome, embraces an area of 108.7 acres, and includes within its limits the Vatican Palace, museums, art galleries, gardens, libraries, radio station, post office, bank, astronomical observatory, offices, apartments, service facilities, St. Peter's Basilica, and neighboring buildings between the Basilica and Viale Vaticano.

The extraterritorial rights of Vatican City extend to more than 10 buildings in Rome, including the major basilicas and office buildings of various congregations of the Roman Curia, and to the **Villa of Castel Gandolfo** 15 miles southeast of the City of Rome. Castel Gandolfo is the summer residence of the Holy Father.

The government of Vatican City is in the hands of the reigning pope, who has full executive, legislative and judicial power. The administration of affairs, however, is handled by the Pontifical Commission for the State of Vatican City. The legal system is based on Canon Law; in cases where this code does not obtain, the laws of the City of Rome apply. The City is an absolutely neutral state and enjoys all the rights and privileges of a sovereign power. The Secretariat of State (Papal Secretariat) maintains diplomatic relations with other nations. The citizens of Vatican City, and they alone, owe allegiance to the pope as a temporal head of state.

Cardinals of the Roman Curia residing outside Vatican City enjoy the privileges of extraterritoriality.

The normal population is approximately 1,000. While the greater percentage is made up of priests and religious, there are several hundred lay persons living in Vatican City. They are housed in their own apartments in the City and are engaged in secretarial, domestic, trade and service occupations. About 4,000 persons are employed by the Vatican.

Services of honor and order are performed by the Swiss Guards, who have been charged with responsibility for the personal safety of popes since 1506. Additional police and ceremonial functions are under the supervision of a special office. These functions were formerly handled by the Papal Gendarmes, the Palatine Guard of Honor, and the Guard of Honor of the Pope (Pontifical Noble Guard) which Pope Paul disbanded Sept. 14, 1970.

The **Basilica of St. Peter,** built between 1506 and 1626, is the largest church in Christendom and the site of most papal ceremonies. The pope's own patriarchal basilica, however, is **St. John Lateran,** whose origins date back to 324.

**St. Ann's** is the parish church of Vatican City.

The vicar general of the pope for Vatican City, which is part of the diocese of Rome, is Most Rev. Peter Canisius Van Lierde, O.S.A., titular bishop of Porfireone.

The **Vatican Library,** one of five in the City, has among its holdings 70,000 manuscripts, 770,000 printed books, and 7,500 incunabula.

The independent temporal power of the pope, which is limited to the confines of Vatican City and small areas outside, was for many centuries more extensive than it is now. As late as the nineteenth century, the pope ruled 16,000 square miles of Papal States across the middle of Italy, with a population of over 3,000,000. In 1870 forces of the Kingdom of Italy occupied these lands which, with the exception of the small areas surrounding the Vatican and Lateran in Rome and the Villa of Castel Gandolfo, became part of the Kingdom by the Italian law of May 13, 1871.

The **Roman Question,** occasioned by this seizure and the voluntary confinement of the pope to the limited papal lands, was finally settled with ratification of the Lateran Agreement on June 7, 1929, by the Italian government and Vatican City and provided a financial indemnity for the former Papal States, which became recognized as part of Italy. The Lateran Agreement became Article 7 of the Italian Constitution on Mar. 26, 1947. It was revised in 1984 (see Index).

### Papal Flag

The papal flag consists of two equal vertical stripes of yellow and white, charged with the insignia of the papacy on the white stripe — a triple crown or tiara over two crossed keys, one of gold and one of silver, tied with a red cord and two tassels. The divisions of the crown represent the teaching, sanctifying and ruling offices of the pope. The keys symbolize his jurisdictional authority.

The papal flag is a national flag inasmuch as it is the standard of the Supreme Pontiff as the sovereign of the state of Vatican City. It is also universally accepted by the faithful as a symbol of the supreme spiritual authority of the Holy Father.

In a Catholic church, the papal flag is displayed on a staff on the left side of the sanctuary (facing the congregation), and the American flag is displayed on the right.

## Vatican Radio

The declared purpose of Vatican Radio Station HVJ is "that the voice of the Supreme Pastor may be heard throughout the world by means of the ether waves, for the glory of Christ and the salvation of souls." Designed by Guglielmo Marconi, the inventor of radio, and supervised by him until his death, the station was inaugurated by Pope Pius XI in 1931. The original purpose has been extended to a wide variety of programming.

Vatican Radio operates on international wave lengths, transmits programs in 35 languages, and serves as a channel of communication between the Vatican, church officials and listeners in general in many parts of the world. The station broadcasts about 280 hours a week throughout the world.

The staff of 350 broadcasters and technicians includes 40 Jesuits and is directed by Father Robert Tucci, S.J. Headquarters are located in Vatican City. Studios and offices are at Palazzo Pio, Piazza Pia, 3. The transmitters are situated at Santa Maria di Galeria, a short distance north of Rome.

## 1984 Vatican Stamps

The Vatican Philatelic Office scheduled the following issues of stamps and postal stationery for 1984. (Issue date is given where available.)

• Series commemorating the centenary of the death of the Augustinian biologist, Johann Gregor Mendel. Issued Feb. 28, 1984, in two values (450 and 1,500 lire) on a single subject.

• Series commemorating the fifth centenary of the death of St. Casimir, patron of Lithuania. Issued Feb. 28, 1984, in two values (550 and 1,200 lire) on a single subject.

• Regular issue: the Journeys of Pope John Paul II throughout the world in 1981 and 1982.

• Series commemorating the 1600th anniversary of the death of Pope St. Damasus.

• Series in honor of cultural and scientific institutions of the Holy See. Issued June 18, 1984, in four values: 150 lire (external view of Pontifical Academy of Sciences), 450 lire (seals on a document preserved in the Secret Vatican Archives), 550 lire (entrance to Vatican Library), 1,500 lire (Vatican Observatory at Castel Gandolfo).

• Aerogramme. Issued June 18, 1984.

• Illustrated stamped postcards.

## Vatican Coins

The Vatican Numismatics Office issued a series of coins Mar. 29, 1984, for the fifth year of the pontificate of Pope John Paul II. The set consisted of seven coins (10, 20, 50, 100, 200, 500 and 1,000 lire).

## Papal Audiences

General audiences are scheduled weekly, on Wednesday.

In Vatican City, they are held in the Audience Hall on the south side of St. Peter's Basilica or, weather permitting, in St. Peter's Square. The hall, which was opened in 1971, has a seating capacity of 6,800 and a total capacity of 12,000.

Audiences are also held during the summer at Castel Gandolfo when the pope is there on a working vacation.

General audiences last from about 60 to 90 minutes, during which the pope gives a talk and his blessing. A résumé of the talk, which is usually in Italian, is given in several languages.

Arrangements for papal audiences are handled by an office of the Prefecture of the Apostolic Household.

American visitors can obtain passes for general audiences by applying to the Bishops' Office for United States Visitors to the Vatican, Casa Santa Maria, Via dell'Umilita, 30, 00187 Rome.

Private and group audiences are reserved for dignitaries of various categories and for special occasions.

## Publications

**Acta Apostolicae Sedis:** The only "official commentary" of the Holy See, was established in 1908 for the publication of activities of the Holy See, laws, decrees and acts of congregations and tribunals of the Roman Curia. The first edition was published in January, 1909.

St. Pius X made *AAS* an official organ in 1908. Laws promulgated for the Church ordinarily take effect three months after the date of their publication in this commentary.

The publication, mostly in Latin, is printed by the Vatican Polyglot Press.

The immediate predecessor of this organ was *Acta Sanctae Sedis,* founded in 1865 and given official status by the Congregation for the Propagation of the Faith in 1904.

**Annuario Pontificio:** The yearbook of the Holy See. It is edited by the Central Statistics Office of the Church and is printed in Italian, with some portions in other languages, by the Vatican Polyglot Press. It covers the worldwide organization of the Church, lists members of the hierarchy, and includes a wide range of statistical information.

The publication of a statistical yearbook of the Holy See dates back to 1716, when a volume called *Notizie* appeared. Publication under the present title began in 1860, was suspended in 1870, and resumed again in 1872 under the title *Catholic Hierarchy.* This volume was printed privately at first, but has been issued by the Vatican Press since 1885. The title *Annuario Pontificio* was restored in 1912, and the yearbook was called an "official publication" until 1924.

**L'Osservatore Romano:** The daily newspaper of the Holy See. It began publication July 1, 1861, as an independent enterprise under the ownership and direction of four Catholic laymen headed by Marcantonio Pacelli, vice minister of the interior under Pope Pius IX and a grandfather of the late Pius XII. Leo XIII bought the publication in 1890, making it the "pope's" own newspaper.

The only official material in *L'Osservatore Romano* is that which appears under the heading, "Nostre Informazioni." This includes notices of appointments made by the Holy See, the texts of papal encyclicals and addresses by the Holy Father and others, various types of documents, accounts of decisions and rulings of administrative bodies, and similar items. Additional material includes news and comment on developments in the Church and the world. Italian is the language most used.

The editorial board is directed by Valerio Volpini. A staff of about 15 reporters covers Rome news sources. A corps of correspondents provides foreign coverage.

A weekly roundup edition in English was inaugurated in 1968. Other weekly editions are printed in French, Spanish, Portuguese and German. Publication of a Polish edition was begun in February, 1980.

**Vatican Press Office:** The establishment of a single Vatican Press Office was announced Feb. 29, 1968, to replace service agencies formerly operated by *L'Osservatore Romano* and an office created for press coverage of the Second Vatican Council. Rev. Romeo Panciroli is the director.

**Vatican Polyglot Press:** The official printing plant of the Vatican.

The Vatican press was conceived by Marcellus II and Pius IV but was actually founded by Sixtus V on Apr. 27, 1587, to print the Vulgate and the writings of the Fathers of the Church and other authors. A Polyglot Press was established in 1626 by the Congregation for the Propagation of the Faith to serve the needs of the Oriental Church. St. Pius X merged both presses under this title.

The plant has facilities for the printing of a wide variety of material in about 30 languages.

**Activities of the Holy See:** An annual documentary volume covering the activities of the pope — his daily work, general and special audiences, discourses and messages on special occasions, visits outside the Vatican, missionary and charitable endeavors, meetings with diplomats, heads of state and others — and activities of the congregations, commissions, tribunals and offices of the Roman Curia.

**Statistical Yearbook of the Church:** Issued by the Central Statistics Office of the Church, it contains principal data concerning the presence and work of the Church in the world. The first issue was published in 1972 under the title *Collection of Statistical Tables, 1969*. It is printed in corresponding columns of Italian and Latin. Some of the introductory material is printed in other languages.

## VATICAN REPRESENTATIVES

(Sources: *Annuario Pontificio;* NC News Service.)

The Vatican has representatives to a number of quasi-governmental and international organizations.

**Governmental Organizations:** United Nations (Abp. Giovanni Cheli, permanent observer); UN Office in Geneva and Specialized Institutes (Abp. Edoardo Rovida, permanent observer); International Atomic Energy Agency (Msgr. Giovanni Ceirano, permanent representative); UN Organization for Industrial Development (Msgr. Giovanni Ceirano, permanent observer); UN Food and Agriculture Organization (Bp. Agostino Ferrari-Toniolo, permanent observer); UN Educational, Scientific and Cultural Organization (Msgr. Renzo Frana, permanent observer);

Council of Europe (Msgr. Luigi Bressan, special envoy with function of permanent observer); Council for Cultural Cooperation of the Council of Europe (Msgr. Luigi Bressan, delegate); Organization of American States (Abp. Pio Laghi, permanent observer); International Institute for the Unification of Private Law (Prof. Pio Ciprotti, delegate); International Committee of Military Medicine and Pharmacy (Adolphe Vander Perre, delegate), World Organization of Tourism (Rev. Giovanni Arrighi, O.P., permanent observer).

Universal Postal Union; International Telecommunications Union; International Council on Grain; World Organization of Intellectual Property; International Union for the Protection of Literary and Artistic Works; International Union for the Protection of Industrial Property; International Organization of Telecommunication via Satellite (Intelsat); European Conference of Postal and Telecommunication Administration (CEPT).

**Non-Governmental Organizations:** International Committee of Historical Sciences (Msgr. Michele Maccarrone); International Committee of Paleography (Msgr. Jose Ruysschaert, delegate); International Committee of the History of Art (Prof. Carlo Pietrangeli, delegate); International Committee of Anthropological and Ethnological Sciences;

International Committee for the Neutrality of Medicine (Rev. Michel Riquet, S.J., permanent observer); International Center of Study for the Preservation and Restoration of Cultural Goods (Prof. Carlo Pietrangeli, permanent observer); International Council of Monuments and Sites (Prof. Carlo Pietrangeli, delegate); International Alliance on Tourism; International Astronomical Union; International Institute of Administrative Sciences; International Technical Committee for Prevention and Extinction of Fires; World Medical Association.

## NATIONAL SHRINE

The National Shrine of the Immaculate Conception is dedicated to the honor of the Blessed Virgin Mary, who was declared patroness of the United States in 1846.

The shrine is the seventh largest religious building in the world and the largest Catholic church in the Western Hemisphere, with normal seating and standing accommodations for 6,000 persons. The shrine contains some of the largest mosaics in the world.

Approximately one million persons visit the shrine each year. Open daily, it is located adjacent to the Catholic University of America, Michigan Ave. and Fourth St. N.E., Washington, D.C., 20017.

The shrine director is Rev. Msgr. Harold Murray.

# DOCTRINE OF THE CATHOLIC CHURCH

*Following are excerpts from the first two chapters of the "Dogmatic Constitution on the Church" promulgated by the Second Vatican Council. They describe the relation of the Catholic Church to the Kingdom of God, the nature and foundation of the Church, the People of God, the necessity of membership and participation in the Church for salvation. Additional subjects in the constitution are treated in other Almanac entries.*

## I. MYSTERY OF THE CHURCH

By her relationship with Christ, the Church is a kind of sacrament or sign of intimate union with God, and of the unity of all mankind (No. 1).

He (the eternal Father) planned to assemble in the holy Church all those who would believe in Christ. Already from the beginning of the world the foreshadowing of the Church took place. She was prepared for in a remarkable way throughout the history of the people of Israel and by means of the Old Covenant. Established in the present era of time, the Church was made manifest by the outpouring of the Spirit. At the end of time she will achieve her glorious fulfillment. Then . . . all just men from the time of Adam, "from Abel, the just one, to the last of the elect," will be gathered together with the Father in the universal Church (No. 2).

When the work which the Father had given the Son to do on earth (cf. Jn. 17:4) was accomplished, the Holy Spirit was sent on the day of Pentecost in order that he might forever sanctify the Church, and thus all believers would have access to the Father through Christ in the one Spirit (cf. Eph. 2:18).

The Spirit dwells in the Church and in the hearts of the faithful as in a temple (cf. 1 Cor. 3:16; 6:19). . . . The Spirit guides the Church into the fullness of truth (cf. Jn. 16:13) and gives her a unity of fellowship and service. He furnishes and directs her with various gifts, both hierarchical and charismatic, and adorns her with the fruits of His grace (cf. Eph. 4:11-12; 1 Cor. 12:4; Gal. 5:22). By the power of the Gospel he makes the Church grow, perpetually renews her, and leads her to perfect union with her Spouse (No. 4).

## Foundation of the Church

The mystery of the holy Church is manifest in her very foundation, for the Lord Jesus inaugurated her by preaching the Good News, that is, the coming of God's Kingdom, which, for centuries, had been promised in the Scriptures. . . . In Christ's word, in his works, and in his presence this Kingdom reveals itself to men.

The miracles of Jesus also confirm that the Kingdom has already arrived on earth.

Before all things, however, the Kingdom is clearly visible in the very Person of Christ, Son of God and Son of Man.

When Jesus rose up again after suffering death on the cross for mankind, he manifested that he had been appointed Lord, Messiah, and Priest forever (cf. Acts 2:36; Heb. 5:6; 7:17-21), and he poured out on his disciples the Spirit promised by the Father (cf. Acts 2:33). The Church, consequently, equipped with the gifts of her Founder and faithfully guarding his precepts . . . receives the mission to proclaim and to establish among all peoples the Kingdom of Christ and of God. She becomes on earth the initial budding forth of that Kingdom. While she slowly grows, the Church strains toward the consummation of the Kingdom and, with all her strength, hopes and desires to be united in glory with her King (No. 5).

## Figures of the Church

In the Old Testament the revelation of the Kingdom had often been conveyed by figures of speech. In the same way the inner nature of the Church was now to be made known to us through various images.

The Church is a sheepfold . . . a flock . . . a tract of land to be cultivated, the field of God . . . his choice vineyard . . . the true vine is Christ . . . the edifice of God . . . the house of God . . . the holy temple (whose members are) . . . living stones . . . this holy city . . . a bride . . . our Mother . . . the spotless spouse of the spotless Lamb . . . an exile (No. 6).

In the human nature which he united to himself, the Son of God redeemed man and transformed him into a new creation (cf. Gal. 6:15; 2 Cor. 5:17) by overcoming death through his own death and resurrection. By communicating his Spirit to his brothers, called together from all peoples, Christ made them mystically into his own body.

In that body, the life of Christ is poured into the believers, who, through the sacraments, are united in a hidden and real way to Christ who suffered and was glorified. Through baptism we are formed in the likeness of Christ.

Truly partaking of the body of the Lord in the breaking of the eucharistic bread, we are taken up into communion with him and with one another (No. 7).

## One Body in Christ

As all the members of the human body, though they are many, form one body, so also are the faithful in Christ (cf. 1 Cor. 12:12). Also, in the building up of Christ's body there is a flourishing variety of members and functions. There is only one Spirit who . . . distributes his different gifts for the welfare of the Church (cf. 1 Cor. 12:1-11). Among these gifts stands out the grace given to the apostles. To their authority, the Spirit himself subjected even those who were endowed with charisms (cf. 1 Cor. 14).

The head of this body is Christ (No. 7).

## Mystical Body of Christ

Christ, the one Mediator, established and ceaselessly sustains here on earth his holy Church, the community of faith, hope, and charity, as a visible structure. Through her he communicates truth and grace to all. But the society furnished with hierarchical agencies and the Mystical Body of Christ are not to be considered as two realities, nor are the visible assembly and the spiritual community, nor the earthly Church and the Church enriched with heavenly things. Rather they form one interlocked reality which is comprised of a divine and a human element. For this reason . . . this reality is compared to the mystery of the incarnate Word. Just as the assumed nature inseparably united to the divine Word serves him as a living instrument of salvation, so, in a similar way, does the communal structure of the Church serve Christ's Spirit, who vivifies it by way of building up the body (cf. Eph. 4:16).

This is the unique Church of Christ which in the Creed we avow as one, holy, catholic, and apostolic. After his Resurrection our Savior handed her over to Peter to be shepherded (Jn. 21:17), commissioning him and the other apostles to propagate and govern her (cf. Mt. 28:18, ff.). Her he erected for all ages as "the pillar and mainstay of the truth" (1 Tm. 3:15). This Church, constituted and organized in the world as a society, subsists in the Catholic Church, which is governed by the successor of Peter and by the bishops in union with that successor, although many elements of sanctification and of truth can be found outside of her visible structure. These elements, however, as gifts properly belonging to the Church of Christ, possess an inner dynamism toward Catholic unity.

The Church, embracing sinners in her bosom, is at the same time holy and always in need of being purified, and incessantly pursues the path of penance and renewal.

The Church, "like a pilgrim in a foreign land, presses forward . . ." announcing the cross and death of the Lord until he comes (cf. 1 Cor. 11:26) (No. 8).

## II. THE PEOPLE OF GOD

At all times and among every people, God has given welcome to whosoever fears him and does what is right (cf. Acts 10:35). It has pleased God, however, to make men holy and save them not merely as individuals without any mutual bonds, but by making them into a single people, a people which acknowledges him in truth and serves him in holiness. He therefore chose the race of Israel as a people unto himself. With it he set up a covenant. Step by step he taught this people by manifesting in its history both himself and the decree of his will, and by making it holy unto himself. All these things, however, were done by way of preparation and as a figure of that new and perfect covenant which was to be ratified in Christ.

Christ instituted this New Covenant, that is to say, the New Testament, in his blood (cf. 1 Cor. 11:25), by calling together a people made up of Jew and Gentile, making them one, not according to the flesh but in the Spirit.

This was to be the new People of God . . . reborn . . . through the Word of the living God (cf. 1 Pt. 1:23) . . . from water and the Holy Spirit (cf. Jn. 3:5-6) . . . "a chosen race, a royal priesthood, a holy nation, a purchased people. . . . You who in

times past were not a people, but are now the People of God" (1 Pt. 2:9-10).

That messianic people has for its head Christ. . . . Its law is the new commandment to love as Christ loved us (cf. Jn. 13:34). Its goal is the Kingdom of God, which has been begun by God himself on earth, and which is to be further extended until it is brought to perfection by him at the end of time.

This messianic people, although it does not actually include all men, and may more than once look like a small flock, is nonetheless a lasting and sure seed of unity, hope, and salvation for the whole human race. Established by Christ as a fellowship of life, charity, and truth, it is also used by him as an instrument for the redemption of all, and is sent forth into the whole world as the light of the world and the salt of the earth (cf. Mt. 5:13-16).

Israel according to the flesh . . . was already called the Church of God (Neh. 13:1; cf. Nm. 20:4; Dt. 23:1, ff.). Likewise the new Israel . . . is also called the Church of Christ (cf. Mt. 16:18). For he has bought it for himself with his blood (cf. Acts 20:28), has filled it with his Spirit, and provided it with those means which befit it as a visible and social unity. God has gathered together as one all those who in faith look upon Jesus as the author of salvation and the source of unity and peace, and has established them as the Church, that for each and all she may be the visible sacrament of this saving unity (No. 9).

## Priesthood

The baptized, by regeneration and the anointing of the Holy Spirit, are consecrated into . . . a holy priesthood.

[All members of the Church participate in the priesthood of Christ, through the common priesthood of the faithful. See Priesthood of the Laity.]

Though they differ from one another in essence and not only in degree, the common priesthood of the faithful and the ministerial or hierarchical priesthood are nonetheless interrelated. Each of them in its own special way is a participation in the one priesthood of Christ (No. 10).

It is through the sacraments and the exercise of the virtues that the sacred nature and organic structure of the priestly community is brought into operation (No. 11). (See Role of the Sacraments.)

## Prophetic Office

The holy People of God shares also in Christ's prophetic office. It spreads abroad a living witness to him, especially by means of a life of faith and charity and by offering to God a sacrifice of praise. . . . The body of the faithful as a whole, anointed as they are by the Holy One (cf. Jn. 2:20, 27), cannot err in matters of belief. Thanks to a supernatural sense of faith which characterizes the People as a whole, it manifests this unerring quality when, "from the bishops down to the last member of the laity," it shows universal agreement in matters of faith and morals.

God's People accepts not the word of men but the very Word of God (cf. 1 Thes. 2:13). It clings

without fail to the faith once delivered to the saints
(cf. Jude 3), penetrates it more deeply by accurate
insights, and applies it more thoroughly to life. All
this it does under the lead of a sacred teaching authority to which it loyally defers.

It is not only through the sacraments and Church
ministries that the same Holy Spirit sanctifies and
leads the People of God. . . . He distributes special
graces among the faithful of every rank. By these
gifts he makes them fit and ready to undertake the
various tasks or offices advantageous for the renewal and upbuilding of the Church. . . . These
charismatic gifts . . . are to be received with
thanksgiving and consolation, for they are exceedingly suitable and useful for the needs of the
Church.

Judgment as to their genuineness and proper use
belongs to those who preside over the Church, and
to whose special competence it belongs . . . to test
all things and hold fast to that which is good (cf. 1
Thes. 5:12; 19-21) (No. 12).

## All Are Called

All men are called to belong to the new People of
God. Wherefore this People, while remaining one
and unique, is to be spread throughout the whole
world and must exist in all ages, so that the purpose of God's will may be fulfilled. In the beginning God made human nature one. After his
children were scattered, he decreed that they
should at length be united again (cf. Jn. 11:52). It
was for this reason that God sent his Son . . . that
he might be Teacher, King, and Priest of all, the
Head of the new and universal People of the sons
of God. For this God finally sent his Son's Spirit as
Lord and Lifegiver. He it is who, on behalf of the
whole Church and each and every one of those who
believe, is the principle of their coming together
and remaining together in the teaching of the
apostles and in fellowship, in the breaking of bread
and in prayers (cf. Acts 2:42) (No. 13).

## One People of God

It follows that among all the nations of earth
there is but one People of God, which takes its
citizens from every race, making them citizens of
a Kingdom which is of a heavenly and not an
earthly nature. For all the faithful scattered
throughout the world are in communion with each
other in the Holy Spirit. . . . the Church or People
of God . . . foster(s) and take(s) to herself, insofar
as they are good, the ability, resources and customs of each people. Taking them to herself, she
purifies, strengthens, and ennobles them . . . This
characteristic of universality which adorns the
People of God is a gift from the Lord himself. By
reason of it, the Catholic Church strives
energetically and constantly to bring all humanity
with all its riches back to Christ its Head in the
unity of his Spirit.

In virtue of this catholicity each individual part
of the Church contributes through its special gifts
to the good of the other parts and of the whole
Church. Thus through the common sharing of gifts
. . . the whole and each of the parts receive increase.

All men are called to be part of this catholic
unity of the People of God. . . . And there belong to
it or are related to it in various ways, the Catholic
faithful as well as all who believe in Christ, and indeed the whole of mankind. For all men are called
to salvation by the grace of God (No. 13).

## The Catholic Church

This sacred Synod turns its attention first to the
Catholic faithful. Basing itself upon sacred Scripture and tradition, it teaches that the Church . . . is
necessary for salvation. For Christ, made present
to us in his Body, which is the Church, is the one
Mediator and the unique Way of salvation. In explicit terms he himself affirmed the necessity of
faith and baptism (cf. Mk. 16:16; Jn. 3:5) and
thereby affirmed also the necessity of the Church,
for through baptism as through a door men enter
the Church. Whosoever, therefore, knowing that
the Catholic Church was made necessary by God
through Jesus Christ, would refuse to enter her or
to remain in her could not be saved.

They are fully incorporated into the society
Church who, possessing the Spirit of Christ, accept
her entire system and all the means of salvation
given to her, and through union with her visible
structure are joined to Christ, who rules her
through the Supreme Pontiff and the bishops. This
joining is effected by the bonds of professed faith,
of the sacraments, of ecclesiastical government,
and of communion. He is not saved, however, who,
though he is part of the body of the Church, does
not persevere in charity. He remains indeed in the
bosom of the Church, but . . . only in a "bodily"
manner and not "in his heart."

Catechumens who, moved by the Holy Spirit,
seek with explicit intention to be incorporated into
the Church, are by that very intention joined to
her. . . . Mother Church already embraces them as
her own (No. 14).

## Other Christians, The Unbaptized

The Church recognizes that in many ways she is
linked with those who, being baptized, are honored
with the name of Christian, though they do not profess the faith in its entirety or do not preserve
unity of communion with the successor of Peter.

We can say that in some real way they are joined
with us in the Holy Spirit, for to them also he gives
his gifts and graces, and is thereby operative
among them with his sanctifying power (No. 15).

Finally, those who have not yet received the
Gospel are related in various ways to the People of
God. In the first place there is the people to whom
the covenants and the promises were given and
from whom Christ was born according to the flesh
(cf. Rom. 9:4-5). On account of their fathers, this
people remains most dear to God, for God does not
repent of the gifts he makes nor of the calls he issues (cf. Rom. 11:28-29).

But the plan of salvation also includes those who
acknowledge the Creator. In the first place among
these are the Moslems. . . . Nor is God himself far
distant from those who in shadows and images
seek the unknown God.

Those also can attain to everlasting salvation

who through no fault of their own do not know the Gospel of Christ or his Church, yet sincerely seek God and, moved by grace, strive by their deeds to do his will as it is known to them through the dictates of conscience. Nor does divine Providence deny the help necessary for salvation to those who, without blame on their part, have not yet arrived at an explicit knowledge of God, but who strive to live a good life, thanks to his grace. Whatever goodness or truth is found among them is looked upon by the Church as a preparation for the Gospel. She regards such qualities as given by him who enlightens all men so that they may finally have life (No. 16).

## THE POPE, TEACHING AUTHORITY, COLLEGIALITY

The Roman Pontiff — the successor of St. Peter as the Vicar of Christ and head of the Church on earth — has full and supreme authority over the universal Church in matters pertaining to faith and morals (teaching authority), discipline and government (jurisdictional authority).

The primacy of the pope is real and supreme power. It is not merely a prerogative of honor — that is, of his being regarded as the first among equals. Neither does primacy imply that the pope is just the presiding officer of the collective body of bishops. The pope is the head of the Church.

Catholic belief in the primacy of the pope was stated in detail in the dogmatic constitution on the Church, *Pastor Aeternus,* approved in 1870 by the fourth session of the First Vatican Council. Some elaboration of the doctrine was made in the *Dogmatic Constitution on the Church* which was approved and promulgated by the Second Vatican Council Nov. 21, 1964. The entire body of teaching on the subject is based on Scripture and tradition and the centuries-long experience of the Church.

### Infallibility

The essential points of doctrine concerning infallibility in the Church and the infallibility of the pope were stated by the Second Vatican Council in the *Dogmatic Constitution on the Church,* as follows:

"This infallibility with which the divine Redeemer willed his Church to be endowed in defining a doctrine of faith and morals extends as far as extends the deposit of divine revelation, which must be religiously guarded and faithfully expounded. This is the infallibility which the Roman Pontiff, the head of the college of bishops, enjoys in virtue of his office, when, as the supreme shepherd and teacher of all the faithful who confirms his brethren in their faith (cf. Lk. 22:32), he proclaims by a definitive act some doctrine of faith or morals. Therefore his definitions, of themselves, and not from the consent of the Church, are justly styled irreformable, for they are pronounced with the assistance of the Holy Spirit, an assistance promised to him in blessed Peter. Therefore they need no approval of others, nor do they allow an appeal to any other judgment. For then the Roman Pontiff is not pronouncing judgment as a private person. Rather, as the supreme teacher of the universal Church, as one in whom the charism of the infallibility of the Church herself is individually present, he is expounding or defending a doctrine of Catholic faith.

"The infallibility promised to the Church resides also in the body of bishops when that body exercises supreme teaching authority with the successor of Peter. To the resultant definitions the assent of the Church can never be wanting, on account of the activity of that same Holy Spirit, whereby the whole flock of Christ is preserved and progresses in unity of faith.

"But when either the Roman Pontiff or the body of bishops together with him defines a judgment, they pronounce it in accord with revelation itself. All are obliged to maintain and be ruled by this revelation, which, as written or preserved by tradition, is transmitted in its entirety through the legitimate succession of bishops and especially through the care of the Roman Pontiff himself.

"Under the guiding light of the Spirit of truth, revelation is thus religiously preserved and faithfully expounded in the Church. The Roman Pontiff and the bishops, in view of their office and of the importance of the matter, strive painstakingly and by appropriate means to inquire properly into that revelation and to give apt expression to its contents. But they do not allow that there could be any new public revelation pertaining to the divine deposit of faith" (No. 25).

### Authentic Teaching

The pope rarely speaks *ex cathedra* — that is, "from the chair" of St. Peter, for the purpose of making an infallible pronouncement. More often and in various ways he states authentic teaching in line with Scripture, tradition, the living experience of the Church, and the whole analogy of faith. Of such teaching, the Second Vatican Council said in its *Dogmatic Constitution on the Church* (No. 25):

"Religious submission of will and of mind must be shown in a special way to the authentic teaching authority of the Roman Pontiff, even when he is not speaking *ex cathedra.* That is, it must be shown in such a way that his supreme magisterium is acknowledged with reverence, the judgments made by him are sincerely adhered to, according to his manifest mind and will. His mind and will in the matter may be known chiefly either from the character of the documents, from his frequent repetition of the same doctrine, or from his manner of speaking."

With respect to bishops, the constitution states: "They are authentic teachers, that is, teachers endowed with the authority of Christ, who preach to the people committed to them the faith they must believe and put into practice. By the light of the Holy Spirit, they make that faith clear, bringing forth from the treasury of revelation new things and old (cf. Mt. 13:52), making faith bear fruit and vigilantly warding off any errors which threaten their flock (cf. 2 Tm. 4:1-4).

"Bishops, teaching in communion with the Roman Pontiff, are to be respected by all as witnesses to divine and Catholic truth. In matters of faith and morals, the bishops speak in the name of Christ and the faithful are to accept their teaching and adhere to it with a religious assent of soul."

## Magisterium—Teaching Authority

Responsibility for teaching doctrine and judging orthodoxy belongs to the official teaching authority of the Church.

This authority is personalized in the pope, the successor of St. Peter as head of the Church, and in the bishops together and in union with the pope, as it was originally committed to Peter and to the whole college of apostles under his leadership. They are the official teachers of the Church.

Others have auxiliary relationships with the magisterium: theologians, in the study and clarification of doctrine; teachers — priests, religious, lay persons — who cooperate with the pope and bishops in spreading knowledge of religious truth; the faithful, who by their sense of faith and personal witness contribute to the development of doctrine and the establishment of its relevance to life in the Church and the world.

The magisterium, Pope Paul VI noted in an address at a general audience Jan. 11, 1967, "is a subordinate and faithful echo and secure interpreter of the divine word." It does not reveal new truths, "nor is it superior to sacred Scripture." Its competence extends to the limits of divine revelation manifested in Scripture and tradition and the living experience of the Church, with respect to matters of faith and morals and related subjects.

Official teaching in these areas is infallible when it is formally defined, for belief and acceptance by all members of the Church, by the pope, acting in the capacity of supreme shepherd of the flock of Christ; also, when doctrine is proposed and taught with moral unanimity of bishops with the pope in a solemn collegial manner, as in an ecumenical council, and/or in the ordinary course of events. Even when not infallibly defined, official teaching in the areas of faith and morals is authoritative and requires religious assent.

The teachings of the magisterium have been documented in creeds, formulas of faith, decrees and enactments of ecumenical and particular councils, various kinds of doctrinal statements, encyclical letters and other teaching instruments. They have also been incorporated into the liturgy, with the result that the law of prayer is said to be a law of belief.

## Collegiality

The bishops of the Church, in union with the pope, have supreme teaching and pastoral authority over the whole Church in addition to the authority of office they have for their own dioceses.

This collegial authority is exercised in a solemn manner in an ecumenical council and can be exercised in other ways as well, "provided that the head of the college calls them to collegiate action, or at least so approves or freely accepts the united action of the dispersed bishops that it is made a true collegiate act."

This doctrine is grounded on the fact that: "Just as, by the Lord's will, St. Peter and the other apostles constituted one apostolic college, so in a similar way the Roman Pontiff as the successor of Peter, and the bishops as the successors of the apostles are joined together."

Doctrine on collegiality was stated by the Second Vatican Council in the *Dogmatic Constitution on the Church* (Nos. 22 and 23).

# REVELATION

*Following are excerpts from the "Constitution on Revelation" promulgated by the Second Vatican Council. They describe the nature and process of divine revelation, inspiration and interpretation of Scripture, the Old and New Testaments, and the role of Scripture in the life of the Church.*

## I. REVELATION ITSELF

God chose to reveal himself and to make known to us the hidden purpose of his will (cf. Eph. 1:9) by which through Christ, the Word made flesh, man has access to the Father in the Holy Spirit and comes to share in the divine nature (cf. Eph. 2:18; 2 Pt. 1:4). Through this revelation, therefore, the invisible God (cf. Col. 1:15; 1 Tm. 1:17) . . . speaks to men as friends (cf. Ex. 33:11; Jn. 15:14-15) and lives among them (cf. Bar. 3:38) so that he may invite and take them into fellowship with himself. This plan of revelation is realized by deeds and words having an inner unity: the deeds wrought by God in the history of salvation manifest and confirm the teaching and realities signified by the words, while the words proclaim the deeds and clarify the mystery contained in them. By this revelation then, the deepest truth about God and the salvation of man is made clear to us in Christ, who is the Mediator and at the same time the fullness of all revelation (No. 2).

God . . . from the start manifested himself to our first parents. Then after their fall his promise of redemption aroused in them the hope of being saved (cf. Gn. 3:15), and from that time on he ceaselessly kept the human race in his care, in order to give eternal life to those who perseveringly do good in search of salvation (cf. Rom. 2:6-7). . . . He called Abraham in order to make of him a great nation (cf. Gn. 12:2). Through the patriarchs, and after them through Moses and the prophets, he taught this nation to acknowledge himself as the one living and true God . . . and to wait for the Savior promised by him. In this manner he prepared the way for the Gospel down through the centuries (No. 3).

## Revelation in Christ

Then, after speaking in many places and varied ways through the prophets, God "last of all in these days has spoken to us by his Son" (Heb. 1:1-2). . . . Jesus perfected revelation by fulfilling it through his whole work of making himself present and manifesting himself: through his words and deeds, his signs and wonders, but especially through his death and glorious resurrection from the dead and final sending of the Spirit of truth. Moreover, he confirmed with divine testimony what revelation proclaimed: that God is with us to free us from the darkness of sin and death, and to raise us up to life eternal.

The Christian dispensation, therefore, as the new and definitive covenant, will never pass away, and we now await no further new public revelation before the glorious manifestation of our Lord Jesus Christ (cf. 1 Tm. 6:14; Ti. 2:13) (No. 4).

## II. TRANSMISSION OF REVELATION

God has seen to it that what he had revealed for the salvation of all nations would abide perpetually in its full integrity and be handed on to all generations. Therefore Christ the Lord, in whom the full revelation of the supreme God is brought to completion (cf. 2 Cor. 1:20; 3:16; 4:6), commissioned the apostles to preach to all men that Gospel which is the source of all saving truth and moral teaching, and thus to impart to them divine gifts. This Gospel had been promised in former times through the prophets, and Christ himself fulfilled it and promulgated it with his own lips. This commission was faithfully fulfilled by the apostles who, by their oral preaching, by example, and by ordinances, handed on what they had received from ... Christ ... or what they had learned through the prompting of the Holy Spirit. The commission was fulfilled, too, by those apostles and apostolic men who under the inspiration of the same Holy Spirit committed the message of salvation to writing (No. 7).

### Tradition

But in order to keep the Gospel forever whole and alive within the Church, the apostles left bishops as their successors, "handing over their own teaching role" to them. This sacred tradition, therefore, and sacred Scripture of both the Old and the New Testament are like a mirror in which the pilgrim Church on earth looks at God (No. 7).

The apostolic preaching, which is expressed in a special way in the inspired books, was to be preserved by a continuous succession of preachers until the end of time. Therefore the apostles, handing on what they themselves had received, warn the faithful to hold fast to the traditions which they have learned. ... Now what was handed on by the apostles includes everything which contributes to the holiness of life, and the increase in faith of the People of God; and so the Church, in her teaching, life, and worship, perpetuates and hands on to all generations all that she herself is, all that she believes (No. 8).

### Development of Doctrine

This tradition which comes from the apostles develops in the Church with the help of the Holy Spirit. For there is a growth in the understanding of the realities and the words which have been handed down. This happens through the contemplation and study made by believers ... through the intimate understanding of spiritual things they expe-

rience, and through the preaching of those who have received through episcopal succession the sure gift of truth. For, as the centuries succeed one another, the Church constantly moves forward toward the fullness of divine truth until the words of God reach their complete fulfillment in her.

The words of the holy Fathers witness to the living presence of this tradition, whose wealth is poured into the practice and life of the believing and praying Church. Through the same tradition the Church's full canon of the sacred books is known, and the sacred writings themselves are more profoundly understood and unceasingly made active in her; ... and the Holy Spirit, through whom the living voice of the Gospel resounds in the Church, and through her, in the world, leads unto all truth those who believe and makes the word of Christ dwell abundantly in them (cf. Col. 3:16) (No. 8).

### Tradition and Scripture

Hence there exist a close connection and communication between sacred tradition and sacred Scripture. For both of them, flowing from the same divine wellspring, in a certain way merge into a unity and tend toward the same end. For sacred Scripture is the word of God inasmuch as it is consigned to writing under the inspiration of the divine Spirit. To the successors of the apostles, sacred tradition hands on in its full purity God's word, which was entrusted to the apostles by Christ the Lord and the Holy Spirit. Thus, led by the light of the Spirit of truth, these successors can in their preaching preserve this word of God faithfully, explain it, and make it more widely known. Consequently, it is not from sacred Scripture alone that the Church draws her certainty about everything which has been revealed. Therefore both sacred tradition and sacred Scripture are to be accepted and venerated with the same sense of devotion and reverence (No. 9).

Sacred tradition and sacred Scripture form one sacred deposit of the word of God, which is committed to the Church (No. 10).

### Teaching Authority of Church

The task of authentically interpreting the word of God, whether written or handed on, has been entrusted exclusively to the living teaching office of the Church, whose authority is exercised in the name of Jesus Christ. This teaching office is not above the word of God, but serves it, teaching only what has been handed on ... it draws from this one deposit of faith everything which it presents for belief as divinely revealed.

It is clear, therefore, that sacred tradition, sacred Scripture, and the teaching authority of the Church ... are so linked and joined together that one cannot stand without the others, and that all together and each in its own way under the action of the one Holy Spirit contribute effectively to the salvation of souls (No. 10).

### III. INSPIRATION, INTERPRETATION

Those ... revealed realities ... contained and presented in sacred Scripture have been committed to writing under the inspiration of the Holy

Spirit. Holy Mother Church, relying on the belief of the apostles, holds that the books of both the Old and New Testament in their entirety, with all their parts, are sacred and canonical because, having been written under the inspiration of the Holy Spirit (cf. Jn. 20:31; 2 Tm. 3:16; 2 Pt. 1:19-21; 3:15-16) they have God as their author and have been handed on as such to the Church herself. In composing the sacred books, God chose men and, while employed by him, they made use of their powers and abilities, so that, with him acting in them and through them, they, as true authors, consigned to writing everything and only those things which he wanted (No. 11).

## Inerrancy

Therefore, since everything asserted by the inspired authors or sacred writers must be held to be asserted by the Holy Spirit, it follows that the books of Scripture must be acknowledged as teaching firmly, faithfully, and without error that truth which God wanted put into the sacred writings for the sake of our salvation. Therefore "all Scripture is inspired by God and useful for teaching, for reproving, for correcting, for instruction in justice; that the man of God may be perfect, equipped for every good work" (2 Tm. 3:16-17) (No. 11).

## Literary Forms

However, since God speaks in sacred Scripture through men in human fashion, the interpreter of sacred Scripture, in order to see clearly what God wanted to communicate to us, should carefully investigate what meaning the sacred writers really intended, and what God wanted to manifest by means of their words.

The interpreter must investigate what meaning the sacred writer intended to express and actually expressed in particular circumstances as he used contemporary literary forms in accordance with the situation of his own time and culture. For the correct understanding of what the sacred author wanted to assert, due attention must be paid to the customary and characteristic styles of perceiving, speaking, and narrating which prevailed at the time of the sacred writer, and to the customs men normally followed at that period in their everyday dealings with one another (No. 12).

## Analogy of Faith

No less serious attention must be given to the content and unity of the whole of Scripture, if the meaning of the sacred texts is to be correctly brought to light. The living tradition of the whole Church must be taken into account along with the harmony which exists between elements of the faith. . . . All of what has been said about the way of interpreting Scripture is subject finally to the judgment of the Church, which carries out the divine commission and ministry of guarding and interpreting the word of God (No. 12).

## IV. THE OLD TESTAMENT

In carefully planning and preparing the salvation of the whole human race, the God of supreme love,

by a special dispensation, chose for himself a people to whom he might entrust his promises. First he entered into a covenant with Abraham (cf. Gn. 15:18) and, through Moses, with the people of Israel (cf. Ex. 24:8). To this people which he had acquired for himself, he so manifested himself through words and deeds as the one true and living God that Israel came to know by experience the ways of God with men. . . . The plan of salvation, foretold by the sacred authors, recounted and explained by them, is found as the true word of God in the books of the Old Testament: these books, therefore, written under divine inspiration, remain permanently valuable (No. 14).

## Principal Purpose

The principal purpose to which the plan of the Old Covenant was directed was to prepare for the coming both of Christ, the universal Redeemer, and of the messianic Kingdom. . . . Now the books of the Old Testament, in accordance with the state of mankind before the time of salvation established by Christ, reveal to all men the knowledge of God and of man and the ways in which God . . . deals with men. These books . . . show us true divine pedagogy (No. 15).

The books of the Old Testament with all their parts, caught up into the proclamation of the Gospel, acquire and show forth their full meaning in the New Testament (cf. Mt. 5:17; Lk. 24:27; Rom. 16:25-26; 2 Cor. 3:14-16) and in turn shed light on it and explain it (No. 16).

## V. THE NEW TESTAMENT

The word of God . . . is set forth and shows its power in a most excellent way in the writings of the New Testament. For when the fullness of time arrived (cf. Gal. 4:4), the Word was made flesh and dwelt among us in the fullness of grace and truth (cf. Jn. 1:14). Christ established the Kingdom of God on earth, manifested his Father and himself by deeds and words, and completed his work by his death, resurrection, and glorious ascension and by the sending of the Holy Spirit. Having been lifted up from the earth, he draws all men to himself (cf. Jn. 12:32). . . . This mystery had not been manifested to other generations as it was now revealed to his holy apostles and prophets in the Holy Spirit (cf. Eph. 3:4-6), so that they might preach the Gospel, stir up faith in Jesus, Christ and Lord, and gather the Church together. To these realities, the writings of the New Testament stand as a perpetual and divine witness (No. 17).

## The Gospels and Other Writings

The Gospels have a special preeminence . . . for they are the principal witness of the life and teaching of the incarnate Word, our Savior.

The Church has always and everywhere held and continues to hold that the four Gospels are of apostolic origin. For what the apostles preached . . . afterwards they themselves and apostolic men, under the inspiration of the divine Spirit, handed on to us in writing: the foundation of faith, namely, the fourfold Gospel, according to Matthew, Mark, Luke, and John (No. 18).

The four Gospels, . . . whose historical character the Church unhesitatingly asserts, faithfully hand on what Jesus Christ, while living among men, really did and taught for their eternal salvation until the day he was taken up into heaven (see Acts 1:1-2). Indeed, after the ascension of the Lord the apostles handed on to their hearers what he had said and done. . . . The sacred authors wrote the four Gospels, selecting some things from the many which had been handed on by word of mouth or in writing, reducing some of them to a synthesis, explicating some things in view of the situation of their churches, and preserving the form of proclamation but always in such fashion that they told us the honest truth about Jesus. For their intention in writing was that . . . we might know "the truth" concerning those matters about which we have been instructed (cf. Lk. 1:2-4) (No. 19).

Besides the four Gospels, the canon of the New Testament also contains the Epistles of St. Paul and other apostolic writings, composed under the inspiration of the Holy Spirit. In these writings . . . those matters which concern Christ the Lord are confirmed, his true teaching is more and more fully stated, the saving power of the divine work of Christ is preached, the story is told of the beginnings of the Church and her marvelous growth, and her glorious fulfillment is foretold (No. 20).

## VI. SCRIPTURE IN CHURCH LIFE

The Church has always venerated the divine Scriptures just as she venerates the body of the Lord. . . . She has always regarded the Scriptures together with sacred tradition as the supreme rule of faith, and will ever do so. For, inspired by God and committed once and for all to writing, they impart the word of God himself without change, and make the voice of the Holy Spirit resound in the words of the prophets and apostles. Therefore, like the Christian religion itself, all the preaching of the Church must be nourished and ruled by sacred Scripture (No. 21).

Easy access to sacred Scripture should be provided for all the Christian faithful. That is why the Church from the very beginning accepted as her own that very ancient Greek translation of the Old Testament which is named after seventy men (the Septuagint); and she has always given a place of honor to other translations, Eastern and Latin, especially the one known as the Vulgate. But since the word of God should be available at all times, the Church with maternal concern sees to it that suitable and correct translations are made into different languages, especially from the original texts of the sacred books. And if, given the opportunity and the approval of Church authority, these translations are produced in cooperation with the separated brethren as well, all Christians will be able to use them (No. 22).

### Biblical Studies, Theology

The constitution encouraged the development and progress of biblical studies "under the watchful care of the sacred teaching office of the Church."

It noted also: "Sacred theology rests on the written word of God, together with sacred tradition, as its primary and perpetual foundation," and that "the study of the sacred page is, as it were, the soul of sacred theology" (Nos. 23, 24).

## THE BIBLE

The Canon of the Bible is the Church's official list of sacred writings. These works, written by men under the inspiration of the Holy Spirit, contain divine revelation and, in conjunction with the tradition and teaching authority of the Church, constitute the rule of Catholic faith. The Canon was fixed and determined by the tradition and teaching authority of the Church.

### The Catholic Canon

The Old Testament Canon of 45 books is as follows.
• **The Pentateuch,** the first five books: Genesis (Gn.), Exodus (Ex.), Leviticus (Lv.), Numbers (Nm.), Deuteronomy (Dt.).
• **Historical Books:** Joshua (Jos.), Judges (Jgs.), Ruth (Ru.) 1 and 2 Samuel (Sm.), 1 and 2 Kings (Kgs.), 1 and 2 Chronicles (Chr.), Ezra (Ezr.), Nehemiah (Neh.), Tobit (Tb.), Judith (Jdt.), Esther (Est.), 1 and 2 Maccabees (Mc.).
• **Wisdom Books:** Job (Jb.), Psalms (Ps.), Proverbs (Prv.), Ecclesiastes (Eccl.), Song of Songs (Song), Wisdom (Wis.), Sirach (Sir.).
• **The Prophets:** Isaiah (Is.), Jeremiah (Jer.), Lamentations (Lam.), Baruch (Bar.), Ezechiel (Ez.), Daniel (Dn.), Hosea (Hos.), Joel (Jl.), Amos (Am.), Obadiah (Ob.), Jonah (Jon.), Micah (Mi.), Nahum (Na.), Habakkuk (Hb.), Zephaniah

(Zep.), Haggai (Hg.), Zechariah (Zec.) Malachi (Mal.).

The New Testament Canon of 27 books is as follows.
• **The Gospels** of Matthew (Mt.), Mark (Mk.), Luke (Lk.), John (Jn.)
• **The Acts of the Apostles** (Acts).
• **The Pauline Letters** — Romans (Rom.), 1 and 2 Corinthians (Cor.), Galatians (Gal.), Ephesians (Eph.), Philippians (Phil.), Colossians (Col.), 1 and 2 Thessalonians (Thes.) 1 and 2 Timothy (Tm.), Titus (Ti.), Philemon (Phlm.), Hebrews (Heb.).
• **The Catholic Letters** — James (Jas.), 1 and 2 Peter (Pt.), 1, 2 and 3 John (Jn.), Jude (Jude).
• **Revelation** (Rv.).

### Developments

The Canon of the Old Testament was firm by the fifth century despite some questioning by scholars. It was stated by a council held at Rome in 382, by African councils held in Hippo in 393 and in Carthage in 397 and 419, and by Innocent I in 405.

All of the New Testament books were generally known and most of them were acknowledged as inspired by the end of the second century. The Muratorian Fragment, dating from about 200, listed most of the books recognized as canonical in later decrees. Prior to the end of the fourth century, however, there was controversy over the inspired character of several works — the Letter to the Hebrews, James, Jude, 2 Peter, 2 and 3 John and Revelation. Controversy ended in the fourth century and these books, along with those about which there was no dispute, were enumerated in the canon stated by the councils of Hippo and Carthage and affirmed by Innocent I in 405.

The Canon of the Bible was solemnly defined by the Council of Trent in the dogmatic decree *De Canonicis Scripturis,* Apr. 8, 1546.

## Hebrew and Other Canons

The Hebrew Canon of sacred writings was fixed by tradition and the consensus of rabbis, probably by about 100 A.D. by the Synod or Council of Jamnia and certainly by the end of the second or early in the third century. It consists of the following works in three categories.

• **The Law (Torah),** the five books of Moses: Genesis, Exodus, Leviticus, Numbers, Deuteronomy.

• **The Prophets:** former prophets — Joshua, Judges, 1 and 2 Samuel, 1 and 2 Kings; latter prophets — Isaiah, Jeremiah, Ezekiel, and 12 minor prophets (Hosea, Joel, Amos, Obadiah, Jonah, Micah, Nahum, Habakkuk, Zephaniah, Haggai, Zechariah, Malachi).

• **The Writings:** 1 and 2 Chronicles, Ezra, Nehemiah, Job, Psalms, Proverbs, Ecclesiastes, Song of Songs, Ruth, Esther, Daniel.

This Canon, embodying the tradition and practice of the Palestine community, did not include a number of works contained in the Alexandrian version of sacred writings translated into Greek between 250 and 100 B.C. and in use by Greek-speaking Jews of the Dispersion (outside Palestine). The rejected works, called apocrypha and not regarded as sacred, are: Tobit, Judith, Wisdom, Sirach, Baruch, 1 and 2 Maccabees, the last six chapters of Esther and three passages of Daniel (3:24-90; 13; 14). These books have also been rejected from the Protestant Canon, although they are included in bibles under the heading, Apocrypha.

The aforementioned books are held to be inspired and sacred by the Catholic Church. In Catholic usage, they are called deuterocanonical because they were under discussion for some time before questions about their canonicity were settled. Books regarded as canonical with little or no debate were called protocanonical. The status of both categories of books is the same in the Catholic Bible.

The Protestant Canon of the Old Testament is the same as the Hebrew.

The Old Testament Canon of some separated Eastern churches differs from the Catholic Canon.

Christians are in agreement on the Canon of the New Testament.

## Languages

Hebrew, Aramaic and Greek were the original languages of the Bible. Most of the Old Testament books were written in Hebrew. Portions of Daniel, Ezra, Jeremiah, Esther, and probably the books of Tobit and Judith were written in Aramaic. The Book of Wisdom, 2 Maccabees and all the books of the New Testament were written in Greek.

## Manuscripts and Versions

The original writings of the inspired authors have been lost. The Bible has been transmitted through ancient copies called manuscripts and through translations or versions.

Authoritative Greek manuscripts include the Sinaitic and Vatican manuscripts of the fourth century and the Alexandrine of the fifth century A.D.

The Septuagint and Vulgate translations are in a class by themselves.

The Septuagint version, a Greek translation of the Old Testament for Greek-speaking Jews, was begun about 250 and completed about 100 B.C. The work of several Jewish translators at Alexandria, it differed from the Hebrew Bible in the arrangement of books and included several, later called deuterocanonical, which were not acknowledged as sacred by the community in Palestine.

The Vulgate was a Latin version of the Old and New Testaments produced from the original languages by St. Jerome from about 383 to 404. It became the most widely used Latin text for centuries and was regarded as basic long before the Council of Trent designated it as authentic and suitable for use in public reading, controversy, preaching and teaching. Because of its authoritative character, it became the basis for many translations into other languages. A critical revision was completed by a pontifical commission in 1977.

Hebrew and Aramaic manuscripts of great antiquity and value have figured more significantly than before in recent scriptural work by Catholic scholars, especially since their use was strongly encouraged, if not mandated, in 1943 by Pius XII in the encyclical *Divino Afflante Spiritu.*

The English translation of the Bible in general use among Catholics until well into the 20th century was the *Douay-Rheims,* so called because of the places where it was prepared and published, the New Testament at Rheims in 1582 and the Old Testament at Douay in 1609. The translation was made from the Vulgate text. As revised and issued by Bishop Richard Challoner in 1749 and 1750, it became the standard Catholic English version for about 200 years.

A revision of the Challoner New Testament, made on the basis of the Vulgate text by scholars of the Catholic Biblical Association of America, was published in 1941 in the United States under the sponsorship of the Episcopal Committee of the Confraternity of Christian Doctrine.

## New American Bible

A new translation of the entire Bible. the first ever made directly into English from the original languages under Catholic auspices, was projected in 1944 and completed in the fall of 1970 with publication of the *New American Bible.* The Episcopal Committee of the Confraternity of Christian Doctrine sponsored the NAB. The translators were members of the Catholic Biblical Association of America and several fellow scholars of other faiths. The typical edition was produced by St. Anthony Guild Press, Paterson, N.J.

Old Testament portions of the NAB were published in separate volumes before undergoing final revision and being bound in one cover. Genesis and Psalms were issued in 1948 and 1950; Genesis to Ruth, in 1952; Job to Sirach, in 1955; the Prophets, in 1961; Samuel to the Maccabees, in 1969. The new translation of the New Testament was issued for the first time in 1970.

The *Jerusalem Bible* is an English translation of a French version based on the original languages. It was published by Doubleday & Co., Inc., which is also working toward completion of the *Anchor Bible.*

The Protestant counterpart of the *Douay-Rheims Bible* was the *King James Bible,* called the *Authorized Version* in England. Originally published in 1611, it was in general use for more than three centuries. Its modern revisions include the *English Revised Version,* published between 1881 and 1885; the *American Revised Version,* 1901, and revisions of the New Testament (1946) and the Old Testament (1952) published in 1957 in the United States as the *Revised Standard Version.* The latest revision, a translation in the language of the present day made from Greek and Hebrew sources, is the *New English Bible,* published Mar. 16, 1970. Its New Testament portion was originally published in 1961.

### Biblical Federation

In November, 1966, Pope Paul commissioned the Secretariat for Promoting Christian Unity to start work for the widest possible distribution of the Bible and to coordinate endeavors toward the production of Catholic-Protestant Bibles in all languages.

The World Catholic Federation for the Biblical Apostolate, established in 1969, sponsors a program designed to create greater awareness among Catholics of the Bible and its use in everyday life.

The U. S. Center for the Catholic Biblical Apostolate, under the direction of Father Stephen Hartdegen, O.F.M., is related to the Department of Education, U.S. Catholic Conference. Address: 1312 Massachusetts Ave. N.W., Washington, D.C. 20005.

### APOCRYPHA

In Catholic usage, Apocrypha are books which have some resemblance to the canonical books in subject matter and title but which have not been recognized as canonical by the Church. They are characterized by a false claim to divine authority; extravagant accounts of events and miracles alleged to be supplemental revelation; material favoring heresy (especially in "New Testament" apocrypha); minimal, if any, historical value.

Among examples of this type of literature itemized by J. McKenzie, S.J., in *Dictionary of the Bible* are: *the Books of Adam and Eve, Martyrdom of Isaiah, Testament of the Patriarchs, Assumption of Moses, Sibylline Oracles; Gospel of James, Gospel of Thomas, Arabic Gospel of the Infancy, History of Joseph the Carpenter; Acts of John, Acts of Paul, Acts of Peter, Acts of Andrew,* and numerous epistles.

Books of this type are called pseudepigrapha by Protestants.

In Protestant usage, some books of the Catholic Bible (deuterocanonical) are called apocrypha because their inspired character is rejected.

### DEAD SEA SCROLLS

The Qumran Scrolls, popularly called the Dead Sea Scrolls, are a collection of manuscripts, all but one of them in Hebrew, found since 1947 in caves in the Desert of Juda west of the Dead Sea.

Among the findings were a complete text of Isaiah dating from the second century, B.C., more or less extensive fragments of other Old Testament texts (including the deuterocanonical Tobit), and a commentary on Habakkuk. Until the discovery of these materials, the oldest known Hebrew manuscripts were from the 10th century, A.D.

Also found were messianic and apocalyptic texts, and other writings describing the beliefs and practices of the Essenes, a rigoristic Jewish sect.

The scrolls, dating from about the first century before and after Christ, are important sources of information about Hebrew literature, Jewish history during the period between the Old and New Testaments, and the history of Old Testament texts. They established the fact that the Hebrew text of the Old Testament was fixed before the beginning of the Christian era and have had definite effects in recent critical studies and translations of the Old Testament. Together with other scrolls found at Masada, they are still the subject of intensive study.

## BOOKS OF THE BIBLE

### OLD TESTAMENT
*(Dates are before Christ.)*

#### Pentateuch

The Pentateuch is the collective title of the first five books of the Bible. Substantially, they identify the Israelites as Yahweh's Chosen People, cover their history from Egypt to the threshold of the Promised Land, contain the Mosaic Law and Covenant, and disclose the promise of salvation to come. Principal themes concern the divine promise of salvation, Yahweh's fidelity and the Covenant. Work on the composition of the Pentateuch was completed in the sixth century.

**Genesis:** The book of origins, according to its title in the Septuagint. In two parts, covers: religious prehistory, including accounts of the origin of the world and man, the original state of innocence and the fall, the promise of salvation, patriarchs before and after the Deluge, the Tower of Babel narrative, genealogies (first 11 chapters);

the Covenant with Abraham and patriarchal history from Abraham to Joseph (balance of the 50 chapters). Significant are the themes of Yahweh's universal sovereignty and mercy.

**Exodus:** Named with the Greek word for departure, is a religious epic which describes the oppression of the 12 tribes in Egypt and their departure, liberation or passover therefrom under the leadership of Moses; Yahweh's establishment of the Covenant with them, making them his Chosen People, through the mediation of Moses at Mt. Sinai; instructions concerning the tabernacle, the sanctuary and Ark of the Covenant; the institution of the priesthood. The book is significant because of its theology of liberation and redemption. In Christian interpretation, the Exodus is a figure of baptism.

**Leviticus:** Mainly legislative in theme and purpose, contains laws regarding sacrifices, ceremonies of ordination and the priesthood of Aaron, legal purity, the holiness code, atonement, the redemption of offerings and other subjects. Summarily, Levitical laws provided directives for all aspects of religious observance and for the manner in which the Israelites were to conduct themselves with respect to Yahweh and each other. Leviticus was the liturgical handbook of the priesthood.

**Numbers:** Taking its name from censuses recounted at the beginning and near the end, is a continuation of Exodus. It combines narrative of the Israelites' desert pilgrimage from Sinai to the border of Canaan with laws related to and expansive of those in Leviticus.

**Deuteronomy:** The concluding book of the Pentateuch, recapitulates, in the form of a testament of Moses, the Law and much of the desert history of the Israelites; enjoins fidelity to the Law as the key to good or bad fortune for the people; gives an account of the commissioning of Joshua as the successor of Moses. Notable themes concern the election of Israel by Yahweh, observance of the Law, prohibitions against the worship of foreign gods, worship of and confidence in Yahweh, the power of Yahweh in nature. The Deuteronomic Code or motif, embodying all of these elements, was the norm for interpreting Israelite history.

### Joshua, Judges, Ruth

**Joshua:** Records the fulfillment of Yahweh's promise to the Israelites in their conquest, occupation and division of Canaan under the leadership of Joshua. It also contains an account of the return of Transjordanian Israelites and of a renewal of the Covenant. It was redacted in final form probably in the sixth century or later.

**Judges:** Records the actions of charismatic leaders, called judges, of the tribes of Israel between the death of Joshua and the time of Samuel, and a crisis of idolatry among the people. The basic themes are sin and punishment, repentance and deliverance; its purpose was in line with the Deuteronomic motif, that the fortunes of the Israelites were related to their observance or non-observance of the Law and the Covenant. It was redacted in final form probably in the sixth century.

**Ruth:** Named for the Gentile (Moabite) woman who, through marriage with Boaz, became an Israelite and an ancestress of David (her son, Obed, became his grandfather). Themes are filial piety, faith and trust in Yahweh, the universality of messianic salvation. Dates ranging from c. 950 to the seventh century have been assigned to the origin of the book, whose author is unknown.

### Historical Books

These books, while they contain a great deal of factual material, are unique in their preoccupation with presenting and interpreting it, in the Deuteronomic manner, in primary relation to the Covenant on which the nation of Israel was founded and in accordance with which community and personal life were judged.

The books are: Samuel 1 and 2, from the end of Judges (c. 1020) to the end of David's reign (c. 961); Kings 1 and 2, from the last days of David to the start of the Babylonian Exile and the destruction of the Temple (587); Chronicles 1 and 2, from the reign of Saul (c. 1020-1000) to the return of the people from the Exile (538); Ezra and Nehemiah, covering the reorganization of the Jewish community after the Exile (458-397); Maccabees 1 and 2, recounting the struggle against attempted suppression of Judaism (168-142).

Three of the books listed below — Tobit, Judith and Esther — are categorized as religious novels.

**Samuel 1 and 2:** A single work in concept and contents, containing episodic history of the last two Judges, Eli and Samuel, the establishment and rule of the monarchy under Saul and David, and the political consequences of David's rule. The royal messianic dynasty of David was the subject of Nathan's oracle in 2 Sm. 7. The books were edited in final form probably late in the seventh century or during the Exile.

**Kings 1 and 2:** Cover the last days of David and the career of Solomon, including the building of the Temple and the history of the kingdom during his reign; stories of the prophets Elijah and Elisha; the history of the divided kingdom to the fall of Israel in the North (721) and the fall of Judah in the South (587), the destruction of Jerusalem and the Temple. They reflect the Deuteronomic motif in attributing the downfall of the people to corruption of belief and practice in public and private life. They were completed probably in the sixth century.

**Chronicles 1 and 2:** A collection of historical traditions interpreted in such a way as to present an ideal picture of one people governed by divine law and united in one Temple worship of the one true God. Contents include genealogical tables from Adam to David, the careers of David and Solomon, coverage of the kingdom of Judah to the Exile, and the decree of Cyrus permitting the return of the people and rebuilding of Jerusalem. Both are related to and were written about 400 by the same author, the Chronicler, who composed Ezra and Nehemiah.

**Ezra and Nehemiah:** A running account of the return of the people to their homeland after the Exile and of practical efforts, under the leadership of Ezra and Nehemiah, to restore and reorganize the religious and political community on the basis of Israelite traditions, divine worship and observance of the Law. Events of great significance were the building of the second Temple, the building of a wall around Jerusalem and the proclamation of the Law by Ezra. This restored community was the start of Judaism. Both are related to and were written about 400 by the same author, the Chronicler, who composed Chronicles 1 and 2.

**Tobit:** Written in the literary form of a novel and having greater resemblance to wisdom than to historical literature, narrates the personal history of Tobit, a devout and charitable Jew and, persons connected with him, viz., his son Tobiah, his kinsman Raguel and Raguel's daughter Sarah. Its purpose was to teach people how to be good Jews. One of its principal themes is patience under trial, with trust in divine Providence which is symbolized by the presence and action of the angel Raphael. It was written about 200.

**Judith:** Recounts, in the literary form of a historical novel or romance, the preservation of the Israelites from conquest and ruin through the action of Judith. The essential themes are trust in God for deliverance from danger and emphasis on observance of the Law. It was written probably during the Maccabean period.

**Esther:** Relates, in the literary form of a historical novel or romance, the manner in which Jews in Persia were saved from annihilation through the central role played by Esther, the Jewish wife of Ahasuerus; a fact commemorated by the Jewish feast of Purim. Like Judith, it has trust in divine Providence as its theme and indicates that God's saving will is sometimes realized by persons acting in unlikely ways. Its origin and date are uncertain; it may have been written about 200 near the beginning of the period of strong Hellenistic influence on the Jews.

**Maccabees 1 and 2:** While related to some extent because of common subject matter, are quite different from each other.

The first book recounts the background and events of the 40-year (175-135) struggle for religious and political freedom led by Judas Maccabaeus and his brothers against the Hellenist Seleucid kings and some Hellenophiles among the Jews. Victory was symbolized by the rededication of the Temple. Against the background of opposition between Jews and Gentiles, the author equated the survival of belief in the one true God with survival of the Jewish people, thus identifying religion with patriotism. It was written probably by a Palestinian Jew after 104.

The second book supplements the first to some extent, covering and giving a theological interpretation to events from 180 to 162. It explains the feast of the Dedication of the Temple, a key event in the survival of Judaism which is commemorated in the feast of Hanukkah; stresses the primacy of God's action in the struggle for survival; and indicates belief in an afterlife and the resurrection of the body. It was written probably by a Jew of Alexandria after 120.

## Wisdom Books

With the exceptions of Psalms and the Song of Songs, the titles listed under this heading are called wisdom books because their purpose was to formulate the fruits of human experience in the context of meditation on sacred Scripture and to present them as an aid toward understanding the problems of life. Hebrew wisdom literature was distinctive from pagan literature of the same type, but it had limitations; these were overcome in the New Testament, which added the dimensions of the New Covenant to those of the Old. Solomon was regarded as the archetype of the wise man.

**Job:** A dramatic, didactic poem consisting mainly of several dialogues between Job and his friends concerning the mystery involved in the coexistence of the just God, evil and the suffering of the just. It describes an innocent man's experience of suffering and conveys the truth that faith in and submission to God rather than complete understanding, which is impossible, make the experience bearable; also, that the justice of God cannot be defended by affirming that it is realized in this world. Of uncertain authorship, it was written probably between the fifth and third centuries.

**Psalms:** A collection of 150 religious songs or lyrics reflecting Israelite belief and piety dating from the time of the monarchy to the post-Exilic period, a span of well over 500 years. The psalms, which are a compendium of Old Testament theology, were used in the temple liturgy and were of several types suitable for the king, hymns, lamentations, expressions of confidence and thanksgiving, prophecy, historical meditation and reflection, and the statement of wisdom. About one-half of them are attributed to David; many, by unknown authors, date from the early post-Exilic period.

**Proverbs:** The oldest book of the wisdom type in the Bible, consisting of collections of sayings attributed to Solomon and other persons regarding a wide variety of subjects including wisdom and its nature, rules of conduct, duties with respect to one's neighbor, the conduct of daily affairs. It reveals many details of Jewish life. Its nucleus dates from the period before the Exile, but no definite date can be assigned for its final compilation.

**Ecclesiastes:** A treatise about many subjects whose unifying theme is the vanity of strictly human efforts and accomplishments with respect to the achievement of lasting happiness; the only things which are not vain are fear of the Lord and observance of his commandments. The pessimistic tone of the book is due to the absence of a concept of afterlife. It was written by an unknown author about 250.

**Song of Songs:** A collection of erotic lyrics reflecting various themes, including the celebration of fidelity and love between man and woman. According to one interpretation, the book is a parable of the love of Yahweh for Israel. It was written by an unknown author after the Exile.

**Wisdom:** Deals with many subjects including the reward of justice; praise of wisdom, a gift of Yahweh proceeding from belief in him and the practice of his Law; the part played by him in the history of his people, especially in their liberation from Egypt; the folly and shame of idolatry. Its contents are taken from the whole sacred literature of the Jews and represent a distillation of its wisdom based on the law, beliefs and traditions of Israel. The last book of the Old Testament to be written, it was probably composed about 100 years before Christ by an unknown author to confirm the faith of the Jewish community at Alexandria.

**Sirach:** Resembling Proverbs, is a collection of sayings handed on by a grandfather to his grandson. It contains a variety of moral instruction and eulogies of patriarchs and other figures in Israelite history. Its moral maxims apply to individuals, the family and community, relations with God, friendship, education, wealth, the Law, divine worship. Its theme is that true wisdom consists in the Law. (It was formerly called Ecclesiasticus, the Church Book, because of its extensive use by the Church for moral instruction.) It was written in Hebrew between 200 and 175, during a period of strong Hellenistic influence, and was translated into Greek after 132.

### The Prophets

These books and the prophecies they contain "express judgments of the people's moral conduct, on the basis of the Mosaic alliance between God and Israel. They teach sublime truths and lofty morals. They contain exhortations, threats, announcements of punishment, promises of deliverance. . . . In the affairs of men, their prime concern is the interests of God, especially in what pertains to the Chosen People through whom the Messiah is to come; hence their denunciations of idolatry and of that externalism in worship which exclude the interior spirit of religion. They are concerned also with the universal nature of the moral law, with personal responsibility, with the person and office of the Messiah, and with the conduct of foreign nations" (*The Holy Bible*, Prophetic Books, CCD Edition, 1961; Preface). There are four major (Isaiah, Jeremiah, Ezekiel, Daniel) and 12 minor prophets (distinguished by the length of books), Lamentations and Baruch. Earlier prophets, mentioned in historical books, include Samuel, Gad, Nathan, Elijah and Elisha.

Before the Exile, prophets were the intermediaries through whom God communicated revelation to the people. Afterwards, prophecy lapsed and the written word of the Law served this purpose.

**Isaiah:** Named for the greatest of the prophets whose career spanned the reigns of three Hebrew kings from 742 to the beginning of the seventh century, in a period of moral breakdown in Judah and threats of invasion by foreign enemies. It is an anthology of poems and oracles credited to him and a number of followers deeply influenced by him. Of special importance are the prophecies concerning Immanuel (6 to 12), including the prophecy of the virgin birth (7:14). Chapters 40 to 55, called Deutero-Isaiah, are attributed to an anonymous poet toward the end of the Exile; this portion contains the Songs of the Servant. The concluding part of the book (56-66) contains oracles by later disciples.

One of many themes in Isaiah concerned the saving mission of the remnant of Israel in the divine plan of salvation. It was edited in its present form by 180.

**Jeremiah:** Combines history, biography and prophecy in a setting of crisis caused by internal and external factors, viz., idolatry and general infidelity to the Law among the Israelites and external threats from the Assyrians, Egyptians and Babylonians. Jeremiah prophesied the promise of a new covenant as well as the destruction of Jerusalem and the Temple. His career began in 626 and ended some years after the beginning of the Exile. The book, the longest in the Bible, was edited in final form after the Exile.

**Lamentations:** A collection of five laments or elegies over the fall of Jerusalem and the fate of the people in Exile, written by an unknown eyewitness not long after 587. They convey the message that Yahweh struck the people because of their sins and reflect confidence in his love and power to restore his converted people.

**Baruch:** Against the background of the already begun Exile, it consists of an introduction and several parts: an exile's prayer of confession and petition for forgiveness and the restoration of Israel; a poem praising wisdom and the Law of Moses; a lament in which Jerusalem, personified, bewails the fate of her people and consoles them with the hope of blessings to come; and a polemic against idolatry. Although ascribed to Baruch, Jeremiah's secretary, it was written by several authors probably in the second century.

**Ezekiel:** Named for the priest-prophet who prophesied in Babylon from 593 to 571, during the first phase of the Exile. To prepare his fellow early exiles for the impending fall of Jerusalem, he reproached the Israelites for past sins and predicted woes to come upon them. After the destruction of the city, the burden of his message was hope and promise of restoration. Ezekiel had great influence on the religion of Israel after the Exile. The book, which contains the substance of his teaching, had a number of authors and editors.

**Daniel:** The protagonist is a fictional young Jew, taken early to Babylon where he lived until 537, who figured in a series of edifying stories. The stories, which originated from Israelite tradition, recount the trials and triumphs of Daniel and his three companions, and other episodes including those concerning Susannah, Bel, and the Dragon. The book is more apocalyptic than prophetic: it envisions Israel in glory to come and conveys the message that men of faith can resist temptation and overcome adversity. It states the prophetic themes of right conduct, divine control of men and events, and the final triumph of the kingdom. It was written by an unknown author in the 160's to give moral support to Jews during the persecutions of the Maccabean period.

**Hosea:** Consists of a prophetic parallel between Hosea's marriage and Yahweh's relations with his people. As the prophet was married to a faithless wife whom he would not give up, Yahweh was bound in Covenant with an idolatrous and unjust Israel whom he would not desert but would chastise for purification. Hosea belonged to the Northern Kingdom of Israel and began his career about the middle of the eighth century. He inaugurated the tradition of describing Yahweh's relation to Israel in terms of marriage.

**Joel:** Is apocalyptic and eschatological regarding divine judgment, the Day of the Lord, which is symbolized by a ravaging invasion of locusts, the judgment of the nations in the Valley of Josaphat and the outpouring of the Spirit in the messianic era to come. Its message is that God will vindicate and save Israel, in view of the prayer and repentance of the people, and will punish their enemies. It was composed after the period of Nehemiah.

**Amos:** Consists of an indictment against foreign enemies of Israel; a strong denunciation of the people of Israel, whose infidelity, idolatry and injustice made them subject to divine judgment and punishment; and a messianic oracle regarding Israel's restoration. Amos prophesied in the Northern Kingdom of Israel, at Bethel, in the first half of the eighth century; chronologically, he was the first of the canonical prophets.

**Obadiah:** A 21-verse prophecy, the shortest and one of the sternest in the Bible, against the Edomites, invaders of southern Judah and enemies of those returning from the Exile to their homeland. It was redacted in final form no later than the end of the fourth century.

**Jonah:** A parable of divine mercy with the theme that Yahweh wills the salvation of all, not just a few, men who respond to his call. Its protagonist is a disobedient prophet; forced by circumstances beyond his control to preach penance among Gentiles, he is highly successful in his mission but baffled by the divine concern for those who do not belong to the Chosen People. It was written after the Exile.

**Micah:** Attacks the injustice and corruption of priests, false prophets, officials and people; announces judgment and punishment to come; foretells the restoration of Israel; refers to the saving remnant of Israel. Micah was a contemporary of Isaiah.

**Nahum:** Dating from about 613, concerns the destruction of Nineveh in 612 and the overthrow of the Assyrian Empire by the Babylonians.

**Habakkuk:** Dating from about 605-597, concerns sufferings to be inflicted by oppressors on the people of Judah because of their infidelity to the Lord. It also sounds a note of confidence in the Lord, the Savior, and declares that the just will not perish.

**Zephaniah:** Exercising his ministry in the second half of the seventh century, during a time of widespread idolatry, superstition and religious degradation, he prophesied impending judgment and punishment for Jerusalem and its people. He prophesied too that a holy remnant of the people (*anawim*, mentioned also by Amos) would be spared. Zephaniah was a forerunner of Jeremiah.

**Haggai:** One of the first prophets after the Exile, Haggai in 520 encouraged the returning exiles to reestablish their community and to complete the second Temple (dedicated in 515), for which he envisioned greater glory, in a messianic sense, than that enjoyed by the original Temple of Solomon.

**Zechariah:** A contemporary of Haggai, he prophesied in the same vein. A second part of the book, called Deutero-Zechariah and composed by one or more unknown authors, relates a vision of the coming of the Prince of Peace, the Messiah of the Poor.

**Malachi:** Written by an anonymous author, presents a picture of life in the post-Exilic community between 516 and the initiation of reforms by Ezra and Nehemiah about 432. Blame for the troubles of the community is placed mainly on priests for failure to carry out ritual worship and to instruct the people in the proper manner; other factors were religious indifference and the influence of doubters who were scandalized at the prosperity of the wicked. The vision of a universal sacrifice to be offered to Yahweh (1:11) is interpreted in Catholic theology as a prophecy of the sacrifice of the Mass. Malachi was the last of the minor prophets.

## OLD TESTAMENT DATES

**c. 1800 — c. 1600:** Period of the patriarchs (Abraham, Isaac, Jacob).

**c. 1600:** Israelites in Egypt.

**c. 1250:** Exodus of Israelites from Egypt.

**c. 1210:** Entrance of Israelites into Canaan.

**c. 1210 — c. 1020:** Period of the Judges.

**c. 1020 — c. 1000:** Reign of Saul, first king.

**c. 1000 — c. 961:** Reign of David.

**c. 961 — 922:** Reign of Solomon. Temple built during his reign.

**922:** Division of the Kingdom into Israel (North) and Judah (South).

**721:** Conquest of Israel by Assyrians.

**587-538:** Conquest of Judah by Babylonians. Babylonian Captivity and Exile. Destruction of Jerusalem and the Temple, 587. Captivity ended with the return of exiles, following the decree of Cyrus permitting the rebuilding of Jerusalem.

**515:** Dedication of the Second Temple.

**458-397:** Restoration and reform of the Jewish religious and political community; building of the Jerusalem wall, 439. Leaders in the movement were Ezra and Nehemiah.

**168-142:** Period of the Maccabees; war against Syrians.

**142:** Independence granted to Jews by Demetrius II of Syria.

**135-37:** Period of the Hasmonean dynasty.

**63:** Beginning of Roman rule.

**37-4:** Period of Herod the Great.

---

## ST. CYRIL OF ALEXANDRIA

St. Cyril was born in Egypt about 376. He was bishop of Alexandria from 412 to 444, when he died. He was the author of treatises on the Trinity, the Incarnation and other subjects, mostly in refutation of Nestorian errors concerning the real unity of divine and human natures in the single divine Person of Christ. He made key contributions to the development of Christology. He presided at the Council of Ephesus (431), which condemned the heresies of Nestorianism and Pelagianism. He was proclaimed a Doctor of the Church in 1882. His feast is observed June 27.

## NEW TESTAMENT BOOKS

### Gospels

The term Gospel is derived from the Anglo-Saxon *god-spell* and the Greek *euangelion*, meaning good news, good tidings. In Christian use, it means the good news of salvation proclaimed by Christ and the Church, and handed on in written form in the Gospels of Matthew, Mark, Luke and John.

The initial proclamation of the coming of the kingdom of God was made by Jesus in and through his Person, teachings and actions, and especially through his Passion, death and resurrection. This proclamation became the center of Christian faith and the core of the oral Gospel tradition with which the Church spread the good news by apostolic preaching for some 30 years before it was committed to writing by the Evangelists.

### Nature of the Gospels

The historical truth of the Gospels was the subject of an instruction issued by the Pontifical Commission for Biblical Studies Apr. 21, 1964.

• The sacred writers selected from the material at their disposal (the oral Gospel tradition, some written collections of sayings and deeds of Jesus, eyewitness accounts) those things which were particularly suitable to the various conditions (liturgical, catechetical, missionary) of the faithful and the aims they had in mind, and they narrated these things in such a way as to correspond with those circumstances and their aims.

• The life and teaching of Jesus were not simply reported in a biographical manner for the purpose of preserving their memory but were "preached" so as to offer the Church the basis of doctrine concerning faith and morals.

• In their works, the Evangelists presented the true sayings of Jesus and the events of his life in the light of the better understanding they had following their enlightenment by the Holy Spirit. They did not transform Christ into a "mythical" Person, nor did they distort his teaching.

Passion narratives are the core of all the Gospels, covering the suffering, death and resurrection of Jesus as central events in bringing about and establishing the New Covenant. Leading up to them are accounts of the mission of John the Baptizer and the ministry of Jesus, especially in Galilee and finally in Jerusalem before the Passion. The infancy of Jesus is covered by Luke and Matthew with narratives inspired in part by appropriate Old Testament citations.

Matthew, Mark and Luke, while different in various respects, have so many similarities that they are called Synoptic; their relationships are the subject of the Synoptic Problem.

**Matthew:** Written in the 70's or 80's for Jewish Christians, with clear reference to Jewish background and identification of Jesus as the divine Messiah, the fulfillment of the Old Testament. Distinctive are the use of Old Testament citations regarding the Person, activity and teaching of Jesus, and the presentation of doctrine in sermons and discourses. The canonical Matthew was written in Greek, with dependence on Mark.

**Mark:** The first of the Gospels, dating from about 65. Written for Gentile Christians, it is noted for the realism and wealth of concrete details with which it reveals Jesus as Son of God and Savior more by his actions and miracles than by his discourses. Theologically, it is less refined than the other Gospels.

**Luke:** Written in the 70's or 80's for Gentile Christians. It is noted for the universality of its address, the insight it provides into the Christian way of life, the place it gives to women, the manner in which it emphasizes Jesus' friendship with sinners and compassion for the suffering.

**John:** Written sometime in the 90's, is the most sublime and theological of the Gospels, and is different from the Synoptics in plan and treatment. Combining accounts of signs with longer discourses and reflections, it progressively reveals the Person and mission of Jesus — as Word, Way, Truth, Life, Light — in line with the purpose, "to help you believe that Jesus is the Messiah, the Son of God, so that through this faith you may have life in his name" (Jn. 20:31). There are questions about the authorship but no doubt about the Johannine tradition behind the Gospel.

### Acts of the Apostles

**Acts of the Apostles:** Written by Luke in the 70's or 80's as a supplement to his Gospel. It describes the origin and spread of Christian communities through the action of the Holy Spirit from the resurrection of Christ to the time when Paul was placed in custody in Rome in the early 60's.

### Letters (Epistles)

These letters, many of which antedated the Gospels, were written in response to existential needs of the early Christian communities for doctrinal and moral instruction, disciplinary action, practical advice, and exhortation to true Christian living.

### Pauline Letters

These letters, which comprise approximately one-fourth of the New Testament, are primary and monumental sources of the development of Christian theology. Several of them may not have had Paul as their actual author, but evidence of the Pauline tradition behind them is strong. The letters to the Colossians, Philippians, Ephesians and Philemon have been called the "Captivity Letters" because of a tradition that they were written while Paul was under house arrest in Rome from 61 to 63.

**Romans:** Written in the late 50's from Corinth on the central significance of Christ and faith in him for salvation, and the relationship of Christianity to Judaism; the condition of mankind without Christ; justification and the Christian life; duties of Christians.

**Corinthians 1:** Written near the beginning of 57 from Ephesus to counteract factionalism and disorders, it covers community dissensions, moral irregularities, marriage and celibacy, conduct at religious gatherings, the Eucharist, spiritual gifts (charisms) and their function in the Church, charity, the resurrection of the body.

**Corinthians 2:** Written later in the same year as 1 Cor., concerning Paul's defense of his apostolic life and ministry, and an appeal for a collection to aid poor Christians in Jerusalem.

**Galatians:** Written probably between 54 and 57 (perhaps earlier, according to some scholars) to counteract Judaizing opinions and efforts to undermine his authority, it asserts the divine origin of Paul's authority and doctrine, states that justification is not through Mosaic Law but through faith in Christ, insists on the practice of evangelical virtues, especially charity.

**Ephesians:** Written probably between 61 and 63, or perhaps in the 70's, mainly on the Church as the Mystical Body of Christ.

**Philippians:** Written between 61 and 63 primarily to thank the Philippians for their kindness to him while he was under house arrest in Rome.

**Colossians:** Written while he was under house arrest in Rome from 61 to 63 to counteract the influence of self-appointed teachers who were watering down doctrine concerning Christ. It includes two highly important Christological passages, a warning against false teachers, and an instruction on the ideal Christian life.

**Thessalonians 1 and 2:** Written within a short time of each other probably in 51 from Corinth, mainly on doctrine concerning the Parousia, the second coming of Christ.

**Timothy 1 and 2, Titus:** Written between 65 and 67, or perhaps in the 70's, giving pastoral counsels to Timothy and Titus who were in charge of churches in Ephesus and Crete, respectively. 1 Tm. emphasizes pastoral responsibility for preserving unity of doctrine; 2 Tm. describes Paul's imprisonment in Rome.

**Philemon:** A private letter written between 61 and 63 to a wealthy Colossian concerning a slave, Onesimus, who had escaped from him; Paul appealed for kind treatment of the man.

**Hebrews:** Dating from sometime between the mid 60's and the 80's, a complex theological treatise on Christology, the priesthood and sacrifice of Christ, the New Covenant, and the pattern for Christian living. Critical opinion is divided as to whether it was addressed to Judaeo or Gentile Christians.

### Catholic Letters, Revelation

These seven letters have been called "catholic" because it was thought for some time, not altogether correctly, that they were not addressed to particular communities.

**James:** Written sometime between the mid-60's and the 80's (although datable before 62 according to some scholars) in the spirit of Hebrew wisdom literature and the moralism of Tobit. An exhortation to practical Christian living, it is also noteworthy for the doctrine it states on good works and its citation regarding anointing of the sick.

**Peter 1 and 2:** The first letter may have been written in the mid-60's; the second dates from 100 to 125. Addressed to Christians in Asia Minor, both are exhortations to perseverance in the life of faith despite trials and difficulties arising from pagan influences, isolation from other Christians and false teaching.

**John 1:** Written sometime in the 90's and addressed to Asian churches, its message is that God is made known to us in the Son and that fellowship with the Father is attained by living in the light, justice and love of the Son.

**John 2:** Written sometime in the 90's and addressed to a church in Asia, it commends the people for standing firm in the faith and urges them to perseverance.

**John 3:** Written sometime in the 90's, it appears to represent an effort to settle a jurisdictional dispute in one of the churches.

**Jude:** Written sometime between the 70's and 90's, it is a brief treatise against erroneous teachings and practices opposed to law, authority and true Christian freedom.

**Revelation:** Written in the 90's along the lines of Johannine thought, it is a symbolic and apocalyptic treatment of things to come and of the struggle between the Church and evil combined with warning but hope and assurance to the Church regarding the coming of the Lord in glory.

## BIBLICAL AUTHORSHIP

Some books of the Bible were not written by the authors whose names they bear; New Testament examples are the Gospels of Matthew and John, Hebrews, 1 and 2 Timothy, Titus, James, Jude.

This fact, which has never been the subject of dogmatic definition by the Church, does not militate against the canonicity of the books, since canonicity concerns the theological matter of inspiration rather than the historical question of human authorship.

Questions concerning authorship are explained in various ways: (1) according to an old custom whereby literary works of importance were sometimes attributed to famous persons so they would get a reading; (2) authorship, by a disciple or school of disciples, of works derived from the doctrine of a master; (3) authorship by persons writing in the spirit and tradition of a master.

## INTERPRETATION OF THE BIBLE

According to the *Constitution on Revelation* issued by the Second Vatican Council, "the interpreter of Sacred Scripture, in order to see clearly what God wanted to communicate to us, should carefully investigate what meaning the sacred writers really intended, and what God wanted to manifest by means of their words" (No. 12).

### Hermeneutics, Exegesis

This careful investigation proceeds in accordance with the rules of hermeneutics, the normative science of biblical interpretation and explanation. Hermeneutics in practice is called exegesis.

The principles of hermeneutics are derived from

various disciplines and many factors which have to be considered in explaining the Bible and its parts. These include: the original languages and languages of translation of the sacred texts, through philology and linguistics; the quality of texts, through textual criticism; literary forms and genres, through literary and form criticism; cultural, historical, geographical and other conditions which influenced the writers, through related studies; facts and truths of salvation history; the truths and analogy of faith.

Distinctive to biblical hermeneutics, which differs in important respects from literary interpretation in general, is the premise that the Bible, though written by human authors, is the work of divine inspiration in which God reveals his plan for the salvation of men through historical events and persons, and especially through the Person and mission of Christ.

## Textual, Form Criticism

Textual criticism is the study of biblical texts, which have been transmitted in copies several times removed from the original manuscripts, for the purpose of establishing the real state of the original texts. This purpose is served by comparison of existing copies; by application to the texts of the disciplines of philology and linguistics; by examination of related works of antiquity; by study of biblical citations in works of the Fathers of the Church and other authors; and by other means of literary study.

Since about 1920, the sayings of Christ have been a particular object of New Testament study, the purpose being to analyze the forms of expression used by the Evangelists in order to ascertain the words actually spoken by him.

## Literary Criticism

Literary criticism aims to determine the origin and kinds of literary composition, called forms or genres, employed by the inspired authors. Such determinations are necessary for decision regarding the nature and purpose and, consequently, the meaning of biblical passages. Underlying these studies is the principle that the manner of writing was conditioned by the intention of the authors, the meaning they wanted to convey, and the then-contemporary literary style, mode or medium best adapted to carry their message — e.g., true history, quasi-historical narrative, poems, prayers, hymns, psalms, aphorisms, allegories, discourses. Understanding these media is necessary for the valid interpretation of their message.

## Literal Sense

The key to all valid interpretation is the literal sense of biblical passages. Regarding this matter and the relevance to it of the studies and procedures described above, Pius XII wrote the following in the encyclical *Divino Afflante Spiritu*.

"What the literal sense of a passage is, is not always as obvious as it is in the speeches and writings of ancient authors of the East as it is in the works of our own time. For what they wished to express is not to be determined by the rules of grammar and

philology alone nor solely by the context; the interpreter must, as it were, go back wholly in spirit to those remote centuries of the East and with the aid of history, archeology, ethnology, and other sciences accurately determine what modes of writing, so to speak, the authors of that ancient period would be likely to use and in fact did use. . . . In explaining the Sacred Scripture and in demonstrating and proving its immunity from all error (the Catholic interpreter) should make a prudent use of this means, determine to what extent the manner of expression or literary mode adopted by the sacred writer may lead to a correct and genuine interpretation; and let him be convinced that this part of his office cannot be neglected without serious detriment to Catholic exegesis."

The literal sense of the Bible is the meaning in the mind and intended by the inspired writer of a book or passage of the Bible. This is determined by the application to texts of the rules of hermeneutics. It is not to be confused with word-for-word literalism.

## Typical Sense

The typical sense is the meaning which a passage has not only in itself but also in reference to something else of which it is a type or foreshadowing. A clear example is the account of the Exodus of the Israelites: in its literal sense, it narrates the liberation of the Israelites from death and oppression in Egypt; in its typical sense, it foreshadowed the liberation of men from sin through the redemptive death and resurrection of Christ. The typical sense of this and other passages emerged in the working out of God's plan of salvation history. It did not have to be in the mind of the author of the original passage.

## Accommodated Senses

Accommodated, allegorical and consequent senses are figurative and adaptive meanings given to books and passages of the Bible for moral and other purposes. Such interpretations involve the danger of stretching the literal sense beyond proper proportions. Hermeneutical principles require that interpretations like these respect the integrity of the literal sense of the passages in question.

In the Catholic view, the final word on questions of biblical interpretation belongs to the teaching authority of the Church. In other views, generally derived from basic principles stated by Martin Luther, John Calvin and other reformers, the primacy belongs to individual judgment acting in response to the inner testimony of the Holy Spirit, the edifying nature of biblical subject matter, the sublimity and simplicity of the message of salvation, the intensity with which Christ is proclaimed.

## Biblical Studies

The first center for biblical studies, in some strict sense of the term, was the School of Alexandria, founded in the latter half of the second century. It was noted for allegorical exegesis. Literal interpretation was a hallmark of the School of Antioch.

St. Jerome, who produced the Vulgate, and St.

Augustine, author of numerous commentaries, were the most important figures in biblical studies during the patristic period. By the time of the latter's death, the Old and New Testament canons had been stabilized. For some centuries afterwards, there was little or no progress in scriptural studies, although commentaries were written, collections were made of scriptural excerpts from the writings of the Fathers of the Church, and the systematic reading of Scripture became established as a feature of monastic life.

Advances were made in the 12th and 13th centuries with the introduction of new principles and methods of scriptural analysis stemming from renewed interest in Hebraic studies and the application of dialectics.

By the time of the Reformation, the Bible had become the first book set in movable type, and more than 100 vernacular editions were in use throughout Europe.

## The Council of Trent

In the wake of the Reformation, the Council of Trent formally defined the Canon of the Bible; it also reasserted the authoritative role of tradition and the teaching authority of the Church as well as Scripture with respect to the rule of faith. In the heated atmosphere of the 16th and 17th centuries, the Bible was turned into a polemical weapon; Protestants used it to defend their doctrines, and Catholics countered with citations in support of the dogmas of the Church. One result of this state of affairs was a lack of substantial progress in biblical studies during the period.

Rationalists from the 18th century on and later Modernists denied the reality of the supernatural and doctrine concerning inspiration of the Bible, which they generally regarded as a strictly human production expressive of the religious sense and experience of mankind. In their hands, the tools of positive critical research became weapons for biblical subversion. The defensive Catholic reaction to their work had the temporary effect of alienating scholars of the Church from solid advances in archeology, philology, history, textual and literary criticism.

## Catholic Developments

Major influences in bringing about a change in Catholic attitude toward use of these disciplines in biblical studies were two papal encyclicals and two institutes of special study, the Ecole Biblique, founded in Jerusalem in 1890, and the Pontifical Biblical Institute established in Rome in 1909. The encyclical *Providentissimus Deus,* issued by Leo XIII in 1893, marked an important breakthrough; in addition to defending the concept of divine inspiration and the formal inspiration of the Scriptures, it encouraged the study of allied and ancillary sciences and techniques for a more fruitful understanding of the sacred writings. The encyclical *Divino Afflante Spiritu,* 50 years later, gave encouragement for the use of various forms of criticism as tools of biblical research. The documents encouraged the work of scholars and stimulated wide communication of the fruits of their study.

Great changes in the climate and direction of biblical studies have occurred in recent years. One of them has been an increase in cooperative effort among Catholic, Protestant, Orthodox and Jewish scholars. Their common investigation of the Dead Sea Scrolls is well known. Also productive has been the collaboration of Catholics and Protestants in turning out various editions of the Bible.

The development and results of biblical studies in this century have directly and significantly affected all phases of the contemporary renewal movement in the Church. Their influence on theology, liturgy, catechetics, and preaching indicate the importance of their function in the life of the Church.

## BIBLICAL STUDIES

*The nature, scope and purpose of biblical studies were the subjects of an address delivered by Pope John Paul May 17, 1984, before an assembly of 400 professors, students and collaborators of the Pontifical Biblical Institute. The occasion for the address was the celebration of the 75th anniversary of the founding of the institute by St. Pius X.*

*The excerpt below is from the text published in the May 28, 1984, English edition of "L'Osservatore Romano." Subheads have been added.*

Your study involves a serious and austere commitment. Your knowledge of the sacred languages and of the ambience in which the Bible was born requires persevering efforts, readiness to understand a world, so different from ours, in which the word of God took literary shape. This study is therefore a specific service rendered to the Church, a ministry, an apostolate.

It requires . . . the effort of the entire man: his memory, his sensitivity, his intellect and will. You cannot fully respond to your ecclesial responsibility without being totally committed. Therefore, good will, faith, prayer and love of God and his Church cannot be absent from your commitment to the inspired word. Besides, how can a scholar approach the Sacred Books without the effort to listen sincerely and himself put into practice what he reads or seeks to understand?

### Testimony about Christ

The profound respect that you nourish for Sacred Scripture leads you to touch more closely the unique testimonies about him who stands at the centre of our faith, Jesus Christ our Savior, foretold by the prophets, proclaimed by the Apostles. The sacred witnesses are the privileged place where there is manifested the mysterious reality of salvation which God offers us in Jesus Christ.

Do not stop searching these witnesses with your philological, linguistic, literary and historical research; these, even if arduous and wearisome, are more useful than ever for a better understanding of the word of God.

### Fidelity to the Text

Fidelity to the sacred text that has been handed down to us remains and must remain one of your traits. It is true, in researching the meaning of the texts, as in researching the historical ambience where they originated, obscurities still remain, which scientific works are gradually clarifying. Even more refined hypotheses are proposed in order to reflect even more faithfully the data offered by the text itself. In all these researches, which are necessary today, prudence, discretion and sobriety are always required of the one who analyzes the texts.

This is all the more so with regard to the biblical writings that express the faith of the Church and are the rule of its faith. Inspired by these virtues and in the wake of your predecessors, . . . continue to give your contribution for a "better understanding and explanation of the meaning of Sacred Scripture, so that through preparatory study the judgment of the Church may mature" *(Dogmatic Constitution on the Church,* Second Vatican Council; No. 12).

### Ecclesial Service

Scientific work and a work of faith, your commitment is indeed essentially an ecclesial service. Each day the Church more clearly feels the need to draw from Sacred Scripture in order to read in it what she is and what she is called to be. There is no spiritual life, catechesis or apostolate that does not demand this constant return to the Sacred Books. Even the other sacred sciences, fundamental for the life of the Church, require from you today a collaboration that you cannot avoid.

These sciences, especially dogmatic and moral theology, echo the need for a methodical, thorough study of their biblical foundations. The Second Vatican Council, taking up the statement of the Fathers, affirms that Scripture is as it were the soul of theology (Ibid., No. 24).

### To Explain and Clarify

Your ecclesial mission must not, therefore, stop at the explanation of the sacred text but must contribute to the clarification of dogmatic and moral questions — to mention only these two more urgent fields — so that the unity of the faith and of Christian morality may be ever more evidenced.

### Ecumenical, Cultural Importance

I add also that in the dialogue with our separated brethren, as well as in the dialogue with the children of Abraham according to the flesh, your active presence is very often of primary importance in rediscovering what unites us in the one Lord and God.

Finally, since today so many cultures flank the Biblical Institute, be ever more aware, in your exegetical commitment, of the demands of a new challenge laid down to the Church of our time: help her to put at the disposal of all cultures the treasure of the Scripture that the Church entrusts to your laborious dedication.

### Exhortation

Dear Brothers, for seventy-five years the Biblical Institute has been at the service of the Church and the Apostolic See in the spirit of the mandate entrusted to it by Saint Pius X and his successors. In renewing this assignment to you today, I exhort you to make shine in the Church and in the entire world, with ever new fidelity, the knowledge and love of the Sacred Books, in serene allegiance to the living magisterium of the Church, to which has been entrusted the office of authentically interpreting the word of God, written or handed down, and whose authority is exercised in the name of Jesus Christ.

As a sign of encouragement for your specific vocation, with all my heart I impart to you my special blessing.

## APOSTLES AND EVANGELISTS

The Apostles were the men selected, trained and commissioned by Christ to preach the Gospel, to baptize, to establish, direct and care for his Church as servants of God and stewards of his mysteries. They were the first bishops of the Church.

St. Matthew's Gospel lists the Apostles in this order: Peter, Andrew, James the Greater, John, Philip, Bartholomew, Thomas, Matthew, James the Less, Jude, Simon and Judas Iscariot. Matthias was elected to fill the place of Judas. Paul became an Apostle by a special call from Christ. Barnabas was called an Apostle.

Two of the Evangelists, John and Matthew, were Apostles. The other two, Luke and Mark, were closely associated with the apostolic college.

**Andrew:** Born in Bethsaida, brother of Peter, disciple of John the Baptist, a fisherman, the first Apostle called; according to legend, preached the Gospel in northern Greece, Epirus and Scythia, and was martyred at Patras about 70; in art, is represented with an x-shaped cross, called St. Andrew's Cross; feast, Nov. 30; is honored as the patron of Russia and Scotland.

**Barnabas:** Originally called Joseph but named Barnabas by the Apostles, among whom he is ranked because of his collaboration with Paul; a Jew of the Diaspora, born in Cyprus; a cousin of Mark and member of the Christian community at Jerusalem, influenced the Apostles to accept Paul, with whom he became a pioneer missionary outside Palestine and Syria, to Antioch, Cyprus and southern Asia Minor; legend says he was martyred in Cyprus during the Neronian persecution; feast, June 11.

**Bartholomew (Nathaniel):** A friend of Philip; according to various traditions, preached the Gospel in Ethiopia, India, Persia and Armenia, where he was martyred by being flayed and beheaded; in art, is depicted holding a knife, an instrument of his death; feast, Aug. 24 in the Roman Rite, Aug. 25 in the Byzantine Rite.

# 204 Apostles and Evangelists

James the Greater: A Galilean, son of Zebedee, brother of John (with whom he was called a "Son of Thunder"), a fisherman; with Peter and John, witnessed the raising of Jairus' daughter to life, the transfiguration, the agony of Jesus in the Garden of Gethsemani; first of the Apostles to die, by the sword in 44 during the rule of Herod Agrippa; there is doubt about a journey legend says he made to Spain and also about the authenticity of relics said to be his at Santiago de Compostela; in art, is depicted carrying a pilgrim's bell; feast, July 25 in the Roman Rite, Apr. 30 in the Byzantine Rite.

James the Less: Son of Alphaeus, called "Less" because he was younger in age or shorter in stature than James the Greater; one of the Catholic Epistles bears his name; was stoned to death in 62 or thrown from the top of the temple in Jerusalem and clubbed to death in 66; in art, is depicted with a club or heavy staff; feast, May 3 in the Roman Rite, Oct. 9 in the Byzantine Rite.

John: A Galilean, son of Zebedee, brother of James the Greater (with whom he was called a "Son of Thunder"), a fisherman, probably a disciple of John the Baptist, one of the Evangelists, called the "Beloved Disciple"; with Peter and James the Greater, witnessed the raising of Jairus' daughter to life, the transfiguration, the agony of Jesus in the Garden of Gethsemani; Mary was commended to his special care by Christ; the fourth Gospel, three Catholic Epistles and Revelation bear his name; according to various accounts, lived at Ephesus in Asia Minor for some time and died a natural death about 100; in art, is represented by an eagle, symbolic of the sublimity of the contents of his Gospel; feast, Dec. 27 in the Roman Rite, May 8 in the Byzantine Rite.

Jude Thaddeus: One of the Catholic Epistles, the shortest, bears his name; various traditions say he preached the Gospel in Mesopotamia, Persia and elsewhere, and was martyred; in art, is depicted with a halberd, the instrument of his death; feast, Oct. 28 in the Roman Rite, June 19 in the Byzantine Rite.

Luke: A Greek convert to the Christian community, called "our most dear physician" by Paul, of whom he was a missionary companion; author of the third Gospel and Acts of the Apostles; the place — Achaia, Bithynia, Egypt — and circumstances of his death are not certain; in art, is depicted as a man, a writer, or an ox (because his Gospel starts at the scene of temple sacrifice); feast, Oct. 18.

Mark: A cousin of Barnabas and member of the first Christian community at Jerusalem; a missionary companion of Paul and Barnabas, then of Peter; author of the Gospel which bears his name; according to legend, founded the Church at Alexandria, was bishop there and was martyred in the streets of the city; in art, is depicted with his Gospel and a winged lion, symbolic of the voice of John the Baptist crying in the wilderness, at the beginning of his Gospel; feast, Apr. 25.

Matthew: A Galilean, called Levi by Luke and John and the son of Alphaeus by Mark, a tax collector, one of the Evangelists; according to various accounts, preached the Gospel in Judea, Ethiopia,

Persia and Parthia, and was martyred; in art, is depicted with a spear, the instrument of his death, and as a winged man in his role as Evangelist; feast, Sept. 21 in the Roman Rite, Nov. 16 in the Byzantine Rite.

Matthias: A disciple of Jesus whom the faithful 11 Apostles chose to replace Judas before the Resurrection; uncertain traditions report that he preached the Gospel in Palestine, Cappadocia or Ethiopia; in art, is represented with a cross and a halberd, the instruments of his death as a martyr; feast, May 14 in the Roman Rite, Aug. 9 in the Byzantine Rite.

Paul: Born at Tarsus, of the tribe of Benjamin, a Roman citizen; participated in the persecution of Christians until the time of his miraculous conversion on the way to Damascus; called by Christ, who revealed himself to him in a special way; became the Apostle of the Gentiles, among whom he did most of his preaching in the course of three major missionary journeys through areas north of Palestine, Cyprus, Asia Minor and Greece; 14 epistles bear his name; two years of imprisonment at Rome, following initial arrest in Jerusalem and confinement at Caesarea, ended with martyrdom, by beheading, outside the walls of the city in 64 or 67 during the Neronian persecution; in art, is depicted in various ways with St. Peter, with a sword, in the scene of his conversion; feasts, June 29, Jan. 25 (Roman Rite).

Peter: Simon, son of Jona, born in Bethsaida, brother of Andrew, a fisherman; called Cephas or Peter by Christ who made him the chief of the Apostles and head of the Church as his vicar; named first in the listings of Apostles in the Synoptic Gospels and the Acts of the Apostles; with James the Greater and John, witnessed the raising of Jairus' daughter to life, the transfiguration, the agony of Jesus in the Garden of Gethsemani; was the first to preach the Gospel in and around Jerusalem and was the leader of the first Christian community there; established a local church in Antioch; presided over the Council of Jerusalem in 51; wrote two Catholic Epistles to the Christians in Asia Minor; established his see in Rome where he spent his last years and was martyred by crucifixion in 64 or 65 during the Neronian persecution; in art, is depicted carrying two keys, symbolic of his primacy in the Church; feasts, June 29, Feb. 22 (Roman Rite).

Philip: Born in Bethsaida; according to legend, preached the Gospel in Phrygia where he suffered martyrdom by crucifixion; feast, May 3 in the Roman Rite, Nov. 14 in the Byzantine Rite.

Simon: Called the Cananean or the Zealot; according to legend, preached in various places in the Middle East and suffered martyrdom by being sawed in two; in art, is depicted with a saw, the instrument of his death, or a book, symbolic of his zeal for the Law; feast, Oct. 28 in the Roman Rite, May 10 in the Byzantine Rite.

Thomas (Didymus): Notable for his initial incredulity regarding the Resurrection and his subsequent forthright confession of the divinity of Christ risen from the dead; according to legend, preached the Gospel in places from the Caspian Sea to the Persian Gulf and eventually reached India where he was martyred near Madras; Thomas Christians trace their origin to him; in art, is depicted kneeling before the risen Christ, or with a carpenter's rule and square; feast, July 3 in the Roman Rite, Oct. 6 in the Byzantine Rite.

## Judas

The Gospels record only a few facts about Judas, the Apostle who betrayed Christ.

The only non-Galilean among the Apostles, he was from Carioth, a town in southern Judah. He was keeper of the purse in the apostolic band. He was called a petty thief by John. He voiced dismay at the waste of money, which he said might have been spent for the poor, in connection with the anointing incident at Bethany. He took the initiative in arranging the betrayal of Christ. Afterwards, he confessed that he had betrayed an innocent man and cast into the Temple the money he had received for that action. Of his death, Matthew says that he hanged himself; the Acts of the Apostles states that he swelled up and burst open; both reports deal more with the meaning than the manner of his death — the misery of the death of a sinner.

The consensus of speculation over the reason why Judas acted as he did in betraying Christ focuses on disillusionment and unwillingness to accept the concept of a suffering Messiah and personal suffering of his own as an Apostle.

## APOSTOLIC FATHERS, FATHERS, DOCTORS OF THE CHURCH

The writers listed below were outstanding and authoritative witnesses to authentic Christian belief and practice, and played significant roles in giving them expression.

The Apostolic Fathers were Christian writers of the first and second centuries whose writings echo genuine apostolic teaching. Chief in importance are: St. Clement (d.c. 97), bishop of Rome and third successor of St. Peter in the papacy; St. Ignatius (50-c. 107), bishop of Antioch and second successor of St. Peter in that see, reputed to be a disciple of St. John; St. Polycarp (69-155), bishop of Smyrna and a disciple of St. John. The authors of the *Didache* and the *Epistle of Barnabas* are also numbered among the Apostolic Fathers.

Other early ecclesiastical writers included: St. Justin, martyr (100-165), of Asia Minor and Rome, a layman and apologist; St. Irenaeus (130-202), bishop of Lyons, who opposed Gnosticism; and St. Cyprian (210-258), bishop of Carthage, who opposed Novatianism.

The Fathers of the Church were theologians and writers of the first eight centuries who were outstanding for sanctity and learning. They were such authoritative witnesses to the belief and teaching of the Church that their unanimous acceptance of doctrines as divinely revealed has been regarded as evidence that such doctrines were so received by the Church in line with apostolic tradition and Sacred Scripture. Their unanimous rejection of doctrines branded them as heretical. Their writings, however, were not necessarily free of error in all respects.

The greatest of these Fathers were: Sts. Ambrose, Augustine, Jerome and Gregory the Great in the West; Sts. John Chrysostom, Basil the Great, Gregory of Nazianzen and Athanasius in the East.

The Doctors of the Church were ecclesiastical writers of eminent learning and sanctity who have been given this title because of the great advantage the Church has derived from their work. Their writings, however, were not necessarily free of error in all respects.

**Albert the Great, St.** (c. 1200-1280): Born in Swabia, Germany; Dominican; bishop of Regensburg (1260-1262); wrote extensively on logic, natural sciences, ethics, metaphysics, Scripture, systematic theology; contributed to development of Scholasticism; teacher of St. Thomas Aquinas; canonized and proclaimed doctor, 1931; named patron of natural scientists, 1941; called Doctor Universalis, Doctor Expertus; feast, Nov. 15.

**Alphonsus Liguori, St.** (1696-1787): Born near Naples, Italy; bishop of Saint Agatha of the Goths (1762-1775); founder of the Redemptorists; in addition to his principal work, *Theologiae Moralis*, wrote on prayer, the spiritual life and doctrinal subjects in response to controversy; canonized, 1839; proclaimed doctor, 1871; named patron of confessors and moralists, 1950; feast, Aug. 1.

**Ambrose, St.** (c. 340-397): Born in Trier, Germany; bishop of Milan (374-397); one of the strongest opponents of Arianism in the West; his homilies and other writings — on faith, the Holy Spirit, the Incarnation, the sacraments and other subjects — were pastoral and practical; influenced the development of a liturgy at Milan which was named for him; Father and Doctor of the Church; feast, Dec. 7.

**Anselm, St.** (1033-1109): Born in Aosta, Piedmont, Italy; Benedictine; archbishop of Canterbury (1093-1109); in addition to his principal work, *Cur Deus Homo*, on the atonement and reconciliation of man with God through Christ, wrote about the existence and attributes of God and defended the *Filioque* explanation of the procession of the Holy Spirit from the Father and the Son; proclaimed doctor, 1720; called Father of Scholasticism; feast, Apr. 21.

**Anthony of Padua, St.** (1195-1231): Born in Lisbon, Portugal; first theologian of the Franciscan Order; preacher; canonized, 1232; proclaimed doctor, 1946; called Evangelical Doctor; feast, June 13.

**Athanasius, St.** (c. 297-373): Born in Alexandria, Egypt; bishop of Alexandria (328-373); participant in the Council of Nicaea I while still a deacon; dominant opponent of Arians whose errors regarding Christ he refuted in *Apology against the Arians, Discourses against the Arians* and other works; Father and Doctor of the Church; called Father of Orthodoxy; feast, May 2.

**Augustine, St.** (354-430): Born in Tagaste, North Africa; bishop of Hippo (395-430) after conversion from Manichaeism; works include the auto-biographical and mystical *Confessions*, *City of God*, treatises on the Trinity, grace, passages of the Bible and doctrines called into question and denied by Manichaeans, Pelagians and Donatists; had strong and lasting influence on Christian theology and philosophy; Father and Doctor of the Church; called Doctor of Grace; feast, Aug. 28.

**Basil the Great, St.** (c. 329-379): Born in Caesarea, Cappadocia, Asia Minor; bishop of Caesarea (370-379); wrote three books *Contra Eunomium* in refutation of Arian errors, a treatise on the Holy Spirit, many homilies and several rules for monastic life, on which he had lasting influence; Father and Doctor of the Church; called Father of Monasticism in the East; feast, Jan. 2.

**Bede the Venerable, St.** (c. 673-735): Born in Northumberland, England; Benedictine; in addition to his principal work, *Ecclesiastical History of the English Nation* (covering the period 597-731), wrote scriptural commentaries; regarded as probably the most learned man in Western Europe of his time; called Father of English History; feast, May 25.

**Bernard of Clairvaux, St.** (c. 1090-1153): Born near Dijon, France; abbot; monastic reformer, called the second founder of the Cistercian Order; mystical theologian with great influence on devotional life; opponent of the rationalism brought forward by Abelard and others; canonized, 1174; proclaimed doctor, 1830; called Mellifluous Doctor because of his eloquence; feast, Aug. 20.

**Bonaventure, St.** (c. 1217-1274): Born near Viterbo, Italy; Franciscan; bishop of Albano (1273-1274); cardinal; wrote *Itinerarium Mentis in Deum*, *De Reductione Artium ad Theologiam*, *Breviloquium*, scriptural commentaries, additional mystical works affecting devotional life and a life of St. Francis of Assisi; canonized, 1482; proclaimed doctor, 1588; called Seraphic Doctor; feast, July 15.

**Catherine of Siena, St.** (c. 1347-1380): Born in Siena, Italy; member of the Third Order of St. Dominic; mystic; authored a long series of letters, mainly concerning spiritual instruction and encouragement, to associates, and *Dialogue*, a spiritual testament in four treatises; was active in support of a crusade against the Turks and efforts to end war between papal forces and the Florentine allies; had great influence in inducing Gregory XI to return himself and the Curia to Rome in 1376, to end the Avignon period of the papacy; canonized, 1461; proclaimed the second women doctor, Oct. 4, 1970; feast, Apr. 29.

**Cyril of Jerusalem, St.** (c. 315-387): Bishop of Jerusalem (350-387); vigorous opponent of Arianism; principal work, *Catecheses*, a pre-baptismal explanation of the creed of Jerusalem; proclaimed doctor, 1882; feast, Mar. 18.

**Ephraem, St.** (c. 306-373): Born in Nisibis, Mesopotamia; counteracted the spread of Gnostic and Arian errors with poems and hymns of his own composition; wrote also on the Eucharist and Mary; proclaimed doctor, 1920; called Deacon of Edessa and Harp of the Holy Spirit; feast, June 9.

**Francis de Sales, St.** (1567-1622): Born in Savoy; bishop of Geneva (1602-1622); spiritual writer with strong influence on devotional life through treatises such as *Introduction to a Devout Life*, and *The Love of God*; canonized, 1665; proclaimed doctor, 1877;. patron of Catholic writers and the Catholic press; feast, Jan. 24.

**Gregory Nazianzen, St.** (c. 330-c. 390): Born in Arianzus, Cappadocia, Asia Minor; bishop of Constantinople (381-390); vigorous opponent of Arianism; in addition to five theological discourses on the Nicene Creed and the Trinity for which he is best known, wrote letters and poetry; Father and Doctor of the Church; called the Christian Demosthenes because of his eloquence and, in the Eastern Church, The Theologian; feast, Jan. 2.

**Gregory I, the Great, St.** (c. 540-604): Born in Rome; pope (590-604): wrote many scriptural commentaries, a compendium of theology in the *Book of Morals* based on Job, *Dialogues* concerning the lives of saints, the immortality of the soul, death, purgatory, heaven and hell, and 14 books of letters; enforced papal supremacy and established the position of the pope vis-a-vis the emperor; worked for clerical and monastic reform and the observance of clerical celibacy; Father and Doctor of the Church; feast, Sept. 3.

**Hilary of Poitiers, St.** (c. 315-368): Born in Poitiers, France; bishop of Poitiers (c. 353-368); wrote *De Synodis*, with the Arian controversy in mind, and *De Trinitate*, the first lengthy study of the doctrine in Latin; introduced Eastern theology to the West; contributed to the development of hymnology; proclaimed doctor, 1851; called the Athanasius of the West because of his vigorous defense of the divinity of Christ against Arians; feast, Jan. 13.

**Isidore of Seville, St.** (c. 560-636): Born in Cartagena, Spain; bishop of Seville (c. 600-636); in addition to his principal work, *Etymologiae*, an encyclopedia of the knowledge of his day, wrote on theological and historical subjects; regarded as the most learned man of his time; proclaimed doctor, 1722; feast, Apr. 4.

**Jerome, St.** (c. 343-420): Born in Stridon, Dalmatia; translated the Old Testament from Hebrew into Latin and revised the existing Latin translation of the New Testament to produce the Vulgate version of the Bible; wrote scriptural commentaries and treatises on matters of controversy; regarded as Father and Doctor of the Church from the eighth century; called Father of Biblical Science; feast, Sept. 30.

**John Chrysostom, St.** (c. 347-407): Born in Antioch, Asia Minor; archbishop of Constantinople (398-407); wrote homilies, scriptural commentaries and letters of wide influence in addition to a classical treatise on the priesthood; proclaimed doctor by the Council of Chalcedon, 451; called the greatest of the Greek Fathers; named patron of preachers, 1909; called Golden-Mouthed because of his eloquence; feast, Sept. 13.

**John Damascene, St.** (c. 675-c. 749): Born in Damascus, Syria; monk; wrote *Fountain of Wisdom*, a three-part work including a history of heresies and an exposition of the Christian faith, three *Discourses against the Iconoclasts,* homilies on Mary, biblical commentaries and treatises on moral subjects; proclaimed doctor, 1890; called Golden Speaker because of his eloquence; feast, Dec. 4.

**John of the Cross, St.** (1542-1591): Born in Old Castile, Spain; Carmelite; founder of Discalced Carmelites; one of the greatest mystical theologians, wrote *The Ascent of Mt. Carmel — The Dark Night, The Spiritual Canticle, The Living Flame of Love;* canonized, 1726; proclaimed doctor, 1926; called Doctor of Mystical Theology; feast, Dec. 14.

**Lawrence of Brindisi, St.** (1559-1619): Born in Brindisi, Italy; Franciscan (Capuchin); vigorous preacher of strong influence in the post-Reformation period; 15 tomes of collected works include scriptural commentaries, sermons, homilies and doctrinal writings; canonized, 1881; proclaimed doctor, 1959; feast, July 21.

**Leo I, the Great, St.** (c. 400-461): Born in Tuscany, Italy; pope (440-461); wrote the *Tome of Leo,* to explain doctrine concerning the two natures and one Person of Christ, against the background of the Nestorian and Monophysite heresies; other works included sermons, letters and writings against the errors of Manichaeism and Pelagianism; was instrumental in dissuading Attila from sacking Rome in 452; proclaimed doctor, 1574; feast, Nov. 10.

**Peter Canisius, St.** (1521-1597): Born in Nijmegen, Holland; Jesuit; wrote popular expositions of the Catholic faith in several catechisms which were widely circulated in 20 editions in his lifetime alone; was one of the moving figures in the Counter-Reformation period, especially in southern and western Germany; canonized and proclaimed doctor, 1925; feast, Dec. 21.

**Peter Chrysologus, St.** (c. 400-450): Born in Imola, Italy; served as archbishop of Ravenna (c. 433-450); his sermons and writings, many of which were designed to counteract Monophysitism, were

pastoral and practical; proclaimed doctor, 1729; feast, July 30.

**Peter Damian, St.** (1007-1072): Born in Ravenna, Italy; Benedictine; cardinal; his writings and sermons, many of which concerned ecclesiastical and clerical reform, were pastoral and practical; proclaimed doctor, 1828; feast, Feb. 21.

**Robert Bellarmine, St.** (1542-1621): Born in Tuscany, Italy; Jesuit; archbishop of Capua (1602-1605); wrote *Controversies,* a three-volume exposition of doctrine under attack during and after the Reformation, two catechisms and the spiritual work, *The Art of Dying Well;* was an authority on ecclesiology and Church-state relations; canonized, 1930; proclaimed doctor, 1931; feast, Sept. 17.

**Teresa of Jesus (Avila), St.** (1515-1582): Born in Avila, Spain; entered the Carmelite Order, in the early 1560's, initiated a primitive Carmelite, discalced-Alcantarine reform which greatly influenced men and women religious, especially in Spain; wrote extensively on spiritual and mystical subjects; principal works included her *Autobiography, Way of Perfection, The Interior Castle, Meditations on the Canticle, The Foundations, Visitation of the Discalced Nuns;* canonized, 1614; proclaimed first woman doctor, Sept. 27, 1970; feast, Oct. 15.

**Thomas Aquinas, St.** (1225-1274): Born near Naples, Italy; Dominican; teacher and writer on virtually the whole range of philosophy and theology; principal works were *Summa contra Gentiles,* a manual and systematic defense of Christian doctrine, and *Summa Theologiae,* a new (at that time) exposition of theology on philosophical principles; canonized, 1323; proclaimed doctor, 1567; called Doctor Communis, Doctor Angelicus, the Great Synthesizer because of the way in which he related faith and reason, theology and philosophy (especially that of Aristotle), and systematized the presentation of Christian doctrine; named patron of Catholic schools and education, 1880; feast, Jan. 28.

## CREEDS

Creeds are formal and official statements of Christian doctrine. As summaries of the principal truths of faith, they are standards of orthodoxy and are useful for instructional purposes, for actual profession of the faith and for expression of the faith in the liturgy.

The classical creeds are the Apostles' Creed and the Creed of Nicaea-Constantinople. Two others are the Athanasian Creed and the Creed of Pius IV.

### Apostles' Creed

**Text:** I believe in God, the Father almighty, Creator of heaven and earth.

And in Jesus Christ, his only Son, our Lord; who was conceived by the Holy Spirit, born of the Virgin Mary, suffered under Pontius Pilate, was crucified, died, and was buried. He descended into hell; the third day he arose again from the dead; he ascended into heaven, sits at the right hand of God, the Father almighty; from thence he shall come to judge the living and the dead.

I believe in the Holy Spirit, the holy Catholic Church, the communion of saints, the forgiveness of sins, the resurrection of the body, and life everlasting. Amen.

**Background:** The Apostles' Creed reflects the teaching of the Apostles but is not of apostolic origin. It probably originated in the second century as a rudimentary formula of faith professed by catechumens before the reception of baptism. Baptismal creeds in fourth-century use at Rome and elsewhere in the West closely resembled the present text, which was quoted in a handbook of Christian doctrine written between 710 and 724. This text was in wide use throughout the West by the ninth century. The Apostles' Creed is common to all Christian confessional churches in the West, but is not used in Eastern Churches.

### Nicene Creed

The following translation of the Latin text of the

creed was prepared by the International Committee on English in the Liturgy.

**Text:** We believe in one God, the Father, the Almighty, maker of heaven and earth, of all that is seen and unseen.

We believe in one Lord, Jesus Christ, the only Son of God, eternally begotten of the Father, God from God, Light from Light, true God from true God, begotten, not made, one in Being with the Father. Through him all things were made. For us men and for our salvation he came down from heaven: by the power of the Holy Spirit he was born of the Virgin Mary, and became man. For our sake he was crucified under Pontius Pilate; he suffered, died, and was buried. On the third day he rose again in fulfillment of the Scriptures; he ascended into heaven and is seated at the right hand of the Father. He will come again in glory to judge the living and the dead, and his kingdom will have no end.

We believe in the Holy Spirit, the Lord, the giver of life, who proceeds from the Father and the Son. With the Father and the Son he is worshiped and glorified. He has spoken through the prophets.

We believe in one holy catholic and apostolic Church. We acknowledge one baptism for the forgiveness of sins. We look for the resurrection of the dead, and the life of the world to come. Amen.

**Background:** The Nicene Creed (Creed of Nicaea-Constantinople) consists of elements of doctrine contained in an early baptismal creed of Jerusalem and enactments of the Council of Nicaea (325) and the Council of Constantinople (381). Its strong trinitarian content reflects the doctrinal errors, especially of Arianism, it served to counteract. Theologically, it is much more sophisticated than the Apostles' Creed. Since late in the fifth century, the Nicene Creed has been the only creed in liturgical use in the Eastern Churches. The Western Church adopted it for liturgical use by the end of the eighth century.

### The Athanasian Creed

The Athanasian Creed, which has a unique structure, is a two-part summary of doctrine concerning the Trinity and the Incarnation-Redemption bracketed at the beginning and end with the statement that belief in the cited truths is necessary for salvation; it also contains a number of anathemas or condemnatory clauses regarding doctrinal errors. Although attributed to St. Athanasius, it was probably written after his death, between 381 and 428, and may have been authored by St. Ambrose. It is not accepted in the East; in the West, it formerly had place in the Roman-Rite Liturgy of the Hours and in the liturgy for the Solemnity of the Holy Trinity.

### Creed of Pius IV

The Creed of Pius IV, also called the Profession of Faith of the Council of Trent, was promulgated in the bull *Injunctum Nobis,* Nov. 13, 1564. It is a summary of doctrine defined by the council concerning: Scripture and tradition, original sin and justification, the Mass and sacraments, veneration of the saints, indulgences, the primacy of the See of Rome. It was slightly modified in 1887 to include doctrinal formulations of the First Vatican Council.

### Redditio of the Creed

The "giving back," by profession, of a baptismal creed by candidates for baptism to a bishop or his representative was one of the immediate preliminaries to reception of the sacrament at the conclusion of the catechumenate in the early Church.

The interrogation concerning truths of faith in the present baptismal rite is reminiscent of this ancient practice.

## MORAL OBLIGATIONS

The basic norm of Christian morality is life in Christ. This involves, among other things, the observance of the Ten Commandments, their fulfillment in the twofold law of love of God and neighbor, the implications of the Sermon on the Mount and the whole New Testament, and membership in the Church established by Christ.

### The Ten Commandments

The Ten Commandments, the Decalogue, were given by God through Moses to his Chosen People for the guidance of their moral conduct in accord with the demands of the Covenant he established with them as a divine gift.

In the traditional Catholic enumeration and according to Dt. 5:6-21, the Commandments are:

1. "I, the Lord, am your God . . . You shall not have other gods besides me. You shall not carve idols. . . ."
2. "You shall not take the name of the Lord, your God, in vain. . . ."
3. "Take care to keep holy the Sabbath day. . . ."
4. "Honor your father and your mother. . . ."
5. "You shall not kill."
6. "You shall not commit adultery."
7. "You shall not steal."
8. "You shall not bear dishonest witness against your neighbor."
9. "You shall not covet your neighbor's wife."
10. "You shall not desire your neighbor's house or field, nor his male or female slave, nor his ox or ass, nor anything that belongs to him" (summarily, his goods).

Another version of the Commandments, substantially the same, is given in Ex. 20:1-17.

The traditional enumeration of the Commandments in Protestant usage differs from the above. Thus: two commandments are made of the first, as above; the third and fourth are equivalent to the second and third, as above, and so on; and the 10th includes the ninth and 10th, as above.

### Love of God and Neighbor

The first three of the commandments deal directly with man's relations with God, viz.: acknowledgment of one true God and the rejection of false gods and idols; honor due to God and his name; observance of the Sabbath as the Lord's day.

The rest cover interpersonal relationships, viz.: the obedience due to parents and, logically, to other persons in authority, and the obligations of parents to children and of persons in authority to those under their care; respect for life and physical integrity; fidelity in marriage, and chastity; justice and rights; truth; internal respect for faithfulness in marriage, chastity, and the goods of others.

## Perfection in Christian Life

The moral obligations of the Ten Commandments are complemented by others flowing from the twofold law of love, the whole substance and pattern of Christ's teaching, and everything implied in full and active membership and participation in the community of salvation formed by Christ in his Church. Some of these matters are covered in other sections of the Almanac under appropriate headings.

## Precepts of the Church

These are moral precepts binding Roman Catholics in conscience. They originated in the Middle Ages; five of them were mentioned in the writings of St. Peter Canisius and St. Robert Bellarmine in the second half of the 16th century.

1. Assist at Mass on Sundays and holy days of obligation. (Also, to avoid work and involvement in business which impede participation in divine worship and enjoyment of rest and relaxation from unnecessary servile work on these days.)

2. Fast and abstain on the days appointed. (The fasting obligation binds persons from the 18th until the 59th birthday; the days of fast are Ash Wednesday and Good Friday. The abstinence obligation binds from the 14th birthday on these days, and is obligatory for all Fridays in Lent in the U.S.) These regulations, which have been modified in recent years, are penitential in purpose but do not exhaust the obligations of penance. Other ways of doing penance are left to personal option.

3. Confess their sins at least once a year.

4. Receive Holy Communion during the Easter season.

5. Contribute to the support of the Church.

6. Observe the laws of the Church concerning marriage.

## SOCIAL DOCTRINE

Since the end of the last century, Catholic social doctrine has been formulated in a progressive manner in a number of authoritative documents. Outstanding examples are the encyclicals: *Rerum Novarum*, issued by Leo XIII in 1891; *Quadragesimo Anno*, by Pius XI in 1931; *Mater et Magistra* ("Christianity and Social Progress") and *Pacem in Terris* ("Peace on Earth"), by John XXIII in 1961 and 1963, respectively; *Populorum Progressio* ("Development of Peoples"), by Paul VI in 1967; and *Laborem Exercens* ("On Human Work"), by John Paul II in 1981. Pius XII, among other accomplishments of ideological importance in the social field, made a distinctive contribution with his formulation of a plan for world peace and order in Christmas messages from 1939 to 1941, and in other documents.

These documents represent the most serious attempts in modern times to systematize the social implications of the Gospel and the rest of divine revelation as well as the socially relevant writings of the Fathers and Doctors of the Church. Their contents are theological penetrations into social life, with particular reference to human rights, the needs of the poor and those in underdeveloped countries, and humane conditions of life, freedom, justice and peace. In some respects, they read like juridical documents; underneath, however, they are Gospel-oriented and pastoral in intention.

### Nature of the Doctrine

Pope John XXIII, writing in *Christianity and Social Progress*, made the following statement about the nature and scope of the doctrine stated in the encyclicals in particular and related writings in general.

"What the Catholic Church teaches and declares regarding the social life and relationships of men is beyond question for all time valid.

"The cardinal point of this teaching is that individual men are necessarily the foundation, cause, and end of all social institutions . . . insofar as they are social by nature, and raised to an order of existence that transcends and subdues nature.

"Beginning with this very basic principle whereby the dignity of the human person is affirmed and defended, Holy Church — especially during the last century and with the assistance of learned priests and laymen, specialists in the field — has arrived at clear social teachings whereby the mutual relationships of men are ordered. Taking general norms into account, these principles are in accord with the nature of things and the changed conditions of man's social life, or with the special genius of our day. Moreover, these norms can be approved by all."

### The Church in the World

Even more Gospel-oriented and pastoral in a distinctive way is the *Pastoral Constitution on the Church in the Modern World* promulgated by the Second Vatican Council in 1965.

Its purpose is to search out the signs of God's presence and meaning in and through the events of this time in human history. Accordingly, it deals with the situation of men in present circumstances of profound change, challenge and crisis on all levels of life.

The first part of the constitution develops the theme of the Church and man's calling, and focuses attention on the dignity of the human person, the problem of atheism, the community of mankind, man's activity throughout the world, and the serving and saving role of the Church in the world. This portion of the document, it has been said, represents the first presentation by the Church in an official text of an organized Christian view of man and society.

The second part of the document considers several problems of special urgency: fostering the nobility of marriage and the family (see Marriage Doctrine), the proper development of culture, socio-economic life, the life of the political community, the fostering of peace (see Peace and War), and the promotion of a community of nations.

In conclusion, the constitution calls for action to implement doctrine regarding the role and work of the Church for the total good of mankind.

### Excerpts

*Following are a number of key excerpts from the ideological heart of the constitution.*

**One Human Family and Community:** God, who has fatherly concern for everyone, has willed that all men should constitute one family and treat one another in a spirit of brotherhood.

For this reason, love for God and neighbor is the first and greatest commandment. Sacred Scripture . . . teaches us that the love of God cannot be separated from love of neighbor. . . . To men growing daily more dependent on one another, and to a world becoming more unified every day, this truth proves to be of paramount importance (No. 24).

**Human Person Is Central:** Man's social nature makes it evident that the progress of the human person and the advance of society itself hinge on each other. For the beginning, the subject and the goal of all social institutions is and must be the human person, which for its part and by its very nature stands completely in need of social life. This social life is not something added on to man. Hence, through his dealings with others, through reciprocal duties and through fraternal dialogue, he develops all his gifts and is able to rise to his destiny.

**Influence of Social Circumstances:** But if by this social life the human person is greatly aided in responding to his destiny, even in its religious dimensions, it cannot be denied that men are often diverted from doing good and spurred toward evil by the social circumstances in which they live and are immersed from their birth. To be sure, the disturbances which so frequently occur in the social order result in part from the natural tensions of economic, political and social forms. But at a deeper level they flow from man's pride and selfishness, which contaminate even the social sphere. When the structure of affairs is flawed by the consequences of sin, man, already born with a bent toward evil, finds there new inducements to sin which cannot be overcome without strenuous efforts and the assistance of grace (No. 25).

**Human Necessities:** Every social group must take account of the needs and legitimate aspirations of other groups, and even of the general welfare of the entire human family.

At the same time, however, there is a growing awareness of the exalted dignity proper to the human person, since he stands above all things and his rights and duties are universal and inviolable. Therefore, there must be made available to all men everything necessary for leading a life truly human, such as food, clothing, and shelter; the right to choose a state of life freely and to found a family; the right to education, to employment, to a good reputation, to respect, to appropriate information, to activity in accord with the upright norm of one's own conscience, to protection of privacy and to rightful freedom in matters religious too.

Hence, the social order and its development must unceasingly work to the benefit of the human person if the disposition of affairs is to be subordinate to the personal realm and not contrariwise, as the Lord indicated when he said that the Sabbath was made for man, and not man for the Sabbath.

**Improvement of Social Order:** This social order requires constant improvement. It must be founded on truth, built on justice and animated by love; in freedom it should grow every day toward a more humane balance. An improvement in attitudes and widespread changes in society will have to take place if these objectives are to be gained.

God's Spirit, who with a marvelous providence directs the unfolding of time and renews the face of the earth, is not absent from this development. The ferment of the Gospel, too, has aroused and continues to arouse in man's heart the irresistible requirements of his dignity (No. 26).

**Regard for Neighbor as Another Self:** Coming down to practical and particularly urgent consequences, this Council lays stress on reverence for man; everyone must consider his every neighbor without exception as another self, taking into account first of all his life and the means necessary to living it with dignity.

In our times a special obligation binds us to make ourselves the neighbor of absolutely every person and to actively help him when he comes across our path.

**Inhuman Evils:** . . . Whatever is opposed to life itself, such as any type of murder, genocide, abortion, euthanasia, or willful self-destruction; whatever violates the integrity of the human person, such as mutilation, torments inflicted on body or mind, attempts to coerce the will itself; whatever insults human dignity, such as subhuman living conditions, arbitrary imprisonment, deportation, slavery, prostitution, the selling of women and children; as well as disgraceful working conditions, where men are treated as mere tools for profit rather than as free and responsible persons: all these things and others of their like are infamies indeed. They poison human society, but they do more harm to those who practice them than those who suffer from the injury. Moreover, they are a supreme dishonor to the Creator (No. 27).

**Respect for Those Who Are Different:** Respect and love ought to be extended also to those who think or act differently than we do in social, political and religious matters. In fact, the more deeply we come to understand their ways of thinking through such courtesy and love, the more easily will we be able to enter into dialogue with them.

**Distinction between Error and Persons in Error:** This love and good will, to be sure, must in no way render us indifferent to truth and goodness. Indeed, love itself impels the disciples of Christ to speak the saving truth to all men. But it is necessary to distinguish between error, which always merits repudiation, and the person in error, who never loses the dignity of being a person, even when he is flawed by false or inadequate religious notions. God alone is the judge and searcher of hearts; for that reason he forbids us to make judgments about the internal guilt of anyone.

The teaching of Christ even requires that we forgive injuries, and extends the law of love to include every enemy (No. 28).

**Men Are Equal but Different:** Since all men possess a rational soul and are created in God's likeness; since they have the same nature and origin, have been redeemed by Christ, and enjoy the same divine calling and destiny: the basic equality of all must receive increasingly greater recognition.

True, all men are not alike from the point of view of varying physical power and the diversity of intellectual and moral resources. Nevertheless, with respect to the fundamental rights of the person, every type of discrimination, whether social or cultural, whether based on sex, race, color, social condition, language or religion, is to be overcome and eradicated as contrary to God's intent.

**Humane Conditions for All:** Although rightful differences exist between men, the equal dignity of persons demands that a more humane and just condition of life be brought about. For excessive economic and social differences between the members of the one human family . . . cause scandal and militate against social justice, equity and the dignity of the human person as well as social and international peace.

Human institutions, both private and public, must labor to minister to the dignity and purpose of man. At the same time, let them put up a stubborn fight against any kind of slavery, whether social or political, and safeguard the basic rights of man under every political system. Indeed, human institutions themselves must be accommodated by degrees to the highest of all realities, spiritual ones, even though, meanwhile, a long enough time will be required before they arrive at the desired goal (No. 29).

Profound and rapid changes make it particularly urgent that no one, ignoring the trend of events or drugged by laziness, content himself with a merely individualistic morality. It grows increasingly true that the obligations of justice and love are fulfilled only if each person, contributing to the common good according to his own abilities and the needs of others, also promotes and assists the public and private institutions dedicated to bettering the conditions of human life.

**Social Necessities Are Prime Duties:** Let everyone consider it his sacred obligation to count social necessities among the primary duties of modern man and to pay heed to them. For the more unified the world becomes, the more plainly do the offices of men extend beyond particular groups and spread by degrees to the whole world. But this challenge cannot be met unless individual men and their associations cultivate in themselves the moral and social virtues and promote them in society.

Thus, with the needed help of divine grace, men who are truly new and artisans of a new humanity can be forthcoming (No. 30).

In order for individual men to discharge with greater exactness the obligations of their conscience toward themselves and the various groups to which they belong, they must be carefully educated to a higher degree of culture through the use of the immense resources available today to the human race.

**Living Conditions and Freedom:** A man can scarcely arrive at the needed sense of responsibility unless his living conditions allow him to become conscious of his dignity and to rise to his destiny by spending himself for God and for others. But human freedom is often crippled when a man falls into extreme poverty, just as it withers when he indulges in too many of life's comforts and imprisons himself in a kind of splendid isolation. Freedom acquires new strength, by contrast, when a man consents to the unavoidable requirements of social life, takes on the manifold demands of human partnership and commits himself to the service of the human community.

Hence, the will to play one's role in common endeavors should be everywhere encouraged (No. 31).

**Communitarian Character of Life:** God did not create man for life in isolation but for the formation of social unity. So also "it has pleased God to make men holy and save them not merely as individuals, without any mutual bonds, but by making them into a single people, a people which acknowledges him in truth and serves him in holiness" (*Dogmatic Constitution on the Church*, No. 9). So from the beginning of salvation history he has chosen men not just as individuals but as members of a certain community. Revealing his mind to them, God called these chosen ones "his people" (Ex. 3:7-12) and, furthermore, made a covenant with them on Sinai.

This communitarian character is developed and consummated in the work of Jesus Christ. For the very Word made flesh willed to share in the human fellowship. He was present at the wedding of Cana, visited the house of Zacchaeus, ate with publicans and sinners. He revealed the love of the Father and the sublime vocation of man in terms of the most common of social realities and by making use of the speech and the imagery of plain everyday life. Willingly obeying the laws of his country, he sanctified those human ties, especially family ones, from which social relationships arise. He chose to lead the life proper to an artisan of his time and place.

In his preaching he clearly taught the sons of God to treat one another as brothers. In his prayers he pleaded that all his disciples might be "one." Indeed, as the Redeemer of all, he offered himself for all even to the point of death. He commanded his Apostles to preach to all peoples the Gospel message so that the human race might become the Family of God, in which the fullness of the Law would be love.

**The Community Founded by Christ:** As the first-born of many brethren and through the gift of his Spirit, he founded after his death and resurrection a new brotherly community composed of all those who receive him in faith and in love. This he did through his Body, which is the Church. There everyone, as members one of the other, would render mutual service according to the different gifts bestowed on each.

This solidarity must be constantly increased until that day on which it is brought to perfection. Then, saved by grace, men will offer flawless glory to God as a family beloved of God and of Christ their Brother (No. 32).

## WORK

The nature of work, its relation to social issues and its significance, along with prayer, as the "way of sanctification," are among key subjects treated in Pope John Paul's third encyclical letter, *Laborem Exercens*. Following are several paragraphs from the encyclical delineating a definition of work together with capsule coverge of a number of salient points in the letter.

### Definition

"Through work man must earn his daily bread and contribute to the continual advance of science and technology and, above all, to elevating unceasingly the cultural and moral level of the society within which he lives in community with those who belong to the same family.

"And work means any activity by man, whether manual or intellectual, whatever its nature or circumstances; it means any human activity that can and must be recognized as work, in the midst of all the many activities of which man is capable and to which he is predisposed by his very nature, by virtue of humanity itself.

"Man is made to be in the visible universe an image and likeness of God himself, and he is placed in it in order to subdue the earth. From the beginning, therefore, he is called to work.

"Work is one of the characteristics that distinguish man from the rest of creatures, whose activity for sustaining their lives cannot be called work. Only man is capable of work and only man works, at the same time by work occupying his existence on earth. Thus, work bears a particular mark of man and of humanity, the mark of a person operating within a community of persons. And this mark decides its interior characteristics; in a sense, it constitutes its very nature."

### Salient Points

**Fundamental Criterion of Economics:** "Respect for the objective rights of the worker . . . must constitute the adequate and fundamental criterion for shaping the whole economy, both on the level of the individual society and state and within the whole of the world economic policy as well as the systems of international relationships that derive from it."

**Work and Family:** "Work constitutes a foundation of the formation of family life" by providing the economic means necessary to maintain a family.

**Just Wage:** "A just wage is the concrete means

of verifying the justice of the whole socio-economic system and, in any case, of checking that it is functioning justly."

**Family Wage:** A "family wage" is needed, "a single salary given to the head of the family for his work, sufficient for the needs of the family without the other spouse having to take up gainful employment outside the home," or without the need of recourse to other social provisions for aid.

**Women:** Women who work "should be able to fulfill their tasks in accordance with their own nature without being discriminated against and without being excluded from jobs for which they are capable." Respect is due "for their family aspirations and for their specific role in contributing, together with men, to the good of society."

**Mothers:** Provisions should be made for "measures such as family allowances or grants to mothers devoting themselves exclusively to their families."

**Unions:** Workers have the right to form a union to protect their vital interests and to be "a mouthpiece for the struggle for social justice."

"Union activity undoubtedly enters the field of politics, understood as prudent concern for the common good." But unions should not engage in partisan politics; otherwise, "they become an instrument used for other purposes."

**Strike:** Workers should be assured the right to strike without being subject to personal sanctions, but have the responsibility of not striking if a strike "is contrary to requirements of the common good."

**Unemployment Benefits:** "The obligation to provide unemployment benefits . . . is a duty springing from the fundamental principle of the common use of goods or, to put it in another way, the right to life and subsistence."

**Disabled Persons:** Society should provide work for disabled persons in keeping with their physical disabilities. Failure to do so means "a serious form of discrimination, that of the strong and healthy against the weak and sick."

**Health Care:** "The expenses involved in health care, especially in the case of accidents at work, demand that medical assistance should be easily available for workers."

**Technology:** It is meant to be the worker's ally but can become his enemy when mechanization supplants him or takes away "all personal satisfaction and the incentive to creativity and responsibility," thus reducing "man to the status of slave."

**Haves and Have-Nots:** "A disconcerting fact of immense proportions" occurs on the world scene. "While conspicuous natural resources remain unused, there are huge numbers of people who are unemployed or underemployed, and countless multitudes of people suffering from hunger." This means that there is "something wrong with the organization of work and employment" on national and international levels.

**Foreign Workers:** People have a right to emigrate in search of work. "The person working away from his native land, whether as a permanent emigrant or as a seasonal worker, should not be placed at a disadvantage in comparison with the workers in that society in the matter of working rights. Emigration in search of work must in no way become an opportunity for financial or social exploitation."

**Marxism:** Catholic social teaching "diverges radically from the program of collectivism proclaimed by Marxism and put into practice in various countries."

**Private Property and Capitalism:** "Christian tradition has never upheld" the right to private property "as absolute and untouchable. On the contrary, it has always understood this right common to all to use the goods of the whole creation."

"Deeply desired reforms" of capitalism "cannot be achieved by an *a priori* elimination of private ownership of the means of production." This is not sufficient to insure "satisfactory socialization" because new managers form another special group "from the fact of exercising power in society. This group . . . may carry out this task badly by claiming for itself a monopoly of the administration and disposal of the means of production and not refraining even from offending basic human rights."

**Exploitation by Multinationals:** "The highly industrialized countries, and even more so the businesses that direct on a large scale the means of industrial production, fix the highest possible prices for their products while trying at the same time to fix the lowest possible prices for raw materials or semi-manufactured goods."

## PEACE AND WAR

*The following excerpts, stating principles and objectives of social doctrine concerning peace and war, are from the "Pastoral Constitution on the Church in the Modern World" (Nos. 77 to 82) promulgated by the Second Vatican Council.*

*(See also: "The Challenge of Peace: God's Promise and Our Purpose.")*

**Call to Peace:** This Council fervently desires to summon Christians to cooperate with all men in making secure among themselves a peace based on justice and love, and in setting up agencies of peace. This Christians should do with the help of Christ, the Author of peace (No. 77).

**Conditions for Peace:** Peace is not merely the absence of war. Nor can it be reduced solely to the maintenance of a balance of power between enemies. Nor is it brought about by dictatorship. Instead, it is rightly and appropriately called "an enterprise of justice" (Is. 32:7). Peace results from that harmony built into human society by its divine Founder and actualized by men as they thirst after ever greater justice.

The common good of men is in its basic sense determined by the eternal law. Still the concrete demands of this common good are constantly changing as time goes on. Hence peace is never attained once and for all, but must be built up ceaselessly. Moreover, since the human will is unsteady and wounded by sin, the achievement of peace requires that everyone constantly master his passions and that lawful authority keep vigilant.

But such is not enough. This peace cannot be obtained on earth unless personal values are safeguarded and men freely and trustingly share with one another the riches of their inner spirits and their talents. A firm determination to respect other men and peoples and their dignity, as well as the studied practice of brotherhood, are absolutely necessary for the establishment of peace. Hence peace is likewise the fruit of love, which goes beyond what justice can provide.

**Renunciation of Violence:** We cannot fail to praise those who renounce the use of violence in the vindication of their rights and who resort to methods of defense which are otherwise available to weaker parties too, provided that this can be done without injury to the rights and duties of others or of the community itself (No. 78).

**Mass Extermination:** The Council wishes to recall first of all the permanent binding force of universal natural law and its all-embracing principles. Man's conscience itself gives ever more emphatic voice to these principles. Therefore, actions which deliberately conflict with these same principles, as well as orders commanding such actions, are criminal. Blind obedience cannot excuse those who yield to them. Among such must first be counted those actions designed for the methodical extermination of an entire people, nation, or ethnic minority. These actions must be vehemently condemned as horrendous crimes. The courage of those who openly and fearlessly resist men who issue such commands merits supreme commendation.

**International Agreements:** On the subject of war, quite a large number of nations have subscribed to various international agreements aimed at making military activity and its consequences less inhuman. Such are conventions concerning the handling of wounded or captured soldiers, and various similar agreements. Agreements of this sort must be honored. They should be improved upon.

**Conscientious Objectors:** It seems right that laws make humane provisions for the case of those who for reasons of conscience refuse to bear arms, provided, however, that they accept some other form of service to the human community.

**Legitimate Defense:** Certainly, war has not been rooted out of human affairs. As long as the danger of war remains and there is no competent and sufficiently powerful authority at the international level, governments cannot be denied the right to legitimate defense once every means of peaceful settlement has been exhausted. Therefore, government authorities and others who share public responsibility have the duty to protect the welfare of the people entrusted to their care and to conduct such grave matters soberly.

But it is one thing to undertake military action for the just defense of the people, and something else again to seek the subjugation of other nations. Nor does the possession of war potential make every military or political use of it lawful. Neither does the mere fact that war has unhappily begun mean that all is fair between the warring parties.

**Nature of Military Service:** Those who are pledged to the service of their country as members of its armed forces should regard themselves as agents of security and freedom on behalf of their people. As long as they fulfill this role properly, they are making a genuine contribution to the establishment of peace (No. 79).

**Total War Condemned:** This most holy Synod makes its own the condemnations of total war already pronounced by recent popes, and issues the following declaration:

Any act of war aimed indiscriminately at the destruction of entire cities or of extensive areas along with their population is a crime against God and man himself. It merits unequivocal and unhesitating condemnation.

The unique hazard of modern warfare consists in this: it provides those who possess modern scientific weapons with a kind of occasion for perpetrating just such abominations. Moreover, through a certain inexorable chain of events, it can urge men on to the most atrocious decisions. That such in fact may never happen in the future, the bishops of the whole world, in unity assembled, beg all men, especially government officials and military leaders, to give unremitting thought to the awesome responsibility which is theirs before God and the entire human race (No. 80).

**Retaliation and Deterrence:** Scientific weapons, to be sure, are not amassed solely for use in war. The defensive strength of any nation is considered to be dependent upon its capacity for immediate retaliation against an adversary. Hence this accumulation of arms, which increases each year, also serves, in a way heretofore unknown, as a deterrent to possible enemy attack. Many regard this state of affairs as the most effective way by which peace of a sort can be maintained between nations at the present time.

**Arms Race:** Whatever be the case with this method of deterrence, men should be convinced that the arms race in which so many countries are engaged is not a safe way to preserve a steady peace. Nor is the so-called balance resulting from this race a sure and authentic peace. Rather than being eliminated thereby, the causes of war threaten to grow gradually stronger.

While extravagant sums are being spent for the furnishing of ever new weapons, an adequate remedy cannot be provided for the multiple miseries afflicting the whole modern world. Disagreements between nations are not really and radically healed. On the contrary, other parts of the world are infected with them. New approaches initiated by reformed attitudes must be adopted to remove this trap and to restore genuine peace by emancipating the world from its crushing anxiety.

Therefore, it must be said again: the arms race is an utterly treacherous trap for humanity, and one which injures the poor to an intolerable degree. It is much to be feared that, if this race persists, it will eventually spawn all the lethal ruin whose path it is now making ready (No. 81).

**Outlaw War:** It is our clear duty, then, to strain every muscle as we work for the time when all war can be completely outlawed by international consent. This goal undoubtedly requires the establishment of some universal public authority acknowledged as such by all, and endowed with effective power to safeguard, on behalf of all, security, regard for justice, and respect for rights.

**Multilateral and Controlled Disarmament:** But before this hoped-for authority can be set up, the highest existing international centers must devote themselves vigorously to the pursuit of better means for obtaining common security. Peace must be born of mutual trust between nations rather than imposed on them through fear of one another's weapons. Hence everyone must labor to put an end at last to the arms race, and to make a true beginning of disarmament, not indeed a unilateral disarmament, but one proceeding at an equal pace according to agreement, and backed up by authentic and workable safeguards.

In the meantime, efforts which have already been made and are still under way to eliminate the danger of war are not to be underrated. On the contrary, support should be given to the good will of the very many leaders who work hard to do away with war, which they abominate.

**Public Opinion:** Men should take heed not to entrust themselves only to the efforts of others, while remaining careless about their own attitudes. For government officials, who must simultaneously guarantee the good of their own people and promote the universal good, depend on public opinion and feeling to the greatest possible extent. It does them no good to work at building peace so long as feelings of hostility, contempt, and distrust, as well as racial hatred and unbending ideologies, continue to divide men and place them in opposing camps.

Hence arises a surpassing need for renewed education of attitudes and for new inspiration in the area of public opinion. Those who are dedicated to the work of education . . . should regard as their most weighty task the effort to instruct all in fresh sentiments of peace (No. 82).

## COMMUNISM

The substantive principles of modern Communism, a theory and system of economics and social organization, were stated about the middle of the 19th century by Karl Marx, author of *The Communist Manifesto* and, with Friedrich Engels, *Das Kapital*.

The elements of Communist ideology include: radical materialism; dialectical determinism; the inevitability of class struggle, which is to be furthered for the ultimate establishment of a worldwide, classless society; common ownership of productive and other goods; the subordination of all persons and institutions to the dictatorship of the collectivity; denial of the rights, dignity and liberty of persons; militant atheism and hostility to religion; utilitarian morality.

Communism in theory and practice has been the subject of many papal documents and statements. Pius IX condemned it in 1846. Leo XIII dealt with it at length in the encyclicals *Quod Apostolici Muneris* in 1878 and *Rerum Novarum* in 1891. Pius XI wrote on the same subject the encyclicals *Quadragesimo Anno* in 1931 and *Divini Redemptoris* in 1937. These writings were updated and developed in new directions by Pius XII, John XXIII, Paul VI and John Paul II.

## THE CHALLENGE OF PEACE:
## GOD'S PROMISE AND OUR RESPONSE

*Following is an excerpt from a summary of the pastoral letter, "The Challenge of Peace: God's Promise and Our Response," copyright* © *1983 by the United States Catholic Conference, all rights reserved. A copy of the complete text can be ordered from the Office of Publishing Services, USCC, 1312 Massachusetts Ave. N.W., Washington, D.C. 20005. The letter was approved by a vote of 238 to 9 at a special meeting of U.S. bishops May 2 and 3, 1983, in Chicago.*

## I. SOME PRINCIPLES, NORMS AND PREMISES OF CATHOLIC TEACHING

### A. On War

1. Catholic teaching begins in every case with a presumption against war and for peaceful settlement of disputes. In exceptional cases, determined by the moral principles of the just-war tradition, some uses of force are permitted.

2. Every nation has a right and duty to defend itself against unjust aggression.

3. Offensive war of any kind is not morally justifiable.

4. It is never permitted to direct nuclear or conventional weapons to "the indiscriminate destruction of whole cities or vast areas with their populations. . . ." *(Pastoral Constitution on the Church in the Modern World*, No. 80.) The intentional killing of innocent civilians or non-combatants is always wrong.

5. Even defensive response to unjust attack can cause destruction which violates the principle of proportionality, going far beyond the limits of legitimate defense. This judgment is particularly important when assessing planned use of nuclear weapons. No defensive strategy, nuclear or conventional, which exceeds the limits of proportionality is morally permissible.

### B. On Deterrence

1. "In current conditions 'deterrence' based on balance, certainly not as an end in itself but as a step on the way toward a progressive disarmament, may still be judged morally acceptable. Nonetheless, in order to ensure peace, it is indispensable not to be satisfied with this minimum which is always susceptible to the real danger of explosion." (Pope John Paul II, Message to U.N. Special Session on Disarmament, No. 8, June, 1982.)

2. No *use* of nuclear weapons which would violate the principles of discrimination or proportionality may be *intended* in a strategy of deterrence. The moral demands of Catholic teaching require resolute willingness not to intend or to do moral evil even to save our own lives or the lives of those we love.

3. Deterrence is not an adequate strategy as a long-term basis for peace; it is a transitional strategy justifiable only in conjunction with resolute determination to pursue arms control and dis-

armament. We are convinced that "the fundamental principle on which our present peace depends must be replaced by another, which declares that the true and solid peace of nations consists not in equality of arms but in mutual trust alone." (Pope John XXIII, Encyclical *Peace on Earth*, No. 113.)

### C. The Arms Race and Disarmament

1. The arms race is one of the greatest curses on the human race; it is to be condemned as a danger, an act of aggression against the poor, and a folly which does not provide the security it promises. (Cf. *Pastoral Constitution*, No. 81; Statement of the Holy See to the United Nations, 1976.)

2. Negotiations must be pursued in every reasonable form possible; they should be governed by the "demand that the arms race should cease; that the stockpiles which exist in various countries should be reduced equally and simultaneously by the parties concerned; that nuclear weapons should be banned; and that a general agreement should eventually be reached about progressive disarmament and an effective method of control." (Pope John XXIII, *Peace on Earth*, No. 112.)

### D. On Personal Conscience

1. *Military Service:* "All those who enter the military service in loyalty to their country should look upon themselves as the custodians of the security and freedom of their fellow countrymen; and when they carry out their duty properly, they are contributing to the maintenance of peace." *(Pastoral Constitution*, No. 79.)

2. *Conscientious Objection:* "Moreover, it seems just that laws should make humane provision for the case of conscientious objectors who refuse to carry arms, provided they accept some other form of community service." *(Pastoral Constitution*, No. 79.)

3. *Non-violence:* "In this same spirit we cannot but express our admiration for all who forego the use of violence to vindicate their rights and resort to other means of defense which are available to weaker parties, provided it can be done without harm to the rights and duties of others and of the community." *(Pastoral Constitution*, No. 78.)

4. *Citizens and Conscience:* "Once again we deem it opportune to remind our children of their duty to take an active part in public life, and to contribute towards the attainment of the common good of the entire human family as well as to that of their own political community. . . . In other words, it is necessary that human beings, in the intimacy of their own consciences, should so live and act in their temporal lives as to create a synthesis between scientific, technical and professional elements on the one hand, and spiritual values on the other." (Pope John XXIII, *Peace on Earth*, Nos. 146, 150.)

## II. MORAL PRINCIPLES AND POLICY CHOICES

As bishops in the United States, assessing the concrete circumstances of our society, we have made a number of observations and recommendations in the process of applying moral principles to specific policy choices.

## A. On the Use of Nuclear Weapons

1. *Counter Population Use:* Under no circumstances may nuclear weapons or other instruments of mass slaughter be used for the purpose of destroying population centers or other predominantly civilian targets. Retaliatory action which would indiscriminately and disproportionately take many wholly innocent lives, lives of people who are in no way responsible for reckless actions of their government, must also be condemned.

2. *The Initiation of Nuclear War:* We do not perceive any situation in which the deliberate initiation of nuclear war, on however restricted a scale, can be morally justified. Non-nuclear attacks by another state must be resisted by other than nuclear means. Therefore, a serious moral obligation exists to develop non-nuclear defensive strategies as rapidly as possible. In this letter we urge NATO to move rapidly toward the adoption of a "no first use" policy, but we recognize this will take time to implement and will require the development of an adequate alternative defense posture.

3. *Limited Nuclear War:* Our examination of the various arguments on this question makes us highly skeptical about the real meaning of "limited." One of the criteria of the just-war teaching is that there must be a reasonable hope of success in bringing about justice and peace. We must ask whether such a reasonable hope can exist once nuclear weapons have been exchanged. The burden of proof remains on those who assert that meaningful limitation is possible. In our view the first imperative is to prevent any use of nuclear weapons and we hope that leaders will resist the notion that nuclear conflict can be limited, contained or won in any traditional sense.

## B. On Deterrence

In concert with the evaluation provided by Pope John Paul II, we have arrived at a strictly conditional moral acceptance of deterrence. In this letter we have outlined criteria and recommendations which indicate the meaning of conditional acceptance of deterrence policy. We cannot consider such a policy adequate as a long-term basis for peace.

## C. On Promoting Peace

1. We support immediate, bilateral, verifiable agreements to halt the testing, production and deployment of new nuclear weapons systems. This recommendation is not to be identified with any specific political initiative.

2. We support efforts to achieve deep cuts in the arsenals of both superpowers; efforts should concentrate first on systems which threaten the retaliatory forces of either major power.

3. We support early and successful conclusion of negotiations of a comprehensive test ban treaty.

4. We urge new efforts to prevent the spread of nuclear weapons in the world, and to control the conventional arms race, particularly the conventional arms trade.

5. We support, in an increasingly interdependent world, political and economic policies designed to protect human dignity and to promote the human rights of every person, especially the least among us. In this regard, we call for the establishment of some form of global authority adequate to the needs of the international common good.

This letter includes many judgments from the perspective of ethics, politics and strategy needed to speak concretely and correctly to the "moment of supreme crisis" identified by Vatican II. We stress again that readers should be aware, as we have been, of the distinction between our statement of moral principles and of official Church teaching and our application of these to concrete issues. We urge that special care be taken not to use passages out of context; neither should brief portions of this document be cited to support positions it does not intend to convey or which are not truly in accord with the spirit of its teaching.

---

## JUBILEE YEAR 1983-84

The 394-day celebration of the 1950th anniversary of the Redemption came to a close on Easter Sunday, Apr. 22, 1984, as Pope John Paul closed the Holy Door of St. Peter's Basilica before a throng of 250,000 people. As he did so, the Holy Father said that, even though the Holy Door was being closed, "we know with certainty that the door of (God's) mercy is never closed for those who believe in (his) love."

The extended Holy Year brought record crowds of tourists to Rome, totaling an estimated 15 million, more than during any other similar observance. Some of the largest crowds were those which attended special celebrations, like those for youths (250,000), families (100,000) and workers (60,000). The greatest surge in attendance came during the last three months of the Jubilee. About 20 per cent of the non-Italian pilgrims during the year were Americans.

The Jubilee observance was unique inasmuch as it was celebrated at the same time in Rome and throughout the world — not in Rome first for a year and then in the rest of the world, in the ordinary manner of observance. The Jubilee Indulgence, however, was the same — full remission of temporal punishment due for sins already forgiven, to be gained by members of the faithful free of all attachment to sin and fulfilling the required conditions.

Celebrations in 22 U.S. dioceses during the first six months of the Jubilee were singled out for recognition and praise in the Sept. 28, 1983, edition of *L'Osservatore Romano.*

It would be difficult to estimate the spiritual benefits accruing to individuals and the Church during and subsequent to the Jubilee celebration.

The nature and purpose of the liturgy, along with norms for its revision, were the subject matter of the "Constitution on the Sacred Liturgy" promulgated by the Second Vatican Council. The principles and guidelines stated in this document, the first issued by the Council, are summarized here and/or are incorporated in other Almanac entries on liturgical subjects.

## Nature and Purpose of Liturgy

The paragraphs under this and the following subhead are quoted directly from the "Constitution on the Sacred Liturgy."

"It is through the liturgy, especially the divine Eucharistic Sacrifice, that 'the work of our redemption is exercised.' The liturgy is thus the outstanding means by which the faithful can express in their lives, and manifest to others, the mystery of Christ and the real nature of the true Church . . ." (No. 2).

"The liturgy is considered as an exercise of the priestly office of Jesus Christ. In the liturgy the sanctification of man is manifested by signs perceptible to the senses, and is effected in a way which is proper to each of these signs; in the liturgy full public worship is performed by the Mystical Body of Jesus Christ, that is, by the Head and his members.

"From this it follows that every liturgical celebration, because it is an action of Christ the priest and of his Body the Church, is a sacred action surpassing all others. No other action of the Church can match its claim to efficacy, nor equal the degree of it" (No. 7).

"The liturgy is the summit toward which the activity of the Church is directed; at the same time it is the fountain from which all her power flows. For the goal of apostolic works is that all who are made sons of God by faith and baptism should come together to praise God in the midst of his Church, to take part in her sacrifice, and to eat the Lord's Supper.

". . . From the liturgy, therefore, and especially from the Eucharist, as from a fountain, grace is channeled into us; and the sanctification of men in Christ and the glorification of God, to which all other activities of the Church are directed as toward their goal, are most powerfully achieved" (No. 10).

## Full Participation

"Mother Church earnestly desires that all the faithful be led to that full, conscious, and active participation in liturgical celebrations which is demanded by the very nature of the liturgy. Such participation by the Christian people as 'a chosen race, a royal priesthood, a holy nation, a purchased people' (1 Pt. 2:9; cf. 2:4-5), is their right and duty by reason of their baptism.

"In the restoration and promotion of the sacred liturgy, this full and active participation by all the people is the aim to be considered before all else; for it is the primary and indispensable source from which the faithful are to derive the true Christian spirit . . ." (No. 14).

"In order that the Christian people may more securely derive an abundance of graces from the sacred liturgy, holy Mother Church desires to undertake with great care a general restoration of the liturgy itself. For the liturgy is made up of unchangeable elements divinely instituted, and elements subject to change. The latter not only may but ought to be changed with the passing of time if features have by chance crept in which are less harmonious with the intimate nature of the liturgy, or if existing elements have grown less functional.

"In this restoration, both texts and rites should be drawn up so that they express more clearly the holy things which they signify. Christian people, as far as possible, should be able to understand them with ease and to take part in them fully, actively, and as befits a community . . ." (No. 21).

## Norms

Norms regarding the reforms concern the greater use of Scripture; emphasis on the importance of the sermon or homily on biblical and liturgical subjects; use of vernacular languages for prayers of the Mass and for administration of the sacraments; provision for adaptation of rites to cultural patterns.

Approval for reforms of various kinds — in liturgical texts, rites, etc. — depends on the Holy See, regional conferences of bishops and individual bishops, according to provisions of law. No priest has authority to initiate reforms on his own. Reforms may not be introduced just for the sake of innovation, and any that are introduced in the light of present-day circumstances should embody sound tradition.

To assure the desired effect of liturgical reforms, training and instruction are necessary for the clergy, religious and the laity. The functions of diocesan and regional commissions for liturgy, music and art are to set standards and provide leadership for instruction and practical programs in their respective fields.

Most of the constitution's provisions regarding liturgical reforms have to do with the Roman Rite. The document clearly respects the equal dignity of all rites, leaving to the Eastern Churches control over their ancient liturgies.

(For coverage of the **Mystery of the Eucharist,** see The Mass; **Other Sacraments,** see separate entries.)

## Sacramentals

Sacramentals, instituted by the Church, "are sacred signs which bear a resemblance to the sacraments: they signify effects, particularly of a spiritual kind, which are obtained through the Church's intercession. By them men are disposed to receive the chief effect of the sacraments, and various occasions in life are rendered holy" (No. 60).

"Thus, for well-disposed members of the faithful, the liturgy of the sacraments and sacramentals sanctifies almost every event in their lives; they are given access to the stream of divine grace which flows from the paschal mystery of the passion, death, and resurrection of Christ, the fountain from which all sacraments and sacramentals draw their power. There is hardly any proper use of material things which cannot thus be directed toward the sanctification of men and the praise of God" (No. 61).

Some common sacramentals are priestly blessings, blessed palm, candles, holy water, medals, scapulars, prayers and ceremonies of the Roman Ritual.

### Liturgy of the Hours

The Liturgy of the Hours (Divine Office) is the public prayer of the Church for praising God and sanctifying the day. Its daily celebration is required as a sacred obligation by men in holy orders and by men and women religious who have professed solemn vows. Its celebration by others is highly commended and is to be encouraged in the community of the faithful.

"By tradition going back to early Christian times, the Divine Office is arranged so that the whole course of the day and night is made holy by the praises of God. Therefore, when this wonderful song of praise is worthily rendered by priests and others who are deputed for this purpose by Church ordinance, or by the faithful praying together with the priest in an approved form, then it is truly the voice of the bride addressing her bridegroom; it is the very prayer which Christ himself, together with his Body, addresses to the Father" (No. 84).

"Hence all who perform this service are not only fulfilling a duty of the Church, but also are sharing in the greatest honor accorded to Christ's spouse, for by offering these praises to God they are standing before God's throne in the name of the Church their Mother" (No. 85).

The Liturgy of the Hours, revised since 1965, was the subject of Pope Paul VI's apostolic constitution *Laudis Canticum,* dated Nov. 1, 1970. The master Latin text was published in 1971; its four volumes have been published in authorized English translation since May, 1975.

One-volume, partial editions of the Liturgy of the Hours containing Morning and Evening Prayer and other elements, have been published in approved English translation.

The revised Liturgy of the Hours consists of:

• Office of Readings, for reflection on the word of God. The principal parts are three psalms, biblical and non-biblical readings.

• Morning and Evening Prayer, called the "hinges" of the Liturgy of the Hours. The principal parts are a hymn, two psalms, an Old or New Testament canticle, a brief biblical reading, Zechariah's canticle (the *Benedictus,* morning) or Mary's canticle (the *Magnificat,* evening), responsories, intercessions and a concluding prayer.

• Daytime Prayer. The principal parts are a hymn, three psalms, a brief biblical reading and one of three concluding prayers corresponding to

the time at which the prayer is offered (midmorning, midday, midafternoon).

• Night Prayer: The principal parts are one or two psalms, a brief biblical reading, Simeon's canticle *(Nunc Dimittis),* a concluding prayer and an antiphon in honor of Mary.

In the revised Liturgy of the Hours, the hours are shorter than they had been, with greater textual variety, meditation aids, and provision for intervals of silence and meditation. The psalms are distributed over a four-week period instead of a week; some psalms, entirely or in part, are not included. Additional canticles from the Old and New Testaments are assigned for Morning and Evening Prayer. Additional scriptural texts have been added and variously arranged for greater internal unity, correspondence to readings at Mass, and relevance to events and themes of salvation history. Readings include some of the best material from the Fathers of the Church and other authors, and improved selections on the lives of saints.

The book used for recitation of the Office is the **Breviary.**

For coverage of the **Liturgical Year,** see Church Calendar.

### Sacred Music

"The musical tradition of the universal Church is a treasure of immeasurable value, greater even than that of any other art. The main reason for this pre-eminence is that, as sacred melody united to words, it forms a necessary or integral part of the solemn liturgy.

". . . Sacred music increases in holiness to the degree that it is intimately linked with liturgical action, winningly expresses prayerfulness, promotes solidarity, and enriches sacred rites with heightened solemnity. The Church indeed approves of all forms of true art, and admits them into divine worship when they show appropriate qualities" (No. 112).

The constitution decreed:

• Vernacular languages for the people's parts of the liturgy, as well as Latin, may be used.

• Participation in sacred song by the whole body of the faithful, and not just by choirs, is to be encouraged and brought about.

• Provisions should be made for proper musical training for clergy, religious and lay persons.

• While Gregorian Chant has a unique dignity and relationship to the Latin liturgy, other kinds of music are acceptable.

• Native musical traditions should be used, especially in mission areas.

• Various instruments compatible with the dignity of worship may be used.

**Gregorian Chant:** A form and style of chant called Gregorian was the basis and most highly regarded standard of liturgical music for centuries. It originated probably during the formative period of the Roman liturgy and developed in conjunction with Gallican and other forms of chant. Gregory the Great's connection with it is not clear, although it is known that he had great concern for and interest in church music. The earliest extant written versions of Gregorian Chant date from the ninth century. A thousand years later, the Benedictines of Solesmes, France, initiated a revival of chant which gave impetus to the modern liturgical movement.

### Sacred Art and Furnishings

"Very rightly the fine arts are considered to rank among the noblest expressions of human genius. This judgment applies especially to religious art and to its highest achievement, which is sacred art. By their very nature both of the latter are related to God's boundless beauty, for this is the reality which these human efforts are trying to express in some way. To the extent that these works aim exclusively at turning men's thoughts to God persuasively and devoutly, they are dedicated to God and to the cause of his greater honor and glory" (No. 122).

The objective of sacred art is "that all things set apart for use in divine worship should be truly worthy, becoming, and beautiful, signs and symbols of heavenly realities. . . . The Church has . . . always reserved to herself the right to pass judgment upon the arts, deciding which of the works of artists are in accordance with faith, piety, and cherished traditional laws, and thereby suited to sacred purposes.

". . . Sacred furnishings should worthily and beautifully serve the dignity of worship . . ." (No. 122).

According to the constitution:

• Contemporary art, as well as that of the past, shall "be given free scope in the Church, provided that it adorns the sacred buildings and holy rites with due honor and reverence . . ." (No. 123).

• Noble beauty, not sumptuous display, should be sought in art, sacred vestments and ornaments.

• "Let bishops carefully exclude from the house of God and from other sacred places those works of artists which are repugnant to faith, morals, and Christian piety, and which offend true religious sense either by their distortion of forms or by lack of artistic worth, by mediocrity or by pretense.

• "When churches are to be built, let great care be taken that they be suitable for the celebration of liturgical services and for the active participation of the faithful" (No. 124).

• "The practice of placing sacred images in churches so that they may be venerated by the faithful is to be firmly maintained. Nevertheless, their number should be moderate and their relative location should reflect right order. Otherwise they may create confusion among the Christian people and promote a faulty sense of devotion" (No. 125).

• Artists should be trained and inspired in the spirit and for the purposes of the liturgy.

• The norms of sacred art should be revised. "These laws refer especially to the worthy and well-planned construction of sacred buildings, the shape and construction of altars, the nobility, location, and security of the Eucharistic tabernacle, the suitability and dignity of the baptistery, the proper use of sacred images, embellishments, and vestments . . ." (No. 128).

## RITES

Rites are the forms and ceremonial observances of liturgical worship coupled with the total expression of the theological, spiritual and disciplinary heritages of particular churches of the East and the West.

Different rites have evolved in the course of church history, giving to liturgical worship and church life in general forms and usages peculiar and proper to the nature of worship and the culture of the faithful in various circumstances of time and place. Thus, there has been development since apostolic times in the prayers and ceremonies of the Mass, in the celebration of the sacraments, sacramentals and the Liturgy of the Hours, and in observances of the liturgical calendar. The principal sources of rites in present use were practices within the patriarchates of Rome (for the West) and Antioch, Alexandria and Constantinople (for the East). Rites are identified as Eastern or Western on the basis of their geographical area of origin in the Roman Empire.

### Eastern and Roman

Eastern Rites are proper to Eastern Catholic Churches (see separate entry). The principal rites are Byzantine, Alexandrian, Antiochene, Armenian and Chaldean.

The Latin or Roman Rite prevails in the Western Church. It was derived from Roman practices and the use of Latin from the third century onward, and has been the rite in general use in the West since the eighth century. Other rites in limited use in the Western Church have been the Ambrosian (in the Archdiocese of Milan), the Mozarabic (in the Archdiocese of Toledo), the Lyonnais, the Braga, and rites peculiar to some religious orders like the Dominicans, Carmelites and Carthusians.

The purpose of the revision of rites in progress since the Second Vatican Council is to renew them, not to eliminate the rites of particular churches or to reduce all rites to uniformity. The Council reaffirmed the equal dignity and preservation of rites as follows.

"It is the mind of the Catholic Church that each individual church or rite retain its traditions whole and entire, while adjusting its way of life to various needs of time and place. Such individual churches, whether of the East or the West, although they differ somewhat among themselves in what are called rites (that is, in liturgy, ecclesiastical discipline and spiritual heritage), are, nevertheless, equally entrusted to the pastoral guidance of the Roman Pontiff, the divinely appointed successor of St. Peter in supreme government over the universal Church. They are, consequently, of equal dignity, so that none of them is superior to the others by reason of rite."

### Determination of Rite

Determination of a person's rite is regulated by church law. Through baptism, a child becomes a member of the rite of his or her parents. If the parents are of different rites, the child's rite is decided by mutual consent of the parents; if there is lack of mutual consent, the child is baptized in the rite of the father. A candidate for baptism over the age of 14 can choose to be baptized in any approved rite. Catholics baptized in one rite may receive the sacraments in any of the approved ritual churches; they may transfer to another rite only with the permission of the Holy See and in accordance with other provisions of the Code of Canon Law.

## MASS, EUCHARISTIC SACRIFICE AND BANQUET

### Declarations of Vatican II

The Second Vatican Council made the following declarations, among others, with respect to the Mass.

"At the Last Supper, on the night when he was betrayed, our Savior instituted the Eucharistic Sacrifice of his Body and Blood. He did this in order to perpetuate the Sacrifice of the Cross throughout the centuries until he should come again, and so to entrust to his beloved spouse, the Church, a memorial of his death and resurrection: a sacrament of love, a sign of unity, a bond of charity, a paschal banquet in which Christ is consumed, the mind is filled with grace, and a pledge of future glory is given to us" (*Constitution on the Sacred Liturgy,* No. 47).

". . . As often as the Sacrifice of the Cross in which 'Christ, our Passover, has been sacrificed' (1 Cor. 5:7) is celebrated on an altar, the work of our redemption is carried on. At the same time, in the sacrament of the Eucharistic bread the unity of all believers who form one body in Christ (cf. 1 Cor. 10:17) is both expressed and brought about. All men are called to this union with Christ . . ." (*Dogmatic Constitution on the Church.* No. 3).

". . . The ministerial priest, by the sacred power he enjoys, molds and rules the priestly people. Acting in the person of Christ, he brings about the Eucharistic Sacrifice, and offers it to God in the name of all the people. For their part, the faithful join in the offering of the Eucharist by virtue of their royal priesthood . . ." (*Ibid.,* No. 10).

### Declarations of Trent

Among its decrees on the Holy Eucharist, the Council of Trent stated the following points of doctrine on the Mass.

1. There is in the Catholic Church a true Sacrifice, the Mass instituted by Jesus Christ. It is the Sacrifice of his Body and Blood, Soul and Divinity, himself, under the appearances of bread and wine.

2. This Sacrifice is identical with the Sacrifice of the Cross, inasmuch as Christ is the Priest and Victim in both. A difference lies in the manner of offering, which was bloody upon the Cross and is bloodless on the altar.

3. The Mass is a propitiatory Sacrifice, atoning for sins of the living and dead for whom it is offered.

4. The efficacy of the Mass is derived from the Sacrifice of the Cross, whose superabundant merits it applies to men.

5. Although the Mass is offered to God alone, it may be celebrated in honor and memory of the saints.

6. Christ instituted the Mass at the Last Supper.

7. Christ ordained the Apostles priests, giving them power and the command to consecrate his Body and Blood to perpetuate and renew the Sacrifice.

### ORDER OF MASS

The Mass consists of two principal divisions called the **Liturgy of the Word**, which features the proclamation of the Word of God, and the **Eucharistic Liturgy**, which focuses on the central act of sacrifice in the Consecration and on the Eucharistic Banquet in Holy Communion. (Formerly, these divisions were called, respectively, the **Mass of the Catechumens** and the **Mass of the Faithful.**) In addition to these principal divisions, there are ancillary introductory and concluding rites.

The following description covers the Mass as celebrated with participation by the people. This Order of the Mass was approved by Pope Paul VI in the apostolic constitution *Missale Romanum* dated Apr. 3, 1969, and promulgated in a decree issued Apr. 6, 1969, by the Congregation for Divine Worship. The assigned effective date was Nov. 30, 1969.

### Introductory Rites

**Entrance:** The introductory rites begin with the singing or recitation of an entrance song consisting of one or more scriptural verses stating the theme of the mystery, season or feast commemorated in the Mass.

**Greeting:** The priest and people make the Sign of the Cross together. The priest then greets them in one of several alternative ways and they reply in a corresponding manner.

**Introductory Remarks:** At this point, the priest or another of the ministers may introduce the theme of the Mass.

**Penitential Rite:** The priest and people together acknowledge their sins as a preliminary step toward worthy celebration of the sacred mysteries. This rite includes a brief examination of conscience, a general confession of sin and plea for divine mercy in one of several ways, and a prayer for forgiveness by the priest.

**Glory to God:** A doxology, a hymn of praise to God, sung or said on festive occasions.

**Opening Prayer:** A prayer of petition offered by the priest on behalf of the worshipping community.

### I. Liturgy of the Word

**Readings:** The featured elements of this liturgy are readings of passages from the Bible. If three readings are in order, the first is usually from the Old Testament, the second from the New Testament (Epistles, Acts, Revelation), and the third from one of the Gospels; the final reading is always a selection from a Gospel. The first reading(s) is concluded with the formula, "This is the Word of the Lord," to which the people respond, "Thanks be to God." The Gospel reading is concluded with the formula, "This is the Gospel of the Lord," to which the people respond, "Praise to you, Lord Jesus Christ," Between the readings, psalm verses and a Gospel acclamation are sung or said.

**Homily:** Sermon on a scriptural or liturgical subject; ideally, it should be related to the liturgical service in progress.

**Creed:** The Nicene profession of faith, by priest and people, on certain occasions.

**Prayer of the Faithful:** Litany-type prayers of petition, with participation by the people. Called general intercessions, they concern needs of the Church, the salvation of the world, public authorities, persons in need, the local community.

## II. Eucharistic Liturgy

**Offertory Song:** Scriptural verses related to the theme of the Mass, or a suitable hymn, may be sung or said while things are prepared at the altar for the Eucharistic Liturgy and while the offerings of bread and wine are brought to the altar.

**Offertory Procession:** Presentation to the priest of the gifts of bread and wine, principally, by participating members of the congregation.

**Offering of and Prayer over the Gifts:** Consists of the prayers and ceremonies with which the priest offers bread and wine as the elements of the sacrifice to take place during the Eucharistic Prayer and of the Lord's Supper to be shared in Holy Communion.

**Washing of Hands:** After offering the bread and wine, the priest cleanses his fingers with water in a brief ceremony of purification.

**Pray, Brethren:** Prayer that the sacrifice to take place will be acceptable to God. The first part of the prayer is said by the priest; the second, by the people.

**Prayer over the Gifts:** A prayer of petition offered by the priest on behalf of the worshipping community.

### Eucharistic Prayer

**Preface:** A hymn of praise, introducing the Eucharistic Prayer or Canon, sung or said by the priest following responses by the people. The Order of the Mass contains a variety of prefaces, for use on different occasions.

**Holy, Holy, Holy; Blessed Is He:** Divine praises sung or said by the priest and people.

**Canon:** The Eucharistic Prayer of the Mass whose central portion is the Consecration, when the essential act of sacrificial offering takes place with the changing of bread and wine into the Body and Blood of Christ. The prayers of the Canon, which are said by the celebrant only, commemorate principal mysteries of salvation history and include petitions for the Church, the living and dead, and remembrances of saints. There are four Eucharistic Prayers, for use on various occasions and at the option of the priest. (Additional Canons

for Masses with children and for reconciliation were approved in 1975.)

**Doxology:** A formula of divine praise sung or said by the priest while he holds aloft the chalice containing the consecrated wine in one hand and the paten containing the consecrated host in the other.

### Communion Rite

**Lord's Prayer:** Sung or said by the priest and people.

**Prayer for Deliverance** from evil: Called an **embolism** because it is a development of the final petition of the Lord's Prayer; said by the priest. It concludes with a memorial of the return of the Lord to which the people respond, "For the kingdom, the power, and the glory are yours, now and forever."

**Prayer for Peace:** Said by the priest, with corresponding responses by the people. The priest can, in accord with local custom, bid the people to exchange a greeting of peace with each other.

**Lamb of God:** A prayer for divine mercy sung or said while the priest breaks the consecrated host and places a piece of it into the consecrated wine in the chalice.

**Communion:** The priest, after saying a preparatory prayer, administers Holy Communion to himself and then to the people, thus completing the sacrifice-banquet of the Mass. (This completion is realized even if the celebrant alone receives the Eucharist.) On giving the Eucharist to the people, the priest says, "The Body of Christ," to each recipient; the customary response is "Amen." If the Eucharist is administered under the forms of bread and wine, the priest says, "The Body and Blood of Christ."

**Communion Song:** Scriptural verses or a suitable hymn sung or said during the distribution of Holy Communion. After Holy Communion is received, some moments may be spent in silent meditation or in the chanting of a psalm or hymn of praise.

**Prayer after Communion:** A prayer of petition offered by the priest on behalf of the worshipping community.

### Concluding Rite

**Announcements:** Brief announcements to the people are in order at this time.

**Dismissal:** Consists of a final greeting by the priest, a blessing, and a formula of dismissal. This rite is omitted if another liturgical action immediately follows the Mass; e.g., a procession, the blessing of the body during a funeral rite.

Some parts of the Mass are changeable with the liturgical season or feast, and are called the **proper** of the Mass. Other parts are said to be **common** because they always remain the same.

### Additional Mass Notes

Catholics are seriously obliged to attend Mass in a worthy manner on Sundays and holy days of obligation. Failure to do so without a proportionately serious reason is gravely wrong.

It is the custom for priests to celebrate Mass

daily whenever possible. To satisfy the needs of the faithful on Sundays and holy days of obligation, they are authorized to say Mass twice (**bination**) or even three times (**trination**). Bination is also permissible on weekdays. On Christmas and All Souls' Day every priest may say three Masses. Mass may be celebrated at any time.

The **fruits of the Mass**, which in itself is of infinite value, are: **general**, for all the faithful; **special (ministerial)**, for the intentions or persons specifically intended by the celebrant; **most special (personal)**, for the celebrant himself. On Sundays and certain other days pastors are obliged to offer Mass for their parishioners, or to have another priest do so. If a priest accepts a stipend or offering for a Mass, he is obliged in justice to apply the Mass for the designated intention. Mass may be applied for the living and the dead, or for any good intention.

Mass can be celebrated in several ways: e.g., with people present, without their presence (privately), with two or more priests as co-celebrants (concelebration), with greater or less solemnity.

Some of the various types of Masses are: **for the dead** (Funeral Mass or Mass of Christian Burial, Mass for the Dead — formerly called Requiem Mass); **ritual**, in connection with celebration of the sacraments, religious profession, etc.; **nuptial**, for married couples, with or after the wedding ceremony; **votive**, to honor a Person of the Trinity, a saint, or for some special intention. A **red Mass** is a Votive Mass of the Holy Spirit, celebrated for members of the legal profession that they might exercise prudence and equity in their official capacities. **Gregorian Masses** are a series of 30 Masses celebrated on 30 consecutive days for a deceased person.

Mass is not celebrated on Good Friday. In its place, there is a Celebration of the Lord's Passion consisting of a Liturgy of the Word, Veneration of the Cross and Holy Communion.

### Places, Altars for Mass

The ordinary place for celebrating the Eucharist is a church or other sacred place, at a fixed or movable altar.

The altar is a table at which the Eucharistic Sacrifice is celebrated.

A *fixed altar* is attached to the floor of the church. It should be of stone, preferably, and should be consecrated. The Code of Canon Law orders observance of the custom of placing under a fixed altar relics of martyrs or other saints.

A *movable altar* can be made of any solid and suitable material, and should be blessed or consecrated.

Outside of a sacred place, Mass may be celebrated in an appropriate place at a suitable table covered with a linen cloth and corporal. An altar stone containing the relics of saints, which was formerly prescribed, is not required by regulations in effect since the promulgation Apr. 6, 1969, of *Institutio Generalis Missalis Romani*.

## LITURGICAL VESTMENTS

In the early years of the Church, vestments worn by the ministers at liturgical functions were the same as the garments in ordinary popular use. They became distinctive when their form was not altered to correspond with later variations in popular style. Liturgical vestments are symbolic of the sacred ministry and add appropriate decorum to divine worship.

### Mass Vestments

**Alb:** A body-length tunic of white fabric; a vestment common to all ministers of divine worship.

**Amice:** A rectangular piece of white cloth worn about the neck, tucked into the collar and falling over the shoulders; prescribed for use when the alb does not completely cover the ordinary clothing at the neck.

**Chasuble:** Originally, a large mantle or cloak covering the body, it is the outer vestment of a priest celebrating Mass or carrying out other sacred actions connected with the Mass.

**Cincture:** A cord which serves the purpose of a belt, holding the alb close to the body.

**Dalmatic:** The outer vestment worn by a deacon in place of a chasuble.

**Stole:** A long, band-like vestment worn about the neck and falling to about the knees. (A stole is used for other functions also.)

The material, form and ornamentation of the aforementioned and other vestments are subject to variation and adaptation, according to norms and decisions of the Holy See and concerned conferences of bishops. The overriding norm is that they should be appropriate for use in divine worship. The customary ornamented vestments are the chasuble, dalmatic and stole.

The minimal vestments required for a priest celebrating Mass are the alb, stole and chasuble.

**Chasuble-Alb:** A vestment combining the features of the chasuble and alb; for use with a stole by concelebrants and, by way of exception, by celebrants in certain circumstances.

### Liturgical Colors

The colors of outer vestments vary with liturgical seasons, feasts and other circumstances. The colors and their use are:

**Green:** For the season of Ordinary Time; symbolic of hope and the vitality of the life of faith.

**Purple:** For Advent and Lent; may also be used in Masses for the dead; symbolic of penance.

**Red:** For the Sunday of the Passion, Good Friday, Pentecost; feasts of the Passion of Our Lord, the Apostles and Evangelists, martyrs; symbolic of the supreme sacrifice of life for the love of God.

**Rose:** May be used in place of purple on the Third Sunday of Advent (Gaudete Sunday) and the Fourth Sunday of Lent (Laetare Sunday); symbolic of anticipatory joy during a time of penance.

**White:** For the seasons of Christmas and Easter; feasts and commemorations of Our Lord, except those of the Passion; feasts and commemorations of the Blessed Virgin Mary, angels, saints who are not martyrs, All Saints (Nov. 1), St. John the Baptist (June 24), St. John the Evangelist (Dec. 27), the Chair of St. Peter (Feb. 22), the Conversion of St. Paul (Jan. 25). White, symbolic of purity and integrity of the life of faith, may generally be substituted for other colors, and can be used for funeral and other Masses for the dead.

Options are provided regarding the color of vestments used in offices and Masses for the dead. The newsletter of the U.S. Bishops' Committee on the Liturgy, in line with No. 308 of the General Instruction of the Roman Missal, announced in July, 1970: "In the dioceses of the United States, white vestments may be used, in addition to violet (purple) and black, in offices and Masses for the dead."

On more solemn occasions, better than ordinary vestments may be used, even though their color (e.g., gold) does not match the requirements of the day.

### Other Vestments

**Cappa Magna:** Flowing vestment with a train, worn by bishops and cardinals.

**Cassock:** A non-liturgical, full-length, close-fitting robe for use by priests and other clerics under liturgical vestments and in ordinary use; usually black for priests, purple for bishops and other prelates, red for cardinals, white for the pope. In place of a cassock, priests belonging to religious institutes wear the habit proper to their institute.

**Cope:** A mantle-like vestment open in front and fastened across the chest; worn by sacred ministers in processions and other ceremonies, as prescribed by appropriate directives.

**Habit:** The ordinary (non-liturgical) garb of members of religious institutes, analogous to the cassock of diocesan priests; the form of habits varies from institute to institute.

**Humeral Veil:** A rectangular vestment worn about the shoulders by a deacon. or priest in Eucharistic processions and for other prescribed liturgical ceremonies.

**Mitre:** A headdress worn at some liturgical functions by bishops, abbots and, in certain cases, other ecclesiastics.

**Pallium:** A circular band of white wool about two inches wide, with front and back pendants, marked with six crosses, worn about the neck. It is a symbol of the fullness of the episcopal office. Pope Paul VI, in a document issued July 20, 1978, on his own initiative and entitled *Inter Eximia Episcopalis*, restricted its use to the pope and archbishops of metropolitan sees. In 1984, Pope John Paul II decreed that the pallium would ordinarily be conferred on metropolitans by the pope on the solemnity of Sts. Peter and Paul, June 29. The pallium is made from the wool of lambs blessed by the pope on the feast of St. Agnes (Jan. 21).

**Rochet:** A knee-length, white linen-lace garment of prelates worn under outer vestments.

**Surplice:** A loose, flowing vestment of white fabric with wide sleeves. For some functions, it is interchangeable with an alb.

**Zucchetto:** A skullcap worn by bishops and other prelates.

## SACRED VESSELS, LINENS

### Vessels

**Chalice and Paten:** The principal sacred vessels required for the celebration of Mass are the chalice (cup) and paten (plate) in which wine and bread, respectively, are offered, consecrated and consumed. Both should be made of solid and noble material which is not easily breakable or corruptible. Gold coating is required of the interior parts of sacred vessels subject to rust. The cup of a chalice should be made of non-absorbent material.

Vessels for containing consecrated hosts (see below) can be made of material other than solid and noble metal — e.g., ivory, more durable woods — provided the substitute material is locally regarded as noble or rather precious and is suitable for sacred use.

Sacred vessels should be blessed, according to prescribed requirements.

Vessels, in addition to the paten, for containing consecrated hosts are:

**Ciborium:** Used to hold hosts for distribution to the faithful and for reservation in the tabernacle.

**Luna, Lunula, Lunette:** A small receptacle which holds the sacred host in an upright position in the monstrance.

**Monstrance, Ostensorium:** A portable receptacle so made that the sacred host, when enclosed therein, may be clearly seen, as at Benediction or during extended exposition of the Blessed Sacrament.

**Pyx:** A watch-shaped vessel used in carrying the Eucharist to the sick.

### Linens

**Altar Cloth:** A white cloth, usually of linen, covering the table of an altar. One cloth is sufficient. Three were used according to former requirements.

**Burse:** A square, stiff flat case, open at one end, in which the folded corporal can be placed; the outside is covered with material of the same kind and color as the outer vestments of the celebrant.

**Corporal:** A square piece of white linen spread on the altar cloth, on which rest the vessels holding the Sacred Species — the consecrated host(s) and wine — during the Eucharistic Liturgy. The corporal is similarly used whenever the Blessed Sacrament is removed from the tabernacle; e.g., during Benediction the vessel containing the Blessed Sacrament rests on a corporal.

**Finger Towel:** A white rectangular napkin used by the priest to dry his fingers after cleansing them following the offering of gifts at Mass.

**Pall:** A square piece of stiff material, usually covered with linen, which can be used to cover the chalice at Mass.

**Purificator:** A white rectangular napkin used for cleansing sacred vessels after the reception of Communion at Mass.

**Veil:** The chalice intended for use at Mass can be covered with a veil made of the same material as the outer vestments of the celebrant.

# THE CHURCH BUILDING

A church is a building set aside and dedicated for purposes of divine worship, the place of assembly for a worshiping community.

A Catholic church is the ordinary place in which the faithful assemble for participation in the Eucharistic Liturgy and other forms of divine worship.

In the early years of Christianity, the first places of assembly for the Eucharistic Liturgy were private homes (Acts 2:46; Rom. 16:5; 1 Cor. 16:5; Col. 4:15) and, sometimes, catacombs. Church building began in the latter half of the second century during lulls in persecution and became widespread after enactment of the Edict of Milan in 313, when it finally became possible for the Church to emerge completely from the underground. The oldest and basic norms regarding church buildings date from about that time.

The essential principle underlying all norms for church building was reformulated by the Second Vatican Council, as follows: "When churches are to be built, let great care be taken that they be suitable for the celebration of liturgical services and for the active participation of the faithful" *(Constitution on the Sacred Liturgy,* No. 124).

This principle was subsequently elaborated in detail by the Congregation for Divine Worship in a document entitled *Institutio Generalis Missalis Romani,* which was approved by Paul VI Apr. 3 and promulgated by a decree of the congregation dated Apr. 6, 1969. Coverage of the following items reflects the norms stated in Chapter V of this document.

## Main Features

**Sanctuary:** The part of the church where the altar of sacrifice is located, the place where the ministers of the liturgy lead the people in prayer, proclaim the word of God and celebrate the Eucharist. It is set off from the body of the church by a distinctive structural feature — e.g., elevation above the main floor — or by ornamentation. (The traditional communion rail, removed in recent years in many churches, served this purpose of demarcation.) The customary location of the sanctuary is at the front of the church; it may, however, be centrally located.

**Altar:** The main altar of sacrifice and table of the Lord is the focal feature of the sanctuary and entire church. It stands by itself, so that the ministers can move about it freely, and is so situated that they face the people during the liturgical action. In addition to this main altar, there may also be others; in new churches, these are ideally situated in side chapels or alcoves removed to some degree from the body of the church.

**Adornment of the Altar:** The altar table is covered with a suitable linen cloth. Required candelabra and a cross are placed upon or near the altar in plain sight of the people and are so arranged that they do not obscure their view of the liturgical action.

**Seats of the Ministers:** The seat of the celebrant, corresponding with his role as the presiding minister of the assembly, is best located behind the altar and facing the people; it is raised a bit above the level of the altar but must not have the appearance of a throne. The seats of other ministers are also located in the sanctuary.

**Ambo, Pulpit, Lectern:** The stand at which scriptural lessons and psalm responses are read, the word of God preached, and the prayer of the faithful offered. It is so placed that the ministers can be easily seen and heard by the people.

**Places for the People:** Seats and kneeling benches (pews) and other accommodations for the people are so arranged that they can participate in the most appropriate way in the liturgical action and have freedom of movement for the reception of Holy Communion. Reserved seats are out of order.

**Place for the Choir:** Where it is located depends on the most suitable arrangement for maintaining the unity of the choir with the congregation and for providing its members maximum opportunity for carrying out their proper function and participating fully in the Mass.

**Tabernacle:** The best place for reserving the Blessed Sacrament is in a chapel suitable for the private devotion of the people. If this is not possible, reservation should be at a side altar or other appropriately adorned place. In either case, the Blessed Sacrament should be kept in a tabernacle, i.e., a safe-like, secure receptacle.

**Statues:** Images of the Lord, the Blessed Virgin Mary and the saints are legitimately proposed for the veneration of the faithful in churches. Their number and arrangement, however, should be ordered in such a way that they do not distract the people from the central celebration of the Eucharistic Liturgy. There should be only one statue of one and the same saint in a church.

**General Adornment and Arrangement of Churches:** Churches should be so adorned and fitted out that they serve the direct requirements of divine worship and the needs and reasonable convenience of the people.

## Other Items

**Ambry:** A box containing the holy oils, attached to the wall of the sanctuary in some churches.

**Baptistery:** The place for administering baptism. Some churches have baptisteries adjoining or near the entrance, a position symbolizing the fact that persons are initiated in the Church and incorporated in Christ through this sacrament. Contemporary liturgical practice favors placement of the baptistery near the sanctuary and altar, or the use of a portable font in the same position, to emphasize the relationship of baptism to the Eucharist, the celebration in sacrifice and banquet of the death and resurrection of Christ.

**Candles:** Used more for symbolical than illuminative purposes, they represent Christ, the light and life of grace, at liturgical functions. They are made of beeswax. (See Index: Paschal Candle.)

**Confessional, Reconciliation Room:** A booth-like structure for the hearing of confessions, with separate compartments for the priest and penitents and a grating or screen between them. The use of confessionals became general in the Roman Rite after the Council of Trent. Since the Second Vatican Council, there has been a trend in the U.S. to replace or supplement confessionals with small reconciliation rooms so arranged that priest and penitent can converse face-to-face.

**Crucifix:** A cross bearing the figure of the body of Christ, representative of the Sacrifice of the Cross.

**Cruets:** Vessels containing the wine and water used at Mass. They are placed on a credence table in the sanctuary.

**Holy Water Fonts:** Receptacles containing holy water, usually at church entrances, for the use of the faithful.

**Sanctuary Lamp:** A lamp which is kept burning continuously before a tabernacle in which the Blessed Sacrament is reserved, as a sign of the Real Presence of Christ.

## LITURGICAL DEVELOPMENTS

The principal developments covered in this article are enactments of the Holy See and actions related to their implementation in the United States.

### Modern Movement

Origins of the modern movement for renewal in the liturgy date back to the 19th century. The key contributing factor was a revival of liturgical and scriptural studies. Of special significance was the work of the Benedictine monks of Solesmes, France, who aroused great interest in the liturgy through the restoration of Gregorian Chant. St. Pius X approved their work in a motu proprio of 1903 and gave additional encouragement to liturgical study and development.

St. Pius X did more than any other single pope to promote early first Communion and the practice of frequent Communion, started the research behind a revised breviary, and appointed a group to investigate possible revisions in the Mass.

The movement attracted some attention in the 1920's and 30's but made little progress.

Significant pioneering developments in the U.S. during the 20's, however, were the establishment of the Liturgical Press, the beginning of publication of *Orate Fratres* (now *Worship*), and the inauguration of the League of the Divine Office by the Benedictines at St. John's Abbey, Collegeville, Minn. Later events of influence were the establishment of the Pius X School of Liturgical Music at Manhattanville College of the Sacred Heart and the organization of a summer school of liturgical music at Mary Manse College by the Gregorian Institute of America. The turning point toward real renewal was reached during and after World War II.

Pius XII gave it impetus and direction, principally through the background teaching in his encyclicals on the *Mystical Body* (1943), *Sacred Liturgy* (1947), and the *Discipline of Sacred Music* (1955), and by means of specific measures affecting the liturgy itself. His work was continued during the pontificates of John XXIII and Paul VI. The Second Vatican Council, in virtue of its *Constitution on the Sacred Liturgy,* inaugurated changes of the greatest significance.

### Before and After Vatican II

The most significant liturgical changes made in the years immediately preceding the Second Vatican Council were the following:

(1) Revision of the Rites of Holy Week, for universal observance from 1956.

(2) Modification of the Eucharistic fast and permission for afternoon and evening Mass, in effect from 1953 and extended in 1957.

(3) The Dialogue Mass, introduced in 1958.

(4) Use of popular languages in administration of the sacraments.

(5) Calendar-missal-breviary reform, in effect from Jan. 1, 1961.

(6) Seven-step administration of baptism for adults, approved in 1962.

The *Constitution on the Sacred Liturgy* approved (2,174 to 4) and promulgated by the Second Vatican Council Dec. 4, 1963, marked the beginning of a profound renewal in the Church's corporate worship. Implementation of some of its measures was ordered by Paul VI Jan. 25, 1964, in the motu proprio *Sacram Liturgiam.* On Feb. 29, a special commission, the Consilium for Implementing the Constitution on the Sacred Liturgy, was formed to supervise the execution of the entire program of liturgical reform. Implementation of the program on local and regional levels was left to bishops acting through their own liturgical commissions and in concert with their fellow bishops in national conferences.

Liturgical reform in the United States has been carried out under the direction of the Liturgy Committee, National Conference of Catholic Bishops. Its secretariat, established early in 1965, is located at 1312 Massachusetts Ave. N.W., Washington, D.C. 20005.

### Stages of Development

Liturgical development after the Second Vatican Council proceeded in several stages. It started with the formulation of guidelines and directives, and with the translation into vernacular languages of virtually unchanged Latin ritual texts. Then came structural changes in the Mass, the sacraments, the calendar, the Divine Office and other phases of the liturgy. These revisions were just about completed with the publication of a new order for the sacrament of penance in February, 1974. A continuing phase of development, in progress from the beginning, involves efforts to deepen the liturgical sense of the faithful, to increase their participation in worship and to relate it to full Christian life.

### Texts and Translations

The master texts of all documents on liturgical reform were in Latin. Effective dates of their implementation depended on the completion and approval of appropriate translations into vernacular languages. English translations were made by the International Committee for English in the Liturgy.

The principal features of liturgical changes and the effective dates of their introduction in the United States are covered below under topical headings. (For expanded coverage of various items, especially the sacraments, see additional entries.)

## The Mass

A new Order of the Mass, supplanting the one authorized by the Council of Trent in the 16th century, was introduced in the U.S. Mar. 22, 1970. It had been approved by Paul VI in the apostolic constitution *Missale Romanum,* dated Apr. 3, 1969.

Preliminary and related to it were the following developments.

**Mass in English:** Introduced Nov. 29, 1964. In the same year, Psalm 42 was eliminated from the prayers at the foot of the altar.

**Incidental Changes:** The last Gospel (prologue of John) and vernacular prayers following Mass were eliminated Mar. 7, 1965. At the same time, provision was made for the celebrant to say aloud some prayers formerly said silently.

**Rubrics:** An instruction entitled *Tres Abhinc Annos,* dated May 4 and effective June 29, 1967, simplified directives for the celebration of Mass, approved the practice of saying the canon aloud, altered the Communion and dismissal rites, permitted purple instead of black vestments in Masses for the dead, discontinued wearing of the maniple, and approved in principle the use of vernacular languages for the canon, ordination rites, and lessons of the Divine Office when read in choir.

**Canons or Eucharistic Prayers:** Three additional Eucharistic prayers authorized May 23, 1968, were approved for use in vernacular translation the following Aug. 15. They have the same basic structure as the traditional Roman Canon, whose use in English was introduced Oct. 22, 1967.

The customary Roman Canon, which dates at least from the beginning of the fifth century and has remained substantially unchanged since the seventh century, is the first in the order of listing of the Eucharistic prayers. It can be used at any time, but is the one of choice for most Sundays, some special feasts like Easter and Pentecost, and for feasts of the Apostles and other saints who are commemorated in the canon. Any preface can be used with it.

The second Eucharistic prayer, the shortest and simplest of all, is best suited for use on weekdays and various special circumstances. It has a preface of its own, but others may be used with it. This canon bears a close resemblance to the one framed by St. Hippolytus about 215.

The third Eucharistic prayer is suitable for use on Sundays and feasts as an alternative to the Roman Canon. It can be used with any preface and has a special formula for remembrance of the dead.

The fourth Eucharistic prayer, the most sophis-

ticated of them all, presents a broad synthesis of salvation history. Based on the Eastern tradition of Antioch, it is best suited for use at Masses attended by persons versed in Sacred Scripture. It has an unchangeable preface.

Five additional Eucharistic prayers — three for Masses with children and two for Masses of reconciliation — were approved in 1974 and 1975, respectively, by the Congregation for the Sacraments and Divine Worship. The original approval for a limited period of experimentation was extended indefinitely, until further notice, according to a letter issued by the congregation Dec. 15, 1980.

**Lectionary:** A new compilation of scriptural readings and psalm responsories for Mass was published in 1969. The *Lectionary* contains a three-year cycle of readings for Sundays and solemn feasts, a two-year weekday cycle, and a one-year cycle for the feasts of saints, in addition to readings for a great variety of Masses, ritual Masses and Masses for various needs. There are also responsorial psalms to follow the first readings, and gospel or alleluia versicles to follow the second readings.

A second edition of the *Lectionary,* substantially the same as the first, was published in 1981. New features included an expanded introduction, extensive scriptural references and additional readings for a number of solemnities and feasts.

**Sacramentary (Missal):** The Vatican Polyglot Press began distribution in June, 1970, of the Latin text of a new *Roman Missal,* the first revision published in 400 years. The English translation was authorized for optional use beginning July 1, 1974; the mandatory date for use was Dec. 1, 1974.

The missal is the celebrant's book of prayers and sacramental formulas and does not include the readings of the Mass, such as the Gospel and the Epistle. It contains the texts of entrance songs, prefaces and other prayers of the Mass. The number of prefaces is four times greater than it had been. There are 10 commons (or sets of Mass prayers) of martyrs, two of doctors of the Church, and a dozen for saints or groups of saints of various kinds, such as religious, educators and mothers of families. There are Masses during which certain sacraments are administered and others for religious profession, the Church, the pope, priests, Christian unity, the evangelization of nations, persecuted Christians, and other intentions.

**Mass for Special Groups:** Reasons and norms for the celebration of Mass at special gatherings of the faithful were the subject of an instruction issued May 15, 1969. Two years earlier, the U.S. Bishops' Liturgy Committee went on record in support of the celebration of Mass in private homes.

**Sunday Mass on Saturday:** The Congregation for the Clergy, under date of Jan. 10, 1970, granted the request that the faithful, where bishops consider it pastorally necessary or useful, may satisfy the precept of participating in Mass in the late afternoon or evening hours of Saturdays and the days before holy days of obligation.

**Trination:** The Congregation for the Sacraments, under date of Jan. 20, 1970, granted to all

U.S. bishops the authority to permit priests to celebrate Mass three times on Saturdays and days preceding holy days of obligation, on condition that the first and second Masses are celebrated for weddings and/or funerals and the third Mass is celebrated in the evening so that the precept (of participating in Mass) will be satisfied by the faithful.

**Mass in Latin:** According to notices issued by the Congregation for Divine Worship June 1, 1971, and Oct. 28, 1974: (1) Bishops may permit the celebration of Mass in Latin for mixed-language groups. (2) Bishops may permit the celebration of one or two Masses in Latin on weekdays or Sundays in any church, irrespective of mixed-language groups involved (1971). (3) Priests may celebrate Mass in Latin when people are not present. (4) The approved revised Order of the Mass is to be used in Latin as well as vernacular languages . (5) By way of exception, bishops may permit older and handicapped priests to use the Council of Trent's Order of the Mass in private celebration of the holy Sacrifice.

**Inter-Ritual Concelebration:** The Apostolic Delegation in Washington, D.C., announced in June, 1971, that it had received authorization to permit priests of Roman and Eastern rites to celebrate Mass together in the rite of the host church. It was understood that the inter-ritual concelebrations would always be "a manifestation of the unity of the Church and of communion among particular churches."

**Ordo of the Sung Mass:** In a decree dated June 24 and made public Aug. 24, 1972, the Congregation for Divine Worship issued a new *Ordo of the Sung Mass* — containing Gregorian chants in Latin — to replace the *Graduale Romanum.*

**Mass for Children:** Late in 1973, the Congregation for Divine Worship issued special guidelines for children's Masses, providing accommodations to the mentality and spiritual growth of pre-adolescents while retaining the principal parts and structures of the Mass. The *Directory for Masses with Children* was approved by Paul VI Oct. 22 and was dated Nov. 1, 1973. Three Eucharistic prayers for Masses with children were approved by the congregation in 1974; English versions were approved June 5, 1975. Their use, authorized originally for a limited period of experimentation, was extended indefinitely Dec. 15, 1980.

### Sacraments

The general use of English in administration of the sacraments was approved for the U.S. Sept. 14, 1964. Structural changes of the rites were subsequently made and introduced in the U.S. as follows.

**Pastoral Care of the Sick:** Revised rites, covering also administration of the Eucharist to sick persons, were approved Nov. 30,. 1972, and published Jan. 18, 1973. The effective date for use of the provisional English prayer formula was Dec. 1, 1974. The mandatory effective date for use of the ritual, Pastoral Care of the Sick in English, was Nov. 27, 1983.

**Baptism:** New rites for the baptism of infants, approved Mar. 19, 1969, were introduced June 1, 1970.

**Christian Initiation of Adults:** Revised rites were issued Jan. 6, 1972, for the Christian initiation of adults — affecting preparation for and reception of baptism, the Eucharist and confirmation; also, the reception of already baptized adults into the Church. These rites, which were introduced in the U.S. on the completion of English translation, nullified a seven-step baptismal process approved in 1962.

**Confirmation:** Revised rites, issued Aug. 15, 1971, became mandatory in the U.S. Jan. 1, 1973.

**Eucharist:** Several enactments concerning the Eucharist have been issued since 1966 when permission was given for the superiors of convents to administer Holy Communion in the absence of priests. Paul VI issued an instruction on *Worship of the Eucharistic Mystery* May 25, 1967, and another on the manner of administering Holy Communion May 20, 1969. Limited permission for lay persons to serve as special ministers of the Eucharist was given in 1971 and extended in 1972. Also in 1972, instructions were issued regarding administration of the Eucharist to other Christians, and in particular circumstances.

**Holy Orders:** Revised ordination rites for deacons, priests and bishops, validated by prior experimental use, were approved in 1970. The sacrament of holy orders underwent further revision in 1972 with the elimination of the Church-instituted orders of porter, reader, exorcist, acolyte and subdeacon, and of the tonsure ceremony symbolic of entrance into the clerical state. The former minor orders of reader and acolyte were changed from orders to ministries.

**Matrimony:** New rites, issued Mar. 19, 1969, were introduced June 1, 1970. Minor revisions had been made in 1964 in conjunction with a directive for imparting the nuptial blessing at all weddings.

**Penance:** Ritual revision of the sacraments was completed with the approval by Paul VI Dec. 2, 1973, of new directives for the sacrament of penance or reconciliation. The U.S. Bishops' Committee on the Liturgy set Feb. 27, 1977, as the mandatory date for use of the new rite. The committee also declared that it could be used from Mar. 7, 1976, after adequate preparation of priests and people. Earlier, authorization was given by the Holy See in 1968 for the omission of any reference to excommunication or other censures in the formula of absolution unless there was some indication that a censure had actually been incurred by a penitent.

### Additional Developments

**Calendar:** A revised liturgical calendar, approved by Paul VI Feb. 14 and made public May 9, 1969, went into effect in the U.S. in 1972.

**Funeral Rites:** Revised rites oriented to the resurrection theme went into effect Nov. 1, 1971.

**Holy Week:** The English version of revised Holy Week rites went into effect in 1971. They introduced concelebration of Mass, placed new emphasis on commemorating the institution of the

## 228                                          *Liturgical Developments*

priesthood on Holy Thursday, and modified Good Friday prayers for other Christians, Jews and other non-Christians.

**Liturgy of the Hours:** The background, contents, scope and purposes of the revised Divine Office, called the Liturgy of the Hours, were described by Paul VI in the apostolic constitution *Laudis Canticum,* dated Nov. 1, 1970. A provisional English version, incorporating basic features of the master Latin text, was published in 1971. The four complete volumes of the Hours in English have been published since May, 1975. One-volume, partial editions, intended for use by Religious and lay persons not bound to pray the Liturgy of the Hours, have also been published in approved form. Nov. 27, 1977, was set by the Congregation for Divine Worship and the National Conference of Catholic Bishops as the effective date for exclusive use in liturgical worship of the translation of the Latin text of the Office approved by the International Committee on English in the Liturgy.

**Music:** An *Instruction on Music in the Liturgy,*dated Mar. 5 and effective May 14, 1967, encouraged congregational singing during liturgical celebrations and attempted to clarify the role of choirs and trained singers. More significantly, the instruction indicated that a major development under way in the liturgy was a gradual erasure of the distinctive lines traditionally drawn between the sung liturgy and the spoken liturgy, between what had been called the high Mass and the low Mass.

In the same year, the U.S. Bishops' Liturgy Committee approved the use of contemporary music, as well as guitars and other suitable instruments, in the liturgy. The Holy See authorized in 1968 the use of musical instruments other than the organ in liturgical services, "provided they are played in a manner suitable to worship."

**Oils:** The Congregation for Divine Worship issued a directive in 1971 permitting the use of other oils — from plants, seeds or coconuts — instead of the traditional olive oil in administering some of the sacraments. The directive also provided that oils could be blessed at other times than at the usual Mass of Chrism on Holy Thursday, and authorized bishops' conferences to permit priests to bless oils in cases of necessity.

**Environment and Art in Catholic Worship:** A booklet with this title was issued by the U.S. Bishops' Committee on the Liturgy in March, 1978.

**Eucharistic Ministers:** Approval by the Congregation for Divine Worship was reported in August, 1978, of a provisional translation of a "Rite of Commissioning Special Ministers of Holy Communion." Note was made of the fact that such ministers should be called "special" instead of "extraordinary."

**Doxology:** The bishops' committee called attention in August, 1978, to the directive that the Doxology concluding the Eucharistic Prayer is said or sung by the celebrant (concelebrants) alone, to which the people respond, "Amen."

**Churches, Altars, Chalices:** The *Newsletter* of the U.S. Bishops' Committee on the Liturgy reported in November, 1978, that the Congregation for Divine Worship had given provisional approval of a new English translation for the rite of dedicating churches and altars, and of a new form for the blessing of chalices.

**Study of the Mass:** The Bishops' Committee on the Liturgy, following approval of the project by the National Conference of Catholic Bishops in May, 1979, began a study of the function and position of some elements of the Mass, including the Gloria, the sign of peace, the penitential rite and the readings. Completion of the first phase of the study was reported in July, 1980; its product was a 175-page study document. The second phase of the project got under way in the spring of 1981 with publication of a work book entitled *The Mystery of Faith: A Study of the Structural Elements of the Order of Mass.* Another draft of the study was circulated late in 1983, for recommendations and final proposals.

**Eucharistic Hosts:** Father Thomas Krosnicki, a staff member of the Bishops' Committee on the Liturgy, reported in July, 1979, that the committee was preparing new guidelines on the preparation of hosts, in compliance with a request from the Congregation for the Doctrine of the Faith. He said the congregation had "questioned the contents of some of the recipes" used in this country. Cardinal Franjo Seper, prefect of the congregation, stressed the importance of carefully observing traditional theological principles relating to the making of hosts — which should be of wheat, unleavened, with the appearance of food, and capable of being broken and distributed to communicants. In 1980, the congregation ruled definitely against changes in the preparation of hosts, and so informed the bishops' committee. The same prohibition was stated in the "Instruction on Certain Norms concerning Worship of the Eucharistic Mystery" approved by the Pope Apr. 17, and released May 23, 1980.

**Eucharistic Worship:** This was the subject of two documents issued in 1980. *Dominicae Coenae* was a letter addressed by Pope John Paul to bishops throughout the world in connection with the celebration of Holy Thursday; it was dated Feb. 24 and released Mar. 18. It was more doctrinal in content than the "Instruction on Certain Norms concerning Worship of the Eucharistic Mystery" (*Inaestimabile Donum,* "The Priceless Gift"), which was approved by the Pope Apr. 17 and published by the Congregation for the Sacraments and Divine Worship May 23. Its stated purpose was to reaffirm and clarify teaching on liturgical renewal contained in enactments of the Second Vatican Council and in several related implementing documents.

**Marian Statues:** A new rite (order) for the coronation of statues of the Blessed Virgin Mary was approved and published in 1981 by the Congregation for the Sacraments and Divine Worship.

### Sunday Communion

More than two-thirds of the U.S. bishops voted (187 to 82) during the general meeting of their national conference in November, 1978, or afterwards for allowing the reception of Holy Communion under the forms of bread and wine on Sundays and holy days — subject to the options of bishops of dioceses, priests celebrating Mass and persons receiving the Eucharist. (Reception of Communion in this manner on certain occasions was already provided for in directives of the Congregation for Divine Worship, but Sundays and holy days were not mentioned.)

## Report on Liturgical Books, Rites

The Bishops' Committee on the Liturgy published in August, 1981, a compendium of information on the status of liturgical books and rites revised since 1965.

The *BCL Report: Ritual Revisions — A Status Report*, covered *The Roman Ritual, The Roman Pontifical, The Roman Missal* and *The Liturgy of the Hours*. The contents also included a chronological review of the revisions of rites initiated by the Second Vatican Council, from decrees of promulgation through publication in Latin, translations into English and adaptations authorized for use in the U.S.

## Dancing and Worship

Dancing and worship was the subject of an essay which appeared in a 1975 edition of Notitiae (11, pp. 202-205), the official journal of the Congregation for the Sacraments and Divine Worship. The article was called a "qualified and authoritative sketch," and should be considered "an authoritative point of reference for every discussion of the matter."

The principal points of the essay were:

• "The dance has never been made an integral part of the official worship of the Latin Church."

• "If the proposal of the religious dance in the West is really to be made welcome, care will have to be taken that in its regard a place be found outside of the liturgy, in assembly areas which are not strictly liturgical. Moreover, the priests must always be excluded from the dance."

## Ongoing Renewal

This was the theme of an address delivered by Archbishop Virgilio Noe, secretary of the Congregation for Divine Worship, June 7, 1984, at The Catholic University of America.

"It would be a grave mistake," he said, "to think that the work of liturgical renewal has been completed apart from a few minor details." Renewal "is an ongoing process because it is growth and development."

He encouraged scholarly study of the liturgy, as well as less specialized liturgical courses for clergy and laity "who have not the capacity or time for scientific work but who want a solid foundation in the subject." Without such a foundation, well-meaning efforts in the liturgy often come either "to nothing or end in disaster, creating division in the local community."

He also encouraged liturgical work by musicians, artists and architects.

The ministry and role of women in the liturgy, he said, "is an area which needs deep study."

Archbishop Noe called liturgical renewal a part of the Second Vatican Council's "aim to throw into greater relief the truth which the Church has to proclaim."

# CANON LAW AND LITURGICAL LAW

*Canon 2 states that, for the most part, the Code of Canon Law does not regulate liturgical rites and ceremonies, and that existing liturgical norms retain the force of law unless they are contrary to legislation in the code.*

*The Newsletter of the Bishops' Committee on the Liturgy (May, 1983) observed in comment:*

The norms in the (approved) liturgical books and in the decrees of the Roman Pontiff, the Roman Congregations and, in matters where they have a right to legislate, the National Conference of Catholic Bishops, are truly liturgical law and not just suggestions. This should be kept in mind, especially since the new Code contains only a minimum of liturgical law. Highlights from that law contained in the code follow.

## Right to Correct Celebration

All the Christian faithful (the laity, religious and those ordained) have a right to the spiritual goods of the Church, especially the Word of God and the sacraments. They also have a right to divine worship according to the prescriptions of the proper rite, which is approved by the legitimate pastors of the Church. (They have a right not only to the liturgy but to correctly celebrated liturgy.) (Canons 213 and 214)

Liturgical actions are not private actions but are celebrations of the Church itself. . . . Individual

members of the faithful are related to the liturgical actions in different ways, depending on the variety of orders, duties and actual participation. (Canon 837)

The regulation of the liturgy depends solely on the authority of the Church, and this rests with the Holy See and, according to the norms of law, with the conference of bishops or the individual diocesan bishop. (Canon 838)

Under certain limited circumstances non-Catholic Christians may receive the sacraments of penance, Holy Eucharist and the anointing of the sick. (Canon 844)

In celebrating the sacraments the liturgical books approved by the competent authority must be faithfully followed. No one may add, delete or change anything on one's own initiative. (Canon 846)

Lay men can assume the instituted ministry of lector and acolyte. By temporary deputation all the laity can perform in liturgical ceremonies the duties of lector, commentator, cantor, and other ministries permitted by the law. And where proper ministers are lacking and necessity urges it, the laity (even if they are not lectors or acolytes) may fulfill other offices, namely, exercising the ministry of the word, presiding over liturgical prayer, conferring baptism and distributing Holy Communion, according to the prescripts of the law. (Canon 230)

The sacraments are actions of Christ and his Church (itself a kind of sacrament) which signify grace, cause it in the act of signifying it, and confer it upon persons properly disposed to receive it. They perpetuate the redemptive activity of Christ, making it present and effective. They infallibly communicate the fruit of that activity — namely grace — to responsive persons with faith. Sacramental actions consist of the union of sensible signs (matter of the sacraments) with the words of the minister (form of the sacraments).

Christ himself instituted the seven sacraments of the New Law by determining their essence and the efficacy of their signs to produce the grace they signify.

Christ is the principal priest or minister of every sacrament; human agents — an ordained priest, baptized persons contracting marriage with each other, any person conferring emergency baptism in a proper manner — are secondary ministers. Sacraments have efficacy from Christ, not from the personal dispositions of their human ministers.

Each sacrament confers sanctifying grace for the special purpose of the sacrament; this is, accordingly, called sacramental grace. It involves a right to actual graces corresponding to the purposes of the respective sacraments.

While sacraments infallibly produce the grace they signify, recipients benefit from them in proportion to their personal dispositions. One of these is the intention to receive sacraments as sacred signs of God's saving and grace-giving action. The state of grace is also necessary for fruitful reception of the Holy Eucharist, confirmation, matrimony, holy orders and anointing of the sick. Baptism is the sacrament in which grace is given in the first instance and original sin is remitted. Penance is the secondary sacrament of reconciliation, in which persons guilty of serious sin after baptism are reconciled with God and the Church, and in which persons already in the state of grace are strengthened in that state.

## Role of Sacraments

The Second Vatican Council prefaced a description of the role of the sacraments with the following statement concerning participation by all the faithful in the priesthood of Christ and the exercise of that priesthood by receiving the sacraments (*Dogmatic Constitution on the Church*, Nos. 10 and 11).

"The baptized by regeneration and the anointing of the Holy Spirit are consecrated into a spiritual house and a holy priesthood. Thus through all those works befitting Christian men they can offer spiritual sacrifice and proclaim the power of him who has called them out of darkness into his marvelous light (cf. 1 Pt. 2:4-10)."

"Though they differ from one another in essence and not only in degree, the common priesthood of the faithful and the ministerial or hierarchical priesthood (of those ordained to holy orders) are nonetheless interrelated. Each of them in its own special way is a participation in the one priesthood of Christ. The ministerial priest, by the sacred power he enjoys, molds and rules the priestly people. Acting in the Person of Christ, he brings about the Eucharistic Sacrifice, and offers it to God in the name of all the people. For their part, the faithful join in the offering of the Eucharist by virtue of their royal priesthood. They likewise exercise that priesthood by receiving the sacraments, by prayer and thanksgiving, by the witness of a holy life, and by self-denial and active charity."

"It is through the sacraments and the exercise of the virtues that the sacred nature and organic structure of the priestly community is brought into operation."

**Baptism:** "Incorporated into the Church through baptism, the faithful are consecrated by the baptismal character to the exercise of the cult of the Christian religion. Reborn as sons of God, they must confess before men the faith which they have received from God through the Church."

**Confirmation:** "Bound more intimately to the Church by the sacrament of confirmation, they are endowed by the Holy Spirit with special strength. Hence they are more strictly obliged to spread and defend the faith both by word and by deed as true witnesses of Christ."

**Eucharist:** "Taking part in the Eucharistic Sacrifice, which is the fount and apex of the whole Christian life, they offer the divine Victim to God, and offer themselves along with It. Thus, both by the act of oblation and through holy Communion, all perform their proper part in this liturgical service, not, indeed, all in the same way but each in that way which is appropriate to himself. Strengthened anew at the holy table by the Body of Christ, they manifest in a practical way that unity of God's People which is suitably signified and wondrously brought about by this most awesome sacrament."

**Penance:** "Those who approach the sacrament of penance obtain pardon from the mercy of God for offenses committed against him. They are at the same time reconciled with the Church, which they have wounded by their sins, and which by charity, example, and prayer seeks their conversion."

**Anointing of the Sick:** "By the sacred anointing of the sick and the prayer of her priests, the whole Church commends those who are ill to the suffering and glorified Lord, asking that he may lighten their suffering and save them (cf. Jas. 5:14-16). She exhorts them, moreover, to contribute to the welfare of the whole People of God by associating themselves freely with the passion and death of Christ (cf. Rom. 8:17; Col. 1:24; 2 Tm. 2:11-12; 1 Pt. 4:13)."

**Holy Orders:** "Those of the faithful who are consecrated by holy orders are appointed to feed the Church in Christ's name with the Word and the grace of God."

**Matrimony:** "Christian spouses, in virtue of the sacrament of matrimony, signify and partake of the mystery of that unity and fruitful love which exists between Christ and his Church (cf. Eph. 5:32). The spouses thereby help each other to attain to holiness in their married life and by the rearing and education of their children. And so, in their state and way of life, they have their own special gift among the People of God (cf. 1 Cor. 7:7).

"For from the wedlock of Christians there comes the family, in which new citizens of human society are born. By the grace of the Holy Spirit received in baptism these are made children of God, thus perpetuating the People of God through the centuries. The family is, so to speak, the domestic Church. In it parents should, by their word and example, be the first preachers of the faith to their children. They should encourage them in the vocation which is proper to each of them, fostering with special care any religious vocation."

"Fortified by so many and such powerful means of salvation, all the faithful, whatever their condition or state, are called by the Lord, each in his own way, to that perfect holiness whereby the Father himself is perfect."

## Baptism

Baptism is the sacrament of spiritual regeneration by which a person is incorporated in Christ and made a member of his Mystical Body, given grace, and cleansed of original sin. Actual sins and the punishment due for them are remitted also if the person baptized was guilty of such sins (e.g., in the case of a person baptized after reaching the age of reason). The theological virtues of faith, hope and charity are given with grace. The sacrament confers a character on the soul and can be received only once.

The matter is the pouring of water. The form is: "I baptize you in the name of the Father and of the Son and of the Holy Spirit."

The minister of solemn baptism is a bishop, priest or deacon, but in case of emergency anyone, including a non-Catholic, can validly baptize. The minister pours water on the forehead of the person being baptized and says the words of the form while the water is flowing. The water used in solemn baptism is blessed during the rite.

Baptism is conferred in the Roman Rite by immersion or infusion (pouring of water), depending on the directive of the appropriate conference of bishops, according to the Code of Canon Law. The Church recognizes as valid baptisms properly performed by non-Catholic ministers. The baptism of infants has always been considered valid and the general practice of infant baptism was well established by the fifth century. Baptism is conferred conditionally when there is doubt about the validity of a previous baptism.

Baptism is necessary for salvation. If a person cannot receive the baptism of water described above, this can be supplied by baptism of blood (martyrdom suffered for the Catholic faith or some Christian virtue) or by baptism of desire (perfect contrition joined with at least the implicit intention of doing whatever God wills that men should do for salvation).

A sponsor is required for the person being baptized. (See Godparents, below).

A person must be validly baptized before he can receive any of the other sacraments.

**Christian Initiation of Infants:** Infants should be solemnly baptized as soon after birth as conveniently possible. In danger of death, anyone may baptize an infant. If the child survives, the ceremonies of solemn baptism should be supplied.

The sacrament is ordinarily conferred by a priest or deacon of the parents' parish.

Catholics 16 years of age and over who have received the sacraments of confirmation and the Eucharist and are practicing their faith are eligible to be sponsors or godparents. Only one is required. Two, one of each sex, are permitted. A non-Catholic Christian cannot be a godparent for a Catholic child, but may serve as a witness to the baptism. A Catholic may not be a godparent for a child baptized in a non-Catholic religion, but may be a witness.

The role of godparents in baptismal ceremonies is secondary to the role of the parents. They serve as representatives of the community of faith and with the parents request baptism for the child and perform other ritual functions. Their function after baptism is to serve as proxies for the parents if the parents should be unable or fail to provide for the religious training of the child.

At baptism every child should be given a name with Christian significance, usually the name of a saint, to symbolize newness of life in Christ.

**Christian Initiation of Adults:** According to the *Ordo Initiationis Christianae Adultorum* ("Rite of the Christian Initiation of Adults") issued by the Congregation for Divine Worship under date of Jan. 6, 1972, adults are prepared for baptism and reception into the Church in several stages:

• An initial period of inquiry, instruction and evangelization.

• The catechumenate, a period of formal instruction and progressive formation in and familiarity with Christian life. It starts with a statement of purpose and includes a rite in which the catechumen is signed with the cross, blessings, exorcisms, and introduction into church for celebration of the word of God.

• Immediate preparation, called a period of purification and enlightenment, from the beginning of Lent to reception of the sacraments of initiation — baptism, confirmation, Holy Eucharist — at Easter. The period is marked by scrutinies, formal giving of the creed and the Lord's Prayer, the choice of a Christian name, and a final statement of intention.

• A final phase whose objective is greater familiarity with Christian life in the Church through observances of the Easter season and association with the community of the faithful.

The priest who baptizes a catechumen can also administer the sacrament of confirmation.

A sponsor is required for the person being baptized.

The *Ordo* also provides a simple rite of initiation for adults in danger of death and for cases in which all stages of the initiation process are not necessary, and guidelines for: (1) the preparation of adults for the sacraments of confirmation and Holy Eucharist in cases where they have been baptized but have not received further formation in the Christian life; (2) for the formation and initiation of children of catechetical age.

The Church recognizes the right of anyone over the age of seven to request baptism and to receive the sacrament after completing a course of instruction and giving evidence of good will. Practically, in the case of minors in a non-Catholic family or environment, the Church accepts them when other circumstances favor their ability to practice the faith — e.g., well-disposed family situation, the presence of another or several Catholics in the family. Those who are not in such favorable circumstances are prudently advised to defer reception of the sacrament until they attain the maturity necessary for independent practice of the faith.

**Reception of Baptized Christians:** Procedure for the reception of already baptized Christians into full communion with the Catholic Church is distinguished from the catechumenate, since they have received some Christian formation. Instruction and formation are provided as necessary, however; and conditional baptism is administered if there is reasonable doubt about the validity of the person's previous baptism.

In the rite of reception, the person is invited to join the community of the Church in professing the Nicene Creed and is asked to state: "I believe and profess all that the holy Catholic Church believes, teaches, and proclaims as revealed by God." The priest places his hand on the head of the person, states the formula of admission to full communion, confirms (in the absence of a bishop), gives a sign of peace, and administers Holy Communion during a Eucharistic Liturgy.

### Confirmation

Confirmation is the sacrament by which a baptized person, through anointing with chrism and the imposition of hands, is endowed with the gifts and special strength of the Holy Spirit for mature Christian living. The sacrament, which completes the Christian initiation begun with baptism, confers a character on the soul and can be received only once.

According to the apostolic constitution *Divinae Consortium Naturae* dated Aug. 15, 1971, in conjunction with the *Ordo Confirmationis* ("Rite of Confirmation"): "The sacrament of confirmation is conferred through the anointing with chrism on the forehead, which is done by the imposition of the hand (matter of the sacrament), and through the words: 'N . . . . , receive the seal of the Holy Spirit, the Gift of the Father' " (form of the sacrament). On May 5, 1975, bishops' conferences in English-speaking countries were informed by the Congregation for Divine Worship that Pope Paul had approved this English version of the form of the sacrament: "Be sealed with the gift of the Holy Spirit."

The ordinary minister of confirmation in the Roman Rite is a bishop. Priests may be delegated for the purpose. A pastor can confirm a parishioner in danger of death, and a priest can confirm in ceremonies of Christian initiation and at the reception of a baptized Christian into union with the Church.

Ideally, the sacrament is conferred during the Eucharistic Liturgy. Elements of the rite include renewal of the promises of baptism, which confirmation ratifies and completes, and the laying on of hands by the confirming bishop and priests participating in the ceremony.

"The entire rite," according to the *Ordo;* "has a twofold meaning. The laying of hands upon the candidates, done by the bishop and the concelebrating priests, expresses the biblical gesture by which the gift of the Holy Spirit is invoked. . . . The anointing with chrism and the accompanying words clearly signify the effect of the Holy Spirit. Signed with the perfumed oil by the bishop's hand, the baptized person receives the indelible character, the seal of the Lord, together with the Spirit who is given and who conforms the person more perfectly to Christ and gives him the grace of spreading the Lord's presence among men."

A sponsor is required for the person being confirmed. Eligible is any Catholic 16 years of age or older who has received the sacraments of confirmation and the Eucharist and is practicing the faith. The baptismal sponsor, preferably, can also be the sponsor for confirmation. Parents may present their children for confirmation but cannot be sponsors.

In the Roman Rite, it has been customary for children to receive confirmation within a reasonable time after first Communion and confession. There is a developing trend, however, to defer confirmation until later when its significance for mature Christian living becomes more evident. In the Eastern Rites, confirmation is administered at the same time as baptism.

### Eucharist

The Holy Eucharist is a sacrifice (see The Mass) and the sacrament in which Christ is present and is received under the appearances of bread and wine.

The matter is bread of wheat, unleavened in the Roman Rite and leavened in the Eastern Rites, and wine of grape. The form consists of the words of consecration said by the priest at Mass: "This is my body. . . . This is the cup of my blood" (according to the traditional usage of the Roman Rite).

Only a priest can consecrate bread and wine so they become the body and blood of Christ. After consecration, however, the Eucharist can be administered by deacons and, for various reasons, by religious and lay persons.

Priests celebrating Mass receive the Eucharist under the appearances of bread and wine. In the Roman Rite, others receive under the appearances of bread only, i.e., the consecrated host, or in some circumstances they may receive under the appearances of both bread and wine. In Eastern-Rite practice, the faithful generally receive a piece of consecrated leavened bread which has been dipped into consecrated wine (i.e., by intinction).

Conditions for receiving the Eucharist, commonly called Holy Communion, are the state of grace, the right intention and observance of the Eucharistic fast.

The faithful of Roman Rite are required by a precept of the Church to receive the Eucharist at least once a year, ordinarily during the Easter time.

(See Eucharistic Fast, Mass, Transubstantiation, Viaticum.)

**First Communion and Confession:** Children are to be prepared for and given opportunity for receiving both sacraments (Eucharist and reconciliation, or penance) on reaching the age of discretion, at which time they become subject to general norms concerning confession and Communion. This, together with a stated preference for first confession before first Communion, was the central theme of a document entitled *Sanctus Pontifex* and published May 24, 1973, by the Congregation for the Discipline of the Sacraments and the Congregation for the Clergy, with the approval of Pope Paul VI.

What the document prescribed was the observance of practices ordered by St. Pius X in the decree *Quam Singulari* of Aug. 8, 1910. Its purpose was to counteract pastoral and catechetical experiments virtually denying children the opportunity of receiving both sacraments at the same time. Termination of such experiments was ordered by the end of the 1972-73 school year.

At the time the document was issued, two- or three-year experiments of this kind — routinely deferring reception of the sacrament of penance until after the first reception of Holy Communion — were in effect in more than half of the dioceses of the U.S. They have remained in effect in many places, despite the advisory from the Vatican.

One reason stated in support of such experiments is the view that children are not capable of serious sin at the age of seven or eight, when Communion is generally received for the first time, and therefore prior reception of the sacrament of penance is not necessary. Another reason is the purpose of making the distinctive nature of the two sacraments clearer to children.

The Vatican view reflected convictions that the principle and practice of devotional reception of penance are as valid for children as they are for adults, and that sound catechetical programs can avoid misconceptions about the two sacraments.

A second letter on the same subject and in the same vein was released May 19, 1977, by the aforementioned congregations. It was issued in response to the question:

" 'Whether it is allowed after the declaration of May 24, 1973, to continue to have, as a general rule, the reception of first Communion precede the reception of the sacrament of penance in those parishes in which this practice developed in the past few years.'

"The Sacred Congregations for the Sacraments and Divine Worship and for the Clergy, with the approval of the Supreme Pontiff, reply: Negative, and according to the mind of the declaration.

"The mind of the declaration is that one year after the promulgation of the same declaration, all experiments of receiving first Communion without the sacrament of penance should cease so that the discipline of the Church might be restored, in the spirit of the decree, *Quam Singulari*."

The two letters from the Vatican congregations have not produced uniformity of practice in this country. Simultaneous preparation for both sacraments is provided in some dioceses where a child has the option of receiving either sacrament first, with the counsel of parents, priests and teachers. Programs in other dioceses are geared first to reception of Communion and later to reception of the sacrament of reconciliation.

Commentators on the letters note that: they are disciplinary rather than doctrinal in content; they are subject to pastoral interpretation by bishops; they cannot be interpreted to mean that a person who is not guilty of serious sin must be required to receive the sacrament of penance before (even first) Communion.

Canon 914 of the Code of Canon Law states that sacramental confession should precede first Communion.

**Holy Communion under the Forms of Bread and Wine** (by separate taking of the consecrated bread and wine or by intinction, the reception of the host dipped in the wine): Such reception is permitted under conditions stated in instructions issued by the Congregation for Divine Worship (May 25, 1967; June 29, 1970), the *General Instruction on the Roman Missal* (No. 242), and directives of bishops' conferences and individual bishops.

Accordingly, Communion can be administered in this way to: persons being baptized, received into communion with the Church, confirmed, receiving anointing of the sick; couples at their wedding or jubilee; religious at profession or renewal of profession; lay persons receiving an ecclesiastical assignment (e.g., lay missionaries); participants at concelebrated Masses, retreats, pastoral commission meetings, daily Masses and on other occasions.

**Holy Communion Twice a Day:** The reception of Holy Communion at Mass a second time on the same day is permitted. A person in danger of death is urged to receive Communion a second time, even outside of Mass.

**Holy Communion and Eucharistic Devotion outside of Mass:** These were the subjects of an instruction (*De Sacra Communione et de Cultu Mysterii Eucharistici extra Missam*) dated June 21 and made public Oct. 18, 1973, by the Congregation for Divine Worship.

Holy Communion can be given outside of Mass to persons unable for a reasonable cause to receive it during Mass on a given day. The ceremonial rite is modeled on the structure of the Mass, consisting of a penitential act, a scriptural reading, the Lord's Prayer, a sign or gesture of peace, giving of the Eucharist, prayer and final blessing. Viaticum and Communion to the sick can be given by extraordinary ministers (authorized lay persons) with appropriate rites.

Forms of devotion outside of Mass are exposition of the Blessed Sacrament (by men or women religious, especially, or lay persons in the absence of a priest; but only a priest can give the blessing), processions and congresses with appropriate rites.

**Intercommunion:** Church policy on intercommunion was stated in an "Instruction on the Admission of Other Christians to the Eucharist," dated June 1 and made public July 8, 1972, against the background of the *Decree on Ecumenism* approved by the Second Vatican Council, and the *Directory on Ecumenism* issued by the Secretariat for Promoting Christian Unity in 1967.

Basic principles related to intercommunion are:

• "There is an indissoluble link between the mystery of the Church and the mystery of the Eucharist, or between ecclesial and Eucharistic communion; the celebration of the Eucharist of itself signifies the fullness of profession of faith and ecclesial communion" (1972 Instruction).

• "Eucharistic communion practiced by those who are not in full ecclesial communion with each other cannot be the expression of that full unity which the Eucharist of its nature signifies and which in this case does not exist; for this reason such communion cannot be regarded as a means to be used to lead to full ecclesial communion" (1972 Instruction).

• The question of reciprocity "arises only with those churches which have preserved the substance of the Eucharist, the sacrament of orders and apostolic succession" (1967 Directory).

• "A Catholic cannot ask for the Eucharist except from a minister who has been validly ordained" (1967 Directory).

The policy distinguishes between separated Eastern Christians and other Christians.

*With Separated Eastern Christians* (e.g., Orthodox): These may be given the Eucharist (as well as penance and anointing of the sick) at their request. Catholics may receive these same sacraments from priests of separated Eastern churches if they experience genuine spiritual necessity, seek spiritual benefit, and access to a Catholic priest is morally or physically impossible. This policy (of reciprocity) derives from the facts that the separated Eastern churches have apostolic succession through their bishops, valid priests, and sacramental beliefs. and practices in accord with those of the Catholic Church .

*With Other Christians* (e.g., members of Reformation-related churches, others): Admission to the Eucharist in the Catholic Church, according to the *Directory on Ecumenism,* "is confined to particular cases of those Christians who have a faith in the sacrament in conformity with that of the Church, who experience a serious spiritual need for the Eucharistic sustenance, who for a prolonged period are unable to have recourse to a minister of their own community and who ask for the sacrament of their own accord; all this provided that they have proper dispositions and lead lives worthy of a Christian." The spiritual need is defined as "a need for an increase in spiritual life and a need for a deeper involvement in the mystery of the Church and of its unity."

Circumstances under which Communion may be given to other properly disposed Christians are danger of death, imprisonment, persecution, grave spiritual necessity coupled with no chance of recourse to a minister of their own community.

Catholics cannot ask for the Eucharist from ministers of other Christian churches who have not been validly ordained to the priesthood.

## Penance

Penance is the sacrament by which sins committed after baptism are forgiven and a person is reconciled with God and the Church.

Individual and integral confession and absolution are the only ordinary means for the forgiveness of serious sin and for reconciliation with God and the Church.

(Other than ordinary means are perfect contrition and general absolution without prior confession, both of which require the intention of subsequent confession and absolution.)

A revised ritual for the sacrament — *Ordo Paenitentiae,* published by the Congregation of Divine Worship Feb. 7, 1974, and made mandatory in the U.S. from the first Sunday of Lent, 1977 — reiterates standard doctrine concerning the sacrament; emphasizes the social (communal and ecclesial) aspects of sin and conversion, with due regard for personal aspects and individual reception of the sacrament; prescribes three forms for celebration of the sacrament; and presents models for community penitential services.

The basic elements of the sacrament are sorrow for sin because of a supernatural motive, confession (of previously unconfessed mortal or grave sins, required; of venial sins also, but not of necessity), and reparation (by means of prayer or other act enjoined by the confessor), all of which comprise the matter of the sacrament; and absolution, which is the form of the sacrament.

The traditional words of absolution — "I absolve you from your sins in the name of the Father, and of the Son, and of the Holy Spirit" — remain unchanged at the conclusion of a petition in the new rite that God may grant pardon and peace through the ministry of the Church.

The minister of the sacrament is an authorized priest — i.e., one who, besides having the power of orders to forgive sins, also has faculties of jurisdiction granted by an ecclesiastical superior and/or by canon law.

The sacrament can be celebrated in three ways.

• For individuals: The traditional manner remains acceptable but is enriched with additional elements including: reception of the penitent and making of the Sign of the Cross; an exhortation by the confessor to trust in God; a reading from Scripture; confession of sins; manifestation of repentance; petition for God's forgiveness through the ministry of the Church and the absolution of the priest; praise of God's mercy, and dismissal in peace. Some of these elements are optional.

• For several penitents, in the course of a community celebration including a Liturgy of the Word of God and prayers, individual confession and absolution, and an act of thanksgiving.

• For several penitents, in the course of a community celebration, with general confession and general absolution. In extraordinary cases, reconciliation may be attained by general absolution without prior individual confession as, for example, under these circumstances: (1) danger of death, when there is neither time nor priests available for hearing confessions; (2) grave necessity of a number of penitents who, because of a shortage of confessors, would be deprived of sacramental grace or Communion for a lengthy period of time through no fault of their own. Persons receiving general absolution are obliged to be properly disposed and resolved to make an individual confession of the grave sins from which they have been absolved; this confession should be made as soon as the opportunity to confess presents itself and before any second reception of general absolution.

Norms regarding general absolution, issued by the Congregation for the Doctrine of the Faith in 1972, are not intended to provide a basis for convoking large gatherings of the faithful for the purpose of imparting general absolution, in the absence of extraordinary circumstances. Judgment about circumstances that warrant general absolution belongs principally to the bishop of the place, with due regard for related decisions of appropriate episcopal conferences.

Communal celebrations of the sacrament are not held in connection with Mass.

The place of individual confession, as determined by episcopal conferences in accordance with given norms, can be the traditional confessional or another appropriate setting.

A precept of the Church obliges the faithful guilty of grave sin to confess at least once a year.

The Church favors more frequent reception of the sacrament not only for the reconciliation of persons guilty of serious sins but also for reasons of devotion. Devotional confession — in which venial sins or previously forgiven sins are confessed — serves the purpose of confirming persons in penance and conversion.

**Penitential Celebrations:** Communal penitential celebrations are designed to emphasize the social dimensions of Christian life — the community aspects and significance of penance and reconciliation.

Elements of such celebrations are community prayer, hymns and songs, scriptural and other readings, examination of conscience, general confession and expression of sorrow for sin, acts of penance and reconciliation, and a form of non-sacramental absolution resembling the one in the penitential rite of the Mass.

If the sacrament is celebrated during the service, there must be individual confession and absolution of sin.

(See Absolution, Confession, Confessional, Confessor, Contrition, Faculties, Forgiveness of Sin, Power of the Keys, Seal of Confession, Sin.)

### Anointing of the Sick

This sacrament, promulgated by St. James the Apostle (Jas. 5:13-15), can be administered to the faithful after reaching the age of reason who begin to be in danger because of illness or old age. By the anointing with blessed oil and the prayer of a priest, the sacrament confers on the person comforting grace; the remission of venial sins and inculpably unconfessed mortal sins, together with at least some of the temporal punishment due for sins; and, sometimes, results in an improved state of health.

The matter of this sacrament is the anointing with blessed oil (of the sick — olive oil, or vegetable oil if necessary) of the forehead and hands; in cases of necessity, a single anointing of another portion of the body suffices. The form is: "Through this holy anointing and his most loving mercy, may the Lord assist you by the grace of the Holy Spirit so that, when you have been freed from your sins, he may save you and in his goodness raise you up."

Anointing of the sick, formerly called extreme unction, may be received more than once, e.g., in new or continuing stages of serious illness. Ideally, the sacrament should be administered while the recipient is conscious and in conjunction with the sacraments of penance and the Eucharist. It should be administered in cases of doubt as to whether the person has reached the age of reason, is dangerously ill or dead.

The sacrament can be administered during a communal celebration in some circumstances, as in a home for the aged.

### Matrimony

Coverage of the sacrament of matrimony is given in the articles, Marriage Doctrine, *Humanae Vitae*, Marriage Laws, Pastoral Ministry for Divorced and Remarried.

### Holy Orders

Holy orders is the sacrament by which spiritual power and grace are given to constitute and enable an ordained minister to consecrate the Eucharist, forgive sins, perform other pastoral and ecclesiastical functions, and form the community of the People of God. Holy orders confers a character on the soul and can be received only once. The minister of the sacrament is a bishop.

Holy orders, like matrimony but in a different way, is a social sacrament. As the Second Vatican Council declared in the *Dogmatic Constitution on the Church:*

'For the nurturing and constant growth of the People of God, Christ the Lord instituted in his Church a variety of ministries, which work for the good of the whole body. For those ministers who are endowed with sacred power are servants of their brethren, so that all who are of the People of God, and therefore enjoy a true Christian dignity, can work toward a common goal freely and in an orderly way, and arrive at salvation" (No. 18).

**Bishop:** The fullness of the priesthood belongs to those who have received the order of bishop. Bishops, in hierarchical union with the pope and their fellow bishops, are the successors of the Apostles as pastors of the Church: they have individual responsibility for the care of the local churches they serve and collegial responsibility for the care of the universal Church (see Collegiality). In the ordination or consecration of bishops, the essential form is the imposition of hands by the consecrator(s) and the assigned prayer in the preface of the rite of ordination.

"With their helpers, the priests and deacons, bishops have . . . taken up the service of the community presiding in place of God over the flock whose shepherds they are, as teachers of doctrine, priests of sacred worship, and officers of good order" (No. 20).

**Priests:** A priest is an ordained minister with the power to celebrate Mass, administer the sacraments, preach and teach the word of God, impart blessings, and perform additional pastoral functions, according to the mandate of his ecclesiastical superior.

Concerning priests, the Second Vatican Council stated in the *Dogmatic Constitution on the Church* (No. 28):

"The divinely established ecclesiastical ministry is exercised on different levels by those who from antiquity have been called bishops, priests, and deacons. Although priests do not possess the highest degree of the priesthood, and although they are dependent on the bishops in the exercise of their power, they are nevertheless united with the bishops in sacerdotal dignity. By the power of the sacrament of orders, and in the image of Christ the eternal High Priest (Hb. 5:1-10; 7:24; 9:11-28), they are consecrated to preach the Gospel, shepherd the faithful, and celebrate divine worship as true priests of the New Testament. . . .

"Priests, prudent cooperators with the episcopal order as well as its aides and instruments, are called to serve the People of God. They constitute one priesthood with their bishop, although that priesthood is comprised of different functions."

In the ordination of a priest of Roman Rite, the essential matter is the imposition of hands on the heads of those being ordained by the ordaining bishop. The essential form is the accompanying prayer in the preface of the ordination ceremony. Other elements in the rite are the presentation of the implements of sacrifice — the chalice containing wine and the paten containing a host — with accompanying prayers.

**Deacon:** There are two kinds of deacons: those who receive the order and remain in it permanently, and those who receive the order while advancing to ordination to the priesthood. The following quotation — from Vatican II's *Dogmatic Constitution on the Church* (No. 29) — describes the nature and role of the diaconate, with emphasis on the permanent diaconate.

"At a lower level of the hierarchy are deacons, upon whom hands are imposed 'not unto the priesthood, but unto a ministry of service.' For strengthened by sacramental grace, in communion with the bishop and his group of priests, they serve the People of God in the ministry of the liturgy, of the word, and of charity. It is the duty of the deacon, to the extent that he has been authorized by competent authority, to administer baptism solemnly, to be custodian and dispenser of the Eucharist, to assist at and bless marriages in the name of the Church, to bring Viaticum to the dying, to read the sacred Scripture to the faithful, to instruct and ex-

hort the people, to preside at the worship and prayer of the faithful, to administer sacramentals, and to officiate at funeral and burial services. (Deacons are) dedicated to duties of charity and administration."

"The diaconate can in the future be restored as a proper and permanent rank of the hierarchy. It pertains to the competent territorial bodies of bishops, of one kind or another, to decide, with the approval of the Supreme Pontiff, whether and where it is opportune for such deacons to be appointed for the care of souls. With the consent of the Roman Pontiff, this diaconate will be able to be conferred upon men of more mature age, even upon those living in the married state. It may also be conferred upon suitable young men. For them, however, the law of celibacy must remain intact" (No. 29).

The Apostles ordained the first seven deacons (Acts 6:1-6): Stephen, Philip, Prochorus, Nicanor, Timon, Parmenas, Nicholas.

**Other Ministries:** The Church later assigned ministerial duties to men in several other orders, as:

Subdeacon, with specific duties in liturgical worship, especially at Mass. The order, whose first extant mention dates from about the middle of the third century, was regarded as minor until the 13th century; afterwards, it was called a major order in the West but not in the East.

Acolyte, to serve in minor capacities in liturgical worship; a function now performed by Mass servers.

Exorcist, to perform services of exorcism for expelling evil spirits; a function which came to be reserved to specially delegated priests.

Lector, to read scriptural and other passages during liturgical worship; a function now generally performed by lay persons.

Porter, to guard the entrance to an assembly of Christians and to ward off undesirables who tried to gain admittance; an order of early origin and utility but of present insignificance.

Long after it became evident that these positions and functions had fallen into general disuse or did not require clerical ordination, the Holy See started a revision of the orders in 1971. By an indult of Oct. 5, the bishops of the United States were permitted to omit ordaining porters and exorcists. Another indult, dated three days later, permitted the use of revised rites for ordaining acolytes and lectors, and authorized the use of a service celebrating admission to the clerical state in place of the ceremony of tonsure which had previously served this purpose.

To complete the revision, Pope Paul VI abolished Sept. 14, 1972, the orders of porter, exorcist and subdeacon; decreed that laymen, as well as candidates for the diaconate and priesthood, can be installed (rather than ordained) in the ministries (rather than orders) of acolyte and lector; reconfirmed the suppression of tonsure and its replacement with a service of dedication to God and the Church; and stated that a man enters the clerical state on ordination to the diaconate.

## PERMANENT DIACONATE

Authorization for restoration of the permanent diaconate in the Roman Rite — making it possible for men to become deacons permanently, without going on to the priesthood — was promulgated by Pope Paul VI June 18, 1967, in a document entitled *Sacrum Diaconatus Ordinem* ("Sacred Order of the Diaconate").

The Pope's action implemented the desire expressed by the Second Vatican Council for reestablishment of the diaconate as an independent order in its own right not only to supply ministers for carrying on the work of the Church but also to complete the hierarchical structure of the Church of Roman Rite.

Permanent deacons have been traditional in the Eastern Church. The Western Church, however, since the fourth or fifth century, generally followed the practice of conferring the diaconate only as a sacred order preliminary to the priesthood, and of restricting the ministry of deacons to liturgical functions.

The Pope's document, issued on his own initiative, provided:

• Qualified unmarried men 25 years of age or older may be ordained permanent deacons. They cannot marry after ordination.

• Qualified married men 35 years of age or older may be ordained permanent deacons. The consent of the wife of a prospective deacon is required. A married deacon cannot remarry after the death of his wife.

• Preparation for the diaconate includes a course of study and formation over a period of at least three years.

• Candidates who are not Religious must be affiliated with a diocese. Reestablishment of the permanent diaconate among Religious is reserved to the Holy See.

• Deacons will practice their ministry under the direction of a bishop and with the priests with whom they will be associated. (For functions, see the description of deacon, under Holy Orders.)

Restoration of the permanent diaconate in the United States was approved by the Holy See in October, 1968. Shortly afterwards the U.S. bishops established a committee of the same name, which is chaired by Bishop John F. Kinney of Bismarck. The committee operates through a secretariat, with offices at 1312 Massachusetts Ave. N. W., Washington, D.C. 20005.

### Status and Functions

Reports filed by 124 program directors in response to an October, 1983, questionnaire indicated that there were in the U.S. 6,598 permanent deacons (722 more than in 1982) and 2,203 candidates (137 less than in 1982). Hispanic deacons numbered 794; Blacks, 265. Fifty-nine per cent of the deacons had a college education.

Sixteen dioceses had 100 or more deacons; the leaders were Chicago with 417 and Newark with 219. Thirty-one deacons and six candidates were members of religious communities.

Training programs of spiritual, doctrinal and pastoral formation are generally based on *Permanent Deacons in the United States: Guidelines on Their Formation and Ministry*, published by the Bishops' Committee on the Permanent Diaconate in September, 1971.

Deacons have various functions, depending on the nature of their assignments. Liturgically, they can officiate at baptisms, weddings, wake services and funerals, can preach and distribute Holy Communion. Some are engaged in religious education work. All are intended to carry out works of charity and pastoral service of one kind or another.

The majority of permanent deacons, 94 per cent of whom are married, continue in their secular work. Their ministry of service is developing in three dimensions: of liturgy, of the word, and of charity. Depending on the individual deacon's abilities and preference, he is assigned by his bishop to either a parochial ministry or to one particular field of service. The latter is the most challenging ministry to develop. Deacons are active in a variety of ministries including those to prison inmates and their families, the sick in hospitals, nursing homes and homes for the aged, alienated youth, the elderly and the poor, and in various areas of legal service to the indigent, of education and campus ministry. Some deacons have been assigned as administrators of parishes. The possibilities for diaconal ministry are under realistic assessment, diocese by diocese.

**National Association of Permanent Diaconate Directors:** Membership organization of directors, vicars and other staff personnel of permanent diaconate programs. Established in 1977 to promote effective communication and facilitate the exchange of information and resources of members; to develop professional expertise and promote research, training and self evaluation; to foster accountability and seek ways to promote means of implementing solutions to problems. NAPDD is governed by an executive board of elected officers. President for the 1984-85 term: Rev. Timothy Shugrue, 97 Ridge Rd., Newark, N.J. 07104.

## NORTH AMERICAN COLLEGE

The North American College was founded by the bishops of the United States in 1859 as a residence and house of formation for U.S. seminarians and graduate students in Rome. The first ordination of an alumnus took place June 14, 1862. Pontifical status was granted the college by Leo XIII Oct. 25, 1884. Students living at the college study theology and related subjects in the various pontifical universities and institutes in Rome, principally at the Pontifical Gregorian University.

The college is directed by an American rector (Msgr. Lawrence Purcell of San Diego) and staff, and operates under the auspices of a U.S. bishops' committee which was set up in 1924.

# MARRIAGE DOCTRINE

*The following excerpts, stating key points of doctrine on marriage, are from the "Pastoral Constitution on the Church in the Modern World" (Nos. 48 to 51) promulgated by the Second Vatican Council.*

## Conjugal Covenant

The intimate partnership of married life and love has been established by the Creator and qualified by his laws. It is rooted in the conjugal covenant of irrevocable personal consent.

God himself is the author of matrimony, endowed as it is with various benefits and purposes. All of these have a very decisive bearing on the continuation of the human race, on the personal development and eternal destiny of the individual members of a family, and on the dignity, stability, peace, and prosperity of the family itself and of human society as a whole. By their very nature, the institution of matrimony itself and conjugal love are ordained for the procreation and education of children, and find in them their ultimate crown.

Thus a man and a woman . . . render mutual help and service to each other through an intimate union of their persons and of their actions. Through this union they experience the meaning of their oneness and attain to it with growing perfection day by day. As a mutual gift of two persons, this intimate union, as well as the good of the children, imposes total fidelity on the spouses and argues for an unbreakable oneness between them (No. 48).

## Sacrament of Matrimony

Christ the Lord abundantly blessed this many-faceted love. . . . The Savior of men and the Spouse of the Church comes into the lives of married Christians through the sacrament of matrimony. He abides with them thereafter so that, just as he loved the Church and handed himself over on her behalf, the spouses may love each other with perpetual fidelity through mutual self-bestowal.

Graced with the dignity and office of fatherhood and motherhood, parents will energetically acquit themselves of a duty which devolves primarily on them; namely, education, and especially religious education.

The Christian family, which springs from marriage as a reflection of the loving covenant uniting Christ with the Church, and as a participation in that covenant, will manifest to all men the Savior's living presence in the world, and the genuine nature of the Church (No. 48).

## Conjugal Love

The biblical Word of God several times urges the betrothed and the married to nourish and develop their wedlock by pure conjugal love and undivided affection.

This love is an eminently human one since it is directed from one person to another through an affection of the will. It involves the good of the whole person. Therefore it can enrich the expressions of body and mind with a unique dignity, ennobling these expressions as special ingredients and signs of the friendship distinctive of marriage. This love the Lord has judged worthy of special gifts, healing, perfecting, and exalting gifts of grace and of charity.

Such love, merging the human with the divine, leads the spouses to a free and mutual gift of themselves, a gift proving itself by gentle affection and by deed. Such love pervades the whole of their lives. Indeed, by its generous activity it grows better and grows greater. Therefore it far excels mere erotic inclination, which, selfishly pursued, soon enough fades wretchedly away.

This love is uniquely expressed and perfected through the marital act. The actions within marriage by which the couple are united intimately and chastely are noble and worthy ones. Expressed in a manner which is truly human, these actions signify and promote that mutual self-giving by which spouses enrich each other with a joyful and a thankful will.

Sealed by mutual faithfulness and hallowed above all by Christ's sacrament, this love remains steadfastly true in body and in mind, in bright days or dark. It will never be profaned by adultery or divorce. Firmly established by the Lord, the unity of marriage will radiate from the equal personal dignity of wife and husband, a dignity acknowledged by mutual and total love.

The steady fulfillment of the duties of this Christian vocation demands notable virtue. For this reason, strengthened by grace for holiness of life, the couple will painstakingly cultivate and pray for constancy of love, largeheartedness, and the spirit of sacrifice (No. 49).

## Fruitfulness of Marriage

Marriage and conjugal love are by their nature ordained toward the begetting and educating of children. Children are really the supreme gift of marriage and contribute very substantially to the welfare of their parents. . . . God himself . . . wished to share with man a certain special participation in his own creative work. Thus he blessed male and female, saying: "Increase and multiply" (Gn. 1:28).

Hence, while not making the other purposes of matrimony of less account, the true practice of conjugal love, and the whole meaning of the family life which results from it, have this aim: that the couple be ready with stout hearts to cooperate with the love of the Creator and the Savior, who through them will enlarge and enrich his own family day by day.

Parents should regard as their proper mission the task of transmitting human life and educating those to whom it has been transmitted. They should realize that they are thereby cooperators with the love of God the Creator, and are, so to speak, the interpreters of that love. Thus they will fulfill their task with human and Christian responsibility (No. 50).

## Norms of Judgment

They will thoughtfully take into account both their own welfare and that of their children, those already born and those who may be foreseen. For this accounting they will reckon with both the material and the spiritual conditions of the times as well as of their state in life. Finally, they will consult the interests of the family group, of temporal society, and of the Church herself.

The parents themselves should ultimately make this judgment in the sight of God. But in their manner of acting, spouses should be aware that they cannot proceed arbitrarily. They must always be governed according to a conscience dutifully conformed to the divine law itself, and should be submissive toward the Church's teaching office, which authentically interprets that law in the light of the Gospel. That divine law reveals and protects the integral meaning of conjugal love, and impels it toward a truly human fulfillment.

Marriage, to be sure, is not instituted solely for procreation. Rather, its very nature as an unbreakable compact between persons, and the welfare of the children, both demand that the mutual love of the spouses, too, be embodied in a rightly ordered manner, that it grow and ripen. Therefore, marriage persists as a whole manner and communion of life, and maintains its value and indissolubility, even when offspring are lacking — despite, rather often, the very intense desire of the couple (No. 50).

## Love and Life

This Council realizes that certain modern conditions often keep couples from arranging their married lives harmoniously, and that they find themselves in circumstances where at least temporarily the size of their families should not be increased. As a result, the faithful exercise of love and the full intimacy of their lives are hard to maintain. But where the intimacy of married life is broken off, it is not rare for its faithfulness to be imperiled and its quality of fruitfulness ruined. For then the upbringing of the children and the courage to accept new ones are both endangered.

To these problems there are those who presume to offer dishonorable solutions. Indeed, they do not recoil from the taking of life. But the Church issues the reminder that a true contradiction cannot exist between the divine laws pertaining to the transmission of life and those pertaining to the fostering of authentic conjugal love.

For God, the Lord of Life, has conferred on men the surpassing ministry of safeguarding life — a ministry which must be fulfilled in a manner which is worthy of men. Therefore from the moment of its conception life must be guarded with the greatest care, while abortion and infanticide are unspeakable crimes. The sexual characteristics of man and the human faculty of reproduction wonderfully exceed the dispositions of lower forms of life. Hence the acts themselves which are proper to conjugal love and which are exercised in accord with genuine human dignity must be honored with great reverence (No. 51).

## Church Teaching

Therefore when there is question of harmonizing conjugal love with the responsible transmission of life, the moral aspect of any procedure does not depend solely on the sincere intentions or on an evaluation of motives. It must be determined by objective standards. These, based on the nature of the human person and his acts, preserve the full sense of mutual self-giving and human procreation in the context of true love. Such a goal cannot be achieved unless the virtue of conjugal chastity is sincerely practiced. Relying on these principles, sons of the Church may not undertake methods of regulating procreation which are found blameworthy by the teaching authority of the Church in its unfolding of the divine law.

Everyone should be persuaded that human life and the task of transmitting it are not realities bound up with this world alone. Hence they cannot be measured or perceived only in terms of it, but always have a bearing on the eternal destiny of men (No. 51).

# HUMANAE VITAE

*Marriage doctrine and morality were the subjects of the encyclical "Humanae Vitae" ("Of Human Life") issued by Pope Paul, July 29, 1968. Following are a number of key excerpts from the document, which was framed in the pattern of traditional teaching and statements by the Second Vatican Council.*

Each and every marriage act ("quilibet matrimonii usus") must remain open to the transmission of life (No. 11).

Indeed, by its intimate structure, the conjugal act, while most closely uniting husband and wife, capacitates them for the generation of new lives, according to laws inscribed in the very being of man and of woman. By safeguarding both these essential aspects, the unitive and the procreative, the conjugal act preserves in its fullness the sense of true mutual love and its ordination toward man's most high calling to parenthood (No. 12).

It is, in fact, justly observed that a conjugal act imposed upon one's partner without regard for his or her condition and lawful desires is not a true act of love, and therefore denies an exigency of right moral order in the relationships between husband and wife. Hence, one who reflects well must also recognize that a reciprocal act of love which jeopardizes the responsibility to transmit life — which God the Creator, according to particular laws, inserted therein — is in contradiction with the design constitutive of marriage and with the will of the Author of life. To use this divine gift, destroying, even if only partially, its meaning and its purpose, is to contradict the nature both of man and of woman and of their most intimate relationship, and therefore it is to contradict also the plan of God and his will (No. 13).

## Forbidden Actions

The direct interruption of the generative process already begun, and, above all, directly willed and procured abortion, even if for therapeutic reasons, are to be absolutely excluded as licit means of regulating birth.

Equally to be excluded . . . is direct sterilization, whether perpetual or temporary, whether of the man or of the woman. Similarly excluded is every action which, either in anticipation of the conjugal act, or in its accomplishment, or in the development of its natural consequences, proposes, whether as an end or as a means, to render procreation impossible.

## Inadmissible Principles

To justify conjugal acts made intentionally infecund, one cannot invoke as valid reasons the lesser evil, or the fact that such acts would constitute a whole together with the fecund acts already performed or to follow later and hence would share in one and the same moral goodness. In truth, if it is sometimes licit to tolerate a lesser evil in order to avoid a greater evil or to promote a greater good, it is not licit, even for the gravest reasons, to do evil so that good may follow therefrom; that is, to make into the object of a positive act of the will something which is intrinsically disorder, and hence unworthy of the human person, even when the intention is to safeguard or promote individual, family or social well-being.

Consequently, it is an error to think that a conjugal act which is deliberately made infecund, and so is intrinsically dishonest, could be made honest and right by the ensemble of a fecund conjugal life (No. 14).

## Family Planning

If, then, there are serious motives to space out births, which derive from the physical or psychological conditions of husband and wife, or from external conditions, the Church teaches that it is then licit to take into account the natural rhythms immanent in the generative functions, for the use of marriage in the infecund periods only, and in this way to regulate birth without offending earlier stated principles (No. 16).

## Pastoral Concern

We do not at all intend to hide the sometimes serious difficulties inherent in the life of Christian married persons; for them, as for everyone else, "the gate is narrow and the way is hard that leads to life." But the hope of that life must illuminate their way, as with courage they strive to live with wisdom, justice and piety in this present time, knowing that the figure of this world passes away.

Let married couples, then, face up to the efforts needed, supported by the faith and hope which "do not disappoint . . . because God's love has been poured into our hearts through the Holy Spirit, who has been given to us." Let them implore divine assistance by persevering prayer; above all, let them draw from the source of grace and charity in the Eucharist. And, if sin should still keep its hold over them, let them not be discouraged but rather have recourse with humble perseverance to the mercy of God, which is poured forth in the sacrament of penance (No. 25).

## STATEMENTS OF POPE JOHN PAUL

Teaching enunciated by Pope Paul VI in *Humanae Vitae* and by the Second Vatican Council in the *Pastoral Constitution on the Church in the Modern World* has been reaffirmed time after time by Pope John Paul since the beginning of his pontificate. Following are several of his statements.

### Objectively Wrong

Addressing 50 priests attending a seminar on responsible procreation Sept. 17, 1983, he said: "Contraception is to be judged objectively so profoundly illicit that it can never, for any reason, be justified. To think, or to say, anything to the contrary is tantamount to saying that in human life there can be situations where it is legitimate not to recognize God as God."

Users of contraception "attribute to themselves a power that belongs only to God; the power to decide in the final instance the coming into existence of a human being."

The Pope also said that the sexual act should symbolize in marriage the complete donation of the essential beings of two persons to each other. But: "The contraceptive act introduces a substantial limitation . . . of this reciprocal donation and expresses an objective refusal to give to the other all the good of femininity or masculinity."

### Encyclical and Council

In one of a series of about a dozen talks on *Humanae Vitae* at general audiences during the summer of 1984, Pope John Paul said July 11 that in the encyclical letter "we are reminded of the Church's teaching that each marriage act must remain open to the transmission of life.

"The inseparable connection between the unitive and procreative aspects of marriage is founded on the intimate structure of the conjugal act itself, which enables husband and wife to generate new life, according to laws inscribed in the very being of man and of woman. By safeguarding both of these essential aspects, the conjugal act preserves in its fullness the sense of true mutual love. At the same time, it remains faithful to God's design for the purposes of marriage in directing husband and wife toward their high calling of parenthood."

On July 25, the Holy Father continued: "Today we continue our reflection on the ethical dimension of conjugal love by linking the teaching of the encyclical *Humanae Vitae* to our whole treatment of the theology of the body. The encyclical serves as a complement to the doctrine expressed in the pastoral constitution *Gaudium et Spes* of the Second Vatican Council. We find clear emphasis on the importance of harmonizing human love with a respect for life. The Church teaches that there can be no conflict between the divine laws which govern the transmission of life and which foster authentic married love.

"The council document and the encyclical of Pope Paul VI have the same aim, namely, to respond to the moral questions of the people of our time. Both documents seek to show the Church's great pastoral concern for the welfare of contemporary man and woman. To many people, the Church's teaching on the regulation of birth will appear difficult to put into practice. Indeed, its observance would not be possible without the help of God, who upholds and strengthens the human will. Yet, to anyone who reflects well, it will be very clear that efforts to put this teaching into practice make the human person more noble and are truly beneficial to the human community.

"Our biblical theology of the body provides a key to understanding the basis of the Church's pastoral concern for the true good of the human person, and for the defense and promotion of authentic human values. Here we come to understand that the only true good of the human person consists in discovering ever more clearly God's plan concerning human love and putting this divine plan into practice, as God has willed it."

### Authoritative Teaching

Once again, on Aug. 1, the conciliar and papal documents keyed the Pontiff's remarks.

"The council document reminds us that, when it is a question of harmonizing married love with the responsible transmission of life, it is not enough to take into account one's own good intention and motivations. Objective criteria must be used, criteria drawn from the nature of the human person and human action, criteria which respect the total meaning of self-giving and human procreation in the context of true love. All this is possible only if the virtue of married chastity is seriously practiced. ... Members of the Church cannot use methods of birth control which are disapproved of by the Church's teaching authority.

"Responsible parenthood, according to the Second Vatican Council and the encyclical *Humanae Vitae,* calls for a careful reflection on the physical, psychological, economic and social conditions whereby the good of the individual, the good of the children already born or yet to come, as well as the good of the family, of society and of the Church, are properly taken into account. However, married people are called to realize that in their consideration of all these factors they must arrive at a judgment before God. In their behavior they must be ruled by conscience, that is, they must make their decisions in the light of the teaching authority of the Church, which is the authentic interpreter of divine law. For the divine law throws light on the meaning of married love, protects it and leads it to truly human fulfillment.

"In this way, the married couple remains faithful to the fundamental principle of the inseparable connection between the unitive and procreative meanings of the marriage act, a connection which conforms to the intimate structure of conjugal love as willed by God in his plan for the human race."

## MARRIAGE LAWS

The Catholic Church claims jurisdiction over its members in matters pertaining to marriage, which is a sacrament. Church legislation on the subject is stated principally in 111 canons of the Code of Canon Law.

Marriage laws of the Church provide juridical norms in support of the marriage covenant. In 10 chapters, the revised Code covers: pastoral directives for preparing men and women for marriage; impediments in general and in particular; matrimonial consent; form for the celebration of marriage; mixed marriages; secret celebration of marriage; effects of marriage; separation of spouses; and convalidation of marriage.

Catholics are bound by all marriage laws of the Church. Non-Catholics, whether baptized or not, are not considered bound by these ecclesiastical laws except in cases of marriage with a Catholic. Certain natural laws, in the Catholic view, bind all men and women, irrespective of their religious beliefs; accordingly, marriage is prohibited before the time of puberty, without knowledge and free mutual consent, in the case of an already existing valid marriage bond, in the case of antecedent and perpetual impotence.

### Formalities

These include, in addition to arrangements for the time and place of the marriage ceremony, doctrinal and moral instruction concerning marriage and the recording of data which verifies in documentary form the eligibility and freedom of the persons to marry. Records of this kind, which are confidential, are preserved in the archives of the church where the marriage takes place.

Premarital instructions are the subject matter of Pre-Cana Conferences.

### Marital Consent

The exchange of consent to the marriage covenant, which is essential for valid marriage, must be rational, free, true and mutual.

Matrimonial consent can be invalidated by an essential defect, substantial error, the strong influence of force and fear, the presence of a condition or intention against the nature of marriage.

### Form of Marriage

A Catholic is required, for validity and lawfulness, to contract marriage — with another Catholic or with a non-Catholic — in the presence of a competent priest or deacon and two witnesses.

There are two exceptions to this law. A Roman Rite Catholic (since Mar. 25, 1967) or an Eastern Rite Catholic (since Nov. 21, 1964) can contract marriage validly in the presence of a priest of a separated Eastern Rite Church, provided other requirements of law are complied with. With permission of the competent Roman-Rite or Eastern-Rite bishop, this form of marriage is lawful, as well as valid. (See Eastern Rite Laws, below.)

With these two exceptions, and aside from cases covered by special permission, the Church does not regard as valid any marriages involving Catholics which take place before non-Catholic ministers of religion or civil officials.

(An excommunication formerly in force against Catholics who celebrated marriage before a non-

Catholic minister was abrogated in a decree issued by the Sacred Congregation for the Doctrine of the Faith on Mar. 18, 1966.)

The ordinary place of marriage is the parish of either Catholic party or of the Catholic party in case of a mixed marriage.

Church law regarding the form of marriage does not affect non-Catholics in marriages among themselves. The Church recognizes as valid the marriages of non-Catholics before ministers of religion and civil officials, unless they are rendered null and void on other grounds.

The canonical form is not to be observed in the case of a marriage between a non-Catholic and a baptized Catholic who has left the Church by a formal act.

## Impediments

**Diriment Impediments** to marriage are factors which render a marriage invalid.

• age, which obtains before completion of the 14th year for a woman and the 16th year for a man;

• impotency, if it is antecedent to the marriage and permanent (this differs from sterility, which is not an impediment);

• the bond of an existing valid marriage;

• disparity of worship, which obtains when one party is a Catholic and the other party is unbaptized;

• sacred orders;

• religious profession of the perpetual vow of chastity;

• abduction, which impedes the freedom of the person abducted;

• crime, variously involving elements of adultery, promise or attempt to marry, conspiracy to murder a husband or wife;

• blood relationship in the direct line (father-daughter, mother-son, etc.) and to the fourth degree inclusive of the collateral line (brother-sister, first, second and third cousins);

• affinity, or relationship resulting from a valid marriage, in any degree of the direct line;

• public honesty, arising from an invalid marriage or from public or notorious concubinage; it renders either party incapable of marrying blood relatives of the other in the first degree of the direct line.

• legal relationship arising from adoption; it renders either party incapable of marrying relatives of the other in the direct line or in the second degree of the collateral line.

**Dispensations from Impediments:** Persons hindered by impediments either may not or cannot marry unless they are dispensed therefrom in view of reasons recognized in canon law. Local bishops can dispense from the impediments most often encountered (e.g., disparity of worship) as well as others.

Decision regarding some dispensations is reserved to the Holy See.

## Separation

A valid and consummated marriage of baptized persons cannot be dissolved by any human author-

ity or any cause other than the death of one of the persons.

In other circumstances:

• 1. A valid but unconsummated marriage of baptized persons, or of a baptized and an unbaptized person, can be dissolved:

a. by the solemn religious profession of one of the persons, made with permission of the pope. In such a case, the bond is dissolved at the time of profession, and the other person is free to marry again;

b. by dispensation from the pope, requested for a grave reason by one or both of the persons. If the dispensation is granted, both persons are free to marry again.

Dispensations in these cases are granted for reasons connected with the spiritual welfare of the concerned persons.

• 2. A legitimate marriage, even consummated, of unbaptized persons can be dissolved in favor of one of them who subsequently receives the sacrament of baptism. This is the Pauline Privilege, so called because it was promulgated by St. Paul (1 Cor. 7:12-15) as a means of protecting the faith of converts. Requisites for granting the privilege are:

a. marriage prior to the baptism of either person;

b. reception of baptism by one person;

c. refusal of the unbaptized person to live in peace with the baptized person and without interfering with his or her freedom to practice the Christian faith. The privilege does not apply if the unbaptized person agrees to these conditions.

• 3. A legitimate and consummated marriage of a baptized and an unbaptized person can be dissolved by the pope in virtue of the Privilege of Faith, also called the Petrine Privilege.

## Civil Divorce

Because of the unity and the indissolubility of marriage, the Church denies that civil divorce can break the bond of a valid marriage, whether the marriage involves two Catholics, a Catholic and a non-Catholic, or non-Catholics with each other.

In view of serious circumstances of marital distress, the Church permits an innocent and aggrieved party, whether wife or husband, to seek and obtain a civil divorce for the purpose of acquiring title and right to the civil effects of divorce, such as separate habitation and maintenance, and the custody of children. Permission for this kind of action should be obtained from proper church authority. The divorce, if obtained, does not break the bond of a valid marriage.

Under other circumstances — as would obtain if a marriage was invalid (see Annulment, below) — civil divorce is permitted for civil effects and as a civil ratification of the fact that the marriage bond really does not exist.

## Annulment

This is a decision by a competent church authority — e.g., a bishop, a diocesan marriage tribunal, the Sacred Roman Rota — that an apparently valid marriage was actually invalid from the beginning because of the unknown or concealed existence, from the beginning, of a diriment impediment, an essential defect in consent, radical incapability for marriage, or a condition placed by one or both of the parties against the very nature of marriage.

## Eastern Rite Laws

Marriage laws of the Eastern Church differ in several respects from the legislation of the Roman Rite. The regulations in effect since May 2, 1949, were contained in the motu proprio *Crebre Allatae* issued by Pius XII the previous February.

According to both the Roman Code of Canon Law and the Oriental Code, marriages between Roman Rite Catholics and Eastern Rite Catholics ordinarily take place in the rite of the groom and have canonical effects in that rite.

Regarding the form for the celebration of marriages between Eastern Catholics and baptized Eastern non-Catholics, the Second Vatican Council declared:

"By way of preventing invalid marriages between Eastern Catholics and baptized Eastern non-Catholics, and in the interests of the permanence and sanctity of marriage and of domestic harmony, this sacred Synod decrees that the canonical 'form' for the celebration of such marriages obliges only for lawfulness. For their validity, the presence of a sacred minister suffices, as long as the other requirements of law are honored" *(Decree on Eastern Catholic Churches,* No. 18).

Marriages taking place in this manner are lawful, as well as valid, with permission of a competent Eastern Rite bishop.

## The Rota

The Sacred Roman Rota is the ordinary court of appeal for marriage, and some other cases, which are appealed to the Holy See from lower church courts. Appeals are made to the Rota if decisions by diocesan and archdiocesan courts fail to settle the matter in dispute.

## MIXED MARRIAGES

"Mixed Marriages" *(Matrimonia Mixta)* was the subject of: (1) a letter issued under this title by Pope Paul VI Mar. 31, 1970, and (2) a statement, *Implementation of the Apostolic Letter on Mixed Marriages,* approved by the National Conference of Catholic Bishops Nov. 16, 1970.

One of the key points in the bishops' statement referred to the need for mutual pastoral care by ministers of different faiths for the sacredness of marriage and for appropriate preparation and con-

tinuing support of parties to a mixed marriage.

Pastoral experience, which the Catholic Church shares with other religious bodies, confirms the fact that marriages of persons of different beliefs involve special problems related to the continuing religious practice of the concerned persons and to the religious education and formation of their children.

Pastoral measures to minimize these problems include instruction of a non-Catholic party in essentials of the Catholic faith for purposes of understanding. Desirably, some instruction should also be given the Catholic party regarding his or her partner's beliefs.

## Requirements

The Catholic party to a mixed marriage is required to declare his (her) intention of continuing practice of the Catholic faith and to promise to do all in his (her) power to share his (her) faith with children born of the marriage by having them baptized and raised as Catholics. No declarations or promises are required of the non-Catholic party, but he (she) must be informed of the declaration and promise made by the Catholic.

Notice of the Catholic's declaration and promise is an essential part of the application made to a bishop for (1) permission to marry a baptized non-Catholic, or (2) a dispensation to marry an unbaptized non-Catholic.

A mixed marriage can take place with a Nuptial Mass. (The bishops' statement added this caution: "To the extent that Eucharistic sharing is not permitted by the general discipline of the Church, this is to be considered when plans are being made to have the mixed marriage at Mass or not.")

The ordinary minister at a mixed marriage is an authorized priest, and the ordinary place is the parish church of the Catholic party. A non-Catholic minister may not only attend the marriage ceremony but may also address, pray with and bless the couple.

For appropriate pastoral reasons, a bishop can grant a dispensation from the Catholic form of marriage and can permit the marriage to take place in a non-Catholic Church with a non-Catholic minister as the officiating minister. A priest may not only attend such a ceremony but may also address, pray with and bless the couple.

"It is not permitted," however, the bishops' statement declared, "to have two religious services or to have a single service in which both the Catholic marriage ritual and a non-Catholic marriage ritual are celebrated jointly or successively."

## PASTORAL MINISTRY FOR DIVORCED AND REMARRIED

Ministry to divorced and remarried Catholics is a difficult field of pastoral endeavor, situated as it is in circumstances tantamount to the horns of a dilemma.

### At Issue

On the one side is firm church teaching on the permanence of marriage and norms against reception of the Eucharist and full participation in the

life of the Church by Catholics in irregular unions.

On the other side are men and women with broken unions followed by second and perhaps happier attempts at marriage which the Church does not recognize as valid and which may not be capable of being validated because of the existence of an earlier marriage bond.

The forces at work in these circumstances are those of the Church, upholding its doctrine and practice regarding the permanence of marriage, and those of many men and women in irregular second marriages who desire full participation in the life of the Church.

Sacramental participation is not possible for those whose first marriage was valid, although there is no bar to their attendance at Mass, to sharing in other activities of the Church, or to their efforts to have children baptized and raised in the Catholic faith.

An exception to this rule is the condition of a divorced and remarried couple living in a brother-sister relationship.

There is no ban against sacramental participation by separated or divorced persons who have not attempted a second marriage.

Unverified estimates of the number of U.S. Catholics who are divorced and remarried vary between six and eight million.

## Tribunal Action

What can the Church do for them and with them in pastoral ministry, is an old question charged with new urgency because of the rising number of divorced and remarried Catholics.

One way to help is through the agency of marriage tribunals charged with responsibility for investigating and settling questions concerning the validity or invalidity of a prior marriage. There are reasons in canon law justifying the Church in declaring a particular marriage null and void from the beginning, despite the short- or long-term existence of an apparently valid union.

Decrees of nullity (annulments) are not new in the history of the Church. If such a decree is issued, a man or woman is free to validate a second marriage and live in complete union with the Church.

U.S. tribunals issued 450 annulments in 1968 and approximnately 48,000 in 1981. The increase was a result not just of new tribunal procedures but, more significantly, of judgments regarding the radical incapability of persons to contract valid marriage in the first place.

## Reasons behind Decrees

Pastoral experience reveals that some married persons, a short or long time after contracting an apparently valid marriage, exhibit signs that point back to the existence, at the time of marriage, of latent and serious personal deficiencies which made them incapable of valid consent and sacramental commitment.

Such deficiencies might include gross immaturity and those affecting in a serious way the capacity to love, to have a true interpersonal and conjugal relationship, to fulfill marital obligations, to accept the faith aspect of marriage.

Psychological and behavioral factors like these have been given greater attention by tribunals in recent years and have provided grounds for numerous decrees of nullity.

Decisions of this type do not indicate any softening of the Church's attitude regarding the permanence of marriage. They affirm, rather, that some persons who have married were really not capable of doing so.

Serious deficiencies in the capacity for real interpersonal relationship in marriage were the reasons behind a landmark decree of nullity issued in 1973 by the Roman Rota, the Vatican high court of appeals in marriage cases. Pope John Paul referred to such deficiencies — the "grave lack of discretionary judgment," incapability of assuming "essential matrimonial rights and obligations," for example — in an address Jan. 26, 1984, to personnel of the Rota.

## Decree Not Always Possible

The tribunal way to a decree of nullity regarding a previous marriage is not open to many persons in second marriages — because grounds are either lacking or, if present, cannot be verified in tribunal process.

Many men and women in this second category are aligned and in sympathy with aims of the North American Conference of Separated and Divorced Catholics, which has several hundred support groups in various parts of the United States and Canada. Formed early in 1972, the conference seeks a special pastoral ministry for divorced Catholics in second irregular unions.

This purpose is shared by the Judeans (founded in 1952) and by official ministries in many U.S. dioceses, by other church agencies and by hosts of priests.

The principal problem involved in such ministry is the lack of sacramental participation open to persons in irregular unions.

## Unacceptable Solution

One unacceptable solution of the problem, called "good conscience procedure," involves administration of the sacraments of penance and the Eucharist to divorced and remarried Catholics unable to obtain a decree of nullity for a first marriage who are living in a subsequent marriage "in good faith."

This procedure, despite the fact that it has no standing or recognition in church law, is being advocated and practiced by some priests and remarried Catholics.

## MARRIAGE ENCOUNTER

Marriage Encounter brings couples together for a weekend program of events directed by a team of several couples and a priest for the purpose of developing their abilities to communicate with each other in their life together as husband and wife. ME originated in Spain between the early 1950s and 1962 through the efforts of Father Gabriel Calvo and others interested in ministry to married couples.

The address of National Marriage Encounter is P.O. Box 4508, Ithaca, N.Y. 14852.

The national office of Worldwide Marriage Encounter is located at 1025 W. 3rd Ave., Columbus, O. 43212.

Commentators insist that ME is not a retreat, not for troubled marriages, and not an exercise in group dynamics.

The calendar of the Roman Church consists of an arrangement throughout the year of a series of liturgical seasons, commemorations of divine mysteries and commemorations of saints for purposes of worship.

The purposes of this calendar were outlined in the "Constitution on the Sacred Liturgy" (Nos. 102-105) promulgated by the Second Vatican Council.

Within the cycle of a year . . . (the Church) unfolds the whole mystery of Christ, not only from his incarnation and birth until his ascension, but also as reflected in the day of Pentecost, and the expectation of a blessed, hoped-for return of the Lord.

Recalling thus the mysteries of redemption, the Church opens to the faithful the riches of her Lord's powers and merits, so that these are in some way made present at all times, and the faithful are enabled to lay hold of them and become filled with saving grace (No. 102).

In celebrating this annual cycle of Christ's mysteries, holy Church honors with special love the Blessed Mary, Mother of God (No. 103).

The Church has also included in the annual cycle days devoted to the memory of the martyrs and the other saints. . . . (who) sing God's perfect praise in heaven and offer prayers for us. By celebrating the passage of these saints from earth to heaven the Church proclaims the paschal mystery as achieved in the saints who have suffered and been glorified with Christ; she proposes them to the faithful as examples who draw all to the Father through Christ, and through their merits she pleads for God's favors (No. 104).

In the various seasons of the year and according to her traditional discipline, the Church completes the formation of the faithful by means of pious practices for soul and body, by instruction, prayer, and works of penance and mercy (No. 105).

## THE ROMAN CALENDAR

Norms for a revised calendar for the Western Church as decreed by the Second Vatican Council were approved by Paul VI in the *motu proprio Mysterii Paschalis* dated Feb. 14, 1969. The revised calendar was promulgated a month later by a decree of the Congregation for Divine Worship and went into effect Jan. 1, 1970, with provisional modifications. Full implementation of all its parts was delayed in 1970 and 1971, pending the completion of work on related liturgical texts. The U.S. bishops ordered the calendar into effect for 1972.

### The Seasons

**Advent:** The liturgical year begins with the first Sunday of Advent, which introduces a season of four weeks or slightly less duration with the theme of expectation of the coming of Christ. During the first two weeks, the final coming of Christ as Lord and Judge at the end of the world is the focus of attention. From Dec. 17 to 24, the emphasis shifts to anticipation of the celebration of his Nativity on the solemnity of Christmas.

Advent has four Sundays. Since the 10th century, the first Sunday has marked the beginning of the liturgical year in the Western Church. In the Middle Ages, a kind of pre-Christmas fast was in vogue during the season.

**Christmas Season:** The Christmas season begins with the vigil of Christmas and lasts until the Sunday after January 6, inclusive.

The period between the end of the Christmas season and the beginning of Lent belongs to the Ordinary Time of the year. Of variable length, the pre-Lenten phase of this season includes what were formerly called the Sundays after Epiphany and the suppressed Sundays of Septuagesima, Sexagesima and Quinquagesima.

**Lent:** The penitential season of Lent begins on Ash Wednesday, which occurs between Feb. 4 and Mar. 11, depending on the date of Easter, and lasts until the Mass of the Lord's Supper (Holy Thursday). It has six Sundays. The sixth Sunday marks the beginning of Holy Week and is known as Passion (formerly called Palm) Sunday.

The origin of Lenten observances dates back to the fourth century or earlier.

**Easter Triduum:** The Easter Triduum begins with evening Mass of the Lord's Supper and ends with Evening Prayer on Easter Sunday.

**Easter Season:** The Easter season whose theme is resurrection from sin to the life of grace, lasts for 50 days, from Easter to Pentecost. Easter, the first Sunday following the vernal equinox, occurs between Mar. 22 and Apr. 25. The terminal phase of the Easter season, between the solemnities of the Ascension of the Lord and Pentecost, stresses anticipation of the coming and action of the Holy Spirit.

**Ordinary Time:** The season of Ordinary Time begins on the Monday after the Sunday following January 6 and continues until the day before Ash Wednesday, inclusive. It begins again on the Monday after Pentecost and ends on the Saturday before the first Sunday of Advent. It consists of 33 or 34 weeks. The last Sunday is celebrated as the Solemnity of Christ the King. The overall purpose of the season is to elaborate the themes of salvation history.

The various liturgical seasons are characterized in part by the scriptural readings and Mass prayers assigned to each of them. During Advent, for example, the readings are messianic; during the Easter season, from the Acts of the Apostles, chronicling the Resurrection and the original proclamation of Christ by the Apostles, and from the Gospel of John; during Lent, baptismal and penitential passages. Mass prayers reflect the meaning and purpose of the various seasons.

### Commemorations of Saints

The commemorations of saints are celebrated concurrently with the liturgical seasons and feasts of our Lord. Their purpose is to illustrate the paschal mysteries as reflected in the lives of saints, to honor them as heroes of holiness, and to appeal for their intercession.

In line with revised regulations, some former feasts were either abolished or relegated to observance in particular places by local option for one of two reasons: (1) lack of sufficient historical evidence for observance of the feasts; (2) lack of universal significance.

The commemoration of a saint, as a general rule, is observed on the day of death (*dies natalis,* day of birth to glory with God in heaven). Exceptions to this rule include the feasts of St. John the Baptist, who is honored on the day of his birth; Sts. Basil the Great and Gregory Nazianzen, and the brother Saints, Cyril and Methodius, who are commemorated in joint feasts.

Application of this general rule in the revised calendar resulted in date changes of some observances.

### Sundays and Other Holy Days

Sunday is the original Christian feast day and holy day of obligation because of the unusually significant events of salvation history which took place and are commemorated on the first day of the week — viz., the Resurrection of Christ, the key event of his life and the fundamental fact of Christianity; and the descent of the Holy Spirit upon the Apostles on Pentecost, the birthday of the Church. The transfer of observance of the Lord's Day from the Sabbath to Sunday was made in apostolic times. The Mass and Liturgy of the Hours (Divine Office) of each Sunday reflect the themes and set the tones of the various liturgical seasons.

Holy days of obligation are special occasions on which Catholics who have reached the age of reason are seriously obliged, as on Sundays, to assist at Mass and to avoid unnecessary servile work. Serious reasons excuse from the observance of either or both of these obligations.

The holy days of obligation observed in the United States are: Christmas, the Nativity of Jesus, Dec. 25; Solemnity of Mary the Mother of God, Jan. 1; Ascension of the Lord; Assumption of Blessed Mary the Virgin, Aug. 15; All Saints' Day, Nov. 1; Immaculate Conception of Blessed Mary the Virgin, Dec. 8.

In addition to these, there are four other holy days of obligation prescribed in the general law of the Church which are not so observed in the U.S.: Epiphany, Jan. 6; St. Joseph, Mar. 19; Corpus Christi; Sts. Peter and Paul, June 29. The solemnities of Epiphany and Corpus Christi are transferred to a Sunday in countries where they are not observed as holy days of obligation.

### Feasts and Commemorations

**Categories of observances** according to dignity and manner of observance are: solemnity (highest, corresponding to former first-class feasts); feast (corresponding to former second-class feasts); memorial (corresponding to former third-class feasts); optional memorial (observable by choice). Observances of the first three categories are universal in the Roman Rite.

**Fixed observances** are those which are regularly celebrated on the same calendar day each year.

**Movable observances** are those which are not observed on the same calendar day each year. Examples of these are Easter (the first Sunday after the first full moon following the vernal equinox),

Ascension (40 days after Easter), Pentecost (50 days after Easter), Trinity Sunday (first after Pentecost), Christ the King (last Sunday of the liturgical year).

### Weekdays, Days of Prayer

**Weekdays** are those on which no proper feast or vigil is celebrated in the Mass or Liturgy of the Hours (Divine Office). On such days, the Mass may be that of the preceding Sunday, which expresses the liturgical spirit of the season, an optional memorial, a votive Mass, or a Mass for the dead. Weekdays of Advent and Lent are in a special category of their own.

**Days of Prayer:** Dioceses, at times to be designated by local bishops, should observe "days or periods of prayer for the fruits of the earth, prayer for human rights and equality, prayer for world justice and peace, and penitential observance outside of Lent." So stated the *Instruction on Particular Calendars* (No. 331) issued by the Congregation for the Sacraments and Divine Worship June 24, 1970.

These days are contemporary equivalents of what were formerly called ember and rogation days.

Ember days originated at Rome about the fifth century, probably as Christian replacements for seasonal festivals of agrarian cults. They were observances of penance, thanksgiving, and petition for divine blessing on the various seasons; they also were occasions of special prayer for clergy to be ordained. These days were observed four times a year.

Rogation days originated in France about the fifth century. They were penitential in character and also occasions of prayer for a bountiful harvest and protection against evil.

### Days of Penance

The Code of Canon law states that all the Christian faithful are bound by divine law to do penance, and prescribes times for the common observance of penance. These times are Fridays throughout the year and the season of Lent.

Abstinence from meat or another kind of food is to be observed on all Fridays except those on which a solemnity (e.g., Christmas) is celebrated, subject to directives from an appropriate conference of bishops. Whether or not such abstinence is ordered by a conference, the obligation to do penance still binds and can be discharged by alternative works of penance, like voluntary abstinence, prayer, self-denial, works of charity.

Ash Wednesday and Good Friday are days of fast and abstinence.

In the United States, in accord with provisions of the Code and decisions of the National Conference of Catholic Bishops, Ash Wednesday and Good Friday are days of fast and abstinence, and all Fridays of Lent are days of abstinence.

The obligation to abstain from meat binds Catholics from the age of 14 throughout life. The obligation to fast, limiting onself to one full meal and two lighter meals in the course of a day, binds adults (from 18 in the U.S.) to the beginning of their 60th year.

## JANUARY 1985

**1—Tues. Solemnity of Mary, Mother of God. Holy day of obligation.** (Nm. 6:22-27; Gal. 4:4-7; Lk. 2:16-21.)

2—Wed. Sts. Basil the Great and Gregory Nazianzen, bishops-doctors; memorial.

3—Thurs. Weekday.

4—Fri. St. Elizabeth Ann Seton; memorial (in U.S.).

5—Sat. St. John Neumann, bishop; memorial (in U.S.).

**6—Sun. Epiphany of the Lord; solemnity.** (Is. 60:1-6; Eph. 3:2-3a, 5-6; Mt. 2:1-12.) [Bl. Andre Bessette, religious; optional memorial in U.S.]

7—Mon. Weekday. St. Raymond of Peñafort, priest; optional memorial.

8—Tues. Weekday.

9—Wed. Weekday.

10—Thurs. Weekday.

11—Fri. Weekday.

12—Sat. Weekday.

**13—Sun. Baptism of the Lord; feast.** (Is. 42:1-4, 6-7; Acts. 10:34-38; Mk. 1:6b-11.) [St. Hilary, bishop-doctor; optional memorial.]

14—Mon. Weekday. (First Week of the Year.)

15—Tues. Weekday.

16—Wed. Weekday.

17—Thurs. St. Anthony, abbot; memorial.

18—Fri. Weekday.

19—Sat. Weekday.

**20—Second Sunday of the Year.** (1 Sm. 3:3b-10, 19; 1 Cor. 6:13c-15a, 17-20; Jn. 1:35-42.) [St. Fabian, pope-martyr, or St. Sebastian, martyr; optional memorials.]

21—Mon. St. Agnes, virgin-martyr; memorial.

22—Tues. Weekday. St. Vincent, deacon-martyr; optional memorial.

23—Wed. Weekday.

24—Thurs. St. Francis de Sales, bishop-doctor; memorial.

25—Fri. Conversion of St. Paul, apostle; feast.

26—Sat. Sts. Timothy and Titus, bishops; memorial.

**27—Third Sunday of the Year.** (Jon. 3:1-5, 10; 1 Cor. 7:29-31; Mk. 1:14-20). [St. Angela Merici, virgin; optional memorial.]

28—Mon. St. Thomas Aquinas, priest-doctor; memorial.

29—Tues. Weekday.

30—Wed. Weekday.

31—Thurs. St. John Bosco, priest; memorial.

GENERAL PRAYER INTENTION: The Jewish People — For a special remembrance of them during the Week of Prayer for Unity, Jan. 18 to 25.

MISSION PRAYER INTENTION: The Pontifical Mission Work of the Holy Childhood — For greater appreciation and support of this work under the auspices of the Pope and bishops. This mission-aid society provides assistance to children in nearly 100 foreign countries and mission-education materials at home.

## FEBRUARY 1985

1—Fri. Weekday.

2—Sat. Presentation of the Lord; feast.

**3—Fourth Sunday of the Year.** (Dt. 18:15-20; 1 Cor. 7:32-35; Mk. 1:21-28.) [St. Blase, bishop-martyr, or St. Ansgar, bishop; optional memorials.]

4—Mon. Weekday.

5—Tues. St. Agatha, virgin-martyr; memorial.

6—Wed. Sts. Paul Miki and Companions, martyrs; memorial.

7—Thurs. Weekday.

8—Fri. Weekday. St. Jerome Emiliani; optional memorial.

9—Sat. Weekday.

**10—Fifth Sunday of the Year.** (Jb. 7:1-4, 6-7; 1 Cor. 9:16-19, 22-23; Mk. 1:29-39.) [St. Scholastica, virgin; memorial.]

11—Mon. Weekday. Our Lady of Lourdes; optional memorial.

12—Tues. Weekday.

13—Wed. Weekday.

14—Thurs. Sts. Cyril, monk, and Methodius, bishop; memorial.

15—Fri. Weekday.

16—Sat. Weekday.

**17—Sixth Sunday of the Year.** (Lv. 13:1-2, 45-46; 1 Cor. 10:31 to 11:1; Mk. 1:40-45.) [Seven Holy Founders of the Servite Order; optional memorial.]

18—Mon. Weekday.

19—Tues. Weekday.

**20—Ash Wednesday. Beginning of Lent.** *Fast and abstinence.* Ashes are blessed on this day and imposed on the forehead of the faithful to remind them of their obligation to do penance for sin and to seek spiritual renewal by means of prayer, fasting, good works, and by bearing with patience and for God's purposes the trials and difficulties of everyday life.

21—Thurs. Weekday of Lent. [St. Peter Damien, bishop-doctor; optional memorial.]

22—Fri. Chair of Peter, apostle; feast. *Abstinence.*

23—Sat. St. Polycarp, bishop-martyr; memorial.

**24—First Sunday of Lent.** (Gn. 9:8-15; 1 Pt. 3:18-22; Mk. 1:12-15.)

25—Mon. Weekday of Lent.

26—Tues. Weekday of Lent.

27—Wed. Weekday of Lent.

28—Thurs. Weekday of Lent.

GENERAL PRAYER INTENTION: The Young, Builders of a New World — The intention is in accord with the U.N. proclamation of 1985 as the "Year of the Young." Pope John Paul II has singled out the young for their role in spreading the Gospel.

MISSION PRAYER INTENTION: The Catholic Church in Islamic Countries — For courage and vigor of the faithful in giving testimony to their faith in places, like Sudan, and circumstances in which they and their way of life are suspect, in effect, and barely tolerated.

## MARCH 1985

1—Fri. Weekday of Lent. *Abstinence.*

2—Sat. Weekday of Lent.

**3—Second Sunday of Lent.** (Gn. 22:1-2, 10-13, 15-18; Rom. 8:31b-34; Mk. 9:2-10.)

4—Mon. Weekday of Lent. [St. Casimir; optional memorial.]

5—Tues. Weekday of Lent.

6—Wed. Weekday of Lent.

7—Thurs. Weekday of Lent. [Sts. Perpetua and Felicity, martyrs; memorial.]

8—Fri. Weekday of Lent. *Abstinence.* [St. John of God, religious; optional memorial.]

9—Sat. Weekday of Lent. [St. Frances of Rome, religious; optional memorial.]

**10—Third Sunday of Lent.** (Ex. 20:1-17; 1 Cor. 1:22-25; Jn. 2:13-25.)

11—Mon. Weekday of Lent.

12—Tues Weekday of Lent.

13—Wed. Weekday of Lent.

14—Thurs. Weekday of Lent.

15—Fri. Weekday of Lent. *Abstinence.*

16—Sat. Weekday of Lent.

**17—Fourth Sunday of Lent.** (2 Chr. 36:14-16, 19-23; Eph. 2:4-10; Jn. 3:14-21.) [St. Patrick, bishop; optional memorial.]

18—Mon. Weekday of Lent. [St. Cyril of Jerusalem, bishop-doctor; optional memorial.]

19—Tues. St. Joseph; solemnity. Weekday of Lent.

20—Wed. Weekday of Lent.

21—Thurs. Weekday of Lent.

22—Fri. Weekday of Lent. *Abstinence.*

23—Sat. Weekday of Lent. [St. Turibius, bishop; optional memorial.]

**24—Fifth Sunday of Lent.** (Jer. 31:31-34; Heb. 5:7-9; Jn. 12:20-33.)

25—Mon. Annunciation of the Lord; solemnity. Weekday of Lent.

26—Tues. Weekday of Lent.

27—Wed. Weekday of Lent.

28—Thurs. Weekday of Lent.

29—Fri. Weekday of Lent. *Abstinence.*

30—Sat. Weekday of Lent.

**31—Sunday of the Passion (Palm Sunday).** (Procession — Mt. 11:1-10, or Jn. 12:12-16. Mass — Is. 50:4-7; Phil. 2:6-11; Mk. 14:1 to 15:47.)

GENERAL PRAYER INTENTION: Recognition of the Rights of the Family — This intention is in accord with the "Charter of the Rights of the Family" published by the Vatican Nov. 24, 1983. The Charter states: "The rights enunciated . . . are expressed in the conscience of the human being and in the common values of all humanity. . . . These rights arise, in the ultimate analysis, from that law which is inscribed by the Creator in the heart of every human being. Society is called to defend those rights against all violations and to respect and promote them in their entirety."

MISSION PRAYER INTENTION: Migrant Workers of the Third World — They are rarely accepted and understood in the countries where they work.

## APRIL 1985

1—Monday of Holy Week.

2—Tuesday of Holy Week. [St. Francis of Paola, hermit; optional memorial.]

3—Wednesday of Holy Week.

4—Thursday of Holy Week. Holy Thursday. The Paschal Triduum begins with the evening Mass of the Supper of the Lord. [St. Isidore of Seville, bishop-doctor; optional memorial.]

5—Friday of the Passion of the Lord. Good Friday. *Fast and abstinence.* [St. Vincent Ferrer, priest; optional memorial.]

6—Holy Saturday. The Easter Vigil.

**7—Easter Sunday; solemnity.** (Acts 10:34a, 37-43; Col. 3:1-4 or 1 Cor. 5:6b-8; Jn. 20:1-9 or Mt. 28:1-10 or (Evening) Lk. 24:13-35.) [St. John Baptist de la Salle, priest; memorial.]

8—Monday of Easter Octave.

9—Tuesday of Easter Octave.

10—Wednesday of Easter Octave.

11—Thursday of Easter Octave. [St. Stanislaus, bishop-martyr; memorial.]

12—Friday of Easter Octave.

13—Saturday of Easter Octave. [St. Martin I, pope-martyr; optional memorial.]

**14—Second Sunday of Easter.** (Acts 4:32-35; 1 Jn. 5:1-6; Jn. 20:19-31.)

15—Mon. Weekday.

16—Tues. Weekday.

17—Wed. Weekday.

18—Thurs. Weekday.

19—Fri. Weekday.

20—Sat. Weekday.

**21—Third Sunday of Easter.** (Acts 3:13-15, 17-19; 1 Jn. 2:1-5a; Lk. 24:35-48.) [St. Anselm, bishop-doctor; optional memorial.]

22—Mon. Weekday.

23—Tues. Weekday. St. George, martyr; optional memorial.

24—Wed. Weekday. St. Fidelis of Sigmaringen, priest-martyr; optional memorial.

25—Thurs. St. Mark, evangelist; feast.

26—Fri. Weekday.

27—Sat. Weekday.

**28—Fourth Sunday of Easter.** (Acts 4:8-12; 1 Jn. 3:1-2; Jn. 10:11-18.) [St. Peter Chanel, priest-martyr; optional memorial.]

29—Mon. St. Catherine of Siena, virgin-doctor; memorial.

30—Tues. Weekday. St. Pius V, pope; optional memorial.

GENERAL PRAYER INTENTION: The Faith of the Slavic Peoples — This intention is in accord with the celebration during the year of the 11th centenary of the missionary work of Sts. Cyril and Methodius, apostles of the Slavs.

MISSION PRAYER INTENTION: The Church in Asia, Communities of Faith — This was the theme of the message issued in 1983 by the Third General Conference of the Bishops of Asia. Their unique problems involve relations with predominant majorities of non-Christian peoples.

## MAY 1985

1—Wed. Weekday. St. Joseph the Worker; optional memorial.
2—Thurs. St. Athanasius, bishop-doctor; memorial.
3—Fri. Sts. Philip and James, apostles; feast.
4—Sat. Weekday.
5—**Fifth Sunday of Easter.** (Acts 9:26-31; 1 Jn. 3:18-24; Jn. 15:1-8.)
6—Mon. Weekday.
7—Tues. Weekday.
8—Wed. Weekday.
9—Thurs. Weekday.
10—Fri. Weekday.
11—Sat. Weekday.
12—**Sixth Sunday of Easter.** (Acts 10:25-26, 34-35, 44-48; 1 Jn. 4:7-10; Jn. 15:9-17.) [Sts. Nereus and Achilleus, martyrs, or St. Pancras, martyr; optional memorials.]
13—Mon. Weekday.
14—Tues. St. Matthias, apostle; feast.
15—Wed. Weekday.
16—**Thurs. Ascension of the Lord; solemnity. Holy day of obligation.** (Acts 1:1-11; Eph. 1:17-23; Mk. 16:15-20.)
17—Fri. Weekday.
18—Sat. Weekday. St. John I, pope-martyr; optional memorial.
19—**Seventh Sunday of Easter.** (Acts 1:15-17, 20a, 20c-26; 1 Jn. 4:11-16; Jn. 17:11b-19.)
20—Mon. Weekday. St. Bernardine of Siena, priest; optional memorial.
21—Tues. Weekday.
22—Wed. Weekday.
23—Thurs. Weekday.
24—Fri. Weekday.
25—Sat. Weekday. St. Bede the Venerable, priest-doctor, or St. Gregory VII, pope, or St. Mary Magdalene de Pazzi, virgin; optional memorials.
26—**Sun. Pentecost; solemnity.** (Acts 2:1-11; 1 Cor. 12:3b-7, 12-13; Jn. 20:19-23.) [St. Philip Neri, priest; memorial.]
27—Mon. Weekday. St. Augustine of Canterbury, bishop; optional memorial. (Eighth Week of the Year.)
28—Tues. Weekday.
29—Wed. Weekday.
30—Thurs. Weekday.
31—Fri. Visitation of Blessed Mary the Virgin; feast.

GENERAL PRAYER INTENTION: Acceptance of Mary as the Model of Our Faith — Pope John Paul II, in a statement of July 31, 1983, called Mary the prototype of the Church and of every Christian. In the Second Vatican Council's *Dogmatic Constitution on the Church,* she is "Mother of the Church."

MISSION PRAYER INTENTION: The Young People of the Third World — The youth of the Third World, with their increasing numbers and influence, should have a leading role in the 1985 U.N.-sponsored Year of the Young.

## JUNE 1985

1—Sat. St. Justin, martyr; memorial.
2—**Trinity Sunday; solemnity.** (Dt. 4:32-34; 39-40; Rom. 8:14-17; Mt. 28:15-20.) [Sts. Marcellinus and Peter, martyrs; optional memorial.]
3—Mon. Sts. Charles Lwanga and Companions, martyrs; memorial. (Ninth Week of the Year.)
4—Tues. Weekday.
5—Wed. St. Boniface, bishop-martyr; memorial.
6—Thurs. Weekday. St. Norbert, bishop; optional memorial.
7—Fri. Weekday.
8—Sat. Weekday.
9—**Sun. Corpus Christi (in U.S.); solemnity.** (Ex. 24:3-8; Heb. 9:11-15; Mk. 14:12-16, 22-26.) [St. Ephraem, deacon-doctor; optional memorial.]
10—Mon. Weekday. (Tenth Week of the Year.)
11—Tues. St. Barnabas, apostle; memorial.
12—Wed. Weekday.
13—Thurs. St. Anthony of Padua, priest-doctor; memorial.
14—Fri. Sacred Heart of Jesus; solemnity.
15—Sat. Weekday. Immaculate Heart of Mary; optional memorial.
16—**Eleventh Sunday of the Year.** (Ez. 17:22-24; 2 Cor. 5:6-10; Mk. 4:26-34.)
17—Mon. Weekday.
18—Tues. Weekday.
19—Wed. Weekday. St. Romuald, abbot; optional memorial.
20—Thurs. Weekday.
21—Fri. St. Aloysius Gonzaga, religious; memorial.
22—Sat. Weekday. St. Paulinus of Nola, bishop, or Sts. John Fisher, bishop-martyr, and Thomas More, martyr; optional memorials.
23—**Twelfth Sunday of the Year.** (Jb. 38:1, 8-11; 2 Cor. 5:14-17; Mk. 4:35-41.)
24—Mon. Birth of St. John the Baptist; solemnity.
25—Tues. Weekday.
26—Wed. Weekday.
27—Thurs. Weekday. St. Cyril of Alexandria, bishop-doctor; optional memorial.
28—Fri. St. Irenaeus, bishop-martyr; memorial.
29—Sat. Sts. Peter and Paul, apostles; solemnity.
30—**Thirteenth Sunday of the Year.** (Wis. 1:13-15 and 2:23-24; 2 Cor. 8:7, 9, 13-15; Mk. 5:21-43.) [First Martyrs of the Roman Church; optional memorial.]

GENERAL PRAYER INTENTION: A Lasting Peace in the Middle East — This intention has been a recurrent theme in addresses and appeals of Pope John Paul II since early in his pontificate. He has not ceased to urge efforts to resolve the serious and painful problem posed to world peace by hostilities in the region.

MISSION PRAYER INTENTION: Insertion of the Gospel into the Culture of New Christian Communities — Inculturation is a pressing need and problem in mission areas.

## JULY 1985

1—Mon. Weekday.
2—Tues. Weekday.
3—Wed. St. Thomas, apostle; feast.
4—Thurs. Weekday. St. Elizabeth of Portugal; optional memorial. Independence Day Votive Mass (permitted in U.S.).
5—Fri. Weekday. St. Anthony Zaccaria, priest; optional memorial.
6—Sat. Weekday. St. Maria Goretti, virgin-martyr; optional memorial.
**7—Fourteenth Sunday of the Year.** (Ez. 2:2-5; 2 Cor. 12:7-10; Mk. 6:1-6.)
8—Mon. Weekday.
9—Tues. Weekday.
10—Wed. Weekday.
11—Thurs. St. Benedict, abbot; memorial.
12—Fri. Weekday.
13—Sat. Weekday. St. Henry; optional memorial.
**14—Fifteenth Sunday of the Year.** (Am. 7:12-15; Eph. 1:3-14; Mk. 6:7-13.) [Bl. Kateri Tekakwitha, virgin; memorial in U.S. St. Camillus de Lellis, priest; optional memorial.]
15—Mon. St. Bonaventure, bishop-doctor; memorial.
16—Tues. Weekday. Our Lady of Mt. Carmel; optional memorial.
17—Wed. Weekday.
18—Thurs. Weekday.
19—Fri. Weekday.
20—Sat. Weekday.
**21—Sixteenth Sunday of the Year.** (Jer. 23:1-6; Eph. 2:13-18; Mk. 6:30-34. [St. Lawrence of Brindisi, priest-doctor; optional memorial.]
22—Mon. St. Mary Magdalene; memorial.
23—Tues. Weekday. St. Bridget, religious; optional memorial.
24—Wed. Weekday.
25—Thurs. St. James, apostle; feast.
26—Fri. Sts. Joachim and Anne, parents of Blessed Mary the Virgin; memorial.
27—Sat. Weekday.
**28—Seventeenth Sunday of the Year.** (1 Kgs. 4:42-44; Eph. 4:1-6; Jn. 6:1-15).
29—Mon. St. Martha; memorial.
30—Tues. Weekday. St. Peter Chrysologus, bishop-doctor; optional memorial.
31—Wed. St. Ignatius of Loyola, priest; memorial.

GENERAL PRAYER INTENTION: Those Suffering Injustice and Persecution for Their Faith — The Holy Father, at Lourdes Aug. 14, 1983, asked people to concentrate attention on these people, who have been called "The Church of Silence" and "Modern-Day Martyrs."

MISSION PRAYER INTENTION: The Suffering Church in Vietnam — This heroic Church, which constantly lives in grave difficulties, cries out for solidarity with the rest of the Church. In 1984, the Pope expressed concern over reported efforts of the government to sponsor a dissident church of "patriotic" Catholics.

## AUGUST 1985

1—Thurs. St. Alphonsus Liguori, bishop-doctor; memorial.
2—Fri. Weekday. St. Eusebius of Vercelli, bishop; optional memorial.
3—Sat. Weekday.
**4—Eighteenth Sunday of the Year.** (Ex. 16:2-4, 12-15; Eph. 4:17, 20-24; Jn. 6:24-35.) [St. John Vianney, priest; memorial.]
5—Mon. Weekday. Dedication of St. Mary Major Basilica; optional memorial.
6—Tues. Transfiguration of the Lord; feast.
7—Wed. Weekday. Sts. Sixtus II, pope, and Companions, martyrs; or St. Cajetan, priest; optional memorials.
8—Thurs. St. Dominic, priest; memorial.
9—Fri. Weekday.
10—Sat. St. Lawrence, deacon-martyr; feast.
**11—Nineteenth Sunday of the Year.** (1 Kgs. 19:4-8; Eph. 4:30 to 5:2; Jn. 6:41-51.) [St. Clare, virgin; memorial.]
12—Mon. Weekday.
13—Tues. Weekday. Sts. Pontian, pope, and Hippolytus, priest, martyrs; optional memorial.
14—Wed. St. Maximilian Kolbe, priest-martyr; memorial.
**15—Thurs. Assumption of Blessed Mary the Virgin; solemnity. Holy day of obligation.** (Rv. 11:19a and 12:1-6a, 10ab; 1 Cor. 15:20-26; Lk. 1:39-56.)
16—Fri. Weekday. St. Stephen of Hungary; optional memorial.
17—Sat. Weekday.
**18—Twentieth Sunday of the Year.** (Prv. 9:1-6; Eph. 5: 15-20; Jn. 6:51-58.)
19—Mon. Weekday. St. John Eudes, priest; optional memorial.
20—Tues. St. Bernard of Clairvaux, abbot-doctor; memorial.
21—Wed. St. Pius X, pope; memorial.
22—Thurs. Queenship of Mary; memorial.
23—Fri. Weekday. St. Rose of Lima; optional memorial.
24—Sat. St. Bartholomew, apostle; feast.
**25—Twenty-First Sunday of the Year.** (Jos. 24:1-2a, 15-17, 18b; Eph. 5:21-32; Jn. 6:60-69.) [St. Louis, or St. Joseph Calasanz, priest; optional memorials.]
26—Mon. Weekday.
27—Tues. St. Monica, memorial.
28—Wed. St. Augustine, bishop-doctor; memorial.
29—Thurs. Beheading of St. John the Baptist; memorial.
30—Fri. Weekday.
31—Sat. Weekday.

GENERAL PRAYER INTENTION: For a Greater Eucharistic Devotion — This is the purpose of the 43rd International Eucharistic Congress to be held this month.

MISSION PRAYER INTENTION: That the Eucharistic Congress in Nairobi might be an occasion for vigorous evangelization and catechesis.

## SEPTEMBER 1985

**1—Twenty-Second Sunday of the Year.** (Dt. 4:1-2, 6-8; Jas. 1:17-18, 21b-22, 27; Mk. 7:1-8, 14-15, 21-23.)
2—Mon. Labor Day Votive Mass (prescribed in U.S.).
3—Tues. St. Gregory the Great, pope-doctor; memorial.
4—Wed. Weekday.
5—Thurs. Weekday.
6—Fri. Weekday.
7—Sat. Weekday.
**8—Twenty-Third Sunday of the Year.** (Is. 35:4-7a; Jas. 2:1-5; Mk. 7:31-37.) [Birth of Mary; feast.]
9—Mon. St. Peter Claver, priest; memorial (in U.S.). Weekday.
10—Tues. Weekday.
11—Wed. Weekday.
12—Thurs. Weekday.
13—Fri. St. John Chrysostom, bishop-doctor; memorial.
14—Sat. Triumph of the Cross; feast.
**15—Twenty-Fourth Sunday of the Year.** (Is. 50:5-9a; Jas. 2:14-18; Mk. 8:27-35.) [Our Lady of Sorrows; memorial.]
16—Mon. Sts. Cornelius, pope, and Cyprian, bishop, martyrs; memorial.
17—Tues. Weekday. St. Robert Bellarmine, bishop-doctor; optional memorial.
18—Wed. Weekday.
19—Thurs. Weekday. St. Januarius, bishop-martyr; optional memorial.
20—Fri. Weekday.
21—Sat. St. Matthew, apostle-evangelist; feast.
**22—Twenty-Fifth Sunday of the Year.** (Wis. 2:12, 17-20; Jas. 3:16 to 4:3; Mk. 9:30-37.)
23—Mon. Weekday.
24—Tues. Weekday.
25—Wed. Weekday.
26—Thurs. Weekday. Sts. Cosmas and Damian, martyrs; optional memorial.
27—Fri. St. Vincent de Paul, priest; memorial.
28—Sat. Weekday. St. Wenceslaus, martyr; optional memorial.
**29—Twenty-Sixth Sunday of the Year.** (Nm. 11:25-29; Jas. 5:1-6; Mk. 9:38-43, 45, 47-48.) [Sts. Michael, Gabriel and Raphael, archangels; feast.]
30—Mon. St. Jerome, priest-doctor; memorial.

GENERAL PRAYER INTENTION: All Our Bishops — "They are signs of mercy, of fidelity and of contradiction," said Pope John Paul II Sept. 5, 1983.

MISSION PRAYER INTENTION: Peace and Vocations for the Church in Chad — The archbishop of N'Djamena, president of the Episcopal Conference of Chad, considers these two problems the most pressing in the country. Less than 20 of more than 150 priests in the nation are natives. The quarter of a million Catholics comprise about six per cent of the total population of 4.5 million.

## OCTOBER 1985

1—Tues. St. Therese of the Child Jesus, virgin; memorial.
2—Wed. Guardian Angels; memorial.
3—Thurs. Weekday.
4—Fri. St. Francis of Assisi; memorial.
5—Sat. Weekday.
**6—Twenty-Seventh Sunday of the Year.** (Gn. 2:18-24; Heb. 2:9-11; Mk. 10:2-16.) [Bl. Marie-Rose Durocher, virgin; optional memorial in U.S.; St. Bruno, priest; optional memorial.]
7—Mon. Our Lady of the Rosary; memorial.
8—Tues. Weekday.
9—Wed. Weekday. Sts. Denis, bishop, and Companions, martyrs; or St. John Leonard, priest; optional memorials.
10—Thurs. Weekday.
11—Fri. Weekday.
12—Sat. Weekday.
**13—Twenty-Eighth Sunday of the Year.** (Wis. 7:7-11; Heb. 4:12-13; Mk. 10:17-30.)
14—Mon. Weekday. St. Callistus I, pope-martyr; optional memorial.
15—Tues. St. Teresa of Jesus (Avila), virgin-doctor; memorial.
16—Wed. Weekday. St. Hedwig, religious, or St. Margaret Mary Alacoque, virgin; optional memorials.
17—Thurs. St. Ignatius of Antioch, bishop-martyr; memorial.
18—Fri. St. Luke, evangelist; feast.
19—Sat. Sts. Isaac Jogues, John de Brebeuf, priests, and Companions, martyrs; memorial (in U.S.). Weekday. St. Paul of the Cross; optional memorial.
**20—Twenty-Ninth Sunday of the Year.** (Is. 53:10-11; Heb. 4:14-16; Mk. 10:34-45.)
21—Mon. Weekday.
22—Tues. Weekday.
23—Wed. Weekday. St. John of Capistrano, priest; optional memorial.
24—Thurs. Weekday. St. Anthony Mary Claret, bishop; optional memorial.
25—Fri. Weekday.
26—Sat. Weekday.
**27—Thirtieth Sunday of the Year.** (Jer. 31:7-9; Heb. 5:1-6; Mk. 10:46-52.)
28—Mon. Sts. Simon and Jude, apostles; feast.
29—Tues. Weekday.
30—Wed. Weekday.
31—Thurs. Weekday.

GENERAL PRAYER INTENTION: Men and Women Religious as Examples to the World of Lives of Total Dedication — The Church insists on their radical fidelity to the Gospel.

MISSION PRAYER INTENTION: A Greater Sense of Missionary Responsibility on the Part of All Christians — Pope John Paul II has stressed this intention in addresses to personnel of the superior council of the Commission on Pontifical Missionary Works, and also in statements for the observance of Mission Sunday this month.

## NOVEMBER 1985

**1—Fri. All Saints; solemnity. Holy day of obligation.** (Rv. 7:2-4, 9-14; 1 Jn. 3:1-3; Mt. 5:1-12a.)

2—Sat. Commemoration of All the Faithful Departed. (All Souls' Day). Three Masses proper.

**3—Thirty-First Sunday of the Year.** (Dt. 6:2-6; Heb. 7:23-28; Mk. 12:28b-34.) [St. Martin de Porres, religious; optional memorial.]

4—Mon. St. Charles Borromeo, bishop; memorial.

5—Tues. Weekday.

6—Wed. Weekday.

7—Thurs. Weekday.

8—Fri. Weekday.

9—Sat. Dedication of St. John Lateran (Archbasilica of Most Holy Savior); feast.

**10—Thirty-Second Sunday of the Year.** (1 Kgs. 17:10-16; Heb. 9:24-28; Mk. 12:38-44.) [St. Leo the Great, pope-doctor; memorial.]

11—Mon. St. Martin of Tours, bishop; memorial.

12—Tues. St. Josaphat, bishop-martyr; memorial.

13—Wed. St. Frances Xavier Cabrini, virgin; memorial (in U.S.).

14—Thurs. Weekday.

15—Fri. Weekday. St. Albert the Great, bishop-doctor; optional memorial.

16—Sat. Weekday. St. Margaret of Scotland, or St. Gertrude, virgin; optional memorials.

**17—Thirty-Third Sunday of the Year.** (Dn. 12:1-3; Heb. 10:11-14, 18; Mk. 13:24-32.) [St. Elizabeth of Hungary, religious; memorial.]

18—Mon. Weekday. Dedication of Basilicas of Sts. Peter and Paul, apostles; optional memorial.

19—Tues. Weekday.

20—Wed. Weekday.

21—Thurs. Presentation of Blessed Mary the Virgin; memorial.

22—Fri. St. Cecilia, virgin-martyr; memorial.

23—Sat. Weekday. St. Clement I, pope-martyr, or St. Columban, abbot; optional memorials.

**24—Sun. Christ the King; solemnity.** (Dn. 7:13-14; Rv. 1:5-8; Jn. 18:33b-37.)

25—Mon. Weekday. (Thirty-Fourth [Last] Week of the Year.)

26—Tues. Weekday.

27—Wed. Weekday.

28—Thurs. Weekday.

29—Fri. Weekday.

30—Sat. St. Andrew, apostle; feast.

GENERAL PRAYER INTENTION: Those Who Suffer because of Society's Neglect — The subjects of this intention are those who are neglected in prisons, hospitals, homes for the aged, slums of larger cities and other situations.

MISSION PRAYER INTENTION: Afro-Americans in Latin America — The bishops of Latin America, at their 1979 plenary conference in Puebla, Mexico, emphasized the need for the presence and influence of the Church among these people in so many places of dire deprivation throughout their territories.

## DECEMBER 1985

**1—First Sunday of Advent.** (Jer. 33:14-16; 1 Thes. 3:12 to 4:2; Lk. 21:25-28, 34-36.)

2—Mon. Weekday.

3—Tues. St. Francis Xavier, priest; memorial.

4—Wed. Weekday of Advent. St. John Damascene, priest-doctor; optional memorial.

5—Thurs. Weekday of Advent.

6—Fri. Weekday of Advent. St. Nicholas, bishop; optional memorial.

**7—Sat. Immaculate Conception of Blessed Mary the Virgin** (transferred from Dec. 8; Mass obligation not transferred); solemnity. (Gn. 3:9-15, 20; Eph. 1:3-6, 11-12; Lk. 1:26-38.) [St. Ambrose, bishop-doctor; memorial.]

**8—Second Sunday of Advent.** (Bar. 5:1-9; Phil. 1:4-6, 8-11; Lk. 3:1-6.)

9—Mon. Weekday of Advent.

10—Tues. Weekday of Advent.

11—Wed. Weekday of Advent. St. Damasus I, pope; optional memorial.

12—Thurs. Our Lady of Guadalupe; memorial (in U.S.). Weekday of Advent. St. Jane Frances de Chantal, religious; optional memorial.

13—Fri. St. Lucy, virgin-martyr; memorial.

14—Sat. St. John of the Cross, priest-doctor; memorial.

**15—Third Sunday of Advent.** (Zep. 3:14-18a; Phil. 4:4-7; Lk. 3:10-18.)

16—Mon. Weekday of Advent.

17—Tues. Weekday of Advent.

18—Wed. Weekday of Advent.

19—Thurs. Weekday of Advent.

20—Fri. Weekday of Advent.

21—Sat. Weekday of Advent. [St. Peter Canisius, priest-doctor; optional memorial.]

**22—Fourth Sunday of Advent.** (Mi 5:1-4a; Heb. 10:5-10; Lk. 1:39-45.)

23—Mon. Weekday of Advent. [St. John of Kanty, priest; optional memorial.]

24—Tues. Weekday of Advent.

**25—Wed. Christmas. Birth of the Lord; solemnity. Holy day of obligation.** (Midnight—Is. 9:1-6; Ti. 2:11-14; Lk. 2:1-14. Dawn—Is. 62:11-12; Ti. 3:4-7; Lk. 2:15-20. During the Day—Is. 57:7-10; Heb. 1:1-6; Jn. 1:1-18.)

26—Thurs. St. Stephen, first martyr; feast.

27—Fri. St. John, apostle-evangelist; feast.

28—Sat. Holy Innocents, martyrs; feast.

**29—Sun. Holy Family; feast.** (Sir. 3:2-6, 12-14; Col. 3:12-21; Lk. 2:41-52.) [St. Thomas Becket, bishop-martyr; optional memorial.]

30—Mon. Sixth Day of Christmas Octave.

31—Tues. Seventh Day of Christmas Octave. St. Sylvester I, pope; optional memorial.

GENERAL PRAYER INTENTION: A Greater Esteem for Confirmation.

MISSION PRAYER INTENTION: A More Conscious and Generous Missionary Commitment in All Dioceses — A diocese should be prepared not only to give but also to receive from the diocese it helps.

## TABLE OF MOVABLE FEASTS

| Year | Ash Wednesday | Easter | Ascension | Pentecost | Weeks of Ordinary Time | | | | First Sunday of Advent |
|---|---|---|---|---|---|---|---|---|---|
| | | | | | Before Lent | | After Pent. | | |
| | | | | | Week | Ends | Week | Begins | |
| 1985 | Feb. 20 | Apr. 7 | May 16 | May 26 | 6 | Feb. 19 | 8 | May 27 | Dec. 1 |
| 1986 | Feb. 12 | Mar. 30 | May 8 | May 18 | 5 | Feb. 11 | 7 | May 19 | Nov. 30 |
| 1987 | Mar. 4 | Apr. 19 | May 28 | June 7 | 9 | Mar. 3 | 10 | June 8 | Nov. 29 |
| 1988 | Feb. 17 | Apr. 3 | May 12 | May 22 | 6 | Feb. 16 | 8 | May 23 | Nov. 27 |
| 1989 | Feb. 8 | Mar. 26 | May 4 | May 14 | 5 | Feb. 7 | 6 | May 15 | Dec. 3 |
| 1990 | Feb. 28 | Apr. 15 | May 24 | June 3 | 8 | Feb. 27 | 9 | June 4 | Dec. 2 |
| 1991 | Feb. 13 | Mar. 31 | May 9 | May 19 | 5 | Feb. 12 | 7 | May 20 | Dec. 1 |
| 1992 | Mar. 4 | Apr. 19 | May 28 | June 7 | 9 | Mar. 3 | 10 | June 8 | Nov. 29 |
| 1993 | Feb.24 | Apr. 11 | May 20 | May 30 | 7 | Feb. 23 | 9 | May 31 | Nov. 28 |
| 1994 | Feb. 16 | Apr. 3 | May 12 | May 22 | 6 | Feb. 15 | 8 | May 23 | Nov. 27 |
| 1995 | Mar. 1 | Apr. 16 | May 25 | June 4 | 8 | Feb. 28 | 9 | June 5 | Dec. 3 |
| 1996 | Feb. 21 | Apr. 7 | May 16 | May 26 | 7 | Feb. 20 | 8 | May 27 | Dec. 1 |
| 1997 | Feb. 12 | Mar. 30 | May 8 | May 18 | 5 | Feb. 11 | 7 | May 19 | Nov. 30 |
| 1998 | Feb. 25 | Apr. 12 | May 21 | May 31 | 7 | Feb. 24 | 9 | June 1 | Nov. 29 |
| 1999 | Feb. 17 | Apr. 4 | May 13 | May 23 | 6 | Feb. 16 | 8 | May 24 | Nov. 28 |
| 2000 | Mar. 8 | Apr. 23 | June 1 | June 11 | 9 | Mar. 7 | 10 | June 12 | Dec. 3 |
| 2001 | Feb. 28 | Apr. 15 | May 24 | June 3 | 8 | Feb. 27 | 9 | June 4 | Dec. 2 |
| 2002 | Feb. 13 | Mar. 31 | May 9 | May 19 | 5 | Feb. 12 | 7 | May 20 | Dec. 1 |
| 2003 | Mar. 5 | Apr. 20 | May 29 | June 8 | 8 | Mar. 4 | 10 | June 9 | Nov. 30 |
| 2004 | Feb. 25 | Apr. 11 | May 20 | May 30 | 7 | Feb. 24 | 9 | May 31 | Nov. 28 |
| 2005 | Feb. 9 | Mar. 27 | May 5 | May 15 | 5 | Feb. 8 | 7 | May 16 | Nov. 27 |
| 2006 | Mar. 1 | Apr. 16 | May 25 | June 4 | 8 | Feb. 28 | 9 | June 5 | Dec. 3 |
| 2007 | Feb. 21 | Apr. 8 | May 17 | May 27 | 7 | Feb. 20 | 8 | May 28 | Dec. 2 |
| 2008 | Feb. 6 | Mar. 23 | May 1 | May 11 | 5 | Feb. 5 | 6 | May 12 | Nov. 30 |

### Season of Ordinary Time

Weeks between the end of the Christmas season and the beginning of Lent, and from the day after Pentecost to the last Sunday of the liturgical year, belong to the season of Ordinary Time. The table indicates the number and terminal date of the week ending the first part, and the number and starting date of the week beginning the second part, of this season. In some years, a week of this season is eliminated because of calendar conditions.

### Holiday Masses

Liturgical experiments in recent years have led to the development of votive Masses for national holidays, like those introduced in the U.S. for Thanksgiving Day in 1969 and July 4 in 1972. This development is in line with a custom whereby "from the earliest times the Church has crowned many non-Christian feasts with Christian fulfillment by instituting its own liturgical festivals" to coincide with them.

Labor Day, in lieu of a special votive Mass, may be observed with celebration of the Mass of St. Joseph the Worker.

### Readings at Mass

The texts of scriptural readings for Mass on Sundays, holy days and some other days are indicated under the respective dates. The second (B) cycle of readings in the Lectionary is prescribed for the 1985 liturgical year (Dec. 2, 1984, to Nov. 30, 1985); the third (C) cycle is prescribed for the 1986 liturgical year which begins with the first Sunday of Advent, Dec. 1, 1985.

Weekday cycles of readings are the first and second, respectively, for liturgical years 1985 and 1986.

### Monthly Prayer Intentions

General and mission intentions chosen and recommended by Pope John Paul II to the prayers of the Apostles of Prayer are given under each month of the calendar. He has expressed his desire that all Catholics make these intentions their own "in the certainty of being united with the Holy Father and praying according to his intentions and desires." These intentions represent the worldwide needs of the Church and its missions as seen through the eyes of the Pope.

## HOLY DAYS AND OTHER FEASTS

The following list includes the six holy days of obligation observed in the United States and additional observances of devotional and historical significance. The dignity or rank of observances is indicated by the terms: **solemnity** (highest in rank); **feast; memorial** (for universal observance); **optional memorial** (for celebration by choice).

**All Saints,** Nov. 1, holy day of obligation, solemnity. Commemorates all the blessed in heaven, and is intended particularly to honor the blessed who have no special feasts. The background of the feast dates to the fourth century when groups of martyrs, and later other saints, were honored on a common day in various places. In 609 or 610, the Pantheon, a pagan temple at Rome, was consecrated as a Christian church for the honor of Our Lady and the martyrs (later all saints). In 835, Gregory IV fixed Nov. 1 as the date of observance.

**All Souls,** Commemoration of the Faithful Departed, Nov. 2. The dead were prayed for from the earliest days of Christianity. By the sixth century it was customary in Benedictine monasteries to hold a commemoration of deceased members of the order at Pentecost. A common commemoration of all the faithful departed on the day after All Saints was instituted in 998 by St. Odilo, of the Abbey of Cluny, and an observance of this kind was accepted in Rome in the 14th century. In 1915, Benedict XV granted priests throughout the world permission to celebrate three Masses for this commemoration. He also granted a special indulgence for the occasion.

**Annunciation of the Lord** (formerly, Annunciation of the Blessed Virgin Mary), Mar. 25, solemnity. A feast of the Incarnation which commemorates the announcement by the Archangel Gabriel to the Virgin Mary that she was to become the Mother of Christ (Lk. 1:26-38), and the miraculous conception of Christ by her. The feast was instituted about 430 in the East. The Roman observance dates from the seventh century, when celebration was said to be universal.

**Ascension of the Lord,** movable observance held 40 days after Easter, holy day of obligation, solemnity. Commemorates the Ascension of Christ into heaven 40 days after his Resurrection from the dead (Mk. 16:19; Lk. 24:51; Acts 1:2). The feast recalls the completion of Christ's mission on earth for the salvation of all people and his entry into heaven with glorified human nature. The Ascension is a pledge of the final glorification of all who achieve salvation. Documentary evidence of the feast dates from early in the fifth century, but it was observed long before that time in connection with Pentecost and Easter.

**Ash Wednesday,** movable observance, six and one-half weeks before Easter. It was set as the first day of Lent by Pope St. Gregory the Great (590-604) with the extension of an earlier and shorter penitential season to a total period including 40 weekdays of fasting before Easter. It is a day of fast and abstinence. Ashes, symbolic of penance, are blessed and distributed among the faithful during the day. They are used to mark the forehead with the Sign of the Cross, with the reminder: "Remember, man, that you are dust, and unto dust you shall return," or: "Repent, and believe the Good News."

**Assumption** Aug. 15, holy day of obligation, solemnity. Commemorates the taking into heaven of Mary, soul and body, at the end of her life on earth, a truth of faith that was proclaimed a dogma by Pius XII on Nov. 1, 1950. One of the oldest and most solemn feasts of Mary, it has a history dating back to at least the seventh century when its celebration was already established at Jerusalem and Rome.

**Baptism of the Lord,** movable, usually celebrated on the Sunday after January 6, feast. Recalls the baptism of Christ by John the Baptist (Mk. 1:9-11), an event associated with the liturgy of the Epiphany. This baptism was the occasion for Christ's manifestation of himself at the beginning of his public life.

**Birth of Mary,** Sept. 8, feast. This is a very old feast which originated in the East and found place in the Roman liturgy in the seventh century.

**Candlemas Day,** Feb. 2. See Presentation of the Lord.

**Chair of Peter,** The feast, which has been in the Roman calendar since 336, is a liturgical expression of belief in the episcopacy and hierarchy of the Church.

**Christmas, Birth of Our Lord Jesus Christ,** Dec. 25, holy day of obligation, solemnity. Commemorates the birth of Christ (Lk. 2:1-20). This event was originally commemorated in the East on the feast of Epiphany or Theophany. The Christmas feast itself originated in the West; by 354 it was certainly kept on Dec. 25. This date may have been set for the observance to offset pagan ceremonies held at about the same time to commemorate the birth of the sun at the winter solstice. There are texts for three Christmas Masses — at midnight, dawn and during the day.

**Christ the King,** movable, celebrated on the last Sunday of the liturgical year, solemnity. Commemorates the royal prerogatives of Christ and is equivalent to a declaration of his rights to the homage, service and fidelity of men in all phases of individual and social life. Pius XI instituted the feast Dec. 11, 1925.

**Conversion of St. Paul,** Jan. 25, feast. An observance mentioned in some calendars from the 8th and 9th centuries. Pope Innocent III (1198-1216) ordered its observance with great solemnity.

**Corpus Christi,** movable, celebrated on the Thursday (or Sunday, as in the U.S.) following Trinity Sunday, solemnity. Commemorates the institution of the Holy Eucharist (Mt. 26:26-28). The feast originated at Liege in 1246 and was extended throughout the Church in the West by Urban IV in 1264. St. Thomas Aquinas composed the Liturgy of the Hours for the feast.

**Dedication of St. John Lateran,** Nov. 9, feast. Commemorates the first public consecration of a church, that of the Basilica of the Most Holy Savior by Pope St. Sylvester Nov. 9, 324. The church, as well as the Lateran Palace, was the gift of Emperor Constantine. Since the 12th century it has been known as St. John Lateran, in honor of John the Baptist after whom the adjoining baptistery was named. It was rebuilt by Innocent X (1644-55), reconsecrated by Benedict XIII in 1726, and enlarged by Leo XIII (1878-1903). This basilica is regarded as the church of highest dignity in Rome and throughout the Roman Rite.

**Dedication of St. Mary Major,** Aug. 5, optional memorial. Commemorates the rebuilding and dedication by Pope Sixtus III (432-40) of a church in honor of Blessed Mary the Virgin. This is the Basilica of St. Mary Major on the Esquiline Hill in Rome. An earlier building was erected during the pontificate of Liberius (352-66); according to legend, it was located on a site covered by a miraculous fall of snow seen by a nobleman favored with a vision of Mary.

**Easter,** movable celebration held on the first Sunday after the full moon following the vernal equinox (between Mar. 22 and Apr. 25), solemnity with an octave. Commemorates the Resurrection of Christ from the dead (Mk. 16:1-7). The observance of this mystery, kept since the first days of the Church, extends throughout the Easter season which lasts until the feast of Pentecost, a period of 50 days. Every Sunday in the year is regarded as a "little" Easter. The date of Easter determines the dates of movable feasts, such as Ascension and Pentecost, and the number of weeks before Lent and after Pentecost.

**Easter Vigil,** called by St. Augustine the "Mother of All Vigils," the night before Easter. Ceremonies are all related to the Resurrection and renewal-in-grace theme of Easter: blessing of the new fire, procession with the Easter Candle, singing of the Easter Proclamation (Exsultet), Liturgy of the Word with at least three Old Testament readings, the Litany of Saints, blessing of water, baptism of converts and infants, renewal of baptismal promises, Liturgy of the Eucharist. The vigil ceremonies are held after sundown.

**Epiphany of Our Lord,** Jan. 6 or (in the U.S.) a Sunday between Jan. 2 and 8, solemnity. Commemorates the manifestations of the divinity of Christ. It is one of the oldest Christian feasts, with an Eastern origin traceable to the beginning of the third century and antedating the Western feast of Christmas. Originally, it commemorated the manifestations of Christ's divinity — or Theophany — in his birth, the homage of the Magi, and baptism by John the Baptist. Later, the first two of these commemorations were transferred to Christmas when the Eastern Church adopted that feast between 380 and 430. The central feature of the Eastern observance now is the manifestation or declaration of Christ's divinity in his baptism and at the beginning of his public life. The Epiphany was adopted by the Western Church during the same period in which the Eastern Church accepted Christmas. In the Roman Rite, commemoration is made in the Mass of the homage of the wise men from the East (Mt. 2:1-12).

**Good Friday,** the Friday before Easter, the second day of the Easter Triduum. Liturgical elements of the observance are commemoration of the Passion and Death of Christ in the reading of the Passion (according to John), special prayers for the Church and people of all ranks, the veneration of the Cross, and a Communion service. The celebration takes place in the afternoon, preferably at 3:00 p.m.

**Guardian Angels,** Oct. 2, memorial. Commemorates the angels who protect people from spiritual and physical dangers and assist them in doing good. A feast in their honor celebrated in Spain in the 16th century was extended to the whole Church by Paul V in 1608. In 1670, Clement X set Oct. 2 as the date of observance. Earlier, guardian angels were honored liturgically in conjunction with the feast of St. Michael.

**Holy Family,** movable observance on the Sunday after Christmas, feast. Commemorates the Holy Family of Jesus, Mary and Joseph as the model of domestic society, holiness and virtue. The devotional background of the feast was very strong in the 17th century. In the 18th century, in prayers composed for a special Mass, a Canadian bishop likened the Christian family to the Holy Family. Leo XIII consecrated families to the Holy Family. In 1921, Benedict XV extended the Divine Office and Mass of the feast to the whole Church.

**Holy Innocents,** Dec. 28, feast. Commemorates the infants who suffered death at the hands of Herod's soldiers seeking to kill the child Jesus (Mt. 2:13-18). A feast in their honor has been observed since the fifth century.

**Holy Saturday,** the day before Easter. The Sacrifice of the Mass is not celebrated, and Holy Communion may be given only as Viaticum. If possible the Easter fast should be observed until the Easter Vigil.

**Holy Thursday,** the Thursday before Easter. Commemorates the institution of the sacraments of the Eucharist and holy orders, and the washing of the feet of the Apostles by Jesus at the Last Supper. The Mass of the Lord's Supper in the evening marks the beginning of the Easter Triduum. Following the Mass, there is a procession of the Blessed Sacrament to a place of reposition for adoration by the faithful. At an earlier Mass of Chrism, bishops bless oils (of catechumens, chrism, the sick) for use during the year. (For pastoral reasons, diocesan bishops may permit additional Masses, but these should not overshadow the principal Mass of the Lord's Supper.)

**Immaculate Conception,** Dec. 8, holy day of obligation, solemnity. Commemorates the fact that Mary, in view of her calling to be the Mother of Christ and in virtue of his merits, was preserved from the first moment of her conception from original sin and was filled with grace from the very beginning of her life. She was the only person so preserved from original sin. The present form of the feast dates from Dec. 8, 1854, when Pius IX defined the dogma of the Immaculate Conception. An earlier feast of the Conception, which testified to long-existing belief in this truth, was observed in the East by the eighth century, in Ireland in the ninth, and subsequently in European countries. In 1846, Mary was proclaimed patroness of the U.S. under this title.

**Immaculate Heart of Mary,** Saturday following the second Sunday after Pentecost, optional memorial. On May 4, 1944, Pius XII ordered this feast observed throughout the Church in order to obtain Mary's intercession for "peace among nations, freedom for the Church, the conversion of sinners, the love of purity and the practice of virtue." Two years earlier, he consecrated the entire human race to Mary under this title. Devotion to Mary under the title of her Most Pure Heart originated during the Middle Ages. It was given great impetus in the 17th century by the preaching of St. John Eudes, who was the first to celebrate a Mass and Divine Office of Mary under this title. A feast, celebrated in various places and on different dates, was authorized in 1799.

**Joachim and Ann,** July 26, memorial. Commemorates the parents of Mary. A joint feast, celebrated Sept. 9, originated in the East near the end of the sixth century. Devotion to Ann, introduced in the eighth century at Rome, became widespread in Europe in the 14th century; her feast was extended throughout the Latin Church in 1584. A feast of Joachim was introduced in the West in the 15th century.

**John the Baptist, Birth,** June 24, solemnity. The precursor of Christ, whose cousin he was, was commemorated universally in the liturgy by the fourth century. He is the only saint, except the Blessed Virgin Mary, whose birthday is observed as a feast. Another feast, on Aug. 29, commemorates his passion and death at the order of Herod (Mk. 6:14-29).

**Joseph,** Mar. 19, solemnity. Joseph is honored as the husband of the Blessed Virgin Mary, the patron and protector of the universal Church and workman. Devotion to him already existed in the eighth century in the East, and in the 11th in the West. Various feasts were celebrated before the 15th century when Mar. 19 was fixed for his commemoration; this feast was extended to the whole Church in 1621 by Gregory XV. In 1955, Pius XII instituted the feast of St. Joseph the Workman for observance May 1; this feast, which may be celebrated by local option, supplanted the Solemnity or Patronage of St. Joseph formerly observed on the third Wednesday after Easter. St. Joseph was proclaimed protector and patron of the universal Church in 1870 by Pius IX.

**Michael, Gabriel and Raphael, Archangels,** Sept. 29, feast. A feast bearing the title of Dedication of St. Michael the Archangel formerly commemorated on this date the consecration in 530 of a church near Rome in honor of Michael, the first angel given a liturgical feast. For a while, this feast was combined with a commemoration of the Guardian Angels. The separate feasts of Gabriel (Mar. 24) and Raphael (Oct. 24) were suppressed by the calendar in effect since 1970 and this joint feast of the three archangels was instituted.

**Octave of Christmas,** Jan. 1. See Solemnity of Mary, Mother of God.

**Our Lady of Sorrows,** Sept. 15, memorial. Recalls the sorrows experienced by Mary in her association with Christ: the prophecy of Simeon (Lk. 2:34-35), the flight into Egypt (Mt. 2:13-21), the three-day separation from Jesus (Lk. 2:41-50), and four incidents connected with the Passion: her meeting with Christ on the way to Calvary, the crucifixion, the removal of Christ's body from the cross, and his burial (Mt. 27:31-61; Mk. 15:20-47; Lk. 23:26-56; Jn. 19:17-42). A Mass and Divine Office of the feast were celebrated by the Servites, especially, in the 17th century, and in 1817 Pius VII extended the observance to the whole Church.

**Our Lady of the Rosary,** Oct. 7, memorial. Commemorates the Virgin Mary through recall of the mysteries of the Rosary which recapitulate events in her life and the life of Christ. The feast was instituted to commemorate a Christian victory over invading Mohammedan forces at Lepanto on Oct. 7, 1571, and was extended throughout the Church by Clement XI in 1716.

**Passion Sunday** (formerly called **Palm Sunday**), the Sunday before Easter. Marks the start of Holy Week by recalling the triumphal entry of Christ into Jerusalem at the beginning of the last week of his life (Mt. 21:1-9). A procession and other ceremonies commemorating this event were held in Jerusalem from very early Christian times and were adopted in Rome by the ninth century, when the blessing of palm for the occasion was introduced. Full liturgical observance includes the blessing of palm and a procession before the principal Mass of the day. The Passion, by Matthew, Mark or Luke, is read during the Mass.

**Pentecost,** also called **Whitsunday,** movable celebration held 50 days after Easter, solemnity. Commemorates the descent of the Holy Spirit upon the Apostles, the preaching of Peter and the other Apostles to Jews in Jerusalem, the baptism and aggregation of some 3,000 persons to the Christian community (Acts 2:1-41). It is regarded as the birthday of the Catholic Church. The original observance of the feast antedated the earliest extant documentary evidence from the third century.

**Peter and Paul, Sts.,** June 29, solemnity. Commemorates the martyrdoms of Peter by crucifixion and Paul by beheading during the Neronian persecution. This joint commemoration of the chief Apostles dates at least from 258 at Rome.

**Presentation of the Lord** (formerly called Purification of the Blessed Virgin Mary, also Candlemas), Feb. 2, feast. Commemorates the presentation of Jesus in the Temple — according to prescriptions of Mosaic Law (Lv. 12:2-8; Ex. 13:2; Lk. 2:22-32) — and the purification of Mary 40 days after his birth. In the East, where the feast antedated fourth century testimony regarding its existence, it was observed primarily as a feast of Our Lord; in the West, where it was adopted later, it was regarded more as a feast of Mary until the calendar in effect since 1970. Its date was set for Feb. 2 after the celebration of Christmas was fixed for Dec. 25, late in the fourth century. The blessing of candles, probably in commemoration of Christ who was the Light to enlighten the Gentiles, became common about the 11th century and gave the feast the secondary name of Candlemas.

**Queenship of Mary,** Aug. 22, memorial. Commemorates the high dignity of Mary as Queen of heaven, angels and men. Universal observance of the memorial was ordered by Pius XII in the encyclical *Ad Caeli Reginam*, Oct. 11, 1954, near the close of a Marian Year observed in connection with the centenary of the proclamation of the dogma of the Immaculate Conception and four years after the proclamation of the dogma of the Assumption. The original date of the memorial was May 31.

**Resurrection.** See Easter.

**Sacred Heart of Jesus,** movable observance held on the Friday after the second Sunday after Pentecost (Corpus Christi, in the U.S.), solemnity. The object of the devotion is the divine Person of Christ, whose heart is the symbol of his love for men — for whom he accomplished the work of Redemption. The Mass and Office now used on the feast were prescribed by Pius XI in 1929. Devotion to the Sacred Heart was introduced into the liturgy in the 17th century through the efforts of St. John Eudes who composed an Office and Mass for the feast. It was furthered as the result of the revelations of St. Margaret Mary Alacoque after 1675 and by the work of Claude de la Colombiere, S.J. In 1765, Clement XIII approved a Mass and Office for the feast, and in 1856 Pius IX extended the observance throughout the Roman Rite.

**Solemnity of Mary, Mother of God,** Jan. 1, holy day of obligation, solemnity. The calendar in effect since 1970, in accord with Eastern tradition, reinstated the Marian character of this commemoration on the octave day of Christmas. The former feast of the Circumcision, dating at least from the first half of the sixth century, marked the initiation of Jesus (Lk. 2:21) in Judaism and by analogy focused attention on the initiation of persons in the Christian religion and their incorporation in Christ through baptism. The feast of the Solemnity supplants the former feast of the Maternity of Mary observed on Oct. 11.

**Transfiguration of the Lord,** Aug. 6, feast. Commemorates the revelation of his divinity by Christ to Peter, James and John on Mt. Tabor (Mt. 17:1-9). The feast, which is very old, was extended throughout the universal Church in 1457 by Callistus III.

**Trinity, Most Holy,** movable observance held on the Sunday after Pentecost, solemnity. Commemorates the most sublime mystery of the Christian faith, i.e., that there are Three Divine Persons — Father, Son and Holy Spirit — in one God (Mt. 28:18-20). A votive Mass of the Most Holy Trinity dates from the seventh century; an Office was composed in the 10th century; in 1334, John XXII extended the feast to the universal Church.

**Triumph of the Cross,** Sept. 14, feast. Commemorates the finding of the cross on which Christ was crucified, in 326 through the efforts of St. Helena, mother of Constantine; the consecration of the Basilica of the Holy Sepulchre nearly 10 years later; and the recovery in 628 or 629 by Emperor Heraclius of a major portion of the cross which had been removed by the Persians from its place of veneration at Jerusalem. The feast originated in Jerusalem and spread through the East before being adopted in the West. General adoption followed the building at Rome of the Basilica of the Holy Cross "in Jerusalem," so called because it was the place of enshrinement of a major portion of the cross of crucifixion.

**Visitation,** May 31, feast. Commemorates Mary's visit to her cousin Elizabeth after the Annunciation and before the birth of John the Baptist, the precursor of Christ (Lk. 1:39-47). The feast had a medieval origin and was observed in the Franciscan Order before being extended throughout the Church by Urban VI in 1389. It is one of the feasts of the Incarnation and is notable for its recall of the Magnificat, one of the few New Testament canticles, which acknowledges the unique gifts of God to Mary because of her role in the redemptive work of Christ. The canticle is recited at Evening Prayer in the Liturgy of the Hours.

## SAINTS

Biographical sketches of additional saints are under other Almanac titles. See Index.

An asterisk with a feast date indicates that a memorial or feast is observed according to the general Roman-Rite calendars.

**Adjutor, St.** (d. 1131): Norman knight; fought in First Crusade; monk-recluse after his return; legendary accounts of incidents on journey to Crusade probably account for his patronage of yachtsmen; Apr. 30.

**Agatha, St.** (d. c. 250): Sicilian virgin-martyr; her intercession credited in Sicily with stopping eruptions of Mt. Etna; patron of nurses; Feb. 5*.

**Agnes, St.** (d. c. 304): Roman virgin-martyr; martyred at age of 10 or 12; patron of young girls; Jan. 21*.

**Aloysius Gonzaga, St.** (1568-1591): Italian Jesuit; died while nursing plague-stricken; canonized 1726; patron of youth; June 21*.

**Amand, St.** (d. c. 676): Apostle of Belgium; b. France; established monasteries throughout Belgium; Feb. 6.

**Andre Bessette, Bl.** (Bro. Andre) (1845-1937): Canadian Holy Cross Brother; prime mover in building of St. Joseph's Oratory, Montreal; beatified May 23, 1982; Jan. 6* (U.S.).

**Andre Grasset de Saint Sauveur, Bl.** (1758-1792): Canadian priest; martyred in France, Sept. 2, 1792, during the Revolution; one of a group called the Martyrs of Paris who were beatified in 1926; Sept. 2.

**Andrew Corsini, St.** (1302-1373): Italian Carmelite; bishop of Fiesoli; mediator between quarrelsome Italian states; canonized 1629; Feb. 4.

**Andrew Fournet, St.** (1752-1834): French priest; co-founder with St. Jeanne Elizabeth des Anges of the Congregation of Daughters of the Cross; canonized 1933; May 13.

**Angela Merici, St.** (1474-1540): Italian nun; foundress of Institute of St. Ursula, 1535, the first teaching order of nuns in the Church; canonized 1807; Jan. 27*.

**Angelico, Bl.** (Fra Angelico; John of Faesulis) (1378-1455): Dominican; Florentine painter of early Renaissance proclaimed blessed by John Paul II, 1983; patron of artists; Feb. 18.

**Anne Mary Javouhey, Bl.** (1779-1851): French virgin; foundress of Institute of St. Joseph of Cluny, 1812; beatified 1950; July 15.

**Ansgar, St.** (801-865): Bishop, Benedictine monk; b. near Amiens; missionary in Denmark, Sweden, Norway and Northern Germany; apostle of Denmark; Feb. 3*.

**Anthony Abbot, St.** (c. 251-c. 354): Egyptian hermit; patriarch of all monks; established communities for hermits which became models for monastic life, especially in the East; friend and supporter of St. Athanasius in the latter's struggle with the Arians; Jan. 17*.

**Anthony Mary Claret, St.** (1807-1870): Spanish priest; founder of Missionary Sons of the Immaculate Heart of Mary (Claretians), 1849; archbishop of Santiago, Cuba, 1851-57; canonized 1950; Oct. 24*.

**Anthony Mary Zaccaria, St.** (1502-1539): Italian priest; founder of Barnabites (Clerks Regular of St. Paul), 1530; canonized 1897; July 5*.

**Apollonia, St.** (d. 249): Deaconess of Alexandria; martyred during persecution of Decius; her patronage of dentists probably rests on tradition that her teeth were broken by pincers by her persecutors; Feb. 9.

**Augustine of Canterbury, St.** (d. 604 or 605): Italian missionary; apostle of the English; sent by Pope Gregory I with 40 monks to evangelize England; arrived there 597; first archbishop of Canterbury; May 27*.

**Benedict of Nursia, St.** (c. 480-547): Abbot; founder of monasticism in Western Europe; established monastery at Monte Cassino; proclaimed patron of Europe by Paul VI in 1964; July 11*.

**Benedict the Black (il Moro), St.** (1526-1589): Sicilian Franciscan; born a slave; joined Franciscans as lay brother; appointed guardian and novice master; canonized 1807; Apr. 4.

**Bernadette Soubirous, St.** (1844-1879): French peasant girl favored with series of visions of Blessed Virgin Mary at Lourdes (see Lourdes Apparitions); joined Institute of Sisters of Notre Dame at Nevers, 1866; canonized 1933; Apr. 16.

**Bernard of Menthon, St.** (d. 1081): Italian priest; founded Alpine hospices near the two passes named for him; patron of mountaineers; May 28.

**Bernardine of Feltre, Bl.** (1439-1494): Italian Franciscan preacher; a founder of montes pietatis; Sept. 28.

**Bernardine of Siena, St.** (1380-1444): Italian Franciscan; noted preacher and missioner; spread of devotion to Holy Name is attributed to him; represented in art holding to his breast the monogram IHS; canonized 1450; May 20*.

**Blase, St.** (d. c. 316): Armenian bishop; martyr; the blessing of throats on his feast day derives from tradition that he miraculously saved the life of a boy who had half-swallowed a fish bone; Feb. 3*.

**Boniface (Winfrid), St.** (d. 754): English Benedictine; bishop, martyr; apostle of Germany; established monastery at Fulda which became center of German missionary work; archbishop of Mainz; martyred near Dukkum in Holland; June 5*.

**Brendan, St.** (c. 489-583): Irish abbot; founded monasteries; his patronage of sailors probably rests on tradition that he made a seven-year voyage in search of a fabled paradise; called Brendan the Navigator; May 16.

**Bridget (Brigid), St.** (c. 450-525): Irish nun; founded nunnery at Kildare, the first erected on Irish soil; patron, with Sts. Patrick and Columba, of Ireland; Feb. 1.

**Bridget (Birgitta), St.** (c. 1303-1373): Swedish mystic; widow; foundress of Order of Our Savior (Brigittines); canonized 1391; wrote *Revelationes*, accounts of her visions; patroness of Sweden; July 23*.

**Bruno, St.** (1030-1101): German monk; founded Carthusians, 1084, in France; Oct. 6*.

**Cabrini, Mother:** See Index.

**Cajetan of Thiene, St.** (1480-1547): Italian lawyer; religious reformer; a founder of Oratory of Divine Love, forerunner of the Theatines; canonized 1671; Aug. 7*.

**Callistus I, St.** (d. 222): Pope, 217-222; martyr; condemned Sabellianism and other heresies; advocated a policy of mercy toward repentant sinners; Oct. 14*.

**Camillus de Lellis, St.** (1550-1614): Italian priest; founder of Camillians (Ministers of the Sick); canonized 1746; patron of the sick and of nurses; July 14*.

**Casimir, St.** (1458-1484): Polish prince; grand duke of Lithuania; noted for his piety; buried at cathedral in Vilna, Lithuania; canonized 1521; patron of Poland and Lithuania; Mar. 4*.

**Cassian, St.** (d. 298): Roman martyr; an official court stenographer who declared himself a Christian; patron of stenographers; Dec. 3.

**Catherine Laboure, St.** (1806-1876): French nun; favored with series of visions; first Miraculous Medal (see Index) struck as the result of one of the visions; canonized 1947; Dec. 31.

**Catherine of Bologna, St.** (1413-1463): Italian Poor Clare; mystic, writer, artist; canonized 1712; patron of artists; Mar. 9.

**Cecilia, St.** (2nd-3rd century): Roman virgin-martyr; traditional patron of musicians; Nov. 22*.

**Charles Borromeo, St.** (1538-1584): Italian cardinal; nephew of Pope Pius IV; cardinal bishop of Milan; influential figure in Church reform in Italy; promoted education of clergy; canonized 1610; Nov. 4*.

**Charles Lwanga and Companions, Sts.** (d. 1886 and 1887): Martyrs of Uganda; pages of King Mwanga of Uganda; Charles Lwanga and 12 companions were martyred near Rubaga, June 3, 1886; the other nine were martyred between May 26, 1886, and Jan. 27, 1887; canonized 1964; first martyrs of black Africa; June 3*.

**Christopher, St.** (3rd cent.): Early Christian martyr inscribed in Roman calendar about 1550, feast relegated to particular calendars because of legendary nature of accounts of his life; traditional patron of travelers; July 25.

**Clare, St.** (1194-1253): Foundress of Poor Clares; b. at Assisi; later joined in religious life her sisters

Agnes and Beatrice, and her mother Ortolana; canonized 1255; patroness of television; Aug. 11*.

**Clement I, St.** (d. c. 100): Pope, 88-97; third successor of St. Peter; wrote important letter to Church in Corinth settling disputes there; venerated as a martyr; Nov. 23*.

**Columba, St.** (521-597): Irish monk; founded monasteries in Ireland; missionary in Scotland; established monastery at Iona which became the center for conversion of Picts, Scots, and Northern English; Scotland's most famous saint; June 9.

**Columban, St.** (545-615): Irish monk; scholar; founded monasteries in England and Brittany (famous abbey of Luxeuil), forced into exile because of his criticism of Frankish court; spent last years in northern Italy where he founded abbey at Bobbio; Nov. 23*.

**Contardo Ferrini, Bl.** (1859-1902): Italian secular Franciscan; model of the Catholic professor; beatified 1947; patron of universities; Oct. 17.

**Cornelius, St.** (d. 253): Pope, 251-253; promoted a policy of mercy with respect to readmission of repentant Christians who had fallen away during the persecution of Decius (*lapsi*); banished from Rome during persecution of Gallus; regarded as a martyr; Sept. 16 (with Cyprian)*.

**Cosmas and Damian, Sts.** (d. c. 303): Arabian twin brothers; physicians who were martyred during Diocletian persecution; patrons of physicians; Sept. 26*.

**Crispin and Crispinian, Sts.** (3rd cent.): Early Christian martyrs; said to have met their deaths in Gaul; patrons of shoemakers, a trade they pursued; Oct. 25.

**Crispin of Viterbo, St.** (1668-1750); Capuchin brother; beatified 1806; canonized June 20, 1982; May 21.

**Cyprian, St.** (d. 258): Early ecclesiastical writer; b. Africa; bishop of Carthage, 249-258; supported Pope St. Cornelius concerning the readmission of Christians who had apostasized in time of persecution; erred in his teaching that baptism administered by heretics and schismatics was invalid; wrote *De Unitate*; Sept. 16 (with St. Cornelius)*.

**Cyril and Methodius, Sts.:** Greek missionaries; brothers venerated as apostles of the Slavs; Cyril (d. 869) and Methodius (d. 885) began their missionary work in Moravia in 863; developed a Slavonic alphabet; eventually their use of the vernacular in the liturgy was approved; declared patrons of Europe with St. Benedict, Dec. 31, 1980; Feb. 14*.

**Damasus I, St.** (d. 384): Pope, 366-384; opposed Arians and Apollinarians; commissioned St. Jerome to work on Bible translation; developed Roman liturgy; Dec. 11*.

**Damian, St.:** See Cosmas and Damian, Sts.

**David, St.** (5th-6th cent.): Welsh monk; founded monastery at Menevia; patron saint of Wales; Mar. 1.

**Denis and Companions, Sts.** (d. 3rd cent.): Denis, bishop of Paris, and two companions identified by early writers as Rusticus, a priest, and Eleutherius, a deacon; martyred near Paris; Denis is popularly regarded as apostle of France; Oct. 9*.

**Dismas, St.** (1st cent.): Name given to repentant thief (Good Thief) to whom Jesus promised salvation; regarded as patron of prisoners; Mar. 25.

**Dominic, St.** (Dominic de Guzman) (1170-1221): Spanish priest; founder of Dominican Order (Friars Preachers), 1215; preached against the Albigensian heresy; a contemporary of St. Francis of Assisi; canonized 1234; Aug. 8*.

**Dominic Savio, St.** (1842-1857): Italian youth; pupil of St. John Bosco; died before his 15th birthday; canonized 1954; patron of choir boys; Mar. 9.

**Dunstan, St.** (c. 910-988): English monk; archbishop of Canterbury; initiated reforms in religious life; royal counselor to several kings; considered one of greatest Anglo-Saxon saints; patron of armorers, goldsmiths, locksmiths, jewelers; May 17.

**Durocher, Marie-Rose, Bl.** (1811-1849): Canadian religious; foundress of Sisters of Holy Names of Jesus and Mary; beatified May 23, 1982; Oct. 6* (in U.S.).

**Dymphna, St.** (dates uncertain): Nothing certain known of her life; presumably she was an Irish maiden whose relics were discovered at Gheel near Antwerp, Belgium, in the 13th century; since that time many cases of mental illness and epilepsy have been cured at her shrine; patron of those suffering from mental illness; May 15.

**Edmund Campion, St.** (1540-1581): English Jesuit; convert 1573; martyred at Tyburn; canonized 1970, one of the Forty English and Welsh Martyrs; Dec. 1.

**Elizabeth Bayley Seton, St.** (1774-1821): American foundress; convert, 1805; founded Sisters of Charity in the U.S.; beatified 1963; canonized Sept. 14, 1975; the first American-born saint; Jan. 4 (U.S.)*.

**Elizabeth of Hungary, St.** (1207-1231): Queen; became secular Franciscan after death of her husband in 1227; devoted life to poor and destitute; a patron of the Secular Franciscan Order; Nov. 17*.

**Elizabeth of Portugal, St.** (1271-1336): Queen of Portugal; b. Spain; retired to Poor Clare convent as a secular Franciscan after the death of her husband; July 4*.

**Erasmus, St.** (d. 303): Life surrounded by legend; martyred during Diocletian persecution; patron of sailors; June 2.

**Ethelbert, St.** (552-676): King of Kent; baptized by St. Augustine 597; issued legal code; furthered spread of Christianity; Feb. 24.

**Euphrasia Pelletier, St.** (1796-1868): French nun; founded Sisters of the Good Shepherd at Angers, 1829; canonized 1940; Apr. 24.

**Eusebius of Vercelli, St.** (283-370): Italian bishop; exiled from his see for a time because of his opposition to Arianism; considered a martyr because of sufferings he endured; Aug. 2*.

**Fabian, St.** (d. 250): Pope, 236-250; martyred under Decius; Jan. 20*.

**Felicity, St.:** See Perpetua and Felicity, Sts.

**Ferdinand III, St.** (1198-1252): King of Castile and Leon; waged successful crusade against

Mohammedans in Spain; founded university at Salamanca; canonized 1671; May 30.

**Fiacre, St.** (d. c. 670): Irish hermit; patron of gardeners; Aug. 30.

**Fidelis of Sigmaringen, St.** (Mark Rey) (1577-1622): German Capuchin; lawyer before he joined the Capuchins; missionary to Swiss Protestants; stabbed to death by peasants who were told he was agent of Austrian emperor; Apr. 24*.

**Frances of Rome, St.** (1384-1440): Italian model for housewives and widows; happily married for 40 years; after death of her husband in 1436 joined community of Benedictine Oblates she had founded; canonized 1608; patron of motorists; Mar. 9*.

**Frances Xavier Cabrini, St.** (Mother Cabrini) (1850-1917): American foundress; b. Italy; foundress of Missionary Sisters of the Sacred Heart, 1877; settled in the U.S. 1889; became an American citizen at Seattle 1909; worked among Italian immigrants; canonized 1946, the first American citizen so honored; Nov. 13 (U.S.)*.

**Francis Borgia, St.** (1510-1572): Spanish Jesuit; joined Jesuits after death of his wife in 1546; became general of the Order, 1565; Oct. 10.

**Francis of Assisi, St.** (Giovanni di Bernardone) (1182-1226): Founder of the Franciscans, 1209; received stigmata 1224; canonized 1228; one of best known and best loved saints; patron of Italy, Catholic Action and ecologists; Oct. 4*.

**Francis of Paola, St.** (1416-1507): Italian hermit; founder of Minim Friars; Apr. 2*.

**Francis Xavier, St.** (1506-1552): Spanish Jesuit; missionary to Far East; canonized 1602; patron of foreign missions; considered one of greatest Christian missionaries; Dec. 3*.

**Gabriel of the Sorrowful Mother, St.** (Francis Possenti) (1838-1862): Italian Passionist; died while a scholastic; canonized 1920; Feb. 27.

**Genesius, St.** (d. c. 300): Roman actor; according to legend, was converted while performing a burlesque of Christian baptism and was subsequently martyred; patron of actors.

**Genevieve, St.** (422-500): French nun; a patroness and protectress of Paris; events of her life not authenticated; Jan. 3.

**George, St.** (d. c. 300): Martyr, probably during Diocletian persecution in Palestine; all other incidents of his life, including story of the dragon, are legendary; patron of England; Apr. 23*.

**Gerard Majella, St.** (1725-1755): Italian Redemptorist lay brother; noted for supernatural occurrences in his life including bilocation and reading of consciences; canonized 1904; patron of mothers; Oct. 16.

**Gertrude, St.** (1256-1302): German mystic; writer; helped spread devotion to the Sacred Heart; Nov. 16*.

**Gregory VII (Hildebrand), St.** (1020?-1085): Pope, 1075-1085; Benedictine monk; adviser to several popes; as pope, strengthened interior life of Church and fought against lay investiture; driven from Rome by Henry IV; died in exile; May 25*.

**Gregory the Illuminator, St.** (257-332): Martyr; bishop; apostle and patron saint of Armenia; helped free Armenia from the Persians; Sept. 30.

**Hedwig, St.** (1174-1243): Moravian noblewoman; married duke of Silesia, head of Polish royal family; fostered religious life in country; canonized 1266; Oct. 16*.

**Helena, St.** (250-330): Empress; mother of Constantine the Great; associated with discovery of the True Cross; Aug. 18.

**Henry, St.** (972-1024): Bavarian emperor; cooperated with Benedictine abbeys in restoration of ecclesiastical and social discipline; canonized 1146; July 13*.

**Hippolytus, St.** (d. c. 236): Roman priest; opposed Pope St. Callistus I in his teaching about the readmission of Christians who had apostasized during time of persecution; elected antipope; reconciled before his martyrdom; important ecclesiastical writer; Aug. 13*.

**Hubert, St.** (d. 727): Bishop; his patronage of hunters is based on legend that he was converted while hunting; Nov. 3.

**Hugh of Cluny (the Great), St.** (1024-1109): Abbot of Benedictine foundation at Cluny; supported popes in efforts to reform ecclesiastical abuses; canonized 1120; Apr. 29.

**Ignatius of Antioch, St.** (d. c. 107): Early ecclesiastical writer; martyr; bishop of Antioch in Syria for 40 years; Oct. 17*.

**Ignatius of Loyola, St.** (1491-1556): Spanish soldier; renounced military career after recovering from wounds received at siege of Pampeluna (Pamplona) in 1521; founded Society of Jesus (Jesuits), 1534, at Paris; canonized 1622; author *The Book of Spiritual Exercises;* July 31*.

**Irenaeus of Lyons, St.** (130-202): Early ecclesiastical writer; opposed Gnosticism; bishop of Lyons; traditionally regarded as a martyr; June 28*.

**Isidore the Farmer, St.** (d. 1170): Spanish layman; farmer; canonized 1622; patron of farmers; May 15 (U.S.).*

**Jane Frances de Chantal, St.** (1572-1641): French widow; foundress, under guidance of St. Francis de Sales, of Order of the Visitation; canonized 1767; Dec. 12*.

**Januarius (Gennaro), St.** (d. 304): Bishop of Benevento; martyred during Diocletian persecution; fame rests on liquefication of some of his blood preserved in a phial at Naples, an unexplained phenomenon which has occurred regularly several times each year for over 400 years; declared patron of Campania region around Naples, 1980; Sept. 19*.

**Jerome Emiliani, St.** (1481-1537): Venetian priest; founded Somascan Fathers, 1532, for care of orphans; canonized 1767; patron of orphans and abandoned children; Feb. 8*.

**Joan of Arc, St.** (1412-1431): French heroine, called The Maid of Orleans, La Pucelle; led French army against English invaders; captured by Burgundians, turned over to ecclesiastical court on charge of heresy, found guilty and burned at the stake; her innocence was declared in 1456; canonized 1920; patroness of France; May 30.

**John I, St.** (d. 526): Pope, 523-526; martyr; May 18*.

**John Baptist de la Salle, St.** (1651-1719): French

priest; founder of Brothers of the Christian Schools, 1680; canonized 1900; Apr. 7*.

**John Berchmans, St.** (1599-1621): Belgian Jesuit scholastic; patron of Mass servers; canonized 1888; Aug. 13.

**John Bosco, St.** (1815-1888): Italian priest; founded Salesians, 1859, for education of boys and cofounded the Daughters of Mary Help of Christians for education of girls; canonized 1934; Jan. 31*.

**John Capistran, St.** (1386-1456): Italian Franciscan; preacher; papal diplomat; canonized 1690; declared patron of military chaplains, Feb. 10, 1984. Oct. 23*.

**John Eudes, St.** (1601-1680): French priest; founder of Sisters of Our Lady of Charity of Refuge, 1642, and Congregation of Jesus-Mary (Eudists), 1643; canonized 1925; Aug. 19*.

**John Fisher, St.** (1469-1535): English prelate; theologian; martyr; bishop of Rochester, cardinal; refused to recognize validity of Henry VIII's marriage to Anne Boleyn; upheld supremacy of the pope; beheaded for refusing to acknowledge Henry as head of the Church; canonized 1935; June 22 (with St. Thomas More)*.

**John Kanty (Cantius), St.** (1395-1473): Polish theologian; canonized 1767; Dec. 23*.

**John Leonardi, St.** (1550-1609): Italian priest; worked among prisoners and the sick; founded Clerics Regular of the Mother of God; canonized 1938; Oct. 9*.

**John Nepomucene, St.** (1345-1393): Bohemian priest; regarded as a martyr; canonized 1729; patron of Czechoslovakia; May 16.

**John Nepomucene Neumann, St.** (1811-1860): American prelate; b. Bohemia; ordained in New York 1836; missionary among Germans near Niagara Falls before joining Redemptorists, 1840; bishop of Philadelphia, 1852; first bishop in U.S. to prescribe Forty Hours devotion in his diocese; beatified 1963; canonized June 19, 1977; Jan. 5 (U.S.)*.

**John of God, St.** (1495-1550): Portuguese founder; his work among the sick poor led to foundation of Brothers Hospitallers of St. John of God, 1540, in Spain; canonized 1690; patron of sick, hospitals, nurses; Mar. 8*.

**John Vianney (Cure of Ars), St.** (1786-1859): French parish priest; noted confessor, spent 16 to 18 hours a day in confessional; canonized 1925; patron of parish priests; Aug. 4*.

**Josaphat Kuncevyc, St.** (1584-1623): Basilian monk; b. Poland; archbishop of Polotsk, Lithuania; worked for reunion of separated Easterners; martyred by mob of schismatics; canonized 1867; Nov. 12*.

**Joseph Benedict Cottolengo, St.** (1786-1842): Italian priest; established Little Houses of Divine Providence (Piccolo Casa) for care of orphans and the sick; canonized 1934; Apr. 30.

**Joseph Cafasso, St.** (1811-1860): Italian priest; renowned confessor; promoted devotion to Blessed Sacrament; canonized 1947; June 22.

**Joseph Calasanz, St.** (1556-1648): Spanish priest; founder of Piarists (Order of Pious Schools); canonized 1767; Aug. 25*.

**Joseph of Cupertino, St.** (1603-1663): Italian Franciscan; noted for remarkable incidents of levitation; canonized 1767; Sept. 18.

**Jugan, Jeanne Bl.** (1792-1879): French religious; foundress of Little Sisters of the Poor; beatified Oct. 5, 1982; Aug. 29.

**Justin Martyr, St.** (100-165): Early ecclesiastical writer; *Apologies for the Christian Religion, Dialog with the Jew Tryphon;* martyred at Rome; June 1*.

**Kateri Tekakwitha, Bl.** (1656-1680): "Lily of the Mohawks." Indian maiden born at Ossernenon (Auriesville), N.Y.; baptized Christian, Easter, 1676, by Jesuit missionary Father Jacques de Lambertville; lived life devoted to prayer, penitential practices and care of sick and aged in Christian village near Montreal; buried at Caughnawaga, Ont.; beatified June 22, 1980; July 14* (in U.S.).

**Ladislaus, Saint** (1040-1095): King of Hungary; supported Pope Gregory VII against Henry IV; canonized 1192; June 27.

**Lawrence, St.** (d. 258): Widely venerated martyr who suffered death, according to a long-standing but unverifiable legend, by being roasted alive on a gridiron; Aug. 10*.

**Leonard of Port Maurice, St.** (1676-1751); Italian Franciscan; ascetical writer; preached missions throughout Italy; canonized 1867; patron of parish missions; Nov. 26.

**Louis IX, St.** (1215-1270): King of France, 1226-1270; participated in Sixth Crusade; patron of Secular Franciscan Order; canonized 1297; Aug. 25*.

**Louis de Montfort, St.** (1673-1716): French priest; founder of Sisters of Divine Wisdom, 1703, and Missionaries of Company of Mary, 1715; wrote *True Devotion to the Blessed Virgin;* canonized 1947; Apr. 28.

**Louise de Marillac, St.** (1591-1660): French foundress, with St. Vincent de Paul, of the Sisters of Charity; canonized 1934; Mar. 15.

**Lucy, St.** (d. 304): Sicilian maiden; martyred during Diocletian persecution; one of most widely venerated early virgin-martyrs; patron of Syracuse, Sicily; invoked by those suffering from eye diseases (based on legend that she offered her eyes to a suitor who admired them); Dec. 13*.

**Marcellinus and Peter, Sts.** (d.c. 304): Early Roman martyrs; June 2*.

**Margaret Clitherow, St.** (1556-1586): English martyr; convert shortly after her marriage; one of Forty Martyrs of England and Wales; canonized 1970; Mar. 25.

**Margaret Mary Alacoque, St.** (1647-1690): French nun; spread devotion to Sacred Heart in accordance with revelations made to her in 1675 (see Sacred Heart); canonized 1920; Oct. 16*.

**Margaret of Scotland, St.** (1050-1093): Queen of Scotland; noted for solicitude for the poor and promotion of justice; canonized 1251; Nov. 16*.

**Maria Goretti, St.** (1890-1902): Italian virgin-martyr; a model of purity; canonized 1950; July 6*.

**Mariana Paredes of Jesus, St.** (1618-1645): South American recluse; Lily of Quito; canonized 1950; May 26.

**Martha, St.** (1st cent.): Sister of Lazarus and Mary of Bethany; Gospel accounts record her concern for homely details; patron of cooks; July 29*.

**Martin I, St.** (d. 655): Pope, 649; banished from Rome by emperor because of his condemnation of Monothelites; considered a martyr; Apr. 13*.

**Martin of Tours, St.** (316-397): Bishop of Tours; opposed Arianism and Priscillianism; pioneer of Western monasticism, before St. Benedict; Nov. 11*.

**Mary Magdalene, St.** (1st cent.): Gospels record her as devoted follower of Christ to whom he appeared after the Resurrection; her identification with Mary of Bethany (sister of Martha and Lazarus) and the woman sinner (Lk 7:36-50) has been questioned; July 22*.

**Mary Magdalene de Pazzi, St.** (1566-1607): Italian Carmelite nun; recipient of mystical experiences; canonized 1669; May 25*.

**Maximilian Kolbe, St.** (1894-1941): Polish Conventual Franciscan; prisoner at Auschwitz who heroically offered his life in place of a fellow prisoner; beatified 1971, canonized 1982; Aug. 14*.

**Methodius, St.:** See Index.

**Monica, St.** (332-387): Mother of St. Augustine; model of a patient mother; her feast is observed in the Roman calendar the day before her son's; Aug. 27*.

**Nereus and Achilleus, Sts.** (d. c. 100): Early Christian martyrs; soldiers who, according to legend, were baptized by St. Peter; May 12*.

**Nicholas of Myra, St.** (4th cent.): Bishop of Myra in Asia Minor; one of most popular saints in both East and West; most of the incidents of his life are based on legend; patron of Russia; Dec. 6*.

**Nicholas of Tolentino, St.** (1245-1365): Italian hermit; famed preacher; canonized 1446; Sept. 10.

**Norbert, St.** (1080-1134): German bishop; founder of Norbertines or Premonstratensians, 1120; promoted reform of the clergy, devotion to Blessed Sacrament; canonized 1582; June 6*.

**Odilia, St.** (d. c. 720): Benedictine abbess; according to legend she was born blind, abandoned by her family and adopted by a convent where her sight was miraculously restored; patron of blind; Dec. 13.

**Oliver Plunket, St.** (1629-1681): Irish martyr; theologian; archbishop of Armagh and primate of Ireland; beatified 1920; canonized, 1975; July 1.

**Pancras, St.** (d. c. 304): Roman martyr; May 12*.

**Paschal Baylon, St.** (1540-1592): Spanish Franciscan lay brother; spent life as door-keeper in various Franciscan friaries; defended doctrine of Real Presence in Blessed Sacrament; canonized 1690; patron of all Eucharistic confraternities and congresses, 1897; May 17.

**Patrick, St.** (389-461): Famous missionary of Ireland; began missionary work in Ireland about 432; organized the Church there and established it on a lasting foundation; patron of Ireland, with Sts. Bridget and Columba; Mar. 17*.

**Paul Miki and Companions, Sts.** (d. 1597): Martyrs of Japan; Paul Miki, Jesuit, and twenty-five other priests and laymen were martyred at Nagasaki; canonized 1862, the first canonized martyrs of the Far East; Feb. 6*.

**Paul of the Cross, St.** (1694-1775): Italian religious; founder of the Passionists; canonized 1867; Oct. 19*.

**Paulinus of Nola, St.** (d. 451): Bishop of Nola (Spain); writer; June 22*.

**Peregrine, St.** (1260-1347): Italian Servite; invoked against cancer (he was miraculously cured of cancer of the foot after a vision); canonized 1726; May 1.

**Perpetua and Felicity, Sts.** (d. 203): Martyrs; Mar. 7*.

**Peter Chanel, St.** (1803-1841): French Marist; missionary to Oceania, where he was martyred; canonized 1954; Apr. 28*.

**Peter Gonzalez, St.** (1190-1246): Spanish Dominican; worked among sailors; court chaplain and confessor of King St. Ferdinand of Castile; patron of sailors; Apr. 14.

**Peter of Alcantara, St.** (1499-1562): Spanish Franciscan; mystic; initiated Franciscan reform; confessor of St. Teresa of Avila; canonized 1669; Oct. 19.

**Philip Neri, St.** (1515-1595): Italian religious; founded Congregation of the Oratory; considered a second apostle of Rome because of his mission activities there; canonized 1622; May 26*.

**Philip of Jesus, St.** (1571-1597): Mexican Franciscan; martyred at Nagasaki, Japan; canonized 1862; patron of Mexico City; Feb. 6*.

**Pius V, St.** (1504-1572): Pope, 1566-1572; enforced decrees of Council of Trent; organized expedition against Turks resulting in victory at Lepanto; canonized 1712; Apr. 30*.

**Polycarp, St.** (2nd cent.): Bishop of Smyrna; ecclesiastical writer; martyr; Feb. 23*.

**Pontian, St.** (d. c. 235): Pope, 230-235; exiled to Sardinia by the emperor; regarded as a martyr; Aug. 13 (with Hippolytus)*.

**Raymond Nonnatus, St.** (d. 1240): Spanish Mercedarian; cardinal; devoted his life to ransoming captives from the Moors; Aug. 31.

**Raymond of Penyafort, St.** (1175-1275): Spanish Dominican; confessor of Gregory IX; systematized and codified canon law, in effect until 1917; master general of Dominicans, 1238; canonized 1601; Jan. 7*.

**Rita of Cascia, St.** (1381-1457): Widow; cloistered Augustinian religious of Umbria; invoked in impossible and desperate cases; May 22.

**Robert Southwell, St.** (1561-1595): English Jesuit; poet; martyred at Tyburn; canonized 1970, one of the Forty English and Welsh Martyrs; Feb. 21.

**Roch, St.** (1350-1379): French layman; pilgrim; devoted life to care of plague-stricken; widely venerated; invoked against pestilence; Aug. 17.

**Romuald, St.** (951-1027): Italian monk; founded Camaldolese Benedictines; June 19*.

**Rose of Lima, St.** (1586-1617): Peruvian Dominican tertiary; first native-born saint of the New World; canonized 1671; Aug. 23*.

**Scholastica, St.** (d. c. 559): Sister of St. Benedict; regarded as first nun of the Benedictine Order; Feb. 10*.

**Sebastian, St.** (3rd cent.): Roman martyr; traditionally pictured as a handsome youth with arrows; martyred; patron of athletes, archers; Jan. 20*.

**Seven Holy Founders of the Servants of Mary** (Buonfiglio Monaldo, Alexis Falconieri, Benedict dell'Antello, Bartholomew Amidei, Ricovero Uguccione, Gerardino Sostegni, John Buonagiunta Monetti): Florentine youths who founded Servites, 1233, in obedience to a vision; canonized 1888; Feb. 17*.

**Sixtus II and Companions, Sts.** (d. 258): Sixtus, pope 257-258, and four deacons, martyrs; Aug. 7*.

**Stanislaus, St.** (1030-1079): Polish bishop; martyr; canonized 1253; Apr. 11*.

**Stephen, St.** (d. c. 33): First Christian martyr; chosen by the Apostles as the first of the seven deacons; stoned to death; Dec. 26*.

**Stephen, St.** (975-1038): King; apostle of Hungary; welded Magyars into national unity; canonized 1087; Aug. 16*.

**Sylvester I, St.** (d. 335): Pope 314-335; first ecumenical council held at Nicaea during his pontificate; Dec. 31*.

**Tarcisius, St.** (d. 3rd cent.): Early martyr; according to tradition, was martyred while carrying the Blessed Sacrament to some Christians in prison; patron of first communicants; Aug. 15.

**Therese Couderc, St.** (1805-1885): French religious; foundress of the Religious of Our Lady of the Retreat in the Cenacle, 1827; canonized 1970; Sept. 26.

**Therese of Lisieux, St.** (1873-1897): French Carmelite nun; b. Therese Martin; allowed to enter Carmel at 15, died nine years later of tuberculosis; her "little way" of spiritual perfection became widely known through her spiritual autobiography; despite her obscure life, became one of the most popular saints; canonized 1925; patron of foreign missions; Oct. 1*.

**Thomas Becket, St.** (1118-1170): English martyr; archbishop of Canterbury; chancellor under Henry II; murdered for upholding rights of the Church; canonized 1173; Dec. 29*.

**Thomas More, St.** (1478-1535): English martyr; statesman, chancellor under Henry VIII; author of *Utopia;* opposed Henry's divorce, refused to renounce authority of the papacy; beheaded; canonized 1935; June 22 (with St. John Fisher)*.

**Timothy, St.** (d. c. 97): Bishop of Ephesus; disciple and companion of St. Paul; martyr; Jan. 26*.

**Titus, St.** (d. c. 96): Bishop; companion of St. Paul; recipient of one of Paul's epistles; Jan. 26*.

**Valentine, St.** (d. 269): Priest, physician; martyred at Rome; legendary patron of lovers; Feb. 14.

**Vincent, St.** (d. 304): Spanish deacon; martyr; Jan. 22*.

**Vincent de Paul, St.** (1581?-1660): French priest; founder of Congregation of the Mission (Vincentians, Lazarists) and co-founder of Sisters of Charity; declared patron of all charitable organizations and works by Leo XIII; canonized 1737; Sept. 27*.

**Vincent Ferrer, St.** (1350-1418): Spanish Dominican; famed preacher; Apr. 5*.

**Wenceslaus, St.** (d. 935): Duke of Bohemia; martyr; patron of Bohemia; Sept. 28*.

**Zita, St.** (1218-1278): Italian maid; noted for charity to poor; patron of domestics.

## SAINTS—PATRONS AND INTERCESSORS

A patron is a saint who is venerated as a special intercessor before God. Most patrons have been so designated as the result of popular devotion and long-standing custom. In many cases, the fact of existing patronal devotion is clear despite historical obscurity regarding its origin. The Church has made official designation of relatively few patrons; in such cases, the dates of designation are given in the list below. The theological background of the patronage of saints includes the dogmas of the Mystical Body of Christ and the Communion of Saints.

Listed below are patron saints of occupations and professions, and saints whose intercession is sought for special needs.

Accountants: Matthew.
Actors: Genesius.
Advertisers: Bernardine of Siena (May 20, 1960).
Alpinists: Bernard of Menthon (Aug. 20, 1923).
Altar boys: John Berchmans.
Anesthetists: Rene Goupil.
Angina: Swithbert.
Archers: Sebastian.
Architects: Thomas, Apostle.
Armorers: Dunstan.
Art: Catherine of Bologna.

Artists: Luke, Catherine of Bologna, Bl. Angelico (Feb. 21, 1984).
Astronomers: Dominic.
Athletes: Sebastian.
Authors: Francis de Sales.
Aviators: Our Lady of Loreto (1920), Therese of Lisieux, Joseph of Cupertino.
Bakers: Elizabeth of Hungary, Nicholas.
Bankers: Matthew.
Barbers: Cosmas and Damian, Louis.
Barren women: Anthony of Padua, Felicity.
Basket-makers: Anthony, Abbot.
Blacksmiths: Dunstan.
Blind: Odilia, Raphael.
Blood banks: Januarius.
Bodily ills: Our Lady of Lourdes.
Bookbinders: Peter Celestine.
Bookkeepers: Matthew.
Booksellers: John of God.
Boy Scouts: George.
Brewers: Augustine of Hippo, Luke, Nicholas of Myra.
Bricklayers: Stephen.
Brides: Nicholas of Myra.
Brush makers: Anthony, Abbot.
Builders: Vincent Ferrer.
Butchers: Anthony (Abbot), Luke.

Cab drivers: Fiacre.
Cabinetmakers: Anne.
Cancer patients: Peregrine.
Canonists: Raymond of Peñafort.
Carpenters: Joseph.
Catechists: Viator, Charles Borromeo, Robert Bellarmine.
Catholic Action: Francis of Assisi (1916).
Chandlers: Ambrose, Bernard of Clairvaux.
Charitable societies: Vincent de Paul (May 12, 1885).
Children: Nicholas of Myra.
Children of Mary: Agnes, Maria Goretti.
Choir boys: Dominic Savio (June 8, 1956), Holy Innocents.
Church: Joseph (Dec. 8, 1870).
Clerics: Gabriel of the Sorrowful Mother.
Comedians: Vitus.
Communications personnel: Bernardine.
Confessors: Alphonsus Liguori (Apr. 26, 1950), John Nepomucene.
Convulsive children: Scholastica.
Cooks: Lawrence, Martha.
Coopers: Nicholas of Myra.
Coppersmiths: Maurus.
Dairy workers: Brigid.
Deaf: Francis de Sales.
Dentists: Apollonia.
Desperate situations: Gregory of Neocaesarea, Jude Thaddeus, Rita of Cascia.
Dietitians (in hospitals): Martha.
Dyers: Sts. Maurice and Lydia.
Dying: Joseph.
Ecologists: Francis of Assisi (Nov. 29, 1979).
Editors: John Bosco.
Emigrants: Frances Xavier Cabrini (Sept. 8, 1950).
Epilepsy: Vitus.
Engineers: Ferdinand III.
Eucharistic congresses and societies: Paschal Baylon (Nov. 28, 1897).
Expectant mothers: Raymund Nonnatus, Gerard Majella.
Eye diseases: Lucy.
Falsely accused: Raymund Nonnatus.
Farmers: George, Isidore.
Farriers: John the Baptist.
Firemen: Florian.
Fire prevention: Catherine of Siena.
First communicants: Tarcisius.
Fishermen: Andrew.
Florists: Therese of Lisieux.
Forest workers: John Gualbert.
Foundlings: Holy Innocents.
Fullers: Anastasius the Fuller, James the Less.
Funeral directors: Joseph of Arimathea, Dismas.
Gardeners: Adelard, Tryphon, Fiacre, Phocas.
Glassworkers: Luke.
Goldsmiths: Dunstan, Anastasius.
Gravediggers: Anthony, Abbot.
Greetings: Valentine.
Grocers: Michael.
Hairdressers: Martin de Porres.
Happy meetings: Raphael.
Hatters: Severus of Ravenna, James the Less.
Haymakers: Gervase and Protase.

Headache sufferers: Teresa of Jesus (Avila).
Heart patients: John of God.
Hospital administrators: Basil the Great, Frances X. Cabrini.
Hospitals: Camillus de Lellis and John of God (June 22, 1886), Jude Thaddeus.
Housewives: Anne.
Hunters: Hubert, Eustachius.
Infantrymen: Maurice.
Innkeepers: Amand, Martha.
Invalids: Roch.
Jewelers: Eligius, Dunstan.
Journalists: Francis de Sales (Apr. 26, 1923).
Jurists: John Capistran.
Laborers: Isidore, James, John Bosco.
Lawyers: Ivo, Genesius, Thomas More.
Learning: Ambrose.
Librarians: Jerome.
Lighthouse keepers: Venerius.
Locksmiths: Dunstan.
Maids: Zita.
Marble workers: Clement I.
Mariners: Michael, Nicholas of Tolentino.
Medical record librarians: Raymond of Peñafort.
Medical social workers: John Regis.
Medical technicians: Albert the Great.
Mentally ill: Dymphna.
Merchants: Francis of Assisi, Nicholas of Myra.
Messengers: Gabriel.
Metal workers: Eligius.
Military chaplains: John Capistran (Feb. 10, 1984).
Millers: Arnulph, Victor.
Missions, Foreign: Francis Xavier (Mar. 25, 1904), Therese of Lisieux (Dec. 14, 1927).
Missions, Black: Peter Claver (1896, Leo XIII), Benedict the Black.
Missions, Parish: Leonard of Port Maurice (Mar. 17, 1923).
Mothers: Monica.
Motorcyclists: Our Lady of Grace.
Motorists: Christopher, Frances of Rome.
Mountaineers: Bernard of Menthon.
Musicians: Gregory the Great, Cecilia, Dunstan.
Nail makers: Cloud.
Notaries: Luke, Mark.
Nurses: Camillus de Lellis and John of God (1930, Pius XI), Agatha, Raphael.
Nursing and nursing service: Elizabeth of Hungary, Catherine of Siena.
Orators: John Chrysostom (July 8, 1908).
Organ builders: Cecilia.
Orphans: Jerome Emiliani.
Painters: Luke.
Paratroopers: Michael.
Pawnbrokers: Nicholas.
Pharmacists: Cosmas and Damian, James the Greater.
Pharmacists (in hospitals): Gemma Galgani.
Philosophers: Justin.
Physicians: Pantaleon, Cosmas and Damian, Luke, Raphael.
Pilgrims: James the Greater.
Plasterers: Bartholomew.
Poets: David, Cecilia.
Poison sufferers: Benedict.
Policemen: Michael.

Poor: Lawrence, Anthony of Padua.
Poor souls: Nicholas of Tolentino.
Porters: Christopher.
Possessed: Bruno, Denis.
Postal employees: Gabriel.
Priests: Jean-Baptiste Vianney (Apr. 23, 1929).
Printers: John of God, Augustine of Hippo, Genesius.
Prisoners: Dismas, Joseph Cafasso.
Protector of crops: Ansovinus.
Public relations: Bernardine of Siena (May 20, 1960).
Public relations (of hospitals): Paul, Apostle.
Radiologists: Michael (Jan. 15, 1941).
Radio workers: Gabriel.
Retreats: Ignatius Loyola (July 25, 1922).
Rheumatism: James the Greater.
Saddlers: Crispin and Crispinian.
Sailors: Cuthbert, Brendan, Eulalia, Christopher, Peter Gonzales, Erasmus, Nicholas.
Scholars: Brigid.
Schools, Catholic: Thomas Aquinas (Aug. 4, 1880), Joseph Calasanz (Aug. 13, 1948).
Scientists: Albert (Aug. 13, 1948).
Sculptors: Claude.
Seamen: Francis of Paola.
Searchers for lost articles: Anthony of Padua.
Secretaries: Genesius.
Seminarians: Charles Borromeo.
Servants: Martha, Zita.
Shoemakers: Crispin and Crispinian.
Sick: Michael, John of God and Camillus de Lellis (June 22, 1886).
Silversmiths: Andronicus.
Singers: Gregory, Cecilia.
Skaters: Lidwina.
Skiers: Bernard.
Social workers: Louise de Marillac (Feb. 12, 1960).
Soldiers: Hadrian, George, Ignatius, Sebastian, Martin of Tours, Joan of Arc.
Speleologists: Benedict.
Stenographers: Genesius, Cassian.
Stonecutters: Clement.
Stonemasons: Stephen.
Students: Thomas Aquinas.
Surgeons: Cosmas and Damian, Luke.
Swordsmiths: Maurice.
Tailors: Homobonus.
Tanners: Crispin and Crispinian, Simon.
Tax collectors: Matthew.
Teachers: Gregory the Great, John Baptist de la Salle (May 15, 1950).
Telecommunications workers: Gabriel (Jan. 12, 1951).
Telegraph/telephone workers: Gabriel.
Television: Clare of Assisi (Feb. 14, 1958).
Television workers: Gabriel.
Tertiaries (Franciscan): Louis of France, Elizabeth of Hungary.
Theologians: Augustine, Alphonsus Liguori.
Throat sufferers: Blase.
Travelers: Anthony of Padua, Nicholas of Myra, Christopher, Raphael.
Travel hostesses: Bona (Mar. 2, 1962).
Universities: Blessed Contardo Ferrini.
Vocations: Alphonsus.

Watchmen: Peter of Alcantara.
Weavers: Paul the Hermit, Anastasius the Fuller, Anastasia.
Wine merchants: Amand.
Women in labor: Anne.
Women's Army Corps: Genevieve.
Workingmen: Joseph.
Writers: Francis de Sales (Apr. 26, 1923), Lucy.
Yachtsmen: Adjutor.
Young girls: Agnes.
Youth: Aloysius Gonzaga (1729, Benedict XIII; 1926, Pius XI), John Berchmans, Gabriel of the Sorrowful Mother.

## Patron Saints of Places

Alsace: Odilia.
Americas: Our Lady of Guadalupe, Rose of Lima.
Argentina: Our Lady of Lujan.
Armenia: Gregory Illuminator.
Asia Minor: John, Evangelist.
Australia: Our Lady Help of Christians.
Belgium: Joseph.
Bohemia: Wenceslaus, Ludmilla.
Borneo: Francis Xavier.
Brazil: Nossa Senhora de Aparecida, Immaculate Conception, Peter of Alcantara.
Canada: Joseph, Anne.
Chile: James, Our Lady of Mt. Carmel.
China: Joseph.
Colombia: Peter Claver, Louis Bertran.
Corsica: Immaculate Conception.
Czechoslovakia: Wenceslaus, John Nepomucene, Procopius.
Denmark: Ansgar, Canute.
Dominican Republic: Our Lady of High Grace, Dominic.
East Indies: Thomas, Apostle.
Ecuador: Sacred Heart.
England: George.
Europe: Benedict (1964), Cyril and Methodius, co-patrons (Dec. 31, 1980).
Finland: Henry.
France: Our Lady of the Assumption, Joan of Arc, Therese.
Germany: Boniface, Michael.
Gibraltar: Blessed Virgin Mary under title, "Our Lady of Europe" (May 31, 1979).
Greece: Nicholas, Andrew.
Holland: Willibrord.
Hungary: Blessed Virgin, "Great Lady of Hungary," Stephen, King.
India: Our Lady of Assumption.
Ireland: Patrick, Brigid and Columba.
Italy: Francis of Assisi, Catherine of Siena.
Japan: Peter Baptist.
Lesotho: Immaculate Heart of Mary.
Lithuania: Casimir, Bl. Cunegunda.
Malta: Paul, Our Lady of the Assumption.
Mexico: Our Lady of Guadalupe.
Monaco: Devota.
Moravia: Cyril and Methodius.
New Zealand: Our Lady Help of Christians.
Norway: Olaf.
Papua New Guinea (including northern Solomon Islands): Michael the Archangel (May 31, 1979).
Paraguay: Our Lady of Assumption.

Peru: Joseph.
Philippines: Sacred Heart of Mary.
Poland: Casimir, Bl. Cunegunda, Stanislaus of Cracow, Our Lady of Czestochowa.
Portugal: Immaculate Conception, Francis Borgia, Anthony of Padua, Vincent, George.
Russia: Andrew, Nicholas of Myra, Therese of Lisieux.
Scandinavia: Ansgar.
Scotland: Andrew, Columba.
Silesia: Hedwig.
Slovakia: Our Lady of Sorrows.
South Africa: Our Lady of Assumption.
South America: Rose of Lima.
Spain: James the Greater, Teresa.
Sri Lanka (Ceylon): Lawrence.
Sweden: Bridget, Eric.
United States: Immaculate Conception.
Uruguay: Our Lady of Lujan.
Wales: David.
West Indies: Gertrude.

## Emblems, Portrayals of Saints

Agatha: Tongs, veil.
Agnes: Lamb.
Ambrose: Bees, dove, ox, pen.
Andrew: Transverse cross.
Anne, Mother of the Blessed Virgin: Door.
Anthony, Abbot: Bell, hog.
Anthony of Padua: Infant Jesus, bread, book, lily.
Augustine of Hippo: Dove, child, shell, pen.
Barnabas: Stones, ax, lance.
Bartholomew: Knife, flayed and holding his skin.
Benedict: Broken cup, raven, bell, crosier, bush.
Bernard of Clairvaux: Pen, bees, instruments of the Passion.
Bernardine of Siena: Tablet or sun inscribed with IHS.
Blase: Wax, taper, iron comb.
Bonaventure: Communion, ciborium, cardinal's hat.
Boniface: Oak, ax, book, fox, scourge, fountain, raven, sword.
Bridget of Sweden: Book, pilgrim's staff.
Bridget of Kildare: Cross, flame over her head, candle.
Catherine of Ricci: Ring, crown, crucifix.
Catherine of Siena: Stigmata, cross, ring, lily.
Cecilia: Organ.
Charles Borromeo: Communion, coat of arms with word Humilitas.
Christopher: Giant, torrent, tree, Child Jesus on his shoulders.
Clare of Assisi: Monstrance.
Cosmas and Damian: A phial, box of ointment.
Cyril of Alexandria: Blessed Virgin holding the Child Jesus, pen.
Cyril of Jerusalem: Purse, book.
Dominic: Rosary, star.
Edmund the Martyr: Arrow, sword.
Elizabeth of Hungary: Alms, flowers, bread, the poor, a pitcher.
Francis of Assisi: Deer, wolf, birds, fish, skull, the Stigmata.
Francis Xavier: Crucifix, bell, vessel, Negro.
Genevieve: Bread, keys, herd, candle.

George: Dragon.
Gertrude: Crown, taper, lily.
Gervase and Protase: Scourge, club, sword.
Gregory I (the Great): Tiara, crosier, dove.
Helena: Cross.
Hilary: Stick, pen, child.
Ignatius Loyola: Communion, chasuble, book, apparition of Our Lord.
Isidore: Bees, pen.
James the Greater: Pilgrim's staff, shell, key, sword.
James the Less: Square rule, halberd, club.
Jerome: Lion.
John Berchmans: Rule of St. Ignatius, cross, rosary.
John Chrysostom: Bees, dove, pen.
John of God: Alms, a heart, crown of thorns.
John the Baptist: Lamb, head cut off on platter, skin of an animal.
John the Evangelist: Eagle, chalice, kettle, armor.
Josaphat Kuncevyc: Chalice, crown, winged deacon.
Joseph, Spouse of the Blessed Virgin: Infant Jesus, lily, rod, plane, carpenter's square.
Jude: Sword, square rule, club.
Justin Martyr: Ax, sword.
Lawrence: Cross, book of the Gospels, gridiron.
Leander of Seville: A pen.
Liborius: Pebbles, peacock.
Longinus: In arms at foot of the cross.
Louis IX of France: Crown of thorns, nails.
Lucy: Cord, eyes.
Luke: Ox, book, brush, palette.
Mark: Lion, book.
Martha: Holy water sprinkler, dragon.
Mary Magdalene: Alabaster box of ointment.
Matilda: Purse, alms.
Matthew: Winged man, purse, lance.
Matthias: Lance.
Maurus: Scales, spade, crutch.
Meinrad: Two ravens.
Michael: Scales, banner, sword, dragon.
Monica: Girdle, tears.
Nicholas: Three purses or balls, anchor or boat, child.
Patrick: Cross, harp, serpent, baptismal font, demons, shamrock.
Paul: Sword, book or scroll.
Peter: Keys, boat, cock.
Philip, Apostle: Column.
Philip Neri: Altar, chasuble, vial.
Rita of Cascia: Rose, crucifix, thorn.
Roch: Angel, dog, bread.
Rose of Lima: Crown of thorns, anchor, city.
Sebastian: Arrows, crown.
Simon Stock: Scapular.
Teresa of Jesus (Avila): Heart, arrow, book.
Therese of Lisieux: Roses entwining a crucifix.
Thomas, Apostle: Lance, ax.
Thomas Aquinas: Chalice, monstrance, dove, ox, person trampled under foot.
Vincent: Gridiron, boat.
Vincent de Paul: Children.
Vincent Ferrer: Pulpit, cardinal's hat, trumpet, captives.

## THE MOTHER OF JESUS IN CATHOLIC UNDERSTANDING

*This article was written by the Rev. Eamon R. Carroll, O. Carm., member of the theological faculty of Loyola University, Chicago; author of "Understanding the Mother of Jesus" (published by M. Glazier, Wilmington, Del.; 1979).*

Documents of the Second Vatican Council have provided the charter for current Catholic understanding of the Virgin Mary, Mother of Jesus. This conciliar teaching was expanded and applied in the pastoral letter, "Behold Your Mother: Woman of Faith," issued by the U.S. bishops Nov. 21, 1973. Pope Paul VI added guidelines for devotion, in the revised liturgy and with respect to the Rosary, in the letter *Marialis Cultus* ("To Honor Mary"), dated Feb. 2, 1974.

### Conciliar Documents

The first conciliar document, the *Constitution on the Sacred Liturgy*, linked Mary with the life, death and exaltation of Jesus, stating: "In celebrating this annual cycle of Christ's mysteries, holy Church honors with special love blessed Mary, Mother of God, who is joined by an inseparable bond to the saving work of her Son. In her the Church holds up and admires the most excellent fruit of the redemption, and joyfully contemplates, as in a faultless manner, that which she herself wholly desires and hopes to be" (No. 103).

The eighth and final chapter of the *Dogmatic Constitution on the Church* is entitled "The Blessed Virgin Mary, Mother of God, in the Mystery of Christ and the Church." The seventh chapter deals with the communion of saints, the bond between the pilgrim Church on earth and the blessed joined to the risen Christ — what John deSatgé, an English Anglican, describes as the "mutual sharing and caring in Christ for one another." At the Eucharist, above all, "in union with the whole Church we honor Mary, the ever-Virgin Mother of Jesus Christ our Lord and God" (First Eucharistic Prayer; cf. *Constitution on the Church*, No. 50).

What Catholics believe about the Mother of Jesus is the basis for her place in their prayer life, both in the liturgy and particularly the Eucharist, and in other forms of piety, especially the Rosary. The Church's growth in insight about the Blessed Virgin comes about as Christians ponder the meaning of Mary in prayer as well as in study. The Church has come to know Mary's role by experience and by contemplation of her hidden holiness (*Constitution on the Church*, No. 64). The tradition about Mary has been transmitted by doctrinal teaching and also by life and worship, even as in her own life Mary treasured in her heart God's words and deeds (*Dogmatic Constitution on Divine Revelation*, No. 8).

### Mary in the Bible

The possibility of consensus on the Virgin Mary in the Bible was the theme of a book published in 1978, entitled *Mary in the New Testament* (edited by R. E. Brown, J. A. Fitzmyer, J. Reumann and K. P. Donfried). Limiting their study to the New Testament and using critical techniques of interpretation, a team of 12 authors — Catholics, Lutherans, Anglicans and others — agreed on a biblical portrait of Mary the Virgin as the great gospel model of faith commitment.

One valuable insight centers on the "true kinsmen" incident (Mk. 3:31-35; Mt. 12:46-50; Lk. 8:19-21). One day while Jesus was preaching, word was sent to him that his "mother and brethren" wished to see him. In St. Mark, the oldest account, there is a sharp distinction between the circle of the hearers of Jesus, who were "inside" and counted as his "true family," and the relatives "outside," who failed to understand him. St. Mark does not clearly place Mary among the outsiders, but neither does he carefully distinguish her from the other relatives who did not esteem Jesus. St. Luke shifts the focus completely, placing the relatives, especially the Mother of Jesus, among the true followers, as he does also in the Acts of the Apostles by mentioning them in the Upper Room before Pentecost.

St. Luke is fond of speaking of the "word of God." At the Annunciation, Mary consented with the statement, "Be it done to me according to your word" (Lk. 1:26-38), and "the Word was made flesh" (Jn. 1:14). Jesus said in reply to the message about his visitors, "My mother and my brothers are those who hear the word of God and do it" (Lk. 8:21). St. Luke relates this event just after the parables of the sower and the seed and the lamp on the lampstand. Consistent with his high praise of the Virgin Mary in the infancy chapters, he regards Mary as the rich soil — she heard the word and brought forth fruit in abundance, the Holy One who is the Son of God. She is the pure light, rekindled by the coming of the Redeemer; she is the "woman clothed with the sun" (Rv. 12:1), for Jesus is the "sun of justice."

St. Luke alone saved one other mention of Mary during the public ministry of Jesus, in the story of the "enthusiastic woman" (Lk. 11:27-28). One day while Jesus was preaching, a woman cried out, "Blessed is the womb that bore you and the breasts that nursed you." He replied, "Still more blessed are those who hear the word of God and keep it." The obedient Mary, handmaid of the Lord, brought together opposed beatitudes — the anonymous woman's praise of her motherhood and Jesus' tribute to her faith.

In the opening chapter of St. Luke, Elizabeth did the same when, filled with the Holy Spirit, she returned Mary's greeting with the loud cry, "Of all women you are the most blessed, and blessed is the fruit of your womb." Continuing in praise of her young cousin's faith, she added: "Yes, blessed is she who has believed, for the things promised her by the Lord will be fulfilled" (Lk. 1:39-45).

### Mary the Virgin

Both St. Luke and St. Matthew, whose infancy narratives differ so much otherwise, agree that Mary conceived Jesus virginally, that her Son had no human father. The Creed affirms that Jesus was "conceived of the Virgin Mary by the power of the Holy Spirit."

St. Luke writes of the virginal conception of Jesus from the standpoint of Mary. To her question, "How can this be since I know not man?" the angel replied by appealing to God's power.

St. Matthew's viewpoint is that of Joseph, who was informed in a dream-vision that Mary's child was of no human father. God accomplishes his saving purposes without dependence on the will of the flesh and the will of man (Jn. 1:13). God shows his favor where he chooses — whether for the barren Sara, wife of Abraham, or aged Elizabeth, the wife of Zechariah, or the Virgin Mary. In the words of the promise to Abraham, repeated by Gabriel to Mary, "Nothing is impossible to God" (Lk. 1:37; Gn. 18:14).

Mary and Joseph accepted as God's will the virginal conception, an unprecedented event, the sign of God sending his Son to be the Savior. Their lives were henceforth totally dedicated to the service of Jesus.

As various forms of Christian witness developed in the Church, the conviction that Mary remains always a virgin came to be held as Catholic doctrine. The Gospels leave undecided the identity of the "brethren" of Jesus. From lived experience, by the fourth century the Church had come to see Mary's life-long virginity as part of her commitment to her Son and his mission. Such "development of doctrine" remains a point of difference between Catholics and Protestants, although the great Reformers — Luther, Calvin and later John Wesley — all held that Mary was ever-Virgin.

### St. Luke and St. John on Mary

Along with the role of Mary in the childhood of Jesus, St. Luke sees her as part of the fulfillment of messianic prophecy. The Second Vatican Council spoke of "the exalted daughter of Zion in whom the times are fulfilled after the long waiting for the promise, and the new economy inaugurated when the Son of God takes on human nature from her in order to free men from sin by the mysteries of his flesh." The expectations of Israel for the Messiah reach their peak in Mary of Nazareth: "She stands out among the Lord's lowly and poor who confidently look for salvation from him" (*Constitution on the Church*, No. 55).

The Gospel of St. John introduces Mary at the opening and closing of her Son's ministry, which began with the first of his signs at Cana (Jn. 2:1-11) and ended on Calvary (Jn. 19). Both scenes deal with a "third day," both turn on the "hour," not yet come at Cana but achieved in the decisive event of Calvary. In both, Jesus addresses his Mother with the unaccustomed title, "Woman." The request of Mary at Cana is for more than wine to save the wedding feast. She stands for Israel of old, symbolized by the water pots required for religious purifications; Mary stands also for the new Israel, the Church, the bride of Christ, symbolized by the abundant choice wine of the messianic banquet. The marriage feast looks forward to the hour

when Christ, the bridegroom, will lay down his life in love for his bride, the Church.

When Jesus spoke from the cross to his Mother and the beloved disciple, "Woman, behold your son," and "Behold your Mother," more was meant than that the disciple should provide for Mary's care (Jn. 19:26-27). In his farewell discourse at the Last Supper, Jesus spoke of the woman in agony because her hour had come. "But when she has borne her child, she no longer remembers her pain for joy that a man has been born into the world" (Jn. 16:21). The longing of Israel for the coming of the Messiah was sometimes compared to labor pains. The "daughter of Zion" had been promised she would become the mother of all races and all nations. The words of Jesus on Calvary announced the fulfillment of that promise; Mary stands for the "woman" who is mother Church, new Israel, new People of God.

In St. John's Gospel, it is only after his words to his Mother and the disciple that Jesus, knowing "that everything was now finished," said, "I am thirsty," and then, "Now it is finished." "Then he bowed his head and delivered over his spirit" (Jn. 19:28-29).

The giving up of the spirit means both the expiring of Jesus and the giving of the Holy Spirit to the Church. The wine Mary requested at Cana was the wine of the Spirit, to be poured out at the messianic banquet. The prayer for the wine of the Spirit is answered through the self-surrender of Jesus on the cross. The triumphant Christ "gives up his spirit," and the Church comes into being. The Acts of the Apostles describes the effects of the outpouring of the Spirit at Pentecost and afterwards. What Mary requested at Cana, what she prayed for in agony at the cross of Jesus, what she sought before Pentecost in union with the Apostles and relatives and the women — all "with one accord devoted to prayer" — is the gift of the Spirit. At Nazareth Mary conceived her Son, and God became man by the power of the Holy Spirit; in the Upper Room she prayed for the Spirit that Jesus be born again in the members of his Church (*Constitution on the Church*, No. 59).

### The New Eve

To the titles of Mary already familiar from the Gospels — "the Virgin," "Favored One," "Mother of Jesus," "Mother of my Lord" (Elizabeth's greeting, meaning "Mother of the Messianic King") — the early Church added other descriptions. By the mid-second century Mary was being compared to Eve. Eve was deceived by the word of the evil angel and by disobedience brought death; Mary, the obedient Virgin, heeded the message of the good angel and by her consent brought Life to the world. The title of "New Eve" became common for Mary. By the time of St. Jerome (d. 419), it was proverbial to say, "Death through Eve, life through Mary."

### Immaculate Conception

Reflecting on the Blessed Virgin, Christians pondered various aspects of her holiness. The question arose of her freedom from original sin, God's gift of grace that came to be called her Immaculate Conception (not to be confused with the virginal conception of Jesus, for Mary was the child of the father and mother recalled as Joachim and Anne). It took centuries of development before the Immaculate Conception was held to be revealed by God and defined as dogma by Pius IX in 1854. The absence of clear scriptural evidence was one delaying factor; another was lack of clarity about the meaning of original sin; and most cogent was the requirement that Mary be beneficiary of the saving work of Christ. As the English Anglican John deSatgé expresses it, "Mary, who rejoiced in her Savior, was the last person to have no need of one." The Franciscan John Duns Scotus (d. 1308) suggested that Mary was kept free of original sin by a "preservative redemption" — in anticipation of the foreseen merits of Jesus Christ — the explanation eventually recognized as revealed truth.

### The Assumption

The final facet of Mary's holiness is the Assumption, her union body and soul with the risen Christ in the glory of heaven, defined as dogma by Pope Pius XII in 1950. By the sixth century the feast of the Assumption was being celebrated in the East, a development from a still earlier August 15 feast that had been known as the Memory of Mary (like the birthdays into heaven of the martyrs), as the Passing of Mary, and as the Dormition or Falling Asleep of the Mother of God. There is no compelling biblical testimony; the appeal is to the concordant faith of the Church, convinced that the promise of the resurrection of the flesh in union with the risen Savior has already been fulfilled for the Mother of the Lord, who gave him human birth in her pure body and was his loyal disciple unto the end.

### Model of the Church

All beliefs about the Blessed Virgin lead to Christ. God kept her free from original sin for the sake of Jesus, that she might give herself wholeheartedly to his life and work (*Constitution on the Church*, No. 56), and in consideration of his redemptive mission. Mary's Assumption is her reunion with her Son in the power of his resurrection. The Marian privileges of the Immaculate Conception and the Assumption enrich also the self-understanding of the Church, for she is the "most excellent fruit of the redemption, the spotless model of the Church," the one in whom Christians admire God's plan for his Church. "In the most holy Virgin the Church has already reached that perfection whereby she exists without spot or wrinkle (Eph. 5:27)" (*Constitution on the Church*, No. 65).

Mary Immaculate is a sign of the love of Christ for his bride, the Church; the bridegroom purifies her by his blood to make her all-holy. The preface for the Solemnity of the Immaculate Conception (December 8) addresses the Father: "You allowed no stain of sin to touch the Virgin Mary. Full of grace, she was to be a worthy Mother of your Son, your sign of favor to the Church at its beginning, and the promise of its perfection as the bride of Christ, radiantly beautiful."

Faithful to his promise, Christ has prepared a place for his bride, the Church. In Mary, daughter of the Church, now joined to Christ body and soul in glory, the pilgrim Church sees the successful completion of its own journey. The resurrection of Jesus is the central truth; the Assumption of Mary is the living sign of the Church's call to glory, to loving union with the victorious Redeemer. The preface at Mass for August 15 reads: "Today the Virgin Mother of God was taken up into heaven to be the beginning and the pattern of the Church in its perfection, and a sign of sure hope and comfort for your pilgrim people. You would not allow decay to touch her body, for she had given birth in the glory of the Incarnation to your Son, the Lord of all life." (Cf. also *Constitution on the Church*, No. 68.)

### Mother of God

In 325 the first ecumenical council, at Nicaea, proclaimed that Jesus is truly Son of God. Defenders of the faith were the first to call Mary "Mother of God." At the third ecumenical council, Ephesus, in 431, it was solemnly established that the Virgin Mary is indeed "Mother of God," for the Son to whom she gave birth is the pre-existent Second Person of the Blessed Trinity. "Mother of God" had already been used as a popular title in some parts of the Church, and after Ephesus it was adopted in the prayers of the Mass, as is still the practice in the Catholic Church and all Eastern Churches. For example, the current third Eucharistic Prayer reads: "May he (the Holy Spirit) make us an everlasting gift to you (the Father) and enable us to share in the inheritance of your saints, with Mary, the Virgin Mother of God."

### Mother of the Church

When the Church began to celebrate the Assumption of Mary, it did so in the conviction Mary did not leave the members of the Church orphans when her days on earth were ended. She continues her interest for them in union with her Son, the supreme intercessor. By the time of the Council of Ephesus in 431, authors of both the East and West — like St. Ephrem of Syria (d. 373) and St. Ambrose of Italy (d. 397) — proposed Mary as the model of Christian life, and the practice of asking her to pray for her clients on earth began to appear. The feasts of the Nativity of Mary (September 8), the Annunciation (March 25) and the Presentation of Jesus (February 2, also known as the Purification of Mary or Candlemas) have been kept from the sixth and seventh centuries.

When the words of Gabriel and Elizabeth from St. Luke's infancy narrative became part of prayer, the first part of the Hail Mary, their use led to deeper awareness of Mary's holiness as well as to counting on her heavenly help — well expressed in the second part of the Hail Mary — "Holy Mary, Mother of God, pray for us sinners now and at the hour of our death," which reached its fixed form only in the fifteenth century. Mary's place in liturgical prayer and in private prayer reflected and strengthened the sense of her continuing role as loving friend in heaven of the Church on earth. People asked Mary's prayers on their behalf, recalling Mary's own "pilgrimage of faith" and trusting in her abiding maternal care.

Greek homilists like St. John of Damascus (d. ca. 749), St. Andrew of Crete (d. 740) and St. Germanus of Constantinople (d. ca. 733) sang Mary's praises and urged confidence in her loving intercession with Christ. In the West, after the upsurge of the Carolingian times (about 800), remembered for the origin of the Saturday observance in honor of Mary, came the flowering of medieval piety, as evidenced in the writings of St. Anselm (d. 1109), St. Bernard (d. 1153) and his fellow Cistercians, and the great scholastic doctors like St. Thomas Aquinas (d. 1274) and St. Bonaventure (d. 1274). The medieval authors described Mary as Mediatrix of grace, Dispensatrix of grace, spiritual Mother. Blessed Guerric, the Cistercian abbot of Igny (France, d. 1157), emphasized the maternal role of Mary in the formation of Christ in the faithful: "Like the Church of which she is a figure, Mary is Mother of all who are born to life."

## Christian Unity and Mary

At the Reformation, in reaction to abuses, the invocation of the saints was rejected as harmful to confidence in Christ, the unique Mediator. Since the sixteenth century Western Christians have been sharply divided in their understanding of the communion of saints and the legitimacy of "praying to Mary." Recent events, however, hold out hope for a meeting of minds and hearts even in this sensitive area. The Second Vatican Council offered a biblical portrait of Mary without neglecting later developments in doctrine and devotion. The council described the place of Mary in words designed to meet Protestant difficulties; e.g., the much misunderstood word, Mediatrix, was used once only and was explained as com-

pletely dependent on the unique mediatorship of Christ (Constitution on the Church, Nos. 67, 69).

The conciliar Decree on Ecumenism, issued Nov. 21, 1964, spoke of the "order" or "hierarchy of truths" among Catholic doctrines, which differ in their relationship to the foundation of the faith (No. 11). The foundation is Jesus Christ, and here all Christians share a common profession of faith. The document mentioned realistically some differences that still divide Catholics and other Christians, in this "order of truths': the meaning of the Incarnation and Redemption, the mystery and ministry of the Church, and the role of Mary in the work of salvation (No. 20). The decree also said in this context: "We rejoice to see our separated brethren looking to Christ as the source and center of ecclesiastical communion. Inspired by longing for union with Christ, they feel compelled to search for unity ever more ardently, and to bear witness to their faith among all the peoples of the earth."

The formation of the Ecumenical Society of the Blessed Virgin Mary in England in 1967, and of the American branch in 1976, is an encouraging sign. The American bishops' pastoral, "Behold Your Mother," appealed to the "basic reverence" of all Christians for Mary, "a veneration deeper than doctrinal differences and theological disputes" (Nos. 101-112). Pope Paul VI's major document, Marialis Cultus, contains an appeal to other Christians (Nos. 32 and 33). With Christians of the East, said Pope Paul, Catholics honor the Mother of God as "hope of Christians." Catholics join with Anglicans and Protestants in common praise of God, using the Virgin's own words (Lk. 1:46-55).

It may well be that the growing interest in the bonds between the Blessed Virgin and the Holy Spirit will help Christians together. The Spirit of unity inspired Mary's prophecy: "All generations will call me blessed, because he who is mighty has done great things for me" (Lk. 1:48-49).

# APPARITIONS OF THE BLESSED VIRGIN MARY

*Only seven of the best known apparitions of the Blessed Virgin Mary are described briefly below.*

*The sites of the following apparitions have become shrines and centers of pilgrimage. Miracles of the moral and physical orders have been reported as occurring at these places and/or in connection with related practices of prayer and penance.*

**Banneux,** near Liege, Belgium: Mary appeared eight times between Jan. 15 and Mar. 2, 1933, to an 11-year-old peasant girl, Mariette Beco, in a garden behind the family cottage in Banneux, near Liege. She called herself the Virgin of the Poor, and has since been venerated as Our Lady of the Poor, the Sick, and the Indifferent. A small chapel was built by a spring near the site of the apparitions and was blessed Aug. 15, 1933. Approval of devotion to Our Lady of Banneux was given in 1949 by Bishop Louis J. Kerkhofs of Liege, and a statue of that title was solemnly crowned in 1956.

Over 100 sanctuaries throughout the world are dedicated to the honor of Our Lady of Banneux.

**The International Union of Prayer,** for devotion to the Virgin of the Poor, has approximately two million members.

**Beauraing,** Belgium: Mary appeared 33 times between Nov. 29, 1932, and Jan. 3, 1933, to five children in the garden of a convent school in Beauraing. A chapel, which became a pilgrimage center, was erected on the spot. Reserved approval of devotion to Our Lady of Beauraing was given Feb. 2, 1943, and final approbation July 2, 1949, by Bishop Charue of Namur.

**The Marian Union of Beauraing,** a prayer association for the conversion of sinners, has thousands of members throughout the world (see Pro Maria Committee).

**Fatima,** Portugal: Mary appeared six times between May 13 and Oct. 13, 1917, to three children in a field called Cova da Iria near Fatima, north of Lisbon. She recommended frequent recitation of the Rosary; urged works of mortification for the conversion of sinners; called for devotion to herself under the title of her Immaculate Heart; asked that the people of Russia be consecrated to her under this title, and that the faithful make a Communion of reparation on the first Saturday of each month.

The apparitions were declared worthy of belief in October, 1930, after a seven-year canonical investigation, and devotion to Our Lady of Fatima was authorized under the title of Our Lady of the Rosary. In October, 1942, Pius XII consecrated the world to Mary under the title of her Immaculate Heart. Ten years later, in the first apostolic letter addressed directly to the peoples of Russia, he consecrated them in a special manner to Mary.

Fatima, with its sanctuary and basilica, ranks with Lourdes as the greatest of modern Marian shrines.

(See First Saturday Devotion.)

**Guadalupe,** Mexico: Mary appeared four times in 1531 to an Indian, Juan Diego, on Tepeyac hill outside of Mexico City, and instructed him to tell Bishop Zumarraga of her wish that a church be built there. The bishop complied with the request about two years later after being convinced of the genuineness of the apparition by the evidence of a miraculously painted life-size figure of the Virgin on the mantle of the Indian. The mantle bearing the picture has been preserved and is enshrined i' the Basilica of Our Lady of Guadalupe, which has a long history as a center of devotion and pilgrimage in Mexico. The shrine church, originally dedicated in 1709 and subsequently enlarged, has the title of basilica.

Benedict XIV, in a decree issued in 1754, authorized a Mass and Office under the title of Our Lady of Guadalupe for celebration on Dec. 12, and named Mary the patroness of New Spain. Our Lady of Guadalupe was designated patroness of Latin America by St. Pius X in 1910 and patroness of the Americas by Pius XII in 1945.

**La Salette,** France: Mary appeared as a sorrowing and weeping figure Sept. 19, 1846, to two peasant children, Melanie Matthieu, 15, and Maximin Giraud, 11, at La Salette in southern France. The message she confided to them, regarding the necessity of penance, was communicated to Pius IX in 1851 and has since been known at the "secret" of La Salette. Bishop de Bruillard of Grenoble declared in 1851 that the apparition was credible, and devotion to Mary under the title of Our Lady of La Salette was authorized. The devotion has been confirmed by popes since the time of Pius IX, and a Mass and Office with this title were authorized in 1942. The shrine church was given the title of minor basilica in 1879.

**Lourdes,** France: Mary, identifying herself as the Immaculate Conception, appeared 18 times between Feb. 11 and July 16, 1858, to 14-year-old Bernadette Soubirous at the grotto of Massabielle near Lourdes in southern France. Her message concerned the necessity of prayer and penance for the conversion of peoples. Mary's request that a chapel be built at the grotto and spring was fulfilled in 1862 after four years of rigid examination established the credibility of the apparitions. Devotion under the title of Our Lady of Lourdes was authorized later, and a Feb. 11 feast commemorating the apparitions was instituted by Leo XIII. St. Pius X extended this feast throughout the Church in 1907.

The Church of Notre Dame was made a basilica in 1870, and the Church of the Rosary was built later. The underground Church of St. Pius X, consecrated Mar. 25, 1958, is the second largest church in the world, with a capacity of 20,000 persons.

**Our Lady of the Miraculous Medal,** France: Mary appeared three times in 1830 to Catherine Laboure in the chapel of the motherhouse of the Daughters of Charity of St. Vincent de Paul, Rue de Bac, Paris. She commissioned Catherine to have made the medal of the Immaculate Conception, now known as the Miraculous Medal, and to spread devotion to her under this title. In 1832, the medal was struck according to the model revealed to Catherine.

---

## OUR LADY OF CZESTOCHOWA

The Black Madonna, the icon of Our Lady of Czestochowa, is enshrined on the "Hill of Light," Jasna Gora, above the city of Czestochowa in south central Poland. Long the center and focus of Marian devotion since it was brought there in 1382, it is the primary symbol of Polish religious faith and freedom.

The icon is a portrayal of Mary holding the Child Jesus. Their faces and hands are dark, as though they had been burned or stained by smoke. Three cuts are on one of Mary's cheeks, put there by robbers who desecrated the icon in 1430.

The origin of the icon is not clear. Elements of the legend say it was painted by St. Luke on a panel made by St. Joseph for the home of the Holy Family in Nazareth; that it was transported from the Holy Land to Constantinople; that it was given in 988 to a Ukrainian princess, Anna, the wife of Vladimir of Kiev; and that it eventually was brought to Czestochowa in 1382. The *Catholic Encyclopedia* notes another possibility, that the icon was of Greek-Italian origin in the ninth century.

The location of the icon on the hill above Czestochowa was related to the establishment of a priory of Pauline monks there, also in 1382. A shrine was built some time after 1386. A church was erected in 1644, and a 344-foot tower was raised in 1702.

Our Lady of Czestochowa was declared Queen of Poland in 1656, and the icon was solemnly crowned in 1717 during the pontificate of Pope Clement XI.

The shrine has a long history as the greatest pilgrimage and religious center in Central Europe.

The shrine has undergone changes, some of them violent, in the years since 1382. Even in this century it has been a target of search and harassment by officials of the Communist government in control of the country since the end of World War II.

One thing has not changed, however; that is the significance of the icon and Czes-tochowa in the religious and patriotic life of the Polish people.

*The Second Vatican Council, in its "Decree on Eastern Catholic Churches", stated the following points. regarding Eastern heritage, patriarchs, sacraments and worship.*

The Catholic Church holds in high esteem the institutions of the Eastern Churches, their liturgical rites, ecclesiastical traditions, and Christian way of life. For, distinguished as they are by their venerable antiquity, they are bright with that tradition which was handed down from the Apostles through the Fathers, and which forms part of the divinely revealed and undivided heritage of the universal Church (No. 1).

That Church, Holy and Catholic, which is the Mystical Body of Christ, is made up of the faithful who are organically united in the Holy Spirit through the same faith, the same sacraments, and the same government and who, combining into various groups held together by a hierarchy, form separate Churches or rites. . . . It is the mind of the Catholic Church that each individual Church or rite retain its traditions whole and entire, while adjusting its way of life to the various needs of time and place (No. 2).

Such individual Churches, whether of the East or of the West, although they differ somewhat among themselves in what are called rites (that is, in liturgy, ecclesiastical discipline, and spiritual heritage) are, nevertheless, equally entrusted to the pastoral guidance of the Roman Pontiff, the divinely appointed successor of St. Peter in supreme government over the universal Church. They are consequently of equal dignity, so that none of them is superior to the others by reason of rite (No. 3).

**Eastern Heritage:** Each and every Catholic, as also the baptized . . . of every non-Catholic Church or community who enters into the fullness of Catholic communion, should everywhere retain his proper rite, cherish it, and observe it to the best of his ability (No. 4).

The Churches of the East, as much as those of the West, fully enjoy the right, and are in duty bound, to rule themselves. Each should do so according to its proper and individual procedures (No. 5).

All Eastern rite members should know and be convinced that they can and should always preserve their lawful liturgical rites and their established way of life, and that these should not be altered except by way of an appropriate and organic development (No. 6).

**Patriarchs:** The institution of the patriarchate has existed in the Church from the earliest times and was recognized by the first ecumenical Synods.

By the name Eastern Patriarch is meant the bishop who has jurisdiction over all bishops (including metropolitans), clergy, and people of his own territory or rite, in accordance with the norms of law and without prejudice to the primacy of the Roman Pontiff (No. 7).

Though some of the patriarchates of the Eastern Churches are of later origin than others, all are equal in patriarchal dignity. Still the honorary and lawfully established order of precedence among them is to be preserved (No. 8).

In keeping with the most ancient tradition of the Church, the Patriarchs of the Eastern Churches are to be accorded exceptional respect, since each presides over his patriarchate as father and head. This sacred Synod, therefore, decrees that their rights and privileges should be re-established in accord with the ancient traditions of each Church and the decrees of the ecumenical Synods.

The rights and privileges in question are those which flourished when East and West were in union, though they should be somewhat adapted to modern conditions.

The Patriarchs with their synods constitute the superior authority for all affairs of the patriarchate, including the right to establish new eparchies and to nominate bishops of their rite within the territorial bounds of the patriarchate, without prejudice to the inalienable right of the Roman Pontiff to intervene in individual cases (No. 9).

What has been said of Patriarchs applies as well, under the norm of law, to major archbishops, who preside over the whole of some individual Church or rite (No. 10).

**Sacraments:** This sacred Ecumenical Synod endorses and lauds the ancient discipline of the sacraments existing in the Eastern Churches, as also the practices connected with their celebration and administration (No. 12).

With respect to the minister of holy chrism (confirmation), let that practice be fully restored which existed among Easterners in most ancient times. Priests, therefore, can validly confer this sacrament, provided they use chrism blessed by a Patriarch or bishop (No. 13).

In conjunction with baptism or otherwise, all Eastern-Rite priests can confer this sacrament validly on all the faithful of any rite, including the Latin; licitly, however, only if the regulations of both common and particular law are observed. Priests of the Latin rite, to the extent of the faculties they enjoy for administering this sacrament, can confer it also on the faithful of Eastern Churches, without prejudice to rite. They do so licitly if the regulations of both common and particular law are observed (No. 14).

The faithful are bound on Sundays and feast days to attend the divine liturgy or, according to the regulations or custom of their own rite, the celebration of the Divine Praises. That the faithful may be able to satisfy their obligation more easily, it is decreed that this obligation can be fulfilled from the Vespers of the vigil to the end of the Sunday or the feast day (No. 15).

Because of the everyday intermingling of the communicants of diverse Eastern Churches in the same Eastern region or territory, the faculty for hearing confession, duly and unrestrictedly granted by his proper bishop to a priest of any rite, is applicable to the entire territory of the grantor, also to the places and the faithful belonging to any other rite in the same territory, unless an Ordinary of the place explicitly decides otherwise with respect to the places pertaining to his rite (No. 16).

This sacred Synod ardently desires that where it has fallen into disuse the office of the permanent diaconate be restored. The legislative authority of each individual church should decide about the subdiaconate and the minor orders (No. 17).

By way of preventing invalid marriages between Eastern Catholics and baptized Eastern non-Catholics, and in the interests of the permanence and sanctity of marriage and of domestic harmony, this sacred Synod decrees that the canonical 'form' for the celebration of such marriages obliges only for lawfulness. For their validity, the presence of a sacred minister suffices, as long as the other requirements of law are honored (No. 18).

**Worship:** Henceforth, it will be the exclusive right of an ecumenical Synod or the Apostolic See to establish, transfer, or suppress feast days common to all the Eastern Churches. To establish, transfer, or suppress feast days for any of the individual Churches is within the competence not only of the Apostolic See but also of a patriarchal or archiepiscopal synod, provided due consideration is given to the entire region and to other individual Churches (No. 19).

Until such time as all Christians desirably concur on a fixed day for the celebration of Easter, and with a view meantime to promoting unity among the Christians of a given area or nation, it is left to the Patriarchs or supreme authorities of a place to reach a unanimous agreement, after ascertaining the views of all concerned, on a single Sunday for the observance of Easter (No. 20).

With respect to rules concerning sacred seasons, individual faithful dwelling outside the area or territory of their own rite may conform completely to the established custom of the place where they live. When members of a family belong to different rites, they are all permitted to observe sa-

cred seasons according to the rules of any one of these rites (No. 21).

From ancient times the Divine Praises have been held in high esteem among all Eastern Churches. Eastern clerics and religious should celebrate these Praises as the laws and customs of their own traditions require. To the extent they can, the faithful too should follow the example of their forebears by assisting devoutly at the Divine Praises (No. 22).

### Origin

The Church had its beginnings in Palestine, whence it spread to other regions of the world. As it spread, certain cities or jurisdictions became key centers of Christian life and missionary endeavor — notably, Jerusalem, Alexandria, Antioch and Constantinople in the East, and Rome in the West — with the result that their practices became diffused throughout their spheres of influence. Various rites originated from these practices which, although rooted in the essentials of Christian faith, were different in significant respects because of their relationships to particular cultural patterns.

### Patriarchal Jurisdictions

The main lines of Eastern Church organization and liturgy were drawn before the Roman Empire was separated into Eastern and Western divisions in 292. It was originally co-extensive with the boundaries of the Eastern Empire. Its jurisdictions were those of the patriarchates of Alexandria and Antioch (recognized as such by the Council of Nicaea in 325), and of Jerusalem and Constantinople (given similar recognition by the Council of Chalcedon in 451). These were the major parent bodies of the Eastern Rite Churches which for centuries were identifiable only with limited numbers of nationality and language groups in Eastern Europe, the Middle East and parts of Asia and Africa. Their members are now scattered throughout the world.

## RITES AND FAITHFUL OF EASTERN CHURCHES

(Principal source of statistics: *Annuario Pontificio*. The statistics are for Eastern-Rite jurisdictions only, and do not include Eastern-Rite Catholics under the jurisdiction of Roman-Rite bishops. Some of the figures reported are only approximate. Some of the jurisdictions listed may be inactive because of government suppression.)

The Byzantine, Alexandrian, Antiochene, Armenian and Chaldean are the five principal rites used in their entirety or in modified form by the various Eastern churches. The number of Eastern Catholics throughout the world is more than 12 million.

### Alexandrian Rite

Called the Liturgy of St. Mark, the Alexandrian Rite was modified by the Copts and Melkites, and contains elements of the Byzantine Rite of St. Basil and the liturgies of Sts. Mark, Cyril and Gregory of Nazianzen. The liturgy is substantially that of the Coptic Church, which is divided into two

branches — the Coptic or Egyptian, and the Ethiopian or Abyssinian.

The faithful of this rite are:

COPTS: Returned to Catholic unity about 1741; situated in Egypt, the Near East; liturgical languages are Coptic, Arabic. Jurisdictions (located in Egypt): patriarchate of Alexandria, five dioceses; 134,889.

ETHIOPIANS: Returned to Catholic unity in 1846: situated in Ethiopia, Eritrea, Jerusalem, Somalia; liturgical language is Geez. Jurisdictions (located in Ethiopia): one archdiocese two dioceses; 110,260.

### Antiochene Rite

This is the source of more derived rites than any of the other parent rites. Its origin can be traced to the Eighth Book of the *Apostolic Constitutions* and to the Liturgy of St. James of Jerusalem, which ultimately spread throughout the whole patriarchate and displaced older forms based on the *Apostolic Constitutions.*

The faithful of this rite are:

MALANKARESE: Returned to Catholic unity in 1930; situated in India; liturgical languages are Syriac, Malayalam. Jurisdictions (located in India): one archdiocese, two dioceses; 257,233.

MARONITES: United to the Holy See since the time of their founder, St. Maron; have no counterparts among the separated Eastern Christians: situated throughout the world: liturgical languages are Syriac, Arabic. Jurisdictions (located in Lebanon, Cyprus, Egypt, Syria, U.S., Brazil, Australia, Canada): patriarchate of Antioch, 17 archdioceses and dioceses, one patriarchal vicariate; 1,667,340. Where no special jurisdictions exist, they are under jurisdiction of local Roman-Rite bishops.

SYRIANS: Returned to Catholic unity in 1781; situated in Asia, Africa, the Americas, Australia; liturgical languages are Syriac, Arabic. Jurisdictions (located in Lebanon, Iraq, Egypt, Syria and Turkey): patriarchate of Antioch, seven archdioceses and dioceses, three patriarchal vicariates; 188,453.

## Armenian Rite

Substantially, although using a different language, this is the Greek Liturgy of St. Basil; it is considered an older form of the Byzantine Rite, and incorporates some modifications from the Antiochene Rite.

The faithful of this rite are:

ARMENIANS, exclusively: Returned to Catholic unity during the time of the Crusades; situated in the Near East, Europe, Africa, the Americas, Australasia: liturgical language is Classical Armenian. Jurisdictions (located in Lebanon, Iran, Iraq, Egypt, Syria, Turkey, Poland, France, Greece, Rumania, Argentina (for Latin America including Mexico), and the United States (for Canada and the U.S.): patriarchate of Cilicia, eight archdioceses and dioceses, two patriarchal vicariates, three exarchates, two ordinariates; 152,769.

## Byzantine Rite

Based on the Rite of St. James of Jerusalem and the churches of Antioch, and reformed by Sts. Basil and John Chrysostom, the Byzantine Rite is proper to the Church of Constantinople. (The city was called Byzantium before Constantine changed its name; the modern name is Istanbul.) It is now used by the majority of Eastern Catholics and by the Eastern Orthodox Church (which is not in union with Rome). It is, after the Roman, the most widely used rite.

The faithful of this rite are:

ALBANIANS: Returned to Catholic unity about 1628; situated in Albania; liturgical language is Albanian. Jurisdiction (located in Albania): one apostolic administration.

BULGARIANS: Returned to Catholic unity about 1861; situated in Bulgaria; liturgical language is Old Slavonic. Jurisdiction (located in Bulgaria): one apostolic exarchate.

BYELORUSSIANS, also known as WHITE RUS-

SIANS: Returned to Catholic unity in the 17th century; situated in Europe, the Americas, Australia; liturgical language is Old Slavonic. They have an apostolic visitator.

GEORGIANS: Returned to Catholic unity in 1861; situated in Georgia (Southern Russia), France; liturgical language is Georgian. They have an apostolic administrator.

GREEKS: Returned to Catholic unity in 1829; situated in Greece, Asia Minor, Europe; liturgical language is Greek. Jurisdictions (located in Greece and Turkey): two exarchates; 2,560.

HUNGARIANS: Descendants of Ruthenians who returned to Catholic unity in 1646; situated in Hungary, the rest of Europe, the Americas; liturgical languages are Greek, Hungarian, English. Jurisdictions (located in Hungary): one diocese and one exarchate: 322,800.

ITALO-ALBANIANS: Have never been separated from Rome; situated in Italy, Sicily, the Americas; liturgical languages are Greek, Italo-Albanian. Jurisdictions (located in Italy): two dioceses, one abbacy; 70,829.

MELKITES (GREEK CATHOLICS-MELKITES): Returned to Catholic unity during the time of the Crusades, but definitive reunion did not take place until early in the 18th century; situated in the Middle East, Asia, Africa, Europe, the Americas, Australia; liturgical languages are Greek, Arabic, English, Portuguese, Spanish. Jurisdictions (located in Syria, Lebanon, Jordan, Israel, U.S., Brazil, Canada): patriarchate of Antioch (with patriarchal vicariates in Egypt, Sudan, Jerusalem, Iraq and Kuwait), 16 archdioceses and dioceses and one exarchate; 850,894, (*Annuario Pontificio* figures. Some sources estimate 1,000,000).

ROMANIANS: Returned to Catholic unity in 1697; situated in Romania, the rest of Europe, the Americas; liturgical language is Modern Romanian. Jurisdictions (located in Romania and U.S.): one archdiocese, four dioceses, one exarchate. There were 1.5 million members in 1948 when they were forcibly incorporated into the Romanian Orthodox Church. They have an apostolic exarchate in the U.S., where they number approximately 5,000.

RUSSIANS: Returned to Catholic unity about 1905; situated in Europe, the Americas, Australia, China; liturgical language is Old Slavonic. Jurisdictions (located in Russia and China): two exarchates.

RUTHENIANS, or CARPATHO-RUSSIANS (Rusins): Returned to Catholic unity in the Union of Brest-Litovek, 1596, and the Union of Uzhorod, Apr. 24, 1646; situated in Hungary, Czechoslovakia, elsewhere in Europe, the Americas, Australia; liturgical languages are Old Slavonic, English. Jurisdictions (located in Russia and the U.S.): one archdiocese, four dioceses.

SLOVAKS: Jurisdictions (located in Czechoslovakia and Canada): two dioceses.

UKRAINIANS, or GALICIAN RUTHENIANS: Returned to Catholic unity about 1595; situated in Europe, the Americas, Australasia; liturgical languages are Old Slavonic and Ukrainian. Jurisdictions (located in Russian Galicia, Poland, the U.S., Canada, England, Australia, Germany, France, Brazil, Argentina): three archdioceses, 12 dioceses, four apostolic exarchates: 4,683,327. This total includes the 1943 figure of 3.5 million Ukrainian Catholics in jurisdictions subsequently forced into the Russian Orthodox Church.

YUGOSLAVS, SERBS and CROATIANS: Returned to Catholic unity in 1611; situated in Yugoslavia, the Americas; liturgical language is Old Slavonic. Jurisdiction (located in Yugoslavia): one diocese (which also has jurisdiction over all Byzantine-Rite faithful in Yugoslavia); 48,776. They are under the jurisdiction of Ruthenian bishops elsewhere.

## Chaldean Rite

This rite, listed as separate and distinct by the Sacred Congregation for the Oriental Churches, was derived from the Antiochene Rite.

The faithful of this rite are:

CHALDEANS: Descendants of the Nestorians, returned to Catholic unity in 1692; situated throughout the Middle East, in Europe, Africa, the Americas; liturgical languages are Syriac, Arabic. Jurisdictions (located in Egypt, Iraq, Iran, Lebanon, Syria, Turkey, U.S.); patriarchate of Babylonia, 20 archdioceses and dioceses, one apostolic exarchate; 406,723. There are patriarchal vicars for Jordan and Egypt.

SYRO-MALABARESE: Descended from the St. Thomas Christians of India; situated mostly in the Malabar region of India; they use a Westernized and Latinized form of the Chaldean Rite in Syriac and Malayalam. Jurisdictions (located in India): two archdioceses, 16 dioceses; 2,545,977.

## EASTERN JURISDICTIONS

For centuries Eastern-Rite Catholics were identifiable with a limited number of nationality and language groups in certain countries of the Middle East, Eastern Europe, Asia and Africa. The persecution of religion in the Soviet Union since 1917 and in communist-controlled countries since World War II, however — in addition to decimating and destroying the Church in those places — has resulted in the emigration of many Eastern-Rite Catholics from their homelands. This forced emigration, together with voluntary emigration, has led to the spread of Eastern Rites and their faithful to many other countries.

### Europe

(Bishop Vasile Cristea, A.A., is apostolic visitor for Romanian Byzantine Rite Catholics in Europe.)

ALBANIA: Byzantine Rite, apostolic administration.

AUSTRIA: Byzantine Rite, ordinariate.

BULGARIA: Byzantine Rite (Bulgarians), apostolic exarchate.

CZECHOSLOVAKIA: Byzantine Rite (Slovakians and other Byzantine-Rite Catholics), eparchy.

FRANCE: Byzantine Rite (Ukrainians), apostolic exarchate.

Armenian Rite, apostolic exarchate. Ordinariate for all other Eastern-Rite Catholics.

GERMANY: Byzantine Rite (Ukrainians), apostolic exarchate.

GREAT BRITAIN: Byzantine Rite (Ukrainians), apostolic exarchate.

GREECE: Byzantine Rite, apostolic exarchate. Armenian Rite, ordinariate.

HUNGARY: Byzantine Rite (Hungarians), eparchy, apostolic exarchate.

ITALY: Byzantine Rite (Italo-Albanians), two eparchies, one abbacy.

POLAND: Byzantine Rite (Ukrainian), apostolic exarchate.

Armenian Rite, archeparchy.

RUMANIA: Byzantine Rite (Romanians), metropolitan, four eparchies.

Armenian Rite, ordinariate.

RUSSIA: Byzantine Rite (Russians), apostolic exarchate; (Ruthenians), eparchy; (Ukrainians), major archeparchy, two eparchies.

YUGOSLAVIA: Byzantine Rite (Yugoslav and other Byzantine-Rite Catholics), eparchy.

### Asia

CHINA: Byzantine Rite (Russians), apostolic exarchate.

CYPRUS: Antiochene Rite (Maronites), archeparchy.

INDIA: Antiochene Rite (Malankarese), metropolitan see, two eparchies.

Chaldean Rite (Syro-Malabarese), two metropolitan sees, 16 eparchies.

IRAN: Chaldean Rite (Chaldeans), two metropolitan sees, one archeparchy, one eparchy.

Armenian Rite, eparchy.

IRAQ: Antiochene Rite (Syrians), two archeparchies.

Byzantine Rite (Greek-Melkites), patriarchal vicariate.

Chaldean Rite (Chaldeans), patriarchate, two metropolitan sees, eight archeparchies and eparchies.

Armenian Rite, archeparchy.

ISRAEL (includes Jerusalem): Antiochene Rite (Syrians), patriarchal vicariate; (Maronites), patriarchal vicariate.

Byzantine Rite (Greek-Melkites), archeparchy, patriarchal vicariate.

Chaldean Rite (Chaldeans), patriarchal vicariate.

Armenian Rite, patriarchal vicariate.

JORDAN: Byzantine Rite (Greek-Melkites), archeparchy.

KUWAIT: Byzantine Rite (Greek-Melkites), patriarchal vicariate.

LEBANON: Antiochene Rite (Maronites), patriarchate, eight archeparchies and eparchies; (Syrians), patriarchate.

Byzantine Rite (Greek-Melkites), seven metropolitan and archeparchal sees.

Chaldean Rite (Chaldeans), eparchy.

Armenian Rite, patriarchate, eparchy.

SYRIAN ARAB REPUBLIC: Antiochene Rite (Maronites), two archeparchies, one eparchy; (Syrians), four archeparchies.

Byzantine Rite (Greek-Melkites), patriarchate, four metropolitan sees, one archeparchy.
Chaldean Rite (Chaldeans), eparchy.
Armenian Rite, archeparchy, eparchy, patriarchal vicariate.
TURKEY (Europe and Asia): Antiochene Rite (Syrians), patriarchal vicariate.
Byzantine Rite (Greeks), apostolic exarchate.
Chaldean Rite (Chaldeans), one archeparchy, two eparchies.
Armenian Rite, archeparchy.

### Oceania

AUSTRALIA: Byzantine Rite (Ukrainians), eparchy.
Antiochene Rite (Maronites), eparchy.

### Africa

EGYPT, ARAB REPUBLIC OF: Alexandrian Rite (Copts), patriarchate, five eparchies.
Antiochene Rite (Maronites), eparchy; (Syrians), eparchy.
Byzantine Rite (Greek-Melkites), patriarchal vicariate.
Chaldean Rite (Chaldeans), eparchy.
Armenian Rite, eparchy.
ETHIOPIA: Alexandrian Rite (Ethiopians), metropolitan see, two eparchies.
SUDAN: Byzantine Rite (Greek-Melkites), patriarchal vicariate.

### North America

CANADA: Byzantine Rite (Ukrainians), one metropolitan, four eparchies; (Slovaks), eparchy; (Greek-Melkites), apostolic exarchate.
Armenian Rite, apostolic exarchate for Canada and the U.S. (New York is see city).
Antiochene Rite (Maronites), eparchy.
UNITED STATES: Antiochene Rite (Maronites), eparchy.
Byzantine Rite (Ukrainians), one metropolitan see, three eparchies; (Ruthenians), one metropolitan see, three eparchies; (Greek-Melkites), eparchy; (Romanians), apostolic exarchate; (Byelorussians), apostolic visitator.
Armenian Rite, apostolic exarchate for Canada and U.S. (New York is see city).
Chaldean Rite, apostolic exarchate.
Other Eastern-Rite Catholics are under the jurisdiction of local Roman-Rite bishops. (See Eastern-Rite Catholics in the United States.)

### South America

Armenian-Rite Catholics in Latin America (including Mexico) are under the jurisdiction of an apostolic exarchate (see city, Buenos Aires, Argentina).
ARGENTINA: Byzantine Rite (Ukrainians), eparchy.
Armenian Rite, apostolic exarchate (for Latin America)
Ordinariate for all other Eastern-Rite Catholics.
BRAZIL: Antiochene Rite (Maronites), eparchy.
Byzantine Rite (Greek-Melkites), eparchy; (Ukrainians), eparchy.
Ordinariate for all other Eastern-Rite Catholics.

### SYNODS, ASSEMBLIES

These assemblies are collegial bodies which have pastoral authority over members of the Eastern Rite Churches.

**Patriarchal Synods:** Maronites: Cardinal Antoine Khoraiche, patriarch of Antioch of the Maronites.
Melkites: Maximos V Hakim, patriarch of Antioch of the Greek Catholics-Melkites.
Chaldeans: Paul II Cheikho, patriarch of Babylonia of the Chaldeans.
Copts: Cardinal Stephanos I Sidarouss, C.M., patriarch of Alexandria of the Copts.
Syrians: Ignace Antoine II Hayek, patriarch of Antioch of the Syrians.
Armenians: Jean Pierre XVIII Kasparian, patriarch of Cilicia of the Armenians.

**Non-Patriarchal Synod:** The Synod of the Ukrainian Catholic Hierarchy is an extraterritorial synod convoked with the assent of the Pope. Cardinal Josyf Slipyi, major archbishop of Lwow of the Ukrainians, is president.

**Assemblies:** Assembly of Ordinaries of the Arab Republic of Egypt: Cardinal Stephanos I Sidarouss, C.M., patriarch of Alexandria of the Copts, president.
Assembly of Catholic Patriarchs and Bishops of Lebanon: Cardinal Antoine Khoraiche, patriarch of Antioch of the Maronites, president.
Assembly of Ordinaries of the Syrian Arab Republic: Maximos V Hakim, patriarch of Antioch of the Greek Catholics-Melkites, president.
Interritual Union of the Bishops of Iraq: Paul II Cheikho, patriarch of Babylonia of the Chaldeans, president.
Syro-Malabarese Episcopal Conference (June 4, 1970): Cardinal Joseph Parecattil, Ernakulam, president.
Iranian Episcopal Conference (Aug. 11, 1977): Most Rev. Youhannan Semaan Issayi, metropolitan of Teheran of the Chaldeans, president.
Of the collegial bodies listed above, the patriarchal synods have the most authority. In addition to other prerogatives, they have the right to elect bishops and regulate discipline for their respective rites.

### EASTERN RITES IN U.S.

(Statistics, from the *Official Catholic Directory*, are membership figures reported by Eastern-Rite jurisdictions. Additional Eastern-Rite Catholics are included in statistics for Roman-Rite dioceses.)

### Byzantine Rite

**Ukrainians:** There are 231,041 in four jurisdictions in the U.S.: the metropolitan see of Philadelphia (1924, metropolitan 1958) and the suffragan sees of Stamford, Conn. (1956), St. Nicholas of Chicago (1961) and St. Josaphat in Parma (1983).
**Ruthenians:** There are 283,229 in four jurisdictions in the U.S.: the metropolitan see of Pittsburgh (est. 1924 at Pittsburgh; metropolitan and transferred to Munhall, 1969; transferred to Pittsburgh, 1977) and the suffragan sees of Passaic, N.J. (1963), Parma, Ohio (1969) and Van Nuys,

Calif. (1981). Hungarian and Croatian Byzantine Catholics in the U.S. are also under the jurisdiction of Ruthenian-Rite bishops.

**Melkites (Greek Catholics-Melkites):** In 1984, 22,987 (of approximately 55,000) were reported under the jurisdiction of the Melkite eparchy of Newton, Mass. (established as an exarchate, 1965; eparchy, 1976).

**Romanians:** There are approximately 5,000 in 16 Romanian Catholic Byzantine Rite parishes in the U.S., under the jurisdiction of an apostolic exarchate established in 1982 (see city, Canton, Ohio).

**Byelorussians:** Have one parish in the U.S. — Christ the Redeemer, Chicago, Ill. Archimandrite Vladimir Tarasevitch, O.S.B., pastor, was ordained titular bishop of Mariamme, Sept. 8, 1983, and named apostolic visitator of Byelorussian Catholics living outside Byelorussia.

**Russians:** Have parishes in California (St. Andrew, El Segundo, and Our Lady of Fatima Center, San Francisco); Massachusetts (Our Lady of Kazan, Boston); New York (St. Michael's Chapel of St. Patrick's Old Cathedral, Pope John XXIII Ecumenical Center). They are under the jurisdiction of local Roman-Rite bishops.

### Antiochene Rite

In 1984, 50,285 (of approximately 153,000) Maronites were reported under the jurisdiction of the eparchy of St. Maron, Brooklyn (established at Detroit as an exarchate, 1966; eparchy, 1972; transferred to Brooklyn, 1977).

### Armenian Rite

An apostolic exarchate for Canada and the United States (see city, New York) was established July 3, 1981; 30,000 in both countries (*Annuario Pontificio*).

### Chaldean Rite

An apostolic exarchate for the United States (see city, Detroit) was established Jan. 26, 1982; 43,000.

## BYZANTINE DIVINE LITURGY

The Divine Liturgy in all rites is based on the consecration of bread and wine by the narration-reactualization of the actions of Christ at the Last Supper. Aside from this fundamental usage, there are differences between the Roman (Latin) Rite and Eastern Rites, and among the Eastern Rites themselves. Following is a general description of the Byzantine Divine Liturgy which is in widest use in the Eastern-Rite Churches.

In the Byzantine, as in all Eastern Rites, the bread and wine are prepared at the start of the Liturgy. The priest does this in a little niche or at a table in the sanctuary. Taking a round loaf of leavened bread stamped with religious symbols, he cuts out a square host and other particles while reciting verses expressing the symbolism of the action. When the bread and wine are ready, he says a prayer of offering and incenses the oblations, the altar, the icons and the people.

**Liturgy of the Catechumens:** At the altar a litany for all classes of people is sung by the priest. The congregation answers, "Lord, have mercy."

The Little Entrance comes next. In procession, the priest leaves the sanctuary carrying the Book of the Gospels, and then returns. He sings prayers especially selected for the day and the feast. These are followed by the solemn singing of the prayer, "Holy God, Holy Mighty One, Holy Immortal One."

The Epistle follows. The Gospel is sung or read by the priest facing the people at the middle door of the sanctuary.

An interruption after the Liturgy of the Catechumens, formerly an instructional period for those learning the faith, is clearly marked. Catechumens, if present, are dismissed with a prayer. Following this are a prayer and litany for the faithful.

**Great Entrance:** The Great Entrance or solemn Offertory Procession then takes place. The priest first says a long silent prayer for himself, in preparation for the great act to come. Again he incenses the oblations, the altar, the icons and people. He goes to the table on the gospel side for the veil-covered paten and chalice. When he arrives back at the sanctuary door, he announces the intention of the Mass in the prayer: "May the Lord God remember all of you in his kingdom, now and forever."

After another litany, the congregation recites the Nicene Creed.

**Consecration:** The most solemn portion of the sacrifice is introduced by the preface, which is very much like the preface of the Roman Rite. At the beginning of the last phrase, the priest raises his voice to introduce the singing of the Sanctus. During the singing he reads the introduction to the words of consecration.

The words of consecration are sung aloud, and the people sing "Amen" to both consecrations. As the priest raises the Sacred Species in solemn offering, he sings: "Thine of Thine Own we offer unto Thee in behalf of all and for all."

A prayer to the Holy Spirit is followed by the commemorations, in which special mention is made of the all-holy, most blessed and glorious Lady, the Mother of God and ever-Virgin Mary. The dead are remembered and then the living.

**Holy Communion:** A final litany for spiritual gifts precedes the Our Father. The Sacred Body and Blood are elevated with the words, "Holy Things for the Holy." The Host is then broken and commingled with the Precious Blood. The priest recites preparatory prayers for Holy Communion, consumes the Sacred Species, and distributes Holy Communion to the people under the forms of both bread and wine. During this time a communion verse is sung by the choir or congregation.

The Liturgy closes quickly after this. The consecrated Species of bread and wine are removed to the side table to be consumed later by the priest. A prayer of thanksgiving is recited, a prayer for all the people is said in front of the icon of Christ, a blessing is invoked upon all, and the people are dismissed.

## BYZANTINE CALENDAR

The Byzantine-Rite calendar has many distinctive features of its own, although it shares common elements with the Roman-Rite calendar — e.g., general purpose, commemoration of the mysteries of faith and of the saints, identical dates for some feasts. Among the distinctive things are the following.

The liturgical year begins on Sept. 1, the **Day of Indiction,** in contrast with the Latin or Roman start on the First Sunday of Advent late in November or early in December. The Advent season begins on Dec. 10.

### Cycles of the Year

As in the Roman usage, the dating of feasts follows the Gregorian Calendar. Formerly, until well into this century, the Julian Calendar was used. (The Julian Calendar, which is now about 13 days late, is still used by some Eastern-Rite Churches.)

The year has several cycles, which include proper seasons, the feasts of saints, and series of New Testament readings. All of these elements of worship are contained in liturgical books of the rite.

The ecclesiastical calendar, called the **Menologion,** explains the nature of feasts, other observances and matters pertaining to the liturgy for each day of the year. In some cases, its contents include the lives of saints and the history and meaning of feasts.

The Divine Liturgy (Mass) and Divine Office for the proper of the saints, fixed feasts, and the Christmas season are contained in the **Menaion.** The **Triodion** covers the pre-Lenten season of preparation for Easter; Lent begins two days before the Ash Wednesday observance of the Roman Rite. The **Pentecostarion** contains the liturgical services from Easter to the Sunday of All Saints, the first after Pentecost. The **Evangelion** and **Apostolos** are books in which the Gospels, and Acts of the Apostles and the Epistles, respectively, are arranged according to the order of their reading in the Divine Liturgy and Divine Office throughout the year.

The cyclic progression of liturgical music throughout the year, in successive and repetitive periods of eight weeks, is governed by the **Oktoechos,** the Book of Eight Tones.

### Sunday Names

Many Sundays are named after the subject of the Gospel read in the Mass of the day or after the name of a feast falling on the day — e.g., Sunday of the Publican and Pharisee, of the Prodigal Son, of the Samaritan Woman, of St. Thomas the Apostle, of the Fore-Fathers (Old Testament Patriarchs). Other Sundays are named in the same manner as in the Roman calendar — e.g., numbered Sundays of Lent and after Pentecost.

### Holy Days

The calendar lists about 28 holy days. Many of the major holy days coincide with those of the Ro-

man calendar, but the feast of the Immaculate Conception is observed on Dec. 9 instead of Dec. 8, and the feast of All Saints falls on the Sunday after Pentecost rather than on Nov. 1. Instead of a single All Souls' Day, there are five All Souls' Saturdays.

According to regulations in effect in the Byzantine-Rite (Ruthenian) Archeparchy of Pittsburgh and its suffragan sees of Passaic, Parma and Van Nuys, holy days are obligatory, solemn and simple, and attendance at the Divine Liturgy is required on five obligatory days — the feasts of the Epiphany, the Ascension, Sts. Peter and Paul, the Assumption of the Blessed Virgin Mary, and Christmas. Although attendance at the liturgy is not obligatory on 15 solemn and seven simple holy days, it is recommended.

In the Byzantine-Rite (Ukrainian) Archeparchy of Philadelphia and its suffragan sees of St. Josaphat in Parma, St. Nicholas (Chicago) and Stamford, the obligatory feasts are the Circumcision, Epiphany, Annunciation, Easter, Ascension, Pentecost, Dormition (Assumption of Mary), Immaculate Conception and Christmas.

### Lent

The first day of Lent — the Monday before Ash Wednesday of the Roman Rite — and Good Friday are days of strict abstinence for persons in the age bracket of obligation. No meat, eggs, or dairy products may be eaten on these days.

All persons over the age of 14 must abstain from meat on Fridays during Lent, Holy Saturday, and the vigils of the feasts of Christmas and Epiphany; abstinence is urged, but is not obligatory, on Wednesdays of Lent. The abstinence obligation is not in force on certain "free" or "privileged" Fridays.

### Synaxis

An observance without a counterpart in the Roman calendar is the synaxis. This is a commemoration, on the day following a feast, of persons involved with the occasion for the feast — e.g., Sept. 9, the day following the feast of the Nativity of the Blessed Virgin Mary, is the Synaxis of Joachim and Anna, her parents.

### Holy Week

In the Byzantine Rite, Lent is liturgically concluded with the Saturday of Lazarus, the day before Palm Sunday, which commemorates the raising of Lazarus from the dead.

On the following Monday, Tuesday and Wednesday, the Liturgy of the Presanctified is prescribed.

On Holy Thursday, the Liturgy of St. Basil the Great is celebrated together with Vespers.

The Divine Liturgy is not celebrated on Good Friday.

On Holy Saturday, the Liturgy of St. Basil the Great is celebrated along with Vespers.

*The **Church of Santa Susanna** was established as the national church for Americans in Rome Feb. 28, 1922, and entrusted to the Paulist Fathers who have served there continuously since then except for several years during World War II.*

## BYZANTINE FEATURES

**Art:** Named for the empire in which it developed, Byzantine art is a unique blend of imperial Roman and classic Hellenic culture with Christian inspiration. The art of the Greek Middle Ages, it reached a peak of development in the 10th or 11th century. Characteristic of its products, particularly in mosaic and painting, are majesty, dignity, refinement and grace. Its sacred paintings, called icons, are reverenced highly in all Eastern Rites.

**Church Building:** The classical model of Byzantine church architecture is the Church of the Holy Wisdom (Hagia Sophia), built in Constantinople in the first half of the sixth century and still standing. The square structure, extended in some cases in the form of a cross, is topped by a distinctive onion-shaped dome and surmounted by a triple-bar cross. The altar is at the eastern end of building, where the wall bellies out to form an apse. The altar and sanctuary are separated from the body of the church by a fixed or movable screen, the iconostas, to which icons or sacred pictures are attached (see below).

**Clergy:** The Byzantine Rite has married as well as celibate priests. In places other than the US, where married candidates have not been accepted for ordination since about 1929, men already married can be ordained to the diaconate and priesthood and can continue in marriage after ordination. Celibate deacons and priests cannot marry after ordination; neither can a married priest remarry after the death of his wife. Bishops must be unmarried.

**Iconostas:** A large screen decorated with sacred pictures or icons which separates the sanctuary from the nave of a church; its equivalent in the Roman Rite, for thus separating the sanctuary from the nave, is an altar rail.

An iconostas has three doors through which the sacred ministers enter the sanctuary during the Divine Liturgy: smaller (north and south) Deacons' Doors and a large central Royal Door.

The Deacons' Doors usually feature the icons of Sts. Gabriel and Michael; the Royal Door, the icons of the Evangelists — Matthew, Mark, Luke and John. To the right and left of the Royal Door are the icons of Christ the Teacher and of the Blessed Virgin Mary with the Infant Jesus. To the extreme right and left are the icons of the patron of the church and St. John the Baptist (or St. Nicholas of Myra).

Immediately above the Royal Door is a picture of the Last Supper. To the right are six icons depicting the major feasts of Christ, and to the left are six icons portraying the major feasts of the Blessed Virgin Mary. Above the picture of the Last Supper is a large icon of Christ the King.

Some icon screens also have pictures of the 12 Apostles and the major Old Testament prophets surmounted by a crucifixion scene.

**Liturgical Language:** In line with Eastern tradition, Byzantine practice has favored the use of the language of the people in the liturgy. Two great advocates of the practice were Sts. Cyril and Methodius, apostles of the Slavs, who devised the Cyrillic alphabet and pioneered the adoption of Slavonic in the liturgy.

**Sacraments:** Baptism is administered by immersion, and confirmation is conferred at the same time. The Eucharist is administered by intinction, i.e., by giving the communicant a piece of consecrated leavened bread which has been dipped into the consecrated wine. When giving absolution in the sacrament of penance, the priest holds his stole over the head of the penitent. Distinctive marriage ceremonies include the crowning of the bride and groom. Ceremonies for anointing the sick closely resemble those of the Roman Rite. Holy orders are conferred by a bishop.

**Sign of the Cross:** Eastern-Rite Catholics have a distinctive way of making it (see entry in the Glossary). The sign of the cross in conjunction with a deep bow, instead of a genuflection, expresses reverence for the presence of Christ in the Blessed Sacrament.

## VESTMENTS, APPURTENANCES

**Sticharion:** A long white garment of linen or silk with wide sleeves and decorated with embroidery; formerly the vestment for clerics in minor orders, acolytes, lectors, chanters, and subdeacons; symbolic of purity.

**Epitrachelion:** A stole with ends sewn together, having a loop through which the head is passed; its several crosses symbolize priestly duties.

**Zone:** A narrow clasped belt made of the same material as the epitrachelion; symbolic of the wisdom of the priest, his strength against enemies of the Church and his willingness to perform holy duties.

**Epimanikia:** Ornamental cuffs; the right cuff symbolizing strength, the left, patience and good will.

**Phelonion:** An ample cape, long in the back and sides and cut away in front; symbolic of the higher gifts of the Holy Spirit.

**Antimension:** A silk or linen cloth laid on the altar for the Liturgy; it may be decorated with a picture of the burial of Christ and the instruments of his passion; the relics of martyrs are sewn into the front border.

**Eileton:** A linen cloth which corresponds to the Roman-Rite corporal.

**Poterion:** A chalice or cup which holds the wine and Precious Blood.

**Diskos:** A shallow plate, which may be elevated on a small stand, corresponding to the Roman-Rite paten.

**Asteriskos:** Made of two curved bands of gold or silver which cross each other to form a double arch; a star depends from the junction, which forms a cross; it is placed over the diskos holding the consecrated bread and is covered with a veil.

**Veils:** Three are used, one to cover the poterion, the second to cover the diskos, and the third to cover both.

**Spoon:** Used in administering Holy Communion by intinction; consecrated leavened bread is dipped into consecrated wine and spooned onto the tongue of the communicant.

# SEPARATED EASTERN CHURCHES

## Orthodox

Orthodox Churches, the largest and most widespread of the separated Eastern Churches, have much in common with their Eastern Catholic counterparts, including many matters of faith and morals, general discipline, valid orders and sacraments, and liturgy. One important difference is their acceptance of only the first seven ecumenical councils. Another is their rejection of any single supreme head of the Church. They do not acknowledge and hold communion with the pope.

Like their Catholic counterparts, Orthodox Churches are organized in jurisdictions under patriarchs. The patriarchs are the heads of approximately 15 autocephalic and several other autonomous jurisdictions organized along lines of nationality and/or language.

The Ecumenical Patriarch of Constantinople, Dimitrios I, has the primacy of honor among his equal patriarchs but his actual jurisdiction is limited to his own patriarchate. As the spiritual head of worldwide Orthodoxy, he keeps the book of the Holy Canons of the Autocephalous Churches, in which recognized Orthodox Churches are registered, and has the right to call Pan-Orthodox assemblies.

The definitive Orthodox break with Rome dates from 1054.

Top-level relations between the Churches have improved in recent years through the efforts of former Ecumenical Patriarch Athenagoras I, John XXIII, Paul VI and Patriarch Dimitrios I. Pope Paul met with Athenagoras three times before the latter's death in 1972. The most significant action of both spiritual leaders was their mutual nullification of excommunications imposed by the two Churches on each other in 1054.

The largest Orthodox body in the western hemisphere is the Greek Orthodox Archdiocese of North and South America consisting of the Archdiocese of New York, nine dioceses in the U.S., and one diocese each in Canada and South America; it is headed by Archbishop Iakovos and has an estimated membership of 1.9 million. The second largest is the Orthodox Church in America, with approximately one million members; it was given independent status by the Patriarchate of Moscow May 18, 1970, against the will of Athenagoras I who refused to register it in the book of the Holy Canons of Autocephalous Churches. An additional 650,000 or more Orthodox belong to smaller national and language jurisdictions.

Heads of Orthodox jurisdictions in this hemisphere hold membership in the Standing Conference of Canonical Orthodox Bishops in the Americas.

## Jurisdictions

The principal jurisdictions of the Greek, Russian and other Orthodox Churches are as follows.

**Greek:** Patriarchate of Constantinople, with jurisdiction in Turkey, Crete, the Dodecanese, Western Europe, the Americas, Australia; Dimitrios I is Ecumenical Patriarch.

Patriarchate of Alexandria, with jurisdiction in Egypt and the rest of Africa; there is also a native African Orthodox Church in Kenya and Uganda.

Patriarchate of Antioch (Melkites or Syrian Orthodox), with jurisdiction in Syria, Lebanon, Iraq, Australasia, the Americas; Syrian or Arabic, in place of Greek, is the liturgical language.

Patriarchate of Jerusalem, with jurisdiction in Israel and Jordan.

Churches of Greece, Cyprus and Sinai are autocephalic but maintain relations with their fellow Orthodox.

**Russian:** Patriarchate of Moscow with jurisdiction centered in the Soviet Union.

**Other:** Patriarchate of Serbia, with jurisdiction in Yugoslavia, Western Europe, the Americas, Australasia.

Patriarchates of Rumania and Bulgaria.

Katholikate of Georgia, the Soviet Union.

Byelorussians and Ukrainian Byzantines.

Churches of Albania, China, Czechoslovakia, Estonia, Finland, Hungary, Japan, Latvia, Lithuania, Poland.

Other minor communities in various places; e.g., Korea, the U.S., Carpatho-Russia.

The Division of Archives and Statistics of the Eastern Orthodox World Foundation reported a 1970 estimate of more than 200 million Orthodox Church members throughout the world. Other sources estimate the total to be approximately 125 million.

## Nestorians, Monophysites

Unlike the majority of Eastern Christian Churches, several bodies do not acknowledge all of the first seven ecumenical councils. Nestorians acknowledge only the first two councils; they do not accept the doctrinal definition of the Council of Ephesus concerning Mary as the Mother of God. Monophysite Armenians, Syrians, Copts, Ethiopians and Jacobites acknowledge only the first three councils; they do not accept the doctrinal definition of the Council of Chalcedon concerning the two natures in Christ.

The Armenian Church has communicants in the Soviet Union, the Middle and Far East, the Americas.

The Coptic Church has communicants in Egypt and elsewhere.

The Ethiopian or Abyssinian Church has communicants in Africa, the Middle East, the Americas, India.

The Jacobite Church (West Syrians) has communicants in the Middle East, the Americas, India.

Nestorians (Assyrians) are scattered throughout the world.

It is estimated that there are approximately 10 million or more members of these other Eastern Churches throughout the world. For various reasons, a more accurate determination is not possible.

### Conference of Orthodox Bishops

The Standing Conference of Canonical Orthodox Bishops in the Americas was established in 1960 to achieve cooperation among the various ethnic churches. Office: 8-10 East 79th St., New York, N.Y. 10021.

Member churches of the conference are the: Albanian Orthodox Diocese of America (Ecumenical Patriarchate), American Carpatho-Russian Orthodox Greek Catholic Diocese in the U.S.A. (Ecumenical Patriarchate), Antiochian Orthodox Christian Archdiocese of North America, Bulgarian Eastern Orthodox Church, Greek Orthodox Archdiocese of North and South America (Ecumenical Patriarchate), Orthodox Church in America, Romanian Orthodox Missionary Archdiocese in America and Canada, Serbian Orthodox Church in the United States of America and Canada, Ukrainian Orthodox Church in America (Ecumenical Patriarchate).

## EASTERN ECUMENISM

The Second Vatican Council, in the *"Decree on Eastern Catholic Churches,"* pointed out the special role they have to play *"in promoting the unity of all Christians, particularly Easterners."* The document also stated in part as follows.

The Eastern Churches in communion with the Apostolic See of Rome have a special role to play in promoting the unity of all Christians, particularly Easterners, according to the principles of this sacred Synod's *Decree on Ecumenism* first of all by prayer, then by the example of their lives, by religious fidelity to ancient Eastern traditions, by greater mutual knowledge, by collaboration, and by a brotherly regard for objects and attitudes (No. 24).

If any separated Eastern Christian should, under the guidance of grace of the Holy Spirit, join himself to Catholic unity, no more should be required of him than what a simple profession of the Catholic faith demands. A valid priesthood is preserved among Eastern clerics. Hence, upon joining themselves to the unity of the Catholic Church, Eastern clerics are permitted to exercise the orders they possess, in accordance with the regulations established by the competent authority (No. 25).

Divine Law forbids any common worship (*communicatio in sacris*) which would damage the unity of the Church, or involve formal acceptance of falsehood or the danger of deviation in the faith, of scandal, or of indifferentism. At the same time, pastoral experience clearly shows that with respect to our Eastern brethren there should and can be taken into consideration various circumstances affecting individuals, wherein the unity of the Church is not jeopardized nor are intolerable risks involved, but in which salvation itself and the spiritual profit of souls are urgently at issue.

Hence, in view of special circumstances of time, place, and personage, the Catholic Church has often adopted and now adopts a milder policy, offering to all the means of salvation and an example of charity among Christians through participation in the sacraments and in other sacred functions and objects. With these considerations in mind, and "lest because of the harshness of our judgment we prove an obstacle to those seeking salvation," and in order to promote closer union with the Eastern Churches separated from us, this sacred Synod lays down the following policy:

In view of the principles recalled above, Eastern Christians who are separated in good faith from the Catholic Church, if they ask of their own accord and have the right dispositions, may be granted the sacraments of penance, the Eucharist, and the anointing of the sick. Furthermore, Catholics may ask for these same sacraments from those non-Catholic ministers whose Churches possess valid sacraments, as often as necessity or a genuine spiritual benefit recommends such a course of action, and when access to a Catholic priest is physically or morally impossible (Nos. 26, 27).

Again, in view of these very same principles, Catholics may for a just cause join with their separated Eastern brethren in sacred functions, things, and places (No. 28).

This more lenient policy with regard to common worship involving Catholics and their brethren of the separated Eastern Churches is entrusted to the care and execution of the local Ordinaries so that, by taking counsel among themselves and, if circumstances warrant, after consultation also with the Ordinaries of the separated Churches, they may govern relations between Christians by timely and effective rules and regulations (No. 29).

### EASTERN ECUMENICAL BRIEFS
#### Statement on the Church

Catholic and Orthodox theologians, meeting for their 10th consultation since 1966, issued an "Agreed Statement on the Church" Dec. 10, 1974. One of the central points in the statement was the difference of views regarding the position and status of the Pope and the Patriarch of Constantinople in the hierarchy of their churches.

The statement said:

"The Catholic Church recognizes that the position of Peter in the college of the Apostles finds visible expression in the Bishop of Rome who exercises these prerogatives defined by Vatican Council I within the whole church of Christ in virtue of this primacy.

"The Orthodox Church finds this teaching at variance with its understanding of primacy within the whole church. It appears to destroy the tension between independence and collegiality (in the universal and particular churches). For independence, a basic condition for collegiality appears to be removed as a consequence of the jurisdictional teaching role attributed to the Patriarch of the West by Vatican Council I. The Orthodox believe that a necessary primacy in the church depends on the consent of the church and is at present exercised by the Patriarch of Constantinople.

"Our two traditions are not easily harmonized. Yet we believe that the Spirit is ever active to show us the way by which we can live together as one and many. We have the hope that we will be open to his promptings wherever they may lead."

The theological consultation was under the joint sponsorship of the U.S. Bishops' Committee for Ecumenical and Interreligious Affairs and the Standing Conference of Canonical Orthodox Bishops in America.

## Orthodox Guidelines

A 66-page document entitled "Guidelines for Orthodox Churches in Ecumenical Relations" was published in February, 1974, by the Standing Conference of Canonical Orthodox Bishops in the Americas. Among the subjects of guidelines were:

• Marriage: Normally marriage in the Orthodox Church "takes place only between members of that Church." There are, however, occasions in which an Orthodox priest may perform a "mixed marriage," under certain conditions. Clergy of other churches may give a blessing or exhort a couple, but do not actually "assist" or "participate" in the marriage service.

• Baptism: Orthodox Churches accept baptism in the name of the Trinity in another church if "proof of the fact of baptism" can be authenticated.

• Eucharist: "Holy Communion will not be sought by Orthodox Christians outside the Church, nor will it be offered to those who do not confess the Orthodox Church as their mother."

• Reciprocity: The "principle of reciprocity" governs preaching in ecumenical situations, meaning that Orthodox priests may preach in non-Orthodox churches and non-Orthodox may speak in Orthodox churches.

## Bishops and Presbyters

A document published in July, 1976, by the Orthodox-Roman Catholic Consultation in the U.S. Signatories indicated the following points of common understanding: (1) Ordination in apostolic succession is required for pastoral office in the Church. (2) Presiding at the Eucharistic celebration is a task belonging to those ordained to pastoral service. (3) The offices of bishop and presbyter are different realizations of the sacrament of order. (4) Those ordained are claimed permanently for the service of the Church. The statement noted that questions requiring serious study were the possible ordination of women, clerical celibacy, and the compatibility of certain occupations with pastoral office.

## Principle of Economy

A statement issued by the same body at the same time, concerning God's plan and activity in human history for salvation. The concept of "economy" was not completely defined. It appeared that Orthodox understanding precludes recognition of the validity of the sacraments of other Christian churches.

## Ministry

Ministry, especially that of bishop, was the principal subject under discussion at a meeting of an international group of Catholic and Orthodox theologians held in December, 1977, in Chambesy, Switzerland. In the context of a joint statement on the relationship between the incarnational and spiritual aspects of church life, they said: "There is no church of Christ without ministries of the Spirit, but there are no ministries without the church; hence, (there are) no ministries apart from or above the community" of the church.

## Marriage

A statement entitled "The Sanctity of Marriage," issued in December, 1978, by the Eastern Orthodox-Roman Catholic Consultation in the U.S., acknowledged agreement about the sacramental nature and permanence of marriage while noting Orthodox positions regarding divorce (permitted in some circumstances) and validity (the marriage of Orthodox communicants must be blessed by an Orthodox priest).

Another statement related to marriage, regarding the religious faith and training of children of Catholic-Orthodox parents, was approved at a meeting of the consultation Oct. 10 and 11, 1980.

## Russian Orthodox Dialogue

Catholic and Orthodox delegates met for the fifth time, Mar. 13 to 17, 1980, in Odessa for discussions related to the theme, "The Local Church and the Universal Church." In a communique issued at the end of the meeting, they said they "found themselves fully in accord on the following points:

• "The local church, in the ambit of the diocese, represents the people of God united around the bishop, legitimately ordained in the uninterrupted apostolic succession. The bishop, with whom the other members of the clergy collaborate and to whom they are subordinate, is the teacher of the faith, the minister of the sacraments — first of all, of the Eucharist — and the one in charge of the Christian life of this flock."

• "The concept of catholicity, understood as organic wholeness of the Church, as the fullness of the possession of the truth revealed by God and of the means of grace given for men's salvation, was deepened. The presence of the episcopate in the local churches guarantees the fullness of their Eucharistic life in grace."

• Despite their state of separation, the Catholic and Orthodox churches recognize one another as sister churches."

## Catholic-Orthodox Commission

The Coordinating Committee of the Joint Commission for Dialogue between the Roman Catholic Church and the Orthodox Church reported signs of progress at a meeting May 25 to 30, 1981, in Venice. Reviewed at the meeting were Catholic and Orthodox views of the relationship between the mysteries of the Church, the Eucharist and the Holy Trinity.

The 60-member commission, meeting for the second time June 30 to July 6, 1982, in Vienna, focused discussion and study on the central significance of the Eucharist for an understanding of unity within the local church and unity among local churches and the universal Church. A press release issued at the end of the meeting said "large areas of agreement were outlined and foundations were laid for further consideration of questions about which there remain differences." Topics assigned for the next plenary session were baptism, confirmation and the Eucharist, as sacraments related to the unity of the Church.

The commission, the highest ranking and largest of its kind, was established after the meeting of Pope John Paul and Ecumenical Orthodox Patriarch Dimitrios I Nov. 29 and 30, 1979, in Istanbul.

The Orthodox-Roman Catholic dialogue group in the United States released an agreed statement on the Eucharist June 9, 1983.

The coordinating committee of the Joint International Commission for Dialogue between the Roman Catholic Church and the Orthodox Church, at a meeting June 12 to 17, 1983, in Nicosia, Cyprus, began work on a synthesis of three documents — on faith, sacraments and the unity of the church — to be presented to a plenary assembly of the commission in 1984.

The third meeting of the commission, in the spring of 1984 on Crete, did little to advance the cause of unity.

## Key Event

Probably the most significant event of 1984 in relations between the Catholic Church and a separated Eastern Church was the agreement on the doctrine of the Incarnation signed and issued by the Pope and the Syrian Orthodox Patriarch. See the following article for the text.

# JOINT STATEMENT OF THE POPE AND THE SYRIAN ORTHODOX PATRIARCH

*This statement was signed by Pope John Paul II and Syrian Orthodox Patriarch Moran Mar Ignatius Zakka I Iwas of Antioch during an audience at the Vatican June 23, 1984.*

*The text, released by the Vatican, was circulated by NC News Service. Subheads have been added.*

1. His Holiness John Paul II, Bishop of Rome and Pope of the Catholic Church, and His Holiness Moran Mar Ignatius Zakka I Iwas, Patriarch of Antioch and all the East and Supreme Head of the Universal Syrian Orthodox Church, kneel down with full humility in front of the exalted and extolled heavenly throne of our Lord Jesus Christ, giving thanks for this glorious opportunity which has been granted them to meet together in his love in order to strengthen further the relationship between their two sister churches, the Church of Rome and the Syrian Orthodox Church of Antioch — the relationship already excellent through the joint initiative of Their Holinesses of blessed memory, Pope Paul VI and Patriarch Moran Mar Ignatius Jacoub III.

2. Their Holinesses Pope John Paul II and Patriarch Zakka I wish solemnly to widen the horizon of their brotherhood and affirm herewith the terms of the deep spiritual communion which already unites them and the prelates, clergy and faithful of both their churches, to consolidate these ties of faith, hope and love, and to advance in finding a wholly common ecclesial life.

## Agreement on Incarnation

3. First of all, Their Holinesses confess the faith of their two churches, formulated by the Nicene Council of 325 A.D. and generally known as the Nicene Creed. The confusions and schisms that occurred between their churches in the later centuries, they realize today, in no way affect or touch the substance of their faith, since these arose only because of differences in terminology and culture, and in the various formulae adopted by different theological schools to express the same matter. Accordingly, we find today no real basis for the sad divisions and schisms that subsequently arose between us concerning the doctrine of Incarnation. In words and life, we confess the true doctrine concerning Christ our Lord, notwithstanding the differences in interpretation of such a doctrine which arose at the time of the Council of Chalcedon (451).

4. Hence, we wish to reaffirm solemnly our profession of common faith in the Incarnation of our Lord Jesus Christ, as Pope Paul VI and Patriarch Moran Mar Ignatius Jacoub III did in 1971. They denied that there was any difference in the faith they confessed in the mystery of the Word of God made flesh and become truly man. In our turn, we confess that he became incarnate for us, taking to himself a real body with a rational soul. He shared our humanity in all things except sin. We confess that our Lord and our God, our Savior and the King of all, Jesus Christ, is perfect God as to his divinity and perfect man as to his humanity. In him, his divinity is united to his humanity. This union is real, perfect, without blending or mingling, without confusion, without alteration, without division, without the least separation. He who is God eternal and indivisible, became visible in the flesh and took the form of servant. In him are united, in a real, perfect, indivisible and inseparable way, divinity and humanity, and in him all their properties are present and active.

## Sacramental Doctrine

5. Having the same conception of Christ, we confess also the same conception of his mystery. Incarnate, dead and risen again, our Lord, God and Savior has conquered sin and death. Through him during the time between Pentecost and the Second Coming, the period which is also the last phase of time, it is given to man to experience the new creation, the Kingdom of God, the transforming ferment (cf. Mt. 13:33) already present in our midst. For this, God has chosen a new people, his holy Church which is the body of Christ. Through the word and through the sacraments, the Holy Spirit acts in the Church to call everybody and make them members of this body of Christ. Those who believe are baptized in the Holy Spirit in the name of the Holy Trinity to form one body, and through the holy sacrament of the anointing of confirmation their faith is perfected and strengthened by the same Spirit.

6. Sacramental life finds in the holy Eucharist its fulfillment and its summit, in such a way that it is

through the Eucharist that the Church most profoundly realizes and reveals its nature. Through the holy Eucharist, the event of Christ's Pasch expands throughout the Church. Through holy baptism and confirmation, indeed, the members of Christ are anointed by the Holy Spirit, grafted on to Christ; and, through the holy Eucharist, the Church becomes what she is destined to be through baptism and confirmation. By communion with the Body and Blood of Christ, the faithful grow in that mysterious divinization by which the Holy Spirit makes them dwell in the Son as children of the Father.

7. The other sacraments, which the Catholic Church and the Syrian Orthodox Church of Antioch hold together in one and the same succession of apostolic ministry — i.e., holy orders, matrimony, reconciliation of penitents and anointing of the sick — are ordered to that celebration of the holy Eucharist which is the center of sacramental life and the chief visible expression of ecclesial communion. The communion of Christians with each other and of all churches united around their lawful bishops is realized in the gathered community which confesses the same faith, reaches forward in hope of the world to come and in expectation of the savior's return, and is anointed by the Holy Spirit who dwells in it with charity that never fails.

## Pastoral Collaboration

8. Since it is the chief expression of Christian unity between the faithful and between bishops and priests, the holy Eucharist cannot yet be concelebrated by us. Such celebration supposes a complete identity of faith such as does not yet exist between us. Certain questions, in fact, still need to be resolved touching the Lord's will for his Church, as also the doctrinal implications and canonical details of the traditions proper to our communities which have been too long separated.

9. Our identity in faith, though not yet complete, entitles us to envisage collaboration between our churches in pastoral care, in situations which nowadays are frequent both because of the dispersion of our faithful throughout the world and because of the precarious conditions of these difficult times. It is not rare, in fact, for our faithful to find access to a priest of their own church materially or morally impossible. Anxious to meet their needs and with their spiritual benefit in mind, we authorize them in such cases to ask for the sacraments of penance, Eucharist and anointing of the sick from lawful priests of either of our two sister churches, when they need them. It would be a logical corollary of collaboration in pastoral care to cooperate in priestly formation and theological education. Bishops are encouraged to promote sharing of facilities for theological education where they judge it to be advisable. While doing this, we do not forget that we must still do all in our power to achieve full visible communion between the Catholic Church and the Syrian Orthodox Church of Antioch and ceaselessly implore our Lord to grant us that unity which alone will enable us to give to the world a fully unanimous Gospel witness.

10. Thanking the Lord who has allowed us to meet and enjoy the consolation of the faith we hold in common (cf. Rom. 1:12) and to proclaim before the world the mystery of the Person of the Word Incarnate and of his saving work, the unshakeable foundation of that common faith, we pledge ourselves solemnly to do all that in us lies to remove the last obstacles still hindering full communion between the Catholic Church and the Syrian Orthodox Church of Antioch, so that with one heart and voice we may preach the word: "The true light that enlightens every man," and "that all who believe in his name may become the children of God" (cf. Jn. 1:9-12).

## RELATIONS WITH NON-CHRISTIANS

Archbishop Jean Jadot, interviewed Mar. 16, 1984, described three goals of the Vatican Secretariat for Non-Christians, of which he was pro-president.

"The first is to see that Catholics living among non-Christians have better objective knowledge of non-Christian religions so that people are not working from prejudices or impressions."

"The second is to share in social action and cultural activities as far as possible. One specific goal is to improve public education and culturalization by teaching people how to read and write."

The third goal "is to work together against moral and cultural problems."

"Religious groups have to work together, to help people to be concerned about spiritual values and to see people as human beings."

About three weeks before the interview, Archbishop Jadot reported that the secretariat was working on the final draft of a document on dialogue and mission to be sent to bishops' conferences throughout the world.

**Taoism** originated in China several centuries before the Christian era and became a fully developed religious system by the fifth century A.D. As a religion of mystery, it developed extreme polytheism, with the Jade Emperor as the highest deity; sought blessings and long life by means of alchemy; fostered superstition and witchcraft; took on organizational and other aspects of Buddhism, with several categories of priests and nuns; exerted strong ethical influence on the lower classes; split into many sects; adopted features from other religions; became the starting point of many secret societies.

**Shinto** is the way of the gods, the sum total of the cultic beliefs and practices of the ancestral religion of Japan which originated from nature and ancestor worship. Shinto is pantheistic and has many objects of devotion, the highest being the Ruler of Heaven; is practiced with detailed rituals in public shrines, which are cultic centers; has strong social influence. Sectarian Shinto has about 13 recognized sects and many offshoots. Shinto, with principal concern for this-worldly blessing, has been affected by Buddhism and Confucianism.

## MEN, DOCTRINES, CHURCHES OF THE REFORMATION

*Some of the leading figures, doctrines and churches of the Reformation are covered below. A companion article covers Major Protestant Churches in the United States.*

**John Wycliff** (c. 1320-1384): English priest and scholar who advanced one of the leading Reformation ideas nearly 200 years before Martin Luther — that the Bible alone is the sufficient rule of faith — but had only an indirect influence on the 16th century Reformers. Supporting belief in an inward and practical religion, he denied the divinely commissioned authority of the pope and bishops of the Church; he also denied the Real Presence of Christ in the Holy Eucharist, and wrote against the sacrament of penance and the doctrine of indulgences. Nearly 20 of his propositions were condemned by Gregory XI in 1377; his writings were proscribed more extensively by the Council of Constance in 1415. His influence was strongest in Bohemia and Central Europe.

**John Hus** (c. 1369-1415): A Bohemian priest and preacher of reform who authored 30 propositions condemned by the Council of Constance. Excommunicated in 1411 or 1412, he was burned at the stake in 1415. His principal errors concerned the nature of the Church and the origin of papal authority. He spread some of the ideas of Wycliff but did not subscribe to his views regarding faith alone as the condition for justification and salvation, the sole sufficiency of Scripture as the rule of faith, the Real Presence of Christ in the Eucharist, and the sacramental system. In 1457 some of his followers founded the Church of the Brotherhood which later became known as the United Brethren or Moravian Church and is considered the earliest independent Protestant body.

**Martin Luther** (1483-1546): An Augustinian friar, the key figure in the Reformation. In 1517, as a special indulgence was being preached in Germany, and in view of needed reforms within the Church, he published at Wittenberg 95 theses concerning matters of Catholic belief and practice. Leo X condemned 41 statements from Luther's writings in 1520. Luther, refusing to recant, was excommunicated the following year. His teachings strongly influenced subsequent Lutheran theology; its statements of faith are found in the Book of Concord (1580).

Luther's doctrine included the following: The sin of Adam, which corrupted human nature radically (but not substantially), has affected every aspect of man's being. Justification, understood as the forgiveness of sins and the state of righteousness, is by grace for Christ's sake through faith. Faith involves not merely intellectual assent but an act of confidence by the will. Good works are indispensably necessary concomitants of faith, but do not merit salvation. Of the sacraments, Luther retained baptism, penance and the Holy Communion as effective vehicles of the grace of the Holy Spirit; he held that in the Holy Communion the consecrated bread and wine are the Body and Blood of Christ. The rule of faith is the divine revelation in the Sacred Scriptures. He rejected purgatory, indulgences and the invocation of the saints, and held that prayers for the dead have no efficacy.

Lutheran tenets not in agreement with Catholic doctrine were condemned by the Council of Trent.

**Anabaptism:** Originated in Saxony in the first quarter of the 16th century and spread rapidly through southern Germany. Its doctrine included several key Lutheran tenets but was not regarded with favor by Luther, Calvin or Zwingli. Anabaptists believed that baptism is for adults only and that infant baptism is invalid. Their doctrine of the Inner Light, concerning the direct influence of the Holy Spirit on the believer, implied rejection of Catholic doctrine concerning the sacraments and the nature of the Church. Eighteen articles of faith were formulated in 1632 in Holland. Mennonites are Anabaptists.

**Ulrich Zwingli** (1484-1531): A priest who triggered the Reformation in Switzerland with a series of New Testament lectures in 1519, later disputations and by other actions. He held the Gospel to be the only basis of truth; rejected the Mass (which he suppressed in 1525 at Zurich), penance and other sacraments; denied papal primacy and doctrine concerning purgatory and the invocation of saints; rejected celibacy, monasticism and many traditional practices of piety. His symbolic view of the Eucharist, which was at odds with Catholic doctrine, caused an irreconcilable controversy with Luther and his followers. Zwingli was killed in a battle between the forces of Protestant and Catholic cantons in Switzerland.

**John Calvin** (1509-1564): French leader of the Reformation in Switzerland, whose key tenet was absolute predestination of some persons to heaven and others to hell. He rejected Catholic doctrine in 1533 after becoming convinced of a personal mission to reform the Church. In 1536 he published the first edition of *Institutes of the Christian Religion,* a systematic exposition of his doctrine which became the classic textbook of Reformed — as distinguished from Lutheran — theology. To Luther's principal theses — regarding Scripture as the sole rule of faith, the radical corruption of human nature, and justification by faith alone — he added absolute predestination, certitude of salvation for the elect, and the incapability of the elect to lose grace. His Eucharistic theory, which failed to mediate the Zwingli-Luther controversy, was at odds with Catholic doctrine. From 1555 until his death Calvin was the virtual dictator of Geneva, the capital of the non-Lutheran Reformation in Europe.

**Arminianism:** A modification of the rigid predestinationism of Calvin, set forth by Jacob Arminius (1560-1609) and formally stated in the *Remonstrance* of 1610. Arminianism influenced some Calvinist bodies.

**Unitarianism:** A 16th century doctrine which rejected the Trinity and the divinity of Christ in favor of a uni-personal God. It claimed scriptural support for a long time but became generally rationalistic with respect to "revealed" doctrine as well as in ethics and its world-view. One of its principal early proponents was Faustus Socinus (1539-1604), a leader of the Polish Brethren.

A variety of communions developed in England in the Reformation and post-Reformation periods.

**Anglican Communion:** This communion, which regards itself as the same apostolic Church as that which was established by early Christians in England, derived not from Reformation influences but from the renunciation of papal jurisdiction by Henry VIII (1491-1547). His Act of Supremacy in 1534 called Christ's Church an assembly of local churches subject to the prince, who was vested with fullness of authority and jurisdiction. In spite of Henry's denial of papal authority, this Act did not reject substantially other principal articles of faith. Notable changes, proposed and adopted for the reformation of the church, took place in the subsequent reigns of James VI and Elizabeth, with respect to such matters as Scripture as the rule of faith, the sacraments, the nature of the Mass, and the constitution of the hierarchy.

The Anglican Communion is called Episcopal because its prelates have the title and function of bishops. (See Anglican Orders.)

**Puritans:** Extremists who sought church reform along Calvinist lines in severe simplicity. (Use of the term was generally discontinued after 1660.)

**Presbyterians:** Basically Calvinistic, called Presbyterian because church polity centers around assemblies of presbyters or elders. John Knox (c. 1513-1572) established the church in Scotland.

**Congregationalists:** Evangelical in spirit and seeking a return to forms of the primitive church, they uphold individual freedom in religious matters, do not require the acceptance of a creed as a condition for communion, and regard each congregation as autonomous. Robert Browne influenced the beginnings of Congregationalism.

**Quakers:** Their key belief is in internal divine illumination, the inner light of the living Christ, as the only source of truth and inspiration. George Fox (1624-1691) was one of their leaders in England. Called the Society of Friends, the Quakers are noted for their pacifism.

**Baptists:** So called because of their doctrine concerning baptism. They reject infant baptism and consider only baptism by immersion as valid. Leaders in the formation of the church were John Smyth (d. 1612) in England and Roger Williams (d. 1683) in America.

**Methodists:** A group who broke away from the Anglican Communion under the leadership of John Wesley (1703-1791), although some Anglican beliefs were retained. Doctrines include the witness of the Spirit to the individual and personal assurance of salvation. Wesleyan Methodists do not subscribe to some of the more rigid Calvinistic tenets held by other Methodists.

**Universalism:** A product of 18th-century liberal Protestantism in England. The doctrine is not Trinitarian and includes a tenet that all men will ultimately be saved.

## MAJOR PROTESTANT CHURCHES IN THE UNITED STATES

There are more than 250 Protestant church bodies in the United States.

The majority of U.S. Protestants belong to the following denominations: Baptist, Methodist, Lutheran, Presbyterian, Protestant Episcopal, the United Church of Christ, the Christian Church (Disciples of Christ), Holiness Sects.

See Ecumenical Dialogues, Briefs and related entries for coverage of relations between the Catholic Church and other Christian churches.

### Baptist Churches

*(Courtesy of the Division of Communication, American Baptist Churches in the U.S.A.)*

Baptist churches, comprising the largest of all American Protestant denominations, were first established by John Smyth near the beginning of the 17th century in England. The first Baptist church in America was founded at Providence by Roger Williams in 1639.

Largest of the nearly 30 Baptist bodies in the U.S. are:

The Southern Baptist Convention, 460 James Robertson Parkway, Nashville, Tenn. 37219, with 13.6 million members;

The National Baptist Convention, U.S.A., Inc., 915 Spain St., Baton Rouge, La. 70802, with 6.5 million members;

The National Baptist Convention of America, 954 Kings Rd., Jacksonville, Fla. 32204, with 2.6 million members.

The American Baptist Churches in the U.S.A., P.O. Box 851, Valley Forge, Pa. 19482, with 1.5 million members.

The total number of U.S. Baptists is more than 29 million. The world total is 33 million.

Proper to Baptists is their doctrine on baptism. Called an "ordinance" rather than a sacrament, baptism by immersion is a sign that one has experienced and decided in favor of the salvation offered by Christ. It is administered only to persons who are able to make a responsible decision. It is the sole criterion of salvation and involves the obligation to a life of virtue. Baptism is not administered to infants.

Baptists do not have a formal creed but generally subscribe to two professions of faith formulated in 1689 and 1832 and are in general agreement with classical Protestant theology regarding Scripture as the sole rule of faith, original sin, justification through faith in Christ, and the nature of the Church. Their local churches are autonomous.

Worship services differ in form from one congregation to another. Usual elements are the reading of Scripture, a sermon, hymns, vocal and silent prayer. The Lord's Supper, called an "ordinance," is celebrated at various intervals.

## Methodist Churches

*(Courtesy of Joe Hale, General Secretary of the World Methodist Council.)*

John Wesley (1703-1791), an Anglican clergyman, was the founder of Methodism. In 1738, following a period of missionary work in America and strongly influenced by the Moravians, he experienced a new conversion to Christ and shortly thereafter became a leader in a religious awakening in England. By the end of the 18th century, Methodism was strongly rooted also in America.

The United Methodist Church, formed in 1968 by a merger of the Methodist Church and the Evangelical United Brethren Church, is the second largest Protestant denomination in the U.S., with nine million members; its principal agencies are located in New York, Evanston, Ill., Nashville, Tenn., Washington, D.C., Dayton, O., and Lake Junaluska, N.C. (World Methodist Council, P.O. Box 518. 28745). The second largest body, with more than two million communicants, is the African Methodist Episcopal Church. Four other major churches in the U.S. are the African Methodist Episcopal Zion, Christian Methodist Episcopal, Free Methodist Church and the Wesleyan Church. The total Methodist membership in the U.S. is about 14 million.

Worldwide, there are more than 64 autonomous Methodist/Wesleyan churches in 90 countries, with a membership of more than 23 million. All of them participate in the World Methodist Council, which gives global unity to the witness of Methodist communicants.

Methodism, although it has a base in Calvinistic theology, rejects absolute predestination and maintains that Christ offers grace freely to all men, not just to a select elite. Wesley's distinctive doctrine was the "witness of the Spirit" to the individual soul and personal assurance of salvation. He also emphasized the central themes of conversion and holiness. Methodists are in general agreement with classical Protestant theology regarding Scripture as the sole rule of faith, original sin, justification through faith in Christ, the nature of the Church, and the sacraments of baptism and the Lord's Supper. Church polity is structured along episcopal lines in America, with ministers being appointed to local churches by a bishop; churches stemming from British Methodism do not have bishops but vest appointive powers within an appropriate conference. Congregations are free to choose various forms of worship services; typical elements are readings from Scripture, sermons, hymns and prayers.

## Lutheran Churches

*(Courtesy of Thomas Hartley Dorris, editor of Ecumenical Press Service, Box 66, CH-1211 Geneva 20, Switzerland.)*

The origin of Lutheranism is generally traced to Oct. 31, 1517, when Martin Luther tacked "95 Theses" to the door of the castle church in Wittenberg, Germany. This call to debate on the subject of indulgences and related concerns has come to symbolize the beginning of the Reformation. Luther and his supporters intended to reform the Church they knew. Though Lutheranism has come to be visible in separate denominations and national churches, at its heart it professes itself to be a confessional movement within the one, holy, catholic and apostolic Church.

The world's 70 million Lutherans form the third largest grouping of Christians, following Roman Catholics and Eastern Orthodox. About 54 million belong to churches which make up the Lutheran World Federation, headquartered in Geneva; its president is Bishop Zoltan Kaldy of Hungary. Nine countries count more than one million Lutherans each: West Germany (20.7 million), United States (7.9 million), Sweden (7.7 million), East Germany (6.3 million), Denmark (4.7 million), Finland (4.6 million), Norway (3.8 million), Indonesia (2.2 million), India, Brazil and Tanzania (1 million each).

Numbering about 9 million, Lutherans are the fourth largest grouping of North American Christians, exceeded by Roman Catholics, Baptists and Methodists. About 95 per cent of them belong to one of three denominations: Lutheran Church in America, three million members, 231 Madison Avenue, New York, N.Y. 10016; Lutheran Church-Missouri Synod, 2.7 million, 1333 S. Kirkwood Rd., St. Louis, Mo. 63122; American Lutheran Church, 2.3 million, 422 S. Fifth St., Minneapolis, Minn. 55415.

In addition, there are about a dozen other smaller Lutheran denominations in North America. The three largest are: Wisconsin Evangelical Lutheran Synod, 400,000 members, 3512 W. North Ave., Milwaukee, Wis. 53208; the Association of Evangelical Lutheran Churches, 110,000, 12015 Manchester Rd., St. Louis, Mo. 63131; Evangelical Lutheran Church of Canada, 84,000, 247 First Ave. North, Saskatoon, Saskatchewan S7K 4H5. (This is the only independent Canadian denomination; most other Canadian Lutherans belong to the Lutheran Church in America or the Missouri Synod.)

A union of the American Lutheran Church, the Lutheran Church in America and the Association of Evangelical Lutheran Churches is projected for 1988. Their Canadian counterparts are moving toward a merger in 1986. The new denominations would account for about two-thirds of the Lutherans in each country.

The three large bodies, together with the Association of Evangelical Lutheran Churches and the Latvian Evangelical Church in America form the Lutheran Council in the U.S.A., a cooperative agency for work in several fields. The council's main offices are at 360 Park Ave. South, New York, N.Y. 10010. A similar organization, the Lutheran Council in Canada, is headquartered at 500-365 Hargrave St., Winnipeg, Manitoba R3B 2K3.

The Lutheran Church in America, the American Lutheran Church and the Association of Evangelical Lutheran Churches also form Lutheran World Ministries, (the U.S. agency of the Lutheran World Federation), headquartered at 360 Park Ave. South, New York, N.Y. 10010. Its Canadian counterpart is the Canadian National Committee of the Lutheran World Federation, headquartered at

# 288

500-365 Hargrave St., Winnipeg, Manitoba R3B 2K3.

The statements of faith which have shaped the confessional life of Lutheranism are found in the *Book of Concord.* This 1580 collection includes the three ancient ecumenical creeds (Apostles', Nicene and Athanasian), Luther's *Large and Small Catechisms* (1529), the *Augsburg Confession* (1530) and the *Apology* in defense of it (1531), the *Smalcald Articles* (including the "Treatise on the Power and Primacy of the Pope") (1537), and the *Formula of Concord* (1577).

The central Lutheran doctrinal proposition is that Christians "receive forgiveness of sins and become righteous before God by grace, for Christ's sake."

Baptism and the Lord's Supper (Holy Communion, the eucharist) are universally celebrated among Lutherans as sacramental means of grace in which the Word and promise of God are made visible by being bound to earthly elements — water, bread and wine. In baptism, a person is reborn and by God's gracious action is made a member of the Church catholic. Likewise, the eucharist celebrates and re-presents God's gracious action. With the body and blood of Christ — "in, with, and under" the bread and wine — come the gifts of life, salvation, forgiveness.

Lutherans also treasure the Word proclaimed in the reading of the Scriptures, preaching from the pulpit, and pronouncement of absolution. The Word read and preached is always part of the eucharist. Absolution is usually imparted generally, but it may also be given individually in connection with private confession.

Although it was not the wish of the early Lutherans to deny the bishop's place as the ordinary minister of ordination, the general unwillingness of 16th century bishops to ordain Lutheran pastors led to the usual Lutheran system of presbyteral rather than episcopal ordination. Lutherans are concerned to preserve apostolic succession in life and doctrine, and generally concede the value, though not the necessity, of ordination by bishops.

Confirmation among Lutherans has been generally connected with first communion, though recent years have seen a tendency to separate the two. In the U.S., the tendency is to have first communion around grade-five age, though infant communion is not unknown. Confirmation, sometimes called affirmation of the baptismal covenant, generally occurs during the junior high school years, slightly younger than in European practice.

Lutheran jurisdictions corresponding to dioceses are called districts or synods in North America. There are more than 100 of them on the continent. Because they relate to different national denominations, more than one of these jurisdictions includes the same geographic area. The head of a district or synod, chosen by lay and clergy delegates to a convention, is known as a bishop or a president, depending on the denomination and jurisdiction. The terms "diocese" and "bishop" are common among European Lutherans and Asian, African and Latin American Lutherans whose

roots derive from European missionary efforts.

A visitor to a North American Lutheran parish would generally find adornments, vestments, church calendars and an order of service similar to that of Episcopal or Roman Catholic congregations. Weekly celebration of the eucharist is increasingly common and is generally stressed as the desired practice by Lutheran liturgical and sacramental theologians. Lutherans generally like to sing in worship, and successive generations have built up a rich tradition of church music and hymnody. A new North American *Lutheran Book of Worship* was introduced in 1978. The Missouri Synod issued its own revision of the book, *Lutheran Worship,* in 1982.

## Presbyterian Churches

*(Courtesy of Gerald W. Gillette, United Presbyterian Church in the U.S.A.; and Office of the General Assembly, Presbyterian Church in the United States.)*

Presbyterians are so called because of their tradition of governing the church through a system of representative bodies composed of elders (presbyters).

Presbyterianism is a part of the Reformed Family of Churches that grew out of the theological work of John Calvin following the Lutheran Reformation, to which it is heavily indebted. Countries in which it acquired early strength and influence were Switzerland, France, Holland, Scotland and England.

Presbyterianism spread widely in this country in the latter part of the 18th century and afterwards. Presently, it has approximately 4.5 million communicants in nine bodies.

The two largest Presbyterian bodies in the country — the United Presbyterian Church in the U.S.A. and the Presbyterian Church in the United States — were reunited in June, 1983, to form the Presbyterian Church (U.S.A.), with a membership of 3.3 million.

The United Presbyterian Church in the U.S.A., with a membership of 2.5 million, was headquartered at 475 Riverside Drive, New York, N.Y. 10027. It was formed May 28, 1958, by a merger of the Presbyterian Church in the U.S.A. and the United Presbyterian Church of North America.

The Presbyterian Church in the United States, with 815,000 members, had headquarters at 341 Ponce de Leon Avenue N.E., Atlanta, Ga. 30308.

These churches, now merged, are closely allied with the Reformed Church in America, the United Church of Christ, the Cumberland Presbyterian Churches and the Associate Reformed Presbyterian Church.

In Presbyterian doctrine, baptism and the Lord's Supper, viewed as seals of the covenant of grace, are regarded as sacraments. Baptism, which is not necessary for salvation, is conferred on infants and adults The Lord's Supper is celebrated as a covenant of the Sacrifice of Christ. In both sacraments, a doctrine of the real presence of Christ is considered the central theological principle.

The Church is twofold, being invisible and also

visible; it consists of all of the elect and all those Christians who are united in Christ as their immediate head.

Presbyterians are in general agreement with classical Protestant theology regarding Scripture as the sole rule of faith and practice, salvation by grace, and justification through faith in Christ.

Presbyterian congregations are governed by a session composed of elders (presbyters) elected by the communicant membership. On higher levels there are presbyteries, synods and a general assembly with various degrees of authority over local bodies; all such representative bodies are composed of elected elders and ministers in approximately equal numbers.

Worship services, simple and dignified, include sermons, prayer, reading of the Scriptures and hymns. The Lord's Supper is celebrated at intervals.

Doctrinal developments of the past several years included approval in May, 1967, by the General Assembly of the United Presbyterian Church of a contemporary confession of faith to supplement the historic Westminster Confession. The new confession emphasizes the commitment of the Church and its members to reconciliatory and apostolic works in society. A statement entitled "The Declaration of Faith" was approved in 1977 by the Presbyterian Church in the U.S. for teaching and liturgical use.

## Episcopal Church

The Episcopal Church in the U.S.A. regards itself as the same apostolic church as that which was established by early Christians in England. It was established in this country during the Revolutionary period. Its constitution and Prayer Book were adopted at a general convention held in 1789. It has approximately 3 million members.

Offices of the presiding bishop and executive council are located at 815 Second Ave., New York, N.Y. 10017.

This church, which belongs to the Anglican Communion, subscribes to the branch theory of the Church of Christ, holding that it consists of the Church of Rome, the Eastern Orthodox Church, and the Anglican Communion. It accepts the pope as the "first among equals."

Worldwide, the Anglican Communion has 65 million members in 41 provinces. The chief prelate is the Archbishop of Canterbury.

There is considerable variety in Episcopalian beliefs and practices. Official statements of belief and practice are found in the Apostles' Creed, the Nicene Creed and the Book of Common Prayer, but interpretation is not uniform. Scripture has primary importance with respect to the rule of faith, and some authority is attached to tradition.

All seven sacraments, veneration of the saints, and a great many other Catholic teachings are accepted by Episcopalians but are not used by all.

An episcopal system of church government prevails, but clergy of lower rank and lay persons also have an active voice in ecclesiastical affairs. The levels of government are the general convention, the executive council, territorial provinces and dioceses, and local parishes. At the parish level, the congregation has the right to select its own rector or pastor, with the consent of the bishop.

Liturgical worship is according to the Book of Common Prayer as adopted in 1979, but ceremonial practices correspond with the emphases of the various congregations and range from a ceremony similar to the Roman Mass to services of a less elaborate character.

## United Church of Christ

*(Courtesy of the Rev. Carol Joyce Brun, secretary of the United Church of Christ.)*

The 1,726,535-member United Church of Christ was formed in 1957 by a union of the Congregational Christian and the Evangelical and Reformed Churches. The former was originally established by the Pilgrims and the Puritans of the Massachusetts Bay Colony, while the latter was founded in Pennsylvania in the early 1700's by settlers from Central Europe. The denomination has 6,443 congregations throughout the United States.

It considers itself "a united and uniting church" and keeps itself open to all ecumenical options. Its headquarters are located at 105 Madison Ave., New York, N.Y. 10016.

Its statement of faith recognizes Jesus Christ as "our crucified and risen Lord (who) shared our common lot, conquering sin and death and reconciling the world to himself." It believes in the life after death, and the fact that God "judges men and nations by his righteous will declared through prophets and apostles."

The United Church further believes that Christ calls its members to share in his baptism "and eat at his table, to join him in his passion and victory." Ideally, according to its Lord's Day Service, Communion is to be celebrated weekly. Like other Calvinistic bodies, it believes that Christ is spiritually present in the sacrament.

The United Church is governed along congregational lines, and each local church is autonomous. However, the actions of its biennial General Synod are taken with great seriousness by congregations. Between synods, a 43-member executive council oversees the work of the church.

## Christian Church (Disciples of Christ)

*(Courtesy of Robert L. Friedly, Vice President for Communication.)*

The Christian Church (Disciples of Christ) originated early in the 1800's from two movements against rigid denominationalism led by Presbyterians Thomas and Alexander Campbell in western Pennsylvania and Barton W. Stone in Kentucky. The two movements developed separately for about 25 years before being merged in 1832.

The church, which identifies itself with the Protestant mainstream, now has approximately 1.2 million members in the U.S. and Canada. The greatest concentration of members in the U.S. is located roughly along the old frontier line, in an arc sweeping from Ohio and Kentucky through the Midwest and down into Oklahoma and Texas.

The general offices of the church are located at 222 South Downey Ave., Box 1986, Indianapolis, Ind. 46206.

The church's persistent concern for Christian unity is based on a conviction expressed in a basic document, *Declaration and Address,* dating from its founding. The document states: "The church of Christ upon earth is essentially, intentionally and constitutionally one."

The Disciples have no official doctrine or dogma. Their worship practices vary widely from more common informal services to what could almost be described as "high church" services. Membership is granted after a simple statement of belief in Jesus Christ and baptism by immersion; most congregations admit un-immersed transfers from other denominations. The Lord's Supper, generally called Communion, is always open to Christians of all persuasions. Lay men and women routinely preside over the Lord's Supper, which is celebrated each Sunday; they often preach and perform other pastoral functions as well. Distinction between ordained and non-ordained members is blurred somewhat because of the Disciples' emphasis on all members of the church as ministers.

The Christian Church is oriented to congregational government, and has a unique structure in which three levels of polity (general, regional and congregational) operate as equals rather than in a pyramid of authority. At the national or international level, it is governed by a general assembly which has voting representation direct from congregations and regions as well as all ordained clergy.

### Evangelicalism

Evangelicalism, dating from 1735 in England (the Evangelical Revival) and after 1740 in the United States (the Great Awakening), has had and continues to have widespread influence in Protestant churches. It has been estimated that at least 50 per cent of American Protestants — communicants of both large denominations and small bodies — are evangelicals.

The Bible is their rule of faith and religious practice. Being born again in a life-changing experience through faith in Christ is the promise of salvation. Missionary work for the spread of the Gospel is a normal and necessary activity. Additional matters of belief and practice are generally of a conservative character.

Fundamentalists comprise an extreme right-wing subculture of evangelicalism.They are distinguished mainly by militant biblicism, belief in the absolute inerrancy of the Bible and emphasis on the Second Coming of Christ. Fundamentalism developed in the first third of the 20th century in reaction against liberal theology and secularizing trends in mainstream and other Protestant denominations.

The Holiness or Perfectionist wing of evangelicalism evolved from Methodist efforts to preserve, against a contrary trend, the personal-piety and inner-religion concepts of John Wesley. There are at least 30 Holiness bodies in the U.S.

Pentecostals, probably the most demonstrative of evangelicals, are noted for speaking in tongues and the stress they place on healing, prophecy and personal testimony to the practice and power of evangelical faith.

## CHARISMATIC RENEWAL

*(Written with the assistance of the staff of the Service Committee of the Catholic Charismatic Renewal of the U.S.)*

The movement originated with a handful of Duquesne University students and faculty members in the 1966-67 academic year and spread from there to Notre Dame, Michigan State University, the University of Michigan and to other campuses.

According to a Gallup poll reported in the Feb. 22, 1980, issue of *Christianity Today,* 18 per cent of adult Catholics in the U.S. — nearly 6 million — considered themselves charismatic. More than 4,660 U.S. groups are listed in the latest issue of the *International Directory of Catholic Charismatic Prayer Groups.* Findings of a survey conducted by Father Kenneth Metz of the Archdiocese of Milwaukee and reported in August, 1981, estimated that there were 6,364 Catholic charismatic prayer groups in the U.S.

The movement is strong in Canada and some 110 other countries, probably involving more than a million participants.

### Keys to the Movement

Scriptural keys to the renewal are:
• Christ's promise to send the Holy Spirit upon the Apostles;
• the description, in the Acts of the Apostles, of the effects of the coming of the Holy Spirit upon

the Apostles on Pentecost;
• St. Paul's explanation, in the Letter to the Romans, of the charismatic gifts (for the good of the Church and persons) the Holy Spirit would bestow on Christians;
• New Testament evidence concerning the effects of charismatic gifts in and through the early Church.

The personal key to the renewal is baptism of the Holy Spirit. This is not a new sacrament but the personally experienced actualization of grace already sacramentally received.

Among the movement's strongest points of emphasis are prayer, openness to the Holy Spirit, community experience and the sharing of spiritual gifts.

The characteristic form of the renewal is the weekly prayer meeting, a gathering which includes periods of spontaneous prayer, singing, sharing of experience and testimony, fellowship and teaching.

Father Fio Mascarenhas, S.J., is director of the movement's International Communication Office, Via Feruccio, 19, 00185 Rome, Italy. William J. Beatty is executive director of the National Service Committee, 237 N. Michigan St., South Bend, Ind. 46601. Auxiliary Bishop Joseph McKinney of Grand Rapids is episcopal consultant to the National Service Committee.

The modern ecumenical movement, which started about 1910 among Protestants and led to formation of the World Council of Churches in 1948, developed outside the mainstream of Catholic interest for many years. It has now become for Catholics as well one of the great religious facts of our time.

The magna charta of ecumenism for Catholics is a complex of several documents which include, in the first place, the *Decree on Ecumenism* promulgated by the Second Vatican Council Nov. 21, 1964. Other enactments underlying and expanding this decree are the *Dogmatic Constitution on the Church*, the *Decree on Eastern Catholic Churches*, and the *Pastoral Constitution on the Church in the Modern World*.

## VATICAN II DECREE

*The following excerpts from the "Decree on Ecumenism" cover the broad theological background and principles and indicate the thrust of the Church's commitment to ecumenism, under the subheads: Elements Common to Christians, Unity Lacking, What the Movement Involves, Primary Duty of Catholics.*

Men who believe in Christ and have been properly baptized are brought into a certain, though imperfect, communion with the Catholic Church. Undoubtedly, the differences that exist in varying degrees between them and the Catholic Church — whether in doctrine and sometimes in discipline, or concerning the structure of the Church — do indeed create many and sometimes serious obstacles to full ecclesiastical communion. These the ecumenical movement is striving to overcome (No. 3).

### Elements Common to Christians

Moreover some, even very many, of the most significant elements or endowments which together go to build up and give life to the Church herself can exist outside the visible boundaries of the Catholic Church: the written word of God; the life of grace; faith, hope, and charity, along with other interior gifts of the Holy Spirit and visible elements. All of these, which come from Christ and lead back to Him, belong by right to the one Church of Christ (No. 3).

*[In a later passage, the decree singled out a number of elements which the Catholic Church and other churches have in common but not in complete agreement: confession of Christ as Lord and God and as mediator between God and man; belief in the Trinity; reverence for Scripture as the revealed word of God; baptism and the Lord's Supper; Christian life and worship; faith in action; concern with moral questions.]*

The brethren divided from us also carry out many of the sacred actions of the Christian religion. Undoubtedly, in ways that vary according to the condition of each church or community, these actions can truly engender a life of grace, and can be rightly described as capable of providing access to the community of salvation.

It follows that these separated Churches and Communities, though we believe they suffer from defects already mentioned, have by no means been deprived of significance and importance in the mystery of salvation. For the Spirit of Christ has not refrained from using them as means of salvation which derive their efficacy from the very fullness of grace and truth entrusted to the Catholic Church (No. 3).

### Unity Lacking

Nevertheless, our separated brethren, whether considered as individuals or as Communities and Churches, are not blessed with that unity which Jesus Christ wished to bestow on all those whom he has regenerated and vivified into one body and newness of life — that unity which the holy Scriptures and the revered tradition of the Church proclaim. For it is through Christ's Catholic Church alone, which is the all-embracing means of salvation, that the fullness of the means of salvation can be obtained. It was to the apostolic college alone, of which Peter is the head, that we believe our Lord entrusted all the blessings of the New Covenant, in order to establish on earth the one Body of Christ into which all those should be fully incorporated who already belong in any way to God's People (No. 3).

### What the Movement Involves

Today, in many parts of the world, under the inspiring grace of the Holy Spirit, multiple efforts are being expended through prayer, word, and action to attain that fullness of unity which Jesus Christ desires. This sacred Synod, therefore, exhorts all the Catholic faithful to recognize the signs of the times and to participate skillfully in the work of ecumenism.

The "ecumenical movement" means those activities and enterprises which, according to various needs of the Church and opportune occasions, are started and organized for the fostering of unity among Christians. These are:

• First, every effort to eliminate words, judgments, and actions which do not respond to the condition of separated brethren with truth and fairness and so make mutual relations between them more difficult.

• Then, "dialogue" between competent experts from different Churches and Communities [scholarly ecumenism].

• In addition, these Communions cooperate more closely in whatever projects a Christian conscience demands for the common good [social ecumenism].

• They also come together for common prayer, where this is permitted [spiritual ecumenism].

• Finally, all are led to examine their own faithfulness to Christ's will for the Church and, wherever necessary, undertake with vigor the task of renewal and reform.

It is evident that the work of preparing and reconciling those individuals who wish for full Catholic communion is of its nature distinct from ecumenical action. But there is no opposition between the two, since both proceed from the wondrous providence of God (No. 4).

## Primary Duty of Catholics

In ecumenical work, Catholics must assuredly be concerned for their separated brethren, praying for them, keeping them informed about the Church, making the first approaches toward them. But their primary duty is to make an honest and careful appraisal of whatever needs to be renewed and achieved in the Catholic household itself, in order that its life may bear witness more loyally and luminously to the teachings and ordinances which have been handed down from Christ through the Apostles.

Every Catholic must . . . aim at Christian perfection (cf. Jas. 1:4; Rom. 12:1-2) and, each according to his station, play his part so that the Church . . . may daily be more purified and renewed, against the day when Christ will present her to himself in all her glory, without spot or wrinkle (cf. Eph. 5:27).

Catholics must joyfully acknowledge and esteem the truly Christian endowments from our common heritage which are to be found among our separated brethren.

Nor should we forget that whatever is wrought by the grace of the Holy Spirit in the hearts of our separated brethren can contribute to our own edification. Whatever is truly Christian never conflicts with the genuine interests of the faith; indeed, it can always result in a more ample realization of the very mystery of Christ and the Church (No. 4).

## Participation in Worship

Norms concerning participation by Catholics in the worship of other Christian Churches were sketched in this conciliar decree and elaborated in a number of other documents such as: the *Decree on Eastern Catholic Churches,* promulgated by the Second Vatican Council in 1964; *Interim Guidelines for Prayer in Common,* issued June 18, 1965, by the U.S. Bishops' Committee for Ecumenical and Inter-Religious Affairs; a *Directory on Ecumenism,* published in 1967 by the Vatican Secretariat for Promoting Christian Unity; additional communications from the U.S. Bishops' Committee, and numerous sets of guidelines issued locally by and for dioceses throughout the U.S.

The norms encourage common prayer services for Christian unity and other intentions. Beyond that, they draw a distinction between separated churches of the Reformation tradition and separated Eastern churches, in view of doctrine and practice the Catholic Church has in common with the latter concerning the apostolic succession of bishops, holy orders, liturgy, and other credal matters.

Full participation by Catholics in official Protestant liturgies is prohibited, because it implies profession of the faith expressed in the liturgy. Intercommunion by Catholics at Protestant liturgies is prohibited. Under certain conditions, Protestants may be given Holy Communion in the Catholic Church (see Intercommunion). A Catholic may stand as a witness, but not as a sponsor, in baptism, and as a witness in the marriage of separated Christians. Similarly, a Protestant may stand as a witness, but not as a sponsor, in a Catholic baptism, and as a witness in the marriage of Catholics.

## Separated Eastern Churches

The principal norms regarding liturgical participation with separated Eastern Christians are included under Eastern Ecumenism.

# ECUMENICAL AGENCIES

## Vatican Secretariat

The top-level agency for Catholic ecumenical efforts is the Vatican Secretariat for Promoting Christian Unity, which originated in 1960 as a preparatory commission for the Second Vatican Council. Its purposes are to provide guidance and, where necessary, coordination for ecumenical endeavor by Catholics, and to establish and maintain relations with representatives of other Christian Churches for ecumenical dialogue and action.

The secretariat, first under the direction of Cardinal Augustin Bea, S. J., and now of Cardinal Johannes Willebrands, has established firm working relations with representative agencies of other churches and the World Council of Churches. It has joined in dialogue with Orthodox Churches, the Anglican Communion, the Lutheran World Federation, the World Alliance of Reformed Churches, the World Methodist Council and other religious bodies. In the past several years, staff members and representatives of the secretariat have been involved in one way or another in nearly every significant ecumenical enterprise and meeting held throughout the world, including the Fifth General Assembly of the World Council of Churches.

While the secretariat and its counterparts in other churches have focused primary attention on theological and other related problems of Christian unity, they have also begun, and in increasing measure, to emphasize the responsibilities of the churches for greater unity of witness and effort in areas of humanitarian need.

## Bishops' Committee

The U.S. Bishops' Committee for Ecumenical and Interreligious Affairs was established by the American hierarchy in 1964. Its purposes are to maintain relationships with other Christian churches and other religious communities at the national level, to advise and assist dioceses in developing and applying ecumenical policies, and to maintain liaison with corresponding Vatican offices — the Secretariats for Christian Unity and Non-Christian Religions.

This standing committee of the National Conference of Catholic Bishops is chaired by Archbishop John F. Whealon of Hartford. Operationally, the committee is assisted by the Rev. John F. Hotchkin, director; the Rev. Joseph W. Witmer, associate director; Dr. Eugene J. Fisher, executive secretary of the Secretariat for Catholic-Jewish Relations.

The committee co-sponsors several national consultations with other churches and confessional families. These bring together on a regular basis Catholic representatives and their counterparts from the Episcopal Church, the Lutheran World Federation (U.S. Committee), the United Methodist Church, the Orthodox Churches, the Oriental Orthodox Churches, the Alliance of Reformed Churches (North American area), the Interfaith Witness Department of the Home Mission Board of the Southern Baptist Convention. Reports of consultations conducted under committee auspices are published periodically and are available through the Publications Office of the U.S. Catholic Conference. (See Ecumenical Dialogues.)

The committee relates with the National Council of Churches of Christ, through membership in the Faith and Order Commission and through observer relationship with the Commission on Regional and Local Ecumenism, and has sponsored a joint study committee investigating the possibility of Roman Catholic membership in that body.

Advisory and other services are provided by the committee to ecumenical commissions and agencies in dioceses throughout the country.

Through the Secretariat for Catholic-Jewish Relations, the committee is in contact with several national Jewish agencies and bodies. Issues of mutual interest and shared concern are reviewed for the purpose of furthering deeper understanding between the Catholic and Jewish communities.

Through the Secretariat for Non-Christians, the committee promotes activity in wider areas of dialogue. The Rev. John F. Hotchkin serves as executive secretary for this secretariat.

Offices of the committee are located at 1312 Massachusetts Ave. N.W., Washington, D.C. 20005.

## World Council

The World Council of Churches is a fellowship of churches which acknowledge "Jesus Christ as Lord and Savior." It is a permanent organization providing constituent members — 301 churches with some 450 million communicants in 100 countries — with opportunities for meeting, consultation and cooperative action with respect to doctrine, worship, practice, social mission, evangelism and missionary work, and other matters of mutual concern.

The WCC was formally established Aug. 23, 1948, in Amsterdam with ratification of a constitution by 147 communions. This action merged two previously existing movements — Life and Work (social mission), Faith and Order (doctrine) — which had initiated practical steps toward founding a fellowship of Christian churches at meetings held in Oxford, Edinburgh and Utrecht in 1937 and 1938. A third movement for cooperative missionary work, which originated about 1910 and, remotely, led to formation of the WCC, was incorporated into the council in 1971 under the title of the International

Missionary Council (World Mission and Evangelism).

Additional general assemblies of the council have been held since the charter meeting of 1948: in Evanston, Ill. (1954), New Delhi, India (1961), Uppsala, Sweden (1968), Nairobi, Kenya (1975) and Vancouver, British Columbia, Canada (1983).

Between assemblies, the council operates through a central committee which meets every 12 or 18 months, and an executive committee which meets every six months.

The council continues the work of the International Missionary Council, the Commission on Faith and Order, and the Commission on Church and Society. The structure of the council has three program units: Faith and Witness, Justice and Service, Education and Communication.

Liaison between the council and the Vatican has been maintained since 1966 through a joint working group. Roman Catholic membership in the WCC is a question officially on the agenda of this body. The Joint Commission on Society, Development and Peace (SODEPAX) was an agency of the council and the Pontifical Commission for Justice and Peace from 1968 to Dec. 31, 1980, after which another working group was formed. Roman Catholics serve individually as full members of the Commission on Faith and Order and in various capacities on other program committees of the council.

WCC headquarters are located in Geneva, Switzerland. The United States Conference for the World Council of Churches at 475 Riverside Drive, New York, N.Y. 10115, provides liaison between the U.S. churches and Geneva. The WCC also maintains fraternal relations with regional, national and local councils of churches throughout the world.

The Rev. Philip A. Potter, a Methodist from the Island of Dominica, West Indies, was elected secretary general of the WCC in August, 1972.

WCC presidents are: Ms. Annie Jiagge, Ghana; the Rev. J. Miguez-Bonino, Argentina; General T. B. Simatupang, Indonesia; Archbishop O. Sundby, Sweden; Dr. Cynthia Wedel, U.S.A.; His Holiness Ilia, patriarch of the Gregorian Orthodox Church, S.S.R.

## National Council

The National Council of the Churches of Christ in the U.S.A., the largest ecumenical body in the United States, is a cooperative organization of 31 Protestant, Orthodox and Anglican church bodies having about 40 million members.

The NCCC, established by the churches in 1950, was structured through the merger of 12 separate cooperative agencies. Presently, through three main program divisions and five commissions, the NCCC carries on work in behalf of member churches in home and overseas missions, Christian education, communications, disaster relief and rehabilitation, family life, stewardship, regional and local ecumenism, and other areas.

Policies of the NCCC are determined by a governing board of approximately 250 members appointed by the constituent churches. The governing board meets twice a year.

The NCCC's 1983 budget was $43 million, about 80 per cent of which is devoted to compassionate ministries of aid and relief to victims of disasters and endemic poverty in lands overseas.

The acting president and general secretary, respectively, are Bishop Philip R. Cousin and Dr. Claire Randall.

NCCC headquarters are located at 475 Riverside Drive, New York, N.Y. 10115.

## Consultation on Church Union

The Consultation on Church Union, officially begun in 1962, is a venture of American churches seeking a united church "truly catholic, truly evangelical, and truly reformed." The churches engaged in this process, representing 25 million Christians, are the African Methodist Episcopal Church, the African Methodist Episcopal Zion Church, the Christian Church (Disciples of Christ), the Christian Methodist Episcopal Church, the Episcopal Church, the Presbyterian Church (U.S.A); the United Church of Christ, and the United Methodist Church. The National Council of Community Churches is also a member of COCU.

From 1970 to 1973 the member churches studied the first draft of a plan of union for the proposed Church of Christ Uniting. The responses to this plan, on the one hand, gave evidence of an historic consensus on faith, worship, and ministry; on the other hand, they revealed the need for mature involvement in order to discover the structures of a united church. The 11th plenary at Memphis, April, 1973, called for a future agenda involving the congregations more intimately, explored divisive factors such as racism, and affirmed the doctrinal and liturgical rapprochement already achieved.

An affirmation of mutual recognition of membership was accepted and sent to the churches at the 12th plenary held at Cincinnati Nov. 4 to 8, 1974. At the 1976 plenary meeting, six chapters of "an emerging consensus" as a "theological basis for union" were approved for study by COCU members.

A series of Eucharistic texts was published in 1978. The 1979 plenary accepted a series of questions to be posed to each church arising out of the mutual recognition of members, and moved ahead on a draft agreement on the ordained ministry. The 1980 plenary accepted a seventh chapter on ministry.

The 1982 plenary celebrated the 20th anniversary of the Consultation. During the meeting, two commissions — Interim Eucharistic Fellowship and Generating Communities, and the Task Force of Persons with Disabilities — made their final reports and were discharged. The 10 denominations (now nine, with the Presbyterian union) were called upon to "covenant" together until the Uniting Church becomes a reality.

Bishop Arthur Marshall, Jr., of the A.M.E. Zion Church, was elected COCU president in March, 1981. Dr. William D. Watley was appointed associate general secretary in 1982.

Offices are located at 228 Alexander St., Princeton, N.J. 08540.

## Graymoor Institute

The Graymoor Ecumenical Institute provides informational services concerning ecumenism and interfaith developments. One of its publications is *Ecumenical Trends*. The main office is located at the Interchurch Center, 475 Riverside Drive, New York, N.Y. 10115.

# ECUMENICAL DIALOGUES

(Source: Bishops' Committee for Ecumenical and Interreligious Affairs, National Conference of Catholic Bishops.)

Following is a list of principal consultations, from Mar. 16, 1965, involving representatives of the U.S. Catholic Bishops' Committee for Ecumenical and Interreligious Affairs and representatives of other Christian Churches, with names of the churches, places and dates of meetings, and the subject matter of discussions.

**Baptist Convention, American** (Division of Cooperative Christianity): (1) De Witt, Mich., Apr. 3, 1967 — American Baptist and Roman Catholic dialogue; a Baptist view of areas of theological agreement. (2) Green Lake, Wis., Apr. 29, 1968 — Baptism and confirmation; Christian freedom and ecclesiastical authority. (3) Schiller Park, Ill., Apr. 28, 1969 — Nature and communication of grace; Christian freedom and ecclesiastical authority; baptism and confirmation.

(4) Atchison, Kan., Apr. 17, 1970 — Role of the Church, resume of years past and the future; Roman Catholic-American Baptist dialogues; observations concerning bilateral ecumenical conversations and the future course of American Baptist-Roman Catholic conversations.

(5) Detroit, Mich., Apr. 23 to 24, 1971 — Theological perspective on clergy and lay issues and relations; theology of the local church; growth in understanding. (6) Liberty, Mo., Apr. 14 to 15, 1972 — Relationships between Church and State.

**Baptists, Southern** (Ecumenical Institute, Wake Forest University): (1) Winston-Salem, N.C., May 8, 1969 — Impact of biblical criticism on Roman Catholicism and contemporary Christianity in general; holy use of the world; creeds and the Faith; liturgy and spontaneity in worship; retreat, revival and monasticism; world view of ecumenism.

(2) St. Benedict, La., Feb. 4, 1970 — Liturgy and spontaneity in worship; perspectives on Baptist views on Scripture and tradition; the priesthood of all Christians; authority of the Old Testament; Baptist concepts of the Church; retreat, revival and monasticism. (3) Louisville, Ky., May 13, 1970 — The priesthood of all Christians; the ecumenical tide — a pastoral perspective; the enduring meaning of the Old Testament; retreat, revival and monasticism.

(4) Daytona Beach, Fla., Feb. 1 to 3, 1971 — Issues and answers, prepared by the Interfaith Witness Department of the Home Mission Board, Southern Baptist Convention. (5) Houston, Tex.,

Oct. 16 to 18, 1972 — Second regional conference planned in conjunction with the Interfaith Witness Department.

(6) Marriottsville, Md., Feb. 4 to 6, 1974 — Third regional conference, planned in conjunction with the Interfaith and Witness Department, concerning different types of reform and their appropriateness at different levels of church life. (7) Menlo Park, Calif., Oct. 27 to 29, 1975 — Fourth regional conference. The theme: "Conversion to Christ and Life-Long Growth in the Spirit."

(8) Winston-Salem, N.C., Nov. 10-12, 1975 — Fraternal dialogue, planned in conjunction with the Ecumenical Institute of Wake Forest University and Belmont Abbey College, on the abortion issue in Christian perspective, with publication of a statement and proceedings.

(9) Winston-Salem, N.C., Nov. 3-5, 1976 — Dialogue, planned as above, on Church-state issues, with publication of a statement and proceedings.

(10) Kansas City, Mo., Nov. 28 to 30, 1977 — Fifth regional conference on the theology and experience of worship. (11) Cincinnati, O., Apr. 28 to 30, 1978 — Inauguration of a scholars' dialogue, with presentation of papers on the Church in the New Testament and the experience of God in the Church.

(12) Cincinnati, O., Nov. 3 to 5, 1978 — Roman Catholicism in the U.S.A., an historical perspective; Southern Baptist experience in America; overviews of each tradition by the other; the local congregation or church. (13) St. Louis, Mo., Apr. 20 to 22, 1979 — Salvation as understood and taught in both traditions.

(14) Cincinnati, O., Nov. 9 to 11, 1979 — The authority of Scripture from Southern Baptist and Roman Catholic viewpoints. (15) Conyers, Ga., Apr. 11 to 13, 1980 — Spirituality as understood in each tradition, including sacraments, saints and social justice; Roman Catholic teaching on ministry from the Scriptures and the Fathers of the Church.

(16) Kerrville, Tex., Nov. 21 to 23, 1980 — Mission and social action in Southern Baptist life; eschatology; review of previous papers toward publication. (17) Cincinnati, O., Apr. 16 to 18, 1982 — Initial meeting of second round of dialogue, on the life of grace within us.

(18) Atlanta, Ga., Nov. 12 to 14, 1982 — The life of grace within us, continued. (19) Browns, Summit, N.C., Apr. 22 to 24, 1983 — The life of grace within us, continued. (2) Belmont, N.C., Nov. 18 to 20, 1983 — The life of grace within us, continued.

(20) Belmont, N.C., Mar. 30 to Apr. 1 — Discipleship and the life of grace, the communion of saints.

## Christian Church, Disciples of Christ (Council on Christian Unity): (1) Indianapolis, Ind., Mar. 16, 1967 — A look at Disciples for Catholics. (2) Kansas City, Mo., Sept. 25, 1967 — Roman Catholic view of the nature of unity being sought; opportunities in the contemporary ecumenical movement. (3) St. Louis, Mo., Apr. 29, 1968 — Eucharistic sharing.

(4) Washington, D.C., Oct. 16, 1968 — Disciple of Christ inquiry regarding the sacramentality of

marriage; pastoral reflections on mixed marriage. (5) New York, N.Y., Apr. 25, 1969 — Recognition and reconciliation of ministries; theological presuppositions concerning ministry among the Disciples; role of the priest in the Catholic community.

(6) Columbus, O., Nov. 3 to 5, 1970 — The parish concept in a plan of union (Consultation on Church Union); directions emerging in Catholic parish life. (7) New York, N.Y., June 8 to 10, 1971 — Disciples' theology of baptism; meaning of baptism as liberation, incorporation, empowerment.

(8) Indianapolis, Ind., Mar. 8 to 10, 1972 — Ministry of healing and reconciliation as practiced in the two communities. (9) Madison, Wis., June 26 to 28, 1972 — Review and summary of five years of dialogue; planning for future themes.

(10) Pleasant Hill, Shaker Town, Ky., May 22 to 24, 1973 — The Church in the New Testament.

(11) Indianapolis, Ind., Jan. 5-6, 1977 — Planning session, with the Council on Christian Unity of the Christian Church and the International Disciples Ecumenical Consultative Council, for a five-year consultation on apostolicity and catholicity in the visible unity of the church.

(12) Indianapolis, Ind., Sept. 22 to 27, 1977 — First session of a new and international consultation on the nature of the Church and elements of unity relating to it from New Testament and historical perspectives.

(13) Rome, Italy, Dec. 9 to 14, 1978 — Baptism, gift and call in the search for unity; study of various modes of baptism.

(14) Annapolis, Md., Sept. 7 to 12, 1979 — The faith of the individual and the faith of the Church; tradition and the faith of the Church; an agreed account on both subjects.

(15) New Orleans, La., Dec. 5 to 10, 1980 — Unity as gift and call; dynamics of division of the church. (16) Ardfert, Kerry, Ireland, Sept. 10 to 17, 1981 — Completion of final report of this round, "Apostolicity and Catholicity in the Visible Unity of the Church," published June 1, 1982.

**Episcopal** (The Anglican-Roman Catholic Consultation, Joint Commission on Ecumenical Relations): (1) Washington, D.C., June 22, 1965 — Preliminary discussions. (2) Kansas City, Mo., Feb. 2, 1966 — Eucharist as source or expression of community; Eucharist as sign and cause of unity, and the Church as a Eucharistic fellowship.

(3) Providence, R.I., Oct. 10, 1966 — Function of the minister in Eucharistic celebration; minister of the Eucharist. (4) Milwaukee, Wis., May 2, 1967 — Eucharist. (5) Jackson, Miss., Jan. 5, 1968 — Various aspects of the ministerial priesthood and the priesthood of the faithful in Eucharistic celebration; the priest's place and function in the Church's mission of service; the laity in Episcopal Church government.

(6) Liberty, Mo., Dec. 2, 1968 — Directions of the ecumenical movement; episcopal symbol of unity in the Christian community; collegiality; Citizens for Educational Freedom; a layman's view of jurisdictional and cultural factors in division; Church and society in contemporary America.

(7) Boynton Beach, Fla., Dec. 8, 1969 — All in

each place; toward the reconciliation of the Roman Catholic Church and Churches of the Anglican Communion; an approach to designing a Roman Catholic-Episcopal parish; preparation of joint statement on the meeting. (8) Green Bay, Wis., June 17, 1970 — Is the (COCU — Consultation on Church Union) plan of union truly Catholic, with special reference to the priest and the episcopacy; Anglican-Roman Catholic dialogue — achievement and prognostication.

(9) St. Benedict, La., Jan. 26 to 29, 1971 — The primacy of jurisdiction of the Roman Pontiff according to the First Vatican Council; the teaching of the Second Vatican Council concerning the hierarchy of truths; analysis of the ground of "Church Elements: An Ecclesiological Investigation."

(10) Liberty, Mo., June 20 to 23, 1971 — Gift of infallibility; sharing in the teaching authority of the Church; official view of episcopacy in the Episcopal Church in the USA; symposium on Hans Kung's *Infallibility? An Inquiry*; dogma as an ecumenical problem; Revelation and statement in Anglicanism; revised working paper on theological truth, propositions and Christian unity; reflections on the teaching ministry of the Church.

(11) New York, N.Y., Jan 20 to 24, 1972 — Theological truth, propositions and Christian unity; the Protestant Episcopal Church's view of authority, tradition and the Bible; a comment on the Windsor "Statement of Eucharistic Agreement" issued by the International Anglican-Roman Catholic Consultation.

(12) Cincinnati, O., June 12 to 15, 1972 — The notion of *typos* and *typoi* as applied to the forms of the Christian Church; correspondences and differences in the Anglican and Roman Catholic understanding and exercise of teaching authority.

(13) Cincinnati, O., Mar. 18 to 22, 1973 — Formulation of a preliminary draft on the purpose of the Church. (14) Vicksburg, Miss., Jan. 6 to 10, 1974 — Formulation of a response to the "Canterbury Statement" of the International Anglican-Roman Catholic Consultation on ministry and ordination; discussion and amendment of a draft on the purpose of the Church; other subjects in a continuing dialogue on the mission of the Church.

(15) Cincinnati, O., Nov. 10 to 13, 1974 — Discussion on the nature of authority in Anglicanism and Roman Catholicism. Report prepared on the purpose of the Church. (16) Cincinnati, O., June 22 to 25, 1975 — Special ad hoc consultation on women and orders.

(17) Erlanger, Ky., Oct. 21-24, 1975 — Continuation of discussion on women and orders, with release of joint statement on the ordination of women. (18) Overland Park, Kan., Mar. 10-13, 1976 — Continuation of discussion on authority in the Church.

(19) New Orleans, La., Jan. 19-22, 1977 — Presentation and discussion of a paper entitled "Some Implications of a 'Communio Ecclesiology' for the Authority Question"; formulation of an initial response to the "Venice Statement" (see separate entry); near completion of a 12-year report on the consultation.

(20) Cincinnati, O., Aug. 9 to 12, 1977 — Prepara-

tion of a second response to the Venice Statement, "Authority in the Church," and of a 12-year report, "Where We Are: A Challenge for the Future" (planned for publication). (21) Savannah, Ga., Mar. 7 to 10, 1978 — Christian anthropology and discussion of issues raised by the topic of the 12-year report in dialogue.

(22) Cincinnati, O., Jan. 3 to 6, 1979 — Christian anthropology in the patristic period and documents of the Second Vatican Council on the subject; New Testament arguments for and against the ordination of women.

(23) Cincinnati, O., Oct. 29 to Nov. 1, 1979 — Christian anthropology from the viewpoints of biotechnology/bodiliness, and Mariology. (24) Cincinnati, O., June 17 to 20, 1980 — Maleness and femaleness in Christian anthropology.

(25) Cincinnati, O., Mar. 10 to 13, 1981 — Human sexuality in relation to Christology; ordination of women; homosexuality.

(26) Cincinnati, O., Dec. 8 to 11, 1981 — Work on the first draft of a document on Christian anthropology. (27) Savannah, Ga., June 7 to 10, 1982 — additional work on the aforementioned document. (28) Columbus, O., Feb. 22 to 25, 1983 — Completion of final report, "Images of God: Reflections on Christian Anthropology."

(29) Cincinnati, O; Jan. 23 to 26, 1984 — Consideration of the ARCIC-II agenda.

**Lutheran, U.S.A.** (National Committee of the Lutheran World Federation): (1) Baltimore, Md., Mar. 16, 1965 — Exploratory discussion. (2) Baltimore, Md., July 6, 1965 — Nicene Creed as dogma of the Church. (3) Chicago, Ill., Feb. 10, 1966 — Baptism, in the context of the New Testament; Lutheran understanding; teaching of the Council of Trent.

(4) Washington, D.C., Sept. 22, 1966 — Eucharist as sacrifice, in traditional and contemporary Catholic and Lutheran contexts. (5) New York, N.Y., Apr 7, 1967 — Propitiation and five presentations on various aspects of the Eucharist. (6) St. Louis, Mo.. Sept. 29, 1967 — Eucharist. (7) New York, Mar. 8, 1968 — Intercommunion, with respect to Catholic discipline, Lutheran practice, and theological reflections.

(8) Williamsburg, Va., Sept. 27, 1968 — Ministry; the competent minister of the Eucharist; scriptural foundations of diakonia (ministry of service). (9) San Francisco, Calif., Feb. 21, 1969 — Apostolic succession in the patristic era and in a contemporary view; Lutheran view of the validity of Lutheran orders; Christian priesthood in the light of documents of the Second Vatican Council.

(10) Baltimore, Md., Sept. 26, 1969 — The minister of the Eucharist, according to the Council of Trent; the use of "church" as applied to Protestant denominations in the documents of Vatican II; Lutheran doctrine of the ministry — Catholic and Reformed; the ordained minister and layman in Lutheranism. (11) St. George, Bermuda, Feb. 19, 1970 — Preparation of joint statement on the ministry.

(12) New York, N.Y., May, 1970. (13) Chicago, Ill., Oct. 30 to Nov. 1, 1970. (14) Miami, Fla., Feb.

Ecumenical Dialogues                                                            297

19 to 22, 1971 — Peter and the New Testament; the papacy in the late patristic era, Middle Ages, Renaissance; text of the *Dogmatic Constitution on the Church* (Vatican II) with respect to the papacy and infallibility. (15) Seabury, Conn., Sept. 24 to 27, 1971 — An investigation of the concept of divine right *(jus divinum)*; teaching of the First Vatican Council on primacy and infallibility; a Lutheran understanding of what papal primacy in the Church might mean. (16) New Orleans, La., Feb. 18 to 21, 1972 — Further discussion of the concept of divine right; ecumenical projections concerning the Petrine office; teaching authority in the Lutheran Church. (17) Minneapolis, Minn., Sept. 22 to 25, 1972 — Further investigation of the Petrine function; councils and conciliarism. (18) San Antonio, Tex., Feb. 16 to 19, 1973 — Discussion of work and papers of the Petrine panel concerning ministry and the Church universal, Catholic and Lutheran interpretive statements; work on papal primacy papers. (19) Allentown, Pa., Sept. 21 to 24, 1973 — Work on a joint statement concerning ministry and the Church universal, the concluding session on this topic; selection of infallibility as the next topic for consideration. (20) Marriottsville, Md., Feb. 15 to 17, 1974 — Start of discussion on infallibility; commissioning of 16 future research papers. (21) Princeton, N.J., Sept. 19 to 22, 1974 — Scriptural studies re infallibility, inquiries into the teachings of early Lutheranism. (22) St. Louis, Mo., Jan. 30 to Feb. 2, 1975 — Historical and systematic studies of the teaching of infallibility. (23) Washington, D.C., Apr. 2 to 3, 1975 — Special meeting of several Lutheran presidents and Catholic bishops to review the work of the scholars' consultation and propose future directions. Press report issued. (24) Washington, D.C. Sept. 17 to 21, 1975 — Further historical and case studies re infallibility: ecumenical councils and marian definitions. (25) Scottsdale, Ariz., Feb. 19 to 22, 1976 — Infallibility discussion continued. (26) Washington, D.C., Apr. 2-3, 1975 — Meeting of Lutheran presidents and Catholic bishops to evaluate the direction and progress of Lutheran-Catholic dialogue in the U.S., with release of a joint statement. (27) Washington, D.C., Feb. 4-5, 1976 — Continuation of discussion concerning the direction and progress of dialogue. (28) Gettysburg, Pa., Sept. 15-18, 1976 — Presentation of papers entitled: "Draft I — Authority and Doctrine," "The Roman View of the Petrine Office in the Church 366-461," "The Status of the Nicene Creed as Dogma in the Church," "Ecumenical Methodology — Report of Task Force." (29) Washington, D.C., Feb. 16-20, 1977 — Discussion of the second draft of a common statement; presentation of a "Note on the Papacy as an Object of Faith." (30) Columbia, S.C., Sept. 14 to 18, 1977 — Continued discussion of the common statement, "Infallibility and Teaching Authority in the Church."

(31) Lantana, Fla., Feb. 15 to 19, 1978 — Discussion on the fourth draft of a comon statement reporting the findings of dialogue on infallibility. (32) Minneapolis, Minn., Sept. 13 to 17, 1978 — Statement on infallibility produced. (33) Cincinnati, O., Feb. 14 to 18, 1979 — Beginning of study of justification. (34) Princeton, N.J., Sept. 13 to 16, 1979 — Further study of justification. (35) Atlanta, Ga., Mar. 5 to 9, 1980 — Justification by faith, in the Bible and the teaching of the Council of Trent. (36) Gettysburg, Pa., Sept. 18 to 21, 1980 — Justification by faith, patristic and medieval views. (37) Cincinnati, O., Feb. 19 to 22, 1981 — Merit and reward language; additional biblical material on justification by faith. (38) Paoli, Pa., Sept. 23 to 27, 1981 — Drafting session on document on justification by faith. (39) Biloxi, Miss., Feb. 18 to 21, 1982 — Drafting session. (40) New York, N.Y., Sept. 23 to 26, 1982 — Drafting session. (41) Belmont, N.C., Feb. 17 to 20, 1983 — Drafting session. (42) Milwaukee, Wis., Sept. 15 to 18, 1983 — Final report, "Justification by Faith." (43) Sequin, Tex., Feb. 23 to 26, 1984 — Initial discussion concerning Mary and the communion of saints.

**Methodist** (United Methodist Church): (1) Chicago, Ill., June 28, 1966 — Methodists and Roman Catholics: comments for Catholic-Methodist conversation. (2) Chicago, Ill., Dec. 18, 1966 — Salvation, faith and good works; Catholic Church and faith. (3) Lake Junaluska, N.C., June 28, 1967 — Roman Catholic position regarding the Spirit in the Church; mission of the Holy Spirit, in the light of the Second Vatican Council's *Dogmatic Constitution on the Church* and the writings of John Wesley. (4) New York, N.Y., Dec. 17, 1967 — Three generations of Church-State argumentation. (5) San Antonio, Tex., Sept. 30, 1968 — Shared convictions about education. (6) Delaware, O., Oct. 9, 1969 — Major Methodist ecumenical documents; an appraisal of some documents of Vatican II; racial confrontation in Roman Catholicism, Methodism and the National Council of Churches. (7) Chicago, Ill., Jan. 30, 1970 — Review and planning. (8) Washington, D.C., Dec. 16, 1970 — Completion of a statement of shared convictions about education. Task force meetings during 1971. (9) Cincinnati, O., Feb. 25 to 26, 1972 — Ministry in the United Methodist Church and the spirituality of the ordained ministry; problems of ministry. (10) Dayton, O., Oct. 13 to 14, 1972 — Dialogue on the holiness of the Church and Christian holiness. (11) Washington, D.C., Mar. 9 to 10, 1973 — Spirituality of the ministry. (12) Washington, D.C., Nov. 1 to 2, 1973 — Start of preparatory work on a consensus statement on spirituality of the ministry. (13) Washington, D.C., Jan. 30 to Feb. 2, 1975 — Report prepared on Catholic and United Methodist understandings of holiness and spirituality in the ordained ministry; statement on holiness and spirituality of the ordained ministry released in January, 1976. (14) Washington, D.C., May 16, 1977 — Planning session for the next round of dialogue. (15) Washington, D.C., Dec. 4 to 6, 1977 — New phase of dialogue on the Eucharist in both traditions. (16) Marriottsville, Md., Apr. 16 to 18, 1978 — Continuing research on Eucharistic theology as developed in the two churches. (17) Washington, D.C., Oct. 12 to 14, 1978 — Eucharistic practice in both traditions. (18) Marriottsville, Md., May 17 to 19, 1979 — The Eucharist; contemporary eucharistic devotional practices of both traditions. (19) Washington, D.C., Nov. 4 to 6, 1979 — The presence of Christ in the word, related to Eucharistic presence; the notion of sacrifice in the Eucharist. (20) Washington, D.C., May 4 to 6, 1980 — Comparison of liturgical texts of Methodists and Catholics; further exploration of the relationship of word and sacrament. (21) Erlanger, Ky., Dec. 6 to 8, 1981 — Completion of statement, "Eucharistic Celebration: Converging Theology — Divergent Practice."

**Orthodox** (Standing Conference of Canonical Orthodox Bishops of America): Sept. 9, 1965 — Preliminary discussions. (1) New York, N.Y., Sept. 29, 1966 — Consultation led to appointment of task forces to investigate differences in theological methods, questions of sacramental sharing, possible cooperation in theological education and the formation of seminarians. (2) Worcester, Mass., May 5, 1967 — Theological diversity and unity; intercommunion; common witness in theological education. (3) Maryknoll, N.Y., Dec. 7, 1968 — Eucharist and Church; indissolubility of marriage; cooperation in theological education. (4) Worcester, Mass., Dec. 12, 1969 — Orthodox and Catholic views of the Eucharist and membership in the Church; an agreed statement on the Eucharist. (5) New York, N.Y., May 19, 1970 — New Order of the Mass; membership of schismatics and heretics in the ancient Church; current legislation of the Catholic Church and current practices of the Greek Orthodox Church concerning common worship; current legislation of the Catholic Church concerning mixed marriages; Orthodox view of mixed marriages; an agreed statement on mixed marriages. (6) Brookline, Mass., Dec. 4, 1970 — Ministers, doctrine and practice of matrimony in Eastern and Western traditions. (7) Barlin Acres, Mass., Nov. 3 to 4, 1971 — Ethical issues relating to marriage; revision of an agreed statement on mixed marriages; the primacy of Rome as seen by the Eastern Church. (8) New York, N.Y., Dec. 6, 1973 — Study of a draft statement on the sanctity of marriage. (9) Washington, D.C., May 23 to 24, 1974 — Dialogical process; witness of the Church on the American scene; approval of an agreed statement on respect for life; Orthodox and Catholic views of contemporary Orthodoxy and Catholicism. (10) New York, N.Y., Dec. 9 to 10, 1974 — Prepared and issued an agreed statement on the

Church. (11) Washington, D.C., May 19 to 20, 1975 — Dialogue on the local church and on the theology of priesthood. (12) New York, N.Y., Jan. 23 to 24, 1976 — Further dialogue on the theology of priesthood, et al. (13) Washington, D.C., May 18-19, 1976 — Additional discussion of theology of the priesthood, and ecumenical councils; release of joint statements entitled "The Principle of Economy" and "The Pastoral Office." (14) Brookline, Mass., Jan. 13-14, 1977 — Presentations on "Orthodox/Roman Catholic Marriages Revisited" and of two reports on the first pre-synodal Pan-Orthodox Conference in preparation for the coming Great and Holy Council. (15) Washington, D.C., Sept. 28 to 29, 1977 — Presentation and discussion of papers concerning the agenda of the forthcoming Great and Holy Council of the Orthodox Church, the theology of marriage and Orthodox-Roman Catholic marriages. (16) New York, N.Y., Jan. 24 to 25, 1978 — Preparation of a common statement on the sanctity of marriage, authorization for writing a history of the Orthodox-Roman Catholic Consultation. (17) Washington, D.C., May 15 to 16, 1978 — Additional work on a common statement on the sanctity of marriage, and initial discussion concerning the religious upbringing of children in Orthodox-Catholic marriages. (18) New York, N.Y., Dec. 7 to 8, 1978 — Study of the religious formation of children of marriages between Eastern Orthodox and Roman Catholics; release of "An Agreed Statement on the Sanctity of Marriage." (19) Washington, D.C., Mar. 15 to 16, 1979 — Continued study of a draft entitled "Joint Recommendations on the Spiritual Formation of Children of Marriages between Orthodox and Roman Catholics." (20) Pittsburgh, Pa., Nov. 2 to 3, 1979 — Additional work on a document, "Spiritual Formation of Children"; study of early Christian commissioning rites. (21) New York, N.Y., Oct. 10 to 11, 1980 — Study of the theology of ordained ministry; approval of "Joint Recommendations on the Spiritual Formation of Children of Marriages between Orthodox and Roman Catholics." (22) New York, N.Y., Oct. 1 to 3, 1981 — Papers on "The Priest as Icon of Christ" and "The Sacramental Life of the Church in Light of Trinitarian Ecclesiology." (23) Milwaukee, Wis., May 27 to 29, 1982 — Papers on "Aspects of the Theme: Spirit and Sacrament," and "The Theological and Canonical Traditions of Marriage in the Orthodox and Roman Catholic Traditions." (24) Pittsburgh, Pa., Nov. 18 to 20, 1982 — "Pneumatology and Sacramentology: A View of Systematic Theology"; an analysis of the most recent statement issued by the Anglican-Roman Catholic International Commission. (25) New York, N.Y., May 23 to 25, 1983 — Beginning of a theological statement on the relationship of the Holy Spirit to Christ, especially in the Eucharist; preparation of an official reaction to

"The Mystery of the Church and of the Eucharist in Light of the Mystery of the Holy Trinity," a statement issued by the Joint International Commission for Theological Dialogue between the Roman Catholic Church and the Orthodox Church. (26) Milwakee, Wis., Oct. 27 to 29, 1983 — Sacraments of initiation. (27) Crestwood, N.Y., June 4 to 6, 1984 — Joint reflection on baptism, Eucharist and ministry.

**Orthodox, Oriental** (Armenian, Coptic, Ethiopian, Indian Malabar and Syrian Orthodox Churches): (1) New York N.Y., Jan. 27, 1978 — Start of a new consultation, with initial consideration of a historical study of Oriental Orthodoxy. (2) New York, N.Y., May 26 to 27, 1978 — Purpose and method of dialogue; histories of Oriental Orthodox Churches. (3) Washington, D.C., Dec. 1 to 2, 1978 — Presentation of papers on the Council of Chalcedon, Christology and the Church today, concluding that ancient controversy over Christology does not seem to apply at the present time. (4) New York, N.Y., May 25 to 26, 1979 — Roman Catholic Christology; Eucharistic Liturgy of the Syrian Orthodox Church. (5) New York, N.Y., Dec. 27 to 28, 1979 — Paper on Byzantine liturgical commentary; reflection on joint statements of Paul VI with Vasken I, Ignatius Jacoub III and Amba Shenouda III. (6) New York, N.Y., Apr. 18 to 19, 1980 — Paper on Coptic Orthodox Divine Liturgy followed by that Eucharistic Liturgy. (7) Jamaica, N.Y., Nov. 14 to 15, 1980 — Adoption of a statement on the purpose, scope and method of the dialogue between the Oriental Orthodox and Roman Catholic Churches, and a paper on celebration of the Eucharistic liturgy of the Roman Catholic Church. (8) New York, N.Y., Dec. 3 and 4, 1981 — Papers on the role of Christ and the Spirit in the Divine Liturgies of each tradition, and on the development of the Public Office in the Armenian Church. (9) New York, N.Y., Sept. 9 to 11, 1982 — Draft of "An Agreed Statement on the Church Crises in Egypt and Lebanon." (10) New York, N.Y., June 8 to 10, 1983 — Official release of the aforementioned agreed statement and also of an "Agreed Statement on the Eucharist"; discussion of history of the churches' views on mixed marriages, and of the Armenian liturgy. (11) Plymouth, Mich., Jan. 12 to 14, 1984 — Discussion of pastoral practice concerning mixed marriages; theological reflection on the Eucharist as Sacrifice.

**Presbyterian and Reformed** (The Roman Catholic-Presbyterian Consultation Group, North American Council of the World Alliance of Reformed Churches): (1) Washington, D.C., July 27, 1965 — Exploratory discussions. (2) Philadelphia, Pa., Nov. 26, 1965 — Role of the Holy Spirit in renewal and reform of the Church. (3) New York, May 12, 1966 — Roman Catholic view of Scripture and tradition; apostolic and ecclesiastical tradition. (4) Chicago, Ill., Oct. 27, 1966 — Development of

doctrine; dialogue, a program of peace, prayer and study for Roman Catholics and Protestants. (5) Collegeville, Minn., Apr. 26, 1967 — Order and ministry in the Reformed tradition; validity of orders; changes in mixed marriage. (6) Lancaster, Pa., Oct. 26, 1967 — Work was begun on a joint statement on ministry. (7) Bristow, Va., May 9, 1968 — Structures and ministries. (8) Allen Park, Mich., Oct. 24, 1968 — Marriage. (9) Charleston, S.C., May 21, 1969 — Validation of ministries and ministry; theological view of marriage. (10) Macatawa, Mich., Oct. 30, 1969 — Apostles and apostolic succession in the patristic era; report concerning office; divorce and remarriage as understood in the United Presbyterian Church in the USA; the Church and second marriage; recommendations for changes regarding inter-Christian marriages. (11) Morristown, N.J., May 13, 1970 — Joint statements on ministry in the Church and women in Church and society. (12) Princeton, N.J., Oct. 29 to 30, 1970 — Episcopal presbyteral polity; episcopacy. (13) Columbus, O., May 13 to 15, 1971 — Ministry in the Church; man-woman relationships; the future of the Church. (14) Richmond, Va., Oct. 28 to 30, 1971 — Reports finalized on women in the Church and ministry in the Church. (15) Oct. 26 to 29, 1972 — The shape of the unity we seek. (16) Columbus, O., May 30 to June 2, 1973 — Theological and sociological views of the shape of unity we seek. (17) Columbus, O., Oct. 24 to 27, 1973 — Renewed discussion of the previous topic. (18) Columbus, O., May 8 to 11, 1974 — Further discussion of the previous topic in the light of Scripture, tradition, theology and reflection on the total Christian experience; worship and belief; discussion of plans for publication of a book on progress of the dialogue. (17) Cincinnati, O., Oct. 24 to 26, 1974 — Dialogue on the unity we seek in worship and in structures. (18) Washington, D.C., May 22 to 24, 1975 — Report prepared on the mission and nature of the one Church of Christ, with attention to the unity sought in worship, in structure and in common faith. (19) Princeton, N.J., Oct. 20-23, 1976 — Presentation of: an overview of the history of the consultation; a paper covering a Roman Catholic summary of the diversity and unity of current Christian responses to moral issues facing the Church; a paper on ethics and ethos in the Reformed/Presbyterian tradition. (20) Washington, D.C., May 25 to 27, 1977 — Human rights, distributive justice and the abortion issue as faced by the churches. (21) Princeton, N.J., Oct. 6 to 7, 1977 — Discussion of racism in South Africa and continuation of a study on human rights. (22) Washington, D.C., May 30 to June 1, 1978 — Study of the problem of unwanted pregnancies; preparation of statements on abortion and human rights. (23) Washington, D.C., Mar. 4 to 6, 1979 — Re-drafting of proposed statements on abortion and human rights. (24) Washington, D.C., Sept. 27 to 29, 1979 — Statements on abortion and human rights approved along with commentaries, and an interpretative report. (25) Princeton, N.J., May 19 to 21, 1982 — Beginning of the fourth round of dialogue, on the theme, "Church, Society and Kingdom of God," related to the theme of international bilateral dialogue.

(26) Washington, D.C., Nov. 17 to 19, 1982 — Papers on "Church, Society and Kingdom in the Roman Catholic and Reformed Traditions."

(27) Princeton, N.J., Mar. 24 to 26, 1983 — Paper on the Church and society from a political-science point of view; case-study analysis of respective statements on nuclear arms.

(28) Washington, D.C., Oct. 20 to 22, 1983 — Papers on Church-State issues; discussion of initial drafts of statements on "Church, State, Kingdom," and "Convergences and Divergences in Approaches to Nuclear Arms."

## INTERFAITH STATEMENTS

*The ecumenical statements listed below, and others like them, reflect the views of participants in the dialogues which produced them. They have not been formally accepted by the respective churches as formulations of doctrine or points of departure for practical changes in discipline.*

• The "Windsor Statement" on Eucharistic doctrine, published Dec. 31, 1971, by the Anglican-Roman Catholic International Commission of theologians. (For text, see pages 132-33 of the 1973 *Catholic Almanac.*)

• The "Canterbury Statement" on ministry and ordination, published Dec. 13, 1973, by the same commission (For excerpts, see pages 127-30 of the 1975 *Catholic Almanac.*)

• "Papal Primacy / Converging Viewpoints," published Mar. 4, 1974, by the dialogue group sanctioned by the U.S.A. National Convention of the World Lutheran Federation and the U.S. Bishops' Committee for Ecumenical and Interreligious Affairs. (For excerpts, see pages 130-31 of the 1975 *Catholic Almanac.*)

• An "Agreed Statement on the Purpose of the Church," published Oct. 31, 1975, by the Anglican-Roman Catholic Consultation in the U.S., in which the signatories agreed on the purpose and mission of the Church "insofar as it faithfully preaches the Gospel of salvation and manifests the love of God in service." It noted that "Roman Catholics and Episcopalians believe that there is but one Church of Christ," and endorsed social action for human liberation.

• "Christian Unity and Women's Ordination," published Nov. 7, 1975, by the same consultation, in which it was said that the ordination of women (approved in principle by the Anglican Communion but not by the Catholic Church) would "introduce a new element" in dialogue but would not mean the end of consultation nor the abandonment of its declared goal of full communion and organic unity. (A similar view was expressed in an exchange of letters between Pope Paul and Anglican Archbishop Donald Coggan of Canterbury, between July 8, 1975, and Mar. 23, 1976.)

• "Holiness and Spirituality of the Ordained Ministry," issued early in 1976 by theologians of the Catholic Church and the United Methodist Church; the first statement resulting from dialogue begun in 1966.

• "Mixed Marriages," published in the spring of 1976 by the Anglican-Roman Catholic Consultation in the U.S. It was similar in some respects to the statement, "Implementation of the Apostolic Letter on Mixed Marriages," approved by the National Conference of Catholic Bishops Nov. 16, 1970. It differed in softening the statement of a Catholic party's responsibility to do everything possible to raise children in the Catholic faith and favored greater freedom for having the marriage ceremony according to the rite of another Christian church.

• "Bishops and Presbyters," see under Eastern Ecumenical Briefs.

• "The Principle of Economy," see under Eastern Ecumenical Briefs.

• "Venice Statement" on authority in the Church, published Jan. 20, 1977, by the Anglican-Roman Catholic International Commission of theologians. Its major headings were Christian authority, authority of the ordained ministry and of the community, authority in the community of churches, the primacy of the bishop of Rome, authority in matters of faith, conciliar and primatial authority. Differences were cited in Catholic and Anglican views with respect to scriptural passages related to claims of the Roman See to primacy of authority, the divine right of the successors of St. Peter, papal infallibility and universal jurisdiction over the Church. (For text, see pages 145-50 of the *1978 Catholic Almanac.*)

• "Response to the Venice Statement," issued Jan. 4, 1978, by the Anglican-Roman Catholic Consultation in the U.S.A., citing additional questions regarding the sharing of authority in the Church, the nature of the primacy of Rome, and the relation of indefectibility to infallibility.

• "The Presence of Christ in Church and World," published early in 1978 by representatives of the Vatican Secretariat for Promoting Christian Unity and the World Alliance of Reformed Churches. The wide-ranging statement noted considerable degrees of mutual understanding and some agreement, along with substantial differences of view on several subjects — especially papal infallibility.

• "An Ecumenical Approach to Marriage," published in January, 1978, in the form of a report on five or more years of dialogue among representatives of the Catholic Church, the Lutheran World Federation and the World Alliance of Reformed Churches. Significant agreement was reported on doctrinal and pastoral aspects of marriage. Objections continued from the Lutheran and Reformed sides, however, with respect to the sacramental nature of marriage, and to Catholic requirements in cases of mixed marriages: (1) that the marriage normally take place with a priest as the officiating minister, and (2) that the Catholic party promise to do everything possible to raise children in the Catholic faith.

• "Teaching Authority and Infallibility in the Church," released in October, 1978, by the Catholic-Lutheran dialogue group in the U.S., noting similarities and differences between Lutheran understanding of the indefectibility of the Church and the Catholic doctrine of papal infallibility.

• "The Eucharist," reported early in 1979, in which the Roman Catholic-Lutheran Commission indicated developing convergence of views concerning the nature and sacrificial aspect of the Mass, and the significance of believing, active participation in the Eucharist.

• "The Holy Spirit," issued Feb. 12, 1979, by the International Catholic-Methodist Commission, citing points of common faith in the Holy Spirit.

• A statement on "Ministry in the Church," approved in draft form in February, 1980, and published in March, 1981, by the International Roman Catholic-Lutheran Joint Commission, regarding possible mutual recognition of ministries.

• The Final Report of the Anglican-Roman Catholic International Commission, released late in March, 1982, on the results of 12 years of dialogue. (See following article.)

• A report released June 9, 1982, by the Catholic Church-Disciples of Christ international commission concluded after five years of dialogue that the two churches already have a "unity of grace" which is "bearing fruit and which is disposing us for visible unity and urging us to move ahead to it." The report noted, however, that the two churches differ in their views of the relationship between the New Testament and later Catholic treaching embodied in liturgical texts, creeds and conciliar and papal statements.

• "Justification by Faith," issued Sept. 30, 1983, by the U.S. Lutheran-Roman Catholic dialogue group, claiming a "fundamental consensus on the Gospel."

• "Images of God: Reflections on Christian Anthropology," released Dec. 22, 1983, by the Anglican-Roman Catholic Dialogue in the United States, providing "a context in which to approach many of the difficult questions that confront" Catholic and Anglican churches.

## ANGLICAN-CATHOLIC FINAL REPORT

*The report which is the subject of this article is significant because it was one of the first, if not the first, of its kind to elicit critical comment from the Congregation for the Doctrine of the Faith.*

The Anglican-Roman Catholic International Commission of theologians officially published Mar. 31, 1982, a Final Report on 12 years of dialogue concerning subjects of belief and practice which have divided the two churches for more than 400 years.

The report included "Authority in the Church II," a new agreed statement, as well as earlier documents:

• the "Windsor Statement" on Eucharistic doctrine, published Dec. 31, 1971;

• the "Canterbury Statement" on ministry and ordination, published Dec. 13, 1973;

• the "Venice Statement" on authority in the Church, agreed to in 1976 and published Jan. 20, 1977;

• elucidations of these documents issued in 1979 and 1981;

• additional documentary material on the commission and related developments.

### Key Issues

"Controversy between our two communions," the report said, "has centered on the Eucharist, on the meaning and function of ordained ministry, and on the nature and exercise of authority in the Church. Although we are not yet in full communion, what the commission has done has convinced us that substantial agreement on these divisive issues is now possible."

The "divisive issues," subsequently called "four difficulties," were "the interpretation of the Petrine texts, the meaning of the language of 'divine right,' the affirmation of papal infallibility, and the nature of the jurisdiction ascribed to the Bishop of Rome as Universal Primate."

Bishop Raymond W. Lessard of Savannah, chairman of the Anglican-Roman Catholic Consultation in the United States, said in a statement for publication:

"The Final Report maintains that, despite differences of vocabulary and theological emphasis, the Anglican Communion and the Roman Catholic Church are in fundamental agreement in the three areas on which, since the 16th century, Anglicans and Roman Catholics have maintained they differ from one another so sharply that in conscience their Christian communities would have to remain officially separated from each other."

### Catholic Critique

The claim to fundamental agreement made in the Final Report was questioned by Cardinal Joseph Ratzinger, prefect of the Congregation for the Doctrine of the Faith, in a letter addressed to Bishop Alan C. Clark of East Anglia, England, co-president of the Anglican-Roman Catholic International Commission.

The claim was also questioned by the Congregation for the Doctrine of the Faith in the conclusion of a set of observations, dated Mar. 29, 1982, concerning the Final Report.

"At the conclusion of its doctrinal examination, the congregation thinks that the Final Report, which represents a notable ecumenical endeavor and a useful basis for further steps on the road to reconciliation between the Catholic Church and the Anglican Communion, does not yet constitute a substantial and explicit agreement on some essential elements of Catholic faith:

• "a) because the report explicitly recognizes that one or another Catholic dogma is not accepted by our Anglican brethren (for example, Eucharistic adoration, infallibility, the Marian dogmas);

• "b) because one or another Catholic doctrine is accepted only in part by our Anglican brethren (for example, the primacy of the Bishop of Rome);

• "c) because certain formulations in the report are not explicit enough to ensure that they exclude interpretations not in harmony with the Catholic faith (for example, that which concerns the Eucharist as sacrifice, the Real Presence, the nature of the priesthood);

• "d) because certain affirmations in the report are inexact and not acceptable as Catholic doctrine (for example, the relationship between the primacy and the structure of the Church, the doctrine of 'reception' — regarding the validation of doctrine by the acceptance of the people);

• "e) finally, because some important aspects of the teaching of the Catholic Church have either not been dealt with or have been only in an indirect way (for example, apostolic succession, the rule of faith, moral teaching)."

### Recommendation

Regarding next steps to be taken, the congregation said "the results of its examination would recommend:

• "a) that the dialogue be continued, since there are sufficient grounds for thinking its continuation will be fruitful;

• "b) that it be deepened in regard to the points already addressed where the results are not satisfactory;

• "c) that it be extended to new themes, particularly those which are necessary with a view to the restoration of full church unity between the two communions."

## ECUMENICAL BRIEFS

• A statement on Mary, the communion of saints and the intercession of saints was issued Sept. 15, 1983, by a commission of 15 Roman Catholic, Anglican, Lutheran, Reformed and Anglican theologians, at the International Mariological Congress in Malta.

• Catholics participated in various ways in commemorations in November, 1983, of the 500th anniversary of the birth of Martin Luther. Pope John Paul addressed a letter on the subject to Lutherans, and in December visited and addressed Lutherans at a church of their own in Rome.

• Representatives of the Catholic Church and

the Disciples of Christ, meeting in December, 1983, in Venice, released a statement entitled "The Church as Koinonia (Communion) in Christ." The meeting was the first in a planned seven-year cycle, following a five-year cycle completed in 1982.

• Lutheran, Anglican and Orthodox representatives joined Pope John Paul in active participation in an ecumenical scriptural and prayer service in the Basilica of St. Paul Outside the Walls on Jan. 25, 1984, the closing date of the Week of Prayer for Christian Unity.

• "Facing Unity: Models, Forms and Phases of Lutheran-Roman Catholic Unity," was the title of a statement approved at the Feb. 27 to Mar. 3, 1984, meeting of the International Catholic-Lutheran Joint Commission. The group, formed and working since 1973, dissolved itself at this meeting; it called for formation of a new commission and further dialogue and study of justification and the ministry of the bishop of Rome in the service of Christian unity.

### Assessments of Ecumenism

**Msgr. Basil Meeking,** after 15 years of work in the Secretariat for Promoting Christian Unity: A deeper understanding of church, a new Protestant appreciation of Mary, and cooperation between the Catholic Church and the World Council of Churches are positive results, he said Jan. 11, 1984. Christian unity hinges on discussion of the Church. Two critical issues are papal infallibility and doctrine concerning Mary.

**Bishop Raymond Lessard** of Savannah, a member of the second Anglican-Roman Catholic International Commission: He expressed a degree of optimism about Catholic-Anglican dialogue while calling attention to significant obstacles on the way toward unity, and warning against trying to move faster than theological realities would support. He said dialogue statements on the Eucharist and on ministry reflected "substantial agreement," although differences remained concerning the sacrificial aspect of the Eucharist, the representative role of priests, the jurisdiction of the pope and papal infallibility.

## CATHOLIC-JEWISH RELATIONS

*The Second Vatican Council, in addition to the "Decree on Ecumenism" concerning the movement for unity among Christians, stated the mind of the Church on a similar matter in a "Declaration on the Relationship of the Church to Non-Christian Religions." This document, as the following excerpts indicate, backgrounds the reasons and directions of the Church's regard for the Jews. (Other portions of the document, not cited here, refer to Hindus, Buddhists and Moslems.)*

### Spiritual Bond

As this sacred Synod searches into the mystery of the Church, it recalls the spiritual bond linking the people of the New Covenant with Abraham's stock.

For the Church of Christ acknowledges that, according to the mystery of God's saving design, the

beginnings of her faith and her election are already found among the patriarchs, Moses, and the prophets. She professes that all who believe in Christ, Abraham's sons according to faith (cf. Gal. 3:7), are included in the same patriarch's call, and likewise that the salvation of the Church was mystically foreshadowed by the Chosen People's exodus from the land of bondage.

The Church, therefore, cannot forget that she received the revelation of the Old Testament through the people with whom God in his inexpressible mercy deigned to establish the Ancient Covenant. Nor can she forget that she draws sustenance from the root of that good olive tree onto which have been grafted the wild olive branches of the Gentiles (cf. Rom.11:17-24). Indeed, the Church believes that by his cross Christ, our Peace, reconciled Jew and Gentile, making them both one in himself (cf. Eph. 2:14-16).

The Jews still remain most dear to God because of their fathers, for he does not repent of the gifts he makes nor of the calls he issues (cf. Rom. 11:28-29). In company with the prophets and the same Apostle (Paul), the Church awaits that day, known to God alone, on which all peoples will address the Lord in a single voice and "serve him with one accord" (Zeph. 3:9; Cf. Is. 66:23; Ps. 65:4; Rom. 11:11-32).

Since the spiritual patrimony common to Christians and Jews is thus so great, this sacred Synod wishes to foster and recommend that mutual understanding and respect which is the fruit above all of biblical and theological studies, and of brotherly dialogues.

## No Anti-Semitism

True, authorities of the Jews and those who followed their lead pressed for the death of Christ (cf. Jn. 19:6); still, what happened in his passion cannot be blamed upon all the Jews then living, without distinction, nor upon the Jews of today. Although the Church is the new People of God, the Jews should not be presented as repudiated or cursed by God, as if such views followed from the holy Scriptures. All should take pains, then, lest in catechetical instruction and in the preaching of God's Word they teach anything out of harmony with the truth of the Gospel and the spirit of Christ.

The Church repudiates all persecutions against any man. Moreover, mindful of her common patrimony with the Jews, and motivated by the Gospel's spiritual love and by no political considerations, she deplores the hatred, persecutions, and displays of anti-Semitism directed against the Jews at any time and from any source. (No. 4).

The Church rejects, as foreign to the mind of Christ, any discrimination against men or harassment of them because of their race, color, condition of life, or religion. (No. 5).

## Bishops' Secretariat

The American hierarchy's first move toward implementation of the Vatican II *Declaration on the Relationship of the Church to Non-Christian Religions* was to establish, in 1965, a Subcommission for Catholic-Jewish Relations in the framework of its Commission for Ecumenical and Interreligious Affairs. This subcommission was reconstituted and given the title of secretariat in September, 1967. Its moderator is Bishop Francis J. Mugavero of Brooklyn. The Secretariat for Catholic-Jewish Relations is located at 1312 Massachusetts Ave. N.W., Washington, D.C. 20005. The executive director is Dr. Eugene J. Fisher.

According to the key norm of a set of guidelines issued by the secretariat Mar. 16, 1967: "The general aim of all Catholic-Jewish meetings (and relations) is to increase our understanding both of Judaism and the Catholic faith, to eliminate sources of tension and misunderstanding, to initiate dialogue or conversations on different levels, to multiply intergroup meetings between Catholics and Jews, and to promote cooperative social action."

## Vatican Guidelines

In a document issued Jan. 3, 1975, the Vatican Commission for Religious Relations with the Jews offered a number of suggestions and guidelines for implementing the Christian-Jewish portion of the Second Vatican Council's *Declaration on Relations with Non-Christian Religions.*

Among "suggestions from experience" were those concerning dialogue, liturgical links between Christian and Jewish worship, the interpretation of biblical texts, teaching and education for the purpose of increasing mutual understanding, and joint social action.

The document concluded with the statement: "On Oct. 22, 1974, the Holy Father instituted for the universal Church this Commission for Religious Relations with the Jews, joined to the Secretariat for Promoting Christian Unity. This special commission, created to encourage and foster religious relations between Jews and Catholics — and to do so in collaboration with other Christians — will be, within the limits of its competence, at the service of all interested organizations, providing information for them and helping them to pursue their task in conformity with the instructions of the Holy See.

"The commission wishes to develop this collaboration in order to implement, correctly and effectively, the express intentions of the (Second Vatican) Council."

## NCCB Statement

In a statement issued Nov. 20, 1975, in commemoration of the 10th anniversary of the Second Vatican Council's declaration on non-Christian religions, the National Conference of Catholic Bishops welcomed the Vatican guidelines and hailed the "new era in Catholic-Jewish affairs" which "ended a centuries-long silence between Church and Synagogue."

Lamenting the "de-Judaizing process" that set in early in the Church's history — and which "dulled our awareness of our Jewish beginnings," the bishops affirmed that "most essential concepts in the Christian creed grew at first in Judaic soil. Uprooted from that soil, these basic concepts cannot be perfectly understood."

The bishops called on theologians to reconsider the "long-neglected passages" of the Letter to the Romans (Chapters 9 to 11) as a base for "exploring the continuing relationship of the Jewish people with God and their spiritual bonds with the New Covenant" in a positive manner.

Noting also that "an overwhelming majority of Jews see themselves bound in one way or another to the land of Israel," the bishops stated that, "whatever difficulties Christians may experience in sharing this view, they should strive to understand this link between land and people which Jews have expressed in their writings and worship throughout two millennia as a longing for the homeland, holy Zion."

## Papal Statements

*(Courtesy of Dr. Eugene Fisher, Executive Director of the Secretariat for Catholic-Jew-*

*ish Relations, National Conference of Catholic Bishops, and Consultor, since April, 1981, to the Vatican Commission for Religious Relations with the Jews.)*

Pope John Paul, in a remarkable series of addresses beginning in 1979, has sought to promote and give shape to the development of dialogue between Catholics and Jews.

In a homily delivered June 7, 1979, at Auschwitz, which he called the "Golgotha of the Modern World," he prayed movingly for "the memory of the people whose sons and daughters were intended for total extermination."

In a key address delivered Nov. 17, 1980, to the Jewish community in Mainz during his visit to West Germany, the Pope articulated his vision of the three "dimensions" of the dialogue. The first — the meeting between the people of God of the Old Covenant never retracted by God (Rm. 11:29) on the one hand and the people of the New Covenant on the other" — he said, "is at the same time a dialogue within our own Church, so to speak, a dialogue between the first and second part of its Bible." The second dimension is the encounter of "mutual esteem" between today's Christian churches and today's people of the Covenant concluded with Moses." The third is the "holy duty" of witnessing to the one God in the world and "jointly to work for peace and justice."

In addressing representatives of episcopal conferences gathered in Rome by the Vatican Commission from around the world, the Pope again stressed Mar. 6, 1982, the continuing validity of God's covenant with the Jewish people, noting that "our two religious communities are linked at the very level of their identities," forging links between the two that "are grounded in the design of the God of the Covenant." In his 1982 address, the Pope called especially for a renewal of catechesis that "will not only present Jews and Judaism in an honest and objective manner, but will also do so with a lively awareness" of "our common spiritual heritage . . . taking into account the faith and religious life of the Jewish people as professed and lived now as well." The delegates to the meeting began the process of considering the biblical, theological, and contemporary dynamics of such a catechesis.

### International Liaison Committee

The International Catholic-Jewish Liaison Committee, meeting for the ninth time in March, 1981, in London, held discussions on "The Challenge of Secularism to Our Religious Commitments." Speakers warned against "pernicious revisions of the history of the Holocaust," referring pointedly to recent pseudo-scholarly attempts to deny the reality of the Nazi genocide policy against the Jews.

"The Sanctity and Meaning of Human Life in the Present Situation of Violence" was the topic of the 10th meeting, held in September, 1982, in Milan.

Previous meetings discussed such topics as mission and witness (Venice, 1977), religious education (Madrid, 1978), and religious liberty and pluralism (Regensburg, 1979).

### U.S. Dialogue

National Workshops on Christian-Jewish Relations, an increasingly important forum for dialogue, have been held since 1975 in several U.S. cities.

A continuing dialogue on religious tradition and social policy — sponsored by the Synagogue Council of America and the NCCB Secretariat for Catholic-Jewish Relations — has been held annually since 1979.

Ongoing relationships are also maintained by the NCCB Secretariat with other Jewish agencies, such as the American Jewish Committee and the Anti-Defamation League of B'nai B'rith.

### New Institute

The American Jewish Congress announced in January, 1984, the formation of an Institute for Jewish-Christian Relations for promoting dialogue on theological subjects among Jewish and Christian scholars. Named to head the institute was Dr. Michael Wyschogrod, professor and chairman of the philosophy department of Baruch College.

Henry Siegman, executive director of the congress, noted that there was something different about the institute's effort to bring Jews and Christians together.

"Up until now," he said, "the interreligious dialogue has focused primarily on historical issues, specifically, anti-Semitism, Israel and the Middle East, and humanitarian and social-justice concerns. What will distinguish the institute is its focus on theological and scholarly activities."

The first project under auspices of the institute was a conference held in January in Lucerne, Switzerland, on the theme, "The Authority and Interpretation of Scripture in Judaism and Christianity." The Vatican Commission for Catholic-Jewish Relations was among sponsors of the meeting.

The International Jewish Committee, in a letter reported in March, objected to Vatican participation in the conference. Two reasons for controversy appeared to be the opposition of Orthodox Jews to theological dialogue with Christians, and the fact that the dialogue had not been coordinated by the international committee.

## JUDAISM

Judaism is the religion of the Old Testament and of contemporary Jews. Divinely revealed and with a patriarchal background (Abraham, Isaac, Jacob), it originated with the Mosaic Covenant, was identified with the Israelites, and achieved distinctive form and character as the religion of The Law from this Covenant and reforms initiated by Ezra and Nehemiah after the Babylonian Exile.

Judaism does not have a formal creed but its principal points of belief are clear. Basic is belief in one transcendent God who reveals himself through The Law, the prophets, the life of his people and events of history. The fatherhood of God involves the brotherhood of men. Religious faith and practice are equated with just living according to The Law. Moral conviction and practice are regarded as more important than precise doctrinal formulation and profession. Formal worship, whose principal act was sacrifice from Canaanite times to 70 A.D., is by prayer, reading and meditating upon the sacred writings, and observance of the Sabbath and festivals.

Judaism has messianic expectations of the complete fulfillment of the Covenant, the coming of God's kingdom, the ingathering of his people, final judgment and retribution for all men. Views differ regarding the manner in which these expectations will be realized — through a person, the community of God's people, an evolution of historical events, an eschatological act of God himself. Individual salvation expectations also differ, depending on views about the nature of immortality, punishment and reward, and related matters.

### Sacred Books

The sacred books are the 24 books of the Masoretic Hebrew Text of The Law, the Prophets and the Writings (see The Bible). Together, they contain the basic instruction or norms for just living. In some contexts, the term Law or Torah refers only to the Pentateuch (Genesis, Exodus, Leviticus, Numbers, Deuteronomy); in others, it denotes all the sacred books and/or the whole complex of written and oral tradition.

Also of great authority are two Talmuds which were composed in Palestine and Babylon in the fourth and fifth centuries A.D., respectively. They consist of the Mishna, a compilation of oral laws, and the Gemara, a collection of rabbinical commentary on the Mishna. Midrash are collections of scriptural comments and moral counsels.

Priests were the principal official ministers during the period of sacrificial and temple worship. Rabbis were, and continue to be, teachers and leaders of prayer. The synagogue is the place of community worship. The family and home are focal points of many aspects of Jewish worship and practice.

Of the various categories of Jews, Orthodox are the most conservative in adherence to strict religious traditions. Others — Reformed, Conservative, Reconstructionist — are liberal in comparison with the Orthodox. They favor greater or less modification of religious practices in accommodation to contemporary culture and living conditions.

Principal events in Jewish life include the circumcision of males, according to prescriptions of the Covenant; the bar mitzvah which marks the coming-of-age of boys in Judaism at the age of 13; marriage; and observance of the Sabbath and festivals.

### Sabbath and Festivals

Observances of the Sabbath and festivals begin at sundown of the previous calendar day and continue until the following sundown.

**Sabbath:** Saturday, the weekly day of rest prescribed in the Decalogue.

**Booths** (Tabernacles): A seven-to-nine-day festival in the month of Tishri (Sept.-Oct.), marked by some Jews with Covenant-renewal and reading of The Law. It originated as an agricultural feast at the end of the harvest and got its name from the temporary shelters used by workers in the fields.

**Hanukkah** (The Festival of Lights, the Feast of Consecration and of the Maccabees): Commemorates the dedication of the new altar in the Temple at Jerusalem by Judas Maccabeus in 165 B.C. The eight-day festival, during which candles in an eight-branch candelabra are lighted in succession, one each day, occurs near the winter solstice, close to Christmas time.

**Passover:** A seven-day festival commemorating the liberation of the Israelites from Egypt. The narrative of the Exodus, the Haggadah, is read at ceremonial Seder meals on the first and second days of the festival, which begins on the 14th day of Nisan (Mar.-Apr.).

**Pentecost** (Feast of Weeks): Observed 50 days after Passover. Some Jews regard it as commemorative of the anniversary of the revelation of The Law to Moses.

**Purim:** A joyous festival observed on the 14th day of Adar (Feb.-Mar.), commemorating the rescue of the Israelites from massacre by the Persians through the intervention of Esther. The festival is preceded by a day of fasting. A gift- and alms-giving custom became associated with it in medieval times.

**Rosh Hashana** (Feast of the Trumpets, New Year): Observed on the first day of Tishri (Sept.-Oct.), the festival focuses attention on the day of judgment and is marked with meditation on the ways of life and the ways of death. It is second in importance only to the most solemn observance of Yom Kippur, which is celebrated 10 days later.

**Yom Kippur** (Day of Atonement): The highest holy day, observed with strict fasting. It occurs 10 days after Rosh Hashana.

## ISLAM

Islam is the religion of Mohammed and his followers, called Moslems, or Muslims. Islam, meaning submission to God, originated with Mohammed (570-632), an Arabian, who taught that he had received divine revelation and was the last and greatest of the prophets.

Moslems believe in one God. There were six great prophets—Adam, Noah, Abraham, Moses, Jesus and Mohammed—and Mohammed was the greatest. The creed states: "There is no God but Allah and Mohammed is the prophet of Allah."

The principal duties of Moslems are to: profess the faith by daily recitation of the creed; pray five times a day facing in the direction of the holy city of Mecca; give alms; fast daily from dawn to dusk during the month of Ramadan; make a pilgrimage to Mecca once if possible.

Moslems believe in a final judgment, heaven and hell. Polygamy is practiced. Some dietary regulations are in effect. The weekly day of worship is Friday, and the principal service is at noon in a mosque. Moslems do not have an ordained ministry. The general themes of their prayer are adoration and thanksgiving.

The basis of Islamic belief is the Koran, the created word of God revealed to Mohammed by the angel Gabriel over a period of 20 years. The contents of this sacred book are complemented by the Sunna, a collection of sacred traditions, and reinforced by Ijma, the consensus of Moslems which guarantees them against error in matters of belief and practice.

There are several sects of Moslems.

## Conciliar Statement

The attitude of the Church toward Islam was stated as follows in the Second Vatican Council's *Declaration on the Relationship of the Church to Non-Christian Religions* (No. 3).

"Upon the Moslems, too, the Church looks with esteem. They adore one God, living and enduring, merciful and all-powerful, Maker of heaven and earth and Speaker to men. They strive to submit wholeheartedly even to his inscrutable decrees, just as did Abraham, with whom the Islamic faith is pleased to associate itself. Though they do not acknowledge Jesus as God, they revere him as a prophet. They also honor Mary, his virgin mother; at times they call on her, too, with devotion. In addition they await the day of judgment when God will give each man his due after raising him up. Consequently, they prize the moral life, and give worship to God especially through prayer, alms-giving and fasting.

"Although in the course of the centuries many quarrels and hostilities have arisen between Christians and Moslems, this most sacred Synod urges all to forget the past and to strive sincerely for mutual understanding. On behalf of all mankind, let them make common cause of safeguarding and fostering social justice, moral values, peace and freedom."

# NON-REVEALED RELIGIONS

## Hinduism

Hinduism is the traditional religion of India with origins dating to about 5,000 B.C. Its history is complex, including original Vedic Hinduism, with a sacred literature (Veda) of hymns, incantations and other elements, and with numerous nature gods; Brahmanism, with emphasis on ceremonialism and its power over the gods; philosophical speculation, reflected in the Upanishads, with development of ideas concerning Karma, reincarnation, Brahman, and the manner of achieving salvation; the cults of Vishnu, Shiva and other deities; reforms in Hinduism and in relation to Islam and Christianity.

The principal tenets of Hinduism are open to various interpretations. Karma is the law of the deed, of sowing and reaping, of retribution. It determines the progress of a person toward liberation from the cycle of rebirths necessary for salvation. Liberation is accomplished in stages, through successive reincarnations which indicate the previous as well as the existing state of a person. The means of liberation are the practice of ceremonialism and asceticism; faith in, devotion to and worship of the gods Vishnu and Shiva in their several incarnations; and/or knowledge attained through disciplined meditation called Yoga. Salvation, according to philosophical Hinduism, consists in absorption in Brahman, the neuter world-soul. Vishnu, the sun-god, and Shiva, the destroyer or generative force of the universe, are the principal popular deities. Ancient belief in nature gods (pantheism) is reflected in sacred respect for some animals. The concept of reincarnation underlies the caste system in Indian society.

There are many sects in Hinduism, which does not have a definite creed. It lends itself easily to syncretism or amalgamation with other beliefs, as evidenced in the 15th century Sikh movement which adopted the monotheism and militancy of Islam. Hindu rituals are various and elaborate, with respect to foods, festivals, pilgrimages, marriage and other life-events.

## Buddhism

Buddhism originated in the sixth century B.C. in reaction to formalism, pantheism and other trends in Hinduism. The Buddha, the Enlightened One, was Sidartha Gautama, an Indian prince, who sought to explain human suffering and evil and to find a middle way between the extremes of austerity and sensuality.

The four noble truths of Buddhism are: (1) existence involves suffering or pain; (2) suffering comes from craving: (3) craving can be overcome; (4) the way to overcome craving is to follow the "noble eightfold path" of right views, right intention, right speech, right action, right livelihood, right effort, right mindfulness and right concentration.

Karma, the deed-principle of judgment and retribution, and reincarnation are elements of Buddhism. The ultimate objective of life is Nirvana — the absorption of a person in the absolute — which ends the cycles of rebirth.

Buddhism is essentially atheistic and more of a moral philosophy and ethical system than a religion. It has a cultic element in veneration for Buddha. Monasteries, temples and shrines are places of contemplation and ritualistic observance. There are several categories of Buddhist monks and nuns.

Buddhism has many sects. Mahayana Buddhism, with an elaborate ideology, is strong in China, Korea and Japan. Hinayana Buddhism is common in Southeast Asia. Zen Buddhism is highly contemplative. Lamaism in Tibet is a combination of Buddhism and local demonolatry.

## Confucianism

Confucianism is an ethical system based on the teachings of Confucius (c. 551-479 B.C.). It is oriented toward the moral perfection of individuals and society, the attainment of the harmony of individual and social life with the harmony of the universe, through conduct governed by the relationships of humanity, justice, ritual and courtesy, wisdom, and fidelity. Originally and basically humanistic, Confucianism was eventually mingled with elements of Chinese religion.

# GLOSSARY

## A

**Abbess:** The female superior of a monastic community of nuns; e.g., Benedictines, Poor Clares, some others. Elected by members of the community, an abbess has general authority over her community but no sacramental jurisdiction. Earliest evidence of the use of the title, a feminine derivative of the Aramaic *abba* (father), dates from early in the sixth century.

**Abbey:** See Abbot, Monastery.

**Abbot:** The male superior of a monastic community of men religious; e.g., Benedictines, Cistercians, some others. Elected by members of the community, an abbot has ordinary jurisdiction and general authority over his community. He has some episcopal privileges. The title derives from the Aramaic *abba* (father); first given to the spiritual fathers and guides of hermits in Egypt in the fourth century, it was appropriated in the Rule of St. Benedict to the heads of abbeys and monasteries. Eastern-Rite equivalents of an abbot are a *hegumen* and an *archimandrite*.

A regular abbot is the head of an abbey or monastery. An abbot general or archabbot is the head of a congregation consisting of several monasteries. An abbot primate is the head of the modern Benedictine Confederation.

A few regular abbots have had jurisdiction, similar in some respects to that of a bishop in his diocese, over the residents and institutions of districts (*abbacies nullius*) not belonging to a diocese. Pope Paul VI stated in a document issued on his own initiative in 1976 that no more such abbacies would be established, except in cases of extraordinary necessity; also, that such abbacies, with the possible exception of ones of historical significance (like Monte Cassino, the cradle of the Benedictine Order) would be phased out of existence. The only *abbacy nullius* ever in the U.S. was Belmont Abbey, N.C. (1910-1976).

**Abjuration:** Renunciation of apostasy, heresy or schism by a solemn oath.

**Ablution:** A term derived from Latin, meaning washing or cleansing, and referring to the cleansing of the hands of a priest celebrating Mass, after the offering of gifts; and to the cleansing of the chalice with water and wine after Communion.

**Abortion:** The expulsion of a nonviable human fetus from the womb of the mother, with moral implications stemming from the humanity of the fetus from the moment of conception and its consequent right to life.

Accidental expulsion, as in cases of miscarriage, is without moral fault.

Direct abortion, in which a fetus is intentionally removed from the womb, constitutes a direct attack on an innocent human being, a violation of the Fifth Commandment. A person who procures an abortion is automatically excommunicated (Canon 1398 of the Code of Canon Law). Direct abortion is not justifiable for any reason, e.g.: therapeutic, for the physical and/or psychological welfare of the mother; preventive, to avoid the birth of a defective or unwanted child; social, in the interests of family and/or community.

Indirect abortion, which occurs when a fetus is expelled during medical or other treatment of the mother for a reason other than procuring expulsion, is permissible under the principle of double effect for a proportionately serious reason; e.g., when a medical or surgical procedure is necessary to save the life of the mother.

**Absolution:** The act by which an authorized priest, acting as the agent of Christ and minister of the Church, grants forgiveness of sins in the sacrament of penance. The essential formula of absolution is: "I absolve you from your sins; in the name of the Father, and of the Son, and of the Holy Spirit. Amen."

Priests receive the power to absolve in virtue of their ordination and the right to exercise this power in virtue of faculties of jurisdiction given them by their bishop, their religious superior, or by canon law. The faculties of jurisdiction can be limited or restricted regarding certain sins and penalties or censures.

In cases of necessity, and also in cases of the absence of their own confessors, Eastern- and Roman-Rite Catholics may ask for and receive sacramental absolution from a priest of a separated Eastern Church. Separated Eastern Christians may similarly ask for and receive sacramental absolution from an Eastern- or Roman-Rite priest.

Any priest can absolve a person in danger of death; in the absence of a priest with the usual faculties, this includes a laicized priest or a priest under censure.

(See additional entry under Sacraments.)

**Absolution, General:** A blessing of the Church to which a plenary indulgence is attached, given at the hour of death, and at stated times to members of religious institutes and secular (third) orders.

(See also under Penance, Sacrament; Norms on General Absolution.)

**Accessory to Another's Sin:** One who culpably assists another in the performance of an evil action. This may be done by counsel, command, provocation, consent, praise, flattery, concealment, participation, silence, defense of the evil done.

**Adoration:** The highest act and purpose of religious worship, which is directed in love and reverence to God alone in acknowledgment of his infinite perfection and goodness, and of his total dominion over creatures. Adoration, which is also called *latria*, consists of internal and external elements, private and social prayer, liturgical acts and ceremonies, and especially sacrifice.

**Adultery:** (1) Sexual intercourse between a married person and another to whom one is not married; a violation of the obligations of chastity and justice. The Sixth Commandment prohibition against adultery also prohibits all external sins of a sexual nature.

(2) Any sin of impurity (thought, desire, word, action) involving a married person who is not

one's husband or wife has the nature of adultery.

**Adventists:** Members of several Christian sects whose doctrines are dominated by belief in a more or less imminent second advent or coming of Christ upon earth for a glorious 1,000-year reign of righteousness. This reign, following victory by the forces of good over evil in a final Battle of Armageddon, will begin with the resurrection of the chosen and will end with the resurrection of all others and the annihilation of the wicked. Thereafter, the just will live forever in a renewed heaven and earth. A sleep of the soul takes place between the time of death and the day of judgment. There is no hell. The Bible, in fundamentalist interpretation, is regarded as the only rule of faith and practice.

About six sects have developed in the course of the Adventist movement which originated with William Miller (1782-1849) in the United States. Miller, on the basis of calculations made from the Book of Daniel, predicted that the second advent of Christ would occur between 1843 and 1844. After the prophecy went unfulfilled, divisions occurred in the movement and the Seventh Day Adventists, whose actual formation dates from 1860, emerged as the largest single body. The observance of Saturday instead of Sunday as the Lord's Day dates from 1844.

**Advent Wreath:** A wreath of laurel, spruce, or similar foliage with four candles which are lighted successively in the weeks of Advent to symbolize the approaching celebration of the birth of Christ, the Light of the World, at Christmas. The wreath originated among German Protestants.

**Agape:** A Greek word, meaning love, love feast, designating the meal of fellowship eaten at some gatherings of early Christians. Although held in some places in connection with the Mass, the agape was not part of the Mass, nor was it of universal institution and observance. It was infrequently observed by the fifth century and disappeared altogether between the sixth and eighth centuries.

**Age of Reason:** (1) The time of life when one begins to distinguish between right and wrong, to understand an obligation and take on moral responsibility; seven years of age is the presumption in church law.

(2) Historically, the 18th century period of Enlightenment in England and France, the age of the Encyclopedists and Deists. According to a basic thesis of the Enlightenment, human experience and reason are the only sources of certain knowledge of truth; consequently, faith and revelation are discounted as valid sources of knowledge, and the reality of supernatural truth is called into doubt and/or denied.

**Aggiornamento:** An Italian word having the general meaning of bringing up to date, renewal, revitalization, descriptive of the processes of spiritual renewal and institutional reform and change in the Church; fostered by the Second Vatican Council.

**Agnosticism:** A theory which holds that a person cannot have certain knowledge of immaterial reality, especially the existence of God and things

pertaining to him. Immanuel Kant, one of the philosophical fathers of agnosticism, stood for the position that God, as well as the human soul, is unknowable on speculative grounds; nevertheless, he found practical imperatives for acknowledging God's existence, a view shared by many agnostics. The First Vatican Council declared that the existence of God and some of his attributes can be known with certainty by human reason, even without divine revelation. The word agnosticism was first used, in the sense given here, by T. H. Huxley in 1869.

**Agnus Dei:** A Latin phrase, meaning Lamb of God.

(1) A title given to Christ, the Lamb (victim) of the Sacrifice of the New Law (on Calvary and in Mass).

(2) A prayer said at Mass before the reception of Holy Communion.

(3) A sacramental. It is a round paschal-candle fragment blessed by the pope. On one side it bears the impression of a lamb, symbolic of Christ. On the reverse side, there may be any one of a number of impressions; e.g., the figure of a saint, the name and coat of arms of the reigning pope. The *agnus dei* may have originated at Rome in the fifth century. The first definite mention of it dates from about 820.

**Alleluia:** An exclamation of joy derived from Hebrew, All hail to him who is, praise God, with various use in the liturgy and other expressions of worship.

**Allocution:** A formal type of papal address, as distinguished from an ordinary sermon or statement of views.

**Alms:** An act, gift or service of compassion, motivated by love of God and neighbor, for the help of persons in need; an obligation of charity, which is measurable by the ability of one person to give assistance and by the degree of another's need. Almsgiving, along with prayer and fasting, is regarded as a work of penance as well as an exercise of charity. (See Corporal and Spiritual Works of Mercy.)

**Alpha and Omega:** The first and last letters of the Greek alphabet, used to symbolize the eternity of God (Rv. 1:8) and the divinity and eternity of Christ, the beginning and end of all things (Rv. 21:6; 22:13). Use of the letters as a monogram of Christ originated in the fourth century or earlier.

**Amen:** A Hebrew word meaning truly, it is true. In the Gospels, Christ used the word to add a note of authority to his statements. In other New Testament writings, as in Hebrew usage, it was the concluding word to doxologies. As the concluding word of prayers, it expresses assent to and acceptance of God's will.

**Anathema:** A Greek word with the root meaning of cursed or separated and the adapted meaning of excommunication, used in church documents, especially the canons of ecumenical councils, for the condemnation of heretical doctrines and of practices opposed to proper discipline.

**Anchorite:** A kind of hermit living in complete isolation and devoting himself exclusively to exercises of religion and severe penance according to a rule and way of life of his own devising. In early Christian times, anchorites were the forerunners of the monastic life. The closest contemporary approach to the life of an anchorite is that of Carthusian and Camaldolese hermits.

**Angels:** Purely spiritual beings with intelligence and free will, whose name indicates their mission as ministers of God and ministering spirits to men. They were created before the creation of the visible universe; the devil and bad angels, who were created good, fell from glory through their own fault. In addition to these essentials of defined doctrine, it is held that angels are personal beings; they can intercede for persons; fallen angels were banished from God's glory in heaven to hell; bad angels can tempt persons to commit sin. The doctrine of guardian angels, although not explicitly defined as a matter of faith, is rooted in long-standing tradition. No authoritative declaration has ever been issued regarding choirs or various categories of angels: according to theorists, there are nine choirs, consisting of seraphim, cherubim, thrones, dominations, principalities, powers, virtues, archangels and angels. In line with scriptural usage, only three angels can be named—Michael, Raphael and Gabriel.

**Angelus:** A devotion which commemorates the Incarnation of Christ. It consists of three versicles, three Hail Marys and a special prayer, and recalls the announcement to Mary by the Archangel Gabriel that she was chosen to be the Mother of Christ, her acceptance of the divine will, and the Incarnation (Lk. 1:26-38). The Angelus is recited in the morning, at noon and in the evening. The practice of reciting the Hail Mary in honor of the Incarnation was introduced by the Franciscans in 1263. The *Regina Caeli*, commemorating the joy of Mary at Christ's Resurrection, replaces the Angelus during the Easter season.

**Anger:** Passionate displeasure arising from some kind of offense suffered at the hands of another person, frustration or other cause, combined with a tendency to strike back at the cause of the displeasure; a violation of the Fifth Commandment and one of the capital sins if the displeasure is out of proportion to the cause and or if the retaliation is unjust.

**Anglican Orders:** Holy orders conferred according to the rite of the Anglican Church, which Leo XIII declared null and void in the bull *Apostolicae Curae*, Sept. 13, 1896. The orders were declared null because they were conferred according to a rite that was substantially defective in form and intent, and because of a break in apostolic succession that occurred when Matthew Parker became head of the Anglican hierarchy in 1559.

In making his declaration, Pope Leo cited earlier arguments against validity made by Julius III in 1553 and 1554 and by Paul IV in 1555. He also noted related directives requiring absolute ordination, according to the Catholic ritual, of convert ministers who had been ordained according to the Anglican Ordinal.

**Antichrist:** The man of sin, the lawless and wicked antagonist of Christ and the work of God; a mysterious figure of prophecy mentioned in the New Testament. Supported by Satan, submitting to no moral restraints, and armed with tremendous power, Antichrist will set himself up in opposition to God, work false miracles, persecute the People of God, and employ unimaginable means to lead people into error and evil during a period of widespread defection from the Christian faith before the end of time; he will be overcome by Christ. Catholic thinkers have regarded Antichrist as a person, a caricature of Christ, who will lead a final violent struggle against God and his people; they have also applied the title to personal and impersonal forces in history hostile to God and the Church. Official teaching has said little about Antichrist. In 1318, it labeled as partly heretical, senseless, and fanciful the assertions made by the Fraticelli about his coming; in 1415, the Council of Constance condemned the Wycliff thesis that excommunications made by the pope and other prelates were the actions of Antichrist.

**Antiphon:** (1) A short verse or text, generally from Scripture, recited in the Liturgy of the Hours before and after psalms and canticles.

(2) Any verse sung or recited by one part of a choir or congregation in response to the other part, as in antiphonal or alternate chanting.

**Apologetics:** The science and art of developing and presenting the case for the reasonableness of the Christian faith, by a wide variety of means including facts of experience, history, science, philosophy. The constant objective of apologetics, as well as of the total process of pre-evangelization, is preparation for response to God in faith; its ways and means, however, are subject to change in accordance with the various needs of people and different sets of circumstances.

**Apostasy:** (1) The total and obstinate repudiation of the Christian faith. An *apostate* automatically incurs a penalty of excommunication.

(2) Apostasy from orders is the unlawful withdrawal from or rejection of the obligations of the clerical state by a man who has received major orders. An apostate from orders is subject to a canonical penalty.

(3) Apostasy from the religious life occurs when a religious with perpetual vows unlawfully leaves the community with the intention of not returning, or actually remains outside the community without permission. An apostate from religious life is subject to a canonical penalty.

**Apostolate:** The ministry or work of an apostle. In Catholic usage, the word is an umbrella-like term covering all kinds and areas of work and endeavor for the service of God and the Church and the good of people. Thus, the apostolate of bishops is to carry on the mission of the Apostles as pastors of the People of God: of priests, to preach the word of God and to carry out the sacramental and pastoral ministry for which they are ordained; of religious, to follow and do the work of Christ in conformity with the evangelical counsels and their rule of life; of lay persons, as individuals and/or in groups, to give witness to Christ and build up the kingdom of God through practice of their faith, professional competence and the performance of good works in the concrete circumstances of daily life. Apostolic works are not limited to those done within the Church or by specifically Catholic groups, although some apostolates are officially assigned to certain persons or groups and are under the direction of church authorities. Apostolate derives from the commitment and obligation of baptism, confirmation, holy orders, matrimony, the duties of one's state in life, etc.

**Apostolic Succession:** Bishops of the Church, who form a collective body or college, are successors to the Apostles by ordination and divine right; as such they carry on the mission entrusted by Christ to the Apostles as guardians and teachers of the deposit of faith, principal pastors and spiritual authorities of the faithful. The doctrine of apostolic succession is based on New Testament evidence and the constant teaching of the Church, reflected as early as the end of the first century in a letter of Pope St. Clement to the Corinthians. A significant facet of the doctrine is the role of the pope as the successor of St. Peter, the vicar of Christ and head of the college of bishops. The doctrine of apostolic succession means more than continuity of apostolic faith and doctrine; its basic requisite is ordination by the laying on of hands in apostolic succession.

**Archangel:** An angel who carries out special missions for God in his dealings with persons. Three of them are named in the Bible: Michael, leader of the angelic host and protector of the synagogue; Raphael, guide of Tobiah and healer of his father, who is regarded as the patron of travelers; Gabriel, called the angel of the Incarnation because of his announcement to Mary that she was to be the Mother of Christ.

**Archdiocese:** An ecclesiastical jurisdiction headed by an archbishop. An archdiocese is usually a metropolitan see, i.e., the principal one of a group of dioceses comprising a province; the other dioceses in the province are suffragan sees.

**Archives:** Documentary records, and the place where they are kept, of the spiritual and temporal government and affairs of the Church, a diocese, church agencies like the departments of the Roman Curia, bodies like religious institutes, and individual parishes. The collection, cataloguing, preserving, and use of these records are governed by norms stated in canon law and particular regulations. The strictest secrecy is always in effect for confidential records concerning matters of conscience, and documents of this kind are destroyed as soon as circumstances permit.

**Archpriest:** For some time, before and during the Middle Ages, a priest who took the place of a bishop at liturgical worship. In Europe, the term is sometimes used as an honorary title. It is also an honorary title in Eastern-Rite Churches.

**Ark of the Covenant:** The sacred chest of the Israelites in which were placed and carried the tablets of stone inscribed with the Ten Commandments, the basic moral precepts of the Old Covenant (Ex. 25: 10-22; 37:1-9). The Ark was also a symbol of God's presence. The Ark was probably destroyed with the Temple in 587 B.C.

**Asceticism:** The practice of self-discipline. In the spiritual life, asceticism — by personal prayer, meditation, self-denial, works of mortification, and outgoing interpersonal works — is motivated by love of God and contributes to growth in holiness.

**Ashes:** Religious significance has been associated with their use as symbolic of penance since Old Testament times. Thus, ashes of palm blessed on the previous Sunday of the Passion are placed on the foreheads of the faithful on Ash Wednesday to remind them to do works of penance, especially during the season of Lent, and that they are dust and unto dust will return. Ashes are a sacramental.

**Aspergillum:** A vessel or device used for sprinkling holy water. The ordinary type is a metallic rod with a bulbous tip which absorbs the water and discharges it at the motion of the user's hand.

**Aspersory:** A portable metallic vessel, similar to a pail, for carrying holy water.

**Aspiration:** Short exclamatory prayer; e.g., My Jesus, mercy.

**Atheism:** Denial of the existence of God, finding expression in a system of thought (speculative atheism) or a manner of acting (practical atheism) as though there were no God.

The Second Vatican Council, in its *Pastoral Constitution on the Church in the Modern World* (Nos. 19 to 21), noted that a profession of atheism may represent an explicit denial of God. the rejection of a wrong notion of God, an affirmation of man rather than of God, an extreme protest against evil. It said that such a profession might result from acceptance of such propositions as: there is no absolute truth; man can assert nothing, absolutely nothing, about God; everything can be explained by scientific reasoning alone; the whole question of God is devoid of meaning.

The constitution also cited two opinions of influence in atheistic thought. One of them regards recognition of dependence on God as incompatible with human freedom and independence. The other views belief in God and religion as a kind of opiate which sedates man on earth, reconciling him to the acceptance of suffering, injustice, shortcomings, etc., because of hope for greater things after death, and thereby hindering him from seeking and working for improvement and change for the better here and now.

All of these views, in one way or another, have been involved in the No-God and Death-of-God schools of thought in recent and remote history.

**Atonement:** The redemptive activity of Christ, who reconciled man with God through his Incarnation and entire life, and especially by his suffering and Resurrection. The word also applies to prayer and good works by which persons join themselves with and take part in Christ's work of reconciliation and reparation for sin.

**Attributes of God:** Perfections of God. God possesses — and is — all the perfections of being, without limitation. Because he is infinite, all of these perfections are one, perfectly united in him. Man, however, because of the limited power of understanding, views these perfections separately, as distinct characteristics — even though they are not actually distinct in God. God is: almighty, eternal, holy, immortal, immense, immutable, incomprehensible, ineffable, infinite, invisible, just, loving, merciful, most high, most wise, omnipotent, omniscient, omnipresent, patient, perfect, provident, supreme, true.

**Avarice (Covetousness):** A disorderly and unreasonable attachment to and desire for material things; called a capital sin because it involves preoccupation with material things to the neglect of spiritual goods and obligations of justice and charity.

**Ave Maria:** See Hail Mary.

**B**

**Baldachino:** A canopy over an altar.

**Beatification:** A preliminary step toward canonization of a saint. It begins with an investigation of the candidate's life, writings and heroic practice of virtue, and the certification of at least two miracles worked by God through his intercession. If the findings of the investigation so indicate, the pope decrees that the Servant of God may be called *Blessed* and may be honored locally or in a limited way in the liturgy. Additional procedures lead to canonization (see separate entry).

**Beatific Vision:** The intuitive, immediate and direct vision and experience of God enjoyed in the light of glory by all the blessed in heaven. The vision is a supernatural mystery.

**Beatitude:** A literary form of the Old and New Testaments in which blessings are promised to persons for various reasons. Beatitudes are mentioned 26 times in the Psalms, and in other books of the Old Testament. The best known beatitudes — identifying blessedness with participation in the kingdom of God and his righteousness, and descriptive of the qualities of Christian perfection — are those recounted in Mt. 5:3-11 and Lk. 6:20-22.

In Matthew's account, the beatitudes are:

"How blest are the poor in spirit: the reign of God is theirs.

"Blest too are the sorrowing; they shall be consoled.

"(Blest are the lowly; they shall inherit the land.)

"Blest are they who hunger and thirst for holiness; they shall have their fill.

"Blest are they who show mercy; mercy shall be theirs.

"Blest are the single-hearted for they shall see God.

"Blest too are the peacemakers; they shall be called sons of God.

"Blest are those persecuted for holiness' sake; the reign of God is theirs.

"Blest are you when they insult you and persecute you and utter every kind of slander against you because of me."

In Luke's account, the beatitudes are:

"Blest are you poor; the reign of God is yours.

"Blest are you who hunger; you shall be filled.

"Blest are you who are weeping; you shall laugh.

"Blest shall you be when men hate you, when they ostracize you and insult you and proscribe your name as evil because of the Son of Man."

**Benedictus:** The canticle or hymn of Zechariah at the circumcision of St. John the Baptist (Lk. 1:68-79). It is an expression of praise and thanks to God for sending John as a precursor of the Messiah. The *Benedictus* is recited in the Liturgy of the Hours as part of the Morning Prayer.

**Bible Service:** A devotion consisting essentially of common prayer of a biblical or liturgical character, several readings from Scripture, and a homily on the texts.

**Biglietto:** A papal document of notification of appointment to the cardinalate.

**Biretta:** A stiff, square hat with three ridges on top worn by clerics in church and on other occasions.

**Blasphemy:** Any expression of insult or contempt with respect to God, principally, and to holy persons and things, secondarily; a violation of the honor due to God in the context of the First and Second Commandments.

**Blasphemy of the Spirit:** Deliberate resistance to the Holy Spirit, called the unforgivable sin (Mt. 12:31) because it makes his saving action impossible. Thus, the only unforgivable sin is the one for which a person will not seek pardon from God.

**Blessing:** Invocation of God's favor, by official ministers of the Church or by private individuals. Blessings are recounted in the Old and New Testaments, and are common in the Christian tradition. The Church, through its ordained ministers (bishops and priests, especially), invokes divine favor in liturgical blessings; e.g., of the people at Mass, of the gifts to be consecrated at Mass, of persons and things on various occasions. Sacramentals — such as crucifixes, crosses, rosaries, scapulars, medals — are blessed by ministers of the Church for the invocation of God's favor on those who use them in the proper manner. Many types of blessings are listed in the *Roman Ritual*. Private blessings, as well as those of an official kind, are efficacious. Blessings are imparted with the Sign of the Cross and appropriate prayer.

**Boat:** A small vessel used to hold incense which is to be placed in the censer.

**Brief, Apostolic:** A papal letter, less formal than a bull, signed for the pope by a secretary and impressed with the seal of the Fisherman's Ring. Simple apostolic letters of this kind are issued for beatifications and with respect to other matters.

**Bull, Apostolic:** The most solemn form of papal document, beginning with the name and title of the pope (e.g., John Paul II, Servant of the Servants of God), dealing with an important subject, and having attached to it either a leaden seal called a *bulla* or a red ink imprint of the device on the seal. Bulls are known as apostolic letters with the seal. The seal, on one side, has representations of the heads of Sts. Peter and Paul; on the other side, the name of the reigning pope. Bulls are issued to confer the titles of bishops and cardinals, to promulgate canonizations, and for other purposes. A collection of bulls is called a *bullarium*.

**Burial, Ecclesiastical:** Interment with ecclesiastical rites, a right of the Christian faithful. The Church recommends burial of the bodies of the dead, but cremation is permissible if it does not involve reasons against church teaching. Ecclesiastical burial is in order for catechumens; for unbaptized children whose parents intended to have them baptized before death; and even — in the absence of their own ministers — for baptized non-Catholics unless it would be considered against their will.

## C

**Calumny:** Harming the name and good reputation of a person by lies; a violation of obligations of justice and truth. Restitution is due for calumny.

**Calvary:** A knoll about 15 feet high just outside the western wall of Jerusalem where Christ was crucified, so called from the Latin *calvaria* (skull) which described its shape.

**Canon:** A Greek word meaning rule, norm, standard, measure.

(1) The word designates the Canon of Sacred Scripture, which is the list of books recognized by the Church as inspired by the Holy Spirit.

(2) In the sense of regulating norms, the word designates the Code of Canon Law enacted and promulgated by ecclesiastical authority for the orderly and pastoral administration and government of the Church. A revised Code, effective Nov. 27, 1983, consists of 1,752 canons in seven books under the titles of general norms, the people of God, the teaching mission of the Church, the sanctifying mission of the Church, temporal goods of the Church, penal law and procedural law. The antecedent of this Code was promulgated in 1917 and became effective in 1918; it consisted of 2,414 canons in five books covering general rules, ecclesiastical persons, sacred things, trials, crimes and punishments. Eastern-Rite Churches have their own canon law.

(3) The term also designates the four canons, (Eucharistic prayers, anaphoras) of the Mass, the core of the liturgy.

(4) Certain dignitaries of the Church have the title of Canon, and some Religious are known as Canons.

**Canonization:** An infallible declaration by the pope that a person, who died as a martyr and/or practiced Christian virtue to a heroic degree, is now in heaven and is worthy of honor and imitation by all the faithful. Such a declaration is preceded by the process of beatification and another detailed investigation concerning the person's reputation for holiness, writings, and (except in the case of martyrs) miracles ascribed to his or her intercession after death. Miracles are not required for martyrs. The pope can dispense from some of the formalities ordinarily required in canonization procedures (equivalent canonization), as Pope John XXIII did in the canonization of St. Gregory Barbarigo on May 26, 1960. A saint is worthy of honor in liturgical worship throughout the universal Church.

From its earliest years the Church has venerated saints. Public official honor always required the approval of the bishop of the place. Martyrs were the first to be honored. St. Martin of Tours, who died in 397, was an early non-martyr venerated as a saint. The first official canonization by a pope for the universal Church was that of St. Ulrich by John XV in 993. Alexander III reserved the process of canonization to the Holy See in 1171. In 1588 Sixtus V established the Sacred Congregation of Rites for the principal purpose of handling causes for beatification and canonization: this function is now the work of the Congregation for the Causes of Saints.

The essential portion of a canonization decree states:

"For the honor of the holy and undivided Trinity; for the exaltation of the Catholic faith and the increase of Christian life; with the authority of our Lord Jesus Christ, of the blessed Apostles Peter and Paul, and with our own authority; after mature deliberation and with the divine assistance, often implored; with the counsel of many of our brothers.

"We decree and define that (name) is a saint and we inscribe him (her) in the Catalogue of Saints, stating that he (she) shall be venerated in the universal Church with pious devotion.

"In the name of the Father and of the Son and of the Holy Spirit. Amen."

The official listing of saints and blessed is contained in the *Roman Martyrology* and related decrees issued after its last publication. Butler's unofficial *Lives of the Saints* (1956) contains 2,565 entries.

The Church regards all persons in heaven as saints, not just those who have been officially canonized.

(See Beatification, Saints, Canonizations by Leo XIII and His Successors.)

**Canticle:** A scriptural chant or prayer differing from the psalms. Three of the canticles prescribed for use in the Liturgy of the Hours are: the *Magnificat* (Lk. 1:46-55), the *Benedictus* (Lk. 1:68-79), and the *Nunc Dimittis* (Lk. 2:29-32).

**Capital Punishment:** Punishment for crime by means of the death penalty. The political community, which has authority to provide for the common good, has the right to defend itself and its members against unjust aggression and may in extreme cases punish with the death penalty persons found guilty before the law of serious crimes against individuals and a just social order. Such punishment is essentially vindictive. Its value as a crime deterrent is a matter of perennial debate. The prudential judgment as to whether or not there should be capital punishment belongs to the civic community. The U.S. Supreme Court, in a series of decisions dating from June 29, 1972, ruled against the constitutionality of statutes on capital punishment except in specific cases and with appropriate consideration, with respect to sentence, of mitigating circumstances of the crime.

Capital punishment was the subject of a statement issued Mar. 1, 1978, by the Committee on Social Development and World Peace, U.S. Catholic Conference. The statement said, in part: "The use of the death penalty involves deep moral and religious questions as well as political and legal issues. In 1974, out of a commitment to the value and dignity of human life, the Catholic bishops of the United States declared their opposition to capital punishment. We continue to support this position, in the belief that a return to the use of the death penalty can only lead to the further erosion of respect for life in our society. Violent crime in our society is a serious matter which should not be ignored. We do not challenge society's right to punish the serious and violent offender, nor do we wish to debate the merits of the arguments concerning this right. Past history, however, shows that the death penalty in its present application has been discriminatory with respect to the disadvantaged, the indigent and the socially impoverished. Furthermore, recent data from correction sources definitely question the effectiveness of the death penalty as a deterrent to crime."

Additional statements against capital punishment have been issued by Pope John Paul II, numerous bishops and other sources.

**Capital Sins:** Moral faults which, if habitual, give rise to many more sins. They are pride, covetousness, lust, anger, gluttony, envy, sloth.

The opposite virtues are: humility, liberality, chastity, meekness, temperance, brotherly love, diligence.

**Cardinal Virtues:** The four principal moral virtues are prudence, justice, temperance and fortitude.

**Catacombs:** Underground Christian cemeteries in various cities of the Roman Empire and Italy, especially in the vicinity of Rome; the burial sites of many martyrs and other Christians. Developed from aboveground cemeteries, their passageways, burial niches and assembly rooms were dug out of tuffa, a soft clay which hardened into rock-like consistency on drying. The earliest ones date from the third century; in the fourth, they became the scene of memorial services as the veneration of martyrs increased in popularity; in the seventh and eighth centuries, they were plundered by the Lombards and other invaders. The relics of many martyrs were removed to safer places in the ninth century; afterwards, the catacombs fell into neglect and oblivion until interest in them revived in the 16th century. The catacombs have been excavated extensively, yielding considerable information about early Christian symbolism and art, dating from the third century on, and other aspects of Christian life and practice.

**Catechesis:** Religious instruction and formation not only for persons preparing for baptism but also for the faithful in various stages of their spiritual development.

**Catechism:** A summary of Christian doctrine in question and answer form, used for purposes of instruction.

**Catechumen:** A person preparing in a program of instruction and spiritual formation for baptism and reception into the Church. The Church has a special relationship with catechumens. It invites them to lead the life of the Gospel, introduces them to the celebration of the sacred rites, and grants them various prerogatives that are proper to the faithful (one of which is the right to ecclesiastical burial).

**Cathedra:** A Greek word for chair, designating the chair or seat of a bishop in the principal church of his diocese, which is therefore called a cathedral (see separate entry).

**Cathedraticum:** The tax paid to a bishop by all churches and benefices subject to him for the support of episcopal administration and for works of charity.

**Catholic:** A Greek word, meaning universal, first used in the title Catholic Church in a letter written by St. Ignatius of Antioch about 107 to the Christians of Smyrna.

**Celebret:** A Latin word, meaning Let him celebrate, the name of a letter of recommendation issued by a bishop or other superior stating that a priest is in good standing and therefore eligible to celebrate Mass or perform other priestly functions.

**Celibacy:** The unmarried state of life, required in the Roman Church of candidates for holy orders and of men already ordained to holy orders, for the practice of perfect chastity and total dedication to the service of people in the ministry of the Church. Celibacy is enjoined as a condition for ordination by church discipline and law, not by dogmatic necessity.

In the Roman Church, a consensus in favor of celibacy developed in the early centuries while the clergy included both celibates and men who had been married once. The first local legislation on the subject was enacted by a local council held in Elvira, Spain, about 306; it forbade bishops, priests, deacons and other ministers to have wives. Similar enactments were passed by other local councils from that time on, and by the 12th century particular laws regarded marriage by clerics in major orders to be not only unlawful but also null and void. The latter view was translated by the Second Lateran Council in 1139 into what seems to be the first written universal law making holy orders an invalidating impediment to marriage. In 1563 the Council of Trent ruled definitely on the matter and established the discipline in force in the Roman Church.

Some exceptions to this discipline have been made in recent years. Several married Protestant and Episcopalian (Anglican) clergymen who became converts and were subsequently ordained to the priesthood have been permitted to continue in marriage. Married men over the age of 35 can be ordained to the permanent diaconate.

Eastern Church discipline on celibacy differs from that of the Roman Church. In line with legislation enacted by the Synod of Trullo in 692 and still in force, candidates for holy orders may marry before becoming deacons and may continue in marriage thereafter, but marriage after ordination is forbidden. Eastern-Rite bishops in the U.S., however, do not ordain married candidates for the priesthood. Eastern-Rite bishops are unmarried.

**Cenacle:** The upper room in Jerusalem where Christ ate the Last Supper with his Apostles.

**Censer:** A metal vessel with a perforated cover and suspended by chains, in which incense is burned. It is used at some Masses, Benediction of the Blessed Sacrament and other liturgical functions.

**Censorship of Books:** An exercise of vigilance

by the Church for safeguarding authentic religious teaching.

Pertinent legislation in a decree issued by the Congregation for the Doctrine of the Faith Apr. 9, 1975, is embodied in the Code of Canon Law (Book III, Title IV).

(1) Pre-publication clearance is required for: editions of Sacred Scripture, liturgical texts and books of private devotion, catechisms and other writings relating to catechetical instruction. Books dealing with Scripture, theology, canon law, church history and religious or moral disciplines may not be used as basic texts in educational institutions (from elementary to university levels) unless they have been published with the approval of competent church authority.

(2) Pre-publication clearance is recommended for all books on the aforementioned subjects, even though they are not used as basic texts in teaching.

(3) Books or other writings dealing with religion or morals may not be displayed, sold or given out in churches or oratories unless published with the approval of competent ecclesiastical authority.

(4) Except for a just and reasonable cause, Catholics should not write for newspapers, magazines or periodicals which regularly and openly prove to be inimical to the Catholic religion and good morals. The approval of the local bishop is required before clerics or members of religious institutes (who also need the approval of their superior) may write for such publications.

Permission to publish works of a religious character, together with the apparatus of reviewing them beforehand, falls under the authority of the bishop of the place where the writer lives or where the works are published.

Clearance for publication is usually indicated by the terms *Nihil obstat* (Nothing stands in the way) issued by the censor and *Imprimatur* (Let it be printed) authorized by the bishop; an equivalent statement is, Published with ecclesiastical permission. The clearing of works for publication does not necessarily imply approval of an author's viewpoint or his manner of handling a subject.

**Censures:** Spiritual penalties inflicted by the Church on baptized persons for committing certain serious offenses and for being or remaining obstinate therein. Excommunication (exclusion from the community of the faithful, barring a person from sacramental and other participation in the goods and offices of the community of the Church), suspension (prohibition of a cleric to exercise orders) and interdict (personal or territorial deprivation of the sacraments) have been the censures in force since the time of Innocent III (1214). Their intended purposes are to deter persons from committing sins which, more seriously and openly than others, threaten the common good of the Church and its members; to punish and correct offenders; and to provide for the making of reparation for harm done to the community of the Church. Censures may be incurred automatically (*ipso facto*) on the commission of certain offenses for which fixed penalties have been laid down in church law (*latae sententiae*); or they

may be inflicted by sentence of a judge (*ferendae sententiae*). Automatic excommunication is incurred for the offenses of abortion, apostasy, heresy and schism. Obstinacy in crime — also called contumacy, disregard of a penalty, defiance of church authority — is presumed by law in the commission of offenses for which automatic censures are decreed. The presence and degree of contumacy in other cases, for which judicial sentence is required, is subject to determination by a judge. Absolution can be obtained from any censure, provided the person repents and desists from obstinacy. Absolution may be reserved to the pope, the bishop of a place, or the major superior of an exempt clerical religious institute. In danger of death, any priest can absolve from all censures; in other cases, faculties to absolve from reserved censures can be exercised by competent authorities or given to other priests.

The penal law of the Church is contained in Book VI of the Code of Canon Law.

**Ceremonies, Master of:** One who directs the proceedings of a rite or ceremony during the function.

**Chamberlain:** (1) The Chamberlain of the Holy Roman Church is a cardinal who administers the property and revenues of the Holy See. On the death of the pope he becomes head of the College of Cardinals and summons and directs the conclave until a new pope is elected.

(2) The Chamberlain of the Sacred College of Cardinals has charge of the property and revenues of the College and keeps the record of business transacted in consistories.

(3) The Chamberlain of the Roman Clergy is the president of the secular clergy of Rome.

**Chancellor:** Notary of a diocese, who draws up written documents in the government of the diocese; takes care of, arranges and indexes diocesan archives, records of dispensations and ecclesiastical trials.

**Chancery** (1) A branch of church administration that handles written documents used in the government of a diocese.

(2) The administrative office of a diocese, a bishop's office.

**Chapel:** A building or part of another building used for divine worship; a portion of a church set aside for the celebration of Mass or for some special devotion.

**Chaplain:** A priest appointed for the pastoral service of any division of the armed forces, religious communities, institutions, various groups of the faithful.

**Chaplet:** A term, meaning little crown, applied to a rosary or, more commonly, to a small string of beads used for devotional purposes; e.g., the Infant of Prague chaplet.

**Chapter:** A general meeting of delegates of religious orders for elections and the handling of other important affairs of their communities.

**Charisms:** Gifts or graces given by God to persons for the good of others and the Church. Examples are special gifts for apostolic work, prophecy, healing, discernment of spirits, the life of evangelical poverty, here-and-now witness to faith in various circumstances of life.

The Second Vatican Council made the following statement about charisms in the *Dogmatic Constitution on the Church* (No. 12):

"It is not only through the sacraments and Church ministries that the same Holy Spirit sanctifies and leads the People of God and enriches it with virtues. Allotting his gifts 'to everyone according as he will' (1 Cor. 12:11), he distributes special graces among the faithful of every rank. By these gifts he makes them fit and ready to undertake the various tasks or offices advantageous for the renewal and upbuilding of the Church, according to the words of the Apostle: 'The manifestation of the Spirit is given to everyone for profit' (1 Cor. 12:7). These charismatic gifts, whether they be the most outstanding or the more simple and widely diffused, are to be received with thanksgiving and consolation, for they are exceedingly suitable and useful for the needs of the Church.

"Still, extraordinary gifts are not to be rashly sought after, nor are the fruits of apostolic labor to be presumptuously expected from them. In any case, judgment as to their genuineness and proper use belongs to those who preside over the Church, and to whose special competence it belongs, not indeed to extinguish the Spirit, but to test all things and hold fast to that which is good" (cf. 1 Thes. 5:12; 19-21).

**Charity:** Love of God above all things for his own sake, and love of one's neighbor as oneself because and as an expression of one's love for God; the greatest of the three theological virtues. The term is sometimes also used to designate sanctifying grace.

**Chastity:** Properly ordered behavior with respect to sex. In marriage, the exercise of the procreative power is integrated with the norms and purposes of marriage. Outside of marriage, the rule is self-denial of the voluntary exercise and enjoyment of the procreative faculty in thought, word or action.

The vow of chastity, which reinforces the virtue of chastity with the virtue of religion, is an evangelical counsel and one of the three vows professed by Religious.

**Chirograph or Autograph Letter:** A letter written by a pope himself, in his own handwriting.

**Christ:** The title of Jesus, derived from the Greek translation *Christos* of the Hebrew term *Messiah*, meaning the Anointed of God, the Savior and Deliverer of his people. Christian use of the title is a confession of belief that Jesus is the Savior.

**Christianity:** The sum total of things related to belief in Christ — the Christian religion, Christian churches, Christians themselves, society based on and expressive of Christian beliefs, culture reflecting Christian values.

**Christians:** The name first applied about the year 43 to followers of Christ at Antioch, the capital of Syria. It was used by the pagans as a contemptuous term. The word applies to persons who profess belief in the divinity and teachings of Christ and who give witness to him in life.

**Christian Science:** A religious doctrine consisting of Mary Baker Eddy's interpretation and formulation of the actions and teachings of Christ. Its basic tenets reflect Mrs. Eddy's ideas regarding the reality of spirit and its control and domination of what is not spirit. The basic statement of the doctrine is contained in *Science and Health, with Key to the Scriptures,* which she first published in 1875, nine years after being saved from death and healed on reading the New Testament.

Mary Baker Eddy (1821-1910) established the church in 1879, and in 1892 founded at Boston the First Church of Christ, Scientist, of which all other Christian Science churches are branches. The individual churches are self-governing and self-supporting under the general supervision of a board of directors. Services consist of readings of portions of Scripture and *Science and Health.* One of the church's publications, *The Christian Science Monitor,* has a worldwide reputation as a journal of news and opinion.

**Church:** (1) See several entries under Church, Catholic. The universal Church is the Church spread throughout the world. The local Church is the Church in a particular locality; e.g., a diocese. The Church embraces all of its members — on earth, in heaven, in purgatory.

(2) In general, any religious body.

(3) A building set aside and dedicated for divine worship.

**Circumcision:** A ceremonial practice symbolic of initiation and participation in the covenant between God and Abraham.

**Circumincession:** The indwelling of each divine Person of the Holy Trinity in the others.

**Clergy:** Men commissioned for sacred ministries and assigned to pastoral and other duties for the service of the people and the Church.

(1) Diocesan or secular clergy are committed to pastoral ministry in parishes and in other capacities in a particular church (diocese) under the direction of their bishop, to whom they are bound by a promise of obedience.

(2) Regular clergy belong to religious institutes (orders, congregations, societies — institutes of consecrated life) and are so called because they observe the rule (*regula,* in Latin) of their respective institutes. They are committed to the ways of life and apostolates of their institutes. In ordinary pastoral ministry, they are under the direction of local bishops as well as their own superiors.

**Clericalism:** A term generally used in a derogatory sense to mean action, influence and interference by the Church and the clergy in matters with which they allegedly should not be concerned. Anticlericalism is a reaction of antipathy, hostility, distrust and opposition to the Church and clergy arising from real and/or alleged faults of the clergy, overextension of the role of the laity, or for other reasons.

**Cloister:** Part of a monastery, convent or other house of religious reserved for use by members of the institute. Houses of contemplative Religious have a strict enclosure.

**Code:** A digest of rules or regulations, such as the Code of Canon Law.

**Collegiality:** The bishops of the Church, in union with and subordinate to the pope — who has full, supreme and universal power over the Church which he can always exercise independently — have supreme teaching and pastoral authority over the whole Church. In addition to their proper authority of office for the good of the faithful in their respective dioceses or other jurisdictions, the bishops have authority to act for the good of the universal Church. This collegial authority is exercised in a solemn manner in an ecumenical council and can also be exercised in other ways sanctioned by the pope. Doctrine on collegiality was set forth by the Second Vatican Council in the *Dogmatic Constitution on the Church.* (See separate entry.)

By extension, the concept of collegiality is applied to other forms of participation and co-responsibility by members of a community.

**Commissariat of the Holy Land:** A special jurisdiction within the Order of Friars Minor, whose main purposes are the collecting of alms for support of the Holy Places in Palestine and staffing of the Holy Places and missions in the Middle East with priests and brothers. There are about 70 such commissariats in more than 30 countries. One of them has headquarters at Mt. St. Sepulchre, Washington, D.C. Franciscans have had custody of the Holy Places since 1342.

**Communion of Faithful, Saints:** The communion of all the People of God — on earth, in heavenly glory, in purgatory — with Christ and each other in faith, grace, prayer and good works.

**Concelebration:** The liturgical act in which several priests, led by one member of the group, offer Mass together, all consecrating the bread and wine. Concelebration has always been common in churches of Eastern Rite. In the Roman Rite, it was long restricted, taking place only at the ordination of bishops and the ordination of priests. The *Constitution on the Sacred Liturgy* issued by the Second Vatican Council set new norms for concelebration, which is now relatively common in the Roman Rite.

**Concordance, Biblical:** An alphabetical verbal index enabling a user knowing one or more words of a scriptural passage to locate the entire text.

**Concordat:** A Church-state treaty with the force of law concerning matters of mutual concern — e.g., rights of the Church, arrangement of ecclesiastical jurisdictions, marriage laws, education. Approximately 150 agreements of this kind have been negotiated since the Concordat of Worms in 1122.

**Concupiscence:** Any tendency of the sensitive appetite. The term is most frequently used in reference to desires and tendencies for sinful sense pleasure.

**Confession:** Sacramental confession is the act by which a person tells or confesses his sins to a priest who is authorized to give absolution in the sacrament of penance.

**Confessor:** A priest who administers the sacrament of penance.

The title of confessor, formerly given to a category of male saints, was suppressed with publication of the calendar reform of 1969.

**Confraternity:** An association whose members practice a particular form of religious devotion and/or are engaged in some kind of apostolic work.

**Conscience:** Practical judgment concerning the moral goodness or sinfulness of an action. In the Catholic view, this judgment is made by reference of the action, its attendant circumstances and the intentions of the person to the requirements of moral law as expressed in the Ten Commandments, the summary law of love for God and neighbor, the life and teaching of Christ, and the authoritative teaching and practice of the Church with respect to the total demands of divine Revelation.

A person is obliged: (1) to obey a certain and correct conscience; (2) to obey a certain conscience even if it is inculpably erroneous; (3) not to obey, but to correct, a conscience known to be erroneous or lax; (4) to rectify a scrupulous conscience by following the advice of a confessor and by other measures; (5) to resolve doubts of conscience before acting.

It is legitimate to act for solid and probable reasons when a question of moral responsibility admits of argument (see Probabilism).

**Conscience, Examination of:** Self-examination to determine one's spiritual state before God, regarding one's sins and faults. It is recommended as a regular practice and is practically necessary in preparing for the sacrament of penance. The *particular examen* is a regular examination to assist in overcoming specific faults and imperfections.

**Consistory:** An assembly of cardinals presided over by the pope.

**Constitution:** (1) An apostolic or papal constitution is a document in which a pope enacts and promulgates law.

(2) A formal and solemn document issued by an ecumenical council on a doctrinal or pastoral subject, with binding force in the whole Church; e.g., the four constitutions issued by the Second Vatican Council on the Church, liturgy, Revelation, and the Church in the modern world.

(3) The constitutions of institutes of consecrated life and societies of apostolic life spell out details of and norms drawn from the various rules for the guidance and direction of the life and work of their members.

**Consubstantiation:** A theory which holds that the Body and Blood of Christ coexist with the substance of bread and wine in the Holy Eucharist. This theory, also called *impanation,* is incompatible with the doctrine of transubstantiation.

**Contraception:** Anything done by positive interference to prevent sexual intercourse from resulting in conception. Direct contraception is against the order of nature. Indirect contraception — as a secondary effect of medical treatment or other action having a necessary, good, non-contraceptive purpose — is permissible under the principle of the double effect. The practice of periodic continence is not contraception because it does not involve positive interference with the order of nature.

**Contrition:** Sorrow for sin coupled with a purpose of amendment. Contrition arising from a supernatural motive is necessary for the forgiveness of sin.

(1) Perfect contrition is total sorrow for and renunciation of attachment to sin, arising from the motive of pure love of God. Perfect contrition, which implies the intention of doing all God wants done for the forgiveness of sin (including confession in a reasonable period of time), is sufficient for the forgiveness of serious sin and the remission of all temporal punishment due for sin. (The intention to receive the sacrament of penance is implicit — even if unrealized, as in the case of some persons — in perfect contrition.)

(2) Imperfect contrition or attrition is sorrow arising from a quasi-selfish supernatural motive; e.g., the fear of losing heaven, suffering the pains of hell, etc. Imperfect contrition is sufficient for the forgiveness of serious sin when joined with absolution in confession, and sufficient for the forgiveness of venial sin even outside of confession.

**Contumely:** Personal insult, reviling a person in his presence by accusation of moral faults, by refusal of recognition or due respect; a violation of obligations of justice and charity.

**Corporal Works of Mercy:** Feeding the hungry, giving drink to the thirsty, clothing the naked, visiting the imprisoned, sheltering the homeless, visiting the sick, burying the dead.

**Council, Plenary:** A council held for the particular churches belonging to the same episcopal conference. Such a council can be convoked to take action related to the pastoral activity and mission of the Church in the territory. The membership of such councils is fixed by canon law; their decrees, when approved by the Holy See, are binding in the territory (see Index, Plenary Councils of Baltimore).

**Councils:** Bodies representative of various categories of members of the Church which participate with bishops and other church authorities in making decisions and carrying out action programs for the good of the Church and the accomplishment of its mission to its own members and society in general. Examples are priests' senates or councils, councils of Religious and lay persons, parish councils, diocesan pastoral councils.

**Councils, Provincial:** Meetings of the bishops of a province. The metropolitan, or ranking archbishop, of an ecclesiastical province convenes and presides over such councils in a manner prescribed by canon law to take action related to the life and mission of the Church in the province. Acts and decrees must be approved by the Holy See before being promulgated.

**Counsels, Evangelical:** Gospel counsels of perfection, especially voluntary poverty, perfect chastity and obedience, which were recommended by Christ to those who would devote themselves exclusively and completely to the immediate service of God. Religious (members of institutes of consecrated life) bind themselves by public vows to observe these counsels in a life of total consecration to God and service to people through various kinds of apostolic works.

**Counter-Reformation:** The period of approximately 100 years following the Council of Trent, which witnessed a reform within the Church to stimulate genuine Catholic life and to counteract effects of the Reformation.

**Covenant:** A bond of relationship between parties pledged to each other. God-initiated covenants in the Old Testament included those with Abraham, Noah, Moses, Levi, David. The Mosaic (Sinai) covenant made Israel God's Chosen People on terms of fidelity to true faith, true worship, and righteous conduct according to the Decalogue. The New Testament covenant, prefigured in the Old Testament, is the bond persons have with God through Christ. All persons are called to be parties to this perfect and everlasting covenant, which was mediated and ratified by Christ. The marriage covenant seals the closest possible relationship between a man and a woman.

**Creation:** The production by God of something out of nothing. The biblical account of creation is contained in the first two chapters of Genesis.

**Creator:** God, the supreme, self-existing Being, the absolute and infinite First Cause of all things.

**Creature:** Everything in the realm of being is a creature, except God.

**Cremation:** The reduction of a human corpse to ashes by means of fire. Cremation is not in line with Catholic tradition and practice, even though it is not opposed to any article of faith.

The Congregation for the Doctrine of the Faith, under date of May 8, 1963, circulated among bishops an instruction which upheld the traditional practices of Christian burial but modified anti-cremation legislation. Cremation may be permitted for serious reasons, of a private as well as public nature, provided it does not involve any contempt of the Church or of religion, or any attempt to deny, question, or belittle the doctrine of the resurrection of the body. The person may receive the last rites and be given ecclesiastical burial. A priest may say prayers for the deceased at the crematorium, but full liturgical ceremonies may not take place there.

The principal reason behind an earlier prohibition against cremation was the fact that, historically, the practice had represented an attempt to deny the doctrine of the resurrection of the body.

(See Burial, Ecclesiastical.)

**Crib:** A devotional representation of the birth of Jesus. The custom of erecting cribs is generally attributed to St. Francis of Assisi who in 1223 obtained from Pope Honorius III permission to use a crib and figures of the Christ Child, Mary, St. Joseph, and others, to represent the mystery of the Nativity.

**Crosier:** The bishop's staff, symbolic of his pastoral office, responsibility and authority.

**Crypt:** An underground or partly underground chamber; e.g., the lower part of a church used for worship and/or burial.

**Cura Animarum:** A Latin phrase, meaning care

of souls, designating the pastoral ministry and responsibility of bishops and priests.

**Curia:** The personnel and offices through which (1) the pope administers the affairs of the universal Church, the *Roman Curia* (see separate entry), or (2) a bishop the affairs of a diocese, *diocesan curia*. The principal officials of a diocesan curia are the vicar general of the diocese, the chancellor, officials of the diocesan tribunal or court, examiners, consultors, auditors, notaries.

**Custos:** A religious superior who presides over a number of convents collectively called a custody. In some institutes of consecrated life a custos may be the deputy of a higher superior.

# D

**Deaconess:** A woman officially appointed and charged by the Church to carry out service-like functions. Phoebe apparently was one (Rom. 16:1-2); a second probable reference to the office is in Tm. 3:11.

The office — for assistance at the baptism of women, for pastoral service to women and for works of charity — had considerable development in the third and also in the fourth century when the actual term came into use (in place of such designations as *diacona, vidua, virgo canonica*). Its importance declined subsequently with the substitution of infusion in place of immersion as the common method of baptism in the West, and with the increase of the practice of infant baptism. There is no record of the ministry of deaconess in the West after the beginning of the 11th century. The office continued, however, for a longer time in the East.

The Vatican's Theological Commission, in a paper prepared in 1971, noted that there had been in the past a form of diaconal ordination for women. With a rite and purpose distinctive to women, it differed essentially from the ordination of deacons, which had sacramental effects.

Several Christian churches have had revivals of the office of deaconess since the 1830s. There is a contemporary movement in support of such a revival among some Catholics.

**Dean:** (1) A priest with supervisory responsibility over a section of a diocese known as a deanery. The post-Vatican II counterpart of a dean is an episcopal vicar.

(2) The senior or ranking member of a group.

**Dean of the Sacred College:** The president of the College of Cardinals (the ranking cardinal bishop).

**Decision:** A judgment or pronouncement on a cause or suit, given by a church tribunal or official with judicial authority. A decision has the force of law for concerned parties.

**Declaration:** (1) An ecclesiastical document which presents an interpretation of an existing law.

(2) A position paper on a specific subject; e.g., the three declarations issued by the Second Vatican Council on religious freedom, non-Christian religions, and Christian education.

**Decree:** An edict or ordinance issued by a pope and/or by an ecumenical council, with binding force in the whole Church; by a department of the Roman Curia, with binding force for concerned parties; by a territorial body of bishops, with binding force for persons in the area; by individual bishops, with binding force for concerned parties until revocation or the death of the bishop.

The nine decrees issued by the Second Vatican Council were combinations of doctrinal and pastoral statements with executive orders for action and movement toward renewal and reform in the Church.

**Dedication of a Church:** The ceremony whereby a church is solemnly set apart for the worship of God. The custom of dedicating churches had an antecedent in Old Testament ceremonies for the dedication of the Temple, as in the times of Solomon and the Maccabees. The earliest extant record of the dedication of a Christian church dates from early in the fourth century, when it was done simply by the celebration of Mass. Other ceremonies developed later. A church can be dedicated by a simple blessing or a solemn consecration. The rite of consecration is generally performed by a bishop.

**Deism:** A system of natural religion which acknowledges the existence of God but regards him as so transcendent and remote from man and the universe that divine revelation and the supernatural order of things are irrelevant and unacceptable. It developed from rationalistic principles in England in the 17th and 18th centuries, and had Voltaire, Rousseau and the Encyclopedists among its advocates in France.

**Despair:** Abandonment of hope for salvation arising from the conviction that God will not provide the necessary means for attaining it, that following God's way of life for salvation is impossible, or that one's sins are unforgivable; a serious sin against the Holy Spirit and the theological virtues of hope and faith, involving distrust in the mercy and goodness of God and a denial of the truths that God wills the salvation of all persons and provides sufficient grace for it. Real despair is distinguished from unreasonable fear with respect to the difficulties of attaining salvation, from morbid anxiety over the demands of divine justice, and from feelings of despair.

**Detachment:** Control of affection for creatures by two principles: (1) supreme love and devotion belong to God; (2) love and service of creatures should be an expression of love for God.

**Detraction:** Revelation of true but hidden faults of a person without sufficient and justifying reason; a violation of requirements of justice and charity, involving the obligation to make restitution when this is possible without doing more harm to the good name of the offended party. In some cases, e.g., to prevent evil, secret faults may and should be disclosed.

**Devil:** (1) Lucifer, Satan, chief of the fallen angels who sinned and were banished from heaven. Still possessing angelic powers, he can cause such diabolical phenomena as possession and obsession, and can tempt men to sin.

(2) Any fallen angel.

**Devotion:** (1) Religious fervor, piety; dedication.

(2) The consolation experienced at times during prayer; a reverent manner of praying.

**Devotions:** Pious practices of members of the Church include not only participation in various acts of the liturgy but also in other acts of worship generally called popular or private devotions. Concerning these, the Second Vatican Council said in the *Constitution on the Sacred Liturgy* (No. 13): "Popular devotions of the Christian people are warmly commended, provided they accord with the laws and norms of the Church. Such is especially the case with devotions called for by the Apostolic See. Devotions proper to the individual churches also have a special dignity. . . . These devotions should be so drawn up that they harmonize with the liturgical seasons, accord with the sacred liturgy, are in some fashion derived from it, and lead the people to it, since the liturgy by its very nature far surpasses any of them."

Devotions of a liturgical type are Exposition of the Blessed Sacrament, recitation of Evening Prayer and Night Prayer of the Liturgy of the Hours. Examples of paraliturgical devotion are a Bible Service or Vigil, and the Angelus, Rosary and Stations of the Cross, which have a strong scriptural basis.

**Diocese:** A particular church, a fully organized ecclesiastical jurisdiction under the pastoral direction of a bishop as local Ordinary.

**Discalced:** Of Latin derivation and meaning without shoes, the word is applied to religious orders or congregations whose members go barefoot or wear sandals.

**Disciple:** A term used sometimes in reference to the Apostles but more often to a larger number of followers (70 or 72) of Christ mentioned in Lk. 10:1.

**Disciplina Arcani:** A Latin phrase, meaning discipline of the secret and referring to a practice of the early Church, especially during the Roman persecutions, to: (1) conceal Christian truths from those who, it was feared, would misinterpret, ridicule and profane the teachings, and persecute Christians for believing them; (2) instruct catechumens in a gradual manner, withholding the teaching of certain doctrines until the catechumens proved themselves of good faith and sufficient understanding.

**Dispensation:** The relaxation of a law in a particular case. Laws made for the common good sometimes work undue hardship in particular cases. In such cases, where sufficient reasons are present, dispensations may be granted by proper authorities. Bishops, religious superiors and others may dispense from certain laws; the pope can dispense from all ecclesiastical laws. No one has authority to dispense from obligations of the divine law.

**Divination:** Attempting to foretell future or hidden things by means of things like dreams, necromancy, spiritism, examination of entrails, astrology, augury, omens, palmistry, drawing straws, dice, cards, etc. Practices like these attribute to creatural things a power which belongs to God alone and are violations of the First Commandment.

**Divine Praises:** Fourteen praises recited or sung at Benediction of the Blessed Sacrament in reparation for sins of sacrilege, blasphemy and profanity. Some of these praises date from the end of the 18th century.

Blessed be God. / Blessed be his holy Name. / Blessed be Jesus Christ, true God and true Man. / Blessed be the Name of Jesus. / Blessed be his most Sacred Heart. / Blessed be his most Precious Blood. / Blessed be Jesus in the most holy Sacrament of the Altar. / Blessed be the Holy Spirit, the Paraclete. / Blessed be the great Mother of God, Mary most holy. / Blessed be her holy and Immaculate Conception. / Blessed be her glorious Assumption. / Blessed be the name of Mary, Virgin and Mother. / Blessed be St. Joseph, her most chaste Spouse. / Blessed be God in his Angels and in his Saints.

**Double Effect Principle:** Actions sometimes have two effects closely related to each other, one good and the other bad, and a difficult moral question can arise: Is it permissible to place an action from which two such results follow? It is permissible to place the action, if: the action is good in itself and is directly productive of the good effect; the circumstances are good; the intention of the person is good; the reason for placing the action is proportionately serious to the seriousness of the indirect bad effect. For example: Is it morally permissible for a pregnant woman to undergo medical or surgical treatment for a pathological condition if the indirect and secondary effect of the treatment will be the loss of the child? The reply is affirmative, for these reasons: The action, i.e., the treatment, is good in itself, cannot be deferred until a later time without very serious consequences, and is ordered directly to the cure of critically grave pathology. By means of the treatment, the woman intends to save her life, which she has a right to do. The loss of the child is not directly sought as a means for the cure of the mother but results indirectly and in a secondary manner from the placing of the action, i.e., the treatment, which is good in itself.

The double effect principle does not support the principle that the end justifies the means.

**Doxology:** (1) The lesser doxology, or ascription of glory to the Trinity, is the Glory be to the Father. The first part dates back to the third or fourth century, and came from the form of baptism. The concluding words, As it was in the beginning, etc., are of later origin.

(2) The greater doxology, Glory to God in the highest, begins with the words of angelic praise at the birth of Christ recounted in the Infancy Narrative (Lk. 2:14). It is often recited at Mass. Of early Eastern origin, it is found in the *Apostolic Constitutions* in a form much like the present.

(3) The formula of praise at the end of the Eucharistic Prayer at Mass, sung or said by the celebrant while he holds aloft the paten containing the consecrated host in one hand and the chalice containing the consecrated wine in the other.

**Dulia:** A Greek term meaning the veneration or

homage, different in nature and degree from that given to God, paid to the saints. It includes honoring the saints and seeking their intercession with God.

**Duty:** A moral obligation deriving from the binding force of law, the exigencies of one's state in life, and other sources.

## E

**Easter Controversy:** A three-phase controversy over the time for the celebration of Easter.

Some early Christians in the Near East, called Quartodecimans, favored the observance of Easter on the 14th day of Nisan, the spring month of the Hebrew calendar, whenever it occurred. Against this practice, Pope St. Victor I, about 190, ordered a Sunday observance of the feast.

The Council of Nicaea, in line with usages of the Church at Rome and Alexandria, decreed in 325 that Easter should be observed on the first Sunday following the first full moon of spring.

Uniformity of practice in the West was not achieved until several centuries later, when the British Isles, in delayed compliance with measures enacted by the Synod of Whitby in 664, accepted the Roman date of observance.

Unrelated to the controversy is the fact that some Eastern Christians, in accordance with traditional calendar practices, celebrate Easter at a different time than the Roman and Eastern-Rite churches.

**Easter Duty:** The serious obligation binding Catholics of Roman Rite, by a precept of the Church, to receive Holy Communion during the Easter time.

**Easter Water:** Holy water blessed with special ceremonies and distributed on the Easter Vigil; used during Easter Week for blessing the faithful and homes.

**Ecclesiology:** Study of the nature, constitution, members, mission, functions, etc., of the Church.

**Ecstasy:** An extraordinary state of mystical experience in which a person is so absorbed in God that the activity of the exterior senses is suspended.

**Ecumenism:** The movement of Christians and their churches toward the unity willed by Christ. The Second Vatican Council called the movement "those activities and enterprises which, according to various needs of the Church and opportune occasions, are started and organized for the fostering of unity among Christians" (*Decree on Ecumenism,* No. 4). Spiritual ecumenism, i.e., mutual prayer for unity, is the heart of the movement. The movement also involves scholarly and pew-level efforts for the development of mutual understanding and better interfaith relations in general, and collaboration by the churches and their members in the social area.

**Elevation:** The raising of the host after consecration at Mass for adoration by the faithful. The custom was introduced in the Diocese of Paris about the close of the 12th century to offset an erroneous teaching of the time which held that transubstantiation of the bread did not take place until after the consecration of the wine in the chalice.

The elevation of the chalice following the consecration of the wine was introduced in the 15th century.

**End Justifies the Means:** An unacceptable ethical principle which states that evil means may be used to produce good effects.

**Envy:** Sadness over another's good fortune because it is considered a loss to oneself or a detraction from one's own excellence; one of the seven capital sins, a violation of the obligations of charity.

**Epikeia:** A Greek word meaning reasonableness and designating a moral theory and practice, a mild interpretation of the mind of a legislator who is prudently considered not to wish positive law to bind in certain circumstances. Use of the principle is justified in practice when the lawgiver himself cannot be appealed to and when it can be prudently assumed that in particular cases, e.g., because of special hardship, he would not wish the law to be applied in a strict manner. Epikeia may not be applied with respect to acts that are intrinsically wrong or those covered by laws which automatically make them invalid.

**Episcopate:** (1) The office, dignity and sacramental powers bestowed upon a bishop at his ordination.

(2) The body of bishops collectively.

**Equivocation:** (1) The use of words, phrases, or gestures having more than one meaning in order to conceal information which a questioner has no strict right to know. It is permissible to equivocate (have a broad mental reservation) in some circumstances.

(2) A lie, i.e., a statement of untruth. Lying is intrinsically wrong. A lie told in joking, evident as such, is not wrong.

**Eschatology:** Doctrine concerning the last things: death, judgment, heaven and hell, and the final state of perfection of the people and kingdom of God at the end of time.

**Eternity:** The interminable, perfect possession of life in its totality without beginning or end; an attribute of God, who has no past or future but always is. Man's existence has a beginning but no end and is, accordingly, called immortal.

**Ethics:** Moral philosophy, the science of the morality of human acts deriving from natural law, the natural end of man, and the powers of human reason. It includes all the spheres of human activity — personal, social, economic, political, etc. Ethics is distinct from but can be related to moral theology, whose primary principles are drawn from divine revelation.

**Eucharistic Congresses:** Public demonstrations of faith in the Holy Eucharist. Combining liturgical services, other public ceremonies, subsidiary meetings, different kinds of instructional and inspirational elements, they are unified by central themes and serve to increase understanding of and devotion to Christ in the Eucharist, and to relate this liturgy of worship and witness to life.

The first international congress developed from a proposal by Marie Marthe Tamisier of Touraine, organizing efforts of Msgr. Louis Gaston de Segur, and backing by industrialist Philibert Vrau. It was held with the approval of Pope Leo XIII at the University of Lille, France, and was attended by some 800 persons from France, Belgium, Holland, England, Spain and Switzerland.

International congresses are planned and held under the auspices of a permanent committee for international Eucharistic congresses. Participants include clergy, religious and lay persons from many countries, and representatives of national and international Catholic organizations. Popes have usually been represented by legates, but Paul VI attended two congresses personally, the 38th at Bombay and the 39th at Bogota.

Forty-two international congresses were held from 1881 to 1981:

Lille (1881), Avignon (1882), Liege (1883), Freiburg (1885), Toulouse (1886), Paris (1888), Antwerp (1890), Jerusalem (1893), Rheims (1894), Paray-le-Monial (1897), Brussels (1898), Lourdes (1899), Angers (1901), Namur (1902), Angouleme (1904), Rome (1905), Tournai (1906), Metz (1907), London (1908), Cologne (1909), Montreal (1910), Madrid (1911), Vienna (1912), Malta (1913), Lourdes (1914), Rome (1922), Amsterdam (1924), Chicago (1926), Sydney (1928), Carthage (1930), Dublin (1932), Buenos Aires (1934), Manila (1937), Budapest (1938), Barcelona (1952), Rio de Janeiro (1955), Munich, Germany (1960), Bombay, India (1964), Bogota, Colombia (1968), Melbourne, Australia (1973), Philadelphia (1976), Lourdes (1981). The 43rd international congress will be held in 1985 in Nairobi, Kenya.

**Eugenics:** The science of heredity and environment for the physical and mental improvement of offspring. Extreme eugenics is untenable in practice because it advocates immoral means, such as compulsory breeding of the select, sterilization of persons said to be unfit, abortion, and unacceptable methods of birth regulation.

**Euthanasia:** Mercy killing, the direct causing of death for the purpose of ending human suffering. Euthanasia is murder and is totally illicit, for the natural law forbids the direct taking of one's own life or that of an innocent person.

The use of drugs to relieve suffering in serious cases, even when this results in a shortening of life as an indirect and secondary effect, is permissible under conditions of the double effect principle. It is also permissible for a seriously ill person to refuse to follow — or for other responsible persons to refuse to permit — extraordinary medical procedures even though the refusal might entail shortening of life.

**Evolution:** Scientific theory concerning the development of the physical universe from unorganized matter (inorganic evolution) and, especially, the development of existing forms of vegetable, animal and human life from earlier and more primitive organisms (organic evolution). Various ideas about evolution were advanced for some centuries before scientific evidence in support of the main-line theory of organic evolution, which has several formulations, was discovered and verified in the second half of the 19th century and afterwards. This evidence — from the findings of comparative anatomy and other sciences — confirmed evolution within species and cleared the way to further investigation of questions regarding the processes of its accomplishment. While a number of such questions remain open with respect to human evolution, a point of doctrine not open to question is the immediate creation of the human soul by God.

For some time, theologians regarded the theory with hostility, considering it to be in opposition to the account of creation in the early chapters of Genesis and subversive of belief in such doctrines as creation, the early state of man in grace, and the fall of man from grace. This state of affairs and the tension it generated led to considerable controversy regarding an alleged conflict between religion and science. Gradually, however, the tension was diminished with the development of biblical studies from the latter part of the 19th century onwards, with clarification of the distinctive features of religious truth and scientific truth, and with the refinement of evolutionary concepts.

So far as the Genesis account of creation is concerned, the Catholic view is that the writer(s) did not write as a scientist but as the communicator of religious truth in a manner adapted to the understanding of the people of his time. He used anthropomorphic language, the figure of days and other literary devices to state the salvation truths of creation, the fall of man from grace, and the promise of redemption. It was beyond the competency and purpose of the writer(s) to describe creation and related events in a scientific manner.

**Excommunication:** A penalty or censure by which a baptized person is excluded from the communion of the faithful, for committing and remaining obstinate in certain serious offenses specified in canon law. As by baptism a person is made a member of the Church in which there is a communication of spiritual goods, so by excommunication he is deprived of the same spiritual goods until he repents and receives absolution. Even though excommunicated, a person is still responsible for fulfillment of the normal obligations of a Catholic. (See Censures).

**Exposition of the Blessed Sacrament:** "In churches where the Eucharist is regularly reserved, it is recommended that solemn exposition of the Blessed Sacrament for an extended period of time should take place once a year, even though the period is not strictly continuous. . . . Shorter expositions of the Eucharist (**Benediction**) are to be arranged in such a way that the blessing with the Eucharist is preceded by a reasonable time for readings of the word of God, songs, prayers and a period for silent prayer." So stated Vatican directives issued in 1973.

**Existentialism:** A philosophy with radical concern for the problems of individual existence and identity viewed in particular here-and-now patterns of thought which presuppose irrationality and absurdity in human life and the whole universe. It is preoccupied with questions about freedom, moral decision and responsibility against a background of denial of objective truth and universal norms of conduct; is characterized by prevailing anguish, dread, fear, pessimism, despair; is generally atheistic, although its modern originator, Soren Kierkegaard (d. 1855), and Gabriel Marcel (d. 1973) attempted to give it a Christian orientation. Pius XII called it "the new erroneous philosophy which, opposing itself to idealism, immanentism and pragmatism, has assumed the name of existentialism, since it concerns itself only with the existence of individual things and neglects all consideration of their immutable essences" (Encyclical *Humani Generis*, Aug. 12, 1950).

**Exorcism:** (1) Driving out evil spirits; a rite in which evil spirits are charged and commanded on the authority of God and with the prayer of the Church to depart from a person or to cease causing harm to a person suffering from diabolical possession or obsession. The sacramental is officially administered by a priest delegated for the purpose by the bishop of the place. Elements of the rite include the Litany of Saints; recitation of the Our Father, one or more creeds, and other prayers; specific prayers of exorcism; the reading of Gospel passages and use of the Sign of the Cross. Private exorcism for the liberation of a person from the strong influence of evil spirits, through prayer and the use of sacramentals like holy water, can be done by anyone.

(2) Exorcisms which do not imply the conditions of either diabolical possession or obsession form part of the ceremony of baptism, and are also included in formulas for various blessings; e.g., of water.

# F

**Faculties:** Grants of jurisdiction or authority by the law of the Church or superiors (pope, bishop, religious superior) for exercise of the powers of holy orders; e.g., priests are given faculties to hear confessions, officiate at weddings; bishops are given faculties to grant dispensations, etc.

**Faith:** In religion, faith has several aspects. Catholic doctrine calls faith the assent of the mind to truths revealed by God, the assent being made with the help of grace and by command of the will on account of the authority and trustworthiness of God revealing. The term faith also refers to the truths that are believed (content of faith) and to the way in which a person, in response to Christ, gives witness to and expresses belief in daily life (living faith).

All of these elements, and more, are included in the following statement:

" 'The obedience of faith' (Rom. 16:26; 1:5; 2 Cor. 10:5-6) must be given to God who reveals, an obedience by which man entrusts his whole self freely to God, offering 'the full submission of intellect and will to God who reveals' (First Vatican Council, *Dogmatic Constitution on the Catholic Faith,* Chap. 3), and freely assenting to the truth revealed by him. If this faith is to be shown, the grace of God and the interior help of the Holy Spirit must precede and assist, moving the heart and turning it to God, opening the eyes of the mind, and giving 'joy and ease to everyone in assenting to the truth and believing it' " (Second Council of Orange, Canon 7) (Second Vatican Council, *Constitution on Revelation,* No. 5). Faith is necessary for salvation.

**Faith, Rule of:** The norm or standard of religious belief. The Catholic doctrine is that belief must be professed in the divinely revealed truths in the Bible and tradition as interpreted and proposed by the infallible teaching authority of the Church.

**Fast, Eucharistic:** Abstinence from food and drink, except water and medicine, is required for one hour before the reception of the Eucharist. Persons who are advanced in age or suffer from infirmity or illness, together with those who care for them, can receive Holy Communion even if they have not abstained from food and drink for an hour.

A priest celebrating two or three Masses on the same day can eat and drink something before the second or third Mass without regard for the hour limit.

**Father:** A title of priests, who are regarded as spiritual fathers because they are the ordinary ministers of baptism, by which persons are born to supernatural life, and because of their pastoral service to people.

**Fear:** A mental state caused by the apprehension of present or future danger. Grave fear does not necessarily remove moral responsibility for an act, but may lessen it.

**First Friday:** A devotion consisting of the reception of Holy Communion on the first Friday of nine consecutive months in honor of the Sacred Heart of Jesus and in reparation for sin. (See Sacred Heart, Promises.)

**First Saturday:** A devotion tracing its origin to the apparitions of the Blessed Virgin Mary at Fatima in 1917. Those practicing the devotion go to confession and, on the first Saturday of five consecutive months, receive Holy Communion, recite five decades of the Rosary, and meditate on the mysteries for 15 minutes.

**Fisherman's Ring:** A signet ring engraved with the image of St. Peter fishing from a boat, and encircled with the name of the reigning pope. It is not worn by the pope. It is used to seal briefs, and is destroyed after each pope's death.

**Forgiveness of Sin:** Catholics believe that sins are forgiven by God through the mediation of Christ in view of the repentance of the sinner and by means of the sacrament of penance. (See Penance, Contrition.)

**Fortitude:** Courage to face dangers or hardships for the sake of what is good; one of the four cardinal virtues and one of the seven gifts of the Holy Spirit.

**Fortune Telling:** Attempting to predict the future or the occult by means of cards, palm reading, etc.; a form of divination, prohibited by the First Commandment.

**Forty Hours Devotion:** A Eucharistic observance consisting of solemn exposition of the Blessed Sacrament coupled with special Masses and forms of prayer, for the purposes of making reparation for sin and praying for God's blessings of grace and peace. The devotion was instituted in 1534 in Milan. St. John Neumann of Philadelphia was the first bishop in the U.S. to prescribe its observance in his diocese. For many years in this country, the observance was held annually on a rotating basis in all parishes of a diocese. Simplified and abbreviated Eucharistic observances have taken the place of the devotion in some places.

**Forum:** The sphere in which ecclesiastical authority or jurisdiction is exercised.

(1) External: Authority is exercised in the external forum to deal with matters affecting the public welfare of the Church and its members. Those who have such authority because of their office (e.g., diocesan bishops) are called ordinaries.

(2) Internal: Authority is exercised in the internal forum to deal with matters affecting the private spiritual good of individuals. The sacramental forum is the sphere in which the sacrament of penance is administered; other exercises of jurisdiction in the internal forum take place in the non-sacramental forum.

**Franciscan Crown:** A seven-decade rosary used to commemorate the seven Joys of the Blessed Virgin: the Annunciation, the Visitation, the Nativity of Our Lord, the Adoration of the Magi, the Finding of the Child Jesus in the Temple, the Apparition of the Risen Christ to his Mother, the Assumption and Coronation of the Blessed Virgin. Introduced in 1422, the Crown originally consisted only of seven Our Fathers and 70 Hail Marys. Two Hail Marys were added to complete the number 72 (thought to be the number of years of Mary's life), and one Our Father, Hail Mary and Glory be to the Father are said for the intention of the pope.

**Freedom, Religious:** The Second Vatican Council declared that the right to religious freedom in civil society "means that all men are to be immune from coercion on the part of individuals or of social groups and of any human power, in such wise that in matters religious no one is to be forced to act in a manner contrary to his own beliefs. Nor is anyone to be restrained from acting in accordance with his own beliefs, whether privately or publicly, whether alone or in association with others, within due limits" of requirements for the common good. The foundation of this right in civil society is the "very dignity of the human person" (*Declaration on Religious Freedom*, No. 2).

The conciliar statement did not deal with the subject of freedom within the Church. It noted the responsibility of the faithful "carefully to attend to the sacred and certain doctrine of the Church" (No. 14).

**Freemasons:** A fraternal order which originated in London in 1717 with the formation of the first Grand Lodge of Freemasons. From England, the order spread to Europe and elsewhere. Its basic ideology is deistic and nondenominational. Grand Orient Freemasonry, developed in Latin countries, is atheistic, irreligious and anticlerical as well; since 1877, it has been denied recognition by the Scottish and York Rites because of its failure to require belief in God and the immortality of the soul as a condition of membership. In some places, Freemasonry has been regarded as subversive of the state; in Catholic quarters, it has been considered hostile to the Church and its doctrine. In the United States, Freemasonry is generally known as a fraternal and philanthropic order.

For serious doctrinal and pastoral reasons, Catholics have been forbidden to join the Freemasons, under penalty of excommunication. Eight different popes in 17 different pronouncements, and at least six different local councils, condemned Freemasonry. The first condemnation was made by Clement XII in 1738. Eastern Orthodox and many Protestant bodies have also opposed the order.

In the U.S., there was some easing of the ban against Masonic membership by Catholics in view of a letter written in 1974 by Cardinal Franjo Seper, prefect of the Congregation for the Doctrine of the Faith. The letter was interpreted to mean that Catholics might join Masonic lodges which were not anti-Catholic. This was called erroneous in a declaration issued by the Doctrinal Congregation Feb. 17, 1981.

The prohibition against Masonic membership was restated in a declaration issued by the Doctrinal Congregation Nov. 26, 1983, with the approval of Pope John Paul II, as follows.

"The question has been raised whether the Church's position on Masonic associations has been altered, especially since no explicit mention is made of them in the new Code of Canon Law, as there was in the old Code.

"This Sacred Congregation is able to reply that the circumstance is to be attributed to a criterion adopted in drafting. This criterion was observed also in regard to other associations which were likewise passed over in silence, because they were included in broader categories.

"The Church's negative position on Masonic associations, therefore, remains unaltered, since their principles have always been regarded as irreconcilable with the Church's doctrine. Hence, joining them remains prohibited by the Church. Catholics enrolled in Masonic associations are involved in serious sin and may not approach Holy Communion.

"Local ecclesiastical authorities do not have the faculty to pronounce a judgment on the nature of Masonic associations which might include a diminution of the above-mentioned judgment, in accordance with the intention of this congregation's declaration delivered on Feb. 17, 1981.

"The Supreme Pontiff John Paul II approved this declaration, deliberated at an ordinary meeting of this Sacred Congregation, and ordered it to become part of public law."

This latest declaration, like the revised Code of Canon Law, does not include a penalty of excommunication for Catholics who join the Masons. Local bishops are not authorized to grant dispensations from the prohibition. Dispensations must be sought from the Holy See.

**Free Will:** The faculty or capability of making a reasonable choice among several alternatives. Freedom of will underlies the possibility and fact of moral responsibility.

**Friar:** Term applied to members of mendicant orders to distinguish them from members of monastic orders. (See Mendicants.)

**Fruits of the Holy Spirit:** Charity, joy, peace, patience, benignity, goodness, long-animity, mildness, faith, modesty, continence, chastity.

## G

**Gambling:** The backing of an issue with a sum of money or other valuables, which is permissible if the object is honest, if the two parties have the free disposal of their stakes without prejudice to the rights of others, if the terms are thoroughly understood by both parties, and if the outcome is not known beforehand. Gambling often falls into disrepute and may be forbidden by civil law, as well as by divine law, because of cheating, fraud and other accompanying evils.

**Gehenna:** Greek form of a Jewish name, *Gehinnom*, for a valley near Jerusalem, the site of Moloch worship; used as a synonym for hell.

**Genuflection:** Bending of the knee, a natural sign of adoration or reverence, as when persons genuflect with the right knee in passing before the tabernacle to acknowledge the Eucharistic presence of Christ.

**Gethsemani:** A Hebrew word meaning oil press, designating the place on the Mount of Olives where Christ prayed and suffered in agony the night before he died.

**Gifts of the Holy Spirit:** Supernatural habits disposing a person to respond promptly to the inspiration of grace; promised by Christ and communicated through the Holy Spirit, especially in the sacrament of confirmation. They are: wisdom, understanding, counsel, fortitude, knowledge, piety, fear of the Lord.

**Gluttony:** An unreasonable appetite for food and drink; one of the seven capital sins.

**God:** The infinitely perfect Supreme Being, uncaused and absolutely self-sufficient, eternal, the Creator and final end of all things. The one God subsists in three equal Persons, the Father and the Son and the Holy Spirit. God, although transcendent and distinct from the universe, is present and active in the world in realization of his plan for the salvation of men, principally through Revelation, the operations of the Holy Spirit, the life and ministry of Christ, and the continuation of Christ's ministry in the Church.

The existence of God is an article of faith, clearly communicated in divine Revelation. Even without this Revelation, however, the Church teaches, in a declaration by the First Vatican Council, that men can acquire certain knowledge of the existence of God and some of his attributes. This can be done on the bases of principles of reason and reflection on human experience.

Non-revealed arguments or demonstrations for the existence of God have been developed from the principle of causality; the contingency of man and the universe; the existence of design, change and movement in the universe; human awareness of moral responsibility; widespread human testimony to the existence of God.

**Grace:** A free gift of God to men (and angels), grace is a created sharing or participation in the life of God. It is given to men through the merits of Christ and is communicated by the Holy Spirit. It is necessary for salvation. The principal means of grace are the sacraments (especially the Eucharist), prayer and good works.

Sanctifying or habitual grace makes men holy and pleasing to God, adopted children of God, members of Christ, temples of the Holy Spirit, heirs of heaven capable of supernaturally meritorious acts. With grace, God gives men the supernatural virtues and gifts of the Holy Spirit. The sacraments of baptism and penance were instituted to give grace to those who do not have it; the other sacraments, to increase it in those already in the state of grace. The means for growth in holiness, or the increase of grace, are prayer, the sacraments, and good works. Sanctifying grace is lost by the commission of serious sin.

Each sacrament confers sanctifying grace for the special purpose of the sacrament; in this context, grace is called sacramental grace.

Actual grace is a supernatural help of God which enlightens and strengthens a person to do good and to avoid evil. It is not a permanent quality, like sanctifying grace. It is necessary for the performance of supernatural acts. It can be resisted and refused. Persons in the state of serious sin are given actual grace to lead them to repentance.

**Grace at Meals:** Prayers said before meals, asking a blessing of God, and after meals, giving thanks to God. In addition to traditional prayers for these purposes, many variations suitable for different occasions are possible, at personal option.

## H

**Habit:** (1) A disposition to do things easily, given with grace (and therefore supernatural) and/or acquired by repetition of similar acts.

(2) The garb worn by religious.

**Hagiography:** Writings or documents about saints and other holy persons.

**Hail Mary:** A prayer addressed to the Blessed Virgin Mary; also called the *Ave Maria* (Latin equivalent of Hail Mary) and the Angelic Salutation. In three parts, it consists of the words addressed to Mary by the Archangel Gabriel on the occasion of the Annunciation, in the Infancy Narrative (Hail full of grace, the Lord is with you, blessed are you among women.); the words addressed to Mary by her cousin Elizabeth on the occasion of the Visitation (Blessed is the fruit of your womb.); a concluding petition (Holy Mary, Mother of God, pray for us sinners now and at the hour of our death. Amen.). The first two salutations were joined in Eastern Rite formulas by the sixth century, and were similarly used at Rome in the seventh century. Insertion of the name of Jesus at the conclusion of the salutations was probably made by Urban IV about 1262. The present form of the petition was incorporated into the breviary in 1514.

**Heaven:** The state of those who, having achieved salvation, are in glory with God and enjoy the beatific vision.

The phrase, kingdom of heaven, refers to the order or kingdom of God, grace, salvation.

**Hell:** The state of punishment of the damned —

i.e., those who die in mortal sin, in a condition of self-alienation from God and of opposition to the divine plan of salvation. The punishment of hell begins immediately after death and lasts forever.

**Hermit:** See Anchorite.

**Heroic Act of Charity:** The completely unselfish offering to God of one's good works and merits for the benefit of the souls in purgatory rather than for oneself. Thus a person may offer to God for the souls in purgatory all the good works he performs during life, all the indulgences he gains, and all the prayers and indulgences that will be offered for him after his death. The act is revocable at will, and is not a vow. Its actual ratification depends on the will of God.

**Heterodoxy:** False doctrine, teaching or belief; a departure from truth.

**Holy See:** (1) The diocese of the pope, Rome. (2) The pope himself and/or the various officials and bodies of the Church's central administration at Vatican City — the Roman Curia — which act in the name and by authority of the pope.

**Holy Spirit:** God the Holy Spirit, third Person of the Holy Trinity, who proceeds from the Father and the Son and with whom he is equal in every respect; inspirer of the prophets and writers of sacred Scripture; promised by Christ to the Apostles as their advocate and strengthener; appeared in the form of a dove at the baptism of Christ and as tongues of fire at his descent upon the Apostles; soul of the Church and guarantor, by his abiding presence and action, of truth in doctrine; communicator of grace to men, for which reason he is called the sanctifier.

**Holy Water:** Water blessed by the Church and used as a sacramental, a practice which originated in apostolic times.

**Holy Year:** A year during which the pope grants the plenary Jubilee Indulgence to the faithful who fulfill certain conditions. For those who make a pilgrimage to Rome during the year, the conditions are reception of the sacraments of penance and the Eucharist, visits and prayer for the intention of the pope in the basilicas of St. Peter, St. John Lateran, St. Paul and St. Mary Major. For those who do not make a pilgrimage to Rome, the conditions are reception of the sacraments and prayer for the pope during a visit or community celebration in a church designated by the bishop of the locality.

Holy Year observances have biblical counterparts in the Years of Jubilee observed at 50-year intervals by the pre-exilic Israelites — when debts were pardoned and slaves freed (Lv. 25:25-54) — and in sabbatical years observed from the end of the Exile to 70 A.D. — in which debts to fellow Jews were remitted.

The practice of Christians from early times to go on pilgrimage to the Holy Land, the shrines of martyrs and the tombs of the Apostles in Rome influenced the institution of Holy Years. There was also a prevailing belief among the people that every 100th year was a year of "Great Pardon." Accordingly, even before Boniface VIII formally proclaimed the first Holy Year Feb. 22, 1300, scores of thousands of pilgrims were already on the way to or in Rome.

Medieval popes embodied in the observance of Holy Years the practice of good works (reception of the sacraments of penance and the Eucharist, pilgrimages and/or visits to the tombs of the Apostles, and related actions) and spiritual benefits (particularly, special indulgences for the souls in purgatory). These and related practices, with suitable changes for celebrations in local churches, remain staple features of Holy Year observances.

The first three Holy Years were observed in 1300, 1350 and 1390. Subsequent ones were celebrated at 25-year intervals except in 1800 and 1850 when, respectively, the French invasion of Italy and political turmoil made observance impossible. Pope Paul II (1464-1471) set the 25-year timetable. In 1500, Pope Alexander VI prescribed the start and finish ceremonies — the opening and closing of the Holy Doors in the major basilicas on successive Christmas Eves. All but a few of the earlier Holy Years were classified as ordinary. Several — like those of 1933 and 1983-84 to commemorate the 1900th and 1950th anniversaries of the death and resurrection of Christ — were in the extraordinary category.

Holy Year 1975 coincided with the 10th anniversary of the closing of the Second Vatican Council. Its themes also coincided with the renewal emphasis which dominated the council, and were related to the main topic — the evangelization of the modern world — on the 1974 agenda of the Synod of Bishops.

**Homosexuality:** The condition of a person whose sexual orientation is toward persons of the same rather than the opposite sex. The condition, usually discovered during adolescence rather than deliberately caused, is not normal but is not sinful in itself. Homosexual acts against nature are objectively wrong; subjective responsibility for such acts, however, may be conditioned and diminished by compulsion and related factors.

**Hope:** One of the three theological virtues, by which one firmly trusts that God wills his salvation and will give him the means to attain it.

**Hosanna:** A Hebrew word, meaning O Lord, save, we pray.

**Host, The Sacred:** The bread under whose appearances Christ is and remains present in a unique manner after the consecration which takes place during Mass. (See Transubstantiation.)

**Humility:** A virtue which induces a person to evaluate himself at his true worth, to recognize his dependence on God, and to give glory to God for the good he has and can do.

**Hyperdulia:** The special veneration accorded the Blessed Virgin Mary because of her unique role in the mystery of Redemption, her exceptional gifts of grace from God, and her pre-eminence among the saints. Hyperdulia is not adoration; only God is adored.

**Hypnosis:** A mental state resembling sleep, induced by suggestion, in which the subject does the bidding of the hypnotist. Hypnotism is permissible under certain conditions: the existence of a serious reason, e.g., for anesthetic or therapeutic purposes, and the competence and integrity of the hypnotist. Hypnotism may not be practiced for the sake of amusement. Experiments indicate that, contrary to popular opinion, hypnotized subjects may be induced to perform immoral acts which, normally, they would not do.

**Hypostatic Union:** The union of the human and divine natures in the one divine Person of Christ.

**I**

**Icons:** Byzantine-style paintings or representations of Christ, the Blessed Virgin and other saints, venerated in the Eastern Churches where they take the place of statues.

**Idolatry:** Worship of any but the true God; a violation of the First Commandment.

**IHS:** In Greek, the first three letters of the name of Jesus — Iota, Eta, Sigma.

**Immortality:** The survival and continuing existence of the human soul after death.

**Impurity:** Unlawful indulgence in sexual pleasure. (See Chastity.)

**Incardination:** The affiliation of a priest to his diocese. Every secular priest must belong to a certain diocese. Similarly, every priest of a religious community must belong to some jurisdiction of his community; this affiliation, however, is not called incardination.

**Incarnation:** (1) The coming-into-flesh or taking of human nature by the Second Person of the Trinity. He became human as the Son of Mary, being miraculously conceived by the power of the Holy Spirit, without ceasing to be divine. His divine Person hypostatically unites his divine and human natures.

(2) The supernatural mystery coextensive with Christ from the moment of his human conception and continuing through his life on earth; his sufferings and death; his resurrection from the dead and ascension to glory with the Father; his sending, with the Father, of the Holy Spirit upon the Apostles and the Church; and his unending mediation with the Father for the salvation of men.

**Incense:** A granulated substance which, when burnt, emits an aromatic smoke. It symbolizes the zeal with which the faithful should be consumed, the good odor of Christian virtue, the ascent of prayer to God.

**Incest:** Sexual intercourse with relatives by blood or marriage; a sin of impurity and also a grave violation of the natural reverence due to relatives. Other sins of impurity (desire, etc.) concerning relatives have the nature of incest.

**Inculturation:** This was one of the subjects of an address delivered by Pope John Paul II Feb. 15, 1982, at a meeting in Lagos with the bishops of Nigeria.

"An important aspect of your own evangelizing role is the whole dimension of the inculturation of the Gospel into the lives of your people."

"The Church truly respects the culture of each people. In offering the Gospel message, the Church does not intend to destroy or to abolish what is good and beautiful. In fact, she recognizes many cultural values and, through the power of the

Gospel, purifies and takes into Christian worship certain elements of a people's customs. The Church comes to bring Christ; she does not come to bring the culture of another race. Evangelization aims at penetrating and elevating culture by the power of the Gospel."

"It is through the Providence of God that the divine message is made incarnate and is communicated through the culture of each people. It is forever true that the path of culture is the path of man, and it is on this path that man encounters the one who embodies the values of all cultures and fully reveals the man of each culture to himself. The Gospel of Christ, the Incarnate Word, finds its home along the path of culture, and from this path it continues to offer its message of salvation and eternal life."

**Index of Prohibited Books:** A list of books which Catholics were formerly forbidden to read, possess or sell, under penalty of excommunication. The books were banned by the Holy See after publication because their treatment of matters of faith and morals and related subjects were judged to be erroneous or serious occasions of doctrinal error. Some books were listed in the Index by name; others were covered under general norms. The Congregation for the Doctrine of the Faith declared June 14, 1966, that the Index and its related penalties of excommunication no longer had the force of law in the Church. Persons are still obliged, however, to take normal precautions against occasions of doctrinal error.

**Indifferentism:** A theory that any one religion is as true and good — or false — as any other religion, and that it makes no difference, objectively, what religion one professes, if any. The theory is completely subjective, finding its justification entirely in personal choice without reference to or respect for objective validity. It is also self-contradictory, since it regards as equally acceptable — or unacceptable — the beliefs of all religions, which in fact are not only not all the same but are in some cases opposed to each other.

**Indulgence:** According to *The Doctrine and Practice of Indulgences,* an apostolic constitution issued by Paul VI Jan. 1, 1967, an indulgence is the remission before God of the temporal punishment due for sins already forgiven as far as their guilt is concerned, which a follower of Christ — with the proper dispositions and under certain determined conditions — acquires through the intervention of the Church. The Church grants indulgences in accordance with doctrine concerning the superabundant merits of Christ and the saints, the Power of the Keys, and the sharing of spiritual goods in the communion of saints.

An indulgence is partial or plenary, depending on whether it does away with either part or all of the temporal punishment due for sin. Both types of indulgences can always be applied to the dead by way of suffrage; the actual disposition of indulgences applied to the dead rests with God.

(1) Partial indulgence: Properly disposed faithful who perform an action to which a partial indulgence is attached obtain, in addition to the remission of temporal punishment acquired by the

action itself, an equal remission of punishment through the intervention of the Church. (This grant was formerly designated in terms of days and years.) The proper dispositions for gaining a partial indulgence are sorrow for sin and freedom from serious sin, performance of the required good work, and the intention (which can be general or immediate) to gain the indulgence.

In addition to customary prayers and other good works to which partial indulgences are attached, the *Enchiridion Indulgentiarum* published in 1968 included general grants of partial indulgences to the faithful who: (a) with some kind of prayer, raise their minds to God with humble confidence while carrying out their duties and bearing the difficulties of everyday life; (b) motivated by the spirit of faith and compassion, give of themselves or their goods for the service of persons in need; (c) in a spirit of penance, spontaneously refrain from the enjoyment of things which are lawful and pleasing to them.

2) Plenary indulgence: To gain a plenary indulgence, it is necessary for a person to be free of all attachment to sin, to perform the work to which the indulgence is attached, and to fulfill the three conditions of sacramental confession, Eucharistic Communion, and prayer for the intention of the pope. The three conditions may be fulfilled several days before or after the performance of the prescribed work, but it is fitting that Communion be received and prayers for the intentions of the pope be offered on the same day the work is performed. The condition of praying for the pope's intention is fully satisfied by praying one Our Father and one Hail Mary, and sometimes the Creed, but persons are free to choose other prayers.

Four of the several devotional practices for which a plenary indulgence is granted are: (a) adoration of the Blessed Sacrament for at least one-half hour; (b) devout reading of sacred Scripture for at least one-half hour; (c) the Way of the Cross; (d) recitation of the Marian Rosary in a church or public oratory or in a family group, a religious community or pious association. Only one plenary indulgence can be gained in a single day.

**Indult:** A favor or privilege granted by competent ecclesiastical authority, giving permission to do something not allowed by the common law of the Church.

**Infant Jesus of Prague:** An 18-inch-high wooden statue of the Child Jesus which has figured in a form of devotion to the Holy Childhood and Kingship of Christ since the 17th century. Of uncertain origin, the statue was presented by Princess Polixena to the Carmelites of Our Lady of Victory Church, Prague, in 1628.

**Infused Virtues:** The theological virtues of faith, hope, and charity; principles or capabilities of supernatural action, they are given with sanctifying grace by God rather than acquired by repeated acts of a person. They can be increased by practice; they are lost by contrary acts. Natural-acquired moral virtues, like the cardinal virtues of prudence, justice, temperance, and fortitude, can be considered infused in a person whose state of grace gives them supernatural orientation.

**Inquisition:** A tribunal for dealing with heretics, authorized by Gregory IX in 1231 to search them out, hear and judge them, sentence them to various forms of punishment, and in some cases to hand them over to civil authorities for punishment. The Inquisition was a creature of its time when crimes against faith, which threatened the good of the Christian community, were regarded also as crimes against the state, and when heretical doctrines of such extremists as the Cathari and Albigensians threatened the very fabric of society. The institution, which was responsible for many excesses, was most active in the second half of the 13th century.

**Inquisition, Spanish:** An institution peculiar to Spain and the colonies in Spanish America. In 1478, at the urging of King Ferdinand, Pope Sixtus IV approved the establishment of the Inquisition for trying charges of heresy brought against Jewish (Marranos) and Moorish (Moriscos) converts. It acquired jurisdiction over other cases as well, however, and fell into disrepute because of irregularities in its functions, cruelty in its sentences, and the manner in which it served the interests of the Spanish crown more than the accused persons and the good of the Church. Protests by the Holy See failed to curb excesses of the Inquisition, which lingered in Spanish history until early in the 19th century.

**I N R I:** The first letters of words in the Latin inscription atop the cross on which Christ was crucified: (I)esus (N)azaraenus, (R)ex (J)udaeorum — Jesus of Nazareth, King of the Jews.

**Insemination, Artificial:** The implanting of human semen by some means other than consummation of natural marital intercourse. In view of the principle that procreation should result only from marital intercourse, donor insemination is not permissible. The use of legitimate artificial means to further the fruitfulness of marital intercourse is permissible.

**In Sin:** The condition of a person called spiritually dead because he does not possess sanctifying grace, the principle of supernatural life, action and merit. Such grace can be regained through repentance.

**Instruction:** A document containing doctrinal explanations, directive norms, rules, recommendations, admonitions, issued by the pope, a department of the Roman Curia or other competent authority in the Church. To the extent that they so prescribe, instructions have the force of law.

**Intercommunion:** The common celebration and reception of the Eucharist by members of different Christian churches; a pivotal issue in ecumenical theory and practice. Catholic participation and intercommunion in the Eucharistic liturgy of another church without a valid priesthood and with a variant Eucharistic belief is out of order. Under certain conditions, other Christians may receive the Eucharist in the Catholic Church (see additional Intercommunion entry). Intercommunion is acceptable to some Protestant churches and unacceptable to others.

**Interdict:** An ecclesiastical penalty imposed on

persons and places for certain violations of church law. If the interdict is personal, the interdicted persons may not take part in certain liturgical services, administer or receive certain sacraments. If the interdict is local, persons may not take part in certain liturgical services, administer or receive certain sacraments in the interdicted places.

Interdict is different from excommunication, and does not involve exclusion of a person from the community of the faithful.

**Interregnum:** The period of time between the death of a pope and the election of his successor. Another term applied to the period is *Sede vacante,* meaning the See (of Rome) being vacant.

The main concerns during an interregnum are matters connected with the death and burial of the pope, the election of his successor, and the maintenance of ordinary routine for the proper functioning of the Roman Curia and the Diocese of Rome.

Interregnum procedures follow norms contained in the apostolic constitution *Romano Pontifici Eligendo* (concerning the vacancy of the Apostolic See and the election of the Roman Pontiff) issued by Paul VI Oct. 1, 1975. This constitution superseded two others previously in force: *Vacantis Apostolicae Sedis,* issued by Pius XII Dec. 8, 1945, and *Summi Pontificis Electione,* issued by John XXIII Sept. 5, 1962.

"During the vacancy of the Apostolic See," the constitution states, "the government of the Church is entrusted to the Sacred College of Cardinals for the sole dispatch of ordinary business and of matters which cannot be postponed, and for the preparation of everything necessary for the election of the new pope."

The general congregation of the whole college, presided over by the dean, sub-dean or senior cardinal, has responsibility for major decisions during an interregnum. Other decisions of a routine nature are left to a particular congregation consisting of the chamberlain of the Holy Roman Church and three assistant cardinals.

The chamberlain of the Holy Roman Church and the dean of the college are the key officials, with directive responsibilities before and during the electoral conclave. The chamberlain is in general charge of ordinary administration. He — or the dean prior to a chamberlain's election by the cardinals — certifies the death of the pope; orders the destruction of the Fisherman's Ring and personal seals of the pope; and sets in motion procedures, carried out in collaboration with the dean, for informing the world about the pope's death, for funeral preparations, and for summoning and supervising the conclave for the election of a new pope.

Cardinals in charge of departments of the Roman Curia relinquish their offices at the death of the pope. Remaining in office, however, are the vicar of Rome, for ordinary jurisdiction over the diocese, and the major penitentiary. The substitute secretary of state or papal secretariat maintains the secretariat in a status quo. Papal representatives, such as nuncios and apostolic delegates, remain in office.

The congregations, offices and tribunals of the Curia retain ordinary jurisdiction for routine affairs but may not initiate new business during an interregnum.

If the pope should die during sessions of an ecumenical council or the Synod of Bishops, they would automatically be suspended.

The deceased pope is buried in St. Peter's Basilica, following prescribed ceremonies and traditional customs during a mourning period of nine days.

The conclave for the election of a new pope begins no sooner than 15 and no later than 20 days after the death of his predecessor. On the election of the new pope, the interregnum comes to an end. (See Papal Election.)

**Intinction:** A method of administering Holy Communion under the dual appearances of bread and wine, in which the consecrated host is dipped in the consecrated wine before being given to the communicant. The administering of Holy Communion in this manner, which has been traditional in Eastern-Rite liturgies, was authorized in the Roman Rite for various occasions by the *Constitution on the Sacred Liturgy* promulgated by the Second Vatican Council.

**Irenicism:** Peace-seeking, conciliation, as opposed to polemics; an important element in ecumenism, provided it furthers pursuit of the Christian unity willed by Christ without degenerating into a peace-at-any-price disregard for religious truth.

**Irregularity:** An impediment to the lawful reception or exercise of holy orders. The Church instituted irregularities — which include apostasy, heresy, homicide, attempted suicide — out of reverence for the dignity of the sacraments.

**Itinerarium:** Prayers for a spiritually profitable journey.

## J

**Jansenism:** Opinions developed and proposed by Cornelius Jansenius (1585-1638). He held that: human nature was radically and intrinsically corrupted by original sin; some men are predestined to heaven and others to hell; Christ died only for those predestined to heaven; for those who are predestined, the operations of grace are irresistible. Jansenism also advocated an extremely rigorous code of morals and asceticism. The errors were proscribed by Urban VIII in 1642, by Innocent X in 1653, by Clement XI in 1713, and by other popes. Despite these condemnations, the rigoristic spirit of Jansenism lingered for a long time afterwards, particularly in France.

**Jehovah's Witnesses:** The Witnesses, together with the Watchtower and Bible Tract Society, trace their beginnings to a Bible class organized by Charles Taze Russell in 1872 at Allegheny, Pa. They take their name from a passage in Isaiah (43:12): " 'You are my witnesses,' says Jehovah." They are generally fundamentalist and revivalist with respect to the Bible, and believe that Christ is God's Son but is inferior to God. They place great emphasis on the Battle of Armageddon (as a decisive confrontation of good and evil) that is depicted vividly in Revelation, believing that God will then destroy the existing system of things and that, with the establishment of Jehovah's Kingdom, a small band of 144,000 spiritual sons of God will go to heaven, rule with Christ, and share in some way their happiness with some others.

Each Witness is considered by the society to be an ordained minister charged with the duty of spreading the message of Jehovah, which is accomplished through publications, house-to-house visitations, and other methods. The Witnesses refuse to salute the flag of any nation, regarding this as a form of idolatry, or to sanction blood transfusions even for the saving of life. There are approximately one million Witnesses in more than 22,000 congregations in some 80 countries. The freedom and activities of Witnesses are restricted in some places.

**Jesus:** The name of Jesus, meaning Savior in Christian usage, derived from the Aramaic and Hebrew *Yeshua* and *Joshua,* meaning *Yahweh* is salvation.

**Jesus Prayer:** A form of prayer dating back to the fifth century, "Lord Jesus Christ, Son of God, have mercy on me (a sinner)."

**Judgment:** (1) Last or final judgment: Final judgment by Christ, at the end of the world and the general resurrection.

(2) Particular judgment: The judgment that takes place immediately after a person's death, followed by entrance into heaven, hell or purgatory.

**Jurisdiction:** Right, power, authority to rule. Jurisdiction in the Church is of divine institution; has pastoral service for its purpose; includes legislative, judicial and executive authority; can be exercised only by persons with the power of orders.

(1) Ordinary jurisdiction is attached to ecclesiastical offices by law; the officeholders, called Ordinaries, have authority over those who are subject to them.

(2) Delegated jurisdiction is that which is granted to persons rather than attached to offices. Its extent depends on the terms of the delegation.

**Justice:** One of the four cardinal virtues by which a person gives to others what is due to them as a matter of right. (See Cardinal Virtues.)

**Justification:** The act by which God makes a person just, and the consequent change in the spiritual status of a person, from sin to grace; the remission of sin and the infusion of sanctifying grace through the merits of Christ and the action of the Holy Spirit.

### K

**Kerygma:** Proclaiming the word of God, in the manner of the Apostles, as here and now effective for salvation. This method of preaching or instruction, centered on Christ and geared to the facts and themes of salvation history, is designed to dispose people to faith in Christ and or to intensify the experience and practice of that faith in those who have it.

**Keys, Power of the:** Spiritual authority and jurisdiction in the Church, symbolized by the keys of the kingdom of heaven. Christ promised the keys to St. Peter, as head-to-be of the Church (Mt. 16:19), and commissioned him with full pastoral responsibility to feed his lambs and sheep (Jn. 21:15-17), The pope, as the successor of St. Peter, has this power in a primary and supreme manner. The bishops of the Church also have the power, in union with and subordinate to the pope. Priests share in it through holy orders and the delegation of authority.

Examples of the application of the Power of the Keys are the exercise of teaching and pastoral authority by the pope and bishops, the absolving of sins in the sacrament of penance, the granting of indulgences, the imposing of spiritual penalties on persons who commit certain serious sins.

### L

**Laicization:** The process by which a man ordained to holy orders is relieved of the obligations of orders and the ministry and is returned to the status of a lay person.

**Languages of the Church:** The first language in church use, for divine worship and the conduct of ecclesiastical affairs, was Aramaic, the language of the first Christians in and around Jerusalem. As the Church spread westward, Greek was adopted and prevailed until the third century when it was supplanted by Latin for official use in the West.

According to traditions established very early in churches of the Eastern Rites, many different languages were adopted for use in divine worship and for the conduct of ecclesiastical affairs. The practice was, and still is, to use the vernacular or a language closely related to the common tongue of the people.

In the Western Church, Latin prevailed as the general official language until the promulgation on Dec. 4, 1963, of the *Constitution on the Sacred Liturgy* by the second session of the Second Vatican Council. Since that time, vernacular languages have come into use in the Mass, administration of the sacraments, and the Liturgy of the Hours. The change was introduced in order to make the prayers and ceremonies of divine worship more informative and meaningful to all. Latin, however, remains the official language for documents of the Holy See, administrative and procedural matters.

**Law:** An ordinance or rule governing the activity of things.

(1) Natural law: Moral norms corresponding to man's nature by which he orders his conduct toward God, neighbor, society and himself. This law, which is rooted in human nature, is of divine origin, can be known by the use of reason, and binds all men having the use of reason. The Ten Commandments are declarations and amplifications of natural law. The primary precepts of natural law, to do good and to avoid evil, are universally recognized, despite differences with respect to understanding and application resulting from different philosophies of good and evil.

(2) Divine positive law: That which has been revealed by God. Among its essentials are the twin

precepts of love of God and love of neighbor, and the Ten Commandments.

(3) Ecclesiastical law: That which is established by the Church for the spiritual welfare of the faithful and the orderly conduct of ecclesiastical affairs. (See Canon Law.)

(4) Civil law: That which is established by a socio-political community for the common good.

**Liberalism:** A multiphased trend of thought and movement favoring liberty, independence and progress in moral, intellectual, religious, social, economic and political life. Traceable to the Renaissance, it developed through the Enlightenment, the rationalism of the 19th century, and modernist- and existentialist-related theories of the 20th century. Evaluations of various kinds of liberalism depend on the validity of their underlying principles. Extremist positions — regarding subjectivism, libertinarianism, naturalist denials of the supernatural, and the alienation of individuals and society from God and the Church were condemned by Gregory XVI in the 1830's, Pius IX in 1864, Leo XIII in 1899, and St. Pius X in 1907. There is, however, nothing objectionable about forms of liberalism patterned according to sound principles of Christian doctrine.

**Life in Outer Space:** Whether rational life exists on other bodies in the universe besides earth, is a question for scientific investigation to settle. The possibility can be granted, without prejudice to the body of revealed truth.

**Limbo:** The limbo of the fathers was the state of rest and natural happiness after death enjoyed by the just of pre-Christian times until they were admitted to heaven following the Ascension of Christ. Belief in this matter is stated in the Apostles' Creed. The existence of a limbo for unbaptized persons of infant status — a state of rest and natural happiness — has never been formally defined.

**Litany:** A prayer in the form of responsive petition; e.g., St. Joseph, pray for us, etc. Examples are the litanies of Loreto (Litany of the Blessed Mother), the Holy Name, All Saints, the Sacred Heart, the Precious Blood, St. Joseph, Litany for the Dying.

**Loreto, House of:** A Marian shrine in Loreto, Italy, consisting of the home of the Holy Family which, according to an old tradition, was transported in a miraculous manner from Nazareth to Dalmatia and finally to Loreto between 1291 and 1294. Investigations conducted shortly after the appearance of the structure in Loreto revealed that its dimensions matched those of the house of the Holy Family missing from its place of enshrinement in a basilica at Nazareth. Among the many popes who regarded it with high honor was John XXIII, who went there on pilgrimage Oct. 4, 1962. The house of the Holy Family is enshrined in the Basilica of Our Lady.

**Lust:** A disorderly desire for sexual pleasure; one of the seven capital sins.

# M

**Magi:** In the Infancy Narrative of St. Matthew's Gospel (2:1-12), three wise men from the East whose visit and homage to the Child Jesus at Beth-lehem indicated Christ's manifestation of himself to non-Jewish people. The narrative teaches the universality of salvation. The traditional names of the Magi are Caspar, Melchior and Balthasar.

**Magnificat:** The canticle or hymn of the Virgin Mary on the occasion of her visitation to her cousin Elizabeth (Lk. 1:46-55). It is an expression of praise, thanksgiving and acknowledgment of the great blessings given by God to Mary, the Mother of the Second Person of the Blessed Trinity made Man. The Magnificat is recited in the Liturgy of the Hours as part of the Evening Prayer.

**Martyr:** A Greek word, meaning witness, denoting one who voluntarily suffered death for the faith or some Christian virtue.

**Martyrology:** A catalogue of martyrs and other saints, arranged according to the calendar. The *Roman Martyrology* contains the official list of saints venerated by the Church. Additions to the list are made in beatification and canonization decrees of the Congregation for the Causes of Saints.

**Mass for the People:** On Sundays and certain feasts throughout the year pastors are required to offer Mass for the faithful committed to their care. If they cannot offer the Mass on these days, they must do so at a later date or provide that another priest offer the Mass.

**Master of Novices:** The person in charge of the training and formation of candidates for an institute of consecrated life during novitiate.

**Materialism:** Theory which holds that matter is the only reality, and everything in existence is merely a manifestation of matter; there is no such thing as spirit, and the supernatural does not exist. Materialism is incompatible with Christian doctrine.

**Meditation:** Mental, as distinguished from vocal, prayer, in which thought, affections, and resolutions of the will predominate. There is a meditative element to all forms of prayer, which always involves the raising of the heart and mind to God.

**Mendicants:** A term derived from Latin and meaning beggars, applied to members of religious orders without property rights; the members, accordingly, worked or begged for their support. The original mendicants were Franciscans and Dominicans in the early 13th century; later, the Carmelites, Augustinians, Servites and others were given the mendicant title and privileges, with respect to exemption from episcopal jurisdiction and wide faculties for preaching and administering the sacrament of penance. The practice of begging is limited at the present time, although it is still allowed with the permission of competent superiors and bishops. Mendicants are supported by free will offerings and income received for spiritual services and other work.

**Mercy, Divine:** The love and goodness of God, manifested particularly in a time of need.

**Merit:** In religion, the right to a supernatural reward for good works freely done for a supernatural motive by a person in the state of and with the assistance of grace. The right to such reward is from God, who binds himself to give it. Accordingly, good works, as described above, are meritorious for salvation.

**Metempsychosis:** Theory of the passage or migration of the human soul after death from one body to another for the purpose of purification from guilt. The theory denies the unity of the soul and human personality, and the doctrine of individual moral responsibility.

**Millennium:** A thousand-year reign of Christ and the just upon earth before the end of the world. This belief of the Millenarians, Chiliasts, and some sects of modern times is based on an erroneous interpretation of Rv. 20.

**Miracles:** Observable events or effects in the physical or moral order of things, with reference to salvation, which cannot be explained by the ordinary operation of laws of nature and which, therefore, are attributed to the direct action of God. They make known, in an unusual way, the concern and intervention of God in human affairs for the salvation of men. The most striking examples are the miracles worked by Christ. Numbering about 35, they included his own Resurrection; the raising of three persons to life (Lazarus, the daughter of Jairus, the son of the widow of Naim); the healing of blind, leprous and other persons; nature miracles; and prophecies, or miracles of the intellectual order.

The foregoing notion of miracles, which is based on the concept of a fixed order of nature, was not known by the writers of Sacred Scripture. In the Old Testament, particularly, they called some things miraculous which, according to the definition in contemporary use, may or may not have been miracles. Essentially, however, the occurrences so designated were regarded as exceptional manifestations of God's care and concern for the salvation of his people. The miracles of Christ were miracles in the full sense of the term.

The Church believes it is reasonable to accept miracles as manifestations of divine power for purposes of salvation. God, who created the laws of nature, is their master; hence, without disturbing the ordinary course of things, he can — and has in the course of history before and after Christ — occasionally set aside these laws and has also produced effects beyond their power of operation. The Church does not call miraculous anything which does not admit of easy explanation; on the contrary, miracles are admitted only when the events have a bearing on the order of grace and every possible natural explanation has been tried and found wanting.

(The transubstantiation — i.e., the conversion of the whole substance of bread and wine, their sensible appearances alone remaining, into the Body and Blood of Christ in the act of Consecration at Mass — is not an observable event. Traditionally, however, it has been called a miracle.)

**Missal:** A liturgical book of Roman Rite also called the *Sacramentary*, containing the celebrant's prayers of the Mass, along with general instructions and ceremonial directives. The Latin text of the new *Roman Missal*, replacing the one authorized by the Council of Trent in the 16th century, was published by the Vatican Polyglot Press in 1970. Its use in English was made mandatory in the U.S. from Dec. 1, 1974. Readings and scriptural responsories formerly in the missal are contained in the *Lectionary*.

**Missiology:** Study of the missionary nature, constitution and activity of the Church in all aspects: theological reasons for missionary activity, laws and instructions of the Holy See, history of the missions, social and cultural background, methods, norms for carrying on missionary work.

**Mission:** (1) Strictly, it means being sent to perform a certain work, such as the mission of Christ to redeem mankind, the mission of the Apostles and the Church and its members to perpetuate the prophetic, priestly and royal mission of Christ.

(2) A place where: the Gospel has not been proclaimed; the Church has not been firmly established; the Church, although established, is weak.

(3) An ecclesiastical territory with the simplest kind of canonical organization, under the jurisdiction of the Congregation for the Evangelization of Peoples.

(4) A church or chapel without a resident priest.

(5) A special course of sermons and spiritual exercises conducted in parishes for the purpose of renewing and deepening the spiritual life of the faithful and for the conversion of lapsed Catholics.

**Modernism:** The "synthesis of all heresies," which appeared near the beginning of the 20th century. It undermines the objective validity of religious beliefs and practices which, it contends, are products of the subconscious developed by mankind under the stimulus of a religious sense. It holds that the existence of a personal God cannot be demonstrated, the Bible is not inspired, Christ is not divine, nor did he establish the Church or institute the sacraments. A special danger lies in modernism, which is still influential, because it uses Catholic terms with perverted meanings. St. Pius X condemned 65 propositions of modernism in 1907 in the decree *Lamentabili* and issued the encyclical *Pascendi* to explain and analyze its errors.

**Monastery:** The dwelling place, as well as the community thereof, of monks belonging to the Benedictine and Benedictine-related orders like the Cistercians and Carthusians; also, the Augustinians and Canons Regular. Distinctive of monasteries are: their separation from the world; the enclosure or cloister; the permanence or stability of attachment characteristic of their members; autonomous government in accordance with a monastic rule, like that of St. Benedict in the West or of St. Basil in the East; the special dedication of its members to the community celebration of the liturgy as well as to work that is suitable to the surrounding area and the needs of its people. Monastic superiors of men have such titles as abbot and prior; of women, abbess and prioress. In most essentials, an abbey is the same as a monastery.

**Monk:** A member of a monastic order — e.g., the Benedictines, the Benedictine-related Cistercians and Carthusians, and the Basilians, who bind themselves by religious profession to stable attachment to a monastery, the contemplative life and the work of their community. In popular use, the title is wrongly applied to many men religious who really are not monks.

**Monotheism:** Belief in and worship of one God.

**Morality:** Conformity or difformity of behavior to standards of right conduct. (See Moral Obligations, Commandments of God, Precepts of the Church, Conscience, Law.)

**Mormons:** Members of the Church of Jesus Christ of Latter-Day Saints. The church was established by Joseph Smith (1805-1844) at Fayette, N.Y., three years after he said he had received from an angel golden tablets containing the *Book of the Prophet Mormon.* This book, the Bible, *Doctrine and Covenants,* and *The Pearl of Great Price,* are the basic doctrinal texts of the church. Characteristic of the Mormons are strong belief in the revelations of their leaders, among whom was Brigham Young; a strong community of religious-secular concern; a dual secular and spiritual priesthood, and vigorous missionary activity. The headquarters of the church are located at Salt Lake City, Utah, where the Mormons first settled in 1847.

**Mortification:** Acts of self-discipline, including prayer, hardship, austerities and penances undertaken for the sake of progress in virtue.

**Motu Proprio:** A Latin phrase designating a document issued by a pope on his own initiative. Documents of this kind often concern administrative matters.

**Mysteries of Faith:** Supernatural truths whose existence cannot be known without revelation by God and whose intrinsic truth, while not contrary to reason, can never be wholly understood even after revelation. These mysteries are above reason, not against reason. Among them are the divine mysteries of the Trinity, Incarnation and Eucharist.

Some mysteries — e.g., concerning God's attributes — can be known by reason without revelation, although they cannot be fully understood.

## N

**Necromancy:** Supposed communication with the dead; a form of divination.

**Non-Expedit:** A Latin expression. It is not expedient (fitting, proper), used to state a prohibition or refusal of permission.

**Novena:** A term designating public or private devotional practices over a period of nine consecutive days; or, by extension, over a period of nine weeks, in which one day a week is set aside for the devotions.

**Novice:** A man or woman preparing, in a formal period of trial and formation called a novitiate, for membership in an institute of consecrated life. The novitiate lasts a minimum of 12 and a maximum of 24 months; at its conclusion, the novice professes temporary vows of poverty, chastity and obedience. Norms require that certain periods of time be spent in the house of novitiate: the first three months, one solid period of six months, the final month before the profession of temporary

commitment. Periods of apostolic work are also required, to acquaint the novice with the apostolate(s) of the institute. A novice is not bound by the obligations of the professed members of the institute, is free to leave at any time, and may be discharged at the discretion of competent superiors. The immediate superior of a novice is a master or mistress of novices.

**Nun** (1) Strictly, a member of a religious order of women with solemn vows (moniales).

(2) In general, all women religious, even those in simple vows who are more properly called sisters.

**Nunc Dimittis:** The canticle or hymn of Simeon at the sight of Jesus at the Temple on the occasion of his presentation (Lk. 2:29-32). It is an expression of joy and thanksgiving for the blessing of having lived to see the Messiah. It is prescribed for use in the Night Prayer of the Liturgy of the Hours.

## O

**Oath:** Calling upon God to witness the truth of a statement. Violating an oath, e.g., by perjury in court, or taking an oath without sufficient reason, is a violation of the honor due to God.

**Obedience:** Submission to one in authority. General obligations of obedience fall under the Fourth Commandment. The vow of obedience professed by religious is one of the evangelical counsels.

**Obsession, Diabolical:** The extraordinary state of one who is seriously molested by evil spirits in an external manner. Obsession is more than just temptation.

**Occultism:** Practices involving ceremonies, rituals, chants, incantations, other cult-related activities intended to affect the course of nature, the lives of practitioners and others, through esoteric powers of magic, diabolical or other forces; one of many forms of superstition.

**Octave:** A period of eight days given over to the celebration of a major feast such as Easter.

**Oils, Holy:** The oils consecrated by bishops on Holy Thursday or another suitable day, and by priests under certain conditions for use in certain sacraments and consecrations.

(1) The oil of catechumens (olive or vegetable oil), used at baptism; also, poured with chrism into the baptismal water blessed in Easter Vigil ceremonies.

(2) Chrism (olive or vegetable oil mixed with balm), used at baptism, in confirmation, at the ordination of a priest and bishop, in the dedication of churches and altars.

(3) Oil of the sick (olive or vegetable oil) used in anointing the sick.

**Old Catholics** — Several sects, including: (1) the Church of Utrecht, which severed relations with Rome in 1724; (2) the National Polish Church in the U.S., which had its origin near the end of the 19th century; (3) German, Austrian and Swiss Old Catholics, who broke away from union with Rome following the First Vatican Council in 1870 because they objected to the dogma of papal infallibility.

The formation of the Old Catholic communion of Germans, Austrians and Swiss began in 1870 at a public meeting held in Nuremberg under the leadership of A. Dollinger. Four years later episcopal succession was established with the ordination of an Old Catholic German bishop by a prelate of the Church of Utrecht. In line with the "Declaration of Utrecht" of 1889, they accept the first seven ecumenical councils and doctrine formulated before 1054, but reject communion with the pope and a number of other Catholic doctrines and practices. They have a valid priesthood and valid sacraments. *The Oxford Dictionary of the Christian Church* notes that they have recognized Anglican ordinations since 1925, that they have had full communion with the Church of England since 1932, and that their bishops, using their own formula, have taken part in the ordination of Anglican bishops.

This communion does not recognize the "Old Catholic" status of several smaller sects calling themselves such. In turn, connection with it is disavowed by the Old Roman Catholic Church headquartered in Chicago, which contends that it has abandoned the traditions of the Church of Utrecht.

The United States is the only English-speaking country with Old Catholic communities.

**Opus Dei:** Opus Dei was founded by Msgr. Josemaria Escriva de Belaguer in 1928 in Madrid as "an association of the faithful whose members dedicated themselves entirely in the apostolate (of Christian witness and action) and to the practice of an intense spiritual life without abandoning their own social environment or the exercise of their profession or secular occupation." The association was fully approved by the Vatican as a secular institute in 1950. On Aug. 5, 1982, Pope John Paul II confirmed and ordered publication of a declaration concerning the erection of the secular institute into the Prelature of the Holy Cross and Opus Dei.

The 1984 edition of *Annuario Pontificio* reported that the prelacy had 1,112 priests, (69 newly ordained) and 354 major seminarians. Also, there were approximately 72,000 lay persons — men and women, married and single, of every class and social condition — in about 80 countries.

In the United States, members of Opus Dei, along with non-member associates, conduct apostolic works corporately in major cities in the East and Midwest, and on the West Coast. Elsewhere, members are engaged in universities, vocational institutes, training schools for farmers and numerous other apostolic initiatives.

An information office is located at 330 Riverside Drive, New York, N.Y. 10025.

**Oratory:** A chapel.

**Ordinariate:** An ecclesiastical jurisdiction for special purposes and people. Examples are the military ordinariate of the U.S., for service personnel, and Eastern-Rite ordinariates in places where Eastern-Rite dioceses do not exist.

**Ordinary:** One who has the jurisdiction of an office: the pope, diocesan bishops, vicars general, prelates of missionary territories, vicars apostolic, prefects apostolic, vicars capitular during the vacancy of a see, superiors general, abbots

primate and other major superiors of men religious.

**Ordination:** The consecration of sacred ministers for divine worship and the service of people in things pertaining to God. The power of ordination comes from Christ and the Church, and must be conferred by a minister capable of communicating it.

**Organ Transplants:** The transplanting of organs from one person to another is permissible provided it is done with the consent of the concerned parties and does not result in the death or essential mutilation of the donor. Advances in methods and technology have increased the range of transplant possibilities in recent years.

**Original Sin:** The sin of Adam (Gn. 2:8—3:24), personal to him and passed on to all persons as a state of privation of grace. Despite this privation and the related wounding of human nature and weakening of natural powers, original sin leaves unchanged all that man himself is by nature. The scriptural basis of the doctrine was stated especially by St. Paul in 1 Cor. 15:21, ff., and Romans 5:12-21. Original sin is remitted by baptism and incorporation in Christ, through whom grace is given to persons.

**O Salutaris Hostia:** The first three Latin words, O Saving Victim, of a Benediction hymn.

**Ostpolitik:** Policy adopted by Pope Paul VI in an attempt to improve the situation of Eastern European Catholics through diplomatic negotiations with their governments.

**Oxford Movement:** A movement in the Church of England from 1833 to about 1845 which had for its objective a threefold defense of the church as a divine institution, the apostolic succession of its bishops, and the Book of Common Prayer as the rule of faith. The movement took its name from Oxford University and involved a number of intellectuals who authored a series of influential *Tracts for Our Times.* Some of its leading figures — e.g., F. W. Faber, John Henry Newman and Henry Edward Manning — became converts to the Catholic Church. In the Church of England, the movement affected the liturgy, historical and theological scholarship, the status of the ministry, and other areas of ecclesiastical life.

**P**

**Paganism:** A term referring to non-revealed religions, i.e., religions other than Christianity, Judaism and Mohammedanism.

**Palms:** Blessed palms are a sacramental. They are blessed and distributed on the Sunday of the Passion in commemoration of the triumphant entrance of Christ into Jerusalem. Ashes of the burnt palms are used on Ash Wednesday.

**Pange Lingua:** First Latin words, Sing, my tongue, of a hymn in honor of the Holy Eucharist, used particularly on Holy Thursday and in Eucharistic processions.

**Pantheism:** Theory that all things are part of God, divine, in the sense that God realizes himself as the ultimate reality of matter or spirit through being and/or becoming all things that have been, are, and will be. The theory leads to hopeless confusion of the Creator and the created realm of being, identifies evil with good, and involves many inherent contradictions.

**Papal Election:** The pope is elected by members of the College of Cardinals in a secret conclave or meeting convened ordinarily in secluded quarters of the Vatican Palace between 15 and 20 days after the death of his predecessor. Cardinals under the age of 80, totaling no more than 120, are eligible to participate in a papal election.

Following are some of the principal regulations decreed by Paul VI Oct. 1, 1975, in the apostolic constitution *Romano Pontifici Eligendo* (concerning the vacancy of the Apostolic See and the election of the Roman Pontiff).

The ordinary manner of election is by scrutiny, with two votes each morning and afternoon in the Sistine Chapel until one of the candidates receives a two-thirds plus one vote majority.

Alternative methods, which can be adopted by unanimous agreement of the cardinals in difficult cases, are provided for: (1) by delegation, in which the cardinals designate a limited number (nine to 15) to make the choice; (2) by changing the majority rule from two-thirds plus one vote to an absolute majority plus one; (3) by limiting final choice, if the procedure in force becomes protracted, to one between the two candidates who received the largest numbers of votes, but not a required majority, in the most recent balloting.

An unusual manner of election is by acclamation or inspiration — that is, by spontaneous, unanimous choice without any need for normal voting procedure.

The elected candidate is asked by the dean of the college if he accepts the election. If he does so and is already a bishop, he immediately becomes the bishop of Rome and pope, and signifies the name by which he will be called. The cardinals then pledge their obedience to him before the senior cardinal deacon proclaims his election to the world from the main balcony of the Vatican and the new pope imparts his blessing *Urbi et Orbi* (to the City and the World). If the candidate is not a bishop, he is so ordained before receiving the pledge of obedience and being proclaimed pope. The subsequent coronation of the pope is a ceremonial recognition of the fact of his election.

The pope is elected for life. If one should resign, a new pope would be elected in accordance with the foregoing regulations.

Rigid rules govern the conclave — its personnel, freedom from internal and external influence and interference, absolute secrecy (with a ban on recording devices and a prohibition against any disclosures).

Ordinarily, the first indication that a new pope has been elected is a plume of white smoke rising from the Vatican on burning of the last ballots.

(See College of Cardinals, Interregnum.)

Early methods of electing a pope — with various degrees of participation by the clergy and people of Rome and others — were set aside by Pope Nicholas II, who decreed in 1059 that cardinal bishops would be the electors. Further modification of the process was decreed by the Lateran Council in 1179 (that election would take place by a two-thirds majority vote of the cardinals) and by Pope Gregory X in 1274 (regarding a secluded conclave arrangement for elections).

**Paraclete:** A title of the Holy Spirit meaning, in Greek, Advocate, Consoler.

**Parental Duties:** All duties related to the obligation of parents to provide for the welfare of their children. These obligations fall under the Fourth Commandment.

**Parish:** A community of the faithful served by a pastor charged with responsibility for providing them with full pastoral service. Most parishes are territorial, embracing all of the faithful in a certain area of a diocese: some are personal or national, for certain classes of people, without strict regard for their places of residence.

**Parousia:** The coming, or saving presence, of Christ which will mark the completion of salvation history and the coming to perfection of God's kingdom at the end of the world.

**Paschal Candle:** A large candle, symbolic of the risen Christ, blessed and lighted on the Easter Vigil and placed at the Gospel side of the altar until Ascension Day. It is ornamented with five large grains of incense, representing the wounds of Christ, inserted in the form of a cross; the Greek letters Alpha and Omega, symbolizing Christ the beginning and end of all things, at the top and bottom of the shaft of the cross; and the figures of the current year of salvation in the quadrants formed by the cross.

**Paschal Precept:** Church law requiring reception of the Eucharist during the Easter season unless, for a just cause, once-a-year reception takes place at another time.

**Passion of Christ:** Sufferings of Christ, recorded in the four Gospels.

**Pastor:** An ordained minister charged with responsibility for the doctrinal, sacramental and related service of people committed to his care; e.g., a bishop for the people in his diocese, a priest for the people of his parish.

**Pater Noster:** The initial Latin words, Our Father, of the Lord's Prayer.

**Peace, Sign of:** A gesture of greeting — e.g., a handshake — exchanged by the ministers and participants at Mass.

**Pectoral Cross:** A cross worn on a chain about the neck and over the breast by bishops and abbots as a mark of their office.

**Penance or Penitence:** (1) The spiritual change or conversion of mind and heart by which a person turns away from sin, and all that it implies, toward God, through a personal renewal under the influence of the Holy Spirit. In the apostolic constitution *Paenitemini*, Pope Paul VI called it "a religious, personal act which has as its aim love and surrender to God." Penance involves sorrow and contrition for sin, together with other internal and external acts of atonement. It serves the purposes of reestablishing in one's life the order of God's love and commandments, and of making satisfaction to God for sin. A divine precept states the necessity of penance for salvation: "Unless you do penance, you shall all likewise perish" (Lk. 13:3)

. . . "Be converted and believe in the Gospel" (Mk. 1:15).

In the penitential discipline of the Church, the various works of penance have been classified under the headings of prayer (interior), fasting and almsgiving (exterior). The Church has established minimum requirements for the common and social observance of the divine precept by Catholics — e.g., by requiring them to fast and/or abstain on certain days of the year. These observances, however, do not exhaust all the demands of the divine precept, whose fulfillment is a matter of personal responsibility; nor do they have any real value unless they proceed from the internal spirit and purpose of penance.

Related to works of penance for sins actually committed are works of mortification. The purpose of the latter is to develop — through prayer, fasting, renunciations and similar actions — self-control and detachment from things which could otherwise become occasions of sin.

(2) Penance is a virtue disposing a person to turn to God in sorrow for sin and to carry out works of amendment and atonement.

(3) The sacrament of penance and sacramental penance.

**Perjury:** Taking a false oath, lying under oath, a violation of the honor due to God.

**Persecution, Religious:** A campaign waged against a church or other religious body by persons and governments intent on its destruction. The best known campaigns of this type against the Christian Church were the Roman persecutions which occurred intermittently from about 54 to the promulgation of the Edict of Milan in 313, The most extensive persecutions took place during the reigns of Nero, the first major Roman persecutor, Domitian, Trajan, Marcus Aurelius, and Diocletian. Besides the Roman persecutions, the Catholic Church has been subject to many others, including those of the 20th century in Communist-controlled countries.

**Personal Prelature:** A special-purpose jurisdiction — for particular pastoral and missionary work, etc., — consisting of secular priests and deacons and open to lay persons willing to dedicate themselves to its apostolic works. The prelate in charge is an Ordinary, with the authority of office; he can establish a national or international seminary, incardinate its students and promote them to holy orders under the title of service to the prelature. The prelature is constituted and governed according to statutes laid down by the Holy See. Statutes define its relationship and mode of operation with the bishops of territories in which members live and work. Opus Dei is a personal prelature.

**Peter's Pence:** A collection made each year among Catholics for the maintenance of the pope and his works of charity. It was originally a tax of a penny on each house, and was collected on St. Peter's day, whence the name. It originated in England in the eighth century.

**Petition:** One of the four purposes of prayer. In prayers of petition, persons ask of God the blessings they and others need.

**Pharisees:** Influential class among the Jews, referred to in the Gospels, noted for their self-righteousness, legalism, strict interpretation of the Law, acceptance of the traditions of the elders as well as the Law of Moses, and beliefs regarding angels and spirits, the resurrection of the dead and judgment. Most of them were laymen, and they were closely allied with the Scribes; their opposite numbers were the Sadducees. The Pharisaic and rabbinical traditions had a lasting influence on Judaism following the destruction of Jerusalem in 70 A.D.

**Pious Fund:** Property and money originally accumulated by the Jesuits to finance their missionary work in Lower California. When the Jesuits were expelled from the territory in 1767, the fund was appropriated by the Spanish Crown and used to support Dominican and Franciscan missionary work in Upper and Lower California. In 1842 the Mexican government took over administration of the fund, incorporated most of the revenue into the national treasury, and agreed to pay the Church interest of six per cent a year on the capital so incorporated. From 1848 to 1967 the fund was the subject of lengthy negotiations between the U.S. and Mexican governments because of the latter's failure to make payments as agreed. A lump-sum settlement was made in 1967 with payment by Mexico to the U.S. government of more than $700,000, to be turned over to the Archdiocese of San Francisco.

**Polytheism:** Belief in and worship of many gods or divinities, especially prevalent in pre-Christian religions.

**Poor Box:** Alms-box; found in churches from the earliest days of Christianity.

**Pope Joan:** Alleged name of a woman falsely said to have been pope from 855-858, the years of the reign of Benedict III. The myth was not heard of before the 13th century.

**Portiuncula:** (1) Meaning little portion (of land), the Portiuncula was the chapel of Our Lady of the Angels near Assisi, Italy, which the Benedictines gave to St. Francis early in the 13th century. He repaired the chapel and made it the first church of the Franciscan Order. It is now enshrined in the Basilica of St. Mary of the Angels in Assisi.

(2) The Portiuncula Indulgence, or Pardon of Assisi, was authorized by Honorius III. Originally, it could be gained for the souls in purgatory only in the chapel of Our Lady of the Angels; by later concessions, it could be gained also in other Franciscan and parish churches. The Portiuncula Indulgence can be gained once from noon to midnight of Aug. 1 and once on Aug. 2, or on the following Sunday with permission of the bishop of the place. The conditions are, in addition to freedom from attachment to sin: reception of the sacraments of penance and the Eucharist on or near the day; a visit to a parish church on the day, during which the Our Father and Creed are offered for the intentions of the pope.

**Possession, Diabolical:** The extraordinary state of a person who is tormented from within by evil spirits who exercise strong influence over his powers of mind and body.

**Postulant:** One of several names used to designate a candidate for membership in a religious institute during the period before novitiate.

**Poverty:** (1) The quality or state of being poor, in actual destitution and need, or being poor in spirit. In the latter sense, poverty means the state of mind and disposition of persons who regard material things in proper perspective as gifts of God for the support of life and its reasonable enrichment, and for the service of others in need. It means freedom from unreasonable attachment to material things as ends in themselves, even though they may be possessed in small or large measure.

(2) One of the evangelical counsels professed as a public vow by members of an institute of consecrated life. It involves the voluntary renunciation of rights of ownership and of independent use and disposal of material goods; or, the right of independent use and disposal, but not of the radical right of ownership. Religious institutes provide their members with necessary and useful goods and services from common resources. The manner in which goods are received and/or handled by religious is determined by poverty of spirit and the rule and constitutions of their institute.

**Pragmatism:** Theory that the truth of ideas, concepts and values depends on their utility or capacity to serve a useful purpose rather than on their conformity with objective standards; also called utilitarianism.

**Prayer:** The raising of the mind and heart to God in adoration, thanksgiving, reparation and petition. Prayer, which is always mental because it involves thought and love of God, may be vocal, meditative, private and personal, social, and official. The official prayer of the Church as a worshipping community is called the liturgy.

**Precepts:** Commands or orders given to individuals or communities in particular cases; they establish law for concerned parties. Preceptive documents are issued by the pope, departments of the Roman Curia and other competent authority in the Church.

**Presence of God:** A devotional practice of increasing one's awareness of the presence and action of God in daily life.

**Presumption:** A violation of the theological virtue of hope, by which a person striving for salvation either relies too much on his own capabilities or expects God to do things which he cannot do, in keeping with his divine attributes, or does not will to do, according to his divine plan. Presumption is the opposite of despair.

**Preternatural Gifts:** Exceptional gifts, beyond the exigencies and powers of human nature, enjoyed by Adam in the state of original justice: immunity from suffering and death, superior knowledge, integrity or perfect control of the passions. These gifts were lost as the result of original sin; their loss, however, implied no impairment of the integrity of human nature.

**Pride:** Unreasonable self-esteem; one of the seven capital sins.

**Prie-Dieu:** A French phrase, meaning pray God, designating a kneeler or bench suitable for kneeling while at prayer.

**Priesthood of the Laity:** Lay persons share in the priesthood of Christ in virtue of the sacraments of baptism and confirmation. They are not only joined with Christ for a life of union with him but are also deputed by him for participation in his mission, now carried on by the Church, of worship, teaching, witness and apostolic works. St. Peter called Christians "a royal priesthood" (1 Pt. 2:9) in this connection. St. Thomas Aquinas declared: "The sacramental characters (of baptism and confirmation) are nothing else than certain sharings of the priesthood of Christ, derived from Christ himself."

The priesthood of the laity differs from the official ministerial priesthood of ordained priests and bishops — who have the power of holy orders for celebrating the Eucharist, administering the other sacraments, and providing pastoral care. The ministerial priesthood, by divine commission, serves the universal priesthood. (See Role of Sacraments.)

**Primary Option:** The life-choice of a person for or against God which shapes the basic orientation of moral conduct. A primary option for God does not preclude the possibility of serious sin.

**Prior:** A superior or an assistant to an abbot in a monastery.

**Privilege:** A favor, an exemption from the obligation of a law. Privileges of various kinds, with respect to ecclesiastical laws, are granted by the pope, departments of the Roman Curia and other competent authority in the Church.

**Probabilism:** A moral system for use in cases of conscience which involve the obligation of doubtful laws. There is a general principle that a doubtful law does not bind. Probabilism, therefore, teaches that it is permissible to follow an opinion favoring liberty, provided the opinion is certainly and solidly probable. Probabilism may not be invoked when there is question of: a certain law or the certain obligation of a law; the certain right of another party; the validity of an action; something which is necessary for salvation.

**Pro-Cathedral:** A church used as a cathedral.

**Promoter of the Faith:** An official of the Congregation for the Causes of Saints, whose role in beatification and canonization procedures is to establish beyond reasonable doubt the validity of evidence regarding the holiness of prospective saints and miracles attributed to their intercession.

**Prophecies of St. Malachy:** These so-called prophecies, listing the designations of 102 popes and 10 antipopes, bear the name they have because they have been falsely attributed to St. Malachy, bishop of Armagh, who died in 1148. Actually, they are forgeries by an unknown author and came to light only in the last decade of the 16th century.

The first 75 prophecies cover the 65 popes and 10 antipopes from Celestine II (1143-1144) to Gregory XIV (1590-91), and are exact with respect to names, coats of arms, birthplaces, and other identifying characteristics. This portion of the work, far from being prophetic, is the result of historical knowledge or hindsight. The 37 designations following that of Gregory are vague, fanciful, and subject to wide interpretation. According to the prophecies, John Paul II, from the Labor of the Sun, will have only two successors before the end of the world.

**Prophecy:** (1) The communication of divine revelation by inspired intermediaries, called prophets, between God and his people. Old Testament prophecy was unique in its origin and because of its ethical and religious content, which included disclosure of the saving will of Yahweh for the people, moral censures and warnings of divine punishment because of sin and violations of the Law and Covenant, in the form of promises, admonitions, reproaches and threats. Although Moses and other earlier figures are called prophets, the period of prophecy is generally dated from the early years of the monarchy to about 100 years after the Babylonian Exile. From that time on the written Law and its interpreters supplanted the prophets as guides of the people. Old Testament prophets are cited in the New Testament, with awareness that God spoke through them and that some of their oracles were fulfilled in Christ. John the Baptist is the outstanding prophetic figure in the New Testament. Christ never claimed the title of prophet for himself, although some people thought he was one. There were prophets in the early Church, and St. Paul mentioned the charism of prophecy in 1 Cor. 14:1-5. Prophecy disappeared after New Testament times. Revelation is classified as the prophetic book of the New Testament.

(2) In contemporary non-scriptural usage, the term is applied to the witness given by persons to the relevance of their beliefs in everyday life and action.

**Province:** (1) A territory comprising one archdiocese called the metropolitan see and one or more dioceses called suffragan sees. The head of the archdiocese, an archbishop, has metropolitan rights and responsibilities over the province.

(2) A division of a religious order under the jurisdiction of a provincial superior.

**Prudence:** Practical wisdom and judgment regarding the choice and use of the best ways and means of doing good; one of the four cardinal virtues.

**Punishment Due for Sin:** The punishment which is a consequence of sin. It is of two kinds:

(1) Eternal punishment is the punishment of hell, to which one becomes subject by the commission of mortal sin. Such punishment is remitted when mortal sin is forgiven.

(2) Temporal punishment is a consequence of venial sin and/or forgiven mortal sin; it is not everlasting and may be remitted in this life by means of penance. Temporal punishment unremitted during this life is remitted by suffering in purgatory.

**Purgatory:** The state or condition in which those who have died in the state of grace, but with some attachment to sin, suffer for a time before they are admitted to the glory and happiness of heaven. In this state and period of passive suffering, they are purified of unrepented venial sins, satisfy the demands of divine justice for temporal punishment due for sins, and are thus converted to a state of worthiness of the beatific vision.

## R

**Racism:** A theory which holds that any one or several of the different races of the human family are inherently superior or inferior to any one or several of the others. The teaching denies the essential unity of the human race, the equality and dignity of all men because of their common possession of the same human nature, and the participation of all men in the divine plan of redemption. It is radically opposed to the virtue of justice and the precept of love of neighbor. Differences of superiority and inferiority which do exist are the result of accidental factors operating in a wide variety of circumstances, and are in no way due to essential defects in any one or several of the branches of the one human race. The theory of racism, together with practices related to it, is incompatible with Christian doctrine.

**Rash Judgment:** Attributing faults to another without sufficient reason; a violation of the obligations of justice and charity.

**Rationalism:** A theory which makes the mind the measure and arbiter of all things, including religious truth. A product of the Enlightenment, it rejects the supernatural, divine revelation, and authoritative teaching by any church.

**Recollection:** Meditation, attitude of concentration or awareness of spiritual matters and things pertaining to salvation and the accomplishment of God's will.

**Relativism:** Theory which holds that all truth, including religious truth, is relative, i.e., not absolute, certain or unchanging; a product of agnosticism, indifferentism, and an unwarranted extension of the notion of truth in positive science. Relativism is based on the tenet that certain knowledge of any and all truth is impossible. Therefore, no religion, philosophy or science can be said to possess the real truth; consequently, all religions, philosophies and sciences may be considered to have as much or as little of truth as any of the others.

**Relics:** The physical remains and effects of saints, which are considered worthy of veneration inasmuch as they are representative of persons in glory with God. First class relics are parts of the bodies of saints, and instruments of their penance and death; second class relics are objects which had some contact with their persons. Catholic doctrine proscribes the view that relics are not worthy of veneration. In line with norms laid down by the Council of Trent and subsequent enactments, discipline concerning relics is subject to control by the Congregation for the Causes of Saints.

**Religion:** The adoration and service of God as expressed in divine worship and in daily life. Religion is concerned with all of the relations existing between God and man, and between man and man because of the central significance of God. Objectively considered, religion consists of a body of truth which is believed, a code of morality for the guidance of conduct, and a form of divine worship. Subjectively, it is a person's total response, theoretically and practically, to the demands of faith; it is living faith, personal engagement, self-commitment to God. Thus, by creed, code and cult, a person orders and directs his life in reference to God and, through what the love and service of God implies, to his fellow men and all things.

**Reliquary:** A vessel for the preservation and exposition of a relic; sometimes made like a small monstrance.

**Reparation:** The making of amends to God for sin committed; one of the four ends of prayer and the purpose of penance.

**Rescript:** A written reply by an ecclesiastical superior regarding a question or request; its provisions bind concerned parties only. Papal dispensations are issued in the form of rescripts.

**Reserved Case:** A sin or censure, absolution from which is reserved to religious superiors, bishops, the pope, or confessors having special faculties. Reservations are made because of the serious nature and social effects of certain sins and censures.

**Restitution:** An act of reparation for an injury done to another. The injury may be caused by taking and/or retaining what belongs to another or by damaging either the property or reputation of another. The intention of making restitution, usually in kind, is required as a condition for the forgiveness of sins of injustice, even though actual restitution is not possible.

**Ring:** In the Church a ring is worn as part of the insignia of bishops, abbots, et al.; by sisters to denote their consecration to God and the Church. The wedding ring symbolizes the love and union of husband and wife.

**Ritual:** A book of prayers and ceremonies used in the administration of the sacraments and other ceremonial functions. In the Roman Rite, the standard book of this kind is the Roman Ritual.

**Rogito:** The official notarial act or document testifying to the burial of a pope.

**Rosary:** A form of mental and vocal prayer centered on mysteries or events in the lives of Jesus and Mary. Its essential elements are meditation on the mysteries and the recitation of a number of decades of Hail Marys, each beginning with the Lord's Prayer. Introductory prayers may include the Apostles' Creed, an initial Our Father, three Hail Marys and a Glory be to the Father; each decade is customarily concluded with a Glory be to the Father; at the end, it is customary to say the Hail, Holy Queen and a prayer from the liturgy for the feast of the Blessed Virgin Mary of the Rosary.

The **Mysteries of the Rosary,** which are the subject of meditation, are: (1) Joyful — the Annunciation to Mary that she was to be the Mother of Christ, her visit to Elizabeth, the birth of Jesus, the presentation of Jesus in the Temple, the finding of Jesus in the Temple. (2) Sorrowful — Christ's agony in the Garden of Gethsemani, scourging at the pillar, crowning with thorns, carrying of the Cross to Calvary, and crucifixion. (3) Glorious — the Resurrection and Ascension of Christ, the descent of the Holy Spirit upon the Apostles, Mary's Assumption into heaven and her crowning as Queen of angels and men.

The complete Rosary, called the Dominican Rosary, consists of 15 decades. In customary prac-

tice, only five decades are usually said at one time. Rosary beads are used to aid in counting the prayers without distraction.

The Rosary originated through the coalescence of popular devotions to Jesus and Mary from the 12th century onward. Its present form dates from about the 15th century. Carthusians contributed greatly toward its development; Dominicans have been its greatest promoters.

**S**

**Sabbath:** The seventh day of the week, observed by Jews and Sabbatarians as the day for rest and religious observance.

**Sacramentary:** One of the first liturgical books, containing the celebrant's part of the Mass and rites for administration of the sacraments. The earliest book of this kind, the Leonine Sacramentary, dates from the middle or end of the sixth century.

The *Sacramentary* in current use is the same as the *Roman Missal.*

**Sacrarium:** A basin with a drain leading directly into the ground; standard equipment of a sacristy.

**Sacred Heart, Enthronement:** An acknowledgment of the sovereignty of Jesus Christ over the Christian family, expressed by the installation of an image or picture of the Sacred Heart in a place of honor in the home, accompanied by an act of consecration.

**Sacred Heart, Promises:** Twelve promises to persons having devotion to the Sacred Heart of Jesus, which were communicated by Christ to St. Margaret Mary Alacoque in a private revelation in 1675: (1) I will give them all the graces necessary in their state in life. (2) I will establish peace in their homes. (3) I will comfort them in all their afflictions. (4) I will be their secure refuge during life and, above all, in death. (5) I will bestow abundant blessing upon all their undertakings. (6) Sinners shall find in my Heart the source and the infinite ocean of mercy. (7) By devotion to my Heart tepid souls shall grow fervent. (8) Fervent souls shall quickly mount to high perfection. (9) I will bless every place where a picture of my Heart shall be set up and honored. (10) I will give to priests the gift of touching the most hardened hearts. (11) Those who promote this devotion shall have their names written in my Heart, never to be blotted out. (12) I will grant the grace of final penitence to those who communicate (receive Holy Communion) on the first Friday of nine consecutive months.

**Sacrilege:** Violation of and irreverence toward a person, place or thing that is sacred because of public dedication to God; a sin against the virtue of religion. Personal sacrilege is violence of some kind against a cleric or religious, or a violation of chastity with a cleric or religious. Local sacrilege is the desecration of sacred places. Real sacrilege is irreverence with respect to sacred things, such as the sacraments and sacred vessels.

**Sacristy:** A utility room where vestments, church furnishings and sacred vessels are kept and where the clergy vest for sacred functions.

**Sadducees:** The predominantly priestly party

among the Jews in the time of Christ, noted for extreme conservatism, acceptance only of the Law of Moses, and rejection of the traditions of the elders. Their opposite numbers were the Pharisees.

**Saints, Cult of:** The veneration, called dulia, of holy persons who have died and are in glory with God in heaven; it includes honoring them and petitioning them for their intercession with God. Liturgical veneration is given only to saints officially recognized by the Church; private veneration may be given to anyone thought to be in heaven. The veneration of saints is essentially different from the adoration given to God alone; by its very nature, however, it terminates in the worship of God. According to the Second Vatican Council's *Dogmatic Constitution on the Church* (No. 50): "It is supremely fitting . . . that we love those friends and fellow heirs of Jesus Christ, who are also our brothers and extraordinary benefactors, that we render due thanks to God for them and 'suppliantly invoke them and have recourse to their prayers, their power and help in obtaining benefits from God through his Son, Jesus Christ, our Lord, who is our sole Redeemer and Savior.' For by its very nature every genuine testimony of love which we show to those in heaven tends toward and terminates in Christ, who is the 'crown of all saints.' Through him it tends toward and terminates in God, who is wonderful in his saints and is magnified in them."

**Salvation:** The liberation of persons from sin and its effects, reconciliation with God in and through Christ, the attainment of union with God forever in the glory of heaven as the supreme purpose of life and as the God-given reward for fulfillment of his will on earth. Salvation-in-process begins and continues in this life through union with Christ in faith professed and in action; its final term is union with God and the whole community of the saved in the ultimate perfection of God's kingdom. The Church teaches that: God wills the salvation of all men; men are saved in and through Christ; membership in the Church established by Christ, known and understood as the community of salvation, is necessary for salvation; men with this knowledge and understanding who deliberately reject this Church, cannot be saved. The Catholic Church is the Church founded by Christ. (See below, Salvation outside the Church.)

**Salvation History:** The facts and the record of God's relations with men, in the past, present and future, for the purpose of leading them to live in accordance with his will for the eventual attainment after death of salvation, or everlasting happiness with him in heaven.

The essentials of salvation history are: God's love for all men and will for their salvation; his intervention and action in the world to express this love and bring about their salvation; the revelation he made of himself and the covenant he established with the Israelites in the Old Testament; the perfecting of this revelation and the new covenant of grace through Christ in the New Testament; the continuing action-for-salvation carried on in and through the Mystical Body of Christ, the Church;

the communication of saving grace to men through the merits of Christ and the operations of the Holy Spirit in the here-and-now circumstances of daily life and with the cooperation of men themselves.

**Salvation outside the Church:** The Second Vatican Council covered this subject summarily in the following manner: "Those also can attain to everlasting salvation who through no fault of their own do not know the Gospel of Christ or his Church, yet sincerely seek God and, moved by grace, strive by their deeds to do his will as it is known to them through the dictates of conscience. Nor does divine Providence deny the help necessary for salvation to those who, without blame on their part, have not yet arrived at an explicit knowledge of God, but who strive to live a good life, thanks to his grace. Whatever good or truth is found among them is looked upon by the Church as a preparation for the Gospel. She regards such qualities as given by him who enlightens all men so that they may finally have life" *(Dogmatic Constitution on the Church,* No. 16).

**Satanism:** Worship of the devil, a blasphemous inversion of the order of worship which is due to God alone.

**Scandal:** Conduct which is the occasion of sin to another person.

**Scapular:** (1) A part of the habit of some religious orders like the Benedictines and Dominicans; a nearly shoulder-wide strip of cloth worn over the tunic and reaching almost to the feet in front and behind. Originally a kind of apron, it came to symbolize the cross and yoke of Christ.

(2) Scapulars worn by lay persons as a sign of association with religious orders and for devotional purposes are an adaptation of monastic scapulars. Approved by the Church as sacramentals, they consist of two small squares of woolen cloth joined by strings and are worn about the neck. They are given for wearing in a ceremony of investiture or enrollment. There are nearly 20 scapulars for devotional use: the five principal ones are generally understood to include those of Our Lady of Mt. Carmel (the brown Carmelite Scapular), the Holy Trinity, Our Lady of the Seven Dolors, the Passion, the Immaculate Conception.

**Scapular Medal:** A medallion with a representation of the Sacred Heart on one side and of the Blessed Virgin Mary on the other. Authorized by St. Pius X in 1910, it may be worn or carried in place of a scapular by persons already invested with a scapular.

**Scapular Promise:** According to a legend of the Carmelite Order, the Blessed Virgin Mary appeared to St. Simon Stock in 1251 at Cambridge and declared that wearers of the brown Carmelite Scapular would be saved from hell and taken to heaven by her on the first Saturday after death. The validity of the legend has never been the subject of official decision by the Church. Essentially, it expresses belief in the intercession of Mary and the efficacy of sacramentals in the context of truly Christian life.

**Schism:** Derived from a Greek word meaning separation, the term designates formal and obstinate refusal by a baptized person, called a *schismatic,* to be in communion with the pope and the Church. The canonical penalty is excommunication. One of the most disastrous schisms in history resulted in the definitive separation of the Church in the East from union with Rome about 1054.

**Scholasticism:** The term usually applied to the Catholic theology and philosophy which developed in the Middle Ages.

**Scribes:** Hebrew intellectuals noted for their knowledge of the Law of Moses, influential from the time of the Exile to about 70 A.D. Many of them were Pharisees. They were the antecedents of rabbis and their traditions, as well as those of the Pharisees, had a lasting influence on Judaism following the destruction of Jerusalem in 70 A.D.

**Scruple:** A morbid, unreasonable fear and anxiety that one's actions are sinful when they are not, or more seriously sinful than they actually are. Compulsive scrupulosity is quite different from the transient scrupulosity of persons of tender or highly sensitive conscience, or of persons with faulty moral judgment.

**Seal of Confession:** The obligation of secrecy which must be observed regarding knowledge of things learned in connection with the confession of sin in the sacrament of penance. The seal covers matters whose revelation would make the sacrament burdensome. Confessors are prohibited, under penalty of excommunication, from making any direct revelation of confessional matter; this prohibition holds, outside of confession, even with respect to the person who made the confession unless the person releases the priest from the obligation. Persons other than confessors are obliged to maintain secrecy, but not under penalty of excommunication. General, non-specific discussion of confessional matter does not violate the seal.

**Secularism:** A school of thought, a spirit and manner of action which ignores and/or repudiates the validity or influence of supernatural religion with respect to individual and social life. In describing secularism in their annual statement in 1947, the bishops of the United States said in part: ". . . There are many men — and their number is daily increasing — who in practice live their lives without recognizing that this is God's world. For the most part they do not deny God. On formal occasions they may even mention his name. Not all of them would subscribe to the statement that all moral values derive from merely human conventions. But they fail to bring an awareness of their responsibility to God into their thought and action as individuals and members of society. This, in essence, is what we mean by secularism."

**See:** Another name for diocese or archdiocese.

**Seminary:** A house of study and formation for men, called seminarians, preparing for the priesthood. Traditional seminaries date from the Council of Trent in the middle of the 16th century; before that time, candidates for the priesthood were variously trained in monastic schools, universities under church auspices, and in less formal ways. At the present time, seminaries are undergoing considerable change for the improvement of academic and formation programs and procedures.

**Sermon on the Mount:** A compilation of sayings of Our Lord in the form of an extended discourse in Matthew's Gospel (5:1 to 7:27) and, in a shorter discourse, in Luke (6:17-49). The passage in Matthew, called the "Constitution of the New Law," summarizes the living spirit of believers in Christ and members of the kingdom of God. Beginning with the Beatitudes and including the Lord's Prayer, it covers the perfect justice of the New Law, the fulfillment of the Old Law in the New Law of Christ, and the integrity of internal attitude and external conduct with respect to love of God and neighbor, justice, chastity, truth, trust and confidence in God.

**Servile Work:** Work and concern with business which impede participation in divine worship, the spirit of the Lord's Day, and appropriate physical and mental relaxation.

**Seven Last Words of Christ:** Words of Christ on the Cross. (1) "Father, forgive them; for they do not know what they are doing." (2) To the penitent thief: "I assure you: today you will be with me in Paradise." (3) To Mary and his Apostle John: "Woman, there is your son . . . There is your mother." (4) "My God, my God, why have you forsaken me?" (5) "I am thirsty." (6) "Now it is finished." (7) "Father, into your hands I commend my spirit."

**Shrine, Crowned:** A shrine approved by the Holy See as a place of pilgrimage. The approval permits public devotion at the shrine and implies that at least one miracle has resulted from devotion at the shrine. Among the best known crowned shrines are those of the Virgin Mary at Lourdes and Fatima.

**Shroud of Turin:** A strip of brownish linen cloth, 14 feet, three inches in length and three feet, seven inches in width, bearing the front and back imprint of a human body. A tradition dating from the seventh century, which has not been verified beyond doubt, claims that the shroud is the fine linen in which the body of Christ was wrapped for burial. The early history of the shroud is obscure. It was enshrined at Lirey, France, in 1354 and was transferred in 1578 to Turin, Italy, where it has been kept in the cathedral down to the present time. Scientific investigation, which began in 1898, seems to indicate that the markings on the shroud are those of a human body. The shroud, for the first time since 1933, was placed on public view from Aug. 27 to Oct. 8, 1978, and was seen by an estimated 3.3 million people. Scientists conducted intensive studies of it for several days after the end of public viewing.

The shroud, which had been the possession of the House of Savoy, was willed to Pope John Paul II in 1983.

**Sick Calls:** When a person is confined at home by illness or other cause and is unable to go to church for reception of the sacraments, a parish priest should be informed and arrangements made for him to visit the person at home. Such visitations are common in pastoral practice, both for special needs and for providing persons with regular opportunities for receiving the sacraments.

If a priest cannot make the visitation, arrangements can be made for a Eucharistic minister to bring Holy Communion to the homebound or bedridden person.

**Sign of the Cross:** A sign, ceremonial gesture or movement in the form of a cross by which a person confesses faith in the Holy Trinity and Christ, and intercedes for the blessing of himself, other persons, and things. In Roman-Rite practice, a person making the sign touches the fingers of the right hand to his forehead, below the breast, left shoulder and right shoulder while saying: "In the name of the Father, and of the Son, and of the Holy Spirit." The sign is also made with the thumb on the forehead, the lips, and the breast. For the blessing of persons and objects, a large sign of the cross is made by movement of the right hand. In Eastern-Rite practice, the sign is made with the thumb and first two fingers of the right hand joined together and touching the forehead, below the breast, the right shoulder and the left shoulder; the formula generally used is the doxology, "O Holy God, O Holy Strong One, O Immortal One." The Eastern manner of making the sign was general until the first half of the 13th century; by the 17th century, Western practice involved the whole right hand and the reversal of direction from shoulder to shoulder.

**Signs of the Times:** Contemporary events, trends and features in culture and society, the needs and aspirations of people, all the factors that form the context in and through which the Church has to carry on its saving mission. The Second Vatican Council spoke on numerous occasions about these signs and the relationship between them and a kind of manifestation of God's will, positive or negative, and about subjecting them to judgment and action corresponding to the demands of divine revelation through Scripture, Christ, and the experience, tradition and teaching authority of the Church.

**Simony:** The deliberate intention and act of selling and/or buying spiritual goods or material things so connected with the spiritual that they cannot be separated therefrom; a violation of the virtue of religion, and a sacrilege, because it wrongfully puts a material price on spiritual things, which cannot be either sold or bought. In church law, actual sale or purchase is subject to censure in some cases. The term is derived from the name of Simon Magus, who attempted to buy from Sts. Peter and John the power to confirm people in the Holy Spirit (Acts 8:4-24).

**Sin:** (1) Actual sin is rejection of God manifested by free and deliberate violation of his law by thought, word or action. (a) Mortal sin — involving serious matter, sufficient reflection and full consent — results in total alienation from God, making a person dead to sanctifying grace, incapable of performing meritorious supernatural acts and subject to everlasting punishment. (b) Venial sin — involving less serious matter, reflection and consent — does not have such serious consequences.

(2) Original sin is the sin of Adam, with consequences for all men. (See separate entry.)

**Sins against the Holy Spirit:** Despair of salvation, presumption of God's mercy, impugning the known truths of faith, envy at another's spiritual good, obstinacy in sin, final impenitence. Those guilty of such sins stubbornly resist the influence of grace and, as long as they do so, cannot be forgiven.

**Sins, Occasions of:** Circumstances (persons, places, things, etc.) which easily lead to sin. There is an obligation to avoid voluntary proximate occasions of sin, and to take precautions against the dangers of unavoidable occasions.

**Sins That Cry to Heaven for Vengeance:** Willful murder, sins against nature, oppression of the poor, widows and orphans, defrauding laborers of their wages.

**Sister:** Any woman religious, in popular speech; strictly, the title applies only to women Religious belonging to institutes whose members never professed solemn vows. Most of the institutes whose members are properly called Sisters were established during and since the 19th century. Women Religious with solemn vows, or belonging to institutes whose members formerly professed solemn vows, are properly called nuns.

**Sisterhood:** A generic term referring to the whole institution of the life of women religious in the Church, or to a particular institute of women religious.

**Situation Ethics:** A subjective, individualistic ethical theory which denies the binding force of ethical principles as universal laws and preceptive norms of moral conduct, and proposes that morality is determined only by situational conditions and considerations and the intention of the person. In an instruction issued on the subject in May, 1956, the Congregation for the Holy Office said:

"It ignores the principles of objective ethics. This 'New Morality,' it is claimed, is not only the equal of objective morality, but is superior to it.

"The authors who follow this system state that the ultimate determining norm for activity is not the objective order as determined by the natural law and known with certainty from this law. It is instead some internal judgment and illumination of the mind of every individual by which the mind comes to know what is to be done in a concrete situation.

"This ultimate decision of man is, therefore, not the application of the objective law to a particular case after the particular circumstances of a 'situation' have been considered and weighed according to the rules of prudence, as the more important authors of objective ethics teach; but it is, according to them, immediate, internal illumination and judgment.

"With regard to its objective truth and correctness, this judgment, at least in many things, is not ultimately measured, is not to be measured or is not measurable by any objective norm found outside man and independent of his subjective persuasion, but it is fully sufficient in itself. . . .

"Much that is stated in this system of 'Situation Ethics' is contrary to the truth of reality and to the dictate of sound reason. It gives evidence of relativism and modernism, and deviates far from the Catholic teaching handed down through the ages."

**Slander:** Attributing to a person faults which he does not have; a violation of the obligations of justice and charity, for which restitution is due.

**Sloth:** One of the seven capital sins; spiritual laziness, involving distaste and disgust for spiritual things; spiritual boredom, which saps the vigor of spiritual life. Physical laziness is a counterpart of spiritual sloth.

**Sorcery:** A kind of black magic in which evil is invoked by means of diabolical intervention; a violation of the virtue of religion.

**Soteriology:** The division of theology which treats of the mission and work of Christ as Redeemer.

**Species, Sacred:** The appearances of bread and wine (color, taste, smell, etc.) which remain after the substance has been changed at the Consecration of the Mass into the Body and Blood of Christ. (See Transubstantiation.)

**Spiritism:** Attempts to communicate with spirits and departed souls by means of seances, table tapping, ouija boards, and other methods; a violation of the virtue of religion. Spiritualistic practices are noted for fakery.

**Spiritual Works of Mercy:** Works of spiritual assistance, motivated by love of God and neighbor, to persons in need: counseling the doubtful, instructing the ignorant, admonishing sinners, comforting the afflicted, forgiving offenses, bearing wrongs patiently, praying for the living and the dead.

**Stational Churches, Days:** Churches, especially in Rome, where the clergy and lay people were accustomed to gather with their bishop on certain days for the celebration of the liturgy. The 25 early titular or parish churches of Rome, plus other churches, each had their turn as the site of divine worship in practices which may have started in the third century. The observances were rather well developed toward the latter part of the fourth century, and by the fifth they included a Mass concelebrated by the pope and attendant priests. On some occasions, the stational liturgy was preceded by a procession from another church called a collecta. There were 42 Roman stational churches in the eighth century, and 89 stational services were scheduled annually in connection with the liturgical seasons. Stational observances fell into disuse toward the end of the Middle Ages. Some revival was begun by John XXIII in 1959 and continued by Paul VI.

**Stations of the Cross:** A series of meditations on the sufferings of Christ: his condemnation to death and taking up of the Cross; the first fall on the way to Calvary; meeting his Mother; being assisted by Simon of Cyrene, and by Veronica who wiped his face; the second fall; meeting the women of Jerusalem; the third fall; being stripped and nailed to the Cross; his death; the removal of his body from the Cross and his burial. Depictions of these scenes are mounted in most churches, chapels and in some other places, beneath small crosses.

A person making the Way of the Cross passes before these Stations, or stopping points, pausing at each for meditation. If the Stations are made by a group of people, only the leader has to pass from Station to Station. Prayer for the intentions of the pope is required for gaining the indulgence granted for the Stations.

Those unable to make the Stations in the ordinary manner, because they are impeded from visiting a church or other place where the Stations are, can still practice the devotion by meditating on the sufferings of Christ; praying the Our Father, Hail Mary and Glory for each Station and five times in commemoration of the wounds of Christ; and praying for the intentions of the pope. This practice has involved the use of a Stations Crucifix.

The Stations originated, remotely, from the practice of Holy Land pilgrims who visited the actual scenes of incidents in the Passion of Christ. Representations elsewhere of at least some of these scenes were known as early as the fifth century. Later, the Stations evolved in connection with and as a consequence of strong devotion to the Passion in the 12th and 13th centuries. Franciscans, who were given custody of the Holy Places in 1342, promoted the devotion widely; one of them, St. Leonard of Port Maurice, became known as the greatest preacher of the Way of the Cross in the 18th century. The general features of the devotion were fixed by Clement XII in 1731.

**Statutes:** Virtually the same as decrees (see separate entry), they almost always designate laws of a particular council or synod rather than pontifical laws.

**Stigmata:** Marks of the wounds suffered by Christ in his crucifixion, in hands and feet by nails, and side by the piercing of a lance. Some persons, called stigmatists, have been reported as recipients or sufferers of marks like these. The Church, however, has never issued any infallible declaration about their possession by anyone, even in the case of St. Francis of Assisi whose stigmata seem to be the best substantiated and may be commemorated in the Roman-Rite liturgy. Ninety percent of some 300 reputed stigmatists have been women. Judgment regarding the presence, significance, and manner of causation of stigmata would depend, among other things, on irrefutable experimental evidence.

**Stipend, Mass:** An offering given to a priest for applying the fruits of the Mass according to the intention of the donor. The offering is a contribution to the support of the priest. The disposition of the fruits of the sacrifice, in line with doctrine concerning the Mass in particular and prayer in general, is subject to the will of God. In the early Christian centuries, when Mass was not offered for the intentions of particular persons, the participants made offerings of bread and wine for the sacrifice and their own Holy Communion, and of other things useful for the support of the clergy and the poor. Some offerings may have been made as early as the fourth century for the celebration of Mass for particular intentions, and there are indications of the existence of this practice from the sixth century when private Masses began to be offered. The earliest certain proof of stipend practice, however, dates from the eighth century. By the 11th century, along with private Mass, it was established custom.

**Stole Fee:** An offering given on certain occasions; e.g., at a baptism, wedding, funeral, for the support of the clergy who administer the sacraments and perform other sacred rites.

**Stoup:** A vessel used to contain holy water.

**Suffragan See:** Any diocese, except the archdiocese, within a province.

**Suicide:** The taking of one's own life; a violation of God's dominion over human life. Ecclesiastical burial is denied to persons who deliberately commit suicide while in full possession of their faculties; it is permitted in cases of doubt.

**Supererogation:** Good and virtuous actions which go beyond the obligations of duty and the requirements enjoined by God's law as necessary for salvation. Examples of these works are the profession and observance of the evangelical counsels of poverty, chastity, and obedience, and efforts to practice charity to the highest degree.

**Supernatural:** Above the natural; that which exceeds and is not due or owed to the essence, exigencies, requirements, powers and merits of created nature. While man has no claim on supernatural things and does not need them in order to exist and act on a natural level, he does need them in order to exist and act in the higher order or economy of grace established by God for his salvation.

God has freely given to man certain things which are beyond the powers and rights of his human nature. Examples of the supernatural are: grace, a kind of participation by man in the divine life, by which man becomes capable of performing acts meritorious for salvation; divine revelation by which God manifests himself to man and makes known truth that is inaccessible to human reason alone; faith, by which man believes divine truth because of the authority of God who reveals it through Sacred Scripture and tradition and the teaching of his Church.

**Superstition:** A violation of the virtue of religion, by which God is worshipped in an unworthy manner or creatures are given honor which belongs to God alone. False, vain, or futile worship involves elements which are incompatible with the honor and respect due to God, such as error, deception, and bizarre practices. Examples are: false and exaggerated devotions, chain prayers and allegedly unfailing prayers, the mixing of unbecoming practices in worship. The second kind of superstition attributes to persons and things powers and honor which belong to God alone. Examples are: idolatry, divination, magic, spiritism, necromancy.

**Suspension:** A penalty by which a cleric is forbidden to exercise some or all of his powers of orders and jurisdiction, or to accept the financial support of his benefices.

**Swearing:** Taking an oath; calling upon God to witness the truth of a statement; a legitimate thing to do for serious reasons and under proper circumstances, as in a court of law. To swear without sufficient reason is to dishonor God's name; to swear falsely in a court of law is perjury.

**Swedenborgianism:** A doctrine developed in and from the writings of Emmanuel Swedenborg (1688-1772), who claimed that during a number of visions he had in 1745 Christ taught him the spiritual sense of Sacred Scripture and commissioned him to communicate it to others. He held that, just as Christianity succeeded Judaism, so his teaching supplemented Christianity. He rejected belief in the Trinity, original sin, the Resurrection, and all the sacraments except baptism and the Eucharist. His followers are members of the Church of the New Jerusalem or of the New Church.

**Syllabus, The:** (1) When not qualified, the term refers to the list of 80 errors accompanying Pope Pius IX's encyclical *Quanta Cura*, issued in 1864. (2) The *Syllabus* of St. Pius X in the decree *Lamentabili*, issued by the Holy Office July 4, 1907, condemning 65 heretical propositions of modernism. This schedule of errors was followed shortly by that pope's encyclical *Pascendi*, the principal ecclesiastical document against modernism, issued Sept. 8, 1907.

**Synod, Diocesan:** Meeting of representative persons of a diocese — priests, religious, lay persons — with the bishop, called by him for the purpose of considering and taking action on matters affecting the life and mission of the Church in the diocese. Persons taking part in a synod have consultative status; the bishop alone is the legislator, with power to authorize synodal decrees. According to canon law, every diocese should have a synod every 10 years.

## T

**Te Deum:** The opening Latin words, Thee, God, of a hymn of praise and thanksgiving prescribed for use in the Office of Readings of the Liturgy of the Hours on many Sundays, solemnities and feasts.

**Temperance:** Moderation, one of the four cardinal virtues.

**Temptation:** Any enticement to sin, from any source: the strivings of one's own faculties, the action of the devil, other persons, circumstances of life, etc. Temptation itself is not sin. Temptation can be avoided and overcome with the use of prudence and the help of grace.

**Thanksgiving:** An expression of gratitude to God for his goodness and the blessings he grants; one of the four ends of prayer.

**Theism:** A philosophy which admits the existence of God and the possibility of divine revelation; it is generally monotheistic and acknowledges God as transcendent and also active in the world. Because it is a philosophy rather than a system of theology derived from revelation, it does not include specifically Christian doctrines, like those concerning the Trinity, the Incarnation and Redemption.

**Theological Virtues:** The virtues which have God for their direct object: faith, or belief in God's infallible teaching; hope, or confidence in divine assistance; charity, or love of God. They are given to a person with grace in the first instance, through baptism and incorporation in Christ.

**Theology:** Knowledge of God and religion, deriving from and based on the data of divine Revelation, organized and systematized according to some kind of scientific method. It involves systematic study and presentation of the truths of divine Revelation in Sacred Scripture, tradition, and the teaching of the Church.

The Second Vatican Council made the following declaration about theology and its relation to divine Revelation: "Sacred theology rests on the written word of God, together with sacred tradition, as its primary and perpetual foundation. By scrutinizing in the light of faith all truth stored up in the mystery of Christ, theology is most powerfully strengthened and constantly rejuvenated by that word. For the sacred Scriptures contain the word of God and, since they are inspired, really are the word of God; and so the study of the sacred page is, as it were, the soul of sacred theology" *(Constitution on Revelation.* No. 24).

Theology has been divided under various subject headings. Some of the major fields have been: dogma (systematic theology), moral, pastoral, ascetics (the practice of virtue and means of attaining holiness and perfection), mysticism (higher states of religious experience). Other subject headings include ecumenism (Christian unity, interfaith relations), ecclesiology (the nature and constitution of the Church), Mariology (doctrine concerning the Blessed Virgin Mary), the sacraments, etc.

**Tithing:** Contribution of a portion of one's income, originally one-tenth, for purposes of religion and charity. The practice is mentioned 46 times in the Bible. In early Christian times, tithing was adopted in continuance of Old Testament practices of the Jewish people, and the earliest positive church legislation on the subject was enacted in 567. Catholics are bound in conscience to contribute to the support of their church, but the manner in which they do so is not fixed by law. Tithing, which amounts to a pledged contribution of a portion of one's income, has aroused new attention in recent years in the United States.

**Titular Sees:** Dioceses where the Church once flourished but which later were overrun by pagans or Moslems and now exist only in name or title. Bishops without a territorial or residential diocese of their own; e.g., auxiliary bishops, are given titular sees.

**Transfinalization, Transignification:** Terms coined to express the sign value of consecrated bread and wine with respect to the presence and action of Christ in the Eucharistic sacrifice and the spiritually vivifying purpose of the Eucharistic banquet in Holy Communion. The theory behind the terms has strong undertones of existential and "sign" philosophy, and has been criticized for its openness to interpretations at variance with the doctrine of transubstantiation and the abiding presence of Christ under the appearances of bread and wine after the sacrifice of the Mass and Communion have been completed. The terms, if used as substitutes for transubstantiation, are unaccep-

table; if they presuppose transubstantiation, they are acceptable as clarifications of its meaning.

**Transubstantiation:** "The way Christ is made present in this sacrament (Holy Eucharist) is none other than by the change of the whole substance of the bread into his Body, and of the whole substance of the wine into his Blood (in the Consecration at Mass) . . . this unique and wonderful change the Catholic Church rightly calls transubstantiation" (encyclical *Mysterium Fidei* of Paul VI, Sept. 3, 1965). The first official use of the term was made by the Fourth Council of the Lateran in 1215. Authoritative teaching on the subject was issued by the Council of Trent.

**Treasury of the Church:** The superabundant merits of Christ and the saints from which the Church draws to confer spiritual benefits, such as indulgences.

**Triduum:** A three-day series of public or private devotions.

## U-Z

**Usury:** Excessive interest charged for the loan and use of money; a violation of justice.

**Veronica:** A word resulting from the combination of a Latin word for true, *vera*, and a Greek word for image, *eikon*, designating a likeness of the face of Christ or the name of a woman said to have given him a cloth on which he caused an imprint of his face to appear. The veneration at Rome of a likeness depicted on cloth dates from about the end of the 10th century; it figured in a popular devotion during the Middle Ages, and in the Holy Face devotion practiced since the 19th century. A faint, indiscernible likeness said to be of this kind is preserved in St. Peter's Basilica. The origin of the likeness is uncertain, and the identity of the woman is unknown. Before the 14th century, there were no known artistic representations of an incident concerning a woman who wiped the face of Christ with a piece of cloth while He was carrying the Cross to Calvary.

**Viaticum:** Holy Communion given to those in danger of death. The word, derived from Latin, means provision for a journey through death to life hereafter.

**Vicar General:** A priest or bishop appointed by the bishop of a diocese to serve as his deputy, with ordinary executive power, in the administration of the diocese.

**Virginity:** Observance of perpetual sexual abstinence. The state of virginity, which is embraced for the love of God by religious with a public vow or by others with a private vow, was singled out for high praise by Christ (Mt. 19:10-12) and has always been so regarded by the Church. In the encyclical *Sacra Virginitas,* Pius XII stated: "Holy virginity and that perfect chastity which is consecrated to the service of God is without doubt among the most perfect treasures which the founder of the Church has left in heritage to the society which he established."

Paul VI approved in 1970 a rite in which women can consecrate their virginity "to Christ and their brethren" without becoming members of a religious institute. The *Ordo Consecrationis Vir-*

ginum, a revision of a rite promulgated by Clement VII in 1596, is traceable to the Roman liturgy of about 500.

**Virtue:** A habit or established capability for performing good actions. Virtues are *natural* (acquired and increased by repeating good acts) and/or *supernatural* (given with grace by God).

**Vocation:** A call to a way of life. Generally, the term applies to the common call of all men, from God, to holiness and salvation. Specifically, it refers to particular states of life, each called a vocation, in which response is made to this universal call; viz., marriage, the religious life and/or priesthood, the single state freely chosen or accepted for the accomplishment of God's will. The term also applies to the various occupations in which persons make a living. The Church supports the freedom of each individual in choosing a particular vocation, and reserves the right to pass on the acceptability of candidates for the priesthood and religious life. Signs or indicators of particular vocations are many, including a person's talents and interests, circumstances and obligations, invitations of grace and willingness to respond thereto.

**Vow:** A promise made to God with sufficient knowledge and freedom, which has as its object a moral good that is possible and better than its voluntary omission. A person who professes a vow binds himself or herself by the virtue of religion to fulfill the promise. The best known examples of vows are those of poverty, chastity and obedience professed by religious (see Evangelical Counsels, individual entries).

Public vows are made before a competent person, acting as an agent of the Church, who accepts the profession in the name of the Church, thereby giving public recognition to the person's dedication and consecration to God and divine worship. Vows of this kind are either solemn, rendering all contrary acts invalid as well as unlawful; or simple, rendering contrary acts unlawful. Solemn vows are for life; simple vows are for a definite period of time or for life. Vows professed without public recognition by the Church are called private vows. The Church, which has authority to accept and give public recognition to vows, also has authority to dispense persons from their obligations for serious reasons.

**Week of Prayer for Christian Unity:** Eight days of prayer, from Jan. 18 to 25, for the union of all men in the Church established by Christ. On the initiative of Father Paul James Francis, S.A., of Graymoor, N.Y., it originated in 1908 as the Chair of Unity Octave. In recent years, its observance on an interfaith basis has increased greatly.

**Witness, Christian:** Practical testimony or evidence given by Christians of their faith in all circumstances of life — by prayer and general conduct, through good example and good works, etc.; being and acting in accordance with Christian belief; actual practice of the Christian faith.

## HUMAN DEVELOPMENT CAMPAIGN

The Campaign for Human Development was inaugurated by the U.S. Catholic Conference in November, 1969, to combat injustice, oppression, alienation and poverty in this country in three significant ways:

• by making people in this country, especially Catholics, aware of the poverty, oppression and/or injustice afflicting some 35 million persons, through programs of education and public awareness;

• by funding self-help programs begun and carried out by the poor or by the poor and non-poor working together;

• by seeking a re-evaluation of the priorities of individuals, families, the Church and the civic community with respect to the stewardship of God-given goods.

The campaign got under way with a collection taken up in all parishes throughout the country on Nov. 22, 1970. Seventy-five per cent of the money contributed in this and subsequent annual collections was placed in a national fund principally for funding self-help projects and also for educational purposes; 25 per cent remained in the dioceses where it was collected, for similar use on the local levels.

More than $75 million in grants have been allocated by the national office since 1970; grants to 215 projects in 1984 totaled more than $6½ million. Diocesan allocations since 1970 have amounted to approximately $20 million.

Aid requests are reviewed by a broadly representative committee of 40 members which passes its recommendations for funding on to the 13-member Bishops' Committee for the Campaign for Human Development. Requests for aid from the national office are several times greater than the some 200 programs funded each year. Local-level requests and funding are handled by diocesan offices for the Campaign for Human Development.

More than $10 million was contributed to the campaign in 1984.

Father Marvin Mottet is executive director of the campaign; Timothy Collins is assistant director. Bishop William B. Friend of Alexandria-Shreveport, La., is chairman of the bishops' committee.

The national office is located at 1312 Massachusetts Ave. N.W., Washington, D.C. 20005.

### APPALACHIA COMMITTEE

The 600-member Catholic Committee of Appalachia consists of bishops, priests, religious and lay persons engaged in pastoral and social justice ministry in the 13-state region. Appalachia has been defined by Congress as including all of West Virginia and parts of Alabama, Georgia, Kentucky, Maryland, Mississippi, New York, North Carolina, Ohio, Pennsylvania, South Carolina, Tennessee and Virginia. The committee is the Catholic Caucus of the Commission on Religion in Appalachia, an interfaith group.

Address: P.O. Box 953, Whiteburg, Ky 41858.

(Principal sources for statistics: *Annuario Pontificio, 1984; Statistical Yearbook of the Church, 1981* (the latest edition available at press time). Figures are as of Dec. 31, 1982, or Dec. 31 of the year indicated. See Index under names of countries for additional entries on 1984 events.)

*Abbreviation code: archd. — archdiocese; dioc. — diocese; ap. ex. — apostolic exarchate; prel. — prelature; abb. — abbacy; v.a. — vicariate apostolic; p.a. — prefecture apostolic; a.a. — apostolic administration; card. — cardinal; abp. — archbishops; nat. — native; bp. — bishops (diocesan and titular; priests (dioc. — diocesan or secular priests; rel. — those belonging to religious orders); p.d. — permanent deacons; sem. — major seminarians, diocesan and religious; bros. — brothers; srs. — sisters; bap. — baptisms; Caths. — Catholic population; tot. pop. — total population.*

**Afghanistan:** Republic in south-central Asia; capital, Kabul. Christianity antedated Moslem conquest in the seventh century but was overcome by it. All inhabitants are subject to the law of Islam. Christian missionaries are prohibited. Population (est.), 15,540,000.

**Albania:** Communist people's republic in the Balkans, bordering the Adriatic Sea; capital, Tirana. Christianity was introduced before the middle of the fourth century. The Byzantine-Rite Church broke from unity with Rome following the schism of 1054. A large percentage of the population was forcibly Islamized following the invasion (15th century) and long centuries of occupation by the Ottoman Turks. At the time of the communist take-over in 1945, an estimated 68 per cent of the population was Moslem; 19 per cent, Orthodox and 13 per cent, Roman Catholic. The Catholic Church prevailed in the north. It fell victim, as did all religions, to systematic persecution by the government: non-Albanian missionaries were expelled; death, prison sentences and other repressive measures were enacted against church personnel and laity; Catholic schools and churches were closed and used for other purposes, and lines of communication with the Holy See were cut off. In 1967, the government, declaring it had eliminated all religion in the country, proclaimed itself the first atheist state in the world. Despite this, there are reports of a clandestine Catholic community in the country.

*Archd., 2; dioc., 3; abb., 1; a.a. 1; bp., 3 (impeded). [Unconfirmed reports in 1983 stated that Bishop Ernesto Cobo, apostolic administrator of the Shkodre archdiocese and one of the three impeded bishops, had died in a concentration camp. He was still listed in the 1984 Annuario Pontificio.] Tot. pop.* (1982 est.), 2,800,000.

**Algeria:** Republic in northwest Africa: capital, Algiers. Christianity, introduced at an early date, succumbed to Vandal devastation in the fifth century and Moslem conquest in 709, but survived for centuries in small communities into the 12th century. Missionary work was unsuccessful except in service to traders, military personnel and captives along the coast. Church organization was established after the French gained control of the territory in the 1830s. A large number of Catholics were among the estimated million Europeans who left the country after it secured independence from France July 5, 1962. Islam is the state religion. Algeria maintains diplomatic relations with Vatican City.

*Archd., 1; dioc., 3; card., 1; abp., 1; bp., 3 parishes, 82; priests, 199 (83 dioc., 116 rel.); p.d., 3; sem., 18; srs., 482; bap., 41; Caths., 63,500 (.3%); tot. pop., 20,121,000.*

**Andorra:** Autonomous principality in the Pyrenees, under the rule of co-princes — the French head of state and the bishop of Urgel, Spain; capital, Andorra la Vella. Christianity was introduced at an early date. Catholicism is the state religion. The principality is under the ecclesiastical jurisdiction of the Spanish diocese of Urgel.

*Parishes, 7; priests, 19 (13 dioc., 6 rel.); bro., 1; srs., 16; bap., 448; Caths., 26,000; tot. pop., 30,000 (1981).*

**Angola:** Independent (Nov. 11, 1975) republic in west Africa; capital, Luanda. Evangelization by Catholic missionaries, dating from about 1570, reached high points in the 17th and 18th centuries. Independence from Portugal in 1975 left the Church with a heavy loss of personnel when about half of the foreign missionaries fled the country. Two ecclesiastical provinces were established in 1977; all but two of the hierarchy are Angolan; the first Angolan cardinal (Alexandre do Nascimento) was named in 1983. Angola has an apostolic delegate.

*Archd., 3; dioc., 9; card., 1 (nat.); abp., 2 (nat.); bp., 10 (8 nat.); parishes, 250; priests, 324 (141 dioc., 183 rel.); p.d., 1; sem., 127; bros., 59; srs., 731; bap., 67,121; Caths., 3,305,000; tot. pop., 7,250,000.*

**Anguilla:** Self-governing British island territory in the Caribbean; capital, The Valley. Under ecclesiastical jurisdiction of St. John's-Basseterre diocese, Antigua. Statistics included in St. Christopher (Kitts)-Nevis.

**Antigua and Barbuda:** Independent (1981) Caribbean island nation; capital, St. John's, Antigua.

*Dioc., 1; bp., 1; parishes, 2; priests, 5 (2 dioc., 3 rel.); sem., 1; bros., 5; srs., 6; sch., 4; bap., 143; Caths., 7,000 (9.2%); tot. pop., 76,000 (1981).*

**Arabian Peninsula:** Christianity, introduced in various parts of the peninsula in early Christian centuries, succumbed to Islam in the seventh century. The native population is entirely Moslem. The only Christians are foreign workers mainly from the Philippines, India and Korea. Most of the peninsula is under the ecclesiastical jurisdiction of the Vicariate Apostolic of Arabia with its seat in Abu Dhabi, United Arab Emirates. The area has an apostolic delegate (to the Red Sea Region). See individual countries: Bahrain, Oman, Qatar, Saudi Arabia, United Arab Emirates, North Yemen, and South Yemen.

**Argentina:** Republic in southeast South America, bordering on the Atlantic; capital, Buenos Aires. Priests were with the Magellan exploration party and the first Mass in the country was celebrated Apr. 1, 1519. Missionary work began in the 1530s, diocesan organization in the late 1540s, and effective evangelization about 1570. Independence from Spain was proclaimed in 1816. Since its establishment in the country, the Church has been influenced by Spanish cultural and institutional forces, antagonistic liberalism, government interference and opposition; the latter reached a climax during the last five years of the first presidency of Juan Peron (1946-1955). Widespread human rights violations including the disappearance of thousands of people marked the period of military rule from 1976 to December, 1983, when an elected civilian government took over. The bishops' conference published in book form in September, 1983, communiques they had sent to the military government during those years concerning human right abuses. Catholicism is the state religion. Argentina maintains diplomatic relations with Vatican City.

*Archd., 13 (1984); dioc., 45; prel., 3; ap. ex., 1 (for Armenians of Latin America); ord., 1; card., 3; abp., 10; bp., 65; parishes, 2,178; priests, 5,482 (2,500 dioc., 2,982 rel.); p.d., 31; sem., 1,655; bros., 1,188; srs., 12,552; bap., 610,944; Caths., 26,078,000 (92.8%); tot. pop., 28,090,000 (1981).*

**Australia:** Commonwealth; island continent southeast of Asia; capital, Canberra. The first Catholics in the country were Irish under penal sentence, 1795-1804; the first public Mass was celebrated May 15, 1803. Official organization of the Church dates from 1820. The country was officially removed from mission status in March, 1976. Established diplomatic relations with Vatican City, 1973.

*Archd., 7; dioc., 21; card., 1; abp., 9 (1 is titular); bp., 32; parishes, 1,420; priests, 3,629 (2,213 dioc., 1,416 rel.); p.d., 5; sem., 284; bros., 2,132; srs., 10,654; bap., 78,324; Caths., 3,942,000 (26.4%); tot. pop. 14,900,000.*

**Austria:** Republic in central Europe; capital, Vienna. Christianity was introduced by the end of the third century, strengthened considerably by conversion of the Bavarians from about 600, and firmly established in the second half of the eighth century. Catholicism survived and grew stronger as the principal religion in the country in the post-Reformation period, but suffered from Josephinism in the 18th century. Although liberated from much government harassment in the aftermath of the Revolution of 1848, it came under pressure again some 20 years later in the Kulturkampf. During this time the Church became involved with a developing social movement. The Church faced strong opposition from Socialists after World War I and suffered persecution from 1938 to 1945 during the Nazi regime. Some Church-state matters are regulated by a concordat originally concluded in 1934. Austria maintains diplomatic relations with Vatican City.

*Archd., 2; dioc., 7; abb., 1; ord., 1; card., 1; abp., 2; bp., 13; parishes, 3,065; priests, 5,605 (3,370 dioc., 2,235 rel.); p.d., 122; sem., 406; bros., 795; srs., 10,247; bap., 83,387; Caths., 6,383,000 (84.9%); tot. pop., 7,520,000.*

**Azores:** North Atlantic island group 750 miles west of Portugal, of which it is part. Christianity was introduced in the second quarter of the 15th century.

**Bahamas:** Independent (July 10, 1973) island group consisting of some 700 (30 inhabited) small islands southeast of Florida and north of Cuba; capital, Nassau. On Oct. 12, 1492, Columbus landed on one of these islands, where the first Mass was celebrated in the New World. Organization of the Catholic Church in the Bahamas dates from about the middle of the 19th century. Established diplomatic relations with Vatican City in 1979.

*Dioc., 1; bp., 1; parishes, 29; priests, 46 (12 dioc., 34 rel.); p.d., 4; sem., 2; bros., 5; srs., 48; bap., 1,392; Caths., 50,000 (19.2%); tot. pop., 260,000.*

**Bahrain:** Island state in Persian Gulf; capital, Manama. Under ecclesiastical jurisdiction of Arabia vicariate apostolic.

*Priests, 3 (rel); bap., 200; Caths., 6,000; tot. pop., 360,000 (1981).*

**Balearic Islands:** Spanish province consisting of an island group in the western Mediterranean. Statistics are included in those for Spain.

**Bangladesh:** Formerly the eastern portion of Pakistan. Officially constituted as a separate nation Dec. 16, 1971; capital, Dacca (Dhaka). Islam is the principal religion; freedom of religion is granted. There were Jesuit, Dominican and Augustinian missionaries in the area in the 16th century. A vicariate apostolic (of Bengali) was established in 1834; the hierarchy was erected in 1950. Established diplomatic relations with Vatican City, 1972.

*Archd., 1; dioc., 3; abp., 1 (nat.); bp., 3 (nat.); parishes, 53; priests, 165 (47 dioc., 118 rel.); sem., 130; bros., 73; srs., 533; bap., 5,388; Caths., 168,000 (.18%); tot. pop., 93,000,000.*

**Barbados:** Parliamentary democracy (independent since 1966), easternmost of the Caribbean islands; capital, Bridgetown. About 70 per cent of the people are Anglicans. Established diplomatic relations with Vatican City in 1979.

*Dioc., 1; bp., 1; parishes, 7; priests, 10 (4 dioc., 6 rel.); p.d., 2; sem., 4; bros., 5; srs., 31; bap., 227; Caths., 11,000 (4%); tot. pop., 270,000 (1981).*

**Belgium:** Constitutional monarchy in northwestern Europe; capital, Brussels. Christianity was introduced about the first quarter of the fourth century and major evangelization was completed about 730. During the rest of the medieval period the Church had firm diocesan and parochial organization, generally vigorous monastic life, and influential monastic and cathedral schools. Lutherans and Calvinists made some gains during the

Reformation period but there was a strong Catholic restoration in the first half of the 17th century, when the country was under Spanish rule. Jansenism disturbed the Church from about 1640 into the 18th century. Josephinism, imposed by an Austrian regime, hampered the Church late in the same century. Repressive and persecutory measures were enforced during the Napoleonic conquest. Freedom came with separation of Church and state in the wake of the Revolution of 1830, which ended the reign of William I. Thereafter, the Church encountered serious problems with philosophical liberalism and political socialism. Catholics have long been engaged in strong educational, social and political movements. Except for one five-year period (1880-1884), Belgium has maintained diplomatic relations with Vatican City since 1835.

*Archd., 1; dioc., 7; card., 2 (1 heads an archiepiscopal see); bp., 16; parishes, 3,975; priests, 11,510 (7,508 dioc., 4,002 rel.); p.d., 236; sem., 318; bros., 2,350; srs., 27,420; bap., 102,385; Caths., 8,988,000 (91.1%); tot. pop., 9,861,000.*

**Belize** (formerly British Honduras): Independent (Sept. 21, 1981) republic on east coast of Central America; capital, Belmopan. Its history has points in common with Guatemala, where evangelization began in the 16th century. Established diplomatic relations with Vatican City, 1983.

*Dioc., 1; bp., 1; parishes, 12; priests, 38 (13 dioc., 25 rel.); p.d., 1; sem., 1; bros., 15; srs., 82; bap., 2,823; Caths., 93,000; tot. pop., 160,000.*

**Benin** (formerly Dahomey): Republic in west Africa, bordering on the Atlantic; capital, Porto Novo. Missionary work was very limited from the 16th to the 18th centuries. Effective evangelization dates from 1861. The hierarchy was established in 1955. The majority of Christians are Catholics. Benin maintains diplomatic relations with Vatican City.

*Archd., 1; dioc., 5; card., 1 (nat.); abp., 2 (nat.); bp., 5 ( nat.); parishes, 111; priests, 183 (99 dioc., 84 rel.); sem., 71; bros., 20; srs., 342; bap., 14,442; Caths. (1981), 590,000 (16.2%); tot. pop., 3,640,000.*

**Bermuda:** British dependency, consisting of 360 islands (20 of them inhabited) nearly 600 miles east of Cape Hatteras; capital, Hamilton. Catholics were not permitted until about 1800. Occasional pastoral care was provided the few Catholics there by visiting priests during the 19th century. Early in the 1900s priests from Halifax began serving the area. A prefecture apostolic was set up in 1953. The first bishop assumed jurisdiction in 1956.

*Dioc., 1; bp., 1; parishes, 7; priests, 8 (1 dioc., 7 rel.); p.d., 2; srs., 9; bap., 119; Caths., 9,000 (14.4%); tot. pop., 62,100.*

**Bhutan:** Constitutional monarchy in the Himalayas, northeast of India; capital, Thimphu. Most of the population are Buddhists. Jesuits (1963) and Salesians (1965) were invited to country to direct schools. Salesians were expelled in February, 1982, on disputed charges of proselytism. Jesuits and some Sisters remained *(Fides)*. Ecclesiastical jurisdiction is under the Darjeeling diocese, India.

*Priests, 7 (rel.); srs., 4; bap., 15; Caths., 400; tot. pop., 1,328,000 (1981).*

**Bolivia:** Republic in central South America; capital, Sucre; seat of government, La Paz. Catholicism, the official religion, was introduced in the 1530s and the first bishopric was established in 1552. Effective evangelization among the Indians, slow to start, reached high points in the middle of the 18th and the beginning of the 19th centuries and was resumed about 1840. Independence from Spain was proclaimed in 1825, at the end of a campaign that started in 1809. The republic inherited the Spanish right of nominating candidates for bishoprics. Church-state relations are regulated by a 1951 concordat with the Holy See. In recent years, human rights violations in conditions of political, economic and social turmoil have occasioned strong protests by members of the hierarchy and other people of the Church. Bolivia maintains diplomatic relations with Vatican City.

*Archd., 4; dioc., 4; prel., 2; v.a., 6; card., 1; abp., 5; bp., 17; parishes, 440; priests, 872 (214 dioc., 658 rel.); p.d., 23; sem., 165; bros., 232; srs., 1,680; bap., 176,529; Caths., 5,420,000 (94%); tot. pop., 5,760,000 (1981).*

**Botswana:** Republic (independent since 1966) in southern Africa; capital, Gaborone. Botswana has an apostolic delegate (to Southern Africa).

*Dioc., 1; bp., 1 (nat.); priests, 28 (3 dioc., 25 rel.); p.d., 1; sem., 2; bros., 3; srs., 31; bap., 1,771; Caths., 34,200 (3.8%); tot. pop., 900,000*

**Brazil:** Republic in northeast South America; capital, Brasilia. One of several priests with the discovery party celebrated the first Mass in the country Apr. 26, 1500. Evangelization began some years later and the first diocese was erected in 1551. During the colonial period, which lasted until 1822, evangelization made some notable progress — especially in the Amazon region between 1680 and 1750 — but was seriously hindered by government policy and the attitude of colonists regarding Amazon Indians the missionaries tried to protect from exploitation and slavery. The Jesuits were suppressed in 1782 and other missionaries expelled as well. Liberal anti-Church influence grew in strength. The government gave minimal support but exercised maximum control over the Church. After the proclamation of independence from Portugal in 1822 and throughout the regency, government control was tightened and the Church suffered greatly from dissident actions of ecclesiastical brotherhoods, Masonic anti-clericalism and general decline in religious life. Church and state were separated by the constitution of 1891, proclaimed two years after the end of the empire. The Church carried into the 20th century a load of inherited liabilities and problems amid increasingly difficult political, economic and social conditions affecting the majority of the population. A number of bishops, priests, religious and lay persons have been active in movements for social and religious reform. Brazil maintains diplomatic relations with Vatican City.

*Archd., 36; dioc., 188; prel., 16; abb., 2; ord., 1; card., 6; abp., 35; bp., 237; parishes,*

6,713; priests, 13,443 (5,210 dioc., 8,233 rel.);
p.d., 340; sem., 4,606; bros., 2,638; srs.,
36,983; bap., 2,738,381; Caths., 109,540,000
(90.1%); tot. pop., 121,550,000 (1981, except
jurisdictions).

**Brunei:** State under British protection, on the
northern coast of Borneo; scheduled for independence; capital, Bandar Seri Begawan. Under ecclesiastical jurisdiction of Miri diocese, Malaysia.
Parishes, 3; priests, 5 (2 dioc., 3 rel.); srs.,
4; bap., 102; Caths., 5,000; tot. pop., 240,000
(1981).

**Bulgaria:** People's republic in southeastern Europe on the eastern part of the Balkan peninsula;
capital, Sofia. Christianity was introduced before
343 but disappeared with the migration of Slavs
into the territory. The baptism of Boris I about 865
ushered in a new period of Christianity which soon
became involved in switches of loyalty between
Constantinople and Rome. Through it all the
Byzantine, and later Orthodox, element remained
stronger and survived under the rule of Ottoman
Turks into the 19th century. The few modern Latin
Catholics in the country are traceable to 17th century converts from heresy. The Byzantines are
products of a reunion movement of the 19th century. In 1947 the constitution of the new republic
decreed the separation of Church and state. Catholic schools and institutions were abolished and foreign religious banished in 1948. A year later the
apostolic delegate was expelled. Ivan Romanoff,
vicar general of Plovdiv, died in prison in 1952.
Bishop Eugene Bossilkoff, imprisoned in 1948, was
sentenced to death in 1952; his fate remained unknown until 1975 when the Bulgarian government
informed the Vatican that he had died in prison
shortly after being sentenced. Roman and Bulgarian Rite vicars apostolic were permitted to attend
the Second Vatican Council from 1962 to 1965. All
church activity is under surveillance and/or control by the government, which professes to be
atheistic. Pastoral and related activities are
strictly limited. Most of the population is Orthodox. There was some improvement in Bulgar-
ian-Vatican relations in 1975, following a visit of
Bulgarian President Todor Zhivkov to Pope Paul
VI June 19 and talks between Vatican and Bulgarian representatives at the Helsinki Conference in
late July. The needs of the church in Bulgaria were
outlined by Pope John Paul II in a private audience
with the Bulgarian foreign minister in December,
1978. In 1979, the Sofia-Plovdiv vicariate apostolic
was raised to a diocese and a bishop was appointed
for the vacant see of Nicopoli.
Dioc., 2; ap. ex., 1; bp., 2; Caths. (est.),
65,000 (.7%); tot. pop., 8,862,000.

**Burma:** Union of Burma, a republic in southeast
Asia, on the Bay of Bengal; capital, Rangoon.
Christianity was introduced about 1500. Small-
scale evangelization had limited results from the
middle of the 16th century until the 1850s when effective organization of the Church began. The hierarchy was established in 1955. Buddhism was declared the state religion in 1961, but the state is
now officially secular. In 1965, church schools and
hospitals were nationalized. In 1966, all foreign
missionaries who had entered the country after
1948 for the first time were forced to leave when
the government refused to renew their work permits. Despite these setbacks, the Church has
shown some progress in recent years. Burma has
an apostolic delegate (pro-nuncio to Bangladesh).
Archd., 2; dioc., 6; p.a., 1; abp., 2 (nat.);
bp., 7 (5 nat.); parishes, 147; priests, 225 (200
dioc., 25 rel.); sem., 205; bros., 60; srs., 670;
bap., 21,051; Caths., 390,413 (1.1%); tot. pop.,
35,200,000.

**Burundi:** Republic since 1966, near the equator
in east-central Africa; capital, Bujumbura. The
first permanent Catholic mission station was established late in the 19th century. Large numbers
of persons were received into the Church following
the ordination of the first Burundi priests in 1925.
The first native bishop was appointed in 1959. Most
education takes place in schools under Catholic
auspices. In 1972-73, the country was torn by tribal
warfare between the Tutsis, the ruling minority,
and the Hutus. Since 1979, approximately 100 Catholic missionaries have been expelled. Burundi
maintains diplomatic relations with Vatican City.
Archd., 1; dioc., 6; abp., 1 (nat.); bp., 6
(nat.); parishes, 108; priests, 334 (177 dioc.,
157 rel.); sem., 82; bros., 140; srs., 760; bap.,
84,493; Caths., 2,453,000 (55.7%); tot. pop.,
4,400,000.

**Cambodia** (Kampuchea, Peoples Republic of
Kampuchea); Republic (Oct. 9, 1970) in southeast
Asia, bordering on the Gulf of Siam, Thailand,
Laos and Vietnam; capital Phnom Penh. Evangelization dating from the second half of the 16th century had limited results, more among Vietnamese
than Khmers. Thousands of Catholics of Vietnamese origin were forced to flee in 1970 because of
Khmer hostility. The status of the Church remained uncertain following the Khmer Rouge
take-over in April, 1975. Foreign missionaries
were expelled immediately. Local clergy and religious were sent to work the land; whether they
would be able to minister to the faithful was not
known. Buddhism is the state religion.
V.a., 1; p.a., 2. No statistics available.
Catholics numbered 13,835 in 1973. Tot. pop.
(est.), 6,830,000.

**Cameroon:** Republic in west Africa, bordering
on the Gulf of Guinea; capital, Yaounde. Effective
evangelization began in the 1890s, although Catholics had been in the country long before that time.
In the 40-year period from 1920 to 1960, the number
of Catholics increased from 60,000 to 700,000. The
first native priests were ordained in 1935. Twenty
years later the first native bishops were ordained
and the hierarchy established. In 1982, three new
ecclesiastical provinces and one diocese were established. Cameroon maintains diplomatic relations with Vatican City.
Archd., 4; dioc., 12; abp., 4 ( nat.); bp., 12
(9 nat.); parishes, 404; priests, 810 (333 dioc.,
477 rel.); p.d., 24; sem., 335; bros., 301; srs.,
1,348; bap., 67,121; Caths., 2,410,448 (27%);
tot. pop., 8,895,000.

**Canada:** Independent federation comprising the
northern half of North America; capital, Ottawa.

Canada maintains diplomatic relations with Vatican City. (See Index for papal visit and pages 387-97 for Church in Canada.)

*Archd., 18; dioc., 53; abb., 1; ap. ex., 1; card., 4 (1 heads an archdiocese; 3 are retired); abp., 26 (18 are diocesan, 8, retired); bps., 94 (54 diocesan, 18 auxiliaries, 22 retired); parishes 6,007; priests, 12,133 (7,276 dioc., 4,857 rel.); p.d., 372; sem. (1981), 1,021; bros., 3,887; srs., 35,745; bap. (1981), 178,777; Caths., 10,828,343 (43.8%); tot. pop., 24,739,500. (Principal source: 1984 Directory of Canadian Conference of Catholic Bishops.)*

**Canary Islands:** Two Spanish provinces, consisting of seven islands, off the northwest coast of Africa. Evangelization began about 1400. Almost all of the one million inhabitants are Catholics. Statistics are included in those for Spain.

**Cape Verde:** Independent (July 5, 1975) island group in the Atlantic 300 miles west of Senegal; formerly a Portuguese overseas province; capital, Praia, San Tiago Island. Evangelization began some years before the establishment of the first diocese in 1532. Established diplomatic relations with Vatican City in 1976.

*Dioc., 1; bp., 1; parishes, 30; priests, 45 (11 dioc., 34 rel.); bros., 8; srs., 48; bap., 9,949; Caths. (1981), 314,000; tot. pop., 330,000.*

**Carolines and Marshalls, The:** U.S. trust territory in the southwest Pacific; scheduled for independence. Effective evangelization began in the late 1880s.

*Dioc., 1; bp., 1; parishes, 26; priests, 28 (2 dioc., 26 rel.); p.d., 22; sem., 9; bros., 6; srs., 38; bap., 2,168; Caths., 56,000; tot. pop., 120,000.*

**Cayman Islands:** British colony in Caribbean; capital, George Town on Grand Cayman. Under ecclesiastical jurisdiction of Kingston diocese, Jamaica.

*Srs., 2; bap., 19; Caths., 300; tot. pop., 17,000 (1981).*

**Central African Republic:** Former French colony (independent since 1960) in central Africa; capital, Bangui. Effective evangelization dates from 1894. The region was organized as a mission territory in 1909. The first native priest was ordained in 1938. The hierarchy was organized in 1955. Established diplomatic relations with Vatican City in 1975.

*Archd., 1; dioc., 5; abp., 1 (nat.); bp., 4; parishes, 88; priests, 217 (42 dioc., 175 rel.); p.d., 2; sem., 63; bros., 63; srs., 286; bap., 20,426; Caths., 416,489; tot. pop., 2,400,000.*

**Ceuta:** Spanish possession (city) on the northern tip of Africa, south of Gibraltar. Statistics are included in those for Spain.

**Chad:** Republic (independent since 1960) in north-central Africa; former French possession; capital, N'Djamena. Evangelization began in 1929, leading to firm organization in 1947 and establishment of the hierarchy in 1955. Chad has an apostolic delegate (pro-nuncio, Central African Republic).

*Archd., 1; dioc., 3; abp., 1; bp., 3; parishes, 95; priests, 158 (16 dioc., 142 rel.); sem., 29;*

*bros., 45; srs., 184; bap., 10,703; Caths., 255,000 (5.6%); tot. pop., 4,550,000 (1981).*

**Chile:** Republic on the southwestern coast of South America; capital, Santiago. Priests were with the Spanish conquistadores on their entrance into the territory early in the 16th century. The first parish was established in 1547 and the first bishopric in 1561. Overall organization of the Church took place later in the century. By 1650 most of the peaceful Indians in the central and northern areas were evangelized. Missionary work was more difficult in the southern region. Church activity was hampered during the campaign for independence, 1810 to 1818, and through the first years of the new government, to 1830. Later gains were made, into this century, but hindering factors were shortages of native clergy and religious and attempts by the government to control church administration through the patronage system in force while the country was under Spanish control. Separation of Church and state were decreed in the constitution of 1925. Church-state relations were strained during the regime of Marxist president Salvator Allende Gossens (1970-73). He was overthrown in a bloody coup and was reported to have committed suicide Sept. 11, 1973. Conditions have remained unsettled under the military government which assumed control after the coup. The Chilean bishops have issued numerous statements strongly critical of the military government's human rights violations, urging the release of political prisoners and a return to civilian rule. (See Index, News Events.) Chile maintains diplomatic relations with Vatican City.

*Archd., 5; dioc., 14; prel., 3; v.a., 2; card., 1; abp., 3; bp., 24; parishes, 816; priests, 2,046 (802 dioc., 1,244 rel.); p.d., 192; sem., 895; bros., 445; srs., 5,091; bap., 185,091; Caths., 9,652,000 (85.5%); tot. pop., 11,290,000 (1981).*

**China** *(This article concerns mainland China which has been under Communist control since 1949)*: People's Republic in eastern part of Asia; capital, Peking (Beijing), Christianity was introduced by Nestorians who had some influence on part of the area from 635 to 845 and again from the 11th century until 1368. John of Monte Corvino started a Franciscan mission in 1294; he was ordained an archbishop about 1307. Missionary activity involving more priests increased for a while thereafter but the Franciscan mission ended in 1368. The Jesuit Matteo Ricci initiated a remarkable period of activity in the 1580s. By 1700 the number of Catholics was reported to be 300,000. The Chinese Rites controversy, concerning the adaptation of rituals and other matters to Chinese traditions and practices, ran throughout the 17th century, ending in a negative decision by mission authorities in Rome. Bl. Francis de Capillas, the protomartyr of China, was killed in 1648. Persecution, a feature of Chinese history as recurrent as changes in dynasties, occurred several times in the 18th century and resulted in the departure of most missionaries from the country. The Chinese door swung open again in the 1840s and progress in evangelization increased with an extension of legal and social tolerance. At the turn of the 20th century, however, the Boxer Rebellion took one or the other kind of toll among an estimated 30,000 victims. Missionary work in the 1900s reached a new high in every respect before the disaster of persecution initiated by Communists before and especially since they established the republic in 1949. The Reds began a savage persecution as soon as they came into power. Among its results were the expulsion of over 5,000 foreign missionaries, 510 of whom were American priests, brothers and nuns; the arrest, imprisonment and harassment of all members of the native religious, clergy and hierarchy; the forced closing of 3,932 schools, 216 hospitals, 781 dispensaries, 254 orphanages, 29 printing presses and 55 periodicals; denial of the free exercise of religion to all the faithful; the detention of hundreds of priests, religious and lay persons in jail and their employment in slave labor; the proscription of the Legion of Mary and other Catholic Action groups for "counter-revolutionary activities" and "crimes against the new China"; complete outlawing of missionary work and pastoral activity. The government formally established a Patriotic Association of Chinese Catholics in July, 1957. Relatively few priests and lay persons joined the organization, which was condemned by Pius XII in 1958. The government formed the nucleus of what it hoped might become the hierarchy of a schismatic Chinese church in 1958 by "electing" 26 bishops and having them consecrated validly but illicitly between Apr. 13, 1958, and Nov. 15, 1959, without the permission or approval of the Holy See. By 1983, an estimated 60 bishops were consecrated in this manner. In March, 1960, Bishop James E. Walsh, M.M., the last American missionary in China, was sentenced and placed in custody for a period of 20 years. He was released in the summer of 1970. (He died in 1981.) Activity of the Patriotic Association and official policy of the government are in direct opposition to any connection between the Church in China and the Vatican.

*Archd., 20; dioc., 92; p.a., 29. No Catholic statistics are available. In 1949 there were between 3,500,000-4,000,000 Catholics, about .7 per cent of the total population. Tot. pop. (1982 est.), 1,008,175,288.*

**Colombia:** Republic in northwest South America, with Atlantic and Pacific borders; capital, Bogota. Evangelization began in 1508. The first two dioceses were established in 1534. Vigorous development of the Church was reported by the middle of the 17th century despite obstacles posed by the multiplicity of Indian languages, government interference through patronage rights and otherwise, rivalry among religious orders and the small number of native priests among the predominantly Spanish clergy. Some persecution, including the confiscation of property, followed in the wake of the proclamation of independence from Spain in 1819. The Church was affected in many ways by the political and civil unrest of the nation through the 19th century and into the 20th. Various aspects of Church-state relations are regulated by a concordat with the Vatican signed July 12, 1973, and ratified July 2, 1975. The new concordat replaced

one which had been in effect with some modifications since 1887. Guerrilla warfare aimed at Marxist-oriented radical social reform and redistribution of land has plagued the country since the 1960s, posing problems for the Church which backed reforms but rejected actions of radical groups. In 1984, a peace accord — calling for a cease-fire and peaceful implementation of reforms — was signed by Belisario Betancur, president of Colombia, and leaders of guerrilla factions.

*Archd., 11; dioc. (1984), 32; prel., 2; v.a. (1984), 8; p.a., 7; card., 2; abp., 12; bp., 49; parishes, 2,272; priests, 5,196 (3,213 dioc., 1,983 rel.); p.d., 33; sem., 2,174; bros., 939; srs., 18,304; bap., 711,295; Caths., 26,607,000 (95.5%); tot. pop., 27,840,000 (1981).*

**Comoros:** Consists of main islands of Grande Comore, Anjouan, Moheli and Mayotte in Indian Ocean off southeast coast of Africa; capital, Moroni, Grande Comore Island. Former French territory; independent (July 6, 1975) except Mayotte which voted to remain part of France. The majority of the population is Moslem. An apostolic administration was established in 1975.

*A.a., 1; priests, 4 (1 dioc., 3 rel.); srs., 7; bap., 24; Caths., 1,000 (.2%); tot. pop., 370,000.*

**Congo Republic:** Republic (independent since 1960) in west central Africa; former French possession; capital, Brazzaville. Small-scale missionary work with little effect preceded modern evangelization dating from the 1880s. The work of the Church has been affected by political instability, Communist influence, tribalism and hostility to foreigners. The hierarchy was established in 1955. Established diplomatic relations with the Vatican in 1977.

*Archd., 1; dioc., 4; abp., 1 (nat); bp., 5 (nat); parishes, 71; priests, 141 (63 dioc., 78 rel.); p.d., 2; sem., 35; bros., 31; srs., 201; bap., 14,358; Caths., 772,844 (45.5%); tot. pop., 1,696,880.*

**Cook Islands:** Self-governing territory of New Zealand, an archipelago of small islands in Oceania. Evangelization by Protestant missionaries started in 1821, resulting in a predominantly Protestant population. The first Catholic missionary work began in 1894. The hierarchy was established in 1966.

*Dioc., 1; bp., 1; parishes, 11; priests, 12 (4 dioc., 8 rel.); sem., 4; bros., 3; srs., 11; bap., 78; Caths., 3,000; tot. pop., 20,000 (1981).*

**Costa Rica:** Republic in Central America; capital, San Jose. Evangelization began about 1520 and proceeded by degrees to real development and organization of the Church in the 17th and 18th centuries. The republic became independent in 1838. Twelve years later church jurisdiction also became independent with the establishment of a bishopric in the present capital. Costa Rica maintains diplomatic relations with Vatican City.

*Archd., 1; dioc., 3; v.a., 1; abp., 1; bp., 5; parishes, 173; priests, 454 (285 dioc., 169 rel.); sem., 143; bros., 29; srs., 881; bap., 62,158; Caths., 2,144,000 (91.7%); tot. pop., 2,337,000.*

**Cuba:** Republic under Communist dictatorship,

south of Florida; capital, Havana. Effective evangelization began about 1514, leading eventually to the predominance of Catholicism on the island. Native vocations to the priesthood and religious life were unusually numerous in the 18th century but declined in the 19th. The island became independent of Spain in 1902 following the Spanish-American War. Fidel Castro took control of the government Jan. 1, 1959. In 1961, after Cuba was officially declared a socialist state, the University of Villanueva was closed, 350 Catholic schools were nationalized and 136 priests expelled. A greater number of foreign priests and religious had already left the country. Freedom of worship and religious instruction are limited to church premises and no social action is permitted the Church, which survives under surveillance. A new constitution approved in 1976 guaranteed freedom of conscience but restricted its exercise. Cuba maintains diplomatic relations with Vatican City.

*Archd., 2; dioc., 5; abp., 2; bp., 5; parishes, 221; priests, 197 (118 dioc., 79 rel.); sem., 23; bros., 39; srs., 238; bap., 21,145; Caths. 3,969,000; tot. pop., 10,000,000.*

**Cyprus:** Republic in the eastern Mediterranean; capital, Nicosia. Christianity was preached on the island in apostolic times and has a continuous history from the fourth century. Latin and Eastern rites were established but the latter prevailed and became Orthodox after the schism of 1054. Roman and Orthodox Christians have suffered under many governments, particularly during the period of Turkish dominion from late in the 16th to late in the 19th centuries, and from differences between the 80 per cent Greek majority and the Turkish minority. About 80 per cent of the population are Orthodox. Cyprus established diplomatic relations with Vatican City in 1973. Maronite-Rite Catholics are under the jurisdiction of the archdiocese of Cyprus (of the Maronites), whose archbishop resides in Lebanon. Roman-Rite Catholics are under the jurisdiction of the Roman-Rite patriarchate of Jerusalem.

*Archd., 1 (Maronite); abp., 1 (resides in Lebanon); parishes, 10; priests, 23 (7 dioc., 16 rel.); bros., 3; srs., 92; bap., 61; Caths., 8,000 (1.2%); tot. pop., 640,000 (1981).*

**Czechoslovakia:** Federal socialist republic (since 1969) in Central Europe, consisting of the Czech Socialist Republic, capital Prague; and the Slovak Socialist Republic, capital Bratislava. The republics have local autonomy but are subordinate to the Federal Assembly at Prague made up of representatives from both regions. The Czech and Slovak regions of the country have separate religious and cultural backgrounds. Christianity was introduced in Slovakia in the 8th century by Irish and German missionaries and the area was under the jurisdiction of German bishops. In 863, at the invitation of the Slovak ruler Rastislav who wanted to preserve the cultural and liturgical heritage of the people, Sts. Cyril and Methodius began pastoral and missionary work in the region, ministering to the people in their own language. The saints introduced Old Slovak (Old Church Slavonic) into the liturgy and did so much to evangelize the territory that they are venerated as the apostles of Slovakia. A diocese established at Nitra in 880 had a continuous history except for a century ending in 1024. The Church in Slovakia was severely tested by the Reformation and political upheavals. After World War I, when it became part of the Republic of Czechoslovakia, it was 75 per cent Catholic. In the Czech lands, the martyrdom of Prince Wenceslaus in 929 triggered the spread of Christianity. Prague has had a continuous history as a diocese since 973. A parish system was organized about the 13th century in Bohemia and Moravia, the land of the Czechs. Mendicant orders strengthened relations with the Latin Rite in the 13th century. In the next century the teachings of John Hus in Bohemia brought trouble to the Church in the forms of schism and heresy, and initiated a series of religious wars which continued for decades following his death at the stake in 1415. Church property was confiscated, monastic communities were scattered and even murdered, ecclesiastical organization was shattered, and so many of the faithful joined the Bohemian Brethren that Catholics became a minority. The Reformation, with the way prepared by the Hussites and cleared by other factors, affected the Church seriously. A Counter Reformation got under way in the 1560s and led to a gradual restoration through the thickets of Josephinism, the Enlightenment, liberalism and troubled politics. In 1920, two years after the establishment of the Republic of Czechoslovakia, the schismatic Czechoslovak Church was proclaimed at Prague, resulting in numerous defections from the Catholic Church in the Czech region. In Ruthenia, 112,000 became Russian Orthodox between 1918 and 1930. Vigorous persecution of the church began in Slovakia before the end of World War II when Communists mounted a 1944 offensive against bishops, priests and religious. In 1945, church schools were nationalized, youth organizations were disbanded, the Catholic press was curtailed, the training of students for the priesthood was seriously impeded. Msgr. Josef Tiso, president of the Slovak Republic, was tried for "treason" in December, 1947, and was executed the following April. Between 1945 and 1949 approximately 10 per cent of the Slovak population spent some time in jail or a concentration camp. Persecution began later in the Czech part of the country, following the accession of the Gottwald regime to power early in 1948. Hospitals, schools and property were nationalized and Catholic organizations were liquidated. A puppet organization was formed in 1949 to infiltrate the Church and implement an unsuccessful plan for establishing a schismatic church. In the same year Archbishop Josef Beran of Prague was placed under house arrest. (He left the country in 1965, was made a cardinal, and died in 1969 in Rome.) A number of theatrical trials of bishops and priests were staged in 1950. All houses of religious were taken over between March, 1950, and the end of 1951. Pressure was applied on the clergy and faithful of the Eastern Rite in Slovakia to join the Orthodox Church. Diplomatic relations with Vatican City were terminated in 1950. About 3,000 priests were deprived of liberty in 1951 and attempts were made to force "peace priests" on the people. In 1958 it was reported that 450 to 500 priests were in jail; an undisclosed number of religious and Byzantine-Rite priests had been deported; two bishops released from prison in 1956 were under house arrest; one bishop was imprisoned at Leopoldov and two at the Mirov reformatory. In Bohemia, Moravia and Silesia, five of six dioceses were without ruling bishops; one archbishop and two bishops were active but subject to "supervision"; most of the clergy refused to join the "peace priests." In 1962 only three bishops were permitted to attend the first session of the Second Vatican Council. From January to October, 1968, Church-state relations improved to some extent under the Dubcek regime: a number of bishops were reinstated; some 3,000 priests were engaged in the pastoral ministry, although 1,500 were still barred from priestly work; the "peace priests" organization was disbanded; the Eastern-Rite Church, with 147 parishes, was reestablished. In 1969, an end was ordered to rehabilitation trials for priests and religious, but no wholesale restoration of priests and religious to their proper ways of life and work was in prospect. In 1972, the government ordered the removal of nuns from visible but limited apostolates to farms and mental hospitals where they would be out of sight. In 1973, the government allowed the ordination of four bishops — one in the Czech region and three in the Slovak region. Reports from Slovakia late in the same year stated that authorities there had placed severe restrictions on the education of seminarians and the functioning of priests. Government restrictions continued to hamper the work of priests and nuns in recent years. Signatories of the human rights declaration called Charter 77 have been particular objects of government repression and retribution. In December, 1983, the Czechoslovakian foreign minister met with the Pope at Vatican City — the first meeting of a high Czech official with a pope since the country came under communist rule. In 1984, two Vatican officials visited Czechoslovakia. Despite the communication breakthrough, there was no indication of any change of policy toward the Church in the country.

*Archd., 3; dioc., 10; card., 1; bp., 6 (2 impeded); parishes, 4,444; priests, 3,686 (3,381 dioc., 305 rel.); sem., 295; bros., 72; srs., 5,073; bap., 106,367; Caths., 10,530,000 (68.7%); tot. pop., 15,310,000 (1981).*

**Denmark,** including the Faroe Islands and Greenland: Constitutional monarchy in northwestern Europe, north of West Germany; capital, Copenhagen. Christianity was introduced in the ninth century and the first diocese for the area was established in 831. Intensive evangelization and full-scale organization of the Church occurred from the second half of the 10th century and ushered in a period of great development and influence in the 12th and 13th centuries. Decline followed, resulting in almost total loss to the Church during the Reformation when Lutheranism became the national religion. Catholics were considered foreigners until religious freedom was le-

gally assured in 1849. Modern development of the Church dates from the second half of the 19th century. About 95 per cent of the population are Evangelical Lutherans. Established diplomatic relations with Vatican City in 1982.

*Dioc., 1; bp., 1; parishes, 52; priests, 106 (37 dioc., 69 rel.); p.d., 1; sem., 8; bros., 8; srs., 398; bap., 375; Caths., 28,160 (.5%); tot. pop., 5,191,000.*

**Djibouti** (formerly French Territory of Afars and Issas): Independent (1977) republic in east Africa, on the Gulf of Aden; capital, Djibouti. Christianity in the area, formerly part of Ethiopia, antedated but was overcome by the Arab invasion of 1200. Modern evangelization, begun in the latter part of the 19th century, had meager results. The hierarchy was established in 1955. The territory has an apostolic delegate (to the Red Sea Region).

*Dioc., 1; bp., 1; parishes, 7; priests, 9 (2 dioc., 7 rel.); p.d., 1; bros., 7; srs., 30; bap., 25; Caths., 10,000; tot. pop., 350,000.*

**Dominica:** Independent (Nov. 3, 1978) state in Caribbean; capital, Roseau. Evangelization began in 1642. Established diplomatic relations with Vatican City in 1981.

*Dioc., 1; bp., 1; parishes, 18; priests, 26 (2 dioc., 24 rel.); p.d., 1; sem., 5; bros., 7; srs., 33; bap., 1,110; Caths., 65,000 (81.2%); tot. pop., 80,000.*

**Dominican Republic:** Caribbean republic on the eastern two-thirds of the island of Hispaniola, bordering on Haiti; capital, Santo Domingo. Evangelization began shortly after discovery by Columbus in 1492 and church organization, the first in America, was established by 1510. Catholicism is the state religion. The Dominican Republic maintains diplomatic relations with Vatican City.

*Archd., 1; dioc., 7; card., 1; abp., 1; bp., 9; parishes, 216; priests, 485 (128 dioc., 357 rel.); p.d., 28; sem. (1981), 283; bros. (1981), 82; srs., 1,268; bap., 89,256; Caths., 5,478,000 (93.8%); tot. pop., 5,853,000.*

**Ecuador** (includes Galapagos Islands): Republic on the west coast of South America; capital, Quito. Evangelization began in the 1530s. The first diocese was established in 1545. A synod, one of the first in the Americas, was held in 1570 or 1594. Multiphased missionary work, spreading from the coastal and mountain regions into the Amazon, made the Church highly influential during the colonial period. The Church was practically enslaved by the constitution enacted in 1824, two years after Ecuador, as part of Colombia, gained independence from Spain. Some change for the better took place later in the century, but from 1891 until the 1930s the Church labored under serious liabilities imposed by liberal governments. The concordat of 1866 was violated; foreign missionaries were barred from the country for some time; the property of religious orders was confiscated; education was taken over by the state; traditional state support was refused; legal standing was denied; attempts to control church offices were made through insistence on rights of patronage. A period of harmony and independence for the Church began after agreement was reached on Church-state relations in 1937. Ecuador maintains diplomatic relations with Vatican City.

*Archd., 3; dioc., 10; prel., 1; v.a., 5; p.a., 3; card., 1; abp., 3; bp., 18; parishes, 766; priests, 1,524 (660 dioc., 864 rel.); p.d., 9; sem., 180; bros., 367; srs., 4,133; bap., 203,151; Caths., 7,868,000 (91%); tot. pop., 8,640,000 (1981).*

**Egypt, Arab Republic of:** Republic in northeastern Africa, bordering on the Mediterranean; capital, Cairo. Alexandria was the influential hub of a Christian community established by the end of the second century; it became a patriarchate and the center of the Coptic Church, and had great influence on the spread of Christianity in various parts of Africa; Monasticism developed from desert communities of hermits in the third and fourth centuries. Arianism was first preached in Egypt in the 320s. In the fifth century, the Coptic church went Monophysite through failure to accept doctrine formulated by the Council of Chalcedon in 451 with respect to the two natures of Christ. The country was thoroughly Arabized after 640 and was under the rule of Ottoman Turks from 1517 to 1798. English influence was strong during the 19th century. A monarchy established in 1922 lasted about 30 years, ending with the proclamation of a republic in 1953-54. By that time Egypt had become the leader of pan-Arabism against Israel. It waged two unsuccessful wars against Israel in 1948-49 and 1967. Between 1958 and 1961 it was allied with Syria and Yemen, in the United Arab Republic. In 1979, following negotiations initiated by Pres. Anwar el-Sadat in 1977, Egypt and Israel signed a peace agreement. Islam, the religion of some 90 percent of the population, is the state religion. Egypt maintains diplomatic relations with Vatican City.

*Patriarchate, 2 (Alexandria for the Copts and for the Melkites); dioc., 9; v.a., 3; card., 1; abp., 1; bp., 14; parishes, 202; priests, 336 (166 dioc., 170 rel.); p.d., 1; sem., 58; bros., 73; srs., 1,556; bap., 2,221; Caths., 162,000; tot. pop., 43,470,000.*

**El Salvador:** Republic in Central America; capital, San Salvador. Evangelization affecting the whole territory followed Spanish occupation in the 1520s. The country was administered by the captaincy general of Guatemala until 1821 when independence from Spain was declared and it was annexed to Mexico. El Salvador joined the Central American Federation in 1825, decreed its own independence in 1841 and became a republic formally in 1856. In recent years, Church efforts to achieve social justice have resulted in persecution of the Church. Archbishop Oscar Romero of San Salvador, peace advocate and outspoken champion of human rights, was murdered Mar. 24, 1980, while celebrating Mass. El Salvador maintains diplomatic relations with Vatican City. (See Index for coverage of late 1983 and 1984 events.)

*Archd., 1; dioc., 4; abp., 1; bp., 5; parishes, 228; priests, 347 (162 dioc., 185 rel.); sem., 110; bros., 76; srs., 852; bap., 105,791; Caths., 4,495,000 (90.9%); tot. pop., 4,940,000 (1981).*

**England:** Center of the United Kingdom of Great Britain (England, Scotland, Wales) and Northern Ireland, off the northwestern coast of Europe; capital, London. The arrival of St. Augustine of Canterbury and a band of monks in 597 marked the beginning of evangelization. Real organization of the Church took place some years after the Synod of Whitby, held in 663. Heavy losses were sustained in the wake of the Danish invasion in the 780s, but recovery starting from the time of Alfred the Great and dating especially from the middle of the 10th century led to Christianization of the whole country and close Church-state relations. The Norman Conquest of 1066 opened the Church in England to European influence. The 13th century was climactic, but decline had already set in by 1300 when the country had an all-time high of 17,000 religious. In the 14th century, John Wycliff presaged the Protestant Reformation. Henry VIII, failing in 1529 to gain annulment of his marriage to Catherine of Aragon, refused to acknowledge papal authority over the Church in England, had himself proclaimed its head, suppressed all houses of religious, and persecuted persons — Sts. Thomas More and John Fisher, among others — for not subscribing to the Oath of Supremacy and Act of Succession. He held the line on other-than-papal doctrine, however, until his death in 1547. Doctrinal aberrations were introduced during the reign of Edward VI (1547-53), through the Order of Communion, two books of Common Prayer, and the Articles of the Established Church. Mary Tudor's attempted Catholic restoration (1553-58) was a disaster, resulting in the deaths of more than 300 Protestants. Elizabeth (1558-1603) firmed up the Established Church with formation of a hierarchy, legal enactments and multi-phased persecution. One hundred and 11 priests and 62 lay persons were among the casualties of persecution during the underground Catholic revival which followed the return to England of missionary priests from France and The Lowlands. Several periods of comparative toleration ensued after Elizabeth's death. The first of several apostolic vicariates was established in 1685; this form of church government was maintained until the restoration of the hierarchy and diocesan organization in 1850. The revolution of 1688 and subsequent developments to about 1781 subjected Catholics to a wide variety of penal laws and disabilities in religious, civic and social life. The situation began to improve in 1791, and from 1801 Parliament frequently considered proposals for the repeal of penal laws against Catholics. The Act of Emancipation restored citizenship rights to Catholics in 1829. Restrictions remained in force for some time afterwards, however, on public religious worship and activity. The hierarchy was restored in 1850. Since then the Catholic Church, existing side by side with the Established Churches of England and Scotland, has followed a general pattern of growth and development. Great Britain established diplomatic relations with Vatican City in 1982.

*Archd., 4; dioc., 15; ap. ex., 1; card., 1; abp., 3; bp., 32; parishes, 2,406; priests, 5,665 (3,786 dioc., 1,879 rel.); p.d., 84; sem., 481; bros., 602; srs., 9,398; bap., 76,194; Caths., 3,923,000 (8.5%); tot. pop., 46,000,000 (1984*

*Annuario Pontificio).* The 1984 Catholic Directory of England and Wales reported a total Catholic population of 4,242,980 for the two countries.

**Equatorial Guinea:** Republic on the west coast of Africa, consisting of Rio Muni on the mainland and the islands of Fernando Po and Annobon in the Gulf of Guinea: capital, Malabo (Santa Isabel). Evangelization began in 1841. The country became independent of Spain in 1968. The Church was severely repressed during the 11-year rule of Pres. Macias (Masie) Nguema. Developments since his overthrow (August 1979) indicated some measure of improvement. An ecclesiastical province was established in October, 1982. Established diplomatic relations with Vatican City in 1981.

*Archd., 1; dioc., 2; abp., 1 (nat.); bp., 2 (nat.); parishes, 36; priests, 54 (19 dioc., 35 rel.); sem., 21; bros., 33; srs., 143; bap., 10,897; Caths., 332,400; tot. pop., 347,000.*

**Estonia:** Baltic republic forcibly absorbed by the U.S.S.R. in 1941; capital Tallinn. Catholicism was introduced in the 11th and 12th centuries. Jurisdiction over the area was made directly subject to the Holy See in 1215. Lutheran penetration was general in the Reformation period and Russian Orthodox influence was strong from early in the 18th century until 1917 when independence was attained. The first of several apostolic administrators was appointed in 1924. The small Catholic community was hard hit during and since Russian occupation in 1941. The Russian take-over of Estonia has not been recognized by the Holy See or the United States.

**Ethiopia:** Constitutional monarchy in northeast Africa; capital, Addis Ababa. The country was evangelized by missionaries from Egypt in the fourth century and had a bishop by about 340. Following the lead of its parent body, the Egyptian (Coptic) Church, the Church in the area succumbed to the Monophysite heresy in the sixth century. Catholic influence was negligible for centuries. An ordinariate for the Ethiopian Rite was established in Eritrea in 1930. An apostolic delegation was set up in Addis Ababa in 1937 and several jurisdictions were organized, some under the Congregation for the Oriental Churches and others under the Congregation for the Evangelization of Peoples. Most of the Catholics in the country are in the former Italian colony of Eritrea. Ethiopia maintains diplomatic relations with Vatican City.

*Archd., 1; dioc., 2; v.a., 5; p.a., 1; abp., 1; bp., 5; parishes, 223; priests, 505 (152 dioc., 353 rel.); p.d., 5; sem. (1981), 119; bros., 234; srs., 1,039; bap., 12,084; Caths., 235,433 (.7%); tot. pop., 33,167,000.*

**Falkland Islands:** British colony off the southern tip of South America; capital, Stanley. The islands are called Islas Malvinas by Argentina which also claims sovereignty.

*P.a., 1; parish, 1; priests, 2 (rel.); bap., 1; Caths., 210; tot. pop., 1,900.*

**Faroe Islands:** Self-governing island group in North Atlantic; Danish possession. Under ecclesiastical jurisdiction of Copenhagen diocese.

*Priest, 1 (rel.); srs., 12; bap., 1; Caths.,*

*100; tot. pop., 40,000.*

**Fiji:** Independent island group (100 inhabited) in the southwest Pacific; capital, Suva. Marist missionaries began work in 1844 after Methodism had been firmly established. A prefecture apostolic was organized in 1863. The hierarchy was established in 1966. Established diplomatic relations with Vatican City, 1978.

*Archd., 1; abp., 1 (nat.); parishes, 33; priests, 81 (16 dioc., 65 rel.); sem., 23; bros. (1981), 45; srs., 245; bap., 2,330; Caths., 57,100 (8.7%); tot. pop., 650,000.*

**Finland:** Republic in northern Europe; capital, Helsinki. Swedes evangelized the country in the 12th century. The Reformation swept the country, resulting in the prohibition of Catholicism in 1595, general reorganization of ecclesiastical life and affairs, and dominance of the Evangelical Lutheran Church. Catholics were given religious liberty in 1781 but missionaries and conversions were forbidden by law. The first Finnish priest since the Reformation was ordained in 1903 in Paris. A vicariate apostolic for Finland was erected in 1920. A law on religious liberty, enacted in 1923, banned the foundation of monasteries. Finland maintains diplomatic relations with Vatican City.

*Dioc., 1; bp., 1; parishes, 5; priests, 18 (1 dioc., 17 rel.); p.d., 1; bros., 1; srs., 28; bap., 66; Caths., 3,374 (.06%); tot. pop., 4,844,000.*

**France:** Republic in western Europe; capital, Paris. Christianity was known around Lyons by the middle of the second century. By 250 there were 30 bishoprics. The hierarchy reached a fair degree of organization by the end of the fourth century. Vandals and Franks subsequently invaded the territory and caused barbarian turmoil and doctrinal problems because of their Arianism. The Frankish nation was converted following the baptism of Clovis about 496. Christianization was complete by some time in the seventh century. From then on the Church, its leaders and people, figured in virtually every important development — religious, cultural, political and social — through the periods of the Carolingians, feudalism, the Middle Ages and monarchies to the end of the 18th century. The great University of Paris became one of the intellectual centers of the 13th century. Churchmen and secular rulers were involved with developments surrounding the Avignon residence of the popes and curia from 1309 until near the end of the 14th century and with the disastrous Western Schism that followed. Strong currents of Gallicanism and conciliarism ran through ecclesiastical and secular circles in France; the former was an ideology and movement to restrict papal control of the Church in the country, the latter sought to make the pope subservient to a general council. Calvinism invaded the country about the middle of the 16th century and won a strong body of converts. Jansenism with its rigorous spirit and other aberrations appeared in the next century, to be followed by the highly influential Enlightenment. The Revolution which started in 1789 and was succeeded by the Napoleonic period completely changed the status of the Church, taking a toll of numbers by persecution and defection and disenfranchising the Church in practically every way. Throughout the 19th century the Church was caught up in the whirl of imperial and republican developments and made the victim of official hostility, popular indifference and liberal opposition. In this century, the Church has struggled with problems involving the heritage of the Revolution and its aftermath, the alienation of intellectuals, liberalism, the estrangement of the working classes because of the Church's former identification with the ruling class, and the massive needs of contemporary society. France maintains diplomatic relations with Vatican City.

*Archd., 18; dioc., 75; prel., 1; ap. ex., 2; ord., 1; card. (1984), 7; abp., 15; bp., 100; parishes, 38,370; priests, 38,449 (30,837 dioc., 7,612 rel.); p.d., 137; sem., 1,305; bros., 5,306; srs., 84,308; bap., 530,385; Caths., 45,720,000 (84.7%); tot. pop., 53,960,000 (1981).*

**Gabon:** Republic on the west coast of Equatorial Africa; capital, Libreville. Sporadic missionary effort took place before 1881 when effective evangelization began. The hierarchy was established in 1955. Gabon maintains diplomatic relations with Vatican City.

*Archd., 1; dioc., 3; abp., 1 (nat.); bp., 3 (nat.); parishes, 60; priests, 109 (30 dioc., 79 rel.); sem., 11; bros., 39; srs., 153; bap., 8,596; Caths., 453,984 (52.9%); tot. pop., 857,000. (The total population figure, from the Annuario Pontificio, is higher than that given by some other sources.)*

**Gambia, The:** Republic (1970) on the northwestern coast of Africa, smallest state in Africa; capital, Banjui. The country was under the jurisdiction of a vicariate apostolic until 1931. The hierarchy was established in 1957. Established diplomatic relations with Vatican City, 1978.

*Dioc., 1; bp., 1; parishes, 12; priests, 18 (rel.); sem. 8; bros., 2; srs., 25; bap., 388; Caths., 13,500 (2%); tot. pop., 641,000.*

**Germany:** Country in northern Europe partitioned in 1949 into the Communist German Democratic Republic in the East (capital, East Berlin) and the German Federal Republic in the West (capital, Bonn). Christianity was introduced in the third century, if not earlier. Trier, which became a center for missionary activity, had a bishop by 400. Visigoth invaders introduced Arianism in the fifth century but were converted in the seventh century by the East Franks, Celtic and other missionaries. St. Boniface, the apostle of Germany, established real ecclesiastical organization in the eighth century. The Church had great influence during the Carolingian period. Bishops from that time onward began to act in dual roles as pastors and rulers, a state of affairs which led inevitably to confusion and conflict in Church-state relations and perplexing problems of investiture. The Church developed strength and vitality through the Middle Ages but succumbed to abuses which antedated and prepared the ground for the Reformation. Luther's actions from 1517 made Germany a confessional battleground. Religious strife continued until conclusion of the Peace of Westphalia at the end of the Thirty Years' War in 1648. Nearly a

century earlier the Peace of Augsburg (1555) had been designed, without success, to assure a degree of tranquillity by recognizing the legitimacy of different religious confessions in different states, depending on the decisions of princes. The implicit principle that princes should control the churches emerged in practice into the absolutism and Josephinism of subsequent years. St. Peter Canisius and his fellow Jesuits spearheaded a Counter Reformation in the second half of the 16th century. Before the end of the century, however, 70 per cent of the population of north and central Germany were Lutheran. Calvinism also had established a strong presence. The Church gained internal strength in a defensive position. Through much of the 19th century, however, its influence was eclipsed by Protestant intellectuals and other influences. It suffered some impoverishment also as a result of shifting boundaries and the secularization of property shortly after 1800. It came under direct attack in the Kulturkampf of the 1870s but helped to generate the opposition which resulted in a dampening of the campaign of Bismarck against it. Despite action by Catholics on the social front and other developments, discrimination against the Church spilled over into the 20th century and lasted beyond World War I. Catholics in politics struggled with others to pull the country through numerous postwar crises. The dissolution of the Center Party, agreed to by the bishops in 1933 without awareness of the ultimate consequences, contributed negatively to the rise of Hitler to supreme power. Church officials protested the Nazi anti-Church and anti-Semitic actions, but to no avail. After World War II Christian leadership had much to do with the recovery of Western Germany. East Germany, gone Communist under Russian auspices, initiated a program of control and repression of the Church in 1948 and 1949. With no prospect of success for measures designed to split bishops, priests, religious and lay persons, the regime has concentrated most of its attention on mind control, especially of the younger generation, by the elimination of religious schools, curtailment of freedom for religious instruction and formation, severe restriction of the religious press, and the substitution since the mid-50s of youth initiation and Communist ceremonies for the rites of baptism, confirmation, marriage, and funerals. Bishops are generally forbidden to travel outside the Republic. The number of priests is decreasing, partly because of reduced seminary enrollments ordered by the government since 1958. In 1973, the Vatican appointed three apostolic administrators and one auxiliary (all titular bishops) for the areas of three West German dioceses located in East Germany. West Germany maintains diplomatic relations with Vatican City.

*West Germany: Archd., 5; dioc., 16 (also part of the Berlin diocese); ap., ex., 1; card., 3; abp., 4; bp., 55; parishes, 11,826; priests, 22,985 (17,104 dioc., 5,881 rel.); p.d., 747; sem., 2,624; bros., 3,223; srs., 62,100; bap., 258,248; Caths., 28,600,000 (46.3%); tot. pop., 61,670,000 (1981).*

**East Germany:** *Dioc., 2 (Dresden-Meissen and Berlin, since most of its territory lies in East Germany); a.a., 1 (Gorlitz; there are also 3 territories with apostolic administrators); card., 1; bps., 8; parishes, 914; priests, 1,509 (1,272 dioc., 237 rel.); p.d., 37; sem., 145; bros., 52; srs., 2,962; bap., 9,634; Caths., 1,268,000 (7.5%); tot. pop., 16,740,000 (1981).*

**Ghana:** Republic on the western coast of Africa, bordering on the Gulf of Guinea; capital, Accra. Priests visited the country in 1482, 11 years after discovery by the Portuguese, but missionary effort — hindered by the slave trade and other factors — was slight until 1880 when systematic evangelization began. A prefecture apostolic was set up in 1879. The hierarchy was established in 1950. Ghana maintains diplomatic relations with Vatican City.

*Archd., 2; dioc., 7; abp., 2 (nat.); bp., 7 (nat.); parishes, 208; priests, 438 (203 dioc., 235 rel.); sem., 268; bros., 135; srs., 499; bap., 42,525; Caths., 1,440,000 (11.9%); tot. pop., 12,060,000 (1981).*

**Gibraltar:** British colony on the tip of the Spanish Peninsula on the Mediterranean. Evangelization took place after the Moors were driven out near the end of the 15th century. The Church was hindered by the British who acquired the colony in 1713. Most of the Catholics were, and are, Spanish and Italian immigrants and their descendants. A vicariate apostolic was organized in 1817. The diocese was erected in 1910.

*Dioc., 1; bp., 1; parishes, 5; priests, 11 (10 dioc., 1 rel.); sem., 4; srs., 23; bap., 324; Caths., 22,000; tot. pop., 30,000.*

**Greece,** including Crete: Kingdom in southeastern Europe on the Balkan Peninsula; capital, Athens. St. Paul preached the Gospel at Athens and Corinth on his second missionary journey and visited the country again on his third tour. Other Apostles may have passed through also. Two bishops from Greece attended the First Council of Nicaea. After the division of the Roman Empire, the Church remained Eastern in rite and later broke ties with Rome as a result of the schism of 1054. A Latin-Rite jurisdiction was set up during the period of the Latin Empire of Constantinople, 1204-1261, but crumbled afterwards. Unity efforts of the Council of Florence had poor results. The country now has Greek Catholic and Latin jurisdictions. The Greek Orthodox Church is predominant. Established diplomatic relations with Vatican City in 1980.

*Archd., 4; dioc., 4; v.a., 1; ap. ex., 1; ord., 1; abp., 3; bp., 1; parishes, 73; priests, 101 (57 dioc., 44 rel.); sem., 6; bros., 43; srs., 166; bap., 422; Caths., 49,000 (.5%); tot. pop., 9,710,000 (1981).*

**Greenland (Kalaalit Nunaat):** Danish island province northeast of North America; granted self rule in 1979; capital, Nuuk (Godthaab). Catholicism was introduced about 1000. The first diocese was established in 1124 and a line of bishops dated from then until 1537. The first known churches in the western hemisphere, dating from about the 11th century, were on Greenland; the remains of 19 have been unearthed. The departure of Scandinavians and spread of the Reformation reduced the Church to nothing. The Moravian Brethren evangelized the Eskimos from the 1720s to 1901. By 1930 the Danish Church — Evangelical Lutheran — was in full possession. Since 1930 priests have been in Greenland, which is part of the Copenhagen diocese. There are about 60 Catholics in the area.

**Grenada:** Independent island state in the West Indies; capital, St. George's. Established diplomatic relations with Vatican City in 1979.

*Dioc., 1; bp., 1; parishes, 20; priests, 21 (7 dioc., 14 rel.); p.d., 4; sem., 4; bros., 7; srs., 18; bap., 1,207; Caths., 72,000; tot. pop., 110,000.*

**Guadeloupe:** French overseas department in the Leeward Islands of the West Indies; capital, Basse-Terre. Catholicism was introduced in the islands in the 16th century.

*Dioc., 1; bp., 1; parishes, 46; priests, 77 (41 dioc., 36 rel.); sem., 7; bros., 8; srs., 201; bap., 5,387; Caths., 299,000 tot. pop., 330,000 (1981).*

**Guam:** Outlying area of U.S. in the southwest Pacific; capital, Agana. The first Mass was offered in the Mariana Islands in 1521. The islands were evangelized by the Jesuits, from 1668, and other missionaries. The first native Micronesian bishop was ordained in 1970. The Agana diocese, which had been a suffragan of San Francisco, was made a metropolitan see in 1984.

*Archd., 1; archbp., 1 (nat.); parishes, 27; priests, 50 (18 dioc., 32 rel.); p.d., 7; sem., 18; bros., 4; srs., 135; bap., 1,729; Caths., 102,000; tot. pop., 112,000.*

**Guatemala:** Republic in Central America; capital, Guatemala City. Evangelization dates from the beginning of Spanish occupation in 1524. The first diocese, for all Central American territories administered by the captaincy general of Guatemala, was established in 1534. The country became independent in 1839, following annexation to Mexico in 1821, secession in 1823 and membership in the Central American Federation from 1825. In 1870, a government installed by a liberal revolution repudiated the concordat of 1853 and took active measures against the Church. Separation of Church and state was decreed; religious orders were suppressed and their property seized; priests and religious were exiled; schools were secularized. Full freedom was subsequently granted. The country has been in a virtual state of civil war in recent years, with violence and repression directed at all segments of the population, including the Church which has been subjected to persecution. Since 1976, at least nine priests were reported missing or killed. Guatemala maintains diplomatic relations with Vatican City.

*Archd., 1; dioc., 8; prel., 2; v.a., 1 (1984); a.a., 1; bp. (1984), 15; parishes, 346; priests, 652 (184 dioc., 468 rel.); p.d., 1; sem., 251; bros., 124; srs., 1,181; bap., 187,698; Caths. 6,270,000 (83.3%); tot. pop. 7,480,000 (1981).*

**Guiana, French (Cayenne):** French overseas department on the northeast coast of South America; capital, Cayenne. Catholicism was introduced in the 17th century. The Cayenne diocese was established in 1956.

*Dioc., 1; bp., 1; parishes, 22; priests, 30 (9 dioc., 21 rel.); bros., 2; srs., 104; bap., 1,259; Caths., 55,000; tot. pop., 69,000 (1981).*

**Guinea:** Republic on the west coast of Africa; capital, Conakry. Occasional missionary work followed exploration by the Portuguese about the middle of the 15th century; organized effort dates from 1877. The hierarchy was established in 1955. Following independence from France in 1958, Catholic schools were nationalized, youth organizations banned and missionaries restricted. Foreign missionaries were expelled in 1967. Archbishop Tchidimbo of Conakry, sentenced to life imprisonment in 1971 on a charge of conspiring to overthrow the government, was released in August, 1979; he resigned his see. Private schools, suppressed by the government for more than 20 years, were again authorized in 1984. Guinea has an apostolic delegate.

*Archd., 1; dioc., 1; p.a., 1; abp., 1 (nat.); bp., 1 (nat.); parishes, 28; priests, 19 (18 dioc., 1 rel.); sem., 14 (dioc.); bros., 1; srs., 26; bap., 770; Caths., 51,000 (.9%); tot. pop., 5,150,000 (1981).*

**Guinea-Bissau** (formerly Portuguese Guinea): Independent state on the west coast of Africa; capital, Bissau. Catholicism was introduced in the second half of the 15th century but limited missionary work, hampered by the slave trade, had meager results. Missionary work in this century dates from 1933. A prefecture apostolic was established in 1955 (made a diocese in 1977). Guinea-Bissau has an apostolic delegate.

*Dioc., 1; bp., 1; parishes, 17; priests, 41 (1 dioc., 40 rel.); sem., 2; bros., 13; srs., 32; bap., 861; Caths., 49,000; tot. pop., 800,000.*

**Guyana:** Republic on the northern coast of South America; capital, Georgetown. In 1899 the Catholic Church and other churches were given equal status with the Church of England and the Church of Scotland, which had sole rights up to that time. Most of the Catholics are Portuguese. The Georgetown diocese was established in 1956, 10 years before Guyana became independent of England. The first native bishop was appointed in 1971. Schools were nationalized in 1976. Increased government interference was reported in 1980-81. The Catholic newspaper was forced to close and missionaries were denied access to certain areas.

*Dioc., 1; bp., 1; parishes, 25; priests, 50 (8 dioc., 42 rel.); sem., 2; bros., 6; srs., 43; bap., 1,331; Caths., 105,000; tot. pop., 900,000.*

**Haiti:** Caribbean republic on the western third of Hispaniola adjacent to the Dominican Republic; capital, Port-au-Prince. Evangelization followed discovery by Columbus in 1492. Capuchins and Jesuits did most of the missionary work in the 18th century. From 1804, when independence was declared, until 1860, the country was in schism. Relations were regularized by a concordat concluded in 1860, when an archdiocese and four dioceses were established. Factors hindering the development of the Church have been a shortage of native clergy, inadequate religious instruction and the prevalen-

ce of voodoo. Political upheavals in the 1960s had serious effects on the Church. In 1984, a new concordat was concluded replacing the one in effect since 1860. Haiti maintains diplomatic relations with Vatican City.

*Archd., 1; dioc., 6; abp., 1; bp., 6; parishes, 186; priests, 404 (216 dioc., 188 rel.); p.d., 1; sem., 110; bros., 243; srs., 890; bap., 105,051; Caths. (est.), 5,000,000 (82%); tot. pop. 6,100,000.*

**Honduras:** Republic in Central America; capital, Tegucigalpa. Evangelization preceded establishment of the first diocese in the 16th century. Under Spanish rule and after independence from 1823, the Church held a favored position until 1880 when equal legal status was given to all religions. Harassment of priests and nuns working among peasants and Salvadoran refugees was reported in recent years. Honduras maintains diplomatic relations with Vatican City.

*Archd., 1; dioc., 4; prel., 1; abp., 1; bp., 7; parishes, 125; priests, 249 (71 dioc., 178 rel.); p.d. (1982), 4; sem., 29; bros., 16; srs., 341; bap., 97,285; Caths., 3,670,000 (96%); tot. pop., 3,820,000 (1981).*

**Hong Kong:** British crown colony at the mouth of the Canton River, adjacent to the southeast Chinese province of Kwangtung. A prefecture apostolic was established in 1841. Members of the Pontifical Institute for Foreign Missions began work there in 1858. The Hong Kong diocese was erected in 1946.

*Dioc., 1; bp., 1; parishes, 55; priests, 336 (74 dioc., 262 rel.); sem., 13; bros., 95; srs., 764; bap., 4,841; Caths., 266,508; tot. pop., 5,287,800.*

**Hungary:** People's republic in east central Europe; capital, Budapest. The early origins of Christianity in the country, whose territory was subject to a great deal of change, is not known. Magyars accepted Christianity about the end of the 10th century. St. Stephen I (d. 1038) promoted its spread and helped to organize some of its historical dioceses. Bishops early became influential in politics as well as in the Church. For centuries the country served as a buffer for the Christian West against barbarians from the East, notably the Mongols in the 13th century. Religious orders, whose foundations started from the 1130s, provided the most effective missionaries, pastors and teachers. Outstanding for years were the Franciscans and Dominicans; the Jesuits were noted for their work in the Counter-Reformation from the second half of the 16th century onwards. Hussites and Waldensians prepared the way for the Reformation which struck at almost the same time as the Turks. The Reformation made considerable progress after 1526, resulting in the conversion of large numbers to Lutheranism and Calvinism by the end of the century. Most of them or their descendants returned to the Church later, but many Magyars remained staunch Calvinists. Turks repressed the churches, Protestant as well as Catholic, during a reign of 150 years but they managed to survive. Domination of the Church was one of the objectives of government policy during the reigns of Maria Theresa and Joseph II in the second half of the 18th century; their Josephinism affected Church-state relations until the first World War. More than 100,000 Eastern-Rite schismatics were reunited with Rome about the turn of the 18th century. Secularization increased in the second half of the 19th century, which also witnessed the birth of many new Catholic organizations and movements to influence life in the nation and the Church. Catholics were involved in the social chaos and anti-religious atmosphere of the years following World War I, struggling with their compatriots for religious as well as political survival. After World War II Communist strength, which had manifested itself with less intensity earlier in the century, was great long before it forced the legally elected president out of office in 1947 and imposed a Soviet type of constitution on the country in 1949. The campaign against the Church started with the disbanding of Catholic organizations in 1946. In 1948, "Caritas," the Catholic charitable organization, was taken over and all Catholic schools, colleges and institutions were suppressed. Interference in church administration and attempts to split the bishops preceded the arrest of Cardinal Mindszenty on Dec. 26, 1948, and his sentence to life imprisonment in 1949. (He was free for a few days during the unsuccessful uprising of 1956. He then took up residence at the U.S. Embassy in Budapest where he remained until September, 1971, when he was permitted to leave the country. He died in 1975 in Vienna.) In 1950, religious orders and congregations were suppressed and 10,000 religious were interned. At least 30 priests and monks were assassinated, jailed or deported. About 4,000 priests and religious were confined in jail or concentration camps. The government sponsored a national "Progressive Catholic" church and captive organizations for priests and "Catholic Action," which attracted only a small minority. Signs were clear in 1965 and 1966 that a 1964 agreement with the Holy See regarding episcopal appointments had settled nothing. Six bishops were appointed by the Holy See and some other posts were filled, but none of the prelates were free from government surveillance and harassment. Four new bishops were appointed by the Holy See in January and ordained in Budapest in February, 1969; three elderly prelates resigned their sees. Shortly thereafter, peace priests complained that the "too Roman" new bishops would not deal with them. Talks between Vatican and Hungarian representatives during the past several years have resulted in the appointment of diocesan bishops to fill long-vacant sees.

*Archd., 3; dioc., 8; abb., 1; ap. ex., 1; card, 1; abp., 3; bp., 16; parishes, 2,270; priests, 3,193 (3,124 dioc., 69 rel.); p.d., 1; sem., 278; srs., 53; bap., 76,969; Caths., 6,573,000 (61.3%); tot. pop., 10,710,000 (1981).*

**Iceland:** Island republic between Norway and Greenland; capital, Reykjavik. Irish hermits were there in the eighth century. Missionaries subsequently evangelized the island and Christianity was officially accepted about 1000. The first bishop was ordained in 1056. The Black Death had dire effects and spiritual decline set in during the 15th century. Lutheranism was introduced from Denmark between 1537 and 1552 and made the official religion. Some Catholic missionary work was done in the 19th century. Religious freedom was granted to the few Catholics in 1874. A vicariate was erected in 1929 (made a diocese in 1968). Iceland maintains diplomatic relations with Vatican City.

*Dioc., 1; bp., 1; parishes, 2; priests, 8 (3 dioc., 5 rel.); sem., 5; srs., 32; bap., 18; Caths., 2,000; tot. pop., 230,000.*

**India:** Republic on the subcontinent of south central Asia; capital, New Delhi. Long-standing tradition credits the Apostle Thomas with the introduction of Christianity in the Kerala area. Evangelization followed the establishment of Portuguese posts and the conquest of Goa in 1510. Jesuits, Franciscans, Dominicans, Augustinians and members of other religious orders figured in the early missionary history. An archdiocese for Goa, with two suffragan sees, was set up in 1558. Five provincial councils were held between 1567 and 1606. The number of Catholics in 1572 was estimated to be 280,000. This figure rose to 800,000 in 1700 and declined to 500,000 in 1800. Missionaries had some difficulties with the British East India Co. which exercised virtual government control from 1757 to 1858. They also had trouble because of a conflict that developed between policies of the Portuguese government, which pressed its rights of patronage in episcopal and clerical appointments, and the Congregation for the Propagation of the Faith, which sought greater freedom of action in the same appointments. This struggle eventuated in the schism of Goa between 1838 and 1857. In 1886, when the number of Catholics was estimated to be one million, the hierarchy for India and Ceylon was restored. Jesuits contributed greatly to the development of Catholic education from the second half of the 19th century. A large percentage of the Catholic population is located around Goa and Kerala and farther south. The country is predominantly Hindu. So-called anti-conversion laws in effect in several states have had a restrictive effect on pastoral ministry and social service. India maintains diplomatic relations with Vatican City.

*Patriarchate, 1 (titular of East Indies); archd., 19; dioc., 89; p.a., 2; card., 2; abp., 19; bp., 101; parishes, 5,159; priests, 12,001 (7,058 dioc., 4,943 rel.); p.d., 24; sem., 5,011; bros., 2,801; srs., 49,956; bap., 288,826; Caths., 11,707,000 (1.6%); tot. pop. (est.), 713,000,000.*

**Indonesia:** Republic southeast of Asia, consisting of some 3,000 islands including Kalimantan (most of Borneo), Sulawesi (Celebes), Java, the Lesser Sundas, Moluccas, Sumatra, Timor and West Irian (Irian Jaya, western part of New Guinea); capital, Jakarta. Evangelization by the Portuguese began about 1511. St. Francis Xavier, greatest of the modern missionaries, spent some 14 months in the area. Christianity was strongly rooted in some parts of the islands by 1600. Islam's rise to dominance began at this time. The Dutch East Indies Co., which gained effective control in the 17th century, banned evangelization by Catholic missionaries for some time but Dutch secular and religious priests managed to resume the work. A vicariate of Batavia for all the Dutch East Indies was set up in 1841. About 90 per cent of the population is Moslem. The hierarchy was established in 1961. Indonesia maintains diplomatic relations with Vatican City.

*Archd., 7; dioc., 26; card., 1; abp., 6; bp., 26; parishes, 473; priests, 1,731 (249 dioc., 1,482 rel.); p.d., 8; sem., 1,098; bros., 773; srs., 4,106; bap., 164,331; Caths., 3,449,000 (2.2%); tot. pop., 150,520,000 (1981). (Statistics for former Portuguese Timor which was annexed by Indonesia in 1976 are listed separately; see Timor, Eastern.)*

**Iran:** Constitutional monarchy in southwestern Asia, between the Caspian Sea and the Persian Gulf; capital, Teheran. Some of the earliest Christian communities were established in this area outside the (then) Roman Empire. They suffered persecution in the fourth century and were then cut off from the outside world. Nestorianism was generally professed in the late fifth century. Islam became dominant after 640. Some later missionary work was attempted but without success. Religious liberty was granted in 1834, but Catholics were the victims of a massacre in 1918. Islam is the religion of perhaps 98 per cent of the population. In 1964 the country had 100,000 Monophysites, the largest group of Christians, and some 20,000 Nestorians. Catholics belong to the Latin, Armenian and Chaldean rites. Iran (Persia until 1935) maintains diplomatic relations with Vatican City.

*Archd., 4; dioc., 2; abp., 3; bp., 1; parishes, 32; priests, 33 (6 dioc., 27 rel.); p.d., 9; sem., 5; bro., 1; srs., 41, bap., 265; Caths., 20,000 (.05%); tot. pop., 39,320,000 (1981).*

**Iraq:** Republic in southwestern Asia, between Iran and Saudi Arabia; capital, Baghdad. Some of the earliest Christian communities were established in the area, whose history resembles that of Iran. Catholics belong to the Armenian, Chaldean, Latin and Syrian rites; Chaldeans are most numerous. Islam is the religion of some 90 per cent of the population. Iraq maintains diplomatic relations with Vatican City.

*Patriarchate, 1; archd., 9; dioc., 5; patriarch, 1; abp., 7; bp., 3; parishes, 103; priests, 148 (109 dioc., 39 rel.); p.d., 4; sem., 17; bros., 18; srs., 250; bap., 5,435; Caths., 374,000; tot. pop., 13,530,000 (1981).*

**Ireland:** Republic in the British Isles; capital, Dublin. St. Patrick, who is venerated as the apostle of Ireland, evangelized parts of the island for some years after the middle of the fifth century. Conversion of the island was not accomplished, however, until the seventh century or later. Celtic monks were the principal missionaries. The Church was organized along monastic lines at first, but a movement developed in the 11th century for the establishment of jurisdiction along episcopal lines. By that time many Roman usages had been adopted. The Church gathered strength during the period from the Norman Conquest of England to the reign of Henry VIII despite a wide variety of rivalries, wars, and other disturbances. Henry introduced an age of repression of the faith which continued for many years under several of his successors. The Irish suffered from proscription of the Catholic faith, economic and social disabilities, subjection to absentee landlords and a plantation system designed to keep them from owning property, and actual persecution which took an uncertain toll of lives up until about 1714. Most of those living in the northern part of Ireland became Anglican and Presbyterian in the 1600s but the south remained strong in faith. Some penal laws remained in force until emancipation in 1829. Nearly 100 years later Ireland was divided by two enactments which made Northern Ireland, consisting of six counties, part of the United Kingdom (1920) and gave dominion status to the Irish Free State, made up of the other 26 counties (1922). This state (Eire, in Gaelic) was proclaimed the Republic of Ireland in 1949. The Catholic Church predominates but religious freedom is guaranteed for all. Ireland maintains diplomatic relations with Vatican City.

*Archd., 4; dioc., 22; card., 1; abp., 3; bp., 28; parishes, 1,311; priests, 6,091 (3,737 dioc., 2,354 rel.); sem., 1,127; bros., 1,777; srs., 12,504; bap., 88,288 (preceding figures include Northern Ireland); Caths., (approx.), 3,255,000 (93%); tot. pop., 3,440,000 (1981).*

**Ireland, Northern:** Part of the United Kingdom, it consists of six of the nine counties of Ulster in the northeast corner of Ireland; capital, Belfast. History is given under Ireland, above. For recent developments, see Index.

*Caths. (approx.), 505,000 (32%); tot. pop., 1,540,000 (other statistics are included in Ireland).*

**Israel:** Parliamentary democracy in the Middle East, at the eastern end of the Mediterranean; capitals, Jerusalem and Tel Aviv (diplomatic). Israel was the birthplace of Christianity, the site of the first Christian communities. Some persecution was suffered in the early Christian era and again during the several hundred years of Roman control. Moslems conquered the territory in the seventh century and, except for the period of the Kingdom of Jerusalem established by Crusaders, remained in control most of the time up until World War I. The Church survived in the area, sometimes just barely, but it did not prosper greatly or show any notable increase in numbers. The British took over the protectorate of the area after World War I. Partition into Israel for the Jews and Palestine for the Arabs was approved by the United Nations in 1947. War broke out a year later with the proclamation of the Republic of Israel. The Israelis won the war and 50 percent more territory than they had originally been ceded. War broke out again for six days in June, 1967, and in October, 1973, resulting in a Middle East crisis which persists to the present time. Caught in the middle of the conflict are hundreds of thousands of dispossessed Palestinian refugees. Judaism is the faith professed by about 85 percent of the inhabitants; approximately one-third of them are considered observants. Most of the Arab minority are Moslems. The Akka archdiocese for Melkites is situated in Israel. Maronites are subject to the bishop of Tyr, Lebanon. Latins are under the jurisdiction of the Roman patriarchate of Jerusalem. Israel has an apostolic delegate. The *1981 Statistical Yearbook of the Church* reported a Catholic population of 128,000. The total population (1982 est.) is 4,100,000.

**Italy:** Republic in southern Europe; capital, Rome. A Christian community was formed early at Rome, probably by the middle of the first century. St. Peter established his see there. He and St. Paul suffered death for the faith there in the 60s. The early Christians were persecuted at various times there, as in other parts of the empire, but the Church developed in numbers and influence, gradually spreading out from towns and cities in the center and south to rural areas and the north. Organization, in the process of formation in the second century, developed greatly between the fifth and eighth centuries. By the latter date the Church had already come to grips with serious problems, including doctrinal and disciplinary disputes that threatened the unity of faith, barbarian invasions, and the need for the pope and bishops to take over civil responsibilities because of imperial default. The Church has been at the center of life on the peninsula throughout the centuries. It emerged from underground in 313, with the Edict of Milan, and rose to a position of prestige and lasting influence. It educated and converted the barbarians, preserved culture through the early Middle Ages and passed it on to later times, suffered periods of decline and gained strength through recurring reforms, engaged in military combat for political reasons and intellectual combat for the preservation and development of doctrine, saw and patronized the development of the arts, experienced all human strengths and weaknesses in its members, knew triumph and the humiliation of failure. For long centuries, from the fourth to the 19th, the Church was a temporal as well as spiritual power. This temporal aspect complicated its history in Italy. Since the 1870s, however, when the Papal States were annexed by the Kingdom of Italy, the history became simpler — but remained complicated — as the Church, shorn of temporal power, began to find new freedom for the fulfillment of its spiritual mission. In 1984, a new concordat was concluded between the Vatican and Italy, replacing one in effect since 1929. (See Index: Vatican-Italian Concordat.) Italy maintains diplomatic relations with Vatican City.

*Patriarchate, 1; archd., 57; dioc., 210; prel., 4; abb., 8; card. (1984), 33; abp., and bp., 444 (216 residential; 228 titular, including retired); parishes, 28,656; priests, 62,861 (40,256 dioc., 22,605 rel.); p.d., 246; sem., 4,877; bros., 6,532; srs., 142,733; bap., 639,929; Caths., 55,770,000 (97.5%); tot. pop., 57,200,000 (1981).*

**Ivory Coast:** Republic in western Africa; capital, Abidjan. The Holy Ghost Fathers began systematic evangelization in 1895. The first native priests from the area were ordained in 1934. The

hierarchy was set up in 1955; the first native cardinal (Bernard Yago) was named in 1983. Ivory Coast maintains diplomatic relations with Vatican City.

*Archd., 1; dioc., 9; card., 1 (nat.); bp., 10 (nat.); parishes, 172; priests, 371 (135 dioc., 236 rel.); sem., 78; bros., 119; srs., 502; bap., 22,321; Caths., 890,000 (10%); tot. pop., 8,800,000.*

**Jamaica:** Parliamentary democracy in the West Indies; capital, Kingston. Franciscans and Dominicans evangelized the island from about 1512 until 1655. Missionary work was interrupted after the English took possession but was resumed by Jesuits about the turn of the 19th century. A vicariate apostolic was organized in 1837. The hierarchy was established in 1967. Established diplomatic relations with Vatican City in 1979.

*Archd., 1; dioc., 1; abp., 1; bp., 1; parishes, 30; priests, 92 (13 dioc., 79 rel.); p.d., 3; sem., 5; bros., 9; srs., 201; bap., 3,049; Caths., 215,000 (9.6%); tot. pop., 2,229,000 (1981).*

**Japan:** Constitutional monarchy in the northwest Pacific; capital, Tokyo. Jesuits began evangelization in the middle of the 16th century and about 300,000 converts, most of them in Kyushu, were reported at the end of the century. The Nagasaki Martyrs were victims of persecution in 1597. Another persecution took some 4,000 lives between 1614 and 1651. Missionaries, banned for two centuries, returned about the middle of the 19th century and found Christian communities still surviving in Nagasaki and other places in Kyushu. A vicariate was organized in 1866. Religious freedom was guaranteed in 1889. The hierarchy was established in 1891. Japan maintains diplomatic relations with Vatican City.

*Archd., 3; dioc., 13; p.a., 1; card., 1; abp., 2; bp., 14; parishes, 769; priests, 2,000 (517 dioc., 1,483 rel.); p.d., 2; sem., 187; bros., 424; srs., 7,169; bap., 10,346; Caths., 406,000 (.3%); tot. pop., 117,650,000 (1981). (The Catholic population in 1983 was 421,090, according to statistics released in mid-1984.)*

**Jerusalem:** The entire city, site of the first Christian community, has been under Israeli control since the Israeli-Arab war of June, 1967. There are two patriarchates in the city, Melkite and Latin. Jerusalem has an apostolic delegate. (See Index for Pope John Paul's Apostolic Letter on Jerusalem.)

**Jordan:** Constitutional monarchy in the Middle East; capital, Amman. Christianity there dates from apostolic times. Survival of the faith was threatened many times under the rule of Moslems from 636 and Ottoman Turks from 1517 to 1918, and in the Islamic Emirate of Trans-Jordan from 1918 to 1949. Since the creation of Israel, some 500,000 Palestinian refugees, some of them Christians, have been in Jordan. Islam is the state religion but religious freedom is guaranteed for all. The Greek Melkite-Rite Archdiocese of Petra and Philadelphia is located in Jordan. Latin (Roman)-Rite Catholics are under the jurisdiction of the Latin patriarchate of Jerusalem. Jordan has an apostolic delegate.

*Archd., 1; abp., 1; parishes, 59; priests, 61 (52 dioc., 9 rel.); sem. 9; bros., 5; srs., 208; bap., 1,111; Caths., 96,000; tot. pop., 3,360,000 (1981).*

**Kenya:** Republic in eastern Africa bordering on the Indian Ocean; capital, Nairobi. Systematic evangelization by the Holy Ghost Fathers began in 1892, nearly 40 years after the start of work by Protestant missionaries. The hierarchy was established in 1953. Kenya maintains diplomatic relations with Vatican City.

*Archd., 1; dioc., 15; card., 1 (nat.); bp., 14 (10 nat.); parishes, 345; priests, 897 (248 dioc., 649 rel.); p.d., 2; sem., 502; bros., 233; srs., 1,941; bap., 207,597; Caths., 3,354,000 (19.5%); tot. pop., 17,150,000 (1981).*

**Kiribati (Gilbert Islands):** Former British colony in Oceania; became independent July 12, 1979; capital Bairiki on Tarawa. French Missionaries of the Sacred Heart began work in the islands in 1888. A vicariate for the islands was organized in 1897. The hierarchy was established in 1966.

*Dioc., 1; bp., 1; parishes, 22; priests, 13 (2 dioc., 11 rel.); sem., 5; bros., 2; srs., 49; bap., 454; Caths., 30,000; tot. pop., 57,000.*

**Korea:** Peninsula in eastern Asia, east of China, divided into the (Communist) Democratic People's Republic in the North, formed May 1, 1948, with Pyongyang as its capital; and the Republic of Korea in the South, with Seoul as the capital. Some Catholics may have been in Korea before it became a "hermit kingdom" toward the end of the 16th century and closed its borders to foreigners. The real introduction to Catholicism came in 1784 through lay converts. A priest arriving in the country in 1794 found 4,000 Catholics there who had never seen a priest. A vicariate was erected in 1831 but was not manned for several years thereafter. There were 15,000 Catholics by 1857. Four persecutions in the 19th century took a terrible toll; several thousands died in the last one, 1866-69. (One-hundred and three martyrs of this period were canonized by Pope John Paul II during his 1984 apostolic visit to the country.) Freedom of religion was granted in 1883 when Korea opened its borders. Progress was made thereafter. The hierarchy was established in 1962. Since the war of 1950-1953, there have been no signs of Catholic life in the North, which has been blanketed by a news blackout. In July, 1972, both Koreas agreed to seek peaceful means of reunification. The South maintains diplomatic relations with Vatican City. Bishop Tji of Won Ju, South Korea, convicted and sentenced to 15 years' imprisonment in 1974 on a charge of inciting to rebellion, was released in February, 1975. (See Index for papal visit.)

*North Korea: Dioc., 2; abb., 1; bp., 1 (exiled); tot. pop., 18,320,000. No recent Catholic statistics available; there were an estimated 100,000 Catholics reported in 1969.*

*South Korea: Archd., 3; dioc., 11; card., 1; abp., 2; bp., 14; parishes, 637; priests, 1,237 (942 dioc., 295 rel.); sem., 762; bros., 259; srs., 3,646; bap., 133,720; Caths. 1,530,720 (3.8%); tot. pop., 40,347,158.*

**Kuwait:** Constitutional monarchy (sultanate or

sheikdom) in southwest Asia bordering on the Persian Gulf. Remote Christian origins probably date to apostolic times. Islam is the predominant and official religion. Kuwait maintains diplomatic relations with Vatican City.

*V.a., 1; bp., 1; parishes, 3; priests, 7 (3 dioc., 4 rel.); srs., 29; bap., 768; Caths., 47,000; tot. pop., 1,460,000.*

**Laos:** Constitutional monarchy in southeast Asia, surrounded by China, Vietnam, Kampuchea, Thailand and Burma; capital, Vientiane. Systematic evangelization by French missionaries started about 1881; earlier efforts ended in 1688. A vicariate apostolic was organized in 1899 when there were 8,000 Catholics and 2,000 catechumens in the country. Most of the foreign missionaries were expelled following the communist take-over in 1975. Buddhism is the state religion. Laos has an apostolic delegate.

*V.a., 4; bp., 4 (nat.; a coad. vicar apostolic was ordained in 1983). No statistics available. Catholics numbered 35,000 (1% of the total population) in 1974. Tot. pop. (1980), 3,810,000.*

**Latvia:** Baltic republic forcibly absorbed by the U.S.S.R. in the early 1940s; capital, Riga. Catholicism was introduced late in the 12th century. Lutheranism became the dominant religion after 1530. Catholics were free to practice their faith during the long period of Russian control and during independence from 1918 to 1940. The relatively small Catholic community has been repressed since the start of Soviet occupation. The Russian take-over of Latvia has not been recognized by the Holy See or the United States.

*Archd., 1; dioc., 1; card., 1 (Julijans Vaivods, named in 1983); bp., 3 (titular); parishes, 179; priests, 114 (104 dioc., 10 rel.); sem., 49; bap., 4,413; Caths., 250,000; tot. pop. 2,500,000.*

**Lebanon:** Republic in the Middle East, north of Israel; capital, Beirut. Christianity, introduced in apostolic times, was firmly established by the end of the fourth century and has remained so despite heavy Moslem influence since early in the seventh century. The country is the center of the Maronite Rite. During the past 10 years the country has been torn by violence and often heavy fighting among rival political-religious factions drawn along Christian-Moslem lines. (See Index for 1984 developments.) Lebanon maintains diplomatic relations with Vatican City.

*Archd. 10 (3 Maronite, 7 Greek Melkite); dioc., 7 (1 Armenian, 1 Chaldean, 5 Maronite); v.a., 1 (Latin); card., 1 (Patr. Antoine Khoraiche of Maronites); patriarchs, 3 (patriarchs of Antioch of the Maronites, a cardinal; Antioch of the Syrians and Cilicia of the Armenians who reside in Lebanon); abp. and bp., 19; priests, 1,428 (635 dioc., 793 rel.); p.d., 1; sem., 349; bros., 120; srs., 3,453; bap., 14,744; Caths., 1,299,000; tot. pop., 3,000,000 (1981).*

**Lesotho:** Constitutional monarchy, an enclave in the southeastern part of the Republic of South Africa; capital, Maseru. Oblates of Mary Immaculate, the first Catholic missionaries in the area, started evangelization in 1862. A prefecture apostolic was organized in 1894. The hierarchy was established in 1951. Lesotho maintains diplomatic relations with Vatican City.

*Archd., 1; dioc., 3; abp., 1 (nat.); bp., 3 (nat.); parishes, 74; priests, 122 (22 dioc., 100 rel.); sem., 25; bros., 69; srs., 710; bap., 27,372; Caths., 597,662 (43%); tot. pop., 1,400,000.*

**Liberia:** Republic in western Africa, bordering on the Atlantic; capital, Monrovia. Missionary work and influence, dating interruptedly from the 16th century, were slight before the Society of African Missions undertook evangelization in 1906. The hierarchy was established in 1982. Liberia maintains diplomatic relations with Vatican City.

*Archd., 1; dioc., 1; abp., 1 (nat.); bp., 1 (nat.); parishes, 46; priests, 49 (8 dioc., 41 rel.); p.d., 4; sem., 18; bros., 26; srs., 87; bap. 3,025; Caths., 40,000 (1.9%); tot. pop., 2,040,000.*

**Libya:** Arab republic in northern Africa, on the Mediterranean between Egypt and Tunisia; capital, Tripoli. Christianity was probably preached in the area at an early date but was overcome by the spread of Islam from the 630's. Islamization was complete by 1067 and there has been no Christian influence since then. The Catholics in the country belong to the foreign colony. Islam is the state religion. Libya has an apostolic delegate.

*V.a., 3; p.a., 1; bp., 2; parishes, 3; priests, 13 (rel.); srs., 126; bap., 121; Caths., 43,000 (1.3%); tot. pop., 3,100,000.*

**Liechtenstein:** Constitutional monarchy in central Europe, in the Alps and on the Rhine between Switzerland and Austria; capital, Vaduz. Christianity in the country dates from the fourth century; the area has been under the jurisdiction of Chur, Switzerland, since about that time. The Reformation had hardly any influence in the country. Catholicism is the state religion but religious freedom for all is guaranteed by law.

*Parishes, 10; priests, 31 (18 dioc., 13 rel); bros., 11; srs., 102; bap., 350; Caths., 21,000; tot. pop., 30,000.*

**Lithuania:** Baltic republic forcibly absorbed and under Soviet domination since 1945; captial, Vilna (Vilnius). Catholicism was introduced in 1251 and two dioceses were established by 1260. Effective evangelization took place between 1385 and 1417, when Catholicism became the state religion. Losses to Lutheranism in the 16th century were overcome. Efforts of czars to "russify" the Church between 1795 and 1918 were strongly resisted. Concordat relations with the Vatican were established in 1927, nine years after independence from Russia and 13 years before the start of another kind of Russian control with the following results, among others: all convents closed since 1940; four seminaries shut down; appointment to one seminary (Kaunas) only with government approval; priests restricted in pastoral ministry and subject to appointment by government officials; no religious services outside churches; no religious press; religious instruction banned; parish installations and activities controlled by directives

enacted in 1976; two bishops — Vincentas Sladkevicius and Julijonas Steponavicius — forbidden to act as bishops and relegated to remote parishes in 1957 and 1961, respectively; arrest, imprisonment or detention in Siberia for four bishops, 185 priests, 275 lay persons between 1945 and 1955. Despite such developments and conditions, there remains a strong and vigorous underground Church in Lithuania, where the Soviet government finds its repressive potential limited by the solidarity of popular resistance. In July, 1982, two episcopal appointments were made: Rev. Antanas Vaicius was named titular bishop of Cubda and apostolic administrator of the Telsiai diocese and Klaipeda prelature; Bishop Vincentas Sladkevicius, titular bishop of Abora and auxiliary bishop of Kaisiadorys, was named apostolic administrator of that diocese. In 1983, four of the five bishops were allowed to go to Rome for their *ad limina* visit. The Soviet take-over of Lithuania is not recognized by the Holy See or the United States.

*Archd., 2 (Kaunas and Vilna, which includes territory in political confines of Poland); dioc., 4; prel., 1; bp., 5 (none residential); parishes 630; priests, 707 (698 dioc., 9 rel.); p.d., 1; sem., 94; Caths., 2,542,000; tot. pop., 3,178,000 (1981).*

**Luxembourg:** Constitutional monarchy in western Europe, between Belgium, Germany and France; capital, Luxembourg. Christianity, introduced in the fifth and sixth centuries, was firmly established by the end of the eighth century. A full-scale parish system was in existence in the ninth century. Monastic influence was strong until the Reformation, which had minimal influence in the country. The Church experienced some adverse influence from the currents of the French Revolution. Luxembourg maintains diplomatic relations with Vatican City.

*Dioc., 1; bp., 1; parishes, 274; priests, 416 (325 dioc., 91 rel.); sem., 20; bros., 21; srs., 1,175; bap., 3,395; Caths. 350,386 (95.2%); tot. pop., 368,000.*

**Macau:** Portuguese-administered territory in southeast Asia across the Pearl River estuary from Hong Kong. Christianity was introduced by the Jesuits in 1557. Diocese was established in 1576. Macau served as a base for missionary work in Japan and China.

*Dioc., 1; bp., 1; parishes, 6; priests, 64 (33 dioc., 31 rel.); sem., 6; bros., 19; srs., 190; bap., 566; Caths., 19,085; tot. pop., 328,000.*

**Madagascar (Malagasy Republic):** Republic off the eastern coast of Africa; capital, Antananarivo. Missionary efforts were generally fruitless from early in the 16th century until the Jesuits were permitted to start open evangelization about 1845. A prefecture apostolic was set up in 1850 and a vicariate apostolic in the north was placed in charge of the Holy Ghost Fathers in 1898. There were 100,000 Catholics by 1900. The first native bishop was ordained in 1936. The hierarchy was established in 1955. Madagascar maintains diplomatic relations with Vatican City.

*Archd., 3; dioc., 14; card., 1 (nat.); abp., 2*

*(nat.); bp., 16 (14 nat.); parishes, 228; priests, 687 (164 dioc., 523 rel.); sem., 166; bros., 367; srs., 1,889; bap., 74,834; Caths., 1,993,000 (22.2%); tot. pop. 8,960,000 (1981).*

**Madeira Islands:** Portuguese province, an archipelago 340 miles west of the northwestern coast of Africa; capital, Funchal. Catholicism has had a continuous history since the first half of the 15th century. Statistics are included in those for Portugal.

**Malawi:** Republic in the interior of eastern Africa; capital, Lilongwe. Missionary work, begun by Jesuits in the late 16th and early 17th centuries, was generally ineffective until the end of the 19th century. The White Fathers arrived in 1889 and later were joined by others. A vicariate was set up in 1897. The hierarchy was established in 1959. Malawi maintains diplomatic relations with Vatican City.

*Archd., 1; dioc., 6; abp., 1 (nat.); bp., 6 (4 nat.); parishes, 131; priests, 310 (103 dioc., 207 rel.); sem., 140; bros., 93; srs., 628; bap., 41,659; Caths., 1,453,000 (21%); tot. pop., 6,647,000.*

**Malaysia:** Parliamentary democracy in southeastern Asia; federation of former states of Malaya, Sabah (former Br. North Borneo), and Sarawak; capital, Kuala Lumpur. Christianity, introduced by Portuguese colonists about 1511, was confined almost exclusively to Malacca until late in the 18th century. The effectiveness of evangelization increased from then on because of the recruitment and training of native clergy. Singapore (see separate entry), founded in 1819, became a center for missionary work. Seventeen thousand Catholics were in the Malacca diocese in 1888. Effective evangelization in Sabah and Sarawak began in the second half of the 19th century. The hierarchy was established in 1973. Malaysia has an apostolic delegate.

*Archd., 2; dioc., 4; abp., 2 (nat.); bp., 4 (nat.); parishes, 159; priests, 246 (170 dioc., 76 rel.); p.d., 2; sem., 32; bros., 111; srs., 558; bap., 15,974; Caths. (1981), 456,000 (3.1%); tot. pop., 14,700,000.*

**Maldives:** Republic, an archipelago 400 miles southwest of India and Ceylon; capital, Male. No serious attempt was ever made to evangelize the area, which is completely Moslem.

*Tot. pop., 160,000.*

**Mali:** Republic, inland in western Africa; capital, Bamako. Catholicism was introduced late in the second half of the 19th century. Missionary work made little progress in the midst of the predominantly Moslem population. A vicariate was set up in 1921. The hierarchy was established in 1955. Established diplomatic relations with Vatican City in 1979.

*Archd., 1; dioc., 5; abp., 1 (nat.); bp., 5 (3 nat.); parishes, 38; priests, 131 (20 dioc., 111 rel.); sem., 19; bros., 23; srs., 168; bap., 2,392; Caths. (1981), 70,000 (.97%); tot. pop., 7,160,000.*

**Malta:** Parliamentary democracy 58 miles south of Sicily; capital, Valletta. Early catacombs and inscriptions are evidence of the early introduc-

tion of Christianity. St. Paul was shipwrecked on Malta in 60. Saracens controlled the island(s) from 870 to 1090, a period of difficulty for the Church. The line of bishops extends from 1090 to the present. The passage in recent years of government-sponsored legislation affecting Catholic schools and church-owned property has brought charges of harassment by church leaders. (See News Events.) Malta maintains diplomatic relations with Vatican City.

*Archd., 1; dioc., 1; abp., 1; bp., 1; parishes, 79; priests, 1,096 (653 dioc., 443 rel.); sem., 132; bros., 108; srs., 1,552; bap., 5,625; Caths., 340,000 (91%); tot. pop., 370,000 (1981).*

**Marianas, The:** U.S. Trust territory in Pacific (scheduled to become a U.S. commonwealth). Under ecclesiastical jurisdiction of Agana archdiocese, Guam.

*Parishes, 8; priests, 4 (dioc.); p.d., 2; srs., 19; bap., 730; Caths., 18,000; tot. pop., 24,000.*

**Martinique:** French overseas department in the West Indies, about 130 miles south of Guadeloupe; capital, Fort-de-France. Catholicism was introduced in the 16th century. The hierarchy was established in 1967.

*Archd., 1; abp., 1; parishes, 47; priests, 94 (41 dioc., 53 rel.); sem., 8; bros., 12; srs., 220; bap., 3,973; Caths., 290,000; tot. pop., 329,000.*

**Mauritania:** Islamic republic on the northwest coast of Africa; capital, Nouakchott. With few exceptions, the Catholics in the country are members of the foreign colony. Mauritania has an apostolic delegate.

*Dioc., 1; bp., 1; parishes, 6; priests, 9 (2 dioc., 7 rel.); bro., 1; srs., 25; bap., 48; Caths., 4,000 (.2%); tot. pop., 1,700,000.*

**Mauritius:** Self-governing island state 500 miles east of Madagascar; capital, Port Louis. Catholicism was introduced by Vincentians in 1722. Port Louis, made a vicariate in 1819 and a diocese in 1847, was a jumping-off point for missionaries to Australia, Madagascar and South Africa. Mauritius maintains diplomatic relations with Vatican City.

*Dioc., 1; bp., 1; parishes, 44; priests, 163 (85 dioc., 78 rel.); sem., 5; bros., 49; srs., 320; bap., 7,136; Caths., 350,000 (36%); tot. pop., 970,000 (1981).*

**Melilla:** Spanish possession in northern Africa. Statistics are included in those for Spain.

**Mexico** (United States of Mexico): Republic in Middle America. Christianity was introduced early in the 16th century. Mexico City, made a diocese in 1530, became the missionary and cultural center of the whole country. Missionary work, started in 1524 and forwarded principally by Franciscans, Dominicans, Augustinians and Jesuits, resulted in the baptism of all persons in the central plateau by the end of the century. Progress there and in the rest of the country continued in the following century but tapered off and went into decline in the 18th century, for a variety of reasons ranging from diminishing government support to relaxations of Church discipline. The wars of independence, 1810-21, in which some Catholics participated, created serious problems of adjustment for the

Church. Social problems, political unrest and government opposition climaxed in the constitution of 1917 which practically outlawed the Church. Persecution took serious tolls of life and kept the Church underground, under Calles, 1924-1928, again in 1931, and under Cardenas in 1934. President Camacho, 1940-1946, ended persecution and instituted a more lenient policy. The Church, however, still labors under legal and practical disabilities. Mexico has an apostolic delegate; the Mexican president has a personal envoy to the Vatican.

*Archd., 12; dioc., 53; prel., 7; v.a., 2; card., 3; abp., 10; bp., 74; parishes, 4,072; priests, 10,235 (7,162 dioc., 3,073 rel.); p.d., 42; sem., 3,385; bros., 1,155; srs., 25,468; bap., 1,903,594; Caths., 68,600,000; tot. pop., 71,190,000 (1981).*

**Monaco:** Constitutional monarchy, an enclave on the Mediterranean coast of France near the Italian border; capital, Monaco-Ville. Christianity was introduced before 1000. Catholicism is the official religion but freedom is guaranteed for all. Monaco has an ambassador at Vatican City.

*Archd., 1; abp., 1; parishes, 5; priests, 33 (15 dioc., 18 rel.); p.d., 1; sem., 5; bros., 22; srs., 58; bap., 226; Caths., 22,375; tot. pop., 24,861.*

**Mongolia:** Republic in north central Asia; capital Ulaanbaatar. Christianity was introduced by Nestorians. Some Franciscans were in the country in the 13th and 14th centuries, en route to China. Limited evangelization efforts from the 18th century had little success among the Mongols in Outer Mongolia, where Buddhism has predominated for hundreds of years. No Christians were known to be there in 1953. There may be a few Catholics in Inner Mongolia. No foreign missionaries have been in the country since 1953.

*Pop., 1,700,000.*

**Montserrat:** British island possession in Caribbean; capital, Plymouth. Under ecclesiastical jurisdiction of St. John's-Basseterre diocese, Antigua.

*Parishes, 2; priests, 2 (1 dioc., 1 rel.); p.d.; 1; srs., 5; bap., 35; Caths., 1,000; tot. pop., 13,000.*

**Morocco:** Constitutional monarchy in northwest Africa with Atlantic and Mediterranean coastlines; capital, Rabat. Christianity was known in the area by the end of the third century. Bishops from Morocco attended a council at Carthage in 484. Catholic life survived under Visigoth and, from 700, Arab rule; later it became subject to influence from the Spanish, Portuguese and French. Islam is the state religion. The hierarchy was established in 1955. Morocco maintains diplomatic relations with Vatican City.

*Archd., 2; abp., 2; parishes, 57; priests, 97 (26 dioc., 71 rel.); bros., 11; srs., 399; bap., 171; Caths., 64,520 (.3%); tot. pop., 22,300,000.*

**Mozambique:** Independent (June 25, 1975) republic in southeast Africa, bordering on the Indian Ocean; former Portuguese territory; capital, Maputo (formerly Lourenco Marques ). Christianity was introduced by Portuguese Jesuits about the middle of the 16th century. Evangelization continued from then until the 18th century when it went into decline largely because of the Portuguese government's expulsion of the Jesuits. Conditions worsened in the 1830s, improved after 1881, but deteriorated again during the anticlerical period from 1910 to 1925. Conditions improved in 1940, the year Portugal concluded a new concordat with the Holy See and the hierarchy was established. Outspoken criticism by missionaries of Portuguese policies in Mozambique resulted in Church-state tensions in the years immediately preceding independence. Tension continues to be a factor, although to a smaller degree, in relations between the Church and the Marxist-oriented government in power since 1975. The first two native bishops were ordained March 9, 1975. Two ecclesiastical provinces were established in 1984. Mozambique has an apostolic delegate.

*Archd., 3; dioc., 6; abp., 3 (2 nat.); bp., 6 (5 nat.); parishes, 258; priests, 251 (24 dioc., 227 rel.); sem., 19; bros., 72; srs., 488; bap., 28,470; Caths., 1,738,000 (14.4%); tot. pop., 12,000,000.*

**Namibia** (South West Africa): Territory in South Africa in dispute between the Republic of South Africa and the United Nations; capital, Windhoek. The area shares the history of South Africa. Namibia has an apostolic delegate (to Southern Africa).

*V.a., 2; bp., 2 (1 nat); parishes, 61; priests, 65 (2 dioc., 63 rel.); p.d., 15; bros., 55; srs., 277; bap., 7,496; Caths., 180,364; tot. pop., 1,086,000.*

**Nauru:** Independent republic in western Pacific; capital, Yaren. Forms part of the Tarawa and Nauru diocese (Tarawa).

*Srs., 4; bap., 70; Caths., 2,000; tot. pop., 7,000 (1981).*

**Nepal:** Constitutional monarchy, the only Hindu kingdom in the world, in central Asia south of the Himalayas between India and Tibet; capital, Kathmandu. Little is known of the country before the 15th century. Some Jesuits passed through from 1628 and some sections were evangelized in the 18th century, with minimal results, before the country was closed to foreigners. Conversions from Hinduism, the state religion, are not recognized in law. Christian missionary work is not allowed. Nepal established diplomatic relations with Vatican City in 1983.

*Mission "sui juris," 1 (est. 1983); priests, 23 (rel); bros., 7; srs., 30; bap., 18; Caths., 750; tot. pop., 15,000,000.*

**Netherlands:** Kingdom in northwestern Europe; capital, Amsterdam (seat of the government, The Hague). Evangelization, begun about the turn of the sixth century by Irish, Anglo-Saxon and Frankish missionaries, resulted in Christianization of the country by 800 and subsequent strong influence on The Lowlands. Invasion by French Calvinists in 1572 brought serious losses to the Catholic Church and made the Reformed Church dominant. Catholics suffered a practical persecution of official repression and social handicap in the 17th century. The schism of Utrecht occurred in 1724. Only one-third of the population was Catholic in 1726. The Church had only a skeleton organization from 1702 to 1853, when the hierarchy was reestablished. Despite this upturn, cultural isolation was the experience of Catholics until about 1914. From then on new vigor came into the life of the Church, and a whole new climate of interfaith relations began to develop. Before and for some years following the Second Vatican Council, the thrust and variety of thought and practice in the Dutch Church moved it to the vanguard position of "progressive" renewal. A particular synod of Dutch bishops held at the Vatican in January, 1980, and aimed at internal improvement of the Church in the Netherlands, had disappointing results, according to reports in 1981. The Netherlands maintains diplomatic relations with Vatican City.

*Archd., 1; dioc., 6; card., 3; abp., 1; bp., 9; parishes, 1,794; priests 6,199 (2,492 dioc., 3,707 rel.); p.d., 36; sem., 261; bros., 2,691; srs., 19,893; bap., 55,872; Caths., 5,561,412 (39%); tot. pop., 14,270,000.*

**Netherlands Antilles** (Curacao): Autonomous part of the Kingdom of The Netherlands. Consists of two groups of islands in the Caribbean: Curacao, Aruba and Bonaire, off the northern coast of Venezuela; and St. Eustatius, Saba and the southern part of St. Martaan, southeast of Puerto Rico; capital, Willemstad on Curacao. Christianity was introduced in the 16th century. Apostolic delegation was established in 1975.

*Dioc., 1; bp., 1; parishes, 47; priests, 57 (10 dioc., 47 rel.); sem., 1; bros., 51; srs., 130; bap., 3,440; Caths., 221,448 (85.9%); tot. pop., 258,000.*

**New Caledonia:** French territory consisting of several islands in Oceania east of Queensland, Australia; capital, Noumea. Catholicism was introduced in 1843, nine years after Protestant missionaries began evangelization. A vicariate was organized in 1847. The hierarchy was established in 1966.

*Archd., 1; abp., 1; parishes, 36; priests, 59 (11 dioc., 48 rel.); sem., 5; bros., 56; srs., 195; bap., 1,836; Caths., 92,200; tot. pop., 144,000.*

**New Zealand:** Dominion in the British Commonwealth, a group of islands in Oceania 1,200 miles southeast of Australia: capital, Wellington. Protestant missionaries were the first evangelizers. On North Island, Catholic missionaries started work before the establishment of two dioceses in 1848; their work among the Maoris was not organized until about 1881. On South Island, whose first resident priest arrived in 1840, a diocese was established in 1869. These three jurisdictions were joined in a province in 1896. The Marists were the outstanding Catholic missionaries in the area. Established diplomatic relations with Vatican City, 1973.

*Archd., 1; dioc., 5; card., 1; bp., 8; parishes, 286; priests, 756 (415 dioc., 341 rel.); sem., 47; bros., 327; srs., 1,839; bap., 8,788; Caths. 457,516 (14.5%); tot. pop., 3,143,327.*

**Nicaragua:** Republic in Central America: capital, Managua. Evangelization began shortly after the Spanish conquest about 1524 and eight years later the first bishop took over jurisdiction of the Church in the country. Jesuits were leaders in missionary work during the colonial period, which lasted until the 1820s. Evangelization endeavor increased after establishment of the republic in 1838. In this century it was extended to the Atlantic coastal area where Protestant missionaries had begun work about the middle of the 1900s. Many church leaders, clerical and lay, supported the aims but not necessarily all the methods of the revolution which forced the resignation and flight July 17, 1979, of Anastasio Somoza Debayle, whose family had controlled the government since the early 1930s. Nicaragua maintains diplomatic relations with Vatican City. (See Index for 1984 developments.)

*Archd., 1; dioc., 4; prel., 2; v.a., 1; abp., 1; bp., 7; parishes, 182; priests, 313 (121 dioc., 192 rel.); p.d., 37; sem., 46; bros., 89; srs., 651; bap., 64,380; Caths., 2,574,225 (90.9%); 2,831,683.*

**Niger:** Republic in west central Africa; capital, Niamey. The first mission was set up in 1831. A prefecture apostolic was organized in 1942 and the first diocese was established in 1961. The country is predominantly Moslem. Niger maintains diplomatic relations with Vatican City.

*Dioc., 1; bp., 1; parishes, 11; priests, 29 (6 dioc., 23 rel.); sem., 1; bros., 12; srs., 77; bap., 164; Caths., 14,400 (.25%); tot. pop., 5,660,000.*

**Nigeria:** Republic in western Africa; capital, Lagos. The Portuguese introduced Catholicism in the coastal region in the 15th century. Capuchins did some evangelization in the 17th century but systematic missionary work did not get under way along the coast until about 1840. A vicariate for this area was organized in 1870. A prefecture was set up in 1911 for missions in the northern part of the country where Islam was strongly entrenched. From 1967, when Biafra seceded, until early in 1970 the country was torn by civil war. The hierarchy was established in 1950. Nigeria maintains diplomatic relations with Vatican City.

*Archd., 3; dioc., 28; mission "sui juris," 1; card., 1 (nat.); abp., 3 (nat.); bp., 30 (23 nat.); parishes, 473; priests, 1,350 (778 dioc., 572 rel.); p.d., 11; sem., 1,205; bros., 199; srs., 1,240; bap., 256,585; Caths., 5,520,000 (6.9%); tot. pop., 79,680,000 (1981).*

**Niue:** New Zealand self-governing territory in South Pacific. Under ecclesiastical jurisdiction of Rarotonga diocese, Cook Islands.

*Parish, 1; priest, 1 (rel.); srs., 2; Caths., 200; tot. pop., 3,000.*

**Norway:** Constitutional monarchy in northern Europe, the western part of the Scandinavian peninsula; capital, Oslo. Evangelization begun in the ninth century by missionaries from England and Ireland put the Church on a firm footing about the turn of the 11th century. The first diocese was set up in 1153 and development of the Church progressed until the Black Death in 1349 inflicted losses from which it never recovered. Lutheranism, introduced from outside in 1537 and furthered cautiously, gained general acceptance by about 1600 and was made the state religion. Legal and other measures crippled the Church, forcing priests to flee the country and completely disrupting normal activity. Changes for the better came in the 19th century, with the granting of religious liberty in 1845 and the repeal of many legal disabilities in 1897. Norway was administered as a single apostolic vicariate from 1892 to 1932, when it was divided into three jurisdictions under the supervision of the Congregation for the Propagation of the Faith. Established diplomatic relations with Vatican City in 1982.

*Dioc., 1; prel., 2; bp., 2; parishes, 27; priests, 61 (19 dioc., 42 rel.); sem., 3; bros., 9; srs., 344; bap., 254; Caths., 16,482; tot. pop., 4,113,000.*

**Oman:** Independent monarchy in eastern corner of Arabian Peninsula; capital, Muscat. Under ecclesiastical jurisdiction of Arabia vicariate apostolic.

*Parish, 1; priests, 2 (1 dioc., 1 rel.); srs., 9; bap., 45; Caths., 6,000; tot. pop., 948,000.*

**Pakistan:** Islamic republic in southwestern Asia; capital, Islamabad. (Formerly included East Pakistan which became the independent nation of Bangladesh in 1971.) Islam, firmly established in the eighth century, is the state religion. Christian evangelization of the native population began about the middle of the 19th century, years after earlier scattered attempts. The hierarchy was established in 1950. Pakistan maintains diplomatic relations with Vatican City.

*Archd., 1; dioc., 5; card., 1 (nat.); bp., 7 (6 nat.); parishes, 53; priests, 223 (87 dioc., 136 rel.); p.d., 2; sem., 37; bros., 70; srs., 658; bap., 23,639; Caths. (1981), 480,000 (.5%); tot. pop., 84,580,000.*

**Panama:** Republic in Central America; capital, Panama City. Catholicism was introduced by Franciscan missionaries and evangelization started in 1514. The Panama diocese, oldest in the Americas, was set up at the same time. The Catholic Church has favored status and state aid for missions, charities and parochial schools, but religious freedom is guaranteed to all religions. Panama maintains diplomatic relations with Vatican City.

*Archd., 1; dioc., 3; prel., 1; v.a., 1; abp., 1; bp., 6; parishes, 137; priests, 302 (78 dioc., 224 rel.); p.d., 5; sem., 105; bros., 39; srs., 490; bap., 35,247; Caths., 1,727,000 (89%); tot. pop., 1,940,000 (1981).*

**Papua New Guinea:** Independent (Sept. 16, 1975) republic (formerly under Australian administration) in southwest Pacific. Consists of the eastern half of the southwestern Pacific island of New Guinea and the Northern Solomon Islands; capital, Port Moresby. Marists began evangelization about 1844 but were handicapped by many factors, including "spheres of influence" laid out for Catholic and Protestant missionaries. A prefecture apostolic was set up in 1896 and placed in charge of the Divine Word Missionaries. The territory suffered greatly during World War II. Hierarchy was established for New Guinea and adjacent islands in 1966. Papua New Guinea established diplomatic relations with the Vatican in 1977. (See Index for papal visit.)

*Archd., 4; dioc., 14; abp., 4; bp., 15; parishes, 316; priests, 516 (55 dioc., 461 rel.); p.d., 12; sem., 148; bros., 353; srs., 948; bap., 32,963; Caths., 916,000 (30%); tot. pop., 3,010,000 (1981).*

**Paraguay:** Republic in central South America; capital, Asuncion. Catholicism was introduced in 1542, evangelization began almost immediately. A diocese erected in 1547 was occupied for the first time in 1556. On many occasions thereafter dioceses in the country were left unoccupied because of political and other reasons. Jesuits who came into the country after 1609 devised the reductions system for evangelizing the Indians, teaching them agriculture, husbandry, trades and other useful arts, and giving them experience in property use and community life. The reductions were communes of Indians only, under the direction of the missionaries. About 50 of them were established in southern Brazil, Uruguay and northeastern Argentina as well as in Paraguay. They had an average population of three to four thousand. At their peak, some 30 reductions had a population of 100,000. Political officials regarded the reductions with disfavor because they did not control them and feared that the Indians trained in them might foment revolt and upset the established colonial system under Spanish control. The reductions lasted until about 1768 when their Jesuit founders and directors were expelled from Latin America. Church-state relations following independence from Spain in 1811 were tense as often as not because of government efforts to control the Church through continued exercise of Spanish patronage rights and by other means. The Church as well as the whole country suffered a great deal during the War of the Triple Alliance from 1865-70. After that time, the Church had the same kind of experience in Paraguay as in the rest of Latin America with forces of liberalism, anticlericalism, massive educational needs, poverty, a shortage of priests and other personnel. Most recently church leaders have been challenging the government to initiate long-needed economic and social reforms. Paraguay maintains diplomatic relations with Vatican City.

*Archd., 1; dioc., 8; prel., 2; v.a., 2; abp., 1; bp., 14; parishes, 266; priests, 554 (185 dioc., 369 rel.); p.d., 13; sem., 172; bros., 96; srs., 977; bap., 90,572; Caths., 2,992,000 (91.4%); tot. pop., 3,270,000 (1981).*

**Peru:** Republic on the western coast of South America; capital, Lima. An effective diocese became operational in 1537, five years after the Spanish conquest. Evangelization, already under way, developed for some time after 1570 but deteriorated before the end of the colonial period in the 1820s. The first native-born saint of the new world was a Peruvian, Rose of Lima, a Dominican tertiary who died in 1617 and was canonized in 1671. In the new republic founded after the wars of independence the Church experienced problems of adjustment and many of the difficulties that cropped up in other South American countries:

government efforts to control it through continuation of the patronage rights of the Spanish crown; suppression of houses of religious and expropriation of church property; religious indifference and outright hostility. The Church was given special status but was not made the established religion. Repressive measures by the government against labor protests have been condemned by Church leaders in the past several years. Peru maintains diplomatic relations with Vatican City.

*Archd., 7; dioc., 12; prel., 13; v.a., 8; card., 1; abp., 5; bp., 44; parishes, 1,200; priests, 2,198 (920 dioc., 1,278 rel.); p.d., 36; sem., 787; bros., 427; srs., 4,944; bap., 447,724; Caths.,   16,898,000   (92.4%); tot.   pop., 18,280,000 (1981).*

**Philippine Islands:** Republic, an archipelago of 7,000 islands off the southeast coast of Asia; capital, Quezon City. Systematic evangelization was begun in 1564 and resulted in firm establishment of the Church by the 19th century. During the period of Spanish rule, which lasted from the discovery of the islands by Magellan in 1521 to 1898, the Church experienced difficulties with the patronage system under which the Spanish crown tried to control ecclesiastical affairs through episcopal and other appointments. This system ended in 1898 when the United States gained possession of the islands and instituted a policy of separation of Church and state. Anticlericalism flared late in the 19th century. The Aglipayan schism, an attempt to set up a nationalist church, occurred a few years later, in 1902. The government of Ferdinand Marcos has been under attack by people of the church for a number of years for violations of human rights. The republic maintains diplomatic relations with Vatican City.

*Archd., 16; dioc., 41; prel., 5; v.a., 5; card., 1; abp., 15; bp., 69; parishes, 2,037; priests, 4,969 (2,721 dioc., 2,248 rel.); p.d., 9; sem., 3,997; bros., 341; srs., 8,350; bap., 1,277,281; Caths.,    41,520,000    (83.8%);   tot.   pop., 49,530,000 (1981).*

**Poland:** People's republic in eastern Europe; capital, Warsaw. The first traces of Christianity date from the second half of the ninth century. Its spread was accelerated by the union of the Slavs in the 10th century. The first bishopric was set up in 968. The Gniezno archdiocese, with suffragan sees and a mandate to evangelize the borderlands as well as Poland, was established in 1000. Steady growth continued thereafter, with religious orders and their schools playing a major role. Some tensions with the Orthodox were experienced. The Reformation, supported mainly by city dwellers and the upper classes, peaked from about the middle of the 16th century, resulting in numerous conversions to Lutheranism, the Reformed Church and the Bohemian Brethren. A successful Counter-Reformation, with the Jesuits in a position of leadership, was completed by about 1632. The movement served a nationalist as well as religious purpose; in restoring religious unity to a large degree, it united the country against potential invaders, the Swedes, Russians and Turks. The Counter-Reformation had bad side effects, leading to the re-

pression of Protestants long after it was over and to prejudice against Orthodox who returned to allegiance with Rome in 1596 and later. The Church, in the same manner as the entire country, was adversely affected by the partitions of the 18th and 19th centuries. Russification hurt the Orthodox who had reunited with Rome and the Latins who were in the majority. Germans extended their Kulturkampf to the area they controlled. The Austrians exhibited some degree of tolerance. In the republic established after World War I the Church reorganized itself, continued to serve as a vital force in national life, and enjoyed generally harmonious relations with the state. Progressive growth was strong until 1939 when disaster struck in the form of invasion by German and Russian forces and six years of war. In 1945, seven years before the adoption of a Soviet-type of constitution, the Communist-controlled government initiated a policy that included a constant program of atheistic propaganda; a strong campaign against the hierarchy and clergy; the imprisonment in 1948 of 700 priests and even more religious; rigid limitation of the activities of religious; censorship and curtailment of the Catholic press and Catholic Action; interference with church administration and appointments of the clergy; the "deposition" of Cardinal Wyszynski in 1953 and the imprisonment of other members of the hierarchy; the suppression of "Caritas," the Catholic charitable organization; promotion of "Progressive Catholic" activities and a small minority of "patriotic priests." Establishment of the Gomulka regime, the freeing of Cardinal Wyszynski in October, 1956, and the signing of an agreement two months later by bishops and state officials, led to some improvement of conditions. The underlying fact, however, was that the regime conceded to Catholics only so much as was necessary to secure support of the government as a more tolerable evil than the harsh and real threat of a Russian-imposed puppet government like that in Hungary. This has been the controlling principle in Church-state relations. Auxiliary Bishop Ladislaw Rubin of Gniezno sketched the general state of affairs in March, 1968. He said that there was no sign that the government had any intention of releasing its oppressive grip on the Church. As evidence of the "climate of asphyxiation" in the country he cited: persistent questioning of priests by officials concerning their activities; the prohibition against Catholic schools, hospitals and charitable works; the financial burden of a 60 per cent tax on church income. Cardinal Wyszynski denounced "enforced atheism" in a Lenten pastoral in the same year. In May, 1969, the bishops drafted a list of grievances against the government which, they said, were "only some examples of difficulties which demonstrated the situation of the Church in our homeland." The grievances were: refusal of permits to build new churches and establish new parishes; refusal of permission "for the organization of new religion classes"; pressure on Catholics who attend religious ceremonies; censorship and the lack of an independent Catholic daily newspaper; lack of representation in public life; restriction of "freedom to conduct normal pastoral work" in the western portion of the country. There was a move toward improvement in Church-state relations in 1971-72. In 1973, the Polish bishops issued a pastoral letter urging Catholics to resist the official atheism imposed by the government. In 1974 the bishops expressed approval of renewed Vatican efforts at regularizing Church-state relations but insisted that they (the bishops) be consulted on every step of the negotiations. The bishops have continued their sharp criticism of anti-religious policies and human rights violations of the government. Regular contacts on a working level were initiated by the Vatican and Poland in 1974, but regular diplomatic relations have not been established. Cardinal Karol Wojtyla of Cracow was elected to the papacy in 1978. Church support was strong for the independent labor movement, Solidarity, which was recognized by the government in August, 1980, but outlawed in December, 1981, when martial law was imposed. The prevailing church-state condition is one of tension, affected by three principal internal factors: (1) the need of the government for social order, which is impossible to achieve without the moderating influence of the Church; (2) pressure by the Church for freedom from restraints on its pastoral, education, and social mission; (3) mutual resistance to Soviet intervention. (See entries in News Events.)

*Archd., 7; dioc., 21; card., 3; abp., 3; bp., 79; parishes, 7,641; priests, 19,745 (15,255 dioc., 4,490 rel.); sem., 6,566; bros., 1,129; srs., 25,331; bap., 711,351; Caths., 33,720,000 (93.9%); tot. pop., 35,900,000 (1981).*

**Polynesia, French:** French possession in the southern Pacific, including Tahiti and the Marquesas Islands; capital, Papeete. The first phase of evangelization in the Marquesas Islands, begun in 1838, resulted in 216 baptisms in 10 years. A vicariate was organized in 1848 but real progress was not made until after the baptism of native rulers in 1853. Persecution caused missionaries to leave the islands several times. By the 1960s, more than 95 per cent of the population was Catholic. Isolated attempts to evangelize Tahiti were made in the 17th and 18th centuries. Two Picpus Fathers began missionary work in 1831. A vicariate was organized in 1848. By 1908, despite the hindrances of Protestant opposition, disease and other factors, the Church had firm roots.

*Archd., 1; dioc., 1; abp., 1 (nat.); bp., 1; parishes, 78; priests, 35 (9 dioc., 26 rel.); p.d., 7; sem., 4; bros., 29; srs., 65; bap., 1,511; Caths., 52,800; tot. pop., 154,000.*

**Portugal:** Republic in the western part of the Iberian peninsula; capital, Lisbon. Christianity was introduced before the fourth century. From the fifth century to early in the eighth century the Church experienced difficulties from the physical invasion of barbarians and the intellectual invasion of doctrinal errors in the forms of Arianism, Priscillianism and Pelagianism. The Church survived under the rule of Arabs from about 711 and of the Moors until 1249. Ecclesiastical life was fairly vigorous from 1080 to 1185, and monastic influence became strong. A decline set in

about 1450. Several decades later Portugal became the jumping-off place for many missionaries in newly discovered colonies. The Reformation had little effect in the country. Beginning about 1750, Pombal, minister of foreign affairs and prime minister, mounted a frontal attack on the Jesuits whom he succeeded in expelling from Portugal and the colonies. His anti-Jesuit campaign successful Pombal also attempted, and succeeded to some extent, in controlling the Church in Portugal until his fall from power about 1777. Liberal revolutionaries with anti-Church policies made the 19th century a difficult one for the Church. Similar policies prevailed in Church-state relations in this century until the accession of Salazar to power in 1928. In 1940 he concluded a concordat with the Holy See which regularized Church-state relations but still left the Church in a subservient condition. The prevailing spirit of church authorities in Portugal has been conservative. In 1971 several priests were tried for subversion for speaking out against colonialism and for taking part in guerrilla activities in Angola. A military coup of Apr. 25, 1974, triggered a succession of chaotic political developments which led to an attempt by Communists, after receiving only 18 per cent of the votes cast in a national election, to take over the government in the summer of 1975. Portugal maintains diplomatic relations with Vatican City.

*Patriarchate, 1; archd., 2; dioc., 17; card., 1; abp., 2; bp., 24; parishes, 4,278; priests, 4,924 (3,755 dioc., 1,169 rel.); p.d., 2; sem., 520; bros., 524; srs., 7,649; bap., 156,219; Caths., 9,355,000 (94%); tot. pop., 9,930,000 (1981).*

**Puerto Rico:** A U.S. commonwealth, the smallest of the Greater Antilles, 885 miles southeast of the southern coast of Florida; capital, San Juan. Following its discovery by Columbus in 1493, the island was evangelized by Spanish missionaries and remained under Spanish ecclesiastical as well as political control until 1898 when it became a possession of the United States. The original diocese, San Juan, was erected in 1511. The present hierarchy was established in 1960. Puerto Rico has an apostolic delegate (nuncio to Dominican Republic).

*Archd., 1; dioc., 4; card., 1; bp., 8; parishes, 267; priests, 680 (252 dioc., 428 rel.); p.d., 119; sem., 110; bros., 128; srs., 1,503; bap., 49,489; Caths., 2,804,000 (83%); tot. pop., 3,377,000.*

**Qatar:** Independent state in the Persian Gulf; capital, Doha. Under ecclesiastical jurisdiction of Arabia vicariate apostolic.

*Priest, 1 (rel.); bap., 54; Caths., 6,000; tot. pop., 250,000.*

**Reunion:** French overseas department, 450 miles east of Madagascar; capital, Saint-Denis. Catholicism was introduced in 1667 and some intermittent missionary work was done through the rest of the century. A prefecture apostolic was organized in 1712. Vincentians began work there in 1817 and were joined later by Holy Ghost Fathers. Reunion has an apostolic delegate.

*Dioc., 1; bp., 1; parishes, 71; priests, 111 (60*

*dioc., 51 rel.); sem., 10; bros., 47; srs., 425; bap., 11,107; Caths., 468,000; tot. pop., 515,814.*

**Rhodes:** Greek island in the Aegean Sea, 112 miles from the southwestern coast of Asia Minor. A diocese was established about the end of the third century. A bishop from Rhodes attended the Council of Nicaea in 325. Most of the Christians followed the Eastern Churches into schism in the 11th century and became Orthodox. Turks controlled the island from 1522 to 1912. The small Catholic population, for whom a diocese existed from 1328 to 1546, lived in crossfire between Turks and Orthodox. After 1719 Franciscans provided pastoral care for the Catholics, for whom an archdiocese was erected in 1928. Statistics are included in Greece.

**Romania:** Socialist republic in southeastern Europe; capital, Bucharest. Latin Christianity, introduced in the third century, all but disappeared during the barbarian invasions. The Byzantine Rite was introduced by the Bulgars about the beginning of the eighth century and established firm roots. It eventually became Orthodox, but a large number of its adherents returned later to union with Rome. Attempts to reintroduce the Latin Rite on any large scale have been unsuccessful. Communists took over the government following World War II, forced the abdication of Michael I in 1947, and enacted a Soviet type of constitution in 1952. By that time a campaign against religion was already in progress. In 1948 the government denounced a concordat concluded in 1929, nationalized all schools and passed a law on religions which resulted in the disorganization of Church administration. The 1.5 million-member Romanian Byzantine Rite Church, by government decree, was incorporated into the Romanian Orthodox Church, and the Orthodox bishops then seized the cathedrals of Roman Catholic bishops. Five of the six Latin Rite bishops were immediately disposed of by the government, and the last was sentenced to 18 years' imprisonment in 1951, when a great many arrests of priests and laymen were made. Religious orders were suppressed in 1949. Since 1948 more than 50 priests have been executed and 200 have died in prison. One hundred priests were reported in prison at the end of 1958. Some change for the better in Church-state relations was reported after the middle of the summer of 1964, although restrictions were still in effect. About 1,200 priests were engaged in parish work in August, 1965. (See also February News Events, International.)

*Archd., 2; dioc., 8; ord., 1; bp., 2. No recent statistics are available on the number of Catholics. There were an estimated 1,140,000 Catholics (5.9% of the population) in 1969. Tot. pop., 22,600,000.*

**Rwanda:** Republic in east central Africa; capital, Kigali. Catholicism was introduced about the turn of the 20th century. The hierarchy was established in 1959. Intertribal warfare between the ruling Hutus (90 per cent of the population) and the Tutsis (formerly the ruling aristocracy) plagued the country for a number of years. Rwanda maintains diplomatic relations with Vatican City.

*Archd., 1; dioc., 7; abp., 1 (nat.); bp., 7 (6 nat.); parishes, 111; priests, 439 (249 dioc., 190 rel.); sem., 132; bros., 235; srs., 819; bap., 97,275; Caths., 2,359,000 (43.6%); tot. pop., 5,400,000.*

**Saint Christopher (Kitts)-Nevis:** Independent (Sept. 19, 1983) island states in West Indies; capital, Basseterre, on St. Christopher; Charlestown, on Nevis. Under ecclesiastical jurisdiction of St. John's-Basseterre diocese, Antigua.

*Parishes, 5; priests, 3 (rel.); bap., 94; Caths., 4,000; tot. pop., 67,000 (1981). Statistics include Anguilla.*

**Saint Lucia:** Independent (Feb. 22, 1979) island state in West Indies; capital, Castries. Established diplomatic relations with Vatican City in 1984.

*Archd., 1; abp., 1; parishes, 22; priests, 31 (10 dioc., 21 rel.); p.d., 1; sem., 7; bros., 2; srs., 36; bap., 3,243; Caths., 109,000; tot. pop., 120,000.*

**Saint Pierre and Miquelon:** French overseas department, islands near the southwest coast of Newfoundland. Catholicism was introduced about 1689.

*V.a., 1; bp., 1; parishes, 3; priests, 3 (rel.); srs., 12; bap., 128; Caths., 6,000; tot. pop., 6,350.*

**Saint Vincent and the Grenadines:** Independent State in West Indies; capital, Kingstown. Under ecclesiastical jurisdiction of Bridgetown-Kingstown diocese, Barbados.

*Parishes, 7; priests, 4 (rel.); bros., 8; srs., 13; bap., 276; Caths., 14,000; tot. pop., 122,000.*

**Samoa, American:** Unincorporated U.S. territory in southwestern Pacific, consisting of six small islands; seat of government, Pago Pago on the Island of Tutuila. Samoa-Pago Pago diocese established in 1982.

*Dioc., 1; parishes 5; priests, 9 (4 dioc., 5 rel.); bros., 8; srs., 17; bap., 328; Caths., 7,260; tot. pop., 33,000.*

**Samoa, Western:** Independent state in the southwestern Pacific; capital, Apia. Catholic missionary work began in 1845. Most of the missions now in operation were established by 1870 when the Catholic population numbered about 5,000. Additional progress was made in missionary work from 1896. The first Samoan priest was ordained in 1892. A diocese was established in 1966; elevated to a metropolitan see in 1982.

*Archd., 1; card., 1; parishes, 20; priests, 37 (8 dioc., 29 rel.); p.d., 1; sem., 30; bros., 22; srs., 110; bap., 1,682; Caths., 40,800; tot. pop., 165,881.*

**San Marino:** Republic, a 24-square-mile enclave in northeastern Italy; capital, San Marino. The date of initial evangelization is not known, but a diocese was established by the end of the third century. Ecclesiastically, it forms part of the diocese of San Marino-Montefeltro in Italy. San Marino is represented by a minister at Vatican City.

*Parishes, 12; priests, 26 (13 dioc., 13 rel.); bro., 1; srs., 33; bap., 219; Caths., 20,000 (95%); tot. pop., 21,000.*

**Sao Tome and Principe:** Independent republic (July 12, 1975), consisting of two islands off the western coast of Africa in the Gulf of Guinea; former Portuguese territory; capital Sao Tome. Evangelization was begun by the Portuguese who discovered the islands in 1471-72. The Sao Tome diocese was established in 1534.

Dioc., 1; parishes, 12; priests, 9 (rel.); bros., 3; srs., 15; bap., 3,153; Caths. (est.), 90,000; tot. pop., 100,000.

**Saudi Arabia:** Monarchy occupying four-fifths of Arabian peninsula; capital, Riyadh (Taif, summer capital). Under ecclesiastical jurisdiction of Arabia vicariate apostolic.

Priests, 6 (rel.); srs., 3; bap., 309; Caths., 198,000; tot. pop., 9,320,000.

**Scotland:** Part of the United Kingdom, in the northern British Isles; capital, Edinburgh. Christianity was introduced by the early years of the fifth century. The arrival of St. Columba and his monks in 563 inaugurated a new era of evangelization which reached into remote areas by the end of the sixth century. He was extremely influential in determining the character of the Celtic Church, which was tribal, monastic, and in union with Rome. Considerable disruption of church activity resulted from Scandinavian invasions in the late eighth and ninth centuries. By 1153 the Scottish Church took a turn away from its insularity and was drawn into closer contact with the European community. Anglo-Saxon religious and political relations, complicated by rivalries between princes and ecclesiastical superiors, were not always the happiest. Religious orders expanded greatly in the 12th century. From shortly after the Norman Conquest of England to 1560 the Church suffered adverse effects from the Hundred Years' War, the Black Death, the Western Schism and other developments. In 1560 parliament abrogated papal supremacy over the Church in Scotland and committed the country to Protestantism in 1567. The Catholic Church was proscribed, to remain that way for more than 200 years, and the hierarchy was disbanded. Defections made the Church a minority religion from that time on. Presbyterian church government was ratified in 1690. Priests launched the Scottish Mission in 1653, incorporating themselves as a mission body under a prefect apostolic and working underground to serve the faithful in much the same way their confreres did in England. About 100 heather priests, trained in clandestine places in the heather country, were ordained by the early 19th century. Catholics got some relief from legal disabilities in 1793 and more later. Many left the country about that time. Some of their numbers were filled subsequently by immigrants from Ireland. The hierarchy was restored in 1878. Scotland, though predominantly Protestant, has a better record for tolerance than Northern Ireland.

Archd., 2; dioc., 6; card., 1; abp., 1; bp., 9; parishes, 481; priests, 1,025 (787 dioc., 238 rel.); sem., 148; bros., 127; srs., 1,208; bap., 13,780; Caths., 827,068 (16%); tot. pop., 5,150,000.

**Senegal:** Republic in western Africa; capital, Dakar. The country had its first contact with Catholicism through the Portuguese some time after

1460. Some incidental missionary work was done by Jesuits and Capuchins in the 16th and 17th centuries. A vicariate for the area was placed in charge of the Holy Ghost Fathers in 1779. More effective evangelization efforts were accomplished after the Senegambia vicariate was established in 1955. Senegal maintains diplomatic relations with Vatican City.

Archd., 1; dioc., 4; p.a., 1; card., 1 (nat.); bp., 4 (nat.); parishes, 58; priests, 210 (63 dioc., 147 rel.); sem., 60; bros., 118; srs., 519; bap., 9,285 Caths., 255,000 (4.3%); tot. pop., 5,900,000.

**Seychelles:** Independent (1976) group of 92 islands in the Indian Ocean 970 miles east of Kenya; capital, Victoria on Mahe. Catholicism was introduced in the 18th century. A vicariate apostolic was organized in 1852. All education in the islands was conducted under Catholic auspices until 1954. Seychelles established diplomatic relations with Vatican City in 1984.

Dioc., 1; bp., 1 (nat.); parishes, 17; priests, 18 (6 dioc., 12 rel.); sem., 3; bros., 8; srs., 55; bap., 1,433; Caths., 60,903; tot. pop., 67,000.

**Sierra Leone:** Republic on the western coast of Africa; capital, Freetown. Catholicism was introduced in 1858. Members of the African Missions Society, the first Catholic missionaries in the area, were joined by Holy Ghost Fathers in 1864. Protestant missionaries were active in the area before their Catholic counterparts. Educational work had a major part in Catholic endeavor. The hierarchy was established in 1950. Sierra Leone has an apostolic delegate.

Archd., 1; dioc., 2; abp., 1; bp., 1; parishes, 27; priests, 90 (10 dioc., 80 rel.); sem., 29; bros., 9; srs., 91; bap., 3,735; Caths. (1981), 71,000 (1.9%); tot. pop., 3,570,000.

**Singapore:** Independent island republic off the southern tip of the Malay Peninsula; capital, Singapore. Christianity was introduced in the area by Portuguese colonists about 1511. Singapore was founded in 1819; the first parish church was built in 1846. Established diplomatic relations with Vatican City, 1981.

Archd., 1; abp., 1 (nat.); parishes, 26; priests, 101 (64 dioc., 37 rel.); sem., 17; bros., 56; srs., 226; bap., 2,776; Caths., 100,486 (4%); tot. pop., 2,481,000.

**Solomon Islands:** Independent (July 7, 1978) island group in Oceania; capital, Honiara, on Guadalcanal. Evangelization of the Southern Solomons, begun earlier but interrupted because of violence against them, was resumed by the Marists in 1898. A vicariate apostolic was organized in 1912. A similar jurisdiction was set up for the Western Solomons in 1959. World War II caused a great deal of damage to mission installations. The area has an apostolic delegate. (See Index for papal visit.)

Archd., 1; dioc., 2; abp., 1; bp., 3; parishes, 34; priests, 48 (16 dioc., 32 rel.); bros., 37; srs., 226; bap., 2,323; Caths., 61,276; tot. pop., 339,500.

**Somalia:** Republic on the eastern coast of Africa; capital, Mogadishu. The country has been

Moslem for centuries. Pastoral activity has been confined to immigrants. Schools and hospitals were nationalized in 1972, resulting in the departure of some foreign missionaries. Somalia has an apostolic delegate (to the Red Sea Region).

*Dioc., 1; bp., 1; parishes, 2; priests, 6 (rel.); bros., 2; srs., 69; bap., 5; Caths., 2,000; tot. pop., 4,600,000.*

**South Africa:** Republic in the southern part of Africa; capitals, Cape Town (legislative) and Pretoria (administrative). Christianity was introduced by the Portuguese who discovered the Cape of Good Hope in 1488. Boers, who founded Cape Town in 1652, expelled Catholics from the region. There was no Catholic missionary activity from that time until the 19th century. After a period of British opposition, a bishop established residence in 1837 and evangelization got under way thereafter among the Bantus and white immigrants. In recent years church authorities have strongly protested the white supremacy policy of apartheid which seriously infringes the human rights of the native Blacks and impedes the Church from carrying out its pastoral, educational and social service functions. The hierarchy was established in 1951. South Africa has an apostolic delegate.

*Archd., 4; dioc., 19; abb., 1; p.a., 2; card., 1; abp., 3; bp., 20; parishes, 614; priests, 1,194 (301 dioc., 893 rel.); p.d., 70; sem., 165; bros., 364; srs., 3,765; bap., 69,279; Caths., 2,105,000 (6.9%); tot. pop., 30,130,000 (1981). Statistics include autonomous homelands of Transkei, Bophuthatswana, Venda and Ciskei.*

**Spain:** Nominal monarchy on the Iberian peninsula in southwestern Europe; capital, Madrid. Christians were on the peninsula by 200; some of them suffered martyrdom during persecutions of the third century. A council held in Elvira about 304/6 enacted the first legislation on clerical celibacy in the West. Vandals invaded the peninsula in the fifth century, bringing with them an Arian brand of Christianity which they retained until their conversion following the baptism of their king Reccared, in 589. One of the significant developments of the seventh century was the establishment of Toledo as the primatial see. The Visigoth kingdom lasted to the time of the Arab invasion, 711-14. The Church survived under Moslem rule but experienced some doctrinal and disciplinary irregularities as well as harassment. Reconquest of most of the peninsula was accomplished by 1248; unification was achieved during the reign of Ferdinand and Isabella. The discoveries of Columbus and other explorers ushered in an era of colonial expansion in which Spain became one of the greatest mission-sending countries in history. In 1492, in repetition of anti-Semitic actions of 694, the expulsion of unbaptized Jews was decreed, leading to mass baptisms but a questionable number of real conversions in 1502. (The Jewish minority numbered about 165,000.) Activity by the Inquisition followed. Spain was not seriously affected by the Reformation. Ecclesiastical decline set in about 1650. Anti-Church actions authorized by a constitution enacted in 1812 resulted in the suppression of religious and other encroachments on the leaders, people and goods of the Church. Political, religious and cultural turmoil recurred during the 19th century and into the 20th. A revolutionary republic was proclaimed in 1931, triggering a series of developments which led to civil war from 1936 to 1939. During the conflict, which pitted leftist Loyalists against the forces of Francisco Franco, 6,632 priests and religious and an unknown number of lay persons perished in addition to thousands of victims of combat. One-man, one-party rule, established after the civil war and with rigid control policies with respect to personal liberties and social and economic issues, continued for more than 35 years before giving way after the death of Franco to democratic reforms. The Catholic Church, long the established religion, was disestablished under a new constitution providing guarantees of freedom for other religions as well. Disestablishment was ratified with modifications of a 1976 revision of the earlier concordat of 1953. Spain maintains diplomatic relations with Vatican City.

*Archd., 13; dioc., 52; card., 4; abp., 12; bp., 68; parishes, 21,423; priests, 32,328 (21,778 dioc., 10,550 rel.); p.d., 20; sem., 3,039; bros., 7,695; srs., 79,829; bap., 552,937; Caths., 37,100,000 (98.5%); tot. pop., 37,650,000 (1981).*

**Sri Lanka** (formerly Ceylon): Independent socialist republic, island southeast of India; capital, Colombo. Effective evangelization began in 1543 and made great progress by the middle of the 17th century. The Church was seriously hampered during the Dutch period from about 1650 to 1795. Anti-Catholic laws were repealed by the British in 1806. The hierarchy was established in 1886. Leftist governments and other factors have worked against the Church since the country became independent in 1948. The high percentage of indigenous clergy and religious has been of great advantage to the Church. Sri Lanka maintains diplomatic relations with Vatican City.

*Archd., 1; dioc., 8; card., 1 (nat.); abp., 1 (nat.); bp., 9 (nat.); parishes, 315; priests, 618 (375 dioc., 243 rel.); p.d., 1; sem., 186; bros., 218; srs., 2,195; bap., 29,676; Caths., 1,044,496 (6.8%); tot. pop., 15,183,000.*

**Sudan:** Republic in northeastern Africa, the largest country on the continent; capital, Khartoum. Christianity was introduced from Egypt and gained acceptance in the sixth century. Under Arab rule, it was eliminated in the northern region. No Christians were in the country in 1600. Evangelization attempts begun in the 19th century in the south yielded hard-won results. By 1931 there were nearly 40,000 Catholics there, and considerable progress was made by missionaries after that time. In 1957, a year after the republic was established, Catholic schools were nationalized. An act restrictive of religious freedom went into effect in 1962, resulting in the harassment and expulsion of foreign missionaries. By 1964 all but a few Sudanese missionaries had been forced out of the southern region. The northern area, where Islam predominates, is impervious to Christian influence. Late in 1971 some missionaries were allowed to return to work in the South. Southern Sudan was granted regional autonomy within a unified country in March, 1972, thus ending often bitter fighting between the North and South dating back to 1955. The hierarchy was established in 1974. The imposition of Islamic penal codes in 1984 was a cause of concern to all Christian churches. (See Index.) Sudan maintains diplomatic relations with Vatican City.

*Archd., 2; dioc., 6; abp., 2 (nat.); bp., 4 (nat.); parishes, 90; priests, 146 (39 dioc., 107 rel.); p.d., 1; sem., 50; bros., 40; srs., 221; bap., 17,722; Caths., 953,000 (5%); tot. pop., 18,900,000 (1981).*

**Suriname** (formerly Dutch Guiana): Independent (Nov. 25, 1975) state in northern South America; capital, Paramaribo, Catholicism was introduced in 1683. Evangelization began in 1817.

*Dioc., 1; bp., 1; parishes, 19; priests, 33 (3 dioc., 30 rel.); p.d., 1; sem., 3; bros., 28; srs., 95; bap., 2,057; Caths. (1981), 86,000; tot. pop., 400,000.*

**Swaziland:** Constitutional monarchy in southern Africa; almost totally surrounded by South Africa; capital, Mbabane. Missionary work was entrusted to the Servites in 1913. A prefecture apostolic was organized in 1923. The hierarchy was established in 1951. Swaziland has an apostolic delegate (to Southern Africa).

*Dioc., 1; priests, 38 (4 dioc., 34 rel.); sem., 2; bros., 8; srs., 130; bap., 984; Caths., 36,000 (6.3%); tot. pop., 570,000.*

**Sweden:** Kingdom in northwestern Europe; capital, Stockholm. Christianity was introduced by St. Ansgar, a Frankish monk, in 829/30. The Church became well established in the 12th century and was a major influence at the end of the Middle Ages. Political and other factors favored the introduction and spread of the Lutheran Church which became the state religion in 1560. The Augsburg Confession of 1530 was accepted by the government; all relations with Rome were severed; monasteries were suppressed; the very presence of Catholics in the country was forbidden in 1617. A decree of tolerance for foreign Catholics was issued about 1781. Two years later a vicariate apostolic was organized for the country. In 1873 Swedes were given the legal right to leave the Lutheran Church and join another Christian church. (Membership in the Lutheran Church is presumed by law unless notice is given of membership in another church.) In 1923 there were only 11 priests and five churches in the country. Since 1952 Catholics have enjoyed almost complete religious freedom. The hierarchy was reestablished in 1953. Hindrances to growth of the Church are the strongly entrenched established church, limited resources, a clergy shortage and the size of the country. Established diplomatic relations with Vatican City in 1982.

*Dioc., 1; bp., 1; parishes, 31; priests, 95 (35 dioc., 60 rel.); p.d., 6; sem., 7; bros., 7; srs., 228; bap., 829; Caths., 107,533 (1.2%); tot. pop., 8,326,000.*

**Switzerland:** Republic in central Europe; capital, Bern. Christianity was introduced in the fourth century or earlier and was established on a firm footing before the barbarian invasions of the sixth century. Constance, established as a diocese in the seventh century, was a stronghold of the faith against the pagan Alamanni, in particular, who were not converted until some time in the ninth century. During this period of struggle with the barbarians, a number of monasteries of great influence were established. The Reformation in Switzerland was triggered by Zwingli in 1519 and furthered by him at Zurich until his death in battle against the Catholic cantons in 1531. Calvin set in motion the forces that made Geneva the international capital of the Reformation and transformed it into a theocracy. Catholics mobilized a Counter-Reformation in 1570, six years after Calvin's death. Struggle between Protestant and Catholic cantons was a fact of Swiss life for several hundred years. The Helvetic Constitution enacted at the turn of the 19th century embodied anti-Catholic measures and consequences, among them the dissolution of 130 monasteries. The Church was reorganized later in the century to meet the threats of liberalism, radicalism and the Kulturkampf. In the process, the Church, even though on the defensive, gained the strength and cohesion that characterizes it to the present time. The six dioceses in the country are immediately subject to the Holy See. In 1973, constitutional articles banning Jesuits from the country and prohibiting the establishment of convents and monasteries were repealed. There is a papal nuncio to Switzerland, but Switzerland does not have a diplomatic officer accredited to Vatican City. (See Index for papal visit.)

*Dioc., 6; abb., 2; bp., 8; parishes, 1,712; priests, 4,229 (2,495 dioc., 1,734 rel.); p.d., 13; sem., 190; bros., 391; srs., 9,954; bap., 35,348; Caths., 3,066,000 (47%); tot. pop., 6,521,000.*

**Syria:** Arab republic in southwest Asia; capital, Damascus. Christian communities were formed in apostolic times. It is believed that St. Peter established a see at Antioch before going to Rome. Damascus became a center of influence. The area was the place of great men and great events in the early history of the Church. Monasticism developed there in the fourth century. So did the Monophysite and Monothelite heresies to which portions of the Church succumbed. Byzantine Syrians who remained in communion with Rome were given the name Melkites. Christians of various persuasions — Jacobites, Orthodox and Melkites — were subject to various degrees of harassment from the Arabs who took over in 638 and from the Ottoman Turks who isolated the country and remained in control from 1516 to the end of World War II. Syria maintains diplomatic relations with Vatican City.

*Patriarchates, 3 (Antioch of Maronites, Greek Melkites and Syrians; patriarchs of Maronites and Syrians reside in Lebanon); Archd., 12 (1 Armenian, 2 Maronite, 5 Greek-Melkite, 4 Syrian); dioc., 3 (Armenian, Chaldean, Maronite); v.a., 1 (Latin); patr., 1; abp., 15; bp., 2; parishes, 185; priests, 225 (148 dioc., 77 rel.); p.d., 2; sem., 36; bros., 9;*

*srs., 384; bap., 2,745; Caths., 238,000 (2.5%); tot. pop., 9,310,000 (1981).*

**Taiwan** (Formosa): Location of the Nationalist Government of the Republic of China, an island 100 miles off the southern coast of mainland China; capital, Taipei. Attempts to introduce Christianity in the 17th century were unsuccessful. Evangelization in the 19th century resulted in some 1,300 converts in 1895. Missionary endeavor was hampered by the Japanese who occupied the island following the Sino-Japanese war of 1894-95. Nine thousand Catholics were reported in 1938. Great progress was made in missionary endeavor among the Chinese who emigrated to the island following the Communist take-over of the mainland in 1949. The hierarchy was established in 1952. Nationalist China maintains diplomatic relations with Vatican City.

*Archd., 1; dioc., 6; abp., 1; bp., 6; parishes, 449; priests, 729 (212 dioc., 517 rel.); sem., 48; bros., 133; srs., 1,199; bap., 5,127; Caths., 291,167 (1.5%); tot. pop., 18,500,000.*

**Tanzania:** Republic (consisting of former Tanganyika on the eastern coast of Africa and former Zanzibar, an island group off the eastern coast); capital, Dar es Salaam (future capital, Dodoma). The first Catholic mission in the former Tanganyikan portion of the republic was manned by Holy Ghost Fathers in 1868. The hierarchy was established there in 1953. Zanzibar was the landing place of Augustinians with the Portuguese in 1499. Some evangelization was attempted between then and 1698 when the Arabs expelled all priests from the territory. There was no Catholic missionary activity from then until the 1860s. The Holy Ghost Fathers arrived in 1863 and were entrusted with the mission in 1872. Zanzibar was important as a point of departure for missionaries to Tanganyika, Kenya and other places in East Africa. A vicariate for Zanzibar was set up in 1906. Tanzania maintains diplomatic relations with Vatican City.

*Archd., 2; dioc., 24; card., 1 (nat.); abp., 1 (nat.); bp., 23 (21 nat.); parishes, 617; priests, 1,543 (767 dioc., 776 rel.); p.d., 1; sem., 343; bros., 391; srs., 3,993; bap., 155,517; Caths., 3,710,000 (20%); tot. pop., 18,510,000 (1981).*

**Thailand (Siam):** Constitutional monarchy in southeastern Asia; capital, Bangkok. The first Christians in the region were Portuguese traders who arrived early in the 16th century. A number of missionaries began arriving in 1554 but pastoral care was confined mostly to the Portuguese until the 1660s. Evangelization of the natives got under way from about that time. A seminary was organized in 1665, a vicariate was set up four years later, and a point of departure was established for missionaries to Tonkin, Cochin China and China. Persecution and death for some of the missionaries ended evangelization efforts in 1688. It was resumed, however, and made progress from 1824 onwards. In 1881 missionaries were sent from Siam to neighboring Laos. The hierarchy was established in 1965. Abp., Michai Kitbunchu was named the first Thai cardinal in 1983. Thailand

maintains diplomatic relations with Vatican City. (See Index for papal visit.)

*Archd., 2; dioc., 8; card., 1 (nat.); abp., 1 (nat.); bp., 8 (7 nat.); parishes, 251; priests, 385 (181 dioc., 204 rel.); sem., 140; bros., 185; srs., 1,202; bap., 8,315; Caths., 204,250 (.4%); tot. pop., 49,800,000.*

**Timor, Eastern:** Former Portuguese overseas province in the Malay archipelago; annexed by Indonesia in 1976.

*Dioc., 1; parishes, 21; priests, 36 (19 dioc., 17 rel.); sem., 14; bros., 7; srs., 47; bap., 39,070; Caths. (1981), 240,000; tot. pop., 770,000.*

**Togo:** Republic on the western coast of Africa; capital, Lome. The first Catholic missionaries in the area, where slave raiders operated for nearly 200 years, were members of the African Missions Society who arrived in 1563. They were followed by Divine Word Missionaries in 1914, when a prefecture apostolic was organized. At that time the Catholic population numbered about 19,000. The African Missionaries returned after their German predecessors were deported following World War I. The first native priest was ordained in 1922. The hierarchy was established in 1955. Established diplomatic relations with Vatican City, 1981.

*Archd., 1; dioc., 3; abp., 1 (nat.); bp., 3 (2 nat.); parishes, 68; priests, 175 (82 dioc., 93 rel.); sem., 78; bros., 53; srs., 250; bap., 19,713; Caths., 580,799 (21%); tot. pop., 2,800,000.*

**Tokelau:** Pacific islands administered by New Zealand. Forms part of Samoa-Apia and Tokelau archdiocese, Western Samoa.

*Parish, 1; priest, 1 (dioc.); srs., 2; bap., 2; Caths., 900; tot. pop., 2,000.*

**Tonga:** Polynesian monarchy in the southwestern Pacific, consisting of about 150 islands; capital Nuku'alofa. Marists started missionary work in 1842, some years after Protestants had begun evangelization. By 1880 the Catholic population numbered about 1,700. A vicariate was organized in 1937. The hierarchy was established in 1966.

*Dioc., 1; bp., 1 (nat); parishes, 13; priests, 22 (10 dioc., 12 rel.); sem., 9; bros., 10; srs., 53; bap., 591; Caths., 14,213 (14%); tot. pop., 101,000.*

**Trinidad and Tobago:** Independent nation, consisting of two islands in the Caribbean; capital, Port-of-Spain. The first Catholic church in Trinidad was built in 1591, years after several missionary ventures had been launched and a number of missionaries killed. Capuchins were there from 1618 until about 1802. Missionary work continued after the British gained control early in the 19th century. Cordial relations have existed between the Church and state, both of which have manifested their desire for the development of native clergy. Established diplomatic relations with Vatican City in 1978.

*Archd., 1; abp., 1; parishes, 58; priests, 118 (26 dioc., 92 rel.); sem., 13; bros., 32; srs., 179; bap., 8,650; Caths., 377,000 (33.5%); tot. pop., 1,125,000.*

**Tunisia:** Republic on the northern coast of Africa; capital, Tunis. There were few Christians in the territory until the 19th century. A prefecture apostolic was organized in 1843 and the Carthage archdiocese was established in 1884. The Catholic population in 1892 consisted of most of the approximately 50,000 Europeans in the country. When Tunis became a republic in 1956, most of the Europeans left the country. The Holy See and the Tunisian government concluded an agreement in 1964 which changed the Carthage archdiocese into a prelacy and handed over some ecclesiastical property to the republic. A considerable number of Moslem students are in Catholic schools, but the number of Moslem converts to the Church has been small. Tunisia maintains diplomatic relations with Vatican City.

*Prel., 1; abp., 1; parishes, 17; priests, 50 (24 dioc., 26 rel.); p.d., 1; bros., 11; srs., 224; bap., 37; Caths., 20,000 (.3%); tot. pop., 6,700,000.*

**Turkey:** Republic in Asia Minor and southeastern Europe, capital, Ankara. Christian communities were established in apostolic times, as attested in the Acts of the Apostles, some of the Epistles of St. Paul, and Revelation. The territory was the scene of heresies and ecumenical councils, the place of residence of Fathers of the Church, the area in which ecclesiastical organization reached the dimensions of more than 450 sees in the middle of the seventh century. The region remained generally Byzantine except for the period of the Latin occupation of Constantinople from 1204 to 1261, but was conquered by the Ottoman Turks in 1453 and remained under their domination until establishment of the republic in 1923. Christians, always a minority, numbered more Orthodox than Latins; they were all under some restriction during the Ottoman period. They suffered persecution in the 19th and 20th centuries, the Armenians being the most numerous victims. Turkey is overwhelmingly Moslem. Catholics are tolerated to a degree. Turkey maintains diplomatic relations with Vatican City.

*Patriarchate, 1 (Cilicia for the Armenians, the patriarch resides in Lebanon); archd., 3; dioc., 2; v.a., 2; mission "sui juris," 1; ap. ex., 1; abp., 3; bp., 1; parishes, 58; priests, 78 (17 dioc., 61 rel.); p.d., 2; sem., 3; bros., 24; srs., 157; bap., 210; Caths., 17,000; tot. pop., 46,380,000 (1981).*

**Turks and Caicos Islands:** British possession in West Indies; capital, Grand Turk.

*Mission "sui juris," 1 (est. 1984); Caths., 200; tot. pop., 7,000.*

**Tuvalu** (formerly Ellice Islands): Independent state (1978) in Oceania, consisting of 9 islands (8 inhabited); capital, Funafuti.

*Mission "sui juris," 1; Caths., 100; tot. pop., 7,349.*

**Uganda:** Republic in eastern Africa; capital, Kampala. The White Fathers were the first Catholic missionaries, starting in 1879. Persecution broke out from 1885 to 1887, taking a toll of 22 Catholic martyrs, who were canonized in 1964, and a number of Anglican victims. (Pope Paul honored all those who died for the faith during a visit to Kampala in 1969.) By 1888, there were more than 8,000 Catholics. Evangelization was resumed in 1894, after being interrupted by war, and proceeded thereafter. The first native African bishop was ordained in 1939. The hierarchy was established in 1953. The Church was suppressed during the erratic regime of Pres. Idi-Amin, who was deposed in the spring of 1979. Uganda maintains diplomatic relations with Vatican City.

*Archd., 1; dioc., 13; card., 1 (nat.); bp., 14 (12 nat.); parishes, 307; priests, 927 (574 dioc., 353 rel.); p.d., 1; sem., 604; bros., 340; srs., 2,189; bap., 236,592; Caths., 5,504,000 (40%); tot. pop., 13,620,000 (1981).*

**Union of Soviet Socialist Republics:** Union of 15 Soviet Socialist Republics in northern Eurasia, from the Baltic Sea to the Pacific; Russian capital, Moscow. The Orthodox Church has been predominant in Russian history. It developed from the Byzantine Church before 1064. Some of its members subsequently established communion with Rome as the result of reunion movements but most of them remained Orthodox. The government has always retained some kind of general or particular control of this church. Latins, always a minority, had a little more freedom. From the beginning of the Communist government in 1917, all churches of whatever kind — including Jews and Moslems — became the targets of official campaigns designed to negate their influence on society and/or to eliminate them entirely. An accurate assessment of the situation of the Catholic Church in Russia is difficult to make. Its dimensions, however, can be gauged from the findings of a team of research specialists made public by the Judiciary Committee of the U.S. House of Representatives in 1964. It was reported: "The fate of the Catholic Church in the USSR and countries occupied by the Russians from 1917 to 1959 shows the following: (a) the number killed: 55 bishops; 12,800 priests and monks; 2.5 million Catholic believers; (b) imprisoned or deported: 199 bishops; 32,000 priests and 10 million believers; (c) 15,700 priests were forced to abandon their priesthood and accept other jobs; and (d) a large number of seminaries and religious communities were dissolved; 1,600 monasteries were nationalized, 31,779 churches were closed. 400 newspapers were prohibited, and all Catholic organizations were dissolved." Several Latin Rite churches are open; e.g., in Moscow, Leningrad, Odessa and Tiflis. An American chaplain is stationed in Moscow to serve Catholics at the U.S. embassy there. Recent reports indicate that, despite repression and attempts at Sovietization, the strongholds of Catholicism in the USSR are Lithuania (incorporated in the USSR in 1940, together with Estonia and Latvia) and the Ukraine. No Catholic statistics are available for the USSR. See separate entries for Estonia, Latvia, Lithuania.

*Tot. pop., 268,000,000.*

**United Arab Emirates:** Independent state along Persian Gulf; capital, Abu Dhabi.

*V.a., 1; bp., 1; parishes, 4; priests, 9 (3*

*dioc., 6 rel.); sem. 3; srs., 33; bap., 738; Caths., 30,000; tot. pop., 1,200,000.*

**United States:** See Catholic History in the United States, Statistics of the Church in the United States.

**Upper Volta (Burkina-Fasso):** Republic inland in western Africa; capital, Ouagadougou. White Fathers started the first missions in 1900 and 1901. White Sisters began work in 1911. A minor and a major seminary were established in 1926 and 1942, respectively. The first native bishop in modern times from West Africa was ordained in 1956 and the first cardinal created in 1965. The hierarchy was established in 1955. Upper Volta established diplomatic relations with Vatican City in 1973.

*Archd., 1; dioc., 8; card., 1 (nat.); bp., 10 (nat.); parishes, 100; priests, 392 (167 dioc., 225 rel.); sem., 121; bros., 130; srs., 631; bap., 26,237; Caths., 538,848 (8%); tot. pop., 6,700,000.*

**Uruguay:** Republic (called the Eastern Republic of Uruguay) on the southeast coast of South America; capital, Montevideo. The Spanish established a settlement in 1624 and evangelization followed. Missionaries followed the reduction pattern to reach the Indians, form them in the faith and train them in agriculture, husbandry, other useful arts, and the experience of managing property and living in community. Montevideo was made a diocese in 1878. The constitution of 1830 made Catholicism the religion of the state and subsidized some of its activities, principally the missions to the Indians. Separation of Church and state was provided for in the constitution of 1917. Uruguay maintains diplomatic relations with Vatican City.

*Archd., 1; dioc., 9; abp., 1; bp., 11; parishes, 222; priests, 586 (197 dioc., 389 rel.); p.d., 18; sem., 89; bros., 148; srs., 1,595; bap., 40,722; Caths., 2,304,000 (78.6%); tot. pop., 2,930,000 (1981).*

**Vanuatu (New Hebrides):** Independent (July 29, 1980) island group in the southwest Pacific, about 500 miles west of Fiji; formerly under joint British-French administration; capital, Vila. Effective, though slow, evangelization by Catholic missionaries began about 1887. A vicariate apostolic was set up in 1904. The hierarchy was established in 1966.

*Dioc., 1; bp., 1; parishes, 19; priests, 24 (3 dioc., 21 rel.); p.d., 1; sem., 14; bros., 19; srs., 67; bap., 726; Caths., 17,694 (14%); tot. pop., 125,600.*

**Vatican City:** See separate entry.

**Venezuela:** Republic in northern South America; capital, Caracas. Evangelization began in 1513-14 and involved members of a number of religious orders who worked in assigned territories, developing missions into pueblos or towns and villages of Indian converts. Nearly 350 towns originated as missions. Fifty-four missionaries met death by violence from the start of missionary work until 1817. Missionary work was seriously hindered during the wars of independence in the second decade of the 19th century and continued in decline through the rest of the century as dictator followed dictator in a period of political tur-

bulence. Restoration of the missions got under way in 1922. The first diocese was established in 1531. Most of the bishops have been native Venezuelans. The first diocesan synod was held in 1574. Church-state relations are regulated by an agreement concluded with the Holy See in 1964. Venezuela maintains diplomatic relations with Vatican City.

*Archd., 6; dioc., 18; v.a., 4; card. (1984), 1; abp., 5; bp., 31; parishes, 1,000; priests, 2,022 (853 dioc., 1,169 rel.); p.d., 22; sem., 383; bros., 229; srs., 4,270; bap., 350,947; Caths., 13,226,000 (92.4%); tot. pop., 14,310,000 (1981).*

**Vietnam:** Country in southeastern Asia, reunited officially July 2, 1976, as the Socialist Republic of Vietnam; capital, Hanoi. Previously, from 1954, partitioned into the Democratic Peoples' Republic of Vietnam in the North (capital, Hanoi) and the Republic of Vietnam in the South (capital, Saigon). Catholicism was introduced in 1533 but missionary work was intermittent until 1615 when Jesuits arrived to stay. One hundred thousand Catholics were reported in 1639. Two vicariates were organized in 1659. A seminary was set up in 1666 and two native priests were ordained two years later. A congregation of native women religious formed in 1670 is still active. Severe persecution broke out in 1698, three times in the 18th century, and again in the 19th. Between 100,000 and 300,000 persons suffered in some way from persecution during the 50 years before 1883 when the French moved in to secure religious liberty for the Catholics. Most of the 117 beatified Martyrs of Vietnam were killed during this 50-year period. After the French were forced out of Vietnam in 1954, the country was partitioned at the 17th parallel. The North went Communist and the Viet Cong, joined by North Vietnamese regular army troops in 1964, fought to gain control of the South. In 1954 there were approximately 1,114,000 Catholics in the North and 480,000 in the South. More than 650,000 fled to the South to avoid the government repression that silenced the Church in the North. In South Vietnam, the Church continued to develop during the war years. Fragmentary reports about the status of the Church since the end of the war in 1975 have been ominous. Freedom of religious belief, promised by the Revolutionary Government in May, 1975, shortly after its capture of Saigon (Ho Chi Min City), is denied in practice. Late in 1983, the government initiated support for a "patriotic" Catholic church analogous to the communist-sponsored church in China. The hierarchy was established in 1960. The apostolic delegation, formerly in Saigon, was transferred to Hanoi in 1976; it is presently vacant.

*Archd., 3; dioc., 22; card., 1; abp. 4; bp., 37. No statistics are available. There were 2,749,475 Catholics (6.4% of the total population) in 1974. Pop., 56,600,000.*

**Virgin Islands:** Organized unincorporated U.S. territory, about 34 miles east of Puerto Rico; capital, Charlotte Amalie on St. Thomas (one of the three principal islands). The islands were discovered by Columbus in 1493 and named for St. Ursula and her virgin companions. Missionaries began evangelization in the 16th century. A church on St. Croix dates from about 1660; another, on St. Thomas, from 1774. The Baltimore archdiocese had jurisdiction over the islands from 1804 to 1820 when it was passed on to the first of several places in the Caribbean area. Some trouble arose over a pastoral appointment in the 19th century, resulting in a small schism. The Redemptorists took over pastoral care in 1858; normal conditions have prevailed since.

*Dioc., 1 (St. Thomas, suffragan of Washington, D.C.); bp., 1; parishes, 6; priests, 17 (2 dioc., 15 rel.); sem., 2; bros., 2; srs., 19; bap., 729; Caths., 25,000; tot. pop., 100,000.*

**Virgin Islands, British:** British crown colony in Caribbean; capital, Road Town.

*Parish, 1; priest, 1 (rel.); bap., 10; Caths., 300; tot. pop., 13,000.*

**Wales:** Part of the United Kingdom, on the western part of the island of Great Britain. Celtic missionaries completed evangelization by the end of the sixth century, the climax of what has been called the age of saints. Welsh Christianity received its distinctive Celtic character at this time. Some conflict developed when attempts were made — and proved successful later — to place the Welsh Church under the jurisdiction of Canterbury; the Welsh opted for direct contact with Rome. The Church made progress despite the depredations of Norsemen in the eighth and ninth centuries. Norman infiltration occurred near the middle of the 12th century, resulting in a century-long effort to establish territorial dioceses and parishes to replace the Celtic organizational plan of monastic centers and satellite churches. The Western Schism produced split views and allegiances. Actions of Henry VIII in breaking away from Rome had serious repercussions. Proscription and penal laws crippled the Church, resulted in heavy defections and touched off a 150-year period of repression in which more than 91 persons died for the faith. Methodism prevailed by 1750. Modern Catholicism came to Wales with Irish immigrants in the 19th century, when the number of Welsh Catholics was negligible. Catholic emancipation was granted in 1829. The hierarchy was restored in 1850.

*Archd., 1; dioc., 1; abp., 1; bp., 2; parishes, 169; priests, 305 (171 dioc., 134 rel.); p.d., 4; sem., 27; srs., 606; bap., 3,297; Caths., 149,431 (5.2%); tot. pop., 2,866,200.*

**Wallis and Futuna Islands:** French overseas territory in the southwestern Pacific. Marists, who began evangelizing the islands in 1836-7, were the first Catholic missionaries. The entire populations of the two islands were baptized by the end of 1842 (Wallis) and 1843 (Futuna). The first missionary to the latter island was killed in 1841; he was the first martyr of the Pacific. Most of the priests on the islands are native Polynesians. The hierarchy was established in 1966.

*Dioc., 1; bp., 1 (nat.); parishes, 5; priests, 14 (9 dioc., 5 rel.); sem., 1; bros., 8; srs., 47; bap., 419; Caths., 10,000; tot. pop., 11,000.*

**Western Sahara:** Former Spanish overseas province (Spanish Sahara) on the northwestern coast of Africa. Territory is under control of Morocco. Islam is the religion of non-Europeans. A prefecture apostolic was established in 1954 for the European Catholics there.

*P.a., 1; parishes, 2; priests, 3 (rel.); bap., 2; Caths., 400.*

**Yemen, North:** Arab republic in southwestern Arabia; capital, Sanaa. Christians perished in the first quarter of the sixth century. Moslems have been in control since the seventh century. The state religion is Islam. In 1973, for the first time in 1,400 years, Catholic personnel — priests, religious, lay persons — were invited to work in the country as staff of a government hospital; they were not to engage in proselytizing. Under ecclesiastical jurisdiction of Arabia vicariate apostolic.

*Caths., 3,000; tot. pop., 5,940,000.*

**Yemen, South** (People's Democratic Republic of Yemen): Republic in the southern part of the Arabian peninsula; capitals, Aden and Medina as-Shaab. No Christian community has existed there since the Moslem conquest of the seventh century. Catholics are from other countries. Under ecclesiastical jurisdiction of Arabia vicariate apostolic.

*Caths., 1,000; tot. pop., 2,030,000.*

**Yugoslavia:** Socialist republic in southeastern Europe; capital, Belgrade. Christianity was introduced from the seventh to ninth centuries in the regions which were combined to form the nation after World War I. Since these regions straddled the original line of demarcation for the Western and Eastern Empires (and churches), and since the Reformation had little lasting effect, the Christians are nearly all either Roman Catholics or Byzantines (some in communion with Rome, the majority Orthodox). Yugoslavia was proclaimed a Socialist republic in 1945. Repression of religion became government policy. Between May, 1945, and December, 1950, persecution took the following toll: almost two-thirds of 22 dioceses lost their bishops; about 348 priests were killed; 200 priests were under arrest and in prison; 12 of 18 seminaries were closed; the Catholic press was confiscated; religious instruction was suppressed in all schools; 300 religious houses and institutions were confiscated, and nuns and other religious driven out; all Church property was expropriated; the ministry of priests was severely restricted and subject to government interference; many thousands of the faithful shared the fate of priests and religious in death, imprisonment and slave labor. Cardinal Stepinac, arrested in 1946 and the symbol of the Church under persecution in Yugoslavia, died Feb. 10, 1960. In an agreement signed June 25, 1966, the government recognized the Holy See's spiritual jurisdiction over the Church in the country and guaranteed to bishops the possibility of maintaining contact with Rome in ecclesiastical and religious matters. The Holy See confirmed the principle that the activity of ecclesiastics, in the exercise of priestly functions, must take place within the religious and ecclesiastical sphere, and that abuse of these functions for political ends would be illegal. Less than two months after the agreement was signed, a group of exiled Croatian priests issued a statement in which they accused the Yugoslav government of failing to abide by it. According to others, an improvement was noticeable. Yugoslavia maintains diplomatic relations with Vatican City.

*Archd., 8; dioc., 14; a.a., 1, card., 1; abp., 7; bp., 23; parishes, 2,786; priests, 4,216 (2,768 dioc., 1,448 rel.); p.d., 2; sem., 716; bros., 256; srs., 6,355; bap., 81,934; Caths., 7,147,000 (31.7%); tot. pop., 22,520,000 (1981).*

**Zaire** (formerly the Congo): Republic in south central Africa; capital, Kinshasa. Christianity was introduced in 1484 and evangelization began about 1490. The first native bishop in black Africa was ordained in 1518. Subsequent missionary work was hindered by faulty methods of instruction and formation, inroads of the slave trade, wars among the tribes, and Portuguese policy based on the patronage system and having all the trappings of anticlericalism in the 18th and 19th centuries. Modern evangelization started in the second half of the 19th century. The hierarchy was established in 1959. In the civil disorders which followed independence in 1960, some missions and other church installations were abandoned, thousands of people reverted to tribal religions and many priests and religious were killed. Church-state tensions have developed in recent years because of the Church's criticism of the anti-Christian thrust of Pres. Mobutu's "Africanization" policies. Zaire maintains diplomatic relations with Vatican City.

*Archd., 6; dioc., 41; card., 1 (nat.); abp., 5 (nat.); bp., 46 (43 nat.); parishes, 998; priests, 2,584 (726 dioc., 1,858 rel.); p.d., 7; sem., 1,790; bros., 941; srs., 4,401; bap., 401,212; Caths., 12,750,000 (46%); tot. pop., 27,483,000 (1981).*

**Zambia:** Republic in central Africa; capital, Lusaka. Portuguese priests did some evangelizing

in the 16th and 17th centuries but no results of their work remained in the 19th century. Jesuits began work in the south in the 1880s and White Fathers in the north and east in 1895. Evangelization of the western region began for the first time in 1831. The number of Catholics doubled in the 20 years following World War II. Zambia maintains diplomatic relations with Vatican City.

*Archd., 2; dioc., 7; abp., 2 (nat.); bp., 6 (5 nat.); parishes, 223; priests, 472 (105 dioc., 367 rel.); p.d., 1; sem., 124; bros., 143; srs., 625; bap., 48,824; Caths., 1,687,000 (26%); tot. pop., 6,495,000.*

**Zimbabwe** (formerly Rhodesia): Independent republic (Apr. 18, 1980) in south central Africa; capital, Harare (Salisbury). Earlier unsuccessful missionary ventures preceded the introduction of Catholicism in 1879. Missionaries began to make progress after 1893. The hierarchy was established in 1955; the first black bishop was ordained in 1973. In 1969, four years after the government of Ian Smith made a unilateral declaration of independence from England, a new constitution was enacted for the purpose of assuring continued white supremacy over the black majority. Catholic and Protestant prelates in the country protested vigorously against the constitution and related enactments as opposed to human rights of the blacks and restrictive of the Church's freedom to carry out its pastoral, educational and social service functions. The Smith regime was ousted in 1979 after seven years of civil war in which at least 25,000 people were killed. Diplomatic relations with the Vatican were established in 1980.

*Archd., 1; dioc., 4; p.a., 1; abp., 1 (nat.); bp., 5 (3 nat.); priests, 317 (67 dioc., 250 rel.); p.d., 9; sem., 62; bros., 100; srs., 946; bap., 25,077; Caths. (1981), 698,000 (9.1%); tot. pop., 7,600,000.*

## CATHOLIC WORLD STATISTICS

*(Principal sources: Statistical Yearbook of the Church, 1981, the latest edition available at press time; Annuario Pontificio, 1984. Figures are from Dec. 31, 1981, unless indicated otherwise; jurisdictions have been updated to June, 1984, in most cases.)*

**Patriarchates: 13.** Eastern Rites, 8 (Africa, 2; Asia, 6). Roman Rite, 5 (Asia, 2; Europe, 2; West Indies, 1). The West Indies patriarchate has been vacant since 1963.

**Archdioceses: 508** (Africa, 59; North and Middle America, 77; South America, 86; Asia, 123; Europe, 145; Oceania, 18).

**Dioceses: 1,914** (Africa, 309; North and Middle America, 314; South America, 344; Asia, 361; Europe, 535; Oceania, 51).

**Prelatures: 69** (Africa, 1; North and Middle America, 12; South America, 43; Asia, 5; Europe, 8).

**Abbacies: 19** (Africa, 1; North and Middle America, 1; South America, 2; Asia, 1; Europe, 14).

**Vicariates Apostolic: 73** (Africa, 13; North and Middle America, 7; South America, 35; Asia, 17; Europe, 1).

**Prefectures Apostolic: 54** (Africa, 8; South America, 11; Asia, 35).

**Apostolic Administrations: 7** (Africa, 1; North and Middle America, 1; Asia, 1; Europe, 4).

**Missions "Sui Juris": 6** (Africa, 1; Asia, 3; Middle America, 1; Oceania, 1).

**Apostolic Exarchates, Ordinariates: 22** (North and Middle America, 4; South America, 3; Asia, 2; Europe, 13).

**Military Vicariates: 29** (Africa, 3; North and Middle America, 4; South America, 8; Asia, 3; Europe, 9; Oceania, 2).

**Cardinals** (as of Sept. 15, 1984): **125** (Africa, 14; North America, 15; Central and South America, 17; Asia, 11; Europe, 65; Oceania, 3).

**Archbishops: 422** (Africa, 49; North and Middle America, 70; South America, 80; Asia, 94; Europe, 115; Oceania, 14).

*Figures for archbishops and bishops (below) include residential and auxiliary prelates only. Titular archbishops and bishops engaged in other apostolates and retired members of the hierarchy are not included. The total number of archbishops* and bishops was 695 and 3,017, respectively, according to the "1981 Statistical Yearbook of the Church."

**Bishops: 2,435** (Africa, 325; North and Middle America, 486; South America, 510; Asia, 326; Europe, 720; Oceania, 68).

**Priests, Total: 408,945** (Africa, 17,233; North and Middle America, 85,393; South America, 33,909; Asia, 27,731; Euorpe, 239,137; Oceania, 5,542). As of Dec. 31, 1982.

• Diocesan Priests: 254,797 (Africa, 6,538; North and Middle America, 51,563; South America, 14,837; Asia, 14,144; Europe, 164,840; Oceania, 2,875).

• Religious Priests: 154,148 (Africa, 10,695; North and Middle America, 33,830; South America, 19,072; Asia, 13,587; Europe, 74,297; Oceania, 2,667).

**Permanent Deacons: 8,647** (Africa, 156; North and Middle America, 6,026; South America, 716; Asia, 68; Europe, 1,629; Oceania, 52).

**Brothers: 70,621** (Africa, 5,305; North and Middle America, 15,496; South America, 6,744; Asia, 5,892; Europe, 34,051; Oceania, 3,133).

**Sisters: 952,043** (Africa, 36,165; North and Middle America, 202,427; South America, 90,784; Asia, 87,099; Europe, 519,773; Oceania, 15,795).

**Major Seminarians: 73,001** (Africa, 7,495; North and Middle America, 13,554; South America, 11,959; Asia, 13,447; Europe, 25,630; Oceania, 916). As of Dec. 31, 1982.

**Baptisms: 17,466,303** (Africa, 2,142,482; North and Middle America, 4,004,563; South America 5,560,451; Asia, 2,039,400; Europe, 3,592,016; Oceania, 127,391). Includes 16,158,149 baptisms up to the age of seven and 1,308,154 over that age.

**Marriages: 4,134,512** (Africa, 184,507: North and Middle America, 900,450; South America, 1,101,346; Asia, 386,317; Europe, 1,527,584; Oceania, 34,308). Includes 3,796,073 marriages between Catholis and 338,439 between Catholics and non-Catholics.

**Parishes, 207,971** (Africa, 7,412; North and Middle America, 31,150; South America, 15,938; Asia, 12,108; Europe, 139,009; Oceania, 2,354).

**Elementary/Primary Schools and Students:** 75,470 schools; 20,988,965 students. Africa, 19,082 — 6,006,933; North and Middle America, 12,539 — 3,789,203; South America, 8,807 — 3,160,632; Asia, 11,264 — 3,664,528; Europe, 21,365 — 3,882,505; Oceania, 2,413 — 485,164.

**Secondary Schools and Students: 29,919** schools; **11,254,697** students. Africa, 3,609 — 894,712; North and Middle America, 3,608 — 1,468,816; South America, 4,892 — 1,858,045; Asia, 6,235 — 3,310,899; Europe, 10,882 — 3,454,080; Oceania, 693 — 268,145.

**Students in Higher Institutes and Universities: 2,143,481** (Africa, 7,872; North and Middle America, 771,787; South America, 463,217; Asia, 662,328; Europe, 233,924; Oceania, 4,353).

**Hospitals: 6,475** (Africa, 921; North and Middle America, 1,013; South America, 1,269; Asia, 1,168; Europe, 1,943; Oceania, 161).

**Dispensaries: 12,628** (Africa, 3,269; North and Middle America, 1,351; South America, 2,993; Asia, 2,406; Europe, 2,364; Oceania, 245).

**Leprosaria; 798** (Africa, 436; North and Middle America, 9; South America, 48; Asia, 295; Europe, 4; Oceania, 6).

**Homes for Aged, Chronically Ill, Handicapped: 10,085** (Africa, 295; North and Middle America, 1,024; South America, 1,335; Asia, 550; Europe, 6,711; Oceania, 170).

**Orphanages: 6,393** (Africa, 390; North and Middle America, 444; South America, 930; Asia, 1,747; Europe, 2,707; Oceania, 175).

**Nurseries: 5,754** (Africa, 583; North and Middle America, 262; South America, 931; Asia, 1,063; Europe, 2,890; Oceania, 25).

**Catholic Population: 794,380,000** (17.7% of the total world population of 4,485,462,000). Africa, 60,543,000 (12.5%; total population, 482,056,000). North and Middle America, 169,687,000 (44.8%; total population, 378,474,000). South America, 220,829,000 (90.7%; total population 243,331,000). Asia, 64,575,000 (2.4% total population, 2,674,879,000). Europe, 272,881,000 (39.9%; total population, 683,785,000). Oceania, 5,865,000 (25.5%; total population, 22,937,000).

## DEATHS SEPTEMBER 1983 TO SEPTEMBER 1984

**Baroni,** Msgr. Geno, 53, Aug. 27, 1984, Washington, D.C., of cancer; specialist in urban-ethnic affairs; worked to save ethnic neighborhoods; secretary for Housing and Urban Development (HUD) during the Carter administration.

**Burke,** Rev. Eugene M., C.S.P., 72, Jan. 29, 1964, Los Angeles, Calif.; theologian; taught dogmatic theology at Catholic University of America for over 30 years; founded Catholic Theological Society of America in 1947.

**Caillouet,** Bishop L. Abel, 84, Sept. 16, 1984, New Orleans, La.; auxiliary bishop of New Orleans from 1947 to 1976, when he retired.

**Chevalier,** Rev. Pierre, O.S.F.S., 67, Nov. 28, 1983, Geneva, Switzerland; Swiss leader in Catholic press; secretary general of International Catholic Union of the Press from 1974.

**Chu Shu-teh,** Rev. Francis Xavier, S.J., 70,

Dec. 28, 1983, in a labor camp in China; Chinese priest who, from his first arrest in 1953, spent most of his life in prison or in labor camps.

**Conroy,** Msgr. James, 72, Dec. 22, 1983, Kendallville, Ind.; retired columnist; editor, 1967-78, of Fort Wayne-South Bend editon of *Our Sunday Visitor;* founded "The Fighting 69th," a youth organization popular in 1950s and 1960s.

**Corridan,** Rev. John M., S.J., 73, July 1, 1984, Bronx, N.Y.; gained national attention as the "Waterfront Priest"; his crusade against corruption on the docks led to formation of Waterfront Commission; character of priest in film, *On the Waterfront,* modeled after him.

**Dohen,** Dorothy M., 60, Jan. 2, 1984, New York; editor, authority on religious literature; sociology professor at Fordham University; edited, 1952-56, *Integrity,* Catholic literary arts magazine.

**Finnegan,** Rev. James M., S.J., 71, Feb. 26, 1984, Beirut, Lebanon, as a result of shell fire; American Jesuit of New York Province who taught philosophy at Jesuit-run St. Joseph University in Beirut from 1951.

**Fox,** Msgr. Robert J., 54, Apr. 27, 1984, New York, N.Y.; inner-city pastor; coordinator of Spanish community Action Program in the New York Archdiocese in the 1960s; developed programs aimed at revitalizing neighborhoods and easing social tensions.

**Fulcher,** Bishop George A., 61, Jan. 25, 1984, near Lafayette, Ind., in a car accident; auxiliary bishop of Columbus, Ohio, 1976-83; bishop of Lafayette from 1983; chairman of U.S. bishops' follow-up committee on the war and peace pastoral.

**Halas,** George S., 88, Nov. 3, 1983, Chicago, Ill.; one of the founders of pro-football; owner of the Chicago Bears.

**Hoag,** Rev. Donald, O.F.M., 83, June 21, 1984, Totowa, N.J.; minister provincial of the New York-based Franciscan Province of the Most Holy Name, 1961-67, when it was the largest Franciscan province in the world.

**La Velle,** Rev. Malcolm, C.P., 83, Sept. 5, 1984, Chicago, Ill.; superior general of the Passionists, 1952-64, the first North American elected to that position.

**Legrand,** Rev. Francis Xavier, C.I.C.M., 80, Jan. 28, 1984, Belgium; missionary in China from 1929 to 1954, when he was expelled; founder and director until 1977 of the review, *Christ to the World.*

**Ligutti,** Msgr. Luigi, 88, Dec. 28, 1983, Rome, Italy; Italian-born Des Moines diocesan priest whose apostolate was devoted to concerns of rural peoples of the world; a founder of the National Catholic Rural Life Conference in the U.S. and Agrimissio; permanent observer of Holy See at the United Nations FAO, 1948-70.

**McCrory,** Mother M. Angeline Teresa, 91, Jan. 21, 1984, Germantown, N.Y.; foundress of the Carmelite Sisters for the Aged and Infirm, 1929.

**McGucken,** Archbishop Joseph T., 81, Oct. 26, 1983, San Francisco, Calif.; archbishop of San Francisco from 1962 to 1977, when he retired.

**McKenna,** Sister Mary Paul, M.M., 95, Jan. 9, 1984, Maryknoll, N.Y.; missionary; led Maryknoll Sisters to their pioneer mission assignment in China, 1921.

**Maginn,** Bishop Edward J., 87, Aug. 21, 1984, Albany, N.Y.; auxiliary bishop of Albany from 1957 to 1972, when he retired.

**Mardaga,** Bishop Thomas J., 71, May 28, 1984, Wilmington, Del., of cancer; bishop of Wilmington from 1968.

**Medeiros,** Cardinal Humberto S., 67, Sept. 17, 1983, Boston, Mass.; archbishop of Boston from 1970; before that had been bishop of Brownsville, Tex., 1966-70; named to College of Cardinals in 1973.

**Mihalik,** Bishop Emil J., 63, Jan. 27, 1984, Cleveland, O., of cancer; first bishop of Byzantine Ruthenian Diocese of Parma, 1969.

**Mozzoni,** Cardinal Umberto, 79, Nov. 7, 1983, Vatican City; longtime papal diplomat; named to College of Cardinals in 1973.

**Murphy,** Sister Eileen, R.S.M., 48, Dec. 5, 1983, Providence, R.I.; established several facilities for feeding the poor and sheltering homeless of Providence.

**O'Brien,** Pat, 83, Oct. 16, 1983, Los Angeles, Calif.; longtime actor; roles included that of Knute Rockne and Father Duffy.

**O'Connor,** Bishop William A., 79, Nov. 14, 1983, Springfield, Ill.; bishop of Springfield from 1949 to 1975, when he retired.

**Philippe,** Cardinal Pierre Paul, O.P., 79, Apr. 9, 1984, Rome, Italy; French cardinal; curial official from 1959; headed Congregation for Eastern Churches, 1973 (when he was named cardinal) to 1980.

**Pocock,** Archbishop Philip F., 78, Sept., 1984, Toronto, Canada; retired archbishop of Toronto.

**Quintero,** Cardinal Jose Humberto, 81, July 8, 1984, Caracas, Venezuela; named first Venezuelan cardinal in 1961; archbishop of Caracas from 1960 to 1980, when he retired.

**Reedy,** Rev. John, C.S.C., 58, Dec. 2, 1983, South Bend, Ind., of bone marrow disease; columnist in Catholic press; publisher of Ave Maria Press for 30 years.

**Reicher,** Bishop Louis J., 93, Feb. 23, 1984, near Austin, Tex.; first bishop of Austin from 1948 to 1978, when he retired.

**Renard,** Cardinal Alexandre Charles, 77, Oct. 8, 1983, Paris, France; named to College of Cardinals in 1967; archbishop of Lyons from 1967 to 1981, when he retired.

**Schulte,** Archbishop Paul, 93, Feb. 17, 1984, Indianapolis, Ind.; archbishop of Indianapolis from 1946 to 1970, when he retired; oldest American bishop.

**Shehan,** Cardinal Lawrence J., 86, Aug. 26, 1984, Baltimore, Md.; leader in ecumenism and civil rights; archbishop of Baltimore from 1961 to 1974, when he retired; named to College of Cardinals in 1965.

**Stemper,** Bishop Alfred M., M.S.C., 71, Feb. 20, 1984, Kavieng, Papua New Guinea; missionary; bishop of Kavieng from 1957 to 1980, when he retired.

**Swords,** Rev. Raymond, S.J., 64, Jan. 12, 1984, Portland, Me.; president of Holy Cross College, Worcester, Mass., 1960-70.

**Ting Shue Yen,** Msgr. Joseph, 63, May 24, 1984, Rome, Italy; Manchurian-born priest; ministered to Chinese of the diaspora.

**Ward,** Rev. Leo Richard, C.S.C., 91, Sept. 9, 1984, South Bend, Ind.; author; Notre Dame faculty member for more than 40 years.

**Willson,** Meredith, 82, June 15, 1984, Santa Monica, Calif.; composer and lyricist; best known for *The Music Man;* convert, 1974.

**Wurm,** Bishop John D., 56, Apr. 27, 1984, Belleville, Ill., of cancer; bishop of Belleville from 1981; was auxiliary bishop of St. Louis, 1976-81.

**Zablocki,** Rep. Clement, 71, Dec. 3, 1983, Washington, D.C.; U.S. Democratic Representative from Wisconsin since 1949.

**Zilly,** Mrs. Bernice, July 13, 1984, Detroit, Mich.; president of National Council of Catholic Women, 1973-75.

# EPISCOPAL CONFERENCES

(Principal source: *Annuario Pontificio*.)

Episcopal conferences, organized and operating under general norms and particular statutes approved by the Holy See, are official bodies in and through which the bishops of a given country or territory act together as pastors of the Church.

Listed below according to countries or regions are titles and addresses of conferences and names and sees of presidents (archbishops unless otherwise noted).

**Africa, North:** Conference Episcopale d'Afrique du Nord, 13 rue Khelifa Boukhalfa, Algiers, Algeria. Card. Leon-Etienne Duval (Algiers).

**Africa, South:** Southern African Catholic Bishops' Conference (SACBC), P.O. Box 941, Pretoria 0001, S. Africa. Denis Eugene Hurley, O.M.I. (Durban).

**Angola and Sao Tome:** Conferencia Episcopal de Angola e Sao Tome (CEAST), C.P. 10, Huambo, Angola. Manuel F. da Costa (Huambo).

**Antilles:** Antilles Episcopal Conference, 27 Maraval Rd., Port of Spain, Trinidad. Gordon Anthony Pantin (Port of Spain).

**Arab Countries:** Conference des Eveques Latins dans les Regions Arabes (CELRA), Latin Patriarchate, P.O. Box 14152, Jerusalem (Old City). Patriarch Giacomo Beltritti (Jerusalem).

**Argentina:** Conferencia Episcopal Argentina (CEA), Calle Paraguay 1867, Buenos Aires. Card. Juan Carlos Aramburu (Buenos Aires).

**Australia:** Australian Episcopal Conference, P.O. Box 368, Canberra, A.C.T., 2601. Francis Roberts Rush (Brisbane).

**Austria:** Osterreichische Bischofskonferenz, Rotenturmstrasse 2, A1010 Vienna. Card. Franz Koenig (Vienna).

**Bangladesh:** Catholic Bishops' Conference (CBCB), P.O. Box 3, Ramna, Dhaka-2. Michael Rozario (Dhaka).

**Belgium:** Bisschoppenconferentie van Belgie — Conference Episcopale de Belgique, Wollemarkt 15, B-2800 Mechelen. Card. Godfried Danneels (Mechelen-Brussel).

**Benin:** Conference Episcopale du Benin, B.P. 491, Cotonou. Christophe Adimou (Cotonou).

**Bolivia:** Conferencia Episcopal de Bolivia (CEB), Casilla 2309, La Paz. Luis Rodriguez Pardo (Santa Cruz de la Sierra).

**Brazil:** Conferencia Nacional dos Bispos do Brasil (CNBB), C.P. 13-2067, 70000 Brasilia, D.F. Bp. Jose Ivo Lorscheiter (Santa Maria).

**Bulgaria:** Ulitza Pashovi 10-B, Sofia VI. Bp. Metodio Dimitrow Stratiew (Apostolic Exarch, Sofia).

**Burma:** Burma Catholic Bishops' Conference (BCBC), 292 Prome Rd., Sanchaung P.O., Rangoon. Bp. Paul Zinghtung Grawng (Myitkyina).

**Burundi:** Conference Episcopale du Burundi, B. P. 1390, Bujumbura. Joachim Ruhuna (Gitega).

**Cameroon:** Conference Episcopale Nationale du Cameroun, P.O. Box 207, Yaounde. Jean Zoa (Yaounde).

**Canada:** See Canadian Conference of Catholic Bishops.

**Central African Republic:** Conference Episcopale Centrafricaine (CECA), B.P. 1518, Bangui. Joachim N'Dayen (Bangui).

**Chad:** Conference Episcopale du Tchad, B.P., 456, N'Djamena. Charles Vandame, S.J. (N'Djamens).

**Chile:** Conferencia Episcopal de Chile (CECH), Casilla 13191, Correo 21, Santiago de Chile. Bernardino Piñero Carvallo (La Serena).

**China** (Republic of China, Taiwan): Regional Episcopal Conference of China, Lane 32, Kuangfu Rd., Taipeh 34, Taiwan. Stanislaus Lokuang (Taipeh, emeritus).

**Colombia:** Conferencia Episcopal de Colombia, Apartado 7448, Bogota D.E. Mario Revollo Bravo (Nueva Pamplona).

**Congo:** Conference Episcopale du Congo, B.P. 2301, Brazzaville. Bp. Georges Singha (Owanda).

**Costa Rica:** Conferencia Episcopal de Costa Rica (CECOR), Apartado 497, San Jose. Roman Arrieta Villalobos (San Jose de Costa Rica).

**Cuba:** Conferencia Episcopal de Cuba (CEC), Apartado 105, Camaguey. Bp. Adolfo Rodriguez Herrera (Camaguey).

**Dominican Republic:** Conferencia del Episcopado Dominicano (CED), Apartado 1313, Higuey. Abp.-Bp. Hugo Eduardo Polanco Brito (Nuestra Senora de la Altagracia en Higuey).

**Ecuador:** Conferencia Episcopal Ecuatoriana, Apartado 1081, Quito. Card. Pablo Munoz Vega, S.J. (Quito).

**El Salvador:** Conferencia Episcopal de El Salvador (CEDES). Apartado Postal 1310, San Salvador. Bp. Marco Rene Revelo Contreras (Santa Ana).

**Equatorial Guinea:** Apartado 106, Malabo. Rafael Nze Abuy, C.M.F. (Malabo).

**Ethiopia:** Conferenza Episcopale di Etiopia, P.O. Box 21903, Addis Ababa. Paulos Tzadua (Addis Ababa).

**France:** Conference Episcopale Francaise, 106 rue du Bac, 75341 Paris CEDEX 07. Bp. Jean Vilnet (Lille).

**Gabon:** Conference Episcopale du Gabon, B.P. 230, Franceville. Bp. Felicien-Patrice Makouaka (Franceville).

**Gambia, Liberia and Sierra Leone:** Inter-Territorial Episcopal Conference, P.O. Box 893, Freetown, Sierra Leone. Michael Kpakala Francis (Monrovia, Liberia).

**Germany:** Deutsche Bischofskonferenz, Kaiserstrasse 163, D-5300 Bonn. Card. Joseph Hoeffner (Cologne). Berliner Bischofskonferenz, Franzosische Strasse 34, DDR-1086 Berlin. Card. Joachim Meisner (Berlin).

**Ghana:** Ghana Bishops' Conference, P.O. Box 42, Tamale. Peter Poreku Dery (Tamale).

**Great Britain:** Bishops' Conference of England and Wales, Archbishop's House, Westminster, London, SW IP IQ. Card. George Basil Hume, O.S.B. (Westminster). Bishops' Conference of Scotland, 42 Greenhill Gardens, Edinburgh EH 10

**4BJ.** Card. Gordon J. Gray (Saint Andrews and Edinburgh).

**Greece:** Conferenza Episcopale di Grecia, Archeveche Catholique, Corfu. Antonio Varthalitis (Corfu, Zante and Cefalonia.)

**Guatemala:** Conferencia Episcopal de Guatemala (CEG), 4 Calle 9-45, zona 1, Ciudad de Guatemala. Bp. Prospero Penados del Barrio (San Marcos).

**Guinea:** Conference Episcopale de la Guinee, B.P. 1006 Bis, Conakry.

**Haiti:** Conference Episcopale de Haiti (CEH). C.P. 22, Cap Hatien, Haiti. Bp. Francois Gayot, S.M.M. (Cap Haitien).

**Honduras:** Conferencia Episcopal de Honduras (CEH), Arzobispado, Apartado 106, Tegucigalpa. Hector Enrique Santos Hernandez, S.D.B. (Tegucigalpa).

**Hungary:** Magyar Puspoki Kar, Berenyi Zsigmond u. 2, Pf. 25, H-2500 Esztergom. Card. Laszlo Lekai (Esztergom).

**India:** Catholic Bishops' Conference of India (CBCI), CBCI Centre, Goldakkana, New Delhi-110001. Simon Ignatius Pimenta (Bombay).

**Indonesia:** General Conference of the Ordinaries of Indonesia (Majelis Agung Waligerija Indonesia — MAWI), Pusat Jalan Cut Mutiah 10, Jakarta II/14. Bp. Francis Xavier Sudartanto Hadisumarta, O. Carm. (Malang).

**Ireland:** Episcopal Meetings, "Ara Coeli," Armagh. Card. Tomas O'Fiaich (Armagh).

**Italy:** Conferenza Episcopale Italiana (CEI), Circonvallazione Aurelia, 50, 00165 Roma. Card. Anastasio Alberto Ballestrero, O.C.D. (Turin).

**Ivory Coast:** Conference Episcopale de la Cote d'Ivoire, B.P. 1287, Abidjan. Card. Bernard Yago (Abidjan).

**Japan:** Japan Catholic Bishops' Conference, Catholic Center, 10-1 Rokubancho, Chiyoda-Kir, Tokyo 102. Peter Seiichi Shirayanagi (Tokyo).

**Kenya:** Kenya Episcopal Conference (KEC), P.O. Box 938, Nakuru. Bp. Raphael S. Ndingi Mwana's Nzeki (Nakuru).

**Korea:** Catholic Conference of Korea, Box 16, Seoul. Card. Stephen Sou Hwan Kim (Seoul).

**Laos and Cambodia:** Conference Episcopale du Laos et du Cambodge, Centre Catholique, Vientiane, Laos. Bp. Thomas Nantha (vic. ap. Vientiane).

**Latvia:** Pils Jela, 2, Riga. Card. Julijans Vaivods (Ap. Admin., Riga and Liepaja).

**Lesotho:** Lesotho Catholic Bishops' Conference, P.O. Box 200, Maseru 100. Bp. Sebastian Koto Khoarai, O.M.I. (Mohale's Hoek).

**Liberia:** See Gambia, Liberia and Sierra Leone.

**Lithuania:** Vilniaus gatve 4, 233000 Kaunas. Bp. Liudas Povilonis (Ap. Admin., Kaunas and Vilkaviskis).

**Madagascar:** Conference Episcopale du Madagascar, 102 bis, Av. Marechal Joffre Antanimena, B. P 667, Antananarivo. Card. Victor Razafimahatratra, S.J. (Tananarive).

**Malawi:** Episcopal Conference of Malawi, Catholic Secretariat of Malawi, P.O. Box 30384, Lilongwe 3. Bp. Felix Mkhori (Chikwawa).

**Malaysia-Singapore-Brunei:** Catholic Bishops' Conference of Malaysia-Singapore-Brunei, (BCMSB), Archbishop's House, 31 Victoria St., Singapore 0718. Gregory Yong Sooi Nghean (Singapore).

**Mali:** Conference Episcopale du Mali, B.P. 298, Bamako. Luc Auguste Sangare (Bamako).

**Malta:** Conferenza Episcopale Maltese, Archbishop's Curia, Floriana. Joseph Mercieca (Malta).

**Mexico:** Conferencia del Episcopado Mexicano (CEM), Apartado Postal 22-119, Victoria 21, Tlalpan 22, D.F. Sergio Obeso Rivera (Jalapa).

**Mozambique:** Conferencia Episcopal de Mocambique (CEM), C.P. 286, Maputo. Bp. Jaime Pedro Goncalves (Beira).

**Netherlands:** Nederlandse Bisschoppenconferentie, Postbus 13049, NL-3507 La, Utrecht. Adrianus J. Simonis (Utrecht).

**New Zealand:** New Zealand Episcopal Conference, P.O. Box 198, Wellington. Card. Thomas Stafford Williams (Wellington).

**Nicaragua:** Conferencia Episcopal de Nicaragua, Apartado 2148, Managua. Bp. Pablo Antonio Vega (Juigalpa, prelacy).

**Niger:** See Upper Volta.

**Nigeria:** Catholic Bishops Conference of Nigeria, P.O. Box 951, Lagos. Francis Arinze (Onitsha).

**Pacific:** Conference des Eveques du Pacifique (CEPAC), P.O. Box 109, Petero Mataca (Suva).

**Pakistan:** Pakistan Episcopal Conference, St. Patrick's Cathedral, Karachi 3. Card. Joseph Cordeiro (Karachi).

**Panama:** Conferencia Episcopal de Panama (CEP), Apartado 386, Panama 1. Bp. Jose Maria Carrizo Villareal (Chitre).

**Papua New Guinea and Solomon Islands:** Bishops' Conference of Papua New Guinea and Solomon Islands, Southern Highlands, P.O. Box 109, Goroko, Eastern Highlands, Papua New Guinea. Bp. Raymond Rodly Caesar, S.V.D. (Goroko).

**Paraguay:** Conferencia Episcopal Paraguaya (CEP), Calle Alberdi 782, Casilla Correo 1436, Asuncion. Bp. Felipe Santiago Benitez Avalos (Villarrica).

**Peru:** Conferencia Episcopal Peruana, Apartado 310, Lima 1. Card. Juan Landazuri Ricketts, O.F.M. (Lima).

**Philippine Islands:** Catholic Bishops' Conference of the Philippines (CBCP), P.O. Box 1160, Manila. Antonio Mabutas y Lloren (Davao).

**Poland:** Konferencja Episkopatu Polski, Ul. Wronia 84, 01-015 Warsaw. Card. Jozef Glemp (Gniezno and Warsaw).

**Portugal:** Conferencia Episcopal Portuguesa, Campo dos martires de Patria, 43-1 Esq., 1198 Lisbon. Bp. Manuel D'Almeida Trindade (Aveiro).

**Puerto Rico:** Conferencia Episcopal Puertorriquena (CEP), Apartado 5-1967, San Juan de Puerto Rico 00903. Bp. Juan Fremiot Torres Olivier (Ponce).

**Rhodesia:** See Zimbabwe.

**Rumania:** Vacant.

**Rwanda:** Conference Episcopale du Rwanda (C.Ep.R.), B.P. 715, Kigali. Bp. Joseph Ruzindana (Byumba).

**Scandinavia:** Conferentia Episcopalis Scandiae, Akersvejen 5, P.B. 8270 Hammersborg, Oslo 1, Norway. Bp. John W. Gran, O.C.S.O. (Oslo, Norway).

**Senegal-Mauritania:** Conference Episcopale du Senegal-Mauritania, B.P. 5082, Dakar, Fann. Senegal. Card. Hyacinthe Thiandoum (Dakar).

**Sierra Leone:** See Gambia, Liberia and Sierra Leone.

**Spain:** Conferencia Episcopal Espanola, Calle Anastro 1, Madrid 16. Gabino Diaz Merchan (Oviedo).

**Sri Lanka:** Catholic Bishops' Conference of Sri Lanka, Bishop's House, Chilaw. Bp. Frank Marcus Fernando (Chilaw).

**Sudan:** Sudan Episcopal Conference (SEC), P.O. Box 49, Khartoum. Gabriel Zubeir Wako (Khartoum).

**Switzerland:** Conference des Eveques Suisses, Secretariat, av. Moleson 30, CH-1700 Fribourg 1. Bp. Henri Schivery (Sion).

**Tanzania:** Tanzania Episcopal Conference (TEC), P.O. Box 2133, Dar-es-Salaam. Bp. Anthony Mayala (Musoma).

**Thailand:** Conference des Eveques de Thailand, P.O. Box 5, Nakhonsawan. Bp. Joseph Banchong Aribarg (Nakhon Sawan).

**Togo:** Conference Episcopale du Togo, B.P. 348, Lome. Robert Dosseh Anyron (Lome).

**Turkey:** Conferenza Episcopale di Turchia, Olcek Sokak 83, Harbiya, Istanbul. Bp. Gauthier Pierre Dubois, O.F.M. Cap. (V.A., Istanbul).

**Uganda:** Uganda Episcopal Conference, P.O. Box 2886, Kampala. Bp. Barnabas Halem 'Imana (Kabale).

**United States:** See National Conference of Catholic Bishops.

**Upper Volta and Niger:** Conference des Eveques de la Haute-Volta et du Niger, B.P. 1195, Ouagadougou, Upper Volta. Bp. Tatianma Anselm Sanan (Bobo-Dioulasso, Upper Volta).

**Uruguay:** Conferencia Episcopal Uruguaya (CEU), Avenida Uruguay 1319, Montevideo. Carlos Parteli (Montevideo).

**Venezuela:** Conferencia Episcopal de Venezuela (CEV), Apartado Postal 954, Caracas 101. Domingo Roa Perez (Maracaibo).

**Vietnam:** Conference Episcopale du Vietnam, 40 Pho Nha Chung, Hanoi. Card. Joseph-Marie Trinh van-Can (Hanoi).

**Yugoslavia:** Biskupska Konferencija Jugoslavije, Kaptol 1, 41000, Zagreb. Card. Franjo Kuharic (Zagreb).

**Zaire:** Conference Episcopale du Zaire (CEZ), B.P. 3258, Kinshasa-Gombe. Bp. Kaseba (Kalemie-Kirungu).

**Zambia:** Zambian Episcopal Conference, P.O. Box 31965, Lusaka. Bp. Dennis Harold De Jong (Ndola).

**Zimbabwe:** Zimbabwe Catholic Bishops' Conference (ZCBC), P.O. Box 8135, Causeway, Harare. Patrick Chakaipa (Harare).

*Significant statements on concerns of the Church are framed and published by episcopal conferences for appropriate pastoral action.*

## Territorial Conferences

(Sources: Almanac survey; *Annuario Pontificio.*)

*Territorial as well as national episcopal conferences have been established in some places. Some conferences of this kind are still in the planning stage.*

**Africa:** Symposium of Episcopal Conferences of Africa and Madagascar (SECAM) (Symposium des Conferences Episcopales d'Afrique et de Madagascar, SCEAM): Card. Paul Zoungrano, P.A., Ouagadougou, Upper Volta, president. Address: Secretariat, P.O. Box 9156, Airport, Accra, Ghana.

Association of Member Episcopal Conferences in Eastern Africa (AMECEA): Represents Ethiopia, Kenya, Malawi, Sudan, Tanzania, Uganda and Zambia. The Seychelles was accepted as an affiliate member in 1979, Bp. Medardo Joseph Mazombwe, Chipata, Zambia, president. Address: P.O. Box 21191, Nairobi, Kenya.

Regional Episcopal Conference of French-Speaking West Africa (Conference Episcopale Regionale de l'Afrique de l'Ouest Francophone, CERAO): Bp. Diedonne Yougbare, Koupela, Upper Volta, president. Address: Secretariat General, B.P. 22, Abidjan 08, Ivory Coast.

Association of Episcopal Conferences of Anglophone West Africa (AECAWA): Abp. John Kodwo Amissah, Cape Coast, Ghana, president. Address: P.O. Box 502, Monrovia, Liberia.

Association of Episcopal Conferences of Congo, Central African Republic and Chad (ACECCT): Abp. Joachim N'Dayen, Bangui, Central African Republic, president. Address: Secretariat, B.P. 1518, Bangui, Central African Republic.

Inter-Regional Meeting of Bishops of Southern Africa (IMBISA): The Secretariate, P.O. Box 212, Manzini, Swaziland.

**Asia:** Federation of Asian Bishops' Conferences (FABC): Represents 14 Asian episcopal conferences (excluding the Middle East). Headquarters, P.O. Box 2948, Hong Kong. Established in 1970; statutes approved experimentally Dec. 6, 1972. Abp. Mariano Gaviola Garces, Lipa, Philippines, secretary general.

**Europe:** Council of European Bishops' Conferences (Consilium Conferentiarum Episcopalium Europae, CCEE): Card. George Basil Hume, O.S.B., Westminster, England, president. Address of secretariat: Klosterhof 6b, CH-9000 St. Gallen, Switzerland.

Commission of the Episcopates of the European Community (Commissio Episcopatuum Communitatis Europaeae, COMECE): Established in 1980; represents episcopates of states which belong to European Community. Bp. Jean Hengen, Luxembourg, president. Address of secretariat: 13 Avenue Pere Damien, 1150 Brussels, Belgium.

**Central and South America:** Latin American Bishops' Conference (Consejo Episcopal LatinoAmericano, CELAM): Established in 1956; statutes approved Nov. 9, 1974. Represents 22 Latin American national bishops' conferences. Bp. Antonio Quarracino, Avellaneda, Argentina, president. Address of the secretariat: Calle 78, no. 11-17, Apartado Aereo 5278, Bogota, D.E., Colombia.

Episcopal Secretariat of Central America and Panama (Secretariado Episcopal de America Central y Panama, SEDAC): Statutes approved experimentally Sept. 26, 1970. Abp. Roman Arrieta Villalobos, San Jose de Costa Rica, president. Address of secretariat: Apartado 497, San Jose, Costa Rica.

## INTERNATIONAL CATHOLIC ORGANIZATIONS

(Principal sources: Conference of International Catholic Organizations; Pontifical Council for the Laity; Almanac survey.)

### Guidelines

International organizations wanting to call themselves "Catholic" are required to meet standards set by the Vatican's Council for the Laity and to register with and get the approval of the Papal Secretariat of State, according to guidelines dated Dec. 3 and published in *Acta Apostolicae Sedis* under date of Dec. 23, 1971.

Among conditions for the right of organizations to "bear the name Catholic" are:

• leaders "will always be Catholics," and candidates for office will be approved by the Secretariat of State;

• adherence by the organization to the Catholic Church, its teaching authority and teachings of the Gospel;

• evidence that the organization is really international with a universal outlook and that it fulfills its mission through its own management, meetings and accomplishments.

The guidelines also stated that leaders of the organizations "will take care to maintain necessary reserve as regards taking a stand or engaging in public activity in the field of politics or trade unionism. Abstention in these fields will normally be the best attitude for them to adopt during their term of office."

The guidelines were in line with a provision stated by the Second Vatican Council in the *Decree on the Apostolate of the Laity*: "No project may claim the name 'Catholic' unless it has obtained the consent of the lawful church authority."

They made it clear that all organizations are not obliged to apply for recognition, but that the Church "reserves the right to recognize as linked with her mission and her aims those organizations or movements which see fit to ask for such recognition."

### Conference

**Conference of International Catholic Organizations:** A permanent body for collaboration among various organizations which seek to promote the development of international life along the lines of Christian principles. Eleven international Catholic organizations participated in its foundation and first meeting in 1927 at Fribourg, Switzerland. In 1951, the conference established its general secretariat and adopted governing statutes which were approved by the Vatican Secretariat of State in 1953.

The permanent secretariat is located at 37-39 rue de Vermont, CH-1202 Geneva, Switzerland. Other office addresses are: 1 rue de Varembe, C.P. 43, CH-1211 Geneva 20, Switzerland (Information Center); 9, rue Cler, F-75007 Paris, France (International Catholic Center for UNESCO); ICO Information Center, 323 East 47th St., New York, N.Y. 10017.

### International Organizations

International Catholic organizations are listed below. Information includes name, date and place of establishment (when available), address of general secretariat. An asterisk indicates that the organization is a member of the Conference of International Catholic Organizations. Approximately 30 of the organizations have consultative status with other international or regional non-governmental agencies.

**Apostleship of Prayer** (1849): Borgo Santo Spirito 5, I-00193 Rome, Italy. National secretariat in most countries. (See Index.)

**Apostolatus Maris (Apostleship of the Sea)** (1922, Glasgow, Scotland): Pontifical Commission for Migration and Tourism, Palazzo San Calisto, I-00120 Vatican City. (See Index.)

**Associationes Juventutis Salesianae (Associations of Salesian Youth)** (1847): Via della Pisana, 1111, 00163 Rome, Italy.

**Blue Army of Our Lady of Fatima:** (See Index.)

**Caritas Internationalis\*** (1951, Rome, Italy): Piazza San Calisto 16, I-00153, Rome, Italy. Coordinates relief aid on an international level.

**Catholic International Education Office\*** (1952): 60, rue des Eburons, B-1040 Brussels, Belgium.

**Catholic International Federation for Physical and Sports Education** (1911; present name, 1957): 5, rue Cernuschi, F-75017 Paris, France.

**Catholic International Union for Social Service\*** (1925, Milan, Italy): rue de la Poste 111, B-1030 Brussels, Belgium (general secretariat).

**Christian Fraternity of the Sick and Handicapped:** 9, Avenue de la Gare, CH-1630, Bulle, Switzerland.

**"Focolari"** (1943, Trent, Italy): Via di Frascati, 302, I-00040 Rocca di Papa (Rome), Italy. (See Index: Focolare Movement.)

**International Alliance of Joan of Arc** (1911, in England): 15 London Rd., Canterbury (Kent) CT2 LR, England.

**International Association of Charities of St. Vincent de Paul\*** (1617, Chatillon les Dombes, France): 38, rue d'Alsace-Lorraine, B-1050 Brussels, Belgium. (See Index: St. Vincent de Paul Society.)

**International Association of Children of Mary** (1847): 67 rue de Sèvres, F-75006 Paris, France.

**International Catholic Association for Service to Young Women\*** (1897): Case Postale n 22, CH-1211 Geneva 20 CIC, Switzerland. Welfare of Catholic girls living away from home.

**International Catholic Auxiliaries** (1937, Belgium): 91, rue de la Servette, CH-1202 Geneva, Switzerland.

**International Catholic Child Bureau\*** (1947): 65, rue de Lausanne, CH-1202 Geneva, Switzerland.

**International Catholic Conference of Guiding\*** (1965): Rue Paul-Emile Janson, 35, B-1050 Brussels, Belgium. Founded by member bodies of interdenominational World Association of Guides and Girl Scouts.

**International Catholic Conference of Scouting\*** (1948): 21, rue de Dublin, B-1050 Brussels, Belgium.

**International Catholic Film and Audiovisual Organization\*** (1928, The Hague, The Netherlands): 8, rue de l'Orme, B-1040 Brussels, Belgium (general secretariat). Federation of national Catholic film offices.

**International Catholic Migration Commission\*** (1951): 37-39 rue de Vermont, C.P. 96, CH-1211 Geneva 20, Switzerland. Coordinates Catholic activities to help migrants.

**International Catholic Rural Association** (1962, Rome): Palazzo San Calisto, I-00120 Vatican City. International body for agricultural and rural organizations.

**International Catholic Union of the Press\*:** 37-39 rue de Vermont, Case Postale 197 CH-1211 Geneva 20 CIC, Switzerland. Coordinates and represents at the international level the activities of Catholics and Catholic federations or associations in the field of press and information. Has five specialized branches: International Federation of Catholic Dailies and Periodicals (1928); International Federation of Catholic Journalists (1927); International Federation of Catholic Press Agencies (1950); International Catholic Association of Teachers and Scientific or Technical Research Workers on Information (1968); Federation of Church Press Associations (1974).

**International Centre for Studies in Religious Education** (1934-35, Louvain, Belgium, under name Catechetical Documentary Centre; present name, 1956): 184, rue Washington, B-1050 Brussels, Belgium. Also referred to as Lumen Vitae Centre; concerned with all aspects of religious formation.

**International Committee for the Blind:** 8, rue Francois-Elie Dujenne, St. Satur, F-18300 Sancerre, France.

**International Committee of Catholic Nurses and Medical Social Workers\*** (1933): Palazzo San Calisto, 00120 Vatican City.

**International Cooperation for Socio-Economic Development** (1965, Rome, Italy): 104, Avenue Princess Elisabeth, B-1030 Brussels, Belgium.

**International Crusade for the Blind** (1957): Chamblious 18, CH-1700 Fribourg, Switzerland. Coordinates action of Catholic groups and associations for the blind and develops their apostolate.

**International Federation of Catholic Medical Associations** (1954): Palazzo San Calisto, I-00120 Vatican City.

**International Federation of Catholic Men\*** (Unum Omnes) (1948): Palazzo San Calisto, I-00120 Vatican City.

**International Federation of Catholic Parochial**

**Youth Communities\*** (1962, Rome, Italy): Kipdorp 30, B-2000 Antwerp, Belgium.

**International Federation of Catholic Pharmacists\*** (1954): 59, Bergstrasse, B-4700 Eupen, Belgium.

**International Federation of Catholic Rural Movements\*** (1964, Lisbon, Portugal): 92, rue Africaine, B-1050 Brussels, Belgium.

**International Federation of Catholic Universities\*** (1949): 78A, rue de Sevres, F-75341 Paris Cedex 7, France.

**International Federation of Institutes for Social and Socio-Religious Research** (1952): Vlamingenstraat, 116, B-3000 Leuven, Belgium.

**International Military Apostolate** (1967): 20, rue Notre-Dame des Champs, F-75006 Paris, France. Comprised of organizations of military men.

**International Movement of Apostolate of Children\*** (1929, France): 8, rue Duguay-Trouin, F-75006 Paris, France.

**International Movement of Apostolate in Middle and Upper Classes\*** (1963): Palazzo San Calisto, I-00120 Vatican City. Evangelization of adults of the independent milieus (that part of population known as old or recent middle class, aristocracy, bourgeoisie or "white collar").

**International Movement of Catholic Agricultural and Rural Youth** (1954, Annevoie, Belgium): Tiensevest 68, B-3000 Leuven, Belgium (permanent secretariat).

**International Young Catholic Students\*** (1946, Fribourg, Switzerland; present name, 1954): 171 rue de Rennes, F-75006 Paris, France.

**International Young Christian Workers\*** (1925, Belgium): 11, rue Plantin, B-1070 Brussels, Belgium.

**Legion of Mary** (1921, Dublin, Ireland): De Montfort House, North Brunswick St., Dublin, Ireland. (See Index.)

**Medicus Mundi:** P.O. Box 1547, 6501 BN Nijmegen, Netherlands. Place medicine at service of poor.

**Movement for a Better World** (1952): Via Vinovo, 58, 00166, Rome, Italy. (See Index.)

**Our Lady's Teams (Equipes Notre-Dame)** (1937, France): 49, rue de la Glacière, F-75013 Paris, France. Movement for spiritual formation of couples.

**Pax Christi International** (1950): Kerkstraat, 150, B-2000 Antwerp, Belgium. (See Index.)

**Pax Romana\*** (1921, Fribourg, Switzerland, divided into two movements, 1947):

**International Movement of Catholic Students\*** (1921): 171, rue de Rennes, F-75006, Paris, France. For undergraduates.

**International Movement of Catholic Intellectuals\*** (1947): 37-39 rue de Vermont, Case Postale n 85, CH-1211 Geneva 20 CIC, Switzerland. For university graduates.

**Salesian Cooperators** (1876): Don Bosco College, Newton, N.J. 07860. Third Salesian family founded by St. John Bosco. Members commit themselves to an apostolate at the service of the Church, giving particular attention to youth in the Salesian spirit and style.

**Secular Franciscan Order** (1221, first Rule approved): Via Piemonte, 70, 00187, Rome, Italy. (See Index.)

**Serra International** (1953, in U.S.): (See Index.)

**Society of St. Vincent de Paul** (1933): 5, rue Pré-aux-Clercs, F-75007 Paris, France.

**The Grail** (1921, Nijmegen, The Netherlands): Duisburgerstrasse 470, D-4330, Mulheim, West Germany. (See Index.)

**Third Order of St. Dominic** (1285): Convento Santa Sabina, Piazza Pietro d'Illiria, Aventino, I-00153 Rome, Italy. (See Index.)

**Unda: International Catholic Association for Radio and Television** (1928, Cologne, Germany): rue de l'Orme, 12, B-1040 Brussels, Belgium. (See Index.)

**Unio Internationalis Laicorum in Servitio Ecclesiae** (1965, Aachen, Germany): Postfach 990125, Am Kielshof 2, 5000 Cologne, Germany 91. Consists of national and diocesan associations of persons who give professional services to the Church.

**Union of Adorers of the Blessed Sacrament** (1937): Largo dei Monti Parioli 3, I-00197, Rome, Italy.

**World Catholic Federation for the Biblical Apostolate** (1969, Rome): Mittelstrasse, 12, D 7000, Stuttgart 1, Germany.

**World Federation of Christian Life Communities** (1953): 8, Borgo Santo Spirito, C.P.

6139, I-00195, Rome, Italy. First Sodality of Our Lady founded in 1563.

**World Movement of Christian Workers** (1961): 90, rue des Palais, B-1030 Brussels, Belgium.

**World Organization of Former Students of Catholic Schools** (1967, Rome): Largo Nazareno 25, I-00187 Rome, Italy.

**World Union of Catholic Philosophical Societies** (1948, Amsterdam, The Netherlands): The Catholic University of America, Washington, D.C. 20064.

**World Union of Catholic Teachers** (1951): Palazzo San Calisto, I-00120 Vatican City.

**World Union of Catholic Women's Organizations** (1910): 20, rue Notre Dame des Champs, F-75006 Paris, France.

## Regional Organizations

**European Federation for Catholic Adult Education** (1963, Lucerne, Switzerland): Bildunghaus Turnseestrasse 24, D-7800, Freiburg 1. B2, Germany.

**European Forum of National Committees of the Laity** (1968): 12, Brookwood Lawn Artane, Dublin 5, Ireland.

**Movimiento Familiar Cristiano** (1949-50, Montevideo and Buenos Aires): Carrera 17 n. 4671, Bogota, D.E., Colombia. Christian Family Movement of Latin America.

# AMERICAN CATHOLIC AWARDS

**Aquinas Medal,** by the American Catholic Philosophical Association for outstanding contributions to the field of Catholic philosophy. Jean T. Oesterle (1984).

**Bellarmine Medal** (1955), by Bellarmine College (Louisville, Ky.), to persons in national or international affairs who, in controversial matters, exemplify the characteristics of St. Robert Bellarmine in charity, justice and temperateness. Ambassador Philip C. Habib (1984).

**Berakah Award** (1976), by the North American Academy of Liturgy, to recognize distinguished contribution to the professional work of liturgy by a liturgist or person of an allied vocation. Eugene L. Brand (1984).

**Borromeo Award** (1960), by Carroll College (Helena, Mont.), for zeal, courage and devotion in the spirit of St. Charles Borromeo. Sisters of Charity of Leavenworth (1984).

**Brent Award** (1976), by the Diocese of Arlington, Va., for distinguished service to fellowman. Most Rev. Thomas J. Welsh (1984).

**Campion Award** (1955), by the Catholic Book Club for distinguished service in Catholic letters. Raymond E. Brown, S.S. (1984).

**Cardinal Gibbons Medal** (1949) by the Alumni Association of the Catholic University of America for distinguished and meritorious service to the Church, the United States or the Catholic University. Bruce Ritter O.F.M. Conv. (1984).

**Cardinal Spellman Award** (1947), by the Catho-

lic Theological Society for outstanding achievement in the field of theology. Raymond E. Brown, S.S. (1971). For recipients after 1971, see John Courtney Murray Award.

**The Catholic University of America Patronal Medal** (1974), by the University for outstanding contributions to the Catholic Church and in promoting interest and devotion to Mary, patroness of the University. Eugene F. Kennedy and John McShain (1983).

**Cecilia Medal** (1952), by the Music Department of Boys Town (Nebr.) for outstanding work in liturgical music. Evelyn Letter (1980).

**Christian Culture Award** (1941), by Assumption University (Canada) to outstanding lay exponents of Christian ideals. Robert E. Rambusch (1984).

**Collegian Award** (1949), by "The Collegian," weekly student newspaper of La Salle College (Phila.), for public service in the field of communications. Lawrence M. O'Rourke (1978).

**Compostela Award, The** (1982), by the Cathedral-Basilica of St. James (Diocese of Brooklyn) to men and women whose lives represent the noblest ideals of the cathedral tradition of fidelity to justice, truth, beauty and peace. Celeste Holm, Archbishop Iakovos, Joseph Papp and Eudora Welty (1984).

**Damien-Dutton Award** (1953), by the Damien-Dutton Society for service toward conquest of leprosy or for the promotion of better understanding of social problems connected with the disease. Mother Teresa of Calcutta (1984).

# THE CATHOLIC CHURCH IN CANADA

The first date in the remote background of the Catholic history of Canada was July 7, 1534, when a priest in the exploration company of Jacques Cartier celebrated Mass on the Gaspe Peninsula.

Successful colonization and the significant beginnings of the Catholic history of the country date from the foundation of Quebec in 1608 by Samuel de Champlain and French settlers. Montreal was established in 1642.

The earliest missionaries were Franciscan Recollects and Jesuits who arrived in 1615 and 1625, respectively. They provided some pastoral care for the settlers but worked mainly among the 100,000 Indians — Algonquins, Hurons and Iroquois — in the interior and in the Lake Ontario region. Eight of the Jesuit missionaries, killed in the 1640s, were canonized in 1930. (See Index: Jesuit North American Martyrs.) Sulpician Fathers, who arrived in Canada late in the 1640s, played a part in the great missionary period which ended about 1700.

Kateri Tekakwitha, "Lily of the Mohawks," who was baptized in 1676 and died in 1680, was declared "Blessed" June 22, 1980.

The communities of women religious with the longest histories in Canada are the Canonesses of St. Augustine, since 1637; the Ursulines, since 1639; and the Hospitallers of St. Joseph, since 1642. Communities of Canadian origin are the Congregation of Notre Dame, founded by St. Marguerite Bourgeoys in 1658, and the Grey Nuns, formed by Bl. Marie Marguerite d'Youville in 1738.

Mother Marie (Guyard) of the Incarnation, an Ursuline nun, was one of the first three women missionaries to New France; called "Mother of the Church in Canada," she was declared "Blessed" June 22, 1980.

## Start of Church Organization

Ecclesiastical organization began with the appointment in 1658 of Francois De Montmorency-Laval, "Father of the Church in Canada," as vicar apostolic of New France. He was the first bishop of Quebec from 1674 to 1688, with jurisdiction over all French-claimed territory in North America. He was declared "Blessed" June 22, 1980.

In 1713, the French Canadian population numbered 18,000. In the same year, the Treaty of Utrecht ceded Acadia, Newfoundland and the Hudson Bay Territory to England. The Acadians were scattered among the American Colonies in 1755.

The English acquired possession of Canada and its 70,000 French-speaking inhabitants in virtue of the Treaty of Paris in 1763. Anglo-French and Anglican-Catholic differences and tensions developed. The pro-British government at first refused to recognize the titles of church officials, hindered the clergy in their work and tried to install a non-Catholic educational system. Laws were passed which guaranteed religious liberties to Catholics (Quebec Act of 1774, Constitutional Act of 1791, legislation approved by Queen Victoria

in 1851), but it took some time before actual respect for these liberties matched the legal enactments. The initial moderation of government antipathy toward the Church was caused partly by the loyalty of Catholics to the Crown during the American Revolution and the War of 1812.

## Growth

The 15 years following the passage in 1840 of the Act of Union, which joined Upper and Lower Canada, were significant. New communities of men and women religious joined those already in the country. The Oblates of Mary Immaculate, missionaries par excellence in Canada, advanced the penetration of the West which had been started in 1818 by Abbe Provencher. New jurisdictions were established, and Quebec became a metropolitan see in 1844. The first Council of Quebec was held in 1851. The established Catholic school system enjoyed a period of growth.

Laval University was inaugurated in 1854 and canonically established in 1876.

Archbishop Elzear-Alexandre Taschereau of Quebec was named Canada's first cardinal in 1886.

The apostolic delegation to Canada was set up in 1899. It became a nunciature October 16, 1969, with the establishment of diplomatic relations with the Vatican.

Early in this century, Canada had eight ecclesiastical provinces, 23 dioceses, three vicariates apostolic, 3,500 priests, 2.4 million Catholics, about 30 communities of men religious, and 70 or more communities of women religious. The Church in Canada was phased out of mission status and removed from the jurisdiction of the Congregation for the Propagation of the Faith in 1908.

## Diverse Population

The greatest concentration of Catholics is in the eastern portion of the country. In the northern and western portions, outside metropolitan centers, there are some of the most difficult parish and mission areas in the world. Bilingual (English-French) differences in the general population are reflected in the Church; for example, in the parallel structures of the Canadian Conference of Catholic Bishops, which was established in 1943. Quebec is the center of French cultural influence. Many language groups are represented among Catholics, who include about 211,265 members of Eastern Rite in a metropolitan see, six eparchies and an apostolic exarchate.

Education, a past source of friction between the Church and the government, is administered by the civil provinces in a variety of arrangements authorized by the Canadian Constitution. Denominational schools have tax support in one way in Quebec and Newfoundland, and in another way in Alberta, Ontario and Saskatchewan. Several provinces provide tax support only for public schools, making private financing necessary for separate church-related schools.

## ECCLESIASTICAL JURISDICTIONS OF CANADA

### Provinces

Names of ecclesiastical provinces and metropolitan sees in bold face: suffragan sees in parentheses.

**Edmonton** (Calgary, St. Paul).

**Grouard-McLennan** (Mackenzie-Ft. Smith, Prince George, Whitehorse).

**Halifax** (Antigonish, Charlottetown, Yarmouth).

**Keewatin-LePas** (Churchill-Hudson Bay, Labrador-Schefferville, Moosonee).

**Kingston** (Alexandria-Cornwall, Peterborough, Sault Ste. Marie).

**Moncton** (Bathurst, Edmundston, St. John).

**Montreal** (Joliette, St. Jean-Longueuil, St. Jerome, Valleyfield).

**Ottawa** (Gatineau-Hull, Hearst, Mont-Laurier, Pembroke, Rouyn-Noranda, Timmins).

**Quebec** (Amos, Chicoutimi, Ste.-Anne-de-la-Pocatiere, Trois Rivieres).

**Regina** (Gravelbourg, Prince Albert, Saskatoon, Abbey of St. Peter).

**Rimouski** (Gaspe, Hauterive).

**St. Boniface** (no suffragans).

**St. John's** (Grand Falls, St. George).

**Sherbrooke** (Nicolet, St. Hyacinthe).

**Toronto** (Hamilton, London, St. Catharines, Thunder Bay).

**Vancouver** (Kamloops, Nelson, Victoria).

**Winnipeg** — Ukrainian (Edmonton, New Westminster, Saskatoon, Toronto).

**Jurisdictions immediately subject to the Holy See:** Roman-Rite Archdiocese of Winnipeg, Byzantine-Rite Eparchy of Sts. Cyril and Methodius for Slovaks, Byzantine-Rite Apostolic Exarchate for Greek Melkites; Antiochene-Rite Eparchy of St. Maron of Montreal for Maronites.

### Archdioceses, Archbishops

**Edmonton, Alta.** (St. Albert, 1871; archdiocese, transferred Edmonton, 1912): Joseph N. MacNeil, archbishop, 1973.

**Grouard-McLennan, Alta.** (v.a. Athabaska-Mackenzie, 1862; Grouard, 1927; archdiocese Grouard-McLennan, 1967); Henri Legare, O.M.I., archbishop, 1972.

**Halifax, N.S.** (1842; archdiocese, 1852): James M. Hayes, archbishop, 1967.

**Keewatin-Le Pas, Man.** (v.a., 1910; archdiocese, 1967): Paul Dumouchel, O.M.I., archbishop, 1967.

**Kingston, Ont.** (1826; archdiocese, 1889): Francis J. Spence, archbishop, 1982.

**Moncton, N.B.** (1936): Donat Chiasson, archbishop, 1972.

**Montreal, Que.** (1836; archdiocese, 1886): Paul Gregoire, archbishop, 1968. Andre Cimichella, O.S.M., Leonard Crowley, Gerard Tremblay, P.S.S., Jude Saint-Antoine, Jean-Claude Turcotte, auxiliaries.

**Ottawa, Ont.** (Bytown, 1847, name changed, 1854; archdiocese, 1886): Joseph Aurele Plourde, archbishop, 1967. John Beahen, Gilles Belisle, auxiliaries.

**Quebec, Que.** (v.a., 1658; diocese, 1674; archdiocese, 1819; metropolitan, 1844; primatial see, 1956): Louis-Albert Vachon, archbishop, 1981. Jean-Paul Labrie, Maurice Couture, Marc Leclerc, auxiliaries.

**Regina, Sask.** (1910; archdiocese, 1915): Charles A. Halpin, archbishop, 1973.

**Rimouski, Que.** (1867; archdiocese, 1946): Gilles Ouellet, P.M.E., archbishop, 1973.

**St. Boniface, Man.** (1847; archdiocese, 1871): Antoine Hacault, archbishop, 1974.

**St. John's, Nfld.** (p.a., 1784; v.a., 1796; diocese, 1847; archdiocese, 1904): Alphonsus Penney, archbishop, 1979.

**Sherbrooke, Que.** (1874; archdiocese, 1951); J.-M. Fortier, archbishop, 1968.

**Toronto, Ont.** (1841; archdiocese, 1870): Cardinal G. Emmett Carter, archbishop, 1978. Aloysius M. Ambrozic, Michael Pearse Lacey, Robert B. Clune, Leonard J. Wall, auxiliaries.

**Vancouver, B. C.** (v.a. British Columbia, 1863; diocese New Westminster, 1890; archdiocese Vancouver, 1908): James F. Carney, archbishop, 1969.

**Winnipeg, Man.** (1915): Adam Exner, O.M.I, archbishop, 1982.

**Winnipeg, Man. (Ukrainian Byzantine Rite)** (Ordinariate of Canada, 1912; ap. ex. Central Canada, 1948; ap. ex. Manitoba, 1951; archdiocese Winnipeg, 1956): Maxim Hermaniuk, C.SS.R., archbishop, 1956. Myron Daciuk, O.S.B.M., auxiliary.

### Dioceses, Bishops

**Alexandria-Cornwall, Ont.** (1890): Eugene Philippe LaRocque, bishop, 1974.

**Amos, Que.** (1938): Gerard Drainville, bishop, 1978.

**Antigonish, N.S.** (Arichat, 1844; transferred, 1886): William E. Power, bishop, 1960.

**Bathurst, N.B.** (Chatham, 1860; transferred, 1938): Edgar Godin, bishop, 1969.

**Calgary, Alta.** (1912): Paul J. O'Byrne, bishop, 1968.

**Charlottetown, P.E.I.** (1829): James H. MacDonald, C.S.C., bishop, 1982.

**Chicoutimi, Que.** (1878): Jean-Guy Couture, bishop, 1979. Roch Pedneault, auxiliary.

**Churchill-Hudson Bay, Man.** (p.a., 1925; v.a. Hudson Bay, 1931; diocese Churchill, 1967; Churchill-Hudson Bay, 1968): Omer Robidoux, O.M.I., bishop, 1970.

**Edmonton, Alta.** (Ukrainian Byzantine Rite) (ap. ex., 1948; diocese, 1956): Nile Nicholas Savaryn, O.S.B.M., bishop, 1948. Martin Greschuk, apostolic administrator.

**Edmundston, N.B.** (1944): Gerard Dionne, bishop, 1983.

**Gaspe, Que.** (1922): Bertrand Blanchet, bishop, 1973.

**Gatineau-Hull, Que.** (1963 as Hull; name changed, 1982); Adolphe E. Proulx, bishop, 1974.

**Grand Falls, Nfld.** (Harbour Grace, 1856; present title, 1964): Joseph Faber MacDonald, bishop, 1980.

**Gravelbourg, Sask.** (1930): Noel Delaquis, bishop, 1974.

**Hamilton, Ont.** (1856): Anthony Tonnos, bishop, 1984.

**Hauterive, Que.** (p.a., 1882; v.a., 1905; diocese Gulf of St. Lawrence, 1945; name changed, 1960): Roger Ebacher, bishop, 1979.

**Hearst, Ont.** (p.a., 1918; v.a., 1920; diocese, 1938): Roger Despatie, bishop, 1973.

**Joliette, Que.** (1904): Rene Audet, bishop, 1968.

**Kamloops, B.C.** (1945): Lawrence Sabatini, C.S., bishop, 1982.

**Labrador (Nfld.)-Schefferville, Que.** (v.a. Labrador, 1945; diocese, 1967): Peter A. Sutton, O.M.I., bishop, 1974.

**London, Ont.** (1855; transferred Sandwich, 1859; London, 1869): John Sherlock, bishop, 1978. Marcel Gervais, auxiliary.

**Mackenzie-Fort Smith, N.W.T.** (v.a. Mackenzie, 1901; diocese Mackenzie-Fort Smith, 1967): Paul Piché, O.M.I., bishop, 1967.

**Mont-Laurier, Que.** (1913): Jean Gratton, bishop, 1978.

**Moosonee, Ont.** (v.a. James Bay, 1938; diocese Moosonee, 1967): Jules LeGuerrier, O.M.I., bishop, 1967.

**Nelson, B.C.** (1936): Wilfred Emmett Doyle, bishop, 1958.

**New Westminster, B.C.** (Ukrainian Byzantine Rite) (1974): Jerome Chimy, O.S.B.M., bishop, 1974.

**Nicolet, Que.** (1885): Albertus Martin, bishop, 1950.

**Pembroke, Ont.** (v.a. 1882; diocese, 1898): Joseph R. Windle, bishop, 1971.

**Peterborough, Ont.** (1882): James L. Doyle, bishop, 1976.

**Prince Albert, Sask.** (v.a., 1890; diocese, 1907): Blaise Morand, bishop, 1983.

**Prince George, B.C.** (p.a., 1908; v.a. Yukon and Prince Rupert, 1944; diocese Prince George, 1967): J. Fergus O'Grady, O.M.I., bishop, 1967.

**Rouyn-Noranda, Que.** (1973): Jean-Guy Hamelin, bishop, 1974.

**St. Catharines, Ont.** (1958): Thomas B. Fulton, bishop, 1978.

**St. George's, Nfld.** (p.a., 1870; v.a., 1890; diocese, 1904): Richard T. McGrath, bishop, 1970.

**St. Hyacinthe, Que.** (1852): Louis-de-Gonzague Langevin, bishop, 1979.

**Saint-Jean-Longueuil, Que.** (1933 as St.-Jean-de-Quebec; named changed, 1982): Bernard Hubert, bishop, 1978.

**St. Jerome, Que.** (1951): Charles Valois, bishop, 1977. Raymond Saint-Gelais, auxiliary.

**Saint John, N.B.** (1842): Arthur J. Gilbert, bishop, 1974. J. Edward Troy, coadjutor.

**St. Maron of Montreal** (Maronites) (1982); Elias Shaheen, eparch, 1982.

**St. Paul in Alberta** (1948): Raymond Roy, bishop, 1972.

**Sts. Cyril and Methodius, Toronto, Ont.** (Slovakian Byzantine Rite) (1981): Michael Rusnak, C.Ss.R., bishop, 1981.

**Sainte-Anne-de-la-Pocatiere, Que.** (1951): C.-H. Levesque, bishop, 1968.

**Saskatoon, Sask.** (1933): James P. Mahoney, bishop, 1967.

**Saskatoon, Sask.** (Ukrainian Byzantine Rite) (ap. ex., 1951; diocese, 1956): Basil (Wasyl) Filevich, bishop, 1984.

**Sault Ste. Marie, Ont.** (1904): Alexander Carter, bishop, 1958. Bernard F. Pappin, auxiliary.

**Thunder Bay, Ont.** (Ft. William, 1952; transferred, 1970): John A. O'Mara, bishop, 1976.

**Timmins, Ont.** (v.a. Temiskaming, 1908; diocese Haileybury, 1915; present title, 1938): Jacques Landriault, bishop, 1971.

**Toronto, Ont.** (Ukrainian Byzantine Rite) (ap. ex., 1948; diocese, 1956): Isidore Borecky, bishop, 1948.

**Trois-Rivieres, Que.** (1852): Laurent Noel, bishop, 1975.

**Valleyfield, Que.** (1892): Robert Lebel, bishop, 1976.

**Victoria, B.C.** (diocese Vancouver Is., 1846; archdiocese, 1903; diocese Victoria, 1908): Remi J. De Roo, bishop, 1962.

**Whitehorse, Y.T.** (v.a., 1944; diocese 1967): Hubert P. O'Connor, O.M.I., bishop, 1971.

**Yarmouth, N.S.** (1953): Austin-Emile Burke, bishop, 1968.

**Apostolic Exarchate for Greek Melkites** (Montreal, Que.) (1980): Archbishop Michel Hakim, B.S., exarch, 1980.

**Military Vicariate of Canada** (1951): Archbishop Francis J. Spence, military vicar.

**Abbacy of St. Peter, Muenster, Sask.** (1921): Jerome Weber, O.S.B. (blessed, 1960).

An **Apostolic Exarchate for Armenian-Rite Catholics in Canada and the United States** was established in July, 1981, with headquarters in New York City.

### Dioceses with Interprovincial Lines

The following dioceses, indicated by + in the table, have interprovincial lines.

**Churchill-Hudson Bay** includes part of Northwest Territories.

**Keewatin-Le Pas** includes part of Manitoba and Saskatchewan provinces.

**Labrador-Schefferville** includes the Labrador region of Newfoundland and the northern part of Quebec province.

**MacKenzie-Fort Smith, Northwest Territories,** includes part of Alberta and Saskatchewan provinces.

**Moosonee, Ont.,** includes part of Quebec province.

**Pembroke, Ont.,** includes one county of Quebec province.

**Whitehorse, Y.T.,** includes part of British Columbia.

The purpose of the **House of Prayer Experience** is to help active religious, priests and lay persons to acquire a contemporary style of contemplative life for renewal, inner growth and a more joyful personal and communal life in the light of the Gospel. The result sought is an apostolic spirituality integrating prayer with action in ministry and witness, especially for justice and peace.

## STATISTICS OF CATHOLIC CHURCH IN CANADA

(Principal source: *1984 Directory of the Canadian Conference of Catholic Bishops.* Permanent deacon statistics are from the *1984 Annuario Pontificio.* Archdioceses are indicated by an asterisk. For dioceses marked +, see Canadian Dioceses with Interprovincial Lines.)

Canada's 10 civil provinces and two territories are divided into 17 ecclesiastical provinces consisting of 17 metropolitan sees (archdioceses) and 52 suffragan sees (51 dioceses and one abbacy); there are also one archdiocese, one eparchy and one exarchate immediately subject to the Holy See. (See listing of Ecclesiastical Provinces elsewhere in this section.)

This table presents a regional breakdown of Catholic statistics. In some cases, the totals are approximate because diocesan boundaries fall within several civil provinces.

| Civil Province Diocese | Cath. Pop. | Dioc. Priests | Rel. Priests | Total Priests | Perm. Deacs. | Bros. | Srs. | Parishes |
|---|---|---|---|---|---|---|---|---|
| Newfoundland | 202,458 | 122 | 36 | 158 | — | 86 | 502 | 217 |
| *St. John's | 112,698 | 57 | 19 | 76 | — | 57 | 334 | 88 |
| Grand Falls | 35,453 | 30 | 2 | 32 | — | 16 | 75 | 45 |
| Labrador-Schefferville+ | 14,381 | 3 | 14 | 17 | — | 5 | 28 | 24 |
| St. George's | 39,926 | 32 | 1 | 33 | — | 8 | 65 | 60 |
| **Prince Edward Island** | | | | | | | | |
| Charlottetown | 51,504 | 77 | 2 | 79 | 1 | — | 235 | 57 |
| Nova Scotia | 278,554 | 284 | 58 | 342 | 14 | 7 | 1,047 | 221 |
| *Halifax | 115,000 | 74 | 27 | 101 | 14 | 1 | 461 | 51 |
| Antigonish | 127,024 | 189 | 9 | 198 | — | 6 | 523 | 127 |
| Yarmouth | 36,530 | 21 | 22 | 43 | — | — | 63 | 43 |
| New Brunswick | 360,666 | 308 | 114 | 422 | 2 | 47 | 1,153 | 273 |
| *Moncton | 87,330 | 80 | 56 | 136 | — | 24 | 390 | 60 |
| Bathurst | 113,405 | 85 | 27 | 112 | — | 12 | 338 | 69 |
| Edmundston | 54,931 | 56 | 15 | 71 | — | 10 | 190 | 37 |
| St. John | 105,000 | 87 | 16 | 103 | 2 | 1 | 235 | 107 |
| Quebec | 5,693,977 | 4,188 | 2,469 | 6,657 | 144 | 3,204 | 24,381 | 1,909 |
| *Montreal | 1,499,200 | 767 | 965 | 1,732 | 34 | 864 | 7,622 | 283 |
| *Quebec | 996,765 | 821 | 490 | 1,311 | 47 | 581 | 5,890 | 274 |
| *Rimouski | 164,661 | 197 | 44 | 241 | 1 | 47 | 944 | 121 |
| *Sherbrooke | 253,116 | 311 | 133 | 444 | 6 | 185 | 1,430 | 145 |
| Amos | 102,116 | 92 | 22 | 114 | — | 22 | 300 | 81 |
| Chicoutimi | 272,388 | 290 | 80 | 370 | 4 | 119 | 911 | 95 |
| Gaspe | 104,822 | 104 | 18 | 122 | 1 | 15 | 260 | 66 |
| Gatineau-Hull | 186,000 | 85 | 57 | 142 | 2 | — | 368 | 62 |
| Hauterive | 104,652 | 60 | 31 | 91 | 4 | 34 | 266 | 51 |
| Joliette | 162,963 | 140 | 59 | 199 | 1 | 144 | 591 | 58 |
| Mont Laurier | 71,963 | 73 | 33 | 106 | — | 56 | 207 | 59 |
| Nicolet | 170,591 | 225 | 35 | 260 | 9 | 133 | 1,070 | 85 |
| Rouyn-Noranda | 55,125 | 33 | 25 | 58 | — | 16 | 169 | 44 |
| Ste.-Anne-de-la-Pocatiere | 91,958 | 182 | 10 | 192 | — | 12 | 396 | 54 |
| St. Hyacinthe | 306,445 | 237 | 121 | 358 | 22 | 399 | 1,583 | 115 |
| St. Jean-Longueuil | 463,135 | 158 | 87 | 245 | — | 129 | 684 | 89 |
| St. Jerome | 242,620 | 110 | 122 | 232 | 2 | 145 | 323 | 66 |
| Trois Rivieres | 249,030 | 195 | 91 | 286 | 8 | 215 | 1,007 | 96 |
| Valleyfield | 196,427 | 108 | 46 | 154 | 3 | 88 | 360 | 65 |
| Ontario | 2,710,781 | 1,333 | 1,287 | 2,620 | 152 | 343 | 5,005 | 1,174 |
| *Kingston | 65,582 | 76 | 7 | 83 | 1 | — | 260 | 68 |
| *Ottawa | 302,629 | 159 | 211 | 370 | 10 | 126 | 1,107 | 114 |
| *Toronto | 1,100,000 | 241 | 616 | 857 | 86 | 112 | 1,020 | 193 |
| Alexandria-Cornwall | 44,281 | 48 | 8 | 56 | 5 | 12 | 123 | 34 |
| Hamilton | 316,263 | 145 | 147 | 292 | 1 | 29 | 549 | 147 |
| Hearst | 33,686 | 37 | 5 | 42 | — | 1 | 56 | 40 |
| London | 342,021 | 245 | 108 | 353 | — | 18 | 735 | 174 |
| Moosonee+ | 3,000 | — | 10 | 10 | 1 | 7 | 10 | 8 |

| Civil Province Diocese | Cath. Pop. | Dioc. Priests | Rel. Priests | Total Priests | Perm. Deacs. | Bros. | Srs. | Par- ishes |
|---|---|---|---|---|---|---|---|---|
| Ontario | | | 12 | 69 | — | 4 | 294 | 72 |
| Pembroke+ | 55,508 | 57 | 8 | 75 | 1 | 2 | 177 | 77 |
| Peterborough | 56,111 | 67 | 38 | 101 | — | 2 | 84 | 47 |
| St. Catharines | 100,000 | 63 | 65 | 199 | 46 | 12 | 419 | 115 |
| Sault Ste. Marie | 175,000 | 134 | 37 | 66 | — | 3 | 69 | 48 |
| Thunder Bay | 57,000 | 29 | 15 | 47 | 1 | 15 | 102 | 37 |
| Timmins | 59,700 | 32 | | | | | | |
| | | | 187 | 343 | 21 | 53 | 981 | 347 |
| Manitoba | 217,925 | 156 | 31 | 32 | 2 | 7 | 50 | 58 |
| *Keewatin-LePas+ | 35,000 | 1 | 66 | 168 | 6 | 33 | 566 | 111 |
| *St. Boniface | 80,000 | 102 | 73 | 126 | 13 | 10 | 355 | 152 |
| *Winnipeg | 97,500 | 53 | 17 | 17 | — | 3 | 10 | 26 |
| Churchill-Hudson Bay+ | 5,425 | — | | | | | | |
| | | | 139 | 321 | — | 23 | 785 | 382 |
| Saskatchewan | 211,042 | 182 | 40 | 121 | — | 3 | 245 | 198 |
| *Regina | 91,000 | 81 | 6 | 33 | — | — | 84 | 46 |
| Gravelbourg | 13,226 | 27 | 25 | 65 | — | 6 | 181 | 52 |
| Prince Albert | 49,088 | 40 | 42 | 76 | — | 2 | 171 | 62 |
| Saskatoon | 45,228 | 34 | 26 | 26 | — | 12 | 104 | 24 |
| St. Peter Muenster (Abb.) | 12,500 | — | | | | | | |
| Alberta | 405,125 | 214 | 242 | 456 | 1 | 36 | 912 | 466 |
| *Edmonton | 197,000 | 94 | 121 | 215 | — | 22 | 594 | 183 |
| *Grouard-McLennan | 35,000 | 3 | 42 | 45 | — | 5 | 64 | 81 |
| Calgary | 130,000 | 93 | 69 | 162 | 1 | 8 | 184 | 130 |
| St. Paul | 43,125 | 24 | 10 | 34 | — | 1 | 70 | 72 |
| British Columbia | 330,600 | 175 | 174 | 349 | 2 | 44 | 585 | 343 |
| *Vancouver | 175,000 | 92 | 110 | 202 | — | 25 | 313 | 88 |
| Kamloops | 40,000 | 16 | 12 | 28 | 1 | 9 | 40 | 76 |
| Nelson | 41,377 | 30 | 12 | 42 | 1 | 1 | 54 | 60 |
| Prince George | 30,223 | 2 | 21 | 23 | — | 7 | 49 | 60 |
| Victoria | 44,000 | 35 | 19 | 54 | — | 2 | 129 | 59 |
| **Yukon Territory** | | | | | | | | |
| Whitehorse+ | 7,251 | 2 | 17 | 19 | — | 1 | 10 | 15 |
| **Northwest Territories** | | | | | | | | |
| MacKenzie-Ft. Smith+ | 18,404 | 1 | 34 | 35 | — | 21 | 39 | 30 |
| Eastern Rite (Ukrainians) | 195,125 | 175 | 69 | 244 | 35 | 22 | 104 | 495 |
| *Winnipeg | 49,000 | 38 | 14 | 52 | 12 | 2 | 30 | 160 |
| Edmonton | 41,065 | 31 | 15 | 46 | 5 | 15 | 23 | 98 |
| New Westminster | 7,000 | 14 | 4 | 18 | 1 | — | 8 | 20 |
| Saskatoon | 14,860 | 19 | 20 | 39 | 2 | 3 | 18 | 130 |
| Toronto | 83,200 | 73 | 16 | 89 | 15 | 2 | 25 | 87 |
| **Other Eastern Rites** | | | | | | | | |
| Sts. Cyril and Methodius of Toronto (Slovaks) | 15,000 | 7 | 2 | 9 | — | — | — | 12 |
| St. Maron of Montreal (Maronites) | — | — | — | — | — | — | — | — |
| Greek Melkites (Ap. Ex.) | 50,000 | — | 9 | 9 | — | — | — | 6 |
| Military Vicariate | 79,931 | 52 | 18 | 70 | — | — | 6 | 60 |
| TOTALS 1984 | 10,828,343 | 7,276 | 4,857 | 12,133 | 372 | 3,887 | 35,745 | 6,007 |
| Totals 1983 | 10,433,849 | 7,243 | 5,132 | 12,375 | 332 | 3,497 | 37,214 | 5,915 |

## PLEA FOR PEACE

Pope John Paul pleaded for world peace at Mass Sept. 20, 1984, before leaving Ottawa for Rome. "It is necessary," he said before 200,000 people, "to maintain that close link which unites peace and justice, peace and the defense of the inviolable rights of individuals and nations."

## CANADIAN CONFERENCE OF CATHOLIC BISHOPS

The *Canadian Conference of Catholic Bishops was established Oct. 12, 1943, as a permanent voluntary association of the bishops of Canada, was given official approval by the Holy See in 1948, and acquired the status of an episcopal conference after the Second Vatican Council.*

The CCCB acts in two ways: (1) as a strictly ecclesiastical body through which the bishops act together with pastoral authority and responsibility for the Church throughout the country; (2) as an operational secretariat through which the bishops act on a wider scale for the good of the Church and society.

At the top of the CCCB organizational table are the president, an executive committee, an administrative board and a plenary assembly. The membership consists of all the bishops of Canada.

### Departments and Offices

The CCCB's work is planned and co-ordinated by a Pastoral Team of 14 members — six bishops and six staff members (lay and clergy) and the two general secretaries.

The CCCB's nine episcopal commissions undertake study and projects in special areas of pastoral work. Six serve nationally (social affairs, canon law/inter-rite, ministries, missions, ecumenism, theology); three relate to French and English sectors (social communications, Christian education, liturgy).

The general secretariat consists of a French and an English general secretary and their assistants and directors of public relations.

Administrative services for purchasing, archives and library, accounting, personnel, publications, printing and distribution are supervised by directors who relate to the general secretaries.

Various advisory councils and committees with mixed memberships of lay persons, religious, priests and bishops also serve the CCCB on a variety of topics.

### Operations

Meetings for the transaction of business are held at least once a year by the plenary assembly, six times a year by the executive committee, and four times a year by the administrative board.

Bishop John M. Sherlock of London, Ont., is president of the CCCB; Bishop Jean-Guy Hamelin of Rouyn-Noranda, Que., is vice-president.

Headquarters are located at 90 Parent Ave., Ottawa, K1N 7B1, Canada.

### ORGANIZATIONS

**The Catholic Church Extension Society of Canada** supports home missions. Address: 67 Bond St., Toronto, Ontario M5B 1X6.

**The Oblate Indian-Eskimo Council of Canada,** 238 Argyle St., Ottawa.

**The Catholic Women's League of Canada,** with a membership of more than 100,000. Address: 3081 Ness Ave., Winnipeg, Man. R2Y 2G3.

**G. K. Chesterton Society,** 1437 College Dr., Saskatoon, Sask. S7N OW8.

### PERCENTAGE OF CATHOLICS

Catholic population statistics are from the *1984 Directory of the Canadian Conference of Catholic Bishops;* total population figures are 1983 estimates.

The table presents a regional breakdown of Catholic percentage in total population. In some cases, the Catholic totals are approximate because diocesan boundaries fall within several civil provinces. See Index: Canadian Dioceses with Interprovincial Lines.

| Civil Province Territory | Cath. Pop. | Total Pop. | Cath. Pct. |
|---|---|---|---|
| Alberta | 405,125 | 2,340,600 | 17.3 |
| British Columbia | 330,600 | 2,800,500 | 11.8 |
| Manitoba | 217,925 | 1,042,500 | 20.9 |
| New Brunswick | 360,666 | 706,300 | 51.0 |
| Newfoundland | 202,458 | 575,900 | 35.1 |
| Nova Scotia | 278,554 | 857,100 | 32.5 |
| Ontario | 2,710,781 | 8,753,600 | 31.0 |
| Prince Edward Is. | 51,504 | 123,600 | 41.7 |
| Quebec | 5,693,977 | 6,477,800 | 87.9 |
| Saskatchewan | 211,042 | 991,000 | 21.3 |
| Northwest Territories | 18,404 | 47,400 | 38.8 |
| Yukon | 7,251 | 23,200 | 31.2 |
| Eastern Rites | 260,125 | — | — |
| Military Vicariate | 79,931 | — | — |
| **TOTALS 1984** | **10,828,343** | **24,739,500** | **43.8** |
| **Totals 1983** | **10,433,849** | **24,347,400** | **42.9** |

## BIOGRAPHIES OF CANADIAN BISHOPS

(Sources: Almanac survey; *1984 Directory of Canadian Conference of Catholic Bishops; Annuario Pontificio.* Data as of July 10, 1984.)

**Ambrozic, Aloysius M.:** b. Jan. 27, 1930; ord. priest June 4, 1955; ord. titular bishop of Valabria and auxiliary bishop of Toronto, May 27, 1976.

**Audet, Lionel:** b. May 22, 1908, Ste. Marie de Beauce, Que.; ord. priest July 8, 1934; ord. titular bishop of Tibari and auxiliary bishop of Quebec, May 1, 1952; retired Mar. 26, 1983.

**Audet, Rene:** b. Jan. 18, 1920, Montreal, Que.; ord. priest May 30, 1948; ord. titular bishop of Chonochora and auxiliary bishop of Ottawa, July 31, 1963; bishop of Joliette, Jan. 3, 1968.

**Baudoux, Maurice:** b. July 10, 1902, Louviere, Belgium; ord. priest July 17, 1929; ord. bishop of St. Paul in Alberta, Oct. 28, 1948; titular archbishop of Preslavus and coadjutor archbishop of St. Boniface, Mar. 4, 1952; archbishop of St. Boniface, Sept. 14, 1955; retired Sept. 7, 1974.

**Beahen, John:** b. Feb. 14, 1922, Ottawa, Ont.; ord. priest June 15, 1946; ord. titular bishop of Ploaghe and auxiliary bishop of Ottawa, June 21, 1977.

**Belisle, Gilles:** b. Oct. 7, 1923, Clarence Creek, Ont.; ord. priest Feb. 2, 1950; ord. titular bishop of Uccula and auxiliary bishop of Ottawa, June 21, 1977.

**Blais, Leo:** b. Apr. 28, 1904, Dollar Bay, Mich.; ord. priest June 14, 1930; ord. bishop of Prince Albert, Aug. 28, 1952; titular bishop of Geron and auxiliary bishop of Montreal, 1959; retired 1964.

**Blanchet, Bertrand:** b. Sept. 19, 1932, Saint Thomas de Montmagny, Que.; ord. priest May 20, 1956; ord. bishop of Gaspe, Dec. 8, 1973.

**Borecky, Isidore:** b. Oct. 1, 1911, Ostrovec, Ukraine; ord. priest July 17, 1938; ord. titular bishop of Amathus in Cypro and exarch of Toronto, May 27, 1948; bishop of Toronto (Ukrainians), Nov. 3, 1956.

**Brodeur, Rosario L.:** b. Oct. 30, 1889, Acton Vale, Que.; ord. priest June 17, 1916; ord. titular bishop of Mideo and coadjutor bishop of Alexandria, June 30, 1941; bishop of Alexandria, July 27, 1941; retired Oct. 15, 1966.

**Burke, Austin-Emile:** b. Jan. 11, 1922, Sluice Point, N.S.; ord. priest Mar. 25, 1950; ord. bishop of Yarmouth, May 14, 1968.

**Cabana, Georges:** b. Oct. 23, 1894, Notre Dame de Granby, Que; ord. priest July 28, 1918; ord. titular archbishop of Anchialo and coadjutor archbishop of St. Boniface, June 30, 1941; coadjutor archbishop of Sherbrooke, Jan. 20, 1952; archbishop of Sherbrooke, May 28, 1952; retired Feb. 7, 1968.

**Carew, William A.:** b. Oct. 23, 1922, St. John's, Nfld., ord. priest June 15, 1947; ord. titular archbishop of Telde, Jan. 4, 1970; nuncio to Rwanda and Burundi, 1970-74; apostolic delegate to Jerusalem and Palestine and pro-nuncio to Cyprus, 1974-83; pro-nuncio to Japan, Aug. 30, 1983.

**Carney, James F.:** b. June 28, 1915, Vancouver, B.C.; ord. priest Mar. 21, 1942; ord. titular bishop of Obori and auxiliary bishop of Vancouver, Feb. 11, 1966; archbishop of Vancouver, Jan. 8, 1969.

**Carter, Alexander:** b. Apr. 16, 1909, Montreal, Que.; ord. priest June 6, 1936; ord. titular bishop of Sita and coadjutor bishop of Sault Ste. Marie, Feb. 2, 1957; bishop of Sault Ste. Marie, Nov. 22, 1958.

**Carter, G. Emmett:** (See Cardinals, Biographies.)

**Charbonneau, Paul E.:** b. May 4, 1922, Ste. Therese de Blainville, Que.; ord. priest May 31, 1947; ord. titular bishop of Thapsus and auxiliary bishop of Ottawa, Jan. 18, 1961; first bishop of Hull, May 21, 1963; retired Apr. 12, 1973, because of ill health.

**Chiasson, Donat:** b. Jan. 2, 1930, Paquetville, N.B.; ord. priest May 6, 1956; ord. archbishop of Moncton, June 1, 1972.

**Chimy, Jerome I., O.S.B.M.:** b. Mar. 12, 1919, Radway, Alta.; ord. priest, June 29, 1944; ord. first bishop of New Westminster, B.C., for the Ukrainians, Sept. 5, 1974.

**Cimichella, Andre, O.S.M.:** b. Feb. 21, 1921, Grotte Santo Stefano, Italy; ord. priest May 26, 1945; ord. titular bishop of Quiza and auxiliary of Montreal, July 16, 1964.

**Clune, Robert B.:** b. Sept. 18, 1920, Toronto,

Ont.; ord. priest May 26, 1945; ord. titular bishop of Lacubaza and auxiliary bishop of Toronto, June 21, 1979.

**Coderre, Gerard Marie:** b. Dec. 19, 1904, St. Jacques de Montcalm, Que.; ord. priest May 30, 1931; ord. titular bishop of Aegae and coadjutor bishop of St.-Jean-de-Quebec, Sept. 12, 1951; bishop of St.-Jean-de-Quebec, (now Saint-Jean-Longueuil); Feb. 3, 1955; retired May 3, 1978.

**Couture, Jean-Guy:** b. May 6, 1929, St.-Jean-Baptiste de Quebec, Que.; ord. priest May 30, 1953; ord. bishop of Hauterive, Que., Aug. 15, 1975; bishop of Chicoutimi, Apr. 5, 1979.

**Couture, Maurice, R.S.V.:** b. Nov. 3, 1926, Saint-Pierre-de-Broughton, Que.; ord. priest June 17, 1951; ord. titular bishop of Talaptula and auxiliary bishop of Quebec, Oct. 22, 1982.

**Couturier, Gerard:** b. Jan. 12, 1913, St. Louis du Ha Ha, Que; ord. priest Mar. 25, 1938; ord. bishop of Hauterive, Feb. 28, 1957; resigned see Sept. 7, 1974.

**Crowley, Leonard:** b. Dec. 28, 1921, Montreal, Que.; ord. priest May 31, 1947; ord. titular bishop of Mons and auxiliary bishop of Montreal, Mar. 24, 1971.

**Daciuk, Myron, O.S.B.M.:** b. Nov. 16, 1919, Mundare, Alta; ord. priest June 10, 1945; ord. titular bishop of Thyatira and auxiliary bishop of Winnipeg (Ukrainians), Oct. 14, 1982.

**Decosse, Aime:** b. June 21, 1903, Somerset, Man.; ord. priest July 4, 1926; ord. bishop of Gravelbourg, Jan. 20, 1954; retired May 12, 1973.

**Delaquis, Noel:** b. Dec. 25, 1934, Notre-Dame-de-Lourdes, Man.; ord. priest June 5, 1958; ord. bishop of Gravelbourg, Feb. 19, 1974.

**De Roo, Remi J.:** b. Feb. 24, 1924, Swan Lake, Man.; ord. priest June 8, 1950; ord. bishop of Victoria, Dec. 14, 1962.

**Despatie, Roger:** b. Apr. 12, 1927, Sudbury, Ont.; ord. priest Apr. 12, 1952; ord. titular bishop of Usinaza and auxiliary bishop of Sault Ste. Marie, June 28, 1968; bishop of Hearst, Feb. 8, 1973.

**Dionne, Gerard:** b. June 19, 1919, Saint-Basile, N.B.; ord. priest May 1, 1948; ord. titular bishop of Garba and auxiliary bishop of Sault Ste. Marie, Apr. 8, 1975; bishop of Edmundston, Nov. 17, 1983.

**Douville, Arthur:** b. July 22, 1894, St. Casimir de Portneuf, Que.; ord. priest May 25, 1919; ord. titular bishop of Vita and auxiliary bishop of St. Hyacinthe, Jan. 29, 1940; coadjutor bishop of St. Hyacinthe, Mar. 21, 1942; bishop of St. Hyacinthe, Nov. 27, 1942; retired June 13, 1967.

**Doyle, James L.:** b. June 20, 1929, Chatham, Ont.; ord. priest June 12, 1954; ord. bishop of Peterborough June 28, 1976.

**Doyle, W. Emmett:** b. Feb. 18, 1913, Calgary, Alta.: ord. priest June 5, 1938; ord. bishop of Nelson, Dec. 3, 1958.

**Drainville, Gerard:** b. May 20, 1930, L'Isle-du-Pas, Que.; ord. priest May 30, 1953; ord. bishop of Amos, June 12, 1978.

**Dumouchel, Paul, O.M.I.:** b. Sept. 19, 1911, St. Boniface, Man.; ord. priest June 24, 1936; ord. titular bishop of Sufes and vicar apostolic of

Keewatin, May 24, 1955; archbishop of Keewatin-Le Pas, July 13, 1967.

**Ebacher, Roger:** b. Oct. 6, 1936, Amos, Que.; ord. priest May 27, 1961; ord. bishop of Hauterive, July 31, 1979.

**Exner, Adam, O.M.I.:** b. Dec. 24, 1928, Killaly, Sask.; ord. priest July 7, 1957; ord. bishop of Kamloops, B.C., Mar. 12, 1974; archbishop of Winnipeg, April, 1982.

**Filevich, Basil (Wasyl):** b. Jan. 13, 1918; ord. priest Apr. 17, 1942; app. bishop of Ukrainian eparchy of Saskatoon Dec. 5, 1983.

**Flahiff, George F.:** (See Cardinals Biographies.)

**Fortier, Jean-Marie:** b. July 1, 1920, Quebec, Que.; ord. priest June 16, 1944; ord. titular bishop of Pomaria and auxiliary bishop of Ste. Anne-de-la-Pocatiere, Jan. 23, 1961; bishop of Gaspe, Jan. 19, 1965; archbishop of Sherbrooke, Apr. 20, 1968.

**Fulton, Thomas B.:** b. Jan. 13, 1918, St. Catharines, Ont.; ord. priest June 7, 1941; ord. titular bishop of Cursola and auxiliary bishop of Toronto, Jan. 6, 1969; bishop of St. Catharines, July 7, 1978.

**Gagnon, Edouard, P.S.S.:** b. Jan. 15, 1918, Port Daniel, Que.; ord. priest Aug. 15, 1940; ord. bishop Mar. 25, 1969; bishop of St. Paul in Alberta 1969-72; rector of Canadian College in Rome, 1972-77; vice-president and secretary of Vatican Committee for the Family, 1973-80; titular archbishop of Giustiniana Prima, July 7, 1983; pro-president of Pontifical Council for Family, 1983.

**Gervais, Marcel A.:** b. Sept. 21, 1931, Elie, Man.; ord. priest May 31, 1958; ord. titular bishop of Rosmarkaeum and auxiliary bishop of London, Ont., June 11, 1980.

**Gilbert, Arthur J.:** b. Oct. 26, 1915, Oromocto, N.B.; ord. priest June 3, 1943; ord. bishop of St. John, N.B., June 19, 1974.

**Godin, Edgar:** b. May 31, 1911, Neguac, N.B.; ord. priest June 15, 1941; ord. bishop of Bathurst, July 25, 1969.

**Gratton, Jean:** b. Dec. 4, 1924, Wendover, Ont.; ord. priest Apr. 27, 1952; ord. bishop of Mont Laurier, June 29, 1978.

**Gregoire, Paul:** b. Oct. 24, 1911, Verdun, Que.; ord. priest May 22, 1937; ord. titular bishop of Curubis and auxiliary bishop of Montreal, Dec. 27, 1961; archbishop of Montreal, Apr. 20, 1968.

**Greschuk, Martin:** b. Nov. 7, 1923, Innisfree, Alta.; ord. priest June 11, 1950; ord. titular bishop of Nazianus and auxiliary bishop of Edmonton of the Ukrainians, Oct. 3, 1974; apostolic administrator "sede plena" of Edmonton, Apr. 14, 1984.

**Hacault, Antoine:** b. Jan. 17, 1926, Bruxelles, Man.; ord. priest May 20, 1951; ord. titular bishop of Media and coadjutor of St. Boniface, Sept. 8, 1964; archbishop of St. Boniface, Sept. 7, 1974.

**Hains, Gaston:** b. Sept. 10, 1921, Drummondville, Que.; ord. priest June 15, 1946; ord. titular bishop of Belesana and auxiliary bishop of St. Hyacinthe, Oct. 10, 1964; coadjutor bishop of

Amos, 1967; bishop of Amos, Oct. 31, 1968; retired 1978.

**Hakim, Michel:** b. Apr. 21, 1921, Magdouche, South Lebanon; ord. priest Nov. 10, 1947; ord. archbishop of Saida of Greek Melkites, Sept. 10, 1977; app. titular archbishop of Caesarea in Cappadocia and apostolic exarch of Greek Melkite Catholics in Canada, Oct. 13, 1980.

**Halpin, Charles A.:** b. Aug. 30, 1930, St. Eustache, Man.; ord. priest May 27, 1956; ord. archbishop of Regina, Nov. 26, 1973.

**Hamelin, Jean-Guy:** b. Oct. 8, 1925, St. Severin-de-Proulxville, Que.; ord. priest June 11, 1949; ord. first bishop of Rouyn-Noranda, Que., Feb. 9, 1974.

**Hayes, James M.:** b. May 27, 1924, Halifax, N.S.; ord. priest June 15, 1947; ord. titular bishop of Reperi and apostolic administrator of Halifax, Apr. 20, 1965; archbishop of Halifax, June 22, 1967.

**Hermaniuk, Maxim, C.Ss.R.:** b. Oct. 30, 1911, Nove Selo, Ukraine; ord. priest Sept. 4, 1938; ord. titular bishop of Sinna and exarch of Manitoba (Ukrainians), June 29, 1951; archbishop of Winnipeg (Ukrainians), Nov. 3, 1956.

**Hubert, Bernard:** b. June 1, 1929, Beloeil, Que.; ord. priest May 30, 1953; ord. bishop of St. Jerome, Sept. 12, 1971; coadjutor bishop of Saint-Jean-de-Quebec, 1977; succeeded as bishop of Saint-Jean-de-Quebec, May 3, 1978; title of see changed to Saint-Jean-Longueuil, 1982.

**Jette, Edouard:** b. Aug. 9, 1898, St. Jacques, Que.; ord. priest May 31, 1923; ord. titular bishop of Tabe and auxiliary of Joliette, Apr. 14, 1948; retired 1968.

**Labrie, Jean-Paul:** b. Nov. 4, 1922, Laurieville, Que.; ord. priest May 20, 1951; ord. titular bishop of Urci and auxiliary bishop of Quebec, May 14, 1977.

**Lacey, Michael Pearse:** b. Nov. 27, 1916, Toronto, Ont.; ord. priest May 23, 1943; ord. titular bishop of Diana and auxiliary bishop of Toronto, June 21, 1979.

**Lacroix, Fernand, C.J.M.:** b. Oct. 16, 1919, Quebec; ord. priest Feb. 10, 1946; ord. bishop of Edmundston, Oct. 20, 1970; retired May 31, 1983.

**Landriault, Jacques:** b. Sept. 23, 1921, Alfred, Ont.; ord. priest Feb. 9, 1947; ord. titular bishop of Cadi and auxiliary bishop of Alexandria, July 25, 1962; bishop of Hearst, May 27, 1964; app. bishop of Timmins, Mar. 24, 1971.

**Langevin, Louis-de-Gonzague, P.B.:** b. Oct. 31, 1921, Oka, Que.; ord. priest Feb. 2, 1950; ord. titular bishop of Rosemarkie and auxiliary of St. Hyacinthe Sept. 23, 1974; bishop of St. Hyacinthe, July 18, 1979.

**LaRocque, Eugene Philippe:** b. Mar. 27, 1927, Windsor, Ont.; ord. priest June 7, 1952; ord. bishop of Alexandria, Ont., Sept. 3, 1974; title of see changed to Alexandria-Cornwall, 1976.

**Lebel, Robert:** b. Nov. 8, 1924, Trois-Pistoles, Que.; ord. priest June 18, 1950; ord. titular bishop of Alinda and auxiliary of St. Jean de Quebec, May 12, 1974; bishop of Valleyfield, Mar. 26, 1976.

**Le Blanc, Camille A.:** b. Aug. 25, 1898, Barachois, N.B.; ord. priest Apr. 5, 1924; ord. bish-

op of Bathurst, Sept. 8, 1942; retired Jan. 8, 1969.
**Leclerc, Marc:** b. Jan. 9, 1933, Saint-Gregoire de Montmorency, Que; ord. priest, May 31, 1958; ord. titular bishop of Eguga and auxiliary bishop of Quebec, Oct. 22, 1982.

**Legare, Henri, O.M.I.:** b. Feb. 20, 1918, Willow Bunch, Sask.; ord. priest June 29, 1943; ord. first bishop of Labrador-Schefferville, Sept. 9, 1967; archbishop of Grouard-McLennan, Nov. 21, 1972. President of Canadian Conference of Catholic Bishops, 1981-83.

**Leger, Paul-Emile:** (See Cardinals, Biographies).

**Leguerrier, Jules, O.M.I.:** b. Feb. 18, 1915, Clarence Creek, Ont.; ord. priest June 19, 1943; ord. titular bishop of Bavagaliana and vicar apostolic of James Bay, June 29, 1964; first bishop of Moosonee, July 13, 1967.

**Lemieux, Marie Joseph, O.P.:** b. May 10, 1902, Quebec, Que.; ord. priest Apr. 15, 1928; ord. bishop of Sendai, Japan, June 29, 1936; titular bishop of Calydon, 1941; apostolic administrator of Gravelbourg, 1942; bishop of Gravelbourg, Apr. 15, 1944; archbishop of Ottawa, 1953-66; titular archbishop of Salde, Nov. 16, 1966, apostolic nuncio. Retired.

**Levesque, Charles Henri:** b. Dec. 29, 1921, St. Andre de Kamouraska, Que.; ord. priest June 13, 1948; ord. titular bishop of Guzabeta and auxiliary bishop of Ste.-Anne-de-la-Pocatiere, Dec. 27, 1965; bishop of Ste.-Anne-de-la-Pocatiere, Aug. 17, 1968.

**Levesque, Louis:** b. May 27, 1908, Amqui, Que.; ord. priest June 26, 1932; ord. bishop of Hearst, Aug. 15, 1952; titular archbishop of Egnatia and coadjutor of Rimouski, Apr. 13, 1964; archbishop of Rimouski, Feb. 25, 1967; retired May 14, 1973.

**Lussier, Philippe, C.Ss.R.:** b. Oct. 3, 1911, Weedon, Que.; ord. priest Sept. 18, 1937; ord. bishop of St. Paul in Alberta, Aug. 17, 1952; retired Aug. 17, 1968.

**McCarthy, Thomas J.:** b. Oct. 4, 1905, Goderich, Ont.; ord. priest May 25, 1929; ord. bishop of Nelson, Aug. 1, 1955; bishop of St. Catharines, Nov. 9, 1958; retired 1978.

**MacDonald, James H., C.S.C.:** b. Apr. 28, 1925, Wycogama, N.S.; ord. priest June 28, 1953; ord. titular bishop of Gibba and auxiliary bishop of Hamilton April 17, 1978; app. bishop of Charlottetown, Aug. 12, 1982.

**MacDonald, Joseph Faber:** b. Jan. 20, 1932, Little Pond, P.E.I.; ord. priest Mar. 9, 1963; ord. bishop of Grand Falls, Mar. 19, 1980.

**McGrath, Richard T.:** b. June 17, 1912, Oderin, Placentia Bay, Nfld.; ord. priest June 24, 1936; ord. bishop of St. George's, Nfld., July 22, 1970.

**MacNeil, Joseph N.:** b. Apr. 15, 1924, Sydney, N.S.; ord. priest May 23, 1948; ord. bishop of St. John, N.B., June 24, 1969; archbishop of Edmonton, July 6, 1973. President Canadian Conference of Catholic Bishops, 1979-81.

**Mahoney, James P.:** b. Dec. 7, 1927, Saskatoon, Sask.; ord. priest June 7, 1952; ord. bishop of Saskatoon, Dec. 13, 1967.

**Martin, Albertus:** b. Oct. 4, 1913, Southbridge, Mass.; ord. priest May 18, 1939; ord. titular bishop of Bassiana and coadjutor bishop of Nicolet, Oct. 7, 1950; bishop of Nicolet, Nov. 8, 1950.

**Morand, Blaise E.:** b. Sept. 12, 1932, Tecumseh, Ont.; ord. priest Mar. 22, 1958; ord. coadjutor bishop of Prince Albert, June 29, 1981; bishop of Prince Albert, Apr. 9, 1983.

**Morin, Laurent:** b. Feb. 14, 1908, Montreal, Que.; ord. priest May 27, 1934; ord. titular bishop of Arsamosata and auxiliary bishop of Montreal, Oct. 30, 1955; bishop of Prince Albert, Feb. 28, 1959; retired Apr. 9, 1983.

**Noel, Laurent:** b. Mar. 19, 1920, Saint-Just-de-Bretenieres, Que.; ord. priest June 16, 1944; ord. titular bishop of Agathopolis and auxiliary bishop of Quebec, Aug. 29, 1963; bishop of Trois Rivieres, Nov. 5, 1975.

**O'Byrne, Paul J.:** b. Dec. 21, 1922, Calgary, Alta.; ord. priest Feb. 21, 1948; ord. bishop of Calgary, Aug. 22, 1968.

**O'Connor, Hubert P., O.M.I.:** b. Feb. 17, 1928, Huntingdon, Que.; ord. priest June 5, 1955; ord. bishop of Whitehorse, Dec. 8, 1971.

**O'Grady, John Fergus, O.M.I.:** b. July 27, 1908, Macton, Ont.; ord. priest June 29, 1934; ord. titular bishop of Aspendus and vicar apostolic of Prince Rupert, Mar. 7, 1956; first bishop of Prince George, July 13, 1967.

**O'Mara, John A.:** b. Nov. 17, 1924, Buffalo, N.Y.; ord. priest June 1, 1951; ord. bishop of Thunder Bay, June 29, 1976.

**Ouellet, Gilles, P.M.E.:** b. Aug. 14, 1922, Bromptonville, Que.; ord. priest June 30, 1946; ord. bishop of Gaspe, Nov. 23, 1968; app. archbishop of Rimouski, Apr. 27, 1973. President Canadian Conference of Catholic Bishops, 1977-79.

**Ouellette, Andre:** b. Feb. 4, 1913, Salem, Mass.; ord. priest June 11, 1938; ord. titular bishop of Carre and auxiliary bishop of Mont-Laurier, Feb. 25, 1957; bishop of Mont-Laurier, Mar. 27, 1965; retired Feb. 15, 1978.

**Pappin, Bernard F.:** b. July 10, 1928, Westmeath, Ont.; ord. priest May 27, 1954; ord. titular bishop of Aradi and auxiliary bishop of Sault Ste. Marie, Apr. 11, 1975.

**Pare, Marius:** b. May 22, 1903, Montmagny, Que.; ord. priest July 3, 1927; ord. titular bishop of Aegae and auxiliary bishop of Chicoutimi, May 1, 1956; bishop of Chicoutimi, Feb. 18, 1961; retired Apr. 5, 1979.

**Pedneault, Roch:** b. Apr. 10, 1927, Saint Joseph d'Alma, Que.; ord. priest Feb. 8, 1953; ord. titular bishop of Aggersel and auxiliary of Chicoutimi, Que., June 29, 1974.

**Pelletier, Georges Leon:** b. Aug. 19, 1904, Saint-Epiphane, Que.; ord. priest June 24, 1931; ord. titular bishop of Hephaestus and auxiliary bishop of Quebec, Feb. 24, 1943; bishop of Trois Rivieres, July 26, 1947; retired Oct. 31, 1975.

**Penney, Alphonsus L.:** b. Sept. 17, 1924, St. John's, Nfld.; ord. priest June 29, 1949; ord. bishop of Grand Falls, Jan. 18, 1973; archbishop of St. John's, Nfld., Apr. 5, 1979.

**Piche, Paul, O.M.I.:** b. Sept. 14, 1909, Gravelbourg, Sask.; ord. priest Dec. 23, 1934; ord. titular bishop of Orcistus and vicar apostolic of Mackenzie, June 11, 1959; first bishop of Mackenzie-Fort Smith, July 13, 1967.

**Plourde, Joseph Aurele:** b. Jan. 12, 1915, St. Francois de Madawaska, N.B.; ord. priest May 7, 1944; ord. titular bishop of Lapda and auxiliary bishop of Alexandria, Aug. 26, 1964; archbishop of Ottawa, Jan. 2, 1967.

**Pocock, Philip:** b. July 2, 1906, St. Thomas, Ont.; ord. priest June 14, 1930; ord. bishop of Saskatoon, June 29, 1944; titular archbishop of Aprus and coadjutor archbishop of Winnipeg, Aug. 6, 1951; archbishop of Winnipeg, Jan. 14, 1952; titular archbishop of Isauropolis and coadjutor archbishop of Toronto, Feb. 18, 1961; archbishop of Toronto, Mar. 30, 1971; retired Apr. 29, 1978.

**Power, William E.:** b. Sept. 27, 1915; Montreal, Que.; ord. priest June 7, 1941; ord. bishop of Antigonish, July 20, 1960; president Canadian Conference of Catholic Bishops, 1971-73.

**Proulx, Adolphe J.:** b. Dec. 12, 1927, Hanmer, Ont., Canada; ord. priest Apr. 17, 1954; ord. titular bishop of Missua and auxiliary bishop of Sault Ste. Marie, Feb. 24, 1965; bishop of Alexandria, Apr. 28, 1967; bishop of Hull, Feb. 13, 1974; title of see changed to Gatineau-Hull, 1982.

**Robidoux, Omer, O.M.I.:** b. Nov. 19, 1913, Saint-Pierre-Jolys, Man.; ord. priest June 29, 1939; ord. bishop of Churchill-Hudson Bay, May 20, 1970.

**Routhier, Henri, O.M.I.:** b. Feb. 28, 1900, Pincher Creek, Alta.; ord. priest Sept. 7, 1924; ord. titular bishop of Naissus and coadjutor vicar apostolic of Grouard, Sept. 8, 1945; vicar apostolic of Grouard, 1953; archbishop of Grouard-McLennan, July 13, 1967; retired Nov. 21, 1972.

**Roy, Maurice:** (Cardinals, Biographies.)

**Roy, Raymond:** b. May 3, 1919, St. Boniface, Man.; ord. priest May 31, 1947; ord. bishop of St. Paul in Alberta, July 18, 1972.

**Rusnak, Michael, C.Ss.R.:** b. Aug. 21, 1921, Beaverdale, Pa.; ord. priest July 3, 1949; ord. titular bishop of Tzernicus and auxiliary bishop of Toronto eparchy and apostolic visitator to Slovak Catholics of Byzantine rite in Canada, Jan. 2, 1965; first bishop of Sts Cyril and Methoduis Eparchy for Slovaks of Byzantine Rite, Feb. 28, 1981.

**Ryan, Joseph F.:** b. Mar. 1, 1897, Dundas, Ont.; ord. priest May 21, 1921; ord. bishop of Hamilton, Oct. 19, 1937; retired Mar. 27, 1973.

**Sabatini, Lawrence, C.S.:** b. May 15, 1930, Chicago, Ill.; ord. priest Mar. 19, 1957; ord. titular bishop of Nasai and auxiliary bishop of Vancouver, Sept. 21, 1978; bishop of Kamloops, Sept. 30, 1982.

**Saint-Antoine, Jude:** b. Oct. 29, 1930, Montreal, Que.; ord. priest May 31, 1956; ord. titular bishop of Scardona and auxiliary bishop of Montreal, May 22, 1981. Episcopal vicar of west central region.

**Saint-Gelais, Raymond:** b. Mar. 23, 1936, Baie St. Paul, Que.; ord. priest June 12, 1960; ord. titular bishop of Diana and auxiliary bishop of St. Jerome, July 31, 1980.

**Sanschagrin, Albert, O.M.I.:** b. Aug. 5, 1911, Saint-Tite, Que.; ord. priest May 24, 1936; ord.

titular bishop of Bagi and coadjutor bishop of Amos Sept. 14, 1957; bishop of Saint-Hyacinthe, June 13, 1967; retired July 18, 1979.

**Savaryn, Nile Nicholas, O.S.B.M.:** b. May 19, 1905, Stary Sambir, Ukraine; ord. priest Aug. 23, 1931; ord. titular bishop of Jos and auxiliary bishop of the Catholic Ukrainian diocese in Canada, July 1, 1943; bishop of apostolic exarchate for western Canada, 1948; bishop of Edmonton (Ukrainians), Nov. 3, 1956.

**Setian, Nerses Mikael:** Apostolic Exarch of Armenian Catholics in Canada and the U.S. (see Index).

**Shaheen, Elias:** b. July 20, 1914, Ebrine, Patriarchate of Antioch of Maronites; ord. priest Mar. 25, 1939; ord. first eparch of St. Maron of Montreal for the Maronites, Nov. 7, 1982.

**Sherlock, John M.:** b. Jan. 20, 1926, Regina, Sask.; ord. priest June 3, 1950; ord. titular bishop of Macriana and auxiliary of London, Ont., Aug. 28, 1974; bishop of London, July 7, 1978. President of the Canadian Conference of Catholic Bishops, 1983-.

**Skinner, Patrick J., C.J.M.:** b. Mar. 9, 1904, St. John's, Nfld.; ord. priest May 30, 1929; ord. titular bishop of Zenobia and auxiliary bishop of St. John's, Mar. 17, 1950; archbishop of St. John's, Mar. 23, 1951; retired Apr. 5, 1979.

**Smith, William J.:** b. Jan. 2, 1897, Greenfield, Ont.; ord. priest June 16, 1927; ord. bishop of Pembroke, July 25, 1945; retired Feb. 8, 1971.

**Spence, Francis J.:** b. June 3, 1926, Perth, Ont.; ord. priest Apr. 16, 1950; ord. titular bishop of Nova and auxiliary bishop of the military vicariate, June 15, 1967; bishop of Charlottetown, Aug. 15, 1970; military vicar of Canada, March 1982; archbishop of Kingston, May, 1982.

**Sutton, Peter A., O.M.I.:** b. Oct. 18, 1934, Chandler, Que.; ord. priest Oct. 22, 1960; ord. bishop of Labrador-Schefferville, July 18, 1974.

**Tessier, Maxime:** b. Oct. 9, 1906, St. Sebastien, Que.; ord. priest June 14, 1930; ord. titular bishop of Christopolis and auxiliary bishop of Ottawa, Aug. 2, 1951; coadjutor bishop of Timmins, 1953; bishop of Timmins, May 8, 1955; retired Mar. 24, 1971.

**Tonnos, Anthony:** b. Aug. 1, 1935, Port Colborne, Ont.; ord. priest May 27, 1961; ord. titular bishop of Naziona and auxiliary bishop of Hamilton, July 12, 1983; app. bishop of Hamilton, May 5, 1984.

**Tremblay, Gerard, P.S.S.:** b. Oct. 27, 1918, Montreal, Que.; ord. priest June 16, 1946; ord. titular bishop of Trisipa and auxiliary bishop of Montreal, May 22, 1981.

**Troy, J. Edward:** b. 1932, Bathurst, N.B.; ord. priest May 28, 1959; app. coadjutor bishop of St. John, N.B., March, 1984.

**Turcotte, Jean-Claude:** b. June 26, 1936, Montreal, Que.; ord. priest May 24, 1959; ord. titular bishop of Suas and auxiliary bishop of Montreal, June 29, 1982.

**Vachon, Louis-Albert:** b. Feb. 4, 1912, Saint-Frederic, Que.; ord. priest June 11, 1938; ord.

titular bishop of Mesarfelta and auxiliary bishop of Quebec, May 14, 1977; archbishop of Quebec and primate of Canada, Apr. 4, 1981.

**Valois, Charles:** b. Apr. 24, 1924, Montreal, Que.; ord. priest June 3, 1950; ord. bishop of St. Jerome, June 29, 1977.

**Wall, Leonard J.:** b. Sept. 27, 1924, Windsor, Ont.; ord. priest June 11, 1949; ord. titular bishop of Leptiminus and auxiliary bishop of Toronto, June 21, 1979.

**Wilhelm, Joseph L.:** b. Nov. 16, 1909, Walkerton, Ont.; ord. priest June 9, 1934; ord. titular bishop of Saccaea and auxiliary bishop of Calgary, Aug. 22, 1963; archbishop of Kingston, Dec. 14, 1966; retired Mar. 12, 1982.

**Windle, Joseph R.:** b. Aug. 28, 1917, Ashdad, Ont.; ord. priest May 16, 1943; ord. titular bishop of Uzita and auxiliary bishop of Ottawa, Jan. 18, 1961; coadjutor bishop of Pembroke, 1969; bishop of Pembroke, Feb. 15, 1971.

## CANADIAN SHRINES

**Our Lady of the Cape (Cap de la Madeleine), Queen of the Most Holy Rosary:** The Three Rivers, Quebec, parish church, built of fieldstone in 1714 and considered the oldest stone church on the North American continent preserved in its original state, was rededicated June 22, 1888, as a shrine of the Queen of the Most Holy Rosary. Thereafter, the site increased in importance as a pilgrimage and devotional center, and in 1904 St. Pius X decreed the crowning of a statue of the Blessed Virgin which had been donated 50 years earlier to commemorate the dogma of the Immaculate Conception. In 1909, the First Plenary Council of Quebec declared the church a shrine of national pilgrimage. In 1964, the church at the shrine was given the status and title of minor basilica.

**St. Anne de Beaupre:** The devotional history of this shrine in Quebec, began with the reported cure of a cripple, Louis Guimont, on Mar. 16, 1658, the starting date of construction work on a small chapel of St. Anne. The original building was successively enlarged and replaced by a stone church which was given the rank of minor basilica in 1888. The present structure, a Romanesque-Gothic basilica, houses the shrine proper in its north transept. The centers of attraction are an eight-foot-high oaken statue and the great relic of St. Anne, a portion of her forearm.

**St. Joseph's Oratory:** The massive oratory basilica standing on the western side of Mount Royal and overlooking the city of Montreal had its origin in a primitive chapel erected there by Blessed Andre Bessette, C.S.C., in 1904. Eleven years later, a large crypt was built to accommodate an increasing number of pilgrims, and in 1924 construction work was begun on the large church. A belfry, housing a 60-bell carillon and standing on the site of the original chapel, was dedicated May 15, 1955, as the first major event of the jubilee year observed after the oratory was given the rank of minor basilica.

**Martyrs' Shrine:** A shrine commemorating several of the Jesuit Martyrs of North America who were killed between 1642 and 1649 in the Ontario and northern New York area is located on the former site of old Fort Sainte Marie. Before its location was fixed near Midland, Ont., in 1925, a small chapel had been erected in 1907 at old Mission St. Ignace to mark the martyrdom of Fathers Jean de Brebeuf and Gabriel Lalemant. This sanctuary has a U.S. counterpart in the Shrine of the North American Martyrs near Auriesville, N.Y., under the care of the Jesuits.

### Others

Other shrines and historic churches in Canada include the following.

In Quebec City: the Basilica of Notre Dame, dating from 1650, once the cathedral of a diocese stretching from Canada to Mexico; Notre Dame des Victoires, on the waterfront, dedicated in 1690; the Ursuline Convent, built in 1720, on du Parloir St.

In Montreal: Notre Dame Basilica, patterned after the famous basilica of the same name in Paris, constructed in 1829; the Shrine of Mary, Queen of All Hearts.

Near Montreal: the Chapel of Mother d'Youville, foundress of the Grey Nuns; Notre Dame de Lourdes, at Rigaud.

### CONFERENCE OF RELIGIOUS

The Canadian Religious Conference, founded in 1954, is a union of major superiors of men and women in Canada. Offices are located at 324 E. Laurier Ave., Ottawa, Ont. KIN 6P6.

## CANADIAN CATHOLIC PUBLICATIONS

(Sources: *Catholic Press Directory*, Canadian Conference of Catholic Bishops.)

### Newspapers

**British Columbia Catholic, The,** w; 150 Robson St., Vancouver, B.C. V6B 2A7.

**Catholic New Times** (national), biweekly; 80 Sackville St., Toronto, Ont. M5A 3E5.

**Catholic Register, The** (national), w; 110 Church St. (Suite 400), M5C 2S2. Lay edited.

**Catholic Times, The,** 10 times a year; 2005 St. Marc St., Montreal, Que. H3H 2G8.

**Diocesan News,** m; P.O. Box 1689, Charlottetown, P.E.I. CIA 7N4.

**Hamilton Diocesan News,** 3 times a year; 700 King St., West Hamilton, Ont. L8P 1C7.

**L'Informateur Catholique,** semimonthly; 1915 Est-Boulevard Gouin, Montreal, Que. H2B 1W7.

**Monitor, The,** m; P.O. Box 986, St. John's, Nfld. A1C 5M3.

**New Freeman, The,** w; Box 6609, Sta. A, St. John, N.B. E2L 4S1.

**Our Diocese,** bm; 22 Sutherland Dr., Grand Falls, Nfld. A2A 2G1.

**Pastoral Reporter, The,** 4 times a year; 1916 Second St. S.W., Calgary. Alta. T2S 153.

**Prairie Messenger,** w; Box 190, Muenster, Sask. SOK 2Y0.

**Teviskes, Ziburiai** (Lithuanian), w; 2185 Stavebank Rd., Mississauga, Ont. L5C 1T3.

**Western Catholic Reporter,** w; 10562 109th St., Edmonton, Alta. T5H 3B2.

## Magazines

**Annals of St. Anne de Beaupre,** m; Box 1000, St. Anne de Beaupre, Que. GOA 3CO; Basilica of St. Anne.

**Apostolat,** bm; 460, Primiere Rue, Richelieu, Que. J3L 4B5, Oblates of Mary Immaculate.

**Bulletin** (French-English), q; 324 E. Laurier St., Ottawa, Ont. K1N 6P6. Canadian Religious Conference.

**Canadian Catholic Review,** 11 times a year; 1437 College Dr., Saskatoon, Saskatchewan S7N 0W6.

**Canadian League, The,** 4 times a year; 3081 Ness Ave., Winnipeg, Man. R2Y 2G3. Catholic Women's League of Canada.

**Casket, The,** w; 88 College St., Antigonish, N.S. B2G 2LC.

**Chesterton Review,** q; 1437 College Dr., Saskatoon, Sask. S7N 0W6.

**Companion of St. Francis and St. Anthony,** m; P.O. Box 535, Sta. F., Toronto, Ont. M4Y 2L8; Conventual Franciscan Fathers.

**Fatima Crusader, The,** 4 times a year, P.O. Box 3394, Ottawa, Ont. K1Y 4J6.

**Global Village Voice, The,** 4 times a year; 3028 Danforth Ave., Toronto, Ont. M4C IN2. Canadian Catholic Organization for Development and Peace.

**Indian Record,** 4 times a year; 503-480 Aulneau, Winnipeg, Man. R2H 2V2.

**Kateri** (English-French), q; P.O. Box 70, Caughnawaga, Que. JOL 1BO.

**Logos** (Ukrainian, English and French), q; 165 Catherine St., P.O. Box 220, Yorkton, Sask. S3N 2V7.

**Martyrs' Shrine Message,** q; Midland, Ont. L4R 4K5.

**Messager de Saint Antoine, Le,** 10 times a year; Lac-Bouchette, Que. GOW 1VO.

**Messenger of the Sacred Heart,** m; 661 Greenwood Ave., Toronto, Ont. M4J 4B3.

**Missions Etrangeres,** 6 times a year; 160 Place Juge-Desnoyers, Laval, Que. H7G 1A4.

**Oratory,** 6 times a year; 3800 Ch. Reine-Marie, Montreal, Que. H3V 1H6.

**Our Family,** m; P.O. Box 249, Battleford, Sask.; S0M 0E0; Oblates of Mary Immaculate.

**Prete et Pasteur,** m; 4450 St. Hubert St., Montreal, Que. H2J 2W9.

**Redeemer's Voice** (Ukrainian-English), m; 165 Catherine St., P.O. Box 220, Yorkton, Sask. S3N 2V7.

**Regard de Foi,** 6 times a year; 5875 Est. rue Sherbrooke, Montreal, Que. H1N 1B6.

**Relations,** m; 8100 Blvd., Saint-Laurent, Montreal Que. H2P 2L9; Jesuit Fathers.

**Restoration,** m; Madonna House, Combermere, Ont., KOJ 1LO.

**Sainte Anne de Beaupre,** m; Basilica of St. Anne, Que. GOA 3CO.

**Scarboro Missions,** m; 2685 Kingston Rd., Scarboro, Ont. M1M 1M4.

**Spiritan Missionary News,** 4 times a year; 1440 McQueen Rd., Edmonton, Alta. T5N 3L2.

# MISSIONARIES TO THE AMERICAS

**Allouez, Claude Jean** (1622-1689): French Jesuit; missionary in Canada and midwestern U.S.; preached to 20 different tribes of Indians and baptized over 10,000; vicar general of Northwest.

**Altham, John** (1589-1640): English Jesuit; missionary among Indians in Maryland.

**Anchieta, Jose de, Bl.** (1534-1597): Portuguese Jesuit, b. Canary Islands; missionary in Brazil; writer; beatified 1980; feast, June 9.

**Andreis, Felix de** (1778-1820): Italian Vincentian; missionary and educator in western U.S.

**Aparicio, Sebastian, Bl.** (1502-1600): Franciscan brother, born Spain; settled in Mexico, c. 1533; worked as road builder and farmer before becoming Franciscan at about the age of 70; beatified, 1787; feast, Feb. 25.

**Badin, Stephen T.** (1768-1853): French missioner; came to U.S., 1792, when Sulpician seminary in Paris was closed; ordained, 1793, Baltimore, the first priest ordained in U.S.; missionary in Kentucky, Ohio and Michigan; bought land on which Notre Dame University now stands; buried on its campus.

**Baraga, Frederic** (1797-1868): Slovenian missionary bishop in U.S.; studied at Ljubljana and Vienna, ordained, 1823; came to U.S., 1830; missionary to Indians of Upper Michigan; first bishop of Marquette, 1857-1868; wrote Chippewa grammar, dictionary, prayer book and other works.

**Bertran, Louis, St.** (1526-1581): Spanish Domini-

can; missionary in Colombia and Caribbean, 1562-69; canonized, 1671; feast, Oct. 9.

**Betancur, Pedro de San Jose, Bl.** (1626-1667): Secular Franciscan, b. Canary Islands; arrived in Guatemala, 1651; established hospital, school and homes for poor; beatified 1980; feast, Apr. 25.

**Bourgeoys, Marguerite, St.** (1620-1700): French foundress, missionary; settled in Canada, 1653; founded Congregation of Notre Dame de Montreal, 1658; beatified, 1950; canonized 1982; feast, Jan. 19.

**Brebeuf, John de, St.** (1593-1649): French Jesuit; missionary among Huron Indians in Canada; martyred by Iroquois, Mar. 16, 1649; canonized, 1930; one of Jesuit North American martyrs; feast, Oct. 19.

**Cancer de Barbastro, Louis** (1500-1549): Spanish Dominican; began missionary work in Middle America, 1533; killed at Tampa Bay, Fla.

**Castillo, John de, Bl.** (1596-1628): Spanish Jesuit; worked in Paraguay Indian mission settlements (reductions); martyred; beatified, 1934; feast, Nov. 17.

**Catala, Magin** (1761-1830): Spanish Franciscan; worked in California mission of Santa Clara for 36 years.

**Chabanel, Noel, St.** (1613-1649): French Jesuit; missionary among Huron Indians in Canada; murdered by renegade Huron, Dec. 8, 1649; canonized, 1930; one of Jesuit North American martyrs; feast, Oct. 19.

**Chaumonot, Pierre Joseph** (1611-1693): French Jesuit; missionary among Indians in Canada.

**Claver, Peter, St.** (1581-1654): Spanish Jesuit; missionary among Negroes of South America and West Indies; canonized, 1888; patron of Catholic missions among black people; feast, Sept. 9.

**Daniel, Anthony, St.** (1601-1648): French Jesuit; missionary among Huron Indians in Canada; martyred by Iroquois, July 4, 1648; canonized, 1930; one of Jesuit North American martyrs; feast, Oct. 19.

**De Smet, Pierre Jean** (1801-1873): Belgian-born Jesuit; missionary among Indians of northwestern U.S.; served as intermediary between Indians and U.S. government; wrote on Indian culture.

**Duchesne, Rose Philippine, Bl.** (1769-1852): French nun; educator and missionary in the U.S.; established first convent of the Society of the Sacred Heart in the U.S., at St. Charles, Mo. (later Florissant); founded schools for girls; did missionary work among Indians; beatified, 1940; feast, Nov. 17.

**Farmer, Ferdinand** (family name, Steinmeyer) (1720-1786): German Jesuit; missionary in Philadelphia, where he died; one of the first missionaries in New Jersey.

**Flaget, Benedict J.** (1763-1850): French Sulpician bishop; came to U.S., 1792; missionary and educator in U.S.; first bishop of Bardstown, Ky. (now Louisville), 1810-32; 1833-50.

**Gallitzin, Demetrius** (1770-1840): Russian prince, born The Hague; convert, 1787; ordained priest at Baltimore, 1795; frontier missionary, known as Father Smith; Gallitzin, Pa., named for him.

**Garnier, Charles, St.** (c. 1606-1649): French Jesuit; missionary among Hurons in Canada; martyred by Iroquois, Dec. 7, 1649; canonized, 1930; one of Jesuit North American martyrs; feast, Oct. 19.

**Gibault, Pierre** (1737-1804): Canadian missionary in Illinois and Indiana; aided in securing states of Ohio, Indiana, Illinois, Michigan and Wisconsin for the Americans during Revolution.

**Gonzalez, Roch, Bl.** (1576-1628): Paraguayan Jesuit; worked in Paraguay Indian mission settlements (reductions); martyred; beatified, 1934; feast, Nov. 17.

**Goupil, Rene, St.** (1607-1642): French Jesuit brother; missionary companion of St. Isaac Jogues among the Hurons; martyred, Sept. 29, 1642; canonized, 1930; one of Jesuit North American martyrs; feast, Oct. 19.

**Gravier, Jacques** (1651-1708): French Jesuit; missionary among Indians of Canada and midwestern U.S.

**Jesuit North American Martyrs:** Isaac Jogues, Anthony Daniel, John de Brebeuf, Gabriel Lalemant, Charles Garnier, Noel Chabanel (Jesuit priests), and Rene Goupil and John Lalande (lay missionaries) who were martyred between Sept. 29, 1642, and Dec. 9, 1649, in the missions of New France; canonized June 29, 1930; feast, Oct. 19. See separate entries.

**Jogues, Isaac, St.** (1607-1646): French Jesuit; missionary among Indians in Canada; martyred near present site of Auriesville, N.Y., by Mohawks, Oct. 18, 1646; canonized, 1930; one of Jesuit North American martyrs; feast, Oct. 19.

**Kino, Eusebio** (1645-1711): Italian Jesuit; missionary and explorer in U.S.; arrived Southwest, 1681; established 25 Indian missions, took part in 14 exploring expeditions in northern Mexico, Arizona and southern California; helped develop livestock raising and farming in the area. He was selected in 1965 to represent Arizona in Statuary Hall.

**Lalande, John, St.** (d. 1646): French lay missionary, companion of Isaac Jogues; martyred by Mohawks at Auriesville, N.Y., Oct. 19, 1646; canonized, 1930; one of Jesuit North American martyrs; feast, Oct. 19.

**Lalemant, Gabriel, St.** (1610-1649): French Jesuit; missionary among the Hurons in Canada; martyred by the Iroquois, Mar. 17, 1649; canonized, 1930; one of Jesuit North American martyrs; feast, Oct. 19.

**Lamy, Jean Baptiste** (1814-1888): French prelate; came to U.S., 1839; missionary in Ohio and Kentucky; bishop in Southwest from 1850; first bishop (later archbishop) of Santa Fe, 1850-1885. He was nominated in 1951 to represent New Mexico in Statuary Hall.

**Las Casas, Bartolome** (1474-1566): Spanish Dominican; missionary in Haiti, Jamaica and Venezuela; reformer of abuses against Indians and black people; bishop of Chalapas, Mexico, 1544-47; historian.

**Laval, Francoise de Montmorency, Bl.** (1623-1708): French Jesuit; named vicar apostolic of Canada, 1658; first bishop of Quebec, 1674; jurisdiction extended over all French-claimed territory in New World; beatified 1980; feast, May 6.

**Manogue, Patrick** (1831-1895): Missionary bishop in U.S., b. Ireland; migrated to U.S.; miner in California; studied for priesthood at St. Mary's of the Lake, Chicago, and St. Sulpice, Paris; ordained, 1861; missionary among Indians of California and Nevada; coadjutor bishop, 1881-84, and bishop, 1884-86, of Grass Valley; first bishop of Sacramento, 1886-1895, when see was transferred there.

**Margil, Antonio** (1657-1726): Spanish Franciscan; missionary in Middle America; apostle of Guatemala; established missions in Texas.

**Marie of the Incarnation, Bl.** (Marie Guyard Martin) (1599-1672): French widow; joined Ursuline Nuns; arrived in Canada, 1639; first superior of Ursulines in Quebec; missionary to Indians; writer; beatified 1980; feast, Apr. 30.

**Marquette, Jacques** (1637-1675): French Jesuit; missionary and explorer in America; sent to New France, 1666; began missionary work among Ottawa Indians on Lake Superior, 1668; accompanied Joliet down the Mississippi to mouth of the Arkansas, 1673, and returned to Lake Michigan by way of Illinois River; made a second trip over the same route; his diary and map are of historical significance. He was selected in 1895 to represent Wisconsin in Statuary Hall.

**Massias (Macias), John de, St.** (1585-1645): Dominican brother, a native of Spain; entered Dominican Friary at Lima, Peru, 1622; served as doorkeeper until his death; beatified, 1837; canonized 1975; feast, Sept. 16.

**Mazzuchelli, Samuel C.** (1806-1864): Italian Dominican; missionary in midwestern U.S.; called builder of the West; writer.

**Membre, Zenobius** (1645-1687): French Franciscan; missionary among Indians of Illinois; accompanied LaSalle expedition down the Mississippi (1681-1682) and Louisiana colonizing expedition (1684) which landed in Texas; murdered by Indians.

**Nerinckx, Charles** (1761-1824): Belgian priest; missionary in Kentucky; founded Sisters of Loretto at the Foot of the Cross.

**Nobrega, Manoel** (1517-1570): Portuguese Jesuit; leader of first Jesuit missionaries to Brazil, 1549.

**Padilla, Juan de** (d. 1542): Spanish Franciscan; missionary among Indians of Mexico and southwestern U.S.; killed by Indians in Kansas; protomartyr of the U.S.

**Palou, Francisco** (c. 1722-1789): Spanish Franciscan; accompanied Junipero Serra to Mexico, 1749; founded Mission Dolores in San Francisco; wrote history of the Franciscans in California.

**Pariseau, Mother Mary Joseph** (1833-1902): Canadian Sister of Charity of Providence; missionary in state of Washington from 1856; founded first hospitals in northwest territory; artisan and architect. Represents Washington in National Statuary Hall.

**Peter of Ghent** (d. 1572): Belgian Franciscan brother; missionary in Mexico for 49 years.

**Porres, Martin de, St.** (1579-1639): Peruvian Dominican oblate; his father was a Spanish soldier and his mother a black freedwoman from Panama; called wonder worker of Peru; beatified, 1837; canonized, 1962; feast, Nov. 3.

**Quiroga, Vasco de** (1470-1565): Spanish missionary in Mexico; founded hospitals; bishop of Michoacan, 1537.

**Ravalli, Antonio** (1811-1884): Italian Jesuit; missionary in far-western United States, mostly Montana, for 40 years.

**Raymbaut, Charles** (1602-1643): French Jesuit; missionary among Indians of Canada and northern U.S..

**Richard, Gabriel** (1767-1832): French Sulpician; missionary in Illinois and Michigan; a founder of University of Michigan; elected delegate to Congress from Michigan, 1823; first priest to hold seat in the House of Representatives.

**Rodriguez, Alonso, Bl.** (1598-1628): Spanish Jesuit; missionary in Paraguay; martyred; beatified, 1934; feast, Nov. 17.

**Rosati, Joseph** (1789-1843): Italian Vincentian; missionary bishop in U.S. (vicar apostolic of Mississippi and Alabama, 1822; coadjutor of Louisiana and the Two Floridas, 1823-26; administrator of New Orleans, 1826-29; first bishop of St. Louis, 1826-1843).

**Sahagun, Bernardino de** (c. 1500-1590): Spanish Franciscan; missionary in Mexico for over 60 years; expert on Aztec archaeology.

**Seelos, Francis X.** (1819-1867): Redemptorist

missionary, born Bavaria; ordained, 1844, at Baltimore; missionary in Pittsburgh and New Orleans.

**Serra, Junipero** (1713-1784): Spanish Franciscan, b. Majorca; missionary in America; arrived Mexico, 1749, where he did missionary work for 20 years; began work in Upper California in 1769 and established nine of the 21 Franciscan missions along the Pacific coast; baptized some 6,000 Indians and confirmed almost 5,000; a cultural pioneer of California. Represents California in Statuary Hall.

**Seghers, Charles J.** (1839-1886): Belgian missionary bishop in North America; Apostle of Alaska; archbishop of Oregon City (now Portland), 1880-1884; murdered by berserk companion.

**Solanus, St. Francis** (1549-1610): Spanish Franciscan; missionary in Paraguay, Argentina and Peru; wonder worker of the New World; canonized, 1726; feast, July 13.

**Sorin, Edward F.** (1814-1893): French priest; member of Congregation of Holy Cross; sent to U.S. in 1841; founder and first president of the University of Notre Dame; missionary in Indiana and Michigan.

**Todadilla, Anthony de** (1704-1746): Spanish Capuchin; missionary to Indians of Venezuela; killed by Motilones.

**Turibius de Mogrovejo, St.** (1538-1606): Spanish archbishop of Lima, Peru, c. 1580-1606; canonized 1726; feast, Apr. 27.

**Twelve Apostles of Mexico** (early 16th century): Franciscan priests; arrived in Mexico, 1524: Fathers Martin de Valencia (leader), Francisco de Soto, Martin de la Coruna, Juan Suares, Antonio de Ciudad Rodrigo, Toribio de Benevente, Garcia de Cisneros, Luis de Fuensalida, Juan de Ribas, Francisco Ximenes; Brothers Andres de Coroboda, Juan de Palos.

**Valdivia, Luis de** (1561-1641): Spanish Jesuit; defender of Indians in Peru and Chile.

**Vasques de Espinosa, Antonio** (early 17th century): Spanish Carmelite; missionary and explorer in Mexico, Panama and western coast of South America.

**Vieira, Antonio** (1608-1687): Portuguese Jesuit; preacher; missionary in Peru and Chile; protector of Indians against exploitation by slave owners and traders; considered foremost prose writer of 17th-century Portugal.

**White, Andrew** (1579-1656): English Jesuit; missionary among Indians in Maryland.

**Wimmer, Boniface** (1809-1887): German Benedictine; missionary among German immigrants in the U.S..

**Youville, Marie Marguerite d', Bl.** (1701-1771): Canadian widow; foundress of Sisters of Charity (Grey Nuns), 1738, at Montreal; beatified, 1959; feast, Dec. 23.

**Zumarraga, Juan de** (1468-1548): Spanish Franciscan; missionary; first bishop of Mexico; introduced first printing press in New World, published first book in America, a catechism for Aztec Indians; extended missions in Mexico and Central America; vigorous opponent of exploitation of Indians; approved of devotions at Guadalupe; leading figure in early church history in Mexico.

The starting point of the mainstream of Catholic history in the United States was Baltimore at the end of the Revolutionary War, although before that time Catholic explorers had traversed much of the country and missionaries had done considerable work among the Indians in the Southeast, Northeast and Southwest.

## Beginning of Organization

Father John Carroll's appointment as superior of the American missions on June 9, 1784, was the first step toward organization of the Church in this country.

At that time, according to a report he made to Rome in 1785, there were approximately 25,000 Catholics in the general population of four million. Many of them had been in the Colonies for several generations. Among them were such outstanding figures as Charles Carroll, a member of the Continental Congress and signer of the Declaration of Independence; Thomas FitzSimons of Philadelphia and Oliver Pollock, the Virginia agent, who raised funds for the militia; Commander John Barry, father of the American Navy, and numerous high-ranking army officers. For the most part, however, Catholics were an unknown minority laboring under legal and social handicaps.

Father Carroll, the cousin of Charles Carroll, was named the first American bishop in 1789 and placed in charge of the Diocese of Baltimore, whose boundaries were coextensive with those of the United States. He was consecrated in England Aug. 15, 1790, and installed in his see the following Dec. 12.

Ten years later, Father Leonard Neale became his coadjutor and the first bishop ordained in the United States. Bishop Carroll became an archbishop in 1808 when Baltimore was designated a metropolitan see and the new dioceses of Boston, New York, Philadelphia and Bardstown were established. These jurisdictions were later subdivided, and by 1840 there were, in addition to Baltimore, 15 dioceses, 500 priests and 663,000 Catholics in the general population of 17 million.

## Priests and First Seminaries

The number of the 24 original priests was gradually augmented with the arrival of others from France, after the Civil Constitution on the Clergy went into effect there, and other countries. Among the earliest arrivals were several Sulpicians who established the first seminary in the U.S., St. Mary's, Baltimore, in 1791. By 1815, 30 alumni of the school had been ordained to the priesthood. By that time, two additional seminaries were in operation: Mt. St. Mary's, established in 1809 at Emmitsburg, Md., and St. Thomas, founded two years later, at Bardstown, Ky. These and similar institutions founded later played key roles in the development and growth of the American clergy.

## Early Schools

Early educational enterprises included the establishment in 1791 of a school at Georgetown which later became the first Catholic university in the U.S.; the opening of a secondary school for girls, conducted by Visitation Nuns, in 1792 at Georgetown; and the start of a similar school in the first decade of the 19th century at Emmitsburg, Md., by Saint Elizabeth Ann Seton and the Sisters of Charity of St. Joseph, the first religious community of American foundation.

By the 1840s, which saw the beginnings of the present public school system, more than 200 Catholic elementary schools, half of them west of the Alleghenies, were in operation. From this start, the Church subsequently built the greatest private system of education in the world.

## Trusteeism

The initial lack of organization in ecclesiastical affairs, nationalistic feeling among Catholics and the independent action of some priests were factors involved in several early crises.

In Philadelphia, some German Catholics withdrew from one parish in 1789 and founded one of their own, Holy Trinity, which they maintained until 1802. Controversy over the affair reached the point of schism in 1796. Philadelphia was also the scene of the Hogan Schism, which developed in the 1820's when Father William Hogan, with the aid of lay trustees, seized control of St. Mary's Cathedral. His movement, for churches and parishes controlled by other than canonical procedures and run in extra-legal ways, was nullified by a decision of the Pennsylvania Supreme Court in 1822.

Similar troubles seriously disturbed the peace of the Church in other places, principally New York, Baltimore, Buffalo, Charleston and New Orleans.

Dangers arising from the exploitation of lay control were gradually diminished with the extension and enforcement of canonical procedures and with changes in civil law about the middle of the century.

## Bigotry

Bigotry against Catholics waxed and waned during the 19th century and into the 20th. The first major campaign of this kind, which developed in the wake of the panic of 1819 and lasted for about 25 years, was mounted in 1830 when the number of Catholic immigrants began to increase to a noticeable degree. Nativist anti-Catholicism generated a great deal of violence, represented by climaxes in loss of life and property in Charlestown, Mass., in 1834, and in Philadelphia 10 years later. Later bigotry was fomented by the Know-Nothings, in the 1850s; the Ku Klux Klan, from 1866; the American Protective Association, from 1887, and the Guardians of Liberty. Perhaps the last eruption of virulently overt anti-Catholicism occurred during the campaign of Alfred E. Smith for the presidency in 1928. Observers feel the issue was muted to a considerable extent in the political area with the election of John F. Kennedy to the presidency in 1960.

## Growth and Immigration

Between 1830 and 1900, the combined factors of

natural increase, immigration and conversion raised the Catholic population to 12 million. A large percentage of the growth figure represented immigrants: some 2.7 million, largely from Ireland, Germany and France, between 1830 and 1880; and another 1.25 million during the 1880s when Eastern and Southern Europeans came in increasing numbers. By the 1860s the Catholic Church, with most of its members concentrated in urban areas, was one of the largest religious bodies in the country.

The efforts of progressive bishops to hasten the acculturation of Catholic immigrants occasioned a number of controversies, which generally centered around questions concerning national or foreign-language parishes. One of them, called Cahenslyism, arose from complaints that German Catholic immigrants were not being given adequate pastoral care.

Immigration continued after the turn of the century, but its impact was more easily cushioned through the application of lessons learned earlier in dealing with problems of nationality and language.

## Councils of Baltimore

The bishops of the growing U.S. dioceses met at Baltimore for seven provincial councils between 1829 and 1849.

In 1846, they proclaimed the Blessed Virgin Mary patroness of the United States under the title of the Immaculate Conception, eight years before the dogma was proclaimed.

After the establishment of the Archdiocese of Oregon City in 1846 and the elevation to metropolitan status of St. Louis, New Orleans, Cincinnati and New York, the first of the three plenary councils of Baltimore was held.

The first plenary assembly was convoked on May 9, 1852, with Archbishop Francis P. Kenrick of Baltimore as papal legate. The bishops drew up regulations concerning parochial life, matters of church ritual and ceremonies, the administration of church funds and the teaching of Christian doctrine.

The second plenary council, meeting from Oct. 7 to 21, 1866, under the presidency of Archbishop Martin J. Spalding, formulated a condemnation of several current doctrinal errors and established norms affecting the organization of dioceses, the education and conduct of the clergy, the management of ecclesiastical property, parochial duties and general education.

Archbishop (later Cardinal) James Gibbons called into session the third plenary council which lasted from Nov. 9 to Dec. 7, 1884. Among highly significant results of actions taken by this assembly were the preparation of the line of Baltimore catechisms which became a basic means of religious instruction in this country; legislation which fixed the pattern of Catholic education by requiring the building of elementary schools in all parishes; the establishment of the Catholic University of America in Washington, D.C., in 1889; and the determination of six holy days of obligation for observance in this country.

The enactments of the three plenary councils have had the force of particular law for the Church in the United States.

The Holy See established the Apostolic Delegation in Washington, D.C., on Jan. 24, 1893.

### Slavery

In the Civil War period, as before, Catholics reflected attitudes of the general population with respect to the issue of slavery. Some supported it, some opposed it, but none were prominent in the Abolition Movement. Gregory XVI had condemned the slave trade in 1839, but no contemporary pope or American bishop published an official document on slavery itself. The issue did not split Catholics in schism as it did Baptists, Methodists and Presbyterians.

Catholics fought on both sides in the Civil War. Five hundred members of 20 or more sisterhoods served the wounded of both sides.

One hundred thousand of the four million slaves emancipated in 1863 were Catholics; the highest concentrations were in Louisiana, about 60,000, and Maryland, 16,000. Three years later, their pastoral care was one of the subjects covered in nine decrees issued by the Second Plenary Council of Baltimore. The measures had little practical effect with respect to integration of the total Catholic community, predicated as they were on the proposition that individual bishops should handle questions regarding segregation in churches and related matters as best they could in the pattern of local customs.

Long entrenched segregation practices continued in force through the rest of the 19th century and well into the 20th. The first effective efforts to alter them were initiated by Cardinal Joseph Ritter of St. Louis in 1947, Cardinal (then Archbishop) Patrick O'Boyle of Washington in 1948, and Bishop Vincent Waters of Raleigh in 1953.

### Friend of Labor

The Church became known during the 19th century as a friend and ally of labor in seeking justice for the working man. Cardinal Gibbons journeyed to Rome in 1887, for example, to defend and prevent a condemnation of the Knights of Labor by Leo XIII. The encyclical *Rerum Novarum* was hailed by many American bishops as a confirmation, if not vindication, of their own theories. Catholics have always formed a large percentage of union membership, and some have served unions in positions of leadership.

### The American Heresy

Near the end of the century some controversy developed over what was characterized as Americanism or the phantom heresy. It was alleged that Americans were discounting the importance of contemplative virtues, exalting the practical virtues, and watering down the purity of Catholic doctrine for the sake of facilitating convert work.

The French translation of Father Walter Elliott's *Life of Isaac Hecker*, which fired the controversy, was one of many factors that led to the issuance of Leo XIII's *Testem Benevolentiae* in

January, 1899, in an attempt to end the matter. It was the first time the orthodoxy of the Church in the U.S. was called into question.

## Schism

In the 1890s, serious friction developed between Poles and Irish in Scranton, Buffalo and Chicago, resulting in schism and the establishment of the Polish National Church. A central figure in the affair was Father Francis Hodur, who was excommunicated by Bishop William O'Hara of Scranton in 1898. Nine years later, his ordination by an Old Catholic Archbishop of Utrecht gave the new church its first bishop.

Another schism of the period led to formation of the American Carpatho-Russian Orthodox Greek Catholic Church.

## Coming of Age

In 1900, there were 12 million Catholics in the total U.S. population of 76 million, 82 dioceses in 14 provinces, and 12,000 priests and members of about 40 communities of men religious. Many sisterhoods, most of them of European origin and some of American foundation, were engaged in Catholic educational and hospital work, two of their traditional apostolates.

The Church in the United States was removed from mission status with promulgation of the apostolic constitution *Sapienti Consilio* by Pope St. Pius X on June 29, 1908.

Before that time, and even into the early 1920s, the Church in this country received financial assistance from mission-aid societies in France, Bavaria and Austria. Already, however, it was making increasing contributions of its own. At the present time, it is the heaviest national contributor to the worldwide Society for the Propagation of the Faith.

American foreign missionary personnel increased from 14 or less in 1906 to 7,148 by 1975 (197 diocesan priests, 3,692 religious priests and brothers, 2,850 sisters, 65 seminarians, 344 lay persons). The first missionary seminary in the U.S. was in operation at Techny, Ill., in 1909, under the auspices of the Society of the Divine Word. Maryknoll, the first American missionary society, was established in 1911 and sent its first priests to China in 1918. Despite these contributions, the Church in the U.S. has not matched the missionary commitment of some other nations.

## Bishops' Conference

A highly important apparatus for mobilizing the Church's resources was established in 1917 under the title of the National Catholic War Council. Its name was changed to National Catholic Welfare Conference several years later, but its objectives remained the same: to serve as an advisory and coordinating agency of the American bishops for advancing works of the Church in fields of social significance and impact — education, communications, immigration, social action, legislation, youth and lay organizations.

The forward thrust of the bishops' social thinking was evidenced in a program of social re-construction they recommended in 1919. By 1945, all but one of their twelve points had been enacted into legislation.

The NCWC was renamed the United States Catholic Conference (USCC) in November, 1966, when the hierarchy also organized itself as a territorial conference with pastoral-juridical authority under the title, National Conference of Catholic Bishops. The USCC is carrying on the functions of the former NCWC.

## Pastoral Concerns

The potential for growth of the Church in this country by immigration was sharply reduced but not entirely curtailed after 1921 with the passage of restrictive federal legislation. As a result, the Catholic population became more stabilized and, to a certain extent and for many reasons, began to acquire an identity of its own.

Some increase from outside has taken place in the past 50 years, however; from Canada, from Central and Eastern European countries, and from Puerto Rico and Latin American countries since World War II. This influx, while not as great as that of the 19th century and early 20th, has enriched the Church here with a sizable body of Eastern-Rite Catholics for whom eight ecclesiastical jurisdictions were established between 1924 and 1969. It has also created a challenge for pastoral care of millions of Hispanics in urban centers and in agricultural areas where migrant workers are employed.

The Church continues to grapple with serious pastoral problems in rural areas, where about 600 counties are no-priest land. The National Catholic Rural Life Conference was established in 1922 in an attempt to make the Catholic presence felt on the land, and the Glenmary Society since its foundation in 1939 has devoted itself to this single apostolate. Religious communities and diocesan priests are similarly engaged.

Other challenges lie in the cities and suburbs where 75 percent of the Catholic population lives. Conditions peculiar to each segment of the metropolitan area have developed in recent years as the flight to the suburbs has not only altered some traditional aspects of parish life but has also, in combination with many other factors, left behind a complex of special problems in inner city areas.

## Contemporary Factors

The Church in the U.S. is in a stage of transition from a relatively stable and long established order of life and action to a new order of things. Some of the phenomena of this period are:

• differences in trends and emphasis in theology, and in interpretation and implementation of directives of the Second Vatican Council, resulting in situations of conflict;

• the changing spiritual formation, professional education, style of life and ministry of priests and religious (men and women), which are altering influential patterns of pastoral and specialized service;

• vocations to the priesthood and religious life, which are generally in decline;

• departures from the priesthood and religious life which, while small percentage-wise, are numerous enough to be a matter of serious concern;
• decline of traditional devotional practices;
• exercise of authority along the lines of collegiality and subsidiarity;
• structure and administration, marked by a trend toward greater participation in the life and work of the Church by its members on all levels, from the parish on up;
• alienation from the Church, leading some persons into the catacombs of an underground church,

"anonymous Christianity" and religious indifferentism;
• education, undergoing crisis and change in Catholic schools and seeking new ways of reaching out to the young not in Catholic schools and to adults;
• social witness in ministry to the world, which is being shaped by the form of contemporary needs — e.g., race relations, poverty, the peace movement, the Third World;
• ecumenism, involving the Church in interfaith relations on a wider scale than before.

## BACKGROUND DATES IN U.S. CATHOLIC CHRONOLOGY

*Dates in this section refer mostly to earlier "firsts" and developments in the background of Catholic history in the United States. For other dates, see various sections of the Almanac.*

### Alabama

**1540:** Priests crossed the territory with De Soto's expedition.
**1560:** Five Dominicans in charge of mission at Santa Cruz des Nanipacna.
**1682:** La Salle claimed territory for France.
**1704:** First parish church established at Fort Louis de la Mobile under the care of diocesan priests.
**1829:** Mobile diocese established (redesignated Mobile-Birmingham, 1954-69).
**1830:** Spring Hill College, Mobile, established.
**1834:** Visitation Nuns established an academy at Summerville.
**1969:** Birmingham diocese established.
**1980:** Mobile made metropolitan see.

### Alaska

**1779:** Mass celebrated for first time on shore of Port Santa Cruz on lower Bucareli Bay on May 13 by Franciscan Juan Riobo.
**1868:** Alaska placed under jurisdiction of Vancouver Island.
**1879:** Father John Althoff became first resident missionary.
**1886:** Archbishop Charles J. Seghers, "Apostle of Alaska," murdered by a guide; had surveyed southern and northwest Alaska in 1873 and 1877, respectively.
Sisters of St. Ann first nuns in Alaska.
**1887:** Jesuits enter Alaska territory.
**1894:** Alaska made prefecture apostolic.
**1902:** Sisters of Providence opened hospital at Nome.
**1916:** Alaska made vicariate apostolic.
**1917:** In first ordination in territory, Rev. G. Edgar Gallant raised to priesthood.
**1951:** Juneau diocese established.
**1962:** Fairbanks diocese established.
**1966:** Anchorage archdiocese established.

### Arizona

**1539:** Franciscan Marcos de Niza explored the state.
**1540:** Franciscans Juan de Padilla and Marcos de Niza accompanied Coronado expedition through the territory.

**1629:** Spanish Franciscans began work among Moqui Indians.
**1632:** Franciscan Martin de Arvide killed by Indians.
**1680:** Franciscans Jose de Espeleta, Augustin de Santa Maria, Jose de Figueroa and Jose de Trujillo killed in Pueblo Revolt.
**1700:** Jesuit Eusebio Kino established mission at San Xavier del Bac, near Tucson.
**1767:** Jesuits expelled; Franciscans took over 10 missions.
**1828:** Spanish missionaries expelled by Mexican government.
**1863:** Jesuits returned to San Xavier del Bac briefly.
**1869:** Sisters of Loretto arrived to conduct schools at Bisbee and Douglas.
**1897:** Tucson diocese established.
**1969:** Phoenix diocese established.

### Arkansas

**1541:** Priests accompanied De Soto expedition through the territory.
**1673:** Marquette visited Indians in east.
**1686:** Henri de Tonti established trading post, first white settlement in territory.
**1700-1702:** Fr. Nicholas Foucault working among Indians.
**1805:** Bishop Carroll of Baltimore appointed Administrator Apostolic of Arkansas.
**1838:** Sisters of Loretto opened first Catholic school.
**1843:** Little Rock diocese established. There were about 700 Catholics in state, two churches, one priest.
**1851:** Sisters of Mercy founded St. Mary's Convent in Little Rock.

### California

**1542:** Cabrillo discovered Upper (Alta) California; name of priest accompanying expedition unknown.
**1602:** On Nov. 12 Carmelite Andres de la Ascencion offered first recorded Mass in California on shore of San Diego Bay.
**1697:** Missionary work in Lower and Upper Californias entrusted to Jesuits.
**1767:** Jesuits expelled from territory. Spanish Crown confiscated their property, including the Pious Fund for Missions. Upper California missions entrusted to Franciscans.
**1769:** Franciscan Junipero Serra began establish-

ment of Franciscan missions in California, in present San Diego. (See Franciscan Missions of Upper California.)

**1775:** Franciscan Luis Jayme killed by Indians at San Diego Mission.

**1779:** Diocese of Sonora, Mexico, which included Upper California, established.

**1781:** On Sept. 4 an expedition from San Gabriel Mission founded present city of Los Angeles — Pueblo "de Nuestra Senora de los Angeles." Franciscans Francisco Hermenegildo Garces, Juan Antonio Barreneche, Juan Marcello Diaz and Jose Matias Moreno killed by Indians.

**1812:** Franciscan Andres Quintana killed at Santa Cruz Mission.

**1822:** Dedication on Dec. 8 of Old Plaza Church, "Assistant Mission of Our Lady of the Angels."

**1833:** Missions secularized, finally confiscated.

**1840:** Pope Gregory XVI established Diocese of Both Californias.

**1846:** Peter H. Burnett, who became first governor of California in 1849, received into Catholic Church.

**1848:** Mexico ceded California to the United States.

**1850:** Monterey diocese erected; title changed to Monterey-Los Angeles, 1859; and to Los Angeles-San Diego, 1922.

**1851:** University of Santa Clara chartered.

Sisters of Notre Dame de Namur opened women's College of Notre Dame at San Jose; chartered in 1868; moved to Belmont, 1923.

**1852:** Baja California detached from Monterey diocese.

**1853:** San Francisco archdiocese established.

**1855:** Negotiations inaugurated to restore confiscated California missions to Church.

**1868:** Grass Valley diocese established; transferred to Sacramento in 1886.

**1922:** Monterey-Fresno diocese established; became separate dioceses, 1967.

**1934:** Sesquicentennial of Serra's death observed; Serra Year officially declared by Legislature and Aug. 24 observed as Serra Day.

**1936:** Los Angeles made archdiocese. San Diego diocese established.

**1952:** Law exempting non-profit, religious-sponsored elementary and secondary schools from taxation upheld in referendum, Nov. 4.

**1953:** Archbishop James Francis McIntyre of Los Angeles made cardinal by Pius XII.

**1962:** Oakland, Santa Rosa and Stockton dioceses established.

**1973:** Archbishop Timothy Manning of Los Angeles made cardinal by Pope Paul VI.

**1976:** Orange diocese established.

**1978:** San Bernardino diocese established.

**1981:** San Jose diocese established.

Byzantine-Rite eparchy of Van Nuys established.

### Colorado

**1858:** First parish in Colorado established.

**1864:** Sisters of Loretto at the Foot of the Cross, first nuns in the state, established academy at Denver.

**1868:** Vicariate Apostolic of Colorado and Utah established.

**1887:** Denver diocese established.

**1888:** Regis College founded.

**1941:** Denver made archdiocese. Pueblo diocese established.

**1983:** Colorado Springs diocese established.

### Connecticut

**1651:** Probably first priest to enter state was Jesuit Gabriel Druillettes; ambassador of Governor of Canada, he participated in a New England Colonial Council at New Haven.

**1756:** Catholic Acadians, expelled from Nova Scotia, settled in the state.

**1791:** Rev. John Thayer, first native New England priest, offered Mass at the Hartford home of Noah Webster, his Yale classmate.

**1808:** Connecticut became part of Boston diocese.

**1818:** Religious freedom established by new constitution, although the Congregational Church remained, in practice, the state church.

**1829:** Father Bernard O'Cavanaugh became first resident priest in state.

*Catholic Press* of Hartford established.

**1830:** First Catholic church in state dedicated at Hartford.

Father James Fitton (1805-81), New England missionary, was assigned to Hartford for six years. He ministered to Catholics throughout the state.

**1843:** Hartford diocese established.

**1882:** Knights of Columbus founded by Father Michael J. McGivney.

**1942:** Fairfield University founded.

**1953:** Norwich and Bridgeport dioceses established. Hartford made archdiocese.

**1956:** Byzantine Rite Exarchate of Stamford established; made eparchy, 1958.

### Delaware

**1730:** Mount Cuba, New Castle County, the scene of Catholic services.

**1750:** Jesuit mission at Apoquiniminck administered from Maryland.

**1772:** First permanent parish established at Coffee Run.

**1792:** French Catholics from Santo Domingo settled near Wilmington.

**1816:** St. Peter's Church, later the cathedral of the diocese, erected at Wilmington.

**1830:** Daughters of Charity opened school and orphanage at Wilmington.

**1868:** Wilmington diocese established.

**1869:** Visitation Nuns established residence in Wilmington.

### District of Columbia

**1641:** Jesuit Andrew White evangelized Anacosta Indians.

**1774:** Father John Carroll ministered to Catholics.

**1789:** Georgetown, first Catholic college in U.S., established.

**1791:** Pierre Charles L'Enfant designed the Federal City of Washington. His plans were not fully implemented until the early 1900s.

**1792:** James Hoban designed the White House.

**1794:** Father Anthony Caffrey began St. Patrick's Church, first parish church in the new Federal City.

**1801:** Poor Clares opened school for girls in Georgetown; first school established by nuns in U.S..

**1802:** First mayor of Washington, appointed by President Jefferson, was Judge Robert Brent.

**1889:** Catholic University of America founded.

**1893:** Apostolic Delegation established; became an Apostolic Nunciature in 1984 with the establishment of full diplomatic relations between the U.S. and the Vatican.

**1919:** National Catholic Welfare Conference (now the United States Catholic Conference) organized by American hierarchy to succeed National Catholic War Council.

**1920:** Cornerstone of National Shrine of Immaculate Conception laid.

**1939:** Washington made archdiocese of equal rank with Baltimore, under direction of same archbishop.

**1947:** Washington archdiocese received its own archbishop, was separated from Baltimore; became a metropolitan see in 1965.

**1967:** Archbishop Patrick A. O'Boyle of Washington made cardinal by Pope Paul VI.

**1976:** Archbishop William Baum of Washington made a cardinal by Pope Paul VI; transferred to Roman Curia in 1980 as prefect of Sacred Congregation for Catholic Education.

## Florida

**1513:** Ponce de Leon discovered Florida.

**1521:** Missionaries accompanying Ponce de Leon and other explorers probably said first Masses within present limits of U.S..

**1528:** Franciscans landed on western shore.

**1539:** Twelve missionaries landed with De Soto at Tampa Bay.

**1549:** Dominican Luis Cancer de Barbastro and two companions slain by Indians near Tampa Bay.

**1565:** City of St. Augustine, oldest in U.S., founded by Pedro Menendez de Aviles, who was accompanied by four secular priests.

America's oldest mission, Nombre de Dios, was established.

Father Martin Francisco Lopez de Mendoza Grajales became the first parish priest of St. Augustine, where the first parish in the U.S. was established.

**1572:** St. Francis Borgia, general of the Society, withdrew Jesuits from Florida.

**1606:** Bishop Juan de las Cabeyas de Altamirano, O.P., conducted the first episcopal visitation in the U.S..

**1620:** The chapel of Nombre de Dios was dedicated to Nuestra Senora de la Leche y Buen Parto (Our Nursing Mother of the Happy Delivery); oldest shrine to the Blessed Mother in the U.S..

**1704:** Destruction of Florida's northern missions by English and Indian troops led by Governor James Moore of South Carolina. Franciscans Juan de Parga, Dominic Criodo, Tiburcio de Osorio, Augustine Ponze de Leon, Marcos

Delgado and two Indians, Anthony Enixa and Amador Cuipa Feliciano, were slain by the invaders.

**1735:** Bishop Francis Martinez de Tejadu Diaz de Velasco, auxiliary of Santiago, was the first bishop to take up residence in U.S., at St. Augustine.

**1793:** Florida and Louisiana were included in Diocese of New Orleans.

**1857:** Eastern Florida made a vicariate apostolic.

**1870:** St. Augustine diocese established.

**1917:** Convent Inspection Bill passed; repealed 1935.

**1958:** Miami diocese established.

**1968:** Miami made metropolitan see; Orlando and St. Petersburg dioceses established.

**1976:** Pensacola-Tallahassee diocese established.

**1984:** Palm Beach and Venice dioceses established.

## Georgia

**1540:** First priests to enter were chaplains with De Soto. They celebrated first Mass within territory of 13 original colonies.

**1566:** Pedro Martinez, first Jesuit martyr of the New World, was slain by Indians on Cumberland Island.

**1569:** Jesuit mission was opened at Guale Island by Father Antonio Sedeno.

**1572:** Jesuits withdrawn from area.

**1595:** Five Franciscans assigned to Province of Guale.

**1597:** Five Franciscan missionaries (Fathers Pedro de Corpa, Blas de Rodriguez, Miguel de Anon, Francisco de Berascolo and Brother Antonio de Badajoz) killed in coastal missions. Their cause for beatification was formally opened in 1984.

**1606:** Bishop Altamirano, O.P., conducted visitation of the Georgia area.

**1612:** First Franciscan province in U.S. erected under title of Santa Elena; it included Georgia, South Carolina and Florida.

**1655:** Franciscans had nine flourishing missions among Indians.

**1742:** Spanish missions ended as result of English conquest at Battle of Bloody Marsh.

**1796:** Augustinian Father Le Mercier was first post-colonial missionary to Georgia.

**1798:** Catholics granted right of refuge.

**1800:** First church erected in Savannah on lot given by city council.

**1810:** First church erected in Augusta on lot given by State Legislature.

**1850:** Savannah diocese established; became Savannah-Atlanta, 1937; divided into two separate sees, 1956.

**1864:** Father Emmeran Bliemel, of the Benedictine community of Latrobe, Pa., was killed at the battle of Jonesboro while serving as chaplain of the Confederate 10th Tennessee Artillery.

**1962:** Atlanta made metropolitan see.

## Hawaii

**1825:** Pope Leo XII entrusted missionary efforts in Islands to Sacred Hearts Fathers.

**1827:** The first Catholic missionaries arrived —
Fathers Alexis Bachelot, Abraham Armand and
Patrick Short, along with three lay brothers. After three years of persecution, the priests were
forcibly exiled.

**1836:** Father Arsenius Walsh, SS. CC., a British
subject, was allowed to remain in Islands but
was not permitted to proselytize or conduct missions.

**1839:** Hawaiian government signed treaty with
France granting Catholics freedom of worship
and same privileges as Protestants.

**1844:** Vicariate Apostolic of Sandwich Islands (Hawaii) erected.

**1873:** Father Damien de Veuster of the Sacred
Hearts Fathers arrived in Molokai and spent the
remainder of his life working among lepers.

**1941:** Honolulu diocese established, made a suffragan of San Francisco.

### Idaho

**1840:** Jesuit Pierre de Smet preached to the Flathead and Pend d'Oreille Indians; probably offered first Mass in state.

**1842:** Jesuit Nicholas Point opened a mission
among Coeur d'Alene Indians near St. Maries.

**1863:** Secular priests sent from Oregon City to administer to incoming miners.

**1867:** Sisters of Holy Names of Jesus and Mary
opened first Catholic school at Idaho City.

**1868:** Idaho made a vicariate apostolic.

**1870:** First church in Boise established.

Church lost most of missions among Indians of
Northwest Territory when Commission on Indian Affairs appointed Protestant missionaries to
take over.

**1893:** Boise diocese established.

### Illinois

**1673:** Jesuit Jacques Marquette, accompanying
Joliet, preached to Indians.

**1674:** Father Marquette set up a cabin for saying
Mass in what later became City of Chicago.

**1675:** Father Marquette established Mission of the
Immaculate Conception among Kaskaskia Indi-
ans, near present site of Utica; transferred to
Kaskaskia, 1703.

**1679:** La Salle brought with him Franciscans Louis
Hennepin, Gabriel de la Ribourde, and Zenobius
Membre.

**1680:** Father Ribourde was killed by Kickapoo Indians.

**1689:** Jesuit Claude Allouez died after 32 years of
missionary activity among Indians of Midwest;
he had evangelized Indians of 20 different tribes.
Jesuit Jacques Gravier succeeded Allouez as
vicar general of Illinois.

**1699:** Mission established at Cahokia, first permanent settlement in state.

**1730:** Father Gaston, a diocesan priest, was killed
at the Cahokia Mission.

**1763:** Jesuits were banished from the territory.

**1778:** Father Pierre Gibault championed Colonial
cause in the Revolution and aided greatly in securing states of Ohio, Indiana, Illinois, Michigan
and Wisconsin for Americans.

**1827:** The present St. Patrick's Parish at Ruma,
oldest English-speaking Catholic congregation
in state, was founded.

**1833:** Visitation Nuns established residence in
Kaskaskia.

**1843:** Chicago diocese established.

**1853:** Quincy diocese established; transferred to
Alton, 1857; Springfield, 1923.

**1860:** Quincy College founded.

**1877:** Peoria diocese established.

**1880:** Chicago made archdiocese.

**1887:** Belleville diocese established.

**1894:** Franciscan Sisters of Bl. Kunegunda (now
the Franciscan Sisters of Chicago) founded by
Mother Marie Therese (Josephine Dudzik).

**1908:** Rockford diocese established.

First American Missionary Congress held in Chicago.

**1924:** Archbishop Mundelein of Chicago made cardinal by Pope Pius XI.

**1926:** The 28th International Eucharistic Congress,
first held in U.S., convened in Chicago.

**1946:** Blessed Frances Xavier Cabrini, former resident of Chicago, was canonized; first U.S.
citizen raised to dignity of altar.

Archbishop Samuel A. Stritch of Chicago made
cardinal by Pope Pius XII.

**1948:** Joliet diocese established.

**1958:** Cardinal Stritch appointed Pro-Prefect of
the Sacred Congregation for the Propagation of
the Faith — the first U.S.-born prelate to be
named to the Roman Curia.

**1959:** Archbishop Albert G. Meyer of Chicago
made cardinal by Pope John XXIII.

**1961:** Eparchy of St. Nicholas of the Ukrainians established at Chicago.

**1967:** Archbishop John P. Cody of Chicago made
cardinal by Pope Paul VI.

**1983:** Archbishop Joseph L. Bernardin of Chicago
made cardinal by Pope John Paul II.

### Indiana

**1679:** Recollects Louis Hennepin and Gabriel de la
Ribourde passed through state.

**1686:** Land near present Notre Dame University at
South Bend given by French government to
Jesuits for mission.

**1749:** Beginning of the records of St. Francis
Xavier Church, Vincennes. These records continue with minor interruptions to the present.

**1778:** Father Gibault aided George Rogers Clark
in campaign against British in conquest of
Northwest Territory.

**1824:** Sisters of Charity of Nazareth, Ky., opened
St. Clare's Academy in Vincennes.

**1825:** Laying of cornerstone of third church of St.
Francis Xavier, which later (from 1834-98) was
the cathedral of the Vincennes diocese. The
church was designated a minor basilica in 1970
and is still in use as a parish church.

**1834:** Vincennes diocese established with Simon
Gabriel Brute as bishop; title changed to Indianapolis, 1898.

**1840:** Sisters of Providence founded St. Mary-of-
the-Woods College for women.

**1842:** University of Notre Dame founded by Holy

Cross Father Edward Sorin and Brothers of St. Joseph on land given the diocese of Vincennes by Father Stephen Badin.

**1853:** First Benedictine community established in state at St. Meinrad. It became an abbey in 1870 and an archabbey in 1954.

**1857:** Fort Wayne diocese established; changed to Fort Wayne-South Bend, 1960.

**1944:** Indianapolis made archdiocese. Lafayette and Evansville dioceses established.

**1957:** Gary diocese established.

### Iowa

**1673:** A Peoria village on Mississippi was visited by Father Marquette.

**1679:** Fathers Louis Hennepin and Gabriel de la Ribourde visited Indian villages.

**1836:** First permanent church, St. Raphael's, founded at Dubuque by Dominican Samuel Mazzuchelli.

**1837:** Dubuque diocese established.

**1838:** St. Joseph's Mission founded at Council Bluffs by Jesuit Father De Smet.

**1843:** Sisters of Charity of the Blessed Virgin Mary were first sisterhood in state.

Sisters of Charity opened Clarke College, Dubuque.

**1850:** First Trappist Monastery in state, Our Lady of New Melleray, was begun.

**1881:** Davenport diocese established.

**1882:** St. Ambrose College, Davenport, established.

**1893:** Dubuque made archdiocese.

**1902:** Sioux City diocese established.

**1911:** Des Moines diocese established.

### Kansas

**1542:** Franciscan Juan de Padilla, first martyr of the United States, was killed in central Kansas.

**1858:** St. Benedict's College founded.

**1863:** Sisters of Charity opened orphanage at Leavenworth, and St. John's Hospital in following year.

**1877:** Leavenworth diocese established; transferred to Kansas City in 1947.

**1887:** Dioceses of Concordia (transferred to Salina in 1944) and Wichita established.

**1888:** Oblate Sisters of Providence opened an orphanage for Negro boys at Leavenworth, first west of Mississippi.

**1951:** Dodge City diocese established.

**1952:** Kansas City made archdiocese.

### Kentucky

**1775:** First Catholic settlers came to Kentucky.

**1787:** Father Charles Maurice Whelan, first resident priest, ministered to settlers in the Bardstown district.

**1793:** Father Stephen T. Badin began missionary work in Kentucky.

**1806:** Dominican Fathers built Priory at St. Rose of Lima.

**1808:** Bardstown diocese established with Benedict Flaget as its first bishop; transferred to Louisville, 1841.

**1811:** Rev. Guy I. Chabrat first priest ordained west of the Allegheny Mountains.

St. Thomas Seminary founded.

**1812:** Sisters of Loretto founded by Rev. Charles Nerinckx; first religious community in the United States without foreign affiliation.

Sisters of Charity of Nazareth founded, the second native community of women founded in the West.

**1814:** Nazareth College for women established.

**1816:** Cornerstone of St. Joseph's Cathedral, Bardstown, laid.

**1836:** Hon. Benedict J. Webb founded *Catholic Advocate* first Catholic weekly newspaper in Kentucky.

**1848:** Trappist monks took up residence in Gethsemani.

**1849:** Cornerstone of Cathedral of the Assumption laid at Louisville.

**1852:** Know-Nothing troubles in state.

**1853:** Covington diocese established.

**1937:** Louisville made archdiocese. Owensboro diocese established.

### Louisiana

**1682:** La Salle's expedition, accompanied by two priests, completed discoveries of De Soto at mouth of Mississippi. LaSalle named territory Louisiana.

**1699:** French Catholics founded colony of Louisiana.

First recorded Mass offered Mar. 3, by Franciscan Father Anastase Douay.

**1706:** Father John Francis Buisson de St. Cosme was killed near Donaldsonville.

**1717:** Franciscan Anthony Margil established first Spanish mission in north central Louisiana.

**1718:** City of New Orleans founded by Jean Baptiste Le Moyne de Bienville.

**1720:** First resident priest in New Orleans was the French Recollect Prothais Boyer.

**1725:** Capuchin Fathers opened school for boys.

**1727:** Ursuline Nuns founded convent in New Orleans, oldest convent in what is now U.S.; they conducted a school, hospital and orphan asylum.

**1793:** New Orleans diocese established.

**1850:** New Orleans made archdiocese.

**1853:** Natchitoches diocese established; transferred to Alexandria in 1910; became Alexandria-Shreveport in 1977.

**1892:** Sisters of Holy Family, a black congregation, established at New Orleans.

**1912:** Loyola University of South established.

**1918:** Lafayette diocese established.

**1925:** Xavier University established in New Orleans.

**1961:** Baton Rouge diocese established.

**1962:** Catholic schools on all levels desegregated in New Orleans archdiocese.

**1977:** Houma-Thibodaux diocese established.

**1980:** Lake Charles diocese established.

### Maine

**1604:** First Mass in territory celebrated by Father Nicholas Aubry, accompanying De Monts' expedition which was authorized by King of France to begin colonizing region.

**1605:** Colony founded on St. Croix Island; two secular priests served as chaplains.

**1613:** Four Jesuits attempted to establish permanent French settlement near mouth of Kennebec River.

**1619:** French Franciscans began work among settlers and Indians; driven out by English in 1628.

**1630:** New England made a prefecture apostolic in charge of French Capuchins.

**1633:** Capuchin Fathers founded missions on Penobscot River.

**1646:** Jesuits established Assumption Mission on Kennebec River.

**1688:** Church of St. Anne, oldest in New England, built at Oldtown.

**1704:** English soldiers destroyed French missions.

**1724:** English forces again attacked French settlements, killed Jesuit Sebastian Rale.

**1853:** Portland diocese established.

**1854:** Know-Nothing uprising resulted in burning of church in Bath.

**1856:** Anti-Catholic feeling continued; church at Ellsworth burned.

**1864:** Sisters of Congregation of Notre Dame from Montreal opened academy at Portland.

**1875:** James A. Healy, first bishop of Negro blood consecrated in U.S., became second Bishop of Portland.

## Maryland

**1634:** Maryland established by Lord Calvert. Two Jesuits among first colonists.

First Mass offered on Island of St. Clement in Lower Potomac by Jesuit Father Andrew White.

St. Mary's founded by English and Irish Catholics.

**1641:** St. Ignatius Parish founded by English Jesuits at Chapel Point, near Port Tobacco.

**1649:** Religious Toleration Act passed by Maryland Assembly. It was repealed in 1654 by Puritan-controlled government.

**1651:** Cecil Calvert, second Lord Baltimore, gave Jesuits 10,000 acres for use as Indian mission.

**1658:** Lord Baltimore restored Toleration Act.

**1672:** Franciscans came to Maryland under leadership of Father Massius Massey.

**1688:** Maryland became royal colony as a result of the Revolution in England; Anglican Church became the official religion (1692); Toleration Act repealed; Catholics disenfranchised and persecuted until 1776.

**1784:** Father John Carroll appointed prefect apostolic for the territory embraced by new Republic.

**1789:** Baltimore became first diocese established in U.S., with John Carroll as first bishop.

**1790:** Carmelite Nuns founded convent at Port Tobacco, the first in the English-speaking Colonies.

**1791:** First Synod of Baltimore held.

St. Mary's Seminary, first seminary in U.S., established.

**1793:** Rev. Stephen T. Badin first priest ordained by Bishop Carroll.

**1800:** Jesuit Leonard Neale became first bishop consecrated in present limits of U.S..

**1806:** Cornerstone of Assumption Cathedral, Baltimore, was laid.

**1808:** Baltimore made archdiocese.

**1809:** St. Joseph's College, first women's college in U.S., founded.

Sisters of Charity of St. Joseph founded by St. Elizabeth Ann Seton; first native American sisterhood.

**1821:** Assumption Cathedral, Baltimore, formally opened.

**1829:** Oblate Sisters of Providence, a Negro congregation, established at Baltimore.

First Provincial Council of Baltimore held; six others followed, in 1833, 1837, 1840, 1843, 1846 and 1849.

**1836:** Roger B. Taney appointed Chief Justice of Supreme Court by President Jackson.

**1852:** First of the three Plenary Councils of Baltimore convened. Subsequent councils were held in 1866 and 1884.

**1855:** German Catholic Central Verein founded.

**1886:** Archbishop James Gibbons of Baltimore made cardinal by Pope Leo XIII.

**1965:** Archbishop Lawrence Shehan of Baltimore made cardinal by Pope Paul VI.

## Massachusetts

**1630:** New England made a prefecture apostolic in charge of French Capuchins.

**1647:** Massachusetts Bay Company enacted an anti-priest law.

**1732:** Although Catholics were not legally admitted to colony, a few Irish families were in Boston; a priest was reported working among them.

**1755-56:** Acadians landing in Boston were denied services of a Catholic priest.

**1775:** General Washington discouraged Guy Fawkes Day procession in which pope was carried in effigy, and expressed surprise that there were men in his army "so void of common sense as to insult the religious feelings of the Canadians with whom friendship and an alliance are being sought."

**1780:** The Massachusetts State Constitution granted religious liberty, but required a religious test to hold public office and provided for tax to support Protestant teachers of piety, religion and morality.

**1788:** First public Mass said in Boston on Nov. 2 by Abbe de la Poterie, first resident priest.

**1803:** Church of Holy Cross erected in Boston with financial aid given by Protestants headed by John Adams.

**1808:** Boston diocese established.

**1831:** Irish Catholic immigration increased.

**1832:** St. Vincent's Orphan Asylum, oldest charitable institution in Boston, opened by Sisters of Mercy.

**1834:** Ursuline Convent in Charlestown burned by a Nativist mob.

**1843:** Holy Cross College founded.

**1855:** Catholic militia companies disbanded; nunneries' inspection bill passed.

**1859:** St. Mary's, first parochial school in Boston, opened.

**1860:** Portuguese Catholics from Azores settled in New Bedford.

**1870:** Springfield diocese established.

**1875:** Boston made archdiocese.

**1904:** Fall River diocese established.

**1911:** Archbishop O'Connell of Boston made cardinal by Pope Pius X.

**1950:** Worcester diocese established.

**1958:** Archbishop Richard J. Cushing of Boston made cardinal by Pope John XXIII.

**1966:** Apostolic Exarchate for Melkites in the U.S. established, with headquarters in Boston; made an eparchy in 1976.

**1973:** Archbishop Humberto S. Medeiros of Boston made cardinal by Pope Paul VI.

## Michigan

**1641:** Jesuits Isaac Jogues and Charles Raymbaut preached to Chippewas; named the rapids Sault Sainte Marie.

**1660:** Jesuit Rene Menard opened first regular mission in Lake Superior region.

**1668:** Father Marquette founded Sainte Marie Mission at Sault Sainte Marie.

**1671:** Father Marquette founded St. Ignace Mission at Michilimackinac.

**1701:** Fort Pontchartrain founded on present site of Detroit and placed in command of Antoine de la Mothe Cadillac. The Chapel of Sainte-Anne-de-Detroit founded.

**1706:** Franciscan Father Delhalle killed by Indians at Detroit.

**1823:** Father Gabriel Richard elected delegate to Congress from Michigan territory; he was the first priest chosen for the House of Representatives.

**1833:** Father Frederic Baraga celebrated first Mass in present Grand Rapids.

Detroit diocese established, embracing whole Northwest Territory.

**1843:** *Western Catholic Register* founded at Detroit.

**1845:** St. Vincent's Hospital, Detroit, opened by Sisters of Charity.

**1848:** Cathedral of Sts. Peter and Paul, Detroit, consecrated.

**1853:** Vicariate Apostolic of Upper Michigan established.

**1857:** Sault Ste. Marie diocese established; later transferred to Marquette.

**1877:** University of Detroit founded.

**1882:** Grand Rapids diocese established.

**1897:** Nazareth College for women founded.

**1937:** Detroit made archdiocese. Lansing diocese established.

**1938:** Saginaw diocese established.

**1946:** Archbishop Edward Mooney of Detroit created cardinal by Pope Pius XII.

**1949:** Opening of St. John's Theological (major) Seminary at Plymouth; this was first seminary in U.S. serving an entire ecclesiastical province (Detroit).

**1966:** Apostolic Exarchate for Maronites in the United States established, with headquarters in Detroit; made an eparchy in 1972; transferred to Brooklyn, 1977.

**1969:** Archbishop John Dearden of Detroit made cardinal by Pope Paul VI.

**1971:** Gaylord and Kalamazoo dioceses established.

**1982:** Apostolic Exarchate for Chaldean-Rite Catholics in United States established. Detroit designated see city.

## Minnesota

**1680:** Falls of St. Anthony discovered by Franciscan Louis Hennepin.

**1727:** First chapel, St. Michael the Archangel, erected near town of Frontenac and placed in charge of French Jesuits.

**1732:** Fort St. Charles built; Jesuits ministered to settlers.

**1736:** Jesuit Jean Pierre Aulneau killed by Indians.

**1839:** Swiss Catholics from Canada settled near Fort Snelling; Bishop Loras of Dubuque, accompanied by Father Pellamourgues, visited the Fort and administered sacraments.

**1841:** Father Lucian Galtier built Church of St. Paul, thus forming nucleus of modern city of same name.

**1850:** St. Paul diocese established.

**1851:** Sisters of St. Joseph arrived in state.

**1857:** St. John's University founded.

**1888:** St. Paul made archdiocese; name changed to St. Paul and Minneapolis in 1966.

**1889:** Duluth, St. Cloud and Winona dioceses established.

**1909:** Crookston diocese established.

**1957:** New Ulm diocese established.

## Mississippi

**1540:** Chaplains with De Soto expedition entered territory.

**1682:** Franciscans Zenobius Membre and Anastase Douay preached to Taensa and Natchez Indians. Father Membre offered first recorded Mass in the state on Mar. 29, Easter Sunday.

**1698:** Priests of Quebec Seminary founded missions near Natchez and Fort Adams.

**1702:** Father Nicholas Foucault murdered by Indians near Fort Adams.

**1721:** Missions practically abandoned, with only Father Juif working among Yazoos.

**1725:** Jesuit Mathurin de Petit carried on mission work in northern Mississippi.

**1729:** Indians tomahawked Jesuit Paul du Poisson near Fort Rosalie; Father Jean Souel shot by Yazoos.

**1736:** Jesuit Antoine Senat burned at stake by Chickasaws.

**1822:** Vicariate Apostolic of Mississippi and Alabama established.

**1825:** Mississippi made a separate vicariate apostolic.

**1837:** Natchez diocese established; became Natchez-Jackson in 1956; transferred to Jackson in 1977.

**1848:** Sisters of Charity opened orphan asylum and school in Natchez.
**1977:** Biloxi diocese established.

### Missouri

**1700:** Jesuit Gabriel Marest established a mission among Kaskaskia Indians near St. Louis.
**1734:** French Catholic miners and traders settled Old Mines and Sainte Genevieve.
**1750:** Jesuits visited French settlers.
**1762:** Mission established at St. Charles.
**1767:** Carondelet mission established.
**1770:** First church founded at St. Louis.
**1811:** Jesuits established Indian mission school at Florissant.
**1818:** Bishop Dubourg arrived at St. Louis, with Vincentians Joseph Rosati and Felix de Andreis. St. Louis University, the diocesan (Kenrick) seminary and the Vincentian Seminary in Perryville trace their origins to them.
**1826:** St. Louis diocese established.
**1828:** Sisters of Charity opened first hospital west of the Mississippi, at St. Louis.
**1832:** *The Shepherd of the Valley,* first Catholic paper west of the Mississippi.
**1845:** First conference of Society of St. Vincent de Paul in U.S. founded at St. Louis.
**1847:** St. Louis made archdiocese.
**1865:** A Test Oath Law passed by State Legislature (called Drake Convention) to crush Catholicism in Missouri. Law declared unconstitutional by Supreme Court in 1866.
**1867:** College of St. Teresa for women founded at Kansas City.
**1868:** St. Joseph diocese established.
**1880:** Kansas City diocese established.
**1946:** Archbishop John J. Glennon of St. Louis made cardinal by Pope Pius XII.
**1956:** Kansas City and St. Joseph dioceses combined into one see. Jefferson City and Springfield-Cape Girardeau dioceses established.
**1961:** Archbishop Joseph E. Ritter of St. Louis made cardinal by Pope John XXIII.
**1969:** Archbishop John J. Carberry of St. Louis made cardinal by Pope Paul VI.

### Montana

**1743:** Pierre and Francois Verendrye, accompanied by Jesuit Father Coquart, may have explored territory.
**1833:** Indian missions handed over to care of Jesuits by Second Provincial Council of Baltimore.
**1840:** Jesuit Pierre De Smet began missionary work among Flathead and Pend d'Oreille Indians.
**1841:** St. Mary's Mission established by Father De Smet and two companions on the Bitter Root River in present Stevensville.
**1845:** Jesuit Antonio Ravalli arrived at St. Mary's Mission; Ravalli County named in his honor.
**1859:** Fathers Point and Hoecken established St. Peter's Mission near the Great Falls.
**1869:** Sisters of Charity founded a hospital and school in Helena.
**1884:** Helena diocese established.

**1904:** Great Falls diocese established; redesignated Great Falls-Billings in 1980.
**1910:** Carroll College founded.
**1935:** Rev. Joseph M. Gilmore became first Montana priest elevated to hierarchy.

### Nebraska

**1541:** Coronado expedition, accompanied by Franciscan Juan de Padilla, reached the Platte River.
**1673:** Father Marquette visited Nebraska Indians.
**1720:** Franciscan Juan Miguel killed by Indians near Columbus.
**1855:** Father J. F. Tracy administered to Catholic settlement of St. Patrick and to Catholics in Omaha.
**1856:** Land was donated by Governor Alfred Cumming for a church in Omaha.
**1857:** Nebraska vicariate apostolic established.
**1878:** Creighton University established.
**1881:** Poor Clares, first contemplative group in state, arrived in Omaha. Duchesne College established.
**1885:** Omaha diocese established.
**1887:** Lincoln diocese established.
**1912:** Kearney diocese established; name changed to Grand Island, 1917.
**1917:** Father Flanagan founded Boy's Town for homeless boys, an institution which gained national and international recognition in subsequent years.
**1945:** Omaha made archdiocese.

### Nevada

**1774:** Franciscan missionaries passed through Nevada on way to California missions.
**1860:** First parish, serving Genoa, Carson City and Virginia City, established.
**1862:** Rev. Patrick Manogue appointed pastor of Virginia City. He established a school for boys and girls, an orphanage and hospital.
**1871:** Church erected at Reno.
**1931:** Reno diocese established; name changed to Reno-Las Vegas, 1977.

### New Hampshire

**1630:** Territory made part of a prefecture apostolic embracing all of New England.
**1784:** State Constitution included a religious test which barred Catholics from public office; local support was provided for public Protestant teachers of religion.
**1818:** The Barber family of Claremont was visited by their son Virgil (converted to Catholicism in 1816) accompanied by Father Charles Ffrench, O.P. The visit led to the conversion of the entire Barber family.
**1823:** Father Virgil Barber, minister who became a Jesuit priest, built first Catholic church and school at Claremont.
**1830:** Church of St. Aloysius dedicated at Dover.
**1853:** New Hampshire made part of the Portland diocese.
**1858:** Sisters of Mercy began to teach school at St. Anne's, Manchester.

**1877:** Catholics obtained full civil liberty and rights.
**1884:** Manchester diocese established.
**1893:** St. Anselm's College opened; St. Anselm's Abbey canonically erected.
**1937:** Francis P. Murphy became first Catholic governor of New Hampshire.

### New Jersey

**1668:** William Douglass of Bergen was refused a seat in General Assembly because he was a Catholic.
**1672:** Fathers Harvey and Gage visited Catholics in Woodbridge and Elizabethtown.
**1701:** Tolerance granted to all but "papists."
**1744:** Jesuit Theodore Schneider of Pennsylvania visited German Catholics of New Jersey.
**1762:** Fathers Ferdinand Farmer and Robert Harding working among Catholics in state.
**1765:** First Catholic community organized in New Jersey at Macopin in Passaic County.
**1776:** State Constitution tacitly excluded Catholics from office.
**1799:** Foundation of first Catholic school in state, St. John's at Trenton.
**1814:** First church in Trenton erected.
**1820:** Father Richard Bulger, of St. John's, Paterson, first resident pastor in state.
**1844:** Catholics obtained full civil liberty and rights.
**1853:** Newark diocese established.
**1856:** Seton Hall University established.
**1878:** John P. Holland, teacher at St. John's School, Paterson, invented first workable submarine.
**1881:** Trenton diocese established.
**1937:** Newark made archdiocese. Paterson and Camden dioceses established.
**1947:** U.S. Supreme Court ruled on N.J. bus case, permitting children attending non-public schools to ride on buses and be given other health services provided for those in public schools.
**1957:** Seton Hall College of Medicine and Dentistry established: the first medical school in state; it was run by Seton Hall until 1965.
**1963:** Byzantine Eparchy of Passaic established.
**1981:** Metuchen diocese established.

### New Mexico

**1539:** Territory explored by Franciscan Marcos de Niza.
**1581:** Franciscans Agustin Rodriguez, Juan de Santa Maria and Francisco Lopez named the region "New Mexico"; they later died at hands of Indians.
**1598:** Juan de Onate founded a colony at Chamita, where first chapel in state was built.
**1609-10:** Santa Fe founded.
**1631:** Franciscan Pedro de Miranda was killed by Indians.
**1632:** Franciscan Francisco Letrado was killed by Indians.
**1672:** Franciscan Pedro de Avila y Ayala was killed by Indians.
**1675:** Franciscan Alonso Gil de Avila was killed by Indians.

**1680:** Pueblo Indian revolt; 21 Franciscan missionaries massacred; missions destroyed.
**1692:** Franciscan missions refounded and expanded.
**1696:** Indians rebelled, five more Franciscan missionaries killed.
**1850:** Jean Baptiste Lamy appointed head of newly established Vicariate Apostolic of New Mexico.
**1852:** Sisters of Loretto arrived in Santa Fe.
**1853:** Santa Fe diocese established.
**1859:** Christian Brothers arrived, established first school for boys in New Mexico (later St. Michael's College).
**1865:** Sisters of Charity started first orphanage and hospital in Santa Fe. It was closed in 1966.
**1875:** Santa Fe made archdiocese.
**1939:** Gallup diocese established.
**1982:** Las Cruces diocese established.

### New York

**1524:** Giovanni da Verrazano was first white man to enter New York Bay.
**1642:** Jesuits Isaac Jogues and Rene Goupil were mutilated by Mohawks; Rene Goupil was killed by them shortly afterwards. Dutch Calvinists rescued Father Jogues.
**1646:** Jesuit Isaac Jogues and John Lalande were martyred by Iroquois at Ossernenon, now Auriesville.
**1654:** The Onondagas were visited by Jesuits from Canada.
**1655:** First permanent mission established near Syracuse.
**1656:** Church of St. Mary erected on Onondaga Lake, in first French settlement within state.
Kateri Tekakwitha, "Lily of the Mohawks," was born at Ossernenon, now Auriesville (d. in Canada, 1680). She was beatified in 1980.
**1658:** Indian uprisings destroyed missions among Cayugas, Senecas and Oneidas.
**1664:** English took New Amsterdam. Freedom of conscience allowed by the Duke of York, the new Lord Proprietor.
**1667:** Missions were restored under protection of Garaconthie, Onondaga chief.
**1678:** Franciscan Louis Hennepin, first white man to describe Niagara Falls, celebrated Mass there.
**1682:** Thomas Dongan appointed governor by Duke of York.
**1683:** English Jesuits came to New York, later opened a school.
**1700:** Although Assembly enacted a bill calling for religious toleration of all Christians in 1683, other penal laws were now enforced against Catholics; all priests were ordered out of the province.
**1709:** French Jesuit missionaries obliged to give up their central New York missions.
**1741:** Because of an alleged popish plot to burn city of New York, four whites were hanged and 11 blacks burned at stake.
**1774:** Elizabeth Bayley Seton, foundress of the American Sisters of Charity, was born in New York City on Aug. 28. She was canonized in 1975.
**1777:** State Constitution gave religious liberty, but

the naturalization law required an oath to renounce allegiance to any foreign ruler, ecclesiastical as well as civil.

**1785:** Cornerstone was laid for St. Peter's Church, New York City, first permanent structure of Catholic worship in state.

Trusteeism began to cause trouble at New York.

**1806:** Anti-Catholic 1777 Test Oath for naturalization repealed.

**1808:** New York diocese established.

**1828:** New York State Legislature enacted a law upholding sanctity of seal of confession.

**1834:** First native New Yorker to become a secular priest, Rev. John McCloskey, was ordained.

**1836:** John Nepomucene Neumann arrived from Bohemia and was ordained a priest in Old St. Patrick's Cathedral, New York City. He was canonized in 1977.

**1841:** Fordham University and Manhattanville College established.

**1847:** Albany and Buffalo dioceses established.

**1850:** New York made archdiocese.

**1853:** Brooklyn diocese established.

**1856:** Present St. Bonaventure University and Christ the King Seminary founded at Allegany.

**1858:** Cornerstone was laid of second (present) St. Patrick's Cathedral, New York City. The cathedral was completed in 1879.

**1868:** Rochester diocese established.

**1872:** Ogdensburg diocese established.

**1875:** Archbishop John McCloskey of New York made first American cardinal by Pope Pius IX.

**1878:** Franciscan Sisters of Allegany were first native American community to send members to foreign missions.

**1880:** William R. Grace was first Catholic mayor of New York City.

**1886:** Syracuse diocese established.

**1889:** Mother Frances Xavier Cabrini arrived in New York City to begin work among Italian immigrants. She was canonized in 1946.

**1911:** Archbishop John M. Farley of New York made cardinal by Pope Pius X.

Catholic Foreign Mission Society of America (Maryknoll) opened a seminary for foreign missions, the first of its kind in U.S. The Maryknollers were also unique as the first U.S.-established foreign mission society.

**1917:** Military Ordinariate established with headquarters at New York.

**1919:** Alfred E. Smith became first elected Catholic governor.

**1924:** Archbishop Patrick Hayes of New York made cardinal by Pope Pius XI.

**1930:** Jesuit Martyrs of New York and Canada were canonized on June 29.

**1946:** Archbishop Francis J. Spellman of New York made cardinal by Pope Pius XII.

**1957:** Rockville Centre diocese established.

**1969:** Archbishop Terence Cooke of New York made cardinal by Pope Paul VI.

**1981:** Apostolic Exarchate for Armenian-Rite Catholics in the United States and Canada established. New York designated see city.

## North Carolina

**1526:** The Ayllon expedition attempted to establish a settlement on Carolina coast.

**1540:** De Soto expedition, accompanied by chaplains, entered state.

**1776:** State Constitution denied office to "those who denied the truths of the Protestant religion."

**1805:** The few Catholics in state were served by visiting missionaries.

**1821:** Bishop John England celebrated Mass in the ballroom of the home of William Gaston at New Bern, marking the start of organization of the first parish, St. Paul's, in the state.

**1835:** William Gaston, State Supreme Court Justice, succeeded in having repealed the article denying religious freedom.

**1852:** First Catholic church erected in Charlotte.

**1868:** North Carolina vicariate apostolic established.

Catholics obtained full civil liberty and rights.

**1874:** Sisters of Mercy arrived, opened an academy, several schools, hospitals and an orphanage.

**1876:** Benedictine priory and school (later Belmont Abbey College) founded at Belmont; priory designated an abbey in 1884.

**1910:** Belmont Abbey established as an abbacy nullius; abbacy nullius status suppressed in 1977.

**1924:** Raleigh diocese established.

**1971:** Charlotte diocese established.

## North Dakota

**1742:** Pierre and Francois Verendrye, accompanied by Jesuit Father Coquart, explored territory.

**1818:** Canadian priests ministered to Catholics in area.

**1840:** Jesuit Father De Smet made first of several trips among Mandan and Gros Ventre Indians.

**1848:** Father George Belcourt, first American resident priest in territory, reestablished Pembina Mission.

**1874:** Grey Nuns arrived at Fort Totten to conduct a school.

**1889:** Jamestown diocese established; transferred to Fargo in 1897.

**1893:** Benedictines founded St. Gall Monastery at Devil's Lake. (It was moved to Richardton in 1899 and became an abbey in 1903.)

**1909:** Bismarck diocese established.

**1959:** Archbishop Aloysius J. Muench, bishop of Fargo, made cardinal by Pope John XXIII.

## Ohio

**1749:** Jesuits in expedition of Céleron de Blainville preached to Indians.

First religious services were held within present limits of Ohio. Jesuit Joseph de Bonnecamps celebrated Mass at mouth of Little Miami River and in other places.

**1751:** First Catholic settlement founded among Huron Indians near Sandusky by Jesuit Father de la Richardie.

**1790:** Benedictine Pierre Didier ministered to French immigrants.

**1812:** Bishop Flaget of Bardstown visited and baptized Catholics of Lancaster and Somerset Counties.

**1818:** Dominican Father Edward Fenwick (later first bishop of Cincinnati) built St. Joseph's Church and established first Dominican convent in Ohio.

**1821:** Cincinnati diocese established.

**1831:** Xavier University founded.

**1843:** Members of Congregation of Most Precious Blood arrived in Cincinnati from Switzerland.

**1845:** Cornerstone laid for St. Peter's Cathedral, Cincinnati.

**1847:** Cleveland diocese established.

**1850:** Cincinnati made archdiocese.

Marianists opened St. Mary's Institute, now University of Dayton.

**1865:** Sisters of Charity opened hospital in Cleveland, first institution of its kind in city.

**1868:** Columbus diocese established.

**1871:** Ursuline College for women opened at Cleveland.

**1910:** Toledo diocese established.

**1935:** Archbishop John T. McNicholas, O.P., founded the Institutum Divi Thomae in Cincinnati for fundamental research in natural sciences.

**1943:** Youngstown diocese established.

**1944:** Steubenville diocese established.

**1969:** Byzantine Rite Eparchy of Parma (for Ruthenians) established.

**1982:** Apostolic Exarchate for Romanian Byzantine-Rite Catholics in the United States established. Canton designated see city.

**1983:** Byzantine Rite Eparchy of Saint Josaphat in Parma (for Ukrainians) established.

## Oklahoma

**1540:** De Soto expedition, accompanied by chaplains, explored territory.

**1541:** Coronado expedition, accompanied by Franciscan Juan de Padilla, explored state.

**1630:** Spanish Franciscan Juan de Salas labored among Indians.

**1700:** Scattered Catholic families were visited by priests from Kansas and Arkansas.

**1874:** First Catholic church built by Father Smyth at Atoka.

**1876:** Prefecture Apostolic of Indian Territory established with Benedictine Isidore Robot as its head.

**1886:** First Catholic day school for Choctaw and white children opened by Sisters of Mercy at Krebs.

**1891:** Vicariate Apostolic of Oklahoma and Indian Territory established.

**1905:** Oklahoma diocese established; title changed to Oklahoma City and Tulsa, 1930.

**1917:** Benedictine Heights College for women founded.

Carmelite Sisters of St. Theresa of the Infant Jesus founded at Oklahoma City.

**1972:** Oklahoma City made archdiocese. Tulsa diocese established.

## Oregon

**1603:** Vizcaino explored northern Oregon coast.

**1774:** Franciscan missionaries accompanied Juan Perez on his expedition to coast, and Heceta a year later.

**1811:** Catholic Canadian trappers and traders with John J. Astor expedition founded first American settlement — Astoria.

**1834:** Indian missions in Northwest entrusted to Jesuits by Holy See.

**1838:** Abbe Blanchet appointed vicar general to Bishop of Quebec with jurisdiction over area which included Oregon Territory.

**1839:** First Mass celebrated at present site of St. Paul.

**1843:** Oregon vicariate apostolic established.

St. Joseph's College for boys opened.

**1844:** Jesuit Pierre de Smet established Mission of St. Francis Xavier near St. Paul.

Sisters of Notre Dame de Namur, first to enter Oregon, opened an academy for girls.

**1846:** Vicariate made an ecclesiastical province with Bishop Blanchet as first Archbishop of Oregon City (now Portland).

Walla Walla diocese established; suppressed in 1853.

**1847:** First priest was ordained in Oregon.

**1848:** First Provincial Council of Oregon.

**1857:** Death of Dr. John McLoughlin, "Father of Oregon."

**1865:** Rev. H. H. Spalding, a Protestant missionary, published the Whitman Myth to hinder work of Catholic missionaries.

**1874:** Catholic Indian Mission Bureau established.

**1875:** St. Vincent's Hospital, first in state, opened at Portland.

**1903:** Baker diocese established.

**1922:** Anti-private school bill sponsored by Scottish Rite Masons was passed by popular vote, 115,506 to 103,685.

**1925:** U.S. Supreme Court declared Oregon anti-private school bill unconstitutional.

**1953:** First Trappist monastery on West Coast established in Willamette Valley north of Lafayette.

## Pennsylvania

**1673:** Priests from Maryland ministered to Catholics in the Colony.

**1682:** Religious toleration was extended to members of all faiths.

**1720:** Jesuit Joseph Greaton became first resident missionary of Philadelphia.

**1734:** St. Joseph's Church, first Catholic church in Philadelphia, was opened.

**1741:** Jesuit Fathers Schneider and Wappeler ministered to German immigrants.

Conewego Chapel, a combination chapel and dwelling, was built by Father William Wappeler, S.J., a priest sent to minister to the German Catholic immigrants who settled in the area in the 1730's.

**1782:** St. Mary's Parochial School opened at Philadelphia.

**1788:** Holy Trinity Church, Philadelphia, was incorporated; first exclusively national church organized in U.S.

**1797:** Augustinian Matthew Carr founded St. Augustine parish, Philadelphia.

**1799:** Prince Demetrius Gallitzin (Father Augustine Smith) built church in western Pennsylvania, at Loretto.

**1808:** Philadelphia diocese established.

**1814:** St. Joseph's Orphanage was opened at Philadelphia; first Catholic institution for children in U.S.

**1842:** University of Villanova founded by Augustinians.

**1843:** Pittsburgh diocese established.

**1844:** Thirteen persons killed, two churches and a school burned in Know-Nothing riots at Philadelphia.

**1846:** First Benedictine Abbey in New World founded near Latrobe by Father Boniface Wimmer.

**1852:** Redemptorist John Nepomucene Neumann became fourth bishop of Philadelphia. He was beatified in 1963 and canonized in 1977.

**1853:** Erie diocese established.

**1868:** Scranton and Harrisburg dioceses established.

**1871:** Chestnut Hill College, first for women in state, founded.

**1875:** Philadelphia made archdiocese.

**1901:** Altoona-Johnstown diocese established.

**1913:** Byzantine Rite Apostolic Exarchate of Philadelphia established; became metropolitan see, 1958.

**1921:** Archbishop Dennis Dougherty made cardinal by Pope Benedict XV.

**1924:** Byzantine Rite Apostolic Exarchate of Pittsburgh established; made an eparchy in 1963; raised to metropolitan status and transferred to Munhall, 1969; transferred back to Pittsburgh in 1977.

**1951:** Greensburg diocese established.

**1958:** Archbishop John O'Hara, C.S.C., of Philadelphia made cardinal by Pope John.

**1961:** Allentown diocese established.

**1967:** Archbishop John J. Krol of Philadelphia made cardinal by Pope Paul VI.

**1969:** Bishop John J. Wright of Pittsburgh made cardinal by Pope Paul VI and transferred to Curia post.

**1976:** The 41st International Eucharistic Congress, the second held in the U.S. convened in Philadelphia, August 1-8.

## Rhode Island

**1663:** Colonial Charter granted freedom of conscience.

**1719:** Laws denied Catholics the right to hold public office.

**1829:** St. Mary's Church, Pawtucket, was first Catholic church in state.

**1837:** Parochial schools inaugurated in state. First Catholic church in Providence was built.

**1851:** Sisters of Mercy began work in Rhode Island.

**1872:** Providence diocese established.

**1900:** Trappists took up residence in state.

**1917:** Providence College founded.

## South Carolina

**1569:** Jesuit Juan Rogel was the first resident priest in the territory.

**1573:** First Franciscans arrived in southeastern section.

**1606:** Bishop Altamirano conducted visitation of area.

**1655:** Franciscans had two missions among Indians; later destroyed by English.

**1697:** Religious liberty granted to all except "papists."

**1790:** Catholics given right to vote.

**1820:** Charleston diocese established.

**1822:** Bishop England founded *U.S. Catholic Miscellany,* first Catholic paper of a strictly religious nature in U.S.

**1830:** Sisters of Our Lady of Mercy, first in state, took up residence at Charleston.

**1847:** Cornerstone of Cathedral of St. John the Baptist, Charleston, was laid.

**1861:** Cathedral and many institutions destroyed in Charleston fire.

## South Dakota

**1842:** Father Augustine Ravoux began ministrations to French and Indians at Fort Pierre, Vermilion and Prairie du Chien; printed devotional book in Sioux language the following year.

**1867:** Parish organized among the French at Jefferson.

**1878:** Benedictines opened school for Sioux children at Fort Yates.

**1889:** Sioux Falls diocese established.

**1902:** Lead diocese established; transferred to Rapid City, 1930.

**1950:** Mount Marty College for women founded.

**1952:** Blue Cloud Abbey, first Benedictine foundation in state, was dedicated.

## Tennessee

**1541:** Cross planted on shore of Mississippi by De Soto; accompanying the expedition were Fathers John de Gallegos and Louis De Soto.

**1682:** Franciscan Fathers Membre and Douay accompanied La Salle to present site of Memphis; may have offered the first Masses in the territory.

**1800:** Catholics were served by priests from Bardstown, Ky.

**1822:** Non-Catholics assisted in building church in Nashville.

**1837:** Nashville diocese established.

**1843:** Sisters of Charity opened a school for girls in Nashville.

**1921:** Sisters of St. Dominic opened Siena College for women at Memphis; closed in 1971.

**1940:** Christian Brothers College founded at Memphis.

**1970:** Memphis diocese established.

## Texas

**1541:** Missionaries with Coronado expedition probably entered territory.

**1553:** Dominicans Diego de la Cruz, Hernando

Mendez, Juan Ferrer, Brother Juan de Mina killed by Indians.

**1675:** Bosque-Larios missionary expedition entered region; Father Juan Larios offered first recorded high Mass.

**1682:** Mission Corpus Christi de Isleta (Ysleta) founded by Franciscans near El Paso, first mission in present-day Texas.

**1690:** Mission San Francisco de los Tejas founded in east Texas.

**1703:** Mission San Francisco de Solano founded on Rio Grande; rebuilt in 1718 as San Antonio de Valero or the Alamo.

**1717:** Franciscan Antonio Margil founded six missions in northeast.

**1720:** San Jose y San Miguel de Aguayo Mission founded by Fray Antonio Margil de Jesus.

**1721:** Franciscan Brother Jose Pita killed by Indians at Carnezeria.

**1728:** Site of San Antonio settled.

**1738:** Construction of San Fernando Cathedral at San Antonio.

**1744:** Mission church of the Alamo built.

**1750:** Franciscan Francisco Xavier was killed by Indians; so were Jose Ganzabal in 1752, and Alonzo Ferrares and Jose San Esteban in 1758.

**1793:** Mexico secularized missions.

**1825:** Governments of Cohuila and Texas secularized all Indian missions.

**1838-39:** Irish priests ministered to settlements of Refugio and San Patricio.

**1841:** Vicariate of Texas established.

**1847:** Ursuline Sisters established their first academy in territory at Galveston.
Galveston diocese established.

**1852:** Oblate Fathers and Franciscans arrived in Galveston to care for new influx of German Catholics.
St. Mary's College founded at San Antonio.

**1854:** Know-Nothing Party began to stir up hatred against Catholics.

**1858:** Texas Legislature passed law entitling all schools granting free scholarships and meeting state requirements to share in school fund.

**1874:** San Antonio diocese established.
Vicariate of Brownsville established.

**1881:** St. Edward's College founded: became first chartered college in state in 1889.
Sisters of Charity founded Incarnate Word College at San Antonio.

**1890:** Dallas diocese established; changed to Dallas-Ft. Worth, 1953; made two separate dioceses, 1969.

**1912:** Corpus Christi diocese established.

**1914:** El Paso diocese established.

**1926:** San Antonio made archdiocese. Amarillo diocese established.

**1947:** Austin diocese established.

**1959:** Galveston diocese redesignated Galveston-Houston.

**1961:** San Angelo diocese established.

**1965:** Brownsville diocese established.

**1966:** Beaumont diocese established.

**1982:** Victoria diocese established.

**1983:** Lubbock diocese established.

## Utah

**1776:** Franciscans Silvestre de Escalante and Atanasio Dominguez reached Utah (Salt) Lake; first white men known to enter the territory.

**1858:** Jesuit Father De Smet accompanied General Harney as chaplain on expedition sent to settle troubles between Mormons and U.S. Government.

**1866:** On June 29 Father Edward Kelly offered first Mass in Salt Lake City in Mormon Assembly Hall.

**1886:** Utah vicariate apostolic established.

**1891:** Salt Lake City diocese established.

**1926:** College of St. Mary-of-the-Wasatch for women was founded.

## Vermont

**1609:** Champlain expedition passed through territory.

**1666:** Captain La Motte built fort and shrine of St. Anne on Isle La Motte; Sulpician Father Dollier de Casson celebrated first Mass.

**1668:** Bishop Laval of Quebec (beatified in 1980), administered confirmation in region; this was the first area in northeastern U.S. to receive an episcopal visit.

**1710:** Jesuits ministered to Indians near Lake Champlain.

**1793:** Discriminatory measures against Catholics were repealed.

**1830:** Father Jeremiah O'Callaghan became first resident priest in state.

**1853:** Burlington diocese established.

**1854:** Sisters of Charity of Providence arrived to conduct St. Joseph's Orphanage at Burlington.

**1904:** St. Michael's College founded.

**1951:** First Carthusian foundation in America established at Whitingham.

## Virginia

**1526:** Dominican Antonio de Montesinos offered first Mass on Virginia soil.

**1561:** Dominicans visited the coast.

**1571:** Father John Baptist de Segura and seven Jesuit companions killed by Indians.

**1642:** Priests outlawed and Catholics denied right to vote.

**1689:** Capuchin Christopher Plunket was captured and exiled to a coastal island where he died in 1697.

**1776:** Religious freedom granted.

**1791:** Father Jean Dubois arrived at Richmond with letters from Lafayette. The House of Delegates was placed at his disposal for celebration of Mass.

**1796:** A church was built at Alexandria.

**1820:** Richmond diocese established.

**1822:** Trusteeism created serious problems in diocese; Bishop Kelly resigned the see.

**1848:** Sisters of Charity opened an orphan asylum at Norfolk.

**1866:** School Sisters of Notre Dame and Sisters of Charity opened academies for girls at Richmond.

**1974:** Arlington diocese established.

## Washington

**1774:** Spaniards explored the region.

**1838:** Fathers Blanchet and Demers, "Apostles of the Northwest," were sent to territory by archbishop of Quebec.

**1840:** Cross erected on Whidby Island, Puget Sound.

**1843:** Vicariate Apostolic of Oregon, including Washington, was established.

**1844:** Mission of St. Paul founded at Colville.

Six Sisters of Notre Dame de Namur began work in area.

**1850:** Nesqually diocese established; transferred to Seattle, 1907.

**1856:** Providence Academy, the first permanent Catholic school in the Northwest, was built at Fort Vancouver by Mother Joseph Pariseau of the Sisters of Charity of Providence.

**1887:** Gonzaga University founded.

**1913:** Spokane diocese established.

**1951:** Seattle made archdiocese. Yakima diocese established.

## West Virginia

**1749:** Father Joseph de Bonnecamps, accompanying the Bienville expedition, may have offered first Mass in the territory.

**1821:** First Catholic church in Wheeling.

**1838:** Sisters of Charity founded school at Martinsburg.

**1848:** Visitation Nuns established academy for girls in Wheeling.

**1850:** Wheeling diocese established; name changed to Wheeling-Charleston, 1974.

Wheeling Hospital incorporated, the oldest Catholic charitable institution in territory.

**1955:** Wheeling College established.

## Wisconsin

**1661:** Jesuit Rene Menard, first known missionary in the territory, was killed or lost in the Black River district.

**1665:** Jesuit Claude Allouez founded Mission of the Holy Ghost at La Pointe Chegoimegon, now Bayfield; was the first permanent mission in region.

**1673:** Father Marquette and Louis Joliet traveled from Green Bay down the Wisconsin and Mississippi rivers.

**1762:** Suppression of Jesuits in French Colonies closed many missions for 30 years.

**1843:** Milwaukee diocese established.

**1853:** St. John's Cathedral, Milwaukee, was built.

**1864:** State charter granted for establishment of Marquette University. First students admitted, 1881.

**1868:** Green Bay and La Crosse dioceses established.

**1875:** Milwaukee made archdiocese.

**1905:** Superior diocese established.

**1946:** Madison diocese established.

## Wyoming

**1840:** Jesuit Pierre de Smet offered first Mass near Green River.

**1851:** Father De Smet held peace conference with Indians near Fort Laramie.

**1867:** Father William Kelly, first resident priest, arrived in Cheyenne and built first church a year later.

**1873:** Father Eugene Cusson became first resident pastor in Laramie.

**1875:** Sisters of Charity of Leavenworth opened school and orphanage at Laramie.

**1884:** Jesuits took over pastoral care of Shoshone and Arapaho Indians.

**1887:** Cheyenne diocese established.

**1949:** Weston Memorial Hospital opened near Newcastle.

## Puerto Rico

**1493:** Island discovered by Columbus on his second voyage; he named it San Juan de Borinquen (the Indian name for Puerto Rico).

**1509:** Juan Ponce de Leon, searching for gold, colonized the island and became its first governor; present population descended mainly from early Spanish settlers.

**1511:** Diocese of Puerto Rico established as suffragan of Seville, Spain; Bishop Alonso, Manso, sailing from Spain in 1512, became first bishop to take up residence in New World.

**1645:** Synod held in Puerto Rico to regulate frequency of Masses according to distances people had to walk.

**1898:** Puerto Rico ceded to U.S. (became self-governing Commonwealth in 1952); inhabitants granted U.S. citizenship in 1917.

**1924:** Diocese of Puerto Rico renamed San Juan de Puerto Rico and made immediately subject to the Holy See; Ponce diocese established.

**1948:** Catholic University of Puerto Rico founded at Ponce through efforts of Bishop James E. McManus, C.SS.R., 1947-63.

**1960:** San Juan made metropolitan see. Arecibo diocese established.

**1964:** Caguas diocese established.

**1973:** Archbishop Luis Aponte Martinez of San Juan made first native Puerto Rican cardinal by Pope Paul VI.

**1976:** Mayaguez diocese established.

Virgin of Providence officially approved as Patroness of Puerto Rico by Pope Paul VI.

## CATHOLICS IN STATUARY HALL

Statues of 13 Catholics deemed worthy of national commemoration by the donating states are among the more than 90 enshrined in National Statuary Hall and other places in the U.S. Capitol. The Hall, formerly the chamber of the House of Representatives, was erected by Act of Congress July 2, 1864.

Donating states, names and years of placement are listed. An asterisk indicates placement of a statue in the Hall itself.

**Arizona:** Rev. Eusebio Kino, S. J., missionary, 1965.

**California:** Rev. Junipero Serra, O. F. M.* missionary, 1931.

**Hawaii:** Father Damien, missionary, 1969.

**Illinois:** Gen. James Shields, statesman, 1893.
**Louisiana:** Edward D. White, Justice of the U.S. Supreme Court (1894-1921), 1955.
**Maryland:** Charles Carroll,* statesman, 1901.
**Nevada:** Patrick A. McCarran,* statesman, 1960.
**New Mexico:** Dennis Chavez, statesman, 1966. (Archbishop Jean B. Lamy, pioneer prelate of Santa Fe, was nominated for Hall honor in 1951.)
**North Dakota:** John Burke,* U.S. treasurer, 1963.
**Oregon:** Dr. John McLoughlin, pioneer, 1953.
**Washington:** Mother Mary Joseph Pariseau, pioneer missionary and humanitarian.
**West Virginia:** John E. Kenna, statesman, 1901.
**Wisconsin:** Rev. Jacques Marquette, S.J., missionary, explorer, 1895.

### CATHOLICS IN PRESIDENTS' CABINETS

**Roger B. Taney,** Attorney General 1831-33, Secretary of Treasury 1833-34; app. by Andrew Jackson.

**James Campbell,** Postmaster General 1853-57; app. by Franklin Pierce.

**John B. Floyd,** Secretary of War 1857-61; app. by James Buchanan.

**Joseph McKenna,** Attorney General 1897-98; app. by William McKinley.

**Robert J. Wynne,** Postmaster General 1904-05; app. by Theodore Roosevelt.

**Charles Bonaparte,** Secretary of Navy 1905-06, Attorney General 1906-09; app. by Theodore Roosevelt.

**James A. Farley,** Postmaster General 1933-40; app. by Franklin D. Roosevelt.

**Frank Murphy,** Attorney General 1939-40; app. by Franklin D. Roosevelt.

**Frank C. Walker,** Postmaster General 1940-45; app. by Franklin D. Roosevelt.

**Robert E. Hannegan,** Postmaster General 1945-47; app. by Harry S. Truman.

**J. Howard McGrath,** Attorney General 1949-52; app. by Harry S. Truman.

**Maurice J. Tobin,** Secretary of Labor; 1949-53; app. by Harry S. Truman.

**James P. McGranery,** Attorney General 1952-53; app. by Harry S. Truman.

**Martin P. Durkin,** Secretary of Labor 1953; app. by Dwight D. Eisenhower.

**James P. Mitchell,** Secretary of Labor 1953-61; app. by Dwight D. Eisenhower.

**Robert F. Kennedy,** Attorney General 1961-65; app. by John F. Kennedy, reapp. by Lyndon B. Johnson.

**Anthony Celebrezze,** Secretary of Health, Education and Welfare 1962-65; app. by John F. Kennedy, reapp. by Lyndon B. Johnson.

**John S. Gronouski,** Postmaster General 1963-65; app. by John F. Kennedy, reapp. by Lyndon B. Johnson.

**John T. Connor,** Secretary of Commerce 1965-67; app. by Lyndon B. Johnson.

**Lawrence O'Brien,** Postmaster General 1965-68; app. by Lyndon B. Johnson.

**Walter J. Hickel,** Secretary of Interior 1969-71; app. by Richard M. Nixon.

**John A. Volpe,** Secretary of Transportation 1969-72; app. by Richard M. Nixon.

**Maurice H. Stans,** Secretary of Commerce, 1969-72; app. by Richard M. Nixon.

**Peter J. Brennan,** Secretary of Labor, 1973-75; app. by Richard M. Nixon, reapp. by Gerald R. Ford.

**William E. Simon,** Secretary of Treasury, 1974-76; app. by Richard M. Nixon, reapp. by Gerald R. Ford.

**Joseph A. Califano, Jr.,** Secretary of Health, Education and Welfare, 1977-79; app. by Jimmy Carter.

**Benjamin Civiletti,** Attorney General, 1979-81; app. by Jimmy Carter.

**Moon Landrieu,** Secretary of Housing and Urban Development, 1979-81; app. by Jimmy Carter.

**Edmund S. Muskie,** Secretary of State, 1980-81; app. by Jimmy Carter.

**Alexander M. Haig,** Secretary of State, 1981-82; app. by Ronald Reagan.

**Raymond J. Donovan,** Secretary of Labor, 1981; app. by Ronald Reagan.

**Margaret M. Heckler,** Secretary of Health and Human Services, 1983-; app. by Ronald Reagan.

Men who became Catholics after leaving Cabinet posts: Thomas Ewing, Secretary of Treasury under William A. Harrison, and Secretary of Interior under Zachary Taylor; Luke E. Wright, Secretary of War under Theodore Roosevelt; Albert B. Fall, Secretary of Interior under Warren G. Harding.

### CATHOLIC SUPREME COURT JUSTICES

**Roger B. Taney,** Chief Justice 1836-64; app. by Andrew Jackson.

**Edward D. White,** Associate Justice 1894-1910, app. by Grover Cleveland; Chief Justice 1910-21, app. by William H. Taft.

**Joseph McKenna,** Associate Justice 1898-1925; app. by William McKinley.

**Pierce Butler,** Associate Justice 1923-39; app. by Warren G. Harding.

**Frank Murphy,** Associate Justice 1940-49; app. by Franklin D. Roosevelt.

**William Brennan,** Associate Justice 1956-; app. by Dwight D. Eisenhower.

**Sherman Minton,** Associate Justice from 1949 to 1956, became a Catholic several years before his death in 1965.

---

# BIRTHRIGHT

Birthright is a nondenominational guidance and referral service organization offering pregnant women alternatives to abortion, in line with the motto, "It is the right of every pregnant woman to give birth and the right of every child to be born."

Started by Mrs. Louise Summerhill of Toronto, Canada, in 1968, it has chapters in Canada, the United States, the United Kingdom, Ireland, New Zealand, Australia and South Africa.

The executive director of Birthright, U.S.A., is Mrs. D. Cocciolone, 686 N. Broad St., Woodbury, N.J. 08096.

Birthright is independent and nondenominational. Birthright telephone numbers are listed.

## CHURCH-STATE DECISIONS OF THE SUPREME COURT

(Among sources of this listing of U.S. Supreme Court decisions was *The Supreme Court on Church and State,* Joseph Tussman, editor; Oxford University Press, New York, 1962.)

**Terrett v. Taylor,** 9 Cranch 43 (1815): The Court declared unconstitutional an act of the Virginia Legislature which denied property rights to Protestant Episcopal churches in the state. Religious corporations, like other corporations, have rights to their property.

**Vidal v. Girard's Executors,** 2 Howard 205 (1844): The Court upheld the will of Stephen Girard, which barred ministers of any religion from serving as faculty members or visitors in a school he established for orphans.

**Watson v. Jones,** 13 Wallace 679 (1872): The Court declared that a member of a religious organization may not appeal to secular courts against a decision made by a church tribunal within the area of its competence.

**Reynolds v. United States,** 98 US 145 (1879): The Court declared, in reference to the Mormon practice of polygamy, that one may not knowingly violate by external practices the law of the land on religious grounds, since such conduct would make the professed doctrines of belief superior to federal or state law. One must keep the external practice of religion within the framework of laws enacted for the common welfare. This was the first decision rendered on the Free Exercise Clause of the First Amendment.

**Davis v. Beason,** 133 US 333 (1890): The Court upheld the denial of the right of Mormons to vote in Idaho if they refused to sign a registration oath stating that they were not bigamists or polygamists and would not encourage or preach bigamy or polygamy.

**Church of Latter-Day Saints v. United States,** 136 US 1 (1890): The Court upheld an Act of Congress which annulled the charter of the Corporation of the Church of Jesus Christ of Latter-Day Saints, and declared "forfeited to the government all its real estate except a small portion used exclusively for public worship" (Tussman, *op. cit.,* p. 33). The Court held that the Corporation continually used its power to violate US laws prohibiting polygamy.

**Church of the Holy Trinity v. United States,** 143 US 457 (1892): The Court declared it is not "a misdemeanor for a church of this country to contract for the services of a Christian minister residing in another nation" (from the text of the decision).

**Bradfield v. Roberts,** 175 US 291 (1899): The Court denied that an appropriation of government funds for an institution (Providence Hospital, Washington, D.C.) run by Roman Catholic sisters violated the No Establishment Clause of the First Amendment.

**Pierce v. Society of Sisters,** 268 US 510 (1925): The Court denied that a state can require children to attend public schools only. The Court held that the liberty of the Constitution forbids standardization by such compulsion, and that the parochial schools involved had claims to protection under the Fourteenth Amendment.

**Cochran v. Board of Education,** 281 US 370 (1930): The Court upheld a Louisiana statute providing textbooks at public expense for children attending public or parochial schools. The Court held that the children and state were beneficiaries of the appropriations, with incidental secondary benefit going to the schools.

**United States v. MacIntosh,** 283 US 605 (1931): The Court denied that anyone can place allegiance to the will of God above his allegiance to the government, since such a person could make his own interpretation of God's will the decisive test as to whether he would or would not obey the nation's law. The Court stated that the nation, which has a duty to survive, can require citizens to bear arms in its defense.

**Hamilton v. Regents of University of California,** 293 US 245 (1934): The Court rejected a "claim to exemption from R.O.T.C. based on conscientious objection to war" (Tussman *op. cit.,* p. 64). If such an exemption were allowed, the liberties of the objector might be extended to the point of refusal to pay taxes in furtherance of a war or any other end condemned by his conscience. This would be an undue exaltation of the right of private judgment.

**Cantwell v. Connecticut,** 310 US 296 (1940): The Court declared that the right to religious freedom is violated by a statute requiring a person to secure a permit from a government official before soliciting money for alleged religious purposes from someone not of his or her sect. Such a practice would constitute censorship of religion.

**Minersville School District v. Gobitis,** 310 US 586 (1940): The Court upheld the right of a state to require the salute to the national flag from school children, even from those who refused to do so for sincere religious reasons.

**Jones v. City of Opelika,** 316 US 584 (1942): The court upheld licensing ordinances in three municipalities against "the claim by Jehovah's Witnesses that they interfere with the free exercise of religion" (Tussman, *op. cit.,* p. 91).

**Murdock v. Commonwealth of Pennsylvania,** 319 US 105 (1943): In a reversal of the decision handed down in Jones v. City of Opelika, the Court declared the licensing unconstitutional since it violated a freedom guaranteed under the First Amendment. The selling of religious literature by traveling preachers does not make evangelism the equivalent of a commercial enterprise taxable by the State.

**Jones v. City of Opelika,** 316 US 584 105 (1943): The Court declared that the Constitution denies a city the right to control the expression of men's minds and denies also the right of men to win others to their views through a program of taxes levied against such activity.

**Douglas v. City of Jeannette,** 319 US 157 (1943): The Court again upheld the proselytizing rights of Jehovah's Witnesses, ruling unconstitutional the action of any public authority in regulating or taxing such activity.

**West Virginia State Board of Education v. Barnette,** 319 US 624 (1943): In a reversal of the decision handed down in Minersville School District v. Gobitis, the Court declared unconstitutional a state statute requiring of all children a salute to the national flag and a pledge of allegiance which a child may consider contrary to sincere religious beliefs.

**Prince v. Commonwealth of Massachusetts,** 321 US 158 (1944): The Court upheld a "child-labor regulation against the claim that it prevents a child from performing her religious duty" (Tussman, op. cit., p. 170). The Court asserted a general principle that the state has a wide range of power for limiting parental freedom and authority in things affecting the child's welfare.

**United States v. Ballard,** 322 US 78 (1944): The Court upheld the general principle that "the truth of religious claims is not for secular authority to determine" (Tussman, op. cit., p. 181).

**In Re Summers,** 325 US 561 (1945): The Court upheld "the denial, to an otherwise qualified applicant, of admission to the bar on the basis of the applicant's religiously motivated 'conscientious scruples against participation in war' " (Tussman, op. cit., p. 192). The petitioner was barred because he could not in good faith take the prescribed oath to support the Constitution of Illinois which required service in the state militia in times of necessity.

**Girouard v. United States,** 328 US 61 (1946): In a ruling related to that handed down in United States v. MacIntosh, the Court affirmed the opinion that the refusal of an alien to bear arms does not deny him citizenship.

**Everson v. Board of Education,** 330 US 1 (1947): The Court upheld the constitutionality of a New Jersey statute authorizing free school bus transportation for parochial as well as public school students. The Court expressed the opinion that the benefits of public welfare legislation, included under such bus transportation, do not run contrary to the concept of separation of Church and State.

**McCollum v. Board of Education,** 333 US 203 (1948): The Court declared unconstitutional a program for releasing children, with parental consent, from public school classes so they could receive religious instruction on public school premises from representatives of their own faiths.

**Zorach v. Clauson,** 343 US 306 (1952): The Court upheld the constitutionality of a New York statute permitting, on a voluntary basis, the release during school time of students from public school classes for religious instruction given off public school premises.

**Kedroff v. St. Nicholas Cathedral,** 344 US 94 (1952): The Court ruled against an action of New York in taking "control of St. Nicholas Cathedral away from the Moscow hierarchy" (Tussman, op. cit., p. 292), on the ground that the controversy involved a matter of church government.

**Fowler v. Rhode Island,** 345 US 67 (1953): The Court upheld the right of a Jehovah's Witness to preach in a public park against a city ordinance which forbade such preaching. The Court held that the ordinance, as construed and applied, discriminated against the Witness and therefore amounted to preferment by the state of other religious groups.

**Torcaso v. Watkins,** 367 US 488 (1961): The Court declared unconstitutional a Maryland requirement that one must make a declaration of belief in the existence of God as part of the oath of office for notaries public.

**McGowan v. Maryland,** 81 Sp Ct 1101; **Two Guys from Harrison v. McGinley,** 81 Sp Ct 1135; **Gallagher v. Crown Kosher Super Market,** 81 Sp Ct 1128; **Braunfield v. Brown,** 81 Sp Ct 1144 (1961): The Court ruled that Sunday closing laws do not violate the No Establishment of Religion Clause of the First Amendment, even though the laws were religious in their inception and still have some religious overtones. The Court held that, "as presently written and administered, most of them, at least, are of a secular rather than of a religious character, and that presently they bear no relationship to establishment of religion as those words are used in the Constitution of the United States."

**Engel v. Vitale,** 370 US 42 (1962): The Court declared that the voluntary recitation in public schools of a prayer composed by the New York State Board of Regents is unconstitutional on the ground that it violates the No Establishment of Religion Clause of the First Amendment.

**Abington Township School District v. Schempp and Murray v. Curlett,** 83 Sp Ct 1560 (1963): The Court ruled that Bible reading and recitation of the Lord's Prayer in public schools, with voluntary participation by students, are unconstitutional on the ground that they violate the No Establishment of Religion Clause of the First Amendment.

**Sherbert v. Verner,** 83 A Sp Ct 1790 (1963): The Court ruled that individuals of any religious faith may not, because of their faith or lack of it, be deprived of the benefits of public welfare legislation.

**Chamberlin v. Dade County,** 83 Sp Ct 1864 (1964): The Court reversed a decision of the Florida Supreme Court concerning the constitutionality of prayer and devotional Bible reading in public schools during the school day, as sanctioned by a state statute which specifically related the practices to a sound public purpose.

**Board of Education v. Allen,** No. 660 (1968): The Court declared constitutional the New York school book loan law which requires local school boards to purchase books with state funds and lend them to parochial and private school students.

**Flast v. Cohen,** No. 416 (1968): The Court held that individual taxpayers can bring suits to challenge federal expenditures on grounds that they violate the principle of separation of Church and State even though generally taxpayers cannot challenge federal expenditures in court.

**Walz v. Tax Commission of New York** (1970): The Court upheld the constitutionality of a New York statute exempting church-owned property from taxation.

**Earle v. DiCenso, Robinson v. DiCenso, Lemon v. Kurtzman, Tilton v. Richardson** (1971): In Earle v. DiCenso and Robinson v. DiCenso, the Court ruled unconstitutional a 1969 Rhode Island statute which provided salary supplements to teachers of secular subjects in parochial schools; in Lemon v. Kurtzman, the Court ruled unconstitutional a 1968 Pennsylvania statute which authorized the state to purchase services for the teaching of secular subjects in nonpublic schools. The principal argument against constitutionality in these cases was that the statutes and programs at issue entailed excessive entanglement of government with religion. In Tilton v. Richardson, the Court held that this argument did not apply to a prohibitive degree with respect to federal grants, under the Higher Education Facilities Act of 1963, for the construction of facilities for nonreligious purposes by four church-related institutions of higher learning, three of which were Catholic, in Connecticut.

**Amish Decision** (1972): In a case appealed on behalf of Yoder, Miller and Yutzy, the Court ruled that Amish parents were exempt from a Wisconsin statute requiring them to send their children to school until the age of 16. The Court said in its decision that secondary schooling exposed Amish children to attitudes, goals and values contrary to their beliefs, and substantially hindered "the religious development of the Amish child and his integration into the way of life of the Amish faith-community at the crucial adolescent state of development."

**Committee for Public Education and Religious Liberty, et al., v. Nyquist, et al.,** No. 72-694 (1973): The Court ruled that provisions of a 1972 New York statute were unconstitutional on the grounds that they were violative of the No Establishment Clause of the First Amendment and had the "impermissible effect" of advancing the sectarian activities of church-affiliated schools. The programs ruled unconstitutional concerned: (1) maintenance and repair grants, for facilities and equipment, to ensure the health, welfare and safety of students in nonpublic, non-profit elementary and secondary schools serving a high concentration of students from low income families; (2) tuition reimbursement ($50 per grade school child, $100 per high school student) for parents (with income less than $5,000) of children attending nonpublic elementary or secondary schools; tax deduction from adjusted gross income for parents failing to qualify under the above reimbursement plan, for each child attending a nonpublic school.

**Sloan, Treasurer of Pennsylvania, et al., v. Lemon, et al.,** No. 72-459 (1973): The Court ruled unconstitutional a Pennsylvania Parent Reimbursement Act for Nonpublic Education which provided funds to reimburse parents (to a maximum of $150) for a portion of tuition expenses incurred in sending their children to nonpublic schools. The Court held that there was no significant difference between this and the New York tuition reimbursement program (above), and declared that the Equal Protection Clause of the Fourteenth Amendment cannot be relied upon to sustain a program held to be violative of the No Establishment Clause.

**Levitt, et al., v. Committee for Public Education and Religious Liberty, et al.,** No. 72-269 (1973): The Court ruled unconstitutional the Mandated Services Act of 1970 under which New York provided $28 million ($27 per pupil from first to seventh grade, $45 per pupil from seventh to 12th grade) to reimburse nonpublic schools for testing, recording and reporting services required by the state. The Court declared that the act provided "impermissible aid" to religion in contravention of the No Establishment Clause.

In related decisions handed down June 25, 1973, the Court: (1) affirmed a lower court decision against the constitutionality of an Ohio tax credit law benefiting parents with children in nonpublic schools; (2) reinstated an injunction against a parent reimbursement program in New Jersey; (3) affirmed South Carolina's right to grant construction loans to church-affiliated colleges, and dismissed an appeal contesting its right to provide loans to students attending church-affiliated colleges (**Hunt v. McNair, Durham v. McLeod**).

**Wheeler v. Barrera** (1974): The Court ruled that nonpublic school students in Missouri must share in federal funds for educationally deprived students on a comparable basis with public school students under Title I of the Elementary and Secondary Education Act of 1965.

**Norwood v. Harrison** (93 S. Ct. 2804): The Court ruled that public assistance which avoids the prohibitions of the "effect" and "entanglement" tests (and which therefore does not substantially promote the religious mission of sectarian schools) may be confined to the secular functions of such schools.

**Wiest v. Mt. Lebanon School District** (1974): The Court upheld a lower court ruling that invocation and benediction prayers at public high school commencement ceremonies do not violate the principle of separation of Church and state.

**Meek v. Pittenger** (1975): The Court ruled unconstitutional portions of a Pennsylvania law providing auxiliary services for students of nonpublic schools; at the same time, it ruled in favor of provisions of the law permitting textbook loans to students of such schools. In denying the constitutionality of auxiliary services, the Court held that they had the "primary effect of establishing religion" and involved "excessive entanglement" of Church and state officials with respect to supervision; objection was also made against providing such services only on the premises of non-public schools and only at the request of such schools.

**Roemer v. Board of Public Works of Maryland,** 96 S. Ct. 2337 (1976): The Court ruled that a Maryland statute which authorized state funds to any private institution meeting certain minimal criteria was constitutional. The Court said the statute met the test previously outlined in Lemon v. Kurtzman because the colleges were not pervasively sectarian and the aid was in fact intended only for secular purposes.

**Serbian Eastern Orthodox Diocese v. Milivojevich**, 96 S. Ct. 2372 (1976): The Court held unconstitutional the decision of the Illinois Supreme Court that the Serbian Orthodox Church had arbitrarily removed one of its bishops and that its reorganization of the diocese was beyond the power of the church. The Court declared that the First Amendment does not permit civil courts to make ecclesiastical decisions.

**TWA, Inc., v. Hardison**, 75-1126; **International Association of Machinists and Aero Space Workers v. Hardison**, 75-1385 (1977): The Court ruled that federal civil rights legislation does not require employers to make more than minimal efforts to accommodate employees who want a particular working day off as their religion's Sabbath Day, and that an employer cannot accommodate such an employee by violating seniority systems determined by a union collective bargaining agreement. The Court noted that its ruling was not a constitutional judgment but an interpretation of existing law.

**Wolman v. Walter** (1977): The Court ruled constitutional portions of an Ohio statute providing tax-paid textbook loans and some auxiliary services (standardized and diagnostic testing, therapeutic and remedial services, off school premises) for nonpublic school students. It decided that other portions of the law, providing state funds for non-public school field trips and instructional materials (audio-visual equipment, maps, tape recorders), were unconstitutional.

### Decisions since 1977

**Clergymen** (1978): The Court struck down the last state ban against the holding of public office by clergymen, nullifying the 182-year-old provision of the Tennessee constitution which held that involvement in politics might affect the clergy's "dedication to God and the care of souls."

**Lay Teachers** (1979): The Court ruled that lay teachers in church-related schools are not covered by the National Labor Relations Act. The decision was based, not on church-state grounds, but on the lack of any affirmative decision of the Congress to include such teachers in coverage of the law.

**Church Property** (1979): The Court ruled, in Jones v. Wolf, that civil courts are not always bound to yield to decisions of church courts in settling local church property disputes.

**Parochiaid** (1979): The Court decided, in Byrne v. Public Funds for Public Schools, against the constitutionality of a 1976 New Jersey law providing state income tax deductions for tuition paid by parents of students attending parochial and other private schools.

**Religious Belief v. Union** (1979): The Court supported the claim of a San Diego man that his right to religious freedom was violated when he was fired from his job because his Seventh Day Adventist beliefs prevented him from belonging to a union.

**Student Bus Transportation** (1979): The Court upheld a Pennsylvania law providing bus transportation at public expense for students to non-public schools up to 10 miles away from the boundaries of the public school districts in which they lived.

**Reimbursement** (1980): The Court upheld the constitutionality of a 1974 New York law providing direct cash payment to non-public schools for the costs of state-mandated testing and record-keeping.

**Solicitation of Funds** (1980): The Court struck down a Schaumburg, Ill., ordinance permitting the solicitation of funds only by groups spending a specific percentage of their funds for charitable purposes.

**Remedial Teaching** (1980): The Court refused to hear an appeal from a lower court ruling in support of a New York law permitting the use of federal funds to pay for remedial teaching in non-public schools.

**Ten Commandments** (1980): The Court struck down a 1978 Kentucky law requiring the posting of the Ten Commandments in public school classrooms in the state.

**Christmas Carols** (1980): The Court refused to hear an appeal from a lower court ruling permitting the singing of Christmas carols in public school holiday programs in Sioux City, S.D.

**Highway Prayer** (1981): The Court ruled that North Carolina could not publish a prayer for highway safety on official state maps.

**Unemployment Benefits** (1981): The Court decided, in Thomas v. Review Board, that a worker who, for religious reasons, quits his job rather than help to produce armaments cannot be denied state unemployment benefits.

**Unemployment Taxes** (1981): The Court ruled, in St. Martin Evangelical Lutheran Church v. South Dakota, that church-run schools do not have to pay state unemployment compensation taxes for their employees, because the relevant 1976 law did not "reveal any clear intent to repeal" their tax-exempt status.

**Campus Worship** (1981): The Court ruled, in Widmar v. Vincent, that the University of Missouri at Kansas City could not deny student religious groups the use of campus facilities for worship services. The Court also, in Brandon v. Board of Education of Guilderland Schools, declined without comment to hear an appeal for reversal of lower court decisions denying a group of New York high school students the right to meet for prayer on public school property before the beginning of the school day.

**Americans United** (1982): The Court ruled that Americans United for the Separation of Church and State did not have legal standing to challenge in court the transfer of government property to a Protestant college in Pennsylvania.

**Social Security Taxes** (1982): The Court ruled that Amish businessmen must pay Social Security taxes for their employees even if such payments violate their religious beliefs.

**Unification Church** (1982): The Court struck down a Minnesota law, aimed at the Unification Church, which required detailed financial reports from religious groups which raise more than half of their funds from non-members.

**No Meeting on Public School Property** (1983): By refusing to hear an appeal in Lubbock v. Lubbock Civil Liberties Union, the Court upheld a lower court ruling against a public policy of permitting student religious groups to meet on public school property before and after school hours.

**Tuition Tax Deduction** (1983): In Mueller v. Allen, the Court upheld a Minnesota law allowing parents of students in public and non-public (including parochial) schools to take a tax deduction for the expenses of tuition, textbooks and transportation. Maximum allowable deductions were $500 per child in elementary school and $700 per child in grades seven through 12.

**Pay for Chaplain** (1983): The Court ruled in Marsh v. Chambers that it was not against the Constitution for the Nebraska Legislature to pay a chaplain to open each day's session with a prayer.

**Christmas Nativity Scene** (1984): The Court ruled 5-to-4 in Lynch v. Donnelly that the First Amendment does not mandate "complete separation of church and state," and that, therefore, the sponsorship of a Christmas nativity scene by the City of Pawtucket, R.I., was not unconstitutional. The case involved a scene included in a display of Christmas symbols sponsored by the city in a park owned by a non-profit group. The majority opinion said "the Constitution (does not) require complete separation of church and state; it affirmatively mandates accommodation, not merely tolerance, of all religions and forbids hostility toward any. Anything less" would entail callous indifference not intended by the Constitution. Moreover, "such hostility would bring us into 'war with our national tradition as embodied in the First Amendment's guaranty of the free exercise of religion.' " (The additional quotation was from the 1948 decision in McCollum v. Board of Education.)

## THE WALL OF SEPARATION

Thomas Jefferson, in a letter written to the Danbury (Conn.) Baptist Association Jan. 1, 1802, coined the metaphor, "a wall of separation between Church and State," to express a theory concerning interpretation of the religion clauses of the First Amendment: "Congress shall make no law respecting an establishment of religion or prohibiting the free exercise thereof."

The metaphor was cited for the first time in judicial proceedings in 1879, in the opinion by Chief Justice Waite in Reynolds v. United States. It did not, however, figure substantially in the decision.

### Accepted as Rule

In 1947 the wall of separation gained acceptance as a constitutional rule, in the decision handed down in Everson v. Board of Education. Associate Justice Black, in describing the principles involved in the No Establishment Clause, wrote: "Neither a state nor the Federal Government

can set up a church. Neither can pass laws which aid one religion, aid all religions, or prefer one religion over another. Neither can force nor influence a person to go to or to remain away from church against his will or force him to profess a belief or disbelief in any religion. No person can be punished for entertaining or professing religious beliefs or disbeliefs, for church attendance or nonattendance. No tax in any amount, large or small, can be levied to support any religious activities or institutions, whatever they may be called, or whatever form they may adopt to teach or practice religion. Neither a state nor the Federal Government can, openly or secretly, participate in the affairs of any religious organizations or groups and vice versa. In the words of Jefferson, the clause against establishment of religion by law was intended to erect 'a wall of separation between Church and State.' "

Mr. Black's associates agreed with his statement of principles, which were framed without reference to the Freedom of Exercise Clause. They disagreed, however, with respect to application of the principles, as the split decision in the case indicated. Five members of the Court held that the benefits of public welfare legislation — in this case, free bus transportation to school for parochial as well as public school students — did not run contrary to the concept of separation of Church and State embodied in the First Amendment.

### Different Opinions

Inside and outside the legal profession, opinion is divided concerning the wall of separation and the balance of the religion clauses of the First Amendment.

The view of absolute separationists, carried to the extreme, would make government the adversary of religion. The bishops of the United States, following the McCollum decision in 1948, said that the wall metaphor had become for some persons the "shibboleth of doctrinaire secularism."

Proponents of governmental neutrality toward religion are of the opinion that such neutrality should not be so interpreted as to prohibit incidental aid to religious institutions providing secular services.

In the realm of practice, federal and state legislatures have enacted measures involving incidental benefits to religious bodies. Examples of such measures are the tax exemption of church property; provision of bus rides, book loans and lunch programs to students in church-related as well as public schools; military chaplaincies; loans to church-related hospitals; the financing of studies by military veterans at church-related colleges under GI bills of rights.

## CATHOLIC RIGHTS LEAGUE

The Catholic League for Religious and Civil Rights, founded in 1973, serves the Catholic community as an anti-defamation and civil-rights agency. Father Virgil C. Blum, S.J., is president and founder of the league, which is headquartered at 1100 W. Wells St., Milwaukee, Wis. 53233. The

league also has 15 local chapters across the country.

Speakers representing the league address groups which share its concern, interest and preoccupation with the defense and protection of civil and religious rights.

# U.S. CATHOLIC JURISDICTIONS, HIERARCHY, STATISTICS

The organizational structure of the Catholic Church in the United States consists of 33 provinces with as many archdioceses (metropolitan sees), 146 suffragan sees (dioceses), two jurisdictions immediately subject to the Holy See (the Eparchy of St. Maron for the Maronites and the Melkite Eparchy of Newton), two apostolic exarchates (for Chaldean-Rite Catholics and for Romanians of Byzantine Rite) and the Military Ordinariate. An Armenian-Rite apostolic exarchate for the United States and Canada has its seat in New York. Each of these jurisdictions is under the direction of an archbishop or bishop, called an ordinary, who has apostolic responsibility and authority for the pastoral service of the people in his care.

The structure includes the territorial episcopal conference known as the National Conference of Catholic Bishops. In and through this body, which is strictly ecclesiastical and has defined juridical authority, the bishops exercise their collegiate pastorate over the Church in the entire country (see Index).

Related to the NCCB is the United States Catholic Conference, a civil corporation and operational secretariat through which the bishops, in cooperation with other members of the Church, act on a wider-than-ecclesiastical scale for the good of the Church and society in the United States (see Index).

The representative of the Holy See to the Church in this country is an Apostolic Pro-Nuncio.

## ECCLESIASTICAL PROVINCES

(Sources: *The Official Catholic Directory,* NC News Service.)

*The 33 ecclesiastical provinces bear the names of archdioceses, i.e., of metropolitan sees.*

**Anchorage:** Archdiocese of Anchorage and suffragan sees of Fairbanks, Juneau. Geographical area: Alaska.

**Atlanta:** Archdiocese of Atlanta (Ga.) and suffragan sees of Savannah (Ga.), Charlotte and Raleigh (N.C.), Charleston (S.C.). Geographical area: Georgia, North Carolina, South Carolina.

**Baltimore:** Archdiocese of Baltimore (Md.) and suffragan sees of Wilmington (Del.), Arlington and Richmond (Va.), Wheeling-Charleston (W. Va.). Geographical area: Maryland (except five counties), Delaware, Virginia, West Virginia.

**Boston:** Archdiocese of Boston (Mass.) and suffragan sees of Fall River, Springfield and Worcester (Mass.), Portland (Me.), Manchester (N.H.), Burlington (Vt.). Geographical area: Massachusetts, Maine, New Hampshire, Vermont.

**Chicago:** Archdiocese of Chicago and suffragan sees of Belleville, Joliet, Peoria, Rockford, Springfield. Geographical area: Illinois.

**Cincinnati:** Archdiocese of Cincinnati and suffragan sees of Cleveland, Columbus, Steubenville, Toledo, Youngstown. Geographical area: Ohio.

**Denver:** Archdiocese of Denver (Colo.) and suffragan sees of Colorado Springs and Pueblo (Colo.), Cheyenne (Wyo.). Geographical area: Colorado, Wyoming.

**Detroit:** Archdiocese of Detroit and suffragan sees of Gaylord, Grand Rapids, Kalamazoo, Lansing, Marquette, Saginaw. Geographical area: Michigan.

**Dubuque:** Archdiocese of Dubuque and suffragan sees of Davenport, Des Moines, Sioux City. Geographical area: Iowa.

**Hartford:** Archdiocese of Hartford (Conn.) and suffragan sees of Bridgeport and Norwich (Conn.), Providence (R.I.). Geographical area: Connecticut, Rhode Island.

**Indianapolis:** Archdiocese of Indianapolis and suffragan sees of Evansville, Fort Wayne-South Bend, Gary, Lafayette. Geographical area: Indiana.

**Kansas City** (Kans.): Archdiocese of Kansas City and suffragan sees of Dodge City, Salina, Wichita. Geographical area: Kansas.

**Los Angeles:** Archdiocese of Los Angeles and suffragan sees of Fresno, Monterey, Orange, San Bernardino, San Diego. Geographical area: Southern and Central California.

**Louisville:** Archdiocese of Louisville (Ky.) and suffragan sees of Covington and Owensboro (Ky.), Memphis and Nashville (Tenn.). Geographical area: Kentucky, Tennessee.

**Miami:** Archdiocese of Miami and suffragan sees of Orlando, Palm Beach, Pensacola-Tallahassee, St. Augustine, St. Petersburg, Venice. Geographical area: Florida.

**Milwaukee:** Archdiocese of Milwaukee and suffragan sees of Green Bay, La Crosse, Madison, Superior. Geographical area: Wisconsin.

**Mobile:** Archdiocese of Mobile, Ala., and suffragan sees of Birmingham (Ala.) and Biloxi and Jackson (Miss.). Geographical area: Alabama, Mississippi.

**Newark:** Archdiocese of Newark and suffragan sees of Camden, Metuchen, Paterson, Trenton. Geographical area: New Jersey.

**New Orleans:** Archdiocese of New Orleans and suffragan sees of Alexandria-Shreveport, Baton Rouge, Houma-Thibodaux, Lafayette and Lake Charles. Geographical area: Louisiana.

**New York:** Archdiocese of New York and suffragan sees of Albany, Brooklyn, Buffalo, Ogdensburg, Rochester, Rockville Centre, Syracuse. Geographical area: New York.

**Oklahoma City:** Archdiocese of Oklahoma City (Okla.) and suffragan sees of Tulsa (Okla.) and Little Rock (Ark.). Geographical area: Oklahoma, Arkansas.

**Omaha:** Archdiocese of Omaha and suffragan sees of Grand Island, Lincoln. Geographical area: Nebraska.

**Philadelphia:** Archdiocese of Philadelphia and suffragan sees of Allentown, Altoona-Johnstown, Erie, Greensburg, Harrisburg, Pittsburgh, Scranton. Geographical area: Pennsylvania.

**Philadelphia (Byzantine Rite, Ukrainians):** Metropolitan See of Philadelphia (Byzantine Rite) and Eparchies of St. Josaphat in Parma, St. Nicholas of the Ukrainians in Chicago and Stamford, Conn. The jurisdiction extends to all Ukrainian Catholics in the U.S. from the ecclesiastical province of Galicia in the Ukraine.

**Pittsburgh (Byzantine Rite, Ruthenians):** Metropolitan See of Pittsburgh, Pa. and Eparchies of Passaic (N.J.), Parma (Ohio), Van Nuys (Calif.).

**Portland:** Archdiocese of Portland (Ore.) and suffragan sees of Baker (Ore.), Boise (Ida.), Great Falls-Billings and Helena (Mont.). Geographical area: Oregon, Idaho, Montana.

**St. Louis:** Archdiocese of St. Louis and suffragan sees of Jefferson City, Kansas City-St. Joseph, Springfield-Cape Girardeau. Geographical area: Missouri.

**St. Paul and Minneapolis:** Archdiocese of St. Paul and Minneapolis (Minn.) and suffragan sees of Crookston, Duluth, New Ulm, St. Cloud and Winona (Minn.), Bismarck and Fargo (N.D.), Rapid City and Sioux Falls (S.D.). Geographical

area: Minnesota, North Dakota, South Dakota.

**San Antonio:** Archdiocese of San Antonio (Tex.) and suffragan sees of Amarillo, Austin, Beaumont, Brownsville, Corpus Christi, Dallas, El Paso, Fort Worth, Galveston-Houston, Lubbock, San Angelo and Victoria (Tex.). Geographical area: Texas.

**San Francisco:** Archdiocese of San Francisco (Calif.) and suffragan sees of Oakland, Sacramento, San Jose, Santa Rosa and Stockton (Calif.), Honolulu (Hawaii), Reno-Las Vegas (Nev.), Salt Lake City (Utah). Geographical area: Northern California, Nevada, Utah, Hawaii.

**Santa Fe:** Archdiocese of Santa Fe (N.M.) and suffragan sees of Gallup and Las Cruces (N.M.), Phoenix and Tucson (Ariz.). Geographical area: New Mexico, Arizona.

**Seattle:** Archdiocese of Seattle and suffragan sees of Spokane, Yakima. Geographical area: Washington.

**Washington:** Archdiocese of Washington, D.C., and suffragan see of St. Thomas (Virgin Islands). Geographical area: District of Columbia, five counties of Maryland, Virgin Islands.

## ARCHDIOCESES, DIOCESES, ARCHBISHOPS, BISHOPS

(Sources: *The Official Catholic Directory;* NC News Service. As of Aug. 15, 1984.)

Information includes name of diocese, year of foundation (as it appears on the official document erecting the see), present ordinaries and auxiliaries (for biographies, see Index), former ordinaries.

Archdioceses are indicated by an asterisk.

**Albany, N.Y.** (1847): Howard J. Hubbard, bishop, 1977.

Former bishops: John McCloskey, 1847-64; John J. Conroy, 1865-77; Francis McNeirny, 1877-94; Thomas M. Burke, 1894-1915; Thomas F. Cusack, 1915-18; Edmund F. Gibbons, 1919-54; William A. Scully, 1954-69; Edwin B. Broderick, 1969-76.

**Alexandria-Shreveport, La.** (1853): William B. Friend, bishop, 1983.

Established at Natchitoches, transferred to Alexandria 1910; present title 1977.

Former bishops: Augustus M. Martin, 1853-75; Francis X. Leray, 1877-79, administrator, 1879-83; Anthony Durier, 1885-1904; Cornelius Van de Ven, 1904-32; D. F. Desmond, 1933-45; Charles P. Greco, 1946-73; Lawrence P. Graves, 1973-82.

**Allentown, Pa.** (1961): Thomas J. Welsh, bishop, 1983.

Former bishop: Joseph McShea, 1961-83.

**Altoona-Johnstown, Pa.** (1901): James J. Hogan, bishop, 1966.

Established as Altoona, name changed, 1957.

Former bishops: Eugene A. Garvey, 1901-20; John J. McCort, 1920-36; Richard T. Guilfoyle, 1936-57; Howard J. Carroll, 1958-60; J. Carroll McCormick, 1960-66.

**Amarillo, Tex.** (1926): Leroy T. Matthiesen, bishop, 1980.

Former bishops; Rudolph A. Gerken, 1927-33; Robert E. Lucey, 1934-41; Laurence J. Fitzsimon, 1941-58; John L. Morkovsky, 1958-63; Lawrence M. De Falco, 1963-79.

**Anchorage,\* Alaska** (1966): Francis T. Hurley, archbishop, 1976.

Former archbishop: Joseph T. Ryan, 1966-75.

**Arlington, Va.** (1974): John R. Keating, bishop, 1983.

Former bishop: Thomas J. Welsh, 1974-83.

**Atlanta,\* Ga.** (1956; archdiocese, 1962): Thomas A. Donnellan, archbishop, 1968.

Former ordinaries: Francis E. Hyland, 1956-61; Paul J. Hallinan, first archbishop, 1962-68.

**Austin, Tex.** (1947): Vincent M. Harris, bishop, 1971.

Former bishop: Louis J. Reicher, 1947-71.

**Baker, Ore.** (1903): Thomas J. Connolly, bishop, 1971.

Established as Baker City, name changed, 1952.

Former bishops: Charles J. O'Reilly, 1903-18; Joseph F. McGrath, 1919-50; Francis P. Leipzig, 1950-71.

**Baltimore,\* Md.** (1789; archdiocese, 1808): William D. Borders, archbishop, 1974. P. Francis Murphy, William C. Newman, John H. Ricard, auxiliaries.

Former ordinaries: John Carroll, 1789-1815, first archbishop; Leonard Neale, 1815-17; Ambrose Marechal, S.S., 1817-28; James Whitfield, 1828-34; Samuel Eccleston, S.S., 1834-51; Francis P. Kenrick, 1851-63; Martin J. Spalding, 1864-72; James R. Bayley, 1872-77; Cardinal James Gibbons, 1877-1921; Michael J. Curley, 1921-47; Francis P. Keough, 1947-61; Cardinal Lawrence J. Shehan, 1961-74.

**Baton Rouge, La.** (1961): Stanley J. Ott, bishop, 1983.

Former bishops: Robert E. Tracy, 1961-74; Joseph V. Sullivan, 1974-82.

**Beaumont, Tex.** (1966): Bernard J. Ganter, bishop, 1977.

Former bishops: Vincent M. Harris, 1966-71; Warren L. Boudreaux, 1971-77.

**Belleville, Ill.** (1887): Vacant as of Aug. 15, 1984.

Former bishops: John Janssen, 1888-1913; Henry Althoff, 1914-47; Albert R. Zuroweste, 1948-76; William M. Cosgrove, 1976-81; John N. Wurm, 1981-84.

**Biloxi, Miss.** (1977): (Joseph) Lawson E. Howze, bishop, 1977.

**Birmingham, Ala.** (1969): Joseph G. Vath, bishop, 1969.

**Bismarck, N. Dak.** (1909): John F. Kinney, bishop, 1982.

Former bishops: Vincent Wehrle, O.S.B., 1910-39; Vincent J. Ryan, 1940-51; Lambert A. Hoch, 1952-56; Hilary B. Hacker, 1957-82.

**Boise, Ida.** (1893): Sylvester Treinen, bishop, 1962.

Former bishops: Alphonse J. Glorieux, 1893-1917; Daniel M. Gorman, 1918-27; Edward J. Kelly, 1928-56; James J. Byrne, 1956-62.

**Boston,\* Mass.** (1808; archdiocese, 1875): Bernard F. Law, archbishop, 1984. Lawrence J. Riley, John M. D'Arcy, John J. Mulcahy, Daniel A. Hart, Alfred C. Hughes, auxiliaries.

Former ordinaries: John L. de Cheverus, 1810-23; Benedict J. Fenwick, S.J., 1825-46; John B. Fitzpatrick, 1846-66; John J. Williams, 1866-1907, first archbishop; Cardinal William O'Connell, 1907-44; Cardinal Richard Cushing, 1944-70; Cardinal Humberto Medeiros, 1970-83.

**Bridgeport, Conn.** (1953): Walter W. Curtis, bishop, 1961.

Former bishop: Lawrence J. Shehan, 1953-61.

**Brooklyn, N.Y.** (1853): Francis J. Mugavero, bishop, 1968. Joseph M. Sullivan, Rene Valero, auxiliaries.

Former bishops: John Loughlin, 1853-91; Charles E. McDonnell, 1892-1921; Thomas E. Molloy, 1921-56; Bryan J. McEntegart, 1957-68.

**Brownsville, Tex.** (1965): John J. Fitzpatrick, bishop, 1971.

Former bishops: Adolph Marx, 1965; Humberto S. Medeiros, 1966-70.

**Buffalo, N.Y.** (1847): Edward D. Head, bishop, 1973. Pius A. Benincasa, Bernard J. McLaughlin, auxiliaries.

Former bishops: John Timon, C.M., 1847-67; Stephen V. Ryan, C.M., 1868-96; James E. Quigley, 1897-1903; Charles H. Colton, 1903-15; Dennis J. Dougherty, 1915-18; William Turner, 1919-36; John A. Duffy, 1937-44; John F. O'Hara, C.S.C., 1945-51; Joseph A. Burke, 1952-62; James McNulty, 1963-72.

**Burlington, Vt.** (1853): John A. Marshall, bishop, 1972.

Former bishops: Louis De Goesbriand, 1853-99; John S. Michaud, 1899-1908; Joseph J. Rice, 1910-38; Matthew F. Brady, 1938-44; Edward F. Ryan, 1945-56; Robert F. Joyce, 1957-71.

**Camden, N.J.** (1937): George H. Guilfoyle, bishop, 1968. James L. Schad, auxiliary.

Former bishops: Bartholomew J. Eustace, 1938-56; Justin J. McCarthy, 1957-59; Celestine J. Damiano, 1960-67.

**Charleston, S.C.** (1820): Ernest L. Unterkoefler, bishop, 1964.

Former bishops: John England, 1820-42; Ignatius W. Reynolds, 1844-55; Patrick N. Lynch, 1858-82; Henry P. Northrop, 1883-1916; William T. Russell, 1917-27; Emmet M. Walsh, 1927-49; John

J. Russell, 1950-58; Paul J. Hallinan, 1958-62; Francis F. Reh, 1962-64.

**Charlotte, N.C.** (1971): Vacant as of Aug. 15, 1984.

Former bishop: Michael J. Begley (1972-84).

**Cheyenne, Wyo.** (1887): Joseph Hart, bishop, 1978.

Former bishops: Maurice F. Burke, 1887-93; Thomas M. Lenihan, 1897-1901; James J. Keane, 1902-11; Patrick A. McGovern, 1912-51; Hubert M. Newell, 1951-78.

**Chicago,\* Ill.** (1843; archdiocese, 1880): Cardinal Joseph L. Bernardin, archbishop, 1982. Alfred L. Abramowicz, Nevin W. Hayes, O. Carm., Placido Rodriguez, Timothy Lyne, John Vlazny, Wilton D. Gregory, auxiliaries.

Former ordinaries: William Quarter, 1844-48; James O. Van de Velde, S.J., 1849-53; Anthony O'Regan, 1854-58; James Duggan, 1859-70; Thomas P. Foley, administrator, 1870-79; Patrick A. Feehan, 1880-1902, first archbishop; James E. Quigley, 1903-15; Cardinal George Mundelein, 1915-39; Cardinal Samuel Stritch, 1939-58; Cardinal Albert Meyer, 1958-65; Cardinal John Cody, 1965-82.

**Cincinnati,\* Ohio** (1821; archdiocese, 1850): Daniel E. Pilarczyk, archbishop, 1982. Nicholas Elko (titular archbishop), James H. Garland, auxiliaries.

Former ordinaries: Edward D. Fenwick, O.P., 1822-32; John B. Purcell, 1833-83, first archbishop; William H. Elder, 1883-1904; Henry Moeller, 1904-1925; John T. McNicholas, O.P., 1925-50; Karl J. Alter, 1950-69; Paul F. Leibold, 1969-72; Joseph L. Bernardin, 1972-82.

**Cleveland, Ohio** (1847): Anthony M. Pilla, bishop, 1980. Gilbert I. Sheldon, James P. Lyke, O.F.M., A. Edward Pevec, A. James Quinn, auxiliaries.

Former bishops: L. Amadeus Rappe, 1847-70; Richard Gilmour, 1872-91; Ignatius F. Horstmann, 1892-1908; John P. Farrelly, 1909-21; Joseph Schrembs, 1921-45; Edward F. Hoban, 1945-66; Clarence G. Issenmann, 1966-74; James A. Hickey, 1974-80.

**Colorado Springs, Colo.** (1983): Richard C. Hanifen, bishop, 1983.

**Columbus, Ohio** (1868): James A. Griffin, bishop, 1983.

Former bishops: Sylvester H. Rosecrans, 1868-78; John A. Watterson, 1880-99; Henry Moeller, 1900-03; James J. Hartley, 1904-44; Michael J. Ready, 1944-57; Clarence Issenmann, 1957-64; John J. Carberry, 1965-68; Clarence E. Elwell, 1968-73; Edward J. Herrmann, 1973-82.

**Corpus Christi, Tex.** (1912): Rene H. Gracida, bishop, 1983.

Former bishops; Paul J. Nussbaum, C.P., 1913-20; Emmanuel B. Ledvina, 1921-49; Mariano S. Garriga, 1949-65; Thomas J. Drury, 1965-83.

**Covington, Ky.** (1853): William A. Hughes, bishop, 1979. J. Kendrick Williams, auxiliary.

Former bishops: George A. Carrell, S.J., 1853-68; Augustus M. Toebbe, 1870-84; Camillus P. Maes, 1885-1914; Ferdinand Brossart, 1916-23; Francis W. Howard, 1923-44; William T. Mulloy,

1945-59; Richard Ackerman, C.S.Sp., 1960-78.

**Crookston, Minn.** (1909): Victor Balke, bishop, 1976.

Former bishops: Timothy Corbett, 1910-38; John H. Peschges, 1938-44; Francis J. Schenk, 1945-60; Laurence A. Glenn, 1960-70; Kenneth J. Povish, 1970-75.

**Dallas, Tex.** (1890): Thomas Tschoepe, bishop, 1969.

Established 1890, as Dallas, title changed to Dallas-Ft. Worth 1953; redesignated Dallas, 1969, when Ft. Worth was made diocese.

Former bishops: Thomas F. Brennan, 1891-92; Edward J. Dunne, 1893-1910; Joseph P. Lynch, 1911-54; Thomas K. Gorman, 1954-69.

**Davenport, Ia.** (1881): Gerald F. O'Keefe, bishop, 1966.

Former bishops: John McMullen, 1881-83; Henry Cosgrove, 1884-1906; James Davis, 1906-26; Henry P. Rohlman, 1927-44; Ralph L. Hayes, 1944-66.

**Denver,\* Colo.** (1887; archdiocese, 1941): James V. Casey, archbishop, 1967. George R. Evans, auxiliary.

Former ordinaries: Joseph P. Machebeuf, 1887-89; Nicholas C. Matz, 1889-1917; J. Henry Tihen, 1917-31; Urban J. Vehr, 1931-67, first archbishop.

**Des Moines, Ia.** (1911): Maurice J. Dingman, bishop, 1968.

Former bishops: Austin Dowling, 1912-19; Thomas W. Drumm, 1919-33; Gerald T. Bergan, 1934-48; Edward C. Daly, O.P., 1948-64; George J. Biskup, 1965-67.

**Detroit,\* Mich.** (1833; archdiocese, 1937): Edmund C. Szoka, archbishop, 1981. Thomas J. Gumbleton, Walter J. Schoenherr, Moses B. Anderson, S.S.E., Patrick R. Cooney, Dale J. Melczek, auxiliaries.

Former ordinaries: Frederic Rese, 1833-71; Peter P. Lefevere, administrator, 1841-69; Caspar H. Borgess, 1871-88; John S. Foley, 1888-1918; Michael J. Gallagher, 1918-37; Cardinal Edward Mooney, 1937-58, first archbishop; Cardinal John F. Dearden, 1958-80.

**Dodge City, Kans.** (1951): Stanley G. Schlarman, bishop, 1983.

Former bishops: John B. Franz, 1951-59; Marion F. Forst, 1960-76; Eugene J. Gerber, 1976-82.

**Dubuque,\* Iowa** (1837; archdiocese, 1893): Daniel W. Kucera, O.S.B., archbishop, 1984. Francis J. Dunn, auxiliary.

Former ordinaries: Mathias Loras, 1837-58; Clement Smyth, O.C.S.O., 1858-65; John Hennessy, 1866-1900, first archbishop; John J. Keane, 1900-11; James J. Keane, 1911-29; Francis J. Beckman, 1930-46; Henry P. Rohlman, 1946-54; Leo Binz, 1954-61; James J. Byrne, 1962-83.

**Duluth, Minn.** (1889): Robert H. Brom, bishop, 1983.

Former bishops: James McGolrick, 1889-1918; John T. McNicholas, O.P., 1918-25; Thomas A. Welch, 1926-59; Francis J. Schenk, 1960-69; Paul F. Anderson, 1969-82.

**El Paso, Tex.** (1914): Raymundo J. Pena, bishop, 1980.

Former bishops: Anthony J. Schuler, S.J.,

1915-42; Sidney M. Metzger, 1942-78. Patrick F. Flores, 1978-79.

**Erie, Pa.** (1853): Michael J. Murphy, bishop, 1982.

Former bishops: Michael O'Connor, 1853-54; Josue M. Young, 1854-66; Tobias Mullen, 1868-99; John E. Fitzmaurice, 1899-1920; John M. Gannon, 1920-66; John F. Whealon, 1966-69; Alfred M. Watson, 1969-82.

**Evansville, Ind.** (1944): Francis Raymond Shea, bishop, 1970.

Former bishops: Henry J. Grimmelsman, 1944-65; Paul F. Leibold, 1966-69.

**Fairbanks, Alaska** (1962): Robert L. Whelan, S.J., bishop, 1968. Michael Kaniecki, S.J., coadjutor.

Former bishop: Francis D. Gleeson, S.J., 1962-68.

**Fall River, Mass.** (1904): Daniel A. Cronin, bishop, 1970.

Former bishops: William Stang, 1904-07; Daniel F. Feehan, 1907-34; James E. Cassidy, 1934-51; James L. Connolly, 1951-70.

**Fargo, N. Dak.** (1889): Justin A. Driscoll, bishop, 1970.

Established at Jamestown, transferred, 1897.

Former bishops: John Shanley, 1889-1909; James O'Reilly, 1910-34; Aloysius J. Muench, 1935-59; Leo F. Dworschak, 1960-70.

**Fort Wayne-South Bend, Ind.** (1857): William E. McManus, bishop, 1976. Joseph R. Crowley, auxiliary.

Established as Fort Wayne, name changed, 1960.

Former bishops: John H. Luers, 1858-71; Joseph Dwenger, C.Pp. S., 1872-93; Joseph Rademacher, 1893-1900; Herman J. Alerding, 1900-24; John F. Noll, 1925-56; Leo A. Pursley, 1957-76.

**Fort Worth, Tex.** (1969): Joseph P. Delaney, bishop, 1981.

Former bishop: John J. Cassata, 1969-80.

**Fresno, Calif.** (1967): Joseph J. Madera, M.Sp.S., bishop, 1980.

Formerly Monterey-Fresno, 1922.

Former bishops (Monterey-Fresno): John J. Cantwell, administrator, 1922-24; John B. MacGinley, first bishop, 1924-32; Philip G. Sher, 1933-53; Aloysius J. Willinger, 1953-67.

Former bishops (Fresno): Timothy Manning, 1967-69; Hugh A. Donohoe, 1969-80.

**Gallup, N. Mex.** (1939): Jerome J. Hastrich, bishop, 1969.

Former bishop: Bernard T. Espelage, O.F.M., 1940-69.

**Galveston-Houston, Tex.** (1847): Vacant as of Aug. 24, 1984. John E. McCarthy, auxiliary.

Established as Galveston, name changed, 1959.

Former bishops: John M. Odin, C.M., 1847-61; Claude M. Dubuis, 1862-92; Nicholas A. Gallagher, 1892-1918; Christopher E. Byrne, 1918-50; Wendelin J. Nold, 1950-75; John L. Morkovsky, 1975-84.

**Gary, Ind.** (1956): Norbert F. Gaughan, bishop, 1984.

Former bishop: Andrew G. Grutka, 1957-84.

**Gaylord, Mich.** (1971): Robert J. Rose, bishop, 1981.

Former bishop: Edmund C. Szoka, 1971-81.

**Grand Island, Neb.** (1912): Lawrence McNamara, bishop, 1978.
Established at Kearney, transferred, 1917.
Former bishops: James A. Duffy, 1913-31; Stanislaus V. Bona, 1932-44; Edward J. Hunkeler, 1945-51; John L. Paschang, 1951-72; John J. Sullivan, 1972-77.
**Grand Rapids, Mich.** (1882): Joseph M. Breitenbeck, bishop, 1969. Joseph C. McKinney, auxiliary.
Former bishops: Henry J. Richter, 1883-1916; Michael J. Gallagher, 1916-18; Edward D. Kelly, 1919-26; Joseph G. Pinten, 1926-40; Joseph C. Plagens, 1941-43; Francis J. Haas, 1943-53; Allen J. Babcock, 1954-69.
**Great Falls-Billings, Mont.** (1904): Thomas J. Murphy, bishop, 1978.
Established as Great Falls; name changed, 1980.
Former bishops: Mathias C. Lenihan, 1904-30; Edwin V. O'Hara, 1930-39; William J. Condon, 1939-67; Eldon B. Schuster, 1968-77.
**Green Bay, Wis.** (1868): Adam J. Maida, bishop, 1984. Robert F. Morneau, auxiliary.
Former bishops: Joseph Melcher, 1868-73; Francis X. Krautbauer, 1875-85; Frederick X. Katzer, 1886-91; Sebastian G. Messmer, 1892-1903; Joseph J. Fox, 1904-14; Paul P. Rhode, 1915-45; Stanislaus V. Bona, 1945-67; Aloysius J. Wycislo, 1968-83.
**Greensburg, Pa.** (1951): William G. Connare, bishop, 1960.
Former bishop: Hugh L. Lamb, 1951-59.
**Harrisburg, Pa.** (1868): William H. Keeler, bishop, 1984.
Former bishops: Jeremiah F. Shanahan, 1868-86; Thomas McGovern, 1888-98; John W. Shanahan,1899-1916; Philip R. McDevitt, 1916-35; George L. Leech, 1935-71; Joseph T. Daley, 1971-83.
**Hartford,\* Conn.** (1843; archdiocese, 1953): John F. Whealon, archbishop, 1969. John F. Hackett, Peter A. Rosazza, auxiliaries.
Former ordinaries: William Tyler, 1844-49; Bernard O'Reilly, 1850-56; F. P. MacFarland, 1858-74; Thomas Galberry, O.S.A., 1876-78; Lawrence S. McMahon, 1879-93; Michael Tierney, 1894-1908; John J. Nilan, 1910-34; Maurice F. McAuliffe, 1934-44; Henry J. O'Brien, 1945-68, first archbishop.
**Helena, Mont.** (1884): Elden F. Curtiss, bishop, 1976.
Former bishops: John B. Brondel, 1884-1903; John P. Carroll, 1904-25; George J. Finnigan, C.S.C., 1927-32; Ralph L. Hayes, 1933-35; Joseph M. Gilmore, 1936-62; Raymond Hunthausen, 1962-75.
**Honolulu, Hawaii** (1941): Joseph A. Ferrario, bishop, 1982.
Former bishops: James J. Sweeney, 1941-68; John J. Scanlan, 1968-81.
**Houma-Thibodaux, La.** (1977): Warren L. Boudreaux, bishop, 1977.
**Indianapolis,\* Ind.** (1834; archdiocese, 1944): Edward T. O'Meara, archbishop, 1980.
Established at Vincennes, transferred, 1898.
Former ordinaries: Simon G. Bruté, 1834-39; Celestine de la Hailandiere, 1839-47; John S. Bazin, 1847-48; Maurice de St. Palais, 1849-77; Francis S. Chatard, 1878-1918; Joseph Chartrand, 1918-33; Joseph E. Ritter, 1934-46, first archbishop; Paul C.

Schulte, 1946-70; George J. Biskup, 1970-79.
**Jackson, Miss.** (1837): William R. Houck, bishop, 1984.
Established at Natchez; title changed to Natchez-Jackson, 1956; transferred to Jackson, 1977 (Natchez made titular see).
Former bishops: John J. Chanche, S.S., 1841-52; James Van de Velde, S.J., 1853-55; William H. Elder, 1857-80; Francis A. Jansens, 1881-88; Thomas Heslin, 1889-1911; John E. Gunn, S.M., 1911-24; Richard O. Gerow, 1924-67; Joseph B. Brunini, 1968-84.
**Jefferson City, Mo.** (1956): Michael F. McAuliffe, bishop, 1969.
Former bishop: Joseph Marling, C.Pp.S., 1956-69.
**Joliet, Ill.** (1948): Joseph I. Imesch, bishop, 1979. Raymond J. Vonesh, auxiliary.
Former bishops: Martin D. McNamara, 1949-66. Romeo Blanchette, 1966-79.
**Juneau, Alaska** (1951): Michael H. Kenny, bishop, 1979.
Former bishops: Dermot O'Flanagan, 1951-68; Joseph T. Ryan, administrator, 1968-71; Francis T. Hurley, 1971-76, administrator, 1976-79.
**Kalamazoo, Mich.** (1971): Paul V. Donovan, bishop, 1971.
**Kansas City,\* Kans.** (1877; archdiocese, 1952): Ignatius J. Strecker, archbishop, 1969. Marion F. Forst, auxiliary.
Established as vicariate apostolic, 1850, became Diocese of Leavenworth, 1877, transferred to Kansas City 1947.
Former ordinaries: J. B. Miege, vicar apostolic, 1851-74; Louis M. Fink, O.S.B., vicar apostolic, 1874-77, first bishop, 1877-1904; Thomas F. Lillis, 1904-10; John Ward, 1910-29; Francis Johannes, 1929-37; Paul C. Schulte, 1937-46; George J. Donnelly, 1946-50; Edward Hunkeler, 1951-69, first archbishop.
**Kansas City-St. Joseph, Mo.** (Kansas City, 1880; St. Joseph, 1868; united 1956): John J. Sullivan, bishop, 1977.
Former bishops: John J. Hogan, 1880-1913; Thomas F. Lillis, 1913-38; Edwin V. O'Hara, 1939-56; John P. Cody, 1956-61; Charles H. Helmsing, 1962-77.
Former bishops (St. Joseph): John J. Hogan, 1868-80, administrator, 1880-93; Maurice F. Burke, 1893-1923; Francis Gilfillan, 1923-33; Charles H. Le Blond, 1933-56.
**La Crosse, Wis.** (1868): John J. Paul, bishop, 1983.
Former bishops: Michael Heiss, 1868-80; Kilian C. Flasch, 1881-91; James Schwebach, 1892-1921; Alexander J. McGavick, 1921-48; John P. Treacy, 1948-64; Frederick W. Freking, 1965-83.
**Lafayette, Ind.** (1944): William Higi, bishop, 1984.
Former bishops: John G. Bennett, 1944-57; John J. Carberry, 1957-65; Raymond J. Gallagher, 1965-82; George A. Fulcher, 1983-84.
**Lafayette, La.** (1918): Gerard L. Frey, bishop, 1973.
Former bishops: Jules B. Jeanmard, 1918-56; Maurice Schexnayder, 1956-72.

**Lake Charles, La.** (1980): Jude Speyrer, bishop, 1980.

**Lansing, Mich.** (1937): Kenneth J. Povish, bishop, 1975. James Sullivan, auxiliary.

Former bishops: Joseph H. Albers, 1937-65; Alexander Zaleski, 1965-75.

**Las Cruces, N. Mex.** (1982): Ricardo Ramirez, C.S.B., bishop, 1982.

**Lincoln, Neb.** (1887): Glennon P. Flavin, bishop, 1967.

Former bishops: Thomas Bonacum, 1887-1911; J. Henry Tihen, 1911-17; Charles J. O'Reilly, 1918-23; Francis J. Beckman, 1924-30; Louis B. Kucera, 1930-57; James V. Casey, 1957-67.

**Little Rock, Ark.** (1843): Andrew J. McDonald, bishop, 1972.

Former bishops: Andrew Byrne, 1844-62; Edward Fitzgerald, 1867-1907; John Morris, 1907-46; Albert L. Fletcher, 1946-72.

**Los Angeles,\* Calif.** (1840; archdiocese, 1936): Cardinal Timothy Manning, archbishop, 1970. John J. Ward, Juan A. Arzube, William Levada, Donald Montrose, auxiliaries.

Former ordinaries: Francisco Garcia Diego y Moreno, O.F.M., 1840-46; Joseph S. Alemany, O.P., 1850-53; Thaddeus Amat, C.M., 1854-78; Francis Mora, 1878-96; George T. Montgomery, 1896-1903; Thomas J. Conaty, 1903-15; John J. Cantwell, 1917-47, first archbishop; Cardinal James McIntyre, 1948-70.

**Louisville,\* Ky.** (1808; archdiocese, 1937): Thomas C Kelly, O.P., archbishop, 1982. Charles G. Maloney, auxiliary.

Established at Bardstown, transferred, 1841.

Former ordinaries: Benedict J. Flaget, S.S. 1810-32; John B. David, S.S., 1832-33; Benedict J. Flaget, S.S., 1833-50; Martin J. Spalding, 1850-64; Peter J. Lavialle, 1865-67; William G. McCloskey, 1868-1909; Denis O'Donaghue, 1910-24; John A. Floersh, 1924-67, first archbishop; Thomas J. McDonough, 1967-81.

**Lubbock, Tex.** (1983): Michael Sheehan, bishop, 1983.

**Madison, Wis.** (1946): Cletus F. O'Donnell, bishop, 1967. George O. Wirz, auxiliary.

Former bishop: William P. O'Connor, 1946-67.

**Manchester, N.H.** (1884): Odore J. Gendron, bishop, 1974.Robert Mulvee, auxiliary.

Former bishops: Denis M. Bradley, 1884-1903; John B. Delany, 1904-06; George A. Guertin, 1907-32; John B. Peterson, 1932-44; Matthew F. Brady, 1944-59; Ernest J. Primeau, 1960-74.

**Marquette, Mich.** (1857): Mark F. Schmitt, bishop, 1978.

Former bishops: Frederic Baraga, 1857-68; Ignatius Mrak, 1869-78; John Vertin, 1879-99; Frederick Eis, 1899-1922; Paul J. Nussbaum, C.P., 1922-35; Joseph C. Plagens, 1935-40; Francis Magner, 1941-47; Thomas L. Noa, 1947-68; Charles A. Salatka, 1968-77.

**Memphis, Tenn.** (1970): J. Francis Stafford, bishop, 1982.

Former bishop: Carroll T. Dozier, 1971-82.

**Metuchen, N.J.** (1981): Theodore E. McCarrick, bishop, 1981.

**Miami,\* Fla.** (1958; archdiocese, 1968): Edward A. McCarthy, archbishop, 1977. Agustin A. Roman, auxiliary.

Former ordinary: Coleman F. Carroll, 1958-77, first archbishop.

**Milwaukee,\* Wis.** (1843; archdiocese, 1875): Rembert G. Weakland, O.S.B., archbishop, 1977. Leo J. Brust, Richard J. Sklba, auxiliaries.

Former ordinaries: John M. Henni, 1844-81, first archbishop; Michael Heiss, 1881-90; Frederick X. Katzer, 1891-1903; Sebastian G. Messmer, 1903-30; Samuel A. Stritch, 1930-39; Moses E. Kiley, 1940-53; Albert G. Meyer, 1953-58; William E. Cousins, 1959-77.

**Mobile,\* Ala.** (1829; archdiocese, 1980): Oscar H. Lipscomb, first archbishop, 1980.

Former bishops: Michael Portier, 1829-59; John Quinlan, 1859-83; Dominic Manucy, 1884; Jeremiah O'Sullivan, 1885-96; Edward P. Allen, 1897-1926; Thomas J. Toolen, 1927-69; John L. May, 1969-80.

**Monterey in California** (1967): Thaddeus A. Shubsda, bishop, 1982.

Formerly Monterey-Fresno, 1922.

Former bishops (Monterey-Fresno): John J. Cantwell, administrator, 1922-24; John B. MacGinley, first bishop, 1924-32; Philip G. Sher, 1933-53; Aloysius J. Willinger, 1953-67.

Former bishop (Monterey): Harry A. Clinch, 1967-82.

**Nashville, Tenn.** (1837): James D. Niedergeses, bishop, 1975.

Former bishops: Richard P. Miles, O.P., 1838-60; James Whelan, O.P., 1860-64; Patrick A. Feehan, 1865-80; Joseph Rademacher, 1883-93; Thomas S. Byrne, 1894-1923; Alphonse J. Smith, 1924-35; William L. Adrian, 1936-69; Joseph A. Durick, 1969-75.

**Newark,\* N.J.** (1853; archdiocese, 1937): Peter L. Gerety, archbishop, 1974. Jerome Pechillo, T.O.R., Robert F. Garner, Joseph A. Francis, S.V.D., Dominic A. Marconi, David Arias, O.A.R., auxiliaries.

Former ordinaries: James R. Bayley, 1853-72; Michael A. Corrigan, 1873-80; Winand M. Wigger, 1881-1901; John J. O'Connor, 1901-27; Thomas J. Walsh, 1928-52, first archbishop; Thomas A. Boland, 1953-74.

**New Orleans,\* La.** (1793; archdiocese, 1850): Philip M. Hannan, archbishop, 1965. Harold R. Perry, S. V. D., auxiliary.

Former ordinaries: Luis Penalver y Cardenas, 1793-1801; John Carroll, administrator, 1809-15; W. Louis Dubourg, S.S., 1815-25; Joseph Rosati, C.M., administrator, 1826-29; Leo De Neckere, C.M., 1829-33; Anthony Blanc, 1835-60, first archbishop; Jean Marie Odin, C.M., 1861-70; Napoleon J. Perche, 1870-83; Francis X. Leray, 1883-87; Francis A. Janssens, 1888-97; Placide L. Chapelle, 1897-1905; James H. Blenk, S.M., 1906-17; John W. Shaw, 1918-34; Joseph F. Rummel, 1935-64; John P. Cody, 1964-65.

**Newton, Mass.** (Melkite Rite) (1966; eparchy, 1976): Archbishop Joseph Tawil, exarch, 1969, first eparch, 1976.

Former ordinary: Justin Najmy, 1966-68.

**New Ulm, Minn.** (1957): Raymond A. Lucker, bishop, 1975.

Former bishop: Alphonse J. Schladweiler, 1958-75.

**New York,* N.Y.** (1808; archdiocese, 1850): John J. O'Connor, archbishop, 1984. Patrick V. Ahern, James P. Mahoney, Anthony F. Mestice, Austin Vaughan, Francisco Garmendia, Joseph T. O'Keefe, Emerson Moore, auxiliaries.

Former ordinaries: Richard L. Concanen, O.P., 1808-10; John Connolly, O.P., 1814-25; John Dubois, S.S., 1826-42; John J. Hughes, 1842-64, first archbishop; Cardinal John McCloskey, 1864-85; Michael A. Corrigan, 1885-1902; Cardinal John Farley, 1902-18; Cardinal Patrick Hayes, 1919-38; Cardinal Francis Spellman, 1939-67; Cardinal Terence J. Cooke, 1968-83.

**Norwich, Conn.** (1953): Daniel P. Reilly, bishop, 1975.

Former bishops: Bernard J. Flanagan, 1953-59; Vincent J. Hines, 1960-75.

**Oakland, Calif.** (1962): John S. Cummins, bishop, 1977.

Former bishop: Floyd L. Begin, 1962-77.

**Ogdensburg, N.Y.** (1872): Stanislaus J. Brzana, bishop, 1968.

Former bishops: Edgar P. Wadhams, 1872-91; Henry Gabriels, 1892-1921; Joseph H. Conroy, 1921-39; Francis J. Monaghan, 1939-42; Bryan J. McEntegart, 1943-53; Walter P. Kellenberg, 1954-57; James J. Navagh, 1957-63; Leo R. Smith, 1963; Thomas A. Donnellan, 1964-68.

**Oklahoma City,* Okla.** (1905; archdiocese, 1972): Charles A. Salatka, archbishop, 1977.

Former ordinaries: Theophile Meerschaert, 1905-24; Francis C. Kelley, 1924-48; Eugene J. McGuinness, 1948-57; Victor J. Reed, 1958-71; John R. Quinn, 1971-77, first archbishop.

**Omaha,* Nebr.** (1885; archdiocese, 1945): Daniel E. Sheehan, archbishop, 1969. Anthony Milone, auxiliary.

Former ordinaries: James O'Gorman, O.C.S.O., 1859-74, vicar apostolic; James O'Connor, vicar apostolic, 1876-85, first bishop, 1885-90; Richard Scannell, 1891-1916; Jeremiah J. Harty, 1916-27; Francis Beckman, administrator, 1926-28; Joseph F. Rummel, 1928-35; James H. Ryan, 1935-47, first archbishop; Gerald T. Bergan, 1948-69.

**Orange, Calif.** (1976): William R. Johnson, bishop, 1976. John Steinbock, auxiliary.

**Orlando, Fla.** (1968): Thomas J. Grady, bishop, 1974.

Former bishop: William Borders, 1968-74.

**Owensboro, Ky.** (1937): John J. McRaith, bishop, 1982.

Former bishops: Francis R. Cotton, 1938-60; Henry J. Soenneker, 1961-82.

**Palm Beach, Fla.** (1984): Thomas V. Dailey, bishop, 1984.

**Parma, Ohio** (Byzantine Rite) (1969): Andrew Pataki, eparch, 1984.

Former bishop: Emil Mihalik, 1969-84.

**Passaic, N.J.** (Byzantine Rite) (1963): Michael J. Dudick, eparch, 1968.

Former bishop: Stephen Kocisko, 1963-68.

**Paterson, N.J.** (1937): Frank J. Rodimer, bishop, 1978.

Former bishops: Thomas H. McLaughlin, 1937-47; Thomas A. Boland, 1947-52; James A. McNulty, 1953-63; James J. Navagh, 1963-65; Lawrence B. Casey, 1966-77.

**Pensacola-Tallahassee, Fla.** (1975): J. Keith Symons, bishop, 1983.

Former bishop: Rene H. Gracida, 1975-83.

**Peoria, Ill.** (1877): Edward W. O'Rourke, bishop, 1971.

Former bishops: John L. Spalding, 1877-1908; Edmund M. Dunne, 1909-29; Joseph H. Schlarman, 1930-51; William E. Cousins, 1952-58; John B. Franz, 1959-71.

**Philadelphia,* Pa.** (1808; archdiocese, 1875): Cardinal John Krol, archbishop, 1961. John J. Graham, Martin J. Lohmuller, Edward T. Hughes, Francis B. Schulte, Louis A. De Simone, auxiliaries.

Former ordinaries: Michael Egan, O.F.M., 1810-14; Henry Conwell, 1820-42; Francis P. Kenrick, 1842-51; John N. Neumann, C.SS.R., 1852-60; James F. Wood, 1860-83, first archbishop; Patrick J. Ryan, 1884-1911; Edmond F. Prendergast, 1911-18; Cardinal Dennis Dougherty, 1918-51; Cardinal John O'Hara, C.S.C., 1951-60.

**Philadelphia,* Pa.** (Byzantine Rite) (1924; metropolitan, 1958): Stephen Sulyk, archbishop, 1981.

Former ordinaries: Stephen Ortynsky, O.S.B.M., 1907-16; Constantine Bohachevsky, 1924-61; Ambrose Senyshyn, O.S.B.M., 1961-76; Joseph Schmondiuk, 1977-78; Myroslav J. Lubachivsky, 1979-80, apostolic administrator, 1980-81.

**Phoenix, Ariz.** (1969): Thomas J. O'Brien, bishop, 1982.

Former bishops: Edward A. McCarthy, 1969-76; James S. Rausch, 1977-81.

**Pittsburgh,* Pa.** (Byzantine Rite) (1924; metropolitan, 1969): Stephen J. Kocisko, eparch, 1968, first metropolitan, 1969. John M. Bilock, auxiliary.

Former ordinaries: Basil Takach 1924-48; Daniel Ivancho, 1948-54; Nicholas T. Elko, 1955-67.

**Pittsburgh, Pa.** (1843): Anthony J. Bevilacqua, bishop, 1983. John B. McDowell, Anthony G. Bosco, auxiliaries.

Former bishops: Michael O'Connor, 1843-53, 1854-60; Michael Domenec, C.M., 1860-76; J. Tuigg, 1876-89; Richard Phelan, 1889-1904; J.F. Regis Canevin, 1904-20; Hugh C. Boyle, 1921-55; John F. Dearden, 1950-58; John J. Wright, 1959-69; Vincent M. Leonard, 1969-83.

**Portland, Me.** (1853): Edward C. O'Leary, bishop, 1974. Amedee W. Proulx, auxiliary.

Former bishops: David W. Bacon, 1855-74; James A. Healy, 1875-1900; William H. O'Connell, 1901-06; Louis S. Walsh, 1906-24; John G. Murray, 1925-31; Joseph E. McCarthy, 1932-55; Daniel J. Feeney, 1955-69; Peter L. Gerety, 1969-74.

**Portland,* Ore.** (1846): Cornelius M. Power, archbishop, 1974. Paul E. Waldschmidt, C.S.C., Kenneth D. Steiner, auxiliaries.

Established as Oregon City, name changed, 1928.

Former ordinaries: Francis N. Blanchet, 1846-80 vicar apostolic, first archbishop; Charles J. Seghers, 1880-84; William H. Gross, C.SS.R., 1885-98; Alexander Christie, 1899-1925; Edward D. Howard, 1926-66; Robert J. Dwyer, 1966-74.

**Providence, R.I.** (1872): Louis E. Gelineau, bishop, 1972. Kenneth A. Angell, auxiliary.

Former bishops: Thomas F. Hendricken, 1872-86; Matthew Harkins, 1887-1921; William A. Hickey, 1921-33; Francis P. Keough, 1934-47; Russell J. McVinney, 1948-71.

**Pueblo, Colo.** (1941): Arthur N. Tafoya, bishop, 1980.

Former bishops: Joseph C. Willging, 1942-59; Charles A. Buswell, 1959-79.

**Raleigh, N.C.** (1924): F. Joseph Gossman, bishop, 1975. George E. Lynch, auxiliary.

Former bishops: William J. Hafey, 1925-37; Eugene J. McGuinness, 1937-44; Vincent S. Waters, 1945-75.

**Rapid City, S. Dak.** (1902): Harold J. Dimmerling, bishop, 1969.

Established at Lead, transferred, 1930.

Former bishops: John Stariha, 1902-09; Joseph F. Busch, 1910-15; John J. Lawler, 1916-48; William T. McCarty, C.SS.R., 1948-69.

**Reno-Las Vegas, Nev.** (1931): Norman F. McFarland, bishop, 1976.

Established at Reno; title changed to Reno-Las Vegas, 1976.

Former bishops: Thomas K. Gorman, 1931-52; Robert J. Dwyer, 1952-66; Joseph Green, 1967-74.

**Richmond, Va.** (1820): Walter F. Sullivan, bishop, 1974.

Former bishops: Patrick Kelly, 1820-22; Richard V. Whelan, 1841-50; John McGill, 1850-72; James Gibbons, 1872-77; John J. Keane, 1878-88; Augustine Van de Vyver, 1889-1911; Denis J. O'Connell, 1912-26; Andrew J. Brennan, 1926-45; Peter L. Ireton, 1945-58; John J. Russell, 1958-73.

**Rochester, N.Y.** (1868): Matthew H. Clark, bishop, 1979. Dennis W. Hickey, auxiliary.

Former bishops: Bernard J. McQuaid, 1868-1909; Thomas F. Hickey, 1909-28; John F. O'Hern, 1929-33; Edward F. Mooney, 1933-37; James E. Kearney, 1937-66; Fulton J. Sheen, 1966-69; Joseph L. Hogan, 1969-78.

**Rockford, Ill.** (1908): Arthur J. O'Neill, bishop, 1968.

Former bishops: Peter J. Muldoon, 1908-27; Edward F. Hoban, 1928-42; John J. Boylan, 1943-53; Raymond P. Hillinger, 1953-56; Loras T. Lane, 1956-68.

**Rockville Centre, N.Y.** (1957): John R. McGann, bishop, 1976. Gerald Ryan, James Daly, auxiliaries.

Former bishop: Walter P. Kellenberg, 1957-76.

**Sacramento, Calif.** (1886): Francis A. Quinn, bishop, 1979. Alphonse Gallegos, O.A.R., auxiliary.

Former bishops: Patrick Manogue, 1886-95; Thomas Grace, 1896-1921; Patrick J. Keane, 1922-28; Robert J. Armstrong, 1929-57; Joseph T. McGucken, 1957-62; Alden J. Bell, 1962-79.

**Saginaw, Mich.** (1938): Kenneth E. Untener, bishop, 1980.

Former bishops: William F. Murphy, 1938-50; Stephen S. Woznicki, 1950-68; Francis F. Reh, 1969-80.

**St. Augustine, Fla.** (1870): John J. Snyder, bishop, 1979.

Former bishops: Augustin Verot, S.S., 1870-76;

John Moore, 1877-1901; William J. Kenny, 1902-13; Michael J. Curley, 1914-21; Patrick J. Barry, 1922-40; Joseph P. Hurley, 1940-67; Paul F. Tanner, 1968-79.

**St. Cloud, Minn.** (1889): George H. Speltz, bishop, 1968.

Former bishops: Otto Zardetti, 1889-94; Martin Marty, O.S.B., 1895-96; James Trobec, 1897-1914; Joseph F. Busch, 1915-53; Peter Bartholome, 1953-68.

**St. Josaphat in Parma, Ohio** (Byzantine Rite) (1983): Robert Moskal, bishop, 1984.

**St. Louis,*** Mo. (1826; archdiocese, 1847): John L. May, archbishop, 1980. George J. Gottwald, Charles R. Koester, Edward J. O'Donnell, J. Terry Steib, auxiliaries.

Former ordinaries: Joseph Rosati, C.M., 1827-43; Peter R. Kenrick, 1843-95, first archbishop; John J. Kain, 1895-1903; Cardinal John Glennon, 1903-46; Cardinal Joseph Ritter, 1946-67; Cardinal John J. Carberry, 1968-79.

**St. Maron, Brooklyn, N.Y.** (Maronite Rite) (1966; diocese, 1971): Francis Zayek, (titular archbishop), exarch, 1966, first eparch, 1972. John Chedid, auxiliary.

Established at Detroit; transferred to Brooklyn, 1977.

**St. Nicholas in Chicago** (Byzantine Rite Eparchy of St. Nicholas of the Ukrainians) (1961): Innocent H. Lotocky, O.S.B.M., bishop, 1981.

Former bishop: Jaroslav Gabro, 1961-80.

**St. Paul and Minneapolis,*** Minn. (1850; archdiocese, 1888): John R. Roach, archbishop, 1975. William H. Bullock, J. Richard Ham, M.M., Robert J. Carlson, auxiliaries.

Former ordinaries: Joseph Cretin, 1851-57; Thomas L. Grace, O.P., 1859-84; John Ireland, 1884-1918, first archbishop; Austin Dowling, 1919-30; John G. Murray, 1931-56; William O. Brady, 1956-61; Leo Binz, 1962-75.

**St. Petersburg, Fla.** (1968): W. Thomas Larkin, bishop, 1979.

Former bishop: Charles McLaughlin, 1968-78.

**Salina, Kans.** (1887): George K. Fitzsimons, bishop, 1984.

Established at Concordia, transferred, 1944.

Former bishops: Richard Scannell, 1887-91; John J. Hennessy, administrator, 1891-98; John F. Cunningham, 1898-1919; Francis J. Tief, 1921-38; Frank A. Thill, 1938-57; Frederick W. Freking, 1957-64; Cyril J. Vogel, 1965-79; Daniel W. Kucera, O.S.B., 1980-84.

**Salt Lake City, Utah** (1891): William K. Weigand, bishop, 1980.

Former bishops: Lawrence Scanlan, 1891-1915; Joseph S. Glass, C.M., 1915-26; John J. Mitty, 1926-32; James E. Kearney, 1932-37; Duane G. Hunt, 1937-60; J. Lennox Federal, 1960-80.

**San Angelo, Tex.** (1961): Joseph A. Fiorenza, bishop, 1979.

Former bishops: Thomas J. Drury, 1962-65; Thomas Tschoepe, 1966-69; Stephen A. Leven, 1969-79.

**San Antonio,*** Tex. (1874; archdiocese, 1926): Patrick F. Flores, archbishop, 1979. Bernard Popp, auxiliary.

Former ordinaries: Anthony D. Pellicer, 1874-80; John C. Neraz, 1881-94; John A. Forest, 1895-1911; John W. Shaw, 1911-18; Arthur Jerome Drossaerts, 1918-40, first archbishop; Robert E. Lucey, 1941-69; Francis Furey, 1969-79.

**San Bernardino, Calif.** (1978): Phillip F. Straling, bishop, 1978.

**San Diego, Calif.** (1936): Leo T. Maher, bishop, 1969. Gilbert Espinoza Chavez, auxiliary.

Former bishops: Charles F. Buddy, 1936-66; Francis J. Furey, 1966-69.

**San Francisco,\*** **Calif.** (1853): John R. Quinn, archbishop, 1977. Daniel F. Walsh, auxiliary.

Former ordinaries: Joseph S. Alemany, O.P., 1853-84; Patrick W. Riordan, 1884-1914; Edward J. Hanna, 1915-35; John Mitty, 1935-61; Joseph T. McGucken, 1962-77.

**San Jose, Calif.** (1981): R. Pierre DuMaine, first bishop, 1981.

**Santa Fe,\*** **N. Mex.** (1850; archdiocese, 1875): Robert Sanchez, archbishop, 1974.

Former ordinaries: John B. Lamy, 1850-85, first archbishop; John B. Salpointe, 1885-94; Placide L. Chapelle, 1894-97; Peter Bourgade, 1899-1908; John B. Pitaval, 1909-18; Albert T. Daeger, O.F.M., 1919-32; Rudolph A. Gerken, 1933-43; Edwin V. Byrne, 1943-63; James P. Davis, 1964-74.

**Santa Rosa, Calif.** (1962): Mark J. Hurley, bishop, 1969.

Former bishop: Leo T. Maher, 1962-69.

**Savannah, Ga.** (1850): Raymond W. Lessard, bishop, 1973.

Former bishops: Francis X. Gartland, 1850-54; John Barry, 1857-59; Augustin Verot, S.S., 1861-70; Ignatius Persico, O.F.M. Cap., 1870-72; William H. Gross, C.SS.R., 1873-85; Thomas A. Becker, 1886-99; Benjamin J. Keiley, 1900-22; Michael Keyes, S.M., 1922-35; Gerald P. O'Hara, 1935-59; Thomas J. McDonough, 1960-67; Gerard L. Frey, 1967-72.

**Scranton, Pa.** (1868): James C. Timlin, bishop, 1984.

Former bishops: William O'Hara, 1868-99; Michael J. Hoban, 1899-1926; Thomas C. O'Reilly, 1928-38; William J. Hafey, 1938-54; Jerome D. Hannan, 1954-65; J. Carroll McCormick, 1966-83; John J. O'Connor, 1983-84.

**Seattle,\*** **Wash.** (1850; archdiocese, 1951): Raymond G. Hunthausen, archbishop, 1975.

Established as Nesqually, name changed, 1907.

Former ordinaries; Augustin M. Blanchet, 1850-79; Aegidius Junger, 1879-95; Edward J. O'Dea, 1896-1932; Gerald Shaughnessy, S.M., 1933-50; Thomas A. Connolly, first archbishop, 1950-75.

**Sioux City, Ia.** (1902): Lawrence D. Soens, bishop, 1983.

Former bishops: Philip J. Garrigan, 1902-19; Edmond Heelan, 1919-48; Joseph M. Mueller, 1948-70; Frank H. Greteman, 1970-83.

**Sioux Falls, S. Dak.** (1889): Paul V. Dudley, bishop, 1978. Paul F. Anderson, auxiliary.

Former bishops: Martin Marty, O.S.B., 1889-94; Thomas O'Gorman, 1896-1921; Bernard J. Mahoney, 1922-39; William O. Brady, 1939-56; Lambert A. Hoch, 1956-78.

**Spokane, Wash.** (1913): Lawrence H. Welsh, bishop, 1978.

Former bishops: Augustine F. Schinner, 1914-25; Charles D. White, 1927-55; Bernard J. Topel, 1955-78.

**Springfield, Ill.** (1853): Daniel L. Ryan, bishop, 1984.

Established at Quincy, transferred to Alton 1857; transferred to Springfield 1923.

Former bishops: Henry D. Juncker, 1857-68; Peter J. Baltes, 1870-86; James Ryan, 1888-1923; James A. Griffin, 1924-48; William A. O'Connor, 1949-75; Joseph A. McNicholas, 1975-83.

**Springfield, Mass.** (1870): Joseph F. Maguire, bishop, 1977. Leo E. O'Neil, auxiliary.

Former bishops: Patrick T. O'Reilly, 1870-92; Thomas D. Beaven, 1892-1920; Thomas M. O'Leary, 1921-49; Christopher J. Weldon, 1950-77.

**Springfield-Cape Girardeau, Mo.** (1956): Vacant as of Aug. 15, 1984.

Former bishops: Charles Helmsing, 1956-62; Ignatius J. Strecker, 1962-69; William Baum, 1970-73; Bernard F. Law, 1973-84.

**Stamford, Conn.** (Byzantine Rite) (1956); Basil Losten, eparch, 1977.

Former eparchs: Ambrose Senyshyn, O.S.B.M., 1956-61; Joseph Schmondiuk, 1961-77.

**Steubenville, Ohio** (1944): Albert H. Ottenweller, bishop, 1977.

Former bishop: John K. Mussio, 1945-77.

**Stockton, Calif.** (1962): Roger M. Mahony, bishop, 1980.

Former bishops: Hugh A. Donohoe, 1962-69; Merlin J. Guilfoyle, 1969-79.

**Superior, Wis.** (1905): George A. Hammes, bishop, 1960. Raphael M. Fliss, coadjutor.

Former bishops: Augustine F. Schinner, 1905-13; Joseph M. Koudelka, 1913-21; Joseph G. Pinten, 1922-26; Theodore M. Reverman, 1926-41; William P. O'Connor, 1942-46; Albert G. Meyer, 1946-53; Joseph Annabring, 1954-59.

**Syracuse, N.Y.** (1886): Frank J. Harrison, bishop, 1976. Thomas J. Costello, auxiliary.

Former bishops: Patrick A. Ludden, 1887-1912; John Grimes, 1912-22; Daniel J. Curley, 1923-32; John A. Duffy, 1933-37; Walter A. Foery, 1937-70; David F. Cunningham, 1970-76.

**Toledo, Ohio** (1910): James R. Hoffman, bishop, 1980. Robert Donnelly, auxiliary.

Former bishops: Joseph Schrembs, 1911-21; Samuel A. Stritch, 1921-30; Karl J. Alter, 1931-50; George J. Rehring, 1950-67; John A. Donovan, 1967-80.

**Trenton, N.J.** (1881): John C. Reiss, bishop, 1980. Edward U. Kmiec, auxiliary

Former bishops: Michael J. O'Farrell, 1881-94; James A. McFaul, 1894-1917; Thomas J. Walsh, 1918-28; John J. McMahon, 1928-32; Moses E. Kiley, 1934-40; William A. Griffin, 1940-50; George W. Ahr, 1950-79.

**Tucson, Ariz.** (1897): Manuel D. Moreno, bishop, 1982.

Former bishops: Peter Bourgade, 1897-99; Henry Granjon, 1900-22; Daniel J. Gercke, 1923-60; Francis J. Green, 1960-81.

**Tulsa, Okla.** (1972): Eusebius J. Beltran, bishop, 1978.
Former bishop: Bernard J. Ganter, 1973-77.
**Van Nuys, Calif.** (Byzantine Rite) (1981): Thomas Dolinay, bishop, 1982.
**Venice, Fla.** (1984): John J. Nevins, bishop, 1984.
**Victoria, Tex.** (1982): Charles Grahmann, bishop, 1982.
**Washington,\* D.C.** (1939): James A. Hickey, archbishop, 1980. Thomas W. Lyons, Eugene A. Marino, S.S.J., auxiliaries.
Former ordinaries: Michael J. Curley, 1939-47; Cardinal Patrick O'Boyle, 1948-73; Cardinal William Baum, 1973-80.
**Wheeling-Charleston, W. Va.** (1850): Joseph H. Hodges, bishop, 1962. James E. Michaels, S.S.C., auxiliary.
Established as Wheeling; name changed, 1974.
Former bishops: Richard V. Whelan, 1850-74; John J. Kain, 1875-93; Patrick J. Donahue, 1894-1922; John J. Swint, 1922-62.
**Wichita, Kans.** (1887): Eugene J. Gerber, bishop, 1982.
Former bishops: John J. Hennessy, 1888-1920; Augustus J. Schwertner, 1921-39; Christian H. Winkelmann, 1940-46; Mark K. Carroll, 1947-67; David M. Maloney, 1967-82.
**Wilmington, Del.** (1868): Vacant as of Aug. 15, 1984.
Former bishops: Thomas A. Becker, 1868-86; Alfred A. Curtis, 1886-96; John J. Monaghan, 1897-1925; Edmond Fitzmaurice, 1925-60; Michael Hyle, 1960-67; Thomas J. Mardaga, 1968-84.
**Winona, Minn.** (1889): Loras J. Watters, bishop, 1969.
Former bishops: Joseph B. Cotter, 1889-1909; Patrick R. Heffron, 1910-27; Francis M. Kelly, 1928-49; Edward A. Fitzgerald, 1949-69.
**Worcester, Mass.** (1950): Timothy J. Harrington, bishop, 1983.
Former bishops: John J. Wright, 1950-59; Bernard J. Flanagan, 1959-83.

**Yakima, Wash.** (1951): William Skylstad, bishop, 1977.
Former bishops: Joseph P. Dougherty, 1951-69; Cornelius M. Power, 1969-74; Nicholas E. Walsh, 1974-76.
**Youngstown, Ohio** (1943): James W. Malone, bishop, 1968. Benedict C. Franzetta, auxiliary.
Former bishops: James A. McFadden, 1943-52; Emmet M. Walsh, 1952-68.
**Apostolic Exarchate for Armenian-Rite Catholics in the United States and Canada, New York, N.Y.** (1981); Nerses Mikail Setian, exarch, 1981.
**Apostolic Exarchate for Chaldean-Rite Catholics in the United States, Detroit, Mich.** (1982): Ibrahim Ibrahim, exarch, 1982.
**Apostolic Exarchate for Romanians of Byzantine Rite in the United States, Canton, O.** (1982): Louis Puscas, exarch, 1983.
**Military Ordinariate** (1917): Archbishop John J. O'Connor, apostolic administrator, 1984. Joseph T. Ryan, coadjutor archbishop, 1975. Lawrence Kenney, Francis Roque, Joseph T. Dimino, Angelo T. Acerro, O.S.B., auxiliaries.
Former military vicars: Cardinal Patrick Hayes, 1917-38; Cardinal Francis Spellman, 1939-67; Cardinal Terence J. Cooke, 1968-83.

**Military Ordinariate**
The Military Ordinariate or Vicariate, is the diocese which serves members of the armed forces of the United States wherever they are. It has jurisdiction over: military and Veterans Administration hospital chaplains; personnel of the armed forces and members of their families and dependents habitually living with them; members of the Coast Guard, National Guard, Air National Guard and Civil Air Patrol when on active duty; persons living on military installations and/or attached to military offices or VA facilities.
The ordinariate was canonically established on a permanent basis by a decree of the Sacred Consistorial Congregation dated Sept. 8, 1957. Offices of the ordinariate are located at 1011 First Ave., New York, N.Y. 10022.

## MISSIONARY BISHOPS

### Africa

**Namibia (South West Africa):** Keetmanshoop (vicariate apostolic), Edward F. Schlotterback, O.S.F.S.
**Nigeria:** Sokoto (diocese), Michael J. Dempsey, O.P.
**South Africa:** De Aar (diocese), Joseph A. De Palma, S.C.J.
Keimos (diocese), John Minder, O.S.F.S.
**Tanzania:** Arusha (diocese), Dennis V. Durning, C.S.Sp.

### Asia

**India:** Bhagalpur (diocese), Urban McGarry, T.O.R.
**Indonesia:** Agats (diocese), Alphonse A. Sowada, O.S.C.
**Iraq:** Mossul (Chaldean-rite archdiocese), George Garmo.

**Korea:** Inchon (diocese), William J. McNaughton, M.M.
**Pakistan:** Multan (diocese), Ernest B. Boland, O.P.
**Philippine Islands:** Cotabato (archdiocese), Philip F. Smith, O.M.I.
Jolo (vicariate apostolic), Georges Dion, O.M.I.
**Taiwan:** Taichung (diocese), William F. Kupfer, M.M.

### Central America, West Indies

**Dominican Republic:** San Juan de la Maguana (diocese), Ronald G. Connors, C.SS.R.,
**Honduras:** Comayagua (diocese), Gerald Scarpone, O.F.M.
**Nicaragua:** Bluefields (vicariate apostolic), Salvator Schlaefer, O.F.M.Cap. Paul Schmitz, O.F.M. Cap., auxiliary.

**Virgin Islands:** St. Thomas (diocese), Edward Harper, C.SS.R. Sean O'Malley, O.F.M. Cap., coadjutor.

**North America**

**Mexico:** Mexico City (archdiocese), Ricardo Watty Urquidi, M.Sp.S., auxiliary.

**Oceania**

**Caroline and Marshall Islands** (diocese), Martin J. Neylon, S.J.

**Papua New Guinea:** Goroko (diocese), Raymond R. Caesar, S.V.D.

Madang (archdiocese), Leo Arkfeld, S.V.D.

Mendi (diocese), Firmin Schmidt, O.F.M.Cap.

Mount Hagen (archdiocese), George Bernarding, S.V.D.

Wewak (diocese), Raymond P. Kalisz, S.V.D.

**Vanuatu (New Hebrides):** Port Vila (diocese), Francis Lambert, S.M.

**South America**

**Bolivia:** Coroico (diocese), Thomas R. Manning, O.F.M.

La Paz (archdiocese), Luis Morgan Casey, auxiliary.

Pando (vicariate), Andrew B. Schierhoff.

Santa Cruz (archdiocese), Charles A. Brown, M.M., auxiliary.

**Brazil:** Abaetetuba (diocese), Angelo Frosi, S.X.

Belem do Para (archdiocese), Jude Prost, O.F.M., auxiliary.

Borba (prelacy), Adrian J. M. Veigle, T.O.R.

Cristalandia (prelacy), James A. Schuck, O.F.M.

Jatai (diocese), Benedict D. Coscia, O.F.M, Michael P. Mundo, auxiliary.

Paranagua (diocese), Bernard Nolker, C.SS.R.

Rui Barbosa (diocese), Mathias Schmidt, O.S.B.

Santarem (diocese), James C. Ryan, O.F.M.

Sao Paulo (archdiocese), Alfred Novak, C.SS.R., auxiliary.

Sao Salvador da Bahia (archdiocese), Thomas W. Murphy, C.SS.R., auxiliary.

**Peru:** Chulucanas (prelacy), John McNabb, O.S.A.

## CATHOLIC POPULATION OF THE UNITED STATES

(Source: *The Official Catholic Directory, 1984;* figures as of Jan. 1, 1984. Archdioceses are indicated by an asterisk; for dioceses marked +, see Dioceses with Interstate Lines.)

| Section, State Diocese | Catholics | Dioc. Priests | Rel. Priests | Total Priests | Perm. Deacons | Bros. | Sisters | Parishes |
|---|---|---|---|---|---|---|---|---|
| NEW ENGLAND | 5,639,123 | 4,002 | 2,539 | 6,541 | 656 | 720 | 12,609 | 1,704 |
| Maine, Portland | 273,292 | 217 | 117 | 334 | — | 34 | 786 | 145 |
| New Hampshire, Manchester | 298,960 | 281 | 117 | 398 | 14 | 54 | 1,110 | 130 |
| Vermont, Burlington | 150,800 | 159 | 77 | 236 | 27 | 23 | 359 | 100 |
| Massachusetts | 2,955,931 | 1,955 | 1,737 | 3,692 | 228 | 349 | 6,760 | 784 |
| *Boston | 1,936,146 | 1,147 | 1,196 | 2,343 | 141 | 183 | 4,464 | 408 |
| Fall River | 340,000 | 210 | 208 | 418 | 23 | 30 | 719 | 112 |
| Springfield | 351,181 | 262 | 136 | 398 | 20 | 24 | 905 | 136 |
| Worcester | 328,604 | 336 | 197 | 533 | 44 | 112 | 672 | 128 |
| Rhode Island, Providence | 624,141 | 397 | 194 | 591 | 78 | 160 | 1,223 | 159 |
| Connecticut | 1,335,999 | 993 | 297 | 1,290 | 309 | 100 | 2,371 | 386 |
| *Hartford | 798,821 | 587 | 105 | 692 | 232 | 62 | 1,452 | 222 |
| Bridgeport | 335,917 | 254 | 110 | 364 | 36 | 8 | 576 | 88 |
| Norwich+ | 201,261 | 152 | 82 | 234 | 41 | 30 | 343 | 76 |
| MIDDLE ATLANTIC | 13,416,707 | 9,428 | 5,574 | 15,002 | 1,374 | 1,728 | 33,219 | 3,914 |
| New York | 6,684,926 | 4,335 | 3,123 | 7,458 | 655 | 1,072 | 14,853 | 1,714 |
| *New York | 1,839,000 | 1,004 | 1,540 | 2,544 | 224 | 431 | 5,227 | 411 |
| Albany | 408,648 | 391 | 222 | 613 | 58 | 94 | 1,240 | 201 |
| Brooklyn | 1,394,876 | 910 | 490 | 1,400 | 98 | 228 | 2,179 | 221 |
| Buffalo | 813,498 | 583 | 386 | 969 | 56 | 73 | 2,218 | 296 |
| Ogdensburg | 169,845 | 193 | 39 | 232 | 29 | 31 | 312 | 102 |
| Rochester | 377,207 | 368 | 194 | 562 | 40 | 60 | 1,003 | 163 |
| Rockville Centre | 1,286,140 | 497 | 139 | 636 | 108 | 131 | 1,959 | 129 |
| Syracuse | 395,712 | 389 | 113 | 502 | 42 | 24 | 715 | 171 |
| New Jersey | 3,049,769 | 1,909 | 899 | 2,808 | 566 | 298 | 5,288 | 705 |
| *Newark | 1,358,400 | 830 | 455 | 1,285 | 236 | 183 | 2,483 | 245 |
| Camden | 354,692 | 373 | 50 | 423 | 65 | 22 | 544 | 127 |
| Metuchen | 436,998 | 144 | 82 | 226 | 59 | 24 | 512 | 107 |
| Paterson | 365,098 | 290 | 213 | 503 | 83 | 39 | 1,108 | 106 |
| Trenton | 534,581 | 272 | 99 | 371 | 123 | 30 | 641 | 120 |
| Pennsylvania | 3,682,012 | 3,184 | 1,552 | 4,736 | 153 | 358 | 13,078 | 1,495 |
| *Philadelphia | 1,353,691 | 955 | 662 | 1,617 | 25 | 230 | 5,370 | 305 |
| Allentown | 262,714 | 315 | 112 | 427 | 32 | 18 | 896 | 153 |
| Altoona-Johnstown | 146,990 | 181 | 102 | 283 | 1 | 22 | 240 | 122 |
| Erie | 229,998 | 272 | 52 | 324 | 1 | 3 | 715 | 129 |
| Greensburg | 223,971 | 196 | 119 | 315 | — | 9 | 482 | 117 |

| Section, State Diocese | Catholics | Dioc. Priests | Rel. Priests | Total Priests | Perm. Deacons | Bros. | Sisters | Par- ishes |
|---|---|---|---|---|---|---|---|---|
| **Pennsylvania** | | | | | | | | |
| Harrisburg | 207,748 | 184 | 82 | 266 | 68 | 11 | 812 | 110 |
| Pittsburgh | 908,451 | 616 | 301 | 917 | 26 | 56 | 3,443 | 320 |
| Scranton | 348,449 | 465 | 122 | 587 | — | 9 | 1,120 | 239 |
| | | | | | | | | |
| **SOUTH ATLANTIC** | **3,325,837** | **2,285** | **2,136** | **4,421** | **578** | **560** | **6,483** | **1,324** |
| Delaware, Wilmington+ | 125,572 | 120 | 106 | 226 | 20 | 40 | 438 | 55 |
| Maryland, *Baltimore | 440,483 | 331 | 414 | 745 | 123 | 97 | 1,667 | 153 |
| **District of Columbia** | | | | | | | | |
| *Washington+ | 393,601 | 355 | 657 | 1,012 | 122 | 175 | 962 | 132 |
| Virginia | 316,772 | 252 | 140 | 392 | 55 | 28 | 625 | 168 |
| Arlington | 189,371 | 87 | 103 | 190 | 53 | 21 | 298 | 57 |
| Richmond | 127,401 | 165 | 37 | 202 | 2 | 7 | 327 | 111 |
| **West Virginia** | | | | | | | | |
| Wheeling-Charleston | 107,318 | 130 | 73 | 203 | 22 | 13 | 437 | 128 |
| **North Carolina** | 111,084 | 135 | 93 | 228 | 23 | 15 | 324 | 124 |
| Charlotte | 59,537 | 68 | 66 | 134 | 21 | 8 | 215 | 63 |
| Raleigh | 51,547 | 67 | 27 | 94 | 2 | 7 | 109 | 61 |
| **South Carolina, Charleston** | 70,555 | 82 | 55 | 137 | 25 | 29 | 245 | 80 |
| **Georgia** | 176,250 | 158 | 144 | 302 | 35 | 44 | 377 | 103 |
| *Atlanta | 118,908 | 92 | 106 | 198 | 17 | 34 | 161 | 58 |
| Savannah | 57,342 | 66 | 38 | 104 | 18 | 10 | 216 | 45 |
| **Florida** | **1,584,202** | **722** | **454** | **1,176** | **153** | **119** | **1,408** | **381** |
| *Miami | 925,700 | 348 | 222 | 570 | 57 | 65 | 629 | 137 |
| Orlando | 200,000 | 109 | 36 | 145 | 29 | 1 | 174 | 69 |
| Palm Beach | No separate statistics available | | | | | | | |
| Pensacola-Tallahassee | 45,804 | 64 | 14 | 78 | 48 | — | 65 | 39 |
| St. Augustine | 74,486 | 73 | 26 | 99 | 5 | 6 | 104 | 45 |
| St. Petersburg | 338,212 | 128 | 156 | 284 | 14 | 47 | 436 | 91 |
| Venice | No separate statistics available | | | | | | | |
| | | | | | | | | |
| **EAST NORTH CENTRAL** | **10,436,512** | **7,686** | **4,757** | **12,443** | **1,501** | **1,788** | **27,931** | **4,169** |
| **Ohio** | **2,259,097** | **2,001** | **942** | **2,943** | **341** | **456** | **6,927** | **948** |
| *Cincinnati | 488,770 | 453 | 409 | 862 | 76 | 226 | 1,848 | 256 |
| Cleveland | 883,830 | 643 | 280 | 923 | 61 | 137 | 2,356 | 245 |
| Columbus | 190,815 | 227 | 67 | 294 | 39 | 12 | 655 | 108 |
| Steubenville | 63,000 | 149 | 14 | 163 | 1 | 7 | 121 | 73 |
| Toledo | 345,045 | 277 | 116 | 393 | 139 | 26 | 1,512 | 152 |
| Youngstown | 287,637 | 252 | 56 | 308 | 25 | 48 | 435 | 114 |
| **Indiana** | **724,049** | **717** | **547** | **1,264** | **89** | **300** | **2,727** | **445** |
| *Indianapolis | 200,922 | 217 | 191 | 408 | — | 89 | 929 | 142 |
| Evansville | 89,906 | 128 | 21 | 149 | 19 | 3 | 421 | 67 |
| Ft. Wayne-South Bend | 146,466 | 118 | 208 | 326 | 38 | 171 | 983 | 89 |
| Gary | 195,032 | 139 | 75 | 214 | 26 | 27 | 266 | 83 |
| Lafayette | 91,723 | 115 | 52 | 167 | 6 | 10 | 128 | 64 |
| **Illinois** | **3,569,350** | **2,193** | **1,960** | **4,153** | **657** | **651** | **8,660** | **1,181** |
| *Chicago | 2,368,316 | 1,214 | 1,441 | 2,655 | 446 | 407 | 5,162 | 444 |
| Belleville | 121,754 | 165 | 52 | 217 | 25 | 10 | 430 | 130 |
| Joliet | 420,000 | 213 | 164 | 377 | 62 | 171 | 1,090 | 112 |
| Peoria | 231,376 | 249 | 113 | 362 | 54 | 16 | 473 | 169 |
| Rockford | 235,609 | 166 | 84 | 250 | 70 | 16 | 567 | 102 |
| Springfield | 192,295 | 186 | 106 | 292 | — | 31 | 938 | 144 |
| **Michigan** | **2,297,212** | **1,306** | **596** | **1,902** | **219** | **129** | **4,266** | **803** |
| *Detroit | 1,456,965 | 606 | 412 | 1,018 | 136 | 104 | 2,527 | 331 |
| Gaylord | 89,685 | 62 | 20 | 82 | 3 | 2 | 147 | 59 |
| Grand Rapids | 158,947 | 154 | 42 | 196 | 15 | 2 | 585 | 91 |
| Kalamazoo | 96,461 | 60 | 23 | 83 | 19 | 5 | 298 | 47 |
| Lansing | 246,936 | 152 | 54 | 206 | 20 | 14 | 381 | 87 |
| Marquette | 87,147 | 123 | 22 | 145 | 1 | — | 136 | 86 |
| Saginaw | 161,071 | 149 | 23 | 172 | 25 | 2 | 192 | 102 |
| **Wisconsin** | **1,586,804** | **1,469** | **712** | **2,181** | **195** | **252** | **5,351** | **872** |
| *Milwaukee | 684,311 | 617 | 469 | 1,086 | 123 | 147 | 3,321 | 268 |
| Green Bay | 350,233 | 286 | 148 | 434 | 60 | 74 | 644 | 211 |
| La Crosse | 235,031 | 258 | 35 | 293 | 11 | 13 | 509 | 168 |

| Section, State Diocese | Catholics | Dioc. Priests | Rel. Priests | Total Priests | Perm. Deacons | Bros. | Sisters | Par- ishes |
|---|---|---|---|---|---|---|---|---|
| **Wisconsin** | | | | | | | | |
| Madison | 225,946 | 207 | 38 | 245 | — | 16 | 674 | 138 |
| Superior | 91,283 | 101 | 22 | 123 | 1 | 2 | 203 | 87 |
| | | | | | | | | |
| **EAST SOUTH CENTRAL** | **715,414** | **963** | **429** | **1,392** | **201** | **311** | **3,643** | **675** |
| **Kentucky** | **381,113** | **510** | **143** | **653** | **82** | **148** | **2,516** | **299** |
| *Louisville | 213,585 | 241 | 92 | 333 | 82 | 129 | 1,384 | 132 |
| Covington | 113,745 | 191 | 27 | 218 | — | 15 | 813 | 85 |
| Owensboro | 53,783 | 78 | 24 | 102 | — | 4 | 319 | 82 |
| **Tennessee** | **121,475** | **155** | **54** | **209** | **70** | **67** | **315** | **119** |
| Memphis | 44,000 | 66 | 23 | 89 | 33 | 55 | 145 | 38 |
| Nashville | 77,475 | 89 | 31 | 120 | 37 | 12 | 170 | 81 |
| **Alabama** | **114,536** | **153** | **154** | **307** | **31** | **26** | **447** | **138** |
| *Mobile | 61,950 | 87 | 79 | 166 | 14 | 15 | 269 | 77 |
| Birmingham | 52,586 | 66 | 75 | 141 | 17 | 11 | 178 | 61 |
| **Mississippi** | **98,290** | **145** | **78** | **223** | **18** | **70** | **365** | **119** |
| Biloxi | 53,950 | 66 | 33 | 99 | 6 | 50 | 86 | 44 |
| Jackson | 44,340 | 79 | 45 | 124 | 12 | 20 | 279 | 75 |
| | | | | | | | | |
| **WEST NORTH CENTRAL** | **3,383,471** | **3,991** | **1,911** | **5,902** | **525** | **712** | **14,602** | **2,779** |
| **Minnesota** | **1,064,837** | **987** | **438** | **1,425** | **113** | **201** | **4,019** | **694** |
| *St. Paul and Minneapolis | 574,626 | 404 | 196 | 600 | 83 | 84 | 1,860 | 219 |
| Crookston | 46,137 | 51 | 22 | 73 | 1 | 2 | 301 | 43 |
| Duluth | 93,153 | 96 | 33 | 129 | 10 | — | 309 | 79 |
| New Ulm | 71,977 | 111 | 4 | 115 | 2 | — | 154 | 93 |
| St. Cloud | 154,133 | 159 | 168 | 327 | 17 | 82 | 745 | 136 |
| Winona | 124,811 | 166 | 15 | 181 | — | 33 | 650 | 124 |
| **Iowa** | **554,091** | **852** | **129** | **981** | **102** | **51** | **2,209** | **538** |
| *Dubuque | 242,119 | 341 | 81 | 422 | 35 | 33 | 1,360 | 198 |
| Davenport | 110,900 | 189 | 23 | 212 | 18 | 18 | 393 | 116 |
| Des Moines | 89,608 | 117 | 12 | 129 | 27 | — | 193 | 84 |
| Sioux City | 111,464 | 205 | 13 | 218 | 22 | — | 263 | 140 |
| **Missouri** | **768,447** | **940** | **760** | **1,700** | **169** | **338** | **4,136** | **506** |
| *St. Louis | 542,635 | 565 | 513 | 1,078 | 62 | 202 | 3,248 | 248 |
| Jefferson City | 33,032 | 135 | 19 | 154 | 45 | 8 | 160 | 94 |
| Kansas City-St. Joseph | 144,971 | 159 | 158 | 317 | 61 | 54 | 525 | 101 |
| Springfield- Cape Girardeau | 47,809 | 81 | 70 | 151 | 1 | 74 | 203 | 63 |
| **North Dakota** | **179,882** | **216** | **91** | **307** | **38** | **23** | **518** | **180** |
| Bismarck | 78,814 | 79 | 58 | 137 | 10 | 20 | 205 | 69 |
| Fargo | 101,068 | 137 | 33 | 170 | 28 | 3 | 313 | 111 |
| **South Dakota** | **134,019** | **176** | **114** | **290** | **16** | **21** | **612** | **204** |
| Rapid City | 34,143 | 40 | 49 | 89 | 13 | — | 61 | 82 |
| Sioux Falls | 99,876 | 136 | 65 | 201 | 3 | 21 | 551 | 122 |
| **Nebraska** | **334,352** | **419** | **202** | **621** | **79** | **52** | **982** | **276** |
| *Omaha | 209,517 | 214 | 180 | 394 | 79 | 37 | 720 | 139 |
| Grand Island | 54,539 | 86 | 2 | 88 | — | — | 134 | 50 |
| Lincoln | 70,296 | 119 | 20 | 139 | — | 15 | 128 | 87 |
| **Kansas** | **347,843** | **401** | **177** | **578** | **8** | **26** | **2,126** | **381** |
| *Kansas City | 147,059 | 121 | 104 | 225 | — | 24 | 1,059 | 122 |
| Dodge City | 39,747 | 59 | 10 | 69 | 7 | — | 171 | 46 |
| Salina | 61,022 | 80 | 36 | 116 | — | 2 | 387 | 99 |
| Wichita | 100,015 | 141 | 27 | 168 | 1 | — | 509 | 114 |
| | | | | | | | | |
| **WEST SOUTH CENTRAL** | **4,327,466** | **2,109** | **1,662** | **3,771** | **912** | **611** | **6,563** | **1,633** |
| **Arkansas, Little Rock** | **52,137** | **106** | **64** | **170** | **25** | **60** | **333** | **88** |
| **Louisiana** | **1,334,953** | **723** | **537** | **1,260** | **223** | **284** | **1,954** | **486** |
| *New Orleans | 523,651 | 251 | 307 | 558 | 97 | 203 | 1,201 | 140 |
| Alexandria-Shreveport | 83,283 | 112 | 40 | 152 | 4 | 10 | 204 | 83 |
| Baton Rouge | 188,097 | 96 | 69 | 165 | 22 | 18 | 148 | 70 |
| Houma-Thibodaux | 123,153 | 54 | 10 | 64 | 26 | 10 | 65 | 37 |
| Lafayette | 321,201 | 169 | 76 | 245 | 47 | 37 | 284 | 120 |
| Lake Charles | 95,568 | 41 | 35 | 76 | 27 | 6 | 52 | 36 |

| Section, State Diocese | Catholics | Dioc. Priests | Rel. Priests | Total Priests | Perm. Deacons | Bros. | Sisters | Parishes |
|---|---|---|---|---|---|---|---|---|
| Oklahoma | 139,906 | 174 | 75 | 249 | 48 | 27 | 435 | 158 |
| *Oklahoma City | 84,106 | 112 | 30 | 142 | 27 | 19 | 204 | 72 |
| Tulsa | 55,800 | 62 | 45 | 107 | 21 | 8 | 231 | 86 |
| Texas | 2,800,470 | 1,106 | 986 | 2,092 | 616 | 240 | 3,841 | 901 |
| *San Antonio | 491,918 | 148 | 214 | 362 | 112 | 121 | 1,275 | 133 |
| Amarillo | 36,739 | 44 | 18 | 62 | 26 | 1 | 159 | 35 |
| Austin | 135,120 | 95 | 52 | 147 | 8 | 37 | 152 | 84 |
| Beaumont | 83,397 | 56 | 31 | 87 | 23 | — | 116 | 44 |
| Brownsville | 416,348 | 49 | 79 | 128 | 24 | 13 | 168 | 60 |
| Corpus Christi | 314,812 | 89 | 92 | 181 | 36 | 18 | 358 | 77 |
| Dallas | 200,916 | 113 | 95 | 208 | 113 | 3 | 291 | 67 |
| El Paso | 184,632 | 93 | 46 | 139 | 32 | 9 | 270 | 51 |
| Fort Worth | 113,357 | 70 | 58 | 128 | 25 | 14 | 153 | 81 |
| Galveston-Houston | 608,488 | 213 | 240 | 453 | 130 | 20 | 650 | 141 |
| Lubbock | 51,817 | 26 | 14 | 40 | 30 | — | 37 | 34 |
| San Angelo | 71,440 | 56 | 35 | 91 | 54 | 3 | 48 | 48 |
| Victoria | 91,486 | 54 | 12 | 66 | 3 | 1 | 164 | 46 |
| MOUNTAIN | 1,910,433 | 1,227 | 827 | 2,054 | 375 | 268 | 2,911 | 851 |
| Montana | 131,117 | 215 | 57 | 272 | 12 | 10 | 268 | 135 |
| Great Falls-Billings | 66,092 | 93 | 32 | 125 | 3 | 5 | 184 | 75 |
| Helena | 65,025 | 122 | 25 | 147 | 9 | 5 | 84 | 60 |
| Idaho, Boise | 74,356 | 93 | 27 | 120 | 20 | 4 | 96 | 71 |
| Wyoming, Cheyenne+ | 62,000 | 62 | 7 | 69 | 2 | 4 | 76 | 39 |
| Colorado | 422,969 | 278 | 264 | 542 | 79 | 62 | 1,016 | 195 |
| *Denver | 268,686 | 155 | 197 | 352 | 64 | 44 | 591 | 111 |
| Colorado Springs | 65,000 | 26 | 17 | 43 | 12 | — | 231 | 25 |
| Pueblo | 89,283 | 97 | 50 | 147 | 3 | 18 | 194 | 59 |
| New Mexico | 488,261 | 246 | 183 | 429 | 91 | 118 | 609 | 188 |
| *Santa Fe | 323,906 | 150 | 100 | 250 | 60 | 95 | 327 | 87 |
| Gallup+ | 45,411 | 54 | 48 | 102 | 10 | 18 | 196 | 58 |
| Las Cruces | 118,944 | 42 | 35 | 77 | 21 | 5 | 86 | 43 |
| Arizona | 522,001 | 226 | 189 | 415 | 140 | 40 | 608 | 136 |
| Phoenix | 281,515 | 127 | 119 | 246 | 68 | 31 | 259 | 78 |
| Tucson | 240,486 | 99 | 70 | 169 | 72 | 9 | 349 | 58 |
| Utah, Salt Lake City | 65,729 | 58 | 55 | 113 | 30 | 22 | 126 | 43 |
| Nevada, Reno-Las Vegas | 144,000 | 49 | 45 | 94 | 1 | 8 | 112 | 44 |
| PACIFIC | 6,482,429 | 2,895 | 2,767 | 5,662 | 541 | 887 | 9,609 | 1,546 |
| Washington | 428,443 | 377 | 358 | 735 | 118 | 38 | 1,307 | 228 |
| *Seattle | 291,640 | 225 | 241 | 466 | 88 | 34 | 795 | 130 |
| Spokane | 80,003 | 95 | 104 | 199 | 28 | 4 | 447 | 58 |
| Yakima | 56,800 | 57 | 13 | 70 | 2 | — | 65 | 40 |
| Oregon | 323,281 | 223 | 248 | 471 | 6 | 76 | 905 | 155 |
| *Portland | 295,351 | 180 | 238 | 418 | 5 | 75 | 820 | 126 |
| Baker | 27,930 | 43 | 10 | 53 | 1 | 1 | 85 | 29 |
| California | 5,469,475 | 2,205 | 1,997 | 4,202 | 364 | 704 | 6,956 | 1,039 |
| *Los Angeles | 2,374,021 | 613 | 682 | 1,295 | 124 | 143 | 2,642 | 283 |
| *San Francisco | 368,937 | 229 | 279 | 508 | 14 | 62 | 1,182 | 102 |
| Fresno | 321,000 | 122 | 53 | 175 | 2 | 10 | 190 | 86 |
| Monterey | 130,000 | 79 | 41 | 120 | — | 29 | 228 | 44 |
| Oakland | 412,620 | 168 | 290 | 458 | 46 | 217 | 582 | 87 |
| Orange | 413,393 | 138 | 83 | 221 | 29 | 17 | 453 | 51 |
| Sacramento | 265,948 | 185 | 73 | 258 | 32 | 57 | 305 | 93 |
| San Bernardino | 303,201 | 187 | 87 | 274 | 31 | 16 | 227 | 85 |
| San Diego | 336,952 | 250 | 92 | 342 | 53 | 22 | 487 | 90 |
| San Jose | 313,790 | 108 | 258 | 366 | 20 | 80 | 479 | 47 |
| Santa Rosa | 95,852 | 77 | 23 | 100 | 4 | 45 | 113 | 40 |
| Stockton | 133,761 | 49 | 36 | 85 | 9 | 6 | 68 | 31 |
| Alaska | 46,230 | 40 | 53 | 93 | 45 | 13 | 95 | 60 |
| *Anchorage | 25,495 | 20 | 16 | 36 | 11 | 7 | 40 | 18 |
| Fairbanks | 14,775 | 7 | 34 | 41 | 27 | 6 | 42 | 33 |
| Juneau | 5,960 | 13 | 3 | 16 | 7 | — | 13 | 9 |
| Hawaii, Honolulu | 215,000 | 50 | 111 | 161 | 8 | 56 | 346 | 64 |

| Section, State Diocese | Catholics | Dioc. Priests | Rel. Priests | Total Priests | Perm. Deacons | Bros. | Sisters | Par- ishes |
|---|---|---|---|---|---|---|---|---|
| EASTERN RITES ................. | 630,542 | 577 | 126 | 703 | 39 | 11 | 457 | 523 |
| *Philadelphia .................. | 167,800 | 111 | 16 | 127 | — | — | 201 | 117 |
| St. Nicholas ................... | 18,241 | 40 | 13 | 53 | 4 | — | 14 | 32 |
| Stamford ..................... | 45,000 | 63 | 20 | 83 | 4 | 1 | 49 | 48 |
| St. Josaphat (Parma) | No separate statistics available | | | | | | | |
| *Pittsburgh ................... | 152,100 | 85 | 10 | 95 | — | 5 | 133 | 83 |
| Parma ....................... | 27,151 | 46 | 10 | 56 | 1 | — | 25 | 41 |
| Passaic ...................... | 96,439 | 97 | 25 | 122 | 5 | 1 | 21 | 91 |
| Van Nuys ................... | 7,539 | 15 | 2 | 17 | 6 | — | 1 | 14 |
| St. Maron ..................... | 50,285 | 69 | 3 | 72 | 5 | — | — | 52 |
| Newton ...................... | 22,987 | 39 | 27 | 66 | 14 | 4 | 3 | 37 |
| Chaldeans (Ap. Ex.) ........... | 43,000 | 12 | — | 12 | — | — | 10 | 8 |
| Armenians (Ap. Ex.) | No separate statistics available | | | | | | | |
| Romanians (Ap. Ex.) | No separate statistics available | | | | | | | |
| MILITARY ORDINARIATE ........ | 2,125,000 | — | — | — | — | — | — | — |
| TOTALS 1984 ................... | 52,392,934 | 35,163 | 22,728 | 57,891 | 6,702 | 7,596 | 118,027 | 19,118 |
| Totals 1983 .................... | 52,088,744 | 35,356 | 22,514 | 57,870 | 6,066 | 7,658 | 120,699 | 19,039 |
| Totals 1974 .................... | 48,465,438 | 36,058 | 20,654 | 56,712 | — | 9,233 | 139,963 | 18,433 |

## Dioceses with Interstate Lines

Diocesan lines usually fall within a single state and in some cases include a whole state.

The following dioceses, with their statistics as reported in tables throughout the Almanac, are exceptions.

**Norwich,** Conn., includes Fisher's Island, N.Y.

**Wilmington,** Del., includes all of Delaware and nine counties of Maryland.

**Baltimore,** includes all of Maryland except nine counties under the jurisdiction of Wilmington and five under Washington.

**Washington,** D.C., includes five counties of Maryland.

**Gallup,** N.M., has jurisdiction over several counties of Arizona.

**Cheyenne,** Wyo., includes all of Yellowstone National Park.

## PERCENTAGE OF CATHOLICS IN U.S. POPULATION

(Source: *The Official Catholic Directory, 1984*; figures are as of Jan. 1, 1984. Total general population figures at the end of the table are U.S. Census Bureau estimates for Jan. 1 of the respective years. Archdioceses are indicated by an asterisk; for dioceses marked +, see Dioceses with Interstate Lines.)

| Section, State Diocese | Catholic Pop. | Total Pop. | Cath. Pct. |
|---|---|---|---|
| NEW ENGLAND | 5,639,123 | 12,186,788 | 46.27 |
| Maine, Portland | 273,292 | 1,025,030 | 26.67 |
| New Hampshire | | | |
| Manchester | 298,960 | 920,610 | 32.47 |
| Vermont, Burlington | 150,800 | 517,000 | 29.17 |
| Massachusetts | 2,955,931 | 5,622,352 | 52.57 |
| *Boston | 1,936,146 | 3,657,659 | 52.93 |
| Fall River | 340,000 | 530,000 | 64.15 |
| Springfield | 351,181 | 790,725 | 44.41 |
| Worcester | 328,604 | 643,968 | 51.03 |
| Rhode Island, Providence | 624,141 | 947,154 | 65.90 |
| Connecticut | 1,335,999 | 3,154,642 | 42.35 |
| *Hartford | 798,821 | 1,762,941 | 45.31 |
| Bridgeport | 335,917 | 815,740 | 41.18 |
| Norwich+ | 201,261 | 575,961 | 34.94 |
| | | | |
| MIDDLE ATLANTIC | 13,416,707 | 36,975,426 | 36.29 |
| | | | |
| New York | 6,684,926 | 17,737,195 | 37.69 |
| *New York | 1,839,000 | 4,880,000 | 37.68 |
| Albany | 408,648 | 1,472,684 | 27.75 |
| Brooklyn | 1,394,876 | 4,122,261 | 33.84 |
| Buffalo | 813,498 | 1,639,420 | 49.62 |
| Ogdensburg | 169,845 | 395,563 | 42.94 |
| Rochester | 377,207 | 1,419,276 | 26.58 |
| Rockville Centre | 1,286,140 | 2,600,428 | 49.46 |
| Syracuse | 395,712 | 1,207,563 | 32.77 |

| Section, State Diocese | Catholic Pop. | Total Pop. | Cath. Pct. |
|---|---|---|---|
| New Jersey | 3,049,769 | 7,412,509 | 41.14 |
| *Newark | 1,358,400 | 2,750,900 | 49.38 |
| Camden | 354,692 | 1,165,800 | 30.42 |
| Metuchen | 436,998 | 1,004,823 | 43.49 |
| Paterson | 365,098 | 971,370 | 37.59 |
| Trenton | 534,581 | 1,519,616 | 35.18 |
| Pennsylvania | 3,682,012 | 11,825,722 | 31.14 |
| *Philadelphia | 1,353,691 | 3,662,506 | 36.96 |
| Allentown | 262,714 | 1,027,302 | 25.57 |
| Altoona-Johnstown | 146,990 | 654,338 | 22.46 |
| Erie | 229,998 | 901,829 | 25.50 |
| Greensburg | 223,971 | 719,654 | 31.12 |
| Harrisburg | 207,748 | 1,723,961 | 12.05 |
| Pittsburgh | 908,451 | 2,165,361 | 41.95 |
| Scranton | 348,449 | 970,771 | 35.89 |
| | | | |
| SOUTH ATLANTIC | 3,325,837 | 38,284,322 | 8.69 |
| | | | |
| Delaware, Wilmington+ | 125,572 | 890,608 | 14.10 |
| Maryland, *Baltimore | 440,483 | 2,508,418 | 17.56 |
| District of Columbia | | | |
| *Washington+ | 393,601 | 2,098,200 | 18.76 |
| Virginia | 316,772 | 5,428,470 | 5.84 |
| Arlington | 189,371 | 1,472,000 | 12.86 |
| Richmond | 127,401 | 3,956,470 | 3.22 |
| West Virginia | | | |
| Wheeling-Charleston | 107,318 | 1,949,644 | 5.50 |

| Section, State Diocese | Catholic Pop. | Total Pop. | Cath. Pct. |
|---|---|---|---|
| North Carolina | 111,084 | 5,871,202 | 1.89 |
| Charlotte | 59,537 | 3,101,207 | 1.92 |
| Raleigh | 51,547 | 2,769,995 | 1.86 |
| South Carolina | | | |
| Charleston | 70,555 | 3,375,000 | 2.09 |
| Georgia | 176,250 | 5,741,723 | 3.07 |
| *Atlanta | 118,908 | 3,817,173 | 3.12 |
| Savannah | 57,342 | 1,924,550 | 2.98 |
| Florida | 1,584,202 | 10,421,057 | 15.20 |
| *Miami | 925,700 | 3,779,793 | 24.50 |
| Orlando | 200,000 | 2,220,000 | 9.01 |
| Palm Beach | No separate statistics available. | | |
| Pensacola-Tallahassee | 45,804 | 862,237 | 5.31 |
| St. Augustine | 74,486 | 1,090,000 | 6.83 |
| St. Petersburg | 338,212 | 2,469,027 | 13.70 |
| Venice | No separate statistics available. | | |
| **EAST NORTH CENTRAL** | **10,436,512** | **41,631,231** | **25.07** |
| Ohio | 2,259,097 | 10,844,164 | 20.83 |
| *Cincinnati | 488,770 | 2,770,516 | 17.64 |
| Cleveland | 883,830 | 2,841,792 | 31.10 |
| Columbus | 190,815 | 1,940,333 | 9.83 |
| Steubenville | 63,000 | 541,093 | 11.64 |
| Toledo | 345,045 | 1,486,614 | 23.21 |
| Youngstown | 287,637 | 1,263,816 | 22.76 |
| Indiana | 724,049 | 5,439,438 | 13.31 |
| *Indianapolis | 200,922 | 2,127,915 | 9.44 |
| Evansville | 89,906 | 466,821 | 19.26 |
| Ft. Wayne-S. Bend | 146,466 | 1,044,602 | 14.02 |
| Gary | 195,032 | 735,000 | 26.53 |
| Lafayette | 91,723 | 1,065,100 | 8.61 |
| Illinois | 3,569,350 | 11,476,660 | 31.10 |
| *Chicago | 2,368,316 | 5,693,562 | 41.60 |
| Belleville | 121,754 | 859,359 | 14.17 |
| Joliet | 420,000 | 1,250,000 | 32.60 |
| Peoria | 231,376 | 1,501,917 | 15.41 |
| Rockford | 235,609 | 1,027,342 | 22.93 |
| Springfield | 192,295 | 1,144,480 | 16.80 |
| Michigan | 2,297,212 | 9,141,638 | 25.13 |
| *Detroit | 1,456,965 | 4,362,312 | 33.40 |
| Gaylord | 89,685 | 391,840 | 22.89 |
| Grand Rapids | 158,947 | 906,483 | 17.53 |
| Kalamazoo | 96,461 | 863,911 | 11.17 |
| Lansing | 246,936 | 1,583,644 | 15.59 |
| Marquette | 87,147 | 320,028 | 27.23 |
| Saginaw | 161,071 | 713,420 | 22.58 |
| Wisconsin | 1,586,804 | 4,729,331 | 33.55 |
| *Milwaukee | 684,311 | 2,029,553 | 33.72 |
| Green Bay | 350,233 | 736,053 | 47.58 |
| La Crosse | 235,031 | 751,203 | 31.29 |
| Madison | 225,946 | 903,784 | 25.00 |
| Superior | 91,283 | 308,738 | 29.57 |
| **EAST SOUTH CENTRAL** | **715,414** | **14,402,308** | **4.97** |
| Kentucky | 381,113 | 3,657,669 | 10.42 |
| *Louisville | 213,585 | 1,301,024 | 16.42 |
| Covington | 113,745 | 1,591,000 | 7.15 |
| Owensboro | 53,783 | 765,645 | 7.02 |
| Tennessee | 121,475 | 4,278,469 | 2.84 |
| Memphis | 44,000 | 1,000,000 | 4.40 |
| Nashville | 77,475 | 3,278,469 | 2.36 |

| Section, State Diocese | Catholic Pop. | Total Pop. | Cath. Pct. |
|---|---|---|---|
| Alabama | 114,536 | 3,922,670 | 2.92 |
| *Mobile | 61,950 | 1,422,835 | 4.35 |
| Birmingham | 52,586 | 2,499,835 | 2.10 |
| Mississippi | 98,290 | 2,543,500 | 3.86 |
| Biloxi | 53,950 | 633,500 | 8.52 |
| Jackson | 44,340 | 1,910,000 | 2.32 |
| **WEST NORTH CENTRAL** | **3,383,471** | **17,157,364** | **19.72** |
| Minnesota | 1,064,837 | 4,072,371 | 26.15 |
| *St. Paul and Minneapolis | 574,626 | 2,173,572 | 26.44 |
| Crookston | 46,137 | 239,045 | 19.30 |
| Duluth | 93,153 | 425,987 | 21.87 |
| New Ulm | 71,977 | 291,014 | 24.73 |
| St. Cloud | 154,133 | 409,791 | 37.61 |
| Winona | 124,811 | 532,962 | 23.42 |
| Iowa | 554,091 | 2,909,826 | 19.04 |
| *Dubuque | 242,119 | 995,648 | 24.32 |
| Davenport | 110,900 | 733,591 | 15.12 |
| Des Moines | 89,608 | 667,726 | 13.42 |
| Sioux City | 111,464 | 512,861 | 21.73 |
| Missouri | 768,447 | 4,907,409 | 15.66 |
| *St. Louis | 542,635 | 1,919,042 | 28.28 |
| Jefferson City | 33,032 | 730,592 | 4.52 |
| Kansas City-St. Joseph | 144,971 | 1,260,051 | 11.51 |
| Springfield-Cape Girardeau | 47,809 | 997,724 | 4.79 |
| North Dakota | 179,882 | 652,633 | 27.56 |
| Bismarck | 78,814 | 269,310 | 29.27 |
| Fargo | 101,068 | 383,323 | 26.37 |
| South Dakota | 134,019 | 663,208 | 20.21 |
| Rapid City | 34,143 | 178,208 | 19.16 |
| Sioux Falls | 99,876 | 485,000 | 20.59 |
| Nebraska | 334,352 | 1,568,225 | 21.32 |
| *Omaha | 209,517 | 750,582 | 27.91 |
| Grand Island | 54,539 | 306,000 | 17.82 |
| Lincoln | 70,296 | 511,643 | 13.74 |
| Kansas | 347,843 | 2,383,692 | 14.59 |
| *Kansas City | 147,059 | 952,000 | 15.45 |
| Dodge City | 39,747 | 222,784 | 17.84 |
| Salina | 61,022 | 348,387 | 17.52 |
| Wichita | 100,015 | 860,521 | 11.62 |
| **WEST SOUTH CENTRAL** | **4,327,466** | **23,994,890** | **18.03** |
| Arkansas, Little Rock | 52,137 | 2,284,037 | 2.28 |
| Louisiana | 1,334,953 | 4,116,438 | 32.43 |
| *New Orleans | 523,651 | 1,326,512 | 39.48 |
| Alexandria-Shreveport | 83,283 | 1,083,132 | 7.69 |
| Baton Rouge | 188,097 | 717,855 | 26.20 |
| Houma-Thibodaux | 123,153 | 202,000 | 60.97 |
| Lafayette | 321,201 | 560,094 | 57.35 |
| Lake Charles | 95,568 | 226,845 | 42.13 |
| Oklahoma | 139,906 | 3,014,500 | 4.64 |
| *Oklahoma City | 84,106 | 1,757,900 | 4.78 |
| Tulsa | 55,800 | 1,256,600 | 4.44 |
| Texas | 2,800,470 | 14,579,915 | 19.21 |
| *San Antonio | 491,918 | 1,438,000 | 34.21 |
| Amarillo | 36,739 | 354,400 | 10.37 |
| Austin | 135,120 | 1,289,794 | 10.48 |
| Beaumont | 83,397 | 676,746 | 12.32 |

| Section, State Diocese | Catholic Pop. | Total Pop. | Cath. Pct. | Section, State Diocese | Catholic Pop. | Total Pop. | Cath. Pct. |
|---|---|---|---|---|---|---|---|
| Texas | | | | Washington | | | |
| Brownsville | 416,348 | 537,607 | 77.44 | Spokane | 80,003 | 574,023 | 13.94 |
| Corpus Christi | 314,812 | 596,393 | 52.79 | Yakima | 56,800 | 392,500 | 14.47 |
| Dallas | 200,916 | 2,923,460 | 6.87 | Oregon | 323,281 | 2,633,047 | 12.28 |
| El Paso | 184,632 | 540,162 | 34.18 | *Portland | 295,351 | 2,278,947 | 12.96 |
| Fort Worth | 113,357 | 1,541,937 | 7.35 | Baker | 27,930 | 354,100 | 7.89 |
| Galveston-Houston | 608,488 | 3,402,028 | 17.89 | California | 5,469,475 | 24,769,972 | 22.08 |
| Lubbock | 51,817 | 451,330 | 11.48 | *Los Angeles | 2,374,021 | 8,642,900 | 27.47 |
| San Angelo | 71,440 | 604,958 | 11.81 | *San Francisco | 368,937 | 1,523,032 | 24.22 |
| Victoria | 91,486 | 223,100 | 41.01 | Fresno | 321,000 | 1,463,878 | 21.93 |
| **MOUNTAIN** | **1,910,433** | **11,796,135** | **16.20** | Monterey | 130,000 | 650,000 | 20.00 |
| | | | | Oakland | 412,620 | 1,826,717 | 22.59 |
| Montana | 131,117 | 755,465 | 17.36 | Orange | 413,393 | 2,036,390 | 20.30 |
| Great Falls-Billings | 66,092 | 351,858 | 18.78 | Sacramento | 265,948 | 2,095,695 | 12.69 |
| Helena | 65,025 | 403,607 | 16.11 | San Bernardino | 303,201 | 1,774,700 | 17.08 |
| Idaho, Boise | 74,356 | 989,000 | 7.52 | San Diego | 336,952 | 2,015,689 | 16.72 |
| Wyoming, Cheyenne | 62,000 | 460,000 | 13.48 | San Jose | 313,790 | 1,371,300 | 22.88 |
| Colorado | 422,969 | 2,820,905 | 14.99 | Santa Rosa | 95,852 | 628,371 | 15.30 |
| *Denver | 268,686 | 2,036,806 | 13.19 | Stockton | 133,761 | 741,300 | 18.04 |
| Colorado Springs | 65,000 | 325,000 | 20.00 | Alaska | 46,230 | 459,201 | 10.07 |
| Pueblo | 89,283 | 459,099 | 19.45 | *Anchorage | 25,495 | 275,000 | 9.27 |
| New Mexico | 488,261 | 1,520,340 | 32.12 | Fairbanks | 14,775 | 125,000 | 11.82 |
| *Santa Fe | 323,906 | 800,000 | 40.49 | Juneau | 5,960 | 59,201 | 10.07 |
| Gallup+ | 45,411 | 355,340 | 12.78 | Hawaii, Honolulu | 215,000 | 1,000,000 | 21.50 |
| Las Cruces | 118,944 | 365,000 | 32.59 | | | | |
| Arizona | 522,001 | 2,799,700 | 18.64 | **EASTERN RITES** | **630,542** | **—** | **—** |
| Phoenix | 281,515 | 1,870,200 | 15.05 | | | | |
| Tucson | 240,486 | 929,500 | 25.87 | **MILITARY** | | | |
| Utah, Salt Lake City | 65,729 | 1,560,000 | 4.21 | **ORDINARIATE** | **2,125,000** | **—** | **—** |
| Nevada, Reno-Las Vegas | 144,000 | 890,725 | 16.17 | | | | |
| **PACIFIC** | **6,482,429** | **32,919,881** | **19.69** | **TOTALS 1984** | **52,392,934** | **234,883,707** | **22.31** |
| Washington | 428,443 | 4,057,661 | 10.56 | **Totals 1983** | **52,088,744** | **233,267,000** | **22.33** |
| *Seattle | 291,640 | 3,091,138 | 9.43 | **Totals 1974** | **48,465,438** | **211,216,000** | **22.95** |

## INFANT BAPTISMS AND CONVERTS IN THE UNITED STATES

(Source: *The Official Catholic Directory, 1984;* figures as of Jan. 1, 1984. Archdioceses are indicated by an asterisk; for dioceses marked +, see Dioceses with Interstate Lines.)

| Section, State Diocese | Infant Baptisms | Converts | Section, State Diocese | Infant Baptisms | Converts |
|---|---|---|---|---|---|
| | | | New York | | |
| **NEW ENGLAND** | **83,594** | **3,438** | Buffalo | 9,892 | 558 |
| | | | Ogdensburg | 3,359 | 255 |
| Maine, Portland | 4,458 | 486 | Rochester | 3,210 | 634 |
| New Hampshire, Manchester | 5,127 | 319 | Rockville Centre | 19,329 | 284 |
| Vermont, Burlington | 2,551 | 194 | Syracuse | 7,182 | 528 |
| Massachusetts | 44,513 | 1,412 | | | |
| *Boston | 28,677 | 846 | New Jersey | 44,098 | 1,669 |
| Fall River | 5,603 | 153 | *Newark | 17,715 | 458 |
| Springfield | 5,223 | 244 | Camden | 5,276 | 360 |
| Worcester | 5,010 | 169 | Metuchen | 5,749 | 177 |
| Rhode Island, Providence | 7,561 | 312 | Paterson | 6,741 | 219 |
| Connecticut | 19,384 | 715 | Trenton | 8,617 | 455 |
| *Hartford | 11,580 | 380 | | | |
| Bridgeport | 4,736 | 127 | Pennsylvania | 57,185 | 5,359 |
| Norwich+ | 3,068 | 208 | *Philadelphia | 21,282 | 1,840 |
| | | | Allentown | 4,184 | 173 |
| **MIDDLE ATLANTIC** | **216,581** | **11,365** | Altoona-Johnstown | 2,501 | 313 |
| | | | Erie | 4,000 | 561 |
| New York | 115,298 | 4,337 | Greensburg | 3,062 | 441 |
| *New York | 32,168 | 1,388 | Harrisburg | 4,318 | 770 |
| Albany | 6,700 | — | Pittsburgh | 12,205 | 920 |
| Brooklyn | 33,458 | 690 | Scranton | 5,633 | 341 |

| Section, State Diocese | Infant Baptisms | Converts |
|---|---|---|
| **SOUTH ATLANTIC** | **62,368** | **9,835** |
| Delaware, Wilmington+ | 2,895 | 144 |
| Maryland, *Baltimore | 8,933 | 1,262 |
| District of Columbia, *Washington+ | 6,867 | 977 |
| Virginia | 7,176 | 1,278 |
| Arlington | 4,179 | 533 |
| Richmond | 2,997 | 745 |
| West Virginia, Wheeling-Charleston | 1,789 | 613 |
| North Carolina | 2,538 | 861 |
| Charlotte | 1,284 | 502 |
| Raleigh | 1,254 | 359 |
| South Carolina, Charleston | 1,641 | 448 |
| Georgia | 3,831 | 1,097 |
| *Atlanta | 2,661 | 609 |
| Savannah | 1,170 | 488 |
| Florida | 26,698 | 3,155 |
| *Miami | 15,485 | 1,208 |
| Orlando | 3,979 | 676 |
| Palm Beach | No separate statistics available. | |
| Pensacola-Tallahassee | 1,096 | 299 |
| St. Augustine | 1,451 | 271 |
| St. Petersburg | 4,687 | 701 |
| Venice | No separate statistics available. | |
| | | |
| **EAST NORTH CENTRAL** | **176,186** | **25,115** |
| Ohio | 38,490 | 8,287 |
| *Cincinnati | 9,762 | 1,520 |
| Cleveland | 13,251 | 3,900 |
| Columbus | 3,891 | 1,052 |
| Steubenville | 1,250 | 263 |
| Toledo | 6,047 | 932 |
| Youngstown | 4,289 | 620 |
| Indiana | 14,219 | 3,389 |
| *Indianapolis | 4,493 | 1,392 |
| Evansville | 2,069 | 430 |
| Ft. Wayne-South Bend | 2,852 | 630 |
| Gary | 3,113 | 456 |
| Lafayette | 1,692 | 481 |
| Illinois | 59,044 | 5,937 |
| *Chicago | 35,631 | 2,533 |
| Belleville | 2,285 | 689 |
| Joliet | 8,218 | 560 |
| Peoria | 4,366 | 1,040 |
| Rockford | 4,896 | 607 |
| Springfield | 3,648 | 508 |
| Michigan | 37,016 | 5,142 |
| *Detroit | 20,720 | 2,027 |
| Gaylord | 1,546 | 265 |
| Grand Rapids | 3,900 | 782 |
| Kalamazoo | 1,647 | 385 |
| Lansing | 4,627 | 1,083 |
| Marquette | 1,615 | 185 |
| Saginaw | 2,961 | 415 |
| Wisconsin | 27,417 | 2,360 |
| *Milwaukee | 12,301 | 842 |
| Green Bay | 4,994 | 324 |
| La Crosse | 4,490 | 546 |
| Madison | 3,614 | 442 |
| Superior | 2,018 | 206 |
| | | |
| **EAST SOUTH CENTRAL** | **14,491** | **4,081** |
| | | |
| Kentucky | 7,557 | 1,614 |
| *Louisville | 4,091 | 787 |

| Section, State Diocese | Infant Baptisms | Converts |
|---|---|---|
| Kentucky | | |
| Covington | 2,297 | 386 |
| Owensboro | 1,169 | 441 |
| Tennessee | 2,509 | 972 |
| Memphis | 891 | 429 |
| Nashville | 1,618 | 543 |
| Alabama | 2,281 | 858 |
| *Mobile | 1,213 | 435 |
| Birmingham | 1,068 | 423 |
| Mississippi | 2,144 | 637 |
| Biloxi | 1,219 | 274 |
| Jackson | 925 | 363 |
| | | |
| **WEST NORTH CENTRAL** | **75,797** | **12,449** |
| | | |
| Minnesota | 22,944 | 2,242 |
| *St. Paul and Minneapolis | 12,217 | 1,162 |
| Crookston | 956 | 143 |
| Duluth | 1,734 | 183 |
| New Ulm | 1,687 | 182 |
| St. Cloud | 3,520 | 217 |
| Winona | 2,830 | 355 |
| Iowa | 11,845 | 2,055 |
| *Dubuque | 4,602 | 667 |
| Davenport | 2,667 | 527 |
| Des Moines | 1,973 | 528 |
| Sioux City | 2,603 | 333 |
| Missouri | 14,876 | 3,783 |
| *St. Louis | 9,826 | 1,656 |
| Jefferson City | 1,448 | 379 |
| Kansas City-St. Joseph | 2,712 | 1,066 |
| Springfield-Cape Girardeau | 890 | 682 |
| North Dakota | 4,322 | 332 |
| Bismarck | 2,072 | 211 |
| Fargo | 2,250 | 121 |
| South Dakota | 3,303 | 838 |
| Rapid City | 1,105 | 315 |
| Sioux Falls | 2,198 | 523 |
| Nebraska | 7,796 | 1,395 |
| *Omaha | 4,746 | 708 |
| Grand Island | 1,370 | 277 |
| Lincoln | 1,680 | 410 |
| Kansas | 10,711 | 1,804 |
| *Kansas City | 3,088 | 634 |
| Dodge City | 1,049 | 186 |
| Salina | 1,531 | 279 |
| Wichita | 5,043 | 705 |
| | | |
| **WEST SOUTH CENTRAL** | **110,139** | **9,773** |
| | | |
| Arkansas, Little Rock | 1,237 | 473 |
| Louisiana | 28,706 | 2,495 |
| *New Orleans | 10,331 | 840 |
| Alexandria-Shreveport | 2,053 | 455 |
| Baton Rouge | 3,888 | 489 |
| Houma-Thibodaux | 2,620 | 90 |
| Lafayette | 7,452 | 252 |
| Lake Charles | 2,362 | 369 |
| Oklahoma | 3,366 | 1,168 |
| *Oklahoma City | 2,177 | 765 |
| Tulsa | 1,189 | 403 |
| Texas | 76,830 | 5,637 |
| *San Antonio | 13,224 | 405 |
| Amarillo | 1,472 | 142 |

| Section, State Diocese | Infant Baptisms | Converts |
|---|---|---|
| **Texas** | | |
| Austin | 4,357 | 517 |
| Beaumont | 2,376 | 391 |
| Brownsville | 8,436 | 289 |
| Corpus Christi | 7,668 | 210 |
| Dallas | 6,765 | 1,175 |
| El Paso | 6,042 | 85 |
| Fort Worth | 3,633 | 628 |
| Galveston-Houston | 14,731 | 1,411 |
| Lubbock | 2,453 | 80 |
| San Angelo | 3,343 | 165 |
| Victoria | 2,330 | 139 |
| **MOUNTAIN** | **49,561** | **4,783** |
| Montana | 3,153 | 619 |
| Great Falls-Billings | 1,694 | 254 |
| Helena | 1,459 | 365 |
| Idaho, Boise | 2,123 | 448 |
| Wyoming, Cheyenne+ | 1,592 | 226 |
| Colorado | 11,842 | 1,174 |
| *Denver | 9,301 | 973 |
| Colorado Springs | — | — |
| Pueblo | 2,541 | 201 |
| New Mexico | 12,792 | 736 |
| *Santa Fe | 7,358 | 411 |
| Gallup+ | 1,260 | 213 |
| Las Cruces | 4,174 | 112 |
| Arizona | 13,393 | 944 |
| Phoenix | 7,672 | 650 |
| Tucson | 5,721 | 294 |
| Utah, Salt Lake City | 1,986 | 354 |
| Nevada, Reno-Las Vegas | 2,680 | 282 |
| **PACIFIC** | **165,428** | **12,171** |
| Washington | 9,748 | 1,996 |
| *Seattle | 6,192 | 1,447 |
| Spokane | 1,698 | 369 |
| Yakima | 1,858 | 180 |
| Oregon | 4,890 | 1,318 |
| *Portland | 4,137 | 1,075 |
| Baker | 753 | 243 |
| California | 144,503 | 8,300 |
| *Los Angeles | 66,021 | 2,460 |
| *San Francisco | 7,597 | 573 |
| Fresno | 12,197 | 451 |
| Monterey | 3,841 | 225 |
| Oakland | 7,310 | 653 |
| Orange | 10,274 | 828 |
| Sacramento | 6,679 | 805 |
| San Bernardino | 7,728 | 701 |
| San Diego | 9,356 | 645 |
| San Jose | 7,735 | 469 |
| Santa Rosa | 2,265 | 244 |
| Stockton | 3,500 | 246 |
| Alaska | 1,406 | 188 |
| *Anchorage | 761 | 134 |
| Fairbanks | 483 | 33 |
| Juneau | 162 | 21 |
| Hawaii, Honolulu | 4,881 | 369 |
| **EASTERN RITES** | **4,830** | **439** |
| *Philadelphia | 736 | 29 |
| St. Nicholas (Chicago) | 305 | 13 |
| Stamford | 324 | 9 |
| St. Josaphat (Parma) | No separate statistics available. | |
| *Pittsburgh | 590 | 151 |
| Parma | 624 | 87 |
| Passaic | 526 | 46 |
| Van Nuys | 76 | 21 |
| St. Maron | 565 | 40 |
| Newton | 367 | 43 |
| Chaldeans (Ap. Ex.) | 717 | — |
| Armenians (Ap. Ex.) | — | — |
| Romanians (Ap. Ex.) | — | — |
| **MILITARY ORDINARIATE** | **16,042** | **1,897** |
| **TOTALS 1984** | **975,017** | **95,346** |
| Totals 1983 | 965,049 | 94,251 |
| Totals 1974 | 916,564 | 74,741 |

## STATISTICAL SUMMARY OF THE CHURCH IN THE U.S.

(Principal source: *The Official Catholic Directory, 1984*. Comparisons are with figures reported in the previous edition.)

**Catholic Population:** 52,392,934; increase, 304,190. Percent of total population, 22.3 (no change).

**Jurisdictions:** 33 archdioceses, 147 dioceses, 3 apostolic exarchates; the Military Vicariate.

**Cardinals:** 7 (3 head archiepiscopal sees, 1 is a Roman Curia official, 3 are retired). As of Aug. 27, 1984.

**Archbishops:** 58. Diocesan, in U.S., 33 (includes 3 cardinals); coadjutor, 1; titular, 2; retired, 14 (includes 3 cardinals); serving outside U.S., 8. As of Aug. 27, 1984.

**Bishops:** 380. Diocesan, in U.S., 140; coadjutor, 2; exarchs, 3; auxiliaries, 100; retired, 93; serving outside U.S., 41. As of Aug. 27, 1984.

**Priests:** 57,891; increase, 21. Diocesan or secular priests, 35,163 (decrease, 193); religious order priests, 22,728 (increase, 214).

**Permanent Deacons:** 6,702; increase, 636.

**Brothers:** 7,596; decrease, 62.

**Sisters:** 118,027; decrease, 2,672.

**Seminarians:** 11,262; decrease, 792. Diocesan seminarians, 7,486 (decrease, 560); religious order seminarians, 3,776 (decrease, 232).

**Infant Baptisms:** 975,017; increase, 9,968.

**Converts:** 95,346; increase, 1,095.

**Marriages:** 347,973; increase, 528.

**Deaths:** 421,032; increase, 6,572.

**Parishes:** 19,118; increase, 79.

**Seminaries, Diocesan:** 86 (no change).

**Religious Seminaries, Novitiates, Scholasticates:** 233; decrease, 1.

**Colleges and Universities:** 239; students, 560,835.

**High Schools:** 1,456; decrease, 14. Students, 801,440; decrease, 12,628.

**Elementary Schools:** 8,009; increase, 40. Students, 2,220,964; decrease, 47,489.

**Teachers:** 170,714; increase, 2,332. Priests, 4,613 (decrease, 105); scholastics, 151 (decrease, 11); brothers, 2,756 (decrease, 128); sisters, 31,521 (decrease, 1,789); lay teachers, 131,673 (increase, 4,365).

**Public School Students in Religious Instruction Programs:** 4,067,477; decrease, 137,836. High school students, 961,196 (decrease, 25,511); elementary school students, 3,106,281 (decrease, 112,325).

**Hospitals:** 731; increase, 2. Patients treated, 37,204,944; decrease 1,080,249.
**Nurses' Schools:** 124; decrease, 1. Students, 22,915; increase, 1,599.
**Homes for Aged:** 597; increase, 18. Residents, 75,135; increase, 2,428.
**Orphanages:** 174; resident children, 10,860. Children in foster homes, 14,494.

## CATHEDRALS IN THE UNITED STATES

A cathedral is the principal church in a diocese, the one in which the bishop has his seat (*cathedra*). He is the actual rector, although many functions of the church, which usually serves a parish, are the responsibility of a priest serving as the administrator. Because of the dignity of a cathedral, the dates of its dedication and its patronal feast are observed throughout a diocese.

The pope's cathedral, the Basilica of St. John Lateran, is the highest-ranking church in the world.

(Archdioceses are indicated by asterisk.)

**Albany, N.Y.:** Immaculate Conception.
**Alexandria-Shreveport, La.:** St. Francis Xavier. (Alexandria); St. John Berchmans (Shreveport Co-Cathedral).
**Allentown, Pa.:** St. Catherine of Siena.
**Altoona-Johnstown, Pa.:** Blessed Sacrament (Altoona); St. John Gualbert (Johnstown Co-Cathedral).
**Amarillo, Tex.:** St. Laurence.
**Anchorage,\* Alaska:** Holy Family.
**Arlington, Va:** St. Thomas More.
**Atlanta,\* Ga.:** Christ the King.
**Austin, Tex.:** St. Mary (Immaculate Conception).
**Baker, Ore.:** St. Francis de Sales.
**Baltimore,\* Md.:** Mary Our Queen; Basilica of the Assumption of the Blessed Virgin Mary (Co-Cathedral).
**Baton Rouge, La.:** St. Joseph.
**Beaumont, Tex.:** St. Anthony (of Padua).
**Belleville, Ill.:** St. Peter.
**Biloxi, Miss.:** Nativity of the Blessed Virgin Mary.
**Birmingham, Ala.:** St. Paul.
**Bismarck, N.D.:** Holy Spirit.
**Boise, Ida.:** St. John the Evangelist.
**Boston,\* Mass.:** Holy Cross.
**Bridgeport, Conn.:** St. Augustine.
**Brooklyn, N.Y.:** St. James (Minor Basilica).
**Brownsville, Tex.:** Immaculate Conception.
**Buffalo, N.Y.:** St. Joseph.
**Burlington, Vt.:** Immaculate Conception.
**Camden, N.J.:** Immaculate Conception.
**Charleston, S.C.:** St. John the Baptist.
**Charlotte, N.C.:** St. Patrick.
**Cheyenne, Wyo.:** St. Mary.
**Chicago,\* Ill.:** Holy Name (of Jesus).
**Cincinnati,\* Ohio:** St. Peter in Chains.
**Cleveland, Ohio:** St. John the Evangelist.
**Colorado Springs, Colo:** St. Mary
**Columbus, Ohio:** St. Joseph.
**Corpus Christi, Tex.:** Corpus Christi.
**Covington, Ky.:** Basilica of the Assumption.
**Crookston, Minn.:** Immaculate Conception.
**Dallas, Tex.:** Cathedral-Santuario de Guadalupe.
**Davenport, Ia.:** Sacred Heart.

**Denver,\* Colo.:** Immaculate Conception (Minor Basilica).
**Des Moines, Ia.:** St. Ambrose.
**Detroit,\* Mich.:** Blessed Sacrament.
**Dodge City, Kans.:** Sacred Heart.
**Dubuque,\* Ia.:** St. Raphael.
**Duluth, Minn.:** Holy Rosary.
**El Paso, Tex.:** St. Patrick.
**Erie, Pa.:** St. Peter.
**Evansville, Ind.:** Most Holy Trinity (Pro-Cathedral).
**Fairbanks, Alaska:** Sacred Heart.
**Fall River, Mass.:** St. Mary of the Assumption.
**Fargo, N.D.:** St. Mary.
**Fort Wayne-S. Bend, Ind.:** Immaculate Conception (Fort Wayne); St. Matthew (South Bend Co-Cathedral).
**Fort Worth, Tex.:** St. Patrick.
**Fresno, Calif.:** St. John the Baptist.
**Gallup, N.M.:** Sacred Heart.
**Galveston-Houston, Tex.:** St. Mary (Minor Basilica, Galveston); Sacred Heart (Houston Co-Cathedral).
**Gary, Ind.:** Holy Angels.
**Gaylord, Mich.:** St. Mary, Our Lady of Mt. Carmel.
**Grand Island, Nebr.:** Nativity of Blessed Virgin Mary.
**Grand Rapids, Mich.:** St. Andrew.
**Great Falls-Billings, Mont.:** St. Ann (Great Falls); St. Patrick (Billings Co-Cathedral).
**Green Bay, Wis.:** St. Francis Xavier.
**Greensburg, Pa.:** Blessed Sacrament.
**Harrisburg, Pa.:** St. Patrick.
**Hartford,\* Conn.:** St. Joseph.
**Helena, Mont.:** St. Helena.
**Honolulu, Hawaii:** Our Lady of Peace.
**Houma-Thibodaux, La.:** St. Francis de Sales (Houma); St. Joseph (Thibodaux Co-Cathedral).
**Indianapolis,\* Ind.:** Sts. Peter and Paul.
**Jackson, Miss.:** St. Peter.
**Jefferson City, Mo.:** St. Joseph.
**Joliet, Ill.:** St. Raymond Nonnatus.
**Juneau, Alaska:** Nativity of the Blessed Virgin Mary.
**Kalamazoo, Mich.:** St. Augustine.
**Kansas City,\* Kans.:** St. Peter the Apostle.
**Kansas City-St. Joseph, Mo.:** Immaculate Conception (Kansas City); St. Joseph (St. Joseph Co-Cathedral).
**La Crosse, Wis.:** St. Joseph.
**Lafayette, Ind.:** St. Mary.
**Lafayette, La.:** St. John the Evangelist.
**Lake Charles, La.:** Immaculate Conception.
**Lansing, Mich.:** St. Mary.

**Las Cruces, N. Mex.:** Immaculate Heart of Mary.
**Lincoln, Nebr.:** Cathedral of the Risen Christ.
**Little Rock, Ark.:** St. Andrew.
**Los Angeles,\* Calif.:** St. Vibiana.
**Louisville,\* Ky.:** Assumption.
**Lubbock, Tex.:** Christ the King.
**Madison, Wis.:** St. Raphael.
**Manchester, N.H.:** St. Joseph.
**Marquette, Mich.:** St. Peter.
**Memphis, Tenn.:** Immaculate Conception.
**Metuchen, N.J.:** St. Francis (of Assisi).
**Miami,\* Fla.:** St. Mary (Immaculate Conception).
**Milwaukee,\* Wis.:** St. John.
**Mobile,\* Ala.:** Immaculate Conception (Minor Basilica).
**Monterey, Calif.:** San Carlos Borromeo.
**Nashville, Tenn.:** Incarnation.
**Newark,\* N.J.:** Sacred Heart.
**New Orleans,\* La.:** Cathedral (Basilica) of St. Louis.
**Newton, Mass.** (Melkite Rite): Our Lady of the Annunciation (Boston).
**New Ulm, Minn.:** Holy Trinity.
**New York,\* N.Y.:** St. Patrick.
**Norwich, Conn.:** St. Patrick.
**Oakland, Calif.:** St. Francis de Sales.
**Ogdensburg, N.Y.:** St. Mary (Immaculate Conception).
**Oklahoma City,\* Okla.:** Our Lady of Perpetual Help.
**Omaha,\* Nebr.:** St. Cecilia.
**Orange, Calif.:** Holy Family.
**Orlando, Fla.:** St. James.
**Owensboro, Ky.:** St. Stephen.
**Palm Beach, Fla.:** St. Ignatius Loyola, Palm Beach Gardens.
**Parma, Ohio (Byzantine Rite):** St. John the Baptist.
**Passaic, N.J. (Byzantine Rite):** St. Michael.
**Paterson, N.J.:** St. John the Baptist.
**Pensacola-Tallahassee, Fla.:** Sacred Heart (Pensacola); St. Thomas More (Tallahassee Co-Cathedral).
**Peoria, Ill.:** St. Mary.
**Philadelphia,\* Pa.:** Sts. Peter and Paul (Minor Basilica).
**Philadelphia,\* Pa. (Byzantine Rite):** Immaculate Conception.
**Phoenix, Ariz.:** Sts. Simon and Jude.
**Pittsburgh,\* Pa. (Byzantine Rite):** St. John the Baptist, Munhall.
**Pittsburgh, Pa.:** St. Paul.
**Portland, Me.:** Immaculate Conception.
**Portland,\* Ore.:** Immaculate Conception.
**Providence, R.I.:** Sts. Peter and Paul.
**Pueblo, Colo.:** Sacred Heart.
**Raleigh, N.C.:** Sacred Heart.
**Rapid City, S.D.:** Our Lady of Perpetual Help.
**Reno-Las Vegas, Nev.:** St. Thomas Aquinas (Reno), Guardian Angel (Las Vegas Co-Cathedral).
**Richmond, Va.:** Sacred Heart.
**Rochester, N.Y.:** Sacred Heart.
**Rockford, Ill.:** St. Peter.
**Rockville Centre, N.Y.:** St. Agnes.
**Sacramento, Calif.:** Blessed Sacrament.

**Saginaw, Mich.:** St. Mary.
**St. Augustine, Fla.:** St. Augustine (Minor Basilica).
**St. Cloud, Minn.:** St. Mary.
**St. Josaphat in Parma, Ohio (Byzantine Rite):** St. Josaphat.
**St. Louis,\* Mo.:** St. Louis.
**St. Maron, Brooklyn, N.Y. (Maronite Rite):** Our Lady of Lebanon.
**St. Nicholas in Chicago (Byzantine Rite):** St. Nicholas.
**St. Paul and Minneapolis,\* Minn.:** St. Paul (St. Paul); Basilica of St. Mary (Minneapolis Co-Cathedral).
**St. Petersburg, Fla.:** St. Jude the Apostle.
**Salina, Kans.:** Sacred Heart.
**Salt Lake City, Utah:** The Madeleine.
**San Angelo, Tex.:** Sacred Heart.
**San Antonio,\* Tex.:** San Fernando.
**San Bernardino, Calif:** Our Lady of the Rosary.
**San Diego, Calif.:** St. Joseph.
**San Francisco,\* Calif.:** St. Mary (Assumption).
**San Jose, Calif.:** St. Patrick.
**Santa Fe,\* N.M.:** San Francisco de Asis.
**Santa Rosa, Calif.:** St. Eugene.
**Savannah, Ga.:** St. John the Baptist.
**Scranton, Pa.:** St. Peter.
**Seattle,\* Wash.:** St. James.
**Sioux City, Ia.:** Epiphany.
**Sioux Falls, S.D.:** St. Joseph.
**Spokane, Wash.:** Our Lady of Lourdes.
**Springfield, Ill.:** Immaculate Conception.
**Springfield, Mass.:** St. Michael.
**Springfield-Cape Girardeau, Mo.:** St. Agnes (Springfield): St. Mary (Cape Girardeau Co-Cathedral).
**Stamford, Conn. (Byzantine Rite):** St. Vladimir.
**Steubenville, Ohio:** Holy Name.
**Stockton, Calif:** Annunciation.
**Superior, Wis.:** Christ the King.
**Syracuse, N.Y.:** Immaculate Conception.
**Toledo, Ohio:** Blessed Virgin Mary of the Holy Rosary.
**Trenton, N.J.:** St. Mary (Assumption).
**Tucson, Ariz.:** St. Augustine.
**Tulsa, Okla.:** Holy Family.
**Van Nuys, Calif. (Byzantine Rite).** St. Mary.
**Venice, Fla:** Church of the Epiphany.
**Victoria, Tex.:** Our Lady of Victory.
**Washington,\* D.C.:** St. Matthew.
**Wheeling-Charleston, W. Va.:** St. Joseph (Wheeling); Sacred Heart (Charleston Co-Cathedral).
**Wichita, Kans.:** Immaculate Conception.
**Wilmington, Del.:** St. Peter.
**Winona, Minn.:** Sacred Heart.
**Worcester, Mass.:** St. Paul.
**Yakima, Wash.:** St. Paul.
**Youngstown, Ohio:** St. Columba.
**Apostolic Exarchate for Chaldean-Rite Catholics in the United States:** Our Lady of Chaldeans Cathedral (Mother of God Church), Southfield, Mich.
**Apostolic Exarchate for Romanian Catholics of Byzantine Rite in U.S.:** St. George, Canton, O. (Pro-Cathedral).

**Apostolic Exarchate for Armenian-Rite Catholics in the U.S. and Canada:** St. Ann (110 E. 12th St., New York, N.Y. 10003).

## BASILICAS IN U.S. AND CANADA

Basilica is a title assigned to certain churches because of their antiquity, dignity, historical importance or significance as centers of worship. Major basilicas have the papal altar and holy door, which is opened at the beginning of a Jubilee Year; minor basilicas enjoy certain ceremonial privileges.

Among the major basilicas are the patriarchal basilicas of St. John Lateran, St. Peter, St. Paul Outside the Walls and St. Mary Major in Rome; St. Francis and St. Mary of the Angels in Assisi, Italy. The patriarchal basilica of St. Lawrence, Rome, is a minor basilica.

The dates in the listings below indicate when the churches were designated as basilicas.

### Minor Basilicas in U.S., Puerto Rico

**Alabama:** Mobile, Cathedral of the Immaculate Conception (Mar. 10, 1962).

**California:** San Francisco, Mission Dolores (Feb. 8, 1952); Carmel, Old Mission of San Carlos (Feb. 5, 1960); Alameda, St. Joseph (Jan. 21, 1972); San Diego, Mission San Diego de Alcala (Nov. 17, 1975).

**Colorado:** Denver, Cathedral of the Immaculate Conception (Nov. 3, 1979).

**Florida:** St. Augustine, Cathedral of St. Augustine (Dec. 4, 1976).

**Illinois:** Chicago, Our Lady of Sorrows (May 4, 1956), Queen of All Saints (Mar. 26, 1962).

**Indiana:** Vincennes, Old Cathedral (Mar. 14, 1970).

**Iowa:** Dyersville, St. Francis Xavier (May 11, 1956).

**Kentucky:** Trappist, Our Lady of Gethsemani (May 3, 1949); Covington, Cathedral of Assumption (Dec. 8, 1953).

**Louisiana:** New Orleans, St. Louis King of France (Dec. 9, 1964).

**Maryland:** Baltimore, Assumption of the Blessed Virgin Mary (Sept. 1, 1937).

**Massachusetts:** Roxbury, Perpetual Help ("Mission Church") (Sept. 8, 1954).

**Michigan:** Grand Rapids, St. Adalbert (Aug. 22, 1979).

**Minnesota:** Minneapolis. St. Mary (Feb. 1, 1926).

**Missouri:** Conception, Basilica of Immaculate Conception (Sept. 14, 1940); St. Louis, St. Louis King of France (Jan. 27, 1961).

**New York:** Brooklyn, Our Lady of Perpetual Help (Sept. 5, 1969), Cathedral-Basilica of St. James (June 22, 1982); Lackawanna, Our Lady of Victory (1926); Youngstown, Blessed Virgin Mary of the Rosary of Fatima (Oct. 7, 1975).

**Ohio:** Carey, Shrine of Our Lady of Consolation (Oct. 21, 1971).

**Pennsylvania:** Latrobe, St. Vincent Basilica, Benedictine Archabbey (Aug. 22, 1955); Conewago, Basilica of the Sacred Heart (June 30, 1962); Philadelphia, Sts. Peter and Paul (Sept. 27, 1976).

**Texas:** Galveston, St. Mary Cathedral (Aug. 11, 1979).

**Wisconsin:** Milwaukee, St. Josaphat (Mar. 10, 1929).

**Puerto Rico:** San Juan, Cathedral of San Juan (Jan. 25, 1978).

### Minor Basilicas in Canada

**Alberta:** Edmonton, Cathedral Basilica of St. Joseph (Mar. 15, 1984).

**Manitoba:** St. Boniface, Cathedral Basilica of St. Boniface (June 10, 1949).

**Newfoundland:** St. John's, Cathedral Basilica of St. John the Baptist.

**Nova Scotia:** Halifax, St. Mary's Basilica (June 14, 1950).

**Ontario:** Ottawa, Basilica of Notre Dame; London, St. Peter's Cathedral (Dec. 13, 1961).

**Prince Edward Island:** Charlottetown, Basilica of St. Dunstan.

**Quebec:** Sherbrooke, Cathedral Basilica of St. Michael (July 31, 1959). Montreal, Cathedral Basilica of Our Lady Queen of the World; St. Joseph of Mount Royal; Basilica of Notre Dame (Feb. 15, 1982). Cap-de-la-Madeleine, Basilica of Our Lady of the Cape (Aug. 15, 1964). Quebec, Basilica of Notre Dame; St. Anne de Beaupre, Basilica of St. Anne.

## CHANCERY OFFICES OF U.S. ARCHDIOCESES AND DIOCESES

A chancery office, under this or another title, is the central administrative office of an archdiocese or diocese.

(Archdioceses are indicated by asterisk.)

**Albany, N.Y.:** 465 State St., Box 6297, Quail Station. 12206.

**Alexandria-Shreveport, La.:** 4400 Garner Hwy., P.O. Box 7417, Alexandria. 71306.

**Allentown, Pa.:** 202 N. 17th St., P.O. Box F. 18105.

**Altoona-Johnstown, Pa.:** Box 126, Logan Blvd., Hollidaysburg, Pa. 16648.

**Amarillo, Tex.:** 1800 N. Spring St., P.O. Box 5644. 79117.

**Anchorage,\* Alaska:** P.O. Box 2239. 99510.

**Arlington, Va.:** 200 N. Glebe Rd. 22203.

**Atlanta,\* Ga.:** Catholic Center, 680 W. Peachtree St. N.W. 30308.

**Austin, Tex.:** N. Congress and 16th, P.O. Box 13327. Capitol Sta. 78711.

**Baker, Ore.:** Baker and First Sts., P.O. Box 826, 97814.

**Baltimore,\* Md.:** 320 Cathedral St. 21201.

**Baton Rouge, La.:** P.O. Box 2028. 70821.

**Beaumont, Tex.:** 703 Archie St., P.O. Box 3948. 77704.

**Belleville, Ill.:** The Catholic Center, 220 W. Lincoln St. 62221.

**Biloxi, Miss.:** P.O. Box 1189. 39533.

**Birmingham, Ala.:** P.O. Box 2086. 35201.

**Bismarck, N.D.:** 420 Raymond St., Box 1575. 58501.

**Boise, Ida.:** Box 769. 83701.

**Boston,\* Mass.:** 2121 Commonwealth Ave., Brighton, Mass. 02135.

**Bridgeport, Conn.:** The Catholic Center, 238 Jewett Ave. 06606.

**Brooklyn, N.Y.:** 75 Greene Ave., P.O. Box C. 11202.

**Brownsville, Tex.:** P.O. Box 2279. 78520.

**Buffalo, N.Y.:** 35 Lincoln Parkway. 14222.

**Burlington, Vt.:** 351 North Ave. 05401.

**Camden, N.J.:** 1845 Haddon Ave., P.O. Box 709, 01801.

**Charleston, S.C.:** 119 Broad St., P.O. Box 818. 29402.

**Charlotte, N.C.:** P.O. Box 36776. 28236.

**Cheyenne, Wyo.:** Box 426. 82001.

**Chicago,\* Ill,:** 155 E. Superior St. 60611.

**Cincinnati,\* O.:** 100 E. 8th St. 45202.

**Cleveland, O.:** Chancery Bldg., 1027 Superior Ave. 44114.

**Colorado Springs, Colo.:** 29 W. Kiowa. 80903.

**Columbus, O.:** 198 E. Broad St. 43215.

**Corpus Christi, Tex.:** 620 Lipan St. 78401.

**Covington, Ky.:** 1140 Madison Ave., P.O. Box 192. 41012.

**Crookston, Minn.:** 1200 Memorial Dr., P.O. Box 610. 56716.

**Dallas, Tex.:** 3915 Lemmon Ave., P.O. Box 190507. 75219.

**Davenport, Ia.:** St. Vincent Center, 2706 Gaines St. 52804.

**Denver,\* Colo.:** 200 Josephine St. 80206.

**Des Moines, Ia.:** P.O. Box 1816. 50306.

**Detroit,\* Mich.:** 1234 Washington Blvd. 48226.

**Dodge City, Kans.:** 910 Central Ave., P.O. Box 849. 67801.

**Dubuque,\* Ia.:** 1229 Mt. Loretta Ave. 52001.

**Duluth, Minn.:** 215 W. 4th St. 55806.

**El Paso, Tex.:** 499 St. Matthews St. 79907.

**Erie, Pa.:** 205 W. 9th St. 16501.

**Evansville, Ind.:** P.O. Box 4169. 47711.

**Fairbanks, Alaska:** 1316 Peger Rd. 99701.

**Fall River, Mass.:** 47 Underwood St., Box 2577. 02722.

**Fargo, N.D.:** 1310 Broadway, Box 1750. 58107.

**Fort Wayne-South Bend, Ind.:** P.O. Box 390, Fort Wayne. 46801.

**Fort Worth, Tex.:** 411 E. Bolt St. 76110.

**Fresno, Calif.:** P.O. Box 1668, 1550 N. Fresno St. 93717.

**Gallup, N. Mex.:** 711 S. Puerco Dr., P.O. Box 1338. 87301.

**Galveston-Houston, Tex.:** 1700 San Jacinto St., Houston. 77002.

**Gary, Ind.:** 975 W. Sixth Ave., P.O. Box M-474, 46401.

**Gaylord, Mich.:** M-32 West, P.O. Box 700. 49735.

**Grand Island, Nebr.:** 311 W. 17th St., P.O. Box 996. 68802.

**Grand Rapids, Mich.:** 660 Burton St., 49507.

**Great Falls-Billings, Mont.:** P.O. Box 1399, Great Falls. 59403.

**Green Bay, Wis.:** Box 66. 54305.

**Greensburg, Pa.:** 723 E. Pittsburgh St. 15601.

**Harrisburg, Pa.:** P.O. Box 2153. 17105.

**Hartford,\* Conn.:** 134 Farmington Ave. 06105.

**Helena, Mont.:** 515 North Ewing, P.O. Box 1729. 59624.

**Honolulu, Hawaii:** 1184 Bishop St. 96813.

**Houma-Thibodaux, La.:** 1220 Aycock St., P.O. Box 9077, Houma, La. 70361.

**Indianapolis,\* Ind.:** 1400 N. Meridian St., P.O. Box 1410, 46206.

**Jackson, Miss.:** 237 E. Amite St., P.O. Box 2248. 39205.

**Jefferson City, Mo.:** 605 Clark Ave. P.O. Box 417. 65101.

**Joliet, Ill.:** 425 Summit St. 60435.

**Juneau, Alaska:** 419 6th St. 99801.

**Kalamazoo, Mich.:** 215 N. Westnedge. Ave., P.O. Box 949, 49005.

**Kansas City,\* Kans.:** 2220 Central Ave., P.O. Box 2328. 66101.

**Kansas City-St. Joseph, Mo.:** P.O. Box 1037, Kansas City. 64141.

**La Crosse, Wis.:** P.O. Box 69. 54602.

**Lafayette in Indiana:** P.O. Box 260, 47902.

**Lafayette, La.:** P.O. Drawer 3387. 70502.

**Lake Charles, La.:** P.O. Box 3223. 70602.

**Lansing, Mich.:** 300 W. Ottawa. 48933.

**Las Cruces, N. Mex.:** P.O. Box 16318. 88004.

**Lincoln, Nebr.:** 3400 Sheridan Blvd., P.O. Box 80328. 68501.

**Little Rock, Ark.:** 2415 N. Tyler St. 72217.

**Los Angeles,\* Calif.:** 1531 W. 9th St. 90015.

**Louisville,\* Ky.:** 212 E. College St., P.O. Box 1073. 40201.

**Lubbock, Tex.:** P.O. Box 10238. 79408.

**Madison, Wis.:** 15 E. Wilson St. 53701.

**Manchester, N. H.:** 153 Ash St. 03105.

**Marquette, Mich.:** 444 S. Fourth St., P.O. Box 550. 49855.

**Memphis, Tenn.:** 1325 Jefferson Ave., 38104.

**Metuchen, N.J.:** P.O. Box 191. 08840.

**Miami,\* Fla.:** 9401 Biscayne Blvd., Miami Shores. 33138.

**Milwaukee,\* Wis.:** P.O. Box 2018. 53201.

**Mobile,\* Ala.:** 400 Government St., P.O. Box 1966, 36633.

**Monterey, Calif.:** 580 Fremont Blvd., P.O. Box 2048. 93942.

**Nashville, Tenn.:** 2400 21st Ave. S. 37212.

**Newark,\* N.J.:** 31 Mulberry St. 07102.

**New Orleans,\* La.:** 7887 Walmsley Ave. 70125.

**Newton, Mass. (Melkite Rite):** 19 Dartmouth St., W. Newton, Mass. 02165.

**New Ulm, Minn.:** 1400 Chancery Drive. 56073.

**New York,\* N.Y.:** 1011 First Ave. 10022.

**Norwich, Conn.:** 201 Broadway, P.O. Box 587. 06360.

**Oakland, Calif.:** 2900 Lakeshore Ave. 94610.

**Ogdensburg, N.Y.:** 622 Washington St. 13669.

**Oklahoma City,\* Okla.:** P.O. Box 18838. 73154.

**Omaha,\* Nebr.:** 100 N. 62nd St. 68132.

**Orange, Calif.:** 2811 E. Villa Real Dr. 92667.

**Orlando, Fla.:** P.O. Box 1800. 32802.

**Owensboro, Ky.:** 4003 Frederica St. 42301.

**Palm Beach, Fla.:** 9999 N. Military Trail, Palm Beach Gardens 33410 (address of Cathedral of St. Ignatius Loyola).

**Parma, Ohio (Byzantine Rite):** 1900 Carlton Rd, 44134.

**Passaic, N.J. (Byzantine Rite):** 101 Market St. 07055.

**Paterson, N.J.:** 777 Valley Rd., Clifton. 07013.

**Pensacola-Tallahassee, Fla.:** P.O. Drawer 17329, Pensacola. 32522.

**Peoria, Ill.:** 607 N.E. Madison Ave., P.O. Box 1406. 61655.

**Philadelphia,\* Pa.:** 222 N. 17th St. 19103.

**Philadelphia,\* Pa. (Byzantine Rite):** 827 N. Franklin St. 19123.

**Phoenix, Ariz.:** 400 E. Monroe St. 85004.

**Pittsburgh,\* Pa. (Byzantine Rite):** 54 Riverview Ave. 15214.

**Pittsburgh, Pa.:** 111 Blvd. of the Allies. 15222.

**Portland, Me.:** 510 Ocean Ave., Woodfords P.O. Box 6750. 04103.

**Portland in Oregon\*:** P.O. Box 351, 97207.

**Providence, R.I.:** One Cathedral Sq. 02903.

**Pueblo, Colo.:** 1426 Grand Ave. 81003.

**Raleigh, N.C.:** 300 Cardinal Gibbons Dr. 27606.

**Rapid City, S.D.:** 606 Cathedral Dr., P.O. Box 678. 57709.

**Reno-Las Vegas, Nev.:** 515 Court St., Reno 89509. (Mailing address: P.O. Box 1211, Reno. 89504.)

**Richmond, Va.:** 811 Cathedral Pl., Suite C. 23220.

**Rochester, N.Y.:** 1150 Buffalo Rd. 14624.

**Rockford, Ill.:** 1245 N. Court St. 61101.

**Rockville Centre, N.Y.:** 50 N. Park Ave. 11570.

**Sacramento, Calif.:** 1119 K St., P.O. Box 1706. 95808.

**Saginaw, Mich.:** 5800 Weiss St. 48603.

**St. Augustine, Fla.:** P.O. Box 24000, Jacksonville, Fla. 32241.

**St. Cloud, Minn.:** P.O. Box 1248. 56302.

**St. Josaphat in Parma, Ohio (Byzantine Rite):** c/o 5720 State Rd., Parma 44134.

**St. Louis,\* Mo.:** 4445 Lindell Blvd. 63108.

**St. Maron (Maronite Rite), Brooklyn, N.Y.:** 8120 15th Ave., Brooklyn. 11228.

**St. Nicholas in Chicago (Byzantine Rite):** 2245 W. Rice St. 60622.

**St. Paul and Minneapolis,\* Minn.:** 226 Summit Ave., St. Paul. 55102.

**St. Petersburg, Fla.:** 6363 9th Ave. N. 33710. P.O. Box 40200. 33743.

**Salina, Kans.:** P.O. Box 999. 67402.

**Salt Lake City, Utah:** 27 C St., 84103.

**San Angelo, Tex.:** 116 S. Oakes. Box 1829. 76902.

**San Antonio,\* Tex.:** P.O. Box 28410. 78228.

**San Bernardino, Calif.:** 1450 North D St. 92405.

**San Diego, Calif.:** P.O. Box 80428. 92138.

**San Francisco,\* Calif.:** 445 Church St. 94114.

**San Jose, Calif.:** 7600 St. Joseph Ave., Los Altos 94022.

**Santa Fe,\* N. Mex.:** 202 Morningside Dr. S.E., Albuquerque. 87108.

**Santa Rosa, Calif.:** 547 "B" St., P.O. Box 1297. 95402.

**Savannah, Ga.:** 225 Abercorn St., P.O. Box 8789. 31412.

**Scranton, Pa.:** 300 Wyoming Ave. 18503.

**Seattle,\* Wash.:** 910 Marion St. 98104.

**Sioux City, Ia.:** P.O. Box 3379. 51102.

**Sioux Falls, S.D.:** 423 N. Duluth Ave., Box 5033. 57117.

**Spokane, Wash.:** 1023 W. Riverside Ave. 99201.

**Springfield, Illinois:** 524 E. Lawrence Ave., P.O. Box 1667. 62705.

**Springfield, Mass.:** 76 Elliot St. 01105. P.O. Box 1730, 01101.

**Springfield-Cape Girardeau, Mo.:** P.O. Box 1957, SSS, Springfield. 65805.

**Stamford, Conn. (Byzantine Rite):** 161 Glenbrook Rd. 06902.

**Steubenville, Ohio:** 422 Washington St., P.O. Box 969. 43952.

**Stockton, Calif.:** 1105 N. Lincoln St. 95203. P.O. Box 4237. 95204.

**Superior, Wis.:** Box 969, 54880.

**Syracuse, N.Y.:** P.O. Box 511. 13201.

**Toledo, Ohio:** 2544 Parkwood Ave. 43610.

**Trenton, N.J.:** P.O. Box 5309. 08638.

**Tucson, Ariz.:** 192 S. Stone Ave., Box 31, 85702.

**Tulsa, Okla.:** P.O. Box 2009. 74101.

**Van Nuys, Calif. (Byzantine Rite):** 5335 Sepulveda Blvd. 91411.

**Venice, Fla.:** 235 N. Nassau St., P.O. Box 1887, Venice 33595 (address of Cathedral of Epiphany).

**Victoria, Tex.:** P.O. Box 4708. 77903.

**Washington,\* D.C.:** 5001 Eastern Ave., P.O. Box 29260. 20017..

**Wheeling-Charleston, W. Va.:** 1300 Byron St., Wheeling. 26003.

**Wichita, Kans.:** 424 N. Broadway. 67202.

**Wilmington, Del.:** P.O. Box 2030. 19899.

**Winona, Minn.:** P.O. Box 588. 55987.

**Worcester, Mass.:** 49 Elm St. 01609.

**Yakima, Wash.:** 222 Washington Mutual Bldg., P.O. Box 505. 98907.

**Youngstown, Ohio:** 144 W. Wood St. 44503.

**Armenian-Rite Apostolic Exarchate for the United States and Canada:** 155 Long Hill Rd., Little Falls, N.J. 07424.

**Chaldean-Rite Apostolic Exarchate for the United States:** Our Lady of Chaldeans Cathedral, 25585 Berg Rd., Southfield, Mich. 48034.

**Romanian Catholic Apostolic Exarchate for the United States (Byzantine Rite):** 1121 44th St. N.E., Canton, O. 44714.

---

## NCCB-USCC REGIONS

I. Maine, Vermont, New Hampshire, Massachusetts, Rhode Island, Connecticut.

II. New York. III. New Jersey, Pennsylvania.

IV. Delaware, District of Columbia, Florida, Georgia, Maryland, North Carolina, South Carolina, Virgin Islands, Virginia, West Virginia.

V. Alabama, Kentucky, Louisiana, Mississippi, Tennessee.

VI. Michigan, Ohio.

VII. Illinois, Indiana, Wisconsin.

VIII. Minnesota, North Dakota, South Dakota.

IX. Iowa, Kansas, Missouri, Nebraska.

X. Arkansas, Oklahoma, Texas.

XI. California, Hawaii, Nevada. XII. Idaho, Montana, Alaska, Washington, Oregon.

XIII. Utah, Arizona, New Mexico, Colorado, Wyo.

# NATIONAL CATHOLIC CONFERENCES

The two conferences described below are related in membership and directive control but distinct in nature, purpose and function.

The National Conference of Catholic Bishops (NCCB) is a strictly ecclesiastical body in and through which the bishops of the United States act together, officially and with authority as pastors of the Church. It is the sponsoring organization of the United States Catholic Conference.

The United States Catholic Conference (USCC) is a civil corporation and operational secretariat in and through which the bishops, together with other members of the Church, act on a wider scale for the good of the Church and society. It is sponsored by the National Conference of Catholic Bishops.

The principal officers of both conferences are: Bishop James W. Malone, president; Archbishop John L. May, vice president; Archbishop Edmund C. Szoka, treasurer; Archbishop Thomas C. Kelly, O.P., secretary.

The membership of the Administrative Committee of the NCCB and the Administrative Board of the USCC is identical.

Headquarters of both conferences are located at 1312 Massachusetts Ave. N.W., Washington, D.C. 20005.

## NCCB

*The National Conference of Catholic Bishops, established by action of the U.S. hierarchy Nov. 14, 1966, is a strictly ecclesiastical body with defined juridical authority over the Church in this country. It was set up with the approval of the Holy See and in line with directives from the Second Vatican Council. Its constitution was formally ratified during the November, 1967, meeting of the U.S. hierarchy.*

The NCCB is a development from the Annual Meeting of the Bishops of the United States, whose pastoral character was originally approved by Pope Benedict XV Apr. 10, 1919.

The address of the Conference is 1312 Massachusetts Ave. N.W., Washington, D.C. 20005. Rev. Msgr. Daniel F. Hoye is general secretary.

### Pastoral Council

The conference, one of many similar territorial conferences envisioned in the conciliar *Decree on the Pastoral Office of Bishops in the Church* (No. 38), is "a council in which the bishops of a given nation or territory (in this case, the United States) jointly exercise their pastoral office to promote the greater good which the Church offers mankind, especially through the forms and methods of the apostolate fittingly adapted to the circumstances of the age."

Its decisions, "provided they have been approved legitimately and by the votes of at least two-thirds of the prelates who have a deliberative vote in the conference, and have been recognized by the Apostolic See, are to have juridically binding force only in those cases prescribed by the common law or determined by a special mandate of the Apostolic See, given either spontaneously or in response to a petition of the conference itself."

All bishops who serve the Church in the U.S., its territories and possessions, have membership and voting rights in the NCCB.

### Officers, Committees

The conference operates through a number of bishops' committees with functions in specific areas of work and concern. Their basic assignments are to prepare materials on the basis of which the bishops, assembled as a conference, make decisions, and to put suitable action plans into effect.

The principal officers are: Bishop James W. Malone, president; Archbishop John L. May, vice president; Archbishop Edmund C. Szoka, treasurer; Archbishop Thomas C. Kelly, O.P., secretary.

These officers, with several other bishops, hold positions on executive-level committees — Executive Committee, the Committee on Budget and Finance, the Committee on Personnel and Administrative Services, and the Committee on Priorities and Plans. They also, with other bishops, serve on the NCCB Administrative Board.

*The standing committees and their chairmen (Archbishops and Bishops) are as follows.*

American Board of Catholic Missions, Robert F. Sanchez.
Bishops' Welfare Emergency Relief, James W. Malone.
Boundaries of Dioceses and Provinces, James W. Malone.
Canonical Affairs, Anthony J. Bevilacqua.
Church in Latin America, Patrick F. Flores.
Conciliation and Arbitration, Roger M. Mahony.
Doctrine, John R. Quinn.
Ecumenical and Interreligious Affairs, John F. Whealon.
Human Values, Howard J. Hubbard.
Laity, James R. Hoffman.
Liaison with Priests, Religious and Laity, John J. Nevins.
Liturgy, John S. Cummins.
Men Religious, Paul E. Waldschmidt, C.S.C.
Missions, Joseph A. Fiorenza.
American College, Louvain, Eusebius J. Beltran.
North American College, Rome, Oscar H. Lipscomb.
Pastoral Research and Practices, Bernard F. Law.
Permanent Diaconate, John F. Kinney.
Priestly Formation, Thomas J. Murphy
Priestly Life and Ministry, Michael J Murphy.
Selection of Bishops, James W. Malone.
Vocations, Lawrence H. Welsh.
Women Religious, Amedee W. Proulx.
*Ad hoc committees and their chairmen are as follows.*
Bicentennial of Establishment of U.S. Hierarchy, William D. Borders.

Campaign for Human Development, William B. Friend.

Catholic Charismatic Renewal, Joseph McKinney.

Catholic Social Teaching and the American Economy, Rembert G. Weakland, O.S.B.

Economic Concerns of the Holy See, Edward T. O'Meara.

Evangelization, Edward T. O'Meara.

Farm Labor, Roger M. Mahony.

Hispanic Affairs, Robert F. Sanchez.

Inter-Rite, William G. Connare.

Liaison with National Office for Black Catholics, Eugene A. Marino, S.S.J.

Migration and Tourism, Anthony J. Bevilacqua.

Nomination of Conference Offices, F. Joseph Gossman.

Pro-Life Activities, Cardinal Joseph Bernardin.

Sapientia Christiana, Paul E. Waldschmidt, C.S.C.

Women in Society and Church, Joseph L. Imesch.

## USCC

*The United States Catholic Conference, Inc. (USCC), is the operational secretariat and service agency of the National Conference of Catholic Bishops for carrying out the civic-religious work of the Church in this country. It is a civil corporation related to the NCCB and membership and directive control but distinct from it in purpose and function.*

The address of the Conference is 1312 Massachusetts Ave. N.W., Washington, D.C. 20005. Rev. Msgr. Daniel F. Hoye is general secretary.

### Service Secretariat

The USCC, as of Jan. 1, 1967, took over the general organization and operations of the former National Catholic Welfare Conference, Inc., whose origins dated back to the National Catholic War Council of 1917. The council underwent some change after World War I and was established on a permanent basis Sept. 24, 1919, as the National Catholic Welfare Council to serve as a central agency for organizing and coordinating the efforts of U.S. Catholics in carrying out the social mission of the Church in this country. In 1923, its name was changed to National Catholic Welfare Conference, Inc., and clarification was made of its nature as a service agency of the bishops and the Church rather than as a conference of bishops with real

juridical authority in ecclesiastical affairs.

*The Official Catholic Directory* states that the USCC assists "the bishops in their service to the Church in this country by uniting the people of God where voluntary collective action on a broad interdiocesan level is needed. The USCC provides an organizational structure and the resources needed to insure coordination, cooperation, and assistance in the public, educational and social concerns of the Church at the national or interdiocesan level."

### Officers, Departments

The principal officers of the USCC are Bishop James W. Malone, president; Archbishop John L. May, vice president; Archbishop Edmund C. Szoka, treasurer; Archbishop Thomas C. Kelly, O.P., secretary. These officers, with several other bishops, hold positions on executive-level committees — the Executive Committee; the Committee on Priorities and Plans; the Committee on Budget and Finance; the Committee on Personnel and Administrative Services. They also serve on the Administrative Board.

The Executive Committee, organized in 1969, is authorized to handle matters of urgency between meetings of the Administrative Board and the general conference, to coordinate items for the agenda of general meetings, and to speak in the name of the USCC.

The major departments and their chairmen (Archbishops and Bishops) are: Communications, R. Pierre Du Maine; Education, Edward T. Hughes, Committee of Bishops and Catholic College and University Presidents, Edward T. Hughes; Social Development and World Peace, Mark J. Hurley. Each department is supervised by a committee composed of an equal number of episcopal and non-episcopal members, including lay persons.

A national Advisory Council of bishops, priests, men and women religious, lay men and women advises the Administrative Board on overall plans and operations of the USCC.

The administrative general secretariat, in addition to other duties, supervises staff-service offices of Finance and Administration, General Counsel, Government Liaison, and Research, Plans and Programs.

Most of the organizations and associations affiliated with the USCC are covered in separate Almanac entries.

## 1983 MEETING OF THE U.S. BISHOPS

More than 250 bishops attended the annual meeting of the National Conference of Catholic Bishops and the U.S. Catholic Conference Nov. 14 to 17, 1983, in Washington, D.C.

Bishop James W. Malone of Youngstown and Archbishop John L. May of St. Louis were elected, respectively, to three-year terms as president and vice president of the conferences.

### Items of Business

Items on the agenda of the meeting included the following.

**Budget:** With only one dissenting vote, bishops of dioceses approved a $23.9 million budget for operations of the conferences in 1984. A 12.5-cent assessment per Catholic in each diocese was endorsed for 1985.

**Canonical Measures:** The bishops endorsed recommendations of their Committee on Canonical Affairs, in light of the revised Code, to:

• continue, at least temporarily, current practice regarding the age of reception of the sacrament of confirmation;

• allow diocesan bishops the option of limiting tenure for pastors;
• have lay persons as judges on diocesan tribunals;
• permit diocesan bishops to entrust first trials of some diocesan court cases to single judges;
• seek permission of the Holy See to let auxiliary bishops vote on conference statutes.

**Hispanics:** Unanimous approval was given a pastoral letter entitled "The Hispanic Presence: Challenge and Commitment." (See separate coverage for text).

**Holy Days:** Retention of the six holy days of obligation customarily observed in the U.S. was approved.

**Letters in Work:** Reports were presented on plans and progress with respect to the development of pastoral letters on: (1) Catholic social teaching and the American economy, with a first draft due by November, 1984; (2) the role of women in the Church and society, with completion predicted in perhaps four years.

• **Liturgy:** "The Church at Prayer — A Holy Temple of the Lord" marked the 20th anniversary of the Second Vatican Council's *Constitution on the Sacred Liturgy,* evaluated its impact in the life of the Church and sketched unfinished items of liturgical renewal.

**Meetings:** It was agreed to return to two meetings a year, beginning in 1985, and to extend the time of each meeting by a day. Also endorsed was the scheduling of another 10-day, retreat-type of assembly in 1986; the first such assembly was held in 1982.

**Objectives:** A set of 33 objectives was adopted for the guidance of operations of the conferences. The 10 "primary objectives" were listed as follows.

• "to support and promote the Pope's universal teaching authority and leadership;
• "to promote collegial identity and fraternal support among the bishops of the United States;
• "to teach Catholic doctrine where collective teaching by the bishops is needed and to offer the bishops evaluations of theological trends and individual theological positions;
• "to discern, identify and clarify the call of church members to collaborate in carrying out the Church's mission, with particular attention to full participation by lay men and women and to the

sharing of responsibility for this mission by clergy, Religious and laity;
• "to encourage the development and assist in the implementation of pastoral and spiritual programs responsive to changing conditions of the contemporary world;
• "to encourge vocations to the priesthood, diaconate and religious life, and to collaborate with national Catholic organizations concerned with vocations;
• "to engage in ecumenical and interreligious dialogue and cooperation;
• to teach respect for all human life and organize for its protection, especially in behalf of the unborn, the elderly and the handicapped;
• "to educate, sensitize and encourage attitudinal and behavioral change among the members of the Church on issues of justice and peace — especially the need to eradicate injustice based on race or sex — and thereby establish a foundation for their action on such issues, and
• "to advocate and set policy for the NCCB-USCC on social justice problems and structural reform in society, with a preferential option for the poor."

**Reports and Statements** included the following.
• Central America: The bishops pledged solidarity with their fellow bishops, especially in El Salvador and Nicaragua, and appealed for dialogue-for-reconciliation among parties in conflict, free and fair elections of officials, and the withdrawal of outside military and ideological forces.
• Christian Churches in the Middle East: They were said to be "drowning in an ocean of Islam and non-belief."
• Religious: Archbishop John R. Quinn reported that the ongoing, Vatican-mandated study of men and women Religious was intended to be a dialogue of trust, charity and listening, for the purpose of enabling bishops to be of "pastoral service" to Religious.
• Ukrainian Genocide: A 50th anniversary endorsement was given to a statement recalling the unreported or under-reported starvation of seven million Ukrainians by the government of the U.S.S.R. in 1932-33.
• War and Peace Pastoral: "Unprecedented" ecumenical interest in "The Challenge of Peace: God's Promise and Our Response" was reported. Also reported was the printing of between one and 1.5 million copies in the six months following its publication in May, 1983.

# STATE CATHOLIC CONFERENCES

*These conferences are agencies of bishops and dioceses in the various states. Their general purposes are to develop and sponsor cooperative programs designed to cope with pastoral and common-welfare needs, and to represent the dioceses before governmental bodies, the public, and in private sectors. Their membership consists of representatives from the dioceses in the states — bishops, clergy and lay persons in various capacities.*

The **National Association of State Catholic Con-**ference Directors maintains liaison with the general secretariat of the United States Catholic Conference. Bro. Richard Daly, C.S.C., executive director of the Texas Catholic Conference, is president.

**Arizona** Catholic Conference, 400 E. Monroe St., Phoenix, Ariz. 85004; exec. dir., Thomas F. Allt.

**California** Catholic Conference, 926 J St., Suite 1100, Sacramento, Calif. 95814; exec. dir., Most Rev. William J. Levada.

**Colorado** Catholic Conference, 200 Josephine

St., Denver, Colo. 80206; exec. dir., Sr. Loretto Anne Madden, S.L.

**Connecticut** Catholic Conference, 134 Farmington Ave., Hartford, Conn. 06105; exec. dir., William Wholean.

**Florida** Catholic Conference, P.O. Box 1571, Tallahassee, Fla. 32302; exec. dir., Thomas A. Horkan, Jr.

**Georgia** Catholic Conference, Sussex Pl., Suite 2129, First Atlanta Tower, Atlanta, Ga. 30383; exec. dir., Cheatham E. Hodges, Jr.

**Hawaii** Catholic Conference, 1184 Bishop St., Honolulu, H.I. 96813; exec. sec., Rev. Daniel Dever.

**Illinois** Catholic Conference, One East Superior St., Chicago, Ill. 60611; 300 E. Monroe St., Springfield, Ill. 62701; exec. dir., Rev. John J. Quinn.

**Indiana** Catholic Conference, 1400 N. Meridian St., P.O. Box 1410, Indianapolis, Ind. 46206; exec. dir., M. Desmond Ryan.

**Iowa** Catholic Conference, 818 Insurance Exchange Building, Des Moines, Iowa 50309; exec. dir., Timothy McCarthy.

**Kansas** Catholic Conference, 702 Commercial National Bank Bldg., Kansas City, Kan. 66101; exec. dir., Robert Runnels, Jr.

**Kentucky** Catholic Conference, P.O. Box 1073, Louisville, Ky. 40201; exec. dir., Ken Dupre.

**Louisiana** Catholic Conference: P.O. Box 52948, New Orleans, La. 70152; exec. dir., Emile Comar.

**Maryland** Catholic Conference, 5400 Roland Ave., Baltimore, Md. 21210; exec. dir., Rev. Roger A. Emmert.

**Massachusetts** Catholic Conference, 60 School St., Boston, Mass. 02107; exec. dir., Gerald D. D'Avolio, Esq.

**Michigan** Catholic Conference, 505 N. Capitol Ave., Lansing, Mich. 48933.

**Minnesota** Catholic Conference, 296 Chester St., St. Paul, Minn. 55107; exec. dir., Rev. Msgr. James D. Habiger.

**Missouri** Catholic Conference, P.O. Box 1022, Jefferson City, Mo. 65102; exec. dir., Louis C. DeFeo, Jr.

**Montana** Catholic Conference, P.O. Box 1708, Helena, Mont. 59624; exec. dir., John L. Ortwein.

**Nebraska** Catholic Conference, 521 S. 14th St., Lincoln, Nebr. 68508; exec. dir., James R. Cunningham.

**New Jersey** Catholic Conference, 211 N. Warren St., Trenton, N.J. 08618; exec. dir., Edward J. Leadem.

**New York** State Catholic Conference, 11 N. Pearl St., Albany, N.Y. 12207; exec. dir., J. Alan Davitt.

**North Dakota** Catholic Conference, 227 West Broadway Suite No. 2, Bismarck, N. Dak. 58501; exec. dir., Mrs. Corrine Engelstad.

**Ohio,** Catholic Conference of, 35 E. Gay St., Suite 502, Columbus, Ohio 43215; exec. dir., Nelson N. Harper.

**Oregon** Catholic Conference, 2838 E. Burnside, Portland, Ore. 97214; sec., Rev. Gregory Moys.

**Pennsylvania** Catholic Conference, 223 North St., Box 2835, Harrisburg, Pa. 17105; exec. dir., Howard J. Fetterhoff.

**Texas** Catholic Conference, 3001 S. Congress Ave., Austin, Tex. 78704; exec. dir., Bro. Richard Daly, C.S.C.

**Washington** State Catholic Conference, 1402 3rd Ave., Suite 618, Seattle, Wash. 98101; exec. dir. Rev. D. Harvey McIntyre.

**Wisconsin** Catholic Conference, 30 W. Mifflin St., Suite 910, Madison, Wis. 53703; exec. dir., Charles M. Phillips.

# BIOGRAPHIES OF AMERICAN BISHOPS

(Sources: Almanac survey, *The Official Catholic Directory*, NC News Service. As of Aug. 15, 1984.)

## A

**Abramowicz, Alfred L.:** b. Jan. 27, 1919, Chicago, Ill.; educ. St. Mary of the Lake Seminary (Mundelein, Ill.), Gregorian Univ. (Rome); ord. priest May 1, 1943; ord. titular bishop of Paestum and auxiliary bishop of Chicago, June 13, 1968.

**Acerra, Angelo Thomas, O.S.B.:** b. Nov. 7, 1925, Memphis, Tenn.; educ. St. Benedict's (Atchison, Kans.), Catholic Univ. (Washington, D.C.), St. Mary's Univ. (San Antonio, Tex.), Univ. of Northern Colorado (Greeley, Colo.), Angelicum (Rome); ord. priest May 20, 1950; ord. titular bishop of Lete and auxiliary bishop of the Military Vicariate, Nov. 29, 1983; vicar for the Far East.

**Ackerman, Richard Henry, C.S.Sp.:** b. Aug. 30, 1903, Pittsburgh, Pa.; educ. Duquesne Univ. (Pittsburgh, Pa.), St. Mary's Scholasticate (Norwalk, Conn.), Univ. of Fribourg (Switzerland); ord. priest Aug. 28, 1926; ord. titular bishop of Lares and auxiliary bishop of San Diego, May 22,

1956; app. bishop of Covington, Apr. 4, 1960; resigned Nov. 28, 1978.

**Ahern, Patrick V.:** b. Mar. 8, 1919, New York, N.Y.; educ. Manhattan College and Cathedral College (New York City), St. Joseph's Seminary (Yonkers, N.Y.), St. Louis Univ. (St. Louis, Mo.), Notre Dame Univ. (Notre Dame, Ind.); ord. priest Jan. 27, 1945; ord. titular bishop of Naiera and auxiliary bishop of New York, Mar. 19, 1970.

**Ahr, George William:** b. June 23, 1904, Newark, N.J.; educ. St. Vincent College (Latrobe, Pa.), Seton Hall College (S. Orange, N.J.), North American College (Rome); ord. priest July 29, 1928; ord. bishop of Trenton, Mar. 20, 1950; resigned June 23, 1979.

**Anderson, Moses B., S.S.E.:** b. Sept. 9, 1928, Selma, Ala.; educ. St. Michael's College (Winooski, Vt.), St. Edmund Seminary (Burlington, Vt.), Univ. of Legon (Ghana); ord. priest May 30, 1958; ord. titular bishop of Vatarba and auxiliary bishop of Detroit, Jan. 27, 1983.

**Anderson, Paul F.:** b. Apr. 20, 1917, Roslindale, Mass.; educ. Boston College (Chestnut Hill, Mass.), St. John's Seminary (Brighton, Mass.); ord. priest Jan. 6, 1943; ord. titular bishop of

Polignano and coadjutor bishop of Duluth, Oct. 17, 1968; bishop of Duluth, Apr. 30, 1969; resigned August 17, 1982; app. auxiliary bishop of Sioux Falls.

**Angell, Kenneth A.:** b. Aug. 3, 1930, Providence, R.I.; educ. St. Mary's Seminary (Baltimore, Md.); ord. priest May 26, 1956; ord. titular bishop of Septimunicia and auxiliary bishop of Providence, R.I., Oct. 7, 1974.

**Apuron, Anthony Sablan, O.F.M. Cap.:** b. Nov. 1, 1945, Agana, Guam; educ. St. Anthony College and Capuchin Seminary (Hudson, N.H.), Capuchin Seminary (Garrison, N.Y.), Maryknoll Seminary (New York), Notre Dame Univ. (Notre Dame, Ind.); ord. priest Aug. 26, 1972, in Guam; ord. titular bishop of Muzuca in Proconsulari and auxiliary bishop of Agana, Guam, Feb. 19, 1984.

**Arias, David, O.A.R.:** b. July 22, 1929, Leon, Spain; educ. St. Rita's College (San Sebastian, Spain), Our Lady of Good Counsel Theologate (Granada, Spain), Teresianum Institute (Rome, Italy); ord. priest May 31, 1952; ord. titular bishop of Badie and auxiliary bishop of Newark, Apr. 7, 1983; episcopal vicar for Hispanic affairs.

**Arkfeld, Leo, S.V.D.:** b. Feb. 4, 1912, Butte, Nebr.; educ. Divine Word Seminary (Techny, Ill.), Sacred Heart College (Girard, Pa.); ord. priest Aug. 15, 1943; ord. titular bishop of Bucellus and vicar apostolic of Central New Guinea, Nov. 30, 1948; name of vicariate changed to Wewak, May 15, 1952; first bishop of Wewak, Nov. 15, 1966; app. archbishop of Madang, Papua New Guinea, Dec. 19, 1975.

**Arliss, Reginald, C.P.:** b. Sept. 8, 1906, East Orange, N.J.; educ. Immaculate Conception Seminary (Jamaica, N.Y.) and other Passionist houses of study; ord. priest Apr. 28, 1934; missionary in China for 16 years, expelled 1951; missionary in Philippines; rector of the Pontifical Philippine College Seminary in Rome, 1961-69; ord. titular bishop of Cerbali and prelate of Marbel, Philippines (now a diocese), Jan. 30, 1970; resigned from titular see and prelature, Oct. 1, 1981.

**Arzube, Juan A.:** b. June 1, 1918, Guayaquil, Ecuador; educ. Rensselaer Polytechnic Institute (Troy, N.Y.), St. John's Seminary (Camarillo, Calif.); ord. priest May 5, 1954; ord. titular bishop of Civitate and auxiliary bishop of Los Angeles, Mar. 25, 1971.

## B

**Balke, Victor:** b. Sept. 29, 1931, Meppen, Ill.; educ. St. Mary of the Lake Seminary (Mundelein, Ill.), St. Louis Univ. (St. Louis, Mo.); ord. priest May 24, 1958; ord. bishop of Crookston, Sept. 2, 1976.

**Baltakis, Paul Antanas, O.F.M.:** b. Jan. 1, 1925, Troskunai, Lithuania; educ. seminaries of the Franciscan Province of St. Joseph (Belgium); ord. priest Aug. 24, 1952, in Belgium; served in U.S. as director of Lithuanian Cultural Center, New York, and among Lithuanian youth; head of U.S. Lithuanian Franciscan Vicariate, Kennebunkport, Maine, from 1979; ord. titular bishop of Egara, Sept. 24, 1984; assigned to pastoral assistance to Lithuanian Catholics living outside Lithuania.

**Baum, William W.:** (See Cardinals, Biographies.)

**Begley, Michael J.:** b. Mar. 12, 1909, Mattineague, Mass.; educ. Mt. St. Mary Seminary (Emmitsburg, Md.); ord. priest May 26, 1934; ord. first bishop of Charlotte, N.C., Jan. 12, 1972; retired May 29, 1984.

**Beltran, Eusebius J.:** b. Aug. 31, 1934, Ashley, Pa.; educ. St. Charles Seminary (Philadelphia, Pa.); ord. priest May 14, 1960; ord. bishop of Tulsa, Apr. 20, 1978.

**Benincasa, Pius A.:** b. July 8, 1913, Niagara Falls, N.Y.: educ. Propaganda Univ. and Lateran Univ. (Rome); ord. priest Mar. 27, 1937; served in Vatican Secretariat of State, 1954-64; ord. titular bishop of Buruni and auxiliary bishop of Buffalo, June 29, 1964.

**Bernardin, Joseph L.:** (See Cardinals, Biographies.)

**Bernarding, George, S.V.D.:** b. Feb. 15, 1912, Carrick, Pa.; educ. Divine Word Seminary (Girard, Pa.); ord. priest Aug. 13, 1939; ord. titular bishop of Belabitene and first vicar apostolic of Mount Hagen, New Guinea, Apr. 21, 1960; first bishop of Mount Hagen, Nov. 15, 1966; app. first archbishop Mar. 29, 1982, when see was elevated to metropolitan rank.

**Bevilacqua, Anthony J.:** b. June 17, 1923, Brooklyn, N.Y.; educ. Cathedral College (Brooklyn, N.Y.), Immaculate Conception Seminary (Huntington, N.Y.), Gregorian Univ. (Rome), Columbia Univ. and St. John's Univ. (New York); ord. priest June 11, 1949; ord. titular bishop of Aquae Albae in Byzacena and auxiliary bishop of Brooklyn, Nov. 24, 1980; app. bishop of Pittsburgh Oct. 7, 1983, installed Dec. 11, 1983.

**Bilock, John M.:** b. June 20, 1916, McAdoo, Pa.; educ. St. Procopius College and Seminary (Lisle, Ill.); ord. priest Feb. 3, 1946; vicar general of Byzantine archdiocese of Munhall, 1969; ord. titular bishop of Pergamum and auxiliary bishop of Munhall, May 15, 1973; title of see changed to Pittsburgh, 1977.

**Boccella, John H., T.O.R.:** b. June 25, 1912, Castelfranci, Italy; came to U.S. at the age of two; educ. St. Francis College and Seminary (Loretto, Pa.), Angelicum Univ. (Rome), Catholic Univ. (Washington, D.C.); ord. priest Mar. 29, 1941; minister general of Third Order Regular, 1947-65; ord. archbishop of Izmir, Turkey, Apr. 17, 1968; transferred to titular see of Ephesus, Dec. 7, 1978 (resides in Rome).

**Boland, Ernest B., O.P.:** b. July 10, 1925, Providence, R.I.; educ. Providence College (Rhode Island), Dominican Houses of Study (Somerset, Ohio; Washington, D.C.); ord. priest June 9, 1955; ord. bishop of Multan, Pakistan, July 25, 1966.

**Borders, William D.:** b. Oct. 9, 1913, Washington, Ind.; educ. St. Meinrad Seminary (St. Meinrad, Ind.), Notre Dame Seminary (New Orleans, La.), Notre Dame Univ. (Notre Dame, Ind.); ord. priest May 18, 1940; ord. first bishop of Orlando, June 14, 1968; app. archbishop of Baltimore, Apr. 2, 1974, installed June 26, 1974.

**Bosco, Anthony G.:** b. Aug. 1, 1927, New Castle, Pa.; educ. St. Vincent Seminary (Latrobe, Pa.),

Lateran Univ. (Rome); ord. priest June 7, 1952; ord. titular bishop of Labicum and auxiliary of Pittsburgh, June 30, 1970.

**Boudreaux, Warren L.:** b. Jan. 25, 1918, Berwick, La.; educ. St. Joseph's Seminary (St. Benedict, La.), St. Sulpice Seminary (Paris, France), Notre Dame Seminary (New Orleans, La.), Catholic Univ. (Washington, D.C.); ord. priest May 30, 1942; ord. titular bishop of Calynda and auxiliary bishop of Lafayette, La., July 25, 1962; app. bishop of Beaumont, June 5, 1971; app. first bishop of Houma-Thibodaux, installed June 5, 1977.

**Breitenbeck, Joseph M.:** b. Aug. 3, 1914, Detroit, Mich.; educ. University of Detroit, Sacred Heart Seminary (Detroit, Mich.), North American College and Lateran Univ. (Rome), Catholic Univ. (Washington, D.C.); ord. priest May 30, 1942; ord. titular bishop of Tepelta and auxiliary bishop of Detroit, Dec. 20, 1965; app. bishop of Grand Rapids, Oct. 15, 1969, installed Dec. 2, 1969.

**Brizgys, Vincas:** b. Nov. 10, 1903, Plyniai, Lithuania; ord. priest June 5, 1927; ord. titular bishop of Bosano and auxiliary bishop of Kaunas, Lithuania, May 10, 1940; taken into custody and deported to Germany, 1944; liberated by Americans, 1945; U.S. citizen, 1958.

**Broderick, Edwin B.:** b. Jan. 16, 1917, New York, N.Y.; educ. Cathedral College (New York City), St. Joseph's Seminary (Yonkers, N.Y.), Fordham Univ. (New York City); ord. priest May 30, 1942; ord. titular bishop of Tizica and auxiliary of New York, Apr. 21, 1967; bishop of Albany, 1969-76; executive director of Catholic Relief Services, 1976-82.

**Brom, Robert H.:** b. Sept. 18, 1938, Arcadia, Wis.; educ. St. Mary's College (Winona, Minn.), Gregorian Univ. (Rome); ord. priest Dec. 18, 1963, in Rome; ord. bishop of Duluth, May 23, 1983.

**Brown, Charles A., M.M.:** b. Aug. 20, 1919, New York, N.Y.; educ. Cathedral College (New York City), Maryknoll Seminary (Maryknoll, N.Y.); ord. priest June 9, 1946; ord. titular bishop of Vallis and auxiliary bishop of Santa Cruz, Bolivia, Mar. 27, 1957.

**Brunini, Joseph B.:** b. July 24, 1909, Vicksburg, Miss.; educ. Georgetown Univ. (Washington, D.C.), North American College (Rome), Catholic Univ. (Washington, D.C.); ord. priest Dec. 5, 1933; ord. titular bishop of Axomis and auxiliary bishop of Natchez-Jackson, Jan. 29, 1957; apostolic administrator of Natchez-Jackson, 1966; app. bishop of Natchez-Jackson, Dec. 2, 1967, installed Jan. 29, 1968; title of see changed to Jackson, 1977; retired Jan. 24, 1984.

**Brust, Leo J.:** b. Jan. 7, 1916, St. Francis, Wis.; educ. St. Francis Seminary (Milwaukee, Wis.), Canisianum (Innsbruck, Austria), Catholic Univ. (Washington, D.C.); ord. priest May 30, 1942; ord. titular bishop of Suelli and auxiliary bishop of Milwaukee. Oct. 16, 1969.

**Brzana, Stanislaus J.:** b. July 1, 1917, Buffalo, N.Y.; educ. Christ the King Seminary (St. Bonaventure, N.Y.), Gregorian Univ. (Rome); ord. priest June 7, 1941; ord. titular bishop of Cufruta

and auxiliary bishop of Buffalo, June 29, 1964; bishop of Ogdensburg, Oct. 22, 1968.

**Bullock, William H.:** b. Apr. 13, 1927, Maple Lake, Minn.; educ. St. Thomas College and St. Paul Seminary (St. Paul, Minn.), Notre Dame Univ. (Notre Dame, Ind.); ord. priest June 7, 1952; ord. titular bishop of Natchez and auxiliary bishop of St. Paul and Minneapolis, Aug. 12, 1980.

**Burke, James C., O.P.:** b. Nov. 30, 1926, Philadelphia, Pa.; educ. King's College (Wilkes-Barre, Pa.), Providence College (R.I.); ord. priest June 8, 1956; ord. titular bishop of Lamiggiga and prelate of Chimbote, Peru, May 25, 1967, resigned from prelature, June 8, 1978. Vicar for urban affairs, Wilmington, Del., diocese.

**Buswell, Charles A.:** b. Oct. 15, 1913, Homestead, Okla.; educ. St. Louis Preparatory Seminary (St. Louis, Mo.), Kenrick Seminary (Webster Groves, Mo.), American College, Univ. of Louvain (Belgium); ord. priest July 9, 1939; ord. bishop of Pueblo, Sept. 30, 1959; resigned Sept. 18, 1979.

**Byrne, James J.:** b. July 28, 1908, St. Paul, Minn.; educ. Nazareth Hall Preparatory Seminary and St. Paul Seminary (St. Paul, Minn.), Univ. of Minnesota (Minneapolis, Minn.); Louvain Univ. (Belgium); ord. priest June 3, 1933; ord. titular bishop of Etenna and auxiliary bishop of St. Paul, July 2, 1947; app. bishop of Boise, June 16, 1956; app. archbishop of Dubuque, Mar. 19, 1962, installed May 8, 1962; retired Aug. 23, 1983.

## C

**Caesar, Raymond R., S.V.D.:** b. Feb. 14, 1932, Eunice, La.; educ. Divine Word Seminary (Bay St. Louis, Miss.); Catholic Univ. (Washington, D.C.); ord. priest June 4, 1961; missionary in New Guinea from 1962; ord. coadjutor bishop of Goroka, Papua New Guinea, Oct. 25, 1978; bishop of Goroko, Aug. 30, 1980.

**Caillouet, L. Abel.:** b. Aug. 2, 1900, Thibodaux, La.; educ. St. Joseph's Preparatory Seminary (St. Benedict, La.), St. Mary's Seminary (Baltimore, Md.), North American College (Rome); ord. priest Mar. 7, 1925; ord. titular bishop of Setea and auxiliary bishop of New Orleans, Oct. 28, 1947; retired July 7, 1976.

**Carberry, John J.:** (See Cardinals, Biographies.)

**Carlson, Robert J.:** b. June 30, 1944, Minneapolis, Minn.; educ. Nazareth Hall and St. Paul Seminary (St. Paul, Minn.), Catholic Univ. (Washington, D.C.): ord. priest May 23, 1970; ord. titular bishop of Avioccala and auxiliary bishop of St. Paul and Minneapolis, Jan. 11, 1984; vicar of eastern vicariate.

**Carroll, Mark K.:** b. Nov. 19, 1806, St. Louis, Mo.; educ. St. Louis Preparatory Seminary and Kenrick Seminary (St. Louis, Mo.); ord. priest June 10, 1922; ord. bishop of Wichita, Apr. 23, 1947; retired, 1963, but retained title; resigned, 1967.

**Casey, James V.:** b. Sept. 22, 1914, Osage, Ia.; educ. Loras College (Dubuque, Ia.), North American College (Rome), Catholic Univ. (Washington, D.C.); ord. priest Dec. 8, 1939; ord. titular bishop of Citium and auxiliary bishop of Lincoln, Apr. 24, 1957; bishop of Lincoln, June 14, 1957; app. archbishop of Denver, Feb. 22, 1967, installed May 17, 1967.

**Casey, Luis Morgan:** b. June 23, 1935, Portageville, Mo.; ord. priest Apr. 7, 1962; missionary in Bolivia from 1965; app. titular bishop of Mibiarca and auxiliary of La Paz, Nov. 3, 1983.

**Cassata, John J.:** b. Nov. 8, 1908, Galveston, Tex.; educ. St. Mary's Seminary (La Porte, Tex.), North American College, Urban Univ. and Gregorian Univ. (Rome); ord. priest Dec. 8, 1932; ord. titular bishop of Bida and auxiliary bishop of Dallas-Fort Worth, June 5, 1968; app. bishop of Fort Worth, Aug. 27, 1969, installed Oct. 21, 1969; retired Sept. 16, 1980.

**Chavez, Gilbert Espinoza:** b. May 9, 1932, Ontario, Calif.; educ. St. Francis Seminary (El Cajon, Calif.), Immaculate Heart Seminary (San Diego), Univ. of California; ord. priest Mar. 19, 1960; ord. titular bishop of Magarmel and auxiliary of San Diego, June 21, 1974.

**Chedid, John:** b. July 4, 1923, Eddid, Lebanon; educ. seminaries in Lebanon and Pontifical Urban College (Rome); ord. priest Dec. 21, 1951, in Rome; ord. titular bishop of Callinico and auxiliary bishop of St. Maron of Brooklyn for the Maronites, Jan. 25, 1981.

**Clark, Matthew H.:** b. July 15, 1937, Troy, N.Y.; educ. St. Bernard's Seminary (Rochester, N.Y.), Gregorian Univ. (Rome); ord. priest Dec. 19, 1962; ord. bishop of Rochester, May 27, 1979; installed June 26, 1979.

**Clinch, Harry A.:** b. Oct. 27, 1908, San Anselmo, Calif.; educ. St. Joseph's College (Mountain View, Calif.), St. Patrick's Seminary (Menlo Park, Calif.); ord. priest June 6, 1936; ord. titular bishop of Badiae and auxiliary bishop of Monterey-Fresno, Feb. 27, 1957; app. first bishop of Monterey in California, installed Dec. 14, 1967; resigned Jan. 19, 1982.

**Cohill, John Edward, S.V.D.:** b. Dec. 13, 1907, Elizabeth, N.J.; educ. Divine Word Seminary (Techny, Ill.); ord. priest Mar. 20, 1936; ord. first bishop of Goroko, Papua New Guinea, Mar. 11, 1967; resigned Aug. 30, 1980.

**Comber, John W., M.M.:** b. Mar. 12, 1906, Lawrence, Mass.; educ. St. John's Preparatory College (Danvers, Mass.), Boston College (Boston, Mass.), Maryknoll Seminary (Maryknoll, N.Y.); ord. priest Feb. 1, 1931; superior general of Maryknoll, 1956-66; ord. titular bishop of Foratiana, Apr. 9, 1959.

**Connare, William G.:** b. Dec. 11, 1911, Pittsburgh, Pa.; educ. Duquesne Univ. (Pittsburgh, Pa.), St. Vincent Seminary (Latrobe, Pa.); ord. priest June 14, 1936; ord. bishop of Greensburg, May 4, 1960.

**Connolly, James L.:** b. Nov. 15, 1894, Fall River, Mass.; educ. St. Charles College (Catonsville, Md.), St. Mary's Seminary (Baltimore, Md.), Catholic Univ. (Washington, D.C.), Louvain Univ. (Belgium); ord. priest Dec. 21, 1923; rector of St. Paul (Minn.) minor seminary 1940-43, major seminary 1943-45; ord. titular bishop of Mylasa and coadjutor of Fall River, May 24, 1945; bishop of Fall River, May 17, 1951; resigned Oct. 30, 1970.

**Connolly, Thomas Arthur:** b. Oct. 5, 1899, San Francisco, Calif.; educ. St. Patrick's Seminary (Menlo Park, Calif.), Catholic Univ. (Washington, D.C.); ord. priest June 11, 1926; ord. titular bishop of Sila and auxiliary bishop of San Francisco, Aug. 24, 1939; app. coadjutor bishop of Seattle, Feb. 28, 1948; succeeded as bishop of Seattle, May 18, 1950; first archbishop of Seattle, June 23, 1951; retired Feb. 25, 1975.

**Connolly, Thomas J.:** b. July 18, 1922, Tonopah, Nev.; educ. St. Patrick's Seminary (Menlo Park, Calif.), Catholic Univ. (Washington, D.C.), Lateran Univ. (Rome); ord. priest Apr. 8, 1947; ord. bishop of Baker, June 30, 1971.

**Connors, Ronald G., C.SS.R.:** b. Nov. 1, 1915, Brooklyn, N.Y.; ord. priest June 22, 1941; ord. titular bishop of Equizetum and coadjutor bishop of San Juan de la Maguana, Dominican Republic, July 20, 1976; succeeded as bishop of San Juan de la Maguana, July 20, 1977.

**Cooney, Patrick R.:** b. Mar. 10, 1934, Detroit, Mich.; educ. Sacred Heart Seminary (Detroit), Gregorian Univ. (Rome), Notre Dame Univ. (Notre Dame, Ind.); ord. priest Dec. 20, 1959; ord. titular bishop of Hodelm and auxiliary bishop of Detroit, Jan. 27, 1983.

**Coscia, Benedict Dominic, O.F.M.:** b. Aug. 10, 1922, Brooklyn, N.Y.; educ. St. Francis College (Brooklyn, N.Y.), Holy Name College (Washington, D.C.); ord. priest June 11, 1949; ord. bishop of Jataí, Brazil, Sept. 21, 1961.

**Cosgrove, William M.:** b. Nov. 26, 1916, Canton, Ohio; educ. John Carroll Univ. (Cleveland, O.); ord. priest Dec. 18, 1943; ord. titular bishop of Trisipa and auxiliary bishop of Cleveland, Sept. 3, 1968; app. bishop of Belleville, installed Oct. 28, 1976; retired May 19, 1981.

**Costello, Thomas J.:** b. Feb. 23, 1929, Camden, N.Y.; educ. Niagara Univ. (Niagara Falls, N.Y.), St. Bernard's Seminary (Rochester, N.Y.), Catholic Univ. (Washington, D.C.); ord. priest June 5, 1954; ord. titular bishop of Perdices and auxiliary bishop of Syracuse Mar. 13, 1978.

**Cotey, Arnold R., S.D.S.:** b. June 15, 1921, Milwaukee, Wis.; educ. Divine Savior Seminary (Lanham, Md.), Marquette Univ. (Milwaukee, Wis.); ord. priest June 7, 1949; ord. first bishop of Nachingwea, Tanzania, Oct. 20, 1963; retired Nov. 11, 1983.

**Cousins, William E.:** b. Aug. 20, 1902, Chicago, Ill.; educ. Quigley Seminary (Chicago, Ill.), St. Mary of the Lake Seminary (Mundelein, Ill.); ord. priest Apr. 23, 1927; ord. titular bishop of Forma and auxiliary bishop of Chicago, Mar. 7, 1949; app. bishop of Peoria, May 21, 1952; archbishop of Milwaukee, Jan. 27, 1959; retired Jan. 17, 1977.

**Cronin, Daniel A.:** b. Nov. 14, 1927, Newton, Mass.; educ. St. John's Seminary (Boston, Mass.), North American College and Gregorian Univ. (Rome); ord. priest Dec. 20, 1952; attaché apostolic nunciature (Addis Ababa), 1957-61; served in papal Secretariat of State, 1961-68; ord. titular bishop of Egnatia and auxiliary bishop of Boston, Sept. 12, 1968; bishop of Fall River, Dec. 16, 1970.

**Crowley, Joseph R.:** b. Jan. 12, 1915, Fort Wayne, Ind.; educ. St. Mary's College (St. Mary, Ky.), St. Meinrad Seminary (St. Meinrad, Ind.);

served in US Air Force, 1942-46; ord. priest May 1, 1953; editor of *Our Sunday Visitor* 1958-67; ord. titular bishop of Maraguis and auxiliary bishop of Fort Wayne-South Bend, Aug. 24, 1971.

**Cummins, John S.:** b. Mar. 3, 1928, Oakland, Calif.; educ. St. Patrick's Seminary (Menlo Park, Calif.), Catholic Univ. (Washington, D.C.), Univ. of California; ord. priest Jan. 24, 1953; executive director of the California Catholic Conference 1971-76; ord. titular bishop of Lambaesis and auxiliary bishop of Sacramento, May 16, 1974; app. bishop of Oakland, installed June 30, 1977.

**Curtis, Walter W.:** b. May 3, 1913, Jersey City, N.J.; educ. Fordham Univ. (New York City), Seton Hall Univ. (South Orange, N.J.), Immaculate Conception Seminary (Darlington, N.J.), North American College and Gregorian Univ. (Rome), Catholic Univ. (Washington, D.C.); ord. priest Dec. 8, 1937; ord. titular bishop of Bisica and auxiliary bishop of Newark, Sept. 24, 1957; app. bishop of Bridgeport, 1961, installed Nov. 21, 1961.

**Curtiss, Elden F.:** b. June 16, 1932, Baker, Ore.; educ. St. Edward Seminary College and St. Thomas Seminary (Kenmore, Wash.); ord. priest May 24, 1958; ord. bishop of Helena, Mont., Apr. 28, 1976.

## D

**Daily, Thomas V.:** b. Sept. 23, 1927, Belmont, Mass.; educ. Boston College, St. John's Seminary (Brighton, Mass.); ord. priest Jan. 10, 1952; missionary in Peru for five years as a member of the Society of St. James the Apostle; ord. titular bishop of Bladia and auxiliary bishop of Boston, Feb. 11, 1975; app. first bishop of Palm Beach, Fla., July 17, 1984.

**Daly, James:** b. Aug. 14, 1921, New York, N.Y.; educ. Cathedral College (Brooklyn, N.Y.), Immaculate Conception Seminary (Huntington, L.I.); ord. priest May 22, 1948; ord. titular bishop of Castra Nova and auxiliary bishop of Rockville Centre, May 9, 1977.

**Danglmayr, Augustine:** b. Dec. 11, 1898, Muenster, Tex.; educ. Subiaco College (Arkansas), St. Mary's Seminary (La Porte, Tex.), Kenrick Seminary (St. Louis, Mo.); ord. priest June 10, 1922; ord. titular bishop of Olba, Oct. 7, 1942; auxiliary bishop of Dallas-Ft. Worth, 1942-69.

**D'Antonio, Nicholas, O.F.M.:** b. July 10, 1916, Rochester, N.Y.; educ. St. Anthony's Friary (Catskill, N.Y.); ord. priest June 7, 1942; ord. titular bishop of Giufi Salaria and prelate of Olancho, Honduras, July 25, 1966; resigned 1977; app. vicar general of New Orleans archdiocese and episcopal vicar for Spanish Speaking, August, 1977.

**D'Arcy, John M.:** b. Aug. 18, 1932, Brighton, Mass.; educ. St. John's Seminary (Brighton, Mass.), Angelicum Univ. (Rome); ord. priest Feb. 2, 1957; spiritual director of St. John's Seminary; ord. titular bishop of Mediana and auxiliary bishop of Boston, Feb. 11, 1975.

**Davis, James Peter:** b. June 9, 1904, Houghton, Mich.; educ. St. Joseph's College (Mountain View, Calif.), St. Patrick's Seminary (Menlo Park, Calif.); ord. priest May 19, 1929; ord. bishop of San Juan, Puerto Rico, Oct. 6, 1943; app. first arch-

bishop of San Juan, July 30, 1960; app. archbishop of Santa Fe, installed Feb. 25, 1964; resigned June 4, 1974.

**Dearden, John Francis:** (See Cardinals, Biographies.)

**Deksnys, Antanas L.:** b. May 9, 1906, Buteniskiai, Lithuania; educ. Metropolitan Seminary and Theological and Philosophical Faculty at Vytautas the Great Univ. (all at Kaunas, Lithuania), Univ. of Fribourg (Switzerland); ord. priest May 30, 1931; served in U.S. parishes at Mt. Carmel, Pa., and East St. Louis, Ill.; ord. titular bishop of Lavellum, June 15, 1969; assigned to pastoral work among Lithuanians in Western Europe; retired June 5, 1984.

**Delaney, Joseph P.:** b. Aug. 29, 1934, Fall River, Mass.; educ. Cardinal O'Connell Seminary (Boston, Mass.), Theological College (Washington, D.C.), North American College (Rome), Rhode Island College (Providence, R.I.); ord. priest Dec. 18, 1960; ord. bishop of Fort Worth, Tex., Sept. 13, 1981.

**Dempsey, Michael J., O.P.:** b. Feb. 22, 1912, Providence, R.I.; entered Order of Preachers (Dominicans), Chicago province, 1935; ord. priest June 11, 1942; ord. bishop of Sokoto, Nigeria, Aug. 15, 1967.

**Denning, Joseph P.:** b. Jan. 4, 1907, Flushing, L.I.; educ. Cathedral College (Brooklyn, N.Y.), Immaculate Conception Seminary (Huntington, L.I.), St. Mary's Seminary (Baltimore, Md.); ord. priest May 21, 1932; ord. titular bishop of Mallus and auxiliary bishop of Brooklyn, Apr. 22, 1959; resigned Apr. 13, 1982.

**De Palma, Joseph A., S.C.J.:** b. Sept. 4, 1913, Walton, N.Y.; ord. priest May 20, 1944; superior general of Congregation of Priests of the Sacred Heart, 1959-67; ord. first bishop of De Aar, South Africa, July 19, 1967.

**De Paoli, Ambrose:** b. Aug. 19, 1934, Jeannette, Pa., moved to Miami at age of nine; educ. St. Joseph Seminary (Bloomfield, Conn.), St. Mary of the West Seminary (Cincinnati, O.), North American College and Lateran Univ. (Rome); ord. priest Dec. 18, 1960, in Rome; served in diplomatic posts in Canada, Turkey, Africa and Venezuela; ord. titular archbishop of Lares, Nov. 20, 1983, in Miami; apostolic pro-nuncio to Sri Lanka, 1983.

**De Simone, Louis A.:** b. Feb. 21, 1922, Philadelphia, Pa.; educ. Villanova Univ. (Villanova, Pa.), St. Charles Borromeo Seminary (Overbrook, Pa.); ord. priest May 10, 1952; ord. titular bishop of Cillium and auxiliary bishop of Philadelphia, Aug. 12, 1981.

**Dimino, Joseph T.:** b. Jan. 7, 1923, New York, N.Y.; educ. Cathedral College (New York, N.Y.), St. Joseph's Seminary (Yonkers, N.Y.), Catholic Univ. (Washington, D.C.); ord. priest June 4, 1949; ord. titular bishop of Carini and auxiliary bishop of the Military Vicariate, May 10, 1983.

**Dimmerling, Harold J.:** b. Sept. 23, 1914, Braddock, Pa.; educ. St. Fidelis Preparatory Seminary (Herman, Pa.), St. Charles Seminary (Columbus, O.), St. Francis Seminary (Loretto, Pa.); ord. priest May 2, 1940; ord. bishop of Rapid City, Oct. 30, 1969.

**Dingman, Maurice J.:** b. Jan. 20, 1914, St. Paul, Ia.; educ. St. Ambrose College (Davenport, Ia.), North American College and Gregorian Univ. (Rome), Catholic Univ. (Washington, D.C.); ord. priest Dec. 8, 1939; ord. bishop of Des Moines, June 19, 1968.

**Dion, Georges E., O.M.I.:** b. Sept. 25, 1911, Central Falls, R.I.; educ. Holy Cross College (Worcester, Mass.), Oblate Juniorate (Colebrook, N.H.), Oblate Scholasticates (Natick, Mass., and Ottawa, Ont.); ord. priest June 24, 1936; ord. titular bishop of Arpaia and vicar apostolic of Jolo, Philippine Islands, Apr. 23, 1980.

**Dolinay, Thomas V.:** b. July 24, 1923, Uniontown, Pa.; educ. St. Procopius College (Lisle, Ill.); ord. priest May 16, 1948; editor *Eastern Catholic Life*, 1966-82; ord. titular bishop of Tiatira and auxiliary bishop of Byzantine-Rite diocese of Passaic, Nov. 23, 1976; app. first bishop Byzantine-Rite diocese of Van Nuys, Calif., Dec. 3, 1981, installed Mar. 9, 1982.

**Donaghy, Frederick Anthony, M.M.:** b. Jan. 13, 1903, New Bedford, Mass.; educ. Holy Cross College (Worcester, Mass.), St. Mary's Seminary (Baltimore, Md.), Maryknoll Seminary (Maryknoll, N.Y.); ord. priest Jan. 29, 1929; ord. titular bishop of Setea and vicar apostolic of Wuchow, China, Sept. 21, 1939; title changed to bishop of Wuchow, Apr. 11, 1946; expelled by Communists; bishop emeritus of Wuchow.

**Donnellan, Thomas A.:** b. Jan. 24, 1914, New York, N.Y.; educ. Cathedral College and St. Joseph's Seminary (New York, N.Y.), Catholic Univ. (Washington, D.C.); ord. priest June 3, 1939; ord. bishop of Ogdensburg, Apr. 9, 1964; app. archbishop of Atlanta, installed July 16, 1968.

**Donnelly, Robert William:** b. Mar. 22, 1931, Toledo, O.; educ. St. Meinrad Seminary College (St. Meinrad, Ind.), Mount St. Mary's in the West Seminary (Norwood, O.); ord. priest May 25, 1957; ord. titular bishop of Garba and auxiliary bishop of Toledo, May 3, 1984.

**Donohoe, Hugh A.:** b. June 28, 1905, San Francisco, Calif.; educ. St. Patrick's Preparatory and Major Seminaries (Menlo Park, Calif.), Catholic Univ. (Washington, D.C.); ord. priest June 14, 1930; ord. titular bishop of Taium and auxiliary bishop of San Francisco, Oct. 7, 1947; app. first bishop of Stockton, Jan. 27, 1962; app. bishop of Fresno, Aug. 27, 1969, installed Oct. 7, 1969; retired July 1, 1980.

**Donovan, John A.:** b. Aug. 5, 1911, Chatham, Ont., Canada; educ. Sacred Heart Seminary (Detroit, Mich.), North American College and Gregorian Univ. (Rome); ord. priest Dec. 8, 1935; ord. titular bishop of Rhasus and auxiliary bishop of Detroit, Oct. 26, 1954; app. bishop of Toledo, installed Apr. 18, 1967; retired July 29, 1980.

**Donovan, Paul V.:** b. Sept. 1, 1924, Bernard, Iowa; educ. St. Gregory's Seminary (Cincinnati, Ohio), Mt. St. Mary's Seminary (Norwood, Ohio), Lateran Univ. (Rome); ord. priest May 20, 1950; ord. first bishop of Kalamazoo, Mich., July 21, 1971.

**Dougherty, John J.:** b. Sept. 16, 1907, Jersey City, N.J.; educ. Seton Hall Univ. (S. Orange,

N.J.), Immaculate Conception Seminary (Darlington, N.J.), North American College, Gregorian Univ., Pontifical Biblical Institute (Rome); ord. priest July 23, 1933; ord. titular bishop of Cotenna and auxiliary bishop of Newark, Jan. 24, 1963; retired Sept. 18, 1982.

**Dozier, Carroll T.:** b. Aug. 18, 1911, Richmond, Va.; educ. Holy Cross College (Worcester, Mass.), Gregorian Univ. (Rome); ord. priest, Mar. 19, 1937, Rome; ord. first bishop of Memphis, Jan. 6, 1971; resigned July 27, 1982.

**Driscoll, Justin A.:** b. Sept. 30, 1920, Bernard, Ia.; educ. Loras College (Dubuque, Ia.), Catholic Univ. (Washington, D.C.); ord. priest July 28, 1945; president of Loras College, 1967-70; ord. bishop of Fargo, Oct. 28, 1970.

**Drury, Thomas J.:** b. Jan. 4, 1908, Co. Sligo, Ireland; educ. St. Benedict's College (Atchison, Kans.), Kenrick Seminary (St. Louis, Mo.); ord. priest June 2, 1935; ord. first bishop of San Angelo, Tex., Jan. 24, 1962; app. bishop of Corpus Christi, installed Sept. 1, 1965; resigned May 24, 1983.

**Dudick, Michael J.:** b. Feb. 24, 1916, St. Clair, Pa.; educ. St. Procopius College and Seminary (Lisle, Ill.); ord. priest Nov. 13, 1945; ord. bishop of Byzantine Rite Eparchy of Passaic, Oct. 24, 1968.

**Dudley, Paul:** b. Nov. 27, 1926, Northfield, Minn.; educ. Nazareth College and St. Paul Seminary (St. Paul, Minn.); ord. priest June 2, 1951; ord. titular bishop of Ursona and auxiliary bishop of St. Paul and Minneapolis, Jan. 25, 1977; app. bishop of Sioux Falls, installed Dec. 13, 1978.

**Duhart, Clarence James, C.SS.R.:** b. Mar. 23, 1912, New Orleans, La.; ord. priest June 29, 1937; ord. bishop of Udon Thani, Thailand, Apr. 21, 1966; resigned Oct. 2, 1975.

**DuMaine, (Roland) Pierre:** b. Aug. 2, 1931, Paducah, Ky.; educ. St. Joseph's College (Mountain View, Calif.), St. Patrick's College and Seminary (Menlo Park, Calif.), Univ. of California (Berkeley), Catholic Univ. (Washington, D.C.); ord. priest June 15, 1957; ord. titular bishop of Sarda and auxiliary bishop of San Francisco, June 29, 1978; app. first bishop of San Jose, Jan. 27, 1981; installed Mar. 18, 1981.

**Dunn, Francis J.:** b. Mar. 22, 1922, Elkader, Ia.; educ. Loras College (Dubuque, Ia.), Kenrick Seminary (St. Louis, Mo.), Angelicum (Rome, Italy); ord. priest Jan. 11, 1948; chancellor of Dubuque, Aug. 27, 1960; ord. titular bishop of Turris Tamallani and auxiliary bishop of Dubuque, Aug. 27, 1969, app. vicar general, Aug. 28, 1969.

**Durick, Joseph Aloysius:** b. Oct. 13, 1914, Dayton, Tenn.; educ. St. Bernard Minor Seminary (St. Bernard, Ala.), St. Mary's Seminary (Baltimore, Md.), Urban Univ. (Rome); ord. priest May 23, 1940; ord. titular bishop of Cerbal and auxiliary bishop of Mobile-Birmingham, Mar. 24, 1955; app. coadjutor bishop of Nashville, Tenn., installed Mar. 3, 1964; apostolic administrator, 1966; bishop of Nashville, Sept. 10, 1969; resigned Apr. 4, 1975, to work with inmates of Federal correctional institutions and their families.

**Durning, Dennis V., C.S.Sp.:** b. May 18, 1923, Germantown, Pa.; educ. St. Mary's Seminary

(Ferndale, Conn.); ord. priest June 3, 1949; ord. first bishop of Arusha, Tanzania, May 28, 1963.

## E

**Elko, Nicholas T.:** b. Dec. 14, 1909, Donora, Pa.; educ. Duquesne Univ. (Pittsburgh, Pa.), Seminary of Uzhorod (Czechoslovakia) Louvain Univ. (Belgium); ord. priest Sept. 30, 1934; ord. titular bishop of Apollonias and apostolic administrator of Byzantine-Rite exarchy of Pittsburgh, Mar. 6, 1955; succeeded as exarch of Pittsburgh, Sept. 5, 1955; became eparch when Pittsburgh was raised to eparchy, July, 1963; app. titular archbishop of Dara, 1967, and ordaining prelate for Byzantine Rite in Rome; head of Oriental liturgical commission; app. auxiliary bishop of Cincinnati, Aug. 10, 1971.

**Etteldorf, Raymond P.:** b. Aug. 12, 1911, Ossian, Ia.; educ. Loras College (Dubuque, Ia.), Gregorian Univ. (Rome); ord. priest Dec. 8, 1937; secretary general of Supreme Council for direction of Pontifical Missionary Works, 1964-68; secretary of Pontifical Commission for Economic Affairs, 1968-69; ord. titular archbishop of Tindari, Jan. 6, 1969; papal representative to New Zealand and the Pacific Islands, 1968-74; pro-nuncio to Ethiopia, 1974-82; nuncio-at-large; app. consultor to Congregation for Evangelization of Peoples and Secretariat for Promoting Christian Unity, 1983.

**Evans, George R.:** b. Sept. 25, 1922, Denver, Colo.; educ. Notre Dame Univ. (Notre Dame, Ind.), St. Thomas Seminary (Denver, Colo.), Apollinare Univ. (Rome, Italy); ord. priest May 31, 1947; ord. titular bishop of Tubyza and auxiliary bishop of Denver, Apr. 23, 1969.

## F

**Federal, Joseph Lennox:** b. Jan. 13, 1910, Greensboro, N.C.; educ. Belmont Abbey College (Belmont Abbey, N.C.), Niagara Univ. (Niagara Falls, N.Y.), Univ. of Fribourg (Switzerland), North American College and Gregorian Univ. (Rome); ord. priest Dec. 8, 1934; ord. titular bishop of Appiaria and auxiliary bishop of Salt Lake City, Apr. 11, 1951; app. coadjutor with right of succession, May, 1958; bishop of Salt Lake City, Mar. 31, 1960; retired Apr. 22, 1980.

**Ferrario, Joseph A.:** b. Mar. 3, 1926, Scranton, Pa.; educ. St. Charles College (Catonsville, Md.), St. Mary's Seminary (Baltimore, Md.), Catholic Univ. (Washington, D.C.); Univ. of Scranton; ord. priest May 19, 1951; ord. titular bishop of Cuse and auxiliary bishop of Honolulu Jan. 13, 1978; bishop of Honolulu, May 13, 1982.

**Fiorenza, Joseph A.:** b. Jan. 25, 1931, Beaumont, Tex.; educ. St. Mary's Seminary (LaPorte, Tex.); ord. priest May 29, 1954; ord. bishop of San Angelo, Oct. 25, 1979.

**Fitzpatrick, John J.:** b. Oct. 12, 1918, Trenton, Ont., Canada; educ. Urban Univ. (Rome), Our Lady of the Angels Seminary (Niagara Falls, N.Y.); ord. priest Dec. 13, 1942; ord. titular bishop of Cenae and auxiliary bishop of Miami, Aug. 28, 1968; bishop of Brownsville, Tex., May 28, 1971.

**Fitzsimons, George K.:** b. Sept. 4, 1928, Kansas City, Mo.; educ. Rockhurst College (Kansas City,

Mo.), Immaculate Conception Seminary (Conception, Mo.); ord. priest Mar. 18, 1961; ord. titular bishop of Pertusa and auxiliary bishop of Kansas City-St. Joseph, July 3, 1975; app. bishop of Salina, Apr. 3, 1984.

**Flanagan, Bernard Joseph:** b. Mar. 31, 1908, Proctor, Vt.; educ. Holy Cross College (Worcester, Mass.), North American College (Rome), Catholic Univ. (Washington, D.C.); ord. priest Dec. 8, 1931; ord. first bishop of Norwich, Nov. 30, 1953; app. bishop of Worcester, installed Sept. 24, 1959; resigned Apr. 12, 1983.

**Flavin, Glennon P.:** b. Mar. 2, 1916, St. Louis, Mo.; educ. Kenrick Seminary (St. Louis, Mo.); ord. priest Dec. 20, 1941; ord. titular bishop of Joannina and auxiliary bishop of St. Louis, May 30, 1957; app. bishop of Lincoln, installed Aug. 17, 1967.

**Fliss, Raphael M.:** b. Oct. 25, 1930, Milwaukee, Wis.; educ. St. Francis Seminary (Milwaukee, Wis.), Catholic University (Washington, D.C.), Pontifical Lateran Univ. (Rome); ord. priest May 26, 1956; ord. coadjutor bishop of Superior with right of succession, Dec. 20, 1979.

**Flores, Felixberto C.:** b. Jan. 13, 1921, Agana, Guam; educ. St. John's Seminary (Brighton, Mass.), Fordham Univ. (New York); ord. priest Apr. 30, 1949; ord. titular bishop of Stonj, May 17, 1970, and apostolic administrator of the diocese of Agana, Guam; installed second residential bishop of Agana, July 12, 1972; app. first archbishop of Agana, Mar. 24, 1984, when diocese was made a metropolitan see.

**Flores, Patrick F.:** b. July 26, 1929, Ganado, Tex.; educ. St. Mary's Seminary (Houston, Tex.); ord. priest May 26, 1956; ord. titular bishop of Itolica and auxiliary bishop of San Antonio, May 5, 1970 (first Mexican-American bishop); app. bishop of El Paso, Apr. 4, 1978, installed May 29, 1978; app. archbishop of San Antonio 1979; installed Oct. 13, 1979.

**Foley, John Patrick:** b. Nov. 11, 1935, Sharon Hill, Pa.; educ. St. Joseph's Preparatory School (Philadelphia, Pa.), St. Joseph's College (now University) (Philadelphia, Pa.), St. Charles Borromeo Seminary (Overbrook, Pa.), St. Thomas Univ. (Rome), Columbia School of Journalism (New York); ord. priest May 19, 1962; assistant editor (1967-70) and editor (1970-84) of *The Catholic Standard and Times,* Philadelphia archdiocesan paper; ord. titular archbishop of Neapolis in Proconsulari, May 8, 1984, in Philadelphia; app. to five-year term as president of the Pontifical Commission for Social Communications, Apr. 5, 1984.

**Forst, Marion F.:** b. Sept. 3, 1910, St. Louis, Mo.; educ. St. Louis Preparatory Seminary (St. Louis, Mo.), Kenrick Seminary (Webster Groves, Mo.); ord. priest June 10, 1934; ord. bishop of Dodge City, Mar. 24, 1960; app. titular bishop of Scala and auxiliary bishop of Kansas City, Kans. Oct. 16, 1976.

**Francis Joseph A., S.V.D.:** b. Sept. 30, 1923, Lafayette, La.; educ. St. Augustine Seminary (Bay St. Louis, Miss.), St. Mary Seminary (Techny, Ill.), Catholic Univ. (Washington, D.C.); ord. priest Oct. 7, 1950; president Conference of Major

Superiors of Men, 1974-76, and the National Black Catholic Clergy Caucus; ord. titular bishop of Valliposita and auxiliary bishop of Newark, June 25, 1976.

**Franz, John B.:** b. Oct. 29, 1896, Springfield, Ill.; educ. Quincy College (Quincy, Ill.), Kenrick Seminary (Webster Groves, Mo.), Catholic Univ. (Washington, D.C.); ord. priest June 13, 1920; ord. first bishop of Dodge City, Aug. 29, 1951; app. bishop of Peoria, installed Nov. 4, 1959; resigned May 24, 1971.

**Franzetta, Benedict C.:** b. Aug. 1, 1921, East Liverpool, O.; educ. St. Charles College (Catonsville, Md.), St. Mary Seminary (Cleveland, O.); ord. priest Apr. 29, 1950; ord. titular bishop of Oderzo and auxiliary bishop of Youngstown, Sept. 4, 1980.

**Freking, Frederick W.:** b. Aug. 11, 1913, Heron Lake, Minn.; educ. St. Mary's College (Winona, Minn.), North American College and Gregorian Univ. (Rome), Catholic Univ. (Washington, D.C.); ord. priest July 31, 1938; ord. bishop of Salina, Nov. 30, 1957; app. bishop of La Crosse, Dec. 30, 1964, installed Feb. 24, 1965; resigned May 10, 1983.

**Frey, Gerard L.:** b. May 10, 1914, New Orleans, La.; educ. Notre Dame Seminary (New Orleans, La.); ord. priest Apr. 2, 1938; ord. bishop of Savannah, Aug. 8, 1967; app. bishop of Lafayette, La., Nov. 7, 1972, installed Jan, 7, 1973.

**Friend, William B.:** b. Oct. 22, 1931, Miami, Fla.; educ. St. Mary's College (St. Mary, Ky.), Mt. St. Mary Seminary (Emmitsburg, Md.), Catholic Univ. (Washington, D.C.), Notre Dame Univ. (Notre Dame, Ind.); ord. priest May 7, 1959; ord. titular bishop of Pomaria and auxiliary bishop of Alexandria-Shreveport, La., Oct. 30, 1979; app. bishop of Alexandria-Shreveport, Nov. 17, 1982, installed Jan 11, 1983.

**Frosi, Angelo, S. X.:** b. Jan. 31, 1924, Baffano Cremona, Italy; ord. priest May 6, 1948; U.S. citizen; ord. titular bishop of Magneto, May 1, 1970, and prelate of Abaete do Tocantins, Brazil; app. first bishop of Abaetetuba, Brazil, Sept. 17, 1981.

**Furlong, Philip J.:** b. Dec. 8, 1892, New York, N.Y.; educ. Cathedral College (New York, N.Y.), St. Joseph's Seminary (Yonkers, N.Y.); ord. priest May 18, 1918; ord. titular bishop of Araxa and auxiliary to military vicar, Jan, 25, 1956. Retired 1971.

**G**

**Gallagher, Raymond J.:** b. Nov. 19, 1912, Cleveland, Ohio; educ. John Carroll Univ. and Our Lady of the Lake Seminary (Cleveland, O.); ord. priest Mar. 25, 1939; secretary of the National Conference of Catholic Charities 1961-65; ord. bishop of Lafayette in Indiana, Aug. 11, 1965; resigned Oct, 26, 1982.

**Gallegos, Alphonse, O.A.R.:** b. Feb. 20, 1931, Albuquerque, N. Mex., ord. priest May 24, 1958; ord. titular bishop of Sasabe and auxiliary bishop of Sacramento, Nov. 4, 1981.

**Ganter, Bernard J.:** b. July 17,1928, Galveston, Tex.; educ. Texas A & M Univ. (College Sta., Tex.), St. Mary's Seminary (La Porte, Tex.),

Catholic Univ. (Washington, D.C.); ord. priest May 22, 1952; chancellor of Galveston-Houston diocese, 1966-73; ord. first bishop of Tulsa, Feb. 7, 1973; app. bishop of Beaumont, Tex., Oct. 18, 1977, installed Dec. 13, 1977.

**Garland, James H.:** b. Dec. 13, 1931, Wilmington, Ohio; educ. Wilmington College (Ohio), Ohio State Univ. (Columbus, O.); Mt. St. Mary's Seminary (Cincinnati, O.), Catholic Univ. (Washington, D.C.); ord. priest Aug. 15, 1959; ord. titular bishop of Garriana and auxiliary bishop of Cincinnati, July 25, 1984; director department of social services.

**Garmendia, Francisco:** b. Nov. 6, 1924, Lozcano, Spain; ord. priest June 29, 1947, in Spain; came to New York in 1964; became naturalized citizen; ord. titular bishop of Limisa and auxiliary bishop of New York, June 29, 1977. Vicar for Spanish pastoral development in New York archdiocese.

**Garmo, George:** b. Dec. 8, 1921, Telkaif, Iraq; educ. St. Peter Chaldean Patriarchal Seminary (Mossul, Iraq), Pontifical Urban Univ. (Rome); ord. priest Dec. 8, 1945; pastor of Chaldean parish in Detroit archdiocese, 1960-64, 1966-80; ord. archbishop of Chaldean-Rite archdiocese of Mossul, Iraq, Sept. 14, 1980.

**Garner, Robert F.:** b. Apr. 27, 1920, Jersey City, N.J.; educ. Seton Hall Univ. (S. Orange, N.J.), Immaculate Conception Seminary (Darlington, N.J.); ord. priest June 15, 1946; ord. titular bishop of Blera and auxiliary bishop of Newark, June 25, 1976.

**Gaughan, Norbert F.:** b. May 30, 1921, Pittsburgh, Pa.; educ. St. Vincent College (Latrobe, Pa.), Univ. of Pittsburgh; ord. priest Nov. 4, 1945; ord. titular bishop of Taraqua and auxiliary bishop of Greensburg, June 26, 1975; app. bishop of Gary, July 24, 1984.

**Gelineau, Louis E.:** b. May 3, 1928, Burlington, Vt.; educ. St. Michael's College (Winooski, Vt.), St. Paul's Univ. Seminary (Ottawa, Ont.), Catholic Univ. (Washington, D.C.); ord. priest June 5, 1954; ord. bishop of Providence, R.I., Jan. 26, 1972.

**Gendron, Odore:** b. Sept. 13, 1921, Manchester, N.H.; educ. St. Charles Borromeo Seminary (Sherbrooke, Que., Canada), Univ. of Ottawa, St. Paul Univ. Seminary (Ottawa, Ont., Canada); ord. priest May 31, 1947; ord. bishop of Manchester, Feb. 3, 1975.

**Gerber, Eugene J.:** b. Apr. 30, 1931, Kingman, Kans.; educ. St. Thomas Seminary (Denver, Colo.), Wichita State Univ.; Catholic Univ. (Washington, D.C.), Angelicum (Rome); ord. priest May 19, 1959; ord. bishop of Dodge City, Dec. 14, 1976; app. bishop of Wichita, Nov. 17, 1982.

**Gerbermann, Hugo, M.M.:** b. Sept. 11, 1913, Nada, Tex.; educ. St. John's Minor and Major Seminary (San Antonio, Tex.), Maryknoll Seminary (Maryknoll, N.Y.); ord. priest Feb. 7, 1943; missionary work in Ecuador and Guatemala; ord. titular bishop of Amathus and prelate of Huehuetenango, Guatemala, July 22, 1962; first bishop of Huehuetenango, Dec. 23, 1967; app. titular bishop of Pinkel and auxiliary bishop of San Antonio, July 24, 1975; resigned June 30, 1982.

**Gerety, Peter L.:** b. July 19, 1912, Shelton, Conn.;

educ. Sulpician Seminary (Paris, France); ord. priest June 29, 1939; ord. titular bishop of Crepedula and coadjutor bishop of Portland, Me., with right of succession, June 1, 1966; app. apostolic administrator of Portland, 1967; bishop of Portland, Me., Sept. 15, 1969; app. archbishop of Newark, Apr. 2, 1974; installed June 28, 1974.

**Gerrard, James J.:** b. June 9, 1897, New Bedford, Mass.; educ. St. Laurent College (Montreal, Que.), St. Bernard's Seminary (Rochester, N.Y.); ord. priest May 26, 1923; ord. titular bishop of Forma and auxiliary bishop of Fall River, Mar. 19, 1959. Retired January, 1976.

**Glenn, Laurence A.:** b. Aug. 25, 1900, Bellingham, Wash.; educ. St. John's Univ. (Collegeville, Minn.), Catholic Univ. (Washington, D.C.); ord. priest June 11, 1927; ord. titular bishop of Tuscamia and auxiliary bishop of Duluth, Sept. 12, 1956; app. bishop of Crookston, Jan. 27, 1960, installed Apr. 20, 1960; resigned July 24, 1970.

**Glennie, Ignatius T., S.J.:** b. Feb. 5, 1907, Mexico City; educ. Mt. St. Michael's Scholasticate (Spokane, Wash.), Pontifical Seminary (Kandy, Ceylon), St. Mary's College (Kurdeong, India); entered Society of Jesus, 1924; ord. priest Nov. 21, 1938; ord. bishop of Trincomalee, Ceylon, Sept. 21, 1947; title of see changed to Trincomalee-Batticaloa (Sri Lanka), 1967; resigned Feb. 15, 1974.

**Gossman, F. Joseph:** b. Apr. 1, 1930, Baltimore, Md.; educ. St. Charles College (Catonsville, Md.), St. Mary's Seminary (Baltimore, Md.), North American College (Rome), Catholic Univ. (Washington, D.C.); ord. priest Dec. 17, 1955; ord. titular bishop of Agunto and auxiliary bishop of Baltimore, Sept. 11, 1968; named urban vicar, June 13, 1970; app. bishop of Raleigh April 8, 1975.

**Gottwald, George J.:** b. May 12, 1914, St. Louis, Mo.; educ. Kenrick Seminary (Webster Groves, Mo.); ord. priest June 9, 1940; ord. titular bishop of Cedamusa and auxiliary bishop of St. Louis, Aug. 8, 1961.

**Gracida, Rene H.:** b. June 9, 1923, New Orleans, La.; educ. Rice Univ. and Univ. of Houston (Houston, Tex.), Univ. of Fribourg (Switzerland); ord. priest May 23, 1959; ord. titular bishop of Masuccaba and auxiliary bishop of Miami, Jan. 25, 1972; app. first bishop of Pensacola-Tallahassee, Oct. 1, 1975, installed Nov. 6, 1975; app. bishop of Corpus Christi May 24, 1983, installed July 11, 1983.

**Grady, Thomas J.:** b. Oct. 9, 1914, Chicago, Ill.; educ. St. Mary of the Lake Seminary (Mundelein, Ill.), Gregorian Univ. (Rome), Loyola Univ. (Chicago, Ill.); ord. priest Apr. 23, 1938; ord. titular bishop of Vamalla and auxiliary bishop of Chicago, Aug. 24, 1967; app. bishop of Orlando, Fla., Nov. 11, 1974, installed Dec. 16, 1974.

**Graham, John J.:** b. Sept. 11, 1913, Philadelphia, Pa.; educ. St. Charles Borromeo Seminary (Philadelphia, Pa.), Pontifical Roman Seminary (Rome, Italy); ord. priest Feb. 26, 1938; ord. titular bishop of Sabrata and auxiliary bishop of Philadelphia, Jan. 7, 1964.

**Grahmann, Charles V.:** b. July 15, 1931, Halletsville, Tex.; educ. The Assumption-St. John's Seminary (San Antonio, Tex.); ord. priest Mar. 17, 1956; ord. titular bishop of Equilium and auxiliary bishop of San Antonio, Aug. 20, 1981; app. first bishop of Victoria, Tex., Apr. 13, 1982.

**Graves, Lawrence P.:** b. May 4, 1916, Texarkana, Ark.; educ. St. John's Seminary (Little Rock, Ark.), North American College (Rome), Catholic Univ. (Washington, D.C.); ord. priest June 11, 1942; ord. titular bishop of Vina and auxiliary bishop of Little Rock, Apr. 25, 1969; app. bishop of Alexandria, May 22, 1973, installed Sept. 18, 1973; title of see changed to Alexandria-Shreveport, Jan. 12, 1977; resigned July 20, 1982.

**Graziano, Lawrence, O.F.M.:** b. Apr. 5, 1921, Mt. Vernon, N.Y.; educ. Mt. Alvernia Seminary (Wappingers Falls, N.Y.); ord. priest Jan. 26, 1947; ord. titular bishop of Limata and auxiliary bishop of Santa Ana, El Salvador, Sept. 21, 1961; app. coadjutor bishop of San Miguel, El Salvador, with right of succession, 1965; bishop of San Miguel, Jan. 10, 1968; resigned June 27, 1969.

**Greco, Charles Paschal:** b. Oct. 29, 1894, Rodney, Miss.; educ. St. Joseph's Seminary (St. Benedict, La.), Louvain Univ. (Belgium), Dominican Univ. (Fribourg, Switzerland); ord. priest July 25, 1918; ord. bishop of Alexandria (now Alexandria-Shreveport), Feb. 25, 1946; retired May 22, 1973.

**Green, Francis J.:** b. July 7, 1906, Corning, N.Y.; educ. St. Patrick's Seminary (Menlo Park, Calif.); ord. priest May 15, 1932; ord. titular bishop of Serra and auxiliary bishop of Tucson, Sept. 17, 1953; named coadjutor of Tucson with right of succession, May 11, 1960; bishop of Tucson, Oct. 26, 1960; retired July 27, 1981.

**Gregory, Wilton D.:** b. Dec. 7, 1947, Chicago, Ill.; educ. Quigley Preparatory Seminary South, Niles College of Loyola Univ. (Chicago, Ill.), St. Mary of the Lake Seminary (Mundelein, Ill.), Pontifical Liturgical Institute, Sant'Anselmo (Rome); ord. priest May 9, 1973; ord. titular bishop of Oliva and auxiliary bishop of Chicago, Dec. 13, 1983.

**Grellinger, John B.:** b. Nov. 5, 1899, Milwaukee, Wis.; educ. Marquette Univ. and St. Francis Seminary (Milwaukee, Wis.), Urban Univ. and Gregorian Univ. (Rome); ord. priest July 14, 1929; ord. titular bishop of Syene and auxiliary bishop of Green Bay, July 14, 1949; retired Sept. 22, 1974.

**Greteman, Frank H.:** b. Dec. 25, 1907, Willey, Ia.; educ. Loras Academy and Loras College (Dubuque, Ia.), North American College (Rome), Catholic Univ. (Washington, D.C.); ord. priest Dec. 8, 1932; ord. titular bishop of Vissalsa and auxiliary bishop of Sioux City, May 26, 1965; bishop of Sioux City, Dec. 9, 1970; resigned Jan. 23, 1983.

**Griffin, James A.:** b. June 13, 1934, Fairview Park, O.; educ. St. Charles College (Baltimore, Md.), Borromeo College (Wicklife, O.); St. Mary Seminary (Cleveland, O.); Lateran Univ. (Rome); Cleveland State Univ.; ord. priest May 28, 1960; ord. titular bishop of Holar and auxiliary bishop of Cleveland, Aug. 1, 1979; app. bishop of Columbus, Feb. 8, 1983.

**Grutka, Andrew G.:** b. Nov. 17, 1908, Joliet, Ill.; educ. St. Procopius College and Seminary (Lisle, Ill.), Urban Univ. and Gregorian Univ. (Rome); ord. priest Dec. 5, 1933; app. moderator of lay activities in Gary diocese, 1955; ord. first bishop of

Gary, Feb. 25, 1957; app. member of Pontifical Marian Academy, Jan. 5, 1970; retired July 24, 1984.

**Guilfoyle, George H.:** b. Nov. 13, 1913, New York, N.Y.; educ. Georgetown Univ. (Washington, D.C.), Fordham Univ. (New York City), St. Joseph's Seminary (Dunwoodie, N.Y.), Columbia Univ. Law School (New York City); ord. priest Mar. 25, 1944; ord. titular bishop of Marazane and auxiliary bishop of New York, Nov. 30, 1964; app. bishop of Camden, installed Mar. 4, 1968.

**Gumbleton, Thomas J.:** b. Jan. 26, 1930, Detroit, Mich.; educ. St. John Provincial Seminary (Detroit, Mich.), Pontifical Lateran Univ. (Rome); ord. priest June 2, 1956; ord. titular bishop of Ululi and auxiliary bishop of Detroit, May 1, 1968.

## H

**Hacker, Hilary B.:** b. Jan. 10, 1913, New Ulm, Minn.; educ. St. Paul Seminary (St. Paul, Minn.), Gregorian Univ. (Rome); ord. priest June 4, 1938; ord. bishop of Bismarck, N. Dak., Feb. 27, 1957; resigned June 30, 1982.

**Hackett, John F.:** b. Dec. 7, 1911, New Haven, Conn.; educ. St. Thomas Seminary (Bloomfield, Conn.), Seminaire Ste. Sulpice (Paris); ord. priest June 29, 1936; ord. titular bishop of Helenopolis in Palaestina and auxiliary bishop of Hartford, Mar. 19, 1953.

**Hagarty, Paul Leonard, O.S.B.:** b. Mar. 20, 1909, Greene, Ia.; educ. Loras College (Dubuque, Ia.), St. John's Seminary and St. John's Univ. (Collegeville, Minn.); entered Order of St. Benedict, 1931; ord. priest June 6, 1936; ord. titular bishop of Arba and vicar apostolic of the Bahamas, Oct. 19, 1950; first bishop of Nassau, July 5, 1960; retired 1981.

**Ham, J. Richard, M.M.:** b. July 11, 1921, Chicago, Ill.; educ. Maryknoll Seminary (New York); ord. priest June 12, 1948; missionary to Guatemala, 1958; ord. titular bishop of Puzia di Numidia and auxiliary bishop of Guatemala, Jan. 6, 1968; resigned see 1979; app. vicar for Hispanic ministry in St. Paul and Minneapolis archdiocese, January, 1980; auxiliary bishop of St. Paul and Minneapolis, October, 1980.

**Hammes, George A.:** b. Sept. 11, 1911, St. Joseph Ridge, Wis.; educ. St. Lawrence Seminary (Mt. Calvary. Wis.), St. Louis Preparatory Seminary (St. Louis, Mo.), Kenrick Seminary (Webster Groves, Mo.), Sulpician Seminary, Catholic Univ. (Washington, D.C.); ord. priest May 22, 1937; ord. bishop of Superior, May 24, 1960.

**Hanifen, Richard C.:** b. June 15, 1931, Denver, Colo,; educ. Regis College and St. Thomas Seminary (Denver, Colo.), Catholic Univ. (Washington, D.C.), Lateran Univ. (Rome); ord. priest June 6, 1959; ord. titular bishop of Abercorn and auxiliary bishop of Denver, Sept. 20, 1974; app. first bishop of Colorado Springs, 1983; installed Jan. 30, 1984.

**Hannan, Philip M.:** b. May 20, 1913, Washington, D.C.; educ. St. Charles College (Catonsville, Md.), Catholic Univ. (Washington, D.C.), North American College (Rome); ord. priest Dec. 8, 1939; ord. titular bishop of Hieropolis and auxiliary bishop of Washington, D.C., Aug. 28, 1956; app. archbishop of New Orleans, installed Oct. 13, 1965.

**Harper, Edward, C.SS.R.:** b. July 23, 1910, Brooklyn, N.Y.; educ. Redemptorist Houses of Study; ord. priest June 18, 1939; ord. titular bishop of Heraclea Pontica and first prelate of Virgin Islands, Oct. 6, 1960; became first bishop, 1977, when prelacy was made diocese of St. Thomas.

**Harrington, Timothy J.:** b. Dec. 19, 1918, Holyoke, Mass.; educ. Holy Cross College (Worcester, Mass.), Grand Seminary (Montreal, Que.), Boston College School of Social Work; ord. priest Jan. 19, 1946; ord. titular bishop of Rusuca and auxiliary bishop of Worcester, Mass., July 2, 1968; app. bishop of Worcester, Sept. 1, 1983, installed Oct. 13, 1983.

**Harris, Vincent M.:** b. Oct. 14, 1913, Conroe, Tex.; educ. St. Mary's Seminary (La Porte, Tex.), North American College and Gregorian Univ. (Rome), Catholic Univ. (Washington, D.C.); ord. priest Mar. 19, 1938; ord. first bishop of Beaumont, Tex., Sept. 28, 1966; app. titular bishop of Rotaria and coadjutor bishop of Austin, Apr. 27, 1971; bishop of Austin, Nov. 16, 1971.

**Harrison, Frank J.:** b. Aug. 12, 1912; Syracuse, N.Y.; educ. Notre Dame Univ. (Notre Dame, Ind.), St. Bernard's Seminary (Rochester, N.Y.), ord. priest June 4, 1937; ord. titular bishop of Aquae in Numidia and auxiliary bishop of Syracuse, Apr. 22, 1971; app. bishop of Syracuse, Nov. 9, 1976, installed Feb. 6, 1977.

**Hart, Daniel A.:** b. Aug. 24, 1927, Lawrence, Mass.; educ. St. John's Seminary (Brighton, Mass.); ord. priest Feb. 2, 1953; ord. titular bishop of Tepelta and auxiliary bishop of Boston, Oct. 18, 1976.

**Hart, Joseph:** b. Sept. 26, 1931, Kansas City, Missouri; educ. St. John Seminary (Kansas City, Mo.), St. Meinrad Seminary (Indianapolis, Ind.); ord. priest May 1, 1956; ord. titular bishop of Thimida Regia and auxiliary bishop of Cheyenne, Wyo., Aug. 31, 1976; app. bishop of Cheyenne, installed June 12, 1978.

**Hastrich, Jerome J.:** b. Nov. 13, 1914, Milwaukee, Wis.; educ. Marquette Univ., St. Francis Seminary (Milwaukee, Wis.); ord. priest Feb. 9, 1941; ord. titular bishop of Gurza and auxiliary bishop of Madison, Sept. 3, 1963; app. bishop of Gallup, N.Mex., Sept. 3, 1969.

**Hayes, Nevin W., O.Carm:** b. Feb. 17, 1922, Chicago, Ill.; entered Carmelite novitiate Aug. 15, 1939; educ. Mt. Carmel College (Niagara Falls, Canada), Whitefriars Hall and Catholic Univ. (Washington, D.C.); ord. priest June 8, 1946; prelate nullius of Sicuani, Peru, 1959; ord. titular bishop of Nova Sinna and prelate of Sicuani, Aug. 5, 1965; resigned November 1970; app. auxiliary bishop of Chicago, Feb. 2, 1971.

**Head, Edward D.:** b. Aug. 5, 1919, White Plains, N.Y.; educ. Cathedral College, St. Joseph's Seminary, Columbia Univ. (New York City); ord. priest Jan. 27, 1945; director of New York Catholic Charities; ord. titular bishop of Ardsratha and auxiliary bishop of New York, Mar. 19, 1970; app. bishop of Buffalo, Jan. 23, 1973, installed Mar. 19, 1973.

**Helmsing, Charles H.:** b. Mar. 23, 1908,

Shrewsbury, Mo.; educ. St. Louis Preparatory Seminary (St. Louis, Mo.), Kenrick Seminary (Webster Groves, Mo.); ord. priest June 10, 1933; ord. titular bishop of Axomis and auxiliary bishop of St. Louis, Apr. 19, 1949; first bishop of Springfield-Cape Girardeau, Aug. 24, 1956; bishop of Kansas City-St. Joseph, 1962, installed Apr. 3, 1962; resigned June 25, 1977.

**Herrmann, Edward J.:** b. Nov. 6, 1913, Baltimore, Md.; educ. Mt. St. Mary's Seminary (Emmitsburg, Md.), Catholic Univ. (Washington, D.C.); ord. priest June 12, 1947; ord. titular bishop of Lamzella and auxiliary bishop of Washington, D.C., Apr. 26, 1966; app. bishop of Columbus, June 26, 1973; resigned Sept. 18, 1982.

**Hettinger, Edward Gerhard:** b. Oct. 14, 1902, Lancaster, O.; educ. St. Vincent's College (Beatty, Pa.); ord. priest June 2, 1928; ord. titular bishop of Teos and auxiliary bishop of Columbus, Feb. 24, 1942; retired Oct. 18, 1977.

**Hickey, Dennis W.:** b. Oct. 28, 1914, Dansville, N.Y.; educ. Colgate Univ. and St. Bernard's Seminary (Rochester, N.Y.); ord. priest June 7, 1941; ord. titular bishop of Rusuccuru and auxiliary bishop of Rochester, N.Y., Mar. 14, 1968.

**Hickey, James A.:** b. Oct. 11, 1920, Midland, Mich.; educ. Sacred Heart Seminary (Detroit, Mich.), Catholic Univ. (Washington, D.C.), Lateran Univ. and Angelicum (Rome), Michigan State Univ.; ord. priest June 15, 1946; ord. titular bishop of Taraqua and auxiliary bishop of Saginaw, Apr. 14, 1967; rector of North American College, Rome, 1969-74; app. bishop of Cleveland, June 5, 1974; installed July 16, 1974; app. archbishop of Washington, D.C., installed Aug. 5, 1980.

**Higi, William L.:** b. Aug. 29, 1933, Anderson, Ind.; educ. Our Lady of the Lakes Preparatory Seminary (Wawasee, Ind.), Mt. St. Mary of the West Seminary and Xavier Univ. (Cincinnati, O.); ord. priest May 30, 1959; ord. bishop of Lafayette, Ind., June 6, 1984.

**Hines, Vincent J.:** b. Sept. 14, 1912, New Haven, Conn.; educ. St. Thomas Seminary (Bloomfield, Conn.), St. Sulpice Seminary (Paris), Lateran Univ. (Rome); ord. priest May 2, 1937; ord. bishop of Norwich, Conn., Mar. 17, 1960; retired June 17, 1975.

**Hoch, Lambert A.:** b. Feb. 6, 1903, Elkton, S.D.; educ. Creighton Univ. (Omaha, Nebr.), St. Paul Seminary (St. Paul, Minn.); ord. priest May 30, 1928; ord. bishop of Bismarck, Mar. 25, 1952; app. bishop of Sioux Falls Dec. 5, 1956; retired June 13, 1978.

**Hodapp, Robert L, S.J.:** b. Oct. 1, 1910. Mankato, Minn.; educ. St. Stanislaus Seminary (Florissant, Mo.), St. Louis Univ. (St. Louis, Mo.); ord. priest June 18, 1941; ord. bishop of Belize, June 26, 1958; retired Jan. 16, 1984.

**Hodges, Joseph H.:** b. Oct. 8, 1911, Harper's Ferry, W.Va.; educ. St. Charles College (Catonsville, Md.), North American College (Rome); ord. priest Dec. 8, 1935; ord. titular bishop of Rusadus and auxiliary bishop of Richmond, Oct. 15, 1952; named coadjutor bishop of Wheeling with right of succession, May 24, 1961; bishop of Wheeling, Nov. 23, 1962; title of see changed to Wheeling-Charleston 1974.

**Hoffman, James R.:** b. June 12, 1932, Fremont, O.; educ. Our Lady of the Lake Minor Seminary (Wawasee, Ind.), St. Meinrad College (St. Meinrad, Ind.); Mt. St. Mary Seminary (Norwood, O.); Catholic Univ. (Washington, D.C.); ord. priest July 28, 1957; ord. titular bishop of Italica and auxiliary bishop of Toledo, June 23, 1978; bishop of Toledo, Dec. 16, 1980.

**Hogan, James J.:** b. Oct. 17, 1911, Philadelphia, Pa.; educ. St. Charles College (Catonsville, Md.), St. Mary's Seminary (Baltimore), Gregorian Univ. (Rome), Catholic Univ. (Washington, D.C.); ord. priest Dec. 8, 1937; ord. titular bishop of Philomelium and auxiliary bishop of Trenton, Feb. 25, 1960; app. bishop of Altoona-Johnstown, installed July 6, 1966.

**Hogan, Joseph L.:** b. Mar. 11, 1916, Lima, N.Y.; educ. St. Bernard's Seminary (Rochester, N.Y.), Canisius College (Buffalo, N.Y.), Angelicum (Rome); ord. priest June 6, 1942; ord. bishop of Rochester, Nov. 28, 1969; resigned Nov. 28, 1978.

**Houck, William Russell:** b. June 26, 1926, Mobile Ala.; educ. St. Bernard Junior College (Cullman, Ala.), St. Mary's Seminary College and St. Mary's Seminary (Baltimore, Md.), Catholic Univ. (Washington, D.C.); ord. priest May 19, 1951; ord. titular bishop of Alessano and auxiliary bishop of Jackson, Miss., May 27, 1979, by Pope John Paul II; app. bishop of Jackson, Apr. 24, 1984.

**Howze, (Joseph) Lawson E.:** b. Aug. 30, 1923, Daphne, Ala.; convert to Catholicism, 1948; educ. St. Bonaventure Univ. (St. Bonaventure, N.Y.); ord. priest May 7, 1959; ord. titular bishop of Massita and auxiliary bishop of Natchez-Jackson, Jan. 28, 1973; app. first bishop of Biloxi, Miss., Mar. 8, 1977; installed June 6, 1977.

**Hubbard, Howard J.:** b. Oct. 31, 1938, Troy, N.Y.; educ. St. Joseph's Seminary (Dunwoodie, N.Y.); North American College and Gregorian Univ. (Rome), Catholic Univ. (Washington, D.C.); ord. priest Dec. 18, 1963; ord. bishop of Albany, Mar. 27, 1977.

**Hughes, Alfred C.:** b. Dec. 2, 1932, Boston, Mass.; educ. St. John Seminary (Brighton, Mass), Gregorian Univ. (Rome); ord. priest Dec. 15, 1957, in Rome; ord. titular bishop of Maximiana in Byzacena and auxiliary bishop of Boston, Sept. 14, 1981.

**Hughes, Edward T.:** b. Nov. 13, 1920, Landowne, Pa.; educ. St. Charles Seminary, Univ. of Pennsylvania (Philadelphia, Pa.); ord. priest May 31, 1947; ord. titular bishop of Segia and auxiliary bishop of Philadelphia, July 21, 1976.

**Hughes, William A.:** b. Sept. 23, 1921, Youngstown, O.; educ. St. Charles College (Catonsville, Md.), St. Mary's Seminary (Cleveland, O.) Notre Dame Univ. (Notre Dame, Ind.); ord. priest Apr. 6, 1946; ord. titular bishop of Inis Cathaig and auxiliary bishop of Youngstown, Sept. 12, 1974; app. bishop of Covington, installed May 8, 1979.

**Hunthausen, Raymond G.:** b. Aug. 21, 1921, Anaconda, Mont.; educ. Carroll College (Helena, Mont.), St. Edward's Seminary (Kenmore, Wash.), St. Louis Univ. (St. Louis, Mo.), Catholic

Univ. (Washington, D.C.), Fordham Univ. (New York City), Notre Dame Univ. (Notre Dame, Ind.); ord. priest June 1, 1946; ord. bishop of Helena, Aug. 30, 1962; app. archbishop of Seattle, Feb. 25, 1975.

**Hurley, Francis T.:** b. Jan. 12, 1927, San Francisco, Calif.; educ. St. Patrick's Seminary (Menlo Park, Calif.), Catholic Univ. (Washington, D.C.); ord. priest June 16, 1951; assigned to NCWC in Washington, D.C., 1957; assistant (1958) and later (1968) associate secretary of NCCB and USCC; ord. titular bishop of Daimlaig and auxiliary bishop of Juneau, Alaska, Mar. 19, 1970; app. bishop of Juneau, July 20, 1971, installed Sept. 8, 1971; app. archbishop of Anchorage, May 4, 1976, installed July 8, 1976.

**Hurley, Mark J.:** b. Dec. 13, 1919, San Francisco, Calif.; educ. St. Patrick's Seminary (Menlo Park, Calif.), Univ. of California (Berkeley), Catholic Univ. (Washington, D.C.), Lateran Univ. (Rome), Univ. of Portland (Portland, Ore.); ord. priest Sept. 23, 1944; ord. titular bishop of Thunusuda and auxiliary bishop of San Francisco, Jan. 4, 1968; app. bishop of Santa Rosa, Nov. 19, 1969.

### I-J

**Ibrahim, Ibrahim N.:** b. Oct. 1, 1937, Telkaif, Mosul, Iraq.; educ. Patriarchal Seminary (Mosul, Iraq), St. Sulpice Seminary (Paris, France); ord. priest Dec. 30, 1962, in Baghdad, Iraq; ord. titular bishop of Anbar and apostolic exarch for Chaldean-Rite Catholics in the United States, Mar. 8, 1982, in Baghdad; installed in Detroit, Apr. 18, 1982.

**Imesch, Joseph L.:** b. June 21, 1931, Detroit, Mich.; educ. Sacred Heart Seminary (Detroit, Mich.), North American College, Gregorian Univ. (Rome); ord. priest Dec. 16, 1956; ord. titular bishop of Pomaria and auxiliary bishop of Detroit, Apr. 3, 1973; app. bishop of Joliet, June 30, 1979.

**Iranyi, Ladislaus A., Sch.P.:** b. Apr. 9, 1923, Szeged, Hungary; educ. Pazmany Univ. (Budapest, Hungary), Angelicum and Gregorian Univ. (Rome); ord. priest Mar. 13, 1948, in Rome; becamse U.S. citizen, 1958; ord. titular bishop of Castel Mediano, July 27, 1983; responsible for spiritual care of Hungarian Catholics living outside Hungary.

**Johnson, William R.:** b. Nov. 19, 1918, Tonopah, Nev.; educ. Los Angeles College and St. John's Seminary (Camarillo, Calif.), National Catholic School of Social Service, Catholic Univ. (Washington, D.C.); ord. priest May 28, 1944; ord. titular bishop of Blera and auxiliary bishop of Los Angeles, Mar. 25, 1971; app. first bishop of Orange, Calif., Mar. 30, 1976, installed June 18, 1976.

**Joyce, Robert F.:** b. Oct. 7, 1896, Proctor, Vt.; educ. Univ. of Vermont (Burlington, Vt.), Grand Seminary (Montreal, Canada); ord. priest May 26, 1923; ord. titular bishop of Citium and auxiliary bishop of Burlington, Oct. 28, 1954; installed as bishop of Burlington, Feb. 26, 1957; resigned Dec. 14, 1971.

### K

**Kalisz, Raymond P., S.V.D.:** b. Sept. 25, 1927, Melvindale, Mich.; educ. St. Mary's Seminary

(Techny, Ill.); ord. priest Aug. 15, 1954; ord. bishop of Wewak, Papua New Guinea, August 15, 1980.

**Kaniecki, Michael Joseph, S.J.:** b. Apr. 13, 1935, Detroit Mich.; joined Jesuits 1953; educ. Xavier Univ. (Milford, O.), Mt. St. Michael's Seminary (Spokane, Wash.), Regis College (Willowdale, Ont.); ord. priest June 5, 1965; ord. coadjutor bishop of Fairbanks, May 1, 1984.

**Keating, John Richard:** b. July 20, 1934, Chicago, Ill.; educ. Quigley Preparatory Seminary (Chicago, Ill.), St. Mary of the Lake Seminary (Mundelein, Ill.), Gregorian Univ. (Rome); ord. priest Dec. 20, 1958; ord. bishop of Arlington, Aug. 4, 1983.

**Keeler, William Henry:** b. Mar. 4, 1931, San Antonio, Tex.; educ. St. Charles Seminary (Overbrook, Pa.), North American College, Pontifical Gregorian Univ. (Rome); ord. priest July 17, 1955; ord. titular bishop of Ulcinium and auxiliary bishop of Harrisburg, Sept. 21, 1979; app. bishop of Harrisburg, Nov. 15, 1983; installed Jan. 4, 1984.

**Kellenberg, Walter P.:** b. June 3, 1901, New York, N.Y.; educ. Cathedral College (New York, City), St. Joseph Seminary (Dunwoodie, N.Y.); ord. priest June 2, 1928; ord. titular bishop of Joannina and auxiliary bishop of New York, Oct. 5, 1953; app. bishop of Ogdensburg, Jan. 19, 1954; app. first bishop of Rockville Centre Apr. 16, 1957, installed May 27, 1957; retired May 4, 1976.

**Kelly, Thomas C., O.P.:** b. July 14, 1931, Rochester, N.Y.; educ. Providence College (Providence, R.I.), Immaculate Conception College (Washington, D.C.), Angelicum (Rome); professed in Dominicans, Aug. 26, 1952; secretary, apostolic delegation, Washington, D.C., 1965-71; associate general secretary, 1971-77, and general secretary, 1977-81, NCCB/USCC; ord. titular bishop of Tusurus and auxiliary bishop of Washington, D.C., Aug. 15, 1977; app. archbishop of Louisville, Dec. 28, 1981, installed Feb. 18, 1982.

**Kenney, Lawrence J.:** b. Aug. 30, 1930, New Rochelle, N.Y.; educ. Cathedral College (New York, N.Y.), St. Joseph's Seminary (Yonkers, N.Y.), Iona College (New Rochelle, N.Y.); ord. priest June 2, 1956; ord. titular bishop of Holar and auxiliary bishop of the Military Vicariate, May 10, 1983.

**Kenny, Michael H.:** b. June 26, 1937, Hollywood, Calif.; educ. St. Joseph College (Mountain View, Calif.), St. Patrick's Seminary (Menlo Park, Calif.), Catholic Univ. (Washington, D.C.); ord. priest Mar. 30, 1963; ord. bishop of Juneau, May 27, 1979.

**Kinney, John:** b. June 11, 1937, Oelwein, Iowa; educ. Nazareth Hall and St. Paul Seminaries (St. Paul, Minn.); Pontifical Lateran University (Rome); ord. priest Feb. 2, 1963; ord. titular bishop of Caorle and auxiliary bishop of St. Paul and Minneapolis, Jan. 25, 1977; app. bishop of Bismarck June 30, 1982.

**Kmiec, Edward U.:** b. June 4, 1936, Trenton, N.J.; educ. St. Charles College (Catonsville, Md.), St. Mary's Seminary (Baltimore, Md.), Gregorian Univ. (Rome); ord. priest Dec. 20, 1961; ord.

titular bishop of Simidicca and auxiliary bishop of Trenton, Nov. 3, 1982.

**Kocisko, Stephen:** b. June 11, 1915, Minneapolis, Minn.; educ. Nazareth Hall Minor Seminary (St. Paul, Minn.), Pontifical Ruthenian College, Urban Univ. (Rome); ord. priest Mar. 30, 1941; ord. titular bishop of Teveste and auxiliary bishop of apostolic exarchate of Pittsburgh, Oct. 23, 1956; installed as first eparch of the eparchy of Passaic, Sept. 10, 1963; app. eparch of Byzantine-Rite diocese of Pittsburgh, installed Mar. 5, 1968; app. first metropolitan of Munhall, installed June 11, 1969; title of see changed to Pittsburgh, 1977.

**Koester, Charles R.:** b. Sept. 16, 1915, Jefferson City, Mo.; educ. Conception Academy (Conception, Mo.), St. Louis Preparatory Seminary and Kenrick Seminary (St. Louis, Mo.), North American College (Rome); ord. priest Dec. 20, 1941; ord. titular bishop of Suacia and auxiliary bishop of St. Louis, Feb. 11, 1971.

**Krawczak, Arthur H.:** b. Feb. 2, 1913, Detroit, Mich.; educ. Sacred Heart Seminary, Sts. Cyril and Methodius Seminary (Orchard Lake, Mich.), Catholic Univ. (Washington, D.C.); ord. priest May 18, 1940; ord. titular bishop of Subbar and auxiliary bishop of Detroit, Apr. 3, 1973; retired Aug. 17, 1982.

**Krol, John J.:** (See Cardinals, Biographies.)

**Kucera, Daniel, O.S.B.:** b. May 7, 1923, Chicago, Ill.; educ. St. Procopius College (Lisle, Ill.), Catholic Univ. (Washington, D.C.); professed in Order of St. Benedict, June 16, 1944; ord. priest May 26, 1949; abbot, St. Procopius Abbey, 1964-71; pres. Illinois Benedictine College, 1959-65 and 1971-76; ord. titular bishop of Natchez and auxiliary bishop of Joliet, July 21, 1977; app. bishop of Salina, Mar. 5, 1980, installed May 7, 1980; app. archbishop of Dubuque, installed Feb. 23, 1984.

**Kupfer, William F., M.M.:** b. Jan. 28, 1909, Brooklyn, N.Y.; educ. Cathedral College (Brooklyn, N.Y.), Maryknoll Seminary (Maryknoll, N.Y.); ord. priest June 11, 1933; missionary in China; app. prefect apostolic of Taichung, Formosa, 1951; ord. first bishop of Taichung, July 25, 1962.

**L**

**Lambert, Francis, S.M.:** b. Feb. 7, 1921, Lawrence, Mass.; educ. Marist Seminary (Framingham, Mass.); ord. priest, June 29, 1946; served in Marist missions in Oceania; provincial of Marist Oceania province, 1971; ord. bishop of Port Vila, Vanuatu (New Hebrides), Mar. 20, 1977.

**Larkin, W. Thomas:** b. Mar. 31, 1923, Mt. Morris, N.Y.; educ. St. Andrew Seminary and St. Bernard Seminary (Rochester, N.Y.); Angelicum Univ. (Rome); ord. priest May 15, 1947; ord. bishop of St. Petersburg, May 27, 1979.

**Law, Bernard F.:** b. Nov. 4, 1931, Torreon, Mexico; educ. Harvard Univ. (Cambridge, Mass.), St. Joseph Seminary (St. Benedict, La.), Pontifical College Josephinum (Worthington, O.); ord. priest May 21, 1961; editor of *Mississippi Register* (now *Mississippi Today*), 1963-68; director of NCCB Committee on Ecumenical and Interreligious Affairs, 1968-71; vicar general of Natchez-Jackson diocese, 1971-73; ord. bishop of Springfield-Cape Girardeau, Mo., Dec. 5, 1973; app. archbishop of Boston Jan. 24, 1984, installed Mar. 23, 1984.

**Leech, George Leo:** b. May 21, 1890, Ashley, Pa.; educ. St. Charles Borromeo Seminary (Overbrook, Pa.), Catholic Univ. (Washington, D.C.); ord. priest May 29, 1920; ord. titular bishop of Mela and auxiliary bishop of Harrisburg, Oct. 17, 1935; bishop of Harrisburg Dec. 19, 1935; resigned Oct. 19, 1971; app. titular bishop of Allegheny.

**Leonard, Vincent M.:** b. Dec. 11, 1908, Pittsburgh, Pa.; educ. Duquesne Univ. (Pittsburgh, Pa.), St. Vincent Seminary (Latrobe, Pa.); ord. priest June 16, 1935; ord. titular bishop of Arsacal and auxiliary bishop of Pittsburgh, Apr. 21, 1964; app. bishop of Pittsburgh, installed July 2, 1969; resigned June 30, 1983.

**Lessard, Raymond W.:** b. Dec. 21, 1930, Grafton, N.D.; educ. St. Paul Seminary (St. Paul, Minn.), North American College (Rome); ord. priest Dec. 16, 1956; served on staff of the Congregation for Bishops in the Roman Curia, 1964-73; ord. bishop of Savannah, Apr. 27, 1973.

**Levada, William J.:** b. June 15, 1936, Long Beach, Calif.; educ. St. John's College (Camarillo, Calif.), Gregorian Univ. (Rome); ord. priest Dec. 20, 1961; ord. titular bishop of Capri and auxiliary bishop of Los Angeles, May 12, 1983.

**Lipscomb, Oscar H.:** b. Sept. 21, 1931, Mobile, Ala.; educ. McGill Institute, St. Bernard College (Cullman, Ala.), North American College and Gregorian Univ. (Rome), Catholic Univ. (Washington, D.C.); ord. priest July 15, 1956; ord. first archbishop of Mobile, Nov. 16, 1980.

**Lohmuller, Martin J.:** b. Aug. 21, 1919, Philadelphia, Pa.; educ. St. Charles Borromeo Seminary (Philadelphia, Pa.), Catholic Univ. (Washington, D.C.); ord. priest June 3, 1944; ord. titular bishop of Ramsbury and auxiliary bishop of Philadelphia, Apr. 2, 1970.

**Losten, Basil:** b. May 11, 1930, Chesapeake City, Md.; educ. St. Basil's College (Stamford, Conn.), Catholic University (Washington, D.C.); ord. priest June 10, 1957; ord. titular bishop of Arcadiopolis in Asia and auxiliary bishop of Ukrainian archeparchy of Philadelphia, May 25, 1971; app. apostolic administrator of archeparchy, 1976; app. bishop of Ukrainian eparchy of Stamford, Sept. 20, 1977.

**Lotocky, Innocent Hilarius, O.S.B.M.:** b. Nov. 3, 1915, Petlykiwci, Ukraine; educ. seminaries in Ukraine, Czechoslovakia and Austria; ord. priest Nov. 24, 1940; ord. bishop of St. Nicholas of Chicago for the Ukrainians, Mar. 1, 1981.

**Lubachivsky, Myroslav J.:** b. June 24, 1914, Dolynian, Ukraine; educ. Innsbruck Univ. (Austria), Gregorian Univ. and Biblicum (Rome); began pastoral work in U.S. in 1947; ord. archbishop of Ukrainian-Rite archeparchy of Philadelphia, Nov. 12, 1979; app. coadjutor archbishop of Lwow of the Ukrainians, Mar. 27, 1980.

**Lucker, Raymond A.:** b. Feb. 24, 1927, St. Paul, Minn.; educ. St. Paul Seminary (St. Paul, Minn.); University of Minnesota (Minneapolis), Angeli-

cum (Rome); ord. priest June 7, 1952; director of
USCC department of education, 1968-71; ord.
titular bishop of Meta and auxiliary bishop of St.
Paul and Minneapolis, Sept. 8, 1971; app. bishop of
New Ulm, Dec. 23, 1975, installed Feb. 19, 1976.

**Lyke, James Patterson, O.F.M.:** b. Feb. 18, 1939,
Chicago, Ill.; educ. Quincy College (Quincy, Ill.),
Antonianum (Rome), Union Graduate School (Cincinnati, O.); professed in Order of Friars Minor,
June 21, 1963; ord. priest June 24, 1966; president
of National Black Catholic Clergy Caucus; ord.
titular bishop of Furnos Maior and auxiliary bishop of Cleveland, Aug. 1, 1979.

**Lynch, George E.:** b. Mar. 4, 1917, New York,
N.Y.; educ. Fordham Univ. (New York), Mt. St.
Mary's Seminary (Emmitsburg, Md.), Catholic
Univ. (Washington, D.C.); ord. priest May 29,
1943; ord. titular bishop of Satafi and auxiliary
bishop of Raleigh Jan. 6, 1970.

**Lyne, Timothy J.:** b. Mar. 21, 1919, Chicago, Ill.;
educ. Quigley Preparatory Seminary, St. Mary of
the Lake Seminary (Mundelein, Ill.); ord. priest
May 1, 1943; ord. titular bishop of Vamalla and
auxiliary bishop of Chicago, Dec. 13, 1983.

**Lyons, Thomas W.:** b. Sept. 26, 1923, Washington, D.C.; educ. St. Charles College (Catonsville,
Md.), St. Mary's Seminary (Baltimore, Md.); ord.
priest May 22, 1948; ord. titular bishop of Mortlach
and auxiliary bishop of Washington, D.C., Sept. 12,
1974.

## M

**McAuliffe, Michael F.:** b. Nov. 22, 1920, Kansas
City, Mo.; educ. St. Louis Preparatory Seminary
(St. Louis, Mo.), Catholic Univ. (Washington,
D.C.): ord. priest May 31, 1945; ord. bishop of Jef-
ferson City, Aug. 18, 1969.

**McCarrick, Theodore E.:** b. July 7, 1930, New
York, N.Y.; educ. Fordham Univ. (Bronx, N.Y.),
St. Joseph's Seminary (Dunwoodie, N.Y.), Catholic Univ. (Washington, D.C.); ord. priest May 31,
1958; dean of students Catholic Univ. of America,
1961-63; pres., Catholic Univ. of Puerto Rico,
1965-69; secretary to Cardinal Cooke, 1970; ord.
titular bishop of Rusubisir and auxiliary bishop of
New York, June 29, 1977; app. first bishop of
Metuchen, N.J., Nov. 19, 1981, installed Jan. 31,
1982.

**McCarthy, Edward A.:** b. Apr. 10, 1918, Cincinnati, O.; educ. Mt. St. Mary Seminary (Norwood,
O.), Catholic Univ. (Washington, D.C.), Lateran
and Angelicum (Rome); ord. priest May 29, 1943;
ord. titular bishop of Tamascani and auxiliary
bishop of Cincinnati, June 15, 1965; first bishop of
Phoenix, Ariz., Dec. 2, 1969; app. coadjutor archbishop of Miami, Fla., July 7, 1976; succeeded as
archbishop of Miami, July 26, 1977.

**McCarthy, John E.,** b. June 21, 1930, Houston,
Tex.; educ. Univ. of St. Thomas (Houston, Tex.);
ord. priest May 26, 1956; assistant director Social
Action Dept. USCC, 1967-69; executive director
Texas Catholic Conference; ord. titular bishop of
Pedena and auxiliary bishop of Galveston-Hous-
ton, Mar. 14, 1979.

**McCormick, J. Carroll:** b. Dec. 15, 1907, Philadelphia, Pa.; educ. College Ste. Marie (Montreal),

St. Charles Seminary (Overbrook, Pa.), Minor and
Major Roman Seminary (Rome); ord. priest July
10, 1932; ord. titular bishop of Ruspae and auxiliary bishop of Philadelphia, Apr. 23, 1947; app.
bishop of Altoona-Johnstown, installed Sept. 21,
1960; app. bishop of Scranton, installed May 25,
1966; resigned Feb. 15, 1983.

**McDonald, Andrew J.:** b. Oct. 24, 1923, Savannah, Ga.; educ. St. Mary's Seminary (Baltimore,
Md.), Catholic Univ. (Washington, D.C.), Lateran
Univ. (Rome); ord. priest May 8, 1948; ord. bishop
of Little Rock, Sept. 5, 1972.

**McDonald, William J.:** b. June 17, 1904, Moon-
coin, Ireland; educ. St. Kieran's College and Seminary (Kilkenny, Ireland), Catholic Univ. (Washington, D.C.); ord. priest June 10, 1928; rector of
Catholic Univ. of America, 1957-67; ord. titular
bishop of Aquae Regiae and auxiliary bishop of
Washington, May 19, 1964; app. auxiliary bishop of
San Francisco, July 26, 1967; retired June 5, 1979.

**McDonough, Thomas J.:** b. Dec. 5, 1911, Phila-
delphia, Pa.; educ. St. Charles Seminary
(Overbrook, Pa.), Catholic Univ. (Washington,
D.C.); ord. priest May 26, 1938; ord. titular bishop
of Thenae and auxiliary bishop of St. Augustine,
Apr. 30, 1947; app. auxiliary bishop of Savannah,
Jan. 2, 1957; named bishop of Savannah, installed
Apr. 27, 1960; app. archbishop of Louisville, in-
stalled May 2, 1967; resigned Sept. 29, 1981.

**McDowell, John B.:** b. July 17, 1921, New Castle, Pa.; educ. St. Vincent College, St. Vincent
Theological Seminary (Latrobe, Pa.), Catholic
Univ. (Washington, D.C.); ord. priest Nov. 4, 1945;
superintendent of schools, Pittsburgh diocese,
1955-70; ord. titular bishop of Tamazuca, and auxiliary bishop of Pittsburgh, Sept. 8, 1966.

**McEleney, John J., S.J.:** b. Nov. 13, 1895,
Woburn, Mass.; educ. Boston College (Boston,
Mass.), Jesuit Scholasticate (New England Province); entered Society of Jesus, 1918; ord. priest
June 18, 1930; app. provincial of New England
Province, 1944; ord. titular bishop of Zeugma and
vicar apostolic of Jamaica, Apr. 15, 1950; title
changed to bishop of Kingston, Feb. 29, 1956; archbishop of Kingston, Sept. 14, 1967; retired Sept. 1,
1970.

**McFarland, Norman F.:** b. Feb. 21, 1922,
Martinez, Calif.; educ. St. Patrick's Seminary
(Menlo Park, Calif.), Catholic Univ. (Washington,
D.C.); ord. priest June 15, 1946; ord. titular bishop
of Bida and auxiliary bishop of San Francisco,
Sept. 8, 1970; apostolic adminstrator of Reno, 1974;
app. bishop of Reno, Feb. 10, 1976, installed Mar.
31, 1976; title of see changed to Reno-Las Vegas.

**McGann, John R.:** b. Dec. 2, 1924, Brooklyn,
N.Y.; educ. Cathedral College (Brooklyn, N.Y.),
Immaculate Conception Seminary (Huntington,
L.I.); ord. priest June 3, 1950; ord. titular bishop of
Morosbisdus and auxiliary bishop of Rockville
Centre, Jan. 7, 1971; vicar general and episcopal
vicar; app. bishop of Rockville Centre May 3, 1976,
installed June 24, 1976.

**McGarry, Urban, T.O.R.:** b. Nov. 11, 1911, Warren, Pa.; ord. priest Oct. 3, 1942, in India; prefect
apostolic of Bhagalpur, Aug. 7, 1956; ord. first
bishop of Bhagalpur, India, May 10, 1965.

**McKinney, Joseph C.:** b. Sept. 10, 1928, Grand Rapids, Mich.: educ. St. Joseph's Seminary (Grand Rapids, Mich.), Seminaire de Philosophie (Montreal, Canada), Urban Univ. (Rome, Italy); ord. priest Dec. 20, 1953; ord. titular bishop of Lentini and auxiliary bishop of Grand Rapids, Sept. 26, 1968.

**McLaughlin, Bernard J.:** b. Nov. 19, 1912, Buffalo, N.Y.; educ. Urban Univ. (Rome, Italy ); ord. priest Dec. 21, 1935, at Rome; ord. titular bishop of Mottola and auxiliary bishop of Buffalo, Jan. 6, 1969.

**McManus, William E.:** b. Jan. 27, 1914, Chicago, Ill.; educ. St. Mary of the Lake Seminary (Mundelein, Ill.), Catholic Univ. (Washington, D.C.); ord. priest Apr. 15, 1939; ord. titular bishop of Mesarfelta and auxiliary bishop of Chicago, Aug. 24, 1967; app. bishop of Fort Wayne-South Bend, Aug. 31, 1976, installed Oct. 19, 1976.

**McNabb, John C., O.S.A.:** b. Dec. 11, 1925, Beloit, Wis.; educ. Villanova Univ. (Villanova, Pa.), Augustinian College and Catholic Univ. (Washington, D.C.), De Paul Univ. (Chicago, Ill.); ord. priest May 24, 1952; ord. titular bishop of Saia Maggiore, June 17, 1967 (resigned titular see, Dec. 27, 1977); prelate of Chulucanas, Peru, 1967.

**McNamara, Lawrence J.:** b. Aug. 5, 1928, Chicago, Ill.; educ. St. Paul Seminary (St. Paul, Minn.), Catholic Univ. (Washington, D.C.); ord. priest May 30, 1953; executive director of Campaign for Human Development 1973-77; ord. bishop of Grand Island, Nebr., Mar. 28, 1978.

**McNaughton, William J., M.M.:** b. Dec. 7, 1926, Lawrence, Mass.; educ. Maryknoll Seminary (Maryknoll, N.Y.); ord. priest June 13, 1953; ord. titular bishop of Thuburbo Minus and vicar apostolic of Inchon, Korea, Aug. 24, 1961; title changed to bishop of Inchon, Mar. 10, 1962.

**McRaith, John Jeremiah:** b. Dec. 6, 1934, Hutchinson, Minn.; educ. St. John Preparatory School (Collegeville, Minn.), Loras College, St. Bernard Seminary (Dubuque, Ia); ord. priest Feb. 21, 1960; exec. dir. of Catholic Rural Life Conference, 1971-78; ord. bishop of Owensboro, Ky., Dec. 15, 1982.

**McShea, Joseph M.:** b. Feb. 22, 1907, Latimer, Pa.; educ. St. Charles Seminary (Philadelphia, Pa.), Major Pontifical Roman Seminary (Rome); ord. priest Dec. 6, 1931; ord. titular bishop of Mina and auxiliary bishop of Philadelphia, Mar. 19, 1952; app. first bishop of Allentown, installed Apr. 11, 1961; resigned Feb. 8, 1983.

**Madera, Joseph J., M.Sp.S.:** b. Nov. 27, 1927, San Francisco, Calif.; educ. Domus Studiorum of the Missionaries of the Holy Spirit (Coyoacan, D.F. Mexico); ord. priest June 15, 1957; ord. coadjutor bishop of Fresno, Mar. 4, 1980; bishop of Fresno, July 1, 1980.

**Maguire, John J.:** b. Dec. 11, 1904, New York, N.Y.; educ. Cathedral College (New York City), St. Joseph's Seminary (Dunwoodie, N.Y.), North American College (Rome); ord. priest Dec. 22, 1928; ord. titular bishop of Antiphrae and auxiliary bishop of New York, June 29, 1959; app. titular archbishop of Tabalta and coadjutor archbishop of New York, Sept. 15, 1965; retired Jan. 8, 1980.

**Maguire, Joseph F.:** b. Sept. 4, 1919, Boston, Mass.; educ. Boston College, St. John's Seminary (Boston, Mass.); ord. priest June 29, 1945; ord. titular bishop of Macteris and auxiliary bishop of Boston, Feb. 2, 1972; app. coadjutor bishop of Springfield, Mass., Apr. 13, 1976; succeeded as bishop of Springfield, Mass., Oct. 15, 1977.

**Maher, Leo T.:** b. July 1, 1915, Mount Union, Ia.; educ. St. Joseph's College (Mountain View, Calif.); St. Patrick's Seminary (Menlo Park, Calif.); ord. priest Dec. 18, 1943; ord. first bishop of Santa Rosa, April 5, 1962; bishop of San Diego, Oct. 4, 1969.

**Mahoney, James P.:** b. Aug. 16, 1925, Kingston, N.Y.; educ. St. Joseph's Seminary (Dunwoodie, N.Y.); ord. priest May 19, 1951; ord. titular bishop of Ipagro and auxiliary bishop of New York, Sept. 15, 1972.

**Mahony, Roger M.:** b. Feb. 27, 1936, Hollywood, Calif.; educ. St. John's Seminary (Camarillo, Calif.), National Catholic School of Social Service (Catholic Univ., Washington, D.C.); ord. priest May 1, 1962; ord. titular bishop of Tamascani and auxiliary bishop of Fresno, Mar. 19, 1975; app. bishop of Stockton, installed Apr. 25, 1980.

**Maida, Adam J.:** b. Mar. 18, 1930, East Vandergrift, Pa.; educ. St. Vincent College (Latrobe, Pa.). St. Mary Univ. (Baltimore, Md.), Lateran Univ. (Rome), Duquesne Univ. (Pittsburgh, Pa.); ord. priest May 26, 1956; ord. bishop of Green Bay, Jan. 25, 1984.

**Malone, James W.:** b. Mar. 8, 1920, Youngstown, O.; educ. St. Charles Preparatory Seminary (Catonsville, Md.), St. Mary's Seminary (Cleveland, O.), Catholic Univ. (Washington, D.C.); ord. priest May 26, 1945; ord. titular bishop of Alabanda and auxiliary bishop of Youngstown, Mar. 24, 1960; apostolic administrator, 1966; bishop of Youngstown, installed June 20, 1968.

**Maloney, Charles G.:** b. Sept. 9, 1912, Louisville, Ky.; educ. St. Joseph's College (Rensselaer, Ind.), North American College (Rome); ord. priest Dec. 8, 1937; ord. titular bishop of Capsa and auxiliary bishop of Louisville, Feb. 2, 1955.

**Maloney, David M.:** b. Mar. 15, 1912, Littleton, Colo.; educ. St. Thomas Seminary (Denver, Colo.), Gregorian Univ. and Apollinare Univ. (Rome); ord. priest Dec. 8, 1936; ord. titular bishop of Ruspe and auxiliary bishop of Denver, Jan. 4, 1961; app. bishop of Wichita, Kans., Dec. 6, 1967; resigned July 16, 1982.

**Manning, Thomas R., O.F.M.:** b. Aug. 29, 1922, Baltimore, Md.; educ. Duns Scotus College (Southfield, Mich.), Holy Name College (Washington, D.C.); ord. priest June 5, 1948; ord. titular bishop of Arsamosata, July 14, 1959 (resigned titular see Dec. 30, 1977); prelate of Coroico, Bolivia, July 14, 1959; became first bishop, 1983, when prelature was raised to diocese.

**Manning, Timothy:** (See Cardinals, Biographies.)

**Marcinkus, Paul C.:** b. Jan. 15, 1922, Cicero, Ill.; ord. priest May 3, 1947; served in Vatican secretariat from 1952; ord. titular bishop of Orta, Jan. 6, 1969; secretary (1968-71) and president (1971-   ) of Institute for Works of Religion (Vatican Bank);

titular archbishop, Sept. 26, 1981; pro-president of Pontifical Commission for the State of Vatican City.

**Marconi, Dominic A.:** b. Mar. 13, 1927, Newark, N.J.; educ. Seton Hall Univ. (S. Orange, N.J.), Immaculate Conception Seminary (Darlington, N.J.), Catholic Univ. (Washington, D.C.); ord. priest May 30, 1953; ord. titular bishop of Bure and auxiliary bishop of Newark, June 25, 1976.

**Marino, Eugene A., S.S.J.:** b. May 29, 1934, Biloxi, Miss.; educ. Epiphany Apostolic College and Mary Immaculate Novitiate (Newburgh, N.Y.), St. Joseph's Seminary (Washington, D.C.), Catholic Univ. (Washington, D.C.), Loyola Univ. (New Orleans, La.), Fordham Univ. (New York City); ord. priest June 9, 1962; ord. titular bishop of Walla Walla and auxiliary bishop of Washington, D.C., Sept. 12, 1974.

**Marshall, John A.:** b. Apr. 26, 1928, Worcester, Mass.; educ. Holy Cross College (Worcester, Mass.), Sulpician Seminary (Montreal), North American College and Gregorian Univ. (Rome), Assumption College (Worcester); ord. priest Dec. 19, 1953; ord. bishop of Burlington, Jan. 25, 1972.

**Matthiesen, Leroy Theodore:** b. June 11, 1921, Olfen, Tex.; educ. Josephinum College (Columbus, O.), Catholic Univ. (Washington, D.C.), Register School of Journalism; ord. priest Mar. 10, 1946; ord. bishop of Amarillo, May 30, 1980.

**May, John L.:** b. Mar. 31, 1922, Evanston, Ill.; educ. St. Mary of the Lake Seminary (Mundelein, Ill.); ord. priest May 3, 1947; general secretary and vice-president of the Catholic Church Extension Society, 1959; ord. titular bishop of Tagarbala and auxiliary bishop of Chicago, Aug. 24, 1967; bishop of Mobile, Ala., Sept. 29, 1969; app. archbishop of St. Louis, installed Mar. 25, 1980.

**Melczek, Dale J.:** b. Nov. 9, 1938, Detroit, Mich.; educ. St. Mary's College (Orchard Lake, Mich.), St. John's Provincial Seminary (Plymouth, Mich.), Univ. of Detroit; ord. priest June 6, 1964; ord. titular bishop of Trau and auxiliary bishop of Detroit, Jan. 27, 1983; vicar general; regional bishop of northwest region of Detroit archdiocese.

**Mendez, Alfred, C.S.C.:** b. June 3, 1907, Chicago, Ill.; educ. Notre Dame Univ. (Notre Dame, Ind.), Institute of Holy Cross (Washington, D.C.); ord. priest June 24, 1935; ord. first bishop of Arecibo, Puerto Rico, Oct. 28, 1960; resigned Jan. 24, 1974.

**Mestice, Anthony F.:** b. Dec. 6, 1923, New York, N.Y.; educ. St. Joseph Seminary (Yonkers, N.Y.); ord. priest June 4, 1949; ord. titular bishop of Villa Nova and auxiliary bishop of New York Apr. 27, 1973.

**Metzger, Sidney Matthew:** b. July 11, 1902, Fredericksburg, Tex.; educ. St. John's Seminary (San Antonio, Tex.), North American College (Rome); ord. priest Apr. 3, 1926; ord. titular bishop of Birtha and auxiliary bishop of Santa Fe, Apr. 10, 1940; app. coadjutor bishop of El Paso, Dec. 26, 1941; bishop of El Paso, Dec. 1, 1942; retired May 29, 1978.

**Michaels, James E., S.S.C.:** b. May 30, 1926, Chicago, Ill.; educ. Columban Seminary (St. Colum-

ban, Neb.), Gregorian Univ. (Rome); ord. priest Dec. 21, 1951; ord. titular bishop of Verbe and auxiliary bishop of Kwang Ju, Korea, Apr. 14, 1966; app. auxiliary bishop of Wheeling, Apr. 3, 1973; title of see changed to Wheeling-Charleston, 1974.

**Milone, Anthony:** b. Sept. 24, 1932, Omaha, Nebr.; educ. North American College (Rome); ord. priest Dec. 15, 1957, in Rome; ord. titular bishop of Plestia and auxiliary bishop of Omaha, Jan. 6, 1982.

**Minder, John, O.S.F.S.:** b. Nov. 1, 1923, Philadelphia, Pa.; ord. priest June 3, 1950; ord. bishop of Keimos, South Africa, Jan. 10, 1968.

**Montrose, Donald:** b. May 13, 1923, Denver, Colo.; educ. St. John's Seminary (Camarillo, Calif.); ord. priest May 7, 1949; ord. titular bishop of Forum Novum and auxiliary bishop of Los Angeles, May 12, 1983.

**Moore, Emerson John:** b. May 16, 1938, New York, N.Y.; educ. Cathedral College (New York City), St. Joseph's Seminary (Yonkers, N.Y.); New York University, Columbia Univ. School of Social Work (New York City); ord. priest May 30, 1964; ord. auxiliary bishop of Curubi and auxiliary bishop of New York, Sept. 8, 1982.

**Moran, William J.:** b. Jan. 15, 1906, San Francisco, Calif.; educ. St. Patrick's Seminary (Menlo Park, Calif.); ord. priest June 20, 1931; Army chaplain, 1933; ord. titular bishop of Centuria and auxiliary to the military vicar, Dec. 13, 1965; retired Jan. 15, 1981.

**Moreno, Manuel D.:** b. Nov. 27, 1930, Placentia, Calif.; educ. Univ. of California (Los Angeles), Our Lady Queen of Angels (San Fernando, Calif.), St. John's Seminary (Camarillo, Calif.); ord. priest Apr. 25, 1961; ord. titular bishop of Tanagra and auxiliary bishop of Los Angeles, Feb. 19, 1977; bishop of Tucson, Jan. 12, 1982, installed Mar. 11, 1982.

**Morkovsky, John Louis:** b. Aug. 16, 1909, Praha, Tex.; educ. St. John's Seminary (San Antonio, Tex.), North American College, Urban Univ. and Gregorian Univ. (Rome), Catholic Univ. (Washington, D.C.); ord. priest Dec. 5, 1933; ord titular bishop of Hieron and auxiliary bishop of Amarillo, Feb. 22, 1956; app. bishop of Amarillo, Aug. 27, 1958; titular bishop of Tigava and coadjutor bishop of Galveston-Houston with right of succession, June 11, 1963; apostolic administrator; president Texas Conference of Churches, 1970-72; bishop of Galveston-Houston, Apr. 22, 1975; retired Aug. 21, 1984.

**Morneau, Robert F.:** b. Sept. 10, 1938, New London, Wis.; educ. St. Norbert's College (De Pere, Wis.), Sacred Heart Seminary (Oneida, Wis.), Catholic Univ. (Washington, D.C.); ord. priest May 28, 1966; ord. titular bishop of Massa Lubrense and auxiliary bishop of Green Bay, Feb. 22, 1979.

**Morrow, Louis La Ravoire, S.D.B.:** b. Dec. 24, 1892, Weatherford, Tex.; educ. Salesian School and Palafox (Puebla, Mexico); professed in Salesians of St. John Bosco, Sept. 29, 1912; ord. priest May 21, 1921; ord. bishop of Krishnagar, India, Oct. 29, 1939; resigned Oct. 31, 1969.

**Moskal, Robert:** b. Oct. 24, 1937, Carnegie, Pa.;

educ. St. Basil Minor Seminary (Stamford, Conn.), St. Josaphat Seminary and Catholic Univ. (Washington, D.C.); ord. priest Mar. 25, 1963; ord. titular bishop of Agatopoli and auxiliary bishop of the Ukrainian-Rite archeparchy of Philadelphia, Oct. 13, 1981; app. first bishop of St. Josaphat in Parma, Dec. 5, 1983.

**Mugavero, Francis John:** b. June 8, 1914, Brooklyn, N.Y.; educ. Cathedral College (Brooklyn, N.Y.), Immaculate Conception Seminary (Huntington, N.Y.), Fordham Univ. (New York City); ord. priest May 18, 1940; ord. bishop of Brooklyn, Sept. 12, 1968.

**Mulcahy, John J.:** b. June 26, 1922, Dorchester, Mass.; educ. St. John's Seminary (Brighton, Mass.); ord. priest May 1, 1947; rector Pope John XXIII Seminary for Delayed Vocations, 1969-73; ord. titular bishop of Penafiel and auxiliary bishop of Boston, Feb. 11, 1975.

**Mulrooney, Charles R.:** b. Jan. 13, 1906, Brooklyn, N.Y.; educ. Cathedral College (Brooklyn, N.Y.), St. Mary's Seminary (Baltimore, Md.), Sulpician Seminary (Washington, D.C.); ord. priest June 10, 1930; ord. titular bishop of Valentiniana and auxiliary bishop of Brooklyn, Apr. 22, 1959; retired Jan. 13, 1981.

**Mulvee, Robert E.:** b. Feb. 15, 1930, Boston, Mass.; educ. St. Thomas Seminary (Bloomfield, Conn.), University Seminary (Ottawa, Ont., Canada), American College (Louvain, Belgium), Lateran Univ. (Rome); ord. priest June 30, 1957; ord. titular bishop of Summa and auxiliary bishop of Manchester, N.H., Apr. 14, 1977.

**Mundo, Michael P.:** b. July 25, 1937, New York, N.Y.; educ. Fordham Univ. (Bronx, N.Y.), St. Jerome's College (Kitchener, Ont., Canada), St. Francis Seminary (Loretto, Pa.); ord. May 19, 1962; missionary in Brazil from 1963; ord. titular bishop of Blanda Julia and auxiliary bishop of Jatai, Brazil, June 2, 1978.

**Murphy, Michael J.:** b. July 1, 1915, Cleveland, O.; educ. Niagara Univ. (Niagara Falls, N.Y.); North American College (Rome), Catholic Univ. (Washington, D.C.); ord. priest Feb. 28, 1942; ord. titular bishop of Ariendela and auxiliary bishop of Cleveland, June 11, 1976; app. coadjutor bishop of Erie, Nov. 20, 1978; bishop of Erie, July 16, 1982.

**Murphy, Philip Francis:** b. Mar. 25, 1933, Cumberland, Md.; educ. St. Mary Seminary (Baltimore, Md.), North American College (Rome); ord. priest Dec. 20, 1958; ord. titular bishop of Tacarata and auxiliary bishop of Baltimore, Feb. 29, 1976.

**Murphy, T. Austin:** b. May 11, 1911, Baltimore, Md.; educ. St. Charles College (Catonsville, Md.), St. Mary's Seminary (Baltimore, Md.); ord priest June 10, 1937; ord. titular bishop of Appiaria and auxiliary bishop of Baltimore, July 3, 1962; retired May 29, 1984.

**Murphy, Thomas J.:** b. Oct. 3, 1932, Chicago, Ill.; educ. Quigley Preparatory Seminary (Chicago, Ill.), St. Mary of the Lake Seminary (Mundelein, Ill.); ord. priest Apr. 12, 1958; ord. bishop of Great Falls, Mont. Aug. 21, 1978; title of see changed to Great Falls-Billings, 1980.

**Murphy, Thomas W., C.SS.R.:** b. Dec. 17, 1917,

Omaha, Nebr.; educ. St. Joseph's College (Kirkwood, Mo.); ord. priest June 29, 1943; ord. first bishop of Juazeiro, Brazil, Jan. 2, 1963; resigned Dec. 29, 1973; app. titular bishop of Sululos and auxiliary bishop of Sao Salvador da Bahia, Brazil, Jan. 31, 1974.

## N

**Nelson, Knute Ansgar, O.S.B.:** b. Oct. 1, 1906, Copenhagen, Denmark; educ. Abbey of Maria Laach (Germany), Brown Univ. (Providence, R.I.); professed in the Order of St. Benedict, May 30, 1932; ord. priest May 22, 1937; became an American citizen, Mar. 4, 1941; ord. titular bishop of Bilta and coadjutor bishop of Stockholm, Sweden, Sept. 8, 1947; succeeded as bishop of Stockholm, Oct. 1, 1957; retired; titular bishop of Dura, 1962.

**Nevins, John J.:** b. Jan. 19, 1932, New Rochelle, N.Y.; educ. Iona College (New Rochelle, N.Y.), Catholic Univ. (Washington, D.C.); ord. priest June 6, 1959; ord. titular bishop of Rusticana and auxiliary bishop of Miami, Mar. 24, 1979; app. first bishop of Venice, Fla., July 17, 1984; installed Oct. 24, 1984.

**Newell, Hubert M.:** b. Feb. 16, 1904, Denver, Colo.; educ. Regis College and St. Thomas Seminary (Denver, Colo.), Catholic Univ. (Washington, D.C.); ord. priest June 15, 1930; ord. titular bishop of Zapara and coadjutor bishop of Cheyenne, Sept. 24, 1947; bishop of Cheyenne, Nov. 10, 1951; retired Jan. 3, 1978.

**Newman, William C.:** b. Aug. 16, 1928, Baltimore, Md.; educ. St. Mary Seminary (Baltimore, Md.). Catholic Univ. (Washington, D.C.), Loyola College (Baltimore, Md.); ord. priest May 29, 1954; ord. titular bishop of Numluli and auxiliary bishop of Baltimore, July 2, 1984.

**Neylon, Martin J., S.J.:** b. Feb. 13, 1920, Buffalo, N.Y.; ord. priest June 18, 1950; ord. titular bishop of Libertina and coadjutor vicar apostolic of the Caroline and Marshall Islands, Feb. 2, 1970; vicar apostolic of Caroline and Marshall Is., Sept. 20, 1971; first bishop when vicarate apostolic was raised to diocese, 1979.

**Niedergeses, James D.:** b. Feb. 2, 1917, Lawrenceburg, Tenn.; educ. St. Bernard College (St. Bernard, Ala.), St. Ambrose College (Davenport, Ia.), Mt. St. Mary Seminary of the West and Athenaeum (Cincinnati, Ohio); ord. priest May 20, 1944; ord. bishop of Nashville May 20, 1975.

**Nolker, Bernard, C.SS.R.:** b. Sept. 25, 1912, Baltimore, Md.; educ. St. Mary's College (North East, Pa.), St. Mary's College (Ilchester, Md.), Mt. St. Alphonsus Seminary (Esopus, N.Y.); ord. priest June 18, 1939; ord. first bishop of Paranagua, Brazil, Apr. 25, 1963.

**Novak, Alfred, C.SS.R.:** b. June 2, 1930, Dwight, Nebr.; educ. Immaculate Conception Seminary (Oconomowoc, Wis.); ord. priest July 2, 1956; ord. titular bishop of Vardimissa and auxiliary bishop of Sao Paulo, Brazil, May 25, 1979.

## O

**O'Boyle, Patrick A.:** (See Cardinals, Biographies.)

**O'Brien, Thomas Joseph: b.** Nov. 29, 1935, Indianapolis, Ind.; educ. St. Meinrad High School Seminary, St. Meinrad College Seminary (St. Meinrad, Ind); ord. priest May 7, 1961; ord. bishop of Phoenix, Jan. 6, 1982.

**O'Connor, John J.: b.** Jan. 15, 1920, Philadelphia, Pa.; educ. St. Charles Borromeo Seminary (Philadelphia, Pa.), Catholic Univ., Georgetown Univ. (Washington, D.C.); ord. priest Dec. 15, 1945; U.S. Navy chief of chaplains, 1975; ord. titular bishop of Cursola and auxiliary to the military vicar, May 27, 1979; app. bishop of Scranton, May 10, 1983, installed June 29, 1983; app. archbishop of New York, Jan. 31, 1984; installed Mar. 19, 1984.

**O'Connor, Martin J.: b.** May 18, 1900, Scranton, Pa.; educ. St. Thomas College (Scranton, Pa.), St. Mary's Seminary (Baltimore, Md.), North American College, Urban Univ. and Apollinaris (Rome); ord. priest Mar. 15, 1924; ord. titular bishop of Thespia and auxiliary bishop of Scranton, Jan. 27, 1943; rector of North American College 1946-1964; app. titular archbishop of Laodicea in Syria, Sept. 5, 1959; apostolic nuncio to Malta, 1965-69; president emeritus Pontifical Commission for Social Communication.

**O'Donnell, Cletus F.: b.** Aug. 22, 1917, Waukon, Ia.; educ. St. Mary Seminary (Mundelein, Ill.), Catholic Univ. (Washington, D.C.); ord. priest May 3, 1941; ord. titular bishop of Abritto and auxiliary bishop of Chicago, Dec. 21, 1960; app. bishop of Madison, Feb. 22, 1967, installed Apr. 25, 1967.

**O'Donnell, Edward J.: b.** July 4, 1931, St. Louis, Mo.; educ. St. Louis Preparatory Seminary and Kenrick Seminary (St. Louis, Mo.); ord. priest Apr. 6, 1957; ord. titular bishop of Britania and auxiliary bishop of St. Louis, Feb. 10, 1984.

**O'Keefe, Gerald F.: b.** Mar. 30, 1918, St. Paul, Minn.; educ. College of St. Thomas, St. Paul Seminary (St. Paul, Minn.); ord. priest Jan. 29, 1944; ord. titular bishop of Candyba and auxiliary bishop of St. Paul July 2, 1961; bishop of Davenport, Oct. 20, 1966, installed Jan. 4, 1967.

**O'Keefe, Joseph Thomas: b.** Mar. 12, 1919, New York, N.Y.; educ. Cathedral College (New York City), St. Joseph's Seminary (Yonkers, N.Y.), Catholic Univ. (Washington, D.C.); ord. priest Apr. 17, 1948; ord. titular bishop of Tre Taverne and auxiliary bishop of New York, Sept. 8, 1982.

**O'Leary, Edward C.: b.** Aug. 21, 1920, Bangor, Me.; educ. Holy Cross College (Worcester, Mass.), St. Paul's Seminary (Ottawa, Canada); ord. priest June 15, 1946; ord. titular bishop of Moglena and auxiliary bishop of Portland, Me., Jan. 25, 1971; app. bishop of Portland, installed Dec. 18, 1974.

**O'Malley, Sean, O.F.M. Cap.: b.** 1945, Lakewood, O.; educ. St. Fidelis Seminary (Herman, Pa.), Capuchin College and Catholic Univ. (Washington, D.C.); ord. priest Aug. 29, 1970; episcopal vicar of priests serving Spanish speaking in Washington archdiocese, 1978-84; executive director of Spanish Catholic Center, Washington, from 1973; ord. coadjutor bishop of St. Thomas, Virgin Islands, August, 1984.

**O'Meara, Edward T.: b.** Aug. 3, 1921, St. Louis,

Mo.; educ. Cardinal Glennon College and Kenrick Seminary (St. Louis, Mo.), Angelicum (Rome); ord. priest Dec. 21, 1946; app. national director of Society for the Propagation of the Faith, 1967; ord. titular bishop of Thisiduo and auxiliary bishop of St. Louis, Feb. 13, 1972; app. archbishop of Indianapolis, installed Jan. 10, 1980.

**O'Neil, Leo E.: b.** Jan. 31, 1928, Holyoke, Mass.; educ. Maryknoll Seminary (Maryknoll, N.Y.), St. Anselm's College (Manchester, N.H.), Grand Seminary (Montreal, Canada); ord. priest June 4, 1955; ord. titular bishop of Bencenna and auxiliary bishop of Springfield, Mass., Aug. 22, 1980.

**O'Neill, Arthur J.: b.** Dec. 14, 1917, East Dubuque, Ill.; educ. Loras College (Dubuque, Ia.), St. Mary's Seminary (Baltimore, Md.); ord. priest Mar. 27, 1943; ord. bishop of Rockford, Oct. 11, 1968.

**O'Rourke, Edward W.: b.** Oct. 31, 1917, Downs, Ill.; educ. St. Mary's Seminary (Mundelein, Ill.), Aquinas Institute of Philosophy and Theology (River Forest, Ill.); ord. priest May 28, 1944; exec. dir. National Catholic Rural Life Conference, 1960-71; ord. bishop of Peoria, July 15, 1971.

**Ott, Stanley J.: b.** June 29, 1927, Gretna, La.; educ. Notre Dame Seminary (New Orleans, La.), North American College and Gregorian Univ. (Rome); ord. priest Dec. 8, 1951; ord. titular bishop of Nicives and auxiliary bishop of New Orleans, June 29, 1976; app. bishop of Buton Rouge, Jan 17, 1983, installed Mar. 24, 1983.

**Ottenweller, Albert H.: b.** Apr. 5, 1916, Stanford, Mont.; educ. St. Joseph's Seminary (Rensselaer, Ind.), Catholic Univ. (Washington, D.C.); ord. priest June 19, 1943; ord. titular bishop of Perdices and auxiliary bishop of Toledo, May 29, 1974; app. bishop of Steubenville, Oct. 11, 1977, installed Nov. 22, 1977.

**P**

**Paschang, John L.: b.** Oct. 5, 1895, Hemingford, Nebr.; educ. Conception College (Conception, Mo.), St. John Seminary (Collegeville, Minn.), Catholic Univ. (Washington, D.C.); ord. priest June 12, 1921; ord. bishop of Grand Island, Oct. 9, 1951; resigned July 25, 1972.

**Pataki, Andrew: b.** Aug. 30, 1927, Palmerton, Pa.; educ. St. Vincent College (Latrobe, Pa.), St. Procopius College, St. Procopius Seminary (Lisle, Ill.), Sts. Cyril and Methodius Byzantine Catholic Seminary (Pittsburgh, Pa.), Gregorian Univ. and Oriental Pontifical Institute (Rome, Italy); ord. priest Feb. 24, 1952; ord. titular bishop of Telmisso and auxiliary bishop of Byzantine diocese of Passaic, Aug. 23, 1983; vicar general; episcopal vicar of Pennsylvania; app. bishop of Ruthenian Byzantine diocese of Parma, July 3, 1984.

**Paul, John J.: b.** Aug. 17, 1918, La Crosse, Wis.; educ. Loras College (Dubuque, Iowa), St. Mary's Seminary (Baltimore, Md.), Marquette Univ. (Milwaukee, Wis.), ord. priest Jan. 24, 1943; ord. titular bishop of Lambaesis and auxiliary bishop of La Crosse, Aug. 4, 1977; app. bishop of La Crosse, Oct. 18, 1983, installed Dec. 5, 1983.

**Pearce, George H., S.M.: b.** Jan. 9, 1921, Brighton, Mass.; educ. Marist College and Seminary

(Framington, Mass.); ord. priest Feb. 2, 1947; ord. titular bishop of Attalea in Pamphylia and vicar apostolic of the Samoa and Tokelau Islands, June 29, 1956; title changed to bishop of Apia, June 21, 1966; app. archbishop of Suva, Fiji Islands, June 22, 1967; resigned Apr. 10, 1976.

**Pechillo, Jerome, T.O.R.:** b. May 16, 1919, Brooklyn, N.Y.; educ. Catholic Univ. (Washington, D.C.); ord. priest June 10, 1947; ord. titular bishop of Novasparsa and prelate of Coronel Oviedo, Paraguay, Jan. 25, 1966; app. auxiliary bishop of Newark, N.J., Mar. 6, 1976.

**Pena, Raymundo J.:** b. Feb. 19, 1934, Robstown, Tex.; educ. Assumption Seminary (San Antonio, Tex.); ord. priest May 25, 1957; ord. titular bishop of Trisipa and auxiliary bishop of San Antonio, Dec. 13, 1976; app. bishop of El Paso, Apr. 29, 1980.

**Pernicone, Joseph M.:** b. Nov. 4, 1903, Regalbuto, Sicily; educ. Cathedral College (New York City), St. Joseph's Seminary (Dunwoodie, N.Y.), Catholic Univ. (Washington, D.C.); ord. priest Dec. 18, 1926; ord. titular bishop of Hadrianapolis and auxiliary bishop of New York, May 5, 1954; app. episcopal vicar, 1966; retired Nov. 28, 1978.

**Perry, Harold R., S.V.D.:** b. Oct. 9, 1916, Lake Charles, La.; educ. St. Augustine Seminary (Bay St. Louis, Miss.), St. Mary's Seminary (Techny, Ill.); ord. priest Jan. 6, 1944; app. provincial of southern province of Society of the Divine Word, 1964; ord. titular bishop of Mons in Mauretania and auxiliary bishop of New Orleans, Jan. 6, 1966.

**Pevec, A. Edward:** b. Apr. 16, 1925, Cleveland, O.; educ. St. Mary's Seminary, John Carroll Univ. (Cleveland, O.); ord. priest Apr. 29, 1950; ord. titular bishop of Mercia and auxiliary bishop of Cleveland, July 2, 1982.

**Pilarczyk, Daniel E.:** b. Aug. 12, 1934, Dayton, Ohio; educ. St. Gregory's Seminary (Cincinnati, O.), Urban Univ. (Rome), Xavier Univ. and Univ. of Cincinnati (Cincinnati, O.); ord. priest Dec. 20, 1959; ord. titular bishop of Hodelm and auxiliary bishop of Cincinnati, Dec. 20, 1974; app. archbishop of Cincinnati, Oct. 30, 1982; installed Dec. 2, 1982.

**Pilla, Anthony M.:** b. Nov. 12, 1932, Cleveland, O.; educ. St. Gregory College Seminary (Cincinnati, O.), Borromeo College Seminary (Wickliffe, O.), St. Mary Seminary and John Carroll Univ. (Cleveland, O.); ord. priest May 23, 1959; ord. titular bishop of Scardona and auxiliary bishop of Cleveland, Aug. 1, 1979; app. apostolic administrator of Cleveland, 1980; bishop of Cleveland, Nov. 13, 1980.

**Pinger, Henry A., O.F.M.:** b. Aug. 16, 1897, Lindsay, Nebr.; educ. Our Lady of Angels Seminary (Cleveland, O.), St. Anthony's Seminary (St. Louis, Mo.); professed in the Order of Friars Minor, June 18, 1918; ord. priest June 27, 1924; ord. titular bishop of Capitolias and vicar apostolic of Chowtsun, China, Sept. 21, 1937; title changed to bishop of Chowtsun, Apr. 11, 1946; imprisoned by Reds in 1951, released in 1956; expelled; bishop emeritus of Chowtsun.

**Popp, Bernard F.:** b. Dec. 6, 1917, Nada, Tex.; educ. St. John's Seminary and St. Mary's Univ. (San Antonio, Tex.); ord. priest Feb. 24, 1943; ord. titular bishop of Capsus and auxiliary bishop of San Antonio, July 25, 1983.

**Povish, Kenneth J.:** b. Apr. 19, 1924, Alpena, Mich.; educ. St. Joseph's Seminary (Grand Rapids, Mich.), Sacred Heart Seminary (Detroit, Mich.), Catholic Univ. (Washington, D.C.); ord. priest June 3, 1950; ord. bishop of Crookston, Sept. 29, 1970; app. bishop of Lansing, Oct. 8, 1975, installed Dec. 11, 1975.

**Power, Cornelius M.:** b. Dec. 18, 1913, Seattle, Wash.; educ. St. Patrick's College (Menlo Park, Calif.), St. Edward's Seminary (Kenmore, Wash.), Catholic Univ. (Washington, D.C.); ord. priest June 3, 1939; ord. bishop of Yakima, May 1, 1969, installed May 20, 1969; app. archbishop of Portland, Ore., Jan. 22, 1974, installed Apr. 17, 1974.

**Primeau, Ernest J.:** b. Sept. 17, 1909, Chicago, Ill.; educ. Loyola Univ. (Chicago, Ill.), St. Mary of the Lake Seminary (Mundelein, Ill.), Lateran Univ. (Rome); ord. priest Apr. 7, 1934; ord. bishop of Manchester, Feb. 25, 1960; resigned Jan. 30, 1974; director of Villa Stritch, Rome, 1974-79.

**Prost, Jude, O.F.M.:** b. Dec. 6, 1915, Chicago, Ill.; educ. Our Lady of the Angels Seminary (Cleveland, O.), St. Joseph's Seminary (Teutopolis, Ill.); ord. priest June 24, 1942; ord. titular bishop of Fronta and auxiliary bishop of Belem do Para, Brazil, Nov. 1, 1962.

**Proulx, Amedee W.:** b. Aug. 31, 1932, Sanford, Me.; educ. St. Hyacinthe Seminary (Quebec), St. Paul Univ. Seminary (Ottawa), Catholic Univ. (Washington, D.C.); ord. priest May 31, 1958; ord. titular bishop of Clipia and auxiliary bishop of Portland, Me., Nov. 12, 1975.

**Pursley, Leo A.:** b. Mar. 12, 1902, Hartford City, Ind.; educ. Mt. St. Mary's Seminary (Cincinnati, O.); ord. priest June 11, 1927; ord. titular bishop of Hadrianapolis in Pisidia and auxiliary bishop of Fort Wayne, Sept. 19, 1950; app. apostolic administrator of Fort Wayne, Mar. 9, 1955; installed as bishop of Fort Wayne, Feb. 26, 1957; title of see changed to Fort Wayne-South Bend, 1960; resigned Aug. 31, 1976.

**Puscas, Louis:** b. Sept. 13, 1915, Aurora, Ill.; educ. Quigley Preparatory Seminary (Chicago, Ill.), seminary in Oradea-Mare (Romania), Propaganda Fide Seminary (Rome), Illinois Benedictine College (Lisle, Ill.); ord. priest May 14, 1942; ord. titular bishop of Leuce and first exarch of apostolic exarchate for Romanians of the Byzantine Rite in the U.S., June 26, 1983 (seat of the exarchate is Canton, Ohio).

## Q

**Quinn, Alexander James:** b. Apr. 8, 1932, Cleveland, O.; educ. St. Charles College (Catonsville, Md.), St. Mary Seminary (Cleveland, O.), Lateran Univ. (Rome), Cleveland State Univ.; ord. priest May 24, 1958; ord. titular bishop of Socia and auxiliary bishop of Cleveland, Dec. 5, 1983; vicar of western region of Cleveland diocese.

**Quinn, Francis A.:** b. Sept. 11, 1921, Los Angeles, Calif.; educ. St. Joseph's College (Mountain View, Calif.), St. Patrick's Seminary (Menlo Park, Calif.), Catholic Univ. (Washington, D.C.);

Univ. of California (Berkley); ord. priest June 15, 1946; ord. titular bishop of Numana and auxiliary bishop of San Francisco, June 29, 1978; app. bishop of Sacramento Dec. 18, 1979.

**Quinn, John R.:** b. Mar. 28, 1929, Riverside, Calif.; educ. St. Francis Seminary (El Cajon, Calif.), North American College (Rome); ord. priest July 19, 1953; ord. titular bishop of Thisiduo and auxiliary bishop of San Diego, Dec. 12, 1967; bishop of Oklahoma City and Tulsa, Nov. 30, 1971; first archbishop of Oklahoma City, Dec. 19, 1972; app. archbishop of San Francisco Feb. 22, 1977, installed Apr. 26, 1977; president NCCB, USCC, 1977-80.

# R

**Ramirez, Ricardo, C.S.B.:** b. Sept. 12, 1936, Bay City, Tex.; educ. Univ. of St. Thomas (Houston, Tex.), Univ. of Detroit (Detroit, Mich.), St. Basil's Seminary (Toronto, Ont.); Seminario Concilium (Mexico City, Mexico), East Asian Pastoral Institute (Manila, Philippines); ord. priest Dec. 10, 1966; ord titular bishop of Vatarba and auxiliary of San Antonio, Dec. 6, 1981; app. first bishop of Las Cruces, N. Mex., Aug. 17, 1982; installed Oct. 18, 1982.

**Raya, Joseph M.:** b. July 20, 1917, Zahle, Lebanon; educ. St. Louis College (Paris, France), St. Anne's Seminary (Jerusalem); ord. priest July 20, 1941; came to U.S., 1949, became U.S. citizen; ord. archbishop of Acre, Israel, of the Melkites, Oct. 20, 1968; resigned Aug. 20, 1974; assigned titular metropolitan see of Scytopolis.

**Regan, Joseph W., M.M.:** b. Apr. 5, 1905, Boston, Mass.; educ. Boston College (Boston, Mass.), St. Bernard's Seminary (Rochester, N.Y.), Maryknoll Seminary (Maryknoll, N.Y.); ord. priest Jan. 27, 1929; missionary in China 15 years; in Philippines since 1952; ord. titular bishop of Isinda and prelate of Tagum, Philippine Islands, Apr. 25, 1962; resigned May 16, 1980.

**Reh, Francis F.:** b. Jan. 9, 1911, New York, N.Y.; educ. St. Joseph's Seminary (Dunwoodie, N.Y.), North American College and Gregorian Univ. (Rome); ord. priest Dec. 8, 1935; ord. bishop of Charleston, S.C., June 29, 1962; named titular bishop of Macriana in Mauretania, 1964; rector of North American College, 1964-68; bishop of Saginaw, installed Feb. 26, 1969; resigned Apr. 28, 1980.

**Reilly, Daniel P.:** b. May 12, 1928, Providence, R.I.; educ. Our Lady of Providence Seminary (Warwick, R.I.), St. Brieuc Major Seminary (Cotes du Nord, France); ord. priest May 30, 1953; ord. bishop of Norwich, Aug. 6, 1975.

**Reilly, Thomas F., C.SS.R.:** b. Dec. 20, 1908, Boston, Mass.; educ. Mt. St. Alphonsus Seminary (Esopus, N.Y.), Catholic Univ. (Washington, D.C.); ord. priest June 10, 1933; ord. titular bishop of Themisonium and prelate of San Juan de la Maguana, Dominican Republic, Nov. 30, 1956; first bishop of San Juan de la Maguana, Nov. 21, 1969; retired July 20, 1977.

**Reiss, John C.:** b. May 13, 1922, Red Bank, N.J.; educ. Catholic Univ. (Washington, D.C.), Immaculate Conception Seminary (Darlington, N.J.); ord.

priest May 31, 1947; ord. titular bishop of Simidicca and auxiliary bishop of Trenton, Dec. 12, 1967; app. bishop of Trenton, Mar. 11, 1980.

**Ricard, John, S.S.J.:** b. Feb. 29, 1940, Baton Rouge, La.; educ. St. Joseph's Seminary (Washington, D.C.), Tulane Univ. (New Orleans, La.); ord. priest May 25, 1968; ord. titular bishop of Rucuma and auxiliary of Baltimore, July 2, 1984; urban vicar, Baltimore.

**Riley, Lawrence J.:** b. Sept. 6, 1914; Boston, Mass.; educ. Boston College and St. John's Seminary (Boston, Mass.), North American College and Gregorian Univ. (Rome), Catholic Univ. (Washington, D.C.); ord. priest Sept. 21, 1940; ord. titular bishop of Daimlaig and auxiliary bishop of Boston, Feb. 2, 1972.

**Roach, John R.:** b. July 31, 1921, Prior Lake, Minn.; educ. St. Paul Seminary (St. Paul, Minn.), Univ. of Minnesota (Minneapolis); ord. priest June 18, 1946; ord. titular bishop of Cenae and auxiliary bishop of St. Paul and Minneapolis, Sept. 8, 1971; app. archbishop of St. Paul and Minneapolis, May 28, 1975; vice-president NCCB/USCC, 1977-80; president, 1980-83.

**Rodimer, Frank J.:** b. Oct. 25, 1927, Rockaway, N.J.; educ. Seton Hall Prep (South Orange, N.J.), St. Charles College (Catonsville, Md.), St. Mary's Seminary (Baltimore, Md.), Immaculate Conception Seminary (Darlington, N.J.), Catholic Univ. (Washington, D.C.); ord. priest May 19, 1951; ord. bishop of Paterson, Feb. 28, 1978.

**Rodriguez, Migúel, C.SS.R.:** b. Apr. 18, 1931, Mayaguez, P.R.; educ. St. Mary's Minor Seminary (North East, Pa.), Mt. St. Alphonsus Major Seminary (Esopus, N.Y.); ord. priest June 22, 1958; ord. bishop of Arecibo, P.R., Mar. 23, 1974.

**Rodriguez, Placido, C.M.F.:** b. Oct. 11, 1940, Celaya, Guanajuato, Mexico; educ. Claretian Novitate (Los Angeles, Calif.), Claretville Seminary College (Calabasas, Calif.), Catholic Univ. (Washington, D.C.), Loyola Univ. (Chicago, Ill.); ord. priest May 23, 1968; ord. titular bishop of Fuerteventura and auxiliary bishop of Chicago, Dec. 13, 1983.

**Roman, Agustin:** b. May 5, 1928, San Antonio de los Banos, Havana, Cuba; educ. San Alberto Magno Seminary (Matanzas, Cuba), Missions Etrangeres (Montreal, Canada), Barry College (Miami, Fla.); ord. priest July 5, 1959, Cuba; vicar for Spanish speaking in Miami archdiocese, 1976; ord. titular bishop of Sertei and auxiliary bishop of Miami, Mar. 24, 1979.

**Roque, Francis:** b. Oct. 9, 1928, Providence R.I.; educ. St. John's Seminary (Brighton, Mass.); ord. priest Sept. 19, 1953; became chaplain in U.S. Army 1961; ord. titular bishop of Bagai and auxiliary bishop of Military Vicariate, May 10, 1983.

**Rosazza, Peter Anthony:** b. Feb. 13, 1935, New Haven, Conn.; educ. St. Thomas Seminary (Bloomfield, Conn.), Dartmouth College (Hanover, N.H.), St. Bernard's Seminary (Rochester, N.Y.), St. Sulpice (Issy, France); ord. priest June 29, 1961; ord. titular bishop of Oppido Nuovo and auxiliary bishop of Hartford, June 24, 1978.

**Rose, Robert John:** b. Feb. 28, 1930, Grand Rapids, Mich.; educ. St. Joseph's Seminary

(Grand Rapids, Mich.), Seminaire de Philosophie (Montreal, Canada), Pontifical Urban University (Rome), Univ. of Michigan (Ann Arbor, Mich.); ord. priest Dec. 21, 1955; ord. bishop of Gaylord, Dec. 6, 1981.

**Rudin, John J., M.M.:** b. Nov. 27, 1916, Pittsfield, Mass.; educ. Maryknoll Seminary (Maryknoll, N.Y.), Gregorian Univ. (Rome); ord. priest June 11, 1944; ord. first bishop of Musoma, Tanzania, Oct. 3, 1957; retired Jan. 12, 1979.

**Russell, John J.:** b. Dec. 1, 1897, Baltimore, Md.; educ. St. Charles College (Catonsville, Md.), St. Mary's Seminary (Baltimore, Md.), North American College (Rome); ord. priest July 8, 1923; ord. bishop of Charleston, Mar. 14, 1950; bishop of Richmond, July 3, 1958; retired Apr. 30, 1973.

**Ryan, Daniel L.:** b. Sept. 28, 1930, Mankato, Minn.; educ. St. Procopius Seminary (Lisle, Ill.), Lateran Univ. (Rome); ord. priest May 3, 1956; ord. titular bishop of Surista and auxiliary bishop of Joliet, Sept. 30, 1981; app. bishop of Springfield, Ill., Nov. 22, 1983, installed Jan. 18, 1984.

**Ryan, Gerald:** b. Aug. 24, 1923, Brooklyn, N.Y.; educ. Cathedral College (Brooklyn, N.Y.), Immaculate Conception Seminary (Huntington, L.I.), Fordham Univ. Graduate School of Social Work (Bronx, N.Y.); ord. priest June 3, 1950; ord. titular bishop of Munatiana and auxiliary bishop of Rockville Centre, May 9, 1977.

**Ryan, James C., O.F.M.:** b. Nov. 17, 1912, Chicago, Ill.; educ. St. Joseph's Seraphic Seminary (Westmont, Ill.), Our Lady of the Angels Seminary (Cleveland, O.); ord. priest June 24, 1938; ord. titular bishop of Margo and prelate of Santarem, Brazil, April 9, 1958; first bishop of Santarem, Dec. 4, 1979.

**Ryan, Joseph T.:** b. Nov. 1, 1913, Albany, N.Y.; educ. Manhattan College (New York City); ord. priest June 3, 1939; national secretary of Catholic Near East Welfare Assn. 1960-65; ord. first archbishop of Anchorage, Alaska, Mar. 25, 1966; app. titular archbishop of Gabi and coadjutor archbishop of the military ordinariate, Oct. 24, 1975, installed Dec. 13, 1975.

**S**

**Salatka, Charles A.:** b. Feb. 26, 1918, Grand Rapids, Mich.; educ. St. Joseph's Seminary (Grand Rapids, Mich.), Catholic Univ. (Washington, D.C.), Lateran Univ. (Rome); ord. priest Feb. 24, 1945; ord. titular bishop of Cariana and auxiliary bishop of Grand Rapids, Mich., Mar. 6, 1962; app. bishop of Marquette, installed Mar. 25, 1968; app. archbishop of Oklahoma City, Sept. 27, 1977; installed Dec. 15, 1977.

**Sanchez, Robert:** b. Mar. 20, 1934, Socorro, N.M.; educ. Immaculate Heart Seminary (Santa Fe, N.M.), Gregorian Univ. (Rome), Catholic Univ. (Washington, D.C.); ord. priest Dec. 20, 1959; ord. archbishop of Santa Fe, N.M., July 25, 1974.

**Scanlan, John J.:** b. May 24, 1906, County Cork, Ireland; educ. National Univ. of Ireland (Dublin), All Hallows College (Dublin); ord. priest June 22, 1930; U.S. citizen 1938; ord. titular bishop of Cenae and auxiliary bishop of Honolulu, Sept. 21, 1954;

bishop of Honolulu, installed May 1, 1968; retired June 30, 1981.

**Scarpone, Gerald, O.F.M.:** b. Oct. 1, 1928, Watertown, Mass.; ord. priest June 24, 1956; ord. coadjutor bishop of Comayagua, Honduras, Feb. 21, 1979; succeeded as bishop of Comayagua, May 30, 1979.

**Schad, James L.:** b. July 20, 1917, Philadelphia, Pa.; educ. St. Mary's Seminary (Baltimore, Md.); ord. priest Apr. 10, 1943; ord. titular bishop of Panatoria and auxiliary bishop of Camden, Dec. 8, 1966.

**Schierhoff, Andrew B.:** b. Feb. 10, 1922, St. Louis, Mo.; ord. priest Apr. 14, 1948; missionary in Bolivia from 1956; ord. titular bishop of Cerenza and auxiliary of La Paz, Bolivia, Jan. 6, 1969; app. vicar apostolic of Pando, Bolivia, Dec. 17, 1982.

**Schladweiler, Alphonse:** b. July 18, 1902, Milwaukee, Wis.; educ. St. Joseph College (Teutopolis, Ill.), St. Paul's Seminary (St. Paul, Minn.), Univ. of Minnesota (Minneapolis, Minn.); ord. priest June 9, 1929; ord. first bishop of New Ulm, Jan. 29, 1958; retired Dec. 23, 1975.

**Schlaefer, Salvator, O.F.M. Cap.:** b. June 27, 1920, Campbellsport, Wis.; ord. priest June 5, 1946; missionary in Bluefields, Nicaragua from 1947; ord. titular bishop of Fiumepiscense and vicar apostolic of Bluefields, Nicaragua, Aug. 12, 1970.

**Schlarman, Stanley Gerard:** b. July 27, 1933, Belleville, Ill.; educ. St. Henry Prep Seminary (Belleville, Ill.), Gregorian Univ. (Rome), St. Louis Univ. (St. Louis, Mo.); ord. priest July 13, 1958, Rome; ord. titular bishop of Capri and auxiliary bishop of Belleville, May 14, 1979; app. bishop of Dodge City, Mar. 1, 1983.

**Schlotterback, Edward F., O.S.F.S.:** b. Mar. 2, 1912, Philadelphia, Pa.; educ. Catholic Univ. (Washington, D.C.); ord. priest Dec. 17, 1938; ord. titular bishop of Balanea and vicar apostolic of Keetmanshoop, Namibia, June 11, 1956.

**Schmidt, Firmin M., O.F.M.Cap.:** b. Oct. 12, 1918, Catherine, Kans.; educ. Catholic Univ. (Washington, D.C.); ord. priest June 2, 1946; app. prefect apostolic of Mendi, Papua New Guinea, Apr. 3, 1959; ord. titular bishop of Conana and first vicar apostolic of Mendi, Dec. 15, 1965; became first bishop of Mendi when vicariate apostolic was raised to a diocese, Nov. 15, 1966.

**Schmidt, Mathias, O.S.B.:** b. Apr. 21, 1931, Wortonville, Kans.; ord. priest May 30, 1957; missionary in Brazil; ord. titular bishop of Mutugenna and auxiliary bishop of Jatai, Brazil, Sept. 10, 1972; bishop of Rui Barbosa, Brazil, May 14, 1976.

**Schmitt, Mark:** b. Feb. 14, 1923, Algoma, Wis., educ. Salvatorian Seminary (St. Nazianz, Wis.), St. John's Seminary (Collegeville, Minn.); ord. priest May 22, 1948; ord. titular bishop of Ceanannus Mor and auxiliary bishop of Green Bay, June 24, 1970; app. bishop of Marquette, Mar. 21, 1978, installed May 8, 1978.

**Schmitz, Paul, O.F.M. Cap.:** b. December, 1943, Fond du Lac, Wis.; ord. priest 1970; missionary in Nicaragua from 1970; superior of vice province of Capuchins in Central America (headquartered in Managua), 1982-84; app. titular bishop of Elepla

(Spokane, Wash.), Alma College (Alma, Calif.); ord. priest June 17, 1944; ord. titular bishop of Sicilibba and coadjutor bishop of Fairbanks, Alaska, with right of succession, Feb. 22, 1968; bishop of Fairbanks, Nov. 30, 1968.

**Wildermuth, Augustine F., S.J.:** b. Feb. 20, 1904, St. Louis, Mo.; educ. St. Stanislaus Seminary (Florissant, Mo.), St. Michael's Scholasticate (Spokane, Wash.), Sacred Heart College (Shembaganur, S. India), St. Mary's College (Kurseong, India), Gregorian Univ. (Rome); entered Society of Jesus, 1922; ord. priest July 25, 1935; ord. bishop of Patna, India, Oct. 28, 1947; retired Mar. 6, 1980.

**Williams, James Kendrick:** b. Sept. 5, 1936, Larue Co., Ky.; educ. St. Mary's College (St. Mary's, Ky.), St. Maur's School of Theology (South Union, Ky.); ord. priest May 25, 1963; app. titular bishop of Catula and auxiliary bishop of Covington, Apr. 24, 1984.

**Wirz, George O.:** b. Jan. 17, 1929, Monroe, Wis.; educ. St. Francis Seminary and Marquette Univ. (Milwaukee, Wis.); Cath. Univ. (Washington, D.C.); ord. priest May 31, 1952; ord. titular bishop of Municipa and auxiliary bishop of Madison, Mar. 9, 1978.

**Wycislo, Aloysius John:** b. June 17, 1908, Chicago, Ill.; educ. St. Mary's Seminary (Mundelein, Ill.), Catholic Univ. (Washington, D.C.); ord. priest Apr. 4, 1934; ord. titular bishop of Stadia and auxiliary bishop of Chicago, Dec. 21, 1960; app. bishop of Green Bay, installed Apr. 16, 1968; resigned May 10, 1983.

## Z

**Zayek, Francis:** b. Oct. 18, 1920, Manzanillo, Cuba; ord. priest Mar. 17, 1946; ord. titular bishop of Callinicum and auxiliary bishop for Maronites in Brazil, Aug. 5, 1962; named apostolic exarch for Maronites in U.S., with headquarters in Detroit; installed June 11, 1966; first eparch of St. Maron of Detroit, Mar. 25, 1972; see transferred to Brooklyn, June 27, 1977; given personal title of archbishop, Dec. 22, 1982.

**Zuroweste, Albert R.:** b. Apr. 26, 1901, East St. Louis, Ill.; educ. St. Francis College (Quincy, Ill.), Kenrick Seminary (Webster Groves, Mo.), Catholic Univ. (Washington, D.C.); ord. priest June 8, 1924; ord. bishop of Belleville, Jan. 29, 1948; retired Oct. 29, 1976.

## U.S. BISHOPS OVERSEAS

Cardinal William W. Baum, prefect of the Sacred Congregation for Catholic Education; Archbishop Ambrose De Paoli, apostolic pro-nuncio to Sri Lanka; Archbishop Raymond P. Etteldorf, consultor to several Curial bodies; Archbishop John P. Foley, president of the Pontifical Commission for Social Communications; Bishop Ladislaus Iranyi, Sch. P., pastoral care of Hungarian Catholics living outside of Hungary; Archbishop Paul C. Marcinkus, president of Institute for Works of Religion (Vatican Bank) and pro-president of Pontifical Commission for the State of Vatican City.

(See also Missionary Bishops.)

## RETIRED U.S. PRELATES

Information, as of Aug. 27, 1984, includes name of the prelate and see held at the time of retirement or resignation; archbishops are indicated by an asterisk. Most of the prelates listed below resigned their sees because of age in accordance with church law. See Index: Biographies of American Bishops.

Forms of address of retired residential prelates (unless they have a titular see): *Archbishop or Bishop Emeritus of* (last see held); *Former Archbishop or Bishop of* (last see held).

Richard H. Ackerman, C.S.Sp. (Covington), George W. Ahr (Trenton), Reginald Arliss, C.P. (Marbel, Philippines, prelate), Michael J. Begley (Charlotte), John H. Boccella, T.O.R.* (Izmir, Turkey), Joseph Brunini (Jackson), James C. Burke, O.P. (Chimbote, Peru, prelate), Charles A. Buswell (Pueblo), James J. Byrne* (Dubuque), L. Abel Caillouet (New Orleans, auxiliary), Cardinal John Carberry* (St. Louis), Mark K. Carroll (Wichita), John J. Cassata (Fort Worth), Harry A. Clinch (Monterey), John E. Cohill, S.V.D. (Goroka, Papua New Guinea), James L. Connolly (Fall River), Thomas Connolly* (Seattle), William M. Cosgrove (Belleville), Arnold R. Cotey, S.D.S. (Nachingwea, Tanzania), William E. Cousins* (Milwaukee), Augustine Danglmayr (Ft. Worth, auxiliary), Nicholas D'Antonio, O.F.M. (Olancho, Honduras).

James P. Davis* (Santa Fè), Cardinal John F. Dearden* (Detroit), Antanas L. Deksnys (Lavellum, titular see), Joseph P. Denning (Brooklyn, auxiliary), Frederick A. Donaghy (Wuchow, China), Hugh A. Donohoe (Fresno), John A. Donovan (Toledo), John J. Dougherty (Newark, auxiliary), Carroll T. Dozier (Memphis), Thomas J. Drury (Corpus Christi), Clarence J. Duhart, C.SS.R. (Udon Thani, Thailand), Joseph A. Durick (Nashville), J. Lennox Federal (Salt Lake City), Bernard J. Flanagan (Worcester), John B. Franz (Peoria), Frederick W. Freking (La Crosse), Philip J. Furlong (Military Vicariate, delegate).

Raymond J. Gallagher (Lafayette, Ind.), Hugo Gerbermann, M.M. (San Antonio, auxiliary), James J. Gerrard (Fall River, auxiliary), Laurence A. Glenn (Crookston), Ignatius T. Glennie, S.J. (Trincomalee-Batticaloa, Sri Lanka), Lawrence P. Graves (Alexandria-Shreveport), Lawrence Graziano, O.F.M. (San Miguel, El Salvador), Charles P. Greco (Alexandria), Francis J. Green (Tucson), John B. Grellinger, (Green Bay, auxiliary), Frank J. Greteman (Sioux City), Andrew G. Grutka (Gary).

Hilary B. Hacker (Bismarck), Paul L. Hagarty (Nassau, Bahamas), Charles H. Helmsing (Kansas City-St. Joseph), Edward J. Herrmann (Columbus), Edward G. Hettinger (Columbus, auxiliary), Vincent J. Hines (Norwich), Lambert A. Hoch (Sioux Falls), Robert L. Hodapp, S.J. (Belize), Joseph L. Hogan (Rochester), Robert F. Joyce (Burlington), Walter P. Kellenberg (Rockville Centre), Arthur H. Krawczak (Detroit, auxiliary), George L. Leech (Harrisburg; titular bishop of Allegheny), Vincent M. Leonard (Pittsburgh).

J. Carroll McCormick (Scranton), William McDonald (San Francisco, auxiliary), Thomas J. McDonough* (Louisville), John J. McEleney, S.J.* (Kingston, Jamaica), Joseph H. McShea (Allentown), John J. Maguire* (New York, coadjutor), David M. Maloney (Wichita), Alfred Mendez, C.S.C. (Arecibo, P.R.), Sidney M. Metzger (El Paso), John L. Morkovsky (Galveston-Houston), William J. Moran (Military Vicariate, delegate). Louis La Ravoire Morrow, S.D.B. (Krishnagar, India), Charles R. Mulrooney (Brooklyn, auxiliary), T. Austin Murphy (Baltimore, auxiliary), Knute Ansgar Nelson, O.S.B. (Stockholm, Sweden), Hubert M. Newell (Cheyenne), Cardinal Patrick O'Boyle* (Washington, D.C.).

Martin J. O'Connor* (Prefect Emeritus, Pontifical Commission for Social Communications), John L. Paschang (Grand Island), George H. Pearce, S.M.* (Suva, Fiji Islands), Joseph M. Pernicone (New York, auxiliary), Henry A. Pinger (Chowtsun, China), Ernest J. Primeau (Manchester), Leo A. Pursley (Fort Wayne-South Bend), Joseph M. Raya* (Acre), Joseph W. Regan, M.M. (Tagum, P.I., Prelate), Francis F. Reh (Saginaw).

Thomas F. Reilly, C.SS.R. (San Juan de la Maguana, Dominican Republic), John J. Rudin, M.M. (Musoma, Tanzania), John J. Russell (Richmond), John J. Scanlan (Honolulu), Alphonse Schladweiler (New Ulm), Eldon B. Schuster (Great Falls).

Henry J. Soenneker (Owensboro), Edward E. Swanstrom (New York, auxiliary), Paul F. Tanner (St. Augustine), Bernard J. Topel (Spokane), Nicolas Walsh (Seattle, auxiliary), Alfred M. Watson (Erie), Augustine Wildermuth, S.J. (Patna, India), Aloysius J. Wycislo (Green Bay), Albert R. Zuroweste (Belleville).

## BISHOP-BROTHERS

(The asterisk indicates brothers who were bishops at the same time.)

There have been nine pairs of brother-bishops in the history of the U.S. hierarchy.

Living: Francis T. Hurley,* archbishop of Anchorage and Mark J. Hurley* of Santa Rosa.

Deceased: Francis Blanchet* of Oregon City (Portland) and Augustin Blanchet* of Walla Walla; John S. Foley of Detroit and Thomas P. Foley of Chicago; Francis P. Kenrick,* apostolic administrator of Philadelphia, bishop of Philadelphia and Baltimore, and Peter R. Kenrick* of St. Louis; Matthias C. Lenihan of Great Falls and Thomas M. Lenihan of Cheyenne; James O'Connor, vicar apostolic of Nebraska and bishop of Omaha, and Michael O'Connor of Pittsburgh and Erie; Jeremiah F. and John W. Shanahan, both of Harrisburg; Sylvester J. Espelage, O.F.M.,* of Wuchang, China, who died 10 days after the ordination of his brother, Bernard T. Espelage,* O.F.M., of Gallup; Coleman F. Carroll* of Miami and Howard Carroll* of Altoona-Johnstown.

## SECULAR ORDERS

Secular orders (commonly called third orders) are societies of the faithful living in the world who seek to deepen their Christian life and apostolic commitment in association with and according to the spirit of various religious institutes. The orders are called "third" because their foundation followed the establishment of the first (for men) and second (for women) religious orders with which they are associated.

**Augustine, Third Order Secular of St.:** Founded, 13th century; approved Nov. 7, 1400.

**Carmel (The Lay Carmelite Order) (Calced):** Founded, 13th century; approved by Pope Nicholas V, Oct. 7, 1452. Revised rule aproved November, 1977. Address: Aylesford, National Scapular Center, I-55 and Cass Ave. N. Darien, Ill. 60559. Approximately 16,500 members in U.S.

**Carmelites, The Secular Order of Discalced** (formerly the Third Order Secular of the Blessed Virgin Mary of Mt Carmel and of St. Teresa of Jesus): Rule based on the Carmelite reform established by St. Teresa and St. John of the Cross, 16th century; approved Mar. 23, 1594. Revised rule approved May 10, 1979. Office of National Secretariat, U.S.A.; P.O. Box 3079, San Jose, Calif. 95156. Approximately 22,245 throughout the world; 1,800 in U.S.

**Dominican Laity:** Founded in the 13th century.

Addresses of provincial coordinators: 487 Michigan Ave. N.E., Washington, D.C. 20017; 1909 S. Ashland Ave., Chicago, Ill. 60608; 2390 Bush St., San Francisco, Calif. 94115, P.O. Box 3894, Little Rock, Ark. 72203.

**Franciscan Order, Secular (SFO):** Founded, 1209 by St. Francis of Assisi; approved Aug. 30, 1221. National minister, James David Lynch, 4143 "J" St., Juniata Park, Philadelphia, Pa. 19124. Approximately 780,000 throughout the world; 40,000 in U.S.

**Mary, Third Order of:** Founded, Dec. 8, 1850; rule approved by the Holy See, 1857. Addresses of provincial directors: 4408 — 8th St. N.E., Washington, D.C. 20017; 7 Harvard St., P.O. Box 66, Charlestown, Mass. 02129; P.O. Box 158, Kekaha, Kauai, Hawaii 96752. Approximately 14,000 in the world, 5,600 in U.S.

**Mary, Secular Order of Servants of (Servite):** Founded, 1233; approved, 1304. Address: Assistant for Secular Order, 3401 S. Home Ave., Berwyn, Ill. 60402.

**Mercy, Secular Third Order of Our Lady of (Mercedarian):** Founded, 1219 by St. Peter Nolasco; approved the same year.

**Norbert, Third Order of St.:** Founded, 1122 by St. Norbert; approved by Pope Honorius II, 1126. Address: St. Norbert Abbey, De Pere, Wis. 54115.

**Trinity, Third Order Secular of the Most Holy:** Founded 1198; approved, 1219.

## Institutes of Consecrated Life

Religious orders and congregations are special societies in the Church — institutes of consecrated life — whose members, called Religious, commit themselves, by public vows to observance of the evangelical counsels of poverty, chastity and obedience in a community kind of life in accordance with rules and constitutions approved by church authority.

Secular institutes (covered in its own Almanac entry) are also institutes of consecrated life.

The particular goal of each institute and the means of realizing it in practice are stated in the rule and constitutions proper to the institute. Local bishops can give approval for rules and constitutions of institutes of diocesan rank. Pontifical rank belongs to institutes approved by the Holy See. General jurisdiction over all Religious is exercised by the Congregation for Religious and Secular Institutes. General legislation concerning Religious is contained in Canons 573 to 709 in Book II, Part III, of the Code of Canon Law.

All institutes of consecrated life are commonly called religious orders, despite the fact that there are differences between orders and congregations. The best known orders include the Benedictines, Trappists, Franciscans, Dominicans, Carmelites and Augustinians, for men; and the Carmelites, Benedictines, Poor Clares, Dominicans of the Second Order and Visitation Nuns, for women. The orders are older than the congregations, which did not appear until the 16th century.

Contemplative institutes are oriented to divine worship and service within the confines of their communities, by prayer, penitential practices, other spiritual activities and self-supporting work. Examples are the Trappists and Carthusians, the Carmelite and Poor Clare nuns. Active institutes are geared for pastoral ministry and various kinds of apostolic work. Mixed institutes combine elements of the contemplative and active ways of life. While most institutes of men and women can be classified as active, all of them have contemplative aspects.

Clerical communities of men are those whose membership is predominantly composed of priests.

Non-clerical or lay institutes of men are the various brotherhoods.

## Societies of Apostolic Life

Some of the institutes of men listed below have a special kind of status because their members, while living a common life like that which is characteristic of Religious, do not profess the vows of Religious. Examples are the Maryknoll Fathers, the Oratorians of St. Philip Neri, the Paulists and Sulpicians. They are called societies of apostolic life and are the subject of Canons 731 to 746 in the Code of Canon Law.

# RELIGIOUS INSTITUTES OF MEN IN THE UNITED STATES

(Sources: *Official Catholic Directory;* Catholic Almanac survey.)

**African Missions, Society of, S.M.A.:** Founded 1856, at Lyons, France, by Bishop Melchior de Marion Brésillac. Generalate, Rome, Italy; American provincialate, 23 Bliss Ave., Tenafly, N.J. 07670. Missionary work.

**Assumptionists (Augustinians of the Assumption), AA.:** Founded 1845, at Nimes, France, by Rev. Emmanuel d'Alzon; in U.S., 1946. General house, Rome, Italy; U.S. province, 328 Adams St., Milton, Mass. 02186. Educational, parochial, ecumenical, retreat, foreign mission work.

**Atonement, Franciscan Friars of the, S.A.:** Founded as an Anglican Franciscan community in 1898 at Garrison, N.Y., by Rev. Paul Wattson. Community corporately received into the Catholic Church in 1909. Motherhouse, St. Paul Friary, Graymoor, Garrison N.Y. 10524. Ecumenical, mission, retreat and charitable works.

**Augustinian Recollects, O.A.R.:** Founded 1588: in U.S., 1944. General motherhouse, Rome, Italy. Missionary, parochial, education work.

St. Augustine Province (1944), 29 Ridgeway Ave., W. Orange, N.J. 07052.

St. Nicholas Province (Madrid): U.S. Delegate, 2800 Schurz Ave., Bronx, N.Y. 10465.

**Augustinians (Order of St. Augustine), O.S.A.:** Established canonically in 1256 by Pope Alexander IV; in U.S., 1796. General motherhouse, Rome, Italy.

St. Thomas of Villanova Province (1796), Villanova, Pa. 19085.

Our Mother of Good Counsel Province (1941), Tolentine Center, 20300 Governors Hwy., Olympia Fields, Ill. 60461.

St. Augustine Province (1969), 1605 28th St., San Diego, Calif. 92102.

Good Counsel Vice-Province, St. Augustine Priory, Richland, N.J. 08350.

U.S. Vicariate of Castile, Spain, Province, P.O. Box 190, Waxachachie, Tex. 75165.

**Barnabites (Clerics Regular of St. Paul), C.R.S.P.:** Founded 1530, in Milan, Italy, by St. Anthony M. Zaccaria. Generalate, Rome, Italy; American headquarters, 1023 Swann Rd., Youngstown, N.Y. 14174. Parochial, educational, mission work.

**Basil the Great, Order of St. (Basilian Order of St. Josaphat), O.S.B.M.:** General motherhouse, Rome, Italy; U.S. province, 31-12 30th St., Long Island City, N.Y. 11106. Parochial work among Byzantine Ukrainian Rite Catholics.

**Basilian Fathers (Congregation of the Priests of St. Basil), C.S.B.:** Founded 1822, at Annonay, France. General motherhouse, 20 Humewood Dr., Toronto, Ont. M6C 2W2, Canada. Educational, parochial work.

**Basilian Salvatorian Fathers:** Founded 1684, at Saida, Lebanon, by Eftimios Saifi; in U.S., 1953. General motherhouse, Saida, Lebanon; American headquarters, 30 East St., Methuen, Mass. 01844.

Educational, parochial work among Eastern Rite peoples.

**Benedictine Monks (Order of St. Benedict), O.S.B.:** Founded 529, in Italy, by St. Benedict of Nursia; in U.S., 1846.

• **American Cassinese Federation (1855).** Rt. Rev. John Eidenschink, O.S.B., pres., Church of Seven Dolors, Albany, Minn. 56307. Abbeys and Priories belonging to the federation:

St. Vincent Archabbey, Latrobe, Pa. 15650; St. John's Abbey, Collegeville, Minn. 56321; St. Benedict's Abbey, Atchison, Kans. 66002; St. Mary's Abbey, Delbarton, Morristown, N.J. 07960; Belmont Abbey, Belmont, N.C. 28012; St. Bernard Abbey, St. Bernard, Cullman, Ala. 35055; St. Procopius Abbey, 5601 College Rd., Lisle, Ill. 60532; St. Gregory's Abbey, Shawnee, Okla. 74801; St. Leo Abbey, St. Leo, Fla. 33574; Assumption Abbey, Richardton, N. Dak. 58652;

St. Bede Abbey, Peru, Ill. 61354; St. Martin's Abbey, Lacey, Wash. 98503; Holy Cross Abbey, P.O. Box 351, Canon City, Colo. 81212; St. Anselm's Abbey, Manchester, N.H. 03102; St. Andrew's Abbey, 2900 East Blvd., Cleveland, O. 44104; Holy Trinity Monastery, Butler, Pa. 16001; St. Maur Priory, 4545 Northwestern Ave., Indianapolis, Ind. 46208; Newark Abbey, 528 High St., Newark, N.J. 07102; St. Mark's Priory, South Union, Ky. 42283; Benedictine Priory, 6502 Seawright Dr., Savannah, Ga. 31406; Woodside Priory, 302 Portola Rd., Portola Valley, Calif. 94025.

• **Swiss-American Federation (1870),** Rt. Rev. Raphael De Salvo O.S.B., pres., New Subiaco Abbey, New Subiaco, Ark. 72865. Abbeys and priory belonging to the federation:

St. Meinrad Archabbey, St. Meinrad, Ind. 47577; Conception Abbey, Conception, Mo. 64433; Mt. Michael Abbey, Elkhorn, Nebr. 68022; New Subiaco Abbey, Subiaco, Ark. 72865; St. Joseph's Abbey, St. Benedict, La. 70457; Mt. Angel Abbey, St. Benedict, Ore. 97373; Marmion Abbey, Butterfield Rd., Aurora, Ill. 60504;

St. Benedict's Abbey, Benet Lake, Wis. 53102; Glastonbury Abbey, 16 Hull St., Hingham, Mass. 02043; Westminster Abbey, Mission, B.C., Canada; St. Pius X Abbey, Pevely, Mo. 63070; Blue Cloud Abbey, Marvin, S. Dak. 57251; Corpus Christi Abbey, Star Route, Box A-38-A, Sandia, Tex. 78383; Our Lady of Guadalupe Abbey, Pecos N. Mex. 87552; Prince of Peace Abbey, Benet Hill, Oceanside, Calif. 92054.

• **English Benedictine Congregation:** St. Anselm's Abbey, 4501 S. Dakota Ave. N.E., Washington, D.C. 20017; Abbey of St. Gregory, Cory's Lane, Portsmouth, R.I. 02871; Priory of St. Mary and St. Louis, 500 S. Mason Rd., St. Louis, Mo. 63141.

• **Congregation of St. Ottilien for Foreign Missions,** St. Paul's Abbey, Newton, N.J. 07860; Benedictine Mission House, Schuyler, Neb. 68661.

• **Congregation of the Annunciation,** St. Andrew Priory, Valyermo, Calif. 93563.

• **Houses not in Congregations:** Mount Saviour Monastery, Pine City, N.Y. 14871; Conventual Priory of St. Gabriel the Archangel, Weston, Vt. 05161.

**Benedictines, Olivetan, O.S.B.:** General motherhouse, Siena, Italy. U.S. foundation, Our Lady of Mt. Olivet Monastery, 4029 Ave. G, Lake Charles, La. 70601.

**Benedictines, Sylvestrine, O.S.B.:** Founded 1231, in Italy by Sylvester Gozzolini. General motherhouse, Rome, Italy; U.S. foundations; 17320 Rosemont Rd., Detroit, Mich. 48219; 2711 E. Drahner Rd., Oxford, Mich. 48051; 1697 State Highway 3, Clifton, N.J. 07012.

**Bethlehem Missionaries, Society of, S.M.B.:** Founded 1921, at Immensee, Switzerland, by Rt. Rev. Canon Peter Bondolfi. General motherhouse, Immensee, Switzerland; U.S. headquarters, 5630 E. 17th Ave., Denver, Colo. 80220. Foreign mission work.

**Blessed Sacrament, Congregation of the, S.S.S.:** Founded 1856, at Paris, France, by St. Pierre Julien Eymard; in U.S., 1900. General motherhouse, Rome, Italy; U.S. province, 5384 Wilson Mills Rd., Cleveland, O. 44143. Eucharistic apostolate.

**Brigittine Monks (Order of the Most Holy Savior), O.Ss.S.:** Monastery of the Most Holy Savior, 125 Northgate Dr., Woodside, Calif. 94062.

**Camaldolese Congregation, Cam. O.S.B.:** Founded 1012, at Camaldoli, near Arezzo, Italy, by St. Romuald; in U.S. 1958. General motherhouse, Arezzo, Italy; U.S. foundation, Immaculate Heart Hermitage, Big Sur, Calif. 93920.

**Camaldolese Hermits of the Congregation of Monte Corona, Er. Cam.:** Founded 1520, from Camaldoli, Italy, by Bl. Paul Giustiniani. General motherhouse, Frascati (Rome), Italy; U.S. foundation, Holy Family Hermitage, Rt. 2, Box 36, Bloomingdale, O. 43910.

**Camillian Fathers and Brothers (Order of St. Camillus; Order of Ministers of the Sick), O.S.Cam.:** Founded 1582, at Rome, by St. Camillus de Lellis; in U.S., 1923. General motherhouse, Rome, Italy; North American province, 10213 W. Wisconsin Ave., Wauwatosa, Wis. 53226.

**Carmelites (Order of Our Lady of Mt. Carmel), O. Carm.:** General motherhouse, Rome, Italy. Educational, charitable work.

Most Pure Heart of Mary Province (1864), 45 E. Dundee Rd., Barrington, Ill. 60010.

St. Elias Province (1931), 249 9th St., Brooklyn, N.Y. 11215.

Mt. Carmel Hermitage, Pineland, R.D. 1, Box 36, New Florence, Pa. 15944 (immediately subject to Prior General.)

**Carmelites, Order of Discalced, O.C.D.:** Established 1562, a Reform Order of Our Lady of Mt. Carmel; in U.S., 1935. Generalate, Rome, Italy. Spiritual direction, retreat, parochial work.

St. Therese of Oklahoma Province (1935), 1125 S. Walker St., P.O. Box 26127, Oklahoma City, Okla. 73126.

Immaculate Heart of Mary Province (1947), P.O. Box 67, Hubertus, Wis. 53033.

California-Arizona Province (1924), 510 N. El Molino St., Alhambra, Calif. 91801.

Polish Province of the Holy Spirit, 1628 Ridge Rd., Munster, Ind. 46321.

**Carthusians, Order of, O. Cart.:** Founded 1084,

in France, by St. Bruno; in U.S., 1951. General motherhouse, St. Pierre de Chartreuse, France; U.S. charterhouse, Arlington, Vt. 05250. Cloistered contemplatives; semi-eremitic.

**Charity, Servants of, S.C.:** Founded 1908, in Italy, by Bl. Luigi Guanella. General motherhouse, Rome, Italy; U.S. headquarters, Don Guanella School, Sproul Rd., Springfield, Pa. 19064.

**Christ, Society of, S.Ch.:** Founded 1932, General Motherhouse, Poznan, Poland; U.S. address, 3000 Eighteen Mile Rd., Sterling Heights, Mich. 48078.

**Cistercians, Order of, O. Cist.:** Founded 1098, by St. Robert. Headquarters, Rome, Italy.

Our Lady of Spring Bank Abbey, 34639 W. Fairview Rd., Oconomowoc, Wis. 53066.

Our Lady of Gerowval Monastery, Rose Hill, Miss. 39356.

Our Lady of Dallas Monastery, Rt. 2, Box 1, Irving, Tex. 75062.

Cistercian Monastery of Our Lady of Fatima, Hainesport-Mt. Laurel Rd., Mt. Laurel, N.J. 08054.

Cistercian Monastery of Saint Mary, R.D. 1, New Ringgold, Pa. 17960.

**Cistercians of the Strict Observance, Order of (Trappists), O.C.S.O.:** Founded 1098, in France, by St. Robert; in U.S., 1848. Generalate, Rome, Italy.

Our Lady of Gethsemani Abbey (1848), Trappist P.O., Ky. 40073.

Our Lady of New Melleray Abbey (1849), Dubuque, Iowa 52001.

St. Joseph's Abbey (1825), Spencer, Mass. 01562.

Holy Spirit Monastery (1944), Conyers, Ga. 30208.

Our Lady of Guadalupe Abbey (1947), Lafayette, Ore. 97127.

Our Lady of the Holy Trinity Abbey (1947), Huntsville, Utah 84317.

Abbey of the Genesee (1951), Piffard, N.Y. 14533.

Our Lady of Mepkin Abbey (1949), Route 3, Box 800, Moncks Corner, S. Car. 29461.

Our Lady of the Holy Cross Abbey (1950), Berryville, Va. 22611.

Our Lady of the Assumption Abbey (1950), Rt. 5, Box 193, Ava, Mo. 65608.

Abbey of New Clairvaux (1955), Vina, Calif. 96092.

St. Benedict's Monastery (1956), Snowmass, Colo. 81654.

**Claretians (Missionary Sons of the Immaculate Heart of Mary), C.M.F.:** Founded 1849, at Vich, Spain, by St. Anthony Mary Claret. General headquarters, Rome, Italy. Missionary, parochial, educational, retreat work.

Western Province, 1119 Westchester Pl., Los Angeles, Calif. 90019.

Eastern Province, 400 N. Euclid Ave. Oak Park, Ill. 60302.

**Clerics Regular Minor (Adorno Fathers) C.R.M.:** Founded 1588, at Naples, Italy, by Ven. Augustine Adorno and St. Francis Caracciolo. General motherhouse, Rome, Italy; U.S. address, 575 Darlington Ave., Ramsey, N.J. 07446.

**Columban, Society of St. (St. Columban Foreign Mission Society, S.S.C.):** Founded 1918. General headquarters, Dublin, Ireland. U.S. head-

quarters, St. Columbans, Nebr. 68056. Foreign mission work.

**Comboni Missionaries of the Heart of Jesus (Verona Fathers), M.C.C.J.:** Founded 1885, in Italy by Bp. Daniele Comboni. General motherhouse, Rome, Italy; North American headquarters, Comboni Mission Center, 8108 Beechmont Ave., Cincinnati, O. 45230. Mission work in Africa and the Americas.

**Consolata Society for Foreign Missions, I.M.C.:** Founded 1901, at Turin, Italy, by Father Joseph Allamano. General motherhouse, Rome, Italy; U.S. headquarters, P.O. Box C, Lincoln Hwy., Somerset, N.J. 08873.

**Crosier Fathers (Canons Regular of the Order of the Holy Cross), O.S.C.:** Founded 1210, in Belgium by Bl. Theodore De Celles. Generalate, Rome, Italy; U.S. province, 711 Lincoln Ave., St. Paul, Minn. 55105. Mission, retreat, educational work.

**Cross, Priests of the Congregation of Holy, C.S.C.:** Founded 1837, in France; in U.S., 1841. Generalate, Rome, Italy. Educational and pastoral work; home missions and retreats; foreign missions; social services and apostolate of the press.

Indiana Province (1841), 1304 E. Jefferson Blvd., South Bend, Ind. 46617.

Eastern Province (1952), 835 Clinton Ave., Bridgeport, Conn. 06604.

Southern Province (1968), 1828 S. Carrollton Ave., New Orleans, La. 70118.

**Divine Word, Society of the, S.V.D.:** Founded 1875, in Holland, by Bl. Arnold Janssen. North American Province founded 1897 with headquarters in Techny, Ill. General motherhouse, Rome, Italy.

Province of the Blessed Virgin (Northern Province), (1964), Techny, Ill. 60082.

Sacred Heart Province (Eastern Province) (1940), 1025 Michigan Ave. N.E., Washington, D.C. 20017.

St. Augustine's Province (Southern Province) (1940), 201 Ruella Ave., Bay St. Louis, Miss. 39520.

St. Therese Province (Western Province) (1964), 2737 Pleasant Ave., Riverside, Calif. 92507.

**Dominicans (Order of Friars Preachers), O.P.:** Founded early 13th century by St. Dominic de Guzman. General headquarters, Santa Sabina, Rome, Italy. Preaching, teaching, missions, research, parishes.

St. Joseph Province (1806), 141 E. 65th St., New York, N.Y. 10021.

Holy Name of Jesus Province (1912), 5877 Birch Ct., Oakland, Calif. 94618.

St. Albert the Great Province (1939), 1909 S. Ashland Ave., Chicago, Ill. 60608.

Southern Dominican Province (1979), 3407 Napoleon Ave., New Orleans, La. 70125.

St. Dominic Province (1873), 5353 Notre Dame de Grace Ave., Montreal, Que. H4A 1L2, Canada.

Spanish Province, U.S. foundation (1933), P.O. Box 279, San Diego, Tex. 78384.

**Edmund, Society of St., S.S.E.:** Founded 1843, in France, by Fr. Jean Baptiste Muard. General motherhouse, Edmundite Generalate, Fairholt, S.

Prospect St., Burlington, Vt. 05401. Educational, missionary work.

**Eudists (Congregation of Jesus and Mary), C.J.M.:** Founded 1643, in France, by St. John Eudes. General motherhouse, Rome, Italy; North American province, 6125 Première Ave., Charlesbourg, Quebec G1H 2V9, Canada. Parochial, educational, pastoral, missionary work.

**Francis, Third Order Regular of St., T.O.R.:** Founded 1221, in Italy; in U.S., 1910. General motherhouse, Rome, Italy. Educational, parochial, missionary work.

Most Sacred Heart of Jesus Province (1910), 601 Pitcairn Pl., Pittsburgh, Pa. 15232.

Immaculate Conception Province (1925), 2006 Edgewater Parkway, Silver Springs, Md. 20903.

Commissariat of the Spanish Province (1924), 301 Jefferson Ave., Waco, Tex. 76702.

**Francis de Sales, Oblates of St., O.S.F.S.:** Founded 1871, by Fr. Louis Brisson. General motherhouse, Rome, Italy. Educational, missionary, parochial work.

Wilmington-Philadelphia Province (1906), 2200 Kentmere Parkway, Box 1452, Wilmington, Del. 19899.

Toledo-Detroit Province (1966), Box 4683, Toledo, Ohio 43620.

**Franciscans (Order of Friars Minor), O.F.M.:** A family of the First Order of St. Francis (of Assisi) founded in 1209 and established as a separate jurisdiction in 1517; in U.S., 1844. General headquarters, Rome, Italy. Preaching, missionary, educational, parochial, charitable work.

St. John the Baptist Province (1844), 1615 Vine St., Cincinnati, Ohio 45210.

Sacred Heart Province (1858), 3140 Meramec St., St. Louis, Mo. 63118.

Assumption of the Blessed Virgin Mary Province (1887), Pulaski, Wis. 54162.

Most Holy Name of Jesus Province (1901), 135 W. 31st St., New York, N.Y. 10001.

St. Barbara Province (1915), 1500 34th Ave., Oakland, Calif. 94601.

Immaculate Conception Province (1855), 147 Thompson St., New York, N.Y. 10012.

Holy Cross Custody (1912), 1400 Main St., P.O. Box 608, Lemont, Ill. 60439.

Most Holy Savior Custody, 232 S. Home Ave., Pittsburgh, Pa. 15202.

St. John Capistran Custody (1928), 1290 Hornberger Ave., Roebling, N.J. 08554.

St. Stephen Transylvanian Commissariat (1948), 517 S. Belle Vista Ave., Youngstown, Ohio 44509.

Holy Family Croatian Custody, (1927), 4848 S. Ellis Ave., Chicago, Ill. 60615.

St. Casimir Lithuanian Vicariate, Kennebunkport, Me. 04046.

Holy Gospel Province (Mexico), U.S. foundation, 2400 Marr St., El Paso, Tex. 79903.

Saints Francis and James Province (Jalisco, Mexico), U.S. foundation, 504 E. Santa Clara St., Hebbronville, Tex. 78361.

Commissariat of the Holy Land, Mt. St. Sepulchre, 14th and Quincy Sts. N.E., Washington, D.C. 20017.

St. Mary of the Angels Custody, Byzantine Slavonic Rite, P.O. Box 270, Sybertsville, Pa. 18251.

Academy of American Franciscan History, P.O. Box 34440, West Bethesda, Md. 20817.

**Franciscans (Order of Friars Minor Capuchin), O.F.M. Cap.:** A family of the First Order of St. Francis (of Assisi) founded in 1209 and established as a separate jurisdiction in 1528. General motherhouse, Rome, Italy. Missionary, parochial work, chaplaincies.

St. Joseph Province (1857), 1740 Mt. Elliott Ave., Detroit, Mich. 48207.

St. Augustine Province (1873), 220 37th St., Pittsburgh, Pa. 15201.

St. Mary Province (1952), 30 Gedney Park Dr., White Plains, N.Y. 10605.

Province of the Stigmata (1918), St. Francis Friary, Box 549, Orange, N.J. 07051.

Western American Capuchin Province, Our Lady of the Angels, 1721 Hillside Dr., Burlingame, Calif. 94010.

Sts. Adalbert and Stanislaus Province (Warsaw, Poland), Manor Dr., Oak Ridge, N.J. 07438.

Province of Mid-America (1977), St. Elizabeth Friary, 1060 St. Francis Way, Denver, Colo. 80204.

Texas Capuchin Fraternity (Province of Navarre, Spain), 5605 Bernal Dr., Dallas, Tex. 75212.

**Franciscans (Order of Friars Minor Conventual), O.F.M. Conv.:** A family of the First Order of St. Francis (of Assisi) founded in 1209 and established as a separate jurisdiction in 1517; first U.S. foundation, 1852. General curia, Rome, Italy. Missionary, educational, parochial work.

Immaculate Conception Province (1872), P.O. Box 830, Union City, N.J. 07087.

St. Anthony of Padua Province (1905), 1300 Dundalk Ave., Baltimore, Md. 21222.

St. Bonaventure Province (1939), 6107 Kenmore Ave., Chicago, Ill.

Our Lady of Consolation Province (1926), Mt. St. Francis, Ind. 47146.

Our Lady of Guadalupe Custody (vice-province), St. Cecilia Friary, P.O. Box 430, Jal, N. Mex. 88252.

St. Joseph Cupertino Province (1981), P.O. Box 1113, Arroyo Grande, Calif. 93420.

**Glenmary Missioners (The Home Missioners of America):** Founded 1939, in U.S. General headquarters, P.O. Box 46404, Cincinnati, Ohio 45246. Home mission work.

**Holy Family, Congregation of the Missionaries of the, M.S.F.:** Founded 1895, in Holland, by Rev. John P. Berthier. General motherhouse, Rome, Italy; U.S. provincial house, 10415 Midland Blvd., St. Louis, Mo. 63114. Belated vocations for the missions.

**Holy Family, Sons of the, S.F.:** Founded 1864, at Barcelona, Spain, by Joseph Mañanet y Vives; in U.S., 1920. General motherhouse, Barcelona, Spain; U.S. address, 401 Randolph Rd., Silver Spring, Md. 20904.

**Holy Ghost Fathers, C.S.Sp.:** Founded 1703, in Paris, by Claude Francois Poullart des Places; in U.S., 1872. Generalate, Rome, Italy. Missions, education.

Eastern Province (1872), 6230 Brush Run Rd., Bethel Park, Pa. 15102.

Western Province (1968), 919 Briarcliff, San Antonio, Tex. 78213.

Holy Ghost Fathers of Ireland (1971), U.S. delegate (East), 48-49 37th St., Long Island City, N.Y. 11101.

**Holy Spirit, Missionaries of the, M.Sp.S.:** Founded 1914, at Mexico City, Mexico, by Felix Rougier. General motherhouse, Mexico City; U.S. headquarters, 1005 Colonia Rd., Oxnard, Calif. 93030. Missionary work.

**Jesuits (Society of Jesus), S.J.:** Founded 1534, in France, by St. Ignatius of Loyola; received papal approval, 1540; first U.S. province, 1833. Generalate, Rome, Italy. Missionary, educational, literary work.

Maryland Province (1833), 5704 Roland Ave., Baltimore, Md. 21210.

New York Province (1943), 501 E. Fordham Rd., Bronx, N.Y. 10458.

Missouri Province (1823), 4511 W. Pine Blvd., St. Louis, Mo. 63108.

New Orleans Province (1907), 500 S. Jefferson Davis Pkwy., New Orleans, La. 70119.

California Province (1909), College at Prospect Aves., P.O. Box 519, Los Gatos, Calif. 95030.

New England Province (1926), 761 Harrison Ave., Boston, Mass. 02118.

Chicago Province, 2058 N. Clark St., Chicago, Ill. 60614.

Oregon Province (1932), 2222 N.W. Hoyt, Portland, Ore. 97210.

Detroit Province (1955), 7303 W. Seven Mile Rd., Detroit, Mich. 48221.

Wisconsin Province (1955), 1434 W. State St., Milwaukee, Wis. 53233.

**Joseph, Congregation of St., C.S.J.:** General motherhouse, Rome, Italy; U.S. vice province, 12021 Mayfield Rd., Cleveland, O. 44106. Parochial, missionary, educational work.

**Joseph, Oblates of St., O.S.J.:** Founded 1878, in Italy, by Bishop Joseph Marello. General motherhouse, Rome, Italy. Parochial, educational work.

Eastern Province, 62 W. Oak St., Pittston, Pa. 18640.

Western Province, 544 W. Cliff Dr., Santa Cruz, Calif. 95060.

**Josephite Fathers, C.J.:** General motherhouse, Ghent, Belgium; U.S. foundation, 989 Brookside Ave., Santa Maria, Calif. 93454.

**Josephites (St. Joseph's Society of the Sacred Heart), S.S.J.:** Founded 1866, in England, by Cardinal Vaughan; in U.S., 1871. General motherhouse, 1130 N. Calvert St., Baltimore, Md. 21202. Work in black missions.

**LaSalette, Missionaries of Our Lady of, M.S.:** Founded 1852, by Msgr. de Bruillard; in U.S., 1892. Motherhouse, Rome, Italy.

Our Lady of Seven Dolors Province (1933), P.O. Box 6127, Hartford, Conn. 06106.

Immaculate Heart of Mary Province (1945), P.O. Box 538, Attleboro, Mass. 02703.

Mary Queen Province (1958), 4650 S. Broadway, St. Louis, Mo. 63111.

Mary Queen of Peace Vice Province (1967), P.O. Box 95, Georgetown, Ill. 61846.

**Lateran, Canons Regular of the, C.R.L.:** General house, Rome, Italy; U.S. address: 2317 Washington Ave., Bronx, N.Y. 10458.

**Legionaries of Christ, L.C.:** Founded 1941, in Mexico, by Rev. Marcial Maciel. General headquarters, Rome, Italy; U.S. novitiate, 475 Oak Ave., Cheshire, Conn. 06410.

**Marian Fathers and Brothers, M.I.C.:** Founded 1673; U.S. foundation, 1913. General motherhouse, Rome, Italy. Educational, parochial, mission, publication work.

St. Casimir Province (1930), 6336 S. Kilbourn Ave., Chicago, Ill. 60629.

St. Stanislaus Kostka Province (1948), Eden Hill, Stockbridge, Mass. 01262.

**Marianists (Society of Mary; Brothers of Mary), S.M.:** Founded 1817, at Bordeaux, France, by Rev William-Joseph Chaminade; in U.S., 1849. General motherhouse, Rome, Italy. Educational work.

Cincinnati Province (1849), 4435 E. Patterson Rd., Dayton, Ohio 45430.

St. Louis Province (1908), 4538 Maryland Ave., St. Louis, Mo. 63156.

Pacific Province (1948), P.O. Box AC, Cupertino, Calif. 95015.

New York Province (1961), 4301 Roland Ave., Baltimore, Md. 21210.

Province of Meribah (1976), 240 Emory Rd., Mineola, N.Y. 11501.

**Mariannhill, Congregation of the Missionaries of, C.M.M.:** Trappist monastery, begun in 1882 by Abbot Francis Pfanner in Natal, South Africa, became an independent modern congregation in 1909; in U.S., 1920. Generalate, Rome, Italy; U.S.-Canadian province, St. Joseph Mission House, Route 1, Center Valley, Pa. 18034. Foreign mission work.

**Marist Fathers (Society of Mary), S.M.:** Founded 1816, at Lyons, France, by Jean Claude Colin; in U.S., 1863. General motherhouse, Rome, Italy. Educational, foreign mission, pastoral work.

Washington Province (1924), 4408 8th St. N.E., Washington D.C. 20017.

Northeast Province (1924), 72 Beacon St., Chestnut Hill, Mass. 02167.

San Francisco Western Province (1961), 625 Pine St., San Francisco, Calif. 94108.

**Maronite Hermits of St. Francis (of Assisi), O.P.C.:** Holy Trinity Monastery, Dunhamton Rd., Palmer, Mass. 01069.

**Mary Immaculate, Missionary Oblates of, O.M.I.:** Founded 1816, in France, by Bl. Charles Joseph Eugene de Mazenod; in U.S., 1849. General house, Rome, Italy. Parochial, foreign mission, educational work; ministry to marginal.

Southern U.S. Province (1904), 7711 Madonna Rd., San Antonio, Tex. 78216.

Our Lady of Hope, Eastern Province (1883), 350 Jamaicaway, Boston, Mass. 02130.

St. John the Baptist Province (1921), 45 Kenwood Ave., Worcester, Mass. 01605.

Central Province (1924), 267 E. 8th St., St. Paul, Minn. 55101.

Western Province (1953), 290 Lenox Ave., Oakland, Calif. 94610.

Italian Province, U.S. foundation, St. Nicholas Church, 442 Brinkerhoff Ave., Palisades Park, N.J. 07650.

**Maryknoll (Catholic Foreign Mission Society of America), M.M.:** Founded 1911, in U.S., by Frs. Thomas F. Price and James A. Walsh. General Center, Maryknoll, N.Y. 10545.

**Mekhitarist Order of Vienna, C.M.Vd.:** Established 1773. General headquarters, Vienna, Austria. U.S. addresses: Holy Cross Church, 100 Mt. Auburn St., Cambridge, Mass. 02138; Our Lady Queen of Martyrs Church, 1327 Pleasant Ave., Los Angeles, Calif. 90033. Work among Armenians in U.S..

**Mercedarians (Order of Our Lady of Mercy), O. de M.:** Founded 1218, in Spain, by St. Peter Nolasco. General motherhouse, Rome, Italy; U.S. headquarters, 8692 Lake St., LeRoy, N.Y. 14482.

**Mercy, Congregation of Priests of (Fathers of Mercy), C.P.M.:** Founded 1808, in France, by Rev. Jean Baptiste Rauzan; in U.S., 1839. General mission house, Cold Spring, N.Y. 10516. Mission work.

**Mill Hill Missionaries (St. Joseph's Society for Foreign Missions), M.H.M.:** Founded 1866, in England, by Cardinal Vaughan; in U.S., 1951. General motherhouse, London, England; American headquarters, Albany, N.Y. 12203.

**Missionhurst — CICM (Congregation of the Immaculate Heart of Mary):** Founded 1862, at Scheut, Brussels, Belgium, by Very Rev. Theophile Verbist. General motherhouse, Rome, Italy; U.S. province, 4651 N. 25th St., Arlington, Va. 22207. Home and foreign mission work.

**Missionaries of St. Charles, Congregation of the, C.S.:** Founded 1887, at Piacenza, Italy, by Bishop John Baptist Scalabrini. General motherhouse, Rome, Italy.

St. Charles Borromeo Province (1888), 27 Carmine St., New York, N.Y. 10014.

St. John Baptist Province (1903), 546 N. East Ave., Oak Park, Ill. 60302.

**Missionaries of the Holy Apostles, M.Ss.A.:** Founded 1962, Washington, D.C., by Eusebe M. Menard. North American headquarters, 33 Prospect Hill Rd., Cromwell, Conn. 06416.

**Montfort Missionaries (Missionaries of the Company of Mary), S.M.M.:** Founded 1715, by St. Louis Marie Grignon de Montfort; in U.S., 1948. General motherhouse, Rome, Italy; U.S. headquarters, 101-18 104th St., Ozone Park, N.Y. 11416, Mission work.

**Mother Co-Redemptrix, Congregation of, C.M.C.:** Founded 1953 at Lein-Thuy, Vietnam (North), by Fr. Dominic Mary Tran Dinh Thu; in U.S., 1975. General house, Hochiminhville, Vietnam; U.S. provincial house, 1900 Grand Ave., Carthage, Mo. 64836. Work among Vietnamese Catholics in U.S.

**Oratorians (Congregation of the Oratory of St. Philip Neri), C.O.:** Founded 1575, at Rome, by St. Philip Neri. A confederation of autonomous houses. U.S. addresses: P.O. Box 11586, Rock Hill, S.C. 29730; P.O. Box 1688, Monterey, Calif. 93940; 4040 Bigelow Blvd., Pittsburgh, Pa. 15213; P.O.

Box 211, Yarnell, Ariz. 85362; P.O. Drawer J, Pharr, Tex. 78577.

**Pallottines (Society of the Catholic Apostolate), S.A.C.:** Founded 1835, at Rome, by St. Vincent Pallotti. Generalate, Rome, Italy. Charitable, educational, parochial, mission work.

Immaculate Conception Province (1953), P.O. Box 573, Pennsauken, N.J. 08810.

Mother of God Province (1946), 5424 W. Blue Mound Rd., Milwaukee, Wis. 53208.

Irish Province, U.S. address: 3352 4th St., Wyandotte, Mich. 48192.

Queen of Apostles Province (1909), 448 E. 116th St., New York, N.Y. 10029.

Christ the King Province, 3452 Niagara Falls, Blvd., N. Tonawanda, N.Y. 14120.

**Paraclete, Servants of the, s.P.:** Founded 1947, Santa Fe, N.M., archdiocese. General motherhouse, Rome, Italy; U.S. motherhouse, Via Coeli, Jemez Springs, N.M. 87025. Devoted to care of priests.

**Paris Foreign Missions Society, M.E.P.:** Founded 1662, at Paris, France. Headquarters, Paris, France; U.S. establishment, 930 Ashbury St., San Francisco, Calif. 94117. Mission work and training of native clergy.

**Passionists (Congregation of the Passion), C.P.:** Founded 1720, in Italy, by St. Paul of the Cross. General motherhouse, Rome, Italy.

St. Paul of the Cross Province (1852), 80 David St., South River, N.J. 08882.

Holy Cross Province (Western Province), 5700 N. Harlem Ave., Chicago, Ill. 60631.

**Patrick's Missionary Society, St., S.P.S.:** Founded 1932, at Wicklow, Ireland, by Msgr. Patrick Whitney; in U.S., 1953. International headquarters, Kiltegan Co., Wicklow, Ireland. U.S. foundations: 70 Edgewater Rd., Cliffside Park, N.J. 07010; 19536 Eric Dr., Saratoga, Calif. 95070; 1347 W. Granville Ave., Chicago, Ill. 60660.

**Pauline Fathers (Order of St. Paul the First Hermit), O.S.P.:** Founded 1215; established in U.S., 1955. General motherhouse, Czestochowa, Jasna Gora, Poland; U.S. headquarters, P.O. Box 151, Doylestown, Pa. 18901.

**Pauline Fathers and Brothers (Society of St. Paul for the Apostolate of Communications), S.S.P.:** Founded 1914, by Very Rev. James Alberione; in U.S., 1932. Motherhouse, Rome, Italy; American province, 6746 Lake Shore Rd., Derby, N.Y. 14047. Social communications work.

**Paulists (Missionary Society of St. Paul the Apostle), C.S.P.:** Founded 1858, in New York, by Fr. Isaac Thomas Hecker. General offices, 86 Dromore Rd., Scarsdale, N.Y. 10583. Missionary, ecumenical, pastoral work.

**Piarists (Order of the Pious Schools), Sch.P.:** Founded 1617, at Rome, Italy, by St. Joseph Calasanctius. General motherhouse, Rome, Italy. American provincial, 4605 Bayview Dr., Fort Lauderdale, Fla. 33308. New York-Puerto Rico vice-province (Calasanzian Fathers), 88 Convent Ave., New York, N.Y. 10027. Educational work.

**Pontifical Institute for Foreign Missions, P.I.M.E.:** Founded 1850, in Italy, at request of Pope Pius IX. General motherhouse, Rome, Italy; U.S.

headquarters,17330 Quincy Ave., Detroit, Mich. 48221. Foreign mission work.

**Precious Blood, Society of, C.Pp.S.:** Founded 1815, in Italy, by St. Gaspar del Bufalo. General motherhouse, Rome, Italy.
Cincinnati Province, 431 E. Second St., Dayton, O. 45402.
Kansas City Province, Ruth Ewing Rd., Liberty, Mo. 64068.
Pacific Province, 2820 Milvia, Berkeley, Calif. 94703.
Atlantic Vicariate, 381 Robbins Ave., Niles, O. 44446.

**Premonstratensians (Order of the Canons Regular of Premontre; Norbertines), O. Praem.:** Founded 1120, at Premontre, France, by St. Norbert. Generalate, Rome, Italy. Educational, parish work.
St. Norbert Abbey, 1016 N. Broadway, DePere, Wis. 54115.
Daylesford Abbey, 220 S. Valley Rd., Paoli, Pa. 19301.
St. Michael's Priory, 1042 Star Route, Orange, Calif. 92667.

**Providence, Sons of Divine, F.D.P.:** Founded 1893, at Tortona, Italy, by Bl. Luigi Orione; in U.S., 1933. General motherhouse, Tortona, Italy; U.S. address, 111 Orient Ave., E. Boston, Mass. 02128.

**Redemptorists (Congregation of the Most Holy Redeemer), C.SS.R.:** Founded 1732, in Italy, by St. Alphonsus Mary Liguori. Generalate, Rome, Italy. Mission work.
Baltimore Province (1850), 7509 Shore Rd., Brooklyn, N.Y. 11209.
St. Louis Province (1875), Box 6, Glenview, Ill. 60025.
Oakland Province (1952), 3696 Clay St., San Francisco, Calif. 94118.
New Orleans Vice-Province, 1527 3rd St., New Orleans, La., 70130.

**Resurrectionists (Congregation of the Resurrection), C.R.:** Founded 1836, in France, under direction of Bogdan Janski. Motherhouse, Rome, Italy;
Chicago Province, 2250 N. Latrobe Ave., Chicago, Ill. 60639.
Ontario Kentucky Province, Resurrection College, Westmont Rd., N., Waterloo, Ont. N2L 3G7, Canada.

**Rogationist Fathers, R.C.J.:** Founded 1926. General motherhouse, Rome, Italy. U.S. addresses: P.O. Box 248, Mendota, Calif. 93640; P.O. Box 335, Sanger, Calif. 93657.

**Rosminians (Institute of Charity), I.C.:** Founded 1828, in Italy, by Antonio Rosmini-Serbati. General motherhouse, Rome, Italy; U.S. address, 2327 W. Heading Ave., Peoria, Ill. 61604. Charitable work.

**Sacerdotal Fraternity, Congregation of the, C.F.S.:** Founded 1901, at Paris, France. General house, 500 Ave. Claremont, Montreal (Westmount), Que. H3Y 2N5 Canada. Care of priests.

**Sacred Heart, Missionaries of the, M.S.C.:** Founded 1854, by Rev. Jules Chevelier. General motherhouse, Rome, Italy; U.S. province, P.O. Box 270, Aurora, Ill. 60507.

**Sacred Heart of Jesus, Congregation of the (Sacred Heart Fathers and Brothers), S.C.J.:** Founded 1877, in France. General motherhouse, Rome, Italy; U.S. headquarters, Sacred Heart Monastery, Hales Corners, Wis. 53130. Educational, preaching, mission work.

**Sacred Hearts, Fathers of the (Picpus Fathers), SS.CC.:** Founded 1805, in France, by Fr. Coudrin. General motherhouse, Rome, Italy. Mission, educational work.
Eastern Province (1946), 3 Adams St. (Box 111), Fairhaven, Mass. 02719.
Western Province (1970), 32481 Sage Rd., Hemet, Calif. 92343.
Hawaiian Province, Box 797, Kaneohe, Oahu, Hawaii 96744.

**Sacred Hearts of Jesus and Mary, Missionaries of the, M.SS.CC.:** Founded at Naples, Italy, by Ven. Cajetan Errico. General motherhouse, Rome, Italy; U.S. headquarters, 2249 Shore Rd., Linwood, N.J. 08221.

**Salesians of St. John Bosco (Society of St. Francis de Sales), S.D.B.:** Founded 1859, by St. John (Don) Bosco. Generalate, Rome, Italy.
St. Philip the Apostle Province (1902), 148 Main St., New Rochelle, N.Y. 10802.
San Francisco Province (1926), 1100 Franklin St., San Francisco, Calif. 94109.

**Salvatorians (Society of the Divine Savior), S.D.S.:** Founded 1881, in Rome, by Fr. Francis Jordan; in U.S., 1896. General headquarters, Rome, Italy; U.S. province, 1735 Hi-Mount Blvd., Milwaukee, Wis. 53208. Educational, parochial, mission work; campus ministries, chaplaincies.

**Scalabrinians:** See Missionaries of St. Charles, Congregation of the.

**Servites (Order of Friar Servants of Mary), O.S.M.:** Founded 1233, at Florence, Italy, by Seven Holy Founders. Generalate, Rome, Italy. General apostolic ministry.
Eastern Province (1967) 3401 S. Home Ave., Berwyn, Ill. 60402.
Western Province (1967), 5210 Somerset St., Buena Park, Calif. 90621.

**Somascan Fathers, C.R.S.:** Founded 1534, at Somasca, Italy, by St. Jerome Emiliani. General motherhouse, Rome, Italy; U.S. addresses: 628 Hanover St., Manchester, N.H. 03104; Pine Haven Boys Center, River Rd., Allenstown, P.O. Suncook, N.H. 03275.

**Sons of Mary Missionary Society (Sons of Mary, Health of the Sick), F.M.S.I.:** Founded 1952, in the Boston archdiocese, by Rev. Edward F. Garesche, S.J. Headquarters, 567 Salem End Rd., Framingham, Mass. 01701. Dedicated to health of the sick; medical, catechetical and social work in home and foreign missions.

**Stigmatine Fathers and Brothers (Congregation of the Sacred Stigmata), C.S.S.:** Founded 1816, by Bl. Gaspare Bertoni. General motherhouse, Rome, Italy; North American Province, 36 Fairmont Ave., Newton, Mass. 02158. Parish work.

**Sulpicians (Society of Priests of St. Sulpice), S.S.:** Founded 1641, at Paris, by Rev. Jean Jacques Olier. General motherhouse, Paris, France; U.S.

province, 5408 Roland Ave., Baltimore, Md. 21210. Education of seminarians and priests.

**Theatines (Congregation of Clerics Regular): C.R.:** Founded 1524, at Rome, by St. Cajetan. General motherhouse, Rome, Italy; U.S. headquarters, 1050 S. Birch St., Denver, Colo. 80222.

**Trappists:** See Cistercians of the Strict Observance.

**Trinitarians (Order of the Most Holy Trinity), O.SS.T.:** Founded 1198, by St. John of Matha. General motherhouse, Rome, Italy; U.S. headquarters, P.O. Box 5719, Baltimore, Md. 21208.

**Trinity Missions (Missionary Servants of the Most Holy Trinity), S.T.:** Founded 1929, by Fr. Thomas Augustine Judge. Generalate, 1215 N. Scott St., Arlington, Va. 22209. Home mission work.

**Viatorian Fathers (Clerics of St. Viator), C.S.V.:** Founded 1831, in France, by Fr. Louis Joseph Querbes. General motherhouse, Rome, Italy: U.S. headquarters, 1212 E. Euclid St., Arlington Hts., Ill. 60004. Educational work.

**Vincentians (Congregation of the Mission; Lazarists), C.M.:** Founded 1625, in Paris, by St. Vincent de Paul; in U.S., 1817. General motherhouse, Rome, Italy. Educational work.

Eastern Province (1867), 500 E. Chelten Ave., Philadelphia, Pa. 19144.

Midwest Province (1888), 1723 Pennsylvania Ave., St. Louis, Mo. 63104.

New England Province (1975), 1109 Prospect Ave., W. Hartford, Conn. 06105.

American Italian Branch, Our Lady of Pompei Church, 3600 Claremont St., Baltimore, Md. 21224.

American Spanish Branch (Barcelona, Spain), 134 Vernon Ave., Brooklyn, N.Y. 11206.

American Spanish Branch (Zaragoza, Spain), Holy Agony Church, 1834 3rd Ave., New York, N.Y. 10029.

Western Province (1975), 649 W. Adams Blvd., Los Angeles, Calif. 90007.

Southern Province (1975), 1302 Kipling St., Houston, Tex. 77006.

Puerto Rico Province (1955), Box 8361, Santurce, P.R. 00910.

**Vocationist Fathers (Society of Divine Vocations), S.D.V.:** Founded 1920, in Italy; in U.S., 1962. General motherhouse, Naples, Italy; U.S. address, 170 Broad St., Newark, N.J. 07104.

**White Fathers of Africa (Society of Missionaries of Africa), W.F.:** Founded 1868, at Algiers, by Cardinal C.M.A. Lavigerie. Generalate, Rome, Italy; U.S. headquarters, 1624 21st St. N.W., Washington, D.C. 20009. Missionary work in Africa.

**Xaverian Missionary Fathers, S.X.:** Founded 1895, by Archbishop Conforti, at Parma, Italy. General motherhouse, Rome, Italy; U.S. province, 12 Helene Ct., Wayne, N.J. 07470. Foreign mission work.

## INSTITUTES OF BROTHERS

**Alexian Brothers, C.F.A.:** Founded 14th century in western Germany and Belgium during the Black Plague. Motherhouse, Aachen, Germany; generalate, Signal Mountain, Tenn. 37377. Hospital and general health work.

**Carmelite Brothers of the Holy Eucharist, C.F.S.E.:** Founded 1975 by Bro. Aloysius Scafidi. Motherhouse, 2264 Marshall Ave., Elm Grove, Wheeling, W. Va. 26003. Educational, clerical, social, nursing work.

**Charity, Brothers of, F.C.:** Founded 1807, in Belgium, by Canon Peter J. Triest. General motherhouse, Rome, Italy: American District, 7720 Doe Lane, Philadelphia, Pa. 19118. Charitable, educational work.

**Christian Brothers, Congregation of, C.F.C.** (formerly Christian Brothers of Ireland): Founded 1802 at Waterford, Ireland, by Edmund Ignatius Rice. General motherhouse, Rome, Italy. Educational work.

American Province, Eastern U.S. (1916), 21 Pryer Terr., New Rochelle, N.Y. 10804. 354.

American Province, Western U.S. (1966), P.O. Box 85R, Romeoville, Ill. 60441.

**Christian Instruction, Brothers of (La Mennais Brothers), F.I.C.:** Founded 1817, at Ploermel, France, by Abbe Jean Marie de la Mennais and Abbe Gabriel Deshayes. General motherhouse, Rome, Italy; American province, Notre Dame Institute, Alfred, Me. 04002.

**Christian Schools, Brothers of the (Christian Brothers), F.S.C.:** Founded 1680, at Reims, France, by St. Jean Baptiste de la Salle. General motherhouse, Rome, Italy; U.S. Conference, 100 De La Salle Dr., Romeoville, Ill. 60441. Educational, charitable work.

Baltimore Province (1845), Box 29, Adamstown, Md. 21710.

Chicago Province (1966), 200 De La Salle Dr., Romeoville, Ill. 60441.

New York Province (1848), 820 Newman Springs Rd., Lincroft, N.J. 07738.

Long Island-New England Province (1957), Christian Brothers Center, 635 Ocean Ave., Narragansett, R.I. 02882.

St. Louis Province (1849), 1886 Rue de la Salle, Glencoe, Mo. 63038.

San Francisco Province (1868), P.O. Box A-D, Saint Mary's College, Moraga, Calif. 94575.

New Orleans-Santa Fe Province (1921), De La Salle Christian Brothers, 1522 Breaux Bridge Rd., Lafayette, La. 70501.

Winona Province (1963), 807 Summit Ave., St. Paul, Minn. 55105.

**Cross, Congregation of Holy, C.S.C.:** Founded 1837, in France, by Rev. Basil Moreau; U.S. province, 1841. Generalate, Rome, Italy. Educational, social work; missions.

Midwest Province (1841), Box 460, Notre Dame, Ind. 46556.

Southwest Province (1956), St. Edward's University, Austin, Tex. 78704.

Eastern Province (1956), 85 Overlook Circle, New Rochelle, N.Y. 10804.

**Francis, Brothers of Poor of St., C.F.P.:** Founded 1857. Motherhouse, Aachen, Germany; U.S. province, 6942 Windward St., Cincinnati, Ohio. 45227.

Educational work, especially with poor and emotionally disturbed youth.

**Francis Xavier, Brothers of St. (Xaverian Brothers), C.F.X.:** Founded 1839, in Belgium, by Theodore J. Ryken. Generalate, Rome, Italy. Educational work.

Sacred Heart Province, 10516 Summit Ave., Kensington, Md. 20895.

St. Joseph Province, 704 Brush Hill Rd., Milton, Mass. 02186.

**Franciscan Brothers of Brooklyn, O.S.F.:** Founded in Ireland; established at Brooklyn, 1858. Generalate, 135 Remsen St., Brooklyn, N.Y. 11201. Educational work.

**Franciscan Brothers of Christ the King, O.S.F.:** Founded 1961. General motherhouse, 1401 Central Ave., Bettendorf, Iowa 52722.

**Franciscan Brothers of the Good News, O.S.F.:** Founded 1970 in Archdiocese of New York. Central friary, Mount Road, Cummington, Mass. 01026. Combine volunteer works of mercy with contemplative life of prayer in hermitages.

**Franciscan Brothers of the Holy Cross, F.F.S.C.:** Founded 1862, in Germany. Generalate, Hausen, Linz Rhein, West Germany; U.S. region, R.R. 1, Springfield, Ill. 62707. Educational work.

**Franciscan Missionary Brothers of the Sacred Heart of Jesus, O.S.F.:** Founded 1927, in the St. Louis, Mo., archdiocese. Motherhouse, R.R. 3, Box 39, Eureka, Mo. 63025. Care of aged, infirm, homeless men and boys.

**Good Shepherd, Society of Brothers of the, B.G.S.:** Founded 1951, by Bro. Mathias Barrett. Motherhouse, P.O. Box 389, Albuquerque, N.M. 87102. Operate shelters and refuges for aged and homeless; homes for handicapped men and boys, alcoholic rehabilitation center.

**Holy Eucharist, Brothers of the, F.S.E.:** Founded in U.S., 1957. Generalate, P.O. Box 25, Plaucheville, La. 71362. Teaching, social, clerical, nursing work.

**Immaculate Heart of Mary, Brothers of the, F.I.C.M.:** Founded 1948, at Steubenville, Ohio, by Bishop John K. Mussio. Motherhouse, Villa Maria, 609 N. 7th St., Steubenville, Ohio 43952. Educational, charitable work.

**John of God, Brothers of the Hospitaller Order of St., O.H.:** Founded 1537, in Spain. General motherhouse, Rome, Italy; American province, 2425 S. Western Ave., Los Angeles, Calif. 90018; Irish Province of Immaculate Conception, 532

Delsea Dr., Westville Grove, N.J. 08093. Nursing work and related fields.

**Little Brothers of Jesus:** Generalate, London, England; U.S. foundation, 2833 Cochrane, Detroit, Mich. 48216.

**Little Brothers of St. Francis, O.S.F.:** Founded 1970 in Archdiocese of Boston. General fraternity, 789 Parker St., Mission Hill (Boston), Mass. 02120. Combine contemplative life with evangelical street ministry

**Marist Brothers, F.M.S.:** Founded 1817, in France, by Bl. Marcellin Champagnat. General motherhouse, Rome, Italy. Educational, social, catechetical work.

Province of St. Joseph, P.O. Box 186, Esopus, N.Y. 12429.

Poughkeepsie Province, 38 N. Clinton St., Poughkeepsie, N.Y. 12601.

**Mercy, Brothers of, F.M.M.:** Founded 1856, in Germany. General motherhouse, Montabaur, Germany. American headquarters, 4520 Ransom Rd., Clarence, N.Y. 14031. Hospital work.

**Mercy, Brothers of Our Lady of, C.F.M.M.:** Founded 1844, in The Netherlands by Abp. J. Zwijsen. Generalate, Tilburg, The Netherlands; U.S. region, 2336 South "C" St., Oxnard, Calif. 93030.

**Patrician Brothers (Brothers of St. Patrick), F.S.P.:** Founded 1808, in Ireland, by Bishop Daniel Delaney; U.S. novitiate, 7820 Bolsa Ave., Midway City, Calif. 92655. Educational work.

**Pius X, Brothers of St.:** Founded 1952, at La Crosse, Wis., by Bishop John P. Treacy. Motherhouse, 3710 East Ave. S., La Crosse, Wis. 54601. Education.

**Presentation Brothers of Mary, F.P.M.:** Founded 1802, at Waterford, Ireland, by Edmund Ignatius Rice. General motherhouse, Cork, Ireland. U.S. foundation (Canadian Province), 368 S. Ellsworth, Marshall, Mo. 65340.

**Rosary, Brothers of the Holy, F.S.R.:** Founded 1956, in U.S., Motherhouse and novitiate, 1725 S. McCarran Blvd., Reno, Nev. 89502.

**Sacred Heart, Brothers of the, S.C.:** Founded 1821, in France, by Rev. Andre Coindre. General motherhouse, Rome, Italy, Educational work.

New Orleans Province (1847), P.O. Box 89, Bay St. Louis, Miss. 39520.

New England Province (1945), Rt. 98, R.R. 1, Pascoag, R.I. 02859.

New York Province (1960), P.O. Box 68, Belvidere, N.J. 07823.

## AMERICAN CATHOLIC AWARDS

**The De La Salle Medal,** by Manhattan College, for significant contribution to the moral, cultural or educational life of the nation. Charles Wohlstetter (1984), John J. Horan (1985).

**Edith Stein Award** (1955), by the Edith Stein Guild for service toward better understanding between Christians and Jews. Dr. Eugene Fisher (1983).

**Emmanuel D'Alzon Medal** (1954), by Assumptionists to persons exemplifying the ideals of their founder. Mother Helene-Marie Bories, S.A., and

Cardinal Johannes Willebrands (1980).

**Father McKenna Award** (1950), by the national headquarters of the Holy Name Society, for outstanding service to the society's ideals. Rev. John Morley (1981).

**Fidelitas Medal** (1949), by Orchard Lake Schools (Sts. Cyril and Methodius Seminary, St. Mary's College, St. Mary's Preparatory), to an outstanding American Catholic of Polish descent for fidelity in serving God and country. Czeslaw Milosz (1984).

## MEMBERSHIP OF RELIGIOUS INSTITUTES OF MEN

(Principal source: *Annuario Pontificio*. Statistics as of Jan. 1, 1983, unless indicated otherwise.)

Listed below are world membership statistics of institutes of men of pontifical right with 500 or more members; the number of priests is in parentheses. Also listed are institutes with less than 500 members with houses in the United States.

| | |
|---|---|
| Jesuits (19,106) | 25,990 |
| Franciscans (Friars Minor) (14,026) | 20,262 |
| Salesians (10,983) | 16,869 |
| Franciscans (Capuchins) (8,464) | 11,849 |
| Brothers of Christian Schools | 10,039 |
| Benedictines (6,027) | 9,613 |
| Dominicans (5,593) | 7,325 |
| Marist Brothers | 6,662 |
| Redemptorists (4,884) | 6,608 |
| Oblates of Mary Immaculate (4,484) | 5,833 |
| Society of the Divine Word (3,298) | 5,387 |
| Franciscans (Conventuals) (2,675) | 4,065 |
| Vincentians (3,591) | 3,992 |
| Holy Spirit, Congregation (2,693) | 3,726 |
| Augustinians (2,579) | 3,409 |
| Discalced Carmelties (2,365) | 3,338 |
| Trappists (1,418) | 3,013 |
| Passionists (2,285) | 2,983 |
| White Fathers (2,517) | 2,900 |
| Claretians (1,927) | 2,898 |
| Christian Brothers | 2,707 |
| Priests of the Sacred Heart (1,916) | 2,705 |
| Missionaries of the Sacred Heart of Jesus (1,804) | 2,460 |
| Pallottines (1,484) | 2,189 |
| Marianists (613) | 2,042 |
| Holy Cross, Congregation (941) | 2,025 |
| Carmelites (Ancient Observance) (1,547) | 2,021 |
| Marists (1,582) | 1,924 |
| Combonian Missionaries of the Heart of Jesus (1,297) | 1,893 |
| Brothers of the Sacred Heart (58) | 1,878 |
| Hospitallers of St. John of God (120) | 1,680 |
| Piarists (1,320) | 1,668 |
| Brothers of Christian Instruction | 1,556 |
| Congregation of the Immaculate Heart of Mary (1,258) | 1,534 |
| Cistercians (Common Observance) (894) | 1,454 |
| Carmelites of BVM (897) | 1,430 |
| Sacred Hearts, Congregation (Picpus) (1,182) | 1,423 |
| Brothers of Christian Instruction of St. Gabriel (32) | 1,339 |
| Montfort Missionaries (1,024) | 1,327 |
| Society of African Missions (1,185) | 1,309 |
| Premonstratensians (1,014) | 1,307 |
| Augustinians (Recollects) (952) | 1,246 |
| Salvatorians (835) | 1,240 |
| Assumptionists (980) | 1,195 |
| Servants of Mary (925) | 1,194 |
| Blessed Sacrament, Congr. of (798) | 1,154 |
| Society of St. Paul (527) | 1,142 |
| Viatorians (437) | 1,099 |

| | |
|---|---|
| Little Workers of Divine Providence (1981) (747) | 1,075 |
| Missionaries of Holy Family (752) | 1,047 |
| Consolata Missionaries (816) | 1,028 |
| Ministers of Sick (Camillians) (648) | 996 |
| Mill Hill Missionaries (805) | 979 |
| Oblates of St. Francis de Sales (1981) (719) | 958 |
| Franciscans (Third Order Regular) (597) | 891 |
| Maryknollers (749) | 888 |
| LaSalette Missionaries (628) | 884 |
| Xaverian Missionaries (668) | 884 |
| Columbans (830) | 883 |
| Canons Regular of St. Augustine (691) | 858 |
| Legionaries of Christ (159) | 794 |
| Scalabrinians (598) | 751 |
| Congregation of St. Joseph (566) | 746 |
| Mercedarians (523) | 745 |
| Missionaries of the Most Precious Blood (572) | 717 |
| Pontifical Institute for Foreign Missions (584) | 714 |
| Brothers of the Immaculate Conception (6) | 649 |
| Trinitarians (1981) (402) | 603 |
| Brothers of Our Lady of Mercy | 598 |
| Paris Foreign Mission Society (563) | 565 |
| Crosier Fathers and Brothers (424) | 547 |
| Missionaries of St. Francis de Sales of Annecy (322) | 536 |
| Sulpicians (520) | 520 |
| Eudists (446) | 517 |
| Barnabites (381) | 503 |
| Servants of Charity (378) | 497 |
| Resurrection, Congregation of (343) | 459 |
| Congr. of St. Basil (Canada) (414) | 457 |
| Somascan Fathers (309) | 448 |
| Brothers of Our Lady of Lourdes | 446 |
| Mariannhill Missionaries (265) | 444 |
| St. Patrick's Mission Society (395) | 442 |
| Society of Christ (256) | 441 |
| Xaverian Brothers | 437 |
| Oratorians (326) | 424 |
| Stigmatine Fathers and Brothers (343) | 413 |
| Order of St. Basil the Great (Basilians of St. Josaphat) (286) | 401 |
| Carthusians (221) | 400 |
| Rosminians (300) | 397 |
| Oblates of St. Joseph (266) | 389 |
| Marian Fathers and Brothers (223) | 381 |
| Missionaries of the Holy Spirit (224) | 353 |
| Bethlehem Missionaries (247) | 315 |
| Rogationists (188) | 304 |
| Order of St. Paul the First Hermit (133) | 282 |
| Paulists (243) | 278 |
| Little Brothers of Jesus (74) | 265 |
| Brothers of St. Patrick | 220 |
| Vocationist Fathers (159) | 203 |

| | |
|---|---|
| Missionary Servants of the Most Holy Trinity *(1981)* (149) | 201 |
| Atonement Friars (131) | 200 |
| Josephite Fathers (S.S.J.) (171) | 198 |
| Alexian Brothers (1) | 181 |
| Presentation Brothers | 178 |
| Sons of the Holy Family (124) | 171 |
| Josephites (C.J.) (118) | 151 |
| Theatines (105) | 141 |
| Bros. of Poor of St. Francis (3) | 121 |
| Basilian Salvatorian Fathers *(1977)* (84) | 121 |
| Glenmary Missioners (74) | 116 |
| Brothers of Mercy | 112 |
| Society of St. Edmund *(1981)* (86) | 105 |
| Franciscan Bros. of Holy Cross (3) | 95 |
| Camaldolese (30) | 83 |
| Congr. of Sacerdotal Fraternity (40) | 78 |
| Clerics Regular Minor (Adorno Fathers) (33) | 43 |
| Servants of Holy Paraclete (34) | 42 |
| Mekhitarist Order of Vienna (20) | 24 |
| Fathers of Mercy (6) | 7 |

# RELIGIOUS INSTITUTES OF WOMEN IN THE UNITED STATES

(Sources: Catholic Almanac survey; *Official Catholic Directory.*)

**Africa, Missionary Sisters of Our Lady of (Sisters of Africa), S.A.:** Founded 1869, at Algiers, Algeria, by Cardinal Lavigerie; in U.S., 1929. General motherhouse, Frascati, Italy; U.S. headquarters, 5335 16th St., N.W., Washington, D.C. 20011. Medical, educational, catechetical and social work in Africa.

**Agnes, Sisters of St., C.S.A.:** Founded 1858, in U.S., by Caspar Rehrl. General motherhouse, 475 Gillett St., Fond du Lac, Wis. 54935. Education, health care, social services.

**Ann, Sisters of St., S.S.A.:** Founded 1834, in Italy; in U.S., 1952. General motherhouse, Rome, Italy; U.S. headquarters, Mount St. Ann, Ebensburg, Pa. 15931.

**Anne, Sisters of St., S.S.A.:** Founded 1850, at Vaudreuil, Que., Canada; in U.S., 1866. General motherhouse, Lachine, Que., Canada; U.S. address, 720 Boston Post Rd., Marlboro, Mass. 01752. Retreat work, pastoral ministry, religious education.

**Anthony, Missionary Servants of St., M.S.S.A.:** Founded 1929, in U.S., by Rev. Peter Baque. General motherhouse, 100 Peter Baque Rd., San Antonio, Tex. 78209. Social work.

**Apostolate, Sisters Auxiliaries of the, A.A.:** Founded 1903, in Canada; in U.S., 1911. General motherhouse, 689 Maple Terr., Monongah, W. Va. 26554. Education, nursing.

**Assumption, Little Sisters of the, L.S.A.:** Founded 1865, in France; in U.S., 1891. General motherhouse, Paris, France; U.S. provincialate, 1195 Lexington Ave., New York, N.Y. 10028. Social work, nursing, family life education.

**Assumption, Religious of the, R.A.:** Founded 1839, in France; in U.S., 1919. Generalate, Paris, France; U.S. province, 227 N. Bowman Ave., Merion, Pa. 19066. Educational work.

**Assumption of the Blessed Virgin, Sisters of the, S.A.S.V.:** Founded 1853, in Canada; in U.S., 1891. General motherhouse, Nicolet, Que., Canada; American province, North Main St., Box 128, Petersham, Mass. 01366. Education, mission, pastoral ministry.

**Augustinian Sisters, Servants of Jesus and Mary, Congregation of, As.S.J.M.:** Generalate, Rome, Italy; U.S. foundation, St. John School, Brandenburg, Ky. 40108.

**Basil the Great, Sisters of St. (Pittsburgh Byzantine Rite), O.S.B.M.:** Founded fourth century, by St. Basil the Great. Motherhouse, Mount St. Macrina. 500 W. Main St., Uniontown, Pa. 15401. Education, health care.

**Basil the Great, Sisters of the Order of St. (Ukrainian Byzantine Rite), O.S.B.M.:** Founded fourth century, in Cappadocia, by St. Basil the Great and his sister St. Macrina; in U.S., 1911. Generalate, Rome, Italy; U.S. motherhouse, 710 Fox Chase Rd., Philadelphia, Pa. 19111. Education.

**Benedict, Sisters of the Order of St., O.S.B.:** Our Lady of Mount Caritas Monastery (founded 1979, Ashford, Conn.), Seckar Rd., Ashford, Conn. 06278. Contemplative.

**Benedict, Sisters of the Order of St. (of the Congregation of Solesmes), O.S.B.:** U.S. establishment, 1981, in Burlington diocese. Monastery of the Immaculate Heart of Mary, Westfield, Vt. 05874. Cloistered, papal enclosure.

**Benedictine Nuns of the Primitive Observance, O.S.B.;** Founded c. 529, in Italy; in U.S., 1948. Abbey of Regina Laudis, Flanders Rd., Bethlehem, Conn. 06751. Cloistered.

**Benedictine Sisters, O.S.B.:** Founded c. 529, in Italy; in U.S., 1852. General motherhouse, Eichstatt, Bavaria, Germany. U.S. addresses: St. Vincent's Archabbey, Latrobe, Pa. 15650; St. Emma's Retreat House and Convent, 1001 Harvey St., Greensburg, Pa. 15601; St. Walburga Convent, 6717 S. Boulder Rd., Boulder, Colo. 80302.

**Benedictine Sisters (Bedford, N.H.), O.S.B.:** Founded 1627, in Lithuania as cloistered community; reformed 1918 as active community; established in U.S. 1957, by Mother M. Raphaela Simonis. Regina Pacis, 333 Wallace Rd., Bedford, N.H. 03102.

**Benedictine Sisters, Missionary, O.S.B.:** Founded 1885. Generalate, Rome, Italy; U.S. motherhouse, 300 N. 18th St., Norfolk, Nebr. 68701.

**Benedictine Sisters, Olivetan, O.S.B.:** Founded 1887, in U.S.. General motherhouse, Holy Angels Convent, Jonesboro, Ark. 72401. Educational, hospital work.

**Benedictine Sisters of Perpetual Adoration of Pontifical Jurisdiction, Congregation of the, O.S.B.:** Founded in U.S., 1874, from Maria Rickenbach, Switzerland. General motherhouse, 8300 Morganford Rd., St. Louis, Mo. 63123.

**Benedictine Sisters of Pontifical Jurisdiction, O.S.B.:** Founded c. 529, in Italy. No general motherhouse in U.S.. Three federations.

• Federation of St. Scholastica (1922). Pres., Sis-

ter Johnette Putnam, O.S.B., St. Scholastica Priory, Box 1118, Covington, La. 70433. Motherhouses belonging to the federation: Emmanuel Priory, 3812 Fifth St., Baltimore, Md. 21225; Mt. St. Scholastica, Atchison, Kans. 66002; Benedictine Sisters of Elk Co., St. Joseph's Convent, St. Mary's, Pa. 15857; Mt. St. Benedict Priory, 6101 E. Lake Rd., Erie, Pa. 16511; Benedictine Sisters of Chicago, St. Scholastica Priory, 7430 Ridge Blvd., Chicago, Ill. 60645; Benedictine Convent of the Sacred Heart, 1910 Maple Ave., Lisle, Ill. 60532; Our Lady of Sorrows Convent, 5900 W. 147th St., Oak Forest, Ill. 60452; St. Walburga Convent, 851 N. Broad St., Elizabeth, N.J. 07208; Benedictine Sisters, Mt. St. Mary Priory, 4530 Perrysville Ave., Pittsburgh, Pa. 15229;
Red Plains Priory, P.O. Box 60165, Oklahoma City, Okla. 73146; St. Joseph's Convent, 2200 S. Lewis, Tulsa, Okla. 74114; St. Gertrude's Priory, Ridgely P.O., Md. 21660; St. Walburga Convent, Villa Madonna, 2500 Amsterdam Rd., Covington, Ky. 41016; Sacred Heart Convent, Cullman, Ala. 35055; St. Scholastica Priory, Box 1118, Covington, La. 70434; Holy Family Convent, Benet Lake, Wis. 53102; St. Benedict's Convent, Bristow, Va. 22013; St. Scholastica Convent, P.O. Box 700, Boerne, Tex. 78006; St. Lucy's Priory, Glendora, Calif. 91740; Holy Name Priory, St. Leo, Fla. 33574; Benet Hill Priory, 2555 N. Chelton Rd., Colorado Springs, Colo. 80909; Queen of Heaven Convent (Byzantine Rite), 8640 Squires Lane N.E., Warren, O. 44484.

• Federation of St. Gertrude the Great (1937). Pres., Sister Anselm Hammerling, O.S.B. Address: c/o Mount Saint Benedict, Crookston, Minn. 56716. Motherhouses belonging to the federation: Mother of God Priory, Watertown, S. Dak. 57201; Sacred Heart Convent, Yankton, S. Dak. 57078; Mt. St. Benedict Convent, Crookston, Minn. 56716; Sacred Heart Priory, Richardton, N. Dak. 58652; St. Martin's Priory of the Black Hills, R.R. 4, Box 253, Rapid City, S. Dak. 57701; Convent of the Immaculate Conception, 802 E. 10th St., Ferdinand, Ind. 47532; Priory of St. Gertrude, Cottonwood, Ida. 83522;
St. Benedict Priory, Fox Bluff, Box 5070, Madison, Wis. 53705; Queen of Angels Priory, Mt. Angel, Ore. 97362; St. Scholastica's Convent, Albert Pike and Rogers Ave., Fort Smith, Ark. 72913; Our Lady of Peace Convent, 1511 Wilson, Columbia, Mo. 65201; Queen of Peace Priory, 701 Rolla, Belcourt, N. Dak. 58316. Convent of Our Lady of Grace, Beech Grove, Ind. 46107; Holy Spirit Convent, 9725 Pigeon Pass Rd., Sunnymead, Calif. 92388; St. Benedict's Priory, Winnipeg, Manitoba, R3C 4A3, Canada.

• Federation of St. Benedict (1947). Pres., Sister Margaret Michaud, O.S.B., St. Bede Priory, Eau Claire, Wis. 54702. Motherhouses belonging to the federation:
St. Benedict's Convent, St. Joseph, Minn. 56374; St. Scholastica Priory, Kenwood Ave., Duluth, Minn. 55811; St. Bede Priory, Priory Rd., Eau Claire, Wis. 54702; St. Mary Priory, Nauvoo, Ill. 62354; Annunciation, Priory, Apple Creek Rd., Bismarck, N. Dak. 58501; St. Paul's Priory, 2675

Larpenteur Ave. E., St. Paul, Minn. 55109; St. Placid Priory, 4600 Martin Way, Olympia, Wash. 98506.

**Bethany, Sisters of, C.V.D.:** Founded 1928, in El Salvador; in U.S. 1949. General motherhouse, Santa Tecla, El Salvador. U.S. address: 850 N. Hobart Blvd., Los Angeles, Calif. 90029.

**Bethlemita Sisters, Daughters of the Sacred Heart of Jesus, S.C.I.F.:** Founded 1861, in Guatemala. Motherhouse, Bogota, Colombia; U.S. address, St. Joseph Residence, 330 W. Pembroke St., Dallas, Tex. 75208.

**Blessed Virgin Mary, Institute of the (Loreto Sisters), I.B.V.M.:** Founded 17th century in Belgium; in U.S., 1954. Motherhouse, Rathfarnham, Dublin, Ireland; U.S. addresses: 6351 N. 27th Ave., Phoenix, Ariz. 85017; 810 Patrick Lane, Prescott, Ariz. 86301; 202 S. Kendrick, Flagstaff, Ariz. 86001.

**Blessed Virgin Mary, Institute of the (Loretto Sisters), I.B.V.M.:** Founded 1609, in Belgium; in U.S., 1880. U.S. address, Loretto Convent, Box 508, Wheaton, Ill. 60187. Educational work.

**Bon Secours, Sisters of, C.B.S.:** Founded 1824, in France; in U.S., 1881. Generalate, Rome, Italy; U.S. provincial house, Marriottsville Rd., Marriottsville, Md. 21104. Hospital work.

**Brigid, Congregation of St., C.S.B.:** Founded 1807, in Ireland; in U.S., 1953. U.S. regional house, 5118 Loma Linda Dr., San Antonio, Tex. 78201.

**Brigittine Sisters (Order of the Most Holy Savior), O.SS.S.:** Founded 1344, at Vadstena, Sweden, by St. Bridget; in U.S., 1957. General motherhouse, Rome, Italy; U.S. address, Vikingsborg, Darien, Conn. 06820.

**Carmel, Congregation of Our Lady of Mount, O. Carm.:** Founded 1825, in France; in U.S., 1833. Generalate, P.O. Box 476, Lacombe, La. 70445. Education, social services, pastoral ministry, retreat work.

**Carmel, Institute of Our Lady of Mount, O. Carm.:** Founded 1854, in Italy; in U.S., 1947. General motherhouse, Rome, Italy; U.S. novitiate, 5 Wheatland St., Peabody, Mass. 01960. Apostolic work.

**Carmel Community, C.C.:** Founded 1975, Columbus, O. Address, 100 Noe-Bixby Rd., Columbus, O. 43213. Contemplative.

**Carmelite Missionaries of St. Theresa, C.M.S.T.:** Founded 1903, in Mexico. General motherhouse, Mexico City, Mexico; U.S. foundation, 9600 Deertrail Rd., Houston, Tex. 77003.

**Carmelite Nuns, Byzantine:** Holy Annunciation Monastery, R.D. 1, P.O. Box 245, Sugarloaf, Pa. 18249.

**Carmelite Sisters (Corpus Christi), O. Carm.:** Founded 1908, in England; in U.S., 1920. General motherhouse, Tunapuna, Trinidad, W.I. U.S. addresses: Carmelite Retreat House, 21 Battery St., Newport, R.I. 02840; Mt. Carmel Home, 412 W. 18th St., Kearney, Nebr. 68847; Home and foreign mission work.

**Carmelite Sisters for the Aged and Infirm, O. Carm.:** Founded 1929, at New York, by Mother M. Angeline Teresa, O. Carm. Motherhouse, Avila-on-Hudson, Germantown, N.Y. 12526. Social work, nursing and educating in the field of gerontology.

**Carmelite Sisters of Charity, C.a.Ch.:** Founded 1826 at Vich, Spain, by St. Joaquina de Vedruna. General motherhouse, Rome, Italy; U.S. address, 4200 16th St. N.W., Washington, D.C. 20011.

**Carmelite Sisters of St. Therese of the Infant Jesus, C.S.T.:** Founded 1917, in U.S.. General motherhouse, 1300 Classen Dr., Oklahoma City, Okla. 73103. Educational work.

**Carmelite Sisters of the Divine Heart of Jesus, D.C.J.:** Founded 1891, in Germany; in U.S., 1912. General motherhouse, Sittard, Netherlands. U.S. provincial houses: 1230 Kavanaugh Pl., Milwaukee, Wis. 52313 (Northern Province); 10341 Manchester Rd., St. Louis, Mo. 63122 (Central Province); 8585 La Mesa Blvd., La Mesa, Calif. 92041 (South Western Province). Social services, mission work.

**Carmelite Sisters of the Sacred Heart, O.C.D.:** Founded 1904, in Mexico. General motherhouse, Guadalajara, Mexico; U.S. provincialate and novitiate, 920 E. Alhambra Rd., Alhambra, Calif. 91801. Social services, retreat and educational work.

**Carmelites, Calced (Carmelite Nuns of the Ancient Observance), O. Carm.:** Founded 1452, in The Netherlands; in U.S., 1930, from Naples, Italy, convent. U.S. monasteries: Carmel of Mary, Wahpeton, N.D. 58075; Carmel of the Sacred Heart, 430 Laurel Ave., Hudson, Wis. 54016. Papal enclosure.

**Carmelites, Discalced, O.C.D.:** Founded 1562, Spain. First foundation in U.S. in 1790, at Charles County, Md.; this monastery was moved to Baltimore. Monasteries in U.S. are listed below, according to states.

Alabama: 716 Dauphin Island Pkwy., Mobile 36606. Arkansas: 7201 W. 32nd St., Little Rock 72204. California: 215 E. Alhambra Rd., Alhambra 91801; 27601 Highway 1, Carmel 93923; 68 Rincon Rd., Kensington 94707; 3361 E. Ocean Blvd., Long Beach 90803; 6981 Teresian Way, Georgetown 95634; 5158 Hawley Blvd., San Diego 92116; 721 Parker Ave., San Francisco 94118; 530 Blackstone Dr., San Rafael 94903; 1000 Lincoln St., Santa Clara 95050.

Colorado: 6138 S. Gallup St., Littleton 80120. Georgia: Coffee Bluff, 11 W. Back St., Savannah 31406; Illinois: River Rd. and Central, Des Plaines 60016. Indiana: 2500 Cold Springs Rd., Indianapolis 46222; 63 Allendale Pl., Terre Haute 47802. Iowa: Carmelite Rd., Eldridge 52748; 2901 S. Cecilia St., Sioux City 51106. Kansas: 3535 Wood Ave., Kansas City, 66102. Kentucky: 1740 Newburg Rd., Louisville 40205. Louisiana: Carmel Ave., Lafayette 70507; 1611 Mirabeau Ave., New Orleans 70122.

Maryland: 1318 Dulaney Valley Rd., Towson, Baltimore 21204; R.R. 4, Box 4035A, LaPlata, Md. 20646. Massachusetts: 61 Mt. Pleasant Ave., Roxbury, Boston 02119; 15 Mt. Carmel Rd., Danvers 01923; Sol-E-Mar Rd., S. Dartmouth 02748. Michigan: 16630 Wyoming Ave., Detroit 48221; 1036 Valley Ave. N.W., Grand Rapids 49504; U.S. 2 Highway, P.O. Box 397, Iron Mountain 49801; 3501 Silver Lake Rd., Traverse City 49684. Minnesota: 8251 De Montreville Trail N., Lake Elmo 55042.

Mississippi: 2155 Terry Rd., Jackson 39204. Missouri: 2201 W. Main St., Jefferson City 65101; 9150 Clayton Rd., Ladue, St. Louis Co. 63124; 424 E. Republic Rd., Springfield 65807. Nevada: 1950 La Fond Dr., Reno 89509. New Hampshire: 275 Pleasant St., Concord, 03301. New Jersey: P.O. Box 785, Flemington 08822; 189 Madison Ave., Morristown 07960. New Mexico: Mt. Carmel Rd., Santa Fe 87501. New York: 745 St. John's Pl., Brooklyn 11216; 139 De Puyster Ave., Beacon 12508; 75 Carmel Rd., Buffalo 14214; 1931 W. Jefferson Rd., Pittsford 14534; 68 Franklin Ave., Saranac Lake 12983; 428 Duane Ave., Schenectady 12304. Ohio: 3176 Fairmount Blvd., Cleveland Heights 44118. Oklahoma: 4200 N. Meridian Ave., Oklahoma City 73112. Oregon: 87609 Green Hill Rd., Eugene 97402. Pennsylvania: Thornbrow, Elysburg 17824; 510 E. Gore Rd., Erie 16509; R.D. 6, Box 28, Center Dr., Latrobe 15650; P.O. Box 57, Loretto 15940; 66th Ave. and Old York Rd. (Oak Lane), Philadelphia 19126. Rhode Island: Watson Ave. at Nayatt Rd., Barrington 02806.

Texas: 600 South Flowers Ave., Dallas 75211; 1600 Sunset Terr., Ft. Worth 76102; 1100 Parthenon Pl., Roman Forest, New Caney 77357. 6301 Culebra and St. Joseph Way, San Antonio 78238. Utah: 5714 Holladay Blvd., Salt Lake City 84121. Vermont: Beckley Hill, Barre, 05641. Washington: 2215 N.E. 147th St., Seattle 98155. Wisconsin: W267 N2517 Meadowbrook Rd., Pewaukee 53072.

**Casimir, Sisters of St., S.S.C.:** Founded 1907, in U.S. by Mother Maria Kaupas. General motherhouse, 2601 W. Marquette Rd., Chicago, Ill. 60629. Education, missions, social services.

**Cenacle, Congregation of Our Lady of the Retreat in the, R.C.:** Founded 1826, in France; in U.S., 1892. Generalate, Rome, Italy. Eastern Province: 154-27 Horace Harding Expressway, Flushing, N.Y. 11367; Midwestern Province, 513 Fullerton Pkwy., Chicago, Ill. 60614.

**Charity, Daughters of Divine, F.D.C.:** Founded 1868, at Vienna, Austria; in U.S., 1913. General motherhouse, Rome, Italy. U.S. provinces: 56 Meadowbrook Rd., White Plains, N.Y. 10605; 39 N. Portage Path, Akron, O. 44303; 1315 N. Woodward Ave., Bloomfield Hills, Mich. 48013. Education, social services.

**Charity, Little Missionary Sisters of, P.M.C.:** Founded 1915, in Italy; in U.S., 1949. General motherhouse, Rome, Italy; U.S. headquarters, 201 Washington St., S. Groveland, Mass. 01834.

**Charity, Missionaries of, M.C.:** Founded 1950, in Calcutta, India, by Mother Teresa. General motherhouse, 54A Acharya Jagadish C. Bose Road, Calcutta 16, India. U.S. address, 335 E. 145th St., Bronx, N.Y. 10451. Service of the poor.

**Charity, Religious Sisters of, R.S.C.:** Founded 1815, in Ireland; in U.S., 1953. Motherhouse, Dublin, Ireland; U.S. headquarters, Marycrest Manor, 10664 St. James Dr., Culver City, Calif. 90230.

**Charity, Sisters of (of Seton Hill), S.C.:** Founded 1870, at Altoona, Pa., from Cincinnati foundation. Administrative Offices, De Paul Center, Mt. Thor Rd., Greensburg, Pa. 15601. Educational, hospital, social, foreign mission work.

**Charity, Sisters of (Grey Nuns of Montreal), S.G.M.:** Founded 1737, in Canada by Bl. Marie Marguerite d'Youville; in U.S., 1855. General administration, Montreal, Que. H2Y 2L7, Canada; U.S. provincial house, 10 Pelham Rd., Lexington, Mass. 02173.

**Charity, Sisters of (of Leavenworth), S.C.L.:** Founded 1858, in U.S.. Motherhouse, Leavenworth, Kans. 66048.

**Charity, Sisters of (of Nazareth), S.C.N.:** Founded 1812, in U.S.. General motherhouse, Nazareth P. O., Nelson Co., Ky. 40048.

**Charity, Sisters of (of St. Augustine), C.S.A.:** Founded 1851, at Cleveland, O. Motherhouse, 5232 Broadview Rd., Richfield, O. 44286.

**Charity, Sisters of Christian, S.C.C.:** Founded 1849, in Paderborn, Germany; in U.S., 1873. General motherhouse, Rome, Italy. U.S. provinces: Mallinckrodt Convent, Mendham, N.J. 07945; Maria Immaculata Convent, 1041 Ridge Rd., Wilmette, Ill. 60091, Education, health services, other apostolic work.

**Charity, Vincentian Sisters of, V.S.C.:** Founded 1835, in Austria; in U.S., 1902. General motherhouse, 8200 McKnight Rd., Pittsburgh, Pa. 15237.

**Charity, Vincentian Sisters of, V.S.C.:** Founded 1928, at Bedford, O. General motherhouse, 1160 Broadway, Bedford, O. 44146.

**Charity of Cincinnati, Ohio, Sisters of, S.C.:** Founded 1829. General motherhouse, Mt. St. Joseph, Ohio 45051. Educational, hospital, social work.

**Charity of Ottawa, Sisters of (Grey Nuns of the Cross), S.C.O.:** Founded 1845, at Ottawa, Canada; in U.S., 1857. General motherhouse, Ottawa, Canada; U.S. provincial house, 975 Varnum Ave., Lowell, Mass. 01854. Educational, hospital work, extended health care.

**Charity of Our Lady, Mother of Mercy, Sisters of, S.C.M.M.:** Founded 1832, in Holland; in U.S., 1874. General motherhouse, Rome, Italy; U.S. provincialate, 520 Thompson Ave., East Haven Conn. 06512.

**Charity of Our Lady of Mercy, Sisters of, O.L.M.:** Founded 1829, in U.S. Generalate and motherhouse, Charleston, S.C. 29412. Education, campus ministry, social services.

**Charity of Quebec, Sisters of (Grey Nuns), S.C.Q.:** Founded 1849, at Quebec; in U.S., 1890. General motherhouse, 2655 rue Le Pelletier, Beauport, Quebec GIC 3X7, Canada. Social work.

**Charity of St. Elizabeth, Sisters of (Convent, N.J.), S.C.:** Founded 1859, at Newark, N. J. Generalate, Convent Station, N. J. 07961. Education, pastoral ministry, social services.

**Charity of St. Hyacinthe, Sisters of (Grey Nuns), S.C.S.H.:** Founded 1840, at St. Hyacinthe, Canada; in U.S., 1878. General motherhouse, 665 Avenue Bourdages, SUD, St. Hyacinthe, Quebec J2T 4J8, Canada. Regional house, 98 Campus Ave., Lewiston Me. 04240.

**Charity of St. Joan Antida, Sisters of, S.C.S.J.A.:** Founded 1799, in France; in U.S., 1932. General motherhouse, Rome, Italy; U.S. provincial house, 8560 N. 76th Pl., Milwaukee, Wis. 53223.

**Charity of St. Louis, Sisters of, S.C.S.L:** Founded

1803, in France; in U.S., 1910. Generalate, Rome, Italy; U.S. provincial house, 29 Casablanca Court, Clifton Park, N.Y. 12065.

**Charity of St. Vincent de Paul, Daughters of, D.C.:** Founded 1633, in France; in U.S. 1809, at Emmitsburg, Md., by St. Elizabeth Ann Seton. General motherhouse, Paris, France. U.S. provinces: Emmitsburg, Md. 21727; 7800 Natural Bridge Rd., St. Louis, Mo. 63121; 9400 New Harmony Rd., Evansville, Ind. 47712; 96 Menands Rd., Albany, N.Y. 12204; 26000 Altamont Rd., Los Altos Hills, Calif. 94022.

**Charity of St. Vincent de Paul, Sisters of, S.V.Z.:** Founded 1845, in Croatia; in U.S., 1955. General motherhouse, Zagreb, Yugoslavia; U.S. foundation, 171 Knox Ave., West Seneca, N.Y. 14224.

**Charity of St. Vincent de Paul, Sisters of, Halifax, S.C.H.:** Founded 1856, at Halifax, N. S., from Emmitsburg, Md., foundation. Generalate, Mt. St. Vincent, Halifax, N. S., Canada. U.S. addresses: Commonwealth of Massachusetts, 125 Oakland St., Wellesley Hills, Mass. 02181; Boston Province, 26 Phipps St., Quincy, Mass. 02169; New York Province, 410 Grant Ave., Brooklyn, N.Y. 11208. Educational, hospital, social work.

**Charity of St. Vincent de Paul, Sisters of, New York, S.C.:** Founded 1817, from Emmitsburg, Md. General motherhouse, Mt. St. Vincent on Hudson, New York, N.Y. 10471. Educational, hospital work.

**Charity of the Blessed Virgin Mary, Sisters of, B.V.M.:** Founded 1833, in U.S. General motherhouse, Mt. Carmel, Dubuque, Ia. 52001. Education, pastoral ministry, social services.

**Charity of the Immaculate Conception of Ivrea, Sisters of, S.C.I.C.:** General motherhouse, Rome, Italy; U.S. address, Immaculate Virgin of Miracles Convent, R.D. 2, Mt. Pleasant, Pa. 15666.

**Charity of the Incarnate Word, Congregation of the Sisters of, C.C.V.I.:** Founded 1869, at San Antonio, Tex., by Bishop C. M. Dubuis. General motherhouse, 4503 Broadway, San Antonio, Tex. 78209.

**Charity of the Incarnate Word, Congregation of the Sisters of (Houston, Tex.), C.C.V.I.:** Founded 1866, in U.S., by Bishop C. M. Dubuis. General motherhouse, 6510 Lawndale Ave., Houston, Tex. 77023. Educational, hospital, social work.

**Charity of the Sacred Heart, Daughters of, F.C.S.C.J.:** Founded 1823, at La Salle de Vihiers, France; in U.S., 1905. General motherhouse, La Salle de Vihiers, France; U.S. address, Sacred Heart Province, P.O. Box 642, Littleton, N.H. 03561.

**Charles Borromeo, Missionary Sisters of St. (Scalabrini Srs.):** Founded 1895, in Italy; in U.S., 1941. American novitiate, 1414 N. 37th Ave., Melrose Park, Ill. 60601.

**Child Jesus, Sisters of the Poor, P.C.J.:** Founded 1844, at Aix-la-Chapelle, Germany; in U.S., 1924. General motherhouse, Simpelveld, Holland; American provincialate, 4567 Olentangy River Rd., Columbus, O. 43214.

**Chretienne, Sisters of Ste., S.S.CH.:** Founded 1807, in France; in U.S., 1903. General motherhouse, Metz, France; American provincial house,

297 Arnold St., Wrentham, Mass. 02093. Educational, hospital, mission work.

**Christ, Adorers of the Blood of, A.S.C.:** Founded 1834, in Italy; in U.S., 1870. General motherhouse, Rome, Italy. U.S. provinces: Ruma Province, Rt. 1, Box 115, Red Bud, Ill. 62278; 1400 South Sheridan, Wichita, Kans. 67213; Columbia, Pa. 17512. Education, retreats, social services, pastoral ministry.

**Christ the King, Sister Servants of, S.S.C.K.:** Founded 1936, in U.S. General motherhouse, Loretto Convent, Mt. Calvary, Wis. 53057. Social services.

**Christian Doctrine, Sisters of Our Lady of, R.C.D.:** Founded 1910, at New York. Generalate, St. Stephen of Hungary, 414 E. 82nd St., New York, N.Y. 10028.

**Christian Education, Religious of, R.C.E.:** Founded 1817, in France; in U.S., 1905. General motherhouse, Farnborough, England; U.S. provincial residence, 36 Hillcrest Rd., Belmont, Mass. 02178.

**Cistercian Nuns, O. Cist.:** Headquarters, Rome, Italy; U.S. address, Valley of Our Lady Monastery, Rt. 1, Box 136, Prairie du Sac, Wis. 53578.

**Cistercian Nuns of the Strict Observance, Order of, O.C.S.O.:** Founded 1125, in France, by St. Stephen Harding; in U.S., 1949. U.S. addresses: Mt. St. Mary's Abbey, Arnold St., Wrentham, Mass. 02093; Our Lady of the Santa Rita Abbey, Box 97, Sonoita, Ariz. 85637; Our Lady of the Redwoods Abbey, Whitethorn, Calif. 95489; Abbey of Our Lady of the Mississippi, R.R. 3, Dubuque, Ia. 52001.

**Clergy, Congregation of Our Lady, Help of the, C.L.H.C.:** Founded 1961, in U.S. Motherhouse, Maryvale Convent, Rt. 1, Box 164, Vale, N.C. 28168.

**Clergy, Servants of Our Lady Queen of the, S.R.C.:** Founded 1929, in Canada; in U.S., 1936. General motherhouse, Lac-au-Saumon, Que., GOJ 1MO, Canada.

**Colettines:** See Franciscan Poor Clare Nuns.

**Columban, Missionary Sisters of St., S.S.C.:** Founded 1922, in Ireland; in U.S., 1930. General motherhouse, Wicklow, Ireland; U.S. region, 1250 W. Loyola Ave., Chicago, Ill. 60626.

**Comboni Missionary Sisters (Missionary Sisters of Verona), C.M.S.:** Founded 1872, in Italy; in U.S., 1950. U.S. address, 1307 S. Lakeside Ave., Richmond, Va. 23228.

**Consolata Missionary Sisters, M.C.:** Founded 1910, in Italy; in U.S., 1954. General motherhouse, Turin, Italy; U.S. headquarters, 6801 Belmont Rd., Belmont, Mich. 49306.

**Cross, Daughters of the, D.C.:** Founded 1640, in France; in U.S., 1855. General motherhouse, 1000 Fairview St., Shreveport, La. 71104. Educational work.

**Cross, Daughters of, of Liege, F.C.:** Founded 1833, in Liege, Belgium; in U.S., 1958. U.S. address, 165 W. Eaton Ave., Tracy, Calif. 95376.

**Cross, Sisters, Lovers of the Holy (Phat Diem):** Founded 1670, in Vietnam; in U.S. 1976. U.S. address, Mary Immaculate Seminary Convent, Northampton, Pa. 18067.

**Cross, Sisters of the Holy, C.S.C.:** Founded 1841, at Le Mans, France; in U.S., 1843. General motherhouse, Saint Mary's, Notre Dame, Ind. 46556. Education, health care, social services, pastoral ministry.

**Cross, Sisters of the Holy (Sisters of the Holy Cross and Seven Dolors), C.S.C.:** Founded 1841, at La Mans, France, established 1847, in Canada; in U.S., 1881. General motherhouse, St. Laurent, Montreal, Que., Canada; U.S. provincial house, Fairview Rd., Pittsfield, N.H. 03263. Educational work.

**Cross and Passion, Sisters of the (Passionist Sisters), C.P.:** Founded 1852; in U.S., 1924. General motherhouse, Bolton, England; U.S. address: Mt. St. Joseph, 670 Tower Hill Rd., Wakefield, R.I. 02880.

**Cross and Passion of Our Lord Jesus Christ, Nuns of the (Passionist Nuns), C.P.:** Founded 1771, in Italy, by St. Paul of the Cross; in U.S., 1910. U.S. convents: 2715 Churchview Ave., Pittsburgh, Pa. 15227; 631 Griffin Pond Rd., Clarks Summit, Pa. 18411; 1420 Benita Ave., Owensboro, Ky. 42301; 1151 Donaldson Hwy., Erlanger, Ky. 41018; 1032 Clayton Rd., Ellisville, Mo. 63011. Contemplatives.

**Cyril and Methodius, Sisters of Sts., SS.C.M.:** Founded 1909, in U.S., by Rev. Matthew Jankola. General motherhouse, Danville, Pa. 17821. Education, care of aged.

**Disciples of the Divine Master, Sister, P.D.D.M.:** Founded 1924; in U.S., 1948. General motherhouse, Rome, Italy; U.S. headquarters, 60 Sunset Ave., Staten Island, N.Y. 10314.

**Divine Compassion, Sisters of, R.D.C.:** Founded 1886, in U.S. General motherhouse, 52 N. Broadway, White Plains, N.Y. 10603. Education, other ministries.

**Divine Love, Oblates to, Sisters, R.O.D.A.:** Founded 1923, in Italy; in U.S., 1947. General motherhouse, Rome, Italy; U.S. provincial house, St. Clare's Convent, 1925 Hone Ave., Bronx, N.Y. 10461.

**Divine Spirit, Congregation of the, C.D.S.:** Founded 1956, in U.S., by Archbishop John M. Gannon. Motherhouse, 409 W. 6th St., Erie, Pa. 16507. Education, social services.

## Dominicans

**Nuns of the Order of Preachers (Dominican Nuns), O.P.:** Founded 1206 by St. Dominic at Prouille, France. Cloistered, contemplative. Two branches in the United States:

• Dominican Nuns having perpetual adoration. First monastery established 1880, in Newark, N.J., from Oullins, France, foundation (1869). Seven autonomous monasteries.

St. Dominic, 13th Ave. and S. 10th St., Newark, N.J. 07103; Corpus Christi, 1230 Lafayette Ave., Bronx, N.Y. 10474; Blessed Sacrament, 29575 Middlebelt Rd., Farmington Hills, Mich. 48018; Holy Name, 3020 Erie Ave., Hyde Park, Cincinnati, O. 45208; Monastery of the Angels, 1977 Carmen Ave., Los Angeles, Calif. 90068; Corpus Christi, 215 Oak Grove Ave., Menlo Park, Calif. 94025; Infant Jesus, 1501 Lotus Lane, Lufkin, Tex. 75901.

• Dominican Nuns devoted to the perpetual

Rosary. First monastery established 1891, in Union City, N.J., from Calais, France, foundation (1880). Thirteen autonomous monasteries (some also observe perpetual adoration).

Dominican Nuns of Perpetual Rosary, 14th and West Sts., Union City, N.J. 07087; 217 N. 68th St., Milwaukee, Wis. 53213; Dominican Monastery, 720 Maiden Choice Lane, Catonsville, Baltimore, Md. 21228; Perpetual Rosary, 1500 Haddon Ave., Camden, N.J. 08103; Our Lady of the Rosary, 335 Doat St., Buffalo, N.Y. 14211; Our Lady of the Rosary, 543 Springfield Ave., Summit, N.J. 07901; Mother of God, 1430 Riverdale St., W. Springfield, Mass. 01089; Perpetual Rosary, 802 Court St., Syracuse, N.Y. 13208; Immaculate Heart of Mary, 1834 Lititz Pike, Lancaster, Pa. 17601; Mary the Queen, 1310 W. Church St., Elmira, N.Y. 14905; St. Jude, Marbury, Ala. 36051; Our Lady of Grace, North Guilford, Conn. 06437; St. Dominic, 4901 16th St. N.W., Washington, D.C. 20011.

**Dominican Rural Missionaries, O.P.:** Founded 1932, in France; in U.S., 1951, at Abbeville, La. General motherhouse, Luzarches, France; U.S. address, 1318 S. Henry St., Abbeville, La. 70510.

**Dominican Sisters of Bethany, Congregation, O.P.:** Founded 1866, in France. Motherhouse, France; U.S. novitiate, 204 Ridge St., Millis, Mass. 02054.

**Dominican Sisters of the Presentation, O.P.:** Founded 1684, in France; in U.S., 1906. General motherhouse, Tours, France; U.S. headquarters, 3012 Elm St., Dighton, Mass. 02715. Hospital work.

**Dominican Sisters of the Roman Congregation of St. Dominic, O.P.:** Founded 1621, in France; in U.S., 1904. General motherhouse, Rome, Italy; U.S. province, 2624 Fillmore St., Davenport, Ia. 52804. Educational work.

**Eucharistic Missionaries of St. Dominic, O.P.:** Founded 1927, in Louisiana. General motherhouse, 1101 Aline St., New Orleans, La. 70115. Parish work, social services .

**Maryknoll Sisters of St. Dominic, M.M.:** Founded 1912, in New York. Center, Maryknoll, N.Y. 10545.

**Religious Missionaries of St. Dominic, O.P.:** General motherhouse, Rome, Italy. U.S. foundations: 808 S. Wright St., Alice, Texas 78332; 47 E. Gramman St., Beeville, Tex. 78102; 121 Indiana St., Laredo, Tex.; 432 N. Oak St., Santa Paula, Calif. 93060; 445 W. Pleasant Valley Rd., Oxnard, Calif. 93033.

**Sisters of St. Dominic, O.P.:** Thirty congregations in the U.S. Educational, hospital work. Names of congregations are given below, followed by the date of foundation, and location of motherhouse.

St. Catharine of Siena, 1822. St. Catharine, Ky. 40061.

St. Mary of the Springs, 1830. Columbus Ohio 43219.

Most Holy Rosary, 1847. Sinsinawa, Wis. 53824.

Most Holy Name of Jesus, 1850. San Rafael, Calif. 94901.

Holy Cross, 1853. Albany Ave., Amityville, N.Y. 11701.

Most Holy Rosary, 1859. Mt. St. Mary on Hudson, Newburgh, N.Y. 12550.

St. Cecilia, 1860. Eighth Ave. N. and Clay St., Nashville, Tenn. 37208.

St. Mary, 1860. 580 Broadway, New Orleans, La. 70118.

St. Catherine of Siena, 1862. 5635 Erie St., Racine, Wis. 53402.

Our Lady of the Sacred Heart, 1873. 1237 W. Monroe St., Springfield, Ill. 62704.

Our Lady of the Rosary, 1876. Sparkill, N.Y. 10976.

Queen of the Holy Rosary, 1876. Mission San Jose, Calif. 94538.

Most Holy Rosary, 1892. 1257 Siena Heights Dr., Adrian, Mich. 49221.

Our Lady of the Sacred Heart, 1877. 2025 E. Fulton St., Grand Rapids, Mich. 49503.

St. Dominic, 1878. Blauvelt, N.Y. 10913.

Immaculate Conception (Dominican Sisters of the Sick Poor), 1879. Ossining, N.Y. 10562. Social work.

St. Catherine de Ricci, 1880. 2850 N. Providence Rd., Media, Pa. 19063.

Sacred Heart of Jesus, 1881. Mt. St. Dominic, Caldwell, N.J. 07006.

Sacred Heart, 1882. 6501 Almeda Rd., Houston, Tex. 77021.

St. Thomas Aquinas, 1888. 423 E. 152nd St., Tacoma, Wash. 98445.

Holy Cross, 1890. P.O. Box 280, Edmonds, Wash. 98020.

St. Catherine of Siena, 1891. 37 Park St., Fall River, Mass. 02721.

St. Rose of Lima (Servants of Relief for Incurable Cancer), 1896. Hawthorne, N.Y. 10532.

Immaculate Conception, 1902. 3600 Broadway, Great Bend, Kans. 67530.

St. Catherine of Siena, 1911. 4600 93rd St., Kenosha, Wis. 53140.

St. Rose of Lima, 1923. 775 Drahner Rd., Oxford, Mich. 48051.

Immaculate Conception, 1929. 9000 W. 81st St., Justice, Ill. 60458.

Immaculate Heart of Mary, 1929. Akron, Ohio 44313.

Immaculate Heart of Mary Province (Dominican Sisters of Spokane). W. 3102 Fort George Wright Dr., Spokane, Wash. 99204.

Dominican Sisters of Oakford (St. Catherine of Siena), 1889. Motherhouse, Oakford, Natal, South Africa. U.S. regional house, 1965. Villa Siena, 1855 Miramonte Ave., Mountain View, Calif. 94040.

**(End, Listing of Dominicans)**

**Dorothy, Institute of the Sisters of St., S.S.D.:** Founded 1834, in Italy; by St. Paola Frassinetti; in U.S., 1911. General motherhouse, Rome, Italy; U.S. provincialate, Villa Fatima, Taunton, Mass. 02780.

**Eucharist, Religious of the, R.E.:** Founded 1857, in Belgium; in U.S., 1900. General motherhouse, Belgium; U.S. foundation, 2907 Ellicott Terr., N.W., Washington, D.C. 20008.

**Eucharistic Missionary Sisters, E.M.S.:** Founded 1943, in Mexico. Motherhouse, Our Lady of Loretto

Convent, 267 N. Belmont Ave., Los Angeles, Calif. 90026.

**Family, Congregation of the Sisters of the Holy, S.S.F.:** Founded 1842, in U.S. General motherhouse, 6901 Chef Menteur Hwy., New Orleans, La. 70126. Educational, hospital work.

**Family, Little Sisters of the Holy, P.S.S.F.:** Founded 1880, in Canada; in U.S., 1900. General motherhouse, Sherbrooke, Que., Canada. U.S. novitiate, 285 Andover St., Lowell, Mass. 01852.

**Family, Sisters of the Holy, S.H.F.:** Founded 1872, in U.S. General motherhouse, P.O. Box 3248, Mission San Jose, Calif. 94538. Educational, social work.

**Family of Nazareth, Sisters of the Holy, C.S.F.N.:** Founded 1875, in Italy; in U.S., 1885. General motherhouse, Rome, Italy. U.S. provinces: 353 N. River Rd., Des Plaines, Ill. 60016; Grant and Torresdale Aves., Torresdale, Philadelphia, Pa. 19114; 285 Bellevue Rd., Pittsburgh, Pa. 15229; Marian Heights, 1428 Monroe Turnpike, Monroe, Conn. 06468; 1814 Egyptian Way, Box 757, Grand Prairie, Tex. 75050.

**Filippini, Religious Teachers, M.P.F.:** Founded 1692, in Italy; in U.S., 1910. General motherhouse, Rome, Italy; U.S. provinces: St. Lucy Filippini Province, Villa Walsh, Morristown, N.J. 07960; Queen of Apostles Province, 474 East Rd., Bristol, Conn. 06010. Educational work.

**Francis de Sales, Oblate Sisters of St., O.S.F.S.:** Founded 1866, in France; in U.S., 1951. General motherhouse, Troyes, France; U.S. headquarters, Villa Aviat Convent, Childs, Md. 21916. Educational, social work.

## Franciscans

**Bernardine Sisters of the Third Order of St. Francis, O.S.F.:** Founded 1457, at Cracow, Poland; in U.S., 1894. Generalate, 647 Spring Mill Rd., Villanova, Pa. 19085. Educational, hospital, social work.

**Capuchin Sisters of St. Clare (Madres Clarisas Capuchinas):** U.S. establishment, 1981, Amarillo diocese. Convent of the Blessed Sacrament and Our Lady of Guadalupe, 4201 N.E. 18th St., Amarillo, Tex. 79107. Cloistered.

**Congregation of the Servants of the Holy Infancy of Jesus, O.S.F.:** Founded 1855, in Germany; in U.S., 1929. General motherhouse, Wuerzburg, Germany; American motherhouse, Villa Maria, P.O. Box 708, North Plainfield, N.J. 07061.

**Congregation of the Third Order of St. Francis of Mary Immaculate, O.S.F.:** Founded 1865, in U.S., by Fr. Pamphilus da Magliano, O.F.M. General motherhouse, 520 Plainfield Ave., Joliet, Ill. 60435. Educational and pastoral work.

**Daughters of St. Francis of Assisi, D.S.F.:** Founded 1890, in Austria-Hungary; in U.S., 1946. Provincial motherhouse, 507 N. Prairie St., Lacon, Ill. 61540. Nursing, CCD work.

**Felician Sisters (Congregation of the Sisters of St. Felix), C.S.S.F.:** Founded 1855, in Poland; in U.S., 1874. General motherhouse, Rome, Italy. U.S. provinces: 36800 Schoolcraft Rd., Livonia, Mich. 48150; 600 Doat St., Buffalo, N.Y. 14211; 3800 Peterson Ave., Chicago. Ill. 60659; 260 South Main

St., Lodi, N.J. 07644; 1500 Woodcrest Ave., Coraopolis, Pa. 15108; 1315 Enfield St., Enfield, Conn. 06082; 4210 Meadowlark Lane, S.E., Rio Rancho, N. Mex. 87174.

**Franciscan Handmaids of the Most Pure Heart of Mary, F.H.M.:** Founded 1917, in U.S.. General motherhouse, 15 W. 124th St., New York, N.Y. 10027. Educational, social work.

**Franciscan Hospitaller Sisters of the Immaculate Conception, F.H.I.C.:** Founded 1876, in Portugal; in U.S., 1960. General motherhouse, Lisbon, Portugal; U.S. novitiate, 300 S. 17th St., San Jose, Calif. 95112.

**Franciscan Missionaries of Mary, F.M.M.:** Founded 1877, in India; in U.S., 1904. General motherhouse, Rome, Italy; U.S. provincialate, 225 E. 45th St., New York, N.Y. 10017. Mission work.

**Franciscan Missionaries of Our Lady, O.S.F.:** Founded 1854, at Calais, France; in U.S., 1913. General motherhouse, Desvres, France; U.S. motherhouse, 4200 Essen Lane, Baton Rouge, La. 70809. Hospital work.

**Franciscan Missionaries of St. Joseph (Mill Hill Sisters), F.M.S.J.:** Founded 1883, at Rochdale, Lancashire, England; in U.S., 1952. General motherhouse, Eccleshall, Stafford, England; U.S. headquarters, Franciscan House, 1006 Madison Ave., Albany, N.Y. 12208.

**Franciscan Missionaries of the Infant Jesus:** Generalate, Rome, Italy. U.S. provincialate, 1215 Kresson Rd., Cherry Hill, N.J. 08003.

**Franciscan Missionary Sisters for Africa, O.S.F.:** American foundation, 1953. Generalate, Ireland; U.S. headquarters, 172 Foster St., Brighton, Mass. 02135.

**Franciscan Missionary Sisters of Assisi, F.M.S.A.:** First foundation in U.S., 1961. General motherhouse, Assisi, Italy; U.S. address, St. Francis Convent, 1039 Northampton St., Holyoke, Mass. 01040.

**Franciscan Missionary Sisters of Our Lady of Sorrows, O.S.F.:** Founded 1937, in China, by Bishop R. Palazzi, O.F.M.; in U.S., 1949. U.S. address, 2385 Laurel Glen Rd., Santa Cruz, Calif. 95065. Educational, social, domestic, retreat and foreign mission work.

**Franciscan Missionary Sisters of the Divine Child, F.M.D.C.:** Founded 1927, at Buffalo, N.Y., by Bishop William Turner. General motherhouse, 6380 Main St., Williamsville, N.Y. 14221. Educational, social work.

**Franciscan Missionary Sisters of the Immaculate Conception, O.S.F.:** Founded 1874, in Mexico; in U.S., 1926. U.S. provincial house, 11306 Laurel Canyon Blvd., San Fernando, Calif. 91340.

**Franciscan Missionary Sisters of the Immaculate Heart of Mary, F.M.I.H.M.:** Founded at Cairo, Egypt by Mother Catarino di S. Rosa (Costanzo Troiano). Generalate, Rome, Italy; U.S. address, Ave Maria House, 3501 Good Intent Rd., Deptford, N.J. 08096.

**Franciscan Missionary Sisters of the Sacred Heart, F.M.S.C.:** Founded 1860, in Italy; in U.S., 1865. Generalate, Rome, Italy; U.S. provincialate, 250 South St., Peekskill, N.Y. 10566. Educational and social welfare apostolates and specialized services.

**Franciscan Poor Clare Nuns (Poor Clares, Order of St. Clare, Poor Clares of St. Colette), P.C., O.S.C., P.C.C.:** Founded 1212, at Assisi, Italy, by St. Francis of Assisi; in U.S., 1875. Proto-monastery, Assisi, Italy. Addresses of autonomous motherhouses in U.S. are listed below.
3626 N. 65th Ave., Omaha, Nebr. 68104; 720 Henry Clay Ave., New Orleans, La. 70118; 509 S. Kentucky Ave., Evansville, Ind. 47714; 1310 Dellwood Ave., Memphis Tenn. 38127; 920 Centre St., Jamaica Plain, Mass. 02130; 201 Crosswicks St., Bordentown, N.J. 08505; 1271 Langhorne-Newton Rd., Langhorne, Pa. 19047; 4419 N. Hawthorne St., Spokane, Wash. 99205; 142 Hollywood Ave., Bronx, N.Y. 10465; 421 S. 4th St., Sauk Rapids, Minn. 56379; 8650 Russell Ave. S., Minneapolis, Minn. 55431; 3501 Rocky River Dr., Cleveland, O. 44111; 89th and Kean Ave., Hickory Hills, Ill. 60457; 280 State Park Dr., Aptos, Calif. 95003; 2111 S. Main St., Rockford, Ill. 61102; 215 E. Los Olivos St., Santa Barbara, Calif. 93105; 460 River Rd., W. Andover, Mass. 01810. 809 E. 19th St., Roswell, N. Mex. 88201; 28210 Natoma Rd., Los Altos Hills, Calif. 94022; 1916 N. Pleasantburg Dr., Greenville, S.C. 29609; 28 Harpersville Rd., Newport News, Va. 23601; 805 N. Malfalfa Rd., Kokoma, Ind. 46901; 4000 Sherwood Blvd., Delray Beach, Fla. 33445; 200 Marycrest Dr., St. Louis, Mo. 63129.

**Franciscan Sisters, Daughters of the Sacred Hearts of Jesus and Mary, O.S.F.:** Founded 1860, in Germany; in U.S., 1872. Generalate, Rome, Italy; U.S. motherhouse, P.O. Box 667, Wheaton, Ill. 60187. Educational, hospital, foreign mission, social work.

**Franciscan Sisters of Allegany, N.Y., O.S.F.:** Founded 1859, at Allegany, N.Y., by Fr. Pamphilus da Magliano, O.F.M. General motherhouse Allegany, N.Y. 14706. Educational, hospital, foreign mission work.

**Franciscan Sisters of Baltimore, O.S.F.:** Founded 1868, in England; in U.S., 1881. General motherhouse, 3725 Ellerslie Ave., Baltimore, Md. 21218. Educational work; social services.

**Franciscan Sisters of Chicago, O.S.F.:** Founded 1894, in U.S., by Mother Mary Therese (Josephine Dudzik). General motherhouse, 1220 Main St., Lemont, Ill. 60439. Educational work, social services.

**Franciscan Sisters of Christian Charity, O.S.F.:** Founded 1869, in U.S. Holy Family Convent, 2409 S. Alverno Rd., Manitowoc, Wis. 54220. Educational, hospital work.

**Franciscan Sisters of Little Falls, Minn., O.S.F.:** Founded 1891, in U.S. General motherhouse, Little Falls, Minn. 56345. Health, education, social services, pastoral ministry, mission work.

**Franciscan Sisters of Mary Immaculate of the Third Order of St. Francis of Assisi, F.M.I.:** Founded 16th century, in Switzerland; in U.S., 1932. General motherhouse, Bogota, Colombia; U.S. provincial house, 4301 N.E. 18th Ave., Amarillo, Tex. 79107. Education.

**Franciscan Sisters of Our Lady of Perpetual Help, O.S.F.:** Founded 1901, in U.S., from Joliet, Ill., foundation. General motherhouse, 201 Broth-

erton Lane, St. Louis, Mo. 63135. Educational, hospital work.

**Franciscan Sisters of Ringwood, F.S.R.:** Founded 1927, at Passaic, N.J. General motherhouse, Mt. St. Francis, Ringwood, N.J. 07456. Educational work.

**Franciscan Sisters of St. Elizabeth, F.S.S.E.:** Founded 1866, at Naples, Italy; in U.S., 1919. General motherhouse, Rome; U.S. novitiate, 449 Park Rd., Parsippany, N.J. 07054. Educational work, social services.

**Franciscan Sisters of St. Joseph, F.S.S.J.:** Founded 1897, in U.S. General motherhouse, 5286 S. Park Ave., Hamburg, N.Y. 14075. Educational, hospital work.

**Franciscan Sisters of the Atonement, Third Order Regular of St. Francis (Graymoor Sisters), S.A.:** Founded 1898, in U.S., as Anglican community; entered Church, 1909. General motherhouse, Graymoor, Garrison P.O., N.Y. 10524. Mission work.

**Franciscan Sisters of the Blessed Virgin Mary of the Holy Angels, B.M.V.A.:** Founded 1863, at Neuwied, Germany; in U.S., 1923. General motherhouse, Rhine, Germany; U.S. motherhouse, 1388 Prior Ave. S., St. Paul, Minn. 55116. Educational, hospital, social work.

**Franciscan Sisters of the Immaculate Conception, O.S.F.:** Founded in Germany; in U.S., 1928. General motherhouse, Kloster, Bonlanden, Germany; U.S. province, 291 W. North St., Buffalo, N.Y. 14201.

**Franciscan Sisters of the Immaculate Conception, O.S.F.:** Founded 1901, in U.S. General motherhouse, 1000 30th St., Rock Island, Ill. 61201. Health care.

**Franciscan Sisters of the Immaculate Conception, Missionary, O.S.F.:** Founded 1873, in U.S. General motherhouse, Rome, Italy; U.S. address, 790 Centre St., Newton, Mass. 02158. Educational work.

**Franciscan Sisters of the Immaculate Conception and St. Joseph for the Dying, O.S.F.:** Founded 1919, in U.S. General motherhouse, 485 Church St., Monterey, Calif. 93940.

**Franciscan Sisters of the Poor, S.F.P.:** Founded 1845, at Aachen, Germany, by Bl. Frances Schervier; in U.S., 1858. Community service center, 23 Middagh St., Brooklyn, N.Y. 11201. Hospital, social work and foreign missions.

**Franciscan Sisters of the Sacred Heart, O.S.F.:** Founded 1866, in Germany; in U.S., 1876. General motherhouse, St. Francis Woods, R.R. 1, Mokena, Ill. 60448. Education, health care, other service ministries.

**Hospital Sisters of the Third Order of St. Francis, O.S.F.:** Founded 1844, in Germany; in U.S., 1875. General motherhouse, Muenster, Germany; U.S. motherhouse, Box 42, Springfield, Ill. 62705. Hospital work.

**Institute of the Franciscan Sisters of the Eucharist, F.S.E.:** Founded 1973. Motherhouse, 405 Allen Ave., Meriden, Conn. 06450.

**Little Franciscan Sisters of Mary, P.F.M.:** Founded 1889, in U.S. General motherhouse, Baie St. Paul, Que., Canada. U.S. province, 55 Moore Ave.,

Worcester, Mass. 01602. Educational, hospital, social work.

**Little Sisters of St. Francis, O.S.F.:** Founded 1979, in Boston archdiocese. Address, 785 Parker St., Mission Hill, Mass. 02120. Combine contemplative life with street ministry apostolate.

**Missionaries of the Third Order of St. Francis of Our Lady of the Prairies, O.L.P.:** Founded 1960, in U.S. General motherhouse, Powers Lake, N.D. 58773.

**Missionary Sisters of the Immaculate Conception of the Mother of God, S.M.I.C.:** Founded 1910, in Brazil; in U.S., 1922, Generalate, 779 Broadway, Paterson, N.J. 07514; provincialate, P.O. Box 3026, Paterson, N.J. 07509. Mission, educational, health work, social services.

**Mothers of the Helpless, M.D.:** Founded 1873, in Spain; in U.S., 1916. General motherhouse, Valencia, Spain; U.S. address, San Jose Day Nursery, 432 W. 20th St., New York, N.Y. 10011.

**Philip Neri Missionary Teachers, Sisters of St., R.F.:** Founded 1858, in Spain; in U.S., 1956. General house, Madrid, Spain; U.S. address: Sisters of St. Philip Neri, St. Albert's Convent, 1259 St. Alberts St., Reno, Nev. 89503.

**Poor Clares of Perpetual Adoration, P.C.P.A.:** Founded 1854, at Paris, France; in U.S., 1921, at Cleveland, Ohio. U.S. monasteries: 4200 N. Market Ave., Canton, O. 44714; 2311 Timlin Rd., Portsmouth, O. 45662; 4108 Euclid Ave., Cleveland, O. 44103; 3900 13th St. N.E., Washington, D.C. 20017; 5817 Old Leeds Rd., Birmingham, Ala. 35210. Contemplative, cloistered, perpetual adoration.

**School Sisters of St. Francis, O.S.F.:** Founded 1874, in U.S. General motherhouse, 1501 Layton Blvd., Milwaukee, Wis. 53215.

**School Sisters of St. Francis (Bethlehem, Pa.), O.S.F.:** Founded in Austria, 1843; in U.S., 1913. General motherhouse, Rome, Italy; U.S. province, 395 Bridle Path Rd., Bethlehem, Pa. 18017. Educational, mission work.

**School Sisters of St. Francis, (Pittsburgh, Pa.), O.S.F.:** Established 1913, in U.S. Motherhouse, Mt. Assisi Convent, 934 Forest Ave., Pittsburgh, Pa. 15202. Education, health care services and related ministries.

**School Sisters of the Third Order of St. Francis (Panhandle, Tex.), O.S.F.:** Founded 1845, in Austria; in U.S., 1942. General motherhouse, Vienna, Austria; U.S. center and novitiate, Sancta Maria Convent, Panhandle, Tex. 79068. Educational, social work.

**Sisters of Charity of Our Lady, Mother of the Church, S.C.M.C.:** Established 1970, in U.S. Motherhouse, Baltic, Conn. 06330. Teaching, nursing, care of aged, and dependent children.

**Sisters of Mercy of the Holy Cross, S.C.S.C.:** Founded 1856, in Switzerland; in U.S. 1912. General motherhouse, Ingenbohl, Switzerland; U.S. provincial house, 1500 O'Day St., Merrill, Wis. 54452.

**Sisters of Our Lady of Mercy (Mercedarians), S.O.L.M.:** General motherhouse, Rome, Italy; U.S. addresses: 133 27th Ave., Brooklyn, N.Y. 11214; St. Edward School, Pine Hill, N.J. 08021.

**Sisters of St. Elizabeth, S.S.E.:** Founded 1931, at

Milwaukee, Wis. General motherhouse, 745 N. Brookfield Rd., Brookfield, Wis. 53005.

**Sisters of St. Francis (Clinton, Iowa), O.S.F.:** Founded 1868, in U.S. General motherhouse, Bluff Blvd. and Springdale Dr., Clinton, Ia. 57232. Educational, hospital, social work.

**Sisters of St. Francis (Maryville, Mo.), O.S.F.:** Founded 1894, in U.S. Motherhouse, Mt. Alverno Convent, R.R. 3, Box 64, Maryville, Mo. 64468. Hospital work.

**Sisters of St. Francis (Millvale, Pa.), O.S.F.:** Founded 1865, Pittsburgh, Pa. General motherhouse, 146 Hawthorne Rd., Millvale P.O., Pittsburgh, Pa. 15209. Educational, hospital work.

**Sisters of St. Francis, Hastings-on-Hudson, O.S.F.:** Founded 1893, in New York. General motherhouse, Hastings-on-Hudson, N.Y. 10706. Education, parish ministry, social services.

**Sisters of St. Francis of Christ the King, O.S.F.:** Founded 1869, in Austria. General motherhouse, Rome, Italy; U.S. provincial house, 1600 Main St., Lemont, Ill. 60439. Educational work, home for aged.

**Sisters of St. Francis of Penance and Christian Charity, O.S.F.:** Founded 1835, in Holland; in U.S., 1874. General motherhouse, Rome, Italy. U.S. provinces: 4421 Lower River Rd., Stella Niagara, N.Y. 14144; 2851 W. 52nd Ave., Denver, Colo. 80221; 3910 Bret Harte Dr., P.O. Box 1028, Redwood City, Calif. 94064.

**Sisters of St. Francis of Philadelphia, O.S.F.:** Founded 1855, at Philadelphia, by Mother Mary Francis Bachmann and St. John N. Neumann. General motherhouse, Convent of Our Lady of the Angels, Glen Riddle-Aston, Pa. 19014. Education, health care, social services.

**Sisters of St. Francis of Savannah, Mo., O.S.F.:** Founded 1850, in Austria; in U.S., 1922. Provincial house, La Verna Heights, Savannah, Mo. 64485. Educational, hospital work.

**Sisters of St. Francis of the Congregation of Our Lady of Lourdes, O.S.F.:** Founded 1916, in U.S. General motherhouse, 6832 Convent Blvd., Sylvania, O. 43560. Education, health care, social services, pastoral ministry.

**Sisters of St. Francis of the Holy Cross, O.S.F.:** Founded 1881, in U.S., by Rev. Edward Daems, O.S.C. General motherhouse, 3025 Bay Settlement Rd., Green Bay, Wis. 54301. Educational, nursing work, pastoral ministry, foreign missions.

**Sisters of St. Francis of the Holy Eucharist, O.S.F.:** Founded 1424, in Switzerland; in U.S., 1893. General motherhouse, 2100 N. Noland Rd., Independence, Mo. 64050. Education, health care, social services, foreign missions.

**Sisters of St. Francis of the Holy Family, O.S.F.:** Founded 1875, in U.S. Motherhouse, Mt. St. Francis, Dubuque, Ia. 52001. Varied apostolates.

**Sisters of St. Francis of the Immaculate Conception, O.S.F.:** Founded 1890, in U.S. General motherhouse, 2408 W. Heading Ave., Peoria, Ill. 61604. Education, care of aging, pastoral ministry.

**Sisters of St. Francis of the Immaculate Heart of Mary, O.S.F.:** Founded 1241, in Bavaria; in U.S., 1913. General motherhouse, Rome, Italy; U.S.

motherhouse, Hankinson, N.D. 58041. Education, social services.

**Sisters of St. Francis of the Martyr St. George, O.S.F.:** Founded 1859, in Germany; in U.S., 1923. General motherhouse, Thuine, West Germany; U.S. provincial house, Alton, Ill. 62002. Education, social services, foreign mission work.

**Sisters of St. Francis of the Perpetual Adoration, O.S.F.:** Founded 1863, in Germany; in U.S., 1875. General motherhouse, Olpe, Germany. U.S. provinces: Box 766, Mishawaka, Ind. 46544; P.O. Box 1060, Colorado Springs, Colo. 80901. Educational, hospital work.

**Sisters of St. Francis of the Providence of God, O.S.F.:** Founded 1922, in U.S., by Msgr. M. L. Krusas. General motherhouse, Grove and McRoberts Rds., Pittsburgh, Pa. 15234. Education, varied apostolates.

**Sisters of St. Francis of the Third Order Regular, O.S.F.:** Founded 1861, at Buffalo, N.Y., from Philadelphia foundation. General motherhouse, 400 Mill St., Williamsville, N.Y. 14221. Educational, hospital work.

**Sisters of St. Joseph of the Third Order of St. Francis, S.S.J.:** Founded 1901, in U.S. Administrative office, 231 S. Michigan Ave., P.O. Box 688, South Bend, Ind. 46624. Education, health care, social services.

**Sisters of St. Mary of the Third Order of St. Francis, S.S.M.:** Founded 1872, in St. Louis, Mo. General motherhouse, 1100 Bellevue Ave., St. Louis, Mo. 63117. Health care, social services.

**Sisters of the Infant Jesus, I.J.:** Founded 1662, at Rouen, France; in U.S., 1950. Motherhouse, Paris, France. Generalate, Rome, Italy. U.S. addresses: 20 Reiner St., Colma, Calif. 94014; St. John the Baptist School, Healdsburg, Calif. 95448; 60 Bellevue Ave., Daly City, Calif. 94014.

**Sisters of the Sorrowful Mother (Third Order of St. Francis), S.S.M.:** Founded 1883, in Italy; in U.S., 1889. General motherhouse, Rome, Italy. U.S. provinces: 6618 N. Teutonia Ave., Milwaukee, Wis. 53209; 9 Pocono Rd., Denville, N.J. 07834; Tulsa Provincialate, 17600 E. 51st St. S., Broken Arrow, Okla. 74012. Educational, hospital work.

**Sisters of the Third Franciscan Order Minor Conventuals, O.S.F.:** Founded 1860, at Syracuse, N.Y. Generalate offices, 100 Michaels Ave., Syracuse, N.Y. 13208. Educational, hospital work.

**Sisters of the Third Order of St. Francis, O.S.F.:** Founded 1877, in U.S., by Bishop John L. Spalding. Motherhouse, Edgewood Hills, E. Peoria, Ill. 61611. Hospital work.

**Sisters of the Third Order of St. Francis (Oldenburg, Ind.), O.S.F.:** Founded 1851, in U.S. General motherhouse, Convent of the Immaculate Conception, Oldenburg, Ind. 47036. Education, social services, pastoral ministry, foreign missions.

**Sisters of the Third Order of St. Francis of Assisi, O.S.F.:** Founded 1849, in U.S. General motherhouse, 3221 S. Lake Dr., Milwaukee, Wis. 53207. Education, other ministries.

**Sisters of the Third Order of St. Francis of Penance and Charity, O.S.F.:** Founded 1869, in U.S., by Rev. Joseph Bihn. Motherhouse, St. Francis Convent, St. Francis Ave., Tiffin, O. 44883. Education, social services.

**Sisters of the Third Order of St. Francis of the Perpetual Adoration, F.S.P.A.:** Founded 1849, in U.S. Generalate, 912 Market St., La Crosse, Wis. 54601. Education, health care.

**Sisters of the Third Order Regular of St. Francis of the Congregation of Our Lady of Lourdes, O.S.F.:** Founded 1877, in U.S. General motherhouse, Assisi Heights, Rochester, Minn. 55901. Education, health care, social services.

**(End, Listing of Franciscans)**

**Good Shepherd Sisters (Servants of the Immaculate Heart of Mary), S.C.I.M.:** Founded 1850, in Canada; in U.S., 1882. General motherhouse, Quebec, Canada; Provincial House, Bay View, Saco, Maine 04072. Educational, social work.

**Good Shepherd, Sisters of Our Lady of Charity of the, R.G.S.:** Founded 1641, in France; in U.S., 1843. Generalate, Rome, Italy. U.S. provinces: 9517 Leebrook Dr., Cincinnati, O. 45231; 82-31 Doncaster Pl., Jamaica, N.Y. 11432; 504 Hexton Hill Rd., Silver Spring, Md. 20904; 7654 Natural Bridge Rd., St. Louis, Mo. 63121; 2041 Laurel Ave., St. Paul, Minn. 55104.

**Graymoor Sisters:** See Franciscan Sisters of the Atonement.

**Grey Nuns of the Sacred Heart, G.N.S.H.:** Founded 1921, in U.S. General motherhouse, Quarry Rd., Yardley, Pa. 19067.

**Guadalupe, Sisters of, O.L.G.:** Founded 1946, in Mexico City. General motherhouse, Mexico City, Mexico; U.S. address, St. Mary's College, Winona, Minn. 55987.

**Guardian Angels, Sisters of the Holy, S.A.C.:** Founded 1839, in France. General motherhouse, Madrid, Spain; U.S. foundation, 1245 S. Van Ness, Los Angeles, Calif. 90019.

**Handmaids of Mary Immaculate, A.M.I.:** Founded 1952 in Helena, Mont. Address: Ave Maria Institute, Washington, N.J. 07882.

**Handmaids of the Precious Blood, Congregation of, H.P.B.:** Founded 1947, at Jemez Springs, N.M. Motherhouse and novitiate, Cor Jesu Monastery, Jemez Springs, N.M. 87025.

**Helpers, Society of, H.H.S.:** Founded 1856, in France; in U.S., 1892. General motherhouse, Paris, France; American province, 303 W. Barry Ave., Chicago, Ill. 60657.

**Hermanas Catequistas Guadalupanas, H.C.G.:** Founded 1923, in Mexico; in U.S., 1950. General motherhouse, Mexico; U.S. foundation, 4110 S. Flores, San Antonio, Tex. 78214.

**Holy Child Jesus, Society of the, S.H.C.J.:** Founded 1846, in England; in U.S., 1862. General motherhouse, Rome, Italy. U.S. province: 620 Edmonds Ave., Drexel Hill, Pa. 19026.

**Holy Faith, Congregation of the Sisters of the, C.H.F.:** Founded 1856, in Ireland; in U.S. 1953. General motherhouse, Dublin, Ireland; U.S. regional superior, 1205 Corning St., Los Angeles, Calif. 90035.

**Holy Ghost, Sisters of the, C.H.G.:** Founded 1913, in U.S., by Most Rev. J. F. Regis Canevin. General motherhouse, 5246 Clarwin Ave., Ross

Township, Pittsburgh, Pa. 15229. Educational, nursing work; care of aged.

**Holy Ghost and Mary Immaculate, Sister Servants of, S.H.G.:** Founded 1893, in U.S. Motherhouse, 301 Yucca St., San Antonio, Tex. 78203. Education, hospital work.

**Holy Heart of Mary, Servants of the, S.S.C.M.:** Founded 1860, in France; in U.S., 1889. General motherhouse, Montreal, Que., Canada; U.S. province, 145 S. 4th Ave., Kankakee, Ill. 60901. Educational, hospital, social work.

**Holy Names of Jesus and Mary, Sisters of the, S.N.J.M.:** Founded 1843, in Canada; in U.S., 1859. General motherhouse, Pierrefonds H9K 1C6, P.Q., Canada. U.S. addresses: Oregon Province, Marylhurst, Ore. 97036; California Province, P.O. Box 907, Los Gatos, Calif. 95031; New York Province, 1061 New Scotland Rd., Albany, N.Y. 12208; Washington Province, W. 2911 Ft. Wright Dr., Spokane, Wash. 99204.

**Holy Spirit, Daughters of the, D.H.S.:** Founded 1706, in France; in U.S., 1902. Generalate, Rennes, France; U.S. motherhouse, 72 Church St., Putnam, Conn. 06260. Educational work, district nursing; pastoral ministry.

**Holy Spirit, Mission Sisters of the, M.S.Sp.:** Founded 1932, at Cleveland, O. Motherhouse, 1030 N. River Rd., Saginaw, Mich. 48603.

**Holy Spirit, Missionary Sisters, Servants of the:** Founded 1889, in Holland; in U.S., 1901. Generalate, Rome, Italy; U.S. motherhouse, Convent of the Holy Spirit, Techny, Ill. 60082.

**Holy Spirit, Sisters of the, C.S.Sp.:** Founded 1890, in Rome, Italy; in U.S., 1929. General motherhouse, 10102 Granger Rd., Garfield Hts., Ohio 44125. Educational, social, nursing work.

**Holy Spirit of Perpetual Adoration, Sister Servants of the:** Founded 1896, in Holland; in U.S., 1915. General motherhouse, Steyl, Holland; U.S. motherhouse, 2212 Green St., Philadelphia, Pa. 19130.

**Home Mission Sisters of America (Glenmary Sisters):** Founded 1952, in U.S. Motherhouse, Morning Star, P.O. Box 39188, Cincinnati, O. 45239.

**Home Visitors of Mary, Sisters, H.V.M.:** Founded 1949, in Detroit, Mich. Motherhouse, 356 Arden Park, Detroit, Mich. 48202.

**Humility of Mary, Congregation of, C.H.M.:** Founded 1854, in France; in U.S., 1864. U.S. address, Convent of Humility of Mary, Ottumwa, Ia. 52501.

**Humility of Mary, Sisters of the, H.M.:** Founded 1854, in France; in U.S., 1864. U.S. address, Villa Maria, Pa. 16155.

**Immaculate Conception, Little Servant Sisters of the:** Founded 1850, in Poland; in U.S., 1926. General motherhouse, Poland; U.S. provincial house, 184 Amboy Ave., Woodbridge, N.J. 07095. Education, social services, African missions.

**Immaculate Conception, Sisters of the, R.C.M.:** Founded 1892, in Spain; in U.S., 1962. General motherhouse, Madrid, Spain; U.S. foundation, 867 Oxford, Clovis, Calif. 93612.

**Immaculate Conception, Sisters of the, C.I.C.:** Founded 1874, in U.S. General motherhouse, 4920 Kent St., Metairie, La. 70002.

**Immaculate Conception of the Blessed Virgin Mary, Sisters of the (Lithuanian):** Founded 1918, at Mariampole, Lithuania; in U.S., 1936. General motherhouse, Lithuania; U.S. headquarters, Immaculate Conception Convent, Putnam, Conn. 06260.

**Immaculate Heart of Mary, Missionary Sisters, I.C.M.:** Founded 1897, in India; in U.S., 1919. Generalate, Rome, Italy; U.S. address, 1710 N. Glebe Rd., Arlington, Va. 22207. Educational social, foreign mission work.

**Immaculate Heart of Mary, Sisters of the:** Founded 1848, in Spain; in U.S., 1878. General motherhouse, Rome, Italy. U.S. province, 4100 Sabino Canyon Rd., Tucson, Ariz. 85715. Educational work.

**Immaculate Heart of Mary, Sisters of the (California Institute of the Most Holy and Immaculate Heart of the B.V.M.), I.H.M.:** Founded 1848, in Spain; in U.S., 1871. Generalate, 3431 Waverly Dr., Los Angeles, Calif. 90027.

**Immaculate Heart of Mary, Sisters, Servants of the, I.H.M.:** Founded 1845, at Monroe, Mich., by Rev. Louis Florent Gillet. Three independent branches: Generalate, 610 W. Elm St., Monroe, Mich. 48161; Villa Maria, Immaculata, Pa. 19345; Immaculate Heart of Mary Generalate, Marywood, Scranton, Pa. 18509.

**Incarnate Word and Blessed Sacrament, Congregation of, V.I.:** Founded 1625, in France; in U.S., 1853. Incarnate Word Convent, 3400 Bradford Pl., Houston, Tex. 77028.

**Incarnate Word and Blessed Sacrament, Congregation of the, of the Archdiocese of San Antonio, I.W.B.S.:** Motherhouses: 1101 Northeast Water St., Victoria, Tex. 77901; 2930 S. Alameda, Corpus Christi, Tex. 78404.

**Incarnate Word and Blessed Sacrament, Sisters of the, S.I.W.:** Founded 1625, in France; in U.S. 1853. Motherhouse, 6618 Pearl Rd., Parma Heights, Cleveland, O. 44130.

**Infant Jesus, Congregation of the (Nursing Sisters of the Sick Poor), C.I.J.:** Founded 1835, in France; in U.S., 1905. General motherhouse, 310 Prospect Park W., Brooklyn, N.Y. 11215.

**Jeanne d'Arc, Sisters of Ste.:** Founded 1914, in America, by Rev. Marie Clement Staub, A.A. General motherhouse, 1505, rue de l'Assomption Sillery, Que. G1S 4T3, Canada. Spiritual and temporal service of priests.

**Jesus, Daughters of, F.I.:** Founded 1871, in Spain; in U.S., 1950. General motherhouse, Rome, Italy; U.S. address, 410 Grand St., Apt. 24F, New York, N.Y.

**Jesus, Daughters of (Filles de Jesus), F.J.:** Founded 1834, in France; in U.S., 1904. General motherhouse, Kermaria, Locmine, France; American provincial house, 9040 84th Ave., Edmonton, Alberta T6C 1E4, Canada. Educational, hospital, parish and social work.

**Jesus, Little Sisters of:** Founded 1939, in Sahara; in U.S., 1952. General motherhouse, Rome, Italy; U.S. headquarters, 700 Irving St. N.E., Washington, D.C. 20017.

**Jesus, Society of the Sisters, Faithful Companions of, F.C.J.:** Founded 1820, in France; in U.S.,

1896. General motherhouse, Kent, England. U.S. convents: 20 Atkins St., Providence, R.I. 02908; St. Philomena Convent, Cory's Lane, Portsmouth, R.I. 02871.

**Jesus Crucified, Congregation of:** Founded 1930, in France; in U.S., 1955. General motherhouse, Brou, France; U.S. foundations: Regina Mundi Priory, Devon, Pa. 19333; St. Paul's Priory, 61 Narragansett, Newport, R.I. 02840.

**Jesus Crucified and the Sorrowful Mother, Poor Sisters of, C.J.C.:** Founded 1924, in U.S., by Rev. Alphonsus Maria, C.P. Motherhouse, 261 Thatcher St., Brockton, Mass. 02402. Education, nursing homes, catechetical centers.

**Jesus-Mary, Religious of, R.J.M.:** Founded 1818, at Lyons, France; in U.S., 1877. General motherhouse, Rome, Italy; U.S. province, 8908 Riggs Rd., Hyattsville, Md. 20783. Educational work.

**Jesus, Mary and Joseph, Missionaries of, M.J.M.J.:** Founded 1942, in Spain; in U.S., 1956. General motherhouse, Madrid, Spain; U.S. regional house, 12940 Up River Rd., Corpus Christi, Tex. 78410.

**John the Baptist, Sisters of St., C.S.J.B.:** Founded 1878, in Italy; in U.S., 1906. General motherhouse, Rome, Italy; U.S. provincialate, Anderson Hill Rd., Purchase, N.Y. 10577. Education, parish and retreat work; social services.

**Joseph, Missionary Servants of St., M.S.S.J.:** Founded 1874, in Spain; in U.S., 1957. General motherhouse, Salamanca, Spain; U.S. address, 203 N. Spring St., Falls Church, Va. 22046.

**Joseph, Poor Sisters of St.:** Founded 1880, in Argentina. General motherhouse, Muniz, Argentina; U.S. addresses, Casa Belen, 305 E. 4th St., Bethlehem, Pa. 78015; Casa Nazareth, 330 S. Spruce St., Reading, Pa. 19602; St. Gabriel Convent, 4319 Sano St., Alexandria, Va. 22312.

**Joseph, Religious Daughters of St., F.S.J.:** Founded 1875, in Spain. General motherhouse, Spain; U.S. foundation, 319 N. Humphreys Ave., Los Angeles, Calif. 90022.

**Joseph, Religious Hospitallers of St., R.H.S.J.:** Founded 1636, in France; in U.S., 1894. Generalate, 5621 Canterbury Ave., Montreal, Que., H3T 15B, Canada. Hospital work.

**Joseph, Sisters of St., C.S.J.:** Founded 1650, in France; in U.S., 1836, at St. Louis. U.S. independent motherhouses:

637 Cambridge St., Brighton, Mass. 02135; 1515 W. Ogden Ave., La Grange Park, Ill., 60525; 480 S. Batavia St., Orange, Calif. 92668; Mt. St. Joseph Convent, Chestnut Hill, Philadelphia, Pa. 19118.

St. Joseph Convent, Brentwood, N.Y. 11717; 23 Agassiz Circle, Buffalo, N.Y. 14214; Avila Hall, Clement Rd., Rutland, Vt. 05701; 3430 Rocky River Dr., Cleveland, O. 44111; R.R. No. 3, Box 291A, Tipton, Ind. 46072; Nazareth, Mich. 49074; 1425 Washington St., Watertown, N.Y. 13601; St. Joseph Motherhouse, Baden, Pa. 15005; 819 W. 8th St., Erie, Pa. 16502.

4095 East Ave., Rochester, N.Y. 14610; 215 Court St., Concordia, Kans. 66901; Holyoke, Mass. 01040; 1412 E. 2nd St., Superior, Wis. 54880; Pogue Run Rd., Wheeling, W. Va. 26003; 3700 E. Lincoln St., Wichita, Kans. 67218.

**Joseph, Sisters of St. (Lyons, France), C.S.J.:** Founded 1650, in France; in U.S., 1906. General motherhouse, Lyons, France; U.S. provincialate, 93 Halifax St., Winslow, Me. 04901. Educational, hospital work.

**Joseph, Sisters of St., of Peace, C.S.J.:** Founded 1884, in England. Generalate, 1234 Massachusetts Ave. N.W., Washington, D.C. 20005. Educational, hospital, social service work.

**Joseph of Carondelet, Sisters of St., C.S.J.:** Founded 1650, in France; in U.S., 1836, at St. Louis, Mo. U.S. headquarters, 2307 S. Lindbergh Blvd., St. Louis, Mo. 63131.

**Joseph of Chambery, Sisters of St.:** Founded 1650, in France; in U.S., 1885. Generalate, Rome, Italy; U.S. provincial house, 27 Park Rd., West Hartford, Conn. 06119. Educational, hospital, social work.

**Joseph of Cluny, Sisters of St., S.J.C.:** Founded 1807, in France. Generalate, Paris, France; U.S. provincial house, Brenton Rd., Newport, R.I. 02840.

**Joseph of Medaille, Sisters of, C.S.J.:** Founded 1823, in France; in U.S., 1855. Became an American congregation Nov. 30, 1977. Central office, 5108 Reading Rd., Cincinnati, Ohio 45237.

**Joseph of St. Augustine, Fla., Sisters of St., S.S.J.:** General motherhouse, 241 St. George St., St. Augustine, Fla. 32084. Educational, hospital, pastoral, social work.

**Joseph of St. Mark, Sisters of St., S.S.J.S.M.:** Founded 1845, in France; in U.S., 1937. General motherhouse, 21800 Chardon Rd., Euclid, Cleveland, O. 44117. Nursing homes.

**Joseph the Worker, Sisters of St., S.J.W.:** General motherhouse, St. Joseph Convent, 143 S. Main St., Walton, Ky. 41094.

**Lamb of God, Sisters of the, A.D.:** Founded 1945, in France; in U.S., 1958. General motherhouse, France; U.S. address, Rt. 1, No. 260, Philpot, Ky 42366.

**Living Word, Sisters of the, S.L.W.:** Founded 1975, in U.S. Motherhouse, The Center, 7200 N. Osceola Ave., Chicago, Ill. 60648. Education, hospital, parish ministry work.

**Loretto at the Foot of the Cross, Sisters of, S.L.:** Founded 1812 in U.S., by Rev. Charles Nerinckx. General motherhouse, Nerinx, Ky. 40049. Educational work.

**Louis, Congregation of Sisters of St., S.S.L.:** Founded 1842, in France; in U.S., 1949. General motherhouse, Monaghan, Ireland; U.S. regional house, 22300 Mulholland Dr., Woodland Hills, Calif. 91364. Educational, medical, parish, foreign mission work.

**Marian Sisters of the Diocese of Lincoln:** Founded 1954. Motherhouse, Marycrest, Waverly, Nebr. 68462.

**Marian Society of Dominican Catechists, O.P.:** Founded 1954 in Louisiana. General motherhouse, Boyce, La. 71409. Community of Alexandria-Shreveport, La., diocese.

**Marianites of Holy Cross, Congregation of the Sisters, M.S.C.:** Founded 1841, in France; in U.S., 1843. Motherhouse, Le Mans, Sarthe, France. U.S. provinces: 4123 Woodland Dr., New Orleans, La.

70114; Great Rd. and Drakes Corner, Princeton, N.J. 08540; Cresci Blvd., Hazlet, N.J. 07730 (vice province).

**Marist Sisters, Congregation of Mary, S.M.:** Founded 1824, in France. General motherhouse, Rome, Italy; U.S. convents: St. Albert the Great, 4855 Parker, Dearborn Hts., Mich. 48125; St. Barnabas, 16103 Chesterfield, E. Detroit, Mich. 48021; Our Lady of Peace, Oakwood Dr., Wheeling, W. Va. 26002.

**Maronite Antonine Sisters:** Established in U.S., 1966. U.S. address, 2961 N. Lipkey Rd., R.D. 2, North Jackson, Ohio 44451.

**Martha of Prince Edward Island, Sisters of St., C.S.M.:** Founded 1916, in Canada; in U.S., 1961. General motherhouse, 141 Mt. Edward Rd., Charlottetown, P.E.I., CIA 7M8, Canada.

**Marthe, Sisters of Sainte (of St. Hyacinthe), S.M.S.H.:** Founded 1883, in Canada; in U.S., 1929. General motherhouse 675 ouest, rue St.-Pierre, Hyacinthe, Que., Canada J2T IN7.

**Mary, Company of, O.D.N.:** Founded 1607, in France; in U.S., 1926. General motherhouse, Rome, Italy; U.S. motherhouse, 16791 E. Main St., Tustin, Calif. 92680.

**Mary, Daughters of the Heart of, D.H.M.:** Founded 1790, in France; in U.S., 1851. Generalate, Paris, France; U.S. provincialate, 1339 Northampton St., Holyoke, Mass. 01040. Education retreat work.

**Mary, Little Company of, Nursing Sisters, L.C.M.:** Founded 1877, in England; in U.S., 1893. General motherhouse, Rome, Italy; U.S. provincial house, 9350 S. California Ave., Evergreen Park, Ill. 60642.

**Mary, Missionary Sisters of the Society of (Marist Sisters), S.M.S.M.:** Founded 1845, at St. Brieuc, France; in U.S., 1922. General motherhouse, Rome, Italy; U.S. provincial house, 357 Grove St., Waltham, Mass. 02154. Foreign missions.

**Mary, Servants of, O.S.M.:** Founded 13th century, in Italy; in U.S., 1893. Generalate, Rome, Italy; U.S. provincial motherhouse, 7400 Military Ave., Omaha, Nebr. 68134.

**Mary, Servants of (Servite Sisters), O.S.M.:** Founded 13th century, in Italy; in U.S., 1912. General motherhouse, Our Lady of Sorrows Convent, Ladysmith, Wis. 54848.

**Mary, Servants of, of Blue Island (Mantellate Sisters), O.S.M.:** Founded 1861, in Italy; in U.S., 1916. Generalate, Rome, Italy; U.S. motherhouse, 13811 S. Western Ave., Blue Island, Ill. 60406. Educational work.

**Mary, Sisters of St., of Oregon, S.S.M.O.:** Founded 1886, in Oregon, by Bishop William H. Gross, C.Ss.R. General motherhouse, 4440 S.W. 148th Ave., Beaverton, Ore. 97007. Educational, nursing work.

**Mary, Sisters Servants of (Trained Nurses), S.M.:** Founded 1851, at Madrid, Spain; in U.S., 1914. General motherhouse, Rome, Italy; U.S. motherhouse, 800 N. 18th St., Kansas City, Kans. 66102. Home nursing.

**Mary and Joseph, Daughters of, D.M.J.:** Founded 1817, in Belgium; in U.S., 1926. Generalate,

Rome, Italy; American novitiate, 6037 W. 78th St., Los Angeles, Calif. 90045.

**Mary Help of Christians, Daughters of (Salesian Sisters of St. John Bosco), F.M.A.:** Founded 1872, in Italy, by St. John Bosco and St. Mary Dominic Mazzarello; in U.S., 1908. General motherhouse, Rome, Italy; U.S. motherhouse, 655 Belmont Ave., Haledon, N.J. 07508. Education, youth work.

**Mary Immaculate, Daughters of (Marianist Sisters), F.M.I.:** Founded 1816, in France, by Very Rev. William-Joseph Chaminade. General motherhouse, Rome, Italy; U.S. foundation, 251 W. Ligustrum Dr., San Antonio, Tex. 78228. Educational work.

**Mary Immaculate, Religious of, R.M.I.:** Founded 1876, in Spain; in U.S., 1954. General motherhouse, Rome, Italy: U.S. foundations, 719 Augusta St., San Antonio, Tex. 78215; 539 W. 54th St., New York, N.Y. 10019.

**Mary Immaculate, Sister Servants of, S.S.M.I.:** Founded 1878 in Poland. General motherhouse, Mariowka, Poland; American provincialate, 1220 Tugwell Dr., Catonsville, Md. 21228.

**Mary Immaculate, Sisters Servants of, S.M.I:** Founded 1892, in Ukraine; in U.S., 1935. General motherhouse, Rome, Italy; U.S. province, Immaculate Conception Province, Table Rock, Sloatsburg, N.Y. 10974. Educational, hospital work.

**Mary of Namur, Sisters of St., S.S.M.N.:** Founded 1819, at Namur, Belgium; in U.S., 1863. General motherhouse, Namur, Belgium. U.S. provinces: 3756 Delaware Ave., Kenmore, N.Y. 14217; 3300 Hemphill St., Ft. Worth, Tex. 76110.

**Mary of Providence, Daughters of St., D.S.M.P.:** Founded 1872, at Como, Italy; in U.S., 1913. General motherhouse, Rome, Italy; U.S. provincial house, 4200 N. Austin Ave., Chicago, Ill. 60634. Special education for mentally handicapped.

**Mary of the Immaculate Conception, Daughters of, D.M.:** Founded 1904, in U.S., by Msgr. Lucian Bojnowski. General motherhouse, 314 Osgood Ave., New Britain, Conn. 06053. Educational, hospital work.

**Mary Reparatrix, Society of, S.M.R.:** Founded 1857, in France; in U.S., 1908. Generalate, Rome, Italy. U.S. province, 14 E. 29th St., New York, N.Y. 10016.

**Medical Mission Sisters (Society of Catholic Medical Missionaries, Inc.), S.C.M.M.:** Founded 1925, in U.S., by Mother Anna Dengel. Generalate, London, Eng.; U.S. headquarters, 8400 Pine Rd., Philadelphia, Pa. 19111. Medical work, health education, especially in mission areas.

**Medical Missionaries of Mary, M.M.M.:** Founded 1937, in Ireland, by Mother Mary Martin; in U.S., 1950. General motherhouse, Drogheda, Ireland; U.S. headquarters, 563 Minneford Ave., City Island, Bronx, N.Y. 10464. Medical aid in missions.

**Mercedarian Missionaries of Berriz, M.M.B.:** Founded 1930, in Spain; in U.S., 1946. General motherhouse, Rome, Italy. U.S. headquarters, 918 E. 9th St., Kansas City, Mo. 64106.

**Mercy, Daughters of Our Lady of, D.M.:** Founded 1837, in Italy, by St. Mary Joseph Rossello; in U.S., 1919. General motherhouse,

Savona, Italy; U.S. motherhouse, Villa Rossello, Catawba Ave., Newfield, N.J. 08344. Educational, hospital work.

**Mercy, Missionary Sisters of Our Lady of, M.O.M.:** Founded 1938, in Brazil; in U.S., 1955. General motherhouse, Brazil; U.S. address, 388 Franklin St., Buffalo, N.Y. 14202.

**Mercy, Sisters of, R.S.M.:** Founded 1831, in Ireland, by Mother Mary Catherine McAuley. U.S. motherhouses: 634 New Scotland Ave., Albany, N.Y. 12208; 273 Willoughby Ave., Brooklyn, N.Y. 11205; S. 5245 Murphy Rd., Orchard Park, N.Y. 14127; 100 Mansfield Ave., Burlington, Vt. 05401; 1125 Prairie Dr., N.E., Cedar Rapids, Ia. 52402; 444 E. Grandview Blvd., Erie, Pa. 16504; 249 Steele Rd., W. Hartford, Conn. 06117. Windham, N.H. 03087; Merion, Pa. 10966; 3333 Fifth Ave., Pittsburgh, Pa. 15213; 605 Stevens Ave., Portland, Me. 04103; Belmont, N. Car. 28012; 1437 Blossom Rd., Rochester, N.Y. 14610; 535 Sacramento St., Auburn, Calif. 95603.

2300 Adeline Dr., Burlingame, Calif. 94010; U.S. Route 22 at Terrill Rd., Plainfield, N.J. 07061; 101 Barry Rd., Worcester, Mass. 01609.

**Mercy, Sisters of, of the Union in the United States of America, R.S.M.:** Founded 1831 in Ireland, by Mother M. Catherine McAuley; union formed in 1929. U.S. provinces: P.O. Box 11448, Baltimore, Md. 21239; 10024 S. Central Park Ave., Chicago, Ill. 60642; 2301 Grandview Ave., Cincinnati, Ohio 45206; 29000 Eleven Mile Rd., Farmington Hills, Mich. 48024; 541 Broadway, Dobbs Ferry, N.Y. 10522; 1801 S. 72nd St., Omaha, Nebr. 68124; R.D. 3, Cumberland, R.I. 02864; 2039 N. Geyer Rd., St. Louis, Mo. 63131; Dallas, Pa. 18612.

**Mercy, Sisters of, Daughters of Christian Charity of St. Vincent de Paul, S.M.D.C.:** Founded 1842, in Hungary; U.S. foundation, Rt. 1, Box 353, Hewitt, N.J. 07421.

**Mercy of the Blessed Sacrament, Sisters of:** Founded 1910 in Mexico. U.S. foundation, 555 E. Mountain View, Barstow, Calif. 92311.

**Mill Hill Sisters;** See Franciscan Missionaries of St. Joseph.

**Minim Sisters of Mary Immaculate, C.F.M.M.:** Founded 1886, in Mexico; in U.S. 1926. General motherhouse, Leon, Guanajuato, Mexico; U.S. address, St. Joseph Hospital Convent, Target Range Rd., Nogales, Ariz. 85621.

**Misericordia Sisters, S.M.:** Founded 1848, in Canada; in U.S., 1887. General motherhouse. 12435 Ave. Misericorde, Montreal H4J 2G3, Canada. Social work with unwed mothers and their children; hospital work.

**Mission Helpers of the Sacred Heart, M.H.S.H.:** Founded 1890, in U.S. General motherhouse, 1001 W. Joppa Rd., Baltimore, Md. 21204. Religious education, evangelization.

**Missionary Catechists of the Sacred Hearts of Jesus and Mary (Violetas), M.C.:** Founded 1918, in Mexico; in U.S., 1943. Motherhouse, Tlalpan, Mexico; U.S. address, 209 W. Murray St., Victoria, Tex. 77901.

**Missionary Sisters of the Catholic Apostolate (Pallottine Missionary Sisters), S.A.C.:** Founded in Rome, 1843; in U.S., 1912. Generalate, Rome, Italy; U.S. provincialate, Rt. 2, 15270 Old Halls Ferry Rd., Florissant, Mo. 63034.

**Mother of God, Missionary Sisters of the, M.S.M.G.:** Byzantine, Ukrainian Rite, Stamford. Motherhouse, 711-719 N. Franklin St., Philadelphia, Pa. 19123.

**Mother of God, Sisters Poor Servants of the, S.M.G.:** Founded 1869, at London, England; in U.S., 1947. General motherhouse, Maryfield, Roehampton, London. U.S. addresses: Maryfield Nursing Home, Greensboro Rd., High Point, N.C. 27260; St. Mary's Hospital, 916 Virginia Ave., Norton, Va. 24273; Holy Spirit School, 1800 Geary St., Philadelphia, Pa. 19145. Hospital, educational work.

**Nazareth, Poor Sisters of:** Founded in England; U.S. foundation, 1924. General motherhouse, Hammersmith, London, England; U.S. novitiate, 3333 Manning Ave., Los Angeles, Calif. 90064. Social services, education.

**Notre Dame, School Sisters of, S.S.N.D.:** Founded 1833, in Germany; in U.S., 1847. General motherhouse, Rome, Italy. U.S. motherhouse, 1233 N. Marshall St., Milwaukee, Wis. 53202. Provinces: 6401 N. Charles St., Baltimore, Md. 21212; 320 E. Ripa Ave., St. Louis, Mo. 63125; Good Counsel Hill, Mankato, Minn. 56001; 345 Belden Hill Rd., Wilton, Conn. 06897; 1451 E. Northgate, Irving, Tex. 75062; 1431 Euclid Ave., Berwyn, Ill. 60402.

**Notre Dame, Sisters of, S.N.D.:** Founded 1850, at Coesfeld, Germany; in U.S., 1874. General motherhouse, Rome, Italy. U.S. provinces: 13000 Auburn Rd., Chardon, O. 44024; 1601 Dixie Highway, Covington, Ky. 41011; 3837 Secor Rd., Toledo, O. 43623; 1776 Hendrix Ave., Thousand Oaks, Calif. 91360.

**Notre Dame, Sisters of the Congregation of, C.N.D.:** Founded 1653, in Canada; in U.S., 1860. General motherhouse, Montreal, Que., Canada; U.S. province, 223 West Mountain Rd., Ridgefield, Conn. 06877. Education.

**Notre Dame de Namur, Sisters of, S.N.D.:** Founded 1803, in France; in U.S., 1840. General motherhouse, Rome, Italy. U.S. provinces: P.O. Box 112, Boston, Mass. 02117; Jeffrey's Neck Rd., Ipswich, Mass. 01938; 1561 N. Benson Rd., Fairfield, Conn. 06431; Landing Rd., Ilchester, Md. 21083; 701 E. Columbia Ave., Cincinnati, O. 45215; 14800 Bohlman Rd., Saratoga, Calif. 95070. Educational work.

**Notre Dame de Sion, Congregation of, N.D.S.:** Founded 1843, in France; in U.S., 1892. Generalate, Rome, Italy; U.S. provincial house, 3823 Locust St., Kansas City, Mo. 64109. Creation of better understanding and relations between Christians and Jews.

**Notre Dame Sisters:** Founded 1853, in Czechoslovakia; in U.S., 1910. General motherhouse, Javornik, Czechoslovakia; U.S. motherhouse, 3501 State St., Omaha, Nebr. 68112. Educational work.

**Our Lady of Charity, North American Union of Sisters of, Eudist Sisters (Sisters of Our Lady of**

**Charity of the Refuge), O.L.C.:** Founded 1641, in Caen, France, by St. John Eudes; in U.S., 1855. Autonomous houses were federated in 1944 and in May, 1978, the North American Union of the Sisters of Our Lady of Charity was established. General motherhouse and administrative center, Box 327, Wisconsin Dells, Wis. 53965. Primarily devoted to re-education and rehabilitation of women and girls in residential and non-residential settings.

**Our Lady of Sorrows, Sisters of, O.L.S.:** Founded 1839, in Italy; in U.S., 1947. General motherhouse, Rome, Italy; U.S. headquarters, 10450 Ellerbe Rd., Shreveport, La. 71106.

**Our Lady of the Garden, Sisters of, O.L.G.:** Founded 1829, in Italy, by St. Anthony Mary Gianelli. Motherhouse, Rome, Italy; U.S. address, St. Brendan School, 445½ Whalley Ave., New Haven, Conn. 06511.

**Pallottine Sisters of the Catholic Apostolate, C.S.A.C.:** Founded 1843, at Rome, Italy; in U.S., 1889. General motherhouse, Rome; U.S. motherhouse, St. Patrick's Villa, Harriman Heights, Harriman, N.Y. 10926. Educational work.

**Parish Visitors of Mary Immaculate, P.V.M.I.:** Founded 1920, in New York. General motherhouse, Box 658, Monroe, N.Y. 10950. Mission work.

**Passionist Sisters:** See Cross and Passion, Sisters of the.

**Paul, Angelic Sisters of St.:** Founded 1535, in Milan, Italy; U.S. address, Fatima Shrine, Swan Rd., Youngstown, N.Y. 14174.

**Paul, Daughters of St. (Missionary Sisters of the Media of Communication), D.S.P.:** Founded 1915, at Alba, Piedmont, Italy; in U.S., 1932. General motherhouse, Rome, Italy; U.S. provincial house, 50 St. Paul's Ave., Jamaica Plain, Mass. 02130. Apostolate of the communications arts.

**Paul of Chartres, Sisters of St., S.P.C.:** Founded 1696, in France. General house, Rome, Italy; U.S. address, County Road 492, Marquette, Mich. 49855.

**Peter Claver, Missionary Sisters of St., S.S.P.C.:** Founded 1894; in U.S., 1914. General motherhouse, Rome, Italy; U.S. address, 667 Woods Mill Rd. S., Chesterfield, Mo. 63017.

**Pious Schools, Sisters of, Sch. P.:** Founded 1829 in Spain; in U.S., 1954. General motherhouse, Rome, Italy; U.S. headquarters, 9925 Mason Ave., Chatsworth, Calif. 91311.

**Poor, Little Sisters of the, L.S.P.:** Founded 1839, in France; in U.S., 1868. General motherhouse, St. Pern, France. U.S. provinces: 110-30 221st St., Queens Village, N.Y. 11429; 601 Maiden Choice Lane, Baltimore, Md. 21228; 2325 N. Lakewood Ave.; Chicago, Ill. 60614. Care of aged.

**Poor Clare Missionary Sisters (Misioneras Clarisas), M.C.:** Founded Mexico. General motherhouse, Rome, Italy; U.S. novitiate, 1019 N. Newhope, Santa Ana, Calif. 92703.

**Poor Clare Nuns:** See Franciscan Poor Clare Nuns.

**Poor Clares (Sisters of St. Clare), P.C.:** General motherhouse, Dublin, Ireland; U.S. foundation, 37 E. Emerson, Chula Vista, Calif. 92011.

**Poor Handmaids of Jesus Christ (Ancilla Domini Sisters), P.H.J.C.:** Founded 1851, in Germany; in

U.S., 1868. General motherhouse, Dernbach, Westerwald, Germany; U.S. motherhouse, Donaldson, Ind. 46513. Educational, hospital work, social services.

**Precious Blood, Daughters of Charity of the Most:** Founded 1872, at Pagani, Italy; in U.S., 1908. General motherhouse, Rome, Italy; U.S. convent, 1482 North Ave., Bridgeport, Conn. 06604.

**Precious Blood, Missionary Sisters of the, C.P.S.:** Founded 1885, at Mariannhill, South Africa; in U.S., 1925. Generalate, Rome, Italy; U.S. novitiate, New Holland Ave., P.O. Box 97, Shillington, Pa. 19607. Home and foreign mission work.

**Precious Blood, Sisters Adorers of the, A.P.B.:** Founded 1861, in Canada; in U.S., 1890. General motherhouses: 2520, rue Girouard, St. Hyacinthe, Que. J2S 7B8, Canada (French); 301 Ramsay Rd., London, Ont. N6G 1N7, Canada (English). Contemplatives.

**Precious Blood, Sisters of the, C.Pp.S.:** Founded 1834, in Switzerland; in U.S., 1844. Generalate, 4000 Denlinger Rd., Dayton, Ohio 45426. Education, health care, other ministries.

**Precious Blood, Sisters of the Most, C.Pp.S.:** Founded 1845, in Steinerberg, Switzerland; in U.S., 1870. General motherhouse, 204 N. Main St., O'Fallon, Mo. 63366. Education, other ministries.

**Presentation, Sisters of Mary of the, S.M.P.:** Founded 1829, in France; in U.S., 1903. General motherhouse, Broons, Cotes-du-Nord, France. U.S. address, Maryvale Novitiate, Valley City, N. Dak. 58072. Educational, hospital work.

**Presentation of Mary, Sisters of the, P.M.:** Founded 1796, in France; in U.S., 1873. General motherhouse, Castel Gandolfo, Italy. U.S. provincial houses: 495 Mammoth Rd., Manchester, N.H. 03104; 209 Lawrence St., Methuen, Mass. 01844.

**Presentation of the B.V.M., Sisters of the, P.B.V.M.:** Founded 1775, in Ireland; in U.S., 1854, in San Francisco. U.S. motherhouses: 2360 Carter Rd., Dubuque, Ia. 52001; R.D. 2, Box 33, Newburgh, N.Y. 12550; 8931 Callaghan Rd., San Antonio, Tex. 78230; 2340 Turk Blvd., San Francisco, Calif. 94118; Watervliet, N.Y. 12189.

Route 1, Fargo, N. Dak. 58103; 250 S. Davis Dr., P.O. Box 1113, Warner Robbins, Ga. 31093; 1500 N. Main, Aberdeen, S. Dak. 57401; 1300 E. Cedar, Globe, Ariz. 85501; 1555 E. Dana, Mesa, Ariz. 85201; 366 South St., Fitchburg, Mass. 01420; 419 Woodrow Rd., Annadale, Staten Island, N.Y. 10312.

**Providence, Daughters of Divine, F.D.P.:** Founded 1832, Italy; in U.S., 1964. General motherhouse, Rome, Italy; U.S. address, 1625 Missouri St., Chalmette, La. 70043.

**Providence, Missionary Catechists of Divine, M.C.D.P.:** Founded 1930, as a filial society; adjunct branch of Sisters of Divine Providence (Helotes, Tex.). Motherhouse, 2318 Castroville Rd., San Antonio, Tex. 78237.

**Providence, Oblate Sisters of, O.S.P.:** Founded 1829, in U.S. General motherhouse, 701 Gun Rd., Baltimore, Md. 21227. Educational work.

**Providence, Sisters of, S.P.:** Founded 1861, in Canada; in U.S., 1873. General motherhouse, Our

Lady of Victory Convent, Brightside, Holyoke, Mass. 01040.

**Providence, Sisters of, S.P.:** Founded 1843, in Canada; in U.S., 1854. General motherhouse, Montreal, Canada. U.S. provinces: 1511 Third Ave., Seattle, Wash. 98101; 9 E. 9th Ave., Spokane, Wash. 99202.

**Providence, Sisters of (of St. Mary-of-the-Woods), S.P.:** Founded 1806, in France; in U.S., 1840. Generalate, St. Mary-of-the-Woods, Ind. 47876.

**Providence, Sisters of Divine, C.D.P.:** Founded 1762, in France; in U.S., 1866. Generalate, Box 197, Helotes, Tex. 78023. Educational, hospital work.

**Providence, Sisters of Divine, C.D.P.:** Founded 1851, in Germany; in U.S., 1876. Generalate, Rome, Italy. U.S. provinces: 9000 Babcock Blvd., Allison Park, Pa. 15101; 8351 Florissant Rd., St. Louis, Mo. 63121; Box 2, Rte. 80, Kingston, Mass. 02364. Educational, hospital work.

**Providence, Sisters of Divine (of Kentucky), C.D.P.:** Founded 1762, in France; in U.S., 1889. General motherhouse, Moselle, France; U.S. province, Melbourne, Ky. 41059. Education, social services, other ministries.

**Redeemer, Oblates of the Most Holy, O.SS.R.:** Founded 1864, in Spain. General motherhouse, Spain; U.S. foundation, 60-80 Pond St., Jamaica Plain, Mass. 02130.

**Redeemer, Order of the Most Holy, O.SS.R.:** Founded 1731, by St. Alphonsus Liguori; in U.S., 1957. U.S. addresses: Mother of Perpetual Help Monastery, Esopus, N.Y. 12429; St. Alphonsus Monastery, Liguori, Mo. 63057.

**Redeemer, Sisters of the Divine, S.D.R.:** Founded 1849, in Niederbronn, France; in U.S., 1912. General motherhouse, Rome, Italy; U.S. province, 999 Rock Run Road, Elizabeth, Pa. 15037. Educational, hospital work; care of the aged.

**Redeemer, Sisters of the Holy, S.H.R.:** Founded 1849, in Alsace; in U.S., 1924. General motherhouse, Wuerzburg, Germany; U.S. provincial house, Huntingdon Valley, Pa. 19006. Personalized medical care in hospitals, homes for aged, private homes; retreat work.

**Reparation of the Congregation of Mary, Sisters of, S.R.C.M.:** Founded 1903, in U.S. Motherhouse, St. Zita's Villa, Monsey, N.Y. 10952.

**Resurrection, Sisters of the, C.R.:** Founded 1891, in Italy; in U.S., 1900. General motherhouse, Rome, Italy. U.S. provinces: 7432 Talcott Ave., Chicago, Ill. 60631; Mt. St. Joseph, Castleton-on-Hudson, N.Y. 12033. Education, nursing.

**Rita, Sisters of St., O.S.A.:** General motherhouse, Wurzburg, Germany. U.S. foundation, St. Monica's Convent, 3920 Green Bay Rd., Racine, Wis. 53404.

**Rosary, Congregation of Our Lady of the Holy, R.S.R.:** Founded 1874, in Canada; in U.S., 1899. General motherhouse, C.P. 2020, Rimouski, Que., Canada. U.S. regional house, 20 Thomas St., Portland, Me. 04102. Educational work.

**Rosary, Missionary Sisters of Our Lady of the Holy, H.R.S.:** Founded 1924, in Ireland; in U.S., 1954. Motherhouse, Dublin, Ireland. U.S. regional

address, P.O. Box 304, Bryn Mawr, Pa. 19010. African missions.

**Sacrament, Missionary Sisters of the Most Blessed, M.SS.S.:** General motherhouse, Madrid, Spain; U.S. foundation: 1111 Wordin Ave., Bridgeport, Conn. 06605.

**Sacrament, Nuns of the Perpetual Adoration of the Blessed, A.P.:** Founded 1807, in Rome, Italy; in U.S., 1925. U.S. monasteries: 145 N. Cotton Ave., El Paso, Tex. 79901; 771 Ashbury St., San Francisco, Calif. 94117.

**Sacrament, Oblate Sisters of the Blessed, O.S.B.S.:** Founded 1935, in U.S.; motherhouse, St. Sylvester Convent, Marty, S.D. 57361. Care of American Indians.

**Sacrament, Religious Sisters of the Blessed, R.M.S.S.:** Founded 1910, in Mexico; in U.S., 1926. General motherhouse, Mexico City, Mexico; U.S. convent, 222 W. Cevallos St., San Antonio, Tex. 78204.

**Sacrament, Servants of the Blessed, S.S.S.:** Founded 1858, in France, by St. Pierre Julien Eymard; in U.S., 1947. General motherhouse, Rome, Italy; American vice-provincial house, 101 Silver St., Waterville, Me. 04901. Contemplative.

**Sacrament, Sisters of the Blessed, for Indians and Colored People, S.B.S.:** Founded 1891, in U.S., by Katharine Drexel. General motherhouse, Bensalem, Pa. 19020.

**Sacrament, Sisters of the Most Holy, M.H.S.:** Founded 1851, in France; in U.S., 1872. General motherhouse, 409 W. St. Mary Blvd. (P.O. Box 2429), Lafayette, La. 70502.

**Sacrament, Sisters Servants of the Blessed, S.S.B.S.:** Founded 1904, in Mexico. General motherhouse, Guadalajara, Mexico. U.S. address, Our Lady of Guadalupe School, 536 Rockwood Ave., Calexico, Calif. 92231.

**Sacramentine Nuns (Religious of the Order of the Blessed Sacrament and Our Lady), O.S.S.:** Founded 1639, in France; in U.S., 1912. U.S. monasteries: 23 Park Ave., Yonkers, N.Y. 10703; US 31, Conway, Mich. 49722. Perpetual adoration of the Holy Eucharist.

**Sacred Heart, Daughters of Our Lady of the:** Founded 1882, in France; in U.S., 1955. General motherhouse, Rome, Italy; U.S. address, 424 E. Browning Rd., Bellmawr, N.J. 08031. Educational work.

**Sacred Heart, Missionary Sisters of the (Cabrini Sisters), M.S.C.:** Founded 1880, in Italy, by St. Frances Xavier Cabrini; in U.S., 1889. General motherhouse, Rome, Italy; U.S. provinces: 223 E. 19th St., New York, N.Y. 10003 (Eastern); 434 W. Deming Pl., Chicago, Ill. 60614 (Western). Educational, health, social and catechetical work.

**Sacred Heart, Religious of the Apostolate of the, R.A.:** General motherhouse, Madrid, Spain; U.S. address, 1120 6th St., Miami Beach, Fla., 33139.

**Sacred Heart, Society Devoted to the, S.D.S.H.:** Founded 1940, in Hungary; in U.S., 1956. U.S. motherhouse, 2121 W. Olive Dr., Burbank, Calif. 91506. Educational work.

**Sacred Heart, Society of the, R.S.C.J.:** Founded 1800, in France; in U.S., 1818. Generalate, Rome,

Italy. U.S. provincial house, 4389 W. Pine Blvd., St. Louis, Mo. 63108. Educational work.

**Sacred Heart of Jesus, Apostles of, A.S.C.J.:** Founded 1894, in Italy; in U.S., 1902. General motherhouse, Rome, Italy; U.S. motherhouse, 265 Benham St., Hamden, Conn. 06514. Educational, social work.

**Sacred Heart of Jesus, Handmaids of the, A.C.J.:** Founded 1877, in Spain. General motherhouse, Rome, Italy; U.S. province, 616 Coopertown Rd., Haverford, Pa. 19041. Educational, retreat work.

**Sacred Heart of Jesus, Missionary Sisters of the Most (Hiltrup), M.S.C.:** Founded 1899, in Germany; in U.S., 1908. General motherhouse, Rome, Italy; U.S. province, Hyde Park, Reading, Pa. 19605. Education, health care, pastoral ministry.

**Sacred Heart of Jesus, Oblate Sisters of the, O.S.H.J.:** Founded 1894; in U.S., 1949. General motherhouse, Rome, Italy; U.S. headquarters, 50 Warner Rd., Hubbard, Ohio 44425. Educational, social work.

**Sacred Heart of Jesus, Servants of the Most:** Founded 1894, in Poland; in U.S., 1959. General motherhouse, Cracow, Poland; U.S. address, 231 Arch St., Cresson, Pa. 16630. Education, health care, social services.

**Sacred Heart of Jesus, Sisters of the, S.S.C.J.:** Founded 1816, in France; in U.S., 1903. General motherhouse, St. Jacut, Brittany, France; U.S. provincial house, 5922 Blanco Rd., San Antonio, Tex. 78216. Educational, hospital, domestic work.

**Sacred Heart of Jesus and of the Poor, Servants of the (Mexican), S.S.H.J.P.:** Founded 1885, in Mexico; in U.S., 1907. General motherhouse, Apartado 92, Puebla, Pue., Mexico; U.S. regional house, 237 Tobin Pl., El Paso, Tex. 79905.

**Sacred Heart of Jesus for Reparation, Congregation of the Handmaids of the:** Founded 1918, in Italy; in U.S., 1958. U.S. address, Sunshine Park, R.D. 3, Steubenville, Ohio 43952.

**Sacred Heart of Mary, Religious of the, R.S.H.M.:** Founded 1848, in France; in U.S., 1877. Generalate, Rome, Italy. U.S. provinces; 50 Wilson Park Dr., Tarrytown, N.Y. 10591; 8008 Loyola Blvd., Los Angeles, Calif. 90045.

**Sacred Hearts, Religious of the Holy Union of the, S.U.S.C.:** Founded 1826, in France; in U.S., 1886. Generalate, Rome, Italy. U.S. provinces: 550 Rock St., Fall River, Mass. 02720; Main St., Groton, Mass. 01450. Varied ministries.

**Sacred Hearts and of Perpetual Adoration, Sisters of the, SS.CC.:** Founded 1797, in France; in U.S., 1908. General motherhouse, Rome, Italy; U.S. Pacific province, 45-901A Wailele Rd., Kaneohe, Hawaii 96744. Varied ministries.

**Sacred Hearts of Jesus and Mary, Sisters of the, S.H.J.M.:** Established 1953, in U.S. General motherhouse, Essex, England; U.S. address, 310 San Carlos Ave., El Cerrito, Calif. 94530.

**Savior, Company of the, C.S.:** Founded 1952, in Spain; in U.S., 1962. General motherhouse, Madrid, Spain; U.S. foundation, 820 Clinton Ave., Bridgeport, Conn. 06604.

**Savior, Sisters of the Divine, S.D.S.:** Founded 1888, in Italy; in U.S., 1895. General motherhouse,

Rome, Italy; U.S. province, 4311 N. 100th St., Milwaukee, Wis. 53222. Educational, hospital work.

**Social Service, Sisters of, S.S.S.:** Founded in Hungary, 1923, by Sr. Margaret Slachta. U.S. address, 440 Linwood Ave., Buffalo, N.Y. 14209. Social work.

**Social Service, Sisters of, of Los Angeles, S.S.S.:** Founded 1908, in Hungary; in U.S., 1926. General motherhouse, 1120 Westchester Pl., Los Angeles, Calif. 90019.

**Teresa of Jesus, Society of St., S.T.J.:** Founded 1876, in Spain; in U.S., 1910. General motherhouse, Rome, Italy; U.S. provincial house, 154 Fair Ave., San Antonio, Tex. 78223.

**Thomas of Villanova, Congregation of Sisters of St., S.S.T.V.:** Founded 1661, in France; in U.S., 1948. General motherhouse, Neuilly-sur-Seine, France; U.S. foundation W. Rocks Rd., Norwalk, Conn. 06851.

**Trinity, Missionary Servants of the Most Blessed, M.S.B.T.:** Founded 1912, in U.S., by Very Rev. Thomas A. Judge. General motherhouse, 3501 Solly St., Philadelphia, Pa. 19136. Educational, social work; health services.

**Trinity, Sisters of the Most Holy, O.Ss.T.:** Founded 1198, in Rome; in U.S., 1920. General motherhouse, Rome, Italy; U.S. address, Immaculate Conception Province, 21320 Euclid Ave., Euclid, Ohio 44117. Educational work.

**Ursula of the Blessed Virgin, Society of the Sisters of St., S.U.:** Founded 1606, in France; in U.S., 1902. General motherhouse, France; U.S. novitiate, Rhinebeck, N.Y. 12572. Educational work.

**Ursuline Nuns (Roman Union), O.S.U.:** Founded 1535, in Italy; in U.S., 1727. Generalate, Rome, Italy. U.S. provinces: 323 E. 198th St., Bronx, N.Y. 10458; Crystal Heights Rd., Crystal City, Mo. 63019; 639 Angela Dr., Santa Rosa, Calif. 95401; 71 Lowder St., Dedham, Mass. 02026,

**Ursuline Nuns of the Congregation of Paris, O.S.U.:** Founded 1535, in Italy; in U.S., 1727, in New Orleans. U.S. motherhouses: St. Martin, O. 45170; East and Miami Sts., Paola, Kans. 66071; 3115 Lexington Rd., Louisville, Ky. 40206; 2600 Lander Rd., Cleveland, O. 44124; Maple Mount, Ky. 42356; 2413 Collingwood Blvd., Toledo, O. 43620; 4250 Shields Rd., Canfield, O. 44406; 1339 E. McMillan St., Cincinnati, O. 45206.

**Ursuline Nuns of the Congregation of Tildonk, Belgium, R.U.:** Founded 1535, in Italy; in U.S., 1924. Generalate, Tildonk, Belgium; U.S. address, 81-15 Utopia Parkway, Jamaica, N.Y. 11432. Educational, foreign mission work.

**Ursuline Sisters, O.S.U.:** Founded 1535, in Italy; in U.S., 1910. General motherhouse, Mount Calvary, Germany; U.S. central house, 1026 N. Douglas Ave., Belleville, Ill. 62221. Educational work.

**Ursuline Sisters (Irish Ursuline Union), O.S.U.:** General motherhouse, Blackrock, Cork, Ireland; U.S. address, 1973 Torch Hill Rd., Columbus, Ga. 31903.

**Venerini Sisters, Religious, M.P.V.:** Founded 1685, in Italy; in U.S., 1909. General motherhouse, Rome, Italy; U.S. provincialate; 23 Edward St., Worcester, Mass. 01605.

**Victory Missionary Sisters, Our Lady of, O.L.V.M.:** Founded 1922, in U.S. Motherhouse, Victory Noll, Box 109, Huntington, Ind. 46750. Educational, social work.

**Vincent de Paul, Sisters:** See Charity of St. Vincent de Paul, Sisters of.

**Visitation Nuns, V.H.M.:** Founded 1610, in France; in U.S. (Georgetown, D.C.), 1799. Contemplative, educational work. Two federations in U.S.

First Federation of North America. Major pontifical enclosure. Pres., Mother Mary Gabriella Muth, Monastery of the Visitation, 9001 Old Georgetown Rd., Bethesda, Md. 20014. Addresses of monasteries belonging to the federation: 2300 Springhill Ave., Mobile, Ala. 36607; 9001 Old Georgetown Rd., Bethesda, Md. 20014; 2002 Bancroft Pkwy., Wilmington, Del. 19806; 2209 E. Grace St., Richmond, Va. 23223; 5820 City Ave., Philadelphia, Pa. 19131; 1745 Parkside Blvd., Toledo, O. 43607; 2055 Ridgedale Dr., Snellville, Ga. 30278.

Second Federation of North America. Constitutional enclosure. Pres., Rev. Mother Anne Madeline Ernstmann, Visitation Monastery, 3200 S.W. Dash Point Rd., Federal Way, Wash. 98003. Addresses of monasteries belonging to the federation: 1500 35th St., Washington, D.C. 20007; 3020 N. Ballas Rd., St. Louis, Mo. 63131; 200 E. Second St., Frederick, Md. 21701; Mt. St. Chantal Monastery of the Visitation, Wheeling, W. Va. 26003; Ridge Blvd. and 89th St., Brooklyn, N.Y. 11209;

1600 Murdoch Ave., Parkersburg, W. Va. 26101; 2000 Sixteenth Ave., Rock Island, Ill. 61201; 2475 Dodd Rd., Mendota Heights, St. Paul, Minn. 55120; Visitation Monastery, Georgetown, Ky. 40324; 3200 S.W. Dash Point Rd., Federal Way, Wash. 98003.

**Visitation of the Congregation of the Immaculate Heart of Mary, Sisters of the, S.V.M.:** Founded 1952, in U.S. Motherhouse, 900 Alta Vista St., Dubuque, Ia. 52001. Educational work, parish ministry.

**Vocationist Sisters (Sisters of the Divine Vocations):** Founded 1921, in Italy. General motherhouse, Naples, Italy; U.S. foundation, Perpetual Help Nursery, 172 Broad St., Newark, N.J. 07104.

**White Sisters:** See Africa, Missionary Sisters of Our Lady of.

**Wisdom, Daughters of, D.W.:** Founded 1703, in France, by St. Louis Marie Grignion de Montfort; in U.S., 1904. General motherhouse, Vendee, France; U.S. province, 385 S. Ocean Ave., Islip, N.Y. Education, health care, parish ministry, social services.

**Xaverian Missionary Society of Mary, Inc., X.M.M.:** Founded 1945, in Italy; in U.S., 1954. General motherhouse, Parma, Italy; U.S. address, 242 Salisbury St., Worcester, Mass. 01609.

**Xavier Mission Sisters (Catholic Mission Sisters of St. Francis Xavier), X.M.S.:** Founded 1946, at Warren, Mich., by Cardinal Edward Mooney. General motherhouse, 37179 Moravian Dr., Mount Clemens, Mich. 48043. Educational, hospital, social work in missions.

# ORGANIZATIONS OF RELIGIOUS

## Men

**Conference of Major Superiors of Men:** An association of major superiors of religious institutes of men, founded in 1956 and established officially Mar. 23, 1960, by decree of the Congregation for Religious and Secular Institutes. Its purposes are to assist religious to fulfill their proper prophetic role in the Church and the world; to provide liaison opportunities among religious and with church officials; to exert Christian influence through its operations, and to serve as a national voice for the corporate views of superiors. Conference membership consists of 263 major superiors of institutes with a combined total of approximately 30,000 members. The principal officers are Rev. Ronald Carignan, O.M.I., president, and Rev. Donald P. Skwor, S.D.S., executive director. The national office is located at 8808 Cameron St., Silver Spring, Md. 20910.

**National Assembly of Religious Brothers:** Founded in 1972 as a grassroots organization open to members of all-brother institutes as well as mixed institutes of priests and brothers. It is a service organization for its members and those affected by their apostolates. The primary objectives of the NARB are: to publicize the unique vocations of brothers, to encourage the development of the spiritual life of all brothers; to promote increased awareness among brothers of their ministerial power for good; to provide a corporate voice for brothers in shaping the future of religious life; to heighten their concern with and involve-

ment in the needs of the Church and society; and to further communication among brothers and provide liaison with various organizations of the Church. Membership in the assembly is open to brothers in the U.S. and Canada. Passionist Brother Patrick Hanson is president of the assembly. Brother Gerard Clark, C.SS.R., executive secretary, is located at 1 Liguori Drive, P.O. Box 26, Liguori, Mo. 63057.

## Women

**Association of Contemplative Sisters:** Founded by nearly 140 representatives of 57 communities in the U.S. and Canada in August, 1969. Its principal purpose is development of the contemplative lifestyle for effective service to the Church. It has a membership of approximately 400. Sister Annamae Dannes, O.C.D., is president. The central office is located at 3176 Fairmount Blvd., Cleveland Heights, O. 44118.

**Consortium Perfectae Caritatis:** Named Association of Perfect Love after the Latin title of the Second Vatican Council's *Decree on the Appropriate Renewal of Religious Life*, and organized in March, 1971, at a meeting of nearly 150 sisters from 48 communities in the U.S. and Canada. Its purposes are to encourage the development of religious life in line with Vatican II guidelines and related directives, and to share experiences in the renewal of religious life. Sister Mary Elise, S.N.D., is executive director. The association is administered by a group of 14 superiors from 12 states and Canada. The mailing address is P.O. Box 1856, Middleburg, Va. 22117. Rev. James A. Viall is coordinator.

**Leadership Conference of Women Religious:** An association of major superiors of religious communities of women, with the purpose of promoting the spiritual and apostolic calling and works of sisterhoods in the U.S. Organized in the late 50s and approved by the Congregation for Religious and Secular Institutes June 13, 1962, it has a membership of approximately 700. Its original name, changed in 1971, was the Conference of Major Superiors of Women. With its formerly affiliated Sister Formation Conference, it inaugurated measures for the religious and professional development of sisters and has contributed to the renewal of religious life in this country. Sister Catherine Pinkerton, C.S.J., is president; Sister Lora Ann Quinonez, C.D.P., is executive director. The national secretariat is located at 8808 Cameron St., Silver Spring, Md. 20910.

**National Black Sisters' Conference:** Organized in August, 1968, for the purposes of determining priorities in service to black people, of promoting black vocations and the development of religious life in the unique black life-style, and to influence the formational and recruitment practices of white religious communities. Its members include 700 black sisters belonging to 123 religious communities. Sister Marie de Porres Taylor, S.N.J.M., is the executive director. The mailing address of the conference is 6226 Camden St., Oakland, Calif. 94605.

**National Coalition of American Nuns:** Organized under the leadership of Sister Margaret Traxler, S.S.N.D., in July, 1969, for efforts to secure recognition and development of the role of women in the Church and society, along with advocacy for social activism. Sister Lillanna Kopp, S.F.C.C., is president. Offices are located at 1307 S. Wabash Ave., Chicago, Ill 60605.

**National Sisters' Vocation Conference:** Formed in September, 1970, as a national organization dedicated to promoting understanding of the role of women, especially religious, in the Church through work in the vocation apostolate. It coordinates and provides informational and other services to persons and organizations in the vocation apostolate, and assists prospective candidates for religious life. Its membership includes approximately 1,200 women and men. Sister Sarah Marie Sherman, R.S.M., is executive director. The national office is located at 1307 S. Wabash Ave., Chicago, Ill. 60605.

**Religious Formation Conference:** Originally organized with the title of the Sister Formation Conference in 1953, for the purpose of promoting the spiritual and professional formation of sisters in the U.S. In 1976, the name was changed to Religious Formation Conference to reflect openness to a membership including men and persons belonging to non-canonical religious groups. Sister Peggy Nichols, C.S.J., is executive director. The national office is located at 1234 Massachusetts Ave. N.W., Washington, D.C. 20005.

**International Union of Superiors General (Women):** Established in 1965, with approval of its statutes by the Congregation for Religious and Secular Institutes in 1967. Sister Katherine McDonald, N.D.S., is president.

**Latin American Confederation of Religious:** Established in 1959, with approval of its statutes by the Congregation for Religious and Secular Institutes in 1967. Father Mateo Perdia, C.P., is president.

**National Conference of Vicars for Religious:** Established in 1967 as a national organization of diocesan officials concerned with relations between their respective dioceses and religious communities engaged therein. A service and informational agency for vicars, it also carries on liaison with the Congregation for Religious and Secular Institutes, the National Conference of Catholic Bishops and other organizations concerned with religious. The president is Brother Kevin F. Smith, O.S.F., 50 N. Park Ave., Rockville Centre, N.Y. 11570.

**National Conferences:** Conferences of religious superiors, generally separate for men and women, have been established in 19 countries in Europe, 14 in North and Central America, 10 in South America, 25 in Africa, and 20 in Asia and Oceania.

**Union of Superiors General (Men):** Established in 1957, with approval of its statutes by the Congregation for Religious and Secular Institutes in 1967. Father Egidio Vigano, S.D.B., is president. Fathers John Vaughn, superior general of the Order of Friars Minor, and Paul Boyle, superior general of the Passionists, are American councillors of the union.

**World Conference of Secular Institutes:** Established May 23, 1974. Address: Via degli Ombrellari 40, 00193 Rome.

## Vocation Council

The National Catholic Vocation Council replaced the National Center for Church Vocations in 1977. The principal purpose of the council is to give the Church in the U.S. visible witness of the mutual collaboration of national vocation organizations in their effort to promote awareness and understanding of dedication to the Church, especially through the ordained ministry and vowed life. The council also services efforts of mutual concern and benefit to membership organizations in the recruitment and development of vocations to the priesthood, diaconate and vowed life.

Member organizations with representatives on the council are: the National Sisters Vocation Conference, the National Conference of Diocesan Vocation Directors, the National Conference of Religious Vocation Directors, Serra International, the National Conference of Catholic Bishops, the Leadership Conference of Women Religious, the Conference of Major Superiors of Men, the Conference of Secular Institutes and the Knights of Columbus.

Sister Deanna Fouin, M.H.S., is president; Sr. Margaret M. Kopish, A.S.C., is administrator.

Offices are located at 1307 S. Wabash Ave., Suite 350, Chicago, Ill. 60605

# SECULAR INSTITUTES

(Sources: Almanac survey; United States Conference of Secular Institutes; *Annuario Pontificio*.)

Secular institutes are societies of men and women living in the world who dedicate themselves to observe the evangelical counsels and to carry on apostolic works suitable to their talents and opportunities in the areas of their everyday life.

"Secular institutes are not religious communities but they carry with them in the world a profession of evangelical counsels which is genuine and complete, and recognized as such by the Church. This profession confers a consecration on men and women, laity and clergy, who reside in the world. For this reason they should chiefly strive for total self-dedication to God, one inspired by perfect charity. These institutes should preserve their proper and particular character, a secular one, so that they may everywhere measure up successfully to that apostolate which they were designed to exercise, and which is both in the world and, in a sense, of the world" (*Decree on the Appropriate Renewal of Religious Life*, No. 11; Second Vatican Council).

Secular institutes are under the jurisdiction of the Congregation for Religious and Secular Institutes. General legislation concerning them is contained in Canons 710 to 730 of the Code of Canon Law.

A secular institute reaches maturity in several stages. It begins as an association of the faithful, technically called a pious union, with the approval of a local bishop. Once it has proved its viability, he can give it the status of an institute of diocesan right, in accordance with norms and permission emanating from the Congregation for Religious and Secular Institutes. On issuance of a separate decree from this congregation, an institute of diocesan right becomes an institute of pontifical right.

Secular institutes, which originated in the latter part of the 18th century, were given full recognition and approval by Pius XII Feb. 2, 1947, in the apostolic constitution *Provida Mater Ecclesia*. On Mar. 25 of the same year a special commission for secular institutes was set up within the Congregation for Religious. Institutes were commended and confirmed by Pius XII in a motu proprio of Mar. 12, 1948, and were the subject of a special instruction issued a week later, Mar. 19, 1948.

The United States Conference of Secular Institutes (CSI) was established in October, 1972, following the organization of the World Conference of Secular Institutes in Rome. Its membership is open to all canonically erected secular institutes with members living in the United States. The conference was organized to offer secular institutes an opportunity to exchange experiences, to do research in order to help the Church carry out its mission, and to search for ways and means to make known the existence of secular institutes in the U.S. Address: c/o Claudette Cyr, president, 121 Greenwood St., Watertown, Conn. 06795.

## Institutes in the U.S.

**Caritas Christi:** Originated in Marseilles, 1937; for women. Established as a secular institute of pontifical right Mar. 19, 1955. Address: P.O. Box 162, River Forest, Ill. 60305.

**Company of St. Paul:** Originated in Milan, Italy, 1920; for lay people and priests. Approved as a secular institute of pontifical right June 30, 1950. Address: 52 Davis Ave., White Plains, N.Y. 10605.

**Company of St. Ursula, Secular Institute of St. Angela Merici:** Founded in Brescia, Italy, 1535; for women. Approved as a secular institute of pontifical right 1958. Addresses: Lina Moser, President, Via Rosmini 128, 38100 Trento, Italy; Juline Lamb, 2987 Hemphill St., Fort Worth, Tex. 76110. International membership of 3,000.

**DeSales Secular Institute:** Founded in Vienna, Austria, 1940; for women. Pontifical right, 1964. Address: Rev. John Conmy, O.S.F.S., National Assistant, 24 S. Cliffe Ave., Wilmington, Del. 19809.

**Diocesan Laborer Priests:** Approved as a secular institute of pontifical right, 1952. The specific aim of the institute is the promotion, sustenance and cultivation of apostolic, religious and priestly vocations. Address: c/o Rev. Ovid Percharroman, 3706 15th St. N.E., Washington, D.C. 20017.

**Don Bosco Volunteers:** Founded 1917; for women. Approved as a secular institute of pontifical right Aug. 5, 1978. Address: Don Bosco Volunteers, 202 Union Ave., Paterson, N.J. 07502. International membership of over 800 in 25 countries.

**Handmaids of Divine Mercy:** Founded in Bari, Italy, 1951; for women. Approved as an institute of pontifical right 1972. Address: Mary I. DiFonzo, 2410 Hughes Ave., Bronx, N.Y. 10458. International membership of 980.

**Institute of Secular Missionaries:** Founded in Vitoria, Spain, 1939; for women. Approved as a secular institute, 1955. Address: 2710 Ruberg Ave., Cincinnati, O. 45211, Att. E. Dilger.

**Institute of the Heart of Jesus:** Originated in France Feb. 2, 1791; restored Oct. 29, 1918; for diocesan priests and lay people. Received final approval from the Holy See as a secular institute of pontifical right Feb. 2, 1952. Rev. Jean Grebouval, superior general. Addresses: Central House, 202 Avenue du Maine, Paris 14me, France; U.S. address, Rev. Msgr. John A. Esseff, 300 Wyoming Ave., Scranton, Pa. 18503. International membership of approximately 1,400.

**Mission of Our Lady of Bethany:** Founded in Plessis-Chenet, France, 1948; for women. Approved as an institute of diocesan right 1965. Address: Box 207, Jamaica Plain, Mass. 02130.

**Missionaries of the Kingship of Christ the King:** Under this title are included three distinct and juridically separate institutes founded by Agostino Gemelli, O.F.M. (1878-1959).

(1) Women Missionaries of the Kingship of Christ — Founded in 1919, in Italy; definitively approved as an institute of pontifical rite 1953. Established in 15 countries. U.S. branch established 1950. Age at time of entrance, 21 to 40.

(2) Men Missionaries of the Kingship of Christ —

Founded 1928, in Italy, as an institute of diocesan right. U.S. branch established 1962.

(3) Priest Missionaries of the Kingship of Christ — Established in U.S., 1954; approved as institute of pontifical right July 15, 1978. For diocesan priests. Address: Rev. Stephen Hartdegen, O.F.M., 1650 St. Camillus Dr., Silver Spring, Md. 20903.

**Oblate Missionaries of Mary Immaculate:** Founded, 1952; approved as a secular institute of diocesan right Feb. 2, 1962, and of pontifical right Mar. 25, 1984; for women. Addresses: Oblate Missionaries of Mary Immaculate, 49J Forest Acres Dr., Bradford, Mass. 01830; 7535 Boulevard Parent, Trois Rivieres, P. Q. G9A 5E1, Canada. International membership.

**Rural Parish Workers of Christ the King:** Originated in Cottleville, Mo., 1942; for women. An approved lay institute of apostolic action of the Archdiocese of St. Louis. Dedicated to the service of neighbor, especially in rural areas. Address: Box 300, Rt. 1, Cadet, Mo. 63630.

**Schoenstatt Sisters of Mary:** Originated in Schoenstatt, Germany, 1926; for women. Established as a secular institute of diocesan right May 20, 1948; of pontifical right Oct. 18, 1948. Addresses: Schoenstatt Sisters of Mary, W. 284 N. 404 Cherry Lane, Waukesha, Wis. 53186; House Schoenstatt, Star Rt. 1, Box 100, Rockport, Tex. 78382. International membership of more than 2,800.

**Secular Institute of Pius X:** Originated in Manchester, N.H., 1940; for priests and laymen. Approved as a secular institute, 1959 (first secular institute of diocesan right founded in the U.S. to be approved by the Holy See). Also admits married and unmarried men as associate members. Addresses: Lynchville Park, Goffstown, N.H. 03045. C.P. 1815, Quebec City, P.Q. G1K 7K7, Canada.

**Servitium Christi Secular Institute of the Blessed Sacrament:** Founded in Holland, 1952; for women. Approved as a secular institute of diocesan right May 8, 1963. Address: Miss Olympia Panagatos, 250 E. 77th St., Apt. 3B, New York, N.Y. 10021.

**Society of Our Lady of the Way:** Originated, 1936; for women. Approved as a secular institute of pontifical right Jan. 3, 1953. Addresses: 2701 14th Ave., San Francisco, Calif. 94127; 2339 N. Catalina St., Los Angeles, Calif. 90027; P.O. Box 412, Stamford, Conn. 06904; 2738 Noble Rd., No. 13B, Cleveland Heights, O. 44121. International membership, 300.

**Teresian Institute:** Founded in Spain 1911 by Pedro Poveda. Approved as an institute of pontifical right Jan. 11, 1924. Mailing Address: P.O. Box 14-3407, Coral Gables, Fla. 33114.

**Voluntas Dei:** Originated in Canada, 1958; for secular priests, laymen and couples. Approved as a secular institute May 6, 1965. Addresses: Institute Voluntas Dei, 7385, Blvd. Parent, Trois-Rivieres, Que., Canada G9A 5E1. David J. McDonald, 615 West Alturas St., No. 397, Tucson, Ariz. 85705. International membership of approximately 210.

## Associations

**Association of Mary Immaculate:** Founded 1963. Received diocesan approval Jan. 28, 1977. For mature men and women, widows and widowers; separate section for married couples. Training on cassette tape for blind or handicapped. Address: Holy Family Center, New Riegel, Ohio 44853.

**Caritas:** Originated in New Orleans, 1950; for women. Follow guidelines of secular institutes. Small self-supporting groups who live and work among the poor and oppressed; work in Louisiana and Guatemala. Address: Box 308, Abita Springs, La. 70420.

**Daughters of Our Lady of Fatima:** Originated in Lansdowne, Pa., 1949; for women. Received diocesan approval, Jan., 1952. Address: Fatima House, Rolling Hills Rd., Ottsville, Pa. 18942.

**Focolare Movement:** Inaugurated in Trent, Italy, in 1943, by Chiara Lubich and a small group of companions; for men and women. Approved as an association of the faithful, 1962. It is not a secular institute by statute; however, vows are observed by its totally dedicated core membership of 4,000 who live in small communities called Focolare (Italian word for "hearth") centers. There are 15 resident centers in the U.S. and two in Canada. GEN (New Generation) is the youth organization of the movement. An estimated 70,000 are affiliated with the movement in the U.S. and Canada; 3,000,000, worldwide. Publications include *Living City*, monthly; *GEN II* and *GEN III* for young people and children. Five week-long summer conventions, called "Mariapolis" ("City of Mary"), are held annually. Address for information: P.O. Box 496, New York, N.Y. 10021 (indicate men's or women's branch).

**Institute of Apostolic Oblates:** Founded in Rome, Italy, 1947; for women. Address: 2125 W. Walnut Ave., Fullerton, Calif. 92633 (provincial house).

**Jesus Caritas — Fraternity of Priests:** An international association of priests who strive to live in the spirit of Charles de Foucauld, combining an active life with a contemplative calling. U.S. address: Rev. Howard W. Calkins (National Responsible), St. Joseph of the Holy Family, 405 W. 125th St., New York, N.Y. 10027

**Madonna House Apostolate:** Originated in Toronto, Canada, 1930; for priests and lay persons. Diocesan pious union. Address: Madonna House, Combermere, Ontario, Canada KOJ 1LO — Catherine Doherty (women), Jim Guinan (men), Rev. J. Callahan (priests). International membership and missions.

**Pax Christi:** Lay institute of men and women dedicated to witnessing to Christ, with special emphasis on service to the poor in Mississippi. Addresses: St. Francis Center, 708 Ave. I, Greenwood, Miss. 38930; LaVerna House, 2108 Altawoods Blvd., Jackson, Miss. 39204.

*Catholic Engaged Encounter is designed to prepare couples for marriage by focusing on its sacramental aspects and by increasing their potential for communication with each other.*

# MISSIONARY ACTIVITY OF THE CHURCH

## UNITED STATES FOREIGN MISSIONARIES

*Data on U.S. foreign missionary personnel in the following tables were gathered by, and are reproduced with permission of, the United States Catholic Mission Association, 1233 Lawrence St. N.E., Washington, D.C. 20017. For additional information about the Church in mission areas, see News Events and other Almanac entries.*

### Field Distribution, 1984

Under this and following headings, Alaska, Hawaii, etc., are considered abroad because they are outside the 48 contiguous states.

**Africa:** 967 (501 men, 466 women). Largest numbers in Kenya, 183; Tanzania, 159; Ghana, 90; Zambia, 85; Nigeria, 60.

**Near East:** 84 (56 men, 28 women). Largest numbers in Israel, 44; Egypt, 21; Lebanon, 8.

**Far East:** 1,420 (980 men, 440 women). Largest numbers in Philippines, 369; Japan, 308; Taiwan, 163; Korea, 142; India, 110; Hong Kong, 74.

**Oceania:** 644 (324 men, 320 women). Largest groups in Papua New Guinea, 205; Hawaii, 194; Australia, 71; Mariana Islands, 52; Caroline Islands, 39; Samoa, 29.

**Europe:** 29 (16 men, 13 women). Largest groups in Sweden, 11; Finland, 9; Denmark, 6.

**North America:** 329 (141 men, 188 women). Largest group in Alaska, 173; Canada, 148.

**Caribbean Islands:** 513 (277 men, 236 women). Largest groups in Puerto Rico, 230; Jamaica, 110; Bahamas, 45; Haiti, 42.

**Central America:** 650 (383 men, 267 women). Largest groups in Mexico, 199; Guatemala, 157.

**South America:** 1,498 (788 men, 710 women). Largest groups in Peru, 450; Brazil, 440; Bolivia, 220; Chile, 168.

**TOTAL:** 6,134 (3,466 men, 2,668 women).

### Men Religious, 1984

Eighty-seven mission-sending groups had 3,192 priests and brothers in overseas assignments.

**Jesuits:** 552 in 44 countries; largest group, 86 in the Philippines.

**Maryknoll Fathers:** 537 in 26 countries; largest group, 53 in Tanzania.

**Franciscans (O.F.M.):** 201 in 27 countries; largest group, 63 in Brazil.

**Divine Word Missionaries:** 153 in 13 countries; largest group, 53 in Papua New Guinea.

**Redemptorists:** 147 in 8 countries; largest group, 58 in Brazil.

**Oblates of Mary Immaculate:** 135 in 18 countries; largest group, 26 in Brazil.

**Capuchins (O.F.M. Cap):** 135 in 10 countries; largest group, 33 in Papua New Guinea.

**Marianists:** 122 in 15 countries; largest group, 31 in Hawaii.

**Benedictines:** 87 in 15 countries; largest group, 21 in Guatemala.

**Conventual Franciscans (O.F.M. Conv):** 66 in 9 countries; largest group, 16 in Canada.

**Brothers of the Christian Schools:** 64 in 15 countries; largest group, 19 in the Philippines.

**Columbans:** 61 in 11 countries; largest group, 24 in the Philippines.

**Holy Cross Fathers:** 60 in 10 countries; largest group, 19 in Bangladesh.

**Dominicans:** 59 in 9 countries; largest group, 16 in Nigeria.

**Holy Cross Brothers:** 53 in 7 countries; largest group, 19 in Brazil.

**Holy Ghost Fathers:** 50 in 9 countries; largest group, 19 in Tanzania.

**Passionists:** 44 in 5 countries; largest group, 21 in the Philippines.

**Vincentians:** 42 in 7 countries; largest group, 19 in Panama.

**La Salette Missionaries:** 37 in 5 countries; largest group, 12 in Argentina.

**Missionaries of the Sacred Heart:** 32 in 4 countries; largest group, 23 in Papua New Guinea.

**Augustinians:** 31 in 3 countries; largest group, 20 in Peru.

**Marist Fathers:** 30 in 8 countries; largest group, 10 in Hawaii.

**Salesians:** 27 in 10 countries; largest group, 11 in Canada.

**White Fathers:** 24 in 9 countries: largest group, 5 each in Uganda and Ghana.

**Brothers of the Sacred Heart:** 24 in 4 countries; largest group, 11 in Zambia.

**Marist Brothers:** 21 in 6 countries; largest group, 9 in the Philippines.

**Missionhurst-CICM:** 20 in 9 countries; largest group, 7 in the Dominican Republic.

**Congregation of Christian Brothers:** 20 in 3 countries; largest group, 17 in Peru.

Fifty-nine other mission-sending institutes had 19 or less members in overseas assignments.

### Diocesan Priests, 1984

One hundred and 87 diocesan priests from 79 dioceses were in overseas assignments in 1984.

The largest groups were from Boston (18 in 4 countries) and St. Louis (9 in 2 countries).

Forty-five of the diocesan priests in overseas assignments were members of the Missionary Society of St. James the Apostle, founded by Cardinal Richard J. Cushing of Boston in 1958. Its director is Rev. George F. Emerson, 24 Clark St., Boston, Mass. 02109.

Eighteen other diocesan priests in overseas assignments were working as priest associates with the Maryknoll Fathers, whose headquarters are in Maryknoll, New York 10545.

### Sisters, 1984

Two hundred and 20 mission-sending groups had 2,492 sisters in overseas assignments.

**Maryknoll Sisters:** 369 in 25 countries; largest group, 48 in Hawaii.

## U.S. FOREIGN MISSIONARIES, 1960-1984

| Year | Diocesan Priests | Religious Priests | Religious Brothers | Religious Sisters | Seminarians | Lay Persons | Total |
|---|---|---|---|---|---|---|---|
| 1960 | 14 | 3018 | 575 | 2827 | 170 | 178 | 6782 |
| 1962 | 31 | 3172 | 720 | 2764 | 152 | 307 | 7146 |
| 1964 | 80 | 3438 | 782 | 3137 | 157 | 532 | 8126 |
| 1966 | 215 | 3731 | 901 | 3706 | 201 | 549 | 9303 |
| 1968 | 282 | 3727 | 869 | 4150 | 208 | 419 | 9655 |
| 1970 | 373 | 3117 | 666 | 3824 | 90 | 303 | 8373 |
| 1972+ | 246 | 3182 | 634 | 3121 | 97 | 376 | 7656 |
| 1973 | 237 | 3913* | | 3012 | | 529 | 7691 |
| 1974 | 220 | 3084 | 639 | 2916 | 101 | 458 | 7418 |
| 1975 | 197 | 3023 | 669 | 2850 | 65 | 344 | 7148 |
| 1976 | 193 | 2961 | 691 | 2840 | 68 | 257 | 7010 |
| 1977 | 182 | 2882 | 630 | 2781 | 42 | 243 | 6760 |
| 1978 | 166 | 2830 | 610 | 2673 | 43 | 279 | 6601 |
| 1979 | 187 | 2800 | 592 | 2568 | 50 | 258 | 6455 |
| 1980 | 188 | 2750 | 592 | 2592 | 50 | 221 | 6393 |
| 1981 | 187 | 2702 | 584 | 2574 | 43 | 234 | 6324 |
| 1982 | 178 | 2668 | 578 | 2560 | 44 | 217 | 6245 |
| 1983 | 174 | 2668 | 569 | 2540 | 48 | 247 | 6246 |
| 1984 | 187 | 2603 | 549 | 2492 | 40 | 263 | 6134 |

+A corrected total for 1972 should read 7937, indicating losses of 436 from 1970 to 1972 and 246 from 1972 to 1973.
*Includes religious brothers and seminarians.

## FIELD DISTRIBUTION BY AREAS, 1960-1984

| Year | Africa | Far East | Near East | Oce-ania | Europe | N. Amer. | Carib. Is. | Cent. Amer. | S. Amer. | Total |
|---|---|---|---|---|---|---|---|---|---|---|
| 1960 | 781 | 1959 | 111 | 986 | 203 | 337 | 991 | 433 | 981 | 6782 |
| 1962 | 901 | 2110 | 75 | 992 | 93 | 224 | 967 | 537 | 1247 | 7146 |
| 1964 | 1025 | 2332 | 122 | 846 | 69 | 220 | 1056 | 660 | 1796 | 8126 |
| 1966 | 1184 | 2453 | 142 | 953 | 38 | 211 | 1079 | 857 | 2386 | 9303 |
| 1968 | 1157 | 2470 | 128 | 1027 | 33 | 251 | 1198 | 936 | 2455 | 9655 |
| 1970 | 1141 | 2137 | 39 | 900 | 38 | 233 | 1067 | 738 | 2080 | 8373 |
| 1972 | 1107 | 1955 | 59 | 826 | 39 | 234 | 819 | 728 | 1889 | 7656 |
| 1973 | 1229 | 1962 | 54 | 811 | 40 | 253 | 796 | 763 | 1783 | 7691 |
| 1974 | 1121 | 1845 | 60 | 883 | 43 | 241 | 757 | 752 | 1716 | 7418 |
| 1975 | 1065 | 1814 | 71 | 808 | 37 | 252 | 698 | 734 | 1669 | 7148 |
| 1976 | 1042 | 1757 | 68 | 795 | 34 | 313 | 671 | 712 | 1618 | 7010 |
| 1977 | 1003 | 1659 | 62 | 784 | 34 | 296 | 629 | 702 | 1591 | 6760 |
| 1978 | 966 | 1601 | 57 | 769 | 34 | 339 | 593 | 705 | 1537 | 6601 |
| 1979 | 923 | 1562 | 65 | 743 | 37 | 332 | 562 | 686 | 1545 | 6455 |
| 1980 | 909 | 1576 | 65 | 711 | 35 | 294 | 548 | 699 | 1556 | 6393 |
| 1981 | 946 | 1529 | 70 | 696 | 36 | 315 | 511 | 693 | 1528 | 6324 |
| 1982 | 956 | 1501 | 62 | 673 | 32 | 319 | 522 | 669 | 1511 | 6245 |
| 1983 | 990 | 1468 | 68 | 640 | 34 | 346 | 517 | 650 | 1533 | 6246 |
| 1984 | 967 | 1420 | 84 | 644 | 29 | 329 | 513 | 650 | 1498 | 6134 |

**School Sisters of Notre Dame:** 104 in 18 countries; largest group, 15 in Puerto Rico.

**Marists:** 82 in 15 countries; largest group, 17 in Papua New Guinea.

**Daughters of Charity:** 64 in 9 countries; largest group, 33 in Bolivia.

**Medical Mission Sisters:** 59 in 18 countries; largest group, 14 in Ghana.

**Sisters of Notre Dame de Namur:** 59 in 10 countries; largest group, 17 in Kenya.

**Sisters of St. Joseph (Carondelet):** 51 in 4 countries; largest group, 23 in Hawaii.

**Benedictines:** 46 in 11 countries: largest group, 11 in Colombia.

**Servants of the Immaculate Heart of Mary (Philadelphia):** 44 in 2 countries; largest group, 33 in Peru.

**Sisters of the Holy Cross:** 42 in 6 countries; largest group, 15 in Brazil.

**Franciscan Missionaries of Mary:** 37 in 18 countries; largest groups, 5 each in Japan and Liberia.

**Ursulines of the Roman Union:** 36 in 12 countries; largest group, 8 in Thailand.

**Society of the Sacred Heart:** 30 in 6 countries; largest group, 13 in Japan.

**Servants of the Holy Spirit:** 30 in 7 countries; largest group, 9 in Ghana.

**Franciscan Sisters of Allegany:** 26 in 3 countries; largest group, 17 in Jamaica.

**Sisters of St. Joseph (Brentwood):** 26 in 3 countries; largest group, 23 in Puerto Rico.

**Religious Sisters of Mercy of the Union in the**

**U.S.A.:** 25 in 8 countries; largest group, 10 in Jamaica.

**Sisters of the Assumption BVM:** 25 in 3 countries; largest group, 21 in Canada.

**Sisters of the Third Franciscan Order, Minor Conventuals (Syracuse):** 24 in 3 countries; largest group, 16 in Hawaii.

**Sisters of the Holy Family of Nazareth:** 24 in 3 countries; largest group, 18 in Australia.

**Sisters of Notre Dame:** 23 in 2 countries; larger group, 12 in Papua New Guinea.

**Adorers of the Blood of Christ:** 23 in 5 countries; largest group, 9 in Liberia.

**Little Sisters of the Poor:** 21 in 10 countries; largest group, 5 in Hong Kong.

**Sisters of the Presentation B.V.M.:** 21 in 8 countries; largest groups, 4 each in Alaska and Bolivia.

**Dominican Sisters (Adrian):** 20 in 6 countries; largest group, 5 in Puerto Rico.

One hundred and 95 other mission-sending institutes had 19 or less members in overseas assignments.

### Lay Volunteers, 1984

Two hundred and 63 lay volunteers of 27 sponsoring organizations were in overseas assignments in 1984.

**Maryknoll Lay Missioners:** 66 in 17 countries; largest group, 12 in Venezuela.

**Jesuit Volunteer Corps:** 42 in Alaska.

**Lay Mission Helpers:** 36 in 9 countries; largest group, 10 in Samoa.

**Frontier Apostolate:** 32 in Canada.

**Diocese of Davenport:** 10 in 5 countries; largest groups, 3 each in Mexico and St. Lucia.

**Catholic Medical Mission Board:** 9 in 6 countries; largest group in Papua New Guinea. (This figure represents those whose term of service was for at least one year. In addition, 43 short-term volunteers served in 9 countries during the year.)

**Milwaukee Latin American Office:** 9 in 5 countries; largest group, 4 in Colombia.

The other 20 sponsoring organizations had 8 members or less in overseas assignments.

## U.S. MISSION ASSOCIATION

The United States Catholic Mission Association, juridically established Sept. 1, 1981, continues the activities and functions of the former U.S. Catholic Mission Council.

According to existing bylaws approved by the general assembly May 25, 1982, the USCMA is "open to all those who seek to promote global mission in community with others. It is envisioned to be an experience of the renewed Church, in which all members are equal. The methods of decision-making, of financial support, and of committee service reflect the underlying ecclesiology." The purpose of the association is the "promotion of global mission. Its primary focus is cross-cultural mission, with special emphasis on international justice."

Typical activities of the association are educational efforts related to the Church's teaching about its missionary nature, sponsorship of conferences on theological and pastoral foundations of missionary endeavor, liaison and cooperation with missionary bodies of other Christian churches, training programs and refresher courses for departing and returning missionaries, and general mission animation. The USCMA is also responsible for gathering and publishing annual statistical data on U.S. missionary personnel overseas. It publishes the data in the annual, *Mission Handbook*. The association also publishes ten times a year *Mission Intercom*, a newsletter with brief information on the life and activities of the Church in the six continents.

The president of the association is Sister Mary Louise Lynch, S.C.M.M. The office is located at 1233 Lawrence St. N.E., Washington, D.C. 20017.

## HOME MISSIONS

The expression "home missions" is applied to places in the U.S. where the local church does not have its own resources, human and otherwise, which are needed to begin or, if begun, to survive and grow. These areas share the name "missions" with their counterparts in foreign lands because they too need outside help to provide the personnel and means for making the Church present and active there in carrying out its mission for the salvation of people.

Dioceses in the Southeast, the Southwest, and the Far West are most urgently in need of outside help to carry on the work of the Church. Millions of persons live in counties in which there are no resident priests. Many others live in rural areas beyond the reach and influence of a Catholic center. According to recent statistics compiled by the Glenmary Research Center, there are approximately 545 priestless counties in the United States. Many states generally thought to be well off from a pastoral standpoint include areas in

which the Catholic Church and the ministry of priests are virtually unknown.

About 20 per cent of the total U.S. population and less than three per cent of the Catholic population live within the boundaries of the 17 "most missionary" dioceses of the country. A "Survey of the Catholic Weakness" conducted by the National Catholic Rural Life Conference disclosed that the Catholic Church ranked near the bottom of about 40 religious bodies in percentage of rural membership.

### Mission Workers

A number of forces are at work to meet the pastoral needs of these missionary areas and to establish permanent churches and operating institutions where they are required. In many dioceses, one or more missions and stations are attended from established parishes and are gradually growing to independent status. Priests, brothers and sisters belonging to scores of religious institutes are engaged full-time in the home missions. Lay persons, some of them in affiliation with special groups and movements, are also involved.

The Society for the Propagation of the Faith, which conducts an annual collection for mission support in all parishes of the U.S., allocates 40 per cent of this sum for disbursement to home missions through the American Board of Catholic Missions.

The Catholic Church Extension Society provides one million dollars or more a year for the building of mission installations and related needs.

Special mission support is the purpose of the Commission for the Catholic Missions among the Colored People and the Indians.

Various mission-aid societies frequently undertake projects in behalf of the home missions.

The **Glenmary Home Missioners,** founded by Father W. Howard Bishop in 1939, is the only home mission society established for the sole purpose of carrying out the pastoral ministry in small towns and the rural districts of the United States. Glenmary serves in areas where at least 20 per cent of the people live in poverty and less than one per cent are Catholic. With 71 priests and 24 professed brothers as of May 23, 1984, the Glenmary Missioners had 38 mission bases and 39 satellite missions in the archdioceses of Atlanta and Cincinnati, and in the dioceses of Birmingham, Charlotte, Covington, Dallas, Little Rock, Nashville, Jackson, Tulsa, Owensboro, Savannah, Richmond and Wheeling-Charleston. National headquarters are located in Fairfield, O. The mailing address is P.O. Box 46404, Cincinnati, O. 45246.

## Organizations

**The Catholic Church Extension Society:** This society was established for the purpose of preserving and extending the Church in the U.S. and its dependencies principally through the collection and disbursement of funds for missions. Since the time of its founding in 1905, approximately $102 million have been received and expended for this purpose. Disbursements in fiscal year 1983 were in excess of $9 million.

Works of the society are supervised by a board of governors consisting of twelve members: Cardinal Joseph Bernardin, archbishop of Chicago, chancellor; Very Rev. Edward J. Slattery, president; five bishops or priests, and five laymen. Society headquarters are located at 35 E. Wacker Drive, Chicago, Ill. 60601.

**Commission for Catholic Missions among the Colored People and the Indians:** Organized in 1886, this commission provides several million dollars annually in financial support for religious works among Blacks and Indians in nearly 130 dioceses. Funds are raised by an annual collection in all parishes of the country.

Cardinal John J. Krol is head of the board of directors. Msgr. Paul A. Lenz is secretary. Commission headquarters are located at 2021 H St. N.W., Washington, D.C. 20006.

**Bureau of Catholic Indian Missions:** Established in 1874 as the representative of Catholic Indian missions before the federal government and the public; made permanent organization in 1883 by Third Plenary Council of Baltimore. After a remarkable history of rendering important services to the Indian people, the bureau continues to represent the Catholic Church in the U.S. in her apostolate to the American Indian. Concerns are evangelization, catechesis, liturgy, family life, education, advocacy. Cardinal John Krol is president of the board; Msgr. Paul A. Lenz is secretary. Address: 2021 H St., Washington, D.C. 20006.

**Rural Ministry Institute:** The Edwin Vincent O'Hara Institute for Rural Ministry Education was founded in 1978 to provide training and other resource services for priests, seminarians religious and lay persons beginning or already involved in rural ministry. Brother David Andrews, C.S.C., is director. Address: 3700 Oakview Terr., N.E., Washington, D.C. 20017.

**Tekakwitha Conference:** Established in 1939, the Conference includes active and former Catholic missionaries among Native American people and Native American people recognized as leaders in their respective communities. The primary focus is evangelization in these areas of concern: development of Native American ministry, catechesis, liturgy, family life, social justice ministry, education, ecumenical cooperation, urban ministry spirituality and vocations. The annual Conference serves as an opportunity for exchange of ideas, approaches and mutual support. Publications include a quarterly Newsletter and the annual Proceedings. The conference has a nine-member board of directors. Most Rev. John F. Kinney of Bismarck is episcopal moderator; Rev. Gilbert F. Hemauer, O.F.M. Cap., is president. Address: 1818 Ninth Ave., South No. 5, Great Falls, Mont. 59405.

## BLACK CATHOLICS
### National Office

The National Office for Black Catholics, organized in July, 1970, is a central agency with the general purposes of promoting active and full participation by Black Catholics in the Church and of making more effective the presence and ministry of the Church in the Black community.

Its operations are in support of the aspirations and calls of Black Catholics for a number of objectives, including the following:

• representation and voice for Blacks among bishops and others with leadership and decision-making positions in the Church;

• promoting vocations to the priesthood and religious life;

• sponsoring programs of evangelization, pastoral ministry, education and liturgy on a national level;

• recognition of the Black heritage in liturgy, community life, theology and education.

James McConduit is president of the NOBC.

The NOBC office is located at 810 Rhode Island Ave. N.E., Washington, D.C. 20018.

The biennial conference of the NOBC was one of a series of meetings which began in Chicago in

1980, when an "Action Agenda for the 80s" was drawn up. A follow-up conference was held in 1982 in Houston, and the 1984 assembly continued discussion and development, along with implementation, of the original agenda.

The National Office for Black Catholics sponsored its 14th annual workshop in Afro-American culture and worship, its own biennial conference and a youth conference in July and August, 1984, in New Orleans.

## Clergy Caucus

The National Black Catholic Clergy Caucus, founded in 1968 in Detroit, is a fraternity of approximately 750 Black priests, permanent deacons and brothers pledged to mutual support in their vocations and ministries.

The Caucus develops programs of spiritual, theological, educational and ministerial growth for its members, to counteract the effects of institutionalized racism within the Church and American society. A bimonthly newsletter is published.

Father Donald M. Clark is president.

The NBCCC office is located at 1419 V St. N.W., Washington, D.C. 20009.

The National Black Sisters' Conference (see separate entry), the National Black Catholic Clergy Caucus and the National Black Catholic Seminarians' Association held a joint conference in New Orleans July 29 to Aug. 3, 1984, on the theme, "To Whomever I Send You . . . Go. Whatever I Command You . . . Speak." Proceedings focused on the vision, ministry and mission of the Church in the future, with special focus on Black people.

Honored during the conference were: Father Thaddeus Posey, O.F.M., for work in high school education, vocation and formation activities, and

service to the NBCCC, with the Joseph Morgan Davis Award; a seminarian, with the first C. Earl Williams Award; and a nun, designated as "Moses to Her People," with the Harriet Tubman Award.

## Statistics

In 1984, there were about a million or more Black Catholics in the U.S., comprising about four per cent of the total Black population and two per cent of the Catholic population. Black priests and Religious numbered, respectively, about 250 and 700. There were ten Black bishops: Bishop Joseph L. Howze, head of the Diocese of Biloxi, and Auxiliary Bishops Joseph A. Francis, S.V.D., of Newark, Eugene A. Marino, S.S.J., of Washington, Harold R. Perry, S.V.D., of New Orleans, James P. Lyke, O.F.M., of Cleveland, Emerson Moore of New York, Moses Anderson of Detroit, Wilton D. Gregory of Chicago, J. Terry Steib, S.V.D., of St. Louis and John H. Ricard, S.S.J., of Baltimore.

Various dioceses have agencies like New York's Office of Black Ministry for pastoral and related service to the Black community.

## Josephite Pastoral Center

The Josephite Pastoral Center was established in September, 1968, as an educational and pastoral service agency for the Josephites in their mission work, specifically in the Black community. St. Joseph's Society of the Sacred Heart, the sponsoring body, has about 185 priests and 20 brothers in 80 mostly southern parishes in 18 dioceses.

The staff of the center includes Father John G. Harfman, S.S.J., director, and Brother Damian Wilson, S.S.J., and Maria M. Lannon, associate directors. The center is located at St. Joseph Seminary, 1200 Varnum St. N.E., Washington, D.C. 20017.

# HISPANICS

U.S. Census Bureau figures indicate that there were 14,605,883 persons of Hispanic origin in the United States in 1980. (Not counted were undocumented Hispanic aliens estimated to number between three and six million).

Between 1970 and 1980, there was a nationwide increase of 5,037,440 persons.

Regional increases for the same period were: Northeast, 709,381 for a total of 2,604,261; North Central, 228,144 for a total of 1,276,405; South, 1,707,365 for a total of 4,473,172; West, 2,884,291 for a total of 6,252,045.

Most persons of Hispanic origin in the United States have been baptized in the Catholic Church and comprise, probably, between 25 and 30 per cent of the Catholic population.

In the U.S., as of April, 1984, there were 16 Hispanic bishops (eight heads of dioceses and eight auxiliaries, all named since 1970).

## Pastoral Patterns

Pastoral ministry to Hispanics varies, depending on differences among the people and the availability of personnel to carry it out.

The pattern in cities with large numbers of Spanish-speaking is built around special churches, cen-

ters or other agencies where pastoral and additional forms of service are provided in a manner suited to the needs, language and culture of the people. Services in some places are extensive and include legal advice, job placement, language instruction, recreational and social assistance, specialized counseling, replacement services. In many places, however, even where there are special ministries, the needs are generally greater than the means required to meet them.

Some of the urban dwellers have been absorbed into established parishes and routines of church life and activity. Many Spanish-speaking communities, especially those with migrants, remain in need of special ministries.

An itinerant form of ministry best meets the needs of the thousands of migrant workers who follow the crops.

Special ministries for the Spanish-speaking have been in operation for a long time in dioceses of the Southwest. The total number of dioceses with such ministries is more than 75.

Pastoral care for Hispanics was the central concern of two national meetings, *Encuentros,* held in 1972 and 1977. In line with recommendations made then, particular emphasis has since been focused on meetings and actions for increasing language capability among persons involved in ministry, awareness of Hispanic cultural elements in liturgy and practice, leadership development, and moves for the formation of basic Christian communities (*comunidades de base*). A task force for implementation is chaired by Archbishop Robert F. Sanchez of Santa Fe, N.M.

At the time of writing, preparations were under way for a third *Encuentro* in 1985.

The U.S. bishops, at their annual meeting in November, 1983, approved and subsequently published a pastoral letter on Hispanic Ministry under the title, "The Hispanic Presence: Challenge and Commitment." (For text, see separate entry.)

### Secretariat for Hispanic Affairs

The national secretariat was established by the U.S. Catholic Conference for service in promoting and coordinating pastoral ministry to the Spanish-speaking. Its basic orientation is toward integral evangelization, combining religious ministry with development efforts in programs geared to the culture and needs of Hispanics. Its concerns are urban and migrant Spanish-speaking people; communications and publications in line with secretariat purposes and the service of people; bilingual and bicultural religious and general education; liaison for and representation of Hispanics with church, civic and governmental agencies.

The secretariat publishes a biweekly newsletter, *En Marcha,* available on request to interested parties. In addition, a weekly column available in English and Spanish, written by a variety of Hispanic Catholic authors, is syndicated to Catholic newspapers.

Paul Sedillo, Jr., is director of the national office at 1312 Massachusetts Ave. N.W., Wasington, D.C. 20005.

The secretariat has working relationships with regional offices in the Northeast, Southeast, Midwest, Southwest, Far West and Northwest. Each office shares the objectives of the secretariat. In addition, the Northeast, Southeast and Midwest offices have established pastoral institutes for formation, training and program development.

The Northeast regional office, officially the Northeast Pastoral Center for Hispanics, was established in 1976 and is supported by bishops in 14 states from Maine to Virginia. The office consists of professional staff members in the fields of pastoral work, communications, evangelization, research, development and publications. It has established the Conference of Diocesan Directors of the Hispanic Apostolate, Association of Hispanic Deacons, Regional Youth Task Force and a regional committee of Diocesan Coordinators of Religious Educators for the Hispanics. The executive director is Mario J. Paredes. The center is located at 1011 First Ave., New York, N.Y. 10022.

The Southeast regional office serves 22 dioceses in Tennessee, North and South Carolina, Florida, Georgia, Mississippi, Alabama and Louisiana. Its South East Pastoral Institute offers an academic degree in pastoral ministry, reaches out to communities throughout the region with its Evangeli-

zation Mobile Team and distributes audio-visual and print resources for Hispanic ministry. Father Mario Vizcaino, Sch. P., is director of the region and institute. The office is located at 2900 S.W. 87th Ave., Miami, Fla. 33165.

Five states of the Midwest are served by a Spanish Speaking Catholic Commission and the Midwest Institute for Hispanic Ministry. The executive director of the commission is Olga Villa Parra. The office is located at P.O. Box 703 (Holy Cross Annex), Notre Dame, Ind. 46556.

In the Southwest, a reorganized regional office serving Arkansas, Oklahoma, and Texas was reopened Feb. 1, 1983. Father Elisa Rodriguez is director of the office which is located at 3019 French Pl., San Antonio, Tex. 78228.

California and Nevada are served by the Far West office, which is a component of the California Catholic Conference. The regional director is Father Ricardo A. Chavez. The office is located at 926 J St., Suite 1100, Sacramento Calif. 95814.

A two-year-old regional office serves the northwestern corner of the U.S. and Alaska. The director of the region is Sister Elisa Martinez. The office is located at P.O. Box 1062, Yakima, Wash. 98907.

### PADRES

In the Southwest, 55 Mexican-American priests organized PADRES in February, 1970, to help the Church identify more closely with the pastoral, social, economic and educational needs of the Spanish-speaking. The present membership exceeds 500, mainly in California, Texas, New Mexico and on the East Coast. PADRES is an acronym for the Spanish title, "Padres Asociados para Derechos Religiosos, Educativos y Sociales."

Leadership development of Hispanos is one of the principal concerns of PADRES, now a national organization with membership open to priests, brothers and deacons working in Hispanic ministry. Seminarians and others interested in working with the Hispanic community are eligible for honorary membership. Father Ramon Gaitan, O.A.R., is the national president. The national office is located at 3310 Garfield Ave., Kansas City. Kan. 66104.

(Two other organizations of priests are *La Asociacion de Sacerdotes Hispanos* in New York and Miami.)

### Mexican American Cultural Center

This center was founded in 1972 as a pastoral institute with a variety of programs focused on the evangelization of Hispanics in the United States, particularly through lay leadership and liaison between North, Central and South America. It has been named a center of liturgical research by the National Conference of Catholic Bishops.

Father Virgil Elizondo is president of the center, which is located at 3019 French Pl., P.O. Box 28185, San Antonio, Tex. 78228.

A National Resource Center for Hispanic Ministry, begun in 1981 at the Cultural Center by initiative of the U.S. Bishops' Committee on Hispanic Affairs, collects information on personnel and resources available to the Hispanic apostolate.

## LEGAL STATUS OF CATHOLIC EDUCATION

The right of private schools to exist and operate in the United States is recognized in law. It was confirmed by the U.S. Supreme Court in 1925 when the tribunal ruled (Pierce v. Society of Sisters, see Church-State Decisions of the Supreme Court) that an Oregon state law requiring all children to attend public schools was unconstitutional.

Private schools are obliged to comply with the education laws in force in the various states regarding such matters as required basic curricula, periods of attendance, and standards for proper accreditation.

The special curricula and standards of private schools are determined by the schools themselves. Thus, in Catholic schools, the curricula include not only the subject matter required by state educational laws but also other fields of study, principally, education in the Catholic faith.

The Supreme Court has ruled that the First Amendment to the U.S. Constitution, in accordance with the No Establishment of Religion Clause of the First Amendment, prohibits direct federal and state aid from public funds to church-affiliated schools. (See several cases in Church-State Decisions of the Supreme Court.)

### Public Aid

This prohibition does not extend to all child-benefit and public-purpose programs of aid to students of non-public elementary and secondary schools.

Statutes authorizing such programs have been ruled constitutional on the grounds that they:

• have a "secular legislative purpose";
• neither inhibit nor advance religion as a "principal or primary effect";
• do not foster "excessive government entanglement with religion."

Aid programs considered constitutional have provided bus transportation, textbook loans, school lunches and health services, and "secular, neutral or non-ideological services, facilities and materials provided in common to all school children," public and non-public.

The first major aid to education program in U.S. history containing provisions benefitting nonpublic school students was enacted by the 89th Congress and signed into law by President Lyndon B. Johnson Apr. 11, 1965. The Elementary and Secondary Education Act was designed to avoid the separation of Church and state impasse which had blocked all earlier aid proposals pertaining to non-public, and especially church-affiliated, schools. The objective of the program, under public control, is to serve the public purpose by aiding disadvantaged pupils in nonpublic as well as public schools.

In a highly significant 5-to-4 decision June 29, 1983, the U.S. Supreme Court upheld the constitutionality of a Minnesota tuition tax credit for the parents of students attending parochial, other private and public schools. The majority opinion rejected arguments that the law benefitted religion in an unconstitutional manner, and said that the program did not involve excessive church-state entanglement. Supporters of the measure called it sound tax policy.

With respect to college and university education in church-affiliated institutions, the Supreme Court has upheld the constitutionality of statutes providing student loans and, under the Federal Higher Education Facilities Act of 1963, construction loans and grants for secular-purpose facilities.

Catholic schools are exempt from real estate taxation in all of the states. Since Jan. 1, 1959, nonprofit parochial and private schools have also been exempt from several federal excise taxes.

### Shared and Released Time

In a shared time program of education, students enrolled in Catholic or other church-related schools take some courses (e.g., religion, social studies, fine arts) in their own schools and others (e.g., science, mathematics, industrial arts) in public schools. Such a program has been given serious consideration in recent years by Catholic and other educators. Its constitutionality has not been seriously challenged, but practical problems — relating to teacher and student schedules, transportation, adjustment to new programs, and other factors — are knotty.

Several million children of elementary and high school age of all denominations have the opportunity of receiving religious instruction on released time. Under released time programs they are permitted to leave their public schools during school hours to attend religious instruction classes held off the public school premises. They are released at the request of their parents. Public school authorities merely provide for their dismissal, and take no part in the program.

---

**The National Catholic Educational Association,** founded in 1904, is a voluntary organization of educational institutions and individuals concerned with Catholic education in the U.S. Its objectives are to promote and encourage the principles and ideals of Christian education and formation by suitable service and other activities.

The NCEA has 14,000 institutional and individual members. Its official publication is *Momentum.* Numerous service publications are issued to members.

Bishop John F. Cummins of Oakland, Calif., is chairman of the association.

Headquarters are located at: 1077 30th St. N.W., Washington, D.C. 20007.

**National Association of Boards of Education,** founded in 1971, was made a department of the National Catholic Educational Association in 1973, to develop and promote policy-making boards for the advancement of Catholic education. Has a national membership of 1,207 diocesan and parish boards. Office: 1077 30th St. N.W., Washington, D.C. 20007.

# CATHOLIC SCHOOLS AND STUDENTS IN THE UNITED STATES

(Source: *The Official Catholic Directory, 1984;* figures as of Jan. 1, 1984. Archdioceses are indicated by an asterisk.)

| Section, State<br>Diocese | Univs.<br>Colleges | Students | High<br>Schools | Students | Elem.<br>Schools | Students |
|---|---|---|---|---|---|---|
| NEW ENGLAND | 26 | 59,863 | 133 | 66,213 | 541 | 144,950 |
| Maine, Portland | 1 | 498 | 3 | 991 | 22 | 5,359 |
| New Hampshire, Manchester | 5 | 5,074 | 6 | 2,492 | 29 | 7,751 |
| Vermont, Burlington | 3 | 3,349 | 3 | 1,118 | 11 | 2,684 |
| Massachusetts | 9 | 30,721 | 78 | 35,040 | 249 | 72,540 |
| *Boston | 4 | 20,172 | 61 | 24,158 | 166 | 48,123 |
| Fall River | 1 | 2,749 | 5 | 3,235 | 24 | 6,981 |
| Springfield | 1 | 814 | 4 | 3,260 | 35 | 10,774 |
| Worcester | 3 | 6,986 | 8 | 4,387 | 24 | 6,662 |
| Rhode Island, Providence | 2 | 8,031 | 13 | 6,330 | 65 | 17,064 |
| Connecticut | 6 | 12,190 | 30 | 20,242 | 165 | 39,552 |
| *Hartford | 3 | 1,878 | 15 | 11,047 | 96 | 22,373 |
| Bridgeport | 2 | 10,214 | 10 | 5,933 | 48 | 12,852 |
| Norwich | 1 | 98 | 5 | 3,262 | 21 | 4,327 |
| MIDDLE ATLANTIC | 62 | 182,318 | 361 | 233,468 | 2,068 | 645,617 |
| New York | 28 | 100,214 | 156 | 103,874 | 901 | 291,418 |
| *New York | 11 | 53,745 | 64 | 38,477 | 272 | 89,853 |
| Albany | 4 | 6,622 | 13 | 4,711 | 59 | 14,900 |
| Brooklyn | 2 | 20,175 | 23 | 25,293 | 175 | 82,732 |
| Buffalo | 6 | 13,333 | 21 | 9,331 | 133 | 30,080 |
| Ogdensburg | 1 | 444 | 3 | 871 | 25 | 5,688 |
| Rochester | — | — | 8 | 6,325 | 87 | 20,279 |
| Rockville Centre | 2 | 3,087 | 16 | 14,758 | 88 | 34,381 |
| Syracuse | 2 | 2,808 | 8 | 4,108 | 62 | 13,505 |
| New Jersey | 8 | 17,484 | 89 | 51,959 | 447 | 132,857 |
| *Newark | 4 | 15,032 | 42 | 21,683 | 199 | 54,717 |
| Camden | — | — | 14 | 9,095 | 67 | 18,795 |
| Metuchen | — | — | 9 | 5,153 | 52 | 19,948 |
| Paterson | 3 | 957 | 13 | 5,995 | 65 | 16,069 |
| Trenton | 1 | 1,495 | 11 | 10,033 | 64 | 23,328 |
| Pennsylvania | 26 | 64,620 | 116 | 77,635 | 738 | 221,342 |
| *Philadelphia | 10 | 31,588 | 51 | 46,767 | 278 | 114,326 |
| Allentown | 2 | 1,879 | 10 | 4,676 | 66 | 14,253 |
| Altoona-Johnstown | 2 | 2,194 | — | 1,794 | 37 | 7,770 |
| Erie | 3 | 6,416 | 10 | 4,054 | 50 | 13,830 |
| Greensburg | 2 | 2,016 | 2 | 1,385 | 51 | 10,475 |
| Harrisburg | — | — | 10 | 4,469 | 57 | 12,483 |
| Pittsburgh | 3 | 8,996 | 22 | 9,320 | 140 | 35,831 |
| Scranton | 4 | 11,531 | 11 | 5,170 | 59 | 12,374 |
| SOUTH ATLANTIC | 16 | 41,629 | 127 | 64,868 | 535 | 158,913 |
| Delaware, Wilmington | — | — | 8 | 5,102 | 30 | 10,826 |
| Maryland, *Baltimore | 4 | 9,814 | 24 | 12,251 | 87 | 28,319 |
| District of Columbia, *Washington | 3 | 19,636 | 25 | 11,583 | 83 | 24,068 |
| Virginia | 3 | 2,145 | 15 | 5,982 | 57 | 16,982 |
| Arlington | 3 | 2,145 | 5 | 3,109 | 30 | 9,601 |
| Richmond | — | — | 10 | 2,873 | 27 | 7,381 |
| West Virginia, Wheeling-Charleston | 1 | 1,046 | 9 | 2,284 | 34 | 5,372 |
| North Carolina | 2 | 1,184 | 3 | 1,204 | 33 | 7,479 |
| Charlotte | 2 | 1,184 | 2 | 955 | 15 | 3,886 |
| Raleigh | — | — | 1 | 249 | 18 | 3,593 |
| South Carolina, Charleston | — | — | 4 | 1,414 | 29 | 5,613 |
| Georgia | — | — | 7 | 3,859 | 29 | 8,822 |
| *Atlanta | — | — | 2 | 1,766 | 13 | 4,437 |
| Savannah | — | — | 5 | 2,093 | 16 | 4,385 |

| Section, State Diocese | Univs. Colleges | Students | High Schools | Students | Elem. Schools | Students |
|---|---|---|---|---|---|---|
| **Florida** | 3 | 7,804 | 32 | 21,189 | 153 | 51,432 |
| *Miami | 2 | 6,696 | 17 | 12,370 | 65 | 24,101 |
| Orlando | — | — | 5 | 2,682 | 28 | 8,473 |
| Palm Beach | No separate statistics available. | | | | | |
| Pensacola-Tallahassee | — | — | 1 | 469 | 10 | 2,633 |
| St. Augustine | — | — | 2 | 1,363 | 15 | 4,867 |
| St. Petersburg | 1 | 1,108 | 7 | 4,305 | 35 | 11,358 |
| Venice | No separate statistics available. | | | | | |
| | | | | | | |
| **EAST NORTH CENTRAL** | 51 | 132,098 | 306 | 193,292 | 2,125 | 579,924 |
| | | | | | | |
| **Ohio** | 11 | 29,526 | 87 | 55,856 | 510 | 162,509 |
| *Cincinnati | 4 | 19,993 | 22 | 16,550 | 120 | 39,798 |
| Cleveland | 3 | 5,625 | 26 | 19,885 | 167 | 61,423 |
| Columbus | 1 | 1,020 | 14 | 5,657 | 52 | 14,478 |
| Steubenville | 1 | 1,043 | 3 | 1,043 | 18 | 2,866 |
| Toledo | 1 | 640 | 16 | 8,638 | 93 | 27,778 |
| Youngstown | 1 | 1,205 | 6 | 4,083 | 60 | 16,166 |
| **Indiana** | 10 | 18,465 | 25 | 13,735 | 205 | 47,016 |
| *Indianapolis | 2 | 1,637 | 9 | 5,152 | 71 | 16,103 |
| Evansville | — | — | 5 | 1,727 | 29 | 5,221 |
| Ft. Wayne-South Bend | 6 | 14,553 | 5 | 3,470 | 43 | 10,263 |
| Gary | 1 | 1,297 | 4 | 2,894 | 41 | 11,457 |
| Lafayette | 1 | 978 | 2 | 492 | 21 | 3,972 |
| **Illinois** | 14 | 44,679 | 97 | 72,627 | 659 | 194,731 |
| *Chicago | 8 | 35,420 | 59 | 51,803 | 375 | 129,852 |
| Belleville | 1 | 1,112 | 4 | 2,164 | 54 | 8,986 |
| Joliet | 3 | 5,856 | 9 | 7,167 | 63 | 18,953 |
| Peoria | — | — | 8 | 3,595 | 58 | 12,919 |
| Rockford | — | — | 8 | 4,075 | 47 | 11,559 |
| Springfield | 2 | 2,291 | 9 | 3,823 | 62 | 12,462 |
| **Michigan** | 8 | 18,661 | 65 | 33,792 | 341 | 94,728 |
| *Detroit | 5 | 13,709 | 42 | 23,896 | 164 | 57,046 |
| Gaylord | — | — | 5 | 843 | 20 | 3,363 |
| Grand Rapids | 1 | 2,787 | 4 | 2,845 | 46 | 9,492 |
| Kalamazoo | 1 | 671 | 3 | 1,191 | 21 | 4,671 |
| Lansing | 1 | 1,494 | 5 | 3,277 | 42 | 10,947 |
| Marquette | — | — | 1 | 82 | 12 | 2,195 |
| Saginaw | — | — | 5 | 1,658 | 36 | 7,014 |
| **Wisconsin** | 9 | 20,767 | 32 | 17,282 | 410 | 80,949 |
| *Milwaukee | 5 | 16,634 | 14 | 9,987 | 173 | 40,466 |
| Green Bay | 2 | 2,158 | 9 | 3,528 | 94 | 15,601 |
| La Crosse | 1 | 1,173 | 7 | 2,744 | 75 | 12,831 |
| Madison | 1 | 802 | 2 | 1,023 | 47 | 8,268 |
| Superior | — | — | — | — | 21 | 3,774 |
| | | | | | | |
| **EAST SOUTH CENTRAL** | 8 | 9,198 | 52 | 23,046 | 285 | 64,767 |
| | | | | | | |
| **Kentucky** | 5 | 6,419 | 27 | 12,608 | 156 | 34,826 |
| *Louisville | 3 | 4,154 | 11 | 7,339 | 77 | 19,543 |
| Covington | 1 | 1,335 | 12 | 3,617 | 52 | 10,415 |
| Owensboro | 1 | 930 | 4 | 1,652 | 27 | 4,868 |
| **Tennessee** | 2 | 1,899 | 10 | 4,520 | 43 | 10,064 |
| Memphis | 1 | 1,575 | 5 | 2,337 | 17 | 4,418 |
| Nashville | 1 | 324 | 5 | 2,183 | 26 | 5,646 |
| **Alabama** | 1 | 880 | 5 | 3,094 | 50 | 12,083 |
| *Mobile | 1 | 880 | 3 | 1,711 | 27 | 6,879 |
| Birmingham | — | — | 2 | 1,383 | 23 | 5,204 |
| **Mississippi** | — | — | 10 | 2,824 | 36 | 7,794 |
| Biloxi | — | — | 5 | 1,911 | 17 | 3,295 |
| Jackson | — | — | 5 | 913 | 19 | 4,499 |

| Section, State Diocese | Univs. Colleges | Students | High Schools | Students | Elem. Schools | Students |
|---|---|---|---|---|---|---|
| WEST NORTH CENTRAL | 35 | 58,449 | 161 | 64,634 | 901 | 197,849 |
| **Minnesota** | 9 | 15,784 | 25 | 11,884 | 225 | 50,098 |
| *St. Paul and Minneapolis | 3 | 8,244 | 14 | 8,947 | 110 | 30,300 |
| Crookston | — | — | 1 | 161 | 11 | 1,764 |
| Duluth | 1 | 1,307 | — | — | 15 | 2,464 |
| New Ulm | — | — | 3 | 554 | 26 | 3,927 |
| St. Cloud | 3 | 4,255 | 3 | 916 | 37 | 6,665 |
| Winona | 2 | 1,978 | 4 | 1,306 | 26 | 4,978 |
| **Iowa** | 7 | 9,528 | 29 | 11,390 | 153 | 31,766 |
| *Dubuque | 3 | 4,074 | 11 | 4,668 | 59 | 14,536 |
| Davenport | 3 | 4,199 | 7 | 1,760 | 38 | 5,196 |
| Des Moines | — | — | 2 | 1,926 | 19 | 4,379 |
| Sioux City | 1 | 1,255 | 9 | 3,036 | 37 | 7,655 |
| **Missouri** | 7 | 18,417 | 47 | 23,432 | 277 | 67,298 |
| *St. Louis | 5 | 13,446 | 34 | 18,099 | 178 | 47,685 |
| Jefferson City | — | — | 2 | 863 | 35 | 6,050 |
| Kansas City-St. Joseph | 2 | 4,971 | 8 | 3,836 | 42 | 10,949 |
| Springfield-Cape Girardeau | — | — | 3 | 634 | 22 | 2,614 |
| **North Dakota** | 2 | 1,288 | 7 | 1,837 | 33 | 5,522 |
| Bismarck | 1 | 1,122 | 6 | 1,341 | 18 | 2,864 |
| Fargo | 1 | 166 | 1 | 496 | 15 | 2,658 |
| **South Dakota** | 2 | 865 | 5 | 1,460 | 27 | 4,785 |
| Rapid City | — | — | 2 | 363 | 3 | 762 |
| Sioux Falls | 2 | 865 | 3 | 1,097 | 24 | 4,023 |
| **Nebraska** | 2 | 7,508 | 33 | 9,002 | 94 | 18,756 |
| *Omaha | 2 | 7,508 | 20 | 6,373 | 62 | 13,686 |
| Grand Island | — | — | 7 | 1,225 | 8 | 996 |
| Lincoln | — | — | 6 | 1,404 | 24 | 4,074 |
| **Kansas** | 6 | 5,059 | 17 | 5,629 | 92 | 19,624 |
| *Kansas City | 3 | 2,871 | 7 | 3,035 | 38 | 9,747 |
| Dodge City | 1 | 676 | — | — | 12 | 1,788 |
| Salina | 1 | 611 | 6 | 724 | 12 | 2,013 |
| Wichita | 1 | 901 | 4 | 1,870 | 30 | 6,076 |
| **WEST SOUTH CENTRAL** | 12 | 22,198 | 120 | 50,624 | 511 | 155,304 |
| **Arkansas**, Little Rock | — | — | 6 | 2,005 | 36 | 5,015 |
| **Louisiana** | 4 | 8,479 | 63 | 29,924 | 201 | 82,140 |
| *New Orleans | 4 | 8,479 | 28 | 17,812 | 95 | 43,721 |
| Alexandria-Shreveport | — | — | 7 | 2,127 | 24 | 6,246 |
| Baton Rouge | — | — | 9 | 4,068 | 28 | 12,640 |
| Houma-Thibodaux | — | — | 3 | 1,355 | 12 | 4,847 |
| Lafayette | — | — | 14 | 3,734 | 32 | 11,178 |
| Lake Charles | — | — | 2 | 828 | 10 | 3,508 |
| **Oklahoma** | 1 | 337 | 5 | 2,470 | 30 | 5,554 |
| *Oklahoma City | 1 | 337 | 2 | 1,000 | 16 | 3,020 |
| Tulsa | — | — | 3 | 1,470 | 14 | 2,534 |
| **Texas** | 7 | 13,382 | 46 | 16,225 | 244 | 62,595 |
| *San Antonio | 4 | 6,555 | 10 | 3,634 | 45 | 13,323 |
| Amarillo | — | — | 1 | 148 | 7 | 1,095 |
| Austin | 1 | 2,165 | 1 | 223 | 15 | 3,456 |
| Beaumont | — | — | 1 | 517 | 10 | 1,989 |
| Brownsville | — | — | 2 | 754 | 8 | 2,044 |
| Corpus Christi | — | — | 2 | 782 | 28 | 5,781 |
| Dallas | 1 | 2,594 | 8 | 3,042 | 34 | 10,187 |
| El Paso | — | — | 3 | 1,131 | 14 | 3,424 |
| Fort Worth | — | — | 4 | 1,506 | 14 | 4,640 |
| Galveston-Houston | 1 | 2,068 | 9 | 3,917 | 50 | 12,507 |
| Lubbock | — | — | 1 | 56 | 3 | 608 |
| San Angelo | — | — | — | — | 4 | 868 |
| Victoria | — | — | 4 | 515 | 12 | 2,673 |

| Section, State Diocese | Univs. Colleges | Students | High Schools | Students | Elem. Schools | Students |
|---|---|---|---|---|---|---|
| MOUNTAIN | 6 | 6,282 | 35 | 14,678 | 195 | 45,304 |
| Montana | 2 | 2,725 | 5 | 1,151 | 21 | 3,108 |
| Great Falls-Billings | 1 | 1,192 | 3 | 541 | 18 | 2,585 |
| Helena | 1 | 1,533 | 2 | 610 | 3 | 523 |
| Idaho, Boise | 1 | 48 | 1 | 426 | 12 | 1,804 |
| Wyoming, Cheyenne | — | — | 1 | 145 | 7 | 1,062 |
| Colorado | 1 | 1,018 | 10 | 3,494 | 53 | 13,621 |
| *Denver | 1 | 1,018 | 6 | 2,756 | 38 | 10,801 |
| Pueblo | — | — | 3 | 408 | 11 | 1,643 |
| New Mexico | 2 | 2,491 | 5 | 1,970 | 37 | 7,317 |
| *Santa Fe | 2 | 2,491 | 3 | 1,790 | 22 | 4,886 |
| Gallup | — | — | 2 | 180 | 9 | 1,483 |
| Las Cruces | — | — | — | — | 6 | 948 |
| Arizona | — | — | 9 | 4,878 | 45 | 12,993 |
| Phoenix | — | — | 6 | 3,568 | 25 | 8,068 |
| Tucson | — | — | 3 | 1,310 | 20 | 4,925 |
| Utah, Salt Lake City | — | — | 2 | 1,048 | 9 | 2,351 |
| Nevada, Reno-Las Vegas | — | — | 2 | 1,566 | 11 | 3,048 |
| PACIFIC | 22 | 48,368 | 156 | 90,071 | 787 | 221,788 |
| Washington | 3 | 9,126 | 12 | 7,331 | 83 | 19,623 |
| *Seattle | 2 | 5,250 | 9 | 5,907 | 57 | 14,472 |
| Spokane | 1 | 3,876 | 2 | 1,158 | 19 | 3,563 |
| Yakima | — | — | 1 | 266 | 7 | 1,588 |
| Oregon | 2 | 3,897 | 10 | 3,858 | 64 | 9,660 |
| *Portland | 2 | 3,897 | 9 | 3,785 | 60 | 9,060 |
| Baker | — | — | 1 | 73 | 4 | 600 |
| California | 16 | 32,924 | 124 | 75,466 | 606 | 181,515 |
| *Los Angeles | 5 | 8,768 | 57 | 35,861 | 231 | 73,137 |
| *San Francisco | 3 | 7,716 | 19 | 10,003 | 74 | 22,263 |
| Fresno | — | — | 2 | 1,371 | 25 | 6,144 |
| Monterey | — | — | 2 | 837 | 14 | 3,695 |
| Oakland | 4 | 3,691 | 11 | 6,395 | 56 | 15,352 |
| Orange | 1 | 100 | 5 | 4,193 | 36 | 13,972 |
| Sacramento | — | — | 8 | 3,839 | 42 | 11,162 |
| San Bernardino | — | — | 2 | 1,358 | 29 | 7,927 |
| San Diego | 1 | 5,129 | 5 | 3,284 | 44 | 12,765 |
| San Jose | 2 | 7,520 | 6 | 4,888 | 28 | 8,842 |
| Santa Rosa | — | — | 5 | 1,962 | 14 | 3,131 |
| Stockton | — | — | 2 | 1,475 | 13 | 3,125 |
| Alaska | — | — | 2 | 257 | 4 | 788 |
| *Anchorage | — | — | — | — | 2 | 286 |
| Fairbanks | — | — | 2 | 257 | 1 | 370 |
| Juneau | — | — | — | — | 1 | 132 |
| Hawaii, Honolulu | 1 | 2,421 | 8 | 3,159 | 30 | 10,202 |
| EASTERN RITES | 2 | 432 | 5 | 546 | 43 | 6,548 |
| *Philadelphia | 1 | 412 | 1 | 224 | 13 | 2,202 |
| St. Nicholas of Chicago | — | — | 1 | 100 | 3 | 570 |
| Stamford | 1 | 20 | 3 | 222 | 9 | 892 |
| St. Josaphat (Parma) | No separate statistics available. | | | | | |
| *Pittsburgh | — | — | — | — | 6 | 1,045 |
| Parma | — | — | — | — | 5 | 1,014 |
| Passaic | — | — | — | — | 7 | 825 |
| Van Nuys | — | — | — | — | — | — |
| St. Maron (Maronites) | — | — | — | — | — | — |
| Newton (Melkites) | — | — | — | — | — | — |
| Romanians (Ap. Ex.) | — | — | — | — | — | — |
| Chaldeans (Ap. Ex.) | — | — | — | — | — | — |
| Armenians (Ap. Ex.) | — | — | — | — | — | — |
| MILITARY VICARIATE | — | — | — | — | — | — |
| TOTALS 1984 | 239 | 560,835 | 1,456 | 801,440 | 8,009 | 2,220,964 |
| Totals 1983 | 238 | 544,136 | 1,470 | 814,068 | 7,969 | 2,268,453 |
| Totals 1974 | 258 | 407,081 | 1,702 | 911,730 | 8,647 | 2,717,898 |

# SCHOOL STATISTICS

*The status of Catholic educational institutions and programs in the United States at the beginning of 1984, 1983 and 1974 was reflected in figures (as of Jan. 1) reported by "The Official Catholic Directory, 1984."*

**Colleges and Universities:** 239 (1 more than in 1983 and 19 less than in 1974).

**College and University Students:** 560,835 (16,699 more than in 1983 and 153,754 more than in 1974).

**High Schools:** 1,456 (14 less than in 1983 and 246 less than in 1974).

**High School Students:** 801,440 (12,628 less than in 1983 and 976,135 less than in 1974).

**Public High School Students Receiving Religious Instruction:** 961,196 (25,511 less than in 1983 and 210,126 less than in 1974).

**Elementary Schools:** 8,009 (40 more than in 1983 and 638 less than in 1974).

**Elementary School Students:** 2,220,964 (47,489 less than in 1983 and 496,934 less than in 1974).

**Public Elementary School Students Receiving Religious Instruction:** 3,106,281 (112,325 less than in 1983 and 976,135 less than in 1974).

**Teachers:** 170,714 (2,332 more than in 1983 and 3,997 less than in 1974).

**Lay Teachers:** 131,673 (4,365 more than in 1983 and 28,083 more than in 1974).

**Sisters Teaching:** 31,521 (1,789 less than in 1983 and 28,238 less than in 1974).

**Priests Teaching** (full time): 4,613 (105 less than in 1983 and 2,463 less than in 1974).

**Brothers Teaching:** 2,756 (128 less than in 1983 and 979 less than in 1974).

**Scholastics Teaching:** 151 (11 less than in 1983 and 400 less than in 1974).

## UNIVERSITIES AND COLLEGES IN THE UNITED STATES

(Sources: Almanac survey; *The Official Catholic Directory.*)

Listed below are institutions of higher learning established under Catholic auspices. Some of them are now independent.

Information includes: name of each institution; indication of male (m), female (w), coeducational (c) student body; name of founding group or group with which the institution is affiliated; year of foundation; number of students, in parentheses.

**Albertus Magnus College** (w): 700 Prospect St., New Haven, Conn. 06511. Dominican Sisters; 1925 (500).

**Albuquerque, University of** (c): St. Joseph Pl. N.W., Albuquerque, N.M. 87140. Sisters of St. Francis; 1920 (1,591).

**Allentown College of St. Francis de Sales** (c): Center Valley, Pa. 18034. Oblates of St. Francis de Sales; 1965 (1,006).

**Alvernia College** (c): Reading, Pa. 19607. Bernardine Sisters; 1958 (854).

**Alverno College** (w): 3401 S. 39th St. Milwaukee, Wis. 53215. School Sisters of St. Francis; 1936; independent (1,438).

**Anna Maria College** (c): Sunset Lane, Paxton, Mass. 01612. Sisters of St. Anne; 1946; independent (1,641).

**Aquinas College** (c): 1607 Robinson Rd. S.E., Grand Rapids, Mich. 49506. Sisters of St. Dominic; 1922 (2,787).

**Assumption College** (c): 500 Salisbury St., Worcester, Mass. 01609. Assumptionist Fathers; 1904 (2,536).

**Avila College** (c): 11901 Wornall Rd., Kansas City, Mo. 64145. Sisters of St. Joseph of Carondelet; 1916 (1,775).

**Barat College** (c): 700 E. Westleigh Rd., Lake Forest, Ill. 60045. Society of the Sacred Heart; 1919; independent (655).

**Barry University** (c): 11300 N.E. 2nd Ave., Miami, Fla. 33161. Dominican Sisters; 1940 (3,612).

**Bellarmine College** (c): Newburg Rd., Louisville, Ky. 40205; Louisville archdiocese, 1950 (2,809).

**Belmont Abbey College** (c): Belmont, N.C. 28012. Benedictine Fathers; 1876 (840).

**Benedictine College** (c): Atchison, Kans. 66002. Benedictines, 1971 (957).

**Boston College** (University Status) (c): Chestnut Hill, Mass. 02167. Jesuit Fathers; 1863 (14,069).

**Brescia College** (c): 120 W. 7th St., Owensboro, Ky. 42301. Ursuline Sisters; 1925 (930).

**Briar Cliff College** (c): 3303 Rebecca St., Sioux City, Ia. 51104. Sisters of St. Francis of the Holy Family; 1930 (1,255).

**Cabrini College** (c): Radnor, Pa. 19087. Missionary Srs. of Sacred Heart; 1957 (659).

**Caldwell College** (w): Caldwell, N.J. 07006. Dominican Sisters; 1939 (690).

**Calumet College** (c): 2400 New York Ave., Whiting, Ind. 46394. Society of the Precious Blood, 1951 (1,287).

**Canisius College** (c): 2001 Main St., Buffalo, N.Y. 14208. Jesuit Fathers; 1870; independent (4,519).

**Cardinal Newman College** (c): 7701 Florissant Rd., St. Louis, Mo. 63121. Catholic college with autonomous board of trustees; 1976 (108).

**Cardinal Stritch College** (c): 6801 N. Yates Rd., Milwaukee, Wis. 53217. Sisters of St. Francis of Assisi; 1932; independent (1,763).

**Carlow College** (w): 3333 5th Ave., Pittsburgh, Pa. 15213. Sisters of Mercy; 1929 (1,085).

**Carroll College** (c): Helena, Mont. 59625. Diocesan; 1909 (1,533).

**Catholic University of America, The** (c): 620 Michigan Ave. N.E., Washington, D.C. 20064. Hierarchy of the United States; 1887. Pontifical University (7,057).

**Catholic University of Puerto Rico** (c): Ponce, P.R. Hierarchy of Puerto Rico; 1948; Pontifical University (13,048).

**Chaminade University** (c): 3140 Waialae Ave., Honolulu, Hawaii 96816. Marianists; 1955 (1,907).

**Chestnut Hill College** (w): Philadelphia, Pa. 19118. Sisters of St. Joseph; 1871 (1,100).

**Christendom College** (c): Rt. 3, Box 87, Front Royal, Va. 22630 (107).

**Christian Brothers College** (c): 650 E. Parkway S., Memphis, Tenn. 38104. Brothers of the Christian Schools; 1871 (1,483).

**Clarke College** (c): 1550 Clarke Dr., Dubuque, Iowa 52001. Sisters of Charity, BVM; 1843 (906).

**Creighton University** (c): 2500 California St., Omaha, Neb. 68178. Jesuit Fathers; 1878 (5,600).

**Dallas, University of** (c): Irving, Tex. 75061. Private; 1956; independent (2,594).

**Dayton, University of** (c): 300 College Park Ave., Dayton, Ohio 45409. Marianists; 1850 (10,700).

**De Lourdes College** (w): 353 N. River Rd., Des Plaines, Ill. 60016. Sisters of the Holy Family of Nazareth; 1927; independent (204).

**DePaul University** (c): 2323 N. Seminary Ave., Chicago, Ill. 60614. Vincentians; 1898 (12,447).

**Detroit, University of** (c): 4001 W. McNichols Rd. at Livernois, Detroit, Mich. 48221. Jesuit Fathers; 1877 (6,270).

**Dominican College of Blauvelt** (c): Orangeburg, N.Y. 10962. Dominican Sisters; 1952; independent (1,731).

**Dominican College of San Rafael** (c): 1520 Grand Ave.; San Rafael, Calif. 94901. Dominican Sisters; 1890; independent (710).

**Duquesne University** (c): Bluff St., Pittsburgh, Pa. 15282. Holy Ghost Fathers; 1878 (6,400).

**D'Youville College** (c): One D'Youville Square, Buffalo, N.Y. 14201. Grey Nuns of the Sacred Heart; 1908; independent (1,200).

**Edgecliff College of Xavier University** (c): 2220 Victory Pkwy., Cincinnati, Ohio 45206. Sisters of Mercy; 1935 (667).

**Edgewood College** (c): 855 Woodrow St., Madison, Wis. 53711. Dominican Sisters; 1927 (793).

**Elms College** (w): Chicopee, Mass. 01013. Sisters of St. Joseph; 1928 (700).

**Emmanuel College** (w): 400 The Fenway, Boston, Mass. 02115. Sisters of Notre Dame de Namur; independent (1,257).

**Fairfield University** (c): North Benson Rd., Fairfield, Conn. 06430. Jesuit Fathers; 1942 (4,960).

**Felician College** (w): S. Main St., Lodi, N.J. 07644. Felician Sisters; 1942 (631). Coed in nursing and evening programs.

**Fontbonne College** (c): 6800 Wydown Blvd., St. Louis, Mo. 63105. Sisters of St. Joseph of Carondelet; 1917 (940).

**Fordham University** (c): Fordham Rd. and Third Ave., New York, N.Y. 10458. Society of Jesus (Jesuits); 1841; independent (13,110).

**Gannon University** (c): University Square, Erie, Pa. 16541. Diocese of Erie; 1933 (4,135).

**Georgetown University** (c): Post Office Box 37455, Washington, D.C. 20013. Jesuit Fathers; 1789 (11,960).

**Georgian Court College** (w): Lakewood, N.J. 08701. Sisters of Mercy; 1908 (1,499). Coed in evening and graduate divisions.

**Gonzaga University** (c): Spokane, Wash. 99258. Jesuit Fathers; 1887 (3,532).

**Great Falls, College of** (c): 1301 20th St. S., Great Falls, Mont. 59405. Sisters of Providence; 1932 (750).

**Gwynedd-Mercy College** (c): Gwynedd Valley, Pa. 19437. Sisters of Mercy; 1948; independent (2,200).

**Holy Cross, College of the** (c): Worcester, Mass. 01610. Jesuit Fathers; 1843 (2,494).

**Holy Family College** (c): Grant and Frankford Aves., Philadelphia, Pa. 19114. Sisters of Holy Family of Nazareth; 1954 (1,309).

**Holy Names College** (c): 3500 Mountain Blvd., Oakland, Calif. 94619. Sisters of the Holy Names of Jesus and Mary; 1868 (655).

**Illinois Benedictine College** (c): Lisle, Ill. 60532. Benedictine Fathers of St. Procopius Abbey; 1887 (1,630).

**Immaculata College** (w): Immaculata, Pa. 19345. Sisters, Servants of the Immaculate Heart of Mary; 1920 (823).

**Incarnate Word College** (c): 4301 Broadway, San Antonio, Tex. 78209. Sisters of Charity of the Incarnate Word; 1881 (1,400).

**Iona College** (c): 715 North Ave., New Rochelle, N.Y. 10801. Congregation of Christian Brothers; 1940; independent (6,304).

**John Carroll University** (c): North Park and Miramar Blvds., Cleveland, Ohio. 44118. Jesuit Fathers; 1886 (3,681).

**Kansas Newman College** (formerly Sacred Heart College) (c): 3100 McCormick Ave., Wichita, Kans. 67213. Sisters Adorers of the Blood of Christ; 1933 (763).

**King's College** (c): Wilkes-Barre, Pa. 18711. Holy Cross Fathers; 1946 (2,306).

**La Roche College** (c): 9000 Babcock Blvd., Pittsburgh, Pa. 15237. Sisters of Divine Providence; 1963 (1,723).

**La Salle College** (c): 20th St. and Olney Ave., Philadelphia, Pa. 19141. Brothers of the Christian Schools; 1863 (6,831).

**Le Moyne College** (c): Syracuse, N.Y. 13214. Jesuit Fathers; 1946; independent (1,800).

**Lewis University** (c): Romeoville, Ill. 60441. Christian Brothers; 1932 (2,811).

**Loras College** (c): 1450 Alta Vista St., Dubuque, Ia. 52001. Archdiocese of Dubuque; 1839 (1,906).

**Lourdes College** (c): Sylvania, Ohio 43560. Franciscan Srs.; 1958 (757).

**Loyola College** (c): 4501 N. Charles St., Baltimore, Md. 21210, Jesuits; 1852; combined with Mt. St. Agnes College, 1971 (5,652).

**Loyola Marymount University** (c): Loyola Blvd. at W. 80th St., Los Angeles, Calif. 90045. Society of Jesus; Religious of Sacred Heart of Mary, Sisters of St. Joseph of Orange; 1911 (6,488).

**Loyola University** (c): 6363 St. Charles Ave., New Orleans, La. 70118. Jesuit Fathers. 1904 (4,831).

**Loyola University of Chicago** (c): 820 N. Michigan Ave., Chicago, Ill. 60611. Jesuit Fathers; 1870 (16,674).

**Madonna College** (c): 36600 Schoolcraft Rd., Livonia, Mich. 48150. Felician Sisters; 1947 (3,752).

**Magdalen College** (c): 270 D.W. Highway So.,

RFD No. 5, Bedford, N.H. 03102; Magdalen College Corporation; 1973 (70).

**Mallinckrodt College** (c): 1041 Ridge Rd., Wilmette, Ill. 60091. Sisters of Christian Chrity; 1918; independent. (270).

**Manhattan College** (c): 4513 Manhattan College Pkwy., New York, N.Y. 10471. Brothers of the Christian Schools; 1853; independent (5,000). Cooperative program with College of Mt. St. Vincent.

**Manhattanville College** (c): Purchase, N.Y. 10577. Society of the Sacred Heart; 1841; independent (1,585).

**Marian College** (c): Fond du Lac, Wis. 54935. Sisters of St. Agnes; 1936 (536).

**Marian College** (c): 3200 Cold Spring Rd., Indianapolis, Ind. 46222. Sisters of St. Francis (Oldenburg, Ind.); 1851 (850).

**Marist College** (c): Poughkeepsie, N.Y. 12601. Marist Brothers of the Schools; 1946; independent (1,899).

**Marquette University** (c): 615 N. 11th St., Milwaukee, Wis. 53233. Jesuit Fathers; 1881; independent (12,000).

**Mary College** (c): Bismarck, N.D. 58501. Benedictine Sisters; 1959 (1.153).

**Marycrest College** (c): 1607 W. 12th St., Davenport, Iowa 52804. Congregation of the Humility of Mary; 1939; independent (1,400).

**Marygrove College** (c): 8425 W. McNicholas Rd., Detroit, Mich. 48221. Sisters, Servants of the Immaculate Heart of Mary; 1910 (1,153).

**Marylhurst Education Center, College for Lifelong Learning** (c): Marylhurst, Ore. 97036. Srs. of Holy Names of Jesus and Mary; 1893; independent (453).

**Marymount College** (w): Tarrytown, N.Y. 10591. Religious of the Sacred Heart of Mary; 1907; independent (1,271). Coed in weekend degree programs.

**Marymount College of Kansas** (c): Salina, Kans. 67401. Salina diocese; 1922 (611).

**Marymount College of Virginia** (w): 2807 N. Glebe Rd., Arlington, Va. 22007. Religious of the Sacred Heart of Mary; 1950; independent (1,864).

**Marymount Manhattan College** (w): 221 E. 71st St., New York, N.Y. 10021. Religious of the Sacred Heart of Mary; 1936; independent (2,214).

**Maryville College** (c): 13550 Conway Rd., St. Louis, Mo. 63141. Religious of the Sacred Heart; 1872; independent (2,052).

**Marywood College** (w): Scranton, Pa. 18509. Sisters, Servants of the Immaculate Heart of Mary; 1915 (3,191). Coed in graduate division.

**Mater Dei College** (c): Riverside Dr., Ogdensburg, N.Y. 13669. Sisters of St. Joseph; 1960; independent (444).

**Mercy College of Detroit** (c): 8200 W. Outer Dr., Detroit, Mich. 48219. Sisters of Mercy; 1941 (2,620).

**Mercyhurst College** (c): 501 E. 38th St., Erie, Pa. 16546. Sisters of Mercy; 1926 (1,685).

**Merrimack College** (c): North Andover, Mass. 01845. Augustinians; 1947 (2,165).

**Misericordia** (College Misericordia) (c): Dallas, Pa. 18612. Religious Sisters of Mercy of the Union; 1924 (1,138).

**Molloy College** (c): 1000 Hempstead Ave., Rockville Centre, N.Y. 11570. Dominican Sisters; 1955 (1,636).

**Mount Marty College** (c): Yankton, S.D. 57078. Benedictine Sisters; 1936 (570).

**Mount Mary College** (w): 2900 W. Menomonee River Pkwy., Milwaukee, Wis. 53222. School Sisters of Notre Dame; 1913 (1,144).

**Mt. Mercy College** (c): 1330 Elmhurst Dr. N.E., Cedar Rapids, Ia. 52402. Sisters of Mercy; 1928 (1,262).

**Mt. St. Clare College** (c): Bluff Blvd. and Springdale Dr., Clinton, Ia. 52732. Clinton Franciscans; 1928 (371).

**Mt. St. Joseph on the Ohio, College of** (w): Mt. St. Joseph, Ohio 45051. Sisters of Charity; 1920 (2,008).

**Mt. St. Mary College** (c): Newburgh, N.Y. 12550. Dominican Sisters; 1959; independent (1,078).

**Mount St. Mary College** (c): Emmitsburg, Md. 21727. Diocesan Clergy; 1808; independent (1,386).

**Mt. St. Mary's College** (w): 12001 Chalon Rd., Los Angeles, Calif. 90049 and 10 Chester Pl., Los Angeles, Calif. 90007 (Doheny Campus). Sisters of St. Joseph of Carondelet; 1925 (1,207). Coed in music, nursing and graduate programs.

**Mt. St. Vincent, College of** (c): Mt. St. Vincent-on-Hudson, New York, N.Y. 10471. Sisters of Charity; 1847; independent (1,200). Cooperative program with Manhattan College.

**Mundelein College** (w): 6363 N. Sheridan Rd., Chicago, Ill. 60660. Sisters of Charity of the Blessed Virgin Mary; 1929 (1,282).

**Nazareth College** (c): Nazareth, Mich. 49074. Sisters of St. Joseph; 1924; independent (671).

**Nazareth College** (c): East Ave., Rochester, N.Y. 14610. Sisters of St. Joseph of Rochester; 1924; independent (2,422).

**Neumann College** (formerly Our Lady of Angels) (c): Aston, Pa. 19014. Sisters of St. Francis; 1965 (1,006).

**New Rochelle, College of** (w): 29 Castle Pl., New Rochelle, N.Y. 10801 (main campus). Ursuline Nuns; 1904; independent (5,450). Coed in nursing, graduate, new resources divisions.

**Niagara University** (c): Niagara Univ., N.Y. 14109. Vincentian Fathers; 1856 (3,596).

**Notre Dame, College of** (c): Belmont, Calif. 94002. Sisters of Notre Dame de Namur; 1868; independent (1,360).

**Notre Dame, University of** (c): Notre Dame, Ind. 46556. Congregation of Holy Cross; 1842 (9,050).

**Notre Dame College** (w): 4545 College Rd., Cleveland, Ohio 44121. Sisters of Notre Dame; 1922 (729).

**Notre Dame College** (w): Manchester, N.H. 03104. Sisters of the Holy Cross; 1950 (716).

**Notre Dame of Maryland, College of** (w): 4701 N. Charles St., Baltimore, Md. 21210. School Sisters of Notre Dame; 1873 (575).

**Ohio Dominican College** (c): Columbus, Ohio 43219. Dominican Sisters of St. Mary of the Springs; 1911 (1,019).

**Our Lady of Holy Cross College** (c): 4123 Woodland Dr., New Orleans, La. 70114. Congregation of Sisters Marianites of Holy Cross (746).

**Our Lady of the Lake University of San Antonio** (c): 411 S.W. 24th St., San Antonio, Tex. 78285. Sisters of Divine Providence; 1911 (1,758).

**Parks College of St. Louis University** (c): Cahokia, Ill. 62206. Jesuits; 1927; independent (1,051).

**Portland, University of** (c): 5000 N. Willamette Blvd., Portland, Ore. 97203. Holy Cross Fathers; 1901; independent (2,872).

**Providence College** (c): River Ave. and Eaton St., Providence, R.I. 02918. Dominican Friars; 1917 (3,400).

**Quincy College** (c): 1831 College Ave., Quincy, Ill. 62301. Franciscan Friars; 1859 (1,940).

**Regis College** (c): W. 50th Ave. and Lowell Blvd. Denver, Colo. 80221. Jesuit Fathers; 1887 (1,018).

**Regis College** (w): Weston, Mass. 02193. Sisters of St. Joseph; 1927; independent (1,347).

**Rivier College** (w): Nashua, N.H. 03060. Sisters of the Presentation of Mary; 1933; independent (2,285). Coed continuing education and graduate school.

**Rockhurst College** (c): 5225 Troost Ave., Kansas City, Mo. 64110. Jesuit Fathers; 1910 (3,196).

**Rosary College** (c): 7900 Division St., River Forest, Ill. 60305. Dominican Sisters; 1901 (1,734).

**Rosemont College** (w): Rosemont, Pa. 19010. Society of the Holy Child Jesus; 1921 (600).

**Sacred Heart College** (c): Belmont, N.C. 28012. Sisters of Mercy; 1935 (344).

**Sacred Heart University** (c): Fairfield (P.O. Bridgeport), Conn. 06606. Diocese of Bridgeport; 1963; independent (5,254).

**St. Ambrose College** (c): Davenport, Ia. 52803. Diocese of Davenport; 1882 (2,160).

**Saint Anselm College** (c): Manchester N.H. 03102. Benedictine Monks; 1889 (1,857).

**St. Basil's College** (m): 195 Glenbrook Rd., Stamford, Conn. 06902. Byzantine-Ukrainian Rite Diocese of Stamford; 1939 (15).

**Saint Benedict, College of** (w): St. Joseph, Minn. 56374. Benedictine Sisters; 1913 (2,217).

**St. Bonaventure University** (c): St. Bonaventure, N.Y. 14778. Franciscan Friars; 1856; independent (2,740).

**St. Catherine, College of** (w): 2004 Randolph St., St. Paul, Minn. 55105. Sisters of St. Joseph of Carondelet; 1905 (2,285).

**St. Edward's University** (c): Austin, Tex. 78704, Holy Cross Brothers; 1885; independent (2,165).

**St. Elizabeth, College of** (w): Convent Station, N.J. 07961. Sisters of Charity; 1899; independent (915).

**St. Francis, College of** (c): 500 N. Wilcox St., Joliet, Ill. 60435. Sisters of St. Francis of Mary Immaculate; 1925; independent (940).

**St. Francis College** (c): 180 Remsen St., Brooklyn, N.Y. 11201. Franciscan Brothers; 1884; private, independent in the Franciscsan tradition (2,882).

**St. Francis College** (c): 2701 Spring St., Fort Wayne, Ind. 46808. Sisters of St. Francis; 1890 (1,275).

**St. Francis College** (c): Loretto, Pa. 15940. Franciscan Fathers; 1847; independent (1,654).

**St. John Fisher College** (c): 3690 East Ave., Rochester, N.Y. 14618. Basilian Fathers; 1951; independent (1,700).

**St. John's University** (c): Grand Central and Utopia Pkwys., Jamaica, N.Y. 11439 (Queens Campus); 300 Howard Ave., Grymes Hill, Staten Island, N.Y. 10301 (Staten Island Campus). Vincentian Fathers; 1870 (18,961).

**St. John's University** (m): Collegeville, Minn. 56321. Benedictines; 1857 (2,000). Coed in graduate school.

**Saint Joseph College** (w): 1678 Asylum Ave., West Hartford, Conn. 06117. Sisters of Mercy; 1932 (1,289). Coed in graduate school.

**Saint Joseph's College** (c): N. Windham, Me. 04062. Sisters of Mercy; 1912 (500).

**Saint Joseph's College** (c): Rensselaer, Ind. 47978. Society of the Precious Blood; 1889 (982).

**St. Joseph's College** (c): 245 Clinton Ave., Brooklyn, N.Y. 11205 (459) and 155 Roe Blvd., Patchogue, N.Y. 11772 (1,397). Sisters of St. Joseph; 1916; independent.

**St. Joseph's University** (c): 5600 City Ave., Philadelphia, Pa. 19131. Jesuit Fathers; 1851 (5,587).

**St. Joseph the Provider, College of** (c): Clement Rd., Rutland, Vt. 05701. Sisters of St. Joseph; 1954; independent (386).

**Saint Leo College** (c): Saint Leo, Fla. 33574. Order of St. Benedict; 1889; independent (1,200).

**St. Louis University** (c): 221 N. Grand Blvd., St. Louis, Mo. 63103. Jesuit Fathers; 1818 (10,179).

**Saint Martin's College** (c): Lacey, Wash. 98503. Benedictine Monks; 1895 (550).

**St. Mary, College of** (w): 1901 S. 72nd St., Omaha, Neb. 68124. Sisters of Mercy; 1923; independent (1,207).

**Saint Mary College** (w): Leavenworth, Kans. 66048. Sisters of Charity of Leavenworth; 1923 (1,009).

**St. Mary of the Plains College** (c): Dodge City, Kans. 67801. Sisters of St. Joseph of Wichita; 1952 (676).

**St. Mary-of-the-Woods College** (w): St. Mary-of-the-Woods, Ind. 47876. Sisters of Providence; 1840 (689).

**St. Mary's College** (w): Notre Dame, Ind. 46556. Sisters of the Holy Cross; 1844 (1,839).

**St. Mary's College** (c): Orchard Lake, Mich. 48033. Secular Clergy; 1885 (267).

**St. Mary's College** (c): Moraga, Calif. 94575. Brothers of the Christian Schools; 1863 (2,868).

**St. Mary's College** (c): Winona, Minn. 55987. Brothers of the Christian Schools; 1912 (1,404).

**St. Mary's Dominican College** (w): 7214 St. Charles Ave., New Orleans, La. 70118. Dominican Sisters; 1910 (708).

**St. Mary's University** (c): One Camino Santa Maria, San Antonio, Tex. 78284. Society of Mary (Marianists); 1852 (3,311).

**St. Michael's College** (c): Winooski, Vt. 05404. Society of St. Edmund; 1904 (2,010).

**St. Norbert College** (c): De Pere, Wis. 54115. Norbertine Fathers; 1898; independent (1,644).

**St. Peter's College** (c): 2641 Kennedy Blvd., Jersey City, N.J. 07306. Jesuit Fathers; independent; 1872 (4,217).

**Saint Rose, College of** (c): 432 Western Ave., Albany, N.Y. 12203. Sisters of St. Joseph of Carondelet; 1920; independent (2,662).

**St. Scholastica, College of** (c): 1200 Kenwood Ave., Duluth, Minn. 55811. Benedictine Sisters; 1912 (1,307).

**Saint Teresa, College of** (w): Winona, Minn. 55987. Sisters of St. Francis; 1907 (609).

**St. Thomas, College of** (c): St. Paul, Minn. 55101. Archdiocese of St. Paul; 1885 (5,959).

**St. Thomas, University of** (c): 3812 Montrose Blvd., Houston, Tex. 77006. Basilian Fathers; 1947 (2,068).

**St. Thomas Aquinas College** (c): Sparkill, N.Y. 10976. Dominican Sisters of Sparkill; 1952; independent, corporate board of trustees (1,973).

**St. Thomas University** (c): 16400 N.W. 32nd Ave., Miami, Fla. 33054. Augustinian Fathers; 1962 (3,000).

**St. Vincent College** (c): Latrobe, Pa. 15650. Benedictine Fathers; 1846 (1,060).

**St. Xavier College** (c): 3700 W. 103rd St., Chicago, Ill. 60655. Sisters of Mercy; chartered 1847 (2,300).

**Salve Regina — The Newport College** (c): Ochre Point Ave., Newport, R.I. 02840. Sisters of Mercy; 1934 (1,960).

**San Diego, University of** (c): Alcala Park, San Diego, Calif. 92110. San Diego diocese and Religious of the Sacred Heart; 1949; independent (5,003).

**San Francisco, University of** (c): Ignation Heights, San Francisco, Calif. 94117. Jesuit Fathers; 1855 (7,065).

**Santa Clara, University of** (c): Santa Clara, Calif. 95053. Jesuit Fathers; 1851 (7,401).

**Santa Fe, College of** (c): Santa Fe, N. Mex. 87501. Brothers of the Christian Schools; 1947 (900).

**Scranton, University of** (c): Scranton, Pa. 18510. Society of Jesus; 1888 (4,620).

**Seattle University** (c): Broadway and East Madison, Seattle, Wash. 98122. Jesuit Fathers; 1891 (4,467).

**Seton Hall University** (c): South Orange, N.J. 07079. Diocesan Clergy; 1856 (9,411).

**Seton Hill College** (w): Greensburg, Pa. 15601. Sisters of Charity of Seton Hill; 1883 (937).

**Siena College** (c): Loudonville, N.Y. 12211. Franciscan Friars; 1937 (2,818).

**Siena Heights College** (c): Adrian, Mich. 49221. Dominican Sisters; 1919; independent (1,485).

**Silver Lake College of Holy Family** (c): 2406 S. Alverno Rd., Manitowoc, Wis. 54220. Franciscan Sisters of Christian Charity; 1935 (425).

**Spalding University** (c): 851 S. 4th Ave., Louisville, Ky. 40203. Sisters of Charity of Nazareth; 1814; independent (1,139).

**Spring Hill College** (c): Mobile, Ala. 36608. Jesuit Fathers; 1830 (880).

**Steubenville, University of** (c): Steubenville, Ohio 43952. Franciscan Fathers; 1946 (915).

**Stonehill College** (c): North Easton, Mass.

02356. Holy Cross Fathers; 1948; independent (2,710).

**Thomas Aquinas College** (c): 1000 N. Ojai Rd., Santa Paula, Calif. 93060. (108).

**Thomas More College** (c): Crestview Hills, Covington, Ky. 41017. Diocese of Covington; 1921 (1,335).

**Trinity College** (w): Colchester Ave., Burlington, Vt. 05401. Sisters of Mercy; 1925 (953).

**Trinity College** (w): Michigan Ave. and Franklin St. N.E., Washington, D.C. 20017. Sisters of Notre Dame de Namur; 1897 (670). Coed in graduate school.

**Ursuline College** (w): 2550 Lander Rd., Cleveland, Ohio 44124. Ursuline Nuns; 1871 (1,337).

**Villa Maria College** (w): 2551 W. Lake Rd., Erie, Pa. 16505. Sisters of St. Joseph; 1925 (620).

**Villanova University** (c): Villanova, Pa. 19085. Order of St. Augustine; 1842 (11,190).

**Viterbo College** (c): La Crosse, Wis. 54601. Franciscan Sisters; 1890 (1,173).

**Walsh College** (c): 2020 Easton St. N.W., Canton, Ohio 44720. Brothers of Christian Instruction; 1958 (1,150).

**Wheeling College** (c): 316 Washington Ave., Wheeling, W. Va. 26003. Jesuit Fathers; 1954 (1,046).

**Xavier University** (c): 3800 Victory Pkwy., Cincinnati, Ohio 45207. Jesuit Fathers; 1831 (6,950).

**Xavier University of Louisiana** (c): 7325 Palmetto St., New Orleans, La. 70125. Sisters of Blessed Sacrament; 1925; lay religious administration board (2,194).

## Catholic Junior Colleges

**Ancilla Domini College** (c): Donaldson, Ind. 46513. Ancilla Domini Sisters; 1937 (420).

**Aquinas Junior College** (c): Harding Rd., Nashville, Tenn. 37205. Dominican Sisters; 1961 (324).

**Assumption College for Sisters:** Hilltop Rd., Mendham, N.J. 07945. Sisters of Christian Charity; 1953 (30).

**Chatfield College** (c): St. Martin, O. 45118. Ursulines; 1971 (314).

**Donnelly College** (c): 1236 Sandusky Ave., Kansas City, Kans. 66102. Archdiocesan College; 1949 (905).

**Don Bosco Technical Institute** (m): 1151 San Gabriel Blvd., Rosemead, Calif. 91770. Salesians; 1969 (307).

**Elizabeth Seton College** (c): 1061 N. Broadway, Yonkers, N.Y. 10701. Sisters of Charity; 1960; independent (1,432).

**Felician College** (c): 3800 W. Peterson Ave., Chicago, Ill. 60659.

**Hilbert College** (c): 5200 S. Park Ave., Hamburg, N.Y. 14075. Franciscan Sisters of St. Joseph; 1957; independent (698).

**Holy Cross Junior College** (c): Notre Dame, Ind. 46556. Brothers of Holy Cross; 1966 (265).

**Manor Junior College** (w): Fox Chase Manor, Jenkintown, Pa. 19046. Sisters of St. Basil the Great; 1947 (390).

**Maria College** (c): 700 New Scotland Ave., Albany, N.Y. 12208. Sisters of Mercy; 1963 (841).

**Maria Regina College** (w): 1024 Court St., Syracuse, N.Y. 13208. Franciscan Sisters; 1963; independent (622).

**Marymount Palos Verdes College** (c): Rancho Palos Verdes, Calif. 90274. Religious of the Sacred Heart of Mary (632).

**Mt. Aloysius Junior College** (c): Cresson, Pa. 16630. Sisters of Mercy; 1939 (541).

**Presentation College** (c): Aberdeen, S.D. 57401. Sisters of the Presentation; 1951 (325).

**St. Catharine College** (c); St. Catharine, Ky. 40061. Dominican Sisters; 1931 (201).

**St. Gertrude, College of** (c): Cottonwood, Ida. 83522. Benedictine Sisters.

**St. Gregory's College** (c): Shawnee, Okla. 74801. Benedictine Monks; 1876 (337).

**St. Mary's College of O'Fallon** (c): 200 N. Main St., O'Fallon, Mo. 63366. Sisters of the Most Precious Blood; 1921 (687).

**St. Mary's Junior College** (c): 2500 S. 6th St., Minneapolis, Minn. 55454. Sisters of St. Joseph of Carondelet (889).

**Springfield College in Illinois** (c): 1500 N. Fifth St., Springfield, Ill. 62702. Ursuline Nuns; 1929 (441).

**Trocaire College** (c): 110 Red Jacket Pkwy., Buffalo, N.Y. 14220. Sisters of Mercy; 1958; independent (1,044).

**Villa Julie College** (c): Green Spring Valley Rd., Stevenson, Md. 21153. Sisters of Notre Dame de Namur; 1952; independent (1,031).

**Villa Maria College of Buffalo** (c): 240 Pine Ridge Rd., Buffalo, N.Y. 14225. Felician Srs.; 1960 (850).

## CAMPUS MINISTRY

"Campus ministry is a pastoral apostolate of service to the members of the entire university and college community through concern and care for persons, the proclamation of the Gospel, and the celebration of the liturgy," according to a set of guidelines drawn up by an eight-member commission of the National Catholic Educational Association. The general purpose of the ministry is to make the Church present and active in the academic community.

Ideally, according to the guidelines, elements of the ministry — carried on by teams of priests, men and women religious, and lay persons — include liturgical leadership; pastoral counseling; coordination of expressions and energies for religious life on campus; Christian witness on social and moral issues; objective and independent mediation between various groups on campus; participation in religious aspects of the work of the administration, faculty and students.

### Status, Agencies

The dimensions and challenge of the campus ministry are evident from estimates that approximately 75 to 80 per cent of 2.4 million Catholics in colleges and universities are on non-Catholic public and private campuses. Serving them are about 1,200 full-time and 700 part-time campus ministry personnel.

The Desk of Campus and Young Adult Ministry, under the Department of Education of the U.S. Catholic Conference, has responsibility for continuing support of ministry in this field. The office, headed by Father Joseph J. Kenna, is located at 1312 Massachusetts Ave. N.W., Washington, D.C. 20005.

The autonomous Catholic Campus Ministry Association, is headquartered at 3700 West 103rd St., Chicago, Ill. 60655. Sister Margaret M. Ivers, I.B.V.M., is executive director.

**National Forum of Catholic Parent Organizations:** Founded in 1976 as a commission of the National Catholic Educational Association, to support and promote the role of parents as primary educators of their children. Has a national membership of diocesan and parish/private parent organizations. Office: 1077 30th St. N.W., Washington, D.C. 20007.

## DIOCESAN AND INTERDIOCESAN SEMINARIES

(Sources: Almanac survey; *Official Catholic Directory;* NC News Service.)

*Information, according to states, includes names of archdioceses and dioceses, and names and addresses of seminaries. Types of seminaries, when not clear from titles, are indicated in most cases. Interdiocesan seminaries are generally conducted by religious orders for candidates for the priesthood from several dioceses. The list does not include houses of study only for members of religious communities. Archdioceses are indicated by an asterisk.*

**California:** Los Angeles* — St. John's Seminary (major), 5012 E. Seminary Rd., Camarillo. 93010; St. John's College Seminary, 5118 E. Seminary Rd., Camarillo. 93010; Seminary of Our Lady, Queen of Angels (minor, high school), Box 1071, San Fernando. 91341.

San Diego — St. Francis Seminary (college residence), 1667 Santa Paula Dr., San Diego 92111.

San Francisco* — St. Patrick's Seminary (major), 320 Middlefield Rd., Menlo Park. 94025.

San Jose — St. Joseph's College, P.O. Box 7009, Mountain View 94039.

**Colorado:** Denver* — St. Thomas Theological Seminary (major), 1300 S. Steele St., Denver 80210.

**Connecticut:** Hartford* — St. Thomas Seminary (minor), 467 Bloomfield Ave., Bloomfield. 06002.

Norwich — Holy Apostles College and Seminary (delayed vocations), 33 Prospect Hill Rd., Cromwell 06416.

Stamford Byzantine Rite — Ukrainian Catholic Seminary: St. Basil College (minor), 195 Glenbrook Rd., Stamford 06902; St. Basil's Preparatory School (minor), 39 Clovelly Rd., Stamford 06902.

**District of Columbia:** Washington* — Theological College, The Catholic University of America, 401 Michigan Ave., N.E. 20017.

**Florida:** Miami*, Pensacola-Tallahassee, St. Augustine, St. Petersburg — St. John Vianney College Seminary, 2900 S.W. 87th Ave., Miami 33165; St.

Vincent de Paul Regional Seminary (major), Military Trail, P.O. Box 460, Boynton Beach. 33435.

**Hawaii:** Honolulu — St. Stephen's Seminary Center, P.O. Box 699, Kaneohe. 96744.

**Illinois:** Chicago* — Quigley Preparatory Seminary (North), 103 East Chestnut St., Chicago 60611; Quigley Preparatory Seminary (South), 7740 South Western Ave., Chicago 60620; Niles College of Loyola University, 7135 N. Harlem Ave., Chicago 60631; St. Mary of the Lake Seminary, Mundelein. 60060.

Springfield — Immaculate Conception Seminary, 1903 E. Lake Dr., Springfield 62707.

**Indiana:** Indianapolis* — St. Meinrad Seminary, College and School of Theology (interdiocesan), St. Meinrad. 47577.

**Iowa:** Davenport — St. Ambrose College Seminary, 518 W. Locust St., Davenport 52803.

Dubuque* — Seminary of St. Pius X, Loras College, Dubuque 52001.

**Kansas:** Kansas City* — Savior of the World Seminary (minor), 12601 Parallel Ave., Kansas City 66109.

**Kentucky:** Covington — Seminary of St. Pius X, Erlanger. 41018.

**Louisiana:** New Orleans* — Notre Dame Seminary Graduate School of Theology, 2901 S. Carrollton Ave., New Orleans 70118; St. John Vianney Preparatory Seminary, 3801 Monroe St., New Orleans 70118; St. Joseph Seminary College (interdiocesan), St. Benedict 70457.

**Maryland:** Baltimore* — St. Mary's Seminary and University, 5400 Roland Ave., Baltimore 21210; Mt. St. Mary's Seminary, Emmitsburg. 21727.

**Massachusetts:** Boston* — St. John's Seminary School of Theology, 127 Lake St., Brighton. 02135; St. John's Seminary, College of Liberal Arts, 197 Foster St., Brighton 02135; Pope John XXIII National Seminary, 558 South Ave., Weston. 02193.

Melkite Eparchy of Newton — St. Gregory the Theologian Seminary, 233 Grant Ave., Newton 02159; St. Basil's Salvatorian Seminary, 30 East St., Methuen 01844.

**Michigan:** Detroit* — Sacred Heart Seminary College, Inc., 2701 Chicago Blvd., Detroit 48206; Sts. Cyril and Methodius Seminary (independent institution primarily serving Polish-American community), Orchard Lake 48033; St. John's Provincial Seminary (major, for dioceses in Detroit province), 44011 Five Mile Rd., Plymouth. 48170.

Grand Rapids — Christopher House, 2001 Robinson Rd., S.E., Grand Rapids 49506.

**Minnesota:** Seminary of the Diocese of St. Cloud, Collegeville. 56321.

St. Paul and Minneapolis* — St. Paul Seminary, 2260 Summit Ave., St. Paul. 55105; St. John Vianney College Seminary, 2115 Summit Ave., St. Paul. 55105.

Winona — Immaculate Heart of Mary Seminary, Terrace Heights, St. Mary's College, Winona 55987.

**Missouri:** Jefferson City — St. Thomas Aquinas Preparatory Seminary, 245 N. Levering Ave., P.O. Box 858, Hannibal. 63401.

St. Louis* — St. Louis Roman Catholic Theological Seminary (Kenrick Seminary), 7800 Kenrick Rd., St. Louis 63119; Cardinal Glennon College, 5200 Glennon Dr., St. Louis 63119; St. Louis Preparatory Seminary, 5200 Shrewsbury Ave., St. Louis 63119 (South), 3500 St. Catherine St., Florissant 63033 (North).

**Montana:** Helena — Diocesan Pre-Seminary Program, Carroll College, Helena 59601.

**New Jersey:** Newark* — Immaculate Conception Seminary (major), Darlington, Mahwah. 07430 (scheduled to be transferred to Seton Hall University in September, 1984); College Seminary, Seton Hall University, South Orange. 07079.

**New Mexico:** Gallup — Cristo Rey College and High School Seminary, 205 E. Wilson, Gallup 87301.

Santa Fe* — Immaculate Heart of Mary Seminary, Mt. Carmel Rd., Santa Fe 87501.

**New York:** Brooklyn — Cathedral Preparatory Seminary of the Immaculate Conception, 555 Washington Ave., Brooklyn 11238; Cathedral Preparatory Seminary of the Immaculate Conception, 56-25 92nd St., Elmhurst. 11373; Cathedral College of the Immaculate Conception, 7200 Douglaston Parkway, Douglaston. 11362.

Buffalo — Christ the King Seminary (interdiocesan), 711 Knox Rd., East Aurora. 14052.

New York* — St. Joseph's Seminary (major), Dunwoodie, Yonkers. 10704: Cathedral Preparatory Seminary, 555 West End Ave., New York 10024.

Ogdensburg — Wadhams Hall, Riverside Dr., Ogdensburg 13669.

Rochester — Becket Hall, 314 Gregory St., Rochester 14620.

Rockville Centre — Seminary of the Immaculate Conception, Lloyd Harbor, Huntington, L.I. 11743; St. Pius X Preparatory Seminary, 1220 Front St., Uniondale, L.I. 11553.

St. Maron Diocese, Brooklyn — Our Lady of Lebanon Maronite Seminary, 7164 Alaska Ave. N.W., Washington, D.C. 20012.

Syracuse — Syracuse-Aquinas House, 702 Danforth St., Syracuse 13208.

**North Dakota:** Fargo — Cardinal Muench Seminary, 100 35th Ave. N.E., Fargo 58102.

**Ohio:** Cincinnati* — Mt. St. Mary's Seminary of the West, 6616 Beechmont Ave., Cincinnati. 45230 (division of the Athenaeum of Ohio).

Cleveland — St. Mary Seminary, 1227 Ansel Rd., Cleveland 44108; Borromeo College of Ohio, 28700 Euclid Ave. Wickliffe. 44092.

Columbus — Pontifical College Josephinum (national), theologate and college, Columbus. 43085.

Toledo — Divine Word High School Seminary (interdiocesan), 26581 W. River Rd., Perrysburg 43551.

**Oregon:** Portland* — Mt. Angel Seminary (college, pre-theology program, graduate school of theology), St. Benedict 97373; St. John Vianney House of Studies, 1538 Southwest Montgomery St., Portland 97201.

**Pennsylvania:** Allentown — Mary Immaculate Seminary (interdiocesan), Northampton 18067.

Erie — St. Mark's Seminary, 429 E. Grandview ℝlvd., Erie 16504.

Greensburg — St. Vincent Seminary (interdiocesan), Latrobe 15650.

Philadelphia* — Theological Seminary of St. Charles Borromeo, Overbrook. 19151.

Philadelphia Byzantine Rite (Ukrainians)* — St. Josaphat's Seminary, 201 Taylor St. N.E., Washington, D.C. 20017.

Pittsburgh Byzantine Rite (Ruthenians)* — Byzantine Catholic Seminary of Sts. Cyril and Methodius, 3605 Perrysville Ave., Pittsburgh. 15214.

Pittsburgh — St. Paul Seminary, 2900 Noblestown Rd. 15205.

Scranton — St. Pius X Seminary (college division), Dalton. 18414.

**Rhode Island:** Providence — House of Formation (college students), 485 Mount Pleasant Ave., Providence 02908.

**Texas:** Corpus Christi — Corpus Christi Minor Seminary, Rt. 1, Box 500. 78415.

Dallas — Holy Trinity Seminary (major), P.O. Box 153068, Irving. 75015.

El Paso — St. Charles Seminary High School, P.O. Box 17548, El Paso 79917.

Galveston-Houston — St. Mary's Seminary (major), 9845 Memorial Dr. Houston. 77024.

San Antonio* — The Assumption-St. John's Seminary (major), 2600 W. Woodlawn Ave., San Antonio 78284.

**Washington:** Spokane — Bishop White Seminary, E. 429 Sharp Ave., Spokane 99202.

**West Virginia:** Wheeling-Charleston — St. Joseph Preparatory Seminary, Rt. 6, Vienna. 26101; Seminary House of Studies (college residence), 1252 National Rd., Wheeling. 26003.

**Wisconsin:** Madison — Holy Name Seminary (High School), 3577 High Point Rd., Madison 53711.

Milwaukee* — St. Francis Seminary, School of Pastoral Ministry, and St. Francis Seminary, College Formation Program, 3257 S. Lake Dr., Milwaukee 53207.

## U.S. SEMINARIES AND STUDENTS, 1962-1984

(Source: *The Official Catholic Directory.*)

| Year | Dioc. Seminaries | Total Dioc. Students | Religious Seminaries Scholasticates | Total Rel. Students | Total Seminarians |
|------|------|------|------|------|------|
| 1962 | 98 | 23,662 | 447 | 22,657 | 46,319 |
| 1963 | 107 | 25,247 | 454 | 22,327 | 47,574 |
| 1964 | 112 | 26,701 | 459 | 22,049 | 48,750 |
| 1965 | 117 | 26,762 | 479 | 22,230 | 48,992 |
| 1966 | 126 | 26,252 | 481 | 21,862 | 48,114 |
| 1967 | 123 | 24,293 | 452 | 21,086 | 45,379 |
| 1968 | 124 | 22,232 | 437 | 17,604 | 39,836 |
| 1969 | 122 | 19,573 | 407 | 14,417 | 33,990 |
| 1970 | 118 | 17,317 | 383 | 11,589 | 28,906 |
| 1971 | 110 | 14,987 | 340 | 10,723 | 25,710 |
| 1972 | 106 | 13,554 | 326 | 9,409 | 22,963 |
| 1973 | 107 | 12,925 | 304 | 8,855 | 21,780 |
| 1974 | 109 | 11,765 | 293 | 7,583 | 19,348 |
| 1975 | 104 | 11,223 | 269 | 6,579 | 17,802 |
| 1976 | 102 | 11,015 | 269 | 6,232 | 17,247 |
| 1977 | 100 | 10,344 | 287 | 5,599 | 15,943 |
| 1978 | 98 | 9,560 | 278 | 5,438 | 14,998 |
| 1979 | 92 | 8,694 | 258 | 5,266 | 13,960 |
| 1980 | 92 | 8,552 | 252 | 4,674 | 13,226 |
| 1981 | 88 | 7,954 | 240 | 4,514 | 12,468 |
| 1982 | 86 | 7,625 | 217 | 4,020 | 11,645 |
| 1983 | 86 | 8,046 | 234 | 4,008 | 12,054 |
| 1984 | 86 | 7,486 | 233 | 3,776 | 11,262 |

## PONTIFICAL UNIVERSITIES

(Principal source: *Annuario Pontificio.*)

These universities, listed according to country of location, have been canonically erected and authorized by the Sacred Congregation for Catholic Education to award degrees in stated fields of study.

New laws and norms governing ecclesiastical universities and faculties were promulgated in the apostolic constitution *Sapientia Christiana*, issued Apr. 15, 1979.

**Argentina:** Pontifical Catholic University of S. Maria of Buenos Aires (June 16, 1960): Juncal 1912, Buenos Aires.

**Belgium:** Catholic University of Louvain (Dec.

9, 1425; 1834), with autonomous institutions for French- (Louvain) and Flemish- (Leuven) speaking: Place de l'Universite I, 1348 Louvain-La-Neuve (French); Naamsestraat 22B, 3000 Leuven 'Flemish).

**Brazil:** Pontifical Catholic University of Rio de Janeiro (Jan. 20, 1947): Rua Marques de Sao Vicente 209, 20000 Rio de Janeiro, Est. de Guanabara.

Pontifical Catholic University of Minas Gerais (June 5, 1983): Av. Dom Jose Gaspar 500, C.P. 2686, 30000 Belo Horizonte MG.

Pontifical Catholic University of Rio Grande do

Sul (Nov. 1, 1950): Praca Dom. Sebastiao 2, Porto Alegre, Estado do Rio Grande do Sul.

Pontifical Catholic University of Sao Paulo (Jan. 25, 1947): Rua Monte Alegre 984, Sao Paulo.

Pontifical University of Campinas (Sept. 8, 1956): Rua Marechal Deodoro 1099, Campinas, Sao Paulo.

**Canada:** Laval University (Mar. 15, 1876): Case Postale 460, Quebec G1K 7P4.

St. Paul University (formerly University of Ottawa) (Feb. 5, 1889): 223, Rue Main, Ottawa, K1S 1C4, Ontario.

University of Sherbrooke (Nov. 21, 1957): Chemin Ste.-Catherine, Cite Universitaire, Sherbrooke, Que. J1K 2R1.

**Chile:** Pontifical Catholic University of Chile (June 21, 1888): Avenida Bernardo O'Higgins 340, Casilla 114D, Santiago de Chile.

Catholic University of Valparaiso (Nov. 1, 1961): Avenida Brasil 2950, Casilla 4059, Valparaiso.

**Colombia:** Bolivarian Pontifical Catholic University (Aug. 16, 1945): Calle 52, N. 43-53, Medellin.

Pontifical Xaverian University (July 31, 1937): Carrera 7, N. 40-62, Bogota D.E.

**Cuba:** Catholic University of St. Thomas of Villanueva (May 4, 1957): Avenida Quenta 16,660, Marianao, Havana. Taken over by the Castro government in May, 1961.

**Ecuador:** Pontifical Catholic University of Ecuador (July 16, 1954): Doce de Octubre, N. 1076, Apartado 2184, Quito.

**Ethiopia:** University of Asmara (Sept. 8, 1960): Via Menelik II, 45, Post Office Box 1220, Asmara.

**France:** Catholic University of Lille (Nov. 18, 1875): Boulevard Vauban 60, 59046 Lille.

Catholic Faculties of Lyon (Nov. 22, 1875): 25, Rue du Plat, 69288 Lyon.

Catholic Institute of Paris (Aug. 11, 1875): 21, Rue d'Assas, 75270 Paris.

Catholic Institute of Toulouse (Nov. 15,1877): Rue de la Fonderie 31, 31068 Toulouse.

Catholic University of the West (Sept. 16, 1875): 3, Place Andre Leroy, B.P. 808, 49005 Angers.

**Germany:** Eichstatt Catholic University (Apr. 1, 1980): Ostenstrasse 26-28, D-8078, Eichstatt.

**Guatemala:** Rafael Landivar University (Oct. 18, 1961): 17 Calle 8-64, Z 10 Guatemala.

**Ireland:** St. Patrick's College (Mar. 29, 1896): Maynooth, Co. Kildare.

**Italy:** Catholic University of the Sacred Heart (Dec. 25, 1920): Largo Gemelli 1, 20123 Milan.

**Japan:** *Jochi Daigaku* (Sophia University) (Mar. 29, 1913): Chiyoda-Ku, Kioi-cho 7, Tokyo.

**Lebanon:** St. Joseph University of Beirut (Mar. 25, 1881): Rue de l'Universite St.-Joseph, Boite Postale 293, Beyrouth.

**Netherlands:** Nijmegen Roman Catholic University (June 29, 1923): Wilhelminasingel 13, Nijmegen.

**Panama:** University of S. Maria la Antigua (May 27, 1965): Apartado 2143, Panama 1.

**Paraguay:** Catholic University of Our Lady of the Assumption (Feb. 2, 1965): Comuneros e Independencia Nacional, Asuncion.

**Peru:** Pontifical Catholic University of Peru (Sept. 30, 1942): Apartado 1761, Lima.

**Philippine Islands:** Pontifical University of Santo Tomas (Nov. 20, 1645): Espana Street, Manila.

**Poland:** Catholic University of Lublin (July 25, 1920): Aleje Raclawickie 14, Skr. Poczt. 279, 20-950, Lublin.

Pontifical Academy of Theology of Krakow (Dec. 8, 1981): Ul. Podzamcze 8, 31-003 Krakow.

**Portugal:** Portuguese Catholic University (Nov. 1, 1967): Palma de Cima, 1600 Lisbon.

**Puerto Rico:** Catholic University of Puerto Rico (Aug. 15, 1972): Ponce, Puerto Rico 00731.

**Spain:** Catholic University of Navarra (Aug. 6, 1960): Ciudad Universitaria, Pamplona.

Pontifical University "Comillas" (Mar. 29, 1904): Canto Blanco, Apartado Postal 3082, Madrid 34.

Pontifical University of Salamanca (Sept. 25, 1940): Compania 1, Apartado 541, Salamanca.

University of Deusto (Aug. 10, 1963): Avenida de las Universidades, 28, Apartado 1, Bilbao.

**Taiwan (China):** Fu Jen Catholic University (Nov. 15, 1923, at Peking; reconstituted at Taipeh, Sept. 8, 1961): Hsinchuang, Taipeh Hsien.

**United States:** Catholic University of America (Mar. 7, 1889): Washington, D.C. 20064.

Georgetown University (Mar. 30, 1833): 37th and O Sts. N.W., Washington, D.C. 20057.

Niagara University (June 21, 1956): Niagara University, N.Y. 14109.

**Venezuela:** Catholic University "Andres Bello" (Sept. 29, 1963): Esquina Jesuitas, Apartado 422, Caracas.

## ECCLESIASTICAL FACULTIES

(Principal Source: *Annuario Pontificio*)

These faculties in Catholic seminaries and universities, listed according to country of location, have been canonically erected and authorized by the Sacred Congregation for Catholic Education to award degrees in stated fields of study. In addition to those listed here, there are other faculties of theology or philosophy in state universities and for members of certain religious orders only.

**Argentina:** Faculties of Philosophy and Theology, San Miguel (Sept. 8, 1932).

**Australia:** Institute of Theology, Sydney (Feb. 2, 1954).

**Austria:** Theological Faculty, Linz (Dec. 25, 1978).

**Brazil:** Ecclesiastical Faculty of Philosophy "John Paul II," Rio de Janeiro Aug. 6, 1981.

Philosophical and Theological Faculties of the Company of Jesus, Belo Horizonte (July 15, 1941 and Mar. 30, 1945).

**Canada:** Pontifical Institute of Medieval Studies, Toronto (Oct. 18, 1939).

Dominican Faculty of Theology of Canada, Ottawa (1965; Nov. 15, 1975).

Regis College — Toronto Section of the Jesuit Faculty of Theology in Canada, Toronto (Feb. 17, 1956; Dec. 25, 1977).

College of Immaculate Conception — Montreal Section of Jesuit Faculties in Canada (Sept. 8, 1932).

**France:** Centre Sevres — Faculties of Theology and Philosophy of the Jesuits, Paris (Sept. 8, 1932).

**Germany:** Theological Faculty, Paderborn (June 11, 1966).

Theological Faculty of the Major Episcopal Seminary, Trier (Sept. 8, 1955)

Philosophical Faculty, Munich (1932; Oct. 25, 1971).

Theological-Philosophical Faculty, Frankfurt (1932; June 7, 1971).

Theological Faculty, Fulda (Dec. 22, 1978).

**Great Britain:** Heythrop College, University of London, London (Nov. 1, 1964). Theology, philosophy.

**India:** "Jnana Deepa" (Pontifical Athenaeum), Institute of Philosophy and Religion, Poona (July 27, 1926).

Pontifical Institute of Theology and Philosophy, Alwaye, Kerala (Feb. 24, 1972).

"Vidyajyoti," Institute of Religious Studies, Faculty of Theology, Delhi (1932; Dec. 9, 1974).

Dharmaran Pontifical Institute of Theology and Philosophy, Bangalore (Jan. 6, 1976). Raised to university status May, 1984.

Faculty of Theology, Ranchi (Aug. 15, 1982).

Pontifical Oriental Institute of Religious Studies, Kottayam (July 3, 1982).

St. Peter's Pontifical Institute of Theology, Bangalore (Jan. 6, 1976).

"Satya Nilayam," Institute of Philosophy and Culture. Faculty of Philosophy, Madras (Sept. 8, 1932; Dec. 15, 1976).

**Israel:** French Biblical and Archeological School, Jerusalem (founded 1890; approved Sept. 17, 1892; canonically approved to confer Doctorate in Biblical Science, June 29, 1983).

**Italy:** Interregional Theological Faculty, Milan (Aug. 8, 1935).

Pontifical Theological Faculty of the Most Sacred Heart of Jesus, Cagliari, of the Pontifical Regional Seminary of Sardinia (July 5, 1927).

Pontifical Ambrosian Institute of Sacred Music, Milan (Mar. 12, 1940).

Theological Faculty of Sicily, Palermo (Dec. 8, 1980).

Theological Faculty of Southern Italy, Naples. Two sections: St. Thomas Aquinas Capodimonte (Oct. 31, 1941) and St. Louis Posillipo (Mar. 16, 1918). Pastoral Ignatian Institute, Messina (July 31, 1972).

Faculty of Philosophy "Aloisianum," Gallarate (1937; Mar. 20, 1974).

**Ivory Coast:** Catholic Institute of West Africa, Abidjan (Aug. 12, 1975).

**Lebanon:** Faculty of Theology, University of the Holy Spirit, Kaslik (May 30, 1982).

**Madagascar:** Superior Institute of Theology, at the Regional Seminary of Antananarivo, Ambatoroka-Antananarivo (Apr. 21, 1960).

**Malta:** Faculty of Theology, Tal-Virtu (Nov. 22, 1769).

**Mexico:** Theological Faculty of Mexico, Mexico City (June 29, 1982).

**Nigeria:** Catholic Institute of West Africa, Port Harcourt (Nov. 30, 1981).

**Peru:** Pontifical and Civil Faculty of Theology, Lima (July 25, 1571).

**Poland:** Theological Faculty, Poznan (1969; pontifical designation, June 2, 1974).

**Spain:** Theological Faculty of Barcelona, of the Major Seminary of Barcelona and the College of St. Francis Borgia of San Cugat del Valles (Mar. 7, 1968).

Theological Faculty, Granada (1940; July 31, 1973).

Theological Faculty of the North, of the Metropolitan Seminary of Burgos and the Diocesan Seminary of Vitoria (Feb. 6, 1967).

Theological Faculty "San Vicente Ferrer" (two sections), Valencia (Jan. 23, 1974).

**Switzerland:** Theological Faculty, Chur (Jan. 1, 1974).

Theological Faculty, Luzerne (Dec. 25, 1973).

**United States:** St. Mary's Seminary and University. School of Theology, Baltimore (May 1, 1822).

St. Mary of the Lake Faculty of Theology, Chicago (Sept. 30, 1929).

The Jesuit School of Theology, Berkeley, Calif. (Feb. 2, 1934, as "Alma College," Los Gatos, Calif.).

Weston School of Theology, Cambridge, Mass. (Oct. 18, 1932).

**Vietnam:** Theological Faculty of the Pontifical National Seminary of St. Pius X, Dalat (July 31, 1965). Activities suppressed.

**The Pontifical College Josephinum** (Theologate and College) at Columbus, Ohio, is a national pontifical seminary. Established Sept. 1, 1888, it is immediately subject to the Holy See.

## PONTIFICAL UNIVERSITIES AND INSTITUTES IN ROME

(Source: *Annuario Pontificio*.)

**Pontifical Gregorian University** (1552): Piazza della Pilotta, 4, 00187 Rome. Associated with the university are:

The **Pontifical Biblical Institute** (May 7, 1909): Via della Pilotta, 25, 00187 Rome.

The **Pontifical Institute of Oriental Studies** (Oct. 15, 1917): Piazza S. Maria Maggiore, 7, 00185 Rome.

**Pontifical Lateran University** (1773). Piazza S. Giovanni in Laterano, 4, 00184 Rome.

**Pontifical Urban University** (1627): Via Urban VIII, 16, 00165 Rome.

**Pontifical University of St. Thomas Aquinas (Angelicum)** (1580), of the Order of Preachers: Largo Angelicum, 1, 00184 Rome.

**Pontifical University Salesianum** (May 3, 1940; university designation May 24, 1973), of the Salesians of Don Bosco: Piazza dell' Ateneo Salesiano, 1, 00139 Rome. Associated with the university is the **Pontifical Institute of Higher Latin Studies,** known as the **Faculty of Christian and Classical Letters** (Feb. 22, 1964).

**Pontifical Athenaeum of St. Anselm** (1687), of the Benedictines: Piazza dei Cavalieri di Malta, 5, 00153 Rome.

**Pontifical Athenaeum "Antonianum"** (of St.

Anthony) (May 17, 1933), of the Order of Friars Minor: Via Merulana, 124, 00185 Rome.

**Pontifical Institute of Sacred Music** (1911; May 24, 1931): Piazza S. Agostino, 20-A, 00186, Rome.

**Pontifical Institute of Christian Archeology** (Dec. 11, 1925): Via Napoleone III, 1, 00185 Rome.

**Pontifical Theological Faculty "St. Bonaventure"** (Dec. 18, 1587), of the Order of Friars Minor Conventual: Via del Serafico, 1, 00142 Rome.

**Pontifical Theological Faculty, Pontifical Institute of Spirituality "Teresianum"** (1935), of the Discalced Carmelites: Piazza San Pancrazio, 5-A, 00152 Rome.

**Pontifical Theological Faculty "Marianum"** (1398), of the Servants of Mary: Viale Trente Aprile, 6, 00153 Rome.

**Pontifical Institute of Arabic and Islamic Studies** (1926), of the White Fathers: Piazza S. Apollinare, 49, 00186 Rome.

**Pontifical Faculty of Educational Science "Auxilium"** (June 27, 1970), of the Daughters of Mary, Help of Christians: Via Cremolino, 141, 00166 Rome.

**Pontifical Institute "Regina Mundi"** (1954): Lungotevere Tor di Nona, 7, 00186 Rome.

## PONTIFICAL ACADEMY OF SCIENCES

(Sources: *Annuario Pontificio*, NC News Service. Membership as of July 1, 1984.)

The Pontifical Academy of Sciences was constituted in its present form by Pius XI Oct. 28, 1936, in virtue of *In Multis Solaciis*, a document issued on his own initiative.

The academy is the only supranational body of its kind in the world, with a pope-selected, life-long membership of outstanding mathematicians and experimental scientists from many countries. The normal complement of members is 70; the total number, however, includes additional honorary and supernumerary members. Non-Catholics as well as Catholics belong to the academy.

Purposes of the academy are to honor pure science and its practitioners, to promote the freedom of pure science and to foster research.

The academy traces its origin to the *Linceorum Academia* (Academy of the Lynxes — its symbol) founded in Rome Aug. 17, 1603. Pius IX reorganized this body and gave it a new name — *Pontificia Accademia dei Nuovi Lincei* — in 1847. It was taken over by the Italian state in 1870 and called the *Accademia Nazionale dei Lincei*. Leo XIII reconstituted it with a new charter in 1887. Pius XI designated the Vatican Gardens as the site of academy headquarters in 1922 and gave it its present title and status in 1936. Four years later he gave the title of Excellency to its members.

### Members in U.S.

Scientists in the U.S. who presently hold membership in the Academy are listed below according to year of appointment.

1936 (Oct. 28): Franco Rasetti, professor emeritus of physics at John's Hopkins University, Baltimore, Md.; George Speri-Sperti, president and director of the Institute Divi Thomae in the Athanaeum of Ohio.

1948 (May 29): Adelbert Doisy, professor emeritus of biochemistry at St. Louis University.

1964 (Sept. 24): William Wilson Morgan, professor emeritus of astronomy at the University of Chicago.

1970 (Apr. 10): Albert Szent-Gyorgyi, director of Institute for Muscle Research at the Marine Biological Laboratory, Woods Hole, Mass.

1974 (June 24): Rita Levi-Montalcini, professor of biology at Washington University, St. Louis, Mo.; Severo Ochoa, professor emeritus of the

Roche Institute of Molecular Biology, Nutley, N.J.; Marshall Warren Nirenberg, professor of genetics and biochemistry at the National Institutes of Health, Bethesda, Md.

1975 (Dec. 2): George Palade, professor of cellular biology at Yale University, New Haven, Conn.; Victor Weisskopf, professor of physics at the Massachusetts Institute of Technology, Cambridge, Mass.

1978 (Apr. 17): David Baltimore, professor of biology, Har Gobind Khorana, professor of biochemistry, and Alexander Rich, professor of biophysics — all at the Massachusetts Institute of Technology, Cambridge, Mass.; Roger Walcott Sperry, professor of psychobiology, California Institute of Technology, Pasadena, Calif.

1981 (May 13): Christian Anfinsen, professor of biochemistry at the National Institutes of Health, Bethesda, Md.

1983 (Feb. 12): Charles Townes, professor of physics at the University of California at Berkeley.

Deceased U.S. members of the Academy were: George D. Birkhoff, Alexis Carrel, Herbert Sidney Langfeld, Robert A. Millikan, Thomas H. Morgan, Theodore von Karman, Victor F. Hess, Peter Debye, Hugh Stott Taylor.

### Members in Other Countries

Other members of the Academy are listed below according to country of location; dates of their selection are given in parentheses.

Argentina: Luis F. Leloir (Apr. 22, 1968).

Austria: Hans Tuppy (Apr. 10, 1970).

Belgium: Christian de Duve (Apr. 10, 1970).

Brazil: Carlos Chagas (Aug. 18, 1961); Johanna Dobereiner (Apr. 17, 1978); Crodowaldo Pavan (Apr. 17, 1978).

Canada: Gerhard Herzberg (Sept. 24, 1964); Karel Wiesner (Apr. 17, 1978).

Chile: Hector Croxatto Rezzio (Dec. 2, 1975).

Denmark: Bengt Georg Stromgren (Dec. 2, 1975); Aage Bohr (Apr. 17, 1978).

France: Louis de Broglie (Apr. 5, 1955); Pierre Raphael Lepine (Sept. 24, 1964); Louis Leprince-Ringuet (Aug. 18, 1961); Jerome Lejeune (June 24, 1974); Andre Blanc-LaPierre (Apr. 17, 1978), Anatole Abragam (May 13, 1981), Andre Lichnerowicz (May 13, 1981), Bernard Pullman (May 13, 1981).

Germany: Rudolf L. Mossbauer (Apr. 10, 1970), Manfried Eigen (May 13, 1981).
Ghana: Daniel Azei Bekoe (Sept. 26, 1983).
Great Britain: Hermann Alexander Bruck (Apr. 5, 1955); Paul Adrien Dirac (Aug. 18, 1961); Alan Lloyd Hodgkin (Apr. 22, 1968); Alfred R. Ubbelohde (Apr. 22, 1968); Percy C. C. Garnham (Apr. 10, 1970); George Porter (June 24, 1974); Martin Ryle (Dec. 2, 1975), Max Ferdinand Perutz (May 13, 1981); Stanley Keith Runcorn (Sept. 13, 1981).
Hungary: Janos Szentagothai (May 13, 1981).
India: Mambilliralathil Govind Kumar Menon (May 13, 1981).
Israel: Michael Sela (Dec. 2, 1975).
Italy: Giovanni Battista Bonino (May 23, 1942); Bettolo Giovanni Battista Marini (Apr. 22, 1968); Giuseppe Colombo (Apr. 17, 1978); Giuseppe Moruzzi (Apr. 17, 1978); Giampietro Puppi (Apr. 17, 1978), Ennio De Giorgi (May 13, 1981), Abdus Salam (May 13, 1981).
Japan: Hamao Umezawa (Sept. 26, 1983).

Kenya: Thomas R. Odhiambo (May 13, 1981).
Netherlands: Jan Hendrik Oort (Aug. 18, 1961).
Pakistan: Salimuzzaman Siddiqui (Sept. 24, 1964).
Poland: Stanislao Lojasiewicz (Feb. 12, 1983).
Portugal: Antonio De Almeida (Apr. 8, 1961).
Spain: Manuel Lora Tomayo (Sept. 24, 1964).
Sweden: Sven Horstadius (Aug. 18, 1961).
Switzerland: John Carew Eccles (Apr. 8, 1961), Thomas Lambo (June 24, 1974), Werner Arber (May 13, 1981).
Venezuela: Marcel Roche (Apr. 10, 1970).
Zaire: Wa Kalengo Malu (Sept. 26, 1983).
Ex officio members: Rev. George V. Coyne, S.J., director of Vatican Observatory; Most Rev. Martino Giusti, prefect emeritus of the Secret Vatican Archives.
Honorary members: Silvio Ranzi, professor emeritus of biology and zoology of the University of Milan (May 13, 1981); Pietro Salviucci, former chancellor of the Pontifical Academy of Sciences (Nov. 18, 1982).
President: Carlos Chagas (Nov. 9, 1972).

# VATICAN-ITALIAN CONCORDAT

A new concordat on relations between the Vatican and Italy, designed to replace the one in effect since 1929, was signed Feb. 18, 1984, by Papal Secretary of State Cardinal Agostino Casaroli and Italian Prime Minister Bettino Craxi. In prospect since 1967 and in active negotiation since 1976, it bears the title, "An Agreement on the Revision of the Lateran Concordat."

The 14 articles of the agreement reflect the effects on church-state relations of several developments, principally: (1) the "process of political and social transformation" in Italy since 1929, and (2) church teaching on the civil rights of all religions, stated by the Second Vatican Council in its *Declaration on Religious Liberty.*

Church and state, "independent and sovereign" in their respective spheres, are committed to collaboration for the common good.

## Provisions

Accordingly, the agreement ends the privileged status of the Catholic Church as the official religion of Italy. It refers, not to "the sacred character of the Eternal City of Rome," but to the "particular significance of Rome for Catholicism." It provides that Catholic religious teaching in state schools shall be optional, and makes marriage annulments by church tribunals subject to civil review before ratification by the state.

The treaty guarantees the rights of the Church to:

- perform its pastoral mission;
- oversee dioceses, other institutions, and priests;
- establish schools;
- minister in public institutions such as hospitals, correctional institutions and the armed forces.

It recognizes Sundays as holidays, along with Catholic religious feast days to be agreed upon.

It provides for the protection of church buildings, and calls on Church and state to safeguard the country's historical and artistic treasures.

The concordat provides also for the continuing exemption of priests, deacons and members of religious orders from military service, but requires them to perform some kind of civil service instead.

It was expected that the tax-exempt status of church organizations outside the Vatican would continue in effect.

## Subsidies To End

Government subsidies to the Church and related financial issues not covered in the concordat were the subjects of agreement reached Aug. 2 in the Italian Parliament. Substantially, the arrangement envisaged the end of subsidies in 1990, coupled with provisions for tax deductible contributions for support of the personnel and institutions of the Church.

Pope John Paul noted the "historic importance" of the concordat the day after it was signed. "This was a treaty that Paul VI had foreseen and encouraged, as a sign of renewed agreement between the Church and the Italian State," he said. He called it a significant legal basis for relations with the state, "an ideal inspiration for the generous and creative contribution that the church community is called on to give toward the moral good and civic progress of the nation."

Cardinal Casaroli said the concordat is "an instrument of agreement, not of privilege."

Final ratification of the concordat by parliament was expected in the fall of 1984.

**The National Conference of Catholic Charities:** Established in 1910 to help advance and promote the charitable programs and activities of Catholic community and social service agencies in the United States. As the central and national organization for this purpose, it services member agencies and institutions by consultation, information and assistance in planning and evaluating social service programs under Catholic auspices.

The principal fields of service in which Catholic Charities agencies are engaged are family counseling, child welfare, services for unmarried mothers, community services, day care centers, neighborhood center programs, and care of the aged. Community organization, social action and parish social ministry are also functions of Catholic Charities.

The NCCC conducts research with respect to service to the aging, community self-help programs, the institutional care of children, and other social service projects. It represents the Catholic philosophy of social service to government agencies and personnel, and to professional organizations in the field. Its publications include *Charities USA*, a monthly membership magazine, and *Social Thought*, a quarterly co-sponsored with the National School of Social Service of the Catholic University of America.

The NCCC membership includes 575 diocesan agencies and branches, 200 institutions and 3,000 individuals.

Rev. Thomas J. Harvey is executive director of the conference, with offices at 1346 Connecticut Ave. N.W., Washington, D.C. 20036.

**The Society of St. Vincent de Paul,** originally called the Conference of Charity: An association of Catholic laity devoted to personal service of the poor through the spiritual and corporal works of mercy. The first conference was formed at Paris in 1833 by Frederic Ozanam and his associates.

The first conference in the U.S. was organized in 1845 at St. Louis. There are now approximately 4,700 units of the society in this country, with a membership of about 36,000.

In the past 50 years, members of the society in this country have distributed among poor persons financial and other forms of assistance valued at approximately $400 million.

U.S. Vincentian councils and conferences participating in "twinning" programs assist their poorer counterparts abroad by sending them correspondence, information and financial aid on a continuing basis.

Under the society's revised regulations, women are being admitted to membership. Increasing emphasis is being given to stores and rehabilitation workshops of the society through which persons with marginal income can purchase refurbished goods at minimal cost. Handicapped persons are employed in renovating goods and store operations.

Amin A. de Tarrazi of Paris, France, is president of the Council General, the governing body of the society. There are approximately 750,000 members in the world.

The office of the U.S. Superior Council is located at 4140 Lindell Blvd., St. Louis, Mo. 63108.

**Catholic Health Association of the United States,** formerly Catholic Hospital Association: Founded in 1915, is a service organization for more than 900 Catholic-sponsored health care facilities located throughout the United States.

The association is dedicated to the healing mission of the Church by promoting health of those who are sick or infirm because of age or disability; by respecting human dignity in the experience of sickness and death; and by fostering physical, psychological, emotional, spiritual and social well-being of people.

John E. Curley, Jr., is president. Executive offices are located at 4455 Woodson Rd., St. Louis, Mo. 63134.

*The Official Catholic Directory, 1984,* reported 638 Catholic general hospitals with 172,015 beds treating 36,538,557 patients; 93 special hospitals with 6,491 beds treating 666,387; and 124 nurses' schools with 22,915 students.

**National Association of Catholic Chaplains:** Founded in 1965. Membership is approximately 3,200.

Rev. Edward Dietrich is executive director. Address: 3257 S. Lake Dr., Milwaukee Wis. 53207.

## FACILITIES FOR RETIRED AND AGED PERSONS

(Sources: Almanac survey, *The Official Catholic Directory.*)

*This list covers residence, health care and other facilities for the retired and aged under Catholic auspices. Information includes name, type of facility if not evident from the title, address, and total capacity (in parentheses); unless noted otherwise, facilities are for both men and women. Many facilities for the aged offer intermediate nursing care.*

**Alabama:** Allen Memorial Home (Skilled Nursing), 735 S. Washington Ave., Mobile 36603 (94).

Sacred Heart Residence Little Sisters of the Poor, 1655 McGill Ave., Mobile 36604 (120).

Villa Mercy (Skilled Nursing Facility, Hospice, Home Health Agency), P.O. Box 1096, Daphne 36526. Specialized hospital, not restricted to elderly.

**Arizona:** Sacred Heart Home for the Aged, Little Sisters of the Poor, 1110 N. 16th St., Phoenix 85006 (128).

Villa Maria de Guadalupe Geriatric Center (Skilled Nursing Facility and Apartments), 4310 E. Grant Rd., Tucson 85712 (93 beds, 50 apartments).

**Arkansas:** Benedictine Manor (Retirement Home), 2nd and Grand Sts., Hot Springs 71901 (100).

**California:** Casa Manana Inn, 3700 N. Sutter St., Stockton 95204 (175).

Cathedral Plaza, 1551 Third Ave., San Diego 92101 (222 apartments).

Ellis Seniors Residence, 3263 First Ave., Sacramento 95817 (18).

Francis of Assisi Community, 148 Guerrero St., San Francisco 94103 (140). For elderly and handicapped.

Guadalupe Plaza, 4142 42nd St., San Diego 92105 (111 apartments).

Little Flower Haven (Residential Care Facility for Retired), 8585 La Mesa Blvd., La Mesa 92041 (93).

Little Sisters of the Poor, 300 Lake St., San Francisco 94118 (120).

Little Sisters of the Poor, Jeanne Jugan Residence, 2100 South Western Ave., San Pedro, Calif. 90732 (120).

Madonna Residence (Retirement Home for Women over 62), 1055 Pine St., San Francisco 94109 (46).

Marian Residence (Retirement Home), 124 S. College Dr., Santa Maria 93454 (58).

Nazareth House, 2121 N. 1st St., Fresno 93703 (91).

Nazareth House, 3333 Manning Ave., Los Angeles 90064 (137).

Nazareth House, 245 Nova Albion Way, Terra Linda, San Rafael 94903 (145).

Nazareth House Retirement Home, 6333 Rancho Mission Rd., San Diego 92108 (122).

Our Lady of Fatima Villa (Skilled Nursing Facility, Women), 20400 Saratoga/Los Gatos Rd., Saratoga 95070 (85).

Our Lady's Home, 3431 Foothill Blvd., Oakland 94601 (130).

St. Francis Home (Elderly and Retired Women), 1718 W. 6th St., Santa Ana 92703 (83).

St. John of God Nursing Hospital and Residence, 2035 W. Adams Blvd., Los Angeles 90018.

Villa Scalabrini (Retirement Center), 10631 Vinedale St., Sun Valley 91352 (125).

Villa Siena (Residence and Intermediate Care), 1855 Miramonte Ave., Mountain View 94040 (50, residence; 20, intermediate care).

**Colorado:** Little Sisters of the Poor, 3629 W. 29th Ave., Denver 80211 (118).

St. Elizabeth Center (Retirement Home), 2825 W. 32nd Ave., Denver 80211 (187).

**Connecticut:** Augustana Homes (Residence), Simeon Rd., Bethel 06801.

Carmel Ridge Estates, Carmelite Sisters for the Aged and Infirm, 6448 Main St., Trumbull, 06611 (36 units).

Matulaitis Nursing Home, Putnam 06260.

Monsignor Bojnowski Manor, Inc. (Skilled Nursing Facility), 50 Pulaski St., New Britain 06053 (60).

Notre Dame Convalescent Home, 76 West Rocks Rd., Norwalk 06851 (60).

Regina Pacis Villa (Residence), RFD No. 1, Pomfret Center 06259 (16).

St. Joseph Guest Home (Women, Employed and Retired), 311 Greene St., New Haven 06511 (80).

St. Joseph's Home for the Aged, 88 Jackson St., Willimantic 06226 (37).

St. Joseph's Manor, Carmelite Srs. for Aged and Infirm, 6448 Main St., Trumbull 06611 (285).

St. Joseph's Residence, Little Sisters of the Poor, 1365 Enfield St., Enfield, Conn. 06082 (94)

St. Lucian's Home for the Aged, 532 Burritt St., New Britain 06053 (54).

St. Mary's Home (Residence and Health Care Facility), 291 Steele Rd., W. Hartford 06117 (177).

Teresian Towers, Carmelite Sisters for Aged and Infirm, 6454 Main St., Trumbull 06611 (50 units).

Villa Maria Rest Home for the Aged, West St., Thompson 06277 (30).

**Delaware:** The Antonian, 1701 W. 10th St., Wilmington 19805 (136).

Jeanne Jugan Residence, Little Sisters of the Poor, 185 Salem Church Rd., Newark 19713 (123).

Marydale, 135 Jeandell Dr., Newark 19713 (108 apartments).

St. Patrick's House, Inc., 14th and French Sts., Wilmington 19801 (14).

**District of Columbia:** Jeanne Jugan Residence — St. Joseph' Villa, Little Sisters of the Poor, 4200 Harewood Rd., N.E. Washington 20017.

**Florida:** All Saints Home for the Aged, 2040 Riverside Ave., Jacksonville 32204 (57).

Carroll Manor (Retirement Apartments), 3667 S. Miami Ave., Miami 33133 (236 apartments).

Casa Calderon, Inc., 800 W. Virginia St., Tallahassee 32304. Apartments (111).

Cor Jesu Retirement Center, 4918 N. Habana Ave., Tampa 33614 (75).

Haven of Our Lady of Peace (Residence and Health Care Facility), 5203 N. 9th Ave., Pensacola 32504 (88).

Maria Manor Health Care Center, 10300 4th St. N., St. Petersburg 33702 (274).

Marian Towers, Inc. (Retirement Apartments), 17505 North Bay Rd., Miami Beach 33160.

Noreen McKeen Residence for Geriatric Care, 315 Flagler Dr. S., W. Palm Beach 33401.

Pennsylvania Retirement Residence, 208 Evernia St., W. Palm Beach 33401 (190).

St. Andrew Towers (Retirement Apartments), 2700 N.W. 99th Ave., Coral Springs 33065.

St. Dominic Gardens, 5849 N.W. 7th St., Miami 33126.

St. Elizabeth Gardens, Inc. (Retirement Apartments), 801 N.E. 33rd St., Pompano Beach 33064.

St. Joseph's Residence, 3485 N.W. 30th St., Ft. Lauderdale 33311.

St. Vincent Residence, Inc. (Retirement Home), 1618 Polk St., Hollywood 33020 (19).

**Illinois:** Addolorato Villa (Home for Aged), Highway 83, McHenry Rd., Wheeling 60090 (98).

Alvernia Manor (Sheltered Care), 1598 Main St., Lemont 60439 (56).

Carlyle Healthcare Center, 501 Clinton St., Carlyle 62231 (124).

Carmelite Carefree Village, 8419 Bailey Rd., Darien 60559 (96 units, 150 residents).

Cortland Manor Retirement Home, 1900 N. Karlow, Chicago 68639. (52).

Holy Family Health Center, 2380 Dempster, Des Plaines 60016 (272).

Holy Family Villa (Residence and Health Care,), Lemont 60439 (102).

Huber Memorial Home (Residence, Women), 1000 30th St., Rock Island 61201 (16).

Jugan Terrace, Little Sisters of the Poor, 2300 N. Racine, Chicago 60614 (50 apartments).

Little Sisters of the Poor Center for the Aging, 2325 N. Lakewood Ave., Chicago, Ill. 60614 (120).

Marian Heights Apartments (Elderly, Handicapped), 20 Oak St., Alton 62002 (133).

Marian Park, Inc., 2126 W. Roosevelt Rd., Wheaton 60187 (117 apartments).

Maryhaven, Inc. (Intermediate Care Facility), 1700 E. Lake Ave., Glenview 60025 (147).

Mayslake Village (Retirement Apartments), 1801 35th St., Oak Brook 60521 (630 apartments).

Meredith Memorial Home, Public Square, Belleville 62220 (90).

Merkle-Knipprath Nursing Home, Rt. 1, Franciscan Brothers. Clifton 60927 (100).

Mother Theresa Home (Sheltered and Intermediate Care), 1270 Main St., Lemont 60439 (57).

Nazarethville (Intermediate Care), 300 River Rd., Des Plaines 60016 (84).

Our Lady of Angels Retirement Home, 1201 Wyoming, Joliet 60435 (100).

Our Lady of the Snows Apartment Community (Retirement Apartment Community; Health Care Program), 9500 W. Ill., Rt. 15, Belleville 62223 (200).

Pope John Paul I Apartments (Elderly and Handicapped), 1 Pope John Paul Plaza, Springfield 62703 (160).

Resurrection Retirement Community, 7266 W. Peterson Ave., Chicago, 60631 (311 apartments).

Rosary Hill Home (Residence), 9000 W. 81st St., Justice 60458 (50).

St. Andrew Home for the Aged, 7000 N. Newark Ave., Niles 60648 (198).

St. Ann's Health Care Center, 770 State St., Chester 62233 (92).

St. Benedict Home, 6930 W. Touhy Ave., Niles 60648 (52).

St. Joseph's Home (Sheltered and Intermediate Care), 3306 S. 6th St. Rd., Springfield 62703 (121).

St. Joseph's Home (Sheltered and Intermediate Care), 2223 W. Heading Ave., Peoria 61604 (200).

St. Joseph's Home for the Aged, 649 E. Jefferson St., Freeport 61032 (109).

St. Joseph's Home for the Elderly, 80 W. Northwest Hwy., Palatine 60067 (130).

St. Joseph's Home of Chicago, Inc., 2650 N. Ridgeway Ave., Chicago 60647 (173).

St. Patrick's Residence (Sheltered and Intermediate Care), 22 E. Clinton St., Joliet 60431 (197).

Villa Saint Cyril (Residence), 1111 St. John's Ave., Highland Park 60035 (80).

Villa Scalabrini (Sheltered, Intermediate and Skilled), 480 N. Wolf Rd., Northlake 60164 (265).

**Indiana:** Little Company of Mary Health Facility, San Pierre 46374 (180).

Providence Retirement Home, 703 E. Spring St., New Albany 47150 (85).

Regina Pacis Home (Skilled Nursing and Intermediate Care Facility), 3900 Washington Ave., Evansville 47715 (154).

Sacred Heart Home (Comprehensive Nursing), R.R. 2, Avilla 46710 (130). LaVerna Terrace, same address; independent living for senior citizens, handicapped and disabled (51 units).

St. Anne Home (Residence and Comprehensive Nursing), 1900 Randalia Dr., Ft. Wayne 46805 (154).

St. Anthony Medical Center and St. Anthony Home, Inc.; 201 Franciscan Rd., Crown Point 46307 (200).

St. Augustine Home for the Aged, Little Sisters of the Poor, 2345 W. 86th St., Indianapolis 46260 (120).

St. John's Home for the Aged, Little Sisters of the Poor, 1236 Lincoln Ave., Evansville 47714 (130).

St. Paul Hermitage, 501 N. 17th St., Beech Grove 46107 (105).

**Iowa:** The Alverno Health Care Facility, 849 13th Ave. N., Clinton 52732 (136).

Bishop Drumm Retirement Center, 5387 Winwood Dr., Johnston 50131 (120 beds; 87 apartments).

Hallmar-Mercy Hospital, 701 Tenth St. S.E., Cedar Rapids 52403 (64 residential; 12 skilled nursing facility).

Holy Spirit Retirement Home (Intermediate Care), 1701 W. 25th St., Sioux City 51103 (94).

Kahl Home for the Aged and Infirm (Intermediate Care Facility), 1101 W. 9th St., Davenport 52804 (125).

The Marian Home, 2400 6th Ave. North, Fort Dodge 50501 (97) and Marian Village (Apartments), 2320 6th Ave. North, Fort Dodge 50501.

Mary of the Angels Home (Women, Employed and Retired), 605 Bluff St., Dubuque 52001 (85).

Padre Pio Health Care Center, Stonehill Care Center (Residence, Nursing Home), 3485 Windsor, Dubuque 52001 (250).

Ritter Home for Retired Women, 1837 Sunnyside Ave., Burlington 52601 (6).

St. Anthony Nursing Home (Intermediate Care), 406 E. Anthony St., Carroll 51401 (80).

St. Francis Continuation Care and Nursing Home Center, Burlington 52601 (29 skilled nursing; 59 intermediate care).

**Kansas:** Catholic Center for the Aging, 3411 E. Zimmerly, Wichita 67218 (150).

Mt. Joseph (Intermediate Care Facility), 1110 W. 11, R.R. 1, Concordia 66901 (100).

St. John Rest Home (Intermediate Care Facility), 701 Seventh St., Victoria 67671 (60).

St. John's of Hays (Skilled Facility), 24th and Canterbury Rd., Hays 67601.

St. Joseph Home (Skilled Care Facility), 759

Vermont Ave., Kansas City 66101 (201 nursing; 36 apartments).

Villa Maria, Inc. (Intermediate Care Facility), 116 S. Central, Mulvane 67110 (66).

**Kentucky:** Cardome Residence for Women, Georgetown 40324 (30).

Carmel Home (Residence, Adult Day Care and Nursing Care), Old Hartford Rd., Owensboro 42301 (84).

Carmel Manor (Personal Care Home), Carmel Manor Rd., Ft. Thomas, 41075 (99).

The Knottsville Home, Rt. 1, Philpot 42366 (65).

Madonna Manor Intermediate Care Nursing Home, 2344 Amsterdam Rd., Covington 41016 (38). (Cottages for Senior Citizens: 9, with 48 apartments).

St. Charles Nursing Home, 500 Farrell Dr., Covington 41011 (147).

St. Margaret of Cortona Home (Women, Personal Care Home), 1310 Leestown Pike, Lexington 40508 (24).

Taylor Manor Nursing Home, Versailles 40383 (82).

**Louisiana:** Annunciation Inn, 1220 Spain St., New Orleans 70117 (106 residential units).

Bethany M.H.S. Health Care Center (Women), P.O. Box 2308, Lafayette 70502 (42).

Chateau de Notre Dame (Residence and Nursing Home), 2832 Burdette St., New Orleans 70125 (110 residential units, 180 nursing beds).

Christopher Inn Apartments, 2110 Royal St., New Orleans 70116 (144 residential units).

Consolata Home (Nursing Home), 2319 E. Main St., New Iberia 70560.

Lafon Nursing Home of the Holy Family, 6900 Chef Menteur Hwy., New Orleans 70126 (171).

Mary-Joseph Residence for the Elderly, 4201 Woodland Dr., New Orleans 70114 (123).

Mater Dolorosa Adult Group Home, 1215 Dublin St., New Orleans 70118.

Metairie Manor, 4929 York St., Metairie 70001 (200 residential units).

Nazareth Inn, 9630 Haynes Blvd., New Orleans 70127 (150 apartments).

Ollie Steele Burden Manor (Nursing Home), 4200 Essen Lane, Baton Rouge 70809 (60).

Our Lady of Prompt Succor Home (Skilled Nursing Care), 751 E. Prudhomme Lane, Opelousas 70570.

Place Dubourg, 201 Rue Dubourg, LaPlace 70068 (115 residential units).

Rouquette Lodge, 4300 Hwy 22, Mandeville 70448 (119 residential units).

St. Charles Nursing Home, P.O. Box 508, Newellton 71357.

St. John Berchman's Manor, 3400 St. Anthony St., New Orleans 70122 (150 residential units).

St. Joseph's Home (Nursing Home), 2301 Sterlington Rd., Monroe 71201 (130).

St. Margaret's Daughters Nursing Home, (Women), 6220 Chartres St., New Orleans 70117 (110).

St. Martin Manor, 1501 N. Johnson St., New Orleans 70116 (140 residential units).

Villa St. Maurice, 500 St. Maurice Ave., New Orleans 70117. (110 residential units).

Wynhoven Apartments (Residence for Senior Citizens), 4600 - 10th St., Marrero 70072 (350).

**Maine:** Deering Pavilion (Apartments for Senior Citizens), 880 Forest Ave., Portland 04103 (200 units).

Marcotte Nursing Home, 100 Campus Ave., Lewiston 04240 (376).

Mt. St. Joseph (Nursing Home), Highwood St., Waterville 04901 (77).

St. Andre Health Care Facility, Inc. (Nursing Home), 407 Pool St., Biddeford 04005 (96).

St. Joseph's Manor, 1133 Washington Ave., Portland 04103 (200).

Seton Village, Inc., 1 Carver St., Waterville 04901 (140 housing units.)

Villa Muir, Home for Women, Bay View, Saco 04072 (15).

**Maryland:** Cardinal Shehan Center for the Aging, Inc., 2300 Dulaney Valley Rd., Towson 21204. Services: 400-bed long-term care facility; Home Health Agency; 13 hospice care beds; 200 apartments for elderly; residence for elderly in urban area; outreach programs to elderly in homes; retirement residence for priests.

Carroll Manor (Residence and Nursing Home), 4922 La Salle Rd., Hyattsville 20782 (232).

Little Sisters of the Poor, St. Martin's Home (for the Aged), 601 Maiden Choice Lane, Baltimore 21228 (120).

Sacred Heart Home (Women), 5805 Queens Chapel Rd., Hyattsville 20782 (102).

St. Joseph Nursing Home, 1222 Tugwell Dr., Baltimore 21228 (40).

Villa Rosa (Nursing Home), 3800 Lottsford Vista Rd., Mitchellville 20716 (99).

**Massachusetts:** Beaven-Kelly Home for Men (Rest Home), 1245 Main St., Brightside, Holyoke 01040 (55).

Catholic Memorial Home (Nursing Home), 2446 Highland Ave., Fall River 02720 (288).

Don Orione Nursing Home, 111 Orient Ave., East Boston 02128 (194). Adult day care center (30).

D'Youville Manor (Nursing Home), 981 Varnum Ave., Lowell 01854 (196). Day care program (20).

Jeanne Jugan Residence, Little Sisters of the Poor (Nursing Home), 186 Highland Ave., Somerville 02143 (120). Jeanne Jugan Pavilion, 190 Highland Ave., Somerville 02143 (apartments, 27; residents, 30).

Madonna Manor (Nursing Home), N. Washington St., N. Attleboro 02760 (121).

Marian Manor, for the Aged and Infirm (Nursing Home), 130 Dorchester St., S. Boston, 02127 (376).

Marian Manor of Taunton (Nursing Home), 33 Summer St., Taunton 02780 (83).

Maristhill Nursing Home, 66 Newton St., Waltham 02154 (120).

Mary Immaculate Nursing Home, Bennington St., Lawrence 01841 (250). Adult Day Health Care Center (30).

Mt. St. Vincent Nursing Home, Holy Family Rd., Holyoke 01040 (120).

Our Lady's Haven (Nursing Home), 71 Center St., Fairhaven 02719 (110).

The Protectory, Inc., 189 Maple St., Lawrence 01841. (111 units). The Second Protectory, Inc., 191 Maple St., Lawrence (106 units). The Third Protectory, Inc., 193 Maple St., Lawrence 01841 (88 units). Congregate housing; apartments.

Sacred Heart Nursing Home, 359 Summer St., New Bedford 02740 (217).

St. Francis Home for Aged, 37 Thorne St., Worcester 01604 (66). Adult Day Health Care (36).

St. Joseph Manor Nursing Home, 215 Thatcher St., Brockton 02402 (120).

St. Joseph's Manor (Rest Home, Women), 321 Centre St., Dorchester, Boston 02122 (77).

St. Luke's Home (Rest Home, Women), 85 Spring St., Springfield 01105 (92).

St. Patrick's Manor (Nursing Home), 863 Central St., Framingham 01701 (292).

**Michigan:** Bishop Noa Home for Senior Citizens, Escanaba 49829 (109).

Burtha M. Fisher Home, Little Sisters of the Poor (Residence and Nursing Home), 17550 Southfield Rd., Detroit 48235 (130).

Casa Maria (Residence), 600 Maple Vista, Imlay City 48444 (96).

Kundig Center (Residence), 3300 Jefferies Freeway, Detroit 48208 (180). Rooms and apartments.

Lourdes Nursing Home (Skilled Facility), 2300 Watkins Lake Rd., Pontiac 48054 (108).

Madonna Villa Senior Residence, 17825 Fifteen Mile Rd., Fraser, 48026 (90).

Marian Hall (Residence), 529 Detroit St., Flint 48502 (124).

Marian-Oakland West, 29250 W. Ten Mile Rd., Farmington Hills 48024 (100).

Marian Place (Residence), 408 W. Front St., Monroe 48161 (52).

Marycrest Manor (Skilled Nursing Facility), 15475 Middlebelt Rd., Livonia 48154 (55).

Marydale Center for Senior Citizens (Board and Apartments), 3147 Tenth Ave., Port Huron 48060 (74).

Maryhaven (Residence), 11350 Reeck Rd., Southgate 48195 (93).

St. Ann's Home, (Residence and Nursing Home), 2161 Leonard St. N.W., Grand Rapids 49504 (112).

St. Catherine Cooperative House for Elderly Women, 1641 Webb Ave., Detroit 48206.

St. Elizabeth Briarbank (Women, Residence), 1315 N. Woodward Ave., Bloomfield Hills 48013 (54).

St. Francis Home (Nursing Home), 915 N. River Rd., Saginaw 48603 (100).

St. Joseph's Home for the Aged, 4800 Cadieux Rd., Detroit 48224 (104).

Stapleton Center (Residence), 9341 Agnes St., Detroit 48214 (65).

Villa Elizabeth (Nursing Home), 2100 Leonard St. N.E., Grand Rapids 49505 (136).

Villa Francesca (Residence, Women), 565 W. Long Lake Rd., Bloomfield Hills 48013 (18).

Villa Marie (Board and Apartments), 15131 Newburgh Rd., Livonia 48154.

**Minnesota:** Assumption Home, Cold Spring 56320 (95).

Bethany Home (Nursing Home), Onamia 56359 (80).

Divine Providence Community Home (Intermediate Care), 700 Third Ave. N.W., Sleepy Eye 56085 (58).

Divine Providence Home (Skilled Nursing Home), Ivanhoe 56142 (51).

John Paul Apartments, Cold Spring 56320 (61). For elderly and handicapped.

Little Sisters of the Poor, Holy Family Residence (Skilled Nursing and Intermediate Care), 330 S. Exchange St., St. Paul 55102 (120).

Madonna Towers (Retirement Apartments and Nursing Home), 4001 19th Ave. N.W., Rochester 55901 (200).

Mary Rondorf Retirement Home, 222 N. 5th St., Staples 56479 (84).

Mother of Mercy Nursing Home, Albany 56307 (62).

Regina Nursing Home and Retirement Residence, Hastings 55033. Nursing home (61); retirement home (86).

Sacred Heart Hospice (Skilled and Intermediate Nursing Care), 1200 Twelfth St. S.W., Austin 55912 (59). Adult day care and home health nursing care.

St. Ann's Residence, 330 E. 3rd St., Duluth 55805 (200).

St. Anne Hospice, Inc. (Nursing Home), 1347 W. Broadway, Winona 55987 (121).

St. Benedict's Center (Nursing Home), 1810 Minnesota Blvd. S.E., St. Cloud 56301 (222).

St. Elizabeth's Hospital and Nursing Home, 1200-5th Grant Blvd., Wabasha 55981 (52).

St. Francis Home, 501 Oak St., Breckenridge 56520 (124).

St. Mary's Home (Nursing Home), 1925 Norfolk Ave., St. Paul 55116 (140).

St. Mary's Hospital and Nursing Home, Winsted 55395 (95).

St. Mary's Nursing Home, Detroit Lakes 56501 (103).

St. Mary's Rehabilitation Center, 2512 S. 7th St., Minneapolis 55454 (65).

St. Mary's Villa (Nursing Home), Pierz 56364 (101).

St. Otto's Home (Nursing Home), Little Falls 56345 (159).

St. Therese Home (Residence and Health Care Facility) (302) and St. Therese Retirement Apartments (220), 8000 Bass Lake Rd., New Hope 55428.

St. William's Nursing Home, Parkers Prairie 56361 (61).

Villa of St. Francis Nursing Home, Morris 56267 (144).

Villa St. Vincent (Skilled Nursing Home and Residence), 516 Walsh St., Crookston 56726. Nursing home (80); residence (95).

**Mississippi:** Santa Maria Retirement Apartments, 305 E. Beach St., Biloxi, 39530.

Villa Maria Retirement Apartments, 921 Porter Ave., Ocean Springs 39564.

**Missouri:** The Alverne (Retirement Home), 1014 Locust St., St. Louis 63101 (242).

Cathedral Square Towers, 444 W. 12th St., Kansas City 64105. Apartments for elderly and handicapped.

Chariton Apartments (Retirement Apartments), 4249 Michigan Ave., St. Louis 63111 (122 units; 143 residents).

DePaul Health Center — St. Anne's Division (Skilled Nursing), 12349 DePaul Dr., Bridgeton 63044 (100).

LaVerna Heights Retirement Home (Women), 104 E. Park Ave., Savannah 64485 (40).

LaVerna Village Apartments, 1000-1005 Hall Ave., Savannah 64485 (20).

LaVerna Village Nursing Home, 904 Hall Ave., Savannah 64485 (120).

Little Sisters of the Poor (Home for Aged), 3225 N. Florissant Ave., St. Louis 63107 (210).

Mary, Queen and Mother Center (Skilled-Intermediate Nursing Care), 7601 Watson Rd., St. Louis 63119 (220).

Mercy Villa (Nursing Home), Division of St. John's Regional Health Center, 1100 E. Montclair, Springfield 65807 (150).

Mother of Good Counsel Home (Skilled Nursing, Women), 6825 Natural Bridge Rd., Northwoods, 63121.

Our Lady of Mercy Home (Residence and Nursing Home), 918-24 E. 9th St., Kansas City 64106 (153).

Our Lady of Mercy Country House, Box 451, R.R. No. 4, Liberty 64038 (39).

Price Memorial Skilled Nursing Facility Forby Rd., P.O. Box 476, Eureka 63025 (120.

St. Agnes Home for the Aged, 10341 Manchester Rd., Kirkwood 63122 (130).

St. Joseph Hill Infirmary, Inc., (Nursing Care Facility, Men), St. Joseph Road, Eureka 63025 (130).

St. Joseph's Home, 723 First Capitol Dr., St. Charles 63301 (101).

St. Joseph's Home for the Aged, 1306 W. Main St., Jefferson City 65101 (75).

**Nebraska:** Bergan Mercy Care Center (Health Care), 1870 S. 75th St., Omaha 68124 (250).

Madonna Professional Care Center, 2200 S. 52nd St., Lincoln 68506 (182).

Mt. Carmel Home, Keens' Memorial (Nursing Home), 412 W. 18th St., Kearney 68847 (76).

New Cassel Retirement Center, 900 N. 90th St., Omaha 68114. (156).

St. Joseph's Home (Domiciliary Care), 320 E. Decatur St., West Point 68788 (48).

St. Joseph's Nursing Home, 401 N. 18th St., Norfolk 68701 (70).

St. Joseph's Villa, David City 68632. (65).

**New Hampshire:** Mount Carmel Nursing Home, 235 Myrtle St., Manchester 03104 (120).

St. Ann Home, 195 Dover Point Rd., Dover 03820 (53).

St. Francis Home (Nursing Home), Court St., Laconia 03246 (51).

St. Teresa Manor (Nursing Home), 519 Bridge St., Manchester 03104 (51).

St. Vincent de Paul Nursing Home, 29 Providence Ave., Berlin 03570 (80).

**New Jersey:** Holy Family Residence (Women), 44 Rifle Camp Rd., P.O. Box 536, W. Paterson 07424 (64).

Little Sisters of the Poor, St. Joseph Home, 140 Shepherd Lane, Totowa 07512 (183; also, 22 independent living units).

Mater Dei Nursing Home, RD 3, Box 164, Rt. 40, P.O. Newfield 08344 (64).

Morris Hall, Home for the Aged (Residence and Skilled Nursing Home), 2361 Lawrenceville Rd., Lawrenceville 08648 (127).

Mount St. Andrew Villa (Residence), 55 W. Midland Ave., Paramus 07652 (56).

Our Lady's Residence (Nursing Home), Glendale and Clematis Aves., Pleasantville 08232 (104).

St. Ann's Home for the Aged (Skilled Nursing Home, Women), 198 Old Bergen Rd., Jersey City 07305 (106). Adult Medical Day Care.

St. Joseph's Home (Women), 240 Longhouse Dr., Hewitt 07421.

St. Joseph's Rest Home for Aged Women, 46 Preakness Ave., Paterson 07522 (35).

St. Joseph's Senior Residence, 1 St. Joseph Terr., Woodbridge 07095.

St. Joseph's Villa (Residence, Women), Peapack 07977 (18).

St. Mary's Catholic Home (Skilled Nursing Home), 1730 Kresson Rd., Cherry Hill 08003 (215).

St. Vincent's Nursing Home, 45 Elm St., Montclair 07042 (135).

Villa Maria (Residence and Infirmary, Women), 641 Somerset St., N. Plainfield 07061 (70).

**New Mexico:** Good Shepherd Manor (Residential Care for Aged Persons), Little Brothers of the Good Shepherd, P.O. Box 10248, Albuquerque 87114 (43).

**New York:** Bernardine Apartments, 417 Churchill Ave., Syracuse 13205.

Consolation Residence, 111 Beach Dr., West Islip 11795 (250).

Ferncliff Nursing Home, P.O. Box 386, River Rd., Rhinebeck 12572 (320).

Frances Schervier Home and Hospital, 2975 Independence Ave., New York 10463 (364).

Good Samaritan Nursing Home (Skilled Nursing), 101 Elm St., Sayville, N.Y. 11782 (100).

Holy Family Home, 410 Mill St. Williamsville 14221 (90).

Kateri Residence (Skilled Nursing), 150 Riverside Dr., New York 10024 (520).

Little Sisters of the Poor, Jeanne Jugan Residence (Skilled Nursing and Health Related), 3200 Baychester Ave., Bronx 10475 (170).

Little Sisters of the Poor, Holy Family Home, 1740-84th St., Brooklyn 11214 (146).

Little Sisters of the Poor, Queen of Peace Residence, 110-30 221st St., Queens Village 11429 (202).

Madonna Home of Mercy Hospital (Nursing Home and Extended Care Facility) (140), and Mercy Hospital Health Related Facility (Residence) (58), Watertown 13601.

Madonna Residence, 1 Prospect Park W., Brooklyn, 11215 (290).

Mary Manning Walsh Home (Nursing Home), 1339 York Ave., New York 10021 (362).

Mercy Healthcare Center (Skilled Nursing Facility), Tupper Lake 12986 (54).

Mt. Loretto Nursing Home, (Skilled Nursing Facility), R.D., 3, Amsterdam 12010 (82).

Nazareth Nursing Home and Health Related Facility (Women), 291 W. North St., Buffalo 14201 (125).

Our Lady of Hope Residence (Home for the Aged), Little Sisters of the Poor, 1 Jeanne Jugan Lane, Latham 12210 (250).

Ozanam Hall of Queens Nursing Home, Inc. (Skilled Nursing and Health-Related Facilities), 42-41 201st St., Bayside 11361 (432).

Providence Rest, 3304 Waterbury Ave., Bronx 10465 (200).

Resurrection Rest Home (Nursing Home and Health Related Facility, Women), Castleton 12033 (48).

Sacred Heart Home (Residence) 4520 Ransom Rd., Clarence 10431 (82). Brothers of Mercy Nursing Home, 10570 Bergtold Rd., Clarence 14031 (240). Brothers of Mercy Housing Co., Inc. (Apartments), 10500 Bergtold Rd., Clarence 14031 (100).

Sacred Heart Nursing Home, 8 Mickle St., Plattsburgh 12901 (89).

St. Ann's Home / The Heritage (Skilled Nursing), 1500 Portland Ave., Rochester 14621.

St. Anthony's Home for the Aged, 5285 S. Park Ave., Hamburg 14075 (70).

St. Clare Manor, 543 Locust St., Lockport 14094 (28).

St. Columban's on the Lake (Retirement Home), Silver Creek 14136 (50).

St. Elizabeth Home (Residence), 5539 Broadway, Lancaster 14086 (102).

St. Francis Home (Nursing and Health Related Facility), 147 Reist St., Williamsville 14221 (98).

St. Joseph Manor, W. State St., Olean 14760 (22).

St. Joseph's Guest Home, Missionary Sisters of St. Benedict,, 350 Cuba Hill Rd., Huntington 11743 (60).

St. Joseph's Home, Table Rock, Sloatsburg 10974 (20).

St. Joseph's Home (Nursing Home), 420 Lafayette St., Ogdensburg 13669 (82).

St. Joseph's Nursing Home, 2535 Genesee St., Utica 13501 (120).

St. Joseph's Villa (Residence), 38 Prospect Ave., Catskill 12414 (60).

St. Luke Manor, 17 Wiard St., Batavia 14020 (20).

St. Mary's Manor, 515 Sixth St., Niagara Falls 14301 (119).

St. Patrick's Home for the Aged and Infirm, 66 Van Cortland Park S., Bronx 10463 (225).

St. Vincent's Home for the Aged, 319 Washington Ave., Dunkirk 14048 (36).

Teresian House, Washington Ave. Extension, Albany 12203 (300).

Uihlein Mercy Center (Nursing Home), Lake Placid 12946 (96).

**North Carolina:** Maryfield Nursing Home (115 beds) and Maryfield Acres (16 retirement homes), Greensboro Rd., High Point 27260 (115).

**North Dakota:** Holy Family Guest Home (Nursing Home), Carrington 58421 (38).

Manor St. Joseph Home for Aged and Infirm; Edgeley 58433 (40).

Marillac Manor (Retirement Apartments), 1016 N. 28th St., Bismarck 58501 (42 apartments).

St. Anne's Guest Home (Retirement), 524 N. 17th St., Grand Forks 58201 (56) Apartments (30).

St. Olaf Guest (Retirement) Home, Powers Lake 58773 (16).

St. Vincent's Nursing Home, 1021 N. 26th St., Bismarck 58501 (98).

**Ohio:** Archbishop Leibold Home for the Aged, Little Sisters of the Poor, 476 Riddle Rd., Cincinnati 45220 (125).

Assumption Nursing Home, 550 W. Chalmers Ave., Youngstown 44511 (126).

Francesca Residence (Retirement), 39 N. Portage Path, Akron 44303 (45).

House of Loreto (Nursing Home), 2812 Harvard Ave. N.W., Canton 44709 (98).

Jennings Hall, Inc. (Intermediate Care Facility), 10204 Granger Rd., Garfield Heights 44125 (100).

Kirby Manor (Retirement Apartments), 11500 Detroit Ave., Cleveland 44102 (202 suites).

Little Sisters of the Poor, Sacred Heart Home, 4900 Navarre Ave., Oregon 43616 (126).

Little Sisters of the Poor, Sts. Joseph and Mary Home for Aged, 4291 Richmond Rd., Cleveland 44122 (140).

The Maria-Joseph Living Care Center, 4830 Salem Ave., Dayton 45416 (397).

Mount Alverna (Residence for Aged), 6765 State Rd., Cleveland 44134 (200).

Mt. St. Joseph (Skilled Nursing Facility, Dual Certified), 21800 Chardon Rd., Cleveland 44117 (100).

Nazareth Towers, 300 E. Rich St., Columbus 43215. Hi-rise apartments for independent living.

St. Augustine Manor (Nursing Home), 7818 Detroit Ave., Cleveland 44102 (194).

St. Clare Center, Inc. (Residence and Nursing Care), 80 Compton Rd., Cincinnati 45215 (90).

St. Edward Nursing Home, 3131 Smith Rd., Akron 44313 (100).

St. Francis Home, Inc., 182 St. Francis Ave., Tiffin 44883 (116).

St. Francis Rehabilitation Hospital and Nursing Home, 401 N. Broadway St., Green Springs 44836 (186).

St. Joseph's Hospice (Nursing Home), 2308 Reno Dr., Louisville 44641 (100).

St. Margaret Hall (Residence and Nursing Facility), 1960 Madison Rd., Cincinnati 45206 (145).

St. Raphael Home (Nursing Home), 1550 Roxbury Rd., Columbus 43212 (80).

St. Rita's Home (Skilled Nursing Home), 880 Greenlawn Ave., Columbus 43223 (100).

St. Theresa Home for the Aged, 6760 Belkenton Pl., Cincinnati 45236 (110).

Schroder Manor (Residence and Skilled Nursing Care), Franciscan Sisters of the Poor, 1302 Millville Ave., Hamilton 45013 (85). Independent living units are under construction.

The Siena Home (Skilled Nursing Home), 235 W. Orchard Spring Dr., Dayton 45415 (99).

The Villa Sancta Anna Home for the Aged, 25000 Chagrin Blvd., Beachwood 44122 (68).

**Oklahoma:** Franciscan Villa, 17110 E. 51st St. S., Broken Arrow 74012. Intermediate nursing care (60); apartments (66).

St. Ann's Nursing Home, 3825 N.W. 19th St., Oklahoma City 73107 (82).

**Oregon:** Benedictine Nursing Center, S. Main St., Mt. Angel 97362 (127).

Maryville Nursing Home, 14645 S.W. Farmington, Beaverton 97007 (132).

Mt. St. Joseph's Residence and Extended Care Center, 3060 S.E. Stark St., Portland 97214 (325).

St. Catherine's Residence and Nursing Center, 3959 Sheridan Ave., North Bend 97459 (166).

St. Elizabeth's Nursing Home, 2365 4th St., Baker 97814 (93).

**Pennsylvania:** Ascension Manor I (Senior Citizen Housing), 911 N. Franklin St., Philadelphia 19123 (140 units).

Ascension Manor II (Senior Citizen Housing), 970 N. 7th St., Philadelphia 19123 (140 units).

Benetwood Apartments for Elderly and Handicapped, 640 Troupe Rd., Erie 16421 (75).

Christ the King Manor, 1100 W. Long Ave., Du Bois 15801 (160).

Corpus Christi Residence, 7165 Churchland St., Pittsburgh 15206 (27).

Drueding Infirmary (Intermediate Nursing), 413 W. Master St., Philadelphia 19122 (52).

Garvey Manor (Nursing Home), Logan Blvd., Hollidaysburg, 16648 (150).

Holy Family Home, Little Sisters of the Poor, 5300 Chester Ave., Philadelphia 19143 (130).

Holy Family Manor (Skilled Nursing Facility), 1200 Spring St., Bethlehem 18018 (200).

Holy Family Residence, 217 Spring Garden St., Easton 18042 (18).

Holy Spirit Guest Home (Women), 4537 Wm. Flynn Hwy., Allison Park 15101 (15).

Immaculate Mary Home, (Skilled and Intermediate Nursing Care), Holme Circle and Welsh Rd., Philadelphia 19136 (300).

John XXIII Home, 2250 Shenango Freeway, Hermitage 16148 (119).

Little Flower Manor Nursing Home (Skilled Nursing), 1201 Springfield Rd., Darby 19023 (122).

Little Flower Manor of Diocese of Scranton, (Long-Term Skilled Nursing Care Facility), 200 S. Meade St., Wilkes-Barre 18702.

Little Sisters of the Poor, 1028 Benton Ave. N.S., Pittsburgh 15212 (140).

Little Sisters of the Poor, Holy Family Resi-

dence, 2500 Adams Ave., Scranton 18509 (82).

Maria Joseph Manor, Danville 17821 (94).

Marian Manor (Intermediate Care), 2695 Winchester Dr., Pittsburgh 15220 (170).

Mount Macrina Manor (Skilled Nursing Facility), 520 W. Main St., Uniontown 15401 (54).

Redeemer Village (Senior Citizen Housing), Huntingdon Pike, Huntingdon Valley 19006 (150 apartments).

Sacred Heart Manor (Nursing Home), 6445 Germantown Ave., Philadelphia 19119 (162).

St. Anne Home (Intermediate and Skilled Nursing Care), R.D. 2, Columbia 17512 (120).

St. Anne Home for the Elderly (Nursing Facility), 685 Angela Dr., Greensburg 15601 (125).

St. Basil's Home for Aged Women (Residential), Box 878, Uniontown 15401 (14).

St. Ignatius Nursing Home, 4401 Haverford Ave., Philadelphia 19104 (176).

St. John Neumann Nursing Home, 10400 Roosevelt Blvd. Philadelphia 19116 (218).

St. Joseph Home for the Aged (Residential and Skilled Nursing Facility), 1182 Holland Rd., Holland 18966 (96).

St. Joseph Nursing and Health Care Center (Skilled Nursing Facility), 5324 Penn Ave., Pittsburgh 15224 (160).

St. Joseph's House of Hospitality (Low Income Senior Citizen Residence for Men and Women), 1635 Bedford Ave., Pittsburgh 15219 (65).

St. Joseph Manor (Skilled Nursing Facility), 1616 Huntingdon Pike, Meadowbrook 19046 (250).

St. Joseph's Residence, 1111 S. Cascade St., New Castle 16101.

St. Leonard's Guest Home, 601 N. Montgomery St., Hollidaysburg 16648 (21).

St. Mary's Home of Erie, 607 E. 26th St., Erie 16504. Residential facility (110); geriatric nursing facility (196).

Saint Mary's Manor, 701 Lansdale Ave., Lansdale 19446 (160).

St. Mary's Villa (Nursing Home), Elmhurst 18416 (121).

Villa de Marillac Nursing Home, 5300 Stanton Ave., Pittsburgh 15206 (50).

Villa St. Teresa (Residence, Women), 1215 Springfield Rd., Darby 19023 (53).

Villa Teresa (Nursing Home), 1051 Avila Rd., Harrisburg 17109 (184).

Vincentian Home for the Chronically Ill., Perrymont Rd., Pittsburgh 15237 (219).

**Rhode Island:** Jeanne Jugan Residence of the Little Sisters of the Poor, 964 Main St., Pawtucket 02860 (120).

L'Hospice St. Antoine (Home for Aged), 400 Mendon Rd., North Smithfield 02895 (244).

St. Clare Home, 309 Spring St., Newport 02840 (44).

Scalabrini Villa (Convalescent, Rest — Nursing Home). 860 N. Quidnessett Rd., North Kingstown 02852 (70).

**South Carolina:** Carter-May Home, 1660 Ingram Rd., Charleston 29407 (12). Personal care home for elderly ladies.

**South Dakota:** Brady Memorial Home (Skilled Nursing Facility), 500 S. Ohlman St., Mitchell 57301 (60). Independent living units (9).

Maryhouse, Inc. (Skilled Nursing Facility), 717 E. Dakota, Pierre 57501 (82).

Mother Joseph Manor (Intermediate Care and Skilled Nursing Facility), 1002 North Jay St., Aberdeen 57401 (30 intermediate; 50 skilled). Apartment units (7). Adult day care program. Respite nursing care.

St. William's Home for the Aged (Intermediate Care, 60), and Angela Hall (Supervised Living, 15), 901 E. Virgil, Box 432, Milbank 57252.

Tekakwitha Nursing Home (Skilled and Intermediate Care). Sisseton 57262 (101). Tekakwitha Housing Corp. (Independent Living), same address (24 units).

**Tennessee:** Alexian Village of Tennessee (Retired Men and Women), Signal Mountain 37377 (150).

Ave Maria Home, 2805 Charles Bryan Rd., Memphis 38134 (73).

St. Mary Manor, 1771 Highway 45 Bypass, Jackson 38301.

St. Peter Manor, 108 N. Aubrundale, Memphis 38104.

St. Peter Villa (Nursing Home), 141 N. McLean, Memphis 38104.

**Texas:** Casa Apartment Complex for Elderly and Handicapped, 3201 Sondra Dr., Fort Worth 76107.

Home for Aged Women-Men, 920 S. Oregon St., El Paso 79901 (24).

Laboure Care Center, 1950 Record Crossing Rd., Dallas 75235.

Mother of Perpetual Help Home (Intermediate Care Facility), 519 E. Madison Ave., Brownsville 78520 (37).

Mt. Carmel Home (Personal Care Home), 4130 S. Alameda St., Corpus Christi 78411 (92).

The Regis Retirement Home and St. Elizabeth Nursing Home, 400 Austin Ave., Waco 76701 (420).

The Retirement Residence, Inc., The Whitestone, 2819 Rio Grande, Austin 78705 (100).

St. Ann's Home (Skilled Nursing Facility), P.O. Box 1179, Panhandle 79068 (52).

St. Anthony Center (Skilled Nursing, Rehabilitation, Geriatric), 6301 Almeda Rd., Houston 77021 (372).

St. Benedict's Nursing Home, Alamo and Johnson Sts., San Antonio 78204 (197).

St. Dominic Nursing Home, 6502 Grand Ave., Houston 77021 (120).

St. Dominic Residence Hall, 2401 E. Holcombe Blvd., Houston 77021 (180).

St. Francis Nursing Home (Home for Aged and Convalescents), 2717 N. Flores St., San Antonio 78212 (143).

St. Francis Village, Inc. (Retired and Elderly), 1 Chapel Plaza, Crowley 76036 (415).

St. Joseph Residence, 330 W. Pembroke St., Dallas 75208 (49).

San Juan Nursing Home, Inc. (Skilled and In-termediate Care Facility), 300 N. Nebraska Ave., P.O. Box 1238, San Juan 78589 (120).

**Utah:** St. Joseph Villa (Skilled Care Facility), 475 Ramona Ave., Salt Lake City 84115 (97). Adjacent residential care facility (51).

**Vermont:** Loretto Home for Aged, 59 Meadow St., Rutland 05701 (54).

Michaud Memorial Manor (Home for Aged), Derby Line 05830 (24).

St. Joseph's Home for Aged, 243 N. Prospect St., Burlington 05401 (53).

**Virginia:** Madonna Home, 814 W. 37th St., Norfolk 23508 (15).

Russell House, 900 First Colonial Rd., Virginia Beach 23454 (127).

St. Francis Home, 2511 Wise St., Richmond 23225 (25).

St. Joseph's Home for the Aged, Little Sisters of the Poor, 1503 Michael Rd., Richmond 23229 (126).

**Washington:** Cathedral Plaza Apartments (Retirement Apartments), W. 1120 Sprague Ave., Spokane 99204 (150).

The Delaney, W. 242 Riverside Ave., Spokane 99201 (84).

The De Paul Retirement Apartments, 4831 35th Ave. S.W., Seattle 98126 (118 units).

Fahy Garden Apartments, W. 1403 Dean Ave., Spokane 99201 (31).

Fahy West Apartments, W. 1523 Dean Ave., Spokane 99201 (55).

The Josephinum (Retirement Home), 1902 2nd Ave., Seattle 98101 (228).

Mt. St. Vincent Nursing Center, 4831 35th Ave., S.W., Seattle 98126 (198).

The O'Malley, E. 707 Mission, Spokane 99202 (100).

St. Joseph Nursing Home, 1006 North H St., Aberdeen 98520 (34).

St. Joseph Care Center (Skilled Long-Term Care), West 20 — 90th Ave., Spokane 99204 (103). Adult day care center (35).

**West Virginia:** Knights of St. George Home, Wellsburg 26070 (44).

Welty Home for the Aged (Women), 21 Washington Ave., Wheeling 26003 (44).

**Wisconsin:** Alexian Village of Milwaukee (Retirement Community/Skilled Nursing Home), 7979 W. Glenbrook Rd., Milwaukee 53223 (331 apartments).

Bethany-St. Joseph Health Care Center, 2507 Shelby Rd., La Crosse 54601 (226).

Clement Manor (Retirement Community and Skilled Nursing), 3939 S. 92nd St., Greenfield 53228 (158 skilled nursing; 99 apartments).

Divine Savior Nursing Home, 715 W. Pleasant St., Portage 53901 (128).

Franciscan Villa (Skilled Nursing Home), 3601 S. Chicago Ave., S. Milwaukee 53172 (150).

Hope Nursing Home, 438 Ashford Ave., Lomira 53048 (40).

McCormick Memorial Home for the Aged, 212 Iroquois St., Green Bay 54301 (72).

Marian Catholic Home, 3333 W. Highland Blvd., Milwaukee 53208 (360).

Maryhill Manor Nursing and Retirement Home, 973 Main St., Niagara 54151 (45).

Milwaukee Catholic Home, Inc., 2462 N. Prospect Ave., Milwaukee 53211 (200).

Nazareth House (Skilled Nursing Facility), Stoughton 53589 (100).

St. Ann Rest Home (Intermediate Care Facility, Women), 2020 S. Muskego Ave., Milwaukee 53204 (54).

St. Anne's Home for the Elderly (Aged Poor), 3800 N. 92nd St., Milwaukee 53222 (156).

St. Camillus Health Center (Skilled Nursing Home), 10100 W. Bluemound Rd., Wauwatosa 53226 (188).

St. Catherine Infirmary (Nursing Home), 5635 Erie St., Racine 53402 (40).

St. Elizabeth Nursing Home, 502 St. Lawrence Ave., Janesville 53545 (43).

St. Elizabeth's Nursing Home (Intermediate Care; Women), 745 N. Brookfield Rd., Brookfield 53005 (16).

St. Francis Home, 620 S. 11th St., La Crosse 54601 (95).

St. Francis Home (Skilled Nursing Facility), 1800 New York Ave., Superior 54880 (192).

St. Francis Home (Skilled Nursing), 365 Gillett St., Fond du Lac 54935 (70).

St. Francis Manor (Retirement Residence), 3553 S. 41st St., Milwaukee 53221 (125).

St. Joan Antida Home (Women), 6640 W. Beloit Rd., W. Allis 53219 (76).

St. Joseph's Home, 705 Clyman St., Watertown 53094 (28).

St. Joseph's Home, 9244 29th Ave., Kenosha 53140 (93).

St. Joseph's Home, 5301 W. Lincoln Ave., W. Allis 53219 (124).

St. Joseph's Nursing Home, 464 S. St. Joseph Ave., Arcadia 54612 (75).

St. Joseph's Nursing Home, 2902 East Ave. S., La Crosse 54601 (80).

St. Joseph's Nursing Home, 400 Water Ave., Hillsboro 54634 (65).

St. Joseph Residence, Inc. (Nursing Home), 1925 Division St., New London 54961 (256).

St. Mary's Home for the Aged (Residence and Nursing Care), 2005 Division St., Manitowoc 54220 (256).

St. Mary's Nursing Home, 3516 W. Center St., Milwaukee 53210 (130).

St. Monica's Senior Citizens Home, 3920 N. Green Bay Rd., Racine 53404 (90).

St. Paul Home (Intermediate and Skilled Nursing Home), 509 W. Wisconsin Ave., Kaukauna 54130 (52).

Villa Clement (Nursing and Convalescent Center), 9047 W. Greenfield Ave., W. Allis 53214 (190).

Villa Loretto Nursing Home, Mount Calvary 53057 (52).

# FACILITIES FOR HANDICAPPED CHILDREN AND ADULTS

Sources: Almanac survey; *Directory of Catholic Special Facilities and Programs for Handicapped Children and Adults,* published by the National Catholic Educational Association; *Official Catholic Directory.*

This listing covers facilities and programs with educational and training orientation. Information about other services for the handicapped can generally be obtained from the Catholic Charities Office or its equivalent (c/o Chancery Office) in any diocese. (See Index for listing of addresses of chancery offices in the U.S.)

Abbreviation code: b, boys; c, coeducational; d, day; g, girls; r, residential. Other information includes chronological age for admission. The number in parentheses at the end of an entry indicates total capacity or enrollment.

### Deaf and Hard of Hearing

**California:** St. Joseph's Center for Deaf and Hard of Hearing (d,c; 3-14 yrs.), 37588 Fremont Blvd., Fremont 94536.

**Illinois:** Holy Trinity Day Classes for the Deaf (c; 3-14 yrs.) 1910 Taylor, Chicago 60612 (45).

**Louisiana:** Chinchuba Institute (d,c; 16 yrs.), 1131 Barataria Blvd., Marrero. 70072 (101).

**Massachusetts:** Boston School for the Deaf (r,d,c; 3-21 yrs.), 800 N. Main St., Randolph. 02368 (236). Psycho-Education Center (PEC) for emotionally disturbed deaf children (r, d; 3-10 yrs.).

**Missouri:** St. Joseph Institute for the Deaf

(r,d,c; birth to 15 yrs.), 1483 82nd Blvd., St. Louis 63132 (150).

**New York:** Cleary School for the Deaf (d,c; infancy through high school), 301 Smithtown Blvd., Lake Ronkonkoma, L.I. 11779 (105).

St. Francis de Sales School for the Deaf (d,c; parent-infant programs through age 14), 260 Eastern Parkway, Brooklyn 11225.

St. Joseph's School for the Deaf (d,c; birth-13 yrs.), 1000 Hutchinson River Pkwy, Bronx. 10465 (230).

St. Mary's School for the Deaf (r,d,c; birth to 21 yrs.), 2253 Main St., Buffalo. 14214 (220).

**Ohio:** St. Rita School for the Deaf (r,c; 4 yrs. and older), 1720 Glendale-Milford Rd., Cincinnati. 45215 (120).

**Pennsylvania:** Abp. Ryan Memorial Institute for Deaf (d,c; parent-infant programs through 8th grade), 3509 Spring Garden St., Philadelphia. 19104 (80).

De Paul Institute (d,c; birth-21 yrs.), Castlegate Ave., Pittsburgh. 15226 (132).

### Emotionally And/Or Socially Maladjusted

This listing includes facilities for abused, abandoned and neglected as well as emotionally disturbed children and youth.

**California:** Hanna Boys Center (r; 9-16 yrs.), Box 100, Sonoma. 95476 (72).

Rancho San Antonio (r,b; 12-16 yrs.), 21000 Plummer St., Chatsworth. 91311 (118).

Stanford Lathrop Memorial Home and Group Homes, Sisters of Social Service, 800 N. Street, Sacramento 95814. Conduct five homes for boys and girls.

**Colorado:** Mt. St. Vincent Home (r,c; 5-13 yrs.), 4159 Lowell Blvd., Denver. 80211 (45).

**Connecticut:** Highland Heights — St. Francis Home for Children (r,d,c; 8-13 yrs.), 651 Prospect St., New Haven. 06505 (38). Also conducts Ken-Mar Group Home (r,d,c; 14-17 yrs.), 682 Prospect St., New Haven 06505 (10).

Mt. St. John (r,b; 11-16 yrs.), Kirtland St., Deep River. 06417 (75).

**Delaware:** Our Lady of Grace Home for Children (r,c; 6-12 yrs.), 487 Chestnut Hill Rd., Newark 19713 (28).

**Florida:** Boystown of Florida (r; 13-17 yrs.), 11400 SW 137th Ave., Miami 33186 (45).

**Georgia:** Village of St. Joseph (r,d,c; 6-16 yrs.), 2969 Butner Rd. S.W., Atlanta 30331 (40 r; 48 d). Residential treatment center and therapeutic special school for children with emotional problems, behavior disorders, learning disabilities.

**Illinois:** Charles I. Doyle, S.J., Center and Day School of Loyola University (d, c; pre-school to 19 yrs.), 1043 Loyola Ave., Chicago 60626 (25 in day school, unlimited in guidance center).

Guardian Angel (r,d,c; 5-15 yrs.), Plainfield at Theodore St., Joliet 60435 (20 r, 30 d).

St. Joseph Carondelet Child Center (r,b; 5-16 yrs. and d,c; 5-15 yrs.); 739 E. 35th St., Chicago 60616 (32 r, 20 d).

**Indiana:** Gibault School for Boys (r; 10-16 yrs.), 5901 Dixie Bee Rd., Terre Haute. 47802 (104).

Hoosier Boys Town (r; 9-18 yrs.), Schererville. 46375 (65).

**Kentucky:** Boys' Haven (r; 13 18 yrs.), 3201 Bardstown Rd., Louisville. 40205 (51).

Maryhurst School (r,g; 13-17 yrs.), 1015 Dorsey Lane, Louisville 40223 (42).

**Louisiana:** Hope Haven — Madonna Manor School and Home (r,b; 6-17 yrs.), 1101 Barataria Blvd., Marrero 70072 (176).

Maison Marie Group Home (r,g; 13-18 yrs.), 3020 Independence St., Metairie 70002 (12).

**Maryland:** Good Shepherd Center (r,d,g; 14-18 yrs.), 4100 Maple Ave., Baltimore. 21227 (90r, 15d).

**Massachusetts:** Cushing Hall (r,b; 11-14½ yrs.), 279 Tilden Rd., Scituate. 02066 (40). Diagnostic treatment center.

McAuley Nazareth Home for Boys (r; 6-14 yrs.), 77 Mulberry St., Leicester. 01524 (27).

Madonna Hall (r,g; 12-17 yrs.), Cushing Hill Dr., Marlboro 01752 (48). Diagnostic treatment program (12) and Secure Assessment Treatment Center (12).

Nazareth Child Care Center (r,d,c; 5-14 yrs.), 420 Pond St., Jamaica Plain, Mass. 02130 (96).

Our Lady of Providence Children's Center (r,d,c; 5-15 yrs.), 2112 Riverdale St., W. Springfield. 01089 (50). Diagnostic treatment program also.

St. Vincent Home (r,c), 2425 Highland Ave., Fall River 02720 (85).

**Michigan:** Barat House, Barat Human Services,

League of Catholic Women (r,g; 13-17 yrs.), 5250 John R. St., Detroit. 48202 (24).

Boysville of Michigan, Inc. (r; 13-18 yrs.), 8744 Clinton-Macon Rd., Clinton. 49236 (180).

Don Bosco Hall (r,b; 13-17 years.), 10001 Petoskey Ave., Detroit. 48204 (38).

St. John's Home (r,c; 9-16 yrs.), 385 E. Leonard N.E., Grand Rapids 49503 (40).

St. Vincent Home for Children (r,c; 5-15 yrs.), 2800 W. Willow St., Lansing 48917 (36).

Villa Maria, Sisters of the Good Shepherd (r,g; 13-17 yrs.), 1315 Walker Ave. N.W., Grand Rapids. 49504 (30).

Vista Maria (r,d, g; 13-17 yrs.), 20651 W. Warren Ave., Dearborn Heights. 48127 (107 r; 20 d).

**Minnesota:** Home of the Good Shepherd, (r.g; 12-17 yrs.), 5100 Hodgson Rd., St. Paul. 55112 (48).

St. Cloud Children's Home (r,c; 8-17 yrs.), 1726 7th Ave. S., St. Cloud. 56301 (72).

St. James Children's Home (r,c), Woodland Hills, Duluth 55803 (60).

Tiffany House Group Home (c), 374 4th Ave. S., St. Cloud 56301 (11).

**Missouri:** Child Center of Our Lady (r,c; 4-12 yrs. — d,c; 4-17 yrs.), 7900 Natural Bridge Rd., St. Louis. 63121 (79).

Marillac Center for Children (r,d,c; 4-14 yrs.), 310 W. 106th St., Kansas City. 64114 (28 r; 60 d).

Marygrove (r,g; d,c; 13-17 yrs.), 2705 Mullanphy Lane, Florissant. 63031 (44).

**Nebraska:** Father Flanagan's Boys' Home (r; 10-18 yrs.), Boys Town, Nebr. 68010 (r, 390; d, 307).

**Nevada:** St. Yves School (r,g; 13-17 yrs.), 7000 North Jones Blvd., Las Vegas, 89131 (60).

**New Jersey:** Christopher House (c; 18 and over), 55 N. Clinton Ave., Trenton 08607 (90). Psychiatric day treatment.

Collier Group Home (r,g; 14-18 yrs.), 47 Reckless Pl., Red Bank 07701 (10).

Collier School (d,c; 13-18 yrs.), Wickatunk 07765.

Guidance Clinic of Catholic Welfare Bureau (c), 39 N. Clinton Ave., Trenton 08607. Psychiatric counseling for children and adults.

Mt. St. Joseph Children's Center (r,d,c; 6-12 yrs.), Shepherd Lane, Totowa 07512 (32).

New Jersey's Boystown (r; adolescents), 499 Belgrove Dr., Kearney 07032 (100).

**New York:** The Astor Home for Children (r,d,c; 5-12 yrs.), 36 Mill St., Rhinebeck 12572 (75). Group Homes (7-18 yrs.), 1200 Zerega Ave., Bronx 10462 (52). Child Guidance Clinics/Day Treatment (Rhinebeck, Poughkeepsie, Beacon, Bronx). Head start — Day Care (Poughkeepsie, Beacon, Hyde Park, Dover, Millerton).

Baker Hall (r,d,b; 10-18 yrs.), 150 Martin Rd., Lackawanna. 14218 (250). Special services, institution, group homes, foster homes, preventive services, special education school.

LaSalle School (r,d,b; 12-18 yrs.), 391 Western Ave., Albany. 12203 (145). Also conducts group homes.

Madonna Heights Services (r,d,g; 11-17 yrs.), Burrs Lane, Huntington. 11743 (110). Also conducts group homes on Long Island and outpatient programs.

Saint Anne Institute (r,d,g; 12-18 yrs.), 160 N.

Main Ave., Albany. 12206 (140). Critical level, preventive services, group home.

St. Helena's Residence (r,g; 12-17 yrs.), 120 W. 60th St., New York. 10023 (20).

St. John's of Rockaway Beach (r,b; 10-18 yrs.), 144 Beach 111th St., Rockaway Park. 11694 (112). Also conducts group homes in Far Rockaway and Richmond Hill.

**North Dakota:** Home on the Range for Boys (r; 12-18 yrs.), Box 41, Sentinel Butte. 58654 (46).

**Ohio:** Diocesan Child Guidance Center, Inc. (d,c; preschool) Outpatient counseling program (c; 2-18 yrs.), 840 W. State St., Columbus 43222.

Marycrest (r,g; 13-18 yrs.), 7800 Brookside Rd., Independence. 44131 (70).

Parmadale/St. Anthony's Youth Services Village (r,c; 7-21 yrs.), 6753 State Rd., Parma 44134.

Rosemont (r,g;d,c; 12-18 yrs.), 2440 Dawnlight Ave., Columbus 43211 (150).

**Oregon:** St. Mary's Home for Boys (r; 9-17 yrs.), 16535 S.W. Tualatin Valley Highway, Beaverton 97006 (43).

**Pennsylvania:** De LaSalle in Towne (d,b; 12-17 yrs.), 25 S. Van Pelt St., Philadelphia 19103 (110).

De LaSalle Vocational Day Treatment (b; 15-17 yrs.), P.O. Box 344 — Street Rd. and Bristol Pike, Bensalem 19020 (120).

Gannondale School for Girls (r; 12-17 yrs.), 4635 E. Lake Rd., Erie 16511 (57).

Harborcreek School for Boys (r; 10-17 yrs.), 5712 Iroquois Ave., Harborcreek 16421 (135). Also conducts group homes.

Lourdesmont Good Shepherd Adolescent Services (r,g;d,c; 13-17 yrs.), 537 Venard Rd., Clarks Summit 18411 (100).

Pauline Auberle Foundation, The Auberle Home for Boys (r,b; 13-18 yrs.), 1101 Hartman St., McKeesport 15132 (50).

St. Gabriel Hall (r,b; 12-17 yrs.), P.O. Box 13, Audobon 19407 (220). Also conducts group homes.

St. Michael's School for Boys (r,b; d,c; 12-17 yrs.), Hoban Heights, Tunkhannock 18657 (120). Also conducts group homes.

**Tennessee:** DeNeuville Heights School for Girls (r; 12-18 yrs.), 3060 Baskin St., Memphis 38127 (52).

**Texas:** St. Joseph Youth Center (r,c; 12-17 yrs.), 901 S. Madison St., Dallas 75208 (48).

**Washington:** Morning Star Boys Ranch (Spokane Boys' Ranch, Inc.), (r,b; 9-18 yrs.), Box 8087 Manito Station, Spokane 99203 (30).

**Wisconsin:** Eudes Corporation at Our Lady of Charity Center (r,c; 10-17 yrs.), 2640 West Point Rd., Green Bay 54303 (50).

St. Aemilian Child Care Center, Inc. (r,b; 6-12 yrs.), 8901 W. Capitol Dr., Milwaukee 53222 (57).

St. Charles Boys Home (r; 12-18 yrs.), 151 S. 84th St., Milwaukee 53214 (56).

**Wyoming:** St. Joseph's Children's Home (r,c; 6-18 yrs.), P.O. Box 1117, Torrington 82240 (48). Also conducts group home.

### Developmentally Handicapped

This listing includes facilities for children, youth and adults with learning disabilities and/or mental retardation.

**Alabama:** Father Walter Memorial Child Care Center (r,c; birth-12 yrs.), 2815 Forbes Dr., Montgomery 36199 (34). Skilled nursing facility.

**California:** Catholic Charities "Empower" Services to Developmentally Disabled Persons, 433 Jefferson St., Oakland 94607. Services include (in various locations): Evergreen Center (d; adults); Concord House (r; adults); C.O.R.E. (d; adults outreach program for homebound); Case Management (d; adults, children — social workers); Religious Nurture Program (d; adults, children).

Child Study Center (d,c; 5-13 yrs.), 1339 - 20th St., Santa Monica. 90404 (80). Also conducts a developmental nursery (18 mos.-3 yrs.) and a preschool for children from culturally deprived areas (3-5 yrs.).

Helpers of the Mentally Retarded, Inc., 2626 Fulton St., San Francisco 94118. Conducts three homes: Helpers Home for Girls (18 years and older), 2608 Fulton St. and 2626 Fulton St., San Francisco 94118; Helpers Home for Men (18 years and older), 2750 Fulton St., San Francisco 94118.

St. Madeleine Sophie's Training Center (d,c; 18 yrs. and older), 2111 E. Madison Ave., El Cajon 92021 (102).

St. Vincent's (r,d,c; 8-21 yrs.), P.O. Drawer V, 4200 Calle Real, Santa Barbara 93102 (116).

Tierra del Sol (d,c; 18 yrs. and older), 9919 Sunland Blvd., Sunland 91040 (100).

**Connecticut:** Gengras Center (d,c; 8-21 yrs.), St. Joseph College, 1678 Asylum Ave., W. Hartford 06117 (70).

Special Education Department, Diocese of Bridgeport, 238 Jewett Ave., Bridgeport 06606.

Villa Maria Education Center (d,c), 159 Sky Meadow Dr., Stamford 06903 (31). For children with learning disabilities.

**District of Columbia:** Lt. Joseph P. Kennedy Jr. Institute (d,c; 5-20 yrs.), 801 Buchanan St. N.E., Washington 20017 (120). Also conducts group homes, continuing education and life skills training programs, contract employment and job placement.

St. Gertrude's School of Arts and Crafts (r,d,g; 6-19 yrs.), 4801 Sargent Rd. N.E., Washington 20017 (40).

**Florida:** Marian Center Services for Developmentally Handicapped and Mentally Retarded (r,d,c), 15701 Northwest 37th Ave., Opa Locka 33054. Offers variety of services.

Marian School for Exceptional Children (d,c; 2-5 yrs.), 326 Pine Terr., W. Palm Beach 33401.

Morning Star School (d,c; 4-12 yrs.), 725 Mickler Rd., Jacksonville 32211 (70).

Morning Star School (d,c; 3-12 yrs.), 954 Leigh Ave., Orlando 32804 (45).

Morning Star School (d,c; 6-13 yrs.), 4661 - 80th Ave., N., Pinellas Park 33565 (50).

Morning Star School (d,c; 6-13 yrs.), 210 E. Linebaugh Ave., Tampa 33612. For children with learning disabilities.

**Illinois:** Bartlett Learning Center (r,d,c; 5-21 yrs.), 801 W. Bartlett Rd., Bartlett 60103 (124).

Good Shepherd Manor (permanent home for men; 18 yrs. and older), P.O. Box 260, Momence, 60954 (120).

Lt. Joseph P. Kennedy, Jr., School (r,b;d,c; 6-21 yrs.) and Job Training Center (c; 16 yrs. and older), 123rd and Wolf Rd., Palos Park. 60464 (101).

Misericordia Home South (r,c; 1 mo.-6 yrs.), 2916 W. 47th St., Chicago 60632 (122).

Misericordia Home North (r,c; 4-21 yrs.), 6300 North Ridge, Chicago 60660 (82).

Mt. St. Joseph (mentally handicapped women; 20-45 yrs.), 24955 N. Highway 12, Lake Zurich 60047 (160).

St. Francis School for Exceptional Children (r,c; 4-12 yrs.), 1209 S. Walnut Ave., Freeport 61032 (32).

St. Jude Special Education Center (d,c), 2nd and Spring Ave., Aviston 62216.

St. Mary of Providence (r,d,g; 4-21 yrs.), 4200 N. Austin Ave., Chicago 60634 (190).

St. Rose Center (d,c; 3-21 yrs.), 4911 S. Hoyne Ave., Chicago 60609 (60).

St. Vincent Residential School (c; 12 yrs. and older) (30), and St. Vincent Community Living Facility (adults) (20), and St. Vincent Supported Living Arrangement (adults) (60), 659 E. Jefferson St., Freeport 61032.

Special Education Program of the East St. Louis Deanery (d,c; 5-16 yrs.), 8213 Church Lane, East St. Louis 62203 (60).

**Indiana:** Marian Day Program (d,c; 6-16 yrs.), 700 Herndon Dr., Evansville 47711 (20).

Providence House (r, men; 18 yrs. and up), 520 W. 9th St., Jasper 47546 (66).

St. Bavo Special Class (d,c; 6-15 yrs.), 512 W. 8th St., Mishawaka 46544 (12).

St. Mary Child Center School (d,c; 3-16 yrs.), 311 N. New Jersey St., Indianapolis 46204 (32). Developmentally Disabled.

**Kansas:** Holy Family Center (d,c; 6-21 yrs.), 619 S. Maize Rd., Wichita 67209 (65).

Lakemary Center, Inc. (r,d,c; 3-16 yrs.), 100 Lakemary Dr., Paola 66071 (72r,35d).

**Kentucky:** Ursuline-Pitt School (d,c), 10715 Ward Ave., Louisville 40223 (62).

Ursuline Speech Clinic (d,c), 3105 Lexington Rd., Louisville 40206 (105).

**Louisiana:** Department of Special Education, Archdiocese of New Orleans, St. Michael Special School, 1522 Chippewa St., New Orleans 70130.

Holy Angels School (r,c; teen-age, 14 yrs. and older; nursery, 2 mo. to kindergarten age), 10450 Ellerbe Rd., Shreveport 71106 (200).

Our Lady of Fatima School (d,c; 6-18 yrs.), 2315 Johnston St., Lafayette 70503 (50).

Padua House (r,c; birth-21 yrs.), 200 Beta St., Belle Chase 70037 (44).

Regina Caeli Center (d,c; 6-16 yrs.), 3903 Kingston, Lake Charles. 70605 (50).

St. Agnes Vocational Evaluation and Training Center (d,c), P.O. Box 53326, 715 East Blvd., Baton Rouge 70802 (140).

St. Mary's Training School (r,c; 3-22 yrs.), P.O. Drawer 7768, Alexandria 71306 (150).

**Maryland:** The Benedictine School for Exceptional Children (r,c; 6-21 yrs.), Ridgely 21660 (100). Also conducts Habilitation Center (r,c; 17 yrs. and older) (50).

Francis X. Gallagher Center (r), 2520 Pot Spring Rd., Timonium 21093 (76).

St. Elizabeth School and Habilitation Center (d,c; 12-21 yrs.), 801 Argonne Dr., Baltimore 21218 (125).

St. Francis School for Special Education (d,c; 3-12 yrs.), 2226 Maryland Ave., Baltimore 21218 (60).

**Massachusetts:** Cardinal Cushing School and Training Center (r,d,c; 6-22 yrs.), Hanover 02339 (130 r; 65 d).

Mercy Centre for Developmental Disabilities (d,c; 3-22 yrs. and over), 25 West Chester St., Worcester 01605 (160).

Nazareth Hall (d,c; 7-22 yrs.), 887 Highland Ave., Fall River, 02720 (45).

Nazareth on the Cape (d,c; 6-15 yrs.), 261 South St., Hyannis 02601 (25).

St. Coletta Day School (d,c; 6-20 yrs., admission age), 85 Washington St., Braintree 02184 (132).

**Michigan:** Our Lady of Providence Center (r,d,g; 5-17 yrs., child caring; 18-26, adult foster care), 16115 Beck Rd., Northville. 48167 (100).

St. Louis Center and School (r,d,b; 6-18 yrs. child care; 18-26 yrs. adult foster care), 16195 Old U.S. 12, Chelsea 48118 (80).

**Minnesota:** Mother Teresa Home (r,c; adults), 101-10th Ave. N., Cold Spring 56320 (14).

St. Elizabeth Home (r,c; adults), 306 15th Ave. N., St. Cloud 56301 (14).

St. Francis Home (r,c; 9-12 yrs.) 25-2nd St. N., Waite Park 56387 (6).

**Missouri:** Department of Special Education, Archdiocese of St. Louis, 4472 Lindell Blvd., St. Louis. 63108. Conducts 31 special day classes (c; 5-16 yrs.).

Good Shepherd Manor (residential for developmentally disabled men; 16 yrs. and up), Little Brothers of the Good Shepherd, 3220 E. 23rd St., Kansas City 64127 (43).

Mt. Carmel Group Home (r,c; 16-21 yrs.), 8757 Annetta Ave., St. Louis 63147.

St. Joseph's Vocational Center (d,c; 15-21 yrs.), 5341 Emerson Ave., St. Louis 63120 (147).

St. Mary's Special School (r,c; 5-16 yrs.), 5341 Emerson Ave., St. Louis 63120 (135).

St. Peter's Special Classes (d,c; 5-21 yrs.), 314 W. High St., Jefferson City 65101 (30).

Universal Sheltered Workshop (c, adults), 6912 W. Florissant Ave., St. Louis 63136. Sheltered employment (80).

**Nebraska:** Madonna School for Exceptional Children (d,c; 5-21 yrs.), 2537 N. 62nd St., Omaha 68104 (65).

Villa Marie School (r,d,c; 7-16 yrs.), P. O. Box 80328, Waverly 68501 (25).

**New Jersey:** Alhambra Child Study Center (d,c; 3-12 yrs.), 31 Centre St., Newark 07102 (35).

Archbishop Boland Rehabilitation Center (d,c; 16-60 yrs.), 450 Market St. Newark 07105 (350).

Archbishop Damiano School (d,c; 5-21 yrs.), 532 Delsea Dr., Westville Grove 08093.

Catholic Community Services, Multi-Service Center, 17 Mulberry St., Newark 07102.

Department of Special Education, Diocese of Camden, 1845 Haddon Ave., Camden 08108. Services include: Archbishop Damiano School (above), and full time programs at 6 Catholic

Schools; adult evening classes (18-65 yrs.); religious education programs.

Department of Special Education, Diocese of Paterson. Murray House (r; adults), 389 Main St., Paterson 07501. Also conducts four other adult group homes and one adult opportunity center.

Felician School for Exceptional Children (r,d,c; 2½-14 yrs.), 260 S. Main St., Lodi 07644 (120).

McAuley School for Exceptional Children (d,c; 5-9 yrs.), 1633 Rt. 22 at Terrill Rd., Plainfield-Watchung 07060 (40).

Mt. Carmel Guild Special Education School (d,c; 6-15 yrs.), 241 Erie St., Jersey City 07302 (80).

Mt. Carmel Guild Special Education School (d,c; 6-12 yrs.), 550 E. Broad St., Westfield 07079 (45).

St. Anthony's Special Education School (d,c; 10-20 yrs.), 25 N. 7th St., Belleville 07109 (60).

Sr. Georgine Learning Center (d,c; 6-17 yrs.), 544 Chestnut Ave., Trenton 08611 (30).

St. John of God Community Services (d,c; birth to adults), 532 Delsea Dr., Westville Grove 05093.

St. Patrick's Special Education School (d,c; 6-17 yrs.), 72 Central Ave., Newark 07109 (60).

**New Mexico:** St. Joseph's Manor (r,b; 18-35 yrs.), P.O. Box 610, Bernalillo 87004. Little Brothers of the Good Shepherd, P.O. Box 610, Bernalillo 87004. Twenty-four-hour adult care center for mentally retarded men.

**New York:** Cantalician Center for Learning (d,c; birth-21 yrs.), 3233 Main St., Buffalo 14214 (300).

Cantalician Center Workshop (d,c; 18 yrs. and older), 129A Central Park Plaza, Buffalo 14214 (150). Also conducts a vocational evaluation and rehabilitation training program.

Catholic Charities, Diocese of Rockville Centre — Services for Retarded Adults, 50 N. Park Ave., Box X, Rockville Centre 11570. Conducts four residences for retarded adults (Christopher Residence; Neumann Residence for Deaf Retarded; Alhambra House; Seton Residence — r,c; 21 yrs. and up).

Cobb Memorial School (r,c; 6-10 yrs.), Altamont 12009 (40).

Friends of L'Arche of Greater Syracuse, Inc. (r, adults), 1701 James St., Syracuse 13206 (12). Long-term facility for mentally retarded adults following philosophy of Jean Vanier and L'Arche movement.

Maryhaven Center of Hope (r,d,c; pre-school to adult), Myrtle Ave., Port Jefferson 11777. Offers variety of services.

Mercy Home for Children (r,c), 273 Willoughby Ave., Brooklyn 11205.

Office for the Handicapped, Diocese of Brooklyn, 191 Joralemon St., Brooklyn 11201. Services include day care center and community residences for retarded adults.

Office of the Handicapped, Archdiocese of New York, 1011 First Ave., New York 10022.

St. Catherine Center for Children (r,c; birth to 12 yrs. and d,c; 3-12 yrs.), 30 N. Main St., Albany 12203 (140). Also conducts group home and specialized foster care programs.

St. Joseph School for Exceptional Children (r,d,c; 5-21 yrs.), 10807 Bennett Rd., Dunkirk 14048 (26 r, 14 d). Residents must return home weekends and vacations.

School of the Holy Childhood (d,c; 5-21 yrs.), 1150 Buffalo Rd., Rochester 14624 (94). Adult program, 18-50 yrs.

**North Carolina:** Holy Angels Nursery (r,c; birth to 12 yrs.), Belmont 28012 (66).

**Ohio:** Good Shepherd Manor (permanent care of men 18 years and older), P.O. Box 387, Wakefield 45687 (104).

Julie Billiart School, 4982 Clubside Rd., Cleveland 44127. Non-graded school for children with learning problems.

Mary Immaculate School (d,c; 7-14 yrs.), 3837 Secor Rd., Toledo 43623 (60). For children with learning disabilities.

Mt. Aloysius (r, men; 21 yrs. and over), Tile Plant Rd., New Lexington 43764 (100).

Our Lady of Angels Special School (d,c; 6-16 yrs.), 3570 Rocky River Dr., Cleveland 44111 (30).

Our Lady of the Elms Special School (d,c; 6-15 yrs.), 1230 W. Market St., Akron 44313 (61).

Rose Mary, The Johanna Graselli Rehabilitation and Education Center (r,c; 3-12 yrs.), 19350 Euclid Ave., Cleveland 44117 (40).

St. John's Villa (r,c,b, 6-14 yrs; g, 6-18 yrs., continued care, g, 18 yrs. and over), 620 Roswell Rd. N.W., Carrollton 44615 (221).

St. Joseph Center (d,c; 6-16 yrs.), 2346 W. 14th St., Cleveland 44113 (60).

Sheltered Workshop and Training Center (c; 16 yrs. and older), 1890 W. 22nd St., Cleveland 44113 (35).

**Oregon:** Emily School for Multi-Handicapped Children (d,c; 2½-5 yrs.), 830 N.E. 47th Ave., Portland 97213 (12).

Providence Children's Nursing Center (r, c; nursing care), 830 N. E. 47th Ave., Portland 97213 (54).

**Pennsylvania:** Clelian Heights School for Exceptional Children (r,d,c; 5-21 yrs.), R.D. 9, Box 607, Greensburg 15601 (140). Also conducts re-socialization program (r,d,c; young adults).

Don Guanella School (r,d,b; 6-21 yrs.) and C. K. Center (r,c; adults, post-school age), Sproul Rd., Springfield 19064.

McGuire Memorial (r,d,c; infancy to 7 yrs.), 2119 Mercer Rd., New Brighton 15066 (99).

Mercy Day School: Center for Special Learning (d,c; 2-21 yrs.), 830 S. Woodward St., Allentown 18103 (69).

Our Lady of Confidence Day School (d,c; 5-18 yrs.), 10th and Lycoming Sts., Philadelphia 19140 (120).

St. Anthony School for Exceptional Children (r,d,c; 5-21 yrs.), 13th St. and Hulton Rd., Oakmont 15139 (135).

St. Joseph Day School Center for Special Learning (d,c; 6-21 yrs.), 619 Mahantongo St., Pottsville 17901 (40).

St. Joseph's Center (r,c; birth-20 yrs.), 2010 Adams Ave., Scranton 18509 (85).

St. Katherine School (d,c; 4-18 yrs.), William Rd. and Bowman Ave., Philadelphia 19151 (150)

St. Mary of Providence Center (r,d,g; 6-14 yrs.), Elverson 19520 (120).

**Tennessee:** Madonna Day School for Retarded Children (d,c; 5-16 yrs.), 4189 Leroy, Memphis 38108 (50).

St. Bernard School for Exceptional Children, (c; 4-8 yrs.), 2021 21st Ave. S., Nashville 37212 (25).

**Texas:** Notre Dame of Dallas Special School (d,c; 3-16 yrs.), 1451 E. Northgate Dr., Irving 75062. (115). Notre Dame Vocational Center (d,c; 16 yrs. and over), same address, provides work-study program for exceptional people over 16 (60).

**Virginia:** St. Coletta School (d,c; 3-25 yrs.), 1305 N. Jackson St., Arlington 22201 (45).

St. Mary's Infant Home (r,c; 3 days-9 yrs.), 317 Chapel St., Norfolk 23504 (50).

**Wisconsin:** St. Coletta School (r,c), Jefferson 53549 (372). Offers the following programs:

a complete program of special education from kindergarten through elementary and advanced levels (r,d,c);

a work training center in preparation for job placement (r,c; 18-25 yrs.);

a residential care center (r,c; 45-85 yrs.);

a half-way house to give guidance and assist with problems (r; 18-24 yrs.);

sheltered workshop employment for the mentally retarded in a homelike environment (r,c; 25-45 yrs.).

St. Coletta Day School (c; 8-16 yrs.), 1725 N. 54th St., Milwaukee. 53208 (12).

## Orthopedically Handicapped

**Alabama:** Father Purcell Memorial (r,c; birth to 14 yrs.), 2048 W. Fairview Ave., Montgomery 36108 (50). Skilled nursing home.

**Kentucky:** Redwood School and Rehabilitation Center (d,c; birth and up), 71 Orphanage Rd., Fort Mitchell 41017 (200).

**Pennsylvania:** St. Edmond's Home for Crippled Children (r,c; 2-10 yrs.)., 320 S. Roberts Rd., Rosemont 19010 (50).

## Visually Handicapped

**Illinois:** Department of Vision, Catholic Charities, 721 N. LaSalle St., Chicago 60610. Itinerant education services for visually impaired students attending regular Catholic elementary and high schools in Chicago archdiocese (30).

**Maine:** Visually Handicapped Services: 87 High St., Portland 04101; 15 Vaughn St., Caribou 04736; 382 Sabattus St., Lewiston 04240; 95 Main St., Orono 04472; 333 Lincoln St., Saco 04072; 224 Main St., Waterville. Itinerant teacher and other services.

**New Jersey:** St. Joseph's School for the Multiple Handicapped Blind (r,d,c; 3-21 yrs.), 253 Baldwin Ave., Jersey City 07306 (25).

**New York:** Catholic Charities Services for Visually Impaired Persons (c), 272 Merrick Rd., Lynbrook 11563. All ages, differing programs.

Lavelle School for the Blind (r,d,c; 3-21 yrs.), 221st St. and Paulding Ave., Bronx 10469 (120).

**Pennsylvania:** St. Lucy Day School (d,c; 3½-14 yrs.), 929 S. Farragut St., Philadelphia. 19143.

# ORGANIZATIONS

*(See separate article for a listing of facilities for the handicapped.)*

## Blind

**The Carroll Center for the Blind** (formerly the Catholic Guild for All the Blind): Located at 770 Centre St., Newton, Mass. 02158, the center conducts diagnostic evaluation and rehabilitation programs for blind people over 16 years of age, and maintains programs in community services for all ages, volunteer and special services, casework and counseling, low-vision training and professional training. It offers a large range of services for blind people who are not in residence, and maintains an office of public education and information. *AAR Review* is the quarterly publication of the center. The executive director is Rachel Rosenbaum.

**Xavier Society for the Blind:** The Society is located at 154 E. 23rd St., New York, 10010. Founded in 1900 by Rev. Joseph Stadelman, S.J., it is a center for publications for the blind and maintains a circulating library of approximately 7,000 volumes in Braille, large type and on tape. Its many publications include *The Catholic Review,* a monthly selection of articles of current interest from the Catholic press presented for the visually handicapped in Braille, on tape, and in large print. The director of Xavier is Rev. Anthony F. La Bau, S.J.

## The Deaf

According to the National Catholic Office for the Deaf, there are approximately 95,000 Catholics among the total deaf population of 410,522. (The deaf were defined by the 1974 National Census of the Deaf Population as "those persons who could not hear and understand speech and who had lost — or never had — that ability prior to 19 years of age.) Reported statistics indicated: Students in Catholic schools for the deaf, 1,969; teachers, 570 (147 were religious). Personnel involved in out-of-school pastoral ministry to the deaf included: priests, 73 (41 full-time, 32 part-time); permanent deacons, 6 (part-time); sisters, 45 (40 full-time, 5 part-time); brothers, 3 (1 full-time, 2 part-time); lay people, 23 (19 full-time, 4 part-time).

Organizations involved in work for the deaf include the following.

**International Catholic Deaf Association:** Established by deaf adults in Toronto, Canada, in 1949, the association has more than 3,000 members in 121 chapters, mostly in the U.S. It is the only international lay association founded and controlled by deaf Catholic adults. It is affiliated with the World Federation of the Deaf. Home office address: 814 Thayer Ave., Silver Spring, Md. 20910. The ICDA publishes *The Deaf Catholic,* a bimonthly, and sponsors regional conferences, workshops and an annual convention.

**National Catholic Office for the Deaf:** Formally established in 1976, at Washington, D.C., to provide pastoral service to those who teach deaf children and adults, to the parents of deaf children, to pastors of deaf persons, and to organizations of the deaf. The office develops liturgical and religious education materials; organizes workshops, pastoral weeks, community weeks, leadership programs, cursillos; and serves as a clearinghouse for information concerning ministry to the deaf. It publishes *Listening,* a pastoral service for the hearing impaired, five times a year. The executive director is Sister Alverna Hollis, O.P. Address: 814 Thayer Ave., Silver Spring, Md. 20910.

## Mentally Retarded

**National Apostolate with Mentally Retarded Persons:** Established in 1968, the apostolate publishes the quarterly *NAMRP Journal* and a monthly newsletter, and has available a bibliography on the religious education of the retarded. Ellen Cook is president of the apostolate; the executive director is Bro. Joseph Moloney, O.S.F., 191 Joralemon St., Brooklyn, N.Y. 11201.

## Service Agencies

**National Catholic Office for Persons with Disabilities:** Established in 1982 to assist dioceses in developing pastoral services with handicapped persons. The executive director is Sister Rita Baum, S.S.J. Address: 1200 5th St. N.W., Suite 102, Washington, D.C. 20005.

**Special Education Department, National Catholic Educational Association:** Established in 1954 to coordinate under one agency information and service functions for all areas of special education under Catholic auspices. The executive director is Sr. Suzanne Hall, S.N.D. de N. Address: 1077 30th St. N.W., Washington, D.C. 20007.

## OTHER SOCIAL SERVICES

**Cancer Hospitals or Homes:** The following homes or hospitals specialize in the care of cancer patients. They are listed according to state.

Penrose Cancer Hospital, Sisters of Charity of Cincinnati, 2215 N. Cascade Ave., Colorado Springs, Colo. 80907.

Our Lady of Perpetual Help Home, Servants of Relief for Incurable Cancer, 760 Washington St., S.W., Atlanta, Ga. 30315 (54).

Rose Hawthorne Lathrop Home, Servants of Relief for Incurable Cancer, 1600 Bay St., Fall River, Mass. 02724 (35).

Our Lady of Good Counsel Free Cancer Home, Servants of Relief for Incurable Cancer, 2076 St. Anthony Ave., St. Paul, Minn. 55104 (40).

Calvary Hospital, Inc., 1740 Eastchester Rd., Bronx, N.Y. 10461 (200). Sponsored by Catholic Charities, Department of Health and Hospitals, Archdiocese of New York.

St. Rose's Free Home for Incurable Cancer, Servants of Relief for Incurable Cancer, 71 Jackson St., New York, N.Y. 10002 (45).

Rosary Hill Home, Servants of Relief for Incurable Cancer, Hawthorne, N.Y. 10532 (72).

Holy Family Home, Servants of Relief for Incurable Cancer, 6707 State Rd., Parma, O. 44134 (50).

Sacred Heart Free Home for Incurable Cancer, Servants of Relief for Incurable Cancer, 1315 W. Hunting Park Ave., Philadelphia, Pa. 19140 (59).

**Drug Abuse:** Rehabilitation centers and outpatient clinics have been established in several dioceses. Facilities include:

Alpha House for Drug Rehabilitation (women) and Dismas House for Drug Rehabilitation (men), 396 Straight St., Paterson, N.J. 07501 (residential rehabilitation programs). Cedar Outpatient Clinic and Cedar Day Care Center, 101-105 Cedar St., Paterson, N.J. 07501 (outpatient services).

Daytop Village, Inc., 54 W. 40th St., New York, N.Y. 10018. Msgr. William B. O'Brien. Five residential facilities and six outreach centers in New York.

New Hope Manor (live in therapeutic community for rehabilitation of female drug addicts), Graymoor, Garrison, N.Y. 10524.

St. Joseph's Hospital, L. E. Phillips Center for the Chemically Dependent, 2661 County Trunk I, Chippewa Falls, Wis. 54729 (46).

St. Luke's Center/Bethesda Manor, 2693 Biscayne Blvd., Miami, Fla. 33137. Residential and outpatient detoxification programs for drug abusers; day care services for children of addicts in treatment. Miami DARE, same address, trains parents, youth, priests and teachers as prevention volunteers in the area of substance abuse.

**Alcoholics:** Some priests and religious throughout the U.S. are committed in a special way to the personal rehabilitation and pastoral care of alcoholics through participation in Alcoholics Anonymous and other programs. Facilities for the rehabilitation of alcoholics include:

Matt Talbot Inn, 2270 Professor St., Cleveland, Ohio 44113 (capacity 23 men; Halfway House; residential treatment for male alcoholics).

Straight and Narrow Hospital for Alcoholism (20 beds), and Straight and Narrow Rehabilitation Center for Male Alcoholics (35 beds), 396 Straight St., Paterson, N.J. 07501. McNulty House for Male Alcoholics (10 beds), 101 Cedar St., Paterson, N.J. 07501. Straight and Narrow Alcohol Abuse Services (outpatient services), 896 E. 19th St., Paterson, N.J. 07501.

Sacred Heart Rehabilitation Center, Inc., 569 E. Elizabeth St., Detroit, Mich. 48201 (9 beds, detoxification; 60 beds, early treatment); 400 Stoddard Rd., Memphis, Mich. 48041 (75 beds, advance treatment). Both facilities serve male and female live-in clients.

The National Clergy Conference on Alcoholism and Related Drug Problems, 3112 - 7th St. N.E., Washington, D.C. 20017, offers educational material to those involved in pastoral ministry on ways of dealing with problems related to alcoholism and medication dependency.

**Convicts:** Priests serve as full- or part-time chaplains in penal and correctional institutions throughout the country. Limited efforts have been made to assist in the rehabilitation of released prisoners in Halfway House establishments.

**Dining Rooms; Facilities for Homeless:** Representative of places where meals are provided, and in some cases lodging and other services as well, are:

St. Anthony's Dining Room, 121 Golden Gate Ave., San Francisco, Calif. 94102. Founded in 1950 by Rev. Alfred Boeddeker, O.F.M. More than 16 million free meals have been served. Director, Rev. Floyd A. Lotito, O.F.M.

St. Vincent de Paul Free Dining Room, 675 23rd St., Oakland, Calif. 94604. Administered by Little Brothers of the Good Shepherd, under sponsorship of St. Vincent de Paul Society. Hot meals served at lunch time 7 days a week; clothing, lodging provided those in need.

St. Vincent's Dining Room, 505 W. 3rd St., Reno, Nev. 89503.

St. Vincent Dining Room, 650 S. Main St., Las Vegas, Nev. 89101. Hot meal every day at noon.

Good Shepherd Refuge, Little Brothers of the Good Shepherd, 601 2nd St. S.W., Albuquerque, N.M. 87103.

Holy Name Centre for Homeless Men, Inc., 18 Bleeker St., New York, N.Y. 10012. A day shelter for alcoholic, homeless men. Provides social services and aid to transients and those in need. Affiliated with New York Catholic Charities.

St. Francis Inn, 2441 Kensington Ave., Philadelphia, Pa. 19125. Serves hot meals. Temporary shelter for men and women.

St. John's Hospice for Men, staffed by Little Brothers of the Good Shepherd, 1221 Race St., Philadelphia, Pa. 19107. Founded in 1963. Hot breakfast and dinner served to all in need; accommodations for 35 men for night shelter; clothing distributed daily to needy.

Camillus House, Little Brothers of the Good Shepherd, 726 N.E. First Ave., Miami, Fla. 33132. Breakfast, lunch and dinner served to all in need; accommodations for 61 men for night lodging; clothing distributed daily.

**Temporary Shelters:** Facilities for runaways, the abused, exploited and homeless include:

Anthony House, under sponsorship of St. Anthony's Guild (see Index). Four locations: 246 2nd St., Jersey City, N.J. 07302 (for homeless women and children); 38 E. Roosevelt Ave., Roosevelt, N.Y. 11575 (with St. Vincent de Paul Society — for homeless men); P.O. Box 880, Zellwood, Fla. 32798 (for migrant workers and their families); 2130 N. Hancock St., Philadelphia, Pa. 19122 (for homeless youth).

Covenant House, 460 W. 41st St., New York, N.Y. 10036. Non-sectarian. President, Rev. Bruce Ritter, O.F.M. Conv. Provides shelter and services for homeless, runaway and exploited youth under the age of 21, in New York, Houston, Toronto (Canada) and Antigua (Guatemala).

Crescent House, 1231 Prytania St., New Orleans, La. 70130. Temporary residence for abused women and their children.

The Dwelling Place, 409 W. 40th St., New York, N.Y. 10018. For homeless women.

Francis House, 1902 Cuming St., Omaha, Nebr. 68102. For homeless men.

The Good Shepherd Shelter, 1126 W. Grace St., Chicago, Ill. 60613. For abused women with children.

Good Shepherd Shelter, 2561 Venice Blvd., Los Angeles, Calif. 90019. For battered women with children.

Gracenter, Convent of the Good Shepherd, 501 Cambridge, San Francisco, Calif. Residence for women in need.

Mercy Hospice, Sisters of Mercy, 334 S. 13th St., Philadelphia, Pa. 19107. Temporary shelter and relocation assistance for homeless women and children.

Mt. Carmel House, Carmelite Sisters, 471 G Pl., N.W., Washington, D.C. 20001. For homeless women.

Ozanam Inn, Little Brothers of the Good Shepherd, 843 Camp St., New Orleans, La. 70130. Under sponsorship of the St. Vincent de Paul Society. Hospice for homeless men.

St. Christopher Inn, Graymoor, Garrison, N.Y. 10524. Temporary shelter for homeless and needy men.

Siena House of Hospitality, 804 N. 19th St., Omaha, Nebr. 68102. For homeless women and children.

**Unwed Mothers:** Residential and care services for unwed mothers are available in many dioceses.

---

## AMERICAN CATHOLIC AWARDS

**Franciscan International Award** (1958), by the Conventual Franciscans (Prior Lake, Minn.) for outstanding contributions to the development of life. Gerald and Patricia Mische (1984).

**George M. Cohan Award** (1970), by the Catholic Actors Guild of America, Inc., for outstanding contribution to Church and the arts. William J. O'Malley (1982).

**Good Samaritan Award** (1968), by the National Catholic Development Conference to recognize the concern for one's fellowman exemplified by the Good Samaritan. Mrs. Joann Zimmerman (1983).

**Hoey Awards** (1942), by the Catholic Interracial Council of New York (225 E. 52nd St., New York, N.Y. 10022). For promoting social and interracial justice. Tony Bennett, Jos. J. Christian, Jos. Wiscovitch, Josie McMillian (1982).

**Honor et Veritas Award** (1959), by the Catholic

War Veterans to outstanding Americans. Congressman Joseph G. Minish (1984).

**Howard R. Marraro Prize** (1973), by the American Catholic Historical Association for a book on Italian history or Italo-American history or relations. Randolph Starn (1983).

**Insignis Medal** (1951), by Fordham University for extraordinary distinction in the service of God and humanity. Harold Mulqueen, S.J., Jack F. Haggerty, Esq. (1984).

**John Courtney Murray Award** (1972), by the Catholic Theological Society for distinguished achievement in theology. Originated in 1947 as the Cardinal Spellman Award. Monika Hellwig (1984).

**John Gilmary Shea Prize** (1944), by the American Catholic Historical Association for scholarly works on the history of the Catholic Church broadly considered. Thomas A. Kselman (1983).

# RETREATS, SPIRITUAL RENEWAL PROGRAMS _____

There is great variety in retreat and renewal programs, with orientations ranging from the traditional to teen encounters. Central to all of them are celebration of the liturgy and deepening of a person's commitment to faith and witness in life. Features of many of the forms are as follows.

**Traditional Retreats:** Centered around conferences and the direction of a retreat master; oriented to the personal needs of the retreatants; including such standard practices as participation in Mass, reception of the sacraments, private and group prayer, silence and meditation, discussions.

**Team Retreat:** Conducted by a team of several leaders or directors (priests, religious, lay persons) with division of subject matter and activities according to their special skills and the nature and needs of the group.

**Closed Retreat:** Involving withdrawal for a period of time — overnight, several days, a weekend — from everyday occupations and activities.

**Open Retreat:** Made without total disengagement from everyday involvements, on a part-time basis.

**Private Retreat:** By one person, on a kind of do-it-yourself basis with the one-to-one assistance of a director.

**Special Groups:** With formats and activities geared to particular groups; e.g., members of Alcoholics Anonymous, vocational groups and apostolic groups.

**Marriage Encounters:** Usually weekend periods of husband-wife reflection and dialogue; introduced into the U.S. from Spain in 1967.

**Charismatic Renewal:** Featuring elements of the movement of the same name; "Spirit-oriented"; communitarian and flexible, with spontane-ous and shared prayer, personal testimonies of faith and witness.

**Christian Community:** Characterized by strong community thrust.

**Teens Encounter Christ (TEC), SEARCH:** Formats adapted to the mentality and needs of youth, involving experience of Christian faith and commitment in a community setting.

**Christian Maturity Seminars:** Similar to teen encounters in basic concept but different to suit persons of greater maturity.

**Cursillo:** see separate entry.

**Movement for a Better World:** see separate entry.

## Conference

**Retreats International Inc.:** The first organization for promoting retreats in the U.S. was started in 1904 in California. Its initial efforts and the gradual growth of the movement led to the formation in 1927 of the National Catholic Laymen's Retreat Conference, the forerunner of the men's division of Retreats International. The women's division developed from the National Laywomen's Retreat Movement which was founded in Chicago in 1936. The men's and women's divisions merged July 9, 1977. The services of the organization include an annual summer institute for retreat and pastoral ministry, regional conferences for retreat center leadership and area meetings of directors and key leadership in the retreat movement. The officers are: Auxiliary Bishop Robert Morneau of Green Bay, episcopal advisor; Mr. John Van den Wymelenberg, president; Rev. Thomas W. Gedeon, S.J., executive director. National office: Box 1067, Notre Dame, Ind. 46556.

## HOUSES OF RETREAT AND RENEWAL

(Principal sources: Almanac survey; *1984 Directory of Retreats International; The Official Catholic Directory.*)

Abbreviation code: m, men; w, women; mc, married couples; y, youth. Houses and centers without code generally offer facilities to most groups. An asterisk after an abbreviation indicates that the facility is primarily for the group designated but that special groups are also accommodated. Houses furnish information concerning the types of programs they offer.

**Alabama:** Blessed Trinity Shrine Retreat, Holy Trinity 36859.
Visitation Sacred Heart Retreat House, 2300 Spring Hill Ave., Mobile 36607.

**Alaska:** Holy Spirit Retreat House, Box 10035, 10980 Hillside Dr., Anchorage 99511.

**Arizona:** Franciscan Renewal Center, 5802 E. Lincoln Dr., Box 220, Scottsdale 85252.
Mount Claret Cursillo Center, 4633 N. 54th St., Phoenix 85018.
Picture Rocks Retreat — A Christian Renewal Center, 7101 W. Picture Rocks Rd., Tucson 85704.

**Arkansas:** The Abbey Retreat (Coury House), Subiaco 72865.

**California:** Angela Center, 535 Angela Dr., Santa Rosa 95401.
Camp Mariastella (y*, families, ecumenical), Wrightwood 92397. Office, 1120 Westchester Pl., Los Angeles 90019.
Cenacle Retreat House 5340 Fair Oaks Blvd., Carmichael 95608.
Christ the King Retreat Center, Box 156, Citrus Heights 95610.
Christian Brothers Retreat House (y*), 2233 Sulphur Springs Ave., St. Helena 94574.
Claretian Retreat Center, 1119 Westchester Pl., Los Angeles 90019.
El Carmelo Retreat House, 926 E. Highland Ave., Redlands 92373.
Holy Spirit Retreat Center, 4316 Lanai Rd., Encino 91436.
Immaculate Heart Retreat House, 3431 Waverly Dr., Los Angeles 90027. (Days of Recollection only.)
Jesuit Retreat House, P.O. Box 128, Los Altos 94022.

Manresa Retreat House (m*), P.O. Box K, Azusa 91702.

Mary and Joseph Retreat Center, 5300 Crest Rd., Rancho Palos Verdes 90274.

Mater Dolorosa Retreat House (m*), 700 N. Sunnyside Ave., Sierra Madre 91024.

Mercy Center (mc, engaged encounter), 2300 Adeline Dr., Burlingame 94010.

Mission San Luis Rey Retreat, P.O. Box 409, San Luis Rey 92068.

Mother of Mercy Convent, 10210 Oakdale Ave., Chatsworth 91311.

Mount Mary Immaculate, 3254 Gloria Terr., Lafayette 94549.

Mt. Tabor Monastery, 17001 Tomki Rd., Redwood Valley 95470.

New Camaldoli Immaculate Heart Hermitage Big Sur 93920.

Our Lady of Trust Spirituality Center, 205 Pine St., Fullerton 92633.

Poverello of Assisi Retreat House, 1519 Woodworth St., San Fernando 91340.

Presentation Education and Retreat Center, 19480 Bear Creek Rd., Los Gatos 95030.

Prince of Peace Abbey, 650 Benet Hill, Oceanside 92054.

Sacred Heart Retreat House (w*), 920 E. Alhambra Rd., Alhambra 91801.

St. Andrew's Priory Retreat House, Valyermo 93563.

St. Anthony's Retreat House, P.O. Box 248, Three Rivers 93271.

St. Clare's Retreat, 2381 Laurel Glen Rd. Soquel 95065.

St. Francis Retreat, P.O. Box 1070, San Juan Bautista 95045.

St. Francis Salesian Retreat House, 2400 E. Lake Ave., Watsonville 95076.

St. Joseph's Salesian Youth Center (St. Dominic Savio Retreat House) (y), 8301 Arroyo Dr., Rosemead 91770.

St. Mary's Center and Retreat House, 1964 Las Conoas Rd., Santa Barbara 93105.

San Damiano Retreat, P.O. Box 767, Danville 94526.

San Miguel Retreat House, P.O. Box 69, San Miguel 93451.

Santa Sabina Center, 1520 Grand Ave., San Rafael 94901.

Serra Retreat, 3401 S. Serra Rd., Malibu 90265.

Starcross Monastery, House of Prayer, Annapolis, Calif. 95412.

Vallombrosa Center, 250 Oak Grove Ave., Menlo Park 94025.

Villa Maria del Mar, Santa Cruz. Mailing address, 2-1918 E. Cliff Dr., Santa Cruz 95062.

**Colorado:** Bethlehem Center, W. 128th Ave. at Zuni, Broomfield 80020.

Convent of St. Walburga, 6717 S. Boulder Rd., Boulder 80303.

El Pomar Center, 1661 Mesa Ave., Colorado Springs 80906.

Sacred Heart Retreat House, Box 185, Sedalia 80135.

Spiritual Life Institute (individuals only), Nada Hermitage, Crestone 81131.

**Connecticut:** Archdiocesan Spiritual Life Center, 467 Bloomfield Ave., Bloomfield 06002.

Cenacle Center for Meditation and Spiritual Renewal, Wadsworth St., P.O. Box 550,Middletown 06457.

Edmundite Apostolate and Conference Center, Enders Island, Mystic 06355.

Holy Family Retreat (m, mc*), 303 Tunxis Rd., West Hartford 06107.

Immaculata Retreat House, Windham Rd., Willimantic 06226.

Mercy Center, P.O. Box 191, 167 Neck Rd., Madison 06443.

Montfort Missionaries Retreat Center, P.O. Box 667, Litchfield 06759.

Our Lady of Calvary Retreat (w*), 31 Colton St., Farmington 06032.

Trinita Ecumenical Retreat Center, Town Hill Rd., New Hartford 06057.

Villa Maria Retreat House, 159 Sky Meadow Dr., Stamford 06903.

**Delaware:** St. Francis Renewal Center, 1901 Prior Rd., Wilmington 19809.

**District of Columbia:** Washington Retreat House (w*), 4000 Harewood Rd. N.E., Washington 20017.

**Florida:** Cenacle Retreat House, 1400 S. Dixie Highway, Lantana 33462.

Dominican Retreat House, Inc., 7275 S.W. 124th St., Miami 33156.

Franciscan Center, 3010 Perry Ave., Tampa 33603.

Holy Name Priory, P.O. Drawer H, St. Leo 33574.

John Neumann Renewal Center, 685 Miccosukee Rd., Tallahassee 32303.

Our Lady of Florida Retreat House, 1300 US Hwy. No. 1, North Palm Beach 33408.

Pilgrim Center of St. Leo Abbey, P.O. Drawer "L," St. Leo 33574.

**Georgia:** Ignatius House, 6700 Riverside Dr. N.W., Atlanta 30328.

**Idaho:** Nazareth, 4450 N. Five Mile Rd., Boise 83704.

**Illinois:** Aylesford Carmelite Spiritual Center, I-55 at Cass Ave. N., Darien 60559.

Bellarmine Hall (m*), Box 268, Barrington 60010.

Bishop Lane Retreat House, R.R. 2, Box 214 A, Rockford 61102.

Cabrini Retreat Center, 9430 Golf Rd., Des Plaines 60016.

Cenacle Retreat House, 513 Fullerton Parkway, Chicago 60614.

Cenacle Retreat and Conference Center, P.O. Box 340, Warrenville 60555.

Childerley Retreat House, 506 McHenry Rd., Wheeling 60090.

Christian Life Center, 1209 W. Ogden Ave., La Grange Park 60525.

Divine Word International, 2001 Waukegan Rd., Techny 60082.

Franciscan Apostolic Center, P.O. Box 42, Sangamon Ave., Springfield 67205.

King's House, N. 66th St., Belleville 62223.

King's House of Retreats, Box 165, Henry 61537.

La Salle Manor, Christian Brothers Retreat House, Plano 60545.

Longwood Cenacle, 11600 Longwood Dr., Chicago 60643.

National Shrine of Our Lady of the Snows, 9500 W. Illinois Route 15, Belleville 62223.

Our Lady of Angels Retreat and Renewal Center, 1901 N. 18th St., Quincy 62301.

Resurrection Center, 2710 S. Country Club Rd., Woodstock 60098.

Sacred Heart Center, 3000 Central Rd., Rolling Meadows 60008.

St. Francis Retreat, House at Mayslake, 1717 31st St., Oak Brook 60521.

St. Joseph Retreat Center, 353 N. River Rd., Des Plaines 60521.

St. Mary's Retreat House, P.O. Box 608, 1400 Main St., Lemont 60439.

Tolentine Center, 20300 Governors Highway, Olympia Fields 60461.

Villa Desiderata Retreat House, 3015 N. Bayview Lane, McHenry 60050.

Villa Center for Renewal, 35 W. 076 Villa Maria Rd., St. Charles 60174.

Villa Redeemer, Box 6, Glenview 60025.

**Indiana:** Alverna Center, 8140 Spring Mill Rd., Indianapolis 46260.

Beech Grove Benedictine Center, 1402 Southern Ave., Beach Grove 46107.

Crosier Center, 2620 E. Wallen Rd., Ft. Wayne 46825.

John XXIII Center, 407 W. McDonald St., Hartford City 47348.

Kordes Enrichment Center, R.R. 3, Box 200, Ferdinand 47532.

Lourdes Retreat House (m*), Box 156, Cedar Lake 46303.

Mount Saint Francis Retreat Center, Mount Saint Francis 47146.

Our Lady of Fatima Retreat House, 5353 E. 56th St., Indianapolis 46226.

Our Lady of Fatima Retreat Center, Notre Dame 46556.

St. Jude Guest House, St. Meinrad 47577.

Saint Maur Hospitality Center, 4545 Northwestern Ave., Indianapolis 46208.

Sarto Retreat House, 4200 N. Kentucky Ave., Evansville 47711.

Solitude of St. Joseph, Notre Dame, Ind. 46556.

**Iowa:** American Martyrs Retreat House, 2209 N. Union Rd., Cedar Falls 50613.

Colette Renewal Center, 3380 Windsor Ave., Dubuque 52001.

Colfax Interfaith Spiritual Center, Box 37, Colfax, 50054.

**Kansas:** St. Augustine Retreat Center, A 3301 Parallel Parkway, Kansas City 66104.

Villa Christi Retreat House, 3033 W. Second St., Wichita 67203.

**Kentucky:** Catherine Spalding Center, P.O. Box 24, Nazareth 40048.

Marydale Retreat Center, 695 Donaldson Rd., Erlanger 41018.

Our Lady of Gethsemani (m, private), The Guestmaster, Abbey of Gethsemani, Trappist 40073.

Saint Thomas Center, 170 Crabbs Lane, Louisville 40206.

**Louisiana:** Abbey Christian Life Center, St. Joseph's Abbey, St. Benedict 70457.

Ave Maria Retreat House, Route 1, Box 0368 AB, Marrero 70072.

Cenacle Retreat House (w*), 5500 St. Mary St., P.O. Box 8115, Metairie 70011.

Jesuit Spirituality Center, P.O. Box C, Grand Coteau 70541.

Manresa House of Retreats (m), P.O. Box 89, Convent 70723.

Maryhill Renewal Center, 600 Maryhill Rd., Pineville 71360.

Our Lady of the Oaks Retreat House, P.O. Drawer D, Grand Coteau 70541.

**Maine:** Marie Joseph Spiritual Center, RFD 2, Biddeford 04005.

St. Paul's Center, Oblate Fathers Retreat House (French-English), 136 State St., Augusta 04330.

**Maryland:** Bon Secours Spiritual Center, Marriottsville 21104.

CYO Retreat Center, 5625 Edson Lane, Rockville 20852.

Christian Brothers Spiritual Center, 2535 Buckeyestown Pike, Adamstown 21710.

Loyola Retreat House-on-Potomac, Faulkner 20632.

Manresa-on-Severn, P.O. Box 9, Annapolis 21404.

Monsignor Clare J. O'Dwyer Youth Retreat House, 15523 York Rd., Sparks 21152.

St. Joseph Spiritual Center, 3800 Frederick Ave., Baltimore 21229.

**Massachusetts:** Calvary Retreat Center, Passionist Community, 59 South St., Shrewsbury 01545.

Campion Renewal Center, 319 Concord Rd., Weston 02193.

Cenacle Retreat House, 200 Lake St., Brighton, Boston 02135.

Eastern Point Retreat House, Gonzaga Hall, Gloucester 01930.

Espousal Center, 554 Lexington St., Waltham 02154.

Esther House of Spiritual Renewal, Sisters of St. Anne, 1015 Pleasant St., Worcester 01602.

Genesis Spiritual Life Center, 53 Mill St., Westfield 01085.

Glastonbury Abbey (Benedictine Monks), 16 Hull St., Hingham 02043.

Holy Cross Fathers Retreat House, 490 Washington St., N. Easton 02356.

Jesuit Center, Sullivan Square, Charlestown, Boston 02129.

Julie Center of Spirituality, Jeffrey's Neck Rd., Ipswich 01938.

La Salette Center for Christian Living, 947 Park St., Attleboro 02703.

Marian Center (w*), 1365 Northampton St., Holyoke 01040.

Mater Dei Retreat House (boys), Old Groveland Rd., Bradford 01830.

Miramar Retreat House, Duxbury, 02332.

Mother of Sorrows Retreat House, 110 Monastery Ave., W. Springfield 01089.

Mt. Carmel Christian Life Center, Oblong Rd., Williamstown 01267.

Sacred Heart Retreat House, Salesians of St. John Bosco, P.O. Box 271, Ipswich 01938.

St. Joseph's Abbey Retreat House (m) (Trappist Monks), Spencer 01562.

St. Stephen Priory (Dominican), 20 Glen St., Box 370, Dover, Mass. 02030.

**Michigan:** Blessed Sacrament Retreat House, Sacramentine Sisters, Conway 49722.

Capuchin Retreat, Box 188, Washington 48094.

Colombiere Retreat/Conference Center, Box 139, 9075 Big Lake Rd., Clarkston 48016.

Manresa Jesuit Retreat House, 1390 Quarton Rd., Bloomfield Hills 48013.

Marygrove Center, Garden 49835.

Portiuncula in the Pines, 703 E. Main St., De Witt 48820.

Queen of Angels Retreat, Box 2026, 3400 S. Washington Blvd., Saginaw 48605.

Retreat Center (w*), Sisters of Mary Reparatrix, 13600 Virgil Ave., Detroit 48223.

St. Basil's Center, 3990 Giddings Rd., Pontiac 48055.

St. Clare Capuchin Retreat, 1975 N. River Rd., St. Clair 48079.

St. Lazare Retreat House, 18600 W. Spring Lake Rd., Spring Lake 49456.

St. Mary's Retreat House (w*), 775 W. Drahner Rd., Oxford 48051.

St. Paul of the Cross Retreat Center, 23333 Schoolcraft, Detroit 48223.

Weber Center, 1257 E. Siena Heights Dr., Adrian 49221.

**Minnesota:** Assisi Heights Christian Community Center, Box 4900, Rochester 55903.

Benedictine Center, St. Paul's Priory, 2675 E. Larpenteur Ave., St. Paul 55109.

The Cenacle, 1221 Wayzata Blvd., Wayzata 55391.

Center for Spiritual Development, Box 538, 211 Tenth St., Bird Island 55310.

Christian Brothers Retreat Center, 15525 St. Croix Trail North, Marine-on-St. Croix 55047.

The Dwelling Place, 216 3rd Ave. S., Sauk Rapids 56379.

Epiphany House of Prayer, 266 Summit Ave., St. Paul 55102.

Franciscan Retreats, Conventual Franciscan Friars, 16385 St. Francis Lane, Prior Lake 55372.

Jesuit Retreat House, 8243 De Montreville Trail North, Lake Elmo 55109.

King's House of Retreats, 621 S. First Ave., Buffalo 55313.

Maryhill Retreat House, Society of Daughters of the Heart of Mary, 260 Summit Ave., St. Paul 55102.

Minneapolis Catholic Youth Center (y, mc), 2120 Park Ave. S., Minneapolis 55404.

Villa Maria Center, Frontenac 55026.

Welch Center, 605 N. Central Ave., Duluth 55807.

**Missouri:** Cenacle Retreat House, 900 S. Spoede Rd., St. Louis 63131.

Maria Fonte Solitude (private), P.O. Box 322, High Ridge 63049.

Marianist Apostolic Center, P.O. Box 127, Glencoe 63038.

Our Lady of Assumption Abbey (m, w), Trappists, Rt. 5, Box 193, Ava 65608.

Pallottine Renewal Center, R.R. 2, 15270 Old Halls Ferry Rd., Florissant 63034.

Passionist Retreat of Our Lady, Retreat House, Passionist Fathers and Brothers, 3036 Bellerive Dr., St. Louis 63121.

Queen of Heaven Solitude (private), Rt. 1, Box 107A, Marionville 65705.

Retreat and Conference Center, Conception Seminary College, Conception 64433.

St. Pius X Abbey, Abbey Rd., Pevely 63070.

The White House Retreat (m), 7400 Christopher Dr., St. Louis 63129.

**Montana:** Emmaus Retreat House, 438 7th Ave., Havre 59501.

Ursuline Retreat Center, 2300 Central Ave., Great Falls 59401.

**Nebraska:** Crosier Renewal Center, 223 E. 14th St., P.O. Box 789, Hastings 68901.

Good Counsel, R.R. 1, Box 110, Waverly 68462.

St. Columbans Foreign Mission Society, St. Columbans 68056.

**New Hampshire:** The Common - St. Joseph Monastery, Discalced Carmelite Friars, Peterborough 03458.

La Salette Conference and Retreat Center, Enfield 03748.

New Hampshire Monastery, Hundred Acres, New Boston 03070.

Oblate Fathers Retreat House, Rt. 3A, Lowell Rd., Hudson 03051.

St. Francis Retreat Center, 860 Central Rd., Rye Beach 03871.

**New Jersey:** Bethlehem Hermitage, Pleasant Hill Rd., Box 315, Chester 07930.

Blackwood Center, St. Pius X House, Box 216, Blackwood 08012.

Carmel Retreat House, 1071 Ramapo Valley Rd., Mahwah 07430.

Cenacle Retreat House, 411 River Rd., Highland Park 08904.

Felician Retreat House, Windemere Ave., Mt. Arlington 07856.

Good Shepherd Center, 74 Kahdena Rd., Morristown 07960.

Loyola House of Retreats, 161 James St., Morristown 07960.

Marianist Christian Family Living Center (families), Cape and Yale Ave., Cape May Point 08212.

Maris Stella, P.O. Box 335, Harvey Cedars 08008.

Mt. St. John Academy, Gladstone, N.J. 07934.

Queen of Peace Retreat House, St. Paul's Abbey, P.O. Box 7, Newton 07860.

St. Joseph's Villa (w), Srs. of St. John the Baptist, Peapack 07977.

San Alfonso Retreat House, 755 Ocean Ave., Long Branch 07740.

Stella Maris Retreat House, 981 Ocean Ave., Elberon 07740.

Villa Pauline Retreat and Guest House (w*), Hilltop Rd., Mendham 07945.

Xavier Center, Convent Station 07961.

**New Mexico:** Holy Cross Retreat House, P.O. Box 158, Mesilla Park 88047.

Our Lady of Guadalupe Monastery (families - pentecostal), Pecos 87552.

Our Lady Queen of Peace, 5825 Coors Rd. S.W., Albuquerque 87105.

**New York:** At Home Retreats, 310 Cenacle Rd., Lake Ronkonkoma 11779.

Bethany Retreat House, County Road 105, Highland Mills 10930.

Bethlehem Retreat House (m*), Abbey of the Genesee, Piffard 14533.

Bishop Molloy Retreat House, 86-45 178th St., Jamaica, L.I. 11432.

Cabrini-on-the Hudson, West Park, N.Y. 12493.

Cardinal Spellman Retreat House, Passionist Fathers, 5801 Palisade Ave., Bronx (Riverdale) 10471.

Cenacle Center for Spiritual Renewal, Cenacle Rd., Lake Ronkonkoma 11779.

The Cenacle: Center for Spiritual Renewal, 693 East Ave., Rochester 14607.

Cenacle Retreat House, State Rd., P.O. Box 467, Bedford Village 10506.

Christ the King Retreat House, 500 Brookford Rd., Syracuse 13224.

Cormaria Retreat House, Sag Harbor, L.I. 11963.

Diocesan Cursillo Center (Spanish), 118 Congress St., Brooklyn 11201.

Dominican Retreat House, 1945 Union St., Schenectady 12309.

Don Bosco Retreat Center, Filor's Lane, West Haverstraw 10993.

Graymoor Christian Unity Center, Graymoor, Garrison 10524.

Island Retreat (June-Sept.), Bluff Island, Tupper Lake 12986.

Jesuit Retreat House, North American Martyrs Shrine, Auriesville 12016.

Mary Reparatrix Retreat Center, 14 E. 29th St., New York 10016.

Monastery of the Precious Blood (w), Ft. Hamilton Parkway and 54th St., Brooklyn 11219.

Mount Alvernia Retreat House, Box 858, Wappingers Falls 12590.

Mount Manresa Retreat House, 239 Fingerboard Rd., Staten Island 10305.

Notre Dame Retreat House, Box 342, Foster Rd., Canandaigua 14424.

Our Lady of Hope Center, 434 River Rd., Newburgh 12550.

Regina Maria Retreat House (w*), 77 Brinkerhoff St., Plattsburgh 12901.

St. Albert's Spiritual Life Center, Carmelite Fathers, Box 868, Middletown 10940.

St. Andrew's House, 89 A St. Andrew's Rd., Walden 12586.

St. Columban's Retreat House, P.O. Box 816, Derby 14047.

St. Gabriel Retreat House, 64 Burns Rd., P.O. Box P, Shelter Island 11965.

St. Ignatius Renewal Center, Diocese of Buffalo, 6969 Strickler Rd., Clarence Center 14032. Poustinia available.

St. Ignatius Retreat House, Searington Rd., Manhasset, L.I. 11030.

St. Josaphat's Retreat House, Basilian Monastery, East Beach Rd., Glen Cove 11542.

St. Joseph Center (Spanish Center), 523 W. 142nd St., New York 10031.

St. Mary's Villa, R.R. 1, Box 59, Sloatsburg 10974.

Stella Maris Retreat House and Center for Renewal, 130 E. Genesee St., Skaneateles 13152.

Stella Niagara Center of Renewal, 4421 Lower River Rd., Stella Niagara 14144.

Tagaste Monastery Retreat House (m, y), Suffern 10901.

**North Carolina:** Avila Retreat Center, Rt. 2, Box 285, Mason Rd., Durham 27712.

Living Waters Catholic Reflection Center, Rt. 1, Box 476, Maggie Valley 28751.

Maryhurst Retreat House, P.O. Box 38, Pinehurst 28374.

**North Dakota:** Queen of Peace Retreat, Redemptorist Fathers, 1310 N. Broadway, Fargo 58102.

**Ohio:** Bergamo Conference Center, 4435 E. Patterson Rd., Dayton 45430.

Friarhurst Retreat House, 8136 Wooster Pike, Cincinnati 45227.

Jesuit Renewal Center, 5361 S. Milford Rd., Milford 45150.

Jesuit Retreat House, 5629 State Rd., Cleveland 44134.

Loyola of the Lake, 700 Killinger Rd., Clinton 44216.

Maria Stein Center, 2365 St. Johns Rd., Maria Stein 45860.

Men of Milford Retreat House, Box 348, Milford 45150.

MSC Center, Rt. 4, Shelby 44875.

Our Lady of Consolation Renewal Center, 320 West St., Carey 43316.

Our Lady of the Pines, 1250 Tiffin St., Fremont 43420.

Sacred Heart, 3128 Logan Ave., Box 6074, Youngstown 44501.

St. Anthony Pilgrim House, 321 Clay St., Carey 43316. (Facilities only.)

St. Joseph Christian Life Center, 18485 Lake Shore Blvd., Cleveland 44119.

Shrine Center for Renewal, Diocese of Columbus, 5277 E. Broad St., Columbus 43213.

**Oklahoma:** St. Gregory's Abbey, Shawnee 74801.

**Oregon:** Franciscan Retreat Center, 0858 S.W. Palatine Hill Rd., Portland 97219.

Loyola Retreat House (Jesuit Center for Spiritual Renewal), 3220 S.E. 43rd St., Portland 97206.

Mt. Angel Abbey Guest-Retreat Center, St. Benedict 97373.

Our Lady of Peace Retreat (m, w); 3600 S. W. 170th Ave., Beaverton 97005.

Shalom Prayer Center, Benedictine Sisters, Mt. Angel 97362.

Trappist Abbey Retreat (m*, private), P.O. Box 97, Lafayette 97127.

**Pennsylvania:** Byzantine Catholic Seminary (m), 3605 Perrysville Ave., Pittsburgh 15214.

Cenacle Retreat House (w*), 4721 Fifth Ave., Pittsburgh 15213.

Dominican Retreat House, Ashbourne Rd. and Juniper Ave., Elkins Park 19117.

Family Life Center, P.O. Box 306, Route 219 North, Ebensburg 15931.

Fatima House, Rolling Hills Rd., Ottsville 18942.

Gilmary Diocesan Center, Flaugherty Run Rd., Coraopolis 15108.

Jesuit Center for Spiritual Growth, Box 223, Church Rd., Wernersville 19565.

Malvern Retreat House (m*), St. Joseph's in the Hills, Malvern 19355.

Maria Wald Retreat House, Convent of the Precious Blood, New Holland Ave., Shillington 19607.

Marian Hall, St. Joseph Convent/Academy, Rt. 2, Columbia 17512.

Mercy Center, Box 370, Dallas 18612.

Mount St. Macrina Retreat Center, Mt. St. Macrina, Box 878, Uniontown 15401.

Our Lady of Fatima Center, Griffin Rd., Box 163, Elmhurst 18416.

St. Alphonsus Retreat House (m*), Box 218, Tobyhanna 18466 (1,200).

St. Emma Retreat House, 1001 Harvey St., Greensburg 15601.

St. Fidelis Retreat Center, Herman 16039.

St. Francis Retreat Center, 3918 Chipman Rd., Easton 18042.

St. Francis Retreat House (w), Monocacy Manor, 395 Bridle Path Rd., Bethlehem 18017.

St. Gabriel's Retreat House (w), 631 Griffin Pond Rd., Clarks Summit 18411.

St. Paul of the Cross Retreat House, 148 Monastery Ave., Pittsburgh 15203.

Saint Raphaela Mary Retreat House, 616 Coopertown Rd., Haverford 19041.

St. Vincent Archabbey (m*, summer), Latrobe 15650.

Trinity Spiritual Center, 3609 Simpson Ferry Rd., Camp Hill 17011.

Villa Maria Retreat Center, Box 208, Wernersville 19565.

Villa of Our Lady Retreat House (w, mc), Mt. Pocono 18344.

**Rhode Island:** Carmel Renewal Center, 21 Battery St., Newport 02840.

Ephpheta House — A Center for Renewal, 10 Manville Hill Rd; mailing address, P.O. Box 1, Manville 02838.

Father Marot CYO Center (y), 53 Federal St., Woonsocket 02895.

Our Lady of Peace Spiritual Life Center, Ocean Rd., Narragansett 02882.

St. Dominic Savio Youth Center (y*), Broad Rock Rd., Box 67, Peace Dale 02883.

**South Carolina:** The Oratory, 434 Charlotte Ave., Box 11586, Rock Hill 29730.

Springbank Christian Center, Dominican Retreat House, Kingstree 29556.

**South Dakota:** St. Martin's Community Center, R.R. 4, Box 253, Rapid City 57701.

Sioux Spiritual Center (for Native Americans), Diocese of Rapid City, Howes Star Route Box 271, Plainview 57748.

**Tennessee:** House of the Lord, 1306 Dellwood Ave., Memphis 38127.

House of the Lord, Rt. 4, Box 251, Paris 38242.

**Texas:** Bishop DeFalco Retreat Center, 2100 N. Spring, Amarillo 79109.

Catholic Renewal Center of North Texas, 4503 Bridge St., Ft. Worth 76103.

Cenacle Retreat House, 420 N. Kirkwood, Houston 77079.

Christian Holiday House and Renewal Center, Oblate Fathers, P.O. Box 635, Dickinson 77539.

Holy Name Retreat Center (m*), 430 Bunker Hill Rd., Houston 77024.

Montserrat Jesuit Retreat House, P.O. Box 398, Lake Dallas 75065.

Mount Tabor Retreat House, 12940 Up River Rd., Corpus Christi 78410.

Our Lady of the Pillar Christian Renewal Center, 2507 N.W. 36th St., San Antonio 78228.

Saint Joseph Retreat House (Casa San Jose), 127 Oblate Dr., San Antonio 78216.

San Juan Retreat House, Diocese of Brownsville, P.O. Box 998, San Juan 78589.

**Utah:** Our Lady of the Holy Trinity Retreat House (m), Huntsville 84317.

Our Lady of the Mountains, 1794 Lake St., Ogden 84401.

**Virginia:** Dominican Retreat, 7103 Old Dominion Dr., McLean 22101.

The Franciscan Center, Rt. 642, Box 825, Winchester 22601.

Holy Family Retreat House, Redemptorist Fathers, 1414 N. Mallory St., Hampton 23363.

Missionhurst CICM Mission Center, 4651 N. 25th St., Arlington 22207.

Spiritual Renewal Center (Genesis House), Rt. 2, Box 388 B, Richmond 23233.

**Washington:** Camp Field Retreat Center, P.O. Box 128, Leavenworth 98826.

Immaculate Heart Retreat House, Route 3, Box 653, Spokane 99203.

Redemptorist Palisades Retreat, P.O. Box 3739, Federal Way 98003.

St. Peter the Apostle Diocesan Retreat Center, Route 1, Box 86, Cowiche 98923.

St. Thomas Center, 14500 Juanita Dr, N.E., Bothell 98011.

Visitation Retreat Center (w), 3200 S,W, Dash Point Rd., Federal Way 98003,

**West Virginia:** Cenacle Retreat House, 1114 Virginia St. E., Charleston 25301.

Paul VI Pastoral Center, 667 Stone and Shannon Rd., Wheeling 26003.

St. Joseph Pastoral Center, Rt. 6, Vienna 26101.

**Wisconsin:** Archdiocesan Retreat Center, 3501 S. Lake Dr., P.O. Box 2018, Milwaukee 53201.

Cardoner Jesuit Retreat Center, 1501 S, Layton Blvd., Milwaukee 53215.

Chapel House of Prayer, Route 1, New Franken, Wis. 54229.

Holy Cross Center for Spiritual Growth, 503 S, Center Ave., Merrill 54452.

Holy Name Retreat House, Chambers Island; mailing address, 1825 Riverside Drive, P.O. Box 337, Green Bay 54305.

Jesuit Retreat House, 4800 Fahrnwald Rd., Oshkosh 54901.

Marynook — House of the Lord, 500 S. 12th St., P.O. Box 6, Galesville 54630.

Monte Alverno Retreat Center, 1000 N. Ballard Rd., Appleton 54911.

Perpetual Help Retreat Center, 1800 N. Timber Trail Lane, Oconomowoc 53066.

St. Anthony Retreat Center, Marathon 54448.

St. Benedict Center (ecumenical retreat and conference center), Fox Bluff, P.O. Box 5070, Madison 53705.

St. Francis Friary and Retreat Center, 503 S, Browns Lake Dr., Burlington 53105.

St. Joseph's Retreat Center, Bailey's Harbor 54202.

St. Vincent Pallotti Center, Rt. 3, Box 61, Elkhorn 53121.

Schoenstatt Center, W. 284 N. 698 Cherry Lane, Waukesha 53186.

---

# AMERICAN CATHOLIC AWARDS

**John La Farge Memorial Award for Interracial Justice** (1965), by the Catholic Interracial Council of New York. Presented annually to a leading citizen of the community regardless of race, color or creed for promoting social and interracial justice. Hon. Mario M. Cuomo (1983).

**King Award** (1971), by the U.S. Catholic Historical Society for significant contribution in the study of the history of the Catholic Church in the U.S. Elisa A. Carrillo (1976).

**Laetare Medal** (1883), by the University of Notre Dame for distinguished accomplishment for Church or nation by an American Catholic. John T. Noonan (1984).

**Lumen Christi Award** (1978) by the Catholic Church Extension Society to persons making an outstanding contribution in service to the American home missions. Sr. Mary Christine Taylor, S.S.J. (1984).

**Marianist Award** (1949), by the University of Dayton for outstanding service in America to the Mother of God (until 1966); for outstanding contributions to mankind (from 1967). Eduardo Frei Montalvo (1967).

**Marian Library Medal** (1953), by the Marian Library of the University of Dayton. Awarded annually (until 1967) to encourage books in English on the Blessed Virgin Mary. Awarded every four years (from 1971), at the time of an International Mariological Congress, to a scholar for Mariological studies. Stefano De Fiores, S.M.M. (1983).

**Mater et Magistra Award** (1963), by the College of Mt. St. Joseph on the Ohio to women for social action in the pattern and spirit of the encyclical *Mater et Magistra.* Mother Teresa (1974).

**Mendel Medal** (1928), by Villanova University for scientists. Dr. Alfred M. Bongiovanni (1968).

**Msgr. John P. Monaghan Social Action Award** by the Assn. of Catholic Trade Unionists; originally (1948), the Quadragesimo Anno Medal. Vincent McDonnell (1970).

**The O'Neil D'Amour Award** (1976), by the National Association of Boards of Education/NCEA, for outstanding contribution of statewide, regional, national or international significance to the Catholic board movement. Bishop William B, Friend (1982).

**O'Reilly-Conway Medal** (1979), by *The Pilot,* Boston archdiocesan newspaper, for distinctive contributions to journalism. James Thistle (1984).

**Peace Award** (1950), by the Secular Franciscan Order. Pres. Anwar Sadat (1980).

**Peter Guilday Prize** (1972), by the American Catholic Historical Association for articles accepted by the editors of the *Catholic Historical Review* which are the first scholarly publications of their authors. Vincent J. McNally (1980).

**Pius XII Marian Award** (1955), by the Montfort Missionaries for promotion of the devotion of consecration to the Immaculate Heart of Mary. Mr, and Mrs. Thomas F. Larkin, Jr. (1973).

**Poverello Medal** (1949), by The University of Steubenville (Ohio), "in recognition of great benefactions to humanity, exemplifying in our age the Christ-like spirit of charity which filled the life of St. Francis of Assisi." Special Olympics (1984).

**Regina Medal** (1959), by the Catholic Library Association for outstanding contributions to children's literature. Madeleine L'Engle (1984).

**St. Bonaventure University Justice and Peace Medal** (1981), by St. Bonaventure University (St, Bonaventure, N.Y.), Sister Joan Malone, O.S.F. (1983).

## SPECIAL AGENCIES

*Some of the following agencies are engaged in carrying out programs of the United States Catholic Conference. Additional agencies are reported in other Almanac entries.*

**Religious Education/Catechesis/CCD** (Confraternity of Christian Doctrine): Its objective is the catechesis of persons from early childhood through adult life.

The modern expansion of catechesis dates from publication of the encyclical letter *Acerbo Nimis* by Pope St. Pius X in 1905. His directive, that CCD programs be established in every parish, was incorporated in the 1917 Code of Canon Law, reaffirmed by the Second Vatican Council in the *Decree on the Bishops' Pastoral Office in the Church*, and given direction by the publication of the *National Catechetical Directory* in 1971.

Programs for catechesis are parish-based. Policies are developed by parish boards or commissions, and responsibility for administering programs rests ideally with a coordinator or director who is a trained professional.

On the diocesan level, religious education is coordinated by a director with a staff operating under the title of an office of religious education or a similar title. The diocesan office coordinates and acts as consultant to the work of local parish and regional programs; it conducts teacher-training courses, issues guidelines for unified programs, provides overall in-service aid and resources for local staffs and programs.

On the national level, Religious Education/ Catechetical Ministry/CCD (formerly called the National Center for the Confraternity of Christian Doctrine, and since 1969 under the Department of Education, U.S. Catholic Conference) provides representation and service for local diocesan staffs and programs. On the international level, it participates in programs which find their roots with the Vatican congregations that deal with religious education or catechesis. Publications include *The Living Light*, Catechetical Sunday material and other related programs.

Sister Mariella Frye, M.H.S.H., is representative for Catechetical Ministry in the Department of Education, U.S. Catholic Conference.

Offices are located at 1312 Massachusetts Ave. N.W., Washington, D.C. 20005.

**National Council of Catholic Men:** A federation of Catholic organizations through which Catholic men may be heard nationally on matters of common interest. NCCM is a constituent of the National Council of Catholic Laity.

Offices are located at 4712 Randolph Dr., Annandale, Va. 22003.

**National Council of Catholic Women:** A federation of some 10,000 organizations of Catholic women in the U.S.; founded in 1920. NCCW unites Catholic organizations and individual Catholic women of the U.S., develops their leadership potential, assists them to act upon current issues in the Church and society, provides a medium through which Catholic women may speak and act upon matters of common interest, and relates to other national and international organizations in the solution of present-day problems. It is an affiliate of the World Union of Catholic Women's Organizations.

The official publication is *Catholic Woman*, issued 6 times a year.

National office: 1312 Massachusetts Ave. N.W., Washington, D.C. 20005.

**National Council of Catholic Laity:** Formed in 1971 by the National Council of Catholic Men and the National Council of Catholic Women to provide direction and guidance to existing and new lay organizations. It sponsors conferences and is a contact agency for information about specialized groups in the Church.

The mailing address is P.O. Box 14525, Cincinnati, Ohio 45214.

**National Catholic Rural Life Conference:** Founded in 1923 through the efforts of Bishop Edwin V. O'Hara for the purpose of promoting the general welfare of rural people by a program of extensive services, publications and rural-related activities. Publications include a newsletter and *Catholic Rural Life.*

The conference has approximately 2,500 members among rural pastors, farmers, teachers, sociologists, economists, agricultural agents and officials. There are 144 officially appointed diocesan rural life directors.

Most Rev. Ignatius J. Strecker, archbishop of Kansas City, Kans., is president. Mr. Gregory Cusack is executive director.

National headquarters are located at 4625 N.W. Beaver Dr., Des Moines, Ia. 50310.

**Catholic Relief Services — USCC:** The official overseas aid and development agency of American Catholics; it is a separately incorporated organization of the U.S. Catholic Conference.

CRS was founded in 1943 by the bishops of the United States to help civilians in Europe and North Africa caught in the disruption and devastation of World War II.

Initially, CRS collected, purchased and shipped to war-torn countries huge quantities of food, clothing, medicines and other relief supplies which were distributed to hundreds of thousands of displaced persons, prisoners of war, bombed-out families, widows, orphans and other war victims.

As conditions in Europe improved in the late 1940s and early 1950s, the works conducted by CRS spread to other continents and areas — Asia, Africa and Latin America.

CRS staffs offices in 40 countries and has local representatives in another 30 countries. The agency works with local counterpart organizations to provide humanitarian assistance and emergency relief. Help is given strictly in response to need; race, creed, color and political affiliation are no consideration.

Although best known for its record of disaster response, compassionate aid to refugees and commitment to reconstruction and rehabilitation, CRS places primary focus on long-term development projects designed to help people to help themselves and to determine their own future.

Administrative funding for CRS comes from an annual collection, the Catholic Relief Services Annual Appeal (known variously as Bishops' Relief or American Catholic Overseas Aid Appeal), held during Lent in most of the 18,000 Catholic parishes of the U.S.

Major support is derived from private, individual donors through direct contributions and through a program of sacrificial giving called Operation Rice Bowl. Funds are also received from philanthropic foundations and humanitarian organizations in the U.S. and Europe. Clothing is collected each year, generally at Thanksgiving, for distribution overseas. More than 7 million pounds of used clothing, blankets and bolt goods are contributed annually through Catholic churches.

Assistance is received from the U.S. Government in several forms: foodstuffs available under Title II of Public Law 480, ocean-freight subsidies for government food and other privately generated relief supplies, and grants for both emergency programs and community development projects.

In 1983, the CRS global program in 70 countries employed 1,100 people and was valued at $325 million.

Lawrence Pezzullo is executive director.

CRS headquarters are located at 1011 First Ave., New York, N.Y. 10022.

## SPECIAL APOSTOLATES AND GROUPS

**Apostleship of the Sea:** An international Catholic organization for the moral, social and spiritual welfare of seafarers and those involved in the maritime industry. It was founded in 1920 in Glasgow, Scotland, and formally approved by the Holy See in 1922. It is promoted and directed by the Pontifical Commission for Migrants and Tourism, Piazza San Calisto 16, Rome, Italy 00153. The U.S. unit is the Apostleship of the Sea in the United States, an affiliate of the NCCB-USCC, established in 1947. It serves 70 port chaplains in 58 U.S. ports on the seacoasts and the Great Lakes. Operations include a hospitality and welcoming program as well as counseling and spiritual services carried on by individual port chaplains through Catholic maritime clubs located in Alabama (Mobile); California (Oakland, San Francisco, Wilmington); Florida (Miami); New Jersey (Newark), New York (Brooklyn); Washington (Seattle); and interfaith clubs located in Alaska (Ketchikan); Florida (Pensacola); Georgia (Savannah); New Jersey (Newark, Port Elizabeth); Texas (Corpus Christi, Galveston, Houston); Washington (Tacoma); Wisconsin (Milwaukee). Recent developments have emphasized the interfaith cooperation on the port level in seamen's ministry. The episcopal promoter of the conference is Most Rev. Rene Gracida, 620 Lipan St., Corpus Christi, Tex. 78401. Rev. James E. Dillenburg is national director. Address of the national office is P.O. Box 4787, Corpus Christi, Tex. 78469. Also affiliated with the Apostleship of the Sea in the United States is the **National Catholic Conference for Seafarers.** The president is Rev. Mario Balbi, S.D.B., 222 E. Harris, P.O. Box 8307, Savannah, Ga. 31412.

**Auxiliaries of Our Lady of the Cenacle** (1878, France): An association of Catholic laywomen, under the direction of the Congregation of Our Lady of the Cenacle, who serve God through their own professions and life styles by means of vows. Members live a fully secular life consecrated according to the spirituality of the Cenacle and pursue individual apostolates. They number approximately 150 throughout the world. U.S. regional director: Sister Barbara Whittemore, r.c., 310 Cenacle Rd., Lake Ronkonkoma, N.Y. 11779.

**Catholic Central Union of America** (1855): One of the oldest Catholic lay organizations in the U.S., the Union is devoted to the development and vigor of Christian principles in personal, social, cultural, economic and civic life. It was the first society ever given an official mandate for Catholic Action by a committee of the American bishops, in 1936. The Central Bureau in St. Louis is the center for the separate but coordinated direction of the National Catholic Women's Union. The headquarters is also a publishing house (*Social Justice Review,* other publications), a library of German-Americana and Catholic Americana, a clearinghouse for information, and a center for works of charity. Aid is given to the missions, and maintenance and direction are provided for St. Elizabeth's Center in St. Louis. Union membership is approximately 9,000. Harvey J. Johnson is director of the Central Bureau located at 3835 Westminster Place, St. Louis, Mo. 63108.

**Catholic Medical Mission Board** (1928): Founded by Dr. Paluel Flagg and the Rev. Edward Garesche, S.J. Its purposes are to gather and ship medical supplies for the sick poor in mission lands, and to recruit and assign medical and paramedical personnel to overseas mission hospitals and dispensaries. Since its foundation, it has shipped approximately 48 million pounds of supplies. In 1983, more than $9.7 million in medicines were shipped to 2,015 mission distribution centers in 54 countries. Also in 1983, 49 medical volunteers were placed in 10 countries. Rev. Joseph J. Walter, S.J., is the director. Office: 10 W. 17th Street, New York, N.Y. 10011.

**Center for Applied Research in the Apostolate (CARA):** A research and development agency in the field of the Church's worldwide religious and social mission. Its purpose is to gather information for the use of decision-makers in evaluating the present status of the Church's mission of service and in planning programs of development toward greater effectiveness of its multiphased ministry in the future. CARA has research and planning programs focused on: church personnel (recruitment, selection training, utilization, effectiveness), overseas areas, diocesan planning, religious life, health care ministry, and other subjects.

CARA was incorporated as a non-profit corporation in the District of Columbia Aug. 5, 1964. Thomas R. Byrne is acting president. Offices are located at 3700 Oakview Terrace, N.E., Washington, D.C. 20017.

**Christian Family Movement (CFM)** (1947): Originating in Chicago and having a membership of married couples and individuals, its purpose is to Christianize family life and create communities conducive to Christian family life. Since 1968, CFM in the U.S. has included couples from all Christian churches. The International Confederation of Christian Family Movements embraces a worldwide membership. National president couple: Gary and Kay Aitchison, Box 272, Ames, Iowa 50010.

**Christian Life Communities:** Formerly known as Sodalities of Our Lady, they are groups of men and women, adults and youth, joined with other people involved in living their full Christian vocation and commitment in the world. The governing principles and operating norms of Sodalities, revised in the spirit of documents of the Second Vatican Council, were promulgated and approved by Pope Paul VI in 1971. The Spiritual Exercises of St. Ignatius remain a specific source and characteristic of the spirituality of the movement. Christian Life Communities are located in more than 50 countries; the U.S. Federation is comprised of approximately 150 communities. Eileen C. Burke is executive director. National office: 3721 Westminster Blvd., St. Louis, Mo. 63108. The World Federation office is located in Rome.

**Cursillo Movement:** An instrument of Christian renewal designed to form and stimulate persons to engage in apostolic action individually and in the organized apostolate, in accordance with the mission which individuals have to transform the environments in which they live into Christian environments. The movement originated in Spain, where the first cursillo was held near Palma, Mallorca, in 1949. It was introduced in the U.S. in 1957 and is functioning in more than 140 dioceses. The method of the movement involves a three-day weekend called a cursillo and a follow-up program known as the post-cursillo.

The weekend is an intensive experience in Christian community living centered on Christ and built around 15 talks (10 by laymen, five by priests), active participation in discussions and related activities, the celebration of the liturgy. The follow-up program focuses on small weekly reunions of three to five persons and larger group reunions, called ultreyas, in which participants share experiences and insights derived from their prayer life, study and apostolic action. The movement operates within the framework of diocesan and parish pastoral plans, and functions autonomously in each diocese under the direction of the bishop. Responsibility for growth and effectiveness rests with a diocesan leaders' school, a diocesan secretariat, or both. Most Rev. James S. Sullivan, auxiliary bishop of Lansing, is episcopal advisor to the movement. Gerald P. Hughes is executive director of the National Cursillo Center, P.O. Box 210226, Dallas, Tex. 75211.

**Frontier Apostolate** (1956): Volunteers for a minimum of two years' service in their professional line (teachers, secretaries, houseparents, etc.) in the Diocese of Prince George, British Columbia, Canada. More than 2,600 have served since the start of the corps by Bishop Fergus O'Grady. There are about 150 men and women from 8 different countries actively engaged in works throughout the diocese. Address: Bishop O'Grady, College Rd., P.O. Box 7000, Prince George, B.C., Canada V2N 3Z2.

**Grail, The** (1921): An international movement of women concerned about the full development of all peoples, working in education, religious, social and cultural areas. Founded by Rev. Jacques van Ginneken, S.J., in The Netherlands, it was introduced in the U.S. in 1940. The Grail is at work in: Australia, Brazil, Canada, Costa Rica, Egypt, France, Germany, India, Italy, Kenya, The Netherlands, Nigeria, Philippines, Portugal, South Africa. Tanzania, Uganda, United States. U.S. headquarters: Grailville, Loveland, Ohio 45140. International Secretariat: Duisburger Strasse 470, 4330 Mulheim, West Germany.

**International Liaison, Inc.** (1963): The U.S. Catholic Coordinating Center for Lay Missioners, an affiliate of the U.S. Catholic Conference, is engaged in the promotion, recruiting and referral of lay missioners with church missions, interdenominational and private volunteer agencies throughout the U.S. The organization also assists mission agencies to facilitate participation by lay persons in ministries of the Church. Publications include *The Response,* an annual directory of lay mission opportunities, and a quarterly newsletter. David J. Suley is the executive director. National office: 1234 Massachusetts Ave. N.W., Washington, D.C. 20005.

**Jesuit Volunteer Corps** (1956): Established by the Oregon Province of the Jesuits, for service to the poor and oppressed throughout the U.S. Men and women volunteers must be 21 years of age and older. A minimum one-year commitment is requested. JVC emphasizes Christian service, community and simple lifestyle. Address for information: JVC/Northwest, P.O. Box 3928, Portland Ore. 97208.

**Lay Mission-Helpers Association** (1955): It trains and assigns men and women for work in overseas apostolates for periods of three years. Approximately 600 members of the association have served in overseas assignments since 1955. The Rev. Msgr. Joseph Alzugaray is director of the association. Headquarters: 1531 West Ninth St., Los Angeles, Calif. 90015.

The **Mission Doctors Association** recruits, trains and sends Catholic physicians and their families to mission hospitals and clinics throughout the world for tours of two to three years. Address: 1531 W. Ninth St., Los Angeles, Calif. 90015.

**Legion of Mary** (1921): Founded in Dublin, its purposes are the sanctification of its members and service to others. It is one of the largest lay organizations in the Church. U.S. address for information: The Legion of Mary, St. Louis Regional Senatus, Box 1313, St. Louis, Mo. 63188. The supreme governing body has offices at De Montfort House, North Brunswick St., Dublin 7, Ireland.

**Movement for a Better World** (1952): An international movement founded by Rev. Riccardo Lombardi, S.J. The U.S. promoting group, like its counterparts in other countries, conducts various types of renewal programs with a distinctive communitarian thrust for the purpose of motivating Christian witness and action for making a better world in accordance with the plan of God. Address for information: Sr. Mary Byrnes, 78 Grand St., Jersey City, N.J. 07302. The movement is a nongovernmental organization with the United Nations and has a U.N. office at 777 U.N. Plaza, New York, N.Y. 10017.

**Movimiento Familiar Cristiano — USA** (MFC) (1969): Movement of Catholic Hispanic families united in their efforts to promote the human and Christian virtues of the family so that it may become a force that forms persons, transmits the faith and contributes to the total development of the community. National president couple, Rey and Alma Enriquez. National office, 1041 Wyatt Dr., El Paso, Tex. 79907. Rev. Rafael Miranda is national spiritual director.

**Pax Christi** (1948): International Catholic peace movement. Originated in Lourdes, France, as a union of French and German Catholics to symbolize a mutual effort to heal wounds inflicted by World War II, spread to Poland and Italy, and acquired its international title when it merged with the English organization Pax. A general secretariat is located at Antwerp, Belgium. **Pax Christi USA**, was founded in 1973 to establish peacemaking as a priority for the American Catholic Church, to work for disarmament, primacy of con-

science, a just world order, education for peace, and alternatives to violence. A newsletter is published bimonthly; membership, 10,000. Paul Mazur is national coordinator. Address: 6337 West Cornelia, Chicago, Ill. 60634.

**Pax Romana — American Graduate and Professional Commission:** The U.S. affiliate of Pax Romana, an international Catholic movement for intellectual and cultural affairs (see Catholic International Organizations). The president is Dr. Thomas P. Melady, president of Sacred Heart University, Bridgeport, Conn. 06606. The Pax Romana representative to the United Nations is Professor W. Hilary Lee, Stevens Institute of Technology, Hoboken, N.J. 07030.

**Regis College Lay Apostolate** (1950): Founded by Sister Mary John Sullivan, C.S.J., it enlists college graduates for a year of teaching service in home and overseas missions. More than 250 lay apostles from Regis College and more than 400 from other colleges have served since the beginning of the program. Headquarters: Regis College, Weston, Mass. 02193

**Southwest Volunteer Apostolate** (1970): Places volunteers for work among the Indians and Spanish-speaking of the Diocese of Gallup. Mailing address: P. O. Box 626, Gallup, N.M. 87301.

**Center of Concern** (1971): An independent, public-interest group engaged in analysis, education and advocacy relating to issues of global concern. Discussion is carried on within the framework of social justice. A newsletter, *Center Focus*, is published bimonthly. Peter J. Henriot, S.J., is director. Address: 3700 13th St. N.E., Washington, D.C. 20017.

# CATHOLIC YOUTH ORGANIZATIONS

**Boy Scouts in the Catholic Church:** The National Catholic Committee on Scouting works with the Boy Scouts of America in developing the character and spiritual life of 600,000 members in units chartered to Catholic and non-Catholic organizations. *Boy's Life*. Committee Chairman, Gerard O. Rocque, West Main Rd., Silver Creek, N.Y. 14136.

**Camp Fire, Inc.** (1910): 4601 Madison Ave., Kansas City, Mo. 64112. The National Catholic Committee for Girl Scouts and Camp Fire, a standing committee of the National Federation for Catholic Youth Ministry, cooperates with Camp Fire. To help young people learn and grow in their individual ways through participation in enjoyable activities. Open to youth up to 21 years of age. Membership: approximately 500,000 (no exact statistics available on number of Catholics participating).

**Catholic Forester Youth Program, Catholic Order of Foresters:** 305 W. Madison Street, Chicago, Ill. 60606. To develop Christian leadership and promote the moral, intellectual, social and physical growth of its youth members. *Catholic Forester*. Membership: youth up to 16 years of age — about 22,000 in 825 local courts in U.S. the High Chief Ranger is John A. Gorski.

**Catholic Youth Organization (CYO):** Name of parish-centered diocesan Catholic youth programs

throughout the country. CYO promotes a program of spiritual, social and physical activities. The original CYO was organized by Bishop Bernard Sheil of Chicago in 1930.

**Columbian Squires** (1925): P.O. Drawer 1670, New Haven, Conn. 06507. Junior organization of the Knights of Columbus. To train and develop leadership through active participation in a well-organized program of activities. Membership: 12- to 18-year-old Catholic boys. More than 20,000 in 1,000 circles (local units) active in the U.S., Canada, Puerto Rico, Mexico, Guam and the Philippines. *Squires Newsletter*, monthly.

**Girl Scouts of the U.S.A.:** 830 Third Ave., New York, N.Y. 10022. Girls from most archdioceses and dioceses in the U.S. and its possessions participate in Girl Scouting. The National Catholic Committee for Girl Scouts and Camp Fire, a standing committee of the National Federation for Catholic Youth Ministry, cooperates with Girl Scouts of the U.S.A. *Girl Scout Leader*. Membership: approximately three million (no exact statistics available on number of Catholic girls participating).

**Holy Childhood Association (Pontifical Association of the Holy Childhood)** (1843): 1720 Massachusetts Ave. N.W., Washington, D.C. 20036. The official children's mission-aid society of the Church; provides assistance to children in 94 mission countries. Furnishes mission education programs and materials to pupils in Catholic elementary schools and religious education programs. *It's Our World,* four times a year. National Director, Rev. Francis W. Wright, C.S.Sp.

**Junior Catholic Daughters of the Americas:** 10 W. 71st St., New York, N.Y. 10023. A major department of the Catholic Daughters of the Americas. To promote development of the whole person, service to others, spiritual growth. Membership: Juniors (11 to 18 years old); Juniorettes (6 to 10 years old).

**Knights of the Altar** (1938): P.O. Drawer 5476, Lakeland, Fla. 33807 (national office). Society for altar boys. *Young Heralds,* 6 times a year. Membership: 3,000 units in the U.S. and foreign countries.

**National Catholic Forensic League** (1952): To develop articulate Catholic leaders through an inter-diocesan program of speech and debate activities. *Newsletter,* quarterly. Membership: 600 schools; membership open to Catholic, private and public schools through the local diocesan league. Secretary-Treasurer, Richard Gaudette, 21 Nancy Rd., Milford, Mass. 01757.

**National Catholic Young Adult Ministry Association** (1982): 4665 Willowbrook Ave., Los Angeles, Calif 90029. To strengthen the professional competence of those engaged in young adult ministry. President, Rev. Paul Ojibway, S.A.

**National Christ Child Society Inc.** (1887): 5100 Wisconsin Ave. N.W., Washington, D.C. 20016. Founder, Mary V. Merrick. A non-profit association of Catholic volunteers dedicated to the service of needy children and youth regardless of race or creed. The service has been expanded to include underprivileged adults. Membership: approximately 8,000 adult and junior members in 34 cities in U.S. President, Mrs. James H. Kavanagh.

**National Federation for Catholic Youth Ministry** (1982): 3025 4th St. N.E., Washington, D.C. 20017. To foster the development of youth ministry in the United States through CYO and other expressions of ministry to, with, by and for youth. *Emmaus Newsletter,* quarterly. Executive Director, Mrs. Maggie Brown.

**St. Dominic Savio Club** (1950): Marian Shrine, Filor's Lane, West Haverstraw, N.Y. 10993. A character-building, leadership and public service program conducted in Catholic schools, CCD classes and home/neighborhood units. *Savio Notes,* six times a year. Membership: students in grades three through twelve — more than 1,500,000 since its founding. Director, Rev. Peter Malloy, S.D.B. members in U.S., Canada and nine foreign countries.

**Young Christian Students:** 7436 W. Harrison, Forest Park, Ill. 60130. A student movement for Christian personal and social change. Membership: 500 in high schools and parishes.

### Fraternities and Sororities

**Alpha Delta Gamma** (1924): P.O. Box 54321, Los Angeles, Calif. 90054. Fraternity. *Alphadelity.* Membership: 7,260 in 12 college chapters and 11 alumni associations.

**Delta Epsilon Sigma** (1939): College of Great Falls, Great Falls, Mont. 59405. National scholastic honor society for students, faculty and alumni of colleges and universities with a Catholic tradition. Membership: 26,500 in 100 chapters. Secretary, Dr. Charles M. Hepburn.

**Kappa Gamma Pi** (1926): A national Catholic college women's honor society for graduates who, in addition to academic excellence, have shown outstanding leadership in extra-curricular activities. *Kappa Gamma Pi News,* quarterly. Membership: approximately 16,000 in 123 colleges; 40 alumnae chapters in metropolitan areas. President, Dr. Sally Ann Vonderbrink, 5747 Colerain Ave., Cincinnati, O. 45239.

**Phi Kappa Theta:** 332 Main St., Worcester, Mass. 01608. National collegiate fraternity with a Catholic heritage. Merger (1959) of Phi Kappa Fraternity, founded at Brown Univ. in 1889, and Theta Kappa Phi Fraternity, founded at Lehigh Univ. in 1919. *The Temple Magazine* quarterly, and newsletter, *The Sun.* Membership: 3,000 undergraduate and 36,000 alumni in 55 collegiate and 15 alumni chapters. Executive Director, Kirk Thomas.

## ASSOCIATIONS, MOVEMENTS, SOCIETIES IN THE U.S.

(Principal source: Almanac survey.)
*See Index for other associations, movements and societies covered elsewhere.*

### A

**Academy of American Franciscan History** (1944), Box 34440, West Bethesda, Md. 20817. Dir., Rev. John-Marie Cassese, O.F.M.

**American Benedictine Academy** (1947). Scholarly Benedictine society. Pres., Sr. Dorothy Neuhofer, O.S.B., Holy Name Priory, San Antonio, Fla. 33574; pres.-elect, Rev. Matthias Neuman, O.S.B., St. Meinrad Archabbey, St. Meinrad, Ind. 47577.

**American Catholic Correctional Chaplains Association** (1952), 275 in 475 institutions. Pres., Rev. Kloman Riggie; Sec., Rev. Dismas Boeff, O.S.B., 2900 East Blvd., Cleveland, O. 44104.

**American Catholic Historical Association** (1919), Catholic University of America, Washington, D.C. 20064. *The Catholic Historical Review,* quarterly. Sec.-Treas., Rev. Robert Trisco.

**American Catholic Philosophical Association** (1926), Catholic University of America, Washington, D.C. 20064. *New Scholasticism,* quarterly, *Proceedings,* annually.

**American Committee on Italian Migration** (1952), 42 E. 23rd St., New York, N.Y. 10010; 6,000. *ACIM Newsletter* and *ACIM Nuova Via,* 6 times a year. Sec., Rev. Joseph A. Cogo, C.S.

**Ancient Order of Hibernians in America, Inc.** (1836); 120,000. *National Hibernian Digest,* bimonthly. Nat. Pres., Joseph A. Roche; Nat. Sec., John K. Henry, 10 Stonehedge Rd., Norwalk, Conn. 06851.

**Apostleship of Prayer** (1849-France; 1861-U.S.):

3 Stephen Ave., New Hyde Park, N.Y. 11040. Promotes Daily Offering and Sacred Heart devotion.

**Apostolate for Family Consecration** (1975), The House of St. Joseph, Box 220, Kenosha, Wis. 53141; 26,000 members. Family reinforcement by transforming neighborhoods into God-centered communities Pres., Jerome F. Coniker.

**Archconfraternity of Christian Mothers (Christian Mothers)** (1881), 220 37th St., Pittsburgh, Pa. 15201; over 3,900 branches. Dir., Rev. Bertin Roll, O.F.M. Cap.

**Archconfraternity of Our Lady of Perpetual Help and St. Alphonsus** (1871), 526 59th St., Brooklyn, N.Y. 11220.

**Archconfraternity of the Holy Ghost** (1912), Holy Ghost Fathers, Bensalem, Pa. 19020 (U.S. headquarters). Nat. Dir., Very Rev. Henry J. Brown, C.S.Sp.

**Association for Religious and Value Issues in Counseling** (1962), division of American Association for Counseling and Development. *Counseling and Values,* 2 times a year. Address, 5999 Stevenson Ave., Alexandria, Va. 22304.

**Association for Social Economics** (formerly the Catholic Economic Association) (1941), De Paul University, 25 E. Jackson Blvd., Chicago, Ill. 60604; 1,300. *Review of Social Economy,* triannually.

**Association of Catholic Diocesan Archivists** (1983), c/o Archives, Archdiocese of Boston, 2121 Commonwealth Ave., Brighton, Mass. 02135; 125 members. To work for establishment of an archival program in every American diocese; to provide for professional training and development of diocesan archivists; to work toward formation of national archival standards for the Church in the U.S. Pres., James M. O'Toole, Archivist, Archdiocese of Boston.

**Association of Catholic Trade Unionists** (1937), 12 Holly Hills Dr., Woodstock, N.Y. 12498. Exec. Sec., John C. Donohue.

**Association of Marian Helpers** (1946), Stockbridge, Mass. 01262; 1,100,000, mostly in U.S. *The Marian Helpers Bulletin,* quarterly.

**Association of Romanian Catholics of America** (1948), 4309 Olcott Ave., E. Chicago, Ind. 46312.

**B**

**Blue Army of Our Lady of Fatima** (1946), Washington, N.J. 07882; worldwide membership. *Soul,* bimonthly. U.S. Pres., Most Rev. Jerome Hastrich, bishop of Gallup, N. Mex.

**C**

**Calix Society** (1947), 7601 Wayzata Blvd., Minneapolis, Minn. 55426; 2,000 members in U.S. and Canada; *Chalice,* bimonthly. Association of Catholic alcoholics maintaining their sobriety through affiliation with and participation in Alcoholics Anonymous. Dir., R. D. Dickinson.

**Campaign for Surplus Rosaries** (1948) and the **Mid-America Rosary Museum** (1976), 1821 W. Short 17th St., North Little Rock, Ark. 72114. Collect rosaries and religious articles for free distribution to the poor throughout the world. Lay Internatl. Chairman, P. Marion Chudy, S.F.O.

**Canon Law Society of America** (1939), Catholic University, Washington, D.C. 20064. To further research and study in canon law; 1,600. Exec. Coord., Rev. James H. Provost.

**Cardinal Mindszenty Foundation (CMF)** (1958), P.O. Box 11321, St. Louis, Mo. 63105. To combat communism with knowledge and facts. Exec. Dir., Eleanor Schlafly.

**Catholic Aid Association** (1878), 49 W. Ninth St., St. Paul, Minn. 55102; 80,000. *Catholic Aid News,* monthly. Fraternal life insurance society. Pres., F. L. Spanier.

**Catholic Alumni Clubs International** (1957), To advance social, cultural and spiritual well-being of members. Membership limited to single Catholics with professional education; 7,000 in 50 clubs in U.S. International Chaplain, Rev. Peter Campbell, M.S.C., P.O. Box 6074, Youngstown, O. 44501.

**Catholic Biblical Association of America** (1936), Catholic University of America, Washington, D.C. 20064; 1,010. *The Catholic Biblical Quarterly.* Pres., Rev. Robert North, S.J.

**Catholic Commission on Intellectual and Cultural Affairs (CCICA)** (1946), P.O. Box 21, Notre Dame, Ind. 46556; 268. Exec. Dir., Dr. Konrad Schaum.

**Catholic Daughters of the Americas** (1903), 10 W. 71st St., New York, N.Y. 10023; 170,000. *Share Magazine.* Nat. Regent, Miss Loretta J. Knebel.

**Catholic Evidence Guild** (1918, in England; 1931, in US), c/o 127 W. 31st St., New York, N.Y. 10001. Lay movement for spread of Catholic truth by means of outdoor speaking.

**Catholic Family Life Insurance** (1868), 1572 E. Capitol Dr., Milwaukee, Wis. 53211; 48,000. *The Family Friend,* quarterly. Pres., David L. Springob.

**Catholic Golden Age:** National Headquarters, Scranton, Pa. 18503; 800,000. *CGA World Magazine,* bimonthly. Assist Catholics over 50 years of age in their religious and secular needs.

**Catholic Guardian Society** (1913), 1011 First Ave., New York, N.Y. 10022. Exec. Dir., James P. O'Neill.

**Catholic Home Bureau for Dependent Children** (1898), 1011 First Ave., New York, N.Y. 10022. Exec. Dir., Sr. Una McCormack.

**Catholic Interracial Council of New York, Inc.** (1934), 286 Fifth Ave., New York, N.Y. 10001. Exec. Dir., John J. Gara.

**Catholic Knights of America** (1877), 217 E. 8th St., Cincinnati, O. 45202; 10,200. *Catholic Knights of America Journal,* monthly. Fraternal insurance society.

**Catholic Kolping Society of America** (1923), 22515 Masonic Blvd., St. Clair Shores, Mich. 48082. *Kolping Banner,* monthly. International society concerned with spiritual, educational and physical development of members.

**Catholic Lawyers' Guild.** Organization usually on a diocesan basis, under different titles.

**Catholic League** (1943), 1200 N. Ashland Ave., Chicago, Ill. 60622. Exec. Dir., Most Rev. Alfred Abramowicz.

**Catholic Library Association** (1921), 461 W. Lancaster Avenue, Haverford, Pa., 19041; 3,162. *Cath-*

olic Library World, monthly (Sept.-April), bimonthly (May-June, July-Aug.); *Catholic Periodical and Literature Index*. Pres., Sr. Dennis Lynch, S.H.C.J., Exec. Dir., Matthew R. Wilt.

**Catholic Near East Welfare Association (Near East Missions)** (1926), 1011 First Ave., New York, N.Y. 10022. *Near East Missions*, weekly column in 132 diocesan and four national newspapers. Aids missionary activity in 18 countries (under jurisdiction of the Sacred Congregation for the Oriental Church) in Europe, Africa and Asia, including the Holy Land. Nat. Sec., Rev. Msgr. John G. Nolan; Assoc. Sec., Rev. Msgr. Edward C. Foster.

**Catholic Negro-American Mission Board** (1907), 2021 H. St. N.W., Washington, D.C. 20006.15,000. *Educating in Faith*, quarterly. Exec. Sec., Msgr. Paul A. Lenz.

**Catholic One Parent Organization (COPO):** To give widows and widowers an opportunity to meet others in the same situation, blending social and spiritual programs. Organized in various dioceses.

**Catholic Order of Foresters** (1883), 305 W. Madison St., Chicago, Ill. 60606; 163,000. *The Catholic Forester*, bimonthly. Fraternal insurance society. High Chief Ranger, John A. Gorski.

**Catholic Pamphlet Society** (1938), 2171 Fillmore Ave., Buffalo, N.Y. 14214. Parish pamphlet rack distributors. Dir., Rev. Walter O. Kern.

**Catholic Peace Fellowship** (1964), 339 Lafayette St., New York, N.Y. 10012; 6,500, *CPF Bulletin*. Peace education and action projects, development of the nonviolent tradition within the Catholic Church; draft counseling. Nat. Sec., Thomas C. Cornell.

**Catholic Press Association of the U.S., Inc.** (1911), 119 N. Park Ave., Rockville Centre, N.Y. 11570. *The Catholic Journalist* monthly; *Catholic Press Directory*, annually. Pres., Rev. Owen F. Campion; Exec. Dir., James A. Doyle.

**Catholic Theological Society of America** (1946), Office of Secretary, St. Mary of the Lake Seminary, Mundelein, Ill. 60060; 1,200. *Proceedings*, annually. Pres. (1984-85), Patrick Granfield.

**Catholic Union of the Sick in America, Inc. (CUSA)** (1947), 63 Wall St., New York, N.Y. 10005 (legal office); 1,200. Admin. Leader, Miss Anna Marie Sopko, 176 W. 8th St., Bayonne, N.J. 07002 (national central office).

**Catholic War Veterans** (1935), 2 Massachusetts Ave. N.W., Washington, D.C. 20001; 500 posts, *Catholic War Veteran*, bimonthly.

**Catholic Worker Movement** (1933), 36 E. First St., New York, N.Y. 10003. *The Catholic Worker*, 8 times a year. Lay apostolate founded by Peter Maurin and Dorothy Day; has Houses of Hospitality in over 60 U.S. cities and several communal farms in various parts of the country. Promotes pacifism personalism, voluntary poverty and anarchism in that it is decentralist, and believes in what the popes have termed the principle of subsidiarity, urging decentralization in the school system, community control, and in the economic field credit unions, cooperatives and unions of workers and mutual aid.

**Catholic Workman (Katolicky Delnik)** (1891),

New Prague, Minn. 56071; 16,967. *Catholic Workman*, monthly. Fraternal and insurance society. Pres. Leslie W. Kosarek.

**Catholic Writers' Guild of America** (1919), 65 East 89th St., New York, N.Y. 10028.

**Catholics United for the Faith** (1968), 222 North Ave., Box S, New Rochelle, N.Y. 10801; 15,000 worldwide, *Lay Witness*, monthly. Lay apostolate founded in response to Vatican II's call to the laity. Pres., Mrs. Madeleine F. Stebbins.

**Center for Pastoral Liturgy** (1975), Catholic University of America, Washington, D.C. 20064. Concerned with promotion of pastoral-liturgical action in the U.S.; sponsors programs, publications, conferences, and workshops oriented toward the service of local churches. Dir., Rev. G. Thomas Ryan.

**Central Association of the Miraculous Medal** (1915), 475 E. Chelten Ave., Philadelphia, Pa. 19144. *Miraculous Medal*, quarterly. Dir., Rev. Robert P. Cawley, C.M.

**Chaplains' Aid Association, Inc.** (1917), 1011 First Ave., New York, N.Y. 10022. Pres., Most Rev. Philip J. Furlong.

**Christopher Movement** (1945), 12 E. 48th St., New York, N.Y. 10017. Without formal organization or meetings, the movement stimulates personal initiative and responsible action in line with Christian principles, particularly in the fields of education, government, industrial relations and communications. Christopher radio and TV programs are broadcast by more than 1,500 radio and TV stations; 750,000 copies of *Christopher News Notes* are distributed seven times a year without subscription fee; 152 weekly and 14 daily newspapers carry Christopher columns. Dir., Rev. John Catoir.

**Citizens for Educational Freedom** (1959): Nonsectarian group concerned with parents' right to educational choice by means of tuition tax credits and vouchers. National office: Suite 854 Washington Bldg., 15th St. and New York Ave. N.W., Washington, D.C. 20005.

**Confraternity of Catholic Clergy** (1976), 21-72 43rd St., Astoria, N.Y. 11105; *C.C.C. Newsletter*, bimonthly. To support priests by mutual prayer for personal holiness, loyalty to Pope and adherence to teaching of magisterium. Pres., Rev. Vincent J. Rigdon.

**Confraternity of the Immaculate Conception of Our Lady of Lourdes** (1874), Box 561, Notre Dame, Ind. 46556. Distributors of Lourdes water.

**Confraternity of the Most Holy Rosary:** See Rosary Altar Society.

**Convert Movement Our Apostolate** (CMOA) (1945), formerly Convert Makers of America, c/o Our Lady of Grace Rectory, 430 Avenue W, Brooklyn, N.Y. 11223. *Bulletin* quarterly. To train and assist lay persons on a parish level to discuss and present the Faith to interested persons on a one-to-one basis. Dir., Msgr. Erwin A. Juraschek.

**Czech Catholic Union of Texas (K.J.T.)** (1889), 214 Colorado St., La Grange, Tex. 78945; 16,927. *Nasinec*, weekly, and *K. J. T. News*, monthly. Fraternal and insurance society. Pres., Amos Pavlik.

**D**

**Damien-Dutton Society for Leprosy Aid, Inc.** (1944), 616 Bedford Ave., Bellmore, N.Y. 11710; 25,000. *Damien Dutton Call*, quarterly. Provides medicine, rehabilitation and research for conquest of leprosy. Pres., Howard E. Crouch, Dir., Sr. Mary Augustine, S.M.S.M.

**Daughters of Isabella** (1897), 375 Whitney Ave., New Haven, Conn. 06511; 120,000.

**E**

**Edith Stein Guild, Inc.** (1955), Our Lady of Victory Church, 60 William St., New York, N.Y. 10005; quarterly newsletter. Promotes Judaeo-Christian understanding, extends friendship to Catholics of Jewish background, spreads knowledge of life and writings of Edith Stein (Sister Benedicta of the Cross).

**Enthronement of the Sacred Heart in the Home** (1907), 3 Adams St., Fairhaven, Mass. 02719; over 2,500,000.

**Eucharistic Guard for Nocturnal Adoration** (1938), 800 North Country Club Rd., Tucson, Ariz. 85716.

**Eymard League** (1948), 194 E. 76 St., New York, N.Y. 10021; approximately 24,000. Dir., Rev. Ralph A. Lavigne, S.S.S.

**F**

**Families for Christ** (1977), 6026 W. Harwood Ave., Orlando, Fla., 32811; 8,000. Promote social reign of Christ. Pres., Albert Barone.

**Families for Prayer** (1982), 775 Madison Ave., Albany, N.Y. 12208. Dir., Rev. John J. Gurley, C.S.C.

**Family Rosary, Inc., The** (1942), Executive Park Drive, Albany, N.Y. 12203. Pres., Rev. Patrick Peyton, C.S.C.

**Federation of Diocesan Liturgical Commissions (FDLC)** (1969), 3033 4th St. N.E., Washington, D.C. 20017. Voluntary association of personnel from diocesan liturgical commissions of the U.S. The main purpose is promotion of the liturgy as the heart of Christian life, especially in the parish community. Exec. Sec., Mr. Lawrence J. Johnson.

**Fellowship of Catholic Scholars** (1977), Msgr. George A. Kelly, Newsletter editor, St. John's University, Jamaica, N.Y. 11439; 600 members. Interdisciplinary research and publications of Catholic scholars in accord with the magisterium of the Catholic Church. Pres., Rev. Earl Weis, S.J.

**First Catholic Slovak Ladies' Association, USA** (1892), 24950 Chagrin Blvd., Beachwood, Ohio 44122; 102,000. *Fraternally Yours*, monthly. Fraternal insurance society. Pres., Anna S. Granchay.

**First Catholic Slovak Union (Jednota)** (1890), 3289 E. 55th St., Cleveland, Ohio 44127; 96,206. *Jednota*, weekly. Exec. Sec., Joseph R. Vehec.

**Franciscan Apostolate of the Way of the Cross** (1949), St. Anthony Friary, 63 Bartholdi Ave., Butter, N.J. 07405. Stations Crucifix available on request. Dir., Rev. Cassian J. Kirk, O.F.M.

**Friendship House** (1938), 1746 W. Division, Chicago, Ill. 60622. *Community*, quarterly. Work for social justice through nonviolence and simple living; promote Catholic interracial apostolate.

**G**

**Gabriel Richard Institute** (1949), 2315 Orleans Ave., Detroit, Mich. 48207. Conducts Christopher leadership courses in 18 dioceses.

**Gelasian Guild** (1976), Association of Catholic attorneys working with the USCC; concerned with scholarly study of legal questions affecting Church-state relations. Pres., Rev. Charles Whelan, S.J., 106 W. 56th St., New York, N.Y. 10019.

**Guard of Honor of the Immaculate Heart of Mary** (1932), 135 West 31st St., New York, N.Y. 10001. An archconfraternity approved by the Holy See whose members cultivate devotion to the Blessed Virgin Mary, particularly through a daily Guard Hour of Prayer.

**Guild of Catholic Lawyers** (1928), 220 E. 23rd St., New York, N.Y. 10010; 600.

**Guild of Our Lady of Ransom** (1948), c/o St. Timothy's Rectory, 650 Nichols St., Norwood, Mass. 02062. Boston archdiocesan ministry for spiritual aid and rehabilitation of inmates of penal institutions. Exec. Dir. and Treas., Rev. Dr. Joseph P. McDermott.

**Guild of St. Paul** (1937), Visitation Monastery, Georgetown, Ky. 40324; Nat. Spir. Dir., Rev. Msgr. Leonard Nienaber; Pres., Bert Oram.

**H**

**Holy Name Society:** Founded in 1274 by Blessed John Vercelli, master general of the Dominicans, to promote reverence for the Holy Name of Jesus; this is still the principal purpose of the society, which also develops lay apostolic programs in line with directives of the Second Vatican Council. Introduced in the U.S. by Dominican Father Charles H. McKenna in 1870-71, the society has about 5 million members on diocesan and parochial levels. With approval of the local bishop and pastor, women as well as men may be members.

**Holy Name Society, National Association (NAHNS)** (1970), 516 N. Front St., Minersville, Pa. 17954 (supply office). *Holy Name Newsletter*, monthly. Association of diocesan and parochial Holy Name Societies. Pres., Kenneth. J. Livaudais.

**Hungarian Catholic League of America, Inc.** (1945), 30 E. 30th St., New York, N.Y. 10016. Member of the National Catholic Resettlement Council. *Catholic Hungarian Sunday*, weekly. Pres., Rev. Msgr. John S. Sabo.

**I**

**Institute on Religious Life** (1974), 4200 N. Austin Ave., Chicago, Ill. 60634. *Consecrated Life*, semiannually; *Religious Life*, 10 issues a year. To foster more effective understanding and implementation of teachings of the Church on religious life, promote vocations to religious life and the priesthood, and promote growth in sanctity of all the faithful according to their state in life.

**International Institute of the Heart of Jesus** (1972), 7700 Blue Mound Rd., Milwaukee Wis. 53213

(corporate headquarters); 14 Borgo Angelico, 00193 Rome, Italy (executive offices). Promote awareness and appreciation of the mystery of the Heart of Christ and establish an international forum for the apostolate. Pres., Harry G. John.

**Italian Catholic Federation of California, Central Council** (1924), 1801 Van Ness Ave., San Francisco, Calif. 94109; 30,000; *Bollettino*, monthly, Sec., Robert Aquistapace.

## J

**John Carroll Society, The** (1951), 4844B South 28th St., Arlington, Va. 22206. Pres., John P. Arness, Esq.

**Judean Society, Inc., The** (1966), 1075 Space Park Way No. 336, Mt. View, Calif. 94043; over 800. International organization for divorced Catholic women. Self-help, mutual-help counseling groups. Foundress/Internatl., Dir., Frances A. Miller.

## K

**Knights of Peter Claver** (1909), 554 Palmetto St., P.O. Box 204, Mobile, Ala. 36601; 17,000. *The Claverite*, biannually. Fraternal and aid society.

**Knights of St. John, Supreme Commandery** (1886), 6517 Charles Ave., Parma, O. 44129; Sup, Sec., Brig. Gen. Salvatore La Bianca.

**Knights of the Immaculata (Militia Immaculatae, M.I.)** (1917), National Center, 1600 W. Park Ave., Libertyville, Ill. 60048; canonically established with international headquarters in Rome. A pious association for evangelization and catechesis beginning with members' own inner renewal, through the intercession of the Blessed Virgin Mary.

## L

**Ladies of Charity of the United States, Association of** (1960), 7806 Natural Bridge Rd., P.O. Box 5730, St. Louis, Mo. 63121; 40,000. International Association founded by St. Vincent de Paul in 1617.

**Las Hermanas** (1971): A national organization of Hispanic women and non-Hispanic associates concerned with being "actively present to the ever-changing needs" of Hispanics in the U.S.

**Lithuanian Groups:** Ateitininkai, members of Lithuanian Catholic Federation Ateitis (1910), 1022 Beau Brummel Dr., Dundee, Ill. 60118; to promote Catholic action and uphold Lithuanian heritage among youth; *Ateitis*, monthly; Pres., Kazys Pemkus, M.D. Knights of Lithuania (1913), educational-fraternal organization; *Vytis*, monthly; Pres., Loretta T. Stukas, 234 Sunlit Dr., Watchung, N.J. 07060. Lithuanian Catholic Alliance (1886), 73 S. Washington St., Wilkes-Barre, Pa. 18701; 118 branches; *Garsas*, monthly; fraternal insurance organization; Pres., Thomas E. Mack. Lithuanian Roman Catholic Federation of America (1906), umbrella organization for Lithuanian parishes and organizations; Pres., Saulius Kuprys, 4545 W. 63rd St., Chicago, Ill. 60629. Lithuanian Roman Catholic Priests' League (1909): religious-professional association, *The Observer*, monthly; Pres., Albert Contons, 50 Orton-Marotta Way, Boston, Mass. 02127. Two organizations with offices at 351 Highland Blvd., Brooklyn, N.Y. 11207 — Lithuanian American Catholic Services (1975); religious, educational, research and service association; Exec. Dir., Rev. Casimir Pugevicius. Lithuanian Catholic Religious Aid, Inc. (1961); to assist persecuted Catholics in Lithuania; Pres., Most Rev. Vincent Brizgys.

**Little Flower Mission League** (1957), P.O. Box 25, Plaucheville, La. 71362. Sponsored by the Brothers of the Holy Eucharist.

**Little Flower Society** (1923), 1313 Frontage Rd.; Darien, Ill. 60559; 200,000 Nat. Dir., Rev. Terrence L. Sempowski, O. Carm.

**Liturgical Conference, The,** 806 Rhode Island Ave. N.E., Washington, D.C. 20018. *Liturgy, Accent on Worship, Homily Service.* Education, research and publication programs for renewing and enriching Christian liturgical life. Ecumenical. Exec. Dir., Rachel Reeder.

**Loyal Christian Benefit Association** (1890), 700 Peach St., Erie, Pa. 16512; 56,623. *The Fraternal Leader*, bimonthly. Pres., Mrs. Catherine T. Kelly.

## M

**Marian Movement of Priests,** Nat. Dir., Rev. Albert G. Roux, P.O. Box 8, St. Francis, Me. 04774.

**Mariological Society of America** (1949), Sec., Rev. Theodore A. Koehler, S.M., Marian Library, University of Dayton, Dayton, O. 45469; 300. *Marian Studies,* annually. Founded by Rev. Juniper B. Carol, O.F.M., and other priest-scholars to promote greater appreciation of and scientific research in Marian theology.

**Maryheart Crusaders, The** (1964), 22 Button St., Meriden, Conn. 06450; 2,000. *The Maryheart Crusader,* 4 times a year. To reunite fallen-away Catholics and promote religious education for adults. Pres., Louise D'Angelo.

**Men of the Sacred Hearts** (1964), Shrine of the Sacred Heart, Harleigh, Pa. 18225. Promote enthronement of Sacred Heart.

**Missionary Association of Catholic Women** (1916), 3521 W. National Ave., Milwaukee, Wis. 53215. Pres., Mrs. Elizabeth Schneider.

**Missionary Cenacle Apostolate (MCA)** (1909), General Office, Holy Trinity, Ala. 36859; 350. To foster spiritual and apostolic life of the laity through prayer, instruction, example and service.

**Missionary Vehicle Association, Inc. (MIVA America)** (1971), 1326 Perry St., N.E., Washington, D.C. 20017. To raise funds and distribute them annually as grants to missionaries working with the poor in Third World countries. Nat. Dir., Rev. Philip De Rea, M.S.C.

**Morality in Media, Inc.** (1962), 475 Riverside Dr., New York, N.Y. 10115; 50,000 members. Newsletter, 8 times a year *The Obscenity Law Reporter,* bimonthly. To stop traffic in pornography constitutionally and effectively, and promote principles of love, truth and taste in the media. A major project is the National Obscenity Law Center which provides legal information for prosecutors and other attorneys. Pres., Rev. Morton A. Hill, S.J.

## N

**National Alliance of Czech Catholics** (1917), 2657-59 S. Lawndale Ave., Chicago, Ill. 60623; 450 parishes. Pres., Mr. Vaclav Hyvnar.

**National Assembly of Religious Women** (1970): Founded as the National Assembly of Women Religious; title changed, 1982. A movement of feminist women committed to prophetic tasks of giving witness, raising awareness and engaging in public action and advocacy for justice. Nat. Coord., Sr. Marjorie Tuite, O.P., 1307 S. Wabash Ave., Chicago, Ill. 60605.

**National Association of Church Personnel Administrators** (1973), 100 E. 8th St., Cincinnati, O. 45202. Pres., Rev. David McDonald; Exec. Dir., Sr. Mary Ann Barnhorn, S.N.D.

**National Association of Diocesan Ecumenical Officers,** Pres., Rev. John H. McDonnell, P.O. Box 230, Wheeling, W. Va. 26003.

**National Association of Pastoral Musicians** (1976), 225 Sheridan St., N.W., Washington, D.C. 20011; 7,000. *Pastoral Music*, six times a year. For clergy and musicians. Pres. and Exec. Dir., Rev. Virgil C. Funk.

**National Association of Priest Pilots** (1964), Pres., Rev. John Hemann, 510 First Ave. N.W., Cedar Rapids, Ia. 52405.

**National Catholic Bandmasters' Association** (1953), Box 523, Notre Dame University, Notre Dame, Ind. 46556. *The School Musician Magazine.*

**National Catholic Cemetery Conference** (1949), 710 N. River Rd., Des Plaines, Ill. 60016. *The Catholic Cemetery,* monthly. Pres., Rev. Joseph P. Minturn.

**National Catholic Conference for Interracial Justice (NCCIJ)** (1960), 1200 Varnum St. N.E., Washington, D.C. 20017. Stresses moral dimension of civil rights, intercultural cooperation and interracial justice programming in each diocese/organization. Exec. Dir. Mr. Jerome B. Ernst.

**National Catholic Development Conference** (1968), 86 Front St., Hempstead, N.Y. 11550. Professional association of organizations and individuals engaged in raising funds for Catholic charitable activities. Pres., Rev. Richard K. Knuge, S.M.; Exec. Dir., George T. Holloway.

**National Catholic Disaster Relief Committee,** 1346 Connecticut Ave. N.W., Suite 307, Washington, D.C. 20036.

**National Catholic Pharmacists Guild of the United States** (1962), 400 members; *The Catholic Pharmacist.* Exec. Dir., John P. Winkelmann, 1012 Surrey Hills Dr., St. Louis, Mo. 63117.

**National Catholic Society of Foresters** (1891), 35 E. Wacker, Chicago, Ill. 60601; 70,951; *National Catholic Forester,* quarterly. A fraternal insurance society. Pres., Mrs. Dolores M. Johnson.

**National Catholic Stewardship Council** (1962), 1 Columbia Place, Albany, N.Y. 12207. To promote the total concept of stewardship. Exec. Dir. Rev. James M. Mackey.

**National Catholic Women's Union** (1916), 3835 Westminster Pl., St. Louis, Mo. 63108; 12,500.

**National Center for Urban Ethnic Affairs**

(1971): P.O. Box 33279, Washington, D.C. 20033. Research and action related to the Church's concern for cultural pluralism and urban neighborhoods. An affiliate of the USCC. Pres., Dr. John A. Kromkowski.

**National Church Goods Association,** 1114 Greenfield Lane, Mt. Prospect, Ill. 60056. Pres., Mark Gould.

**National Clergy Conference on Alcoholism and Related Drug Problems,** 3112-7th St. N.E., Washington, D.C. 20017. Exec. Dir., Rev. John F. X. O'Neill.

**National Conference of Diocesan Vocation Directors (NCDVD)** (1961), 1307 S. Wabash, Suite 350, Chicago, Ill. 60605. To provide diocesan vocation personnel with information and services regarding: awareness and discernment of vocations to the diocesan or religious priesthood and the religious life for both men and women; formation of diocesan priesthood candidates. Exec. Dir., Rev. Henry Mancuso.

**National Conference of Religious Vocation Directors (NCRVD),** 1307 S. Wabash Ave., Suite 350, Chicago, Ill. 60605. *Call to Growth/Ministry, NCRVD Newsletter,* quarterlies. Service organization for men and women religious assigned to vocational ministry.

**National Federation of Catholic Physicians' Guilds** (1927), 850 Elm Grove, Suite 11, Elm Grove, Wis. 53122; 5,500 in 81 autonomous guilds in U.S. and Canada, *Linacre Quarterly.* Pres., Joseph Gambescia, M.D.

**National Federation of Spiritual Directors** (1972). Pres., Rev. David Lichter, St. Francis Seminary, 3257 S. Lake Dr., Milwaukee, Wis. 53207.

**National Guild of Catholic Psychiatrists, Inc.** (1949). Integration of psychiatry and Roman Catholic theology. *The Bulletin.* Pres. (1984-1985), Louis M. Vuksinick, M.D. Mailing address: Exec. Sec., 120 Hill St., Whitinsville, Mass. 01588.

**National Organization for Continuing Education of Roman Catholic Clergy, Inc.** (1973). Membership, 136 dioceses, 65 religious provinces, 37 affiliated institutions. Pres., Rev. Robert Pearson, 304 S. Adams Rd., Spokane, Wash. 99216. Exec. Dir., Rev. Jerome Thompson, Catholic Theological Union, 5401 S. Cornell, Chicago, Ill. 60615 (national office).

**Network** (1971), 806 Rhode Island Ave. N.E., Washington, D.C. 20018. A Catholic social justice lobby.

**Nocturnal Adoration Society of the United States** (1882), 194 E. 76th St., New York, N.Y. 10021; 57,000 in 540 units.

**North American Academy of Liturgy,** c/o David Truemper, Valparaiso Univ., Valparaiso, Ind. 46383. *Proceedings,* annually. Foster liturgical research, publication and dialogue on a scholarly level. Pres., Dr. Gordon Lathrop.

## O

**Order of the Alhambra** (1904), 4200 Leeds Ave., Baltimore, Md. 21229. 11,000 in U.S. and Canada. Fraternal society dedicated to assisting retarded children. Supreme Commander, John Ciccozzi.

P

**Paulist League** (1924), 415 W. 59th St., New York, N.Y. 10019; 23,700. Dir., Rev. John E. Hurley, C.S.P.

**Philangeli (Friends of the Angels)** (1949 in England; 1956 in U.S.), Viatorian Fathers, 1115 E. Euclid St., Arlington Heights, Ill. 60004; approximately 750,000 in 60 countries. To encourage devotion to the angels.

**Pious Union of Prayer** (1898), St. Joseph's Home, P.O. Box 288, Jersey City, N.J. 07303; 50,000. *St. Joseph's Messenger and Advocate of the Blind*, quarterly.

**Pious Union of the Holy Spirit** (1900), 30 Gedney Park Dr., White Plains, N.Y. 10605. Pres., Rev. Jerome McHugh, O.F.M. Cap.

**Pontifical Mission for Palestine** (1949), c/o Catholic Near East Welfare Association, 1011 First Ave., New York, N.Y. 10022. Field offices in Rome, Italy, Beirut, Lebanon, Jerusalem, and Amman, Jordan. The papal relief agency for 1.8 million Palestinian refugees in Lebanon, Syria, Jordan, and the Gaza Strip. Distributes food, clothing, other essentials; maintains medical clinics, orphanages, libraries, refugee camp schools and chapels, the Pontifical Mission Center for the Blind (Gaza), the Pontifical Mission Libraries (Jerusalem, Bethlehem, Nazareth), the Epheta Institute for Deaf-Mutes (Bethlehem). Pres., Rev. Msgr. John G. Nolan, Exec. Vice-Pres., Rev. Msgr. Edward C. Foster.

**Pontifical Missionary Union** (1916), 366 Fifth Ave., New York, N.Y. 10001. To promote mission awareness among clergy, religious, candidates to priestly and religious life, and others engaged in pastoral ministry of the Church. Nat. Dir., Rev. Msgr. William J. McCormack; Nat. Sec., Rev. Roman R. Vanasse, O. Praem.

**Priests' Eucharistic League** (1887), 194 E. 76th St., New York, N.Y. 10021; 17,500. *Emmanuel,* 10 issues a year. Nat. Dir., Rev. Eugene La Verdiere, S.S.S.

**Pro Ecclesia Foundation** (1970), 663 Fifth Ave., New York, N.Y. 10022. *Pro Ecclesia, Talks of Pope John Paul II, Common Good;* Manhattan Cable-TV program. To answer attacks against Church and promote Church teachings. Pres., Dr. Timothy A. Mitchell.

**Pro Maria Committee** (1952), 22 Second Ave., Lowell, Mass. 01854. Promote devotion to Our Lady of Beauraing (See Index).

**Pro Sanctity Movement.** A worldwide force of laity organized to spread God's call of all persons to holiness. Addresses: 205 S. Pine Dr., Fullerton, Calif. 92633; 730 E. 37th St., Brooklyn, N.Y. 11236.

**The Providence Association of the Ukrainian Catholics in America** (Ukrainian Catholic Fraternal Benefit Society) (1912), 817 N. Franklin St., Philadelphia, Pa. 19123. *America* (Ukrainian-English).

R

**Raskob Foundation for Catholic Activities, Inc.** (1945), Kennett Pike and Montchanin Rd., P.O. Box 4019, Wilmington, Del. 19807. Exec. Vice Pres., Gerard S. Garey.

**Reparation Society of the Immaculate Heart of Mary, Inc.** (1946), 100 E. 20th St., Baltimore, Md. 21218. *Fatima Findings,* monthly. Dir. Rev. John Ryan, S.J.

**Rosary Altar Society** (Confraternity of the Most Holy Rosary) (1891, in U.S.), 141 E. 65th St., New York, N.Y. 10021; 3,000,000.

**Rosary League** (1901), Franciscan Sisters of the Atonement, Graymoor, Garrison, N.Y. 10524.

S

**Sacred Heart League,** Walls, Miss. 38686; 700,000. Promote devotion to the Sacred Heart. Its program services include the Sacred Heart Auto League for careful, prayerful driving and the Apostolate of the Printed Word. Pres., Rev. Robert Hess, S.C.J.

**St. Ansgar's Scandinavian Catholic League** (1910), 40 W. 13th St., New York, N.Y. 10011; 1,000. *St. Ansgar's Bulletin,* annually.

**St. Anthony's Guild** (1924), Paterson, N.J. 07509. *Anthonian,* quarterly. Dir., Rev. Salvator Fink, O.F.M.

**St. Jude League** (1929), 221 W. Madison St., Chicago, Ill. 60606. *St. Jude Journal,* bi-monthly. Dir., Rev. Mark J. Brummel, C.M.F.

**St. Margaret of Scotland Guild, Inc.** (1938), Graymoor, Garrison, N.Y. 10524; 2,200. Moderator, Bro. Pius MacIsaac, S.A.

**St. Martin de Porres Guild** (1935), 141 E. 65th St., New York, N.Y. 10021. Dir., Rev. John A. Farren, O.P.

**St. Thomas Aquinas Foundation of the Dominican Fathers of the United States (STAF).** Mod., Very Rev. Thomas H. McBrien, O.P., Providence College, Providence, R.I. 02918

**Serra International** (1938), 22 W. Monroe St., Chicago, Ill. 60603; 15,200 members in 490 clubs in 33 countries. *Serran,* bimonthly. Fosters vocations to the priesthood, and religious life, trains Catholic lay leadership. Formally aggregated to the Pontifical Society for Priestly Vocations, 1951. Pres., Matthew H. McCloskey IV.

**Slovak Catholic Federation** (1911): Founded by Rev. Joseph Murgas to promote and coordinate religious activities among Slovak Catholic fraternal societies, religious communities and Slovak ethnic parishes in their effort to address themselves to the special needs of Slovak Catholics in the U.S. and Canada. Pres., Rev. Joseph V. Adamec, 1515 Cass Ave., Bay City, Mich. 48706; Sec., Mr. John Mizenko, 32283 Sedgefield Oval, Solon, Ohio 44139.

**Slovak Catholic Sokol** (1905), 205 Madison St., Passaic, N.J. 07055; 48,500. *Katolicky Sokol (Catholic Falcon),* weekly; *Priatel Dietok (Children's Friend),* bimonthly.

**Society for the Propagation of the Faith** (1822), 366 Fifth Ave., New York, N.Y. 10001; established in 171 dioceses. Church's principal instrument for promoting mission awareness and generating financial support for the missions. General fund for ordinary and extraordinary subsidies for all mission dioceses. *Mission,* 4 times a year; *Director's Newsletter.* Is subject to Sacred Congregation for the Evangelization of Peoples. Nat. Dir., Rev. Msgr. William J. McCormack.

**Society of St. Peter the Apostle** (1889), 366 Fifth Ave., New York, N.Y. 10001; 171 dioceses. Church's central fund for support of seminaries, seminarians and novices in all mission dioceses. Nat. Dir., Rev. Msgr. William J. McCormack.

**Spiritual Life Institute of America** (1960), Box 260, Crestone, Colo. 81131. *Desert Call*, seasonal. An eremetical movement to foster the contemplative spirit in America. Founder, Rev. William McNamara, O.C.D. Second foundation: Primitive Wilderness Hermitage, Kemptville, Nova Scotia, Canada B0W 1Y0.

**T**

**Theresians of America** (1961), 5326 E. Pershing Ave., Scottsdale, Ariz. 85254; 5,000. Spiritual, intellectual and apostolic organization of Christian women. Exec. Dir., Sr. Patricia Mullen.

**U**

**United Societies of U.S.A.** (1903), 613 Sinclair St., McKeesport, Pa. 15132; 3,700 members. *Prosvita-Enlightenment,* monthly newspaper.

**United States Catholic Historical Society** (1884). 500. *Journal,* quarterly; and *Monograph Series,* annually. Exec. Dir., James J. Mahoney, P.O. Box 498, Yonkers, N.Y. 10702.

**W-Y**

**Western Catholic Union** (1877), W.C.U. Bldg., 506-510 Maine St., Quincy, Ill. 62301; 27,537 members. *Western Catholic Union Record,* bimonthly.

**Word of God Institute** (1972), 487 Michigan Ave. N.E., Washington, D.C. 20017. For renewed biblical preaching, Bible sharing and evangelization. Dir., Rev. John Burke, O.P.

**Young Ladies' Institute** (1887), P.O. Box 99687, San Francisco, Calif. 94109. Grand Sec. Mrs. Sylvia Sharman.

**Young Men's Institute** (1883), 50 Oak St., San Francisco, Calif. 94102; 4,500. *Institute Journal,* bimonthly. Grand Sec., R. A. Bettencourt.

### Knights of Columbus

The Knights of Columbus, which originated as a fraternal benefit society of Catholic men, was founded by Father Michael J. McGivney and chartered by the General Assembly of Connecticut Mar. 29, 1882.

In line with their general purpose to be of ser-vice to the Church, the Knights are active in many apostolic works and community programs.

Since January, 1947, the Knights have sponsored a program of Catholic advertising in secular publications with national circulation. This has brought some 7 million inquiries and led to more than 650,000 enrollments in courses in the Catholic faith. In recent years the Knights have broadened this program to include other media for spreading Christian and religious ideals. As a result substantial contributions have been made to support the work of the John LaFarge Institute in New York, the Catholic Communications Foundation in New York, and the Center for Applied Research in the Apostolate (CARA) in Washington. In 1975 the Knights also undertook funding of the up-link costs for telecasting papal ceremonies throughout the world via satellite.

K. of C. scholarship funds — two at the Catholic University of America, another for disbursement at other Catholic colleges in the U.S., one at Canadian colleges and others for the Philippines, Mexico and Puerto Rico — have provided college educations for some 1,600 students since 1914.

The order promotes youth activity through sponsorship of the Columbian Squires and through co-operation with other organized youth groups.

Recent programs undertaken by the Knights include: promotion of vocations to the priesthood and religious life; promotion of rosary devotion with free distribution of more than 100,000 rosaries a year; efforts to halt the increased killing of the unborn; assistance to the retarded and other disadvantaged people.

In 1982, local units of the Knights contributed more than $52.2 million to charitable and benevolent causes, and gave more than 13.4 million hours of community service.

K. of C. membership, as of Apr. 1, 1984, was 1,395,106 in 7,764 councils in the U.S., Canada, the Philippines, Cuba, Mexico, Puerto Rico, Panama, Guatemala, Guam, the Dominican Republic and the Virgin Islands. Assets, as of Dec. 31, 1983, amounted to $1,310,005,611 and total insurance in force, $8,347,551,180.

The Knights' publication, *Columbia,* has the greatest circulation (over 1.3 million) of any Catholic monthly in North America.

Virgil C. Dechant is Supreme Knight.

International headquarters are located at One Columbus Plaza, New Haven, Conn. 06507.

---

## AMERICAN CATHOLIC AWARDS

**St. Francis de Sales Award** (1959), by the Catholic Press Association for distinguished contribution to Catholic journalism. Msgr. George G. Higgins (1984).

**St. Francis Xavier Medal** (1954), by Xavier University (Cincinnati) to persons exemplifying the spirit of St. Francis Xavier. Vincent T. O'Keefe, S.J. (1983).

**St. Vincent de Paul Medal** (1948), by St. John's University (Jamaica, N.Y.), for outstanding service to Catholic charities. Vito V. Gerardi (1983).

**Serra Award of the Americas** (1947), by the Academy of American Franciscan History for ser-vice to Inter-American good will. Miguel Leon-Portilla (1978).

**Signum Fidei Medal** (1942), by the Alumni Association of La Salle College (Phila.) for noteworthy contributions to the advancement of humanitarian principles in keeping with Christian tradition. Ronald A. Codario, M.D. (1984).

**Soteriological Award** (1967), by the Confraternity of the Passion (Third Order of the Passionists, Corpus Christi Residence, 80 David St., South River, N.J. 08882), for outstanding exemplification of sharing in the Passion of Christ in contemporary society. Ann M. O'Bringer (1983).

# COMMUNICATIONS

## CATHOLIC PRESS STATISTICS

The *1984 Catholic Press Directory,* published by the Catholic Press Association, reported a total of 570 periodicals in North America with a circulation of 29,149,381. The figures included 175 English-language newspapers with a circulation of 5,674,869 and 16 other-language newspapers (including 6 Spanish) with a circulation of approximately 198,000. Magazines numbered 354 in the English language with a circulation of 22,802,948 and 25 in other languages with a circulation of approximately 474,000.

### Newspapers in the U.S.

There were 158 English-language newspapers (circulation 5,397,975); 6 Spanish-language (circulation more than 80,000) and 9 other-languages (circulation, over 109,000). Ten of these had national circulation; 155 (including 3 editions of *Our Sunday Visitor*) were diocesan newspapers. Listed below, according to circulation figures, are the national weekly newspapers and diocesan weekly newspapers with large circulations.

**National:** *Our Sunday Visitor,* 211,198; *National Catholic Register,* 66,934; *Catholic Twin Circle,* 63,000; *National Catholic Reporter,* 45,319; *The Wanderer,* 35,600; *Jednota* (Slovak and English), 36,732; *El Visitante Dominical* (Spanish), 31,000.

**Diocesan:** *Chicago Catholic,* 148,125; *Long Island Catholic* (Rockville Centre), 145,554; *Catholic New York* (New York), 129,149; *Pittsburgh Catholic,* 121,500; *St. Louis Review,*

97,635; *The Tablet* (Brooklyn, N.Y.), 92,978; *Catholic Voice* (Oakland), 83,812; *Catholic Standard and Times* (Philadelphia), 80,814; *Denver Catholic Register,* 80,375; *Clarion Herald* (New Orleans), 75,716; *The Evangelist* (Albany, N.Y.), 71,901; *The Record* (Louisville), 60,018; *The Voice* (Miami), 60,000; *The Monitor* (Trenton and Metuchen), 57,412; *Catholic Voice* (Omaha), 57,307; *Catholic Bulletin* (St. Paul and Minneapolis), 57,139; *Florida Catholic* (Orlando and St. Petersburg), 56,945; *Catholic Herald* (Milwaukee), 55,541; *Catholic Review* (Baltimore), 55,347; *The Pilot* (Boston), 55,304.

The oldest Catholic newspaper in the United States is *The Pilot* of Boston, established in 1829 (under a different title).

### Magazines in U.S.

The *Catholic Press Directory* reported more than 345 English- and other-language magazines in the U.S. with a circulation of more than 22,500,000.

*America* (circulation, 32,734) and *Commonweal* (circulation, 17,753), are the only weekly and biweekly magazines, respectively, of general interest.

The monthly magazine with the largest circulation is *Columbia* (1,357,602), the official organ of the Knights of Columbus.

General-interest monthly magazines with large circulations include: *Catholic Digest* (618,395); *Liguorian* (505,000); *St. Anthony's Messenger* (374,554); *U.S. Catholic* (53,668).

## CATHOLIC NEWSPAPERS AND MAGAZINES IN THE U.S.

(Sources: *Catholic Press Directory, 1984;* Almanac survey; NC News Service.)

*Abbreviation code: a, annual; bm, bimonthly; m, monthly; q, quarterly; w, weekly.*

Circulation figures for some of these newspapers and magazines are given in the article, Catholic Press Statistics.

### Newspapers

**Advocate, The,** w; 37 Evergreen Pl., E. Orange, N.J. 07018; Newark archdiocese.

**Alaskan Shepherd,** 6 times a year; 1312 Peger Rd., Fairbanks, Alaska 99701; Fairbanks diocese.

**America** (Ukrainian-English), daily; 817 N. Franklin St., Philadelphia, Pa. 19123.

**Anchor, The** w; P.O. Box 7, Fall River, Mass. 02722; Fall River diocese.

**Arizona Catholic Lifetime,** biweekly; 64 W. Ochoa St., Tucson, Ariz. 85701; Tucson diocese.

**Arlington Catholic Herald,** w; 200 N. Glebe Rd., Suite 614, Arlington, Va. 22203; Arlington diocese.

**Bayou Catholic, The,** w; P.O. Box 9077, Houma, La. 70361; Houma-Thibodaux diocese.

**Beacon, The,** w; P.O. Box 1887, Clifton, N.J. 07015. Paterson diocese.

**Bishop's Bulletin,** m; P.O. Box 665, Yankton, S. Dak. 57078.

**Bolletino,** m; 1801 Van Ness Ave., San Francisco, Calif. 94109; Central Council of Italian Catholic Federation.

**Byzantine Catholic World,** biweekly; 3643 Perrysville Ave., Pittsburgh, Pa. 15214; Pittsburgh Byzantine archdiocese.

**Catholic Accent,** w; P.O. Box 850, Greensburg, Pa. 15601; Greensburg diocese.

**Catholic Advance, The,** w; 424 N. Broadway, Wichita, Kans. 67202; Wichita diocese.

**Catholic Banner,** w; P.O. Box 818, Charleston, S.C. 29402; Charleston diocese.

**Catholic Bulletin,** w; 244 Dayton Ave., St. Paul, Minn. 55102; St. Paul and Minneapolis archdiocese.

**Catholic Calendar,** bm; 834 Ryan St., Lake Charles, La. 70601; one page in local newspaper; Lake Charles diocese.

**Catholic Chronicle,** biweekly; P.O. Box 1866, Toledo, O. 43603; Toledo diocese.

**Catholic Commentary,** w; P.O. Box 2239, Anchorage, Alaska 99510; one-page supplement in local newspaper; Anchorage archdiocese.

**Catholic Commentator, The,** w; P.O. Box 14746, Baton Rouge, La. 70808; Baton Rouge diocese.

**Catholic Crosswinds,** semi-monthly; 1001 N.

Grand Ave., Pueblo, Colo. 81003; Pueblo diocese.

**Catholic Exponent,** biweekly; 315 Ohio One Bldg., Youngstown, O. 44503; Youngstown diocese.

**Catholic Free Press,** w; 47 Elm St., Worcester, Mass. 01609; Worcester diocese.

**Catholic Herald,** w; P.O. Box 1572, Milwaukee, Wis. 53201; Milwaukee archdiocese.

**Catholic Herald — Madison Edition,** w; P.O. Box 1176, Middleton, Wis. 53701.

**Catholic Herald — Superior Edition,** w; P.O. Box 969, Superior, Wis. 54880.

**Catholic Herald,** w; 5890 Newman Ct., Sacramento, Calif. 95819; Sacramento diocese.

**Catholic Hungarian's Sunday,** w; 1739 Mahoning Ave., Youngstown, O. 44509.

**Catholic Key to the News, The,** w; P.O. Box 1037, Kansas City, Mo. 64141; Kansas City-St. Joseph diocese.

**Catholic Lantern,** m; P.O. Box 4237, Stockton, Calif. 95204; Stockton diocese.

**Catholic Light,** biweekly; 300 Wyoming Ave., Scranton, Pa. 18503; Scranton diocese.

**Catholic Messenger,** w; 201 W. 2nd St., Davenport, Ia. 52801; Davenport diocese.

**Catholic Mirror,** biweekly; P.O. Box 10372, Des Moines, Ia. 50306.

**Catholic Missourian,** w; P.O. Box 1107, Jefferson City, Mo. 65102; Jefferson City diocese.

**Catholic New York,** w; P.O. Box 5133, New York, N.Y. 10150; New York archdiocese.

**Catholic Observer,** biweekly; Box 1570, Springfield, Mass. 01101; Springfield diocese.

**Catholic Outlook,** m; 215 W. 4th St., Duluth, Minn. 55806; Duluth diocese.

**Catholic Post, The,** w; P.O. Box 1722, Peoria, Ill. 61656; Peoria diocese.

**Catholic Register,** biweekly; Box 126-C, Logan Blvd., Hollidaysburg, Pa. 16648; Altoona-Johnstown diocese.

**Catholic Review,** w; 320 Cathedral St., Baltimore, Md. 21203; Baltimore archdiocese.

**Catholic Sentinel,** w; 2816 E. Burnside St., Portland, Ore. 97214; Portland archdiocese, Baker diocese.

**Catholic Spirit, The,** m; P.O. Box 13327, Capitol Sta., Austin, Tex. 78711; Austin diocese.

**Catholic Spirit, The,** w; P.O. Box 951, Wheeling, W. Va. 26003; Wheeling-Charleston diocese.

**Catholic Standard,** w; 5001 Eastern Ave., P.O. Box 4464, Washington, D.C. 20017; Washington archdiocese.

**Catholic Standard and Times,** w; 222 N. 17th St., Philadelphia, Pa. 19103; Philadelphia archdiocese; Allentown diocese.

**Catholic Star Herald,** w; 1845 Haddon Ave., Camden, N.J. 08101; Camden diocese.

**Catholic Sun, The,** w; 257 E. Onondaga St., Syracuse, N.Y. 13202; Syracuse diocese.

**Catholic Telegraph,** w; 100 E. 8th St., Cincinnati, O. 45202; Cincinnati archdiocese.

**Catholic Times,** w; P.O. Box 636, Columbus, O. 43216; Columbus diocese.

**Catholic Transcript,** w; 785 Asylum Ave., Hartford, Conn. 06105; Hartford archdiocese, Bridgeport and Norwich dioceses.

**Catholic Twin Circle,** w; 6404 Wilshire Blvd., Suite 900, Los Angeles, Calif. 90048.

**Catholic Universe Bulletin,** biweekly; 1027 Superior Ave. N.E., Cleveland, O. 44114; Cleveland diocese.

**Catholic Virginian,** biweekly; 14 N. Laurel St., Box 26843, Richmond, Va. 23261; Richmond diocese.

**Catholic Voice, The,** w; 2918 Lakeshore Ave., Oakland, Calif. 94610; Oakland diocese.

**Catholic Voice, The,** w; P.O. Box 4010, Omaha, Nebr. 68104; Omaha archdiocese.

**Catholic Week,** w; P.O. Box 349, Mobile, Ala. 36601; Mobile archdiocese.

**Catholic Weekly, The,** w; P.O. Box 1405, Saginaw, Mich. 48605; Saginaw and Gaylord dioceses.

**Catholic Weekly, The,** w; 1628 Lambden Rd., Flint, Mich. 48501; Lansing diocese.

**Catholic Witness, The,** w; P.O. Box 2555, Harrisburg, Pa. 17105; Harrisburg diocese.

**Central California Register,** biweekly; P.O. Box 1668, 1550 N. Fresno St., Fresno, Calif. 93717; Fresno diocese.

**Central Washington Catholic,** m; P.O. Box 505, Yakima, Wash. 98907. Yakima diocese.

**Challenge, The,** semimonthly; P.O. Box 14082, Jefferson Sta., Detroit, Mich. 48214. St. Maron diocese.

**Chicago Catholic, The** w; 155 E. Superior St., Chicago, Ill. 60611; Chicago archdiocese.

**Church Today,** biweekly; P.O. Box 7417, Alexandria, La. 71306; Alexandria-Shreveport diocese.

**Church World,** w; Industry Rd., Brunswick, Me. 04011; Portland diocese.

**Clarion Herald,** w; 523 Natchez St., New Orleans, La. 70130; New Orleans archdiocese.

**Common Sense,** w; 1325 Jefferson Ave., Memphis, Tenn. 38104; Memphis diocese.

**Community,** w; P.O. Box 24000, Jacksonville, Fla. 32241; one-page weekly in Sunday editions of two daily newspapers; St. Augustine diocese.

**Compass, The,** w; Box 1825, Green Bay, Wis. 54305; Green Bay diocese.

**Courier, The,** m; P.O. Box 949, Winona, Minn. 55987; Winona diocese.

**Courier-Journal,** w; 114 S. Union St., Rochester, N.Y. 14607; Rochester diocese.

**Criterion, The,** w; P.O. Box 1410, Indianapolis, Ind. 46206; Indianapolis archdiocese.

**Dakota Catholic Action,** 9 times a year; P.O. Box 128, Wilton, N.D. 58579; Bismarck diocese.

**Darbininkas (The Worker)** (Lithuanian), w; 341 Highland Blvd., Brooklyn, N.Y. 11207; Lithuanian Franciscan Fathers.

**Denver Catholic Register,** w; P.O. Box 1620, Denver, Colo. 80201; Denver archdiocese.

**Dialog, The,** w; 1925 Delaware Ave., Wilmington, Del. 19806; Wilmington diocese.

**Diocese of Orange Bulletin,** m; 2811 E. Villa Real Dr., Orange, Calif. 92667.

**Diocese of Van Nuys Newsletter,** bm; 5335 Sepulveda Blvd., Van Nuys, Calif. 91411; Van Nuys Byzantine-Rite diocese.

**Draugas** (Lithuanian), daily; 4545 W. 63rd St., Chicago, Ill. 60629; Lithuanian Catholic Press Society.

**East Texas Catholic, The,** biweekly; P.O. Box 3948, Beaumont, Tex. 77704; Beaumont diocese.
**Eastern Catholic Life,** w; 101 Market St., Passaic, N.J. 07055; Passaic Byzantine eparchy.
**Eastern Montana Catholic Register,** w; P.O. Box 2107, Great Falls, Mont. 59403; Great Falls-Billings diocese.
**Eastern Oklahoma Catholic,** biweekly; Box 520, Tulsa, Okla. 74101; Tulsa diocese.
**El Heraldo Catolico** (Spanish), bm; P.O. Box 19312, Sacramento, Calif. 95819; Sacramento diocese.
**El Pregonero** (Spanish), w; 1015 University Blvd. East, Silver Spring, Md. 20930; Centro Catolico Hispano of Washington archdiocese.
**El Visitante Dominical** (Spanish), w; P.O. Box 96, San Antonio, Tex. 78291; Southern Province of Missionary Society of Oblate Fathers.
**Evangelist, The,** w; 39 Philip St., Albany, N.Y. 12207; Albany diocese.

**Fairfield County Catholic,** m; 238 Jewett Ave., Bridgeport, Conn. 06606; Bridgeport diocese.
**Florida Catholic, The,** w; P.O. Box 3551, Orlando, Fla. 32802; Orlando and St. Petersburg dioceses.

**Gary Sunday Visitor,** w; P.O. Box M-356, Gary, Ind. 46401; Gary diocese.
**Georgia Bulletin,** w; 680 W. Peachtree St. N.W., Atlanta, Ga. 30308; Atlanta archdiocese.
**Globe, The,** w; 1825 Jackson St., Sioux City, Ia. 51105; Sioux City diocese.
**Guardian, The,** w; P.O. Box 7417, Little Rock, Ark. 72217; Little Rock diocese.
**Gulf Pine Catholic,** w; P.O. Box 1189, Biloxi, Miss. 39533; Biloxi diocese.

**Harmonizer, The** (Edition O.S.V.), w; Cathedral Center, P.O. Box 11169, Fort Wayne, Ind. 46856; Fort Wayne-S. Bend diocese.
**Hawaii Catholic Herald,** w; 1184 Bishop St., Honolulu, H.I. 96813; Honolulu diocese.
**Hlas Naroda** (Voice of the Nation) (Czech-English), w; 2657-59 S. Lawndale Ave., Chicago. 60623.
**Horizons,** semimonthly; 1900 Carlton Rd., Parma, O. 44134; Parma diocese.

**Idaho Register,** w; P.O. Box 2835, Boise, Idaho 83701; Boise diocese.
**IDEA Ink,** q; 4716 Verona Rd., P.O. Box 4010, Madison, Wis. 53711; Dominican Educational Assn., Inc.
**Inland Catholic, The,** w; P.O. Box 2788, San Bernardino, Calif. 92406. San Bernardino diocese.
**Inland Register,** w; P.O. Box 48, Spokane, Wash. 99210; Spokane diocese.
**Inside Passage,** w; 419 6th St., Juneau, Alaska 99801; Juneau diocese.
**Intermountain Catholic, The,** w; P.O. Box 2489, Salt Lake City, Utah 84110; Salt Lake City diocese.

**Jednota** (Slovak-Eng.), w; Jednota and Rosedale Aves., Middletown, Pa. 17057; First Catholic Slovak Union.
**Joliet Catholic Explorer,** w; St. Charles Borromeo Pastoral Center, Rt. 53 and Airport Rd., Romeoville, Ill. 60441. Joliet diocese.

**Katolicky Sokol** (Catholic Falcon) (Slovak-English), biweekly; 205 Madison St., Passaic, N.J. 07055; Slovak Catholic Sokol.

**Lafayette Sunday Visitor,** w; P.O. Box 1603, Lafayette, Ind. 47902; Lafayette diocese.
**Lake Shore Visitor,** w; P.O. Box 4047, Erie, Pa. 16512; Erie diocese.
**La Voz** (Spanish), w; 9401 Biscayne Blvd., Miami, Fla 33138; Miami archdiocese.
**Leaven, The,** w; 2220 Central, Kansas City, Kans. 66110; Kansas City archdiocese.
**Long Island Catholic, The,** w; P.O. Box 700, Hempstead, N.Y. 11551; Rockville Centre diocese.

**Message, The,** w; P.O. Box 4169, Evansville, Ind. 47711; Evansville diocese.
**Messenger, The,** w; 220 W. Lincoln St., Belleville, Ill. 62221; Belleville diocese.
**Messenger, The,** w; P.O. Box 268, Covington, Ky. 41012; Covington diocese.
**Michigan Catholic, The,** w; 2701 Chicago Blvd., Detroit, Mich. 48206; Detroit archdiocese.
**Mirror, The,** weekly; M.P.O. Box 847, Springfield, Mo. 65801; Springfield-Cape Girardeau diocese.
**Mississippi Today,** w; P.O. Box 2130, Jackson, Miss. 39205; Jackson diocese.
**Monitor, The,** w; P.O. Box 3095, Trenton, N.J. 08619; Trenton and Metuchen dioceses.
**Morning Star, The,** biweekly; P.O. Box 3223, Lafayette, La. 70502; Lafayette diocese.

**Narod Polski (Polish Nation)** (Polish-Eng.) semi-monthly; 984 Milwaukee Ave., Chicago, Ill. 60622.
**National Catholic Register,** w; 6404 Wilshire Blvd., Suite 900, Los Angeles, Calif. 90048.
**National Catholic Reporter, The,** w; P.O. Box 281, Kansas City, Mo. 64141.
**New Earth, The,** m (Oct-June); P.O. Box 1750, Fargo, N.D. 58107; Fargo diocese.
**New Star, The,** w; 2208 W. Chicago Ave., Chicago, Ill. 60622; St. Nicholas of Chicago Ukrainian diocese.
**North Carolina Catholic,** w; 300 Cardinal Gibbons Dr., Raleigh, N.C. 27606 and 1524 E. Morehead St., Charlotte, N.C. 28207; Raleigh and Charlotte dioceses.
**North Country Catholic,** w; Box 326, Ogdensburg, N.Y. 13669; Ogdensburg diocese.
**Northwestern Kansas Register,** w; P.O. Box 958, Salina, Kans. 67401; Salina diocese.
**Nuevo Amanecer,** m; P.O. Box 155, Brooklyn, N.Y. 11243; for Hispanic Catholic community of Brooklyn diocese.

**Observer, The,** w; P.O. Box 2079, Monterey, Calif. 93940; Monterey diocese.

**Observer, The,** biweekly; 921 W. State St., Rockford, Ill. 61102; Rockford diocese.

**One Voice,** w; P.O. Box 10822, Birmingham, Ala. 35202; Birmingham diocese.

**Our Northland Diocese,** 22 issues annually; P.O. Box 610, Crookston, Minn. 56716; Crookston diocese.

**Our Sunday Visitor,** w; 200 Noll Plaza, Huntington, Ind. 46750; national edition and official publication for 4 dioceses.

**P.A.D.R.E.S. National Bulletin,** q; 3310 Garfield Ave., Kansas City, Kans. 66104.

**People of God,** m; 7208 Arvada N.E., Albuquerque, N. Mex. 87110; Santa Fe archdiocese.

**Pilot, The,** w; 49 Franklin St., Boston, Mass. 02110; Boston archdiocese.

**Pittsburgh Catholic, The,** w; 110 Third Ave., Pittsburgh, Pa. 15222; Pittsburgh diocese.

**Polish American Journal,** m; 716 Fillmore Ave., Buffalo, N.Y. 14212.

**Progress, The,** w; 910 Marion St., Seattle, Wash. 98104; Seattle archdiocese.

**Pueblo de Dios** (Spanish), biweekly; 37 Evergreen Pl., E. Orange N.J. 07018; Newark archdiocese.

**Record, The,** w; 701 W. Jefferson St., Louisville, Ky. 40202; Louisville archdiocese.

**Redwood Crozier, The,** biweekly, P.O. Box 1297, Santa Rosa, Calif. 95402; Santa Rosa diocese.

**St. Cloud Visitor,** w; P. O. Box 1068, St. Cloud, Minn. 56302; St. Cloud diocese.

**St. Louis Review,** w; 462 N. Taylor Ave., St. Louis, Mo. 63108; St. Louis archdiocese.

**Shlakh — The Way,** (Ukrainian-Eng.), w; 805 N. Franklin St., Philadelphia, Pa. 19123; Philadelphia archeparchy.

**Sooner Catholic, The,** biweekly; P.O. Box 32180, Oklahoma City, Okla. 73123; Oklahoma City archdiocese.

**South Texas Catholic,** w; 1200 Lantana St., Corpus Christi, Tex. 78407; Corpus Christi diocese.

**Southern Catholic, The,** m; 855 W. Carolina St., Tallahassee, Fla. 32304. Pensacola-Tallahassee diocese.

**Southern Cross, The,** w; P.O. Box 81869, San Diego, Calif. 92138; San Diego diocese.

**Southern Cross, The,** w; 601 E. 6th St., Waynesboro, Ga. 30830; Savannah diocese.

**Southern Nebraska Register,** w; P.O. Box 80329, Lincoln, Nebr. 68501; Lincoln diocese.

**Southwest Kansas Register,** w; P.O. Box 1317, Dodge City, Kans. 67801; Dodge City diocese.

**Steubenville Register,** w; P.O. Box 160, Steubenville, O. 43952; Steubenville diocese.

**Tablet,** w; 1 Hanson Pl., Brooklyn, N.Y. 11243; Brooklyn diocese.

**Tennessee Register, The,** w; 2400 21st Ave. S., Nashville, Tenn. 37212; Nashville diocese.

**Texas Catholic,** w; 3915 Lemmon Ave., Dallas, Tex. 75219; Dallas and Fort Worth dioceses.

**Texas Catholic Herald, The,** semi-monthly; 1700 San Jacinto St., Houston, Tex. 77002; Galveston-Houston diocese.

**Tidings, The,** w; 1530 W. 9th St., Los Angeles, Calif. 90015; Los Angeles archdiocese.

**Time and Eternity,** w; 514 E. Lawrence St., Springfield, Ill. 62703; Springfield diocese.

**Times-Review, The,** w; P.O. Box 937, La Crosse, Wis. 54601; La Crosse diocese.

**Today's Catholic,** biweekly; P.O. Box 28410, San Antonio, Tex. 78228; San Antonio archdiocese.

**Upper Peninsula Catholic,** biweekly; P.O. Box 548, Marquette, Mich. 49855; Marquette diocese.

**Valley Catholic,** m; 7600 Y St. Joseph Ave., Los Altos, Calif. 94022; San Jose diocese.

**Vermont Catholic Tribune,** biweekly; 351 North Ave., Burlington, Vt. 05401; Burlington diocese.

**Visitor, The,** w; 184 Broad St., Providence, R.I. 02903; Providence diocese.

**Voice, The,** w; 9401 Biscayne Blvd., P.O. Box 38-1059, Miami, Fla. 33238; Miami archdiocese.

**Voice of the Southwest,** w; P.O. Box 7, San Fidel, N. Mex. 87049; Gallup diocese.

**Wanderer, The,** w; 201 Ohio St., St. Paul, Minn. 55107.

**WestMont Word,** biweekly; P.O. Box 1729, Helena, Mont. 59624; Helena diocese.

**West Nebraska Register,** w; P.O. Box 608, Grand Island, Nebr. 68802; Grand Island diocese.

**West River Catholic,** m; P.O. Box 678, Rapid City, S. Dak. 57709; Rapid City diocese.

**West Texas Angelus,** biweekly; 116 S. Oakes, San Angelo, Tex. 76903; San Angelo diocese.

**West Texas Catholic,** biweekly; 1800 N. Spring, Amarillo, Tex. 79107; Amarillo and Lubbock dioceses.

**Western Michigan Catholic,** w; 650 Burton S.E., Grand Rapids, Mich. 49507; Grand Rapids diocese.

**Western New York Catholic,** m; 100 S. Elmwood Ave., Buffalo, N.Y. 14202; Buffalo diocese.

**Witness, The,** w; 1229 Mt. Loretta, P.O. Box 917, Dubuque, Ia. 52004; Dubuque archdiocese.

**Wyoming Catholic Register,** w; P.O. Box 4279, Caspar, Wyo. 82604; Cheyenne diocese.

### Magazines, Other Periodicals

**Act,** 8 times a year; 38598 Gainesborough, Mt. Clemens, Mich. 48044; Christian Family Movement.

**ADRIS Newsletter,** q; Department of Theology, Fordham University, Bronx, N.Y. 10458. Association for the Development of Religious Information Services.

**AIM (Aids in Ministry),** q; 1800 W. Winnemac Ave., Chicago, Ill. 60640.

**Albanian Catholic Bulletin (Buletini Katholik Shqiptar),** annually; P.O. Box 1217, Santa Clara, Calif. 95053; Albanian Catholic Information Center.

**America,** w; 106 W. 56th St., New York, N.Y. 10019.

**American Benedictine Review,** q; Assumption Abbey, Richardton, N.D. 58652.

**American Midland Naturalist,** q; Notre Dame, Ind. 46556.

**Americas, The,** q; Box 34440, W. Bethesda, Md. 20817; Academy of American Franciscan History.

**Amerikanski Slovenec** (Slovenian), w; 6117 St. Clair Ave., Cleveland, O. 44103; Slovenian Catholic Union.

**Angel Guardian Home Quarterly, The,** q; 6301 12th Ave., Brooklyn, N.Y. 11219.

**Anthonian,** q; Paterson, N.J. 07509; St. Anthony's Guild.

**Anthropological Quarterly,** q; 620 Michigan Ave. N.E., Washington, D.C. 20064.

**Apostolate of Our Lady,** m; 315 Clay St., Carey, O. 43316; Our Lady of Consolation National Shrine.

**Apostolate of the Little Flower,** bm; P.O. Box 5280, 906 Kentucky Ave., San Antonio, Tex. 78201; Discalced Carmelite Fathers.

**Archeparchal Bulletin,** q; 815 N. Franklin St., Philadelphia, Pa. 19123; Philadelphia archeparchy.

**Atchison Benedictine Community News,** bm; Mount St. Scholastica Convent, 801 S. 8th St., Atchison, Kans. 66002.

**Ateitis** (The Future) (Lithuanian), m; 9610 Singleton Dr., Bethesda, Md. 20807; for youth.

**Ave Maria** (Polish), 6 times a year; 600 Doat St., Buffalo, N.Y. 14211; Felician Srs.

**Benedictine Orient,** bm; 2400 Maple Ave., Lisle, Ill. 60532.

**Benedictines,** semiannually; Mt. St. Scholastica, Atchison, Kans. 66002.

**Bernardine Bulletin, The,** semiannually; 647 Spring Mill Rd., Villanova, Pa. 19085; Bernardine Srs..

**Best Sellers,** m; Univ. of Scranton, Scranton, Pa. 18510.

**Bible Today, The,** bm; Liturgical Press, Collegeville, Minn. 56321.

**Biblical Theology Bulletin,** q; 1723 Delaware Ave., Wilmington, Del. 19806.

**BLUEPRINT for Social Justice,** 10 times a year; Institute of Human Relations, Loyola University, New Orleans, La. 70118.

**Bringing Religion Home,** m; 221 W. Madison St., Chicago, Ill. 60606.

**Brothers,** bm; P.O. Box 26, Liguori, Mo. 63057. National Assembly of Religious Brothers.

**Call Board, The,** 5 times a year; 1501 Broadway, Suite 2400, New York, N.Y. 10036; Catholic Actors' Guild.

**Camillian: Journal of the National Association of Catholic Chaplains,** q; 3257 S. Lake Dr., Milwaukee, Wis. 53207; National Association of Catholic Chaplains.

**Carmelite Review, The,** m; 29 N. Broadway, Joliet, Ill. 60435; Canadian-American Province of Carmelite Order.

**Catechist, The,** m (exc. Dec., June-Aug.); 2451 E. River Rd., Dayton, O. 45439.

**Catholic Aid News,** m; 49 W. 9th St., St. Paul, Minn. 55102.

**Catholic Biblical Quarterly,** q; Catholic University of America, Washington, D.C. 20064; Catholic Biblical Assn.

**Catholic Cemetery, The,** m; 710 N. River Rd., Des Plaines, Ill. 60016; National Catholic Cemetery Conference.

**Catholic Digest, The,** m; P.O. Box 43090, St. Paul, Minn. 55164.

**Catholic Evangelist, The,** six times a year; 119 N.W. 11th St., P. O. Box 1282, Boca Raton, Fla. 33432. Catholic Evangelism, Inc.

**Catholic Forester Magazine,** bm; 305 W. Madison St., Chicago, Ill. 60606; Catholic Order of Foresters.

**CGA World,** bm; National Headquarters, Catholic Golden Age, Scranton, Pa. 18503.

**Catholic Historical Review,** q; 620 Michigan Ave. N.E., Washington, D.C. 20064; American Catholic Historical Assn.

**CHA in Washington, The,** m; 4455 Woodson Rd., St. Louis, Mo. 63134; Catholic Health Association.

**Catholic Journalist, The,** m; 119 N. Park Ave., Rockville Centre, N.Y. 11570; Catholic Press Association.

**C.K. of A. Journal,** m; 1850 Dalton St., Cincinnati, O. 45214; Catholic Knights of America.

**Catholic Lawyer,** q; St. John's University, Jamaica, N.Y. 11439; St. Thomas More Institute for Legal Research.

**Catholic League Newsletter,** m; 1100 W. Wells St., Milwaukee, Wis. 53233; Catholic League for Religious and Civil Rights.

**Catholic Library World,** 10 times a year; 461 W. Lancaster Ave., Haverford, Pa. 19041; Catholic Library Association.

**Catholic Life Magazine,** m (exc. July-Aug.); 35750 Moravian Dr., Fraser, Mich. 48026; PIME Missionaries.

**Catholic Near East Magazine,** q; 1011 First Ave., New York, N.Y. 10022; Catholic Near East Welfare Assn.

**Catholic Periodical and Literature Index,** bm; 461 W. Lancaster Ave., Haverford, Pa. 19041; Catholic Library Association.

**Catholic Pharmacist,** q; 1012 Surrey Hills Dr., St. Louis, Mo. 63117; National Catholic Pharmacists Guild.

**Catholic Press Directory,** a; 119 N. Park Ave. Rockville Centre, N.Y. 11570; Catholic Press Assn.

**Catholic Quote,** m; Valparaiso, Nebr. 68065; Rev. Jerome Pokorny.

**CRS News,** q; 1011 First Ave., New York, N.Y. 10022. Catholic Relief Services.

**Catholic Review** (Braille), m; 154 E. 23rd St., New York, N.Y. 10010; Xavier Society for the Blind.

**Catholic Rural Life,** m; 4625 N.W. Beaver Dr., Des Moines, Ia. 50322; National Catholic Rural Life Conference.

**Catholic Trends,** biweekly; 1312 Massachusetts Ave. N.W. Washington, D.C. 20005; NC News Service.

**Catholic University of America Law Review,** q; Washington, D.C. 20064.

**Catholic Update,** m; 1615 Republic St., Cincinnati, O. 45210.

**Catholic War Veteran,** bm; 2 Massachusetts Ave. N.W., Washington, D.C. 20001.

**Catholic Woman,** bm; 1312 Massachusetts Ave. N.W., Washington, D.C. 20005. National Council of Catholic Women.

**Catholic Worker,** 9 times a year; 36 E. First St., New York, N.Y. 10003.

**Catholic Workman,** m; 111 W. Main, P.O. Box 47, New Prague, Minn. 56071.

**Catholic Youth Ministry,** 10 times a year; 22 Willow St., Mystic, Conn. 06355.

**Catholicism in Crisis,** m; P.O. Box 495, Notre Dame, Ind. 46556; Jacques Maritain Center.

**Celebration,** m; 115 East Armour Blvd., Kansas City, Mo. 64111; National Catholic Reporter Publishing Co.

**Center Journal,** q; 237 N. Michigan St., P.O. Box A, Notre Dame, Ind. 46556; Center for Christian Studies.

**Charities USA,** m; 1346 Connecticut Ave. N.W., Washington, D.C. 20036; National Conference of Catholic Charities.

**Chicago Studies,** 3 times a year; P.O. Box 665, Mundelein, Ill. 60060.

**Christian Life Communities Harvest,** 6 times a year; 3721 Westminster Pl., St. Louis, Mo. 63108; National Federation of Christian Life Communities.

**Christian Renewal News,** P.O. Box 467, La Puente, Calif. 91747. Apostolate of Christian Renewal.

**Christopher News Notes,** 7 times a year; 12 E. 48th St., New York, N.Y. 10017; The Christophers, Inc.

**Cistercian Studies,** q; Abbey of Gethsemani, Trappist, Ky. 40051; international review dedicated to monastic and contemplative spirituality.

**City of God, The,** 3 times a year; 4545 Northwestern Ave., Indianapolis, Ind. 46208; St. Maur Theological Center.

**Clarion, The,** 6 times a year; Brothers Residence, 133B Granite St., Alfred, Maine 04002; Brothers of Christian Instruction.

**Claverite, The,** biannually; 554 Palmetto St., P.O. Box 204, Mobile, Ala. 36601; Knights of Peter Claver.

**Columban Mission,** m (exc. June, Aug.); St. Columbans, Nebr. 68056; Columban Fathers.

**Columbia,** m; One Columbus Plaza, New Haven, Conn. 06507; Knights of Columbus.

**Columbian, The,** w; 188 W. Randolph St., Chicago, Ill. 60601.

**Comboni Missions,** 4 times a year; 8108 Beechmont Ave., Cincinnati, O. 45230.

**Commitment,** q; 1200 Varnum St. N.E., Washington, D.C. 20017; National Catholic Conference for Interracial Justice.

**Commonweal,** biweekly; 232 Madison Ave., New York, N.Y. 10016.

**Communio — International Catholic Review,** q; Gonzaga University, Spokane, Wash. 99202.

**Community,** irregularly; 1746 W. Division St., Chicago, Ill. 60622; Friendship House.

**Company,** q; 3441 N. Ashland Ave., Chicago, Ill. 60657. National Jesuit Magazine.

**Consecrated Life,** semi-annually; 4200 N. Austin Ave., Chicago, Ill. 60634; Institute on Religious Life. English edition of *Informationes,* official publication of Sacred Congregation for Religious and Secular Institutes.

**Consolata, Missionaries,** m; P.O. Box C, Somerset, N.J. 08873.

**Contact,** 10 times a year; 555 Albany Ave., Amityville, N.Y. 11701; Sisters of St. Dominic.

**Contemplative Review,** q; Beckley Hill, Barre, Vt. 05641; Association of Contemplative Sisters.

**Context,** 22 issues a year; 221 W. Madison St., Chicago, Ill. 60606.

**Cord, The,** m; P.O. Drawer F, St. Bonaventure, N.Y. 14778.

**Counseling and Values,** q; 5999 Stevenson Ave., Alexandria, Va. 22304. Association for Religious and Value Issues in Counseling.

**Crescat,** 3 times a year; Belmont Abbey, Belmont, N.C. 28012; Benedictine Monks.

**Cross Currents,** q; Mercy College, 555 Broadway, Dobbs Ferry, N.Y. 10522.

**Crossroads Radio Centre,** bm; 1089 Elm St., W. Springfield, Mass. 01089.

**Crusader's Almanac, The,** biannually; 1400 Quincy St. N.E., Washington, D.C. 20017; Commissariat of the Holy Land.

**CRUX of the News,** w; 75 Champlain St., Albany, N.Y. 12204.

**Damien-Dutton Call,** q; 616 Bedford Ave., Bellmore, N.Y. 11710.

**Damien Report, The,** m; 131 Kuulei Rd., Kailua, H.I. 96734.

**Deaf Blind Weekly, The** (Braille), w; 154 E. 23rd St., New York, N.Y. 10010; Xavier Society for the Blind.

**Desert Call,** q; SLIA-Nada, Box 260, Crestone, Colo. 81131; Spiritual Life Institute of America.

**Diakonia,** 3 times a year; Fordham Univ., Bronx, N.Y. 10458; John XXIII Center for Eastern Christian Studies.

**Dimensions,** m; 86 Front St., Hempstead, N.Y. 11550; National Catholic Development Conference.

**Divine Love,** q; P.O. Box 24, Fresno, Calif. 93707.

**Divine Word Missionaries,** q; Techny, Ill. 60082.

**Ecumenical Trends,** m (exc. Aug.); 475 Riverside Dr., Room 528, New York, N.Y. 10115. Friars of the Atonement.

**Ecumenist, The,** 6 times a year; Paulist Press, 545 Island Rd., Ramsey, N.J. 07446.

**Educating in Faith,** q; 2021 H St. N.W., Washington, D.C. 20006. Catholic Negro-American Mission Board.

**Emmanuel,** m (bm July-Aug.); 194 E. 76th St., New York, N.Y. 10021; Blessed Sacrament Fathers.

**Emmaus Letter,** q; 3025 Fourth St. N.E., Washington, D.C. 20017. Federation for Catholic Youth Ministry.

**Envoy,** q; Office of Public Affairs, Catholic University of America, Washington, D.C. 20064.

**Envoy, Journal of Formative Reading,** bm; Institute of Formative Spirituality, Duquesne Univ., Pittsburgh, Pa. 15282.

**Extension,** m; 35 E. Wacker Dr., Suite 400, Chicago, Ill. 60601; Catholic Church Extension Society.

**Faith and Reason,** q. Route 3, Box 87, Front Royal, Va. 22630; Christendom College.
**Family,** m; 50 St. Paul's Ave., Boston, Mass. 02130; Daughters of St. Paul.
**Family Festivals,** bm; Resource Publications, 160 E. Virginia St., San Jose, Calif. 95112.
**Family Friend,** q; P.O. Box 11563, Milwaukee, Wis. 53211; Catholic Family Life Insurance.
**Fatima Findings,** m; 100 E. 20th St., Baltimore, Md. 21218; Reparation Society of the Immaculate Heart of Mary.
**Fellowship of Catholic Scholars Newsletter,** q; St. John's University, Jamaica, N.Y. 11439.
**Flame, The,** m; Barry Univ., 1130 N.E. 2nd Ave., Miami Shores, Fla. 33161.
**Franciscan Herald,** m; 1434 W. 51st St., Chicago, Ill. 60609.
**F.M.A. Focus,** q; 274-280 W. Lincoln Ave., Mt. Vernon, N.Y. 10550; Franciscan Mission Associates.
**Franciscan Reporter,** q; 3140 Meramec St., St. Louis, Mo. 63118.
**Franciscan Studies,** a; St. Bonaventure, N.Y. 14778; Franciscan Institute.
**Fraternal Leader,** bm; P.O. Box 6196, Erie, Pa. 16512; Loyal Christian Benefit Association.
**Fund Raising Forum,** m; 89 Front St., Hempstead, N.Y. 11550; National Catholic Development Conference.

**Garsas (The Sound)** (Lithuanian-English), m; 341 Highland Blvd., Brooklyn, N.Y. 11207; Lithuanian Roman Catholic Alliance of America.
**Generation,** m; 221 Madison St., Chicago, Ill. 60606.
**Glenmary Challenge, The,** q; P.O. Box 46404, Cincinnati, O. 45246; Glenmary Home Missioners.
**God's Word Today,** m; Box 40664, St. Petersburg, Fla. 33743.
**Good News,** m; 3003 S. Congress Ave., Lake Worth, Fla. 33461; Sunday Publications, Inc.
**Good News for Children,** 24 times during school year; 2451 E. River Rd., Dayton, Ohio 45439.
**Good Shepherd** (Dobry Pastier) (Slovak and English), a; 425 W. 12th Ave., Gary, Ind. 46407; Slovak Catholic Federation of America.
**Goose Corn,** 10 issues a year; 221 W. Madison St., Chicago, Ill. 60606.

**Harmony,** 4 or 5 times a year; 8300 Morganford Rd., St. Louis, Mo. 63123; Benedictine Srs. of Perpetual Adoration.
**Health Progress,** m; 4455 Woodson Rd., St. Louis, Mo. 63134; Catholic Health Association.
**Holy Name Newsletter,** m (exc. July and Dec.); P.O. Box 7244, Rocky Mount, N.C. 27801; National Association of the Holy Name Society.
**Homiletic and Pastoral Review,** m; 86 Riverside Dr., New York, N.Y. 10024.
**Horizons,** biannual; Villanova University, Villanova, Pa. 19085. College Theology Society.

**Human Development,** q; Jesuit Educational Center, 53 Park Pl., New York, N.Y. 10007.
**Human Life Issues,** q; St. John's University. Collegeville, Minn. 56321; Human Life Center.

**I.C. Good News,** q; Loyola Center, 5600 City Ave., Philadelphia, Pa. 19131; North City Catholic Conference, Inc.
**In a Word,** m; Bay Saint Louis, Miss. 39520; Society of the Divine Word.
**In-Formation,** 8 times a year; 1234 Massachusetts Ave., N.W., Washington, D.C. 20005; Religious Formation Conference.
**Institute Journal,** bm; 50 Oak St., San Francisco, Calif. 94102; Young Men's Institute.
**Integrity,** m; 6243 S. Fairfield Ave., Chicago, Ill. 60629; Rev. L. Dudley Day, O.S.A.
**International Philosophical Quarterly;** Fordham University, Bronx, N.Y. 10458.
**International Review — Natural Family Planning,** q; St. John's University, Collegeville, Minn. 56321.
**It's Our World,** 4 times a year; 1720 Massachusetts Ave. N.W., Washington, D.C. 20036. Holy Childhood Association.

**Jesuit Blackrobe,** q; 3601 W. Fond du Lac Ave., Milwaukee, Wis. 53216.
**Jesuit Bulletin,** 4 times a year; 4511 W. Pine Blvd., St. Louis, Mo. 63108; Jesuit Seminary Aid Association.
**Josephite Harvest, The,** q; 1130 N. Calvert St., Baltimore, Md. 21202; Josephite Missionaries.
**Jurist, The,** semiannually; Catholic University of America, Washington, D.C. 20064; School of Canon Law.

**Kinship,** q; P.O. Box 39188, Cincinnati, O. 45239; Glenmary Sisters.
**KIT — Keeping in Touch,** m; 1820 Mt. Elliott Ave., Detroit, Mich. 48207; Capuchin Province of St. Joseph.
**Knights of St. John,** q; 6517 Charles Ave., Cleveland, O. 44129.
**Kolping Banner,** m; 115-14 227th St., Cambria Heights., N.Y. 11411; Catholic Kolping Society.

**Laivas** (Lithuanian), bm; 4545 W. 63rd St., Chicago, Ill. 60629.
**Land of Cotton,** q; 2048 W. Fairview Ave., Montgomery, Ala. 39196; City of St. Jude.
**Law Briefs,** m; 1312 Massachusetts Ave. N.W., Washington, D.C. 20005; Office of General Counsel, USCC.
**Law Reports,** m; 4455 Woodson Rd., St. Louis, Mo. 63134.
**Laywitness,** m; 222 North Avenue, P.O. Box S, New Rochelle, N.Y. 10801; Catholics United for the Faith.
**Leaven,** q; Convent of the Holy Spirit, Techny, Ill. 60082.
**Leaves,** bm; 23715 Ann Arbor Trail, Dearborn Heights, Mich. 48127; Mariannhill Fathers.
**Let's Pray Together,** w; 775 Madison Ave., Albany, N.Y. 12208; Families for Prayer.

**Liguorian,** m; 1 Liguori Rd., Liguori, Mo. 63057; Redemptorist Fathers.

**Linacre Quarterly,** q; 850 Elm Grove Rd., Elm Grove, Wis. 53122; Federation of Catholic Physicians Guilds.

**Link, The,** 8 times a year; 95 Madison Ave., New York, N.Y 10016; Catholic Telecommunications Network of America.

**Listening,** 5 times a year; 814 Thayer Ave., Silver Spring, Md. 20910. National Catholic Office for the Deaf.

**Liturgy,** q; 810 Rhode Island Ave. N.E. Washington, D.C. 20018.

**Living Light, The,** q; 11 Park Place, New York, N.Y. 10007; Department of Education, USCC.

**Marian Helpers Bulletin,** q; Stockbridge, Mass. 01262; Association of Marian Helpers and of the Congregation of Marian Fathers.

**Marriage and Family Living,** m; Abbey Press, St. Meinrad, Ind. 47577.

**Marriage Encounter,** m; 955 Lake Dr., St. Paul, Minn. 55120; National Marriage Encounter.

**Mary Magazine and Aylesford News,** bm; Cass Ave. N. at I-55, P.O. Box 65, Darien Ill. 60559; Carmelite Fathers.

**Maryknoll,** m; Maryknoll, N.Y. 10545; Catholic Foreign Mission Society.

**Media and Values,** q; 1962 S. Shenandoah, Los Angeles, Calif. 90034; Center for Communications Ministry.

**Medical Mission News,** bm; 10 W. 17th St., New York, N.Y. 10011; Catholic Medical Mission Board, Inc.

**Medical Mission Sisters News,** 4 times a year; 8400 Pine Road, Philadelphia, Pa. 19111.

**Men of Malvern,** bm; Malvern, Pa. 19355; Laymen's Retreat League of Philadelphia.

**Messenger of St. Joseph's Union, The,** annual; 108 Bedell St., Staten Island, N.Y. 10309.

**MHS Review** (Franciscanews), q; 232 S. Home Ave., Pittsburgh, Pa. 15202.

**Mid-America,** 3 times a year; Loyola University, Chicago, Ill. 60626.

**Miesiecznik Franciszkanski** (Polish), m; 165 E. Pulaski St., Pulaski, Wis. 54162; Franciscan Fathers.

**Migration Today,** 5 times a year; 209 Flagg Pl., Staten Island, N.Y. 10304; Center for Migration Studies.

**Miraculous Medal, The,** q; 475 E. Chelten Ave., Philadelphia, Pa. 19144; Central Association of the Miraculous Medal.

**Mission,** 4 times a year; 366 Fifth Ave., New York, N.Y. 10001; Society for Propagation of the Faith.

**Mission,** q; 1663 Bristol Pike, Bensalem, Pa. 19020; Sisters of the Blessed Sacrament.

**Mission Handbook,** a; 1233 Lawrence St. N.E.; Washington, D.C. 20017. United States Catholic Mission Association.

**Mission Helper, The,** q; 1001 W. Joppa Rd., Baltimore, Md. 21204; Mission Helpers of the Sacred Heart.

**Missionhurst,** 6 times a year; 4651 N. 25th St., Arlington, Va. 22207; Immaculate Heart of Mary Mission Society, Inc.

**Mission Intercom,** 10 times a year; 1233 Lawrence St., N.E., Washington, D.C. 20017; U.S. Catholic Mission Association.

**Missionaries of Africa Report,** bm; 1622 21st St. N.W., Washington, D.C. 20009; Society of Missionaries of Africa (White Fathers).

**Modern Liturgy,** 9 times a year; Resource Publications, P.O. Box 444, Saratoga, Calif. 95071.

**Modern Schoolman, The,** q; 3700 W. Pine Blvd., St. Louis, Mo. 63108; St. Louis University.

**Momentum,** 4 times a year; Suite 100, 1077 30th St., N.W., Washington, D.C. 20007; National Catholic Educational Asssociation.

**Mother Cabrini Messenger,** bm; 434 W. Deming Pl., Chicago, Ill. 60614; Mother Cabrini League.

**Mountain Spirit, The,** 6 times a year; 322 Crab Orchard Rd., Lancaster, Ky. 40446; ecumenical; Christian Appalachian Project.

**MSC Spotlite,** q; 305 S. Lake St., Aurora, Ill. 60507; Missionaries of the Sacred Heart.

**My Daily Visitor,** bm; 200 Noll Plaza, Huntington, Ind. 46750; Our Sunday Visitor, Inc.

**My Friend,** 10 times a year; 50 St. Paul's Ave., Jamaica Plain, Boston, Mass. 02130; for children.

**National Catholic Forester,** q; 35 E. Wacker Dr., Chicago, Ill. 60601.

**NCSC News,** bm; 1 Columbia Pl., Albany, N.Y. 12207. National Catholic Stewardship Council.

**NFPC Newsnotes,** 8 times a year; 1307 S. Wabash, Chicago, Ill. 60605; National Federation of Priests' Councils.

**National Jesuit News,** m; St. Joseph's University, Philadelphia, Pa. 19131.

**National Service Committee Newsletter,** 10 times a year; 237 N. Michigan St., South Bend, Ind. 46601; Catholic Charismatic Renewal.

**Network,** bm; 806 Rhode Island Ave. N.E., Washington, D.C. 20018; Network.

**New Catholic World,** bm; 545 Island Rd., Ramsey, N.J. 07446.

**New Covenant,** m; P.O. Box 7009, Ann Arbor, Mich. 48107; Catholic Charismatic Renewal.

**New Scholasticism,** q; 715 Memorial Library, Notre Dame, Ind. 46556. American Catholic Philosophical Association.

**News/Views,** 5 times a year; 1307 S. Wabash Ave., Chicago, Ill. 60605; National Sisters Vocation Conference.

**News and Views,** q; 3900 Westminster Pl.; St. Louis, Mo. 63108; Sacred Heart Program.

**Newsletter of the Bureau of Catholic Indian Missions,** 10 times a year; 2021 H St. N.W., Washington, D.C. 20006.

**North American Voice of Fatima,** m; 1023 Swann Rd., Youngstown, N.Y. 14174.

**Notre Dame Magazine,** 5 times a year; Notre Dame Univ., Notre Dame, Ind. 46556.

**Nursing Sisters Today,** q; 310 Prospect Park W., Brooklyn, N.Y. 11215; Congregation of Infant Jesus.

**Oblate World and Voice of Hope,** bm; 350 Jamaica Way, Boston, Mass. 02130; Oblates of Mary Immaculate.

**Oblates,** bm; 15 S. 59th St., Belleville, Ill. 62222; Oblate Fathers.

**Old Testament Abstracts,** 3 times a year; Catholic University of America, Washington, D.C. 20064.

**Origins,** 48 times a year; 1312 Massachusetts Ave., N.W., Washington, D.C. 20005; NC News Service.

**Our Lady's Digest,** q; Box 777, Twin Lakes, Wis. 53181; La Salette Fathers.

**Pacer,** bm; 500 17th Ave., Seattle, Wash. 98124; Providence Medical Center.

**Padres' Trail,** 4 times a year; St. Michael's Mission, St. Michael, Ariz. 86511; Franciscan Fathers.

**Paraclete,** 4 times a year; P.O. Box 2000, Wheaton, Md. 20902; Holy Ghost Fathers.

**Parish Communication,** 10 times a year, 22 Willow St., Mystic, Conn. 06355.

**Pastoral Life,** m; Route 224, Canfield, Ohio 44406; Society of St. Paul.

**Pastoral Music,** 6 times a year; 225 Sheridan St., N.W. Washington, D.C. 20011; National Association of Pastoral Musicians.

**Paulist Fathers News,** 6 times a year; 301 Island Rd., Mahwah, N.J. 07430.

**Perpetual Help World,** q; 294 E. 150th St., Bronx, N.Y. 10451; Redemptorists.

**Philosophy Today,** q; Carthagena Station, Celina, Ohio 45822.

**Pilgrim,** q; Jesuit Fathers, Auriesville, N.Y. 12016; Shrine of North American Martyrs.

**Pope Speaks, The,** q; Our Sunday Visitor, Inc., 200 Noll Plaza, Huntington, Ind. 46750.

**Priatel Dietok** (Children's Friend) (Slovak), bm; 205 Madison St., Passaic, N.J. 07055; Slovak Catholic Sokol.

**Priest, The,** 11 times a year; 200 Noll Plaza, Huntington, Ind. 46750; Our Sunday Visitor, Inc.

**Probe,** bm (Sept.-June); 1307 S. Wabash Ave., Chicago, Ill. 60605; NAWR.

**Professional Placement Newsnotes,** bm; 10 W. 17th St., New York, N.Y. 10011; Catholic Medical Mission Board, Inc.

**Program Supplement,** 18 times a year; Columbus Plaza, New Haven, Conn. 06507; Knights of Columbus.

**Provincial Annals,** annually; Siena College, Loudonville, N.Y. 12211. Holy Name Province, Order of Friars Minor.

**Quarterly, The,** 2021 H St. N.W., Washington, D.C. 20006; Commission for Catholic Missions Among the Colored People and the Indians.

**Queen;** bm; 26 S. Saxon Ave., Bay Shore, N.Y. 11706; Montfort Fathers.

**Reign of the Sacred Heart,** m; Hales Corners, Wis. 53130.

**Religion Teacher's Journal,** m (Sept.-May); P.O. Box 180, Mystic, Conn. 06355.

**Religious Life,** m (bm, May-Aug.); 4200 N. Austin Ave., Chicago, Ill. 60634; Institute on Religious Life.

**Renascence,** q; Marquette University, Milwaukee, Wis. 53233.

**Respect Life Report,** m; 1312 Massachusetts Ave. N.W., Washington, D.C. 20005; Committee for Pro-Life Activities, NCCB.

**Response, The,** annual; 1234 Massachusetts Ave. N.W., Washington, D.C. 20005; International Liaison.

**Review for Religious,** bm; Room 428, 3601 Lindell Blvd., St. Louis, Mo. 63108.

**Review of Politics,** q; Box B, Notre Dame, Ind. 46556.

**Review of Social Economy,** 3 times a year; 25 E. Jackson Blvd., Chicago, Ill. 60604; Association for Social Economics.

**Revista Maryknoll** (Spanish-English), m; Maryknoll, N.Y. 10545; Catholic Foreign Mission Society of America.

**Roze Maryi** (Polish), m; Eden Hill, Stockbridge, Mass. 01262; Marian Fathers.

**Sacred Music,** q; 548 Lafond Ave., St. Paul, Minn. 55103.

**St. Anthony Messenger,** m; 1615 Republic St., Cincinnati, O. 45210; Franciscan Fathers.

**St. Anthony's Newsletter,** m; Mt. St. Francis, Ind. 47146.

**St. Joseph's Messenger and Advocate of the Blind,** q; St. Joseph Home, P.O. Box 288, Jersey City, N.J. 07303.

**Salesian Bulletin,** bm; 148 Main St., New Rochelle, N.Y. 10802; Salesian Fathers.

**Salesian Missions,** q; 148 Main St., New Rochelle, N.Y. 10802; Salesians of St. John Bosco.

**Salt,** m; 221 W. Madison St., Chicago, Ill. 60606; Claretians.

**Salvatorian Newsletter, The,** q; Society of the Divine Savior, Salvatorian Center, Wis. 53062.

**Sandal Prints,** bm; 1820 Mt. Elliott Ave., Detroit, Mich. 48207; Capuchin Fathers.

**Scalabrinians,** 3 times a year; 209 Flagg Pl., Staten Island, N.Y. 10304.

**School Guide,** a; 80 W. Broad St., Mt. Vernon, N.Y. 10552.

**School Sister, The,** q; 1233 N. Marshall St., Milwaukee, Wis. 53202; Sisters of Notre Dame.

**SCRC Vision, The,** m; 5730 W. Manchester Ave., Los Angeles, Calif. 90045; Southern California Renewal Communities.

**Scripture in Church,** 4 times a year; P.O. Box 9, Northport, N.Y. 11768.

**Serenity,** q; 601 Maiden Choice Lane, Baltimore, Md. 21228; Little Sisters of the Poor.

**Serran, The,** bm; 22 W. Monroe St., Chicago, Ill. 60603; Serra International.

**Share,** q; 4545 Connecticut Ave. N.W., Washington, D.C. 20008. Catholic Daughters of the Americas.

**Share the Word,** bm; 3031 Fourth St. N.E., Washington, D.C. 20017; Paulist Catholic Evangelist Center.

**Shepherd's Call, The,** q; P.O. Box 7775, Albuquerque, N.M. 87194; Brothers of Good Shepherd.

**Silent Advocate,** q; St. Rita School for the Deaf, 1720 Glendale-Milford Rd., Cincinnati, O. 45215.

**Sister Miriam Teresa League of Prayer Bulletin,** q; League Headquarters, Convent Station, N.J. 07961.

**SC News,** 9 or 10 times a year; 4400 Churchman

Ave., Louisville, Ky. 40215; Sisters of Charity of Nazareth.

**Sisters Today,** m (exc. July-Aug.); Liturgical Press, Collegeville, Minn. 56321.

**Social Justice Review, bm;** 3835 Westminster Pl., St. Louis, Mo. 63108; Catholic Central Union of America.

**Social Thought,** q; 1346 Connecticut Ave. N.W., Washington, D.C. 20036; National Conference of Catholic Charities.

**Sophia,** bm; P.O. Box 265, Newton Center, Mass. 02159; Newton Melkite eparchy.

**Soul,** bm; Mountain View Rd., Washington, N.J. 07882; Blue Army.

**Spectrum,** q; 1011 First Ave., New York, N.Y. 10022; Catholic Relief Services.

**Spirit,** biannually; Seton Hall University, South Orange, N.J. 07079; poetry magazine.

**Spirit and Life,** 6 times a year; 8300 Morganford Rd., St. Louis, Mo. 63123; Benedictine Srs. of Perpetual Adoration.

**Spirit and the Bride, The,** 9 times a year; 4140 Lindell Blvd., St. Louis, Mo. 63108; Catholic Charismatic Renewal Office.

**Spiritual Book News,** 8 times a year; Notre Dame, Ind. 46556.

**Spiritual Life,** q; 2131 Lincoln Rd. N.E., Washington, D.C. 20002; Discalced Carmelites.

**Spirituality Today** (formerly Cross and Crown), q; 1909 S. Ashland Ave., Chicago, Ill. 60608, Dominican Fathers.

**Squires Newsletter,** m; Columbus Plaza, New Haven, Conn. 06507; Columbian Squires.

**Star,** 10 times a year; 18 W. Bijou, Colorado Springs, Colo. 80903.

**Strain Forward,** 11 times a year; 50 St. Paul's Avenue, Jamaica Plain, Boston, Mass. 02130; Daughters of St. Paul.

**Studies in Formative Spirituality,** 3 times a year; Institute of Formative Spirituality, Duquesne Univ., Pittsburgh, Pa. 15282.

**Studies in the Spirituality of Jesuits,** 5 times a year; 3700 W. Pine Blvd., St. Louis, Mo. 63108.

**Tekakwitha Conference Newsletter,** q; 1818 Ninth Ave. So. No. 5, Great Falls, Mont. 59405.

**Theological Studies,** q: Georgetown Univ., 37th and O Sts., N.W., Washington, D.C. 20057.

**Theology Digest,** q; 3634 Lindell Blvd., St. Louis, Mo. 63108.

**Theresian News, The,** 4 times a year; 5326 E. Pershing Ave., Scottsdale, Ariz. 85254.

**Thirsting for Justice,** q; 1312 Massachusetts Ave. N.W. Washington, D.C. 20005, Campaign for Human Development.

**This Week,** w; 135 W. 31st St., New York, N.Y. 10001; Franciscan Communication Office, Holy Name Province.

**Thomist, The,** q; 487 Michigan Ave. N.E., Washington, D.C. 20017; Dominican Fathers.

**Thought,** q; Fordham University Press, Box L, Bronx, N.Y. 10458; Fordham University.

**Today's Catholic Teacher,** m (Sept.-May); 2451 E. River Ave., Suite 200, Dayton, O. 45439.

**Today's Parish,** m (Sept.-May); P.O. Box 180, Mystic, Conn. 06355.

**To Him She Leads,** q; Michigan Ave. and 4th St. E., Washington, D.C.; National Shrine of the Immaculate Conception.

**Topic,** semi-annually; 38 Michigan Ave., Lynn, Mass. 01902. Secular Franciscan Order, Province of Immaculate Conception.

**Tracings,** q; Gamelin St., Holyoke, Mass. 01040.

**Trinity Missions Magazine,** q; P.O. Box 7130, Silver Springs, Md. 20907.

**Trinity Review,** bm; 3606 Coolcrest Dr., P.O. Box 169, Jefferson, Md. 21755.

**Ultreya Magazine,** m; 4500 W. Davis St., Dallas, Tex. 75211. Cursillo Movement.

**L'Union** (French), bm; 1 Social St., Woonsocket, R.I. 02895.

**UNIREA, The Union** (Romanian and English), m; 4309 Olcott Ave., East Chicago, Ind. 46312.

**Universitas,** q; 221 N. Grand, Room 303, St. Louis, Mo. 63103; St. Louis University.

**U.S. Catholic,** m; 221 W. Madison St., Chicago, Ill. 60606; Claretian Fathers and Brothers.

**U.S. Dominican,** q; 3701 14th St., N.E., Washington, D.C. 20017.

**Venture,** 26 times during school year; 2451 E. River Rd., Dayton, O. 45439, Pflaum Press. Intermediate grades.

**Vision,** 3 times a year; P.O. Box 28185, San Antonio, Tex. 78228. Mexican American Cultural Center.

**Visions,** 26 times during school year; 2451 E. River Rd., Dayton, O. 45439; Pflaum Press.

**Waif's Messenger,** q; 1140 W. Jackson Blvd., Chicago, Ill. 60607; Mission of Our Lady of Mercy.

**Way — of St. Francis,** bm; 109 Golden Gate Ave., San Francisco, Calif. 94102; Franciscan Friars of California, Inc.

**Western Catholic Union Record,** m; 906 W.C.U. Bldg., Quincy, Ill. 62301; Western Catholic Union.

**Wheeling College Chronicle,** 4 times a year; 316 Washington Ave., Wheeling, W. Va. 26003.

**World Lithuanian Catholic Directory,** biannually; 351 Highland Blvd., Brooklyn, N.Y. 11207.

**Word Among Us, The,** m; P.O. Box 3646, Washington, D.C. 20037.

**Word of God,** w; 2187 Victory Blvd., Staten Island, N.Y. 10314; Society of St. Paul.

**Working for Boys,** q; Box A, Danvers, Mass. 01923; Xaverian Brothers.

**Worship,** 6 times a year; St. John's Abbey, Collegeville, Minn. 56321.

**Xaverian Missions Newsletter,** bm; 101 Summer St., Holliston, Mass. 01746; Xaverian Missionary Fathers.

**Your Edmundite Missions Newsletter,** bm; 1428 Broad St., Selma, Ala. 36701; Southern Missions of Society of St. Edmund.

**Youth Update,** m; 1615 Republic St., Cincinnati, Ohio 45210.

**Zeal Magazine,** q; N. Main St., Allegany, N.Y. 14706; Franciscan Sisters of Allegany.

## FOREIGN CATHOLIC PERIODICALS

Principal source: Catholic Almanac survey. Included are English-language Catholic periodicals published outside the U.S.

**African Ecclesial Review (AFER),** bm; Gaba Publications, P.O. Box 908, Eldoret, Kenya.

**Australasian Catholic Record,** q; St. Patrick's Seminary, Manly, New South Wales, Australia.

**Christ to the World,** bm; Via di Propaganda 1-C, 00187, Rome, Italy.

**Clergy Review,** m; 48 Great Peter St., London, SW1P 2HB, England.

**Doctrine and Life,** m, and **Supplement to Doctrine and Life,** bm; Dominican Publications, St. Saviour's, Dublin 1, Ireland.

**Downside Review,** q; Newman Bookshop, 87 St. Aldates, Oxford, England.

**East Asian Pastoral Review,** q; East Asian Pastoral Institute, P.O. Box 1815, Manila, Philippines.

**Eastern Churches Review,** semi-annual; 9 Alfred St., Oxford, England.

**Faith Today,** 10 times a year; Dominican Publications, St. Saviour's, Dublin 1, Ireland.

**Furrow,** m; St. Patrick's College, Maynooth, Ireland.

**Heythrop Journal** q; Heythrop College, 11 Cavendish Sq., London W1M, OAN, England (Editorial Office).

**Irish Biblical Studies,** q; Union Theological College, Belfast BT7 1JT, N. Ireland.

**Irish Theological Quarterly,** q; St. Patrick's College, Maynooth, Ireland.

**L'Osservatore Romano,** w; Vatican City.

**Louvain Studies,** semi-annual; Naamsestraat 100 B-3000, Leuven, Belgium.

**Lumen Vitae** (English and French editions), q; International Center for Studies in Religious Education, 186, rue Washington, 1050 Brussels, Belgium.

**Maynooth Review,** q; St. Patrick's College, Maynooth, Ireland.

**Mediaeval Studies,** annual; Pontifical Institute of Mediaeval Studies, 59 Queen's Park Crescent East, Toronto, Ont., Canada M5S 2C4.

**Month,** m; 114 Mount St., London, WIY, 6AH, England.

**Music and Liturgy,** q; Bamsthorn, Ockham Rd., North, West Horsley, Leatherhead, Surrey, England.

**New Blackfriars,** m; edited by English Dominicans, Blackfriars, Oxford, England.

**One in Christ,** q; Turvey Abbey, Turvey, Beds. MK43 8DE, England.

**Recusant History,** biannual; Catholic Record Society, 114 Mount St., London, W1Y 6AH, England.

**Religion and Society,** q; Christian Institute for the Study of Religion and Society, 17 Miller Rd., P.O. Box 4600, Bangalore 560 046, India.

**Social Studies,** q; St. Patrick's College, Maynooth, Ireland.

**Spearhead,** 5 times a year; Gaba Publications, P.O. Box 908, Eldoret, Kenya.

**Studies in Religion/Sciences Religieuses** (bilingual), q; Wilfrid Laurier University Press, Waterloo, Ont., Canada N2L 3C5.

**Sursum Corda—Lift Up Your Hearts,** bm; Box 79, Box Hill, Victoria, Australia 3128.

**Tablet, The** w; 48 Great Peter St., SW1P 2HB, London, England.

**Teilhard Review, The,** 3 times a year; The Teilhard Centre for the Future of Man, 23 Kensington Square, London W8 5 HN, England.

**Theology,** bm; S.P.C.K. Holy Trinity Church, Marylebone Rd., London, NW1 4DU, England.

**Way, The,** q; and **Supplements to The Way,** triannual: 39 Fitzjohn's Ave., London NW3 5JT, England.

## CATHOLIC NEWS AGENCIES

(Sources: International Catholic Union of the Press, Geneva; Catholic Press Association, U.S.)

**Argentina:** Agencia Informativa Catolica Argentina (AICA), av. Rivadavia, 413,4° Casilla de Correo Central 2886, 1020 Buenos Aires.

**Austria:** Katholische Presse-Agentur (Kathpress), Singerstrasse 6.2, 1010 Vienna 1.

**Belgium:** Centre d'Information de Presse (CIP), 1 Bd. Charlemagne, 1041 Bruxelles (Brussels).

**Germany:** Katholische Nachrichten Agentur (KNA), Adenauer Allee 134, 5300 Bonn 1.

**Great Britain:** Catholic Information Office of England and Wales (CIOEW), 38/40 Eccleston Square, London SW1V 1PD.

**Greece:** Agence TYPOS Rue Acharnon 246, Athenes 815.

**Hong Kong:** UCA-News, P.O. Box 69.626, Kwun Tong (Hong Kong).

**Hungary:** Magyar Kurir, Karolyi w 4-8, Postafiok 41, Budapest V.

**India:** South Asia Religious News (SAR-News), P.O. Box 4228, New Delhi 110.048.

**Italy:** Servizio Informazioni Settimanali (SIS-Roma) 1, via della Conciliazione, I-00193 Roma.

Centrum Informationis Catolicae (CIC-Roma), via Domenico Silveri, 30, I-00165 Roma.

**Spain:** Prensa Asociada (PA), Alfonso XI, 4—Apartado 14530, Madrid 14.

**Switzerland:** Katholische Internationale Presse-Agentur (KIPA), Case Postale 1054 CH 1701, Fribourg.

Centre International de Reportages et d'Information Culturelle (CIRIC), 10, av. de la Gare-des-Eaux Vives, CH-1207 Geneva.

**United States of America:** NC News Service (NC), 1312 Massachusetts Ave. N.W., Washington, D.C. 20005.

**Yugoslavia:** Aktusinosti Krscanska Sadasnjost (AKSA), Marulicev TRG 14, Zagreb p.p. 02-748.

**Zaire:** Documentation et Information Africaine (DIA), B.P. 2598, Kinshasa I.

**Missions:** Agenzia Internationale Fides (AIF), Palazzo di Propagande Fide, Via di Propaganda I-c, 00187 Rome, Italy.

Agencies distributing news related to Catholicism as well as other news are:

**France:** Agence France Presse (AFP), 13 Place de la Bourse, Paris 2e.

**Italy:** Agenzia Nazionale Stampa Associata (ANSA), Via Propaganda 27, Rome.

**United States of America:** Religious News Service (RNS), 106 W. 56th St., New York, N.Y. 10019.

## U.S. PRESS SERVICES

**National Catholic News Service (NC),** established in 1920, provides a worldwide daily news report by wire throughout the U.S. and into several foreign countries, and by mail to other subscribers, serving Catholic publications and broadcasters including Vatican Radio, and institutional subscribers in more than 40 countries. NC also provides feature and photo services and a weekly religious education tabloid insert, "Faith Today." It publishes "Origins," a weekly documentary service, "Catholic Trends," a fortnightly newsletter and produces a weekly half-hour TV newscast. NC maintains a full-time bureau in Rome. It is a division of the United States Catholic Conference, with offices at 1312 Massachusetts Ave. N.W., Washington, D.C. 20005. The director and editor-in-chief is Richard W. Daw.

**Religious News Service (RNS)** provides domestic and foreign religious news in daily photos and features; RNS was inaugurated in 1933 by the National Conference of Christians and Jews as an independent news agency. In 1983, it was taken over by the United Methodist Reporter, a chain of newspapers with headquarters in Dallas, Tex. Its offices are located at 106 W. 56th St., New York, N.Y. 10019.

**Eastern Rite Information Service (ER),** for Eastern Church news; 2208 W. Chicago Ave., Chicago, Ill. 60622.

**Spanish-Language Service:** A weekly news summary, *Resumen Semanal de Noticias,* provided by NC News Service, is used by a number of diocesan newspapers. Some papers carry features of their own in Spanish.

## BOOKS

**The Official Catholic Directory,** annual, P. J. Kenedy and Sons, 3004 Glenview Rd., Wilmette, Ill. 60091. First edition, 1817.

**The Catholic Almanac,** annual; Our Sunday Visitor, Inc., 200 Noll Plaza, Huntington, Ind. 46750, publisher; editorial offices, 620 Route 3, Clifton, N.J. 07014. First edition, 1904.

## BOOK CLUBS

**Catholic Book Club** (1928), 106 W. 56th St., New York, N.Y. 10019. Sponsors the Campion Award.

**Catholic Digest Book Club** (1954), Catholic Digest Magazine, P.O. Box 43090, St. Paul, Minn. 55164.

**Herald Book Club** (1958), Franciscan Herald Press, 1434 W. 51st St., Chicago, Ill. 60609.

**Thomas More Book Club** (1939), Thomas More Association, 223 W. Erie St., Chicago, Ill. 60610.

# CATHOLIC WRITERS' MARKET

(Source: Almanac survey.)

*Editors call the following suggestions to the attention of writers:*

Manuscripts should be typewritten, double-spaced, on one side of the page.

Writers should know the editorial policy, purpose and style of the publication to which they submit manuscripts. Sample copies may easily be obtained, often for the mere cost of postage. Some editors suggest that writers send outlines of proposed material, in order to facilitate editorial decision and direction. "Timely" copy should be submitted considerably in advance of the date of proposed publication; some editors advise a period of three months. Authors are urged to avoid sermonizing. Writers should not expect extensive criticism of their work, although they should profit from advice and direction when these are given. Editors are not required to state their reasons for rejecting manuscripts. Replies regarding the acceptance or rejection of copy are usually made within a few weeks.

All writers should send to editors stamped, self-addressed envelopes for the return of material. Those who write to Canadian editors may use international reply coupons, not U.S. stamps.

Payment is made on acceptance or publication. Rates are sometimes variable because of the reputation of the writer, the quality and length of the manuscript, the amount of editorial work required for its final preparation.

**America:** 106 W. 56th St., New York, N.Y. 10019. Ed., Rev. George W. Hunt, S.J. Weekly, circulation 33,000; $23 per year.

ARTICLES on important public issues evaluated scientifically and morally; serious and authen-

ticated articles on family life, education, religion, and social and political issues with ethical or religious implications; occasionally, "thought" pieces; 1,000-2,000 words — 6¢ a word. VERSE, short and modern, befitting a Catholic publication but not necessarily religious—$7.50 and up. No fiction.

**Annals of St. Anne de Beaupre, The:** P.O. Box 1000, St. Anne de Beaupre, Que., Canada G0A 3C0. Ed., Rev. Roch Achard, C.Ss.R. Monthly, circulation 65,000; $6 per year.

FICTION: Stories of general Catholic interest, preferably with slant on devotion to St. Anne; 700-1,200 words — 2-4¢ a word. ARTICLES of solid general interest to Catholics: on aspects of devotion to St. Anne, relative to history of the devotion in North America or elsewhere; on educational or social problems, or situations that should be of concern to all — especially Christians: 700-1,200 words — 2-4¢ a word, Payment on acceptance.

**BLUEPRINT for Social Justice:** Institute for Human Relations, Loyola University, New Orleans, La. 70118. Ed., John J. Mawhinney, S.J. Ten times a year, circulation 4,500; sent free on request.

ARTICLES analyzing current justice issues in economics, peace and human rights affecting the downtrodden and poor; length, 3,200 words.

**Catechist:** 2451 E. River Rd., Dayton, O. 45439. Ed., Patricia Fischer. Monthly August through April (exc. Dec.), circulation 45,620; $14.95 per year.

ARTICLES of interest to teachers of religion in parochial schools and CCD programs: 1,200-1,800 words — rate varies. PHOTOGRAPHS, black and white — rate varies. Payment on publication.

**Catholic Digest:** P.O. Box 43090, St. Paul, Minn.

55164. Ed., Henry Lexau. Monthly, circulation 637,000; $10.97 per year.

ARTICLES of close-to-home interest for average Catholic — rates vary; most frequent payments are $200 for originals, $100 for reprints; payment on acceptance. FILLERS, short features and jokes — rates vary; payment on publication. Cover pictures — $150. No fiction or verse. No queries necessary.

**Columban Mission:** St. Columbans, Nebr. 68056. Ed., Rev. Richard Steinhilber. Monthly (exc. June, Aug.); circulation 228,975; $3 per year.

ARTICLES mostly from missions or staff written: occasionally accept feature or factual articles on social and religious aspects of Asian and Latin American life: 2,000 words — $100 and up. PHOTOGRAPHS of Asian and Latin American subjects and photo stories — $10 each.

**Columbia:** Columbus Plaza, New Haven, Conn. 06507. Ed., Elmer Von Feldt. Monthly, circulation 1,365,813; $6 per year. Official organ of the Knights of Columbus.

ARTICLES dealing with current events, social problems, Catholic apostolic activities: 2,500-3,500 words (must be accompanied by color glossy photos or transparencies) — $500 to $600. SATIRE: 1,000 words — $200. CARTOONS, pungent, wordless humor — $25. COVERS — $750. No fiction.

**Commonweal:** 232 Madison Ave., New York, N.Y. 10016. Ed., Peter Steinfels. Biweekly, circulation 17,000; $24 per year.

ARTICLES, political, religious and literary subjects: 1,000-3,000 words — 2¢ a word. VERSE, serious poetry of high literary merit — about 40¢ a line.

**Crusader's Almanac:** Franciscan Monastery, 1400 Quincy St. N.E., Washington, D.C. 20017. Ed., Rev. Bartholomew Bengisser, O.F.M. Biannually, circulation 85,000; $1 per year.

ARTICLES about the Holy Land, Bible and Crusades given preference — 1¢ a word.

**Emmanuel:** 194 E. 76th Street, New York, N.Y. 10021. Editor-in-Chief, Rev. Eugene La Verdiere, S.S.S. Monthly (combined Jan.-Feb., July-Aug. issues), circulation 7,000; $15 per year.

ARTICLES, spirituality for those in Church ministry, Eucharistic, pastoral, theological, Scriptural: 2,000-3,000 words — $40-$50.

**Family Festivals:** 106 E. Virginia No. 290, San Jose, Calif. 95112. Ed., Sam Mackintosh. Bimonthly, circulation, 9,000; $16 per year.

ARTICLES, examples of family ritual or customs; background on religious/ethnic feasts; 500-1,000 words. All material should be queried (send S.A.S.E. if reply expected.) Writers' guidelines available with S.A.S.E. Sample copies, $2.50 each.

**Franciscan Herald:** 1434 W. 51st St., Chicago, Ill. 60609. Monthly, circulation 8,000; $11 per year.

ARTICLES concerning St. Francis of Assisi and related subjects; application of Gospel principles to living Catholicism today; 2,000 words — $35. BOOK REVIEWS related to Franciscan topics — $10.

**Health Progress:** 4455 Woodson Rd., St. Louis, Mo. 63134. Ed., C. S. Boyer. Ten issues per year.

Circulation 12,613; $30 per year (U.S. and Canada); $35 (foreign).

Official journal of the Catholic Health Association of the United States.

ARTICLES, health-care oriented; administrative procedures and theories; hospital departmental services: 1,500-3,000 words — payment by agreement. BOOK REVIEWS, hospital oriented — payment by agreement.

**Institute Journal:** 50 Oak St., San Francisco, Calif. 94102. Ed., Thomas P. Brady. Bimonthly, $1 per year.

FICTION — no fixed rate. PHOTOGRAPHS — $15.

**Josephite Harvest, The:** 1130 N. Calvert St., Baltimore, Md. 21202. Ed., Rev. Earle A. Newman, S.S.J. Quarterly; circulation 40,000; $2 per year.

ARTICLES concerning apostolate of Catholic Church in U.S. to the black community.

**Liguorian:** One Liguori Dr., Liguori, Mo. 63057. Ed., Norman J. Muckerman, C.SS.R. Monthly, circulation over 530,000; $12 per year.

FICTION concerning current situations; stories with a Christian influence yet without maudlin sentimentality; 1,500-2,000 words — 7-10¢ a word. ARTICLES on family, Scripture, liturgy; material for older readers and those under 21 needed; 1,500-2,000 words — 7-10¢ a word. POETRY, $25. ILLUSTRATIONS and BOOK REVIEWS on assignment only.

**Living Light, The:** Editorial offices, Department of Education, 1312 Massachusetts Ave. N.W., Washington D.C. 20005. Quarterly, circulation 3,000; $12 per year.

ARTICLES on Catholic religious education, catechesis, pastoral ministry; under 3,000 words — $15 per published page.

**Marriage and Family Living:** St. Meinrad, Ind. 47577. Man. Ed., Kass Dotterweich. Monthly, circulation 45,000; $12.50 per year.

ARTICLES: (1) aimed at enriching the husband-wife and parent-child relationships by expanding religious and psychological insights or sensitivity: (2) informative, aimed at helping couples cope, in practical ways, with problems of modern living; (3) personal essays relating amusing and/or heartwarming incidents that point up the human side of marriage and family life: maximum 2,500 words — 7¢ a word. POETRY: any style and length — $15. PHOTOS: b & w glossies (5 x 7 or larger), color transparencies or 35mm slides. 4-color cover or centerspread photo — $300. Photos of couples especially desired. Model releases required.

Buys North American serial rights only. Report on submissions in 3 to 4 weeks. Sample copy available for 50¢. Payment on acceptance. Suggest query with outline and opening paragraphs.

**Maryknoll:** Maryknoll, N.Y. 10545. Ed., Moises Sandoval. Monthly, circulation more than 1,000,000; $1 per year.

ARTICLES must apply in some way to the hopes and aspirations, the culture, the problems and challenges of peoples in Asia, Africa and Latin America: 1,000-1,500 words — average payment, $100. Outline wanted before submission of material. PHOTOS: More interested in photo stories than in individual black and whites and color transparencies. Photo stories — up to $150, black and white; up to $200, color. Individual photos — $20, black and white; $35, color. Transparencies returned after use. Query to be made before sending photos.

**Messenger of the Sacred Heart, The:** 661 Greenwood Ave., Toronto, Ont., Canada, M4J 4B3. Ed., Rev. F. J. Power, S.J. Monthly, circulation 18,000; $5 per year.

FICTION: stories which appeal to men, written with humor—good family reading: maximum, 1,800 words — 2¢ a word. ARTICLES of Catholic interest: 1,800 words — 2¢ a word. Payment upon acceptance.

**Miraculous Medal, The:** 475 E. Chelten Ave., Philadelphia, Pa. 19144. Ed., Rev. Robert P. Cawley, C.M. Quarterly, circulation 100,000.

FICTION, of general interest. Catholic in principle: 1,500-2,000 words — 2¢ a word and up. VERSE, religious in theme or turn; preferably about Our Lady: maximum 20 lines — 50¢ a line and up. Payment on acceptance. No articles.

**Modern Liturgy:** 160 E. Virginia St., No. 290, San Jose, Calif. 95112. Ed. James Nageotte. Nine issues a year, circulation, 15,000; $27 per year.

FICTION: parables, fantasy, fables; 1,000 words — 3¢ a word. ARTICLES: how-to, sample services, skills for liturgical artists; 1,200 words — 3¢ a word. POETRY, up to 50 lines — $10. BOOK REVIEWS appropriate for liturgy or religious education — $1 plus book.

Writers' guidelines available, send S.A.S.E.; or, for $3, a recent issue of magazine.

**My Daily Visitor:** Noll Plaza, Huntington, Ind. 46750. Ed., Patrick R. Moran. Bimonthly, circulation 16,561; $6.75 per year.

A pocket-sized booklet of reflections for each day of the month.

MATERIAL: Daily reflections based on spiritual meditation, the feast of the day or the liturgical season: maximum 165 words per page (each day's reflection is printed on a separate page) — $100 for series of reflections.

**New Catholic World:** 545 Island Rd., Ramsey, N.J. 07446. Mng. Ed., Robert Heyer. Bimonthly, circulation 14,000; $10 per year. Thematic issues.

ARTICLES, related to themes of issue (query editor): about 1,800-2,000 words. Rates of payment supplied.

**Our Family:** Box 249,Dept. C, Battleford, Sask., Canada SOM OEO. Ed., Rev. Albert Lalonde, O.M.I. Monthly, circulation 17,500; $9 per year; $12 in U.S.

FICTION, adult only; stories that reflect lives, problems and concerns of audience; anything true to human nature; no sentimentality or blatant moralizing; stories with "woven in" Christian message: 1,000-3,000 words — 7¢ to 10¢ a word. ARTICLES related to family living; religion, education, social, biographical, marriage, courtship, domestic, institutional: 1,000-3,000 words — 7¢ to 10¢ a word. POETRY, in the market for many more poems; should deal with man in search for himself, for God, for others, for love, for meaning in life, for commitment: 8-30 lines — 75¢-$1.00 per

line. PHOTOS — purchased with manuscript as package (extra payment for photos); also in search of individual photos for editorial use. FILLERS — anecdotes of inspirational value, straight exposition, short humor. Writers' guide and photo specification sheet available on request (free; please enclose SASE). A sample copy is available for $1.50. Usually buys first North American serial rights; will consider purchasing second or reprint rights.

**Our Sunday Visitor Magazine:** Noll Plaza, Huntington, Ind. 46750. Ed., Robert P. Lockwood. Weekly, circulation 290,000; $16 per year.

ARTICLES, no limitation on subjects other than those imposed by good taste and orthodoxy. Picture and text stories, profiles of individuals and organizations; articles that reflect moral, cultural, historical, social, economic and certain political concerns about the U.S. and the world; articles on current problems. Practical, factual and anecdotal material is sought: 750-1,000 words — $75-$100, usual payment. Queries are preferred to unsolicited completed manuscripts. PHOTOGRAPHS, picture stories preferred rather than individual photos. Picture stories (color) — $100 and up. No fiction or poetry.

**Parish Family Digest:** Noll Plaza, Huntington, Ind. 46750. Ed., Patrick R. Moran. Bimonthly, circulation 150,000.

ARTICLES of timely interest to the young and growing Catholic family as a unit of the Catholic parish — personality profiles, interviews, social concerns, education, humor, inspiration and family and parish-family interrelationships; 1,000 words or less — 5¢ a word. REPRINTS — $25. CARTOONS — $10 each for exclusives. FILLERS — $5 each for exclusives based on personal experience.

**Pastoral Music:** 225 Sheridan St. N.W., Washington, D.C. 20011. Ed. Daniel Connors. Bimonthly, circulation 8,000; $18 per year.

FICTION and ARTICLES — 4¢ a word.

**Priest, The:** 200 Noll Plaza, Huntington, Ind. 46750. Ed., Rev. Vincent J. Giese. Eleven issues a year, circulation 10,000; $16.50 per year.

ARTICLES of benefit to priests and seminarians in any of the following areas: priestly spirituality, contemporary theology, liturgy, apostolate and ministry, pastoral notes, Scripture. Controversial subject matter acceptable provided it does not go beyond the realm of orthodoxy or respect for authority or demands of fraternal charity: 6-15 double-spaced pages — $25 to $100 (about $6 per manuscript page).

**Queen of All Hearts:** 26 S. Saxon Ave., Bay Shore, N.Y. 11706. Ed., Rev. James McMillan, S.M.M.; Mng. Ed., Rev. Roger M. Charest S.M.M. Bimonthly; circulation 8,500; $8 per year (U.S.), $9 (Canada and foreign).

FICTION: short stories, preferably with a Marian theme: 1,000-2,000 words. ARTICLES that bring out the importance of devotion to Mary. Payment varies. VERSE with Marian theme — payment, two years' subscription. No artwork or fillers.

**Religion Teacher's Journal:** Twenty-Third Publications, P.O. Box 180, Mystic, Conn. 06355. Ed., Gwen Costello. Seven issues a year, circulation 40,000; $14 per year.

ARTICLES on catechesis, methods, theology, sample programs, how-to ideas, etc.; maximum length, 6 typewritten, double-spaced pages — $100 maximum. ILLUSTRATIONS, black and white — $15 each; covers/color slides — $50.

**Review for Religious:** Room 428, 3601 Lindell Blvd., St. Louis, Mo. 63108. Ed., D.F.X. Meenan, S.J. Bimonthly, circulation 18,448; $10 per year.

ARTICLES, of interest to religious: 3,000-6,000 words — $6 per printed page.

**St. Anthony Messenger:** 1615 Republic St., Cincinnati, O. 45210. Ed., Rev. Norman Perry, O.F.M. Monthly, circulation 375,000; $10 per year.

FICTION: Written out of a totally Christian background, illuminating the truth of human nature for adults. No preachiness, sentimentality. FACT ARTICLES: 3,000-3,500 words. Outstanding personalities (must be based on personal interview). Information and comment on major movements in the Church: application of Christian faith to daily life; real-life solutions in the areas of a) family life, education; b) personal living (labor, leisure, art, psychology, spirituality). Human interest narrative. Humor. Photos and picture stories. Query letters welcome.

**St. Joseph's Messenger and Advocate of the Blind:** St. Joseph's Home, P.O. Box 288, Jersey City, N.J. 07303. Ed., Sr. Ursula Maphet, C.S.J. Quarterly, circulation 51,000; $2 per year.

FICTION, and ARTICLES, contemporary, mainstream themes, 500-1,500 words — 1¢ to 3¢ a word.

**Salesian Missions:** 148 Main St., New Rochelle, New York 10802. Ed., Rev. Edward J. Cappelletti, S.D.B. Quarterly, circulation 1,000,000; $1 per year.

ARTICLES: mission interest; pertaining to Salesian Society, life, spirit and educational system of St. John Bosco; adolescent interest and education — 5¢ a word and up. PHOTOGRAPHS — $6. Suggest queries before submitting material. Payment on acceptance. Early report.

**Social Justice Review:** 3835 Westminster Pl., St. Louis, Mo. 63108. Ed., Harvey J. Johnson. Bimonthly, circulation 1,100; $12 per year.

ARTICLES: research, editorial and review: 2,000-4,000 words — $5 per column. No fiction.

**Spiritual Life:** 2131 Lincoln Rd., N.E., Washington, D.C. 20002. Ed., Rev. Steven Payne, O.C.D. Quarterly, circulation 18,000; $9 per year.

ARTICLES, must follow scope of magazine: 3,000-5,000 words — rate varies. Sample copy and instructions for writers sent upon request.

**Spirituality Today:** 1909 S. Ashland Ave., Chica-

go, Ill. 60608. Ed., Rev. Christopher Kiesling, O.P. Quarterly, circulation 5,000; $9 per year.

ARTICLES concerning any phase of the spiritual life: minimum 3,000-4,000 words — 1¢ a word. No fiction or poetry.

**Today's Catholic Teacher:** 2451 E. River Rd., Suite 200, Dayton, O. 45439. Monthly Sept. through May (exc. Dec.), circulation 60,000; $14.95 per year.

ARTICLES of professional and personal interest to teachers, administrators, pastors, parish councils and school board members concerning Catholic schools and CCD programs: 600-800 words, 1,500-3,000 words — $15-$75. Premium payment for superior content and writing presentation. Black and white photos helpful. Payment on publication.

**Today's Parish:** Twenty-Third Publications, P.O. Box 180, Mystic, Conn. 06355. Ed., Carol Clark. Seven issues a year, circulation 22,000; $15 per year.

ARTICLES related to all aspects of parish life and ministry; minimum 1,200-1,500 words — $60 to $100. PHOTOS — $20; four-color cover photos $50.

**WAY — of St. Francis:** 109 Golden Gate Ave. San Francisco, Calif. 94102. Ed., Simon Scanlon, O.F.M. Bimonthly, circulation 8,000; $5 per year.

ARTICLES, in keeping with the purpose of the magazine, to bear effective witness to the ideals and aims of the Order of St. Francis: to view the world through Christian eyes; to point up the relationship between abstract belief and concrete action in the modern world: 1,500-2,200 words — $30 to $50. PHOTOGRAPHS: bought with articles.

**Working for Boys:** Box A, Danvers, Mass. 01923. Ed., Brother Alphonsus Dwyer, C.F.X. (Mss. to Bro. Alois, C.F.X., Assoc. Ed., St. John's High School, Shrewsbury, Mass, 01545.) Quarterly, circulation 16,000; $2 per year.

FICTION, preferably seasonal: 800-1,000 words — 4¢ a word. ARTICLES, preferably seasonal: All Souls, Christmas, Easter, Summer: 800-1,000 words — 4¢ a word. VERSE, seasonal, 4-16 lines — 25¢-50¢ a line.

**Worship:** St. John's Abbey, Collegeville, Minn. 56321. Ed., Rev. Aelred Tegels, O.S.B. Bimonthly, circulation 6,661; $15 per year.

ARTICLES related to the engagement of the magazine in ongoing study of both the theoretical and pastoral dimensions of liturgy; examines historical traditions of worship in their doctrinal context, the experience of worship in Christian churches, the findings of contemporary theology, psychology, communications, cultural anthropology, and sociology insofar as they have a bearing on public worship: 5,000-8,000 words. No fiction or poetry.

## AGRIMISSIO

Agrimissio is a service office established for the purpose of assisting missionaries in rural development work. Founded in 1970 by Msgr. Luigi Ligutti, late honorary president, it is sponsored by the Union of Superiors General (of male religious), the International Union of Superiors General (of female religious), and the National Catholic Rural Life Conference in the U.S. It promotes cooperation among missionaries, the Rome headquarters of religious orders, governmental and non-governmental organizations, especially the international Food and Agriculture Organization.

Headquarters are located at the Palazzo S. Calisto, 00120, Vatican City.

# RADIO, TELEVISION, THEATRE

## Radio and Television

**Christopher Radio Program:** 15-minute interview-discussion series, "Christopher Closeup," weekly, on 236 stations; a one-minute "Christopher Thought for Today," daily, on 1,500 stations. Address: 12 E. 48th St., New York, N.Y. 10017.

**Christopher TV Series, "Christopher Closeup":** Originated in 1951. Half-hour and quarter-hour interviews in color, weekly, on 52 commercial stations, American Forces Network outlets, CBN and PTL syndicate stations and 41 cable systems, Address; 12 E. 48th St., New York, N.Y. 10017.

**Crossroads (Radio):** Originated in 1954 as the Hour of the Crucified, produced by the Passionist Priests and Brothers. Weekly, on nearly 130 stations. Address: 1089 Elm St., West Springfield, Mass. 01089.

**Directions (TV):** Premiered as a quarterly special in June, 1984. This one-hour program is a news-oriented approach to reporting the moral and religious issues reflected in the national and international community. The NCCB/USCC Department of Communication consults with ABC News in the production of this program and in the seasonal liturgical programs broadcast each year. Broadcast on approximately 100 stations. (ABC-TV).

**For Our Times (TV):** Originated in April 1979, this weekly half-hour series produced by CBS in a unique joint cooperative consultation with the Department of Communication, NCCB/USCC, the National Council of Churches and the New York Board of Rabbis focuses on the ethical and social challenges confronting American society today. Format: documentary and studio discussion (CBS-TV).

**Guideline (Radio):** Produced in cooperation with the Department of Communication, NCCB/USCC. Weekly program designed to set forth the teachings of the Catholic Church and to discuss issues the Church faces in the contemporary world; heard on approximately 65 stations (NBC).

**On This Rock (Radio):** Originated in 1941, produced in cooperation with the Department of Communication, NCCB/USCC. A 15-minute weekly program currently employing a youth-oriented music and commentary format; heard on more than 950 stations (ABC).

**Sacred Heart Program (Radio, TV):** Originated in 1939, operated by the Jesuits. Produces and syndicates nationally one TV program and twelve radio programs each week on more than 900 stations. Address: 3900 Westminster Place, St. Louis, Mo. 63108.

**Religious Specials (TV):** The NCCB/USCC Department of Communication consults in the production of four one-hour Catholic specials a year and additional seasonal liturgical services. The specials use a variety of formats and are broadcast on 100 stations (NBC-TV).

## Theatre

**Catholic University Drama Department:** Established in 1937. Offers degree courses in theatre arts, produces five plays a year in The Hartke Theatre. Affiliated with National Players and Olney Theatre. Chairman of the department, William H. Graham. Address: Catholic University of America, Washington, D.C. 20064.

**National Players:** An operation of University Players, a non-profit organization affiliated with the Drama Department of the Catholic University. It originated in 1949 and is the oldest classical touring company in the U.S.

**Olney Theatre Corporation:** A non-profit organization affiliated with the Drama Department of Catholic University. It operates Olney Theatre, Olney, Md., an Equity theatre designated the State Summer Theatre of Maryland in 1978.

**Catholic Actors' Guild of America, Inc.:** Established in 1914 to provide material and spiritual assistance to people in the theatre. Has more than 500 members; publishes *The Call Board* bimonthly. Address: 1501 Broadway, Suite 2400, New York, N.Y. 10036.

## Communications Services

**Clemons Productions, Inc.** "That's the Spirit," weekly TV family show. Address, P.O. Box 440, Pelham, N.Y. 10803.

**Cross Current Communications:** Dedicated to producing quality Catholic TV programming covering all phases of movements and personalities in the contemporary Church. Produces and distributes CROSSFIRE, a 13-part documentary series for TV. Address: 3220 Geronimo Dr., Oxnard, Calif. 93033.

**Eternal Word Television Network, Inc.,** 5817 Old Leeds Rd., Birmingham, Ala. 35210. Mother M. Angelica, P.C.P.A., foundress.

**Father Justin Rosary Hour:** Station F — Box 217, Buffalo, N.Y. 14212. Rev. Cornelius Dende, O.F.M. Conv., director.

**Father Peyton's Family Theater Productions:** Films for TV, for sale and rental. Address: 7201 Sunset Blvd., Hollywood, Calif. 90046.

**Franciscan Advertising and Media Enterprises (F.A.M.E.):** Produces and distributes media and advertising programs for religious education and evangelization. Address: 620 Route 3, Clifton, N.J. 07014.

**Franciscan Communications:** An audio-visual media center dedicated to the production of public service broadcasting material and audio-visual media for religious education. Creators and producers of TeleSPOTS and AudioSPOTS, 10- to 60-second public service messages for radio and TV; TeleKETICS films and media kits, filmstrips, slide programs, video cassettes, phonograph records and tapes, for religious, moral and value education. Address: 1229 South Santee St., Los Angeles, Calif. 90015.

**Hispanic Telecommunications Network, Inc. (HTN):** Produces *Nuestra Familia*, a national weekly Spanish-language TV series. Address: 1828 Grandstand Dr., San Antonio, Tex. 78238.

**Mary Productions:** Originated in 1950. Offers royalty-free scripts for stage, film, radio and tape production. Audio and video tapes of lives of the saints and historical characters. Address: Mary Productions Guild, 90 Fielding Ave., East Keansburg, N.J. 07734.

**Oblate Centro de Comunicación, Oblates of Mary Immaculate:** Publishes religious educational books, audio-visual materials and a weekly Spanish newspaper. Address: P.O. Box 96, San Antonio, Tex. 78291.

**Passionist Communications Center,** 117 Harmon Ave., P.O. Box 440, Pelham, N.Y. 10803. Sunday Mass on TV; publish TV Prayer Guide.

**Paulist Communications:** Contracts with dioceses and parishes to provide public service programs and spot series free to radio stations and scripts to priest-broadcasters; contacts stations for dioceses. Address: 2257 Barry Ave., Los Angeles, Calif. 90064.

**Paulist Productions:** Producers and distributors of the INSIGHT Film Series (available for TV) and educational film series. Purchase and rental information available. Address: P.O. Box 1057, Pacific Palisades, Calif. 90272.

**Catholic Telecommunications Network of America (CTNA):** 95 Madison Avenue, Suite 804, New York, N.Y. 10016.

**Catholic Television Network (CTN):** Instructional TV operations have been established in the following archdioceses and dioceses. Archdioceses are indicated by an asterisk.

Boston,* Mass.: Rev. James Hawker, Director, 1 Lake St., Brighton 02135.

Brooklyn, N.Y.: Rev. Msgr. Michael J. Dempsey, Director, 1712 10th Ave., 11215.

Chicago,* Ill.: Mr. Kenneth P. Murr, Director, 2001 W. Devon Ave. 60659.

Los Angeles,* Calif.: Mr. Steven J. Gorski, 1520 W. Ninth St. 90015.

New York,* N.Y.: Sr. M. Irene Fugazy, Director, Seminary Ave., Yonkers, N.Y. 10704.

Rockville Centre, N.Y.: Rev. Thomas Hartman, Director, 1345 Admiral Lane, Uniondale, N.Y. 11553.

San Francisco,* Calif.: Mr. Thomas A. Combellick, 324 Middlefield Rd., Menlo Park, Calif. 94025.

**Unda-USA:** A national professional Catholic association for broadcasters and allied communicators organized in 1972. It succeeded the Catholic Broadcasters Association of America which in 1948 had replaced the Catholic Forum of the Air organized in 1938. It is a member of the international Catholic association for radio and television known as Unda (the Latin word for "wave," symbolic of air waves of communication). Subgroups include Catholic Television Network, the Association of Catholic Radio and Television Syndicators, and the Association of Diocesan Directors. Unda-USA publishes a newsletter six times a year for members, produces "Real to Reel," a Catholic TV magazine, sponsors an annual general assembly and presents the Gabriel Awards annually for excellence in broadcasting. President, Rev. John Geaney, C.S.P. National office: 3035 Fourth St. N.E., Washington, D.C. 20017.

**The Catholic Communications Foundation (CCF)** was established by the Catholic Fraternal Benefit Societies in 1966 to lend support and assistance to development of the communications apostolate of the Church. The CCF promotes the development of diocesan communications capabilities and funds a scholarship program at the Annual Institute for Religious Communications. CCF officers include Bishop Anthony G. Bosco, chairman of the board. Address: Suite 198, Box 9000, Carlsbad, Calif. 92008.

## DIOCESAN COMMUNICATIONS OFFICES, DIRECTORS

(Sources: *1984 Directory of Catholic Communications Personnel,* published by the Office of Public Affairs, USCC; *Official Catholic Directory;* NC News Service. Archdioceses are designated by an asterisk.)

**Alabama:** Birmingham — Rev. Martin Muller (Communications), Box 6147, Birmingham 35209.

Mobile* — Rev. Robert L. Anderson, S.J. (Ed., *The Catholic Week),* 400 Government St., Mobile 36601.

**Alaska:** Anchorage* — Bro. Charles P. McBride, C.S.C. (Communications), 3925 Reka Dr., Anchorage 99508.

Fairbanks — c/o Catholic Bishop of North Alaska, 1316 Peger Rd., Fairbanks 99701. Rev. James Poole, S.J. (Radio-TV), Box 101, Nome 99762.

Juneau — Miss Carol Crater (Ed., *Inside Passage),* 419 Sixth St., Room 221, Juneau 99801.

**Arizona:** Phoenix — Ms. Marge Injasoulian (Communications), 400 E. Monroe St., Phoenix 85004.

Tucson — Mr. Robert Nordmeyer (Ed., *Arizona Catholic Lifetime),* 64 W. Ochoa St., Tucson 85701.

**Arkansas:** Little Rock — Mr. William W. O'Donnell (Assoc. Dir., Communications), 2500 N. Tyler St., Little Rock 72217.

**California:** Fresno — Mr. Joseph Jasmin (Information), Box 1668, Fresno 93717.

Los Angeles* — Rev. Joseph Battaglia (Communications), Sr. Gail Tenney, O.S.F., Mr. Steven Gorski (ETV), 1530 W. 9th St., Los Angeles 90015.

Monterey — Rev. Dennis M. Gilbert (Communications Commission), St. Jude Church, 303 Hilcrest Ave., Marina 93940; Rev. Felix Migliazzo (Ed., *The Observer),* Box 2079, Monterey 93940.

Oakland — Mrs. Reggie Finney (Public Relations), Dan Morris (Ed., *The Catholic Voice),* 2900 Lakeshore Ave., Oakland 94610.

Orange — Mr. Thomas A. Fuentes (Communications), Box 2590, Newport Beach 92663.

Sacramento — Rev. Brendan Considine (Communications and Media), All Hallows Church, 5500 13th Ave., Sacramento 95820.

San Bernardino — Dan E. Pitre (Ed., *Inland Catholic),* Box 2788, San Bernardino 92405. Clare M. Colella (Electronic Media), 1550 North "D" St., San Bernardino 92405.

San Diego — Rev. George A. Byrne (Communications), Box 80428, San Diego 92138.

San Francisco* — Rev. Miles O'Brien Riley (Communications), 441 Church St., San Francisco 94114.

San Jose — Arlene Goetze (Communications), 7600 Y St. Joseph Ave., Los Altos 94022.

Santa Rosa — Rev. Anthony Di Russo (Communications), P.O. Box 1297, Santa Rosa 95402.

Stockton — Yvonne Goodman (Communications), Box 4237, Stockton 95204.

**Colorado:** Colorado Springs — Most Rev. Richard C. Hanifen, 29 W. Kiowa St., Colorado Springs 80903.

Denver* — Rev. C. B. Woodrich (Information), 200 Josephine St., Denver 80206.

Pueblo — Ms. Geraldine Carrigan (Communications; Ed., *Catholic Crosswinds*), 1001 N. Grand Ave., Pueblo 81003.

**Connecticut:** Bridgeport — Rev. Nicholas V. Grieco (Communications), 238 Jewett Ave., Bridgeport 06606; Rev. Alfred J. Sienkiewicz (Radio-TV), 385 Scofieldtown Rd., Stamford 06903.

Hartford* — Rev. Edmund O'Brien (Radio-TV), 785 Asylum Ave., Hartford 06105.

Norwich — Jacqueline M. Keller (Communications), 201 Hickory St., Norwich 06360.

Stamford (Ukrainian Diocese) — Rev. Lew Lubynsky, 303 Eddy Glover Blvd., New Britain 06053.

**Delaware:** Wilmington — Mr. F. Eugene Donnelly (Secretary, Communications), Box 2030, Wilmington 19899.

**District of Columbia:** Washington* — Rev. Maurice T. Fox (Delegate, Communications), Box 29260, Washington 20017.

**Florida:** Miami* — Rev. Donald F. Connolly (Communications), Marjorie Donohue (Public Information), Rev. Jose P. Nickse (Radio-TV), 9401 Biscayne Blvd., Miami 33138.

Orlando — Mr. George Fournier (Communications), Box 2728, Orlando 32802.

Pensacola-Tallahassee — Rev. Michael Mooney (Communications), 855 W. Carolina St., Tallahassee 32304.

St. Augustine — Sr. Carol Stovall, S.S.J. (Communications), Box 24000, Jacksonville 32241. Msgr. R. Joseph James (Chairman, Communications Commission), P.O. Box 285, Williston 32696.

St. Petersburg — David MacNamara (Communications), Jeff Rago (Radio), Peter White (Television), Box 18081, Tampa 33679.

**Georgia:** Atlanta* — Msgr. Noel C. Burtenshaw (Communications), 680 W. Peachtree St. N.W., Atlanta 30308.

Savannah — Rev. Joseph Stranc (Communications), 12 W. Jones Ave., Statesboro 30458. Mrs. Gillian Brown (Information), P.O. Box 8789, Savannah 31412.

**Hawaii:** Honolulu — Rev. James Drew (Communications), 3300 Ala Laulani St., Honolulu 96818.

**Idaho:** Boise — Rev. David L. Riffle (Communications Center), 6003 Overland, Boise 83709.

**Illinois:** Belleville — John T. Myler, (Communications), 220 W. Lincoln St., Belleville 62221.

Chicago* — Sr. Joy Clough (Media Relations),

Rev. Alphonse Spilly (Communications), 155 E. Superior St., Chicago 60611. Mr. Kenneth Murr (Broadcast Services), 2011 W. Devon Ave., Chicago 60659.

Joliet — Rev. William F. Irwin (Communications), St. Charles Borromeo Pastoral Center, Rt. 53 and Airport Rd., Romeoville 60441.

Peoria — Mr. Robert England (Communications), 1301 N.E. Glendale,, Peoria 61603.

Rockford — Rev. David D. Kagan (Communications), 850 N. Church St., Rockford 61103.

St. Nicholas in Chicago for Ukrainians — Msgr. Jaroslav Swyschuk (Eastern Rite Information Bureau), 2208 W. Chicago Ave., Chicago 60622.

Springfield — Rev. Richard L. Paynic (Ed., *Time and Eternity*), Rev. Neal Dee (Radio-TV), 514 E. Lawrence, Springfield 62703.

**Indiana:** Evansville — Rev. Joseph L. Ziliak (Information), P.O. Box 4169, Evansville 47711.

Fort Wayne-South Bend — Becky Haxby (Communications), P.O. Box 390, Fort Wayne 46801.

Gary — Rev. John F. Morales (Communications), P.O. Box M474, Gary 46401.

Indianapolis* — Mr. Charles J. Schisla (Communications), Box 1410, Indianapolis 46206.

Lafayette — Office of Information. 610 Lingle Ave., Box 260, Lafayette 47902.

**Iowa:** Davenport — Rev. Francis C. Henricksen (Communications), Suite 500, First Natl. Bldg., 201 W. 2nd St., Davenport 52801. Sr. Hillary Mullany, O.S.F. (Television), 2706 Gaines St., Davenport 52804.

Des Moines — Sr. Mira Mosle, B.V.M. (Communications), 818 Fifth Ave., Box 1816, Des Moines 50306.

Dubuque* — Sr. Carol Hoverman (Communications), 1229 Mt. Loretta Ave. Dubuque 52001.

Sioux City — Mr. Joe Maher (Ed., *The Globe*), 1825 Jackson St., Sioux City 51105; Msgr. Frank Brady (Radio-TV), 1212 Morningside Ave., Sioux City 51106.

**Kansas:** Dodge City — Rev. Daniel V. Heim, Our Lady of Guadalupe Church, 805 Avenue J, Dodge City 67801.

Kansas City* — Rev. William Maher (Ed., *The Leaven*), Box 2329, Kansas City 66110.

Salina — Joseph A. Warner (Communications), Box 958, Salina 67402.

Wichita — Rev. Arthur A. Busch (Communications), 424 N. Broadway, Wichita 67202.

**Kentucky:** Covington — Sr. Colleen Winston, O.S.B. (Communications), Box 192, Covington 41012.

Louisville* — Rev. George N. Rice (Communications), 1951 Bishop Lane, Suite 351. Louisville 40218.

Owensboro — Msgr. George Hancock (Information), 4005 Frederica St., Owensboro 42301; Rev. Leonard Reisz (Radio-TV), 1001 W. 7th St., Owensboro 42301.

**Louisiana:** Alexandria-Shreveport — Mr. Al Nassif (Information), Box 7417, Alexandria 71306. Rev. Calvin C. Burleigh (Electronic Media), 425 McCormick St., Bossier City 71111.

Baton Rouge — Mr. Thomas Barbarie (Ed.,

Catholic Commentator), Box 14746, Baton Rouge 70898.

Houma-Thibodaux — Mr. Louis Aguirre (Communications, Ed., *The Bayou Catholic*), Box 9077, Houma 70361.

Lafayette — Mr. John Jungkind (Communications), Box 3223, Lafayette 70502.

Lake Charles — Mr. Truman Stacey (Diocesan News), 834 Ryan St., Lake Charles 70601.

New Orleans* — Mr. Thomas M. Finney (Communications, Public Relations), 7887 Walmsley Ave., New Orleans 70125.

**Maine:** Portland — Mr. Clarence F. McKay (Communications), 510 Ocean Ave., Portland 04103.

**Maryland:** Baltimore* — Rev. Leo A. Murray, S.J. (Communications), 320 Cathedral St., Baltimore 21201.

**Massachusetts:** Boston* — Rev. Peter V. Conley (Communications), 49 Franklin St., Boston 02110; Rev. Francis T. McFarland (Radio-TV), 55 Chapel St., Newton 02160.

Fall River — Rev. John F. Moore (Communications), 410 Highland Ave., Fall River 02722; Rev. John F. Hogan, (TV), 494 Slocum Rd., N. Dartmouth 02747.

Springfield — Michael Graziano (Communications), 1089 Elm St., W. Springfield 01089.

Worcester — Rev. John W. Barrett (Communications), 49 Elm St., Worcester 01609.

Melkite Eparchy of Newton — Rev. Albert Gorayeb (Media Communications), 1255 McBride Ave., W. Paterson, N.J. 07424.

**Michigan:** Detroit* — Mr. Jay M. Berman (Communications), 305 Michigan Ave., Detroit 48226.

Gaylord — Betty J. Ballou (Communications), 202 W. Mitchell Ave., Gaylord 49735.

Grand Rapids — Michael G. Ghering (Communications), 660 Burton St. S.E., Grand Rapids 49507.

Kalamazoo — Mrs. Eileen Miller (Communications), 215 N. Westnedge Ave., Kalamazoo 49005.

Lansing — Rev. Donald L. Eder (Communications), 300 W. Ottawa St., Lansing 48933.

Marquette — Gregory B. Bell (Communications), Box 550, Marquette 49855.

Saginaw — Rev. David Parsch (Communications), 5800 Weiss St., Saginaw 48603.

**Minnesota:** Crookston — Rev. Michael Patnode (Information), Rev. Gerald Noesen (Radio-TV), Box 610, Crookston 56716.

Duluth — Mr. Francis J. Shane (Information), 215 W. 4th St., Duluth 55806.

New Ulm — Rev. Dennis Labat (Communications), 1400 Chancery Dr., New Ulm 56073.

St. Cloud — Ms. Rosemary Borgert (Communications), 305 7th Ave. N., Suite 207, St. Cloud 56301.

St. Paul and Minneapolis* — Ms. Joan Bernet (Communications), 226 Summit Ave., St. Paul 55102.

Winona — Ivan Kubista (Communications), 55 West Sanborn, Winona 55987.

**Mississippi:** Biloxi — Rev. James Russell (Communications), P.O. Box 1189, Biloxi 39533.

Jackson — Mrs. Janna Avalon (Ed., *Mississippi Today*), Box 2248, Jackson 39205.

**Missouri:** Jefferson City — Mr. Mark Saucier (Communications), Box 417, Jefferson City 65101.

Kansas City-St. Joseph — Rev. John C. Weiss (Communications), 1357 N.E. 42nd Terr., Kansas City 64116.

St. Louis* — Msgr. Edward O'Donnell (Information), 4445 Lindell Blvd., St. Louis 63108; Mr. Ronald Coleman (Public Relations), 2249 S. Brentwood Blvd., St. Louis 63144. Rev. Joseph M. O'Brien (Radio-TV), 9229 Lackland Rd., St. Louis 63114.

Springfield-Cape Girardeau — Mrs. Marilyn Vydra (Communications), 200 McDaniel Bldg., Springfield 65806.

**Montana:** Great Falls-Billings — Box 2107, Great Falls 59403.

Helena — Rev. Robert J. O'Donnell (Chancellor, Communications), Box 1729, Helena 59624.

**Nebraska:** Grand Island — Rev. Harold R. Kurtenbach (Communications), P.O. Box 2231, Grand Island 68802.

Lincoln — Rev. James D. Dawson (Information), Box 80328, Lincoln 68501.

Omaha* — Rev. Mel Rempe (Communications), 100 N. 62nd St., Omaha 68132.

**Nevada:** Reno-Las Vegas — Msgr. Thomas Meger, Chancellor, Box 1211, Reno 89504; Mr. Gerard E. Sherry (Information), 953 Sahara Ave., Las Vegas 89104.

**New Hampshire:** Manchester — Richard B. Carozza (Communications), Rev. John Poirier (Radio-TV), 153 Ash St., Manchester 03105.

**New Jersey:** Camden — Rev. Roger E. McGrath (Communications), Box 709, Camden 08101.

Newark* — Michael S. McGraw (Information, Public Affairs), 31 Mulberry St., Newark 07102.

Passaic (Byzantine Rite Eparchy) — Msgr. Robert G. Moneta (*Eastern Catholic Life*), 101 Market St., Passaic 07055.

Paterson — Tim Manning (Communications), Box 1887, Clifton, N.J. 07015.

Trenton — Rev. Leonard F. Troiano (Communications), 315 Lowell Ave., Trenton 08619.

**New Mexico:** Gallup — Rev. Cormac Antram, O.F.M. (Communications, Radio-TV), 506 W. 66th Ave., Gallup 87301.

Santa Fe* — Rev. Albert Gallegos (Communications-Media), 202 Morningside Dr. S.E., Albuquerque 87108.

**New York:** Albany — Rev. Michael Farano (Information), P. O. Box 6297, Quail Sta., Albany 12206.

Brooklyn — Mr. Frank DeRosa (Information), Box C, Brooklyn 11202.

Buffalo — Rev. David M. Lee (Communications), 100 S. Elmwood Dr., Buffalo 14202.

New York* — Rev. Peter G. Finn (Communications), Rev. Lester S. Avestruz, O.S.A. (Spanish Media), 1011 First Ave., New York, N.Y. 10022. Sr. Irene Fugazy (Instructional TV), Seminary Ave., Yonkers, 10704.

Military Vicariate — Rev. Msgr. James J. Markham (Communications), 1011 First Ave., New York 10022.

Ogdensburg — Rev. David W. Stinebrickner (Information), 622 Washington St., Ogdensburg 13669;

Rev. Donald Kramberg (Radio-TV), Wadhams Hall, RFD No. 4, Ogdensburg 13669.

Rochester — Rev. Louis A. Vasile (Information), 1150 Buffalo Rd., Rochester 14624.

Rockville Centre — Rev. Msgr. Daniel S. Hamilton (Information), Box 700, Hempstead 11551; Rev. Thomas J. Hartman (Radio-TV), 1345 Admiral Lane, Uniondale 11553.

St. Maron Diocese (Maronite Rite) — Rev. Richard Saad, 836 8th St. S., Birmingham, Ala. 35256.

Syracuse — Mr. Ron Smith (Communications), P.O. Box 511, Syracuse 13201.

**North Carolina:** Charlotte — Frank Cancro (Communications), 1524 E. Moorehead St., Charlotte 28207.

Raleigh — Rev. Joseph G. Vetter (Communications), 300 Cardinal Gibbons Dr., Raleigh 27606.

**North Dakota:** Bismarck — Rev. John J. Owens, Box 128, Wilton 58579.

Fargo — Deacon Matt Lanz (Ed., *The New Earth*), Box 1750, Fargo 58107.

**Ohio:** Cincinnati* — Mr. Daniel J. Kane (Communications), Rev. Theodore Kosse (Radio-TV), 100 E. 8th St., Cincinnati 45202.

Cleveland — Rev. Frank P. Kosem (Communications), Mr. J. Jerome Lackamp (Radio-TV), Mr. Patrick DiSalvatore (Catholic Communications Center), 1027 Superior Ave., Cleveland 44114.

Columbus — Rev. James P. Hanley (Vicar, Communications), Mr. Richard J. Hatem (Radio-TV), Susan Linebaugh (Public Relations, Information), 197 E. Gay St., Columbus 43215.

Parma (Byzantine Rite Eparchy) — Rev. Donald Petyo, 5500 W. 54th St., Parma 44129. Barbara Lizanich (Communications), 1900 Carlton Rd., Parma 44134.

St. Josaphat in Parma (Ukrainian) — P.O. Box 34180, Parma 44134.

Steubenville — Rev. Michael Gromczewski, Box 969, Steubenville 43952.

Toledo — Mr. Jim Richards (Communications), 2544 Parkwood Ave., Toledo 43610.

Youngstown — Rev. Bernard Bonnot (Communications), Miss Jean M. Nero (Public/Media Relations), 144 W. Wood St., Youngstown 44503. Mitch Stanley (Telecommunications Center), Box 430, Canfield 44406.

**Oklahoma:** Oklahoma City* — Rev. David F. Monahan (Communications), Box 32180, Oklahoma City 73123.

Tulsa — Rev. Dennis C. Dorney, Chancellor, 820 S. Boulder St., Box 2009, Tulsa 74101.

**Oregon:** Baker — Rev. Joseph B. Hayes, Sacred Heart Church, 815 High St., Klameth Falls 97601.

Portland* — Robert Riler (Communications), 2838 E. Burnside St., Portland 97214.

**Pennsylvania:** Allentown — Rev. Stanley T. Sosnowski (Information), 202 N. 17th St., Box F, Allentown 18105.

Altoona-Johnstown — Msgr. Philip Saylor (Information), Box 413 Logan Blvd., Hollidaysburg 16648.

Erie — Rev. Thomas McSweeney (Communications), Gannon University, 703 Peach St. Erie 16541.

Greensburg — Mrs. Alice Laurich (Communications), Box 850, Greensburg 15601.

Harrisburg — Sr. Arlene Ronollo, S.S.J. (Communications), 4800 Union Deposit Rd., Box 3557, Harrisburg 17105.

Philadelphia* — Rev. John J. Sibel (Communications), 222 North 17th St., Philadelphia 19103.

Philadelphia* (Ukrainian) — Rev. Ronald Popivchak, Box 126, Bridgeport 19405.

Pittsburgh* (Byzantine Rite) — Msgr. Edward V. Rosack (Information), 624 Park Rd., Ambridge 15003; Most Rev. John M. Bilock (Radio-TV), 54 Riverview Ave., Pittsburgh 15214.

Pittsburgh — Rev. Ronald P. Lengwin (Communications), 111 Boulevard of the Allies, Pittsburgh 15222.

Scranton — Miss Mary Ellen Keating, 300 Wyoming Ave., Scranton 18503.

**Rhode Island:** Providence — Marianne Postiglione, R.S.M. (Communications), Gilles D. Dery (Media Center), One Cathedral Square, Providence 02903.

**South Carolina:** Charleston — Dr. Paul C. Beach (Communications), Box 818, Charleston 29402.

**South Dakota:** Rapid City — Mr. Brian T. Olszewski, Box 678, Rapid City 57709.

Sioux Falls — Rev. Leonard Thury, Holy Family Catholic Church, 321 E. 3rd St., Mitchell 57301; Rev. Thomas J. Ryan, 509 Capitol, Yankton 57078.

**Tennessee:** Memphis — Msgr. Paul W. Clunan (Communications), 203 S. White Station Rd., Memphis 38117.

Nashville — Mr. Joseph A. Sweat (Communications, Public Relations), 2400 21st Ave. S., Nashville 37212.

**Texas:** Amarillo — Leroy Behnke (Information), 1800 N. Spring St., Box 5644, Amarillo 79117.

Austin — Rev. Thomas J. Holohan, C.S.P., Box 13327, Austin 78711.

Beaumont — Rev. James Vanderholt (Communications), P.O. Box 3948, Beaumont 77704.

Brownsville — Rev. Jon McMahon, O.M.I., Box 547, Alamo 78516.

Corpus Christi — Rev. Robert E. Freeman (Communications), Sr. Janie Barrera (Radio-TV), 1200 Lantana St., Corpus Christi 78407.

Dallas — Deacon Steve Landregan (Communications), Patricia Martin (ETV), 3915 Lemmon Ave., Dallas 75219.

El Paso — Mr. Andrew Sparke (Parochial Schools TV), 1101 Birch St., El Paso 79930.

Fort Worth — Rev. Reynold Matus (Communications), 3508 Maurice Ave., Fort Worth 76111.

Galveston-Houston — Msgr. John L. Fos, 1700 San Jacinto St., Box 1878, Houston 77001; Rev. Bert Akers, S.J. (Radio-TV), Box 907, Houston 77001.

Lubbock — Rev. Malcolm Neyland (Communications), 303 Toledo St., Box 10238, Lubbock 79408.

San Angelo — Rev. Maurice J. Voity (Communications), Box 1829, San Angelo 76902.

San Antonio* — Richard J. Hemberger (Television), 2718 W. Woodlawn Ave., San Antonio 78228.

**Utah:** Salt Lake City — Sr. Margaret Andre Stechschulte, O.P. (Communications Media), 27C St., Salt Lake City 84103.

**Vermont:** Burlington — Rev. Joseph T. Sullivan (Communications), 351 North Ave., Burlington 05401.
**Virginia:** Arlington — Ellen McCloskey (Communications), 200 N. Glebe Rd., Arlington 22203.
Richmond — Mr. Bob Edwards (Communications), 811 Cathedral Pl., Richmond 23220.
**Washington:** Seattle* — Dr. Maury Sheridan, 910 Marion St., Seattle 98104.
Spokane — Rev. Michael J. Savelesky (Communications), Box 1453, Spokane 99210.
Yakima — Rev. P. J. Auve, Pastoral Office, Box 505, Yakima 98907.
**West Virginia:** Wheeling-Charleston — Mr. W. C. Hehr, 1300 Byron St., Box 230, Wheeling 26003.
**Wisconsin:** Green Bay — Mr. Tony Kuick (Communications), Box 1825, Green Bay 54305.
La Crosse — Rev. Bernard McGarty (Communications), Box 937, La Crosse 54602.
Madison — Maureen Quinn (Communications), 3577 High Point Rd., Rt. 2, Madison 53711.
Milwaukee* — Sr. Mary Luke Baldwin, S.S.N.D. (Communications), Box 2018, Milwaukee 53201.
Superior — Rev. Robert Urban (Information), 1512 N. 12th St., Superior 54880.
**Wyoming:** Cheyenne — Sally Michalov (Information), P.O. Box 4279, Casper 82604

**Catholic Communications Northwest:** Regional communications center serving dioceses in Alaska, Idaho, Montana, Oregon and Washington. Executive Director, Dr. Maury Sheridan, 910 Marion St., Seattle, Wash. 98104.

**Delaware Valley Catholic Office for Television and Radio:** Interdiocesan agency of the Archdiocese of Philadelphia, the dioceses of Camden and Trenton, N.J. and Wilmington, Del. Address: 222 North 17th St., Philadelphia, Pa. 19103.

**Other Communications Offices**
**International Mission Radio Association:** Rev. Jude Bradley, O.S.B., treasurer-administrator, St. Paul's Abbey, Newton, N.J. 07860.
**Jesuits in Communication in North America (JESCOM):** Rev. Donald R. Campion, S.J., executive secretary, Suite 300, 1424 16th St. N.W., Washington, D.C. 20036.
**Maryknoll Media Relations:** Rev. Paul Newpower, M.M., director, Maryknoll Fathers and Brothers, Maryknoll, N.Y. 10545.
**National Franciscan Communications Conference:** Rev. James J. Gardiner, S.A., president, Good Counsel Church, 30 E. 90th St., New York, N.Y. 10128.
**Oblate Communications:** Rev. Jon McMahon, O.M.I., director, Box 547, Alamo, Tex. 78516.

**National Office**
The National Catholic Office for Information (NCOI), successor to the NCWC Bureau of Information, serves as the official spokesman for both the United States Catholic Conference and the National Conference of Catholic Bishops in relating to the news media. The NCOI is part of the NCCB USCC Office for Public Affairs.
The office prepares and distributes news releases; handles inquiries from the press; arranges news media coverage of bishops' meetings; offers public information and public relations counsel on a day-to-day basis to the office of the general secretary of the USCC and the NCCB, and to other agencies and staff members; performs a number of special research and writing functions on behalf of the conferences and their staffs.
William Ryan is director of the office, which is located at 1312 Massachusetts Ave. N.W., Washington, D.C. 20005.

# HONORS AND AWARDS

## PONTIFICAL ORDERS

The Pontifical Orders of Knighthood are secular orders of merit whose membership depends directly on the pope. Details regarding the various orders are handled by a special agency in the Secretariat of Briefs, an office in the Papal Secretariat of State.

**Supreme Order of Christ (Militia of Our Lord Jesus Christ):** The highest of the five pontifical orders of knighthood, the Supreme Order of Christ was approved Mar. 14, 1319, by John XXII as a continuation in Portugal of the suppressed Order of Templars. Members were religious with vows and a rule of life until the order lost its religious character toward the end of the 15th century. Since that time it has existed as an order of merit. Paul VI, in 1966, restricted awards of the order to Christian heads of state.

**Order of the Golden Spur (Golden Militia):** Although the original founder is not certainly known, this order is one of the oldest knighthoods. Indiscriminate bestowal and inheritance diminished its prestige, however, and in 1841 Gregory XVI replaced it with the Order of St. Sylvester and gave it

the title of Golden Militia. In 1905 St. Pius X restored the Order of the Golden Spur in its own right, separating it from the Order of St. Sylvester. Paul VI, in 1966, restricted awards of the order to Christian heads of state.

**Order of Pius IX:** Founded by Pius IX June 17, 1847, the order is awarded for outstanding services for the Church and society, and may be given to non-Catholics as well as Catholics. The title to nobility formerly attached to membership was abolished by Pius XII in 1939. In 1957 Pius XII instituted the Class of the Grand Collar as the highest category of the order; in 1966, Paul VI restricted this award to heads of state "in solemn circumstances." The other three classes are of Knights of the Grand Cross, Knight Commanders with and without emblem, and Knights. The new class was created to avoid difficulties in presenting papal honors to Christian or non-Christian leaders of high merit.

**Order of St. Gregory the Great:** First established by Gregory XVI in 1831 to honor citizens of the Papal States, the order is conferred on persons who are distinguished for personal character and reputation, and for notable accomplishment. The order has civil and military divisions, and three classes of knights.

**Order of St. Sylvester:** Instituted Oct. 31, 1841, by Gregory XVI to absorb the Order of the Golden Spur, this order was divided into two by St. Pius X in 1905, one retaining the name of St. Sylvester and the other assuming the title of Golden Militia. Membership consists of three degrees: Knights of the Grand Cross, Knight Commanders with and without emblem, and Knights.

## ECCLESIASTICAL ORDER

**Order of the Holy Sepulchre:** Critical opinion is divided regarding various details of the history of the order. It is certain, however, that these knights first appeared in the Holy Land and were in existence at the end of the 11th century. Some assign earlier dates or origin, claiming as founders St. James the Apostle, first bishop of Jerusalem, and St. Helena, builder of the Basilica of the Holy Sepulchre. Others hold that Godfrey of Bouillon instituted the order in 1099 and that it took its name from the Holy Sepulchre where its members were knighted.

## ORDER OF MALTA

The Sovereign Military Hospitaller Order of St. John of Jerusalem of Rhodes and of Malta traces its origin to a group of men who maintained a Christian hospital in the Holy Land in the 11th century. The group was approved as a religious order — the Hospitallers of St. John — by Paschal II in 1113.

The order, while continuing its service to the poor, principally in hospital work, assumed military duties in the twelfth century and included knights, chaplains and sergeants-at-arms among its members. All the knights were professed monks with the vows of poverty, chastity and obedience. Headquarters were located in the Holy Land until the last decade of the 13th century and on Rhodes after 1308 (whence the title, Knights of Rhodes).

After establishing itself on Rhodes, the order became a sovereign power like the sea republics of Italy and the Hanseatic cities of Germany, flying its own flag, coining its own money, floating its own navy, and maintaining diplomatic relations with many nations.

The order was forced to abandon Rhodes in 1522 after the third siege of the island by the Turks under Sultan Suliman I. Eight years later, the Knights were given the island of Malta, where they remained as a bastion of Christianity until near the end of the 18th century. Headquarters have been located in Rome since 1834.

The title of Grand Master of the Order, in abeyance for some time, was restored by Leo XIII in 1879. A more precise definition of both the religious and the sovereign status of the order was embodied in a new constitution of 1961 and a code issued in 1966.

Religious aspects of the order are subject to regulation by the Holy See. At the same time the sovereignty of the order, which is based on interna-

tional law, is recognized by the Holy See and by 43 countries with which full diplomatic relations are maintained.

The four main classifications of members are: Knights of Justice, who are religious with the vows of poverty, chastity and obedience; Knights of Obedience, who make a solemn promise to strive for Christian perfection; Knights of Honor and Devotion and of Grace and Devotion — all of noble lineage; and Knights of Magistral Grace. There are also chaplains, Dames and Donats of the order.

The order, with five grand priories, three subpriories and 38 national associations, is devoted to hospital and charitable work of all kinds in some 77 countries.

The Grand Master, who is the sovereign head of the order, has the title of Most Eminent Highness with the rank of Cardinal. He must be of noble lineage and under solemn vows for a minimum period of 10 years, if under 50.

The present Grand Master is Fra' Angelo de Mojana di Cologna, a lawyer of Milan, who was elected for life May 8, 1962, by the Council of State.

The address of headquarters of the order is Via Condotti, 68, Palazzo Malta, 00187 Roma, Italia.

## PAPAL MEDALS

**Pro Ecclesia et Pontifice:** This decoration ("For the Church and the Pontiff") had its origin in 1888 as a token of the golden sacerdotal jubilee of Leo XIII; he bestowed it on those who had assisted in the observance of his jubilee and on persons responsible for the success of the Vatican Exposition. The medal bears the likeness of Leo XIII on one side; on the other, the tiara, the papal keys, and the words *Pro Ecclesia et Pontifice*. Originally, the medal was issued in gold, silver or bronze. It is awarded in recognition of service to the Church and the papacy.

**Benemerenti:** Several medals ("To a well-deserving person") have been conferred by popes for exceptional accomplishment and service. The medals, which are made of gold, silver or bronze, bear the likeness and name of the reigning pope on one side; on the other, a laurel crown and the letter "B."

These two medals may be given by the pope to both men and women. Their bestowal does not convey any title or honor of knighthood.

---

The *National Federation of Priests' Councils* was organized by 233 delegates from 127 priests' organizations at a charter meeting held in Chicago May 20 and 21, 1968. Its stated purpose is to give priests' councils, official or unofficial, a representative voice in matters of presbyteral, pastoral and ministerial concern to the U.S. and the universal Church. The NFPC has a membership of 102 senates (councils and associations), religious institutes, PADRES and the National Black Catholic Clergy Caucus. Headquarters are located at 1307 S. Wabash Ave., Chicago, Ill. 60605.